Johnson
2?, 30 - 32

Song. 13311 from express

3:45 - Tuesday Aft.

Voice Analysis

ADVENTURES IN
AMERICAN LITERATURE

Edited by

H. C. SCHWEIKERT
Central High School, St. Louis, Missouri

REWEY BELLE INGLIS
University High School, The University of Minnesota

JOHN GEHLMANN
Oak Park High School, Oak Park, Illinois

Illustrated by
R. M. BRINKERHOFF

1934
HARCOURT, BRACE AND COMPANY
NEW YORK · CHICAGO

ACKNOWLEDGMENTS

The editors of *Adventures in American Literature* are indebted to the following authors, periodicals, and publishers for permission to use the selections indicated, all rights in which are in all cases reserved by the owner of the copyright.

George Ade: " The Wonderful Meal of Vittles " by George Ade.

D. Appleton & Company, New York: " The Spirit of Christmas " and " Prison Reform and Poise " from *Hermione and Her Little Group of Serious Thinkers* by Don Marquis; " The Awful Fate of Mr. Wolf " from *Uncle Remus: His Songs and Sayings* by Joel Chandler Harris; *The Trysting Place* by Booth Tarkington.

Walter H. Baker Company, Boston: *Nathan Hale* by Clyde Fitch; copyright (renewal) 1927, by Richard W. Fitch, and reprinted with the permission of Walter H. Baker Company, publishers, Boston.

The Bobbs-Merrill Company, Indianapolis: " When the Frost Is on the Punkin " from *Neighborly Poems* by James Whitcomb Riley. Copyright 1897–1925. Used by special permission of the publishers, The Bobbs-Merrill Company.

Albert & Charles Boni, Inc., New York: " The Reading Boy " from *The Janitor's Boy and Other Poems* by Nathalia Crane; " A Horseman in the Sky " from *In the Midst of Life* by Ambrose Bierce.

Brandt & Brandt, New York: " Lament " from *Second April*, published by Harper & Brothers; copyright 1921 by Edna St. Vincent Millay; " The Spring and the Fall " from the *Harp-Weaver and Other Poems*, published by Harper & Brothers; copyright 1920, 1921, 1922, 1923 by Edna St. Vincent Millay; " Dirge Without Music " from *The Buck in the Snow*, published by Harper & Brothers; copyright 1928 by Edna St. Vincent Millay.

The Century Company, New York: " The Runaway " from *Selected Plays and Poems* by Cale Young Rice.

Dodd, Mead & Company, New York: " Green Fire " and " The Joys of the Road " by Bliss Carman; " Sea Gypsy " and " The Wander Lovers " by Richard Hovey; copyright by Dodd, Mead & Company, Inc.

Doubleday, Doran & Company, Garden City: " Correct Behavior on a Picnic " from *Perfect Behavior* by Donald Ogden Stewart, copyright 1922 by Doubleday, Doran & Company, Inc.; " The Century " from *Off the Deep End* by Christopher Morley, copyright 1928 by Doubleday, Doran & Company, Inc.; " The Post Office Inkwell " from *Chimney Smoke* by

Christopher Morley, copyright 1921 by Doubleday, Doran & Company, Inc.; " Long Pants " from *Prose and Cons* by Irvin S. Cobb, copyright 1926 by Doubleday, Doran & Company, Inc.; " A Municipal Report " from *Strictly Business* by O. Henry, copyright 1909 by Doubleday, Doran & Company, Inc.; " The Ballad of Two Lame Men " and " Those Two Boys " from *By and Large* by F. P. A., copyright 1914 by Doubleday, Doran & Company, Inc.; selections from *Leaves of Grass* by Walt Whitman, copyright 1924 by Doubleday, Doran & Company, Inc.; selection from *John Brown's Body* by Stephen Vincent Benét, copyright 1927 and 1928 by Stephen Vincent Benét, and reprinted by special permission of the publishers, Doubleday, Doran & Company, Inc.; " The Same Old Story " from *More Truth Than Poetry* by James J. Montague, copyright 1920 by Doubleday, Doran & Company, Inc.; " The Durable Bon Mot " and " The Humorist " from *Splinters* by Keith Preston, copyright 1921 by Doubleday, Doran & Company, Inc.

E. P. Dutton & Company, New York: " Real Baseball " taken by permission from Arthur Guiterman's *I Sing the Pioneer,* published and copyright by E. P. Dutton & Company, Inc., New York; " Sheener " taken by permission from Ben Ames Williams' *Thrifty Stock,* published and copyright by E. P. Dutton & Company, Inc., New York.

Dorothy Canfield Fisher: " Vermont " from the *Nation.*

Laura P. Gould: " The Mississippi " by Lafcadio Hearn, from Dr. George M. Gould's *Concerning Lafcadio Hearn.*

Harcourt, Brace & Company, New York: " Once There Was a Furnace Boy " from *Like a Summer's Cloud* by Charles S. Brooks; " Walter Reed " from *Microbe Hunters* by Paul de Kruif; " Clean Curtains," " Wind Song," and " Night Stuff " from *Smoke and Steel* by Carl Sandburg; " Fate " and " Good Morning, America " from *Good Morning, America* by Carl Sandburg; " Two 'Mericana Men " from *Carmina* by Thomas Augustine Daly; " To a Telegraph Pole," " Long Feud," " The Stone's Hymn," and " Prayer " by Louis Untermeyer; " Herman Melville Writes Moby-Dick " from *Herman Melville* by Lewis Mumford; " Hawthorne's Friends at College " from *The Rebellious Puritan* by Lloyd Morris; " It Happens, Often " from *Piping and Panning* by Edwin Meade Robinson.

Harper & Brothers, New York: " An Unexpected Acquaintance " from *A Tramp Abroad* by Mark Twain; " How the Feud Started " from *The Mirthful Lyre* by Arthur Guiterman.

Harvard University Press, Cambridge: " The Banks of the Little Eau Pleine " from *Ballads and Songs of a Shanty Boy* by Franz Rickaby.

Henry Holt & Company, New York: " The Pasture," " A Minor Bird," " Stopping by Woods on a Snowy Evening," " Birches," " The Birthplace," and " The Death of the Hired Man " from *Poems* by Robert Frost; " Chicago," " Buttons," " A Fence," " Child of the Romans," " A Coin," and " In a Back Alley " from *Chicago Poems* by Carl Sandburg; " Grass " and " Prayers of Steel " from *Cornhuskers* by Carl Sandburg.

Houghton Mifflin Company, Boston: "A Lady," "Music," and "Patterns" by Amy Lowell; "Memory" and "A Snowflake" by Thomas Bailey Aldrich; "An Ingénue of the Sierras" and "Plain Language from Truthful James" by Bret Harte; "A Fool's Prayer" by Edward Rowland Sill.

P. J. Kenedy & Sons, New York: "The Conquered Banner" by Rev. Abram J. Ryan.

Stanton H. King: "Leave Her, Johnny, Leave Her."

Alfred A. Knopf, Inc., New York: "Nonsense Rhyme" reprinted from *Angels and Earthly Creatures* by Elinor Wylie; "Escape" and "Sea Lullaby" from *Nets to Catch the Wind* by Elinor Wylie; by and with permission of and special arrangement with Alfred A. Knopf, Inc., authorized publishers.

Little, Brown & Company, Boston: Selections from Emily Dickinson.

Horace Liveright, New York: "Where the Cross Is Made" by Eugene O'Neill; "In the Esplanade des Invalides" from *The White Rooster* by George O'Neil.

John A. Lomax: "The Cowboy's Dream" from *Cowboy Songs and Ballads*.

Lothrop, Lee & Shepard Company, Boston: "The Mocking Bird" and "Aspects of the Pines" by Paul Hamilton Hayne.

The Macmillan Company, New York: "To Build a Fire" by Jack London; "Bewick Finzer" by Edwin Arlington Robinson; "Let Me Live Out My Years" by John G. Neihardt; "The Coin," "I Shall Not Care," "Night Song at Amalfi," and "Long Hill" by Sara Teasdale; "The Santa Fé Trail" by Vachel Lindsay; "School Life" from *A Son of the Middle Border* by Hamlin Garland; "Palmetto Town" from *Carolina Chansons* by Dubose Heyward and Hervey Allen; "The Mountain Woman" from *Skylines and Horizons* by Dubose Heyward.

Edwin Markham: "The Man with the Hoe," "Our Israfel," and "Quatrains" copyright by Edwin Markham and used by permission from *Collected Poems*, 1930.

Edgar Lee Masters: "Silence" and selections from *Spoon River Anthology*.

Margaret Prescott Montague: "England to America."

John G. Neihardt: "The Lyric Deed."

A. M. Robertson: "The Master Mariner" and "Dirge" by George Sterling, copyright by A. M. Robertson.

Charles Scribner's Sons, New York: "The Widow's Cruise" by Frank R. Stockton; "A Sisterly Scheme" and "Candor" by H. C. Bunner; "Miniver Cheevy," "Richard Cory," and "The Master" by Edwin Arlington Robinson; "Song of the Chattahoochee," "From the Flats," "Barnacles," and "The Stirrup-Cup" by Sidney Lanier; "Little Boy Blue" and "The Limitations of Youth" by Eugene Field; "I Have a Rendezvous with Death" by Alan Seeger; "How to Write Short Stories"

by Ring Lardner; " Lee in Defeat " by Thomas Nelson Page; " Practical
Politics " from Theodore Roosevelt's *Autobiography;* " God of the Open
Air " by Henry Van Dyke.

Edgar Valentine Smith and *Harper's Magazine:* " 'Lijah."

Wilbur Daniel Steele: " *Footfalls.*"

James Stevens: " An American Hercules."

Carl Van Doren: " A Note on the Essay."

The Viking Press, New York: " It's Me, O Lord " from *The Book of
American Negro Spirituals* by James Weldon Johnson, copyright 1925 by
the Viking Press, Inc.

Harr Wagner Publishing Company, San Francisco: " Westward Ho! "
by Joaquin Miller.

William Allen White: " Mary White."

W. A. Wilde Company, Boston: " That Bubble Reputation " from
Penguin Persons and Peppermints by Walter Prichard Eaton, copyright,
W. A. Wilde Company.

The Williams & Wilkins Compay, Baltimore, and Dr. J. Arthur Myers:
" Henry David Thoreau " from *Fighters of Fate* by J. Arthur Myers.

Leah Rachel Yoffie: " The Lost Vision " from *Dark Altar Stairs* by
Leah Rachel Yoffie.

CONTENTS

		PAGE
THE AMERICAN TOUR		3
THE SHORT STORY		9
SHEENER	Ben Ames Williams	20
THE DEVIL AND TOM WALKER	Washington Irving	30
THE MINISTER'S BLACK VEIL	Nathaniel Hawthorne	44
THE TELL-TALE HEART	Edgar Allan Poe	58
THE WIDOW'S CRUISE	Frank R. Stockton	65
AN INGÉNUE OF THE SIERRAS	Bret Harte	79
A STRUGGLE FOR LIFE	Thomas Bailey Aldrich	97
A HORSEMAN IN THE SKY	Ambrose Bierce	108
A SISTERLY SCHEME	Henry Cuyler Bunner	116
A MUNICIPAL REPORT	O. Henry	126
'LIJAH	Edgar Valentine Smith	142
TO BUILD A FIRE	Jack London	159
ENGLAND TO AMERICA	Margaret Prescott Montague	176
FOOTFALLS	Wilbur Daniel Steele	193
THE ESSAY		217
THE CENTURY	Christopher Morley	219
MARY WHITE	William Allen White	223
THE AUTHOR'S ACCOUNT OF HIMSELF	Washington Irving	228
GIFTS	Ralph Waldo Emerson	233
SELECTIONS FROM OTHER ESSAYS	Ralph Waldo Emerson	239
BRUTE NEIGHBORS	Henry David Thoreau	244
VALENTINE VAGARIES	Lafcadio Hearn	253
THE BUBBLE REPUTATION	Walter Prichard Eaton	255
ONCE THERE WAS A FURNACE BOY	Charles Stephen Brooks	263
VERMONT	Dorothy Canfield Fisher	267
A NOTE ON THE ESSAY	Carl Van Doren	276
WALTER REED	Paul de Kruif	278
BIOGRAPHY AND AUTOBIOGRAPHY		297
SCHOOL LIFE	Hamlin Garland	301
PROJECT OF ARRIVING AT MORAL PERFECTION	Benjamin Franklin	308
LEE IN DEFEAT	Thomas Nelson Page	319
PRACTICAL POLITICS	Theodore Roosevelt	325
HENRY DAVID THOREAU	J. Arthur Myers	333

CONTENTS

		PAGE
HAWTHORNE AT COLLEGE . . .	Lloyd Morris	340
HERMAN MELVILLE WRITES "MOBY-DICK"	Lewis Mumford . . .	346

HUMOROUS PROSE 358

HERMIONE	Don Marquis	362
SAYINGS OF POOR RICHARD . . .	Benjamin Franklin . . .	365
IN THE DAYS OF WOUTER VAN TWILLER	Washington Irving . .	368
THE AUTOCRAT OF THE BREAKFAST TABLE	Oliver Wendell Holmes . .	373
A BUSINESS LETTER	Artemus Ward	379
AN UNEXPECTED ACQUAINTANCE .	Mark Twain	382
THE FABLE OF A WONDERFUL MEAL OF VITTLES	George Ade	392
LONG PANTS	Irvin S. Cobb	396
HOW TO WRITE SHORT STORIES . .	Ring Lardner	405
CORRECT BEHAVIOR ON A PICNIC . .	Donald Ogden Stewart . .	409

HISTORIC MILESTONES 413

COLONIZATION		415
HER PRIVATE JOURNAL . . .	Sarah Kemble Knight . .	415
A HISTORY OF THE DIVIDING LINE .	William Byrd	424
A NEW NATION		431
SPEECH IN THE VIRGINIA CONVENTION, 1775	Patrick Henry	431
THE DECLARATION OF INDEPENDENCE	Thomas Jefferson . . .	435
FAREWELL ADDRESS (condensed) .	George Washington . .	438
CIVIL STRIFE		449
FAREWELL AT SPRINGFIELD . .	Abraham Lincoln . . .	449
LETTER TO GENERAL JOSEPH HOOKER	Abraham Lincoln . . .	451
PROCLAMATION FOR NATIONAL FAST DAY	Abraham Lincoln . . .	452
PROCLAMATION FOR THANKSGIVING	Abraham Lincoln . . .	454
GETTYSBURG ADDRESS . . .	Abraham Lincoln . . .	455
SECOND INAUGURAL ADDRESS . .	Abraham Lincoln . . .	457
WORLD WAR		461
THE WAR MESSAGE TO CONGRESS .	Woodrow Wilson . . .	461
A LEAGUE FOR PEACE . . .	Woodrow Wilson . . .	471

                                                              PAGE
WORLD PEACE 475

   THE MONROE DOCTRINE . . .   *James Monroe* 475
   PRESIDENT CLEVELAND AND THE
     VENEZUELA BOUNDARY . . .   *Grover Cleveland* . . . 476
   THE PEACE PACT . . . .   *Frank B. Kellogg* . . . 477

FOLK LITERATURE 479

   AN AMERICAN HERCULES (PAUL
     BUNYAN) . . . . . .   *James Stevens* 481
   THE BANKS OF THE LITTLE EAU
     PLEINE . . . . . .   *(Lumberjack Song)* . . . 490
   THE COWBOY'S DREAM . . .   *(Cowboy Song)* . . . 495
   LEAVE HER, JOHNNY, LEAVE HER .   *(Sailor Chantey)* . . . 498
   NATHAN HALE . . . . .   *(War Ballad)* 500
   THE AWFUL FATE OF MR. WOLF .   *Joel Chandler Harris* . . 503
   IT'S ME, O LORD . . . . .   *(Negro Spiritual)* . . 506

POETRY 510

EARLY NORTHERN POETRY 523

   TO THE MEMORY OF THE BRAVE
     AMERICANS . . . . .   *Philip Freneau* . . . 524
   THE WILD HONEYSUCKLE . .   *Philip Freneau* . . . 525
   THE INDIAN BURYING GROUND . .   *Philip Freneau* . . . 526
   THANATOPSIS . . . . . .   *William Cullen Bryant* . . 528
   TO A WATERFOWL . . . .   *William Cullen Bryant* . . 531
   THE BATTLE-FIELD . . . .   *William Cullen Bryant* . . 533
   THE CONCORD HYMN . . .   *Ralph Waldo Emerson* . . 536
   A FABLE . . . .   *Ralph Waldo Emerson* . . 536
   COMPENSATION . . . . .   *Ralph Waldo Emerson* . . 537
   THE RHODORA . . . . .   *Ralph Waldo Emerson* . . 538
   VOLUNTARIES III . . . .   *Ralph Waldo Emerson* . . 538
   EACH AND ALL . . . . .   *Ralph Waldo Emerson* . . 539
   HYMN TO THE NIGHT . . .   *Henry Wadsworth Longfellow* 542
   MAIDENHOOD . . . . .   *Henry Wadsworth Longfellow* 544
   THE ARSENAL AT SPRINGFIELD .   *Henry Wadsworth Longfellow* 546
   IN THE CHURCHYARD AT TARRYTOWN   *Henry Wadsworth Longfellow* 548
   MY LOST YOUTH . . . .   *Henry Wadsworth Longfellow* 548
   THE BUILDING OF THE SHIP . .   *Henry Wadsworth Longfellow* 551
   THE BELLS OF SAN BLAS . .   *Henry Wadsworth Longfellow* 563
   ICHABOD . . . . . .   *John Greenleaf Whittier* . . 567
   TELLING THE BEES . . . .   *John Greenleaf Whittier* . . 569
   SNOWBOUND . . . . .   *John Greenleaf Whittier* . . 571
   DEAR LORD AND FATHER OF MANKIND   *John Greenleaf Whittier* . . 594
   OLD IRONSIDES . . . . .   *Oliver Wendell Holmes* . . 595
   TO AN INSECT . . . . .   *Oliver Wendell Holmes* . . 596
   THE BOYS . . . . .   *Oliver Wendell Holmes* . . 598
   THE CHAMBERED NAUTILUS . .   *Oliver Wendell Holmes* . . 600

PAGE

CONTENTMENT . . . . . Oliver Wendell Holmes . . 602
THE COURTIN' . . . . . James Russell Lowell . . 606
WHAT MR. ROBINSON THINKS . . James Russell Lowell . . 608
THE VISION OF SIR LAUNFAL . . James Russell Lowell . . 610

EARLY SOUTHERN POETRY 624

TO HELEN . . . . . . Edgar Allan Poe . . . 625
ISRAFEL . . . . . . Edgar Allan Poe . . . 626
ELDORADO . . . . . . Edgar Allan Poe . . . 628
THE RAVEN . . . . . . Edgar Allan Poe . . . 629
ULALUME . . . . . . Edgar Allan Poe . . . 633
CHARLESTON . . . . . . Henry Timrod . . . 637
ODE . . . . Henry Timrod . . . 639
THE MOCKING BIRD . . . . Paul Hamilton Hayne . . 641
ASPECTS OF THE PINES . . . Paul Hamilton Hayne . . 642
SONG OF THE CHATTAHOOCHEE . . Sidney Lanier . . . 645
FROM THE FLATS . . . . Sidney Lanier . . . 647
BARNACLES . . . . . Sidney Lanier . . . 648
THE STIRRUP-CUP . . . . Sidney Lanier . . . 649
THE CONQUERED BANNER . . . Abram J. Ryan . . . 650

THE TRANSITION POETS 652

ONE'S SELF I SING . . . . . Walt Whitman . . . 654
I HEAR AMERICA SINGING . . . Walt Whitman . . . 655
MANNAHATTA . . . . . Walt Whitman . . . 656
BEAT! BEAT! DRUMS! . . . . Walt Whitman . . . 657
THE CAROL OF DEATH . . . . Walt Whitman . . . 658
A NOISELESS PATIENT SPIDER . . Walt Whitman . . . 659
GIVE ME THE SPLENDID SILENT SUN Walt Whitman . . . 660
WHEN I HEARD THE LEARNED AS-
  TRONOMER . . . . . . Walt Whitman . . . 662
MIRACLES . . . . . . Walt Whitman . . . 662
DAREST THOU NOW O SOUL . . Walt Whitman . . . 663
I'M NOBODY . . . . . . Emily Dickinson . . . 664
A WORD . . . . . . Emily Dickinson . . . 665
TO MAKE A PRAIRIE . . . . Emily Dickinson . . . 665
THE LITTLE STONE . . . . Emily Dickinson . . . 665
AN ALTERED LOOK ABOUT THE HILLS Emily Dickinson . . . 665
SOME KEEP THE SABBATH . . . Emily Dickinson . . . 666
I NEVER SAW A MOOR . . . . Emily Dickinson . . . 666
THE SOUL SELECTS HER OWN SOCIETY Emily Dickinson . . . 667
MY LIFE CLOSED TWICE . . . Emily Dickinson . . . 667
WE NEVER KNOW HOW HIGH . . Emily Dickinson . . . 668
MEMORY . . . . . . Thomas Bailey Aldrich . 668
A SNOWFLAKE . . . . . Thomas Bailey Aldrich . 669
THE FOOL'S PRAYER . . . . Edward Rowland Sill . . 670
WESTWARD HO! . . . . . Joaquin Miller . . . 672

PAGE

WHEN THE FROST IS ON THE PUNKIN	*James Whitcomb Riley*	673
LITTLE BOY BLUE	*Eugene Field*	675
THE LIMITATIONS OF YOUTH	*Eugene Field*	676
THE JOYS OF THE ROAD	*Bliss Carman*	678
GREEN FIRE	*Bliss Carman*	681
THE SEA GYPSY	*Richard Hovey*	682
THE WANDER LOVERS	*Richard Hovey*	683

TWENTIETH CENTURY POETRY 687

THE MAN WITH THE HOE	*Edwin Markham*	688
QUATRAINS	*Edwin Markham*	690
OUR ISRAFEL	*Edwin Markham*	691
GOD OF THE OPEN AIR	*Henry van Dyke*	696
MINIVER CHEEVY	*Edwin Arlington Robinson*	701
RICHARD CORY	*Edwin Arlington Robinson*	703
BEWICK FINZER	*Edwin Arlington Robinson*	704
THE MASTER	*Edwin Arlington Robinson*	705
ANNE RUTLEDGE	*Edgar Lee Masters*	709
JOHN HORACE BURLESON	*Edgar Lee Masters*	709
MRS. GEORGE REECE	*Edgar Lee Masters*	710
GEORGE GRAY	*Edgar Lee Masters*	710
JACOB GOODPASTURE	*Edgar Lee Masters*	711
SILENCE	*Edgar Lee Masters*	712
THE MASTER-MARINER	*George Sterling*	714
DIRGE	*George Sterling*	716
THE RUNAWAY	*Cale Young Rice*	716
A LADY	*Amy Lowell*	718
MUSIC	*Amy Lowell*	719
PATTERNS	*Amy Lowell*	719
THE PASTURE	*Robert Frost*	724
BIRCHES	*Robert Frost*	724
STOPPING BY WOODS	*Robert Frost*	727
THE BIRTHPLACE	*Robert Frost*	727
A MINOR BIRD	*Robert Frost*	728
THE DEATH OF THE HIRED MAN	*Robert Frost*	728
CHICAGO	*Carl Sandburg*	735
BUTTONS	*Carl Sandburg*	736
GRASS	*Carl Sandburg*	737
A FENCE	*Carl Sandburg*	737
CHILD OF THE ROMANS	*Carl Sandburg*	738
CLEAN CURTAINS	*Carl Sandburg*	739
IN A BACK ALLEY	*Carl Sandburg*	739
A COIN	*Carl Sandburg*	740
FATE	*Carl Sandburg*	740
WIND SONG	*Carl Sandburg*	741
NIGHT STUFF	*Carl Sandburg*	741
PRAYERS OF STEEL	*Carl Sandburg*	742
GOOD MORNING, AMERICA (EXTRACT)	*Carl Sandburg*	742

		PAGE
THE SANTA FE TRAIL	Vachel Lindsay	745
LET ME LIVE OUT MY YEARS	John G. Neihardt	751
THE LYRIC DEED	John G. Neihardt	752
THE COIN	Sara Teasdale	753
I SHALL NOT CARE	Sara Teasdale	753
NIGHT SONG AT AMALFI	Sara Teasdale	754
THE LONG HILL	Sara Teasdale	754
TO A TELEGRAPH POLE	Louis Untermeyer	755
LONG FEUD	Louis Untermeyer	756
THE STONE'S HYMN	Louis Untermeyer	757
PRAYER	Louis Untermeyer	757
THE MOUNTAIN WOMAN	Dubose Heyward	759
SEA LULLABY	Elinor Wylie	760
ESCAPE	Elinor Wylie	761
NONSENSE RHYME	Elinor Wylie	762
I HAVE A RENDEZVOUS WITH DEATH	Alan Seeger	763
PALMETTO TOWN	Hervey Allen	764
TO A POST OFFICE INKWELL	Christopher Morley	765
LAMENT	Edna St. Vincent Millay	766
THE SPRING AND THE FALL	Edna St. Vincent Millay	767
DIRGE WITHOUT MUSIC	Edna St. Vincent Millay	768
IN THE ESPLANADE DES INVALIDES	George O'Neil	769
THE LOST VISION	Leah Rachel Yoffie	770
THE DEATH OF STONEWALL JACKSON	Stephen Vincent Benét	771
THE READING BOY	Nathalia Crane	775

HUMOROUS POETRY		777
THE HEIGHT OF THE RIDICULOUS	Oliver Wendell Holmes	778
PLAIN LANGUAGE FROM TRUTHFUL JAMES	Bret Harte	779
THE AHKOOND OF SWAT	George T. Lanigan	781
CANDOR	H. C. Bunner	782
HOW THE FEUD STARTED	Arthur Guiterman	783
REAL BASEBALL	Arthur Guiterman	784
TWO 'MERICANA MEN	Thomas A. Daly	785
THE SAME OLD STORY	James J. Montague	786
IT HAPPENS, OFTEN	Edwin Meade Robinson	787
THE BALLAD OF TWO LAME MEN	Franklin P. Adams	788
THOSE TWO BOYS	Franklin P. Adams	789
THE DURABLE BON MOT	Keith Preston	789
ANY ONE WILL DO	Anonymous	790
THE HUMORIST	Keith Preston	791
AMERICAN LIMERICKS		791

DRAMA		794
THE TRYSTING PLACE	Booth Tarkington	807
WHERE THE CROSS IS MADE	Eugene O'Neill	831
NATHAN HALE	Clyde Fitch	850

PAGE

HISTORY OF AMERICAN LITERATURE: A REVIEW AND RE-
INTERPRETATION 915

   I. COLONIAL AND REVOLUTIONARY LITERATURE 917
   II. THE BEGINNINGS OF AMERICAN LITERARY PRESTIGE 928
   III. TRANSCENDENTALISM IN THE EARLY NINETEENTH CENTURY . . 940
   IV. THE LITERATURE OF CULTURE AND SCHOLARSHIP 950
   V. AMERICAN LITERATURE AND THE CIVIL WAR 962
   VI. WALT WHITMAN AND EMILY DICKINSON — INDIVIDUALISTS . 973
   VII. THE WESTERN FRONTIER MOVEMENT 980
   VIII. THE BEGINNINGS OF REALISM 997
   IX. THE AMERICAN NOVEL OF THE TWENTIETH CENTURY . . 1008
   X. THE TWENTIETH-CENTURY SHORT STORY 1020
   XI. TWENTIETH-CENTURY POETRY 1032
   XII. OTHER TWENTIETH-CENTURY LITERATURE 1044

NOVELS FOR HOME READING 1054

REFERENCE BOOKS ON AMERICAN LITERATURE 1056

DICTIONARY OF WORDS, NAMES, AND PHRASES 1059

INDEX 1077

PREFACE

Adventures in American Literature is the second book in a series of literature anthologies for the three years of the senior high school. Although this volume is intended for the tenth or eleventh grade, it may be used in the twelfth grade if the course of study calls for such an arrangement.

That the boys and girls of America should know the literature of America needs no defense. But just how that literature can best be presented to them requires careful consideration. Too often American literature has been regarded as an insipid dose in comparison with the more savory swallow of English literature. Such a wrong impression has been largely created by a selection and arrangement of material inadequate to the secondary school situation. Many collections used in high schools are better suited to college students; others have insufficient emphasis upon those twentieth century writings through which a national American literature is rapidly coming into its own.

The traditional conception and organization of American literature is breaking down. A recent volume, *The Reinterpretation of American Literature,* edited by Professor Norman Foerster, presents essays by nine members of a special committee of the Modern Language Association. These point out the newer conceptions of American Literature which should be considered in any presentation. The editors of *Adventures in American Literature* have attempted a reinterpretation of our national literature in accordance with the ideas advanced by these specialists, but adapted to the interests and understanding of high school students. The editors endeavor in this book to provide boys and girls with an experience in literature vital and satisfying in itself and at the same time give them a picture and interpretation of American life. To these ends they have followed certain principles and introduced certain innovations:

1. The selections are arranged by literary types rather than by a single chronology. This gives a natural approach to reading,

affords a good basis for comparison and discussion, readily lends itself to a unit plan of study, and avoids that lack of direction which is so often evident when all types are intermingled.

2. Because young students are more readily attracted to modern writings than to those of an earlier period, each of the types is introduced by one or two modern selections of immediate appeal. Then, with interest aroused, attention is turned to the beginnings of the type in this country and the arrangement becomes strictly chronological, to develop in the pupil a time sense along with enjoyment of the writings themselves.

3. The arrangement by types of literature brings out important elements of our national literature hitherto partially or entirely neglected in high school texts. The most notable innovations are the two sections, Humorous Prose and Folk Lore, each of which shows an exclusively American flavor and makes a strong appeal to the adolescent mind. Biography and Drama, well represented here, have been hitherto treated meagerly, if at all. The section called Historic Milestones gives proper perspective to some of the most significant of the colonial writings and great state papers.

4. In each section, a careful balance has been maintained between the old and the new, the easy and the difficult, and the literature produced by different sections of our country. But in all this wide range of material great care has been taken not to include writings of any but the most noteworthy authors. Four anonymous selections and a few selections by young but promising authors are the only exceptions. Since it was the policy of the editors not to include chapters from novels, outstanding authors who are exclusively novelists could not be directly represented, but have been discussed at length in the literary history at the end of the book, and introduced through the reading lists. Several other authors high in favor with literary critics have been omitted because of too great maturity of style or inappropriateness of subject matter. With these exceptions, the list of eighty-odd writers forms a pretty complete roll-call of the names which have made and are making American literature.

5. There are practically no cut texts. Selections appear in their entirety in the Short Story, Drama, Essay, and Folk Lore sections. Except for a mere half dozen, the poems are printed in their entirety. Chapters, complete in themselves, taken from longer works are used in the Biography and Humorous Prose sections. The only serious cuttings are in the Historic Milestones section

where the nature of the material demands the editorial blue pencil for more effective presentation. Omissions are always clearly indicated.

6. The editorial material is planned to interest and aid the average high school student in his study. The section introductions and the history at the end are written, it is hoped, with such directness as to make the reading a pleasure rather than a task. Some teachers may prefer to have the students read the introductions after part or all of the selections in a group have been discussed, but if read first, the introductions will be found to furnish the context for intelligent interpretation of the selections. The biographical material in the various introductions and the literary history aims either to vivify the author as a person or to explain how he came to write as he did. Details not conducive to either of these purposes have been judiciously omitted and, further, the style is conversational rather than encyclopedic. The suggestions for study following individual selections tend to arouse thoughtful discussion and to suggest topics for themes rather than to test comprehension of the mere facts. The reading and reference lists serve to enrich the course by stimulating individual browsing or providing assignments for the more ambitious students.

Objective tests to determine comprehension and mastery of the selections are available in a separate pad. These employ the various new testing devices — true-false, matching, multiple choice, and completion — in such a way as to test both facts and interpretation, and to enable rapid correction by a key. The advantages of having these tests on detachable sheets in a separate pad are several. First, the tests save an immense amount of time because they eliminate much copying and demand exact answers instead of vague generalities. Second, they enable the teacher to tell which pupils have prepared their assignments properly. Third, they indicate which points in an assignment require class discussion and further enlightenment by the teacher. Fourth, the tests may be used as guides by the pupils in their preparation of assignments.

7. The completeness of the editorial material throughout the sections and the history of American literature at the end of the book make unnecessary any separate literary history text. This running comment along with the readings, rounded out at the end by the unifying story of the development of our literature, will give the student a more valuable conception and direct experience

of American literature than could be obtained by a separate anthology and history planned without relation to each other.

It is the hope of the editors that the boys and girls who read this book will regard it not merely as a textbook in a certain English course, but also as a prized " memory book " of high school days, a pleasant beckoner to the library, and a promoter of many later adventures in American literature.

H. C. S.

R. B. I.

J. G.

ADVENTURES IN
AMERICAN LITERATURE

The American Tour

" I want to know! " These four simple words expressing the curiosity of mankind have led the way from the cave to the skyscraper of modern civilization. Upon them America is founded; for Christopher Columbus discovered America because he " wanted to know " what lay across the deep water from the shores of Spain. Curiosity drove Hendrik Hudson up the great river which now bears his name — where was the northwest passage to the Indies? Curiosity sent Daniel Boone across the wilderness trail — what lay beyond the mountains? Curiosity sent Balboa across savage lands to look out upon the Pacific. To want to know is bred in the blood and bone of America.

How do you satisfy curiosity? Some day perhaps you will travel, but today before you are able to bear the expense or spend the time that is necessary for traveling, how may you begin to see the world? For your answer you turn to the most marvelous of all human inventions, the written word — so potent an invention that without it the world would crumble into savagery in a year. You read. And by reading you travel in a triple sense: you travel over miles that separate you from the place you want to know about; you travel into the minds and hearts of men; and you travel back in history where no train nor ship nor airplane could ever take you.

Before reading a book called *Adventures in American Literature* and embarking on such a strange tour of the United States, it is sensible to find an answer to the riddle of how one can travel and still remain at home. Have you ever noticed at a football game that the people in the bleachers lunge forward with their shoulders when the fullback hits the line? At the back of their minds they are playing football; they have placed themselves in the shoes of the fullback, and vicariously they are having many of the experiences that he is having. It is the same with reading. The reader becomes one with the characters. Their sorrow, terror, joy, or defiance lives again in his mind because of a queer trick of the human mind which melts the reader into the being of the characters. So it is that through another's eyes you may see the snow-covered mountains of Alaska though you never move an inch from your armchair; you may think great thoughts with Abraham Lincoln though his brain is now dust; or you may feel the defiance of Patrick Henry though he died a hundred years before you were born. This book, then, is your ticket for a tour of America which should be nearly as real as a trip on a Pullman train and at the same time is as physically impossible as was Alice's trip through the looking-glass.

In your community there is probably some one who is commonly referred to as a great traveler. " He has been around; you couldn't lose him anywhere," you hear people say. He seems to be on speaking terms with Boston, New Orleans, and the Rockies. He is full of tales and experiences which make him a welcome companion. But your imaginary experiences may become almost as vivid to you as the memory of actual experiences is to the much-traveled person. You too may have mental pictures of the tossing waves of the Atlantic, the rolling prairies of Nebraska, the trim villages of New England, the towering skyscrapers of New York. American literature, like the magic carpet of the Arabian tale, can transport you to any of these places with a speed which shames the railroad train and even the airplane.

Now a great traveler must also be a good traveler. That is, he must be what is commonly termed a " good sport," not complaining if the bed is a bit hard or the cooking not just to his taste. Neither must he be lazy and lie sleeping in the hotel rather than go to the top of the Washington Monument for the view. Especially if he travels with a party must he be a person who is easy to get along with, who submerges some of his personal preferences for the better interests of the group. So you, about to launch out on this tour with the rest of your class, have an opportunity to show that you are a " good sport " and will not whine if an occasional essay is hard or a poem not just to your taste. You will not be too lazy to climb the heights of Washington's *Farewell Address* for a lofty view of our country. Such temporary difficulties are found only occasionally among the many opportunities for satisfying entertainment.

Another characteristic of the good traveler is his ability to read signposts, time-tables, maps, and guidebooks. In the literary tour these are represented by the words of the English language, dictionaries which help you understand them, and the histories which help you to interpret the literature. Through contacts with these signposts you will come to understand increasingly the meanings of words, and to appreciate the skill with which great writers have combined them into sentences to form a style all their own. The extension of your vocabulary will be useful in your everyday life, for it will serve to lift you out of that helpless, inarticulate state in which we so often fall back on the meaningless phrase, " You know what I mean."

On the great tour you are about to undertake, not only will you journey all over our country, but, because you will have the company of experienced travelers, you will also find it possible to enter into the minds and personalities of human beings. With such distinguished guides as Washington Irving, Mark Twain, O. Henry, Jack London, and Edgar Lee Masters, you will see human nature. From New England to the Sierras and in half a dozen nationalities the kinks of the human mind will be exposed. And after you have lived the intense sorrows, the joys, the kindness, and the hilarious wit of other people — even though it is only in a book — you will have become more grown up, more mellowed, and wiser in your judgments. This insight into human nature is another thing that reading gives you.

Along with it comes something a little different but quite as important. Probably you have talked to people who have visited faraway places, and who remember only that they stopped at such-and-such a hotel or left by such-and-such a station. Like their baggage, all they have gained by the trip is a paper sticker which proves they have traveled. But when you see life through the eyes of Hawthorne or Emerson, or hear about it in the verses of poets, you receive help in forming ideals which strengthen your character and make you a more worth-while person. Perhaps you will never again let yourself be so petty, or so childish, or so stupidly silly, or so selfish, or so prejudiced as you have been before.

Through acquaintance with our great poets you will also learn the hidden spiritual beauty of many seemingly commonplace objects. A birch tree, a wild duck, even so small a thing as a spider, will become more significant through a better understanding of it as the handi-work of God; even the slums of our cities, receiving the magic touch of a poet's imagination, become eloquent with spiritual truth. After your trip you will look upon the familiar life around you with new eyes and a realization that nothing is humdrum or commonplace to one who has learned to know the truth and beauty which permeate the universe and glorify all its parts.

Moreover, you will find through your reading a new outlet for emotions. Especially in poetry are places where the genius of a singer has turned into crystalline words an emotion you have felt but never expressed. You will pause to say, " That is just the way I often feel. How perfectly he expresses *my* emotions. I must try to remember his exact words."

Finally, the tour outlined in this book will take you back among the scenes and people of the past. In 1704 a cultivated New Eng-land lady, Sarah Kemble Knight, rides horseback south from Boston through the bright leaves of October. It takes her two weeks to travel 180 miles. As she rides, she has such keen perception for the commonplace or the startling details of her trip that through her eyes you see colonial New England as it was before any one had thought of the United States. A little more than twenty years later, Colonel Byrd penetrates the unsurveyed swamps of Virginia and North Carolina, doubtless impelled among other reasons by the same curiosity which sent his illustrious descendant, Commander Richard Byrd, to the south pole by airplane. By his campfire, after a dinner of wild turkey, Colonel Byrd writes with a deft pen about the adventures of his day. In reading the records left behind by these earlier writers, you are learning something no modern tour could teach you. You are seeing the past not only through eyes which watched the events of yesterday, but through minds which had a part in building the foundations of our country, and this ability to see the past as if it were the present is one of the important things you will gain from reading American lit-erature.

What more should you expect to gain from the tour as a whole? You will gain an understanding of the American heritage. The stream of our national literature which starts from New England and Virginia will widen out for you; you will see how as time passed American authors came to reflect the struggle for independence and to express the ambitions, the ideals, and the emotions of a new and great nation. When you have completed this year's tour through the inexhaustible attractions of our literature you will have found a deeper reason for the love of country which is called patriotism; and, as a loyal American, you will wish to continue such traveling throughout your whole life.

SOME EARLIER EXCURSIONS RECALLED

On this tour of American literature which you and your companions have undertaken, doubtless there will be some places to which you will wish to make excursions of your own, just as there will be places where you will wish to linger longer than the whole party. Still other spots will need to be noted down for future visits when their attractions will make more appeal to your interest than they do now. For the side trips this book — as a guidebook — now and then will make definite suggestions based on the experiences of those who have traveled this way before.

But before we start we should consider some of the interesting places we shall have to omit from this trip because most of our party have visited there before. You will wish at the end of this tour to have seen all the interesting places along the route and because of this you should check up on your previous travels. If you have missed important spots that are universally visited, plan to slip them in as side trips in the regular tour. Here is a list of such places. Perhaps you can tell of other interesting American books with which you have already made friends. Great literature, you must remember, has a universal appeal, and many of the books commonly read by children were not written for them at all; likewise, books written for children are often enjoyed by grown-ups.

Alcott, Louisa May. *Little Women.*
    In spite of the name not a girls' book, but one which relates adventures of young people in a way which interests boys as well as girls.
Aldrich, Thomas Bailey. *The Story of a Bad Boy.*
    An interesting true story of a not-so-bad-after-all boy in a New England village. The snow fight is a classic.
Cooper, James Fenimore. *The Last of the Mohicans.*
    Cooper wrote rattling good adventure stories which have lived a hundred years. You may prefer to read *The Deerslayer* or *The Spy.*
Clemens, Samuel Langhorne (Mark Twain). *Tom Sawyer. Huckleberry Finn.*
    Immortal boys who play pranks, scout along the Mississippi, discover a murder, unearth treasures, fall in love, and get lost in caves. " A laugh a minute."

Eggleston, Edward. *The Hoosier Schoolmaster.*

The exciting adventures of a young schoolmaster who " boarded 'round " in the early pioneer days of Indiana and had to match wits with the community " toughs."

Hale, Edward Everett. *The Man Without a Country.*

An American soldier curses his country and pays a strange penalty. The story is so well told that many still believe it really happened.

Harris, Joel Chandler. *Uncle Remus: His Songs and Sayings.*

The first of several " Uncle Remus " collections of the inimitable Negro folk tales about Br'er Rabbit, Br'er Wolf, Br'er Fox, and the others.

Hawthorne, Nathaniel. *The Great Stone Face.*

Which man among many candidates will turn out to resemble the noble stone face in the mountains? Hawthorne defines for us true beauty of character.

Irving, Washington. *The Legend of Sleepy Hollow. Rip Van Winkle.*

Two of our oldest and best American yarns. Everybody knows them.

London, Jack. *The Call of the Wild.*

A thrilling tale of Alaska and the Eskimo dog.

Longfellow, Henry Wadsworth. *The Song of Hiawatha. The Courtship of Miles Standish. Evangeline.*

Legends of the Indian, the Puritan, and the Acadian. A unique group of long poems which " every child should know."

Poe, Edgar Allan. *The Gold Bug.*

One of our very first " detective " stories, and certainly the most famous.

Stowe, Harriet Beecher. *Uncle Tom's Cabin.*

This vivid though somewhat distorted picture of slavery helped to bring about the Civil War. Uncle Tom, Little Eva, Topsy, and Simon Legree have become a part of the American tradition.

The Short Story

THE DEVELOPMENT OF THE SHORT STORY IN AMERICA

We all read short stories. Magazines, newspapers, books, printed in literally millions of copies every month, regularly supply our demand for satisfactory short fiction. And in America today the short story is overwhelmingly the most popular form of current literature.

Perhaps it is our manner of living that insistently demands that our fiction be short. Telegraph, radio, telephone, and automobile all bow at the altar of speed. We live at the double-quick. And literature shares its place in the favor of the crowd with a dozen amusements undreamed of a hundred years ago. The time for leisurely reading of three- to ten-volume novels appears to have passed with the horse and buggy and the " pony express "; the American fiction reader demands a literary form which suits his moods and habits. Long introductions, leisurely discourses on philosophy, become the special joy of the extraordinary reader, while the crowd chooses the short story. Small wonder, then, that we find many of the brilliant writers of the age turning their talents to the short story. Writers wish to be read; while they may refuse to speak the language of the crowd, at least they write in the form the crowd is most eager to read.

America Develops Short Story to Highest Form

When we have realized that the short story is the literary form best adapted to the American mode of life, it is not at all remarkable that this form has reached its highest development in America. Practice makes the master. It is, however, somewhat surprising to learn that the short story first appeared in America long before the tone of American life seemed to demand its brevity. The short story is America's great contribution to the literary forms of the world. Stories that were short there had been before, some in verse and some in prose, in the old folk legends, in the tales of saints, in Aesop's fables, Bible stories, the *Thousand and One Nights* stories of Arabia, Boccaccio's *Decameron,* and others, but the modern short story first appeared in the United States.

Washington Irving — The First American Short Story Writer

The first American short story is Washington Irving's " Rip Van Winkle," published in 1819. The characteristics of this story, differing so little from those of the story you may read in your latest magazine, demonstrate that during its hundred years of life the short story has never been other than modern in form. One could not think of calling Irving's " Legend of Sleepy Hollow " a museum piece of literature, and the delightful Moorish legends of *The Alhambra* remain as readable today as they were when Irving first published them. Writing at the same time that Scott in England and Cooper in America were feeding exciting romances of the past to an eager public, Irving followed suit with his shorter tales of sentiment and adventure, and earned for himself the title: " Father of the American short story." Irving does not write to teach a lesson, but merely to entertain. Originality, a distinctive prose style, a pervading humor, and a sure sense of romantic entertainment — these are the qualities that have made Irving's stories live for a century. And the reader who is to get the greatest enjoyment from Irving must appreciate especially the unsurpassed mastery of beautiful prose which this first American short story writer learned from the great English stylists of the eighteenth century.

Irving, pioneer in a new form, was followed by two of the greatest of American masters of this new form, Nathaniel Hawthorne and Edgar Allan Poe. These three, Irving, Hawthorne, and Poe, are the only great American short story writers before 1850.

Hawthorne and the New England Influence

To understand Hawthorne necessitates knowing something of the New England of Hawthorne's day. The austere tradition of the

Puritan frowned upon fiction of any sort, novel or short story; theaters were considered places of evil, and the violin an instrument of the devil. Probably because he had this background Hawthorne offered in his stories a deep spiritual insight, and a concern with the moral significance of life that is lacking in the stories of Irving. The good influence of such stories as " The Great Stone Face " was so apparent that it silenced the objections of the Puritan to " made-up " stories which had been considered something of " the world, the flesh, and the devil." Remember this when Hawthorne is pointing the moral of his story; recall that had he not written in this manner his masterpieces would probably have died with him, and his skilful style lost. Remember also that nearly always the moral he points is a truth worth knowing.

Poe Defines the Short Story

When in 1842 Hawthorne published eighteen of his stories in a volume under the title of *Twice-Told Tales,* a young Virginian, Edgar Allan Poe, reviewed the book in what is probably the most important bit of writing in the history of the short story as a literary form. Poe recognized Hawthorne's genius, and tried to define just how the short story should be written. The skilful literary artist, Poe said, does not " fashion his thoughts to accommodate his incidents," but deliberately conceives " a certain unique or single effect to be wrought out " and " then combines such incidents as may best aid him in establishing this preconceived effect." This emphasis upon a single effect, generally accepted through its entire life as the very essence of the short story form, has not

EDGAR ALLAN POE

only made the short story what it is but has kept it intact as a form throughout the years. This one piece of critical writing, as much as his later writing in which he followed out his own principles so com-

pletely, won for Poe the somewhat undeserved title, " the creator of
the short story." Hawthorne and Irving wrote the first American
short stories.

The Far-reaching Effects of Poe's Criticism and Tales

Having seen what was the essence of the short story, Poe in his
own stories consciously undertook the task of making them perfect
in the new form.   Scorning the moral lessons of Hawthorne, Poe
was a believer in " art for art's sake "; to him the story was an
end in itself, requiring no justification further than its own art.   He
took the greatest pains to produce the single effect he had decided
upon, be it horror, terror, or mystery, and whether or not his writing added to the spiritual or moral fiber of his reader did not concern
him.   When you have finished a story by Poe, it is enough if you
are able to say, " That story made the shivers run up and down my
spine," or " I have never read anything so horrible."   To Poe that
meant success.   For many years the American public was unable to
understand or appreciate Poe; but European critics, not under the
influence of the American Puritan heritage, accepted him as a master
at once, and immediately began to imitate him.

Poe's coldly analytical mind created the detective story — not the
crime story, but the story that starts with the crime accomplished
and interests the reader in the processes of thought by which the
detective solves the mystery.   " Tales of ratiocination " Poe called
his stories of this type.   " The Purloined Letter " and " The Gold
Bug " are the most famous.   In these stories Poe again demonstrates
clearly that his attitude toward his material is scientific, analytic,
coldly and deliberately intellectual.

Minor Writers Following Poe

The twenty years which followed the death of Poe failed to produce an American short story writer outstanding enough to be placed
beside the three masters just discussed.   Fitz-James O'Brien (1828–
1862) just missed greatness in his contributions to *Harper's Magazine*.   Herman Melville (1819–1890) is now considered a genius of
the longer story because of such books as *Typee* and *Moby-Dick*,
but his short tales are not well known.   Rose Terry Cooke (1827–
1892) contributed stories, portraying New England life with veracity
and a gentle humor, to the *Atlantic Monthly* during the period; and
Edward Everett Hale (1822–1909) had one flash of greatness in his

famous story " The Man Without a Country," which appeared in the *Atlantic Monthly*. But all of these writers fell short of the earlier masters, and the fourth great name in the history of the short story comes from the far West.

Bret Harte Introduces " Local Color "

In 1870 a new landmark was fixed when Bret Harte (1836–1902) published his volume, *The Luck of Roaring Camp and Other Sketches*. (Francis) Bret Harte immediately took the center of the literary stage in America despite the obvious defects of some of his stories, the worst of which is a melodramatic lack of sincerity. The tremendous interest in great fortunes which were being made overnight in the California gold fields had made the public eager to know more of the pioneers of " forty-nine." Harte struck while the iron was hot, and he turned a corner in the history of the American short story.

His success was due to the use of " local color " as the background of his tales, and his success found many imitators. George Washington Cable (1844–1925) portrayed the old Creole days of New Orleans; Sarah Orne Jewett (1849–1905) recorded the romance of

BRET HARTE

the commonplace in New England life; Thomas Nelson Page (1853–1922) turned back to the aristocracy of ante-bellum days in old Virginia. Like Bret Harte, these writers overplayed the romance and sentiment of their local color. They are not to be confused with the later writers who have presented local color in the terms of strict adherence to actual conditions which we call realism.

Bret Harte and Mark Twain Inject Western Humor

Besides establishing the localized romance, Harte introduced into the short story a new western humor which greatly aided in making him popular. For years his name was coupled with that of his contemporary, Samuel Langhorne Clemens, "Mark Twain" (1835–1910). In 1867 Mark Twain, with the publication of *The Celebrated Jumping Frog of Calaveras County, and Other Sketches,* had started on the career which was to lead him to the place of the greatest of American humorists. Although much of this humor is to be found in Bret Harte's tales, it is principally because he originated the local color story in America that Harte stands with Irving, Hawthorne, and Poe.

WASHINGTON IRVING

Vivid and vigorous as was the humor of Mark Twain and Bret Harte, it was often crude and lacking in restraint, and it remained for another group of eastern writers to keep alive the subtlety of Irving. Thomas Bailey Aldrich (1836–1907), Frank Richard Stockton (1834–1902), and Henry Cuyler Bunner (1855–1896) were the contemporaries of Harte and Mark Twain who carried on the eastern tradition, and added to it in their own manner.

Aldrich Contributes the Surprise Ending

Aldrich was a disciple of Poe in that to him the manner in which the story was told seemed more important than the matter. To Poe's art he added a wholesomeness and a whimsical wit that make his work more pleasant than that of his master. The influence of Poe's art, rejected by America, had traveled to France, and it was from France that the principles of Poe came back to Aldrich, softened and made graceful with the refined touch of the French artist. Aldrich's peculiar contribution to the development of the short story form is the surprise ending. His most famous piece of writing, "Marjorie Daw," appeared in 1873, and caused a stir in American literary circles and a revival of interest in the short story form.

in the development of the American short story. In his style is found a summing up of all the American short story had seen before — Poe's art and craftsmanship, Bret Harte's local color, Mark Twain's robust humor, Aldrich's discriminating wit and surprise endings, and Jack London's zest in life. And nothing has so established the fact of his genius as the failure of his numerous imitators to analyze his style or match him.

Contemporary Masters of the Short Story

Since O. Henry the history of the American short story has been so complicated that it is impossible to try to relate it here. All the student of the form can do is to select from the flood of writing and form his opinions for himself. With this in mind we have chosen representative stories from current writers whose excellence is acknowledged. While many will be disposed to add others to the list, no one will be found to deny the art of Margaret Prescott Montague, Edgar Valentine Smith, Ben Ames Williams, and Wilbur Daniel Steele.

THE SHORT STORY AS A LITERARY FORM

What makes a good modern short story? What are the characteristics of the literary form of the short story at its best? We have traced the short story's history and attempted to show the contributions made in bringing it to its present form; without being too technical, let us see what the elements of short story excellence are.

A Successful Short Story Achieves Its Purpose

In attempting to criticize the work of any writer it is always wise to consider just what his motive in writing has been. By considering what he set out to do you will, in the end, be able to form some judgment as to how well he succeeded in the task he set himself. As a consequence you will be able to form an opinion of him that will not be colored by your own likes and dislikes.

Many modern writers attempt to portray life as it is, truthfully. They are called realists, and their work is to be judged by its picture of reality. A second group, called idealists, are endeavoring to improve life by portraying heroic characters who will inspire the reader to higher living. Such stories are to be judged by their moral effect on the character of the reader, and not by the standards of reality. Still a third group of writers are what we call romanticists, or romancers. Interested neither in portraying life as it is, nor in teaching any moral lesson, they are content to entertain the reader with as good a story as they can invent. Such writers are to be criticized when they fail to entertain. Remember that the motive of the writer is his own affair, whether you like it or dislike it, and that you should never condemn a story for failing to be something which its author never intended it to be. A story is a good story if it achieves the purpose for which it was written.

Plot, Characters, and Setting Defined

A second consideration in our appreciation of a short story involves the three different types of material which go to make it up: setting, characters, and plot. Excellence in any of these types of material may earn an author greatness. He may offer you a true picture of a definite locality at a definite time. He may show keen insight into human emotions by the reality with which he creates his characters. Or he may be a master of plot action and its intricate possibilities of suspense or intensity.

Plot is perhaps the most iron-clad of the requirements of the short story, for without plot the short story wanders and becomes only a narration, a tale. The essential meaning of plot is that two or more forces are opposed to each other, and that the story depicts the struggle between these forces. The two forces may be physical (or material), or they may be mental (or spiritual). Many of our best stories are purely psychological; that is, the action takes place in the minds of the characters, sometimes both forces in the struggle being within the mind of a single character. But whether the struggle is physical or mental, the reader is interested in the outcome, and when the struggle is over, the story ends.

To write perfectly the author should be a master in handling all those materials and in blending them perfectly, but perfection is rare, and often we are willing to bow to the writer who can handle one or two of them with great art.

A Short Story Must Strive for a Single Effect on the Reader

Poe declared that the short story must have one quality above all else: a single emotional effect. By this Poe meant that a single impression must be left on the reader's mind; that from start to finish of the story nothing should be included that did not contribute to produce this effect; that the writer must never digress; that he must never confuse the reader by talking too much. It was Poe's ideal that, after reading a story, the reader must be able to say, " How horrible," or " How completely sad." And Poe was rigid in following his ideal, just as many of the writers who have followed him have been rigid in demanding a single effect. In the main his ideal of effect continues to be an essential quality of the short story; but later authors have seen fit to be less rigid in their demands. Without departing from the ideal of compactness, they have sacrificed some of the atmosphere that characterized Poe, and have placed more emphasis on plot. It is enough that the reader can say after reading their stories: " Hon-

POE'S COTTAGE IN NEW YORK CITY

esty is certainly the best policy," or " Gypsies are strange rogues." Poe insisted on a single emotional impression; later writers are content with a single intellectual impression.

But even the modern more liberal interpretation of unity of impression does not permit the " padding " which spoils so many of the stories in our current magazines. Unfortunately, modern magazine publishers often demand that stories must be unduly lengthened in order to be continued among the advertisements, from which the real income of the magazines is derived. Consequently many of our modern stories are spoilt by rambling digressions, " talkiness," and a confusion of impressions. A good story keeps to its single point.

The Importance of Style and Originality in the Short Story

Like all great literature a good short story has style and originality. The writer must have a distinctive touch of his own in order to achieve greatness. Even though you cannot explain precisely what causes your feeling, you should be able to recognize the writing of a great writer without troubling to glance at the title page; for style distinguishes a story just as personality distinguishes an individual. Novelty or originality is another mark of the truly great writer. He is offering you new incidents, and a different struggle, not the same old happenings and plot with the characters re-named or the color of their skin changed.

SHEENER [1]

By BEN AMES WILLIAMS (1889–   )

The stories of Ben Ames Williams are frankly journa'
and subject matter. In " Sheener " the setting is a nev
the main character being a slangy Jewish newsboy, and t
character of importance the " second assistant janitor." 7
and the realistic dialogue are thoroughly characteristic of
tury news-writing. At the same time, Mr. Williams usual
yarn, and " Sheener " is his finest. The story might ea
spoiled by making it " pretty " and ending it in the sentim
one often finds in stories written for modern magaz
" Sheener " gives the impression of having been taken from
the living New York of the present day.

When he was sober the man always insisted that
Evans, but in his cups he was accustomed to declare
fashion, that his name was not Evans at all. How
went farther than this, and since none of us wer_
interested, we were satisfied to call him Evans, or, more often,
Bum, for short. He was the second assistant janitor; and
whereas, in some establishments, a janitor is a man of power and
place, it is not so in a newspaper office. In such institutions,
where great men are spoken of irreverently and by their first
names, a janitor is a man of no importance. How much less, then,
his second assistant. It was never a part of Evans's work, for
example, to sweep the floors. There is something lordly in the

[1] Taken by permission from Ben Ames Williams' *Thrifty Stock*, published
and copyright by E. P. Dutton & Co., Inc., New York.

gesture of the broom. But the janitor's first assistant attended to
that; and Evans's regular duties were more humble, not uncon-
nected with such things as cuspidors. There was no man so poor
to do him honor; yet he had always a certain loftiness of bearing.
He was tall, rather above the average height, with a long, thin,
bony face like a horse, and an aristocratic stoop about his neck
and shoulders. His hands were slender; he walked in a fashion
that you might have called a shuffle, but which might also have
been characterized as a walk of indolent assurance. His eyes were
wash-blue, and his straggling mustache drooped at the corners.

Sober, he was a silent man, but when he had drunk he was
apt to become mysteriously loquacious. And he drank whenever
the state of his credit permitted. At such times he spoke of his
antecedents in a lordly and condescending fashion which we found
amusing. " You call me Evans," he would say. " That does well
enough, to be sure. Quite so, and all that. Evans! Hah! "

And then he would laugh, in a barking fashion that with his
long, bony countenance always suggested to me a coughing horse.
But when he was pressed for details, the man — though he might
be weaving and blinking with liquor — put a seal upon his lips.
He said there were certain families in one of the Midland Counties
of England who would welcome him home if he chose to go; but
he never named them, and he never chose to go, and we put him
down for a liar by the book. All of us except Sheener.

Sheener was a Jewish newsboy; that is to say, a representative
of the only thoroughbred people in the world. I have known
Sheener for a good many years, and he is worth knowing; also,
the true tale of his life might have inspired Scheherazade.[2] A book
must be made of Sheener some day. For the present, it is enough
to say that he had the enterprise which adversity has taught his
people; he had the humility which they have learned by enduring
insults they were powerless to resent, and he had the courage and
the heart which were his ancient heritage. And — the man Evans
had captured and enslaved his imagination.

He believed in Evans from the beginning. This may have been
through a native credulity which failed to manifest itself in his
other dealings with the world. I think it more probable that
Evans and his pretensions appealed to the love of romance native
to Sheener. I think he enjoyed believing, as we enjoy lending our-

---

[2] **Scheherazade:** the Sultan's bride who related the stories of the *Arabian
Nights.*

selves to the illusion of the theater. Whatever the explanation, a certain alliance developed between the two; a something like friendship. I was one of those who laughed at Sheener's credulity, but he told me, in his energetic fashion, that I was making a mistake.

"You got that guy wrong," he would say. "He ain't always been a bum. A guy with half an eye can see that. The way he talks, and the way he walks, and all. There's class to him, I'm telling you. Class, bo."

"He walks like a splay-footed walrus, and he talks like a drunken old hound," I told Sheener. "He's got you buffaloed, that's all."

"Pull in your horns; you're coming to a bridge," Sheener warned me. "Don't be a goat all your life. He's a gent; that's what this guy is."

"Then I'm glad I'm a roughneck," I retorted; and Sheener shook his head.

"That's all right," he exclaimed. "That's all right. He ain't had it easy, you know. Scrubbing spittoons is enough to take the polish off any guy. I'm telling you he's there. Forty ways. You'll see, bo. You'll see."

"I'm waiting," I said.

"Keep right on," Sheener advised me. "Keep right on. The old stuff is there. It'll show. Take it from me."

I laughed at him. "If I get you," I said, "you're looking for something along the line of *noblesse oblige*.[3] What?"

"Cut the comedy," he retorted. "I'm telling you, the old class is there. You can't keep a fast horse in a poor man's stable."

"Blood will tell, eh?"

"Take it from me," said Sheener.

It will be perceived that Evans had in Sheener not only a disciple; he had an advocate and a defender. And Sheener in these rôles was not to be despised. I have said he was a newsboy; to put it more accurately, he was in his early twenties, with forty years of experience behind him, and with half the newsboys of the city obeying his commands and worshipping him like a minor god. He had full charge of our city circulation and was quite as important, and twice as valuable to the paper, as any news editor could hope to be. In making a friend of him, Evans had found an ally in the

[3] **noblesse oblige:** a French phrase signifying that nobleness of conduct is expected from those who are well born.

high places; and it became speedily apparent that Sheener proposed to be more than a mere friend in name. For instance, I learned one day that he was drawing Evans's wages for him, and had appointed himself in some sort a steward for the other.

"That guy wouldn't ever save a cent," he told me when I questioned him. "I give him enough to get soused on, and I stick five dollars in the bank for him every week. I made him buy a new suit of clothes with it last week. Say, you wouldn't know him if you run into him in his glad rags."

"How does he like your running his affairs?" I asked.

"Like it?" Sheener echoed. "He don't have to like it. If he tries to pull anything on me, I'll poke the old coot in the eye."

I doubt whether this was actually his method of dominating Evans. It is more likely that he used a diplomacy which occasionally appeared in his dealings with the world. Certainly the arrangement presently collapsed, for Sheener confessed to me that he had given his savings back to Evans. We were minus a second assistant janitor for a week as a consequence, and when Evans tottered back to the office and would have gone to work I told him he was through.

He took it meekly enough, but not Sheener. Sheener came to me with fire in his eye.

"Sa-a-ay," he demanded, "what's coming off here, anyhow? What do you think you're trying to pull?"

I asked him what he was talking about, and he said: "Evans says you've given him the hook."

"That's right," I admitted. "He's through."

"He is not," Sheener told me flatly. "You can't fire that guy."

"Why not?"

"He's got to live, ain't he?"

I answered, somewhat glibly, that I did not see the necessity, but the look that sprang at once into Sheener's eyes made me faintly ashamed of myself, and I went on to urge that Evans was failing to do his work and could deserve no consideration.

"That's all right," Sheener told me. "I didn't hear any kicks that his work wasn't done while he was on this bat."

"Oh, I guess it got done all right. Some one had to do it. We can't pay him for work that someone else does."

"Say, don't try to pull that stuff," Sheener protested. "As long as his work is done, you ain't got any kick. This guy has got to have a job, or he'll go bust, quick. It's all that keeps his feet on the ground. If he didn't think he was earning his living, he'd go on the bum in a minute."

I was somewhat impatient with Sheener's insistence, but I was also interested in this developing situation. "Who's going to do his work anyhow?" I demanded.

For the first time in our acquaintance I saw Sheener look confused. "That's all right too," he told me. "It don't take any skin off your back, long as it's done."

In the end I surrendered. Evans kept his job; and Sheener — I once caught him in the act, to his vast embarrassment — did the janitor's work when Evans was unfit for duty. Also Sheener loaned him money, small sums that mounted into an interesting total; and furthermore I know that on one occasion Sheener fought for him.

The man Evans went his pompous way, accepting Sheener's homage and protection as a matter of right, and in the course of half a dozen years I left the paper for other work, saw Sheener seldom, and Evans not at all.

About ten o'clock one night in early summer I was wandering somewhat aimlessly through the South End to see what I might see when I encountered Sheener. He was running, and his dark face was twisted with anxiety. When he saw me he stopped with an exclamation of relief, and I asked him what the matter was.

"You remember old Bum Evans?" he asked, and added: "He's sick. I'm looking for a doctor. The old guy is just about all in."

"You mean to say you're still looking out for that old tramp?" I demanded.

"Sure, I am," he said hotly; "that old boy is there. He's got the stuff. Him and me are pals." He was hurrying me along the street toward the office of the doctor he sought. I asked where Evans was. "In my room," he told me. "I found him on the street last night. He was crazy. The D. T.'s.[4] I ain't been able to get away from him till now. He's asleep. Wait. Here's where the doc hangs out."

Five minutes later the doctor and Sheener and I were retracing our steps toward Sheener's lodging, and presently we crowded into the small room where Evans lay on Sheener's bed. The man's muddy garments were on the floor; he himself tossed and twisted feverishly under Sheener's blankets. Sheener and the doctor bent over him, while I stood by. Evans waked, under the touch of their

---

4 **D. T.'s:** delirium tremens.

hands, and waked to sanity. He was cold sober and desperately
sick.

When the doctor had done what could be done, and gone on his
way, Sheener sat down on the edge of the bed and rubbed the
old man's head with a tenderness of which I could not have believed the newsboy capable. Evans's eyes were open; he watched
the other, and at last he said huskily:

"I say, you know, I'm a bit knocked up."

Sheener reassured him. "That's all right, bo," he said. "You
hit the hay. Sleep's the dose for you. I ain't going away."

"DO I LOOK ALL RIGHT TO SEE MY BOY?"

Evans moved his head on the pillow, as though he were nodding.
"A bit tight, wasn't it, what?" he asked.

"Say," Sheener agreed. "You said something, Bum. I thought
you'd kick off, sure."

The old man considered for a little, his lips twitching and
shaking. "I say, you know," he murmured at last. "Can't have
that. Potter's Field, and all that sort of business. Won't do.
Sheener, when I do take the jump, you write home for me. Pass
the good word. You'll hear from them."

Sheener said: " Sure I will. Who'll I write to, Bum? "

Evans, I think, was unconscious of my presence. He gave Sheener a name; his name. Also, he told him the name of his lawyer, in one of the Midland cities of England, and added certain instructions.

When he had drifted into uneasy sleep Sheener came out into the hall to see me off. I asked him what he meant to do.

" What am I going to do? " he repeated. " I'm going to write to this guy's lawyer. Let them send for him. This ain't no place for him."

" You'll have your trouble for your pains," I told him. " The old soak is plain liar; that's all."

Sheener laughed at me. " That's all right, bo," he told me. " I know. This guy's the real cheese. You'll see."

I asked him to let me know if he heard anything, and he said he would. But within a day or two I forgot the matter, and would hardly have remembered it if Sheener had not telephoned me a month later.

" Say, you're a wise guy, ain't you? " he derided when I answered the phone. I admitted it. " I got a letter from that lawyer in England," he told me. " This Evans is the stuff, just like I said. His wife run away with another man, and he went to the devil fifteen years ago. They've been looking for him ever since his son grew up."

" Son? " I asked.

" Son. Sure! Raising wheat out in Canada somewhere. They gave me his address. He's made a pile. I'm going to write to him."

" What does Bum say? "

" Him? I ain't told him. I won't till I'm sure the kid's coming after him." He said again that I was a wise guy; and I apologized for my wisdom and asked for a share in what was to come. He promised to keep me posted.

Ten days later he telephoned me while I was at supper to ask if I could come to his room. I said: " What's up? "

" The old guy's boy is coming after him," Sheener said. " He's got the shakes waiting. I want you to come and help me take care of him."

" When's the boy coming? "

" Gets in at midnight tonight," said Sheener.

I promised to make haste; and half an hour later I joined them in Sheener's room. Sheener let me in. Evans himself sat in something like a stupor, on a chair by the bed. He was dressed in a cheap suit of ready-made clothes, to which he lent a certain dignity. His cheeks were shaven clean, his mustache was trimmed, his thin hair was plastered down on his bony skull. The man stared straight before him, trembling and quivering. He did not look toward me when I came in; and Sheener and I sat down by the table and talked together in undertones.

" The boy's really coming? " I asked.

Sheener said proudly: " I'm telling you."

" You heard from him? "

" Got a wire the day he got my letter."

" You've told Bum? "

" I told him right away. I had to do it. The old boy was sober by then, and crazy for a shot of booze. That was Monday. He wanted to go out and get pied; but when I told him about his boy, he begun to cry. And he ain't touched a drop since then."

" You haven't let him? "

" Sure I'd let him. But he wouldn't. I always told you the class was there. He says to me: ' I can't let my boy see me in this state, you know. Have to straighten up a bit. I'll need new clothes.' "

" I noticed his new suit."

" Sure," Sheener agreed. " I bought it for him."

" Out of his savings? "

" He ain't been saving much lately."

" Sheener," I asked, " how much does he owe you? For money loaned and spent for him."

Sheener said hotly: " He don't owe me a cent."

" I know. But how much have you spent on him? "

" If I hadn't given it to him, I'd have blowed it somehow. He needed it."

I guessed at a hundred dollars, at two hundred. Sheener would not tell me. " I'm telling you, he's my pal," he said. " I'm not looking for anything out of this."

" If this millionaire son of his has any decency, he'll make it up to you."

" He don't know a thing about me," said Sheener, " except my name. I've just wrote as though I knowed the old guy, here in the house, see. Said he was sick, and all."

" And the boy gets in tonight? "

" Midnight," said Sheener, and Evans, from his chair, echoed:
" Midnight! " Then asked with a certain stiff anxiety: " Do I
look all right, Sheener? Look all right to see my boy? "

" Say," Sheener told him. " You look like the Prince of Wales."
He went across to where the other sat and gripped him by the
shoulder. " You look like the king o' the world."

Old Evans brushed at his coat anxiously; his fingers picked
and twisted; and Sheener sat down on the bed beside him and
began to soothe and comfort the man as though he were a child.

The son was to arrive by way of Montreal, and at eleven
o'clock we left Sheener's room for the station. There was a
flower stand on the corner, and Sheener bought a red carnation
and fixed it in the old man's buttonhole. " That's the way the
boy'll know him," he told me. " They ain't seen each other for —
since the boy was a kid."

Evans accepted the attention querulously; he was trembling
and feeble, yet held his head high. We took the subway, reached
the station, sat down for a space in the waiting room.

But Evans was impatient; he wanted to be out in the train
shed, and we went out there and walked up and down before the
gate. I noticed that he was studying Sheener with some embarrassment in his eyes. Sheener was, of course, an unpre-
possessing figure. Lean, swarthy, somewhat flashy of dress, he
looked what he was. He was my friend, of course, and I was
able to look beneath the exterior. But it seemed to me that sight
of him distressed Evans.

In the end the old man said, somewhat furtively: " I say, you
know, I want to meet my boy alone. You won't mind standing
back a bit when the train comes in."

" Sure," Sheener told him. " We won't get in the way. You'll
see. He'll pick you out in a minute, old man. Leave it to me."

Evans nodded. " Quite so," he said with some relief. " Quite
so, to be sure."

So we waited. Waited till the train slid in at the end of the
long train shed. Sheener gripped the old man's arm. " There
he comes," he said sharply. " Take a brace, now. Stand right
there, where he'll spot you when he comes out. Right there, bo."

" You'll step back a bit, eh, what? " Evans asked.

" Don't worry about us," Sheener told him. " Just you keep
your eye skinned for the boy. Good luck, bo."

We left him standing there, a tall, gaunt, shaky figure. Sheener and I drew back toward the stairs that lead to the elevated structure, and watched from that vantage point. The train stopped, and the passengers came into the station, at first in a trickle and then in a stream, with porters hurrying before them, baggage laden.

The son was one of the first. He emerged from the gate, a tall chap, not unlike his father. Stopped for a moment, casting his eyes about, and saw the flower in the old man's lapel. Leaped toward him hungrily.

They gripped hands, and we saw the son drop his hand on the father's shoulder. They stood there, hands still clasped, while the young man's porter waited in the background. We could hear the son's eager questions, hear the old man's drawled replies. Saw them turn at last, and heard the young man say: " Taxi! " The porter caught up the bag. The taxi stand was at our left, and they came almost directly toward us.

As they approached, Sheener stepped forward, a cheap, somewhat disreputable, figure. His hand was extended toward the younger man. The son saw him, looked at him in some surprise, looked toward his father inquiringly.

Evans saw Sheener too, and a red flush crept up his gaunt cheeks. He did not pause, did not take Sheener's extended hand; instead he looked the newsboy through and through.

Sheener fell back to my side. They stalked past us, out to the taxi stand.

I moved forward. I would have halted them, but Sheener caught my arm. I said hotly: " But see here. He can't throw you like that."

Sheener brushed his sleeve across his eyes. " Hell," he said huskily. " A gent like him can't let on that he knows a guy like me."

I looked at Sheener, and I forgot old Evans and his son. I looked at Sheener, and I caught his elbow and we turned away.

He had been quite right, of course, all the time. Blood will always tell. You can't keep a fast horse in a poor man's stable. And a man is always a man, in any guise.

If you still doubt, do as I did. Consider Sheener.

SUGGESTIONS FOR STUDY

1. Vocabulary: antecedents, thoroughbred, credulity, splay-footed, querulously, furtively.
2. Did the ending spoil the story for you? What is the difference between a " happy " ending and a " right " ending?
3. What is the excuse for the introduction of slang and bad grammar into literature?
4. What would you say is the " single impression " of this story? See the last sentence.
5. Did you find any humor? If so, where?
6. Show that this story is a combination of realism, romanticism, and idealism.
7. What scenes in this story would dramatize well?

FOR FURTHER READING

VOLUME OF STORIES   INDIVIDUAL STORIES

Thrifty Stock   " They Grind Exceeding Small "
             " The Nurse "
             " One Crowded Hour "

THE DEVIL AND TOM WALKER

By WASHINGTON IRVING (1783–1859)

Now we drop back to the beginnings of American literature, and read a tale written by the " father of the American short story." This story, included in *Tales of a Traveler* published in 1824, is more than one hundred years old.

Washington Irving was the first American who successfully adopted literature as a calling. We think of Irving first of all as a New Yorker, for it was in New York that he was born, there he spent most of his years, and there he died. He discovered the beauty of the Hudson and the legends of the Catskills, he immortalized Sleepy Hollow, and he created Diedrich Knickerbocker (see p. 368). But we also think of Irving as a cultivated, traveled man of the world. He spent many years in England and Spain, and his books reflect the charm of the former and the romance of the latter, as well as the flavor of his native America. Besides short stories he wrote essays (see p. 233) and biography and history. All of his works are characterized by his genial humor and clear, easy style.

Imagine yourself a guest at Sunnyside, Irving's home. You are near Sleepy Hollow, and from the windows you may look out over the Hudson River. You have just finished dinner, and before a blazing and crackling log fire you lean back in an easy chair, and wait for your host to tell a story. There are no telephones, no radios to interrupt; no train will roar past toward Albany or New York City. In his charming old-school manner, pausing now and then to chuckle with you at some queer twist of the yarn, Irving weaves into his story the artistry of a master story-teller. Last night perhaps it was a colorful legend of old Spain with a little of the flavor of the Arabian Nights, but tonight he spins a story as American as are the characters of Rip Van Winkle and Ichabod Crane. He takes his time about the telling. Don't interrupt him or hurry him; a long, pleasant evening is before you.

A few miles from Boston in Massachusetts, there is a deep inlet, winding several miles into the interior of the country from Charles Bay, and terminating in a thickly wooded swamp or morass. On one side of this inlet is a beautiful dark grove; on the opposite side the land rises abruptly from the water's edge into a high ridge, on which grow a few scattered oaks of great age and immense size. Under one of these gigantic trees, according to old stories, there was a great amount of treasure buried by Kidd the pirate. The inlet allowed a facility to bring the money in a boat secretly and at night to the very foot of the hill; the elevation of the place permitted a good lookout to be kept that no one was at hand; while the remarkable trees formed good landmarks by which the place might easily be found again. The old stories add, moreover, that the devil presided at the hiding of the money, and took it under his guardianship; but this, it is well known, he always does with buried treasure, particularly when it has been ill-gotten. Be that as it may, Kidd never returned to recover his wealth; being shortly after seized at Boston, sent out to England, and there hanged for a pirate.

About the year 1727, just at the time that earthquakes were prevalent in New England, and shook many tall sinners down upon their knees, there lived near this place a meager, miserly fellow, of the name of Tom Walker. He had a wife as miserly as himself: they were so miserly that they even conspired to cheat each other. Whatever the woman could lay hands on, she hid away; a hen could not cackle but she was on the alert to secure the new-laid egg. Her husband was continually prying about to detect her secret hoards, and many and fierce were the conflicts that took place about what ought to have been common property. They lived in a forlorn-looking house that stood alone, and had an air of starvation. A few straggling savin-trees, emblems of sterility, grew near it; no smoke ever curled from its chimney; no traveler stopped at its door. A miserable horse, whose ribs were as articulate as the bars of a gridiron, stalked about a field, where a thin carpet of moss, scarcely covering the ragged beds of pudding-stone, tantalized and balked his hunger; and sometimes he would lean his head over the fence, look piteously at the passer-by, and seem to petition deliverance from this land of famine.

The house and its inmates had altogether a bad name. Tom's wife was a tall termagant, fierce of temper, loud of tongue, and strong of arm. Her voice was often heard in wordy warfare with her husband; and his face sometimes showed signs that their conflicts were not confined to words. No one ventured, however, to interfere between them. The lonely wayfarer shrunk within himself at the horrid clamor and clapper-clawing; eyed the den of discord askance; and hurried on his way, rejoicing, if a bachelor, in his celibacy.

One day when Tom Walker had been to a distant part of the neighborhood, he took what he considered a short cut homeward, through the swamp. Like most short cuts, it was an ill-chosen route. The swamp was thickly grown with great gloomy pines and hemlocks, some of them ninety feet high, which made it dark at noonday, and a retreat for all the owls of the neighborhood. It was full of pits and quagmires, partly covered with weeds and mosses, where the green surface often betrayed the traveler into a gulf of black, smothering mud; there were also dark and stagnant pools, the abodes of the tadpole, the bull-frog, and the water-snake; where the trunks of pines and hemlocks lay half-drowned, half-rotting, looking like alligators sleeping in the mire.

Tom had long been picking his way cautiously through this treacherous forest; stepping from tuft to tuft of rushes and roots, which afforded precarious footholds among deep sloughs; or pacing carefully, like a cat, along the prostrate trunks of trees; startled now and then by the sudden screaming of the bittern, or the quacking of a wild duck rising on the wing from some solitary pool. At length he arrived at a firm piece of ground, which ran out like a peninsula into the deep bosom of the swamp. It had been one of the strongholds of the Indians during their wars with the first colonists. Here they had thrown up a kind of fort, which they had looked upon as almost impregnable, and had used as a place of refuge for their squaws and children. Nothing remained of the old Indian fort but a few embankments, gradually sinking to the level of the surrounding earth, and already overgrown in part by oaks and other forest trees, the foliage of which formed a contrast to the dark pines and hemlocks of the swamp.

It was late in the dusk of evening when Tom Walker reached the old fort, and he paused there awhile to rest himself. Any one but he would have felt unwilling to linger in this lonely, melancholy place, for the common people had a bad opinion of it, from the stories handed down from the time of the Indian wars; when it was asserted that the savages held incantations here, and made sacrifices to the evil spirit.

Tom Walker, however, was not a man to be troubled with any fears of the kind. He reposed himself for some time on the trunk of a fallen hemlock, listening to the boding cry of the tree-toad, and delving with his walking staff into a mound of black mold at his feet. As he turned up the soil unconsciously, his staff struck against something hard. He raked it out of the vegetable mold and lo, a cloven skull, with an Indian tomahawk buried deep in it, lay before him. The rust on the weapon showed the time that had elapsed since this death-blow had been given. It was a dreary memento of the fierce struggle that had taken place in this last foothold of the Indian warriors.

" Humph! " said Tom Walker, as he gave it a kick to shake the dirt from it.

" Let that skull alone! " said a gruff voice. Tom lifted up his eyes, and beheld a great black man seated directly opposite him, on the stump of a tree. He was exceedingly surprised, having neither heard nor seen any one approach; and he was still more perplexed on observing, as well as the gathering gloom would permit, that the stranger was neither Negro nor Indian. It is true he was dressed in a rude half-Indian garb, and had a red belt or sash swathed round his body; but his face was neither black nor copper-color, but swarthy and dingy, and begrimed with soot, as if he had been accustomed to toil among fires and forges. He had a shock of coarse black hair, that stood out from his head in all directions, and bore an axe on his shoulder.

He scowled for a moment at Tom with a pair of great red eyes.

"What are you doing on my grounds?" said the black man, with a hoarse growling voice.

"Your grounds!" said Tom, with a sneer, "no more your grounds than mine; they belong to Deacon Peabody."

"Deacon Peabody be damned," said the stranger, "as I flatter myself he will be, if he does not look more to his own sins and less to those of his neighbors. Look yonder, and see how Deacon Peabody is faring."

Tom looked in the direction that the stranger pointed, and

"WHAT ARE YOU DOING ON MY GROUNDS?"

beheld one of the great trees, fair and flourishing without, but rotten at the core, and saw that it had been nearly hewn through, so that the first high wind was likely to blow it down. On the bark of the tree was scored the name of Deacon Peabody, an eminent man, who had waxed wealthy by driving shrewd bargains with the Indians. He now looked around, and found most of the tall trees marked with the name of some great man of the colony, and all more or less scored by the axe. The one on which he had been seated, and which had evidently just been hewn down, bore the name of Crowninshield; and he recollected a mighty rich man of that name, who made a vulgar display of wealth, which it was whispered he had acquired by buccaneering.

"He's just ready for burning!" said the black man, with a growl of triumph. "You see I am likely to have a good stock of firewood for winter."

"But what right have you," said Tom, "to cut down Deacon Peabody's timber?"

"The right of a prior claim," said the other. "This woodland belonged to me long before one of your white-faced race put foot upon the soil."

"And pray, who are you, if I may be so bold?" said Tom.

"Oh, I go by various names. I am the wild huntsman in some countries; the black miner in others. In this neighborhood I am known by the name of the black woodsman. I am he to whom the red men consecrated this spot, and in honor of whom they now and then roasted a white man, by way of sweet-smelling sacrifice. Since the red men have been exterminated by you white savages, I amuse myself by presiding at the persecutions of Quakers and Anabaptists [1]; I am the great patron and prompter of slave-dealers, and the grand-master of the Salem witches."

"The upshot of all which is, that, if I mistake not," said Tom, sturdily, "you are he commonly called Old Scratch."

"The same, at your service!" replied the black man, with a half civil nod.

Such was the opening of this interview, according to the old story; though it has almost too familiar an air to be credited. One would think that to meet with such a singular personage, in this wild, lonely place, would have shaken any man's nerves; but Tom was a hard-minded fellow, not easily daunted, and he had lived so long with a termagant wife, that he did not even fear the devil.

It is said that after this commencement they had a long and earnest conversation together, as Tom returned homeward. The black man told him of great sums of money buried by Kidd the pirate, under the oak trees on the high ridge, not far from the morass. All these were under his command, and protected by his power, so that none could find them but such as propitiated his

---

[1] **Anabaptists:** a religious sect which arose in Switzerland in 1523. Its members were subjected to persecution because of their opposition to infant baptism.

favor. These he offered to place within Tom Walker's reach, having conceived an especial kindness for him; but they were to be had only on certain conditions. What these conditions were may be easily surmised, though Tom never disclosed them publicly. They must have been very hard, for he required time to think of them, and he was not a man to stick at trifles when money was in view. When they had reached the edge of the swamp, the stranger paused. "What proof have I that all you have been telling me is true?" said Tom. "There's my signature," said the black man, pressing his finger on Tom's forehead. So saying, he turned off among the thickets of the swamp, and seemed, as Tom said, to go down, down, down, into the earth, until nothing but his head and shoulders could be seen, and so on, until he totally disappeared.

When Tom reached home, he found the black print of a finger burnt, as it were, into his forehead, which nothing could obliterate. The first news his wife had to tell him was the sudden death of Absalom Crowninshield, the rich buccaneer. It was announced in the papers with the usual flourish, that "A great man had fallen in Israel."

Tom recollected the tree, which his black friend had just hewn down, and which was ready for burning. "Let the freebooter roast," said Tom, "who cares!" He now felt convinced that all he had heard and seen was no illusion.

He was not prone to let his wife into his confidence; but as this was an uneasy secret, he willingly shared it with her. All her avarice was awakened at the mention of hidden gold, and she urged her husband to comply with the black man's terms, and secure what would make them wealthy for life. However Tom might have felt disposed to sell himself to the Devil, he was determined not to do so to oblige his wife; so he flatly refused, out of the mere spirit of contradiction. Many and bitter were the quarrels they had on the subject; but the more she talked, the more resolute was Tom not to be damned to please her.

At length she determined to drive the bargain on her own account, and if she succeeded, to keep all the gain to herself. Being of the same fearless temper as her husband, she set off for the old Indian fort towards the close of a summer's day. She was many hours absent. When she came back, she was reserved and sullen in her replies. She spoke something of a black man, whom she had met about twilight hewing at the root of a tall tree. He was sulky, however, and would not come to terms: she was to go again with a propitiatory offering, but what it was she forebore to say.

The next evening she set off for the swamp, with her apron heavily laden. Tom waited and waited for her, but in vain; midnight came, but she did not make her appearance: morning, noon, night returned, but still she did not come. Tom now grew uneasy for her safety, especially as he found she had carried off in her apron the silver tea-pot and spoons, and every portable article of value. Another night elapsed, another morning came, but no wife. In a word, she was never heard of more.

What was her real fate nobody knows, in consequence of so many pretending to know. It is one of those facts which have become confounded by a variety of historians. Some asserted that she lost her way among the tangled mazes of the swamp, and sank into some pit or slough; others, more uncharitable, hinted that she had eloped with the household booty, and made off to some other province; while others surmised that the tempter had decoyed her into a dismal quagmire, on the top of which her hat was found lying. In confirmation of this, it was said a great black man, with an axe on his shoulder, was seen late that very evening coming out of the swamp, carrying a bundle tied in a checked apron, with an air of surly triumph.

The most current and probable story, however, observes that Tom Walker grew so anxious about the fate of his wife and his property, that he set out at length to seek them both at the Indian fort. During a long summer's afternoon he searched about the gloomy place, but no wife was to be seen. He called her name repeatedly, but she was nowhere to be heard. The bittern alone responded to his voice, as he flew screaming by, or the bull-frog croaked dolefully from a neighboring pool. At length, it is said, just in the brown hour of twilight, when the owls began to hoot, and the bats to flit about, his attention was attracted by the clamor of carrion crows hovering about a cypress tree. He looked up, and beheld a bundle tied in a checked apron, and hanging in the branches of the tree, with a great vulture perched hard by, as if keeping watch upon it. He leaped with joy; for he recognized his wife's apron, and supposed it to contain the household valuables.

"Let us get hold of the property," said he, consolingly to himself, " and we will endeavor to do without the woman."

As he scrambled up the tree, the vulture spread its wide wings, and sailed off, screaming, into the deep shadows of the forest. Tom seized the checked apron, but, woeful sight! found nothing but a heart and liver tied up in it!

Such, according to this most authentic old story, was all that was to be found of Tom's wife. She had probably attempted to deal with the black man as she had been accustomed to deal with her husband; but though a female scold is generally considered a match for the devil, yet in this instance she appears to have had the worst of it. She must have died game, however; for it is said Tom noticed many prints of cloven feet deeply stamped about the tree, and found handfuls of hair, that looked as if they had been plucked from the coarse black shock of the woodsman. Tom knew his wife's prowess by experience. He shrugged his shoulders, as he looked at the signs of a fierce clapper-clawing. " Egad," said he to himself, " Old Scratch must have had a tough time of it! "

Tom consoled himself for the loss of his property with the loss of his wife, for he was a man of fortitude. He even felt something like gratitude towards the black woodsman, who, he considered, had done him a kindness. He sought, therefore, to cultivate a further acquaintance with him, but for some time without success; the old black-legs played shy, for whatever people may think, he is not always to be had for calling for; he knows how to play his cards when pretty sure of his game.

At length, it is said, when delay had whetted Tom's eagerness to the quick, and prepared him to agree to anything rather than not gain the promised treasure, he met the black man one evening in his usual woodsman's dress, with his axe on his shoulder, sauntering along the swamp, and humming a tune. He affected to receive Tom's advances with great indifference, made brief replies, and went on humming his tune.

By degrees, however, Tom brought him to business, and they began to haggle about the terms on which the former was to have the pirate's treasure. There was one condition which need not be mentioned, being generally understood in all cases where the devil grants favors; but there were others about which, though of less importance, he was inflexibly obstinate. He insisted that the money found through his means should be employed in his service. He proposed, therefore, that Tom should employ it in the black traffic; that is to say, that he should fit out a slave-ship.

This, however, Tom resolutely refused; he was bad enough in all conscience, but the devil himself could not tempt him to turn slave-trader.

Finding Tom so squeamish on this point, he did not insist upon it, but proposed, instead, that he should turn usurer; the devil being extremely anxious for the increase of usurers, looking upon them as his peculiar people.

To this no objections were made, for it was just to Tom's taste.

" You shall open a broker's shop in Boston next month," said the black man.

" I'll do it tomorrow, if you wish," said Tom Walker.

" You shall lend money at two per cent a month."

" Egad, I'll charge four ! " replied Tom Walker.

" You shall extort bonds, foreclose mortgages, drive the merchants to bankruptcy —— "

" I'll drive them to the devil," cried Tom Walker.

" You are the usurer for my money ! " said black-legs with delight. " When will you want the rhino ? " [2]

" This very night."

" Done ! " said the devil.

" Done ! " said Tom Walker. — So they shook hands and struck a bargain.

A few days' time saw Tom Walker seated behind his desk in a counting-house in Boston.

His reputation for a ready-moneyed man, who would lend money out for a good consideration, soon spread abroad. Everybody remembers the time of Governor Belcher,[3] when money was particularly scarce. It was a time of paper credit. The country had been deluged with government bills; the famous Land Bank [4] had been established; there had been a rage for speculating; the people had run mad with schemes for new settlements; for building cities in the wilderness; land-jobbers went about with maps of grants, and townships, and Eldorados, lying nobody knew where, but which everybody was ready to purchase. In a word, the great speculating fever which breaks out every now and then in the country, had raged to an alarming degree, and everybody

---

[2] **rhino:** money.

[3] Jonathan Belcher was governor of Massachusetts from 1730 to 1741.

[4] **Land Bank:** a system by which the province advanced money on mortgages on land.

was dreaming of making sudden fortunes from nothing. As usual the fever had subsided; the dream had gone off, and the imaginary fortunes with it; the patients were left in doleful plight, and the whole country resounded with the consequent cry of "hard times."

At this propitious time of public distress did Tom Walker set up as usurer in Boston. His door was soon thronged by customers. The needy and adventurous; the gambling speculator; the dreaming land-jobber; the thriftless tradesman; the merchant with cracked credit; in short, every one driven to raise money by desperate means and desperate sacrifices, hurried to Tom Walker.

Thus Tom was the universal friend of the needy, and acted like a " friend in need "; that is to say, he always exacted good pay and good security. In proportion to the distress of the applicant was the highness of his terms. He accumulated bonds and mortgages, gradually squeezed his customers closer and closer, and sent them at length, dry as a sponge, from his door.

In this way he made money hand over hand; became a rich and mighty man, and exalted his cocked hat upon 'Change. He built himself, as usual, a vast house, out of ostentation; but left the greater part of it unfinished and unfurnished, out of parsimony. He even set up a carriage in the fulness of his vainglory, though he nearly starved the horses which drew it; and as the ungreased wheels groaned and screeched on the axle-trees, you would have thought you heard the souls of the poor debtors he was squeezing.

As Tom waxed old, however, he grew thoughtful. Having secured the good things of this world, he began to feel anxious about those of the next. He thought with regret on the bargain he had made with his black friend, and set his wits to work to cheat him out of the condition. He became, therefore, all of a sudden, a violent churchgoer. He prayed loudly and strenuously, as if heaven were to be taken by force of lungs. Indeed, one might always tell when he had sinned most during the week, by the clamor of his Sunday devotion. The quiet Christians who had been modestly and steadfastly traveling Zionward, were struck with self-reproach at seeing themselves so suddenly outstripped in their career by this new-made convert. Tom was as rigid in religious as in money matters; he was a stern supervisor and censurer of his neighbors, and seemed to think every sin entered up to their account became a credit on his own side of the page.

He even talked of the expediency of reviving the persecution of Quakers and Anabaptists. In a word, Tom's zeal became as notorious as his riches.

Still, in spite of all this strenuous attention to forms, Tom had a lurking dread that the devil, after all, would have his due. That he might not be taken unawares, therefore, it is said he always carried a small Bible in his coat pocket. He had also a great folio Bible on his counting-house desk, and would frequently be found reading it when people called on business; on such occasions he would lay his green spectacles in the book, to mark the place, while he turned round to drive some usurious bargain.

Some say that Tom grew a little crack-brained in his old days, and that, fancying his end approaching, he had his horse new shod, saddled and bridled, and buried with his feet uppermost; because he supposed that at the last day the world would be turned upside down; in which case he should find his horse standing ready for mounting, and he was determined at the worst to give his old friend a run for it. This, however, is probably a mere old wives' fable. If he really did take such a precaution, it was totally superfluous; at least so says the authentic old legend, which closes this story in the following manner.

One hot summer afternoon in the dog-days, just as a terrible black thunder-gust was coming up, Tom sat in his counting-house, in his white linen cap and India silk morning-gown. He was on the point of foreclosing a mortgage, by which he would complete the ruin of an unlucky land-speculator for whom he had professed the greatest friendship. The poor land-jobber begged him to grant a few months' indulgence. Tom had grown testy and irritated, and refused another day.

" My family will be ruined, and brought upon the parish," said the land-jobber. " Charity begins at home," replied Tom; " I must take care of myself in these hard times."

" You have made so much money out of me," said the speculator.

Tom lost his patience and his piety. " The devil take me," said he, " if I have made a farthing! "

Just then there were three loud knocks at the street door. He stepped out to see who was there. A black man was holding a black horse, which neighed and stamped with impatience.

" Tom, you're come for," said the black fellow, gruffly. Tom shrank back, but too late. He had left his little Bible at the bottom of his coat pocket, and his big Bible on the desk buried under the mortgage he was about to foreclose: never was sinner taken more unawares. The black man whisked him like a child into the saddle, gave the horse the lash, and away he galloped, with Tom on his back, in the midst of the thunderstorm. The clerks stuck their pens behind their ears, and stared after him from the windows. Away went Tom Walker, dashing down the streets; his white cap bobbing up and down; his morning-gown fluttering in the wind, and his steed striking fire out of the pavement at every bound. When the clerks turned to look for the black man, he had disappeared.

Tom Walker never returned to foreclose the mortgage. A countryman, who lived on the border of the swamp, reported that in the height of the thunder-gust he had heard a great clattering of hoofs and a howling along the road, and running to the window caught sight of a figure, such as I have described, on a horse that galloped like mad across the fields, over the hills, and down into the black hemlock swamp towards the old Indian fort; and that shortly after a thunderbolt falling in that direction seemed to set the whole forest in a blaze.

The good people of Boston shook their heads and shrugged their shoulders, but had been so much accustomed to witches and goblins, and tricks of the devil, in all kinds of shapes, from the first settlement of the colony, that they were not so much horror-struck as might have been expected. Trustees were appointed to take charge of Tom's effects. There was nothing, however, to administer upon. On searching his coffers, all his bonds and mortgages were found reduced to cinders. In place of gold and silver, his iron chest was filled with chips and shavings; two skeletons lay in his stable instead of his half-starved horses, and the very next day his great house took fire and was burnt to the ground.

Such was the end of Tom Walker and his ill-gotten wealth. Let all griping money-brokers lay this story to heart. The truth of it is not to be doubted. The very hole under the oak trees, whence he dug Kidd's money, is to be seen to this day; and the neighboring swamp and old Indian fort are often haunted in stormy nights by a figure on horseback, in morning-gown and white cap, which is doubtless the troubled spirit of the usurer. In fact, the story has resolved itself into a proverb, and is the origin of that popular saying, so prevalent throughout New England, of " The Devil and Tom Walker."

SUGGESTIONS FOR STUDY

1. Vocabulary: termagant, buccaneering, morass, propitiated, carrion, usurer, Eldorados.

2. Did you feel the style on which Irving's fame rests? Can you think of any of the eighteenth century English writers whose manner may have influenced Irving? Point out sentences which illustrate Irving's command of the language.

3. Did the story make you laugh? Did it make you chuckle? How would you characterize Irving's humor? Give some examples.

4. In what spirit does Irving say, " Let all griping money-brokers lay this story to heart " ?

5. Count up the familiar expressions which Irving has made concrete in this story. Examples are " the devil will have his due," and " the devil take me."

6. If you like this story, what reply have you for the realists of your class who did not like it " because it is so impossible and could never have happened "?

7. What other stories by Irving do you know in which there is a touch of the fantastic?

FOR FURTHER READING

The Sketch Book: " Rip Van Winkle," " The Specter Bridegroom," " The Legend of Sleepy Hollow "
Bracebridge Hall: " The Stout Gentleman "
The Alhambra: " The Legend of the Moor's Legacy," " The Legend of the Three Beautiful Princesses," " The Legend of the Two Discreet Statues "
Tales of a Traveler: " The Adventure of My Uncle," " The Adventure of My Aunt," " The Bold Dragoon," " The Adventure of the Mysterious Stranger "

For Irving's essays, see page 233.

THE MINISTER'S BLACK VEIL

A PARABLE

By Nathaniel Hawthorne (1804–1864)

We do not think of Hawthorne as a gracious host like Irving, who tells charming stories before his hearth fire. Hawthorne was reared by a widowed mother who for forty years shut herself completely from normal contacts with the world, even refusing to take her meals with her children. From his mother he inherited a love of solitude and a habit of meditation that made him a stranger to the easy sociability of the world. In the pursuance of his resolve to be an author he shut himself up in a seclusion known to no other American writer. He rarely left his room except for an occasional solitary walk; he ate by himself in his room; he made no friends or acquaintances; he brooded and wrote alone. He published his first stories anonymously and once quite correctly characterized himself as " the obscurest man of letters in America."

Later, encouraged by Longfellow, who had been his classmate at Bowdoin College, and by his wife, whose belief in his genius was genuine and heartening, he gradually assumed a more normal, natural contact with his fellows. It was in this happier later life that he wrote those favorites of our childhood, *The Wonder Book for Boys and Girls* and *Tanglewood Tales*. Finally came a full recognition of his genius as a novelist. An appointment as consul to Liverpool by President Franklin Pierce, another college friend, gave him an opportunity for foreign travel, and his life ended with four happy years in his home, " The Wayside," at Concord. Two other houses are inseparably associated with Hawthorne — the " Old Manse " at Concord, built for Emerson's grandfather and at one time the home of Emerson himself, and the mysterious " House of the Seven Gables," at Salem, now one of the show-places of that historic city.

Hawthorne was a profound thinker; he had probed deep into the impulses of the human heart. His stories are more like sermons than fireside conversations, but for that very reason they have depth of thought, moral values, compactness, climax, and power. Notice how in this story he plunges immediately into its main situation, how the action rolls rapidly and without digressions toward its climax, and how it stops when the climax has been reached. Observe the almost poetic quality of the sentences. And don't be too quick in deciding that you know what the black veil represents. In this story Hawthorne is not skimming the surface of human nature; he is teaching a profound lesson that is almost awful in its implication. Although it was written in 1836, the story carries power that has not diminished through its century of life.

The sexton stood in the porch of Milford [1] meeting-house, pulling busily at the bell-rope. The old people of the village came stooping along the street. Children, with bright faces, tripped merrily beside their parents, or mimicked a graver gait, in the conscious dignity of their Sunday clothes. Spruce bachelors looked sidelong at the pretty maidens, and fancied that the Sabbath sunshine made them prettier than on week days. When the throng had mostly streamed into the porch, the sexton began to toll the bell, keeping his eye on the Rev. Mr. Hooper's door. The first glimpse of the clergyman's figure was the signal for the bell to cease its summons.

" But what has good Parson Hooper got upon his face? " cried the sexton in astonishment.

All within hearing immediately turned about, and beheld the semblance of Mr. Hooper, pacing slowly his meditative way towards the meeting house. With one accord they started, expressing more wonder than if some strange minister were coming to dust the cushions of Mr. Hooper's pulpit.

"Are you sure it is our parson? " inquired Goodman [2] Gray of the sexton.

"Of a certainty it is good Mr. Hooper," replied the sexton. " He was to have exchanged pulpits with Parson Shute, of Westbury; but Parson Shute sent to excuse himself yesterday, being to preach a funeral sermon."

The cause of so much amazement may appear sufficiently slight. Mr. Hooper, a gentlemanly person, of about thirty, though still a bachelor, was dressed with due clerical neatness, as if a careful wife had starched his band, and brushed the weekly dust from his Sunday's garb. There was but one thing remarkable in his appearance. Swathed about his forehead, and hanging down over his face, so low as to be shaken by his breath, Mr. Hooper had on a black veil.[3] On a nearer view it seemed to consist of two folds of crape, which entirely concealed his features, except

---

[1] **Milford:** a town in Massachusetts.
[2] **Goodman:** Mister.
[3] Another clergyman in New England, Mr. Joseph Moody, of York, Maine, who died about eighty years since, made himself remarkable by the same eccentricity that is here related of the Reverend Mr. Hooper. In his case, however, the symbol had a different import. In early life he had accidentally killed a beloved friend, and from that day till the hour of his own death, he hid his face from men. [Author's note.]

the mouth and chin, but probably did not intercept his sight, further than to give a darkened aspect to all living and inanimate things. With this gloomy shade before him, good Mr. Hooper walked onward, at a slow and quiet pace, stooping somewhat, and looking on the ground, as is customary with abstracted men, yet nodding kindly to those of his parishioners who still waited on the meeting-house steps. But so wonderstruck were they that his greeting hardly met with a return.

" I can't really feel as if good Mr. Hooper's face was behind that piece of crape," said the sexton.

" I don't like it," muttered an old woman, as she hobbled into the meeting house. "He has changed himself into something awful, only by hiding his face."

" Our parson has gone mad! " cried Goodman Gray, following him across the threshold.

A rumor of some unaccountable phenomenon had preceded Mr. Hooper into the meeting house, and set all the congregation astir. Few could refrain from twisting their heads towards the door; many stood upright, and turned directly about; while several little boys clambered upon the seats, and came down again with a terrible racket. There was a general bustle, a rustling of the women's gowns and shuffling of the men's feet, greatly at variance with that hushed repose which should attend the entrance of the minister. But Mr. Hooper appeared not to notice the perturbation of his people. He entered with an almost noiseless step, bent his head mildly to the pews on each side, and bowed as he passed his oldest parishioner, a white-haired great-grandsire, who occupied an arm-chair in the center of the aisle. It was strange to observe how slowly this venerable man became conscious of something singular in the appearance of his pastor. He seemed not fully to partake of the prevailing wonder, till Mr. Hooper had ascended the stairs, and showed himself in the pulpit, face to face with his congregation, except for the black veil. That mysterious emblem was never once withdrawn. It shook with his measured breath, as he gave out the psalm; it threw its obscurity between him and the holy page, as he read the Scriptures; and while he prayed, the veil lay heavily on his uplifted countenance. Did he seek to hide it from the dread Being whom he was addressing?

Such was the effect of this simple piece of crape, that more than one woman of delicate nerves was forced to leave the meeting-house. Yet perhaps the pale-faced congregation was almost as fearful a sight to the minister, as his black veil to them.

Mr. Hooper had the reputation of a good preacher, but not an energetic one; he strove to win his people heavenward by mild, persuasive influences, rather than to drive them thither by the thunders of the Word. The sermon which he now delivered was marked by the same characteristics of style and manner as the general series of his pulpit oratory. But there was something, either in the sentiment of the discourse itself, or in the imagination of the auditors, which made it greatly the most powerful effort that they had ever heard from their pastor's lips. It was tinged, rather more darkly than usual, with the gentle gloom of Mr. Hooper's temperament. The subject had reference to secret sin, and those sad mysteries which we hide from our nearest and dearest, and would fain conceal from our own consciousness, even forgetting that the Omniscient can detect them. A subtle power was breathed into his words. Each member of the congregation, the most innocent girl, and the man of hardened breast, felt as if the preacher had crept upon them, behind his awful veil, and discovered their hoarded iniquity of deed or thought. Many spread their clasped hands on their bosoms. There was nothing terrible in what Mr. Hooper said, at least no violence; and yet, with every tremor of his melancholy voice, the hearers quaked. An unsought pathos came hand in hand with awe. So sensible were the audience of some unwonted attribute in their minister, that they longed for a breath of wind to blow aside the veil, almost believing that a stranger's visage would be discovered, though the form, gesture, and voice were those of Mr. Hooper.

At the close of the services, the people hurried out with indecorous confusion, eager to communicate their pent-up amazement, and conscious of lighter spirits the moment they lost sight of the black veil. Some gathered in little circles, huddled closely together, with their mouths all whispering in the center; some went homeward alone, wrapt in silent meditation; some talked loudly, and profaned the Sabbath day with ostentatious laughter. A few shook their sagacious heads, intimating that they could penetrate the mystery; while one or two affirmed that there was no mystery at all, but only that Mr. Hooper's eyes were so weakened by the midnight lamp, as to require a shade. After a brief interval, forth came good Mr. Hooper also, in the rear of his flock. Turning his veiled face from one group to another, he paid due reverence to the hoary heads, saluted the middle-aged with kind dignity as their friend and spiritual guide, greeted the young with mingled authority and love, and laid his hands on the little children's heads to bless them. Such was always his custom on the Sabbath day. Strange and bewildered looks repaid him for his courtesy. None, as on former occasions, aspired to the honor of walking by their pastor's side. Old Squire Saunders, doubtless by an accidental lapse of memory, neglected to invite Mr. Hooper to his table, where the good clergyman had been wont to bless the food, almost every Sunday since his settlement. He returned, therefore, to the parsonage, and, at the moment of closing the door, was observed to look back upon the people, all of whom had their eyes fixed upon the minister. A sad smile gleamed faintly from beneath the black veil, and flickered about his mouth, glimmering as he disappeared.

"How strange," said a lady, "that a simple black veil, such as any woman might wear on her bonnet, should become such a terrible thing on Mr. Hooper's face!"

"Something must surely be amiss with Mr. Hooper's intellects," observed her husband, the physician of the village. "But the strangest part of the affair is the effect of this vagary, even on a sober-minded man like myself. The black veil, though it covers only our pastor's face, throws its influence over his whole person, and makes him ghostlike from head to foot. Do you not feel it so?"

"Truly do I," replied the lady; "and I would not be alone with him for the world. I wonder he is not afraid to be alone with himself!"

"Men sometimes are so," said her husband.

The afternoon service was attended with similar circumstances. At its conclusion, the bell tolled for the funeral of a young lady. The relatives and friends were assembled in the house, and the more distant acquaintances stood about the door, speaking of the good qualities of the deceased, when their talk was interrupted by the appearance of Mr. Hooper, still covered with his black veil. It was now an appropriate emblem. The clergyman stepped into the room where the corpse was laid, and bent over the coffin, to take a last farewell of his deceased parishioner. As he stooped, the veil hung straight down from his forehead, so that, if her eyelids had not been closed forever, the dead maiden might have seen his face. Could Mr. Hooper be fearful of her glance, that he so hastily caught back the black veil? A person who watched the interview between the dead and the living scrupled not to affirm, that, at the instant when the clergyman's features were disclosed, the corpse had slightly shuddered, rustling the shroud and muslin cap, though the countenance retained the composure of death. A superstitious old woman was the only witness of this prodigy. From the coffin Mr. Hooper passed into the chamber of the mourners, and thence to the head of the staircase, to make the funeral prayer. It was a tender and heart-dissolving prayer, full of sorrow, yet so imbued with celestial hopes, that the music of a heavenly harp, swept by the fingers of the dead, seemed faintly to be heard among the saddest accents of the minister. The people trembled, though they but darkly understood him when he prayed that they, and himself, and all of mortal race, might be ready, as he trusted this young maiden had been, for the dreadful hour that should snatch the veil from their faces. The bearers went heavily forth, and the mourners followed, saddening all the street, with the dead before them, and Mr. Hooper in his black veil behind.

"Why do you look back?" said one in the procession to his partner.

"I had a fancy," replied she, "that the minister and the maiden's spirit were walking hand in hand."

"And so had I, at the same moment," said the other.

That night, the handsomest couple in Milford village were to be joined in wedlock. Though reckoned a melancholy man, Mr. Hooper had a placid cheerfulness for such occasions, which often excited a sympathetic smile where livelier merriment would have been thrown away. There was no quality of his disposition which made him more beloved than this. The company at the wedding awaited his arrival with impatience, trusting that the strange awe, which had gathered over him throughout the day, would now be dispelled. But such was not the result. When Mr. Hooper came, the first thing that their eyes rested on was the same horrible black veil, which had added deeper gloom to the funeral, and could portend nothing but evil to the wedding. Such was its immediate effect on the guests that a cloud seemed to have rolled duskily from beneath the black crape, and dimmed the light of the candles. The bridal pair stood up before the minister. But the bride's cold fingers quivered in the tremulous hand of the bridegroom, and her deathlike paleness caused a whisper that the maiden who had been buried a few hours before was come from her grave to be married. If ever another wedding were so dismal, it was that famous one where they tolled the wedding knell.[4] After performing the ceremony, Mr. Hooper raised a glass of wine to his lips, wishing happiness to the new-married couple in a strain of mild pleasantry that ought to have brightened the features of the guests, like a cheerful gleam from the hearth. At that instant, catching a glimpse of his figure in the looking-glass, the black veil involved his own spirit in the horror with which it overwhelmed all others. His frame shuddered, his lips grew white, he spilt the untasted wine upon the carpet, and rushed forth into the darkness. For the Earth, too, had on her Black Veil.

The next day, the whole village of Milford talked of little else than Parson Hooper's black veil. That, and the mystery concealed behind it, supplied a topic for discussion between acquaintances meeting in the street, and good women gossiping at their open windows. It was the first item of news that the tavern-keeper told to his guests. The children babbled of it on their way to school. One imitative little imp covered his face with an old black handkerchief, thereby so affrighting his playmates that the panic seized himself, and he well-nigh lost his wits by his own waggery.

It was remarkable that of all the busybodies and impertinent people in the parish, not one ventured to put the plain question to Mr. Hooper, wherefore he did this thing. Hitherto, whenever there appeared the slightest call for such interference, he had never lacked advisers, nor shown himself averse to be guided by their judgment. If he erred at all, it was by so painful a degree of self-distrust, that even the mildest censure would lead him to consider an indifferent action as a crime. Yet, though so well acquainted with this amiable weakness, no individual among his parishioners chose to make the black veil a subject of friendly remonstrance. There was a feeling of dread, neither plainly confessed nor carefully concealed, which caused each to shift the responsibility upon another, till at length it was found expedient to send a deputation of the church, in order to deal with Mr. Hooper about the mystery, before it should grow into a scandal. Never did an embassy so ill discharge its duties. The minister received them with friendly courtesy, but remained silent, after

---

[4] A reference to "The Wedding Knell," the story that precedes this in *Twice-Told Tales*.

they were seated, leaving to his visitors the whole burden of introducing their important business. The topic, it might be supposed, was obvious enough. There was the black veil swathed round Mr. Hooper's forehead, and concealing every feature above his placid mouth, on which, at times, they could perceive the glimmering of a melancholy smile. But that piece of crape, to their imagination, seemed to hang down before his heart, the symbol of a fearful secret between him and them. Were the veil but cast aside, they might speak freely of it, but not till then. Thus they sat a considerable time, speechless, confused, and shrinking uneasily from Mr. Hooper's eye, which they felt to be fixed upon them with an invisible glance. Finally, the deputies returned abashed to their constituents, pronouncing the matter too weighty to be handled, except by a council of the churches, if, indeed, it might not require a general synod.

But there was one person in the village unappalled by the awe with which the black veil had impressed all beside herself. When the deputies returned without an explanation, or even venturing to demand one, she, with the calm energy of her character, determined to chase away the strange cloud that appeared to be settling round Mr. Hooper, every moment more darkly than before. As his plighted wife, it should be her privilege to know what the black veil concealed. At the minister's first visit, therefore, she entered upon the subject with a direct simplicity, which made the task easier both for him and her. After he had seated himself, she fixed her eyes steadfastly upon the veil, but could discern nothing of the dreadful gloom that had so overawed the multitude; it was but a double fold of crape, hanging down from his forehead to his mouth, and slightly stirring with his breath.

"No," said she aloud, and smiling, "there is nothing terrible in this piece of crape, except that it hides a face which I am always glad to look upon. Come, good sir, let the sun shine from behind the cloud. First lay aside your black veil; then tell me why you put it on."

Mr. Hooper's smile glimmered faintly.

"There is an hour to come," said he, "when all of us shall cast aside our veils. Take it not amiss, beloved friend, if I wear this piece of crape till then."

"Your words are a mystery, too," returned the young lady. "Take away the veil from them, at least."

"Elizabeth, I will," said he, "so far as my vow may suffer me.

Know, then, this veil is a type and a symbol, and I am bound to wear it ever, both in light and darkness, in solitude and before the gaze of multitudes, and as with strangers, so with my familiar friends. No mortal eye will see it withdrawn. This dismal shade must separate me from the world; even you, Elizabeth, can never come behind it!"

"What grievous affliction hath befallen you," she earnestly inquired, "that you should thus darken your eyes forever?"

"If it be a sign of mourning," replied Mr. Hooper, "I, perhaps, like most other mortals, have sorrows dark enough to be typified by a black veil."

"But what if the world will not believe that it is the type of an innocent sorrow?" urged Elizabeth. "Beloved and respected as you are, there may be whispers that you hide your face under the consciousness of secret sin. For the sake of your holy office, do away this scandal!"

"DO AWAY THIS SCANDAL!"

The color rose into her cheeks as she intimated the nature of the rumors that were already abroad in the village. But Mr. Hooper's mildness did not forsake him. He even smiled again — that same sad smile, which always appeared like a faint glimmering of light, proceeding from the obscurity beneath the veil.

"If I hide my face for sorrow, there is cause enough," he merely replied; "and if I cover it for secret sin, what mortal might not do the same?"

And with this gentle, but unconquerable obstinacy did he resist her entreaties. At length Elizabeth sat silent. For a few moments she appeared lost in thought, considering, probably, what new methods might be tried to withdraw her lover from so dark a fantasy, which, if it had no other meaning, was perhaps a symptom of mental disease. Though of a firmer character than his own, the tears rolled down her cheeks. But, in an instant, as it were, a new feeling took the place of sorrow; her eyes were fixed insensibly on the black veil, when, like a sudden twilight in the air, its terrors fell around her. She arose, and stood trembling before him.

"And do you feel it then, at last?" said he mournfully.

She made no reply, but covered her eyes with her hand, and turned to leave the room. He rushed forward and caught her arm.

"Have patience with me, Elizabeth!" cried he, passionately. "Do not desert me, though this veil must be between us here on earth. Be mine, and hereafter there shall be no veil over my face, no darkness between our souls! It is but a mortal veil — it is not for eternity! O! you know not how lonely I am, and how frightened, to be alone behind my black veil. Do not leave me in this miserable obscurity forever!"

"Lift the veil but once, and look me in the face," said she.

"Never! It cannot be!" replied Mr. Hooper.

"Then farewell!" said Elizabeth.

She withdrew her arm from his grasp, and slowly departed, pausing at the door, to give one long shuddering gaze, that seemed almost to penetrate the mystery of the black veil. But, even amid his grief, Mr. Hooper smiled to think that only a material emblem had separated him from happiness, though the horrors which it shadowed forth must be drawn darkly between the fondest of lovers.

From that time no attempts were made to remove Mr. Hooper's black veil, or, by a direct appeal, to discover the secret which it was supposed to hide. By persons who claimed a superiority to popular prejudice, it was reckoned more an eccentric whim, such as often mingles with the sober actions of men otherwise rational, and tinges them all with its own semblance of insanity.

But with the multitude, good Mr. Hooper was irreparably a bug-bear. He could not walk the street with any peace of mind, so conscious was he that the gentle and timid would turn aside to avoid him, and that others would make it a point of hardihood to throw themselves in his way. The impertinence of the latter class compelled him to give up his customary walk at sunset to the burial ground; for when he leaned pensively over the gate, there would always be faces behind the gravestones, peeping at his black veil. A fable went the rounds that the stare of the dead people drove him thence. It grieved him, to the very depth of his kind heart, to observe how the children fled from his approach, breaking up their merriest sports, while his melancholy figure was yet afar off. Their instinctive dread caused him to feel more strongly than aught· else, that a preternatural horror was inter-woven with the threads of the black crape. In truth, his own antipathy to the veil was known to be so great, that he never willingly passed before a mirror, nor stooped to drink at a still fountain, lest, in its peaceful bosom, he should be affrighted by himself. This was what gave plausibility to the whispers, that Mr. Hooper's conscience tortured him for some great crime too horrible to be entirely concealed, or otherwise than so obscurely intimated. Thus, from beneath the black veil, there rolled a cloud into the sunshine, an ambiguity of sin or sorrow, which enveloped the poor minister, so that love or sympathy could never reach him. It was said that ghost and fiend consorted with him there. With self-shudderings and outward terrors, he walked continually in its shadow, groping darkly within his own soul, or gazing through a medium that saddened the whole world. Even the lawless wind, it was believed, respected his dreadful secret, and never blew aside the veil. But still good Mr. Hooper sadly smiled at the pale visages of the worldly throng as he passed by.

Among all its bad influences, the black veil had the one desir-able effect, of making its wearer a very efficient clergyman. By the aid of his mysterious emblem — for there was no other appar-ent cause — he became a man of awful power over souls that were in agony of sin. His converts always regarded him with a dread peculiar to themselves, affirming, though but figuratively, that, before he brought them to celestial light, they had been with him behind the black veil. Its gloom, indeed, enabled him to sympa-thize with all dark affections. Dying sinners cried aloud for Mr. Hooper, and would not yield their breath till he appeared; though ever, as he stooped to whisper consolation, they shuddered at the veiled face so near their own. Such were the terrors of the black veil, even when Death had bared his visage! Strangers came long distances to attend service at his church, with the mere idle purpose of gazing at his figure, because it was forbidden them to behold his face. But many were made to quake ere they departed! Once, during Governor Belcher's administration, Mr. Hooper was appointed to preach the election sermon. Covered with his black veil, he stood before the chief magistrate, the council, and the representatives, and wrought so deep an impression, that the legislative measures of that year were characterized by all the gloom and piety of our earliest ancestral sway.

In this manner Mr. Hooper spent a long life, irreproachable in outward act, yet shrouded in dismal suspicions; kind and loving, though unloved, and dimly feared; a man apart from men, shunned in their health and joy, but ever summoned to their aid in mortal anguish. As years wore on, shedding their snows above his sable veil, he acquired a name throughout the New England churches, and they called him Father Hooper. Nearly all his parishioners, who were of mature age when he was settled, had been borne away by many a funeral; he had one congregation in the church, and a more crowded one in the churchyard; and having wrought so late into the evening, and done his work so well, it was now good Father Hooper's turn to rest.

Several persons were visible by the shaded candlelight, in the death chamber of the old clergyman. Natural connections he had none. But there was the decorously grave, though unmoved physician, seeking only to mitigate the last pangs of the patient whom he could not save. There were the deacons, and other eminently pious members of his church. There, also, was the Reverend Mr. Clark, of Westbury, a young and zealous divine, who had ridden in haste to pray by the bedside of the expiring minister. There was the nurse, no hired handmaiden of death, but one whose calm affection had endured thus long in secrecy, in solitude, amid the chill of age, and would not perish, even at the dying hour. Who, but Elizabeth! And there lay the hoary head of good Father Hooper upon the death pillow, with the black veil still swathed about his brow, and reaching down over his face, so that each more difficult gasp of his faint breath caused it to stir. All through life that piece of crape had hung between him and the world; it had separated him from cheerful brotherhood and woman's love, and kept him in that saddest of all prisons, his own heart; and still it lay upon his face, as if to deepen the gloom of his darksome chamber, and shade him from the sunshine of eternity.

For some time previous, his mind had been confused, wavering doubtfully between the past and the present, and hovering forward, as it were, at intervals, into the indistinctness of the world to come. There had been feverish turns, which tossed him from side to side, and wore away what little strength he had. But in his most convulsive struggles, and in the wildest vagaries of his intellect, when no other thought retained its sober influence, he still showed an awful solicitude lest the black veil should slip aside. Even if his bewildered soul could have forgotten, there was a faithful woman at his pillow, who, with averted eyes, would have covered that aged face, which she had last beheld in the comeliness of manhood. At length the death-stricken old man lay quietly in the torpor of mental and bodily exhaustion, with an imperceptible pulse, and breath that grew fainter and fainter, except when a long, deep, and irregular inspiration seemed to prelude the flight of his spirit.

The minister of Westbury approached the bedside.

"Venerable Father Hooper," said he, " the moment of your release is at hand. Are you ready for the lifting of the veil that shuts in time from eternity? "

Father Hooper at first replied merely by a feeble motion of his head; then, apprehensive, perhaps, that his meaning might be doubtful, he exerted himself to speak.

"Yea," said he, in faint accents, " my soul hath a patient weariness until that veil be lifted."

"And is it fitting," resumed the Reverend Mr. Clark, " that a man so given to prayer, of such a blameless example, holy in deed and thought, so far as mortal judgment may pronounce; is it fitting that a father in the church should leave a shadow on his memory, that may seem to blacken a life so pure? I pray you, my venerable brother, let not this thing be! Suffer us to be gladdened by your triumphant aspect as you go to your reward. Before the veil of eternity be lifted, let me cast aside this black veil from your face! "

And thus speaking the Reverend Mr. Clark bent forward to reveal the mystery of so many years. But, exerting a sudden energy, that made all the beholders stand aghast, Father Hooper snatched both his hands from beneath the bedclothes, and pressed them strongly on the black veil, resolute to struggle, if the minister of Westbury would contend with a dying man.

"Never!" cried the veiled clergyman. "On earth, never!"

"Dark old man!" exclaimed the affrighted minister, "with what horrible crime upon your soul are you now passing to the judgment?"

Father Hooper's breath heaved; it rattled in his throat; but, with a mighty effort, grasping forward with his hands, he caught hold of life, and held it back till he should speak. He even raised himself in bed; and there he sat, shivering with the arms of death around him, while the black veil hung down, awful, at that last moment, in the gathered terrors of a lifetime. And yet the faint, sad smile, so often there, now seemed to glimmer from its obscurity, and linger on Father Hooper's lips.

"Why do you tremble at me alone?" cried he, turning his veiled face round the circle of pale spectators. "Tremble also at each other! Have men avoided me, and women shown no pity, and children screamed and fled, only for my black veil? What, but the mystery which it obscurely typifies, has made this piece of crape so awful? When the friend shows his inmost heart to his friend; the lover to his best beloved; when man does not vainly shrink from the eye of his Creator, loathsomely treasuring up the secret of his sin; then deem me a monster, for the symbol beneath which I have lived, and die! I look around me, and, lo! on every visage a Black Veil."

While his auditors shrank from one another, in mutual affright, Father Hooper fell back upon his pillow, a veiled corpse, with a faint smile lingering on the lips. Still veiled, they laid him in his coffin, and a veiled corpse they bore him to the grave. The grass of many years has sprung up and withered on that grave, the burial stone is moss-grown, and good Mr. Hooper's face is dust; but awful is still the thought that it moldered beneath the Black Veil!

SUGGESTIONS FOR STUDY

1. Vocabulary: Omniscient, profaned, vagary, synod.

2. Are you sure that you got the point of the story? Just what does the black veil signify?

3. One of Hawthorne's characteristics is found in the manner in which

he throws an atmosphere of mystery around his stories by suggesting super-natural explanations for the incidents he relates. He never indorses these explanations; in fact, he often denies their truth, but by relating them he gets his effect. Find examples in this story.

4. Show that Hawthorne's prose has poetic quality by writing some of his sentences in the form of verse:

> If I hide my face for sorrow,
> There is cause enough;
> And if I cover it for secret sin,
> What mortal might not do the same?

5. In a few short sentences, state the plot. After looking up the word "parable," try to explain its connection with the plot.

FOR FURTHER READING

Twice-Told Tales: " The Gray Champion," " The Wedding Knell," " Mr. Higginbotham's Catastrophe," " The Prophetic Pictures," " Dr. Heidegger's Experiment," " Lady Eleanore's Mantle," " The Ambitious Guest "
Mosses from an Old Manse: " The Birthmark," " Drowne's Wooden Image," " Rappaccini's Daughter."
The Snow Image: " The Great Stone Face," " Ethan Brand "

THE TELL–TALE HEART
By Edgar Allan Poe (1809–1849)

Poe is probably the least local of any of our authors. Long before he was granted recognition in America, European critics considered him our most gifted writer. Scarcely a story or poem of his reflects a distinctly American setting, but rather an Old World background or " the misty mid-regions of Weir " — the pure realm of the imagination.

Oddly enough, Poe was born in Boston, but he was in no sense a true Bostonian. The mere chances of theatrical life took his parents there to play in a Boston theater. The father belonged to an old Maryland family, and it was back in Virginia that the father and mother both died before Edgar was three years old. The three destitute children were scattered among various families, Edgar being adopted by a wealthy merchant of Richmond named John Allan. Thus it was that Poe acquired his middle name. Unfortunately Mr. and Mrs. Allan spoiled the boy by too much pampering, too much money, and too spasmodic attempts at discipline. He was brilliant, high-strung, wilful, and extravagant. Five years of his schooling were spent in England, the rest in Virginia at private schools and the University of Virginia. But his college career was cut short at the end of a year because of Mr. Allan's indignation at his gambling debts. Poe proceeded to run away and join the army. Later reconciliation with Mr. Allan secured him an appointment to West Point Military Academy, but Poe neglected his duties until he was dismissed. This caused a final break with Mr. Allan, and Poe, thrown on his own resources, turned to literature. His first success was a prize of one hundred dollars won by the story, " MS. Found in a Bottle." This was followed by other prizes and the editorship of the *Southern Literary Messenger* of Richmond.

About this time Poe married his cousin Virginia Clemm, a girl of fourteen. During their twelve years of married life Poe was shifting from one magazine to another in Richmond, Philadelphia, and New York. In almost every case the brilliance of his contributions made surprising increase in the circulation of the magazine, but his intermittent spells of intoxication inevitably brought about his final dismissal. In the last years before Virginia's early death the couple were living in a tiny cottage at Fordham, then outside of New York but now part of the city itself. (Today this cottage is preserved in a park as a memorial to Poe; here one can see the tiny bare room where Virginia died.) By this time the family was so poor that there was not sufficient bedding to keep the invalid warm. She lay wrapped in her husband's army coat, with a great tortoise-shell cat in her bosom, her husband and mother chafing her hands and feet to preserve some warmth. Poe went from bad to worse in the two remaining years of his life. The exact circumstances of his death have never been fully cleared up, but he died in Baltimore, wretched and alone.

Poe was the type of man who is bound to arouse controversy. During his life he wrote scathing criticisms of many of the New England authors; since his death his character has been variously reviled and defended by his biographers. One point remains undisputed — that he was probably the most original genius in our literature.

" The Tell-Tale Heart " can be read in less than half an hour. If possible you should read it when you are sure of a half hour secure from interruption, for in this story Poe is attempting to produce upon you that " single emotional effect " which can be achieved only when " the soul of the reader is at the writer's control." Each line, almost each word of the story, has been chosen by its author to build up this single effect, and any interruption of the growth of the story to its final horror is unfair to the writer who wrought his effect so carefully. Breaking into the story would be as unfair to Poe as an interruption is to a violinist who is in the midst of building up the emotional power of a beautiful sonata. Each is attempting to play upon your emotions; both require an attention from you that is complete and unbroken.

This is no story for a nervous person to read at night. Poe is trying to make you feel horror at the insanity which has led to murder. As the insane man reveals the working of his mind, the reader grows more and more certain that the speaker is a maniac. From that brilliantly conceived sentence, "I loved the old man," which comes early in the story, the reader becomes more and more revolted until the scream of the maniac at the end gives all away to his visitors.

True! — nervous — very, very dreadfully nervous I had been and am; but why *will* you say that I am mad? The disease had sharpened my senses — not destroyed — not dulled them. Above all was the sense of hearing acute. I heard all things in the heaven and in the earth. I heard many things in hell. How, then, am I mad? Hearken! and observe how healthily — how calmly I can tell you the whole story.

It is impossible to say how first the idea entered my brain; but once conceived, it haunted me day and night. Object there was none. Passion there was none. I loved the old man. He had never wronged me. He had never given me insult. For his gold I had no desire. I think it was his eye! yes, it was this! He had the eye of a vulture — a pale blue eye, with a film over it. Whenever it fell upon me, my blood ran cold; and so by degrees — very gradually — I made up my mind to take the life of the old man, and thus rid myself of the eye forever.

I THINK IT WAS HIS EYE

Now this is the point. You fancy me mad. Madmen know nothing. But you should have seen *me*. You should have seen how wisely I proceeded — with what caution — with what foresight — with what dissimulation I went to work! I was never kinder to the old man than during the whole week before I killed him. And every night, about midnight, I turned the latch of his door and opened it so gently! And then, when I had made an opening sufficient for my head, I put in a dark lantern, all closed, closed, so that no light shone out, and then I thrust in my head. Oh, you would have laughed to see how cunningly I thrust it in! I moved slowly — very, very slowly, so that I might not disturb the old man's sleep. It took me an hour to place my whole head within the opening so far that I could see him as he lay upon his bed. Ha! — would a madman have been so wise as this? And then, when my head was well in the room, I undid the lantern cautiously — oh, so cautiously — cautiously (for the hinges creaked) — I undid it just so much that a single thin ray fell upon the vulture eye. And this I did for seven long nights — every night just at midnight — but I found the eye always closed; and so it was impossible to do the work; for it was not the old man who vexed me, but his Evil Eye. And every morning, when the day broke, I went boldly into the chamber, and spoke courageously to him, calling him by name in a hearty tone, and inquiring how he had passed the night. So you see he would have been a very profound old man, indeed, to suspect that every night, just at twelve, I looked in upon him while he slept.

Upon the eighth night I was more than usually cautious in opening the door. A watch's minute hand moves more quickly than did mine. Never before that night, had I *felt* the extent of my own powers — of my sagacity. I could scarcely contain my feelings of triumph. To think that there I was, opening the door, little by little, and he not even to dream of my secret deeds or thoughts. I fairly chuckled at the idea; and perhaps he heard me; for he moved on the bed suddenly, as if startled. Now you may think that I drew back — but no. His room was as black as pitch with the thick darkness (for the shutters were close fastened, through fear of robbers), and so I knew that he could not see the opening of the door, and I kept pushing it on steadily, steadily.

I had my head in, and was about to open the lantern, when my thumb slipped upon the tin fastening, and the old man sprang up in bed, crying out — " Who's there? "

I kept quite still and said nothing. For a whole hour I did not move a muscle, and in the meantime I did not hear him lie down. He was still sitting up in bed listening; — just as I have done, night after night, hearkening to the death watches[1] in the wall.

Presently I heard a slight groan, and I knew it was the groan

[1] **death watches:** insects that make a ticking sound, regarded by the superstitious as prophesying death.

of mortal terror. It was not a groan of pain or of grief — oh, no!
— it was the low stifled sound that arises from the bottom of
the soul when overcharged with awe. I knew the sound well.
Many a night, just at midnight, when all the world slept, it has
welled up from my own bosom, deepening, with its dreadful echo,
the terrors that distracted me. I say I knew it well. I knew what
the old man felt, and pitied him, although I chuckled at heart.
I knew that he had been lying awake ever since the first slight
noise, when he had turned in the bed. His fears had been ever
since growing upon him. He had been trying to fancy them
causeless, but could not. He had been saying to himself — " It is
nothing but the wind in the chimney — it is only a mouse crossing
the floor," or " it is merely a cricket which has made a single
chirp." Yes, he had been trying to comfort himself with these
suppositions: but he had found all in vain. *All in vain;* because
Death, in approaching him, had stalked with his black shadow
before him, and enveloped the victim. And it was the mournful
influence of the unperceived shadow that caused him to feel —
although he neither saw nor heard — to *feel* the presence of my
head within the room.

When I had waited a long time, very patiently, without hearing
him lie down, I resolved to open a little — a very, very little
crevice in the lantern. So I opened it — you cannot imagine how
stealthily, stealthily — until, at length a single dim ray, like the
thread of the spider, shot from out the crevice and fell full upon
the vulture eye.

It was open — wide, wide open — and I grew furious as I gazed
upon it. I saw it with perfect distinctness — all a dull blue, with
a hideous veil over it that chilled the very marrow of my bones;
but I could see nothing else of the old man's face or person: for
I had directed the ray as if by instinct, precisely upon the
damned spot.

And have I not told you that what you mistake for madness
is but overacuteness of the senses? — now, I say, there came
to my ears a low, dull, quick sound, such as a watch makes when
enveloped in cotton. I knew *that* sound well, too. It was the
beating of the old man's heart. It increased my fury, as the
beating of a drum stimulates the soldier into courage.

But even yet I refrained and kept still. I scarcely breathed.
I held the lantern motionless. I tried how steadily I could maintain the ray upon the eye. Meanwhile the hellish tattoo of the

heart increased. It grew quicker and quicker, and louder and louder every instant. The old man's terror *must* have been extreme! It grew louder, I say, louder every moment! — do you mark me well? I have told you that I am nervous: so I am. And now at the dead hour of the night, amid the dreadful silence of that old house, so strange a noise as this excited me to uncontrollable terror. Yet, for some minutes longer I refrained and stood still. But the beating grew louder, louder! I thought the heart must burst. And now a new anxiety seized me — the sound would be heard by a neighbor! The old man's hour had come! With a loud yell, I threw open the lantern and leaped into the room. He shrieked once — once only. In an instant I dragged him to the floor, and pulled the heavy bed over him. I then smiled gaily, to find the deed so far done. But, for many minutes, the heart beat on with a muffled sound. This, however, did not vex me; it would not be heard through the wall. At length it ceased. The old man was dead. I removed the bed and examined the corpse. Yes, he was stone, stone dead. I placed my hand upon the heart and held it there many minutes. There was no pulsation. He was stone dead. His eye would trouble me no more.

If still you think me mad, you will think so no longer when I describe the wise precautions I took for the concealment of the body. The night waned, and I worked hastily, but in silence. First of all I dismembered the corpse. I cut off the head and the arms and the legs.

I took up three planks from the flooring of the chamber, and deposited all between the scantlings. I then replaced the boards so cleverly, so cunningly, that no human eye — not even *his* — could have detected anything wrong. There was nothing to wash out — no stain of any kind — no blood-spot whatever. I had been too wary for that. A tub had caught all — ha! ha!

When I had made an end of these labors, it was four o'clock — still dark as midnight. As the bell sounded the hour, there came a knocking at the street door. I went down to open it with a light heart — for what had I *now* to fear? There entered three men, who introduced themselves, with perfect suavity, as officers of the police. A shriek had been heard by a neighbor during the night; suspicion of foul play had been aroused; information had been lodged at the police office, and they (the officers) had been deputed to search the premises.

I smiled — for *what* had I to fear? I bade the gentlemen welcome. The shriek, I said, was my own in a dream. The old man, I mentioned, was absent in the country. I took my visitors all over the house. I bade them search — search *well*. I led them, at length, to *his* chamber. I showed them his treasures, secure, undisturbed. In the enthusiasm of my confidence, I brought chairs into the room, and desired them *here* to rest from their fatigues, while I myself, in the wild audacity of my perfect triumph, placed my own seat upon the very spot beneath which reposed the corpse of the victim.

The officers were satisfied. My *manner* had convinced them. I was singularly at ease. They sat, and while I answered cheerily, they chatted of familiar things. But, erelong, I felt myself getting pale and wished them gone. My head ached, and I fancied a ringing in my ears: but they still sat and still chatted. The ringing became more distinct: — it continued and became more distinct: I talked more freely to get rid of the feeling: but it continued and gained definiteness — until, at length, I found that the noise was *not* within my ears.

No doubt I now grew *very* pale; — but I talked more fluently, and with a heightened voice. Yet the sound increased — and what could I do? It was *a low, dull, quick sound — much such a sound as a watch makes when enveloped in cotton.* I gasped for breath — and yet the officers heard it not. I talked more quickly — more vehemently; but the noise steadily increased. I arose and argued about trifles, in a high key and with violent gesticulations; but the noise steadily increased. Why *would* they not be gone? I paced the floor to and fro with heavy strides, as if excited to fury by the observations of the men — but the noise steadily increased. Oh God! what *could* I do? I foamed — I raved — I swore! I swung the chair upon which I had been sitting, and grated it upon the boards, but the noise arose over all and continually increased. It grew louder — louder — *louder!* And still the men chatted pleasantly, and smiled. Was it possible they heard not? Almighty God! — no, no! They heard! — they suspected! — they *knew!* — they were making a mockery of my horror! — this I thought, and this I think. But anything was better than this agony! Anything was more tolerable than this derision! I could bear those hypocritical smiles no longer! I felt that I must scream or die! and now — again! — hark! louder! louder! louder! *louder!*

"Villains!" I shrieked, "dissemble no more! I admit the deed! — tear up the planks! here, here! — it is the beating of his hideous heart!"

SUGGESTIONS FOR STUDY

1. Vocabulary: dissimulation, sagacity, suavity.
2. Did you feel the horror Poe expected you to feel? If not, for you the story is a failure.
3. Point out the details with which Poe builds up the feeling of horror to a climax.
4. Are the two opposing forces physical or mental in the plot of this story? Justify your answer.
5. Would you say that you have learned anything about human nature from reading "The Tell-Tale Heart"? What, specifically, did you learn? Was it worth learning?

FOR FURTHER READING

"The Black Cat"   "The Masque of the Red Death"
"The Cask of Amontillado"   "Murders in the Rue Morgue"
"A Descent into the Maelstrom"   "The Oblong Box"
"The Fall of the House of Usher"   "The Oval Portrait"
"The Gold Bug"   "The Pit and the Pendulum"
"MS. Found in a Bottle"   "The Purloined Letter"

THE WIDOW'S CRUISE

By FRANK RICHARD STOCKTON (1834–1902)

Did you ever play a game of "Who can tell the biggest lie?" Such a contest is most interesting when it is not agreed upon in advance but is the spontaneous development of some natural situation. One fisherman tells about the "big one" he caught, another angler has a better fish story, and whopper follows whopper until at last the least suspected listener unrolls a falsehood so tremendous that every other liar is silenced. The humor of such a situation is found in the fact that every story-teller knows himself to be a liar, and for that reason dares not question the truth of anything he hears lest his own tale be questioned. Mr. Stockton presents such a situation in this story. Four old sailors are pitted against a canny widow, and the widow wins.

Mr. Stockton is another old friend to those who have read *The Casting*

Away of Mrs. Lecks and Mrs. Aleshine, or *Rudder Grange,* or his even more famous " The Lady or the Tiger? " He was for a number of years on the staff of *St. Nicholas,* where his deft pen endeared him to a host of young readers who never outgrew a delight in his charm and originality. In " The Widow's Cruise " Mr. Stockton does not use a surprise ending, although he often employs it in other stories. Here he is content to gain his effect by making the preposterous seem plausible. You know these things could not have happened, but even when the widow Ducket " pours oil on the troubled waters " with such surprising results, everything seems, for the moment, quite possible.

The widow Ducket lived in a small village about ten miles from the New Jersey seacoast. In this village she was born, here she had married and buried her husband, and here she expected somebody to bury her, but she was in no hurry for that, for she had scarcely reached middle age. She was a tall woman with no apparent fat in her composition, and full of activity, both muscular and mental.

She rose at six o'clock in the morning, cooked breakfast, set the table, washed the dishes when the meal was over, milked, churned, swept, washed, ironed, worked in her little garden, attended to the flowers in the front yard, and in the afternoon knitted and quilted and sewed, and after tea she either went to see her neighbors or had them come to see her. When it was really dark she lighted the lamp in her parlor and read for an hour, and if it happened to be one of Miss Mary Wilkins'[1] books that she read she expressed doubts as to the realism of the characters therein described.

These doubts she expressed to Dorcas Networthy, who was a small, plump woman, with a solemn face, who had lived with the widow for many years and who had become her devoted disciple. Whatever the widow did that also did Dorcas; not so well, for her heart told her she could never expect to do that, but with a yearning anxiety to do everything as well as she could. She rose at five minutes past six, and in a subsidiary way she helped to get the breakfast, to eat it, to wash up the dishes, to work in the garden, to quilt, to sew, to visit and receive, and no one could have tried harder than she did to keep awake when the widow read aloud in the evening.

All these things happened every day in the summer time, but

[1] **Miss Mary Wilkins:** Mrs. Mary E. Wilkins Freeman.

in the winter the widow and Dorcas cleared the snow from their little front path instead of attending to the flowers, and in the evening they lighted a fire as well as a lamp in the parlor.

Sometimes, however, something different happened, but this was not often, only a few times in the year. One of the different things occurred when Mrs. Ducket and Dorcas were sitting on their little front porch one summer afternoon, one on the little bench on one side of the door and the other on the little bench on the other side of the door, each waiting, until she should hear the clock strike five, to prepare tea. But it was not yet a quarter to five when a one-horse wagon containing four men came slowly down the street. Dorcas first saw the wagon, and she instantly stopped knitting.

" Mercy on me! " she exclaimed. " Whoever those people are they are strangers here and they don't know where to stop, for they first go to one side of the street and then to the other."

The widow looked around sharply. " Humph! " said she. " Those men are sailor-men. You might see that in a twinkling of an eye. Sailor-men always drive that way because that is the way they sail ships. They first tack in one direction and then in another."

" Mr. Ducket didn't like the sea? " remarked Dorcas, for about the three hundredth time.

" No, he didn't," answered the widow, for about the two hundred and fiftieth time, for there had been occasions when she thought Dorcas put this question inopportunely. " He hated it, and he was drowned in it through trusting a sailor-man, which I never did or shall. Do you really believe those men are coming here? "

" Upon my word I do! " said Dorcas, and her opinion was correct.

The wagon drew up in front of Mrs. Ducket's little white house, and the two women sat rigidly, their hands in their laps, staring at the man who drove.

This was an elderly personage with whitish hair, and under his chin a thin whitish beard, which waved in the gentle breeze and gave Dorcas the idea that his head was filled with hair which was leaking out from below.

" Is this the widow Ducket's? " inquired this elderly man, in a strong, penetrating voice.

" That's my name," said the widow, and laying her knitting

on the bench beside her she went to the gate. Dorcas also laid her knitting on the bench beside her and went to the gate.

"I was told," said the elderly man, "at a house we touched at about a quarter of a mile back, that the widow Ducket's was the only house in this village where there was any chance of me and my mates getting a meal. We are four sailors and we are making from the bay over to Cuppertown, and that's eight miles ahead yet and we are all pretty sharp set for something to eat."

"This is the place," said the widow, "and I do give meals if there is enough in the house and everything comes handy."

"Does everything come handy today?" said he.

"It does," said she, "and you can hitch your horse and come in, but I haven't got anything for him."

"Oh, that's all right," said the man, "we brought along stores for him, so we'll just make fast and then come in."

The two women hurried into the house in a state of bustling preparation, for the furnishing of this meal meant one dollar in cash.

The four mariners, all elderly men, descended from the wagon, each one scrambling with alacrity over a different wheel.

A box of broken ship-biscuit was brought out and put on the ground in front of the horse, who immediately set himself to eating with great satisfaction.

Tea was a little late that day, because there were six persons to provide for instead of two, but it was a good meal, and after the four seamen had washed their hands and faces at the pump in the back yard and had wiped them on two towels furnished by Dorcas, they all came in and sat down. Mrs. Ducket seated herself at the head of the table with the dignity proper to the mistress of the house, and Dorcas seated herself at the other end with the dignity proper to the disciple of the mistress. No service was necessary, for everything that was to be eaten or drunk was on the table.

When each of the elderly mariners had had as much bread and butter, quickly-baked soda biscuit, dried beef, cold ham, cold tongue and preserved fruit of every variety known, as his storage capacity would permit, the mariner in command, Captain Bird, pushed back his chair, whereupon the other mariners pushed back their chairs.

"Madam," said Captain Bird, "we have all made a good meal,

which didn't need to be no better nor more of it, and we're satisfied, but that horse out there has not had time to rest himself enough to go the eight miles that lies ahead of us, so if it's all the same to you and this good lady, we'd like to sit on that front porch awhile and smoke our pipes. I was a-looking at that porch when I came in, and I bethought to myself what a rare good place it was to smoke a pipe in."

"There's pipes been smoked there," said the widow rising, " and it can be done again. Inside the house I don't allow tobacco, but on the porch neither of us minds."

So the four Captains betook themselves to the porch, two of them seating themselves on the little bench on one side of the door and two of them on the little bench on the other side of the door, and lighted their pipes.

"Shall we clear off the table and wash up the dishes," said Dorcas, " or wait until they are gone? "

"We will wait until they are gone," said the widow, " for now that they are here we might as well have a bit of a chat with them. When a sailor-man lights his pipe he is generally willing to talk, but when he is eatin' you can't get a word out of him."

Without thinking it necessary to ask permission, for the house belonged to her, the widow Ducket brought a chair and put it in the hall close to the open front door, and Dorcas brought another chair and seated herself by the side of the widow.

"Do all you sailor-men belong down there at the bay? " asked Mrs. Ducket, and thus the conversation began, and in a few minutes it had reached a point at which Captain Bird thought it proper to say that a great many strange things happen to seamen sailing on the sea which lands-people never dream of.

"Such as anything in particular? " asked the widow, at which remark Dorcas clasped her hands in expectancy.

At this question each of the mariners took his pipe from his mouth and gazed upon the floor in thought.

"There's a good many strange things happened to me and my mates at sea. Would you and that other lady like to hear any of them? " asked Captain Bird.

"We would like to hear them if they are true," said the widow.

"There's nothing happened to me and my mates that isn't true," said Captain Bird, " and here is something that once hap-pened to me: I was on a whaling v'yage when a big sperm whale, just as mad as a fiery bull, came at us, head on, and struck the ship at the stern with such tremendous force that his head crashed right through her timbers and he went nearly half his length into her hull. The hold was mostly filled with empty barrels, for we was just beginning our v'yage, and when he had made kindling wood of these, there was room enough for him. We all expected that it wouldn't take five minutes for the vessel to fill and go to the bottom, and we made ready to take to the boats, but it

" A GOOD MANY STRANGE THINGS HAPPENED "

turned out we didn't need to take to no boats, for as fast as the water rushed into the hold of the ship that whale drank it and squirted it up through the two blow holes in the top of his head, and as there was an open hatchway just over his head the water all went into the sea again, and that whale kept working day and night pumping the water out until we beached the vessel on the island of Trinidad — the whale helping us wonderful on our way over by the powerful working of his tail, which, being outside in the water, acted like a propeller. I don't believe anything stranger than that ever happened to a whaling ship."

"No," said the widow, "I don't believe anything ever did." Captain Bird now looked at Captain Sanderson, and the latter took his pipe out of his mouth and said that in all his sailing around the world he had never known anything queerer than what happened to a big steamship he chanced to be on, which ran into an island in a fog. Everybody on board thought the ship was wrecked, but it had twin screws and was going at such a tremendous speed that it turned the island entirely upside down and sailed over it, and he had heard tell that even now people sailing over the spot could look down into the water and see the roots of the trees and the cellars of the houses.

Captain Sanderson now put his pipe back into his mouth and Captain Burress took out his pipe.

"I was once in an obelisk ship," said he, "that used to trade regular between Egypt and New York carrying obelisks. We had a big obelisk on board. The way they ship obelisks is to make a hole in the stern of the ship and run the obelisk in, p'inted end foremost, and this obelisk filled up nearly the whole of that ship from stern to bow. We was about ten days out and sailing afore a northeast gale with the engines at full speed when suddenly we spied breakers ahead, and our Captain saw we was about to run on a bank. Now if we hadn't had an obelisk on board we might have sailed over that bank, but the Captain knew that with an obelisk on board we drew too much water for that, and that we'd be wrecked in about fifty-five seconds if something wasn't done quick. So he had to do something quick, and this is what he did. He ordered all steam on and drove slam-bang on that bank. Just as he expected we stopped so suddint that that big obelisk bounced for'ard, its p'inted end foremost, and went clean through the bow and shot out into the sea. The minute it did that the vessel was so lightened that it rose in the water and we easily steamed over the bank. There was one man knocked overboard by the shock when we struck, but as soon as we missed him we went back after him and we got him all right. You see when that obelisk went overboard its butt end, which was heaviest, went down first, and when it touched the bottom it just stood there, and as it was such a big obelisk there was about five and a half feet of it stuck out of the water. The man who was knocked overboard he just swum for that obelisk and he climbed up the hiryglyphics. It was a mighty fine obelisk and the Egyptians had cut their hiryglyphics good and deep so that the man could get hand and foot hold. And when we got to him and took him off he was sitting high and dry on the p'inted end of that obelisk. It was a great pity about the obelisk, for it was a good obelisk, but as I never heard the company tried to raise it I expect it is standing there yet."

Captain Burress now put his pipe back into his mouth and looked at Captain Jenkinson, who removed his pipe and said:

" The queerest thing that ever happened to me was about a shark. We was off the Banks and the time of year was July, and the ice was coming down and we got in among a lot of it. Not far away, off our weather bow, there was a little iceberg which had such a queerness about it that the Captain and three men went in a boat to look at it. The ice was mighty clear ice and you could see almost through it, and right inside of it, not more than three feet above the water line, and about two feet, or maybe twenty inches, inside the ice, was a whopping big shark, about fourteen feet long — a regular man-eater — frozen in there hard and fast. ' Bless my soul,' said the Captain, ' this is a wonderful curiosity and I'm going to git him out.' Just then one of the men said he saw that shark wink, but the Captain wouldn't believe him, for he said that shark was frozen stiff and hard and couldn't wink. You see the Captain had his own idees about things, and he knew that whales was warm-blooded and would freeze if they was shut up in ice, but he forgot that sharks was not whales and that they're cold-blooded just like toads. And there is toads that has been shut up in rocks for thousands of years, and they stayed alive, no matter how cold the place was, because they was cold-blooded, and when the rocks was split out hopped the frog. But as I said before, the Captain forgot sharks was cold-blooded and he determined to git that one out.

" Now you both know, being housekeepers, that if you take a needle and drive it into a hunk of ice you can split it. The Captain had a sail-needle with him and so he drove it into the iceberg right alongside of the shark and split it. Now the minute he did it he knew that the man was right when he said he saw the shark wink, for it flopped out of that iceberg quicker nor a flash of lightning."

" What a happy fish he must have been! " ejaculated Dorcas, forgetful of precedent, so great was her emotion.

" Yes," said Captain Jenkinson, " it was a happy fish enough, but it wasn't a happy Captain. You see that shark hadn't had anything to eat, perhaps for a thousand years, until the Captain came along with his sail-needle."

" Surely you sailor-men do see strange things," now said the widow, " and the strangest thing about them is that they are true."

" Yes, indeed," said Dorcas, " that is the most wonderful thing."

" You wouldn't suppose," said the widow Ducket, glancing from one bench of mariners to the other, " that I have a sea-story to tell, but I have, and if you like I will tell it to you."

Captain Bird looked up a little surprised. "We would like to hear it, indeed we would, madam," said he.

" Ay, ay! " said Captain Burress, and the two other mariners nodded.

" It was a good while ago," she said, " when I was living on the shore near the head of the bay, that my husband was away and I was left alone in the house. One mornin' my sister-in-law, who lived on the other side of the bay, sent me word by a boy on a horse that she hadn't any oil in the house to fill the lamp that she always put in the window to light her husband home, who was a fisherman, and if I would send her some by the boy she would pay me back as soon as they bought oil. The boy said he would stop on his way home and take the oil to her, but he never did stop, or perhaps he never went back, and about five o'clock I began to get dreadfully worried, for I knew if that lamp wasn't in my sister-in-law's window by dark she might be a widow before midnight. So I said to myself, ' I've got to get that oil to her, no matter what happens or how it's done.' Of course I couldn't tell what might happen, but there was only one way it could be done, and that was for me to get into the boat that was tied to the post down by the water and take it to her, for it was too far for me to walk around by the head of the bay. Now the trouble was I didn't know no more about a boat and the managin' of it than any one of you sailor-men knows about clear starchin'. But there wasn't no use of thinkin' what I knew and what I didn't know, for I had to take it to her and there was no way of doin' it except in that boat. So I filled a gallon can, for I thought I might as well take enough while I was about it, and I went down to the water and I unhitched that boat and I put the oil-can into her and then I got in, and off I started, and when I was about a quarter of a mile from the shore — "

"Madam," interrupted Captain Bird, "did you row or — or was there a sail to the boat?"

The widow looked at the questioner for a moment. "No," said she, "I didn't row. I forgot to bring the oars from the house, and it didn't matter for I didn't know how to use them, and if there had been a sail I couldn't have put it up, for I didn't know how to use it either. I used the rudder to make the boat go. The rudder was the only thing that I knew anything about. I'd held a rudder when I was a little girl and I knew how to work it. So I just took hold of the handle of the rudder and turned it round and round, and that made the boat go ahead, you know, and — "

"Madam!" exclaimed Captain Bird, and the other elderly mariners took their pipes from their mouths.

"Yes, that is the way I did it," continued the widow briskly; " big steamships are made to go by a propeller turning round and round at their back ends, and I made the rudder work in the same way, and I got along very well, too, until suddenly, when I was about a quarter of a mile from the shore, a most terrible and awful storm rose. There must have been a typhoon or a cyclone out at sea, for the waves came up the bay bigger than houses, and when they got to the head of the bay they turned around and tried to get out to sea again; so in this way they continually met, and made the most awful and roarin' pilin' up of waves that ever was known.

"My little boat was pitched about as if it had been a feather in a breeze, and when the front part of it was cleavin' itself down into the water the hind part was stickin' up until the rudder whizzed around like a patent churn with no milk in it. The thunder began to roar and the lightnin' flashed, and three seagulls, so nearly frightened to death that they began to turn up the whites of their eyes, flew down and sat on one of the seats of the boat, forgettin' in that awful moment that man was their nat'ral enemy. I had a couple of biscuits in my pocket, because I had thought I might want a bite in crossing, and I crumbled up one of these and fed the poor creatures. Then I began to wonder what I was goin' to do, for things were gettin' awfuller and awfuller every instant, and the little boat was a-heavin' and a-pitchin' and a-rollin' and h'istin' itself up, first on one end and then on the other, to such an extent that if I hadn't kept tight hold of the rudder handle I'd slipped off the seat I was sittin' on.

"All of a sudden I remembered that oil in the can, but just

as I was puttin' my fingers on the cork my conscience smote me. 'Am I goin' to use this oil,' I said to myself, 'and let my sister-in-law's husband be wrecked for want of it?' And then I thought that he wouldn't want it all that night and perhaps they would buy oil the next day, and so I poured out about a tumblerful of it on the water, and I can just tell you sailor-men that you never saw anything act as prompt as that did. In three seconds, or perhaps five, the water all around me, for the distance of a small front yard, was just as flat as a table and as smooth as glass, and so invitin' in appearance that the three gulls jumped out of the boat and began to swim about on it, primin' their feathers and looking at themselves in the transparent depths, though I must say that one of them made an awful face as he dipped his bill into the water and tasted kerosene.

"Now I had time to sit quiet in the midst of the placid space I had made for myself and rest from working of the rudder. Truly it was a wonderful and marvelous thing to look at. The waves was roarin' and leapin' up all around me higher than the roof of this house, and sometimes their tops would reach over so that they nearly met and shut out all view of the stormy sky, which seemed as if it was bein' torn to pieces by blazin' lightnin', while the thunder pealed so tremendous that it almost drowned the roar of the waves. Not only above and all around me was everything terrific and fearful, but even under me it was the same, for there was a big crack in the bottom of the boat as wide as my hand, and through this I could see down into the water, beneath, and there was — "

"Madam!" ejaculated Captain Bird, the hand which had been holding his pipe a few inches from his mouth now dropping to his knee, and at this motion the hands which held the pipes of the three other mariners dropped to their knees.

"Of course it sounds strange," continued the widow, "but I know that people can see down into clear water, and the water under me was clear, and the crack was wide enough for me to see through, and down under me was sharks and sword-fishes and other horrible water creatures, which I had never seen before, all driven into the bay, I haven't a doubt, by the violence of the storm out at sea. The thought of my bein' upset and fallin' in among those monsters made my very blood run cold, and involuntary-like I began to turn the handle of the rudder, and in a moment I shot into a wall of ragin' sea water that was towerin'

around me. For a second I was fairly blinded and stunned, but
I had the cork out of that oil-can in no time, and very soon, you'd
scarcely believe it if I told you how soon, I had another placid
mill-pond surroundin' of me. I sat there a-pantin' and fannin'
with my straw hat, for you'd better believe I was flustered, and
then I began to think how long it would take me to make a line
of mill-ponds clean across the head of the bay and how much
oil it would need and whether I had enough. So I sat and calculated that if a tumblerful of oil would make a smooth place about
seven yards across, which I should say was the width of the one
I was in, which I calculated by a measure of my eye as to how
many breadths of carpet it would take to cover it, and if the bay
was two miles across, betwixt our house and my sister-in-law's,
and although I couldn't get the thing down to exact figures,
I saw pretty soon that I wouldn't have oil enough to make a level
cuttin' through all those mountainous billows, and besides,
even if I had enough to take me across, what would be the
good of going if there wasn't any oil left to fill my sister-in-law's
lamp?

"While I was thinkin' and calculatin' a perfectly dreadful
thing happened, which made me think if I didn't get out of this
pretty soon I'd find myself in a mighty risky predicament. The
oil-can, which I had forgotten to put the cork in, toppled over,
and before I could grab it every drop of the oil ran into the hind
part of the boat, where it was soaked up by a lot of dry dust that
was there. No wonder my heart sank when I saw this. Glancin'
wildly around me, as people will do when they are scared, I saw
the smooth place I was in gettin' smaller and smaller, for the
kerosene was evaporatin', as it will do even off woolen clothes
if you give it time enough. The first pond I had come out of
seemed to be covered up, and the great, towerin', throbbin' preci-
pice of sea-water was a-closin' around me.

" Castin' down my eyes in despair I happened to look through
the crack in the bottom of the boat, and oh! what a blessed
relief it was, for down there everything was smooth and still, and
I could see the sand on the bottom as level and hard, no doubt,
as it was on the beach. Suddenly the thought struck me that
that bottom would give me the only chance I had of gettin' out
of the frightful fix I was in. If I could fill that oil-can with air
and then puttin' it under my arm and takin' a long breath, if I
could drop down on that smooth bottom, I might run along

toward shore, as far as I could, and then, when I felt my breath was givin' out, I could take a pull at the oil-can and take another run, and then take another pull and another run, and perhaps the can would hold air enough for me until I got near enough to shore to wade to dry land. To be sure the sharks and other monsters were down there, but then they must have been awfully frightened and perhaps they might not remember that man was their nat'ral enemy. Anyway, I thought it would be better to try the smooth water passage down there than stay and be swallowed up by the ragin' waves on top.

" So I blew the can full of air and corked it, and then I tore up some of the boards from the bottom of the boat so as to make a hole big enough for me to get through — and you sailor-men needn't wriggle so when I say that, for you all know a divin' bell hasn't any bottom at all and the water never comes in — and so when I got the hole big enough I took the oil-can under my arm and was just about to slip down through it when I saw an awful turtle a-walkin' through the sand at the bottom. Now, I might trust sharks and sword-fishes and sea-serpents to be frightened and forget about their nat'ral enemies, but I never could trust a gray turtle as big as a cart, with a black neck a yard long, with yellow bags to its jaws, to forget anything or to remember anything. I'd as lieve get into a bath-tub with a live crab as to go down there. It wasn't of no use even so much as thinkin' of it, so I gave up that plan and didn't once look through that hole again."

" And what did you do, madam?" asked Captain Bird, who was regarding her with a face of stone.

" I used electricity," she said. " Now don't start as if you had a shock of it. That's what I used. When I was younger than I was then and sometimes visited friends in the city, we often amused ourselves by rubbing our feet on the carpet until we got ourselves so full of electricity that we could put up our fingers and light the gas. So I said to myself that if I could get full of electricity for the purpose of lightin' the gas I could get full of it for other purposes, and so, without losin' a moment, I set to work. I stood upon one of the seats, which was dry, and I rubbed the bottoms of my shoes backward and forward on it with such violence and swiftness that they pretty soon got warm and I began fillin' with electricity, and when I was fully charged with it from my toes to the top of my head I just sprang into the water and swam ashore. Of course I couldn't sink, bein' full of electricity."

Captain Bird heaved a long sigh and rose to his feet, whereupon the other mariners rose to their feet. "Madam," said Captain Bird, "what's to pay for the supper and — the rest of the entertainment?"

"The supper is twenty-five cents apiece," said the widow Ducket, "and everything else is free, gratis."

Whereupon each mariner put his hand into his trousers pocket, pulled out a silver quarter, and handed it to the widow. Then with four solemn "Good-evenin's" they went out to the front gate.

"Cast off, Captain Jenkinson," said Captain Bird, "and you, Captain Burress, clew him up for'ard. You can stay in the bow, Captain Sanderson, and take the sheet lines. I'll go aft."

All being ready, each of the elderly mariners clambered over a wheel, and having seated themselves, they prepared to lay their course for Cuppertown.

But just as they were about to start Captain Jenkinson asked that they lay-to a bit, and clambering down over his wheel, he reëntered the front gate and went up to the door of the house, where the widow and Dorcas were still standing.

"Madam," said he, "I just came back to ask what became of your brother-in-law through his wife's not bein' able to put no light in the window?"

"The storm drove him ashore on our side of the bay," said she, "and the next mornin' he came up to our house and I told him all that had happened to me; and when he took our boat and went home and told that story to his wife she just packed up and went West, and got divorced from him; and it served him right, too."

"Thank you, ma'am," said Captain Jenkinson, and going out of the gate he clambered up over the wheel and the wagon cleared for Cuppertown.

When the elderly mariners were gone the widow Ducket, still standing in the door, turned to Dorcas:

"Think of it!" she said, "to tell all that to me, in my own house! And after I had opened my one jar of brandied peaches that I'd been keepin' for special company!"

"In your own house!" ejaculated Dorcas. "And not one of them brandied peaches left!"

The widow jingled the four quarters in her hand before she slipped them into her pocket.

"Anyway, Dorcas," she remarked, "I think we can now say we are square with all the world, and so let's go in and wash the dishes."

"Yes," said Dorcas, "we're square."

SUGGESTIONS FOR STUDY

1. Vocabulary: inopportune, obelisk, "hiryglyphics," rudder.
2. How early in the story did you become aware that it was going to be humorous?
3. Which of the four sailors told the best yarn?
4. What are the two opposing forces in the plot?
5. What is your opinion of Stockton's ability to portray characters?
6. Have you ever read a Baron Munchausen story? Or a Paul Bunyan yarn? How are they like the sailors' yarns you find here?
7. Try to write a story that is preposterous and yet plausible.
8. To appreciate the pun in Stockton's title, read the story of the widow's *cruse* in the Bible, I Kings 17:8–17.

FOR FURTHER READING

SHORT STORIES	LONG STORIES OR NOVELETTES
"The Lady or the Tiger?"	"Rudder Grange"
"The Transferred Ghost"	"The Casting Away of Mrs. Lecks
"The Remarkable Wreck of the	and Mrs. Aleshine"
'Thomas Hyke'"	
"A Christmas Wreck"	
"A Tale of Negative Gravity"	

AN INGÉNUE OF THE SIERRAS

By BRET HARTE (1836–1902)

Enter the far West, and with it "local color" to flavor the short story. Stagecoaches, perilous mountain roads, highwaymen, frontier chivalry, frontier cussin', and above all the full-bodied tang of frontier humor. For Bret Harte became famous for his stories of the California of the "fifties." His characters are taken from the gold mines, and from the camps of the "forty-niners." They are strange, but real. Opening a vein of story material that has increased tremendously in popularity — and decreased as tremendously in its excellence — Bret Harte was first with the localized romance of the wild and woolly West.

As founder and editor of *The Overland Monthly* Bret Harte gave the stimulus which probably started a line of famous writers of the American Far West. And yet, strangely enough, Harte was not a true westerner. During his seventeen years in California he considered himself an exile. To him the " great open spaces " had no such appeal as the literary and artistic circles of the metropolis. He had spent his first twenty years in New York, and it was to New York he gladly returned when public favor brought him relief from financial worries. No American writer has ever had a more spectacular success than Bret Harte. At the height of his career *The Atlantic Monthly* made him a contributing editor with an annual salary of $10,000 for whatever he might condescend to write for that magazine. " An Ingénue of the Sierras " was written in 1893, almost twenty-five years after Bret Harte's first book appeared. In it you will see that Harte had learned a trick or two from his eastern contemporary, Thomas Bailey Aldrich (see page 97).

I

We all held our breath as the coach rushed through the semi-darkness of Galloper's Ridge. The vehicle itself was only a huge, lumbering shadow; its side-lights were carefully extinguished, and Yuba Bill had just politely removed from the lips of an outside passenger even the cigar with which he had been ostentatiously exhibiting his coolness. For it had been rumored that the Ramon Martinez gang of " road agents " were " laying " for us on the second grade, and would time the passage of our lights across Gallopers in order to intercept us in the " brush " beyond. If we could cross the ridge without being seen, and so get through the brush before they reached it, we were safe. If they followed, it would only be a stern chase, with the odds in our favor.

The huge vehicle swayed from side to side, rolled, dipped, and plunged, but Bill kept the track, as if, in the whispered words of the expressman, he could " feel and smell " the road he could no longer see. We knew that at times we hung perilously over the edge of slopes that eventually dropped a thousand feet sheer to the tops of the sugar-pines below, but we knew that Bill knew it also. The half-visible heads of the horses, drawn wedgewise together by the tightened reins, appeared to cleave the darkness like a ploughshare, held between his rigid hands. Even the hoof-beats of the six horses had fallen into a vague, monotonous, distant roll. Then the ridge was crossed, and we plunged into the still blacker obscurity of the brush. Rather, we no longer seemed to move — it was only the phantom night that rushed by us. The horses might have been submerged in some swift Lethean stream [1] ; nothing but the top of the coach and the rigid bulk of Yuba Bill arose above them. Yet even in that awful moment our speed was unslackened; it was as if Bill cared no longer to *guide,* but only to drive; or as if the direction of his huge machine was determined by other hands than his. An incautious whisperer hazarded the paralyzing suggestion of our " meeting another team." To our great astonishment Bill overheard it ; to our greater astonishment he replied. " It 'ud be only a neck and neck race which would get to hell first," he said quietly. But we were relieved — for he had *spoken!* Almost simultaneously the wider turnpike began to glimmer faintly as a visible track before us ; the wayside trees fell out of line, opened up, and dropped off one after another ; we were on the broader tableland, out of danger, and apparently unperceived and unpursued.

Nevertheless in the conversation that broke out again with the relighting of the lamps, and the comments, congratulations, and reminiscences that were freely exchanged, Yuba Bill preserved a dissatisfied and even resentful silence. The most generous praise of his skill and courage awoke no response. " I reckon the old man was just spilin' for a fight, and is feelin' disappointed," said a passenger. But those who knew that Bill had the true fighter's scorn for any purely purposeless conflict were more or less concerned and watchful of him. He would drive steadily for four or five minutes with thoughtfully knitted brows, but eyes still keenly observant under his slouched hat, and then, relaxing his strained attitude, would give way to a movement of impatience. " You ain't uneasy about anything, Bill, are you? " asked the expressman, confidentially. Bill lifted his eyes with a slightly contemptuous surprise. " Not about anything ter *come.* It's what *hez* happened that I don't exackly sabe. I don't see no signs of Ramon's gang ever havin' been out at all, and ef they were out I don't see why they didn't go for us."

" The simple fact is, that our ruse was successful," said an outside passenger. " They waited to see our lights on the ridge, and

<hr>

[1] **Lethean stream:** in Greek mythology, Lethe was the river of oblivion in the lower world.

not seeing them, missed us until we had passed. That's my opinion."

" You ain't puttin' any price on that opinion, air ye? " inquired Bill politely.

" No."

" 'Cos thar's a comic paper in 'Frisco pays for them things, and I've seen worse things in it."

" Come off, Bill! " retorted the passenger, slightly nettled by the tittering of his companions. " Then what did you put out the lights for? "

" Well," returned Bill, grimly, " it mout have been because I didn't keer to hev you chaps blazin' away at the first bush you *thought* you saw move in your skeer, and bringin' down their fire on us."

The explanation, though unsatisfactory, was by no means an improbable one, and we thought it better to accept it with a laugh. Bill, however, resumed his abstracted manner.

"Who got in at the Summit? " he at last asked abruptly of the expressman.

" Derrick and Simpson of Cold Spring, and one of the ' Excelsior ' boys," responded the expressman.

" And that Pike County girl from Dow's Flat, with her bundles. Don't forget her," added the outside passenger, ironically.

" Does anybody here know her? " continued Bill, ignoring the irony.

" You'd better ask Judge Thompson; he was mighty attentive to her, gettin' her a seat by the off window, and lookin' after her bundles and things."

" Gettin' her a seat by the *window?* " repeated Bill.

" Yes; she wanted to see everything, and wasn't afraid of the shooting."

" Yes," broke in a third passenger, "and he was so damned civil that, when she dropped her ring in the straw, he struck a match ag'in' all your rules, you know, and held it for her to find it. And it was just as we were crossin' through the brush, too. I saw the hull thing through the window, for I was hanging over the wheels with my gun, ready for action. And it wasn't no fault of Judge Thompson's if his damned foolishness hadn't shown us up, and got us a shot from the gang."

Bill gave a short grunt, but drove steadily on without further comment, or even turning his eyes to the speaker.

We were now not more than a mile from the station at the crossroads where we were to change horses. The lights already glimmered in the distance, and there was a faint suggestion of the coming dawn on the summits of the ridge to the west. We had plunged into a belt of timber, when suddenly a horseman emerged at a sharp canter from a trail that seemed to be parallel with our own. We were all slightly startled; Yuba Bill alone preserving his moody calm.

"Hullo!" he said.

The stranger wheeled to our side as Bill slackened his speed. He seemed to be a "packer," or freight muleteer.

"Ye didn't get held up on the Divide?" continued Bill, cheerfully.

"No," returned the packer, with a laugh; "I don't carry treasure. But I see you're all right, too. I saw you crossin' over Galloper's."

"*Saw* us?" said Bill sharply. "We had our lights out."

"Yes, but there was suthin' white, a handkerchief or woman's veil, I reckon, hangin' from the window. It was only a movin' spot ag'in' the hillside, but ez I was lookin' out for ye I knew it was you by that. Good night!"

He cantered away. We tried to look at each other's faces, and at Bill's expression in the darkness, but he neither spoke nor stirred until he threw down the reins when we stopped before the station. The passengers quickly descended from the roof; the expressman was about to follow, but Bill plucked his sleeve.

"I'm goin' to take a look over this yer stage and these yer passengers with ye, afore we start."

"Why, what's up?"

"Well," said Bill, slowly disengaging himself from one of his enormous gloves, "when we waltzed down into the brush up there, I saw a man, ez plain ez I see you, rise up from it. I thought our time had come and the band was goin' to play, when he sorter drew back, made a sign, and we just scooted past him."

"Well?"

"Well," said Bill, "it means that this yer coach was *passed through free* tonight."

"You don't object to *that*, surely? I think we were deucedly lucky."

Bill slowly drew off his other glove. "I've been riskin' my everlastin' life on this damned line three times a week," he said with mock humility, " and I'm allus thankful for small mercies. *But,*" he added grimly, " when it comes down to being passed free by some pal of a hoss-thief, and thet called a speshul Providence, *I ain't in it !* No, sir, I ain't in it ! "

II

It was with mixed emotions that the passengers heard that a delay of fifteen minutes, to tighten certain screw-bolts, had been ordered by the autocratic Bill. Some were anxious to get their breakfast at Sugar Pine, but others were not averse to linger for the daylight that promised greater safety on the road. The expressman, knowing the real cause of Bill's delay, was nevertheless at a loss to understand the object of it. The passengers were all well known; any idea of complicity with the road agents was wild and impossible; and, even if there was a confederate of the gang among them, he would have been more likely to precipitate a robbery than to check it. Again, the discovery of such a confederate — to whom they clearly owed their safety — and his arrest, would have been quite against the Californian sense of justice, if not actually illegal. It seemed evident that Bill's quixotic sense of honor was leading him astray.

The station consisted of a stable, a wagon-shed, and a building containing three rooms. The first was fitted up with " bunks," or sleeping-berths, for the employees, the second was the kitchen, and the third and larger apartment was dining-room or sitting-room, and was used as general waiting-room for the passengers. It was not a refreshment station, and there was no " bar." But a mysterious command from the omnipotent Bill produced a demijohn of whisky, with which he hospitably treated the company. The seductive influence of the liquor loosened the tongue of the gallant Judge Thompson. He admitted to having struck a match to enable the fair Pike Countian to find her ring, which, however, proved to have fallen in her lap. She was " a fine, healthy young woman — a type of the Far West, sir ; in fact, quite a prairie blossom, yet simple and guileless as a child." She was on her way to Marysville, he believed, " although she expected to meet friends — a friend, in fact — later on." It was her first visit to a large town — in fact, any civilized center — since she crossed the plains three years ago. Her girlish curiosity was quite touching, and her innocence irresistible. In fact, in a country whose tendency was to produce " frivolity and forwardness in young girls," he " found her a most interesting young person." She was even then out in the stable-yard watching the horses being harnessed, " preferring to indulge a pardonable healthy young curiosity than to listen to the empty compliments of the younger passengers."

The figure which Bill saw thus engaged, without being otherwise distinguished, certainly seemed to justify the judge's opinion. She appeared to be a well-matured country girl, whose frank gray eyes and large laughing mouth expressed a wholesome and abiding gratification in her life and surroundings. She was watching the replacing of luggage in the boot. A little feminine start, as one of her own parcels was thrown somewhat roughly on the roof, gave Bill his opportunity. " Now, there," he growled to the helper, " ye ain't carting stone! Look out, will yer! Some of your things, miss? " he added, with gruff courtesy, turning to her. " These yer trunks, for instance? "

She smiled a pleasant assent, and Bill, pushing aside the helper, seized a large, square trunk in his arms. But from excess of zeal, or some other mischance, his foot slipped, and he came down heavily, striking the corner of the trunk on the ground and loosening its hinges and fastenings. It was a cheap, common-looking affair, but the accident discovered in its yawning lid a quantity of white, lace-edged feminine apparel of an apparently superior quality. The young lady uttered another cry and came quickly forward, but Bill was profuse in his apologies, himself girded the broken box with a strap, and declared his intention of having the company " make it good " to her with a new one. Then he casually accompanied her to the door of the waiting-room, entered, made a place for her before the fire by simply lifting the nearest and most youthful passenger by the coat collar from the stool that he was occupying, and, having installed the lady in it, displaced another man who was standing before the chimney, and, drawing himself up to his full six feet of height in front of her, glanced down upon his fair passenger as he took his waybill from his pocket.

" Your name is down here as Miss Mullins? " he said.

She looked up, became suddenly aware that she and her questioner were the center of interest to the whole circle of passengers, and, with a slight rise of color, returned, " Yes."

" Well, Miss Mullins, I've got a question or two to ask ye. I ask it straight out afore this crowd. It's in my rights to take ye aside and ask it — but that ain't my style; I'm no detective. I needn't ask it at all, but act as ef I knowed the answer, or I might leave it to be asked by others. Ye needn't answer it ef ye don't like; ye've got a friend over ther — Judge Thompson — who is a friend to ye, right or wrong, jest as any other man here

" DID YOU SIGNAL FROM THE COACH? "

is — as though ye'd packed your own jury. Well, the simple question I've got to ask ye is *this* — Did you signal to anybody from the coach when we passed Galloper's an hour ago? "

We all thought that Bill's courage and audacity had reached its climax here. To openly and publicly accuse a " lady " before a group of chivalrous Californians, and that lady possessing the further attractions of youth, good looks, and innocence, was little short of desperation. There was an evident movement of adhesion towards the fair stranger, a slight muttering broke out on the right, but the very boldness of the act held them in stupefied surprise. Judge Thompson, with a bland propitiatory smile, began: " Really, Bill, I must protest on behalf of this young lady — " when the fair accused, raising her eyes to her accuser, to the consternation of everybody answered with the slight but convincing hesitation of conscientious truthfulness:

" *I did.*"

" Ahem! " interposed the judge, hastily, " er — that is — er — you allowed your handkerchief to flutter from the window. I noticed it myself casually — one might say even playfully — but without any particular significance."

The girl, regarding her apologist with a singular mingling of pride and impatience, returned briefly:

" I signaled."

" Who did you signal to? " asked Bill, gravely.

" The young gentleman I'm going to marry."

A start, followed by a slight titter from the younger passengers, was instantly suppressed by a savage glance from Bill.

" What did you signal to him for? " he continued.

" To tell him I was here, and that it was all right," returned the young girl, with a steadily rising pride and color.

" Wot was all right? " demanded Bill.

" That I wasn't followed, and that he could meet me on the road beyond Cass's Ridge Station." She hesitated a moment, and then, with a still greater pride, in which a youthful defiance was still mingled, said: " I've run away from home to marry him. And I mean to! No one can stop me. Dad didn't like him just because he was poor, and dad's got money. Dad wanted me to marry a man I hate, and got a lot of dresses and things to bribe me."

" And you're taking them in your trunk to the other fellow? " said Bill, grimly.

" Yes; he's poor," returned the girl, defiantly.

" Then your father's name is Mullins? " asked Bill.

" It's not Mullins. I —I — took that name," she hesitated, with her first exhibition of self-consciousness.

" Wot *is* his name? "

" Eli Hemmings."

A smile of relief and significance went round the circle. The fame of Eli or "Skinner" Hemmings, as a notorious miser and usurer, had passed even beyond Galloper's Ridge.

"The step that you're taking, Miss Mullins, I need not tell you, is one of great gravity," said Judge Thompson, with a certain paternal seriousness of manner, in which, however, we were glad to detect a glaring affectation, "and I trust that you and your affianced have fully weighed it. Far be it from me to interfere with or question the natural affections of two young people; but may I ask you what you know of the — er — young gentleman for whom you are sacrificing so much, and, perhaps, imperiling your whole future? For instance, have you known him long?"

The slightly troubled air of trying to understand — not unlike the vague wonderment of childhood — with which Miss Mullins had received the beginning of this exordium, changed to a relieved smile of comprehension as she said quickly: "Oh, yes, nearly a whole year."

"And," said the judge, smiling, "has he a vocation — is he in business?"

"Oh, yes," she returned, "he's a collector."

"A collector?"

"Yes; he collects bills, you know, money," she went on, with childish eagerness; "not for himself — *he* never has any money, poor Charley — but for his firm. It's dreadful hard work, too; keeps him out for days and nights, over bad roads and baddest weather. Sometimes, when he's stole over to the ranch just to see me, he's been so bad he could scarcely keep his seat in the saddle, much less stand. And he's got to take mighty big risks, too. Times the folks are cross with him and won't pay; once they shot him in the arm, and he came to me, and I helped do it up for him. But he don't mind. He's real brave, jest as brave as he's good." There was such a wholesome ring of truth in this pretty praise that we were touched in sympathy with the speaker.

"What firm does he collect for?" asked the judge gently.

"I don't know exactly — he won't tell me — but I think it's a Spanish firm. You see" — she took us all into her confidence with a sweeping smile of innocent yet half-mischievous artlessness — "I only know because I peeped over a letter he once got from his firm, telling him he must hustle up and be ready for the road the next day; but I think the name was Martinez — yes, Ramon Martinez."

In the dead silence that ensued — a silence so profound that
we could hear the horses in the distant stable-yard rattling their
harness — one of the younger " Excelsior " boys burst into a
hysterical laugh; but the fierce eye of Yuba Bill was down upon
him, and seemed to instantly stiffen him into a silent, grinning
mask. The young girl, however, took no note of it; following out,
with loverlike diffusiveness, the reminiscences thus awakened,
she went on:

" Yes, it's mighty hard work, but he says it's all for me, and as
soon as we're married he'll quit it. He might have quit it before,
but he won't take no money of me, nor what I told him I could
get out of dad! That ain't his style. He's mighty proud — if he
is poor — is Charley. Why, thar's all ma's money which she
left me in the savin's bank that I wanted to draw out — for I had
the right — and give it to him, but he wouldn't hear of it! Why,
he wouldn't take one of the things I've got with me, if he knew
it. And so he goes on ridin' and ridin', here and there and everywhere, and gettin' more and more played out and sad, and thin and
pale as a spirit, and always so uneasy about his business, and
startin' up at times when we're meetin' out in the south woods or
in the far clearin', and sayin': ' I must be goin' now, Polly,' and
yet always tryin' to be chiffle and chipper afore me. Why, he must
have rid miles and miles to have watched for me thar in the
brush at the foot of Galloper's tonight, jest to see if all was safe,
and Lordy! I'd have given him the signal and showed a light if
I'd died for it the next minit. There! That's what I know of
Charley — that's what I'm running away from home for — that's
what I'm running to him for, and I don't care who knows it! And
I only wish I'd done it afore — and I would — if — if — if —
he'd only *asked me!* There now!" She stopped, panted, and
choked. Then one of the sudden transitions of youthful emotion
overtook the eager, laughing face; it clouded up with the swift
change of childhood, a lightning quiver of expression broke over
it — and — then came the rain!

I think this simple act completed our utter demoralization! We
smiled feebly at each other with that assumption of masculine
superiority which is miserably conscious of its own helplessness
at such moments. We looked out of the window, blew our noses,
said: " Eh — what? " and " I say," vaguely to each other, and
were greatly relieved and yet apparently astonished when Yuba
Bill, who had turned his back upon the fair speaker, and was

kicking the logs in the fireplace, suddenly swept down upon us and bundled us all into the road, leaving Miss Mullins alone. Then he walked aside with Judge Thompson for a few moments; returned to us, autocratically demanded of the party a complete reticence towards Miss Mullins on the subject matter under discussion, reëntered the station, reappeared with the young lady, suppressed a faint, idiotic cheer which broke from us at the spectacle of her innocent face once more cleared and rosy, climbed the box, and in another moment we were under way.

"Then she don't know what her lover is yet?" asked the expressman, eagerly.

"No."

"Are *you* certain it's one of the gang?"

"Can't say *for sure*. It mout be a young chap from Yolo who bucked ag'in' the tiger at Sacramento, got regularly cleaned out and busted, and joined the gang for a flier. They say thar was a new hand in that job over at Keeley's — and a mighty game one, too — and ez there was some buckshot onloaded that trip, he might hev got his share, and that would tally with what the girl said about his arm. See! Ef that's the man, I've heered he was the son of some big preacher in the States, and a college sharp to boot, who ran wild in 'Frisco, and played himself for all he was worth. They're the wust kind to kick when they once get a foot over the traces. For stiddy, comf'ble kempany," added Bill reflectively, "give *me* the son of a man that was *hanged!*"

"But what are you going to do about this?"

"That depends upon the feller who comes to meet her."

"But you ain't going to try to take him? That would be playing it pretty low down on them both."

"Keep your hair on, Jimmy! The judge and me are only going to rastle with the sperrit of that gay young galoot, when he drops down for his girl — and exhort him pow'ful! Ef he allows he's convicted of sin and will find the Lord, we'll marry him and the gal offhand at the next station, and the judge will officiate himself for nothin'. We're goin' to have this yer elopement done on the square — and our waybill clean — you bet!"

"But you don't suppose he'll trust himself in your hands?"

"Polly will signal to him that it's all square."

"Ah!" said the expressman. Nevertheless in those few moments the men seemed to have exchanged dispositions. The expressman looked doubtfully, critically, and even cynically before him. Bill's face had relaxed, and something like a bland smile beamed across it as he drove confidently and unhesitatingly forward.

Day, meantime, although full blown and radiant on the mountain summits around us, was yet nebulous and uncertain in the valleys into which we were plunging. Lights still glimmered in the cabins and few ranch buildings which began to indicate the thicker settlements. And the shadows were heaviest in a little copse, where a note from Judge Thompson in the coach was handed up to Yuba Bill, who at once slowly began to draw up his horses. The coach stopped finally near the junction of a small crossroad. At the same moment Miss Mullins slipped down from the vehicle, and, with a parting wave of her hand to the judge, who had assisted her from the steps, tripped down the crossroad, and disappeared in its semi-obscurity. To our surprise the stage waited, Bill holding the reins listlessly in his hands. Five minutes passed — an eternity of expectation — and, as there was that in Yuba Bill's face which forbade idle questioning, an aching void of silence also! This was at last broken by a strange voice from the road:

" Go on; we'll follow."

The coach started forward. Presently we heard the sound of other wheels behind us. We all craned our necks backward to get a view of the unknown, but by the growing light we could only see that we were followed at a distance by a buggy with two figures in it. Evidently Polly Mullins and her lover! We hoped that they would pass us. But the vehicle, although drawn by a fast horse, preserved its distance always, and it was plain that its driver had no desire to satisfy our curiosity. The expressman had recourse to Bill.

" Is it the man you thought of ? " he asked, eagerly.

" I reckon," said Bill, briefly.

" But," continued the expressman, returning to his former skepticism, " what's to keep them both from levanting together now ? "

Bill jerked his hand toward the boot with a grim smile.

" Their baggage."

" Oh! " said the expressman.

" Yes," continued Bill. " We'll hang on to that gal's little frills and fixin's until this yer job's settled, and the ceremony's over, jest as ef we was her own father. And, what's more, young man," he added, suddenly turning to the expressman, " *you'll* express them trunks of hers *through to Sacramento* with your kempany's labels, and hand her the receipts and checks for them so she *can get 'em there.* That'll keep *him* outer temptation and the reach o' the gang, until they get away among white men and civilization again. When your hoary-headed ole grandfather — or, to speak plainer, that partikler old whisky-soaker known as Yuba Bill, wot sits on this box," he continued, with a diabolical wink at the expressman — " waltzes in to pervide for a young couple jest startin' in life, thar's nothin' mean about his style, you bet. He fills the bill every time! Speshul Providences take a back seat when he's around."

When the station hotel and straggling settlement of Sugar Pine, now distinct and clear in the growing light, at last rose within rifle shot on the plateau, the buggy suddenly darted swiftly by us — so swiftly that the faces of the two occupants were barely distinguishable as they passed — and, keeping the lead by a dozen lengths, reached the door of the hotel. The young girl and her companion leaped down and vanished within as we drew up. They had evidently determined to elude our curiosity, and were successful.

But the material appetites of the passengers, sharpened by the keen mountain air, were more potent than their curiosity, and, as the breakfast-bell rang out at the moment the stage stopped, a majority of them rushed into the dining-room and scrambled for places without giving much heed to the vanished couple or to the Judge and Yuba Bill, who had disappeared also. The through coach to Marysville and Sacramento was likewise waiting, for Sugar Pine was the limit of Bill's ministration, and the coach which we had just left went no farther. In the course of twenty minutes, however, there was a slight and somewhat ceremonious bustling in the hall and on the veranda, and Yuba Bill and the Judge reappeared. The latter was leading, with some elaboration of manner and detail, the shapely figure of Miss Mullins, and Yuba Bill was accompanying her companion to the buggy. We all rushed to the windows to get a good view of the mysterious stranger and probable ex-brigand whose life was now linked with our fair fellow-passenger. I am afraid, however, that we all participated in a certain impression of disappointment and doubt. Handsome and even cultivated looking he assuredly was; young and vigorous in appearance. But there was a certain half-shamed,

half-defiant suggestion in his expression, yet coupled with a watchful, lurking uneasiness which was not pleasant, and hardly becoming in a bridegroom — and the possessor of such a bride. But
the frank, joyous, innocent face of Polly Mullins, resplendent with
a simple, happy confidence, melted our hearts again, and condoned the fellow's shortcomings. We waved our hands; I think
we would have given three rousing cheers as they drove away
if the omnipotent eye of Yuba Bill had not been upon us. It
was well, for the next moment we were summoned to the presence
of that soft-hearted autocrat.

We found him alone with the Judge in a private sitting-room,
standing before a table on which there was a decanter and glasses.
As we filed expectantly into the room and the door closed behind
us, he cast a glance of hesitating tolerance over the group.

" Gentlemen," he said slowly, " you was all present at the begin-
nin' of a little game this mornin', and the Judge thar thinks that
you oughter be let in at the finish. *I* don't see that it's any of
your damned business, so to speak; but ez the Judge here allows
you're all in the secret, I've called you in to take a partin' drink
to the health of Mr. and Mrs. Charley Byng — ez is now comf'ably
off on their bridal tower. What *you* know or what *you* suspects
of the young galoot that's married the gal ain't worth shucks to
anybody, and I wouldn't give it to a yaller pup to play with, but
the Judge thinks you ought all to promise right here that you'll
keep it dark. That's his opinion. Ez far as my opinion goes,
gen'lemen," continued Bill, with greater blandness and apparent
cordiality, " I wanter simply remark, in a keerless, offhand, gin'ral
way, that ef I ketch any God-forsaken, lop-eared, chuckle-headed,
blatherin' idjet airin' *his* opinion — "

" One moment, Bill," interposed Judge Thompson, with a grave
smile, " let me explain. — You understand, gentlemen," he said,
turning to us, " the singular, and I may say affecting, situation
which our good-hearted friend here has done so much to bring
to what we hope will be a happy termination. I want to give here,
as my professional opinion, that there is nothing in his request
which, in your capacity as good citizens and law-abiding men, you
may not grant. I want to tell you, also, that you are condoning no
offense against the statutes; that there is not a particle of legal
evidence before us of the criminal antecedents of Mr. Charles
Byng, except that which has been told you by the innocent lips
of his betrothed, which the law of the land has now sealed for-

ever in the mouth of his wife; and that our own actual experience of his acts has been in the main exculpatory of any previous irregularity, if not incompatible with it. Briefly, no judge would charge, no jury convict, on such evidence. When I add that the young girl is of legal age, that there is no evidence of any previous undue influence, but rather of the reverse, on the part of the bridegroom, and that I was content, as a magistrate, to perform the ceremony, I think you will be satisfied to give your promise, for the sake of the bride, and drink a happy life to them both."

I need not say that we did this cheerfully, and even extorted from Bill a grunt of satisfaction. The majority of the company, however, who were going with the through coach to Sacramento, then took their leave, and, as we accompanied them to the veranda, we could see that Miss Polly Mullins's trunks were already transferred to the other vehicle under the protecting seals and labels of the all-potent express company. Then the whip cracked, the coach rolled away, and the last traces of the adventurous young couple disappeared in the hanging red dust of its wheels.

But Yuba Bill's grim satisfaction at the happy issue of the episode seemed to suffer no abatement. He even exceeded his usual deliberately regulated potations, and, standing comfortably with his back to the center of the now deserted barroom, was more than usually loquacious with the expressman. " You see," he said, in bland reminiscence, " when your old Uncle Bill takes hold of a job like this, he puts it straight through without changin' hosses. Yet thar was a moment, young feller, when I thought I was stompt! It was when we'd made up our mind to make that chap tell the gal fust all what he was! Ef she'd rared or kicked in the traces, or hung back only ez much ez that, we'd hev given him jest five minits' law to get up and get and leave her, and we'd hev toted that gal and her fixin's back to her dad again! But she jest gave a little scream and start, and then went off into hysterics, right on his buzzum, laughin' and cryin' and sayin' that nothin' should part 'em. Gosh! if I didn't think *he* woz more cut up than she about it; a minit it looked as ef *he* didn't allow to marry her arter all, but that passed, and they was married hard and fast — you bet! I reckon he's had enough of stayin' out o' nights to last him, and ef the valley settlements hevn't got hold of a very shining member, at least the foothills hev got shut of one more of the Ramon Martinez gang."

" What's that about the Ramon Martinez gang? " said a quiet, potential voice.

Bill turned quickly. It was the voice of the divisional superintendent of the express company — a man of eccentric determination of character, and one of the few whom the autocratic Bill recognized as an equal — who had just entered the barroom. His dusty pongee cloak and soft hat indicated that he had that morning arrived on a round of inspection.

" Don't care if I do, Bill," he continued, in response to Bill's invitatory gesture, walking to the bar. " It's a little raw out on the road. Well, what were you saying about the Ramon Martinez gang? You haven't come across one of 'em, have you? "

" No," said Bill, with a slight blinking of his eye, as he ostentatiously lifted his glass to the light.

" And you *won't,*" added the superintendent, leisurely sipping his liquor. " For the fact is, the gang is about played out. Not from want of a job now and then, but from the difficulty of disposing of the results of their work. Since the new instructions to the agents to identify and trace all dust and bullion offered to them went into force, you see they can't get rid of their swag. All the gang are spotted at the offices, and it costs too much for them to pay a fence or a middleman of any standing. Why, all that flaky river gold they took from the Excelsior Company can be identified as easy as if it was stamped with the company's mark. They can't melt it down themselves; they can't get others to do it for them; they can't ship it to the Mint or Assay Offices in Marysville and 'Frisco, for they won't take it without our certificate and seals, and *we* don't take any undeclared freight *within* the lines that we've drawn around their beat, except from people and agents known. Why, *you* know that well enough, Jim," he said, suddenly appealing to the expressman, " don't you? "

Possibly the suddenness of the appeal caused the expressman to swallow his liquor the wrong way, for he was overtaken with a fit of coughing, and stammered hastily, as he laid down his glass, " Yes — of course — certainly."

" No, sir," resumed the superintendent cheerfully, " they're pretty well played out. And the best proof of it is, that they've lately been robbing ordinary passengers' trunks. There was a freight wagon held up near Dow's Flat the other day, and a lot of baggage gone through. I had to go down there to look into it. Darned if they hadn't lifted a lot o' woman's wedding things from that rich couple who got married the other day out at Marysville. Looks as if they were playing it rather low down, don't it? Coming down to hard pan and the bed rock — eh?"

The expressman's face was turned anxiously towards Bill, who, after a hurried gulp of his remaining liquor, still stood staring at the window. Then he slowly drew on one of his large gloves. " Ye didn't," he said, with a slow, drawling, but perfectly distinct, articulation, " happen to know old ' Skinner ' Hemmings when you were over there? "

" Yes."

" And his daughter? "

" He hasn't got any."

" A sort o' mild, innocent, guileless child of nature? " persisted Bill, with a yellow face, a deadly calm, and satanic deliberation.

" No. I tell you he *hasn't* any daughter. Old man Hemmings is a confirmed old bachelor. He's too mean to support more than one."

" And you didn't happen to know any o' that gang, did ye? " continued Bill, with infinite protraction.

" Yes. Knew 'em all. There was French Pete, Cherokee Bob, Kanaka Joe, One-eyed Stillson, Softy Brown, Spanish Jack, and two or three Greasers."

" And ye didn't know a man by the name of Charley Byng? "

" No," returned the superintendent, with a slight suggestion of weariness and a distraught glance toward the door.

" A dark, stylish chap, with shifty black eyes and a curled-up merstache? " continued Bill, with dry, colorless persistence.

" No. Look here, Bill, I'm in a little bit of a hurry; but I suppose you must have your little joke before we part. Now, what *is* your little game? "

" Wot you mean? " demanded Bill, with sudden brusqueness.

" Mean? Well, old man, you know as well as I do. You're giving me the very description of Ramon Martinez himself. Ha! ha! No, Bill, you didn't play me this time! You're mighty spry and clever, but you didn't catch on just then."

He nodded and moved away with a light laugh. Bill turned a stony face to the expressman. Suddenly a gleam of mirth came into his gloomy eyes. He bent over the young man, and said in a hoarse, chuckling whisper :

" But I got even after all ! "

" How ? "

" He's tied up to that lying little she-devil, hard and fast ! "

SUGGESTIONS FOR STUDY

1. Vocabulary: ingénue, quixotic, exordium, nebulous.
2. Why is this story romantic and not realistic?
3. To what extent are the characters true to life? How do you know?
4. Do you find any weaknesses in the plot?
5. At what places did Bret Harte make you laugh?
6. In what ways do you consider Harte superior to Poe? Hawthorne? In what ways inferior?
7. Is there " unity of effect " in this story?
8. Whom did the public associate with Bret Harte in this new western humor?
9. Name some of the writers who followed Harte into the field of localized romance.

FOR FURTHER READING

" The Luck of Roaring Camp "   " The Postmistress of Laurel Run "
" The Outcasts of Poker Flat "   " Left Out on Lone Star Mountain "
" Tennessee's Partner "   " M'liss "
          " How Santa Claus Came to Simpson's Bar "

A STRUGGLE FOR LIFE

By THOMAS BAILEY ALDRICH (1836–1907)

Aldrich is an old friend, whom we first met as Tom Bailey in the delightful pages of " The Story of a Bad Boy." In his stories we find the compactness and directness of Poe seasoned with a Gallic spice that suggests the French masters who imitated Poe and whom in turn Aldrich followed.

In spite of the fact that Aldrich held the dignified position of editor of *The Atlantic Monthly* he always remained a boy at heart, and it is therefore not surprising that his two chief contributions to American literature suggest perennial youthfulness. " The Story of a Bad Boy "

is dear to the heart of every American boy; and Aldrich's second contribution, the surprise ending, is a kind of literary practical joke such as a
boy would love to play. In "A Struggle for Life," published in the
Atlantic in 1867, six years before the more famous "Marjorie Daw,"
Aldrich outdid himself with a double-barreled surprise; so as you read be
prepared for anything.

One morning last April, as I was passing through Boston Common, which lies pleasantly between my residence and my office,
I met a gentleman lounging along The Mall. I am generally pre-
occupied when walking, and often thrid my way through crowded
streets without distinctly observing a single soul. But this man's
face forced itself upon me, and a very singular face it was. His
eyes were faded, and his hair, which he wore long, was flecked with
gray. His hair and eyes, if I may say so, were seventy years old,
the rest of him not thirty. The youthfulness of his figure, the
elasticity of his gait, and the venerable appearance of his head,
were incongruities that drew more than one pair of curious eyes
towards him. He was evidently an American — the New England cut of countenance is unmistakable — evidently a man who
had seen something of the world; but strangely old and young.

Before reaching the Park Street gate, I had taken up the thread
of thought which he had unconsciously broken; yet throughout the
day this old young man, with his unwrinkled brow and silvered
locks, glided in like a phantom between me and my duties.

The next morning I again encountered him on The Mall. He
was resting lazily on the green rails, watching two little sloops in
distress, which two ragged ship-owners had consigned to the mimic
perils of the Pond. The vessels lay becalmed in the middle of
the ocean, displaying a tantalizing lack of sympathy with the
frantic helplessness of the owners on shore. As the gentleman
observed their dilemma, a light came into his faded eyes, then
died out, leaving them drearier than before. I wondered if he,
too, in his time, had sent out ships that drifted and drifted and
never came to port; and if these poor toys were to him types of his
own losses.

"I would like to know that man's story," I said, half aloud,
halting in one of those winding paths which branch off from the
quietness of the Pond, and end in the rush and tumult of Tremont
Street.

"Would you?" replied a voice at my side. I turned and faced
Mr. H——, a neighbor of mine, who laughed heartily at finding

me talking to myself. " Well," he added, reflectively, " I can tell
you this man's story; and if you will match the narrative with
anything as curious, I shall be glad to hear it."

" You know him, then ? "

" Yes and no. I happened to be in Paris when he was buried."

" Buried ! "

" Well, strictly speaking, not buried; but something quite like
it. If you've a spare half-hour," continued my interlocutor, " we'll
sit on this bench, and I will tell you all I know of an affair that
made some noise in Paris a couple of years ago. The gentleman
himself, standing yonder, will serve as a sort of frontispiece to the
romance — a full-page illustration, as it were."

The following pages contain the story that Mr. H—— related
to me. While he was telling it, a gentle wind arose ; the miniature
sloops drifted feebly about the ocean ; the wretched owners flew
from point to point, as the deceptive breeze promised to waft
the barks to either shore ; the early robins trilled now and then
from the newly fringed elms ; and the old young man leaned on
the rail in the sunshine, wearily, little dreaming that two gossips
were discussing his affairs within twenty yards of him.

Three people were sitting in a chamber whose one large window
overlooked the Place Vendôme.[1] M. Dorine, with his back half
turned on the other two occupants of the apartment, was reading
the *Moniteur,* pausing from time to time to wipe his glasses, and
taking scrupulous pains not to glance toward the lounge at his
right, on which were seated Mademoiselle Dorine and a young
American gentleman, whose handsome face rather frankly told
his position in the family. There was not a happier man in Paris
that afternoon than Philip Wentworth. Life had become so delicious to him that he shrank from looking beyond today. What
could the future add to his full heart? what might it not take
away? In certain natures the deepest joy has always something
of melancholy in it, a presentiment, a fleeting sadness, a feeling
without a name. Wentworth was conscious of this subtle shadow,
that night, when he rose from the lounge, and thoughtfully held
Julie's hand to his lip for a moment before parting. A careless
observer would not have thought him, as he was, the happiest
man in Paris.

M. Dorine laid down his paper and came forward. " If the

---

[1] **Place Vendôme:** a famous square in Paris.

house." he said, " is such as M. Martin describes it, I advise you
to close with him at once. I would accompany you, Philip, but
the truth is, I am too sad at losing this little bird to assist you in
selecting a cage for her. Remember, the last train for town leaves
at five. Be sure not to miss it; for we have seats for M. Sardou's
new comedy tomorrow night. By tomorrow night," he added
laughingly, " little Julie here will be an old lady — 'tis such an
age from now until then."

The next morning the train bore Philip to one of the loveliest
spots within thirty miles of Paris. An hour's walk through green
lanes brought him to M. Martin's estate. In a kind of dream the
young man wandered from room to room, inspected the conserva-
tory, the stables, the lawns, the strip of woodland through which
a merry brook sang to itself continually; and, after dining with
M. Martin, completed the purchase, and turned his steps towards
the station, just in time to catch the express train.

As Paris stretched out before him, with its million lights twinkling in the early dusk, and its sharp spires here and there pricking
the sky, it seemed to Philip as if years had elapsed since he left
the city. On reaching Paris he drove to his hotel, where he found
several letters lying on the table. He did not trouble himself
even to glance at their superscriptions as he threw aside his
traveling surtout for a more appropriate dress.

If, in his impatience to see Mademoiselle Dorine, the cars had
appeared to walk, the fiacre which he had secured at the station
appeared to creep. At last it turned into the Place Vendôme, and
drew up before M. Dorine's residence. The door opened as
Philip's foot touched the first step. The servant silently took his
cloak and hat, with a special deference, Philip thought; but was
he not now one of the family?

" M. Dorine," said the servant slowly, " is unable to see Monsieur at present. He wishes Monsieur to be shown up to the
salon."

" Is Mademoiselle — "

" Yes, Monsieur."

" Alone? "

"Alone, Monsieur," repeated the man, looking curiously at
Philip, who could scarcely repress an exclamation of pleasure.

It was the first time that such a privilege had been accorded
him. His interviews with Julie had always taken place in
the presence of M. Dorine, or some members of the household.

A well-bred Parisian girl has but a formal acquaintance with her lover.

Philip did not linger on the staircase; his heart sang in his bosom as he flew up the steps, two at a time. Ah! this wine of air which one drinks at twenty, and seldom after! He hastened through the softly lighted hall, in which he detected the faint scent of her favorite flowers, and stealthily opened the door of the *salon*.

The room was darkened. Underneath the chandelier stood a slim black casket on trestles. A lighted candle, a crucifix, and some white flowers were on a table near by. Julie Dorine was dead.

When M. Dorine heard the indescribable cry that rang through the silent house, he hurried from the library, and found Philip standing like a ghost in the middle of the chamber.

IT WAS DEATH

It was not until long afterwards that Wentworth learned the details of the calamity that had befallen him. On the previous night Mademoiselle Dorine had retired to her room in seemingly perfect health. She dismissed her maid with a request to be awakened early the next morning. At the appointed hour the girl entered the chamber. Mademoiselle Dorine was sitting in an armchair, apparently asleep. The candle had burnt down to the socket; a book lay half open on the carpet at her feet. The girl started when she saw that the bed had not been occupied, and that her mistress still wore an evening dress. She rushed to Mademoiselle Dorine's side. It was not slumber. It was death.

Two messages were at once despatched to Philip, one to the station at G——, the other to his hotel. The first missed him on the road, the second he had neglected to open. On his arrival at M. Dorine's house, the servant, under the supposition that Wentworth had been advised of Mademoiselle Dorine's death, broke the intelligence with awkward cruelty, by showing him directly to the *salon*.

Mademoiselle Dorine's wealth, her beauty, the suddenness of her death, and the romance that had in some way attached itself to her love for the young American, drew crowds to witness the final ceremonies which took place in the church in the Rue d'Aguesseau. The body was to be laid in M. Dorine's tomb, in the cemetery of Montmartre.

This tomb requires a few words of description. First, there was a grating of filigraned iron; through this you looked into a small vestibule or hall, at the end of which was a massive door of oak opening upon a short flight of stone steps descending into the tomb. The vault was fifteen or twenty feet square, ingeniously ventilated from the ceiling, but unlighted. It contained two sarcophagi; the first held the remains of Madame Dorine, long since dead; the other was new, and bore on one side the letters J. D., in monogram, interwoven with fleurs-de-lis.

The funeral train stopped at the gate of the small garden that enclosed the place of burial, only the immediate relatives following the bearers into the tomb. A slender wax candle, such as is used in Catholic churches, burnt at the foot of the uncovered sarcophagus, casting a dim glow over the center of the apartment, and deepening the shadows which seemed to huddle together in the corners. By this flickering light the coffin was placed in its granite shell, the heavy slab laid over it reverently, and the oaken door revolved on its rusty hinges, shutting out the uncertain ray of sunshine that had ventured to peep in on the darkness.

M. Dorine, muffled in his cloak, threw himself on the back seat of the carriage, too abstracted in his grief to observe that he was the only occupant of the vehicle. There was a sound of wheels grating on the graveled avenue, and then all was silence again in the cemetery of Montmartre. At the main entrance the carriages parted company, dashing off into various streets at a pace

that seemed to express a sense of relief. The band plays a
dead march going to the grave, but "Fra Diavolo"[2] coming
from it.

It is not with the retreating carriages that our interest lies. Nor
yet wholly with the dead in her mysterious dream; but with
Philip Wentworth.

The rattle of wheels had died out of the air when Philip opened
his eyes, bewildered, like a man abruptly roused from slumber.
He raised himself on one arm and stared into the surrounding
blackness. Where was he? In a second the truth flashed upon
him. He had been left in the tomb! While kneeling on the
farther side of the stone box, perhaps he had fainted, and in the
last solemn rites his absence had been unnoticed.

His first emotion was one of natural terror. But this passed
as quickly as it came. Life had ceased to be so very precious to
him; and if it were his fate to die at Julie's side, was not that the
fulfilment of the desire which he had expressed to himself a hundred times that morning? What did it matter, a few years sooner
or later? He must lay down the burden at last. Why not then?
A pang of self-reproach followed the thought. Could he so lightly
throw aside the love that had bent over his cradle? The sacred
name of mother rose involuntarily to his lips. Was it not cowardly
to yield up without a struggle the life which he should guard for
her sake? Was it not his duty to the living and the dead to face
the difficulties of his position, and overcome them if it were within
human power?

With an organization as delicate as a woman's, he had that spirit
which, however sluggish in repose, can leap with a kind of exultation to measure its strength with disaster. The vague fear of the
supernatural, that would affect most men in a similar situation,
found no room in his heart. He was simply shut in a chamber
from which it was necessary that he should obtain release within
a given period. That this chamber contained the body of the
woman he loved, so far from adding to the terror of the case, was
a circumstance from which he drew consolation. She was a beautiful white statue now. Her soul was far hence; and if that
pure spirit could return, would it not be to shield him with her
love? It was impossible that the place should not engender some
thought of the kind. He did not put the thought entirely from

2 **"Fra Diavolo":** an opera with gay, vivacious music, based on the life of
a famous Italian brigand.

him as he rose to his feet and stretched out his hands in the darkness; but his mind was too healthy and practical to indulge long in such speculations.

Philip chanced to have in his pocket a box of wax tapers which smokers use. After several ineffectual attempts, he succeeded in igniting one against the dank wall, and by its momentary glare perceived that the candle had been left in the tomb. This would serve him in examining the fastenings of the vault. If he could force the inner door by any means, and reach the grating, of which he had an indistinct recollection, he might hope to make himself heard. But the oaken door was immovable, as solid as the wall itself, into which it fitted air-tight. Even if he had had the requisite tools, there were no fastenings to be removed; the hinges were set on the outside.

Having ascertained this, he replaced the candle on the floor, and leaned against the wall thoughtfully, watching the blue fan of flame that wavered to and fro, threatening to detach itself from the wick. " At all events," he thought, " the place is ventilated." Suddenly Philip sprang forward and extinguished the light. His existence depended on that candle!

He had read somewhere, in some account of shipwreck, how the survivors had lived for days upon a few candles which one of the passengers had insanely thrown into the long-boat. And here he had been burning away his very life.

By the transient illumination of one of the tapers, he looked at his watch. It had stopped at eleven — but at eleven that day or the preceding night? The funeral, he knew, had left the church at ten. How many hours had passed since then? Of what duration had been his swoon? Alas! It was no longer possible for him to measure those hours which crawl like snails to the wretched, and fly like swallows over the happy.

He picked up the candle, and seated himself on the stone steps. He was a sanguine man, this Wentworth, but, as he weighed the chances of escape, the prospect did not seem encouraging. Of course he would be missed. His disappearance under the circumstances would surely alarm his friends; they would instigate a search for him; but who would think of searching for a live man in the cemetery of Montmartre? The Prefect of Police would set a hundred intelligences at work to find him; the Seine might be dragged, *les misérables* [3] turned over at the dead house; a

---

[3] **les misérables:** the unfortunates.

minute description of him would be in every detective's pocket
and he — in M. Dorine's family tomb!

Yet, on the other hand, it was here he was last seen; from this
point a keen detective would naturally work up the case. Then
might not the undertaker return for the candlestick, probably not
left by design? Or, again, might not M. Dorine send fresh wreaths
of flowers, to take the place of those which now diffused a pungent,
aromatic odor throughout the chamber? Ah! what unlikely
chances! But if one of these things did not happen speedily,
it had better never happen. How long could he keep life in
himself?

With unaccelerated pulse, he quietly cut the half-burned candle
into four equal parts. "Tonight," he meditated, "I will eat the
first of these pieces; tomorrow, the second; tomorrow evening, the
third; the next day, the fourth; and then — then I'll wait!"

He had taken no breakfast that morning, unless a cup of coffee
can be called a breakfast. He had never been very hungry before.
He was ravenously hungry now. But he postponed the meal as
long as practicable. It must have been near midnight, according
to his calculation, when he determined to try the first of his four
singular repasts. The bit of white wax was tasteless; but it served
its purpose.

His appetite for the time appeased, he found a new discomfort.
The humidity of the walls, and the wind that crept through the
unseen ventilator, chilled him to the bone. To keep walking was
his only resource. A sort of drowsiness, too, occasionally came
over him. It took all his will to fight it off. To sleep, he felt
was to die: and he had made up his mind to live.

Very strange fancies flitted through his head as he groped up
and down the stone floor of the dungeon, feeling his way along
the wall to avoid the sepulchers. Voices that had long been silent
spoke words that had long been forgotten; faces he had known in
childhood grew palpable against the dark. His whole life in detail was unrolled before him like a panorama; the changes of a
year, with its burden of love and death, its sweets and its bitter-
nesses, were epitomized in a single second. The desire to sleep had
left him. But the keen hunger came again.

It must be near morning now, he mused; perhaps the sun is just
gilding the pinnacles and domes of the city; or, may be, a dull,
drizzling rain is beating on Paris, sobbing on these mounds above
me. Paris! it seems like a dream. Did I ever walk in its gay

streets in the golden air? O the delight and pain and passion of that sweet human life!

Philip became conscious that the gloom, the silence, and the cold were gradually conquering him. The feverish activity of his brain brought on a reaction. He grew lethargic, he sank down on the steps, and thought of nothing. His hand fell by chance on one of the pieces of candle; he grasped it and devoured it mechanically. This revived him. "How strange," he thought, "that I am not thirsty. Is it possible that the dampness of the walls, which I must inhale with every breath, has supplied the need of water? Not a drop has passed my lips for two days, and still I experience no thirst. That drowsiness, thank Heaven, has gone. I think I was never wide awake until this hour. It would be an anodyne like poison that could weigh down my eyelids. No doubt the dread of sleep has something to do with this."

The minutes were like hours. Now he walked as briskly as he dared up and down the tomb; now he rested against the door. More than once he was tempted to throw himself upon the stone coffin that held Julie, and make no further struggle for his life.

Only one piece of candle remained. He had eaten the third portion, not to satisfy hunger, but from a precautionary motive. He had taken it as a man takes some disagreeable drug upon the result of which hangs safety. The time was rapidly approaching when even this poor substitute for nourishment would be exhausted. He delayed that moment. He gave himself a long fast this time. The half-inch of candle which he held in his hand was a sacred thing to him. It was his last defense against death.

At length, with such a sinking at heart as he had not known before, he raised it to his lips. Then he paused, then he hurled the fragment across the tomb, then the oaken door was flung open, and Philip, with dazzled eyes, saw M. Dorine's form sharply outlined against the blue sky.

When they led him out, half blinded, into the broad daylight, M. Dorine noticed that Philip's hair, which a short time since was as black as a crow's wing, had actually turned gray in places. The man's eyes, too, had faded; the darkness had spoiled their luster.

"And how long was he really confined in the tomb?" I asked, as Mr. H—— concluded the story.

"*Just one hour and twenty minutes!*" replied Mr. H——, smiling blandly.

As he spoke, the little sloops, with their sails all blown out like white roses, came floating bravely into port, and Philip Wentworth lounged by us, wearily, in the pleasant April sunshine.

Mr. H——'s narrative made a deep impression on me. Here was a man who had undergone a strange ordeal. Here was a man whose sufferings were unique. His was no threadbare experience. Eighty minutes had seemed like two days to him! If he had really been immured two days in the tomb, the story, from my point of view, would have lost its tragic element.

After this it was but natural I should regard Mr. Wentworth with deepened interest. As I met him from day to day, passing through the Common with that same abstracted air, there was something in his loneliness which touched me. I wondered that I had not before read in his pale meditative face some such sad history as Mr. H—— had confided to me. I formed the resolution of speaking to him, though with what purpose was not very clear to my mind. One May morning we met at the intersection of two paths. He courteously halted to allow me the precedence.

" Mr. Wentworth — " I began.

He interrupted me.

" My name, sir," he said, in an off-hand manner, " is Jones."

" Jo-Jo-Jones! " I gasped.

" Not Joe Jones," he returned coldly, " Frederick."

Mr. Jones, or whatever his name is, will never know, unless he reads these pages, why a man accosted him one morning as " Mr. Wentworth," and then abruptly rushed down the nearest path, and disappeared in the crowd.

The fact is, I had been duped by Mr. H——, who is a gentleman of literary proclivities, and has, it is whispered, become somewhat demented in brooding over the Great American Novel — not yet hatched. He had actually tried the effect of one of his chapters on me!

My hero, as I subsequently learned, is no hero at all, but a commonplace young man who has some connection with the building of that pretty granite bridge which will shortly span the crooked little lake in the Public Garden.

When I think of the cool ingenuity and readiness with which Mr. H—— built up his airy fabric on my credulity, I am half inclined to laugh; though I feel not slightly irritated at having been the unresisting victim of his Black Art.

SUGGESTIONS FOR STUDY

1. Vocabulary: Mall, dilemma, interlocutor, subtle, surtout, fiacre, lethargic.

2. Is there a moral in this story? If so, what?

3. In your case how successful was the double surprise?

4. Have you ever seen George M. Cohan's play, " Seven Keys to Baldpate "? In what way is the play similar to Aldrich's story?

5. Of the French writers who influenced Aldrich the best known is Guy de Maupassant. You might be interested in his collection, *The Odd Number.*

6. Name two of Aldrich's successors who made use of the surprise ending.

FOR FURTHER READING

Marjorie Daw and Other Stories: " Marjorie Daw," " Mlle. Olympe Zabriski," " Miss Mehetable's Son," " Quite So," " Père Antoine's Date Palm "

Two Bites at a Cherry: " Two Bites at a Cherry," " Goliath "

A HORSEMAN IN THE SKY

By AMBROSE BIERCE (1842–1913)

Ambrose Bierce was born in Ohio and attended a country school, which was the only formal education he had. At the outbreak of the Civil War he enlisted as a private, served the full duration, and came out a major. He went to San Francisco and eventually drifted into journalism. His temperament was distinctly pessimistic, but he had a caustic wit which opened the way for conducting what purported to be a humorous column. It was then the fashion to write devastating personal satire on prominent persons, and Bierce was by nature fitted for that. He spent some years in London on the editorial staff of *Fun,* an English humorous paper. On his return to America he went back to California and began to write short stories dealing with experiences and impressions of the Civil War. His first volume of these appeared in 1891, but it made little impression on the reading public, although it contained the two best stories he ever wrote, " A Horseman in the Sky " and " An Occurrence at Owl Creek Bridge." Besides stories he wrote poetry and essays, but in no field did he ever achieve the recognition he thought he deserved. In November, 1913, he went to Mexico, then in the midst of the Carranza-Villa struggle, and nothing definite was ever heard of him again. It was reported that he was shot at the orders of Villa or one of his subordinates. Two biographies of Bierce were published in 1929, and his best stories, *In the Midst of Life,* may be had in a popular edition.

I

One sunny afternoon in the autumn of the year 1861 a soldier lay in a clump of laurel by the side of a road in western Virginia. He lay at full length upon his stomach, his feet resting upon the toes, his head upon the left forearm. His extended right hand loosely grasped his rifle. But for the somewhat methodical disposition of his limbs and a slight rhythmic movement of the cartridge-box at the back of his belt he might have been thought to be dead. He was asleep at his post of duty. But if detected he would be dead shortly afterward, death being the just and legal penalty of his crime.

The clump of laurel in which the criminal lay was in the angle of a road which after ascending southward a steep declivity to that point turned sharply to the west, running along the summit for perhaps one hundred yards. There it turned southward again and went zigzagging downward through the forest. At the salient of that second angle was a large flat rock, jutting out northward, overlooking the deep valley from which the road ascended. The rock capped a high cliff; a stone dropped from its outer edge would have fallen sheer downward one thousand feet to the tops of the pines. The angle where the soldier lay was on another spur of the same cliff. Had he been awake he would have commanded a view, not only of the short arm of the road and the jutting rock, but of the entire profile of the cliff below it. It might well have made him giddy to look.

The country was wooded everywhere except at the bottom of the valley to the northward, where there was a small natural meadow, through which flowed a stream scarcely visible from the valley's rim. This open ground looked hardly larger than an ordinary door-yard, but was really several acres in extent. Its green was more vivid than that of the inclosing forest. Away beyond it rose a line of giant cliffs similar to those upon which we are supposed to stand in our survey of the savage scene, and through which the road had somehow made its climb to the summit. The configuration of the valley, indeed, was such that from this point of observation it seemed entirely shut in, and one

could but have wondered how the road which found a way out of
it had found a way into it, and whence came and whither went
the waters of the stream that parted the meadow more than a
thousand feet below.

No country is so wild and difficult but men will make it a
theater of war; concealed in the forest at the bottom of that
military rat-trap, in which half a hundred men in possession of
the exits might have starved an army to submission, lay five
regiments of Federal infantry. They had marched all the previous day and night and were resting. At nightfall they would
take to the road again, climb to the place where their unfaithful
sentinel now slept, and descending the other slope of the ridge
fall upon a camp of the enemy at about midnight. Their hope
was to surprise it, for the road led to the rear of it. In case
of failure, their position would be perilous in the extreme; and
fail they surely would should accident or vigilance apprise the
enemy of the movement.

II

The sleeping sentinel in the clump of laurel was a young Virginian named Carter Druse. He was the son of wealthy parents,
an only child, and had known such ease and cultivation and high
living as wealth and taste were able to command in the mountain
country of western Virginia. His home was but a few miles from
where he now lay. One morning he had risen from the breakfast-
table and said, quietly but gravely: " Father, a Union regiment
has arrived at Grafton. I am going to join it."

The father lifted his leonine head, looked at the son a moment
in silence, and replied: " Well, go, sir, and whatever may occur
do what you conceive to be your duty. Virginia, to which you
are a traitor, must get on without you. Should we both live to
the end of the war, we will speak further of the matter. Your
mother, as the physician has informed you, is in a most critical
condition; at the best she cannot be with us longer than a few
weeks, but that time is precious. It would be better not to
disturb her."

So Carter Druse, bowing reverently to his father, who returned
the salute with a stately courtesy that masked a breaking heart,
left the home of his childhood to go soldiering. By conscience
and courage, by deeds of devotion and daring, he soon com-
mended himself to his fellows and his officers; and it was to these

qualities and to some knowledge of the country that he owed his
selection for his present perilous duty at the extreme outpost.
Nevertheless, fatigue had been stronger than resolution and he
had fallen asleep. What good or bad angel came in a dream to
rouse him from his state of crime, who shall say? Without a
movement, without a sound, in the profound silence and the
languor of the late afternoon, some invisible messenger of fate
touched with unsealing finger the eyes of his consciousness —
whispered into the ear of his spirit the mysterious awakening
word which no human lips ever have spoken, no human memory

THE FATHER LIFTED HIS LEONINE HEAD

ever has recalled. He quietly raised his forehead from his arm
and looked between the masking stems of the laurels, instinctively closing his right hand about the stock of his rifle.

His first feeling was a keen artistic delight. On a colossal
pedestal, the cliff — motionless at the extreme edge of the capping
rock and sharply outlined against the sky — was an equestrian
statue of impressive dignity. The figure of the man sat the
figure of the horse, straight and soldierly, but with the repose of
a Grecian god carved in the marble which limits the suggestion
of activity. The gray costume harmonized with its aërial background; the metal of accouterment and caparison was softened
and subdued by the shadow; the animal's skin had no points of
high light. A carbine strikingly foreshortened lay across the

pommel of the saddle, kept in place by the right hand grasping it at the "grip"; the left hand, holding the bridle rein, was invisible. In silhouette against the sky the profile of the horse was cut with the sharpness of a cameo; it looked across the heights of air to the confronting cliffs beyond. The face of the rider, turned slightly away, showed only an outline of temple and beard; he was looking downward to the bottom of the valley. Magnified by its lift against the sky and by the soldier's testifying sense of the formidableness of a near enemy the group appeared of heroic, almost colossal, size.

For an instant Druse had a strange, half-defined feeling that he had slept to the end of the war and was looking upon a noble work of art reared upon that eminence to commemorate the deeds of an heroic past of which he had been an inglorious part. The feeling was dispelled by a slight movement of the group: the horse, without moving its feet, had drawn its body slightly backward from the verge; the man remained immobile as before. Broad awake and keenly alive to the significance of the situation, Druse now brought the butt of his rifle against his cheek by cautiously pushing the barrel forward through the bushes, cocked the piece, and glancing through the sights covered a vital spot of the horseman's breast. A touch upon the trigger and all would have been well with Carter Druse. At that instant the horseman turned his head and looked in the direction of his concealed foeman — seemed to look into his very face, into his eyes, into his brave, compassionate heart.

Is it then so terrible to kill an enemy in war — an enemy who has surprised a secret vital to the safety of one's self and comrades — an enemy more formidable for his knowledge than all his army for its numbers? Carter Druse grew pale; he shook in every limb, turned faint, and saw the statuesque group before him as black figures, rising, falling, moving unsteadily in arcs of circles in a fiery sky. His hand fell away from his weapon, his head slowly dropped until his face rested on the leaves in which he lay. This courageous gentleman and hardy soldier was near swooning from intensity of emotion.

It was not for long; in another moment his face was raised from earth, his hands resumed their places on the rifle, his forefinger sought the trigger; mind, heart, and eyes were clear, conscience and reason sound. He could not hope to capture that enemy; to alarm him would but send him dashing to his camp with his fatal news. The duty of the soldier was plain: the man must be shot dead from ambush — without warning, without a moment's spiritual preparation, with never so much as an unspoken prayer, he must be sent to his account. But no — there is a hope; he may have discovered nothing — perhaps he is but admiring the sublimity of the landscape. If permitted, he may turn and ride carelessly away in the direction whence he came. Surely it will be possible to judge at the instant of his withdrawing whether he knows. It may well be that his fixity of attention — Druse turned his head and looked through the deeps of air downward, as from the surface to the bottom of a translucent sea. He saw creeping across the green meadow a sinuous line of figures of men and horses — some foolish commander was permitting the soldiers of his escort to water their beasts in the open, in plain view from a dozen summits!

Druse withdrew his eyes from the valley and fixed them again upon the group of man and horse in the sky, and again it was through the sights of his rifle. But this time his aim was at the horse. In his memory, as if they were a divine mandate, rang the words of his father at their parting: "Whatever may occur, do what you conceive to be your duty." He was calm now. His teeth were firmly but not rigidly closed; his nerves were as tranquil as a sleeping babe's — not a tremor affected any muscle of his body; his breathing, until suspended in the act of taking aim, was regular and slow. Duty had conquered; the spirit had said to the body: "Peace, be still." He fired.

III

An officer of the Federal force, who in a spirit of adventure or in quest of knowledge had left the hidden bivouac in the valley, and with aimless feet had made his way to the lower edge of a small open space near the foot of the cliff, was considering what he had to gain by pushing his exploration further. At a distance of a quarter-mile before him, but apparently at a stone's throw, rose from its fringe of pines the gigantic face of rock, towering to so great a height above him that it made him giddy to look up to where its edge cut a sharp, rugged line against the sky. It presented a clean, vertical profile against a background of blue sky to a point half the way down, and of distant hills, hardly less blue, thence to the tops of the trees at its base. Lifting his eyes to the dizzy altitude of its summit the officer saw an astonishing sight — a man on horseback riding down into the valley through the air!

Straight upright sat the rider, in military fashion, with a firm seat in the saddle, a strong clutch upon the rein to hold his charger from too impetuous a plunge. From his bare head his long hair streamed upward, waving like a plume. His hands were concealed in the cloud of the horse's lifted mane. The animal's body was as level as if every hoof-stroke encountered the resistant earth. Its motions were those of a wild gallop, but even as the officer looked they ceased, with all the legs thrown sharply forward as in the act of alighting from a leap. But this was a flight!

Filled with amazement and terror by this apparition of a horseman in the sky — half believing himself the chosen scribe of some new Apocalypse, the officer was overcome by the intensity of his emotions; his legs failed him and he fell. Almost at the same instant he heard a crashing sound in the trees — a sound that died without an echo — and all was still.

The officer rose to his feet, trembling. The familiar sensation of an abraded shin recalled his dazed faculties. Pulling himself together he ran rapidly obliquely away from the cliff to a point distant from its foot; thereabout he expected to find his man; and thereabout he naturally failed. In the fleeting instant of his vision his imagination had been so wrought upon by the apparent grace and ease and intention of the marvelous performance that it did not occur to him that the line of march of aërial cavalry is directly downward, and that he could find the objects of his search at the very foot of the cliff. A half-hour later he returned to camp.

This officer was a wise man; he knew better than to tell an incredible truth. He said nothing of what he had seen. But when the commander asked him if in his scout he had learned anything of advantage to the expedition he answered:

"Yes, sir; there is no road leading down into this valley from the southward."

The commander, knowing better, smiled.

IV

After firing his shot, Private Carter Druse reloaded his rifle and resumed his watch. Ten minutes had hardly passed when a Federal sergeant crept cautiously to him on hands and knees. Druse neither turned his head nor looked at him, but lay without motion or sign of recognition.

" Did you fire? " the sergeant whispered.

" Yes."

" At what? "

" A horse. It was standing on yonder rock — pretty far out. You see it is no longer there. It went over the cliff."

The man's face was white, but he showed no other sign of emotion. Having answered, he turned away his eyes and said no more. The sergeant did not understand.

" See here, Druse," he said, after a moment's silence, " it's no use making a mystery. I order you to report. Was there anybody on the horse? "

" Yes."

" Well? "

" My father."

The sergeant rose to his feet and walked away. " Good God! " he said.

SUGGESTIONS FOR STUDY

1. What tragic keynote is struck in the parting between father and son?

2. Is this an adequate preparation for what followed?

3. Do you think that the detailed description of the scene is an essential feature of the story? Comment.

4. Why didn't the officer give a correct report of what he had seen?

5. Is the conclusion of the story satisfactory artistically? Give reasons, one way or the other.

FOR FURTHER READING

In the Midst of Life: " An Occurrence at Owl Creek Bridge," " Chicka-mauga," " The Man and the Snake," " The Affair at Coulter's Notch," " Killed at Resaca "

A SISTERLY SCHEME

By HENRY CUYLER BUNNER (1855–1896)

A story based on a summer resort flirtation must necessarily be light entertainment. But in this story you will learn that mere entertainment may be artistically written and have originality, and that it may contain both the daring unexpectedness of O. Henry and the careful craftsmanship cf Poe. Although Bunner was greatly influenced by the French masters in matters of style and manner, this is a thoroughly American story, and a thoroughly modern one. Replace the dogcart with an automobile, and the story might almost have occurred yesterday. For almost twenty-five years Bunner was editor of *Puck;* both his verse and his stories were fashioned for that humorous weekly, which demanded condensation, originality, and sparkle. Notice how skilfully Bunner manipulates language to achieve his effects. But keep your eye on the thread of the story, or the author may catch you unaware with a swift turn of action.

Away up in the very heart of Maine there is a mighty lake among the mountains. It is reached after a journey of many hours from the place where you " go in." That is the phrase of the country, and when you have once " gone in," you know why it is not correct to say that you have gone *through* the woods, or, simply, *to* your destination. You find that you have plunged into a new world — a world that has nothing in common with the world that you live in ; a world of wild, solemn, desolate grandeur, a world of space and silence ; a world that oppresses your soul — and charms you irresistibly. And after you have once " come out " of that world, there will be times, to the day of your death, when you will be homesick for it, and will long with a childlike longing to go back to it.

Up in this wild region you will find a fashionable summer hotel, with electric bells and seven-course dinners, and " guests " who dress three times a day. It is perched on a little flat point, shut off from the rest of the mainland by a huge rocky cliff. It is an impertinence in that majestic wilderness, and Leather-Stocking would doubtless have had a hankering to burn such an affront to Nature ; but it is a good hotel, and people go to it and breathe the generous air of the great woods.

On the beach near this hotel, where the canoes were drawn up in line, there stood one summer morning a curly-haired, fair young man — not so very young, either — whose cheeks were uncomfort-

ably red as he looked first at his own canoe, high and dry, loaded
with rods and landing net and luncheon basket, and then at another canoe, fast disappearing down the lake wherein sat a young
man and a young woman.

" Dropped again, Mr. Morpeth? "

The young man looked up and saw a saucy face laughing at
him. A girl was sitting on the stringpiece of the dock. It was
the face of a girl between childhood and womanhood. By the
face and the figure, it was a woman grown. By the dress, you
would have judged it a girl.

And you would have been confirmed in the latter opinion by
the fact that the young person was doing something unpardon-
able for a young lady, but not inexcusable in the case of a youthful
tomboy. She had taken off her canvas shoe, and was shaking
some small stones out of it. There was a tiny hole in her black
stocking, and a glimpse of her pink toe was visible. The girl was
sunburnt, but the toe was prettily pink.

" Your sister," replied the young man with dignity, " was to
have gone fishing with me; but she remembered at the last
moment that she had a prior engagement with Mr. Brown."

" She hadn't," said the girl. " I heard them make it up last
evening, after you went upstairs."

The young man clean forgot himself.

" She's the most heartless coquette in the world," he cried, and
clinched his hands.

" She is all that," said the young person on the stringpiece of
the dock, " and more too. And yet, I suppose, you want her all
the same? "

" I'm afraid I do," said the young man miserably.

" Well," said the girl, putting her shoe on again, and beginning to tie it up, " I'll tell you what it is, Mr. Morpeth.
You've been hanging around Pauline for a year, and you are the
only one of the men she keeps on a string who hasn't snubbed me.
Now, if you want me to, I'll give you a lift."

" A — a — what? "

" A lift. You're wasting your time. Pauline has no use for
devotion. It's a drug in the market with her — has been for five
seasons. There's only one way to get her worked up. Two fellows
tried it, and they nearly got there; but they weren't game enough
to stay to the bitter end. I think you're game, and I'll tell you.
You've got to make her jealous."

"Make her jealous of me?"

"No," said his friend, with infinite scorn; "make her jealous of the other girl. *Oh!* but you men are stupid!"

The young man pondered a moment.

"Well, Flossy," he began, and then he became conscious of a sudden change in the atmosphere, and perceived that the young

"WHAT'S THE MATTER WITH — ME?"

lady was regarding him with a look that might have chilled him.

"Miss Flossy — Miss Belton —" he hastily corrected himself. Winter promptly changed to summer in Miss Flossy Belton's expressive face.

"Your scheme," he went on, "is a good one. Only — it involves the discovery of another girl."

"Yes," assented Miss Flossy cheerfully.

"Well," said that young man, "doesn't it strike you that if I were to develop a sudden admiration for any one of these other young ladies whose charms I have hitherto neglected, it would come tardy off — lack artistic verisimilitude, so to speak?"

"Rather," was Miss Flossy's prompt and frank response; "especially as there isn't one of them fit to flirt with."

"Well, then, where am I to discover the girl?"

Miss Flossy untied and retied her shoe. Then she said, calmly:

" What's the matter with — " a slight hesitation — " *me?* "

" With *you?* " Mr. Morpeth was startled out of his manners.

" Yes ! "

Mr. Morpeth simply stared.

" Perhaps," suggested Miss Flossy, " I'm not good-looking enough? "

" You are good-looking enough," replied Mr. Morpeth, recovering himself, " for *anything* — " and he threw a convincing emphasis into the last word as he took what was probably his first real inspection of his adored one's junior — " but — aren't you a trifle — young? "

" How old do you suppose I am? "

" I know. Your sister told me. You are sixteen."

" Sixteen ! " repeated Miss Flossy, with an infinite and uncontrollable scorn, " yes, and I'm the kind of sixteen that stays sixteen till your elder sister's married. I was eighteen years old on the 3d of last December — unless they began to double on me before I was old enough to know the difference — it would be just like mamma to play it on me in some such way," she concluded, reflectively.

" Eighteen years old ! " said the young man. " The deuce ! " Do not think that he was an ill-bred young man. He was merely astonished, and he had much more astonishment ahead of him. He mused for a moment.

" Well," he said, " what's your plan of campaign? I am to — to discover you."

" Yes," said Miss Flossy calmly, " and to flirt with me like fun."

" And may I ask what attitude you are to take when you are — discovered? "

" Certainly," replied the imperturbable Flossy. " I am going to dangle you."

" To — to dangle me? "

" As a conquest, don't you know. Let you hang around and laugh at you."

" Oh, indeed? "

" There, don't be wounded in your masculine pride. You might as well face the situation. You don't think that Pauline's in love with you, do you? "

" No ! " groaned the young man.

" But you've got lots of money. Mr. Brown has got lots more. You're eager. Brown is coy. That's the reason that Brown is in

the boat and you are on the cold, cold shore, talking to Little
Sister. Now if Little Sister jumps at you, why, she's simply taking Big Sister's leavings; it's all in the family, anyway, and there's
no jealousy, and Pauline can devote her whole mind to Brown.
There, *don't* look so limp. You men are simply childish. Now,
after you've asked me to marry you — "

" Oh, I'm to ask you to marry me? "

" Certainly. You needn't look frightened, now. I won't accept
you. But then you are to go around like a wet cat, and mope, and
hang on worse than ever. Then Big Sister will see that she can't
afford to take that sort of thing from Little Sister, and then —
there's your chance."

" Oh, there's my chance, is it? " said Mr. Morpeth. He seemed
to have fallen into the habit of repetition.

" There's your *only* chance," said Miss Flossy, with decision.

Mr. Morpeth meditated. He looked at the lake, where there
was no longer sign or sound of the canoe, and he looked at Miss
Flossy, who sat calm, self-confident, and careless on the stringpiece of the dock.

" I don't know how feasible — " he began.

" It's feasible," said Miss Flossy, with decision. " Of course
Pauline will write to mamma, and of course mamma will
write and scold me. But she's got to stay in New York and nurse
papa's gout; and the Miss Redingtons are all the chaperons
we've got up here, and they don't amount to anything — so I don't
care."

" But why," inquired the young man, and his tone suggested a
complete abandonment to Miss Flossy's idea, " why should you
take so much trouble for *me?* "

" Mr. Morpeth," said Miss Flossy solemnly, " I'm two years
behind the time-table, and I've got to make a strike for liberty, or
die. And besides," she added, " if you are *nice,* it needn't be such
an *awful* trouble."

Mr. Morpeth laughed.

" I'll try to make it as little of a bore as possible," he said, extending his hand. The girl did not take it.

" Don't make any mistake," she cautioned him, searching his
face with her eyes; " this isn't to be any little-girl affair. Little
Sister doesn't want any kind, elegant, supercilious encouragement
from Big Sister's young man. It's got to be a *real* flirtation —
devotion no end, and ten times as much as ever Pauline could get

out of you — and you've got to keep your end 'way — 'way — 'way up ! ' "

The young man smiled.

" I'll keep my end up," he said, " but are you certain that you can keep yours up ? "

" Well, I think so," replied Miss Flossy. " Pauline will raise an awful row; but if she goes too far, I'll tell my age, *and hers, too.*"

Mr. Morpeth looked at Flossy's calm face.   Then he extended his hand once more.

" It's a bargain, so far as I am concerned," he said.

This time a soft and small hand met his with a firm, friendly, honest pressure.

" And I'll refuse you," said Miss Flossy.

Within two weeks, Mr. Morpeth found himself entangled in a flirtation such as he had never dreamed of.   Miss Flossy's scheme had succeeded only too brilliantly.   The whole hotel was talking about the outrageous behavior of " that little Belton girl " and Mr. Morpeth, who certainly ought to know better.

Mr. Morpeth had carried out his instructions.   Before the week was out, he found himself giving the most lifelike imitation of an infatuated lover that ever delighted the old gossips of a summer resort.   And yet he had only done what Flossy told him to do.

He got his first lesson just about the time that Flossy, in the privacy of their apartments, informed her elder sister that if she, Flossy, found Mr. Morpeth's society agreeable, it was nobody's concern but her own, and that she was prepared to make some interesting additions to the census statistics if any one thought differently.

The lesson opened his eyes.

" Do you know," she said, " that it wouldn't be a bit of a bad idea to telegraph to New York for some real nice candy and humbly present it for my acceptance ? I *might* take it — if the bonbonnière was pretty enough."

He telegraphed to New York, and received, in the course of four or five days, certain marvels of sweets in a miracle of an uphol-stered box.   The next day he found her on the veranda, flinging the bonbons on the lawn for the children to scramble for.

" Awfully nice of you to send me these things," she said lan-guidly, but loud enough for the men around her to hear — she had men around her already: she had been discovered — " but I never eat sweets, you know. Here, you little mite in the blue sash, don't you want this pretty box to put your doll's clothes in? "

And Maillard's finest bonbonnière went to a yellow-haired brat of three.

But this was the slightest and lightest of her caprices. She made him send for his dogcart and his horses, all the way from New York, only that he might drive her over the ridiculous little mile and a half of road that bounded the tiny peninsula. And she christened him " Muffets," a nickname presumably suggested by " Morpeth "; and she called him " Muffets " in the hearing of all the hotel people.

And did such conduct pass unchallenged? No. Pauline scolded, raged, raved. She wrote to mamma. Mamma wrote back and reproved Flossy. But mamma could not leave papa. His gout was worse. The Miss Redingtons must act. The Miss Redingtons merely wept, and nothing more. Pauline scolded; the flirtation went on; and the people at the big hotel enjoyed it immensely.

And there was more to come. Four weeks had passed. Mr. Morpeth was hardly on speaking terms with the elder Miss Belton; and with the younger Miss Belton he was on terms which the hotel gossips characterized as " simply scandalous." Brown glared at him when they met, and he glared at Brown. Brown was having a hard time. Miss Belton the elder was not pleasant of temper in those trying days.

" And now," said Miss Flossy to Mr. Morpeth, " it's time you proposed to me, Muffets."

They were sitting on the hotel veranda, in the evening darkness. No one was near them, except an old lady in a Shaker chair.

" There's Mrs. Melby. She's pretending to be asleep, but she isn't. She's just waiting for us. Now walk me up and down and ask me to marry you so that she can hear it. It'll be all over the hotel inside of half an hour. Pauline will just *rage*."

With this pleasant prospect before him, Mr. Morpeth marched Miss Flossy Belton up and down the long veranda. He had passed Mrs. Melby three times before he was able to say, in a choking, husky, uncertain voice: —

" Flossy — I — I — I *love* you! "

Flossy's voice was not choking nor uncertain. It rang out clear and silvery in a peal of laughter.

"Why, of course you do, Muffets, and I wish you didn't. That's what makes you so stupid half the time."

"But—" said Mr. Morpeth vaguely; "but I—"

"But you're a silly boy," returned Miss Flossy; and she added in a swift aside: "*You haven't asked me to marry you!*"

"W-W-W-Will you be my wife?" stammered Mr. Morpeth.

"No!" said Miss Flossy, emphatically, "I will not. You are too utterly ridiculous. The idea of it! No, Muffets, you are charming in your present capacity; but you aren't to be considered seriously."

They strolled on into the gloom at the end of the great veranda.

"That's the first time," he said, with a feeling of having only the ghost of a breath left in his lungs, "that I ever asked a woman to marry me."

"I should think so," said Miss Flossy, "from the way you did it. And you were beautifully rejected, weren't you? Now — look at Mrs. Melby, will you? She's scudding off to spread the news."

And before Mr. Morpeth went to bed, he was aware of the fact that every man and woman in the hotel knew that he had "proposed" to Flossy Belton, and had been "beautifully rejected."

Two sulky men, one sulky woman, and one girl radiant with triumphant happiness started out in two canoes, reached certain fishing grounds known only to the elect, and began to cast for trout. They had indifferent luck. Miss Belton and Mr. Brown caught a dozen trout; Miss Flossy Belton and Mr. Morpeth caught eighteen or nineteen, and the day was wearing to a close. Miss Flossy made the last cast of the day, just as her escort had taken the paddle. A big trout rose — just touched the fly — and disappeared.

"It's this wretched rod!" cried Miss Flossy; and she rapped it on the gunwale of the canoe so sharply that the beautiful split bamboo broke sharp off in the middle of the second joint. Then she tumbled it overboard, reel and all.

"I was tired of that rod, anyway, Muffets," she said; "row me home, now; I've got to dress for dinner."

Miss Flossy's elder sister, in the other boat, saw and heard this exhibition of tyranny; and she was so much moved that she stamped her small foot, and endangered the bottom of the canoe. She resolved that mamma should come back, whether papa had the gout or not.

Mr. Morpeth, wearing a grave expression, was paddling Miss Flossy toward the hotel. He had said nothing whatever, and it was a noticeable silence that Miss Flossy finally broke.

"You've done pretty much everything that I've wanted you to do, Muffets," she said; "but you haven't saved my life yet, and I'm going to give you a chance."

It is not difficult to overturn a canoe. One twist of Flossie's supple body did it, and before he knew just what had happened, Morpeth was swimming toward the shore, holding up Flossy Belton with one arm, and fighting for life in the icy water of a Maine lake.

The people were running down, bearing blankets and brandy, as he touched bottom in his last desperate struggle to keep the two of them above water. One yard further, and there would have been no strength left in him.

He struggled up on shore with her, and when he got breath enough, he burst out:

"Why did you do it? It was wicked! It was cruel!"

"There!" she said, as she reclined composedly in his arms, "that will do, Muffets. I don't want to be scolded."

A delegation came along, bringing blankets and brandy, and took her from him.

At five o'clock of that afternoon, Mr. Morpeth presented himself at the door of the parlor attached to the apartments of the Belton sisters. Miss Belton, senior, was just coming out of the room. She received his inquiry after her sister's health with a white face and a quivering lip.

"I should think, Mr. Morpeth," she began, "that you had gone far enough in playing with the feelings of a m-m-mere child, and that — oh! I have no words to express my *contempt* for you!"

And in a most unladylike rage Miss Pauline Belton swept down the hotel corridor.

She had left the door open behind her. Morpeth heard a voice, weak, but cheery, addressing him from the far end of the parlor.

"You've got her!" it said. "She's crazy mad. She'll make up to you tonight — see if she don't."

Mr. Morpeth looked up and down the long corridor. It was empty. He pushed the door open, and entered. Flossy was lying on the sofa, pale, but bright-eyed.

"You can get her," she whispered, as he knelt down beside her.

"Flossy," he said, "don't you know that that is all ended? Don't you know that I love you and you only? Don't you know that I haven't thought about any one else since — since —oh, Flossy, don't you — is it possible that you don't understand?"

Flossy stretched out two weak arms, and put them around Mr. Morpeth's neck.

"Why have I had you in training all summer?" said she. "Did you think it was for Pauline?"

SUGGESTIONS FOR STUDY

1. Vocabulary: verisimilitude, imperturbable. Does this story have "artistic verisimilitude"?

2. Did the story surprise you? Remember that a clever surprise ending must meet certain standards. No author is justified in telling his readers one thing and then at the end saying, "April Fool! This is a good joke on you. I didn't mean a word of it." The good surprise ending is one which follows a story in which the author has told the truth so subtly as to suggest the wrong interpretation. And at the end of such a story the reader laughs at himself and says to himself, "Of course! What a fool I was not to have seen that!" A clever author plays the game fairly. He surprises the reader, but at the same time he leaves the feeling that, had the reader been keen enough, the ending would not have surprised him. Was Bunner fair to you in this story?

3. Accepting this standard, compare the surprise ending in this story with the one in "An Ingénue of the Sierras."

4. Did you notice that in one paragraph the author obtained his effect by using a series of short sentences? Point out other places where words were used cleverly.

5. Why not try your hand at writing a story with a surprise ending that lives up to the standards given above?

FOR FURTHER READING

Short Sixes: "The Love-Letters of Smith," "Colonel Brereton's Aunty," "The Tenor," "The Nine-Cent Girls," "The Nice People," "The Two Churches of 'Quawket," "Zenobia's Infidelity"
Love in Old Cloathes: "Our Aromatic Uncle"

A MUNICIPAL REPORT

By O. HENRY (1862–1910)

It is fortunate that readers of short stories are usually familiar with the work of O. Henry before they find it in a textbook; otherwise they might be repelled by a title such as " A Municipal Report." As it happens, this particular story is generally credited as being the author's best, and many critics think that it has rarely, if ever, been excelled in American literature. Its style is as unconventional as its subject; it has all the traditional earmarks of the typical O. Henry story — wit, humor, satire, pathos, cleverness, individuality, and local color. As usual, the plot is there, but it has to be disentangled from the apparently hit-or-miss mannerisms of the author.

O. Henry (William Sidney Porter) had a short but exceedingly varied life. Born in North Carolina, he migrated to a Texas cattle ranch in search of health; edited a paper; worked in a bank; became entangled on a charge of embezzlement which caused him to flee to South America; returned to this country to pay the penalty of his lack of business sense; and eventually landed in New York where success but not fortune awaited him. He had a strong story sense and an extraordinary ability to capitalize it. Most of his stories are brief, and as many of them were written for a newspaper it is small wonder that they smack of journalism.

> " The cities are full of pride,
>   Challenging each to each —
> This from her mountainside,
>   That from her burthened beach."
>
> — KIPLING.

" Fancy a novel about Chicago or Buffalo, let us say, or Nashville, Tennessee! There are just three big cities in the United States that are ' story cities ' — New York, of course, New Orleans, and, best of the lot, San Francisco." — FRANK NORRIS.

East is East, and West is San Francisco, according to Californians. Californians are a race of people; they are not merely inhabitants of a State. They are the Southerners of the West. Now, Chicagoans are no less loyal to their city; but when you ask them why, they stammer and speak of lake fish and the new Odd Fellows Building. But Californians go into detail.

Of course they have, in the climate, an argument that is good for half an hour while you are thinking of your coal bills and heavy underwear. But as soon as they come to mistake your silence for conviction, madness comes upon them, and they picture the city of the Golden Gate as the Bagdad of the New World. So far, as a matter of opinion, no refutation is necessary. But, dear cousins all (from Adam and Eve descended), it is a rash one who will lay his finger on the map and say: " In this town there can be no romance — what could happen here?" Yes, it is a bold and a rash deed to challenge in one sentence history, romance, and Rand and McNally.

" NASHVILLE. — A city, port of delivery, and the capital of the State of Tennessee, is on the Cumberland River and on the N. C. & St. L. and the L. & N. railroads. This city is regarded as the most important educational center in the South."

I stepped off the train at 8 P. M. Having searched the thesaurus in vain for adjectives, I must, as a substitution, hie me to comparison in the form of a recipe.

Take of London fog 30 parts; malaria 10 parts; gas leaks 20 parts; dewdrops gathered in a brickyard at sunrise, 25 parts; odor of honeysuckle 15 parts. Mix.

The mixture will give you an approximate conception of a Nashville drizzle. It is not so fragrant as a moth-ball nor so thick as pea soup; but 'tis enough — 'twill serve.

I went to a hotel in a tumbril. It required strong self-suppression for me to keep from climbing to the top of it and giving an imitation of Sidney Carton. The vehicle was drawn by beasts of a bygone era and driven by something dark and emancipated.

I was sleepy and tired, so when I got to the hotel I hurriedly paid it the fifty cents it demanded (with approximate lagniappe, I assure you). I knew its habits; and I did not want to hear it prate about its old " marster " or anything that happened " befo' de wah."

The hotel was one of the kind described as " renovated." That means $20,000 worth of new marble pillars, tiling, electric lights and brass cuspidors in the lobby, and a new L. & N. time table and a lithograph of Lookout Mountain in each one of the great rooms above. The management was without reproach, the attention full of exquisite southern courtesy, the service as slow as the progress of a snail and as good-humored as Rip Van Winkle. The food was worth traveling a thousand miles for. There is no other hotel in the world where you can get such chicken livers *en brochette.*

At dinner I asked a Negro waiter if there was anything doing in town. He pondered gravely for a minute, and then replied: " Well, boss, I don't really reckon there's anything at all doin' after sundown."

Sundown had been accomplished; it had been drowned in the drizzle long before. So that spectacle was denied me. But I went forth upon the streets in the drizzle to see what might be there.

" It is built on undulating grounds; and the streets are lighted by electricity at a cost of $32,470 per annum."

As I left the hotel there was a race riot. Down upon me charged a company of freedmen, or Arabs, or Zulus, armed with — no, I saw with relief that they were not rifles, but whips. And I saw dimly a caravan of black, clumsy vehicles; and at the reassuring shouts, " Kyar you anywhere in the town, boss, fuh fifty cents," I reasoned that I was merely a " fare " instead of a victim.

I walked through long streets, all leading uphill. I wondered how those streets ever came down again. Perhaps they didn't until they were " graded." On a few of the " main streets " I saw lights in stores here and there; saw street cars go by conveying worthy burghers hither and yon; saw people pass engaged in the art of conversation, and heard a burst of semi-lively laughter issuing from a soda-water and ice-cream parlor. The streets other than " main " seemed to have enticed upon their borders houses consecrated to peace and domesticity. In many of them lights shone behind discreetly drawn window shades; in a few pianos tinkled orderly and irreproachable music. There was, indeed, little " doing." I wished I had come before sundown. So I returned to my hotel.

" In November, 1864, the Confederate General Hood advanced against Nashville, where he shut up a National force under General Thomas. The latter then sallied forth and defeated the Confederates in a terrible conflict."

All my life I have heard of, admired, and witnessed the fine marksmanship of the South in its peaceful conflicts in the tobacco-chewing regions. But in my hotel a surprise awaited me. There were twelve bright, new, imposing, capacious brass cuspidors in the great lobby, tall enough to be called urns and so wide-mouthed that the crack pitcher of a lady baseball team should have been able to throw a ball into one of them at five paces distant. But, although a terrible battle had raged and was still raging, the enemy had not suffered. Bright, new, imposing, capacious, untouched, they stood. But, shades of Jefferson Brick! the tile floor — the beautiful tile floor! I could not avoid thinking of the battle of Nashville, and trying to draw, as is my foolish habit, some deductions about hereditary marksmanship.

Here I first saw Major (by misplaced courtesy) Wentworth Caswell. I knew him for a type the moment my eyes suffered from the sight of him. A rat has no geographical habitat. My old friend, A. Tennyson, said, as he so well said almost everything:

> Prophet, curse me the blabbing lip,
> And curse me the British vermin, the rat.

Let us regard the word "British" as interchangeable *ad lib.* A rat is a rat.

This man was hunting about the hotel lobby like a starved dog that had forgotten where he had buried a bone. He had a face of great acreage, red, pulpy, and with a kind of sleepy massiveness like that of Buddha. He possessed one single virtue — he was very smoothly shaven. The mark of the beast is not indelible upon a man until he goes about with a stubble. I think that if he had not used his razor that day I would have repulsed his advances, and the criminal calendar of the world would have been spared the addition of one murder.

I happened to be standing within five feet of a cuspidor when Major Caswell opened fire upon it. I had been observant enough to perceive that the attacking force was using Gatlings instead of squirrel rifles; so I side-stepped so promptly that the major seized the opportunity to apologize to a noncombatant. He had the blabbing lip. In four minutes he had become my friend and had dragged me to the bar.

I desire to interpolate here that I am a Southerner. But I am not one by profession or trade. I eschew the string tie, the slouch hat, the Prince Albert, the number of bales of cotton destroyed by Sherman, and plug chewing. When the orchestra plays Dixie I do not cheer. I slide a little lower on the leather-cornered seat and, well, order another Würzburger and wish that Longstreet had — but what's the use?

Major Caswell banged the bar with his fist, and the first gun at Fort Sumpter re-echoed. When he fired the last one at Appomattox I began to hope. But then he began on family trees, and demonstrated that Adam was only a third cousin of a collateral branch of the Caswell family. Genealogy disposed of, he took up, to my distaste, his private family matters. He spoke of his wife, traced her descent back to Eve, and profanely denied any possible rumor that she may have had relations in the land of Nod.

By this time I began to suspect that he was trying to obscure by noise the fact that he had ordered the drinks, on the chance that I would be bewildered into paying for them. But when they were down he crashed a silver dollar loudly upon the bar. Then, of course, another serving was obligatory. And when I had paid for that I took leave of him brusquely; for I wanted no more of him. But before I had obtained my release he had prated loudly of an income that his wife received, and showed a handful of silver money.

When I got my key at the desk the clerk said to me courteously: " If that man Caswell has annoyed you, and if you would like to make a complaint, we will have him ejected. He is a nuisance, a loafer, and without any known means of support, although he seems to have some money most of the time. But we don't seem to be able to hit upon any means of throwing him out legally."

" Why, no," said I, after some reflection; " I don't see my way clear to making a complaint. But I would like to place myself on record as asserting that I do not care for his company. Your town," I continued, " seems to be a quiet one. What manner of entertainment, adventure, or excitement have you to offer to the stranger within your gates? "

" Well, sir," said the clerk, " there will be a show here next Thursday. It is — I'll look it up and have the announcement sent up to your room with the ice water. Good night."

After I went up to my room I looked out the window. It was only about ten o'clock, but I looked upon a silent town. The drizzle continued, spangled with dim lights, as far apart as currants in a cake sold at the Ladies' Exchange.

" A quiet place," I said to myself, as my first shoe struck the ceiling of the occupant of the room beneath mine. " Nothing of the life here that gives color and variety to the cities in the East and West. Just a good, ordinary, humdrum, business town."

" Nashville occupies a foremost place among the manufacturing centers of the country. It is the fifth boot and shoe market in the United States, the largest candy and cracker manufacturing city in the South, and does an enormous wholesale drygoods, grocery, and drug business."

I must tell you how I came to be in Nashville, and I assure you the digression brings as much tedium to me as it does to you. I was traveling elsewhere on my own business, but I had a commission from a northern literary magazine to stop over there and establish a personal connection between the publication and one of its contributors, Azalea Adair.

Adair (there was no clue to the personality except the handwriting) had sent in some essays (lost art!) and poems that had made the editors swear approvingly over their one o'clock luncheon. So they had commissioned me to round up said Adair and corner by contract his or her output at two cents a word before some other publisher offered her ten or twenty.

At nine o'clock the next morning, after my chicken livers *en brochette* (try them if you can find that hotel), I strayed out into the drizzle, which was still on for an unlimited run. At the first corner I came upon Uncle Caesar. He was a stalwart Negro, older than the pyramids, with gray wool and a face that reminded me of Brutus, and a second afterwards of the late King Cettiwayo. He wore the most remarkable coat that I ever had seen or expect to see. It reached to his ankles and had once been a Confederate gray in color. But rain and sun and age had so variegated it that Joseph's coat, beside it, would have faded to a pale monochrome. I must linger with that coat, for it has to do with the story — the story that is so long in coming, because you can hardly expect anything to happen in Nashville.

Once it must have been the military coat of an officer. The cape of it had vanished, but all adown its front it had been frogged and tasseled magnificently. But now the frogs and tassels were gone. In their stead had been patiently stitched (I surmised by some surviving " black mammy ") new frogs made of cunningly twisted common hempen twine. This twine was frayed and disheveled. It must have been added to the coat as a substitute for vanished splendors, with tasteless but painstaking devotion, for it followed faithfully the curves of the long-missing frogs. And, to complete the comedy and pathos of the garment, all its buttons were gone save one. The second button from the top alone remained. The coat was fastened by other twine strings tied through the buttonholes and other holes rudely pierced in the opposite side. There was never such a weird garment so fantas-

tically bedecked and of so many mottled hues. The lone button
was the size of a half-dollar, made of yellow horn and sewed on
with coarse twine.

This Negro stood by a carriage so old that Ham himself might
have started a hack line with it after he left the ark with the two

HE WAVED IT WITHOUT USING IT

animals hitched to it. As I approached he threw open the door,
drew out a feather duster, waved it without using it, and said in
deep, rumbling tones:

"Step right in, suh; ain't a speck of dust in it — jus' got back from a funeral, suh."

I inferred that on such gala occasions carriages were given an extra cleaning. I looked up and down the street and perceived that there was little choice among the vehicles for hire that lined the curb. I looked in my memorandum book for the address of Azalea Adair.

"I want to go to 861 Jessamine Street," I said, and was about to step into the hack. But for an instant the thick, long, gorilla-like arm of the old Negro barred me. On his massive and saturnine face a look of sudden suspicion and enmity flashed for a moment. Then, with quickly returning conviction, he asked blandishingly: "What are you gwine there for, boss?"

"What is that to you?" I asked, a little sharply.

"Nothin', suh, jus' nothin'. Only it's a lonesome kind of part of town and few folks ever has business out there. Step right in. The seats is clean — jes' got back from a funeral, suh."

A mile and a half it must have been to our journey's end. I could hear nothing but the fearful rattle of the ancient hack over the uneven brick paving; I could smell nothing but the drizzle, now further flavored with coal smoke and something like a mixture of tar and oleander blossoms. All I could see through the streaming windows were two rows of dim houses.

"The city has an area of 10 square miles; 181 miles of streets, of which 137 miles are paved; a system of water-works that cost $2,000,000, with 77 miles of mains."

Eight-sixty-one Jessamine Street was a decayed mansion. Thirty yards back from the street it stood, outmerged in a splendid grove of trees and untrimmed shrubbery. A row of box bushes overflowed and almost hid the paling fence from sight; the gate was kept closed by a rope noose that encircled the gate post and the first paling of the gate. But when you got inside you saw that 861 was a shell, a shadow, a ghost of former grandeur and excellence. But in the story, I have not yet got inside.

When the hack had ceased from rattling and the weary quadrupeds came to a rest I handed my jehu his fifty cents with an additional quarter, feeling a glow of conscious generosity, as I did so. He refused it.

"It's two dollars, suh," he said.

"How's that?" I asked. "I plainly heard you call out at the hotel: 'Fifty cents to any part of the town.'"

"It's two dollars, suh," he repeated obstinately. "It's a long ways from the hotel."

"It is within the city limits and well within them," I argued. "Don't think that you have picked up a greenhorn Yankee. Do you see those hills over there?" I went on, pointing toward the east (I could not see them, myself, for the drizzle); "well, I was born and raised on their other side. You old fool nigger, can't you tell people from other people when you see 'em?"

The grim face of King Cettiwayo softened. "Is you from the South, suh? I reckon it was them shoes of yourn fooled me. They is somethin' sharp in the toes for a southern gen'l'man to wear."

"Then the charge is fifty cents, I suppose?" said I inexorably.

His former expression, a mingling of cupidity and hostility, returned, remained ten seconds, and vanished.

"Boss," he said, "fifty cents is right; but I *needs* two dollars, suh; I'm *obleeged* to have two dollars. I ain't *demandin'* it now, suh; after I knows whar you's from; I'm jus' sayin' that I *has* to have two dollars tonight, and business is mighty po'."

Peace and confidence settled upon his heavy features. He had been luckier than he had hoped. Instead of having picked up a greenhorn, ignorant of rates, he had come upon an inheritance.

"You confounded old rascal," I said, reaching down to my pocket, "you ought to be turned over to the police."

For the first time I saw him smile. He knew; *he knew;* HE KNEW.

I gave him two one-dollar bills. As I handed them over I noticed that one of them had seen parlous times. Its upper right-hand corner was missing, and it had been torn through in the middle, but joined again. A strip of blue tissue paper, pasted over the split, preserved its negotiability.

Enough of the African bandit for the present: I left him happy, lifted the rope and opened the creaky gate.

The house, as I said, was a shell. A paint brush had not touched it in twenty years. I could not see why a strong wind should not have bowled it over like a house of cards until I looked again at the trees that hugged it close — the trees that saw the battle of Nashville and still drew their protecting branches around it against storm and enemy and cold.

Azalea Adair, fifty years old, white-haired, a descendant of the cavaliers, as thin and frail as the house she lived in, robed in the cheapest and cleanest dress I ever saw, with an air as simple as a queen's, received me.

The reception room seemed a mile square, because there was nothing in it except some rows of books, on unpainted white-pine bookshelves, a cracked marble-top table, a rag rug, a hairless horsehair sofa, and two or three chairs. Yes, there was a picture on the wall, a colored crayon drawing of a cluster of pansies. I looked around for the portrait of Andrew Jackson and the pine-cone hanging basket but they were not there.

Azalea Adair and I had conversation, a little of which will be repeated to you. She was a product of the old South, gently nurtured in the sheltered life. Her learning was not broad, but was deep and of splendid originality in its somewhat narrow scope. She had been educated at home, and her knowledge of the world was derived from inference and by inspiration. Of such is the precious, small group of essayists made. While she talked to me I kept brushing my fingers, trying, unconsciously, to rid them guiltily of the absent dust from the half-calf backs of Lamb, Chaucer, Hazlitt, Marcus Aurelius, Montaigne, and Hood. She was exquisite, she was a valuable discovery. Nearly everybody nowadays knows too much — oh, so much too much — of real life.

I could perceive clearly that Azalea Adair was very poor. A house and a dress she had, not much else, I fancied. So, divided between my duty to the magazine and my loyalty to the poets and essayists who fought Thomas in the valley of the Cumberland, I listened to her voice, which was like a harpsichord's, and found that I could not speak of contracts. In the presence of the nine Muses and the three Graces one hesitated to lower the topic to two cents. There would have to be another colloquy after I had regained my commercialism. But I spoke of my mission, and three o'clock of the next afternoon was set for the discussion of the business proposition.

"Your town," I said, as I began to make ready to depart (which is the time for smooth generalities), "seems to be a quiet, sedate place. A home town, I should say, where few things out of the ordinary ever happen."

"It carries on an extensive trade in stoves and hollow ware with the West and South, and its flouring mills have a daily capacity of more than 2,000 barrels."

Azalea Adair seemed to reflect.

"I have never thought of it that way," she said, with a kind of sincere intensity that seemed to belong to her. "Isn't it in the still, quiet places that things do happen? I fancy that when God began to create the earth on the first Monday morning one could have leaned out one's window and heard the drops of mud splashing from His trowel as He built up the everlasting hills. What did the noisiest project in the world — I mean the building of the tower of Babel — result in finally? A page and a half of Esperanto in the *North American Review*."

"Of course," said I platitudinously, "human nature is the same everywhere; but there is more color — er — more drama and movement and — er — romance in some cities than in others."

"On the surface," said Azalea Adair. "I have traveled many times around the world in a golden airship wafted on two wings — print and dreams. I have seen (on one of my imaginary tours) the Sultan of Turkey bowstring with his own hands one of his wives who had uncovered her face in public. I have seen a man in Nashville tear up his theater tickets because his wife was going out with her face covered — with rice powder. In San Francisco's Chinatown I saw the slave girl Sing Yee dipped slowly, inch by inch, in boiling almond oil to make her swear she would never see her American lover again. She gave in when the boiling oil had reached three inches above her knee. At a euchre party in East Nashville the other night I saw Kitty Morgan cut dead by seven of her schoolmates and lifelong friends because she had married a house painter. The boiling oil was sizzling as high as her heart; but I wish you could have seen the fine little smile that she carried from table to table. Oh, yes, it is a humdrum town. Just a few miles of red brick houses and mud and stores and lumber yards."

Some one knocked hollowly at the back of the house. Azalea Adair breathed a soft apology and went to investigate the sound. She came back in three minutes with brightened eyes, a faint flush on her cheeks, and ten years lifted from her shoulders.

"You must have a cup of tea before you go," she said, "and a sugar cake."

She reached and shook a little iron bell. In shuffled a small Negro girl about twelve, barefoot, not very tidy, glowering at me with thumb in mouth and bulging eyes.

Azalea Adair opened a tiny, worn purse and drew out a dollar bill, a dollar bill with the upper right-hand corner missing, torn in two pieces and pasted together again with a strip of blue tissue paper. It was one of the bills I had given the piratical Negro — there was no doubt of it.

"Go up to Mr. Baker's store on the corner, Impy," she said, handing the girl the dollar bill, "and get a quarter of a pound of tea — the kind he always sends me — and ten cents' worth of sugar cakes. Now, hurry. The supply of tea in the house happens to be exhausted," she explained to me.

Impy left by the back way. Before the scrape of her hard, bare feet had died away on the back porch, a wild shriek — I was sure it was hers — filled the hollow house. Then the deep, gruff tones of an angry man's voice mingled with the girl's further squeals and unintelligible words.

Azalea Adair rose without surprise or emotion and disappeared. For two minutes I heard the hoarse rumble of the man's voice; then something like an oath and a slight scuffle, and she returned calmly to her chair.

"This is a roomy house," she said, "and I have a tenant for part of it. I am sorry to have to rescind my invitation to tea. It was impossible to get the kind I always use at the store. Perhaps tomorrow Mr. Baker will be able to supply me."

I was sure that Impy had not had time to leave the house. I inquired concerning street-car lines and took my leave. After I was well on my way I remembered that I had not learned Azalea Adair's name. But tomorrow would do.

That same day I started in on the course of iniquity that this uneventful city forced upon me. I was in the town only two days, but in that time I managed to lie shamelessly by telegraph, and to be an accomplice — after the fact, if that is the correct legal term — to a murder.

As I rounded the corner nearest my hotel the Afrite coachman of the polychromatic, nonpareil coat seized me, swung open the dungeony door of his peripatetic sarcophagus, flirted his feather duster and began his ritual: "Step right in, boss. Carriage is clean — jus' got back from a funeral. Fifty cents to any — "

And then he knew me and grinned broadly. "'Scuse me, boss; you is de gen'l'man what rid out with me dis mawnin'. Thank you kindly, suh."

"I am going out to 861 again tomorrow afternoon at three," said I, "and if you will be here, I'll let you drive me. So you know Miss Adair?" I concluded, thinking of my dollar bill.

" I belonged to her father, Judge Adair, suh," he replied.

" I judge that she is pretty poor," I said. " She hasn't much money to speak of, has she? "

For an instant I looked again at the fierce countenance of King Cettiwayo, and then he changed back to an extortionate old Negro hack driver.

" She ain't gwine to starve, suh," he said slowly. " She has reso'ces, suh; she has reso'ces."

" I shall pay you fifty cents for the trip," said I.

" Dat is puffeckly correct, suh," he answered humbly. " I jus' *had* to have dat two dollars dis mawnin', boss."

I went to the hotel and lied by electricity. I wired the magazine: " A. Adair holds out for eight cents a word."

The answer that came back was: " Give it to her quick, you duffer."

Just before dinner " Major " Wentworth Caswell bore down upon me with the greetings of a long-lost friend. I have seen few men whom I have so instantaneously hated, and of whom it was so difficult to be rid. I was standing at the bar when he invaded me; therefore I could not wave the white ribbon in his face. I would have paid gladly for the drinks, hoping, thereby, to escape another; but he was one of those despicable, roaring, advertising bibbers who must have brass bands and fireworks attend upon every cent that they waste in their follies.

With an air of producing millions he drew two one-dollar bills from a pocket and dashed one of them upon the bar. I looked once more at the dollar bill with the upper right-hand corner missing, torn through the middle, and patched with a strip of blue tissue paper. It was my dollar bill again. It could have been no other.

I went up to my room. The drizzle and the monotony of a dreary, eventless southern town had made me tired and listless. I remember that just before I went to bed I mentally disposed of the mysterious dollar bill (which might have formed the clew to a tremendously fine detective story of San Francisco) by saying to myself sleepily: " Seems as though a lot of people here own stock in the Hack-Driver's Trust. Pays dividends promptly, too. Wonder if — " Then I fell asleep.

King Cettiwayo was at his post the next day, and rattled my bones over the stones out to 861. He was to wait and rattle me back again when I was ready.

Azalea Adair looked paler and cleaner and frailer than she had looked on the day before. After she had signed the contract at eight cents per word she grew still paler and began to slip out of her chair. Without much trouble I managed to get her up on the antediluvian horsehair sofa and then I ran out to the sidewalk and yelled to the coffee-colored Pirate to bring a doctor. With a wisdom that I had not suspected in him, he abandoned his team and struck off up the street afoot, realizing the value of speed. In ten minutes he returned with a grave, gray-haired and capable man of medicine. In a few words (worth much less than eight cents each) I explained to him my presence in the hollow house of mystery. He bowed with stately understanding, and turned to the old Negro.

"Uncle Caesar," he said calmly, " run up to my house and ask Miss Lucy to give you a cream pitcher full of fresh milk and half a tumbler of port wine. And hurry back. Don't drive — run. I want you to get back some time this week."

It occurred to me that Dr. Merriman also felt a distrust as to the speeding power of the land-pirate's steeds. After Uncle Caesar was gone, lumberingly, but swiftly, up the street, the doctor looked me over with great politeness and as much careful calculation until he had decided that I might do.

"It is only a case of insufficient nutrition," he said. "In other words, the result of poverty, pride, and starvation. Mrs. Caswell has many devoted friends who would be glad to aid her, but she will accept nothing except from that old Negro, Uncle Caesar, who was once owned by her family."

"Mrs. Caswell!" said I, in surprise. And then I looked at the contract and saw that she had signed it " Azalea Adair Caswell."

"I thought she was Miss Adair," I said.

"Married to a drunken, worthless loafer, sir," said the doctor. " It is said that he robs her even of the small sums that her old servant contributes toward her support."

When the milk and wine had been brought the doctor soon revived Azalea Adair. She sat up and talked of the beauty of the autumn leaves that were then in season, and their height of color. She referred lightly to her fainting seizure as the outcome of an old palpitation of the heart. Impy fanned her as she lay on the sofa. The doctor was due elsewhere, and I followed him to the door. I told him that it was within my power and intentions to make a reasonable advance of money to Azalea Adair on future contributions to the magazine, and he seemed pleased.

" By the way," he said, " perhaps you would like to know that you have had royalty for a coachman. Old Caesar's grandfather was a king in Congo. Caesar himself has royal ways, as you may have observed."

As the doctor was moving off I heard Uncle Caesar's voice inside: " Did he git bofe of dem two dollars from you, Mis' Zalea? "

" Yes, Caesar," I heard Azalea Adair answer weakly. And then I went in and concluded business negotiations with our contributor. I assumed the responsibility of advancing fifty dollars, putting it as a necessary formality in binding our bargain. And then Uncle Caesar drove me back to the hotel.

Here ends all of the story as far as I can testify as a witness. The rest must be only bare statements of facts.

At about six o'clock I went out for a stroll. Uncle Caesar was at his corner. He threw open the door of his carriage, flourishing his duster, and began his depressing formula: " Step right in, suh. Fifty cents to anywhere in the city — hack's puffickly clean, suh — jus' got back from a funeral — "

And then he recognized me. I think his eyesight was getting bad. His coat had taken on a few more faded shades of color, the twine strings were more frayed and ragged, the last remaining button — the button of yellow horn — was gone. A motley descendant of kings was Uncle Caesar!

About two hours later I saw an excited crowd besieging the front of a drug store. In a desert where nothing happens this was manna; so I edged my way inside. On an extemporized couch of empty boxes and chairs was stretched the mortal corporeality of Major Wentworth Caswell. A doctor was testing him for the immortal ingredient. His decision was that it was conspicuous by its absence.

The erstwhile Major had been found dead on a dark street and brought by curious and ennuied citizens to the drug store. The late human being had been engaged in terrific battle — the details showed that. Loafer and reprobate though he had been, he had been also a warrior. But he had lost. His hands were yet clinched so tightly that his fingers would not be opened. The gentle citizens who had known him stood about and searched their vocabularies to find some good words, if it were possible, to speak of him. One kind-looking man said, after much thought: "When 'Cas' was about fo'teen he was one of the best spellers in school."

While I stood there the fingers of the right hand of "the man that was," which hung down at the side of a white pine box, relaxed, and dropped something at my feet. I covered it with one foot quietly, and a little later on I picked it up and pocketed it. I reasoned that in his last struggle his hand must have seized that object unwittingly and held it in a death grip.

At the hotel that night the main topic of conversation, with the possible exceptions of politics and prohibition, was the demise of Major Caswell. I heard one man say to a group of listeners:

"In my opinion, gentlemen, Caswell was murdered by some of these no-account niggers for his money. He had fifty dollars this afternoon which he showed to several gentlemen in the hotel. When he was found the money was not on his person."

I left the city next morning at nine, and as the train was crossing the bridge over the Cumberland River I took out of my pocket a yellow horn overcoat button the size of a fifty-cent piece, with frayed ends of coarse twine hanging from it, and cast it out of the window into the slow, muddy waters below.

I wonder what's doing in Buffalo!

SUGGESTIONS FOR STUDY

1 As usual, the author uses a number of unusual words. Find six and explain them to the class.

2. In not more than three short sentences, state the plot of the story.

3. Of the various O. Henry ingredients mentioned in the introduction, which stand out particularly in this story?

4. Which do you find most interesting?

5. Can you justify the title? Does it fit the idea in the mind of the author? Does he make his point?

FOR FURTHER READING

The Four Million: " The Gift of the Magi," " The Cop and the Anthem," " Mammon and the Archer," " Springtime à la Carte," " The Green Door," " After Twenty Years," " Lost on Dress Parade "

The Heart of the West: " The Handbook of Hymen," " Hygeia at the Solito "

Roads of Destiny: " Phoebe," " A Retrieved Reformation "

Whirligigs: " The Ransom of Red Chief," " A Blackjack Bargainer "
The Voice of the City: " A Lickpenny Lover," " Transients in Arcadia "
Sixes and Sevens: " At Arms with Morpheus," " The Duplicity of Har-
graves "
Cabbages and Kings: " Shoes "

'LIJAH

By EDGAR VALENTINE SMITH (1875–   )

The chivalry, romance, and the glory of the aristocratic Old South have been beautifully recorded by Thomas Nelson Page. Here is a story of the new South of modern industry and agricultural development. But as the new South is building prosperity on the ruins of the old, we appreciate perhaps more than ever the innate dignity and fine sense of honor of the old aristocratic code. In this story Judge Holmsted with his almost disastrous hospitality, and 'Bama with her unconditional devotion to her master, bring us a charming reminder of the culture destroyed by the Civil War. The author, who is a member of the staff of the *Birmingham News,* represents a rising group of the new South. He has won recognition by his studies of the southern characters of today. " 'Lijah " appeared originally in *Harper's Magazine,* and was later fashioned into a one-act play, in which form it was awarded first prize over fifty other Alabama plays by the Birmingham Little Theater in 1925. Observe that one of the characters is named after the author's native state.

Fortune had long since ceased to smile on the last master of Holmacres. Then, suddenly, with the advent of the strangers and the coincident creation of 'Lijah, came, too, the visit of the angels.

The two strangers — being strangers — of course, knew nothing of the evil days that had befallen Judge Holmsted, nor were they particularly interested, since their mission concerned not the fortunes, either good or ill, of others, but the betterment of their own. What they knew concerning the Judge and Holmacres —other than the fact that the two were intimately connected with the business which was bringing them to the place — was furnished by the aged Negro, who, with his ramshackle surrey and ancient nag, eked out a precarious existence driving occasional transients about the countryside. They had found him at the railway station in Wynnesborough, the county seat, and he had driven them along the five miles of deep-rutted road that stretched from the town to Holmacres. Being old, he was naturally garrulous.

For a long time he had sat fidgeting on the front seat of the vehicle, one ancient ear cocked rearward, listening to the unfamiliar accent of the strangers' speech. Finally, during a lull in their conversation, curiosity overpowered him and he halffaced about.

" 'Scuse me, gen'lemens," he observed, ingratiatingly, " I don't mean no hahm by astin' it, but — you all is Yankees, ain't you? "

" Northerners — yes," one of them answered, smiling. " Why do you ask? "

" Yessuh. I thought so. You jus' don't talk like white folks — I *means* like *us's* white folks, Boss."

The stranger who had answered the query — the younger and less grave-appearing of the two — smiled again. " We'd heard so much of your southern hospitality that we thought we'd come down and see what it is like."

" Hawspitality? Well, suhs, you is comin' to de place wheah it was invented at — when you comes to see de Judge."

Then the old man — product of a bygone day and still living in the memory of its glories — described the hospitality of Holmacres as it had been and as he still saw it. It was the most fertile plantation in the country, and its owner, Judge Holmsted, by odds the richest man, the most learned lawyer, the noblest gentleman, and the most open-handed host who ever breathed. His house was the finest that had ever been built; he set the most sumptuous table in the land; niggers fought for the privilege of working for him, even accepting the humblest tasks merely for the honor of being counted among the Judge's retinue. Judge Holmsted, to sum it up, was real " quality "; not like some of the trash which had sprung up with the last generation.

Thus the strangers were prepared in a measure for the picture which greeted them a few moments later: a grove of broad-topped live oaks, with the house in the near distance, a mansion of cement-walled, slate-roofed dignity, with the huge-columned, two-storied veranda reaching in stately welcome across its entire front. And as they stepped from the conveyance and came up the cape-jasmine-bordered walk, another picture was limned before them: a man well past threescore who had risen from his chair. He had removed his broad-brimmed hat, baring a mane of iron-gray hair, and now stood, despite the dingy frock coat that he wore, a figure as imposing as one of his own Ionic columns, courteously expectant at the visitors' approach.

The young stranger introduced his companion and himself. They were from the North, as he had explained to the ancient driver, and their business was that of timberland investors. One of their agents had sent reports of hardwood acreage adjacent to the Tombigbee, and they were making a personal trip of inspection. They wished to find a place — a boarding or lodging house, perhaps — closer to the river than the county seat. Did Judge Holmsted know of such a place? They would be in the vicinity for several days.

Masters of Holmacres, since that first one who had erected a mansion in what was at that time a wilderness, had been famed for their hospitality. Nor had they been content with the thought that the neighboring gentry only should be the recipients of their bounty, for that first one, a little strangely perhaps for one of cavalier forbears, had caused to be carved beneath the broad fire mantel in the central hall this inscription:

" Be not forgetful to entertain strangers: for thereby some have entertained angels unawares."

Judge Holmsted was of that breed. " I couldn't think of letting you gentlemen stay anywhere but here." He spoke with a soft slurring of r's and a dropping of final g's which any attempt to put into print serves only to distort and make grotesque. " You must do me the honor of becoming my guests during your stay."

The older stranger demurred. " Why . . . that's awfully kind of you, Judge. But we really couldn't take advantage of your hosp — "

" You'll be taking no advantage at all, sir." There was no hint of subservience in the way the Judge said " sir." It was the courteous form of address toward strangers which had been the custom during his youth. " On the contrary, you'll really be doing me a favor. I'm an old man, gentlemen " — his smile would have won them had they really been hesitant at accepting his hospitality — " a little lonely at times, and I like company. And visitors, nowadays, are rare."

The strangers accepted the invitation with suspicious readiness. They hailed the ancient driver of the surrey, who had remained waiting in the driveway and who now brought in their luggage. For just a moment Judge Holmsted seemed ever so slightly embarrassed, a slight flush mantled his cheeks. And then, without stopping to think what it might mean, he created — 'Lijah.

"Be seated, gentlemen," he invited, "while I call someone to bring in your baggage." He took a step toward the broad doorway. "'Lijah!" he called. There was no answer. He called again, more loudly, "'Lijah!" and still no one answered. Frowning, he walked to the end of the veranda, and peering about, shouted the name for the third time, with the same result as before.

He turned apologetically to his guests. "That trifling rascal," he explained, "is never about, particularly at this season of the year, when I need him." He glanced about for the driver of the surrey, but the old man had gone. "Come with me, gentlemen." Taking up their luggage, he led them within the house.

"'LIJAH!" HE CALLED

Though his welcome to the strangers had been extended in all sincerity (he had not been a Holmsted had it been otherwise) their coming brought a problem — another one — to the Judge. And, somehow, in his declining years life seemed to hold little else save problems, and all of them as yet unsolved.

Time had been when Holmacres threw its doors wide open to the countryside, for its masters had lived in the traditions handed down by its founder. Even now Judge Holmsted, daydreaming at times, permitted his thoughts to stray back to the days when servants swarmed about the place, when there were stable boys who seemed actually to get underfoot, and house boys who fairly haunted the guests, eager to be of the slightest service. The big stable had contained riding and driving horses, which were not merely to be had for the asking but were almost forced on one. There had been dogs for the fall quail shooting, and master and guests had ridden to hounds. But now . . . it seemed that there remained little of misfortune that could happen. For of the hospitality for which Holmacres had been famous there existed but a shell, a shell so fragile that it might be crushed at any moment.

Had he belonged to that modern school which placed the mere god of commercialism above neighborliness, he might still have kept himself from actual want. But a friend in financial straits had come to him, and it was a neighborly act to indorse a note for a large sum of money. It was a hideous fate, though, that caused the friend to die, leaving an estate heavily encumbered, and forced the Judge to pay the indebtedness by mortgaging the home of his ancestors.

Even before this, though, the soil of Holmacres, planted for generations exclusively to cotton, had been growing less and less fruitful. Judge Holmsted had seen the yield dwindle year by year. He had divided the plantations into small farms for tenants. Then the northern exodus had begun, one by one the tenants had left, until now, with the few hired " hands " that he could secure, he was cultivating perhaps one-tenth of his tillable lands.

Still, for a time he had not experienced want. His salary as judge of the circuit — which position he had graced for thirty years — while not munificent had enabled him to make a pretense of the hospitality that had brought fame to Holmacres.

Then a new order of things came to pass. Politics was played with the precision — and the heart — of a machine. Those in control of the political destinies of the counties composing the circuit banded themselves together — that is, all of them save Judge Holmsted. Old-fashioned jurist that he was, he refused to lend himself to what he considered certain questionable pre-election machinations. Then the ultimatum went forth: he could submit or take the consequences — political oblivion. He accepted the gage, for he came not only of a hospitable but of a combative breed.

Hitherto his mere announcement that he would be a candidate for nomination at the Democratic primaries had assured his re-election. Now, for the first time in his life, he entered upon a vigorous campaign. He traveled incessantly about the various counties of his circuit, spending, legitimately, of his slender means. He made countless speeches, he met hundreds of friends and received — promises

He returned to the practice of law in Wynnesborough, but it seemed that his methods, like himself, had become old-fashioned. Friends insisted that he retained too much conscience to compete with more modern and, in certain instances, as he maintained, less ethical procedures than met his ideals.

" The practice of law," he had said once, when the matter came up, " is an honorable profession. It was never intended that it should degenerate into a display of legal acrobatics."

Clients were few and those who came were not always of the soundest financial standing. But there was always more or less bickering and litigation between the poorer class of hill-farmers, and some of these brought their troubles to Judge Holmsted. They paid their accounts in various ways: some brought small lots of cotton, others poultry and pigs, while one, an aged bachelor recluse of uncertain temper, just before his death had willed to the judge forty acres of land. This, people inclined to be humorous asserted, was in the way of a subtle revenge, for the Judge, suing for the old man, had lost his case, and the hill forty, as it was known, was not considered worth the tax payments.

There had been excessively poor crops. Years, too, when the cotton raised had not paid operating expenses. Twice the Judge had borrowed money — which he still owed — in advance on his crops. And the present outlook, with the late spring rains and cultivation sadly hampered, was now worse than ever.

Even his plainly dwindling income did not cause him to forsake his ideals. These, he insisted, one must cling to, even though he go down with them. Certain other changes, though, had forced themselves on him. Horses and other stock had been sold, since the plantation would not longer support them in numbers. Now all that remained were a few work mules and the Judge's own mount, Grover Cleveland. Servants were dispensed with until all of them, save one, had gone. She stayed.

Christened Alabama, she was variously called Miz' 'Bama, Sis 'Bama, and 'Bama, the form of address depending on the degree of intimacy she permitted the speaker, the Judge and those of her race whom she considered her equals using the last named. She had remained at Holmacres after all the others had left, though her wage was more often a mirage than a reality. Latterly, continued urging by certain of her friends that she leave Judge Holmsted's service and go to the city always met with scornful rebuff.

" But he ain't payin' you nothin'," the tempter would insist.

" 'Sposin' he ain't? " 'Bama, hands on her ample hips, would face the speaker. " You is fergittin' somep'm, ain't you? What 'bout my social p'sition? "

Usually this ended the discussion, for 'Bama, born and reared in the atmosphere of Holmacres, was the recognized leader of her people in the vicinity. No wedding was complete without her in the rôle of general adviser and master of ceremonies, nor was any funeral fittingly held without her presence to lend due solemnity to the occasion. But sometimes argument failed to convince those who tried to tempt her. Then 'Bama would fall back on flat refusal.

" Go 'way, nigguhs! " she would command. " I wouldn't leave 'is heah plantation foh — foh a *hund'ed dolluhs a yeah!* "

So she remained steadfast at Holmacres as general house factotum for the Judge. It was 'Bama who tactfully reminded him, at those times when the larder became more depleted than usual, that supplies were needed. And it was she who, out of the merest nothing, could serve food fit for a king's banquet. It was 'Bama who attended to the laundry — carefully washing the Judge's shirts to save the frayed cuffs as much as possible — and looked after the scanty supply of household linen. She darned Judge Holmsted's socks, saw that his shiny coat was occasionally brushed, and kept him generally from being out at elbows in the matter of clothing.

Her manifold duties had brought her to the front of the house that afternoon when the Judge summoned the mythical 'Lijah. For a moment she listened in open-mouthed amazement. Then understanding of a sort came to her, as she peeped between the curtains and saw the strangers. For some reason Judge Holmsted wanted it understood that a personage who answered — or should answer — to the name of 'Lijah belonged about the place. And any undertaking that the Judge set on foot was worth seeing to its conclusion. While she lacked the Judge's creative ability, she could, at least, embellish that which he had made. Her first attempt was in evidence that evening when she served a supper that would have tickled the palate of a gourmand.

" Judge," she remarked, taking the privilege of an old servant, " does you know, suh, 'at triflin' 'Lijah ain't got back till yit? "

Judge Holmsted choked momentarily; he seemed to experience sudden difficulty with his food, but recovered his self-control.

" He hasn't? " he demanded, sternly. " Won't he ever learn to come in on time? Tell him that I wish to speak with him the moment he gets in."

" Yessuh. I knows wheah he's at. He's down to 'at river, settin' out catfish lines."

'Bama had cast the die. Judge Holmsted's creation of 'Lijah had been the result of a sudden — and now inexplicable — impulse; probably, upon reflection, he would have made no further reference to him. But 'Bama had given entity to the myth; with a word or two she had made of it an outstanding personality: a house servant who, by implication at least, took whatsoever liberties he chose.

And suddenly the realization came to the Judge that his creation had been nothing short of inspiration. With the present state of affairs at Holmacres, numberless things were sure to happen which might cause embarrassment to one who sought to fill the rôle of dutiful host; and the lack of a perfect hospitality, in many instances, could be blamed on the erring — though mythical — 'Lijah.

" He's one of the older servants about the place," the Judge explained casually to his guests. " Does pretty much as he pleases."

He followed this with a laughing remark about 'Lijah's fondness for fishing. It was almost impossible to keep a Negro and a river apart when the catfish were biting.

" I'd like very much to see 'Lijah." It was the younger stranger speaking. " I've read so many stories dealing with southern plantation life — and especially the old family servants — that I've often wanted to see one of them. And your man, 'Lijah, seems to be typical."

" Oh, he'll be about the place — off and on," the Judge assured, carelessly. " And if you're interested in types, sir, you'll probably like 'Lijah."

Thus for the moment he dismissed 'Lijah. But 'Bama, apparently, was determined not to let the errant one off so easily, for later, as the Judge and his portraits of earlier Holmsteds gave greeting from their oval walnut frames, she came to the doorway.

" Judge," she observed, meaningly, " I don't s'pect you'll hahdly find no seegars. I seed 'Lijah sof'-footin' it round 'at sec'ta'y whilse I was dustin' 'is mawnin'."

Mechanically, Judge Holmsted's eyes sought the old rosewood secretary in one corner of the room, but before he could speak the younger stranger broke in with:

"Oh, that's all right, Judge." He was laughing heartily as he extended a cigar case. "Take one of these. So, he 'borrows' your cigars, does he? I've simply *got* to see him."

The strangers spoke of their business in the vicinity. The timber which they wished to inspect lay some miles away and, although their actual cruising of it would be done on foot, they would need some kind of conveyance to take them to their starting point. They supposed an automobile could be obtained in Wynnesborough?

Guests beneath Holmacres' roof had never been compelled to hire conveyances. It would have been unthinkable. The Judge explained that the swamp roads were in such condition that an automobile would be impracticable. He had never bought a car himself for this reason. His guests must use one of the numerous horses about the place. He would have 'Lijah hitch one of them to the buggy. It would be the very thing for their trips.

When one of them, giving as an excuse their long railroad journey, suggested retiring, Judge Holmsted, first ascertaining that 'Lijah was nowhere to be found, led them up the broad, winding stairway to their room. He lighted the kerosene lamp. Then, carelessly turning back the bed covering, he stopped in sudden horror. There was only one sheet on the bed!

He turned, his face crimsoning, to his guests. They had seen. "That trifling, worthless —" he began, and stopped. "It's 'Lijah — of course, gentlemen — as usual," he said, helplessly. "Come with me."

He led them to another room — his own — which for more than forty years no one save himself had occupied. This, he knew, would be in readiness. It always was, for he was fastidious about certain things, among them fresh bed linen. 'Bama attended to that.

"Just leave your shoes outside the door, gentlemen," he said in parting. "'Lijah will polish them."

He found 'Bama in the kitchen. Her answer to his question about the sheets brought home to him dishearteningly the scarcity of household linen.

In the library he picked up the latest issue of the Wynnesborough *Clarion*, a weekly newspaper published in the county seat, but he could not fasten his thoughts on the printed page. There were weightier things to be considered. Plainly, the visit of the strangers — should it prove of some duration — meant a still further drain on the slender resources of Holmacres. Since he had promised his guests the use of a horse, they would have to take Grover Cleveland. The Judge sighed. All of the work-mules were sadly needed, but he must use one of them for his daily trips to his office. By waiting until the strangers had left every morning, though, and remaining at his office till he was sure they had returned, they need never know of the subterfuge he had resorted to for their convenience.

Another matter claimed his attention: the disquieting letter — rather the letter that spelled doom — which had come that morning. The interest payment on the mortgage would be due shortly, and the letter stated brusquely that the mortgage had passed into other hands. Hereafter all payments must be met at maturity. Covetous eyes, Judge Holmsted knew, had long looked toward Holmacres. Once or twice he had succeeded in having his payments extended, but now . . . alien owners — people with no reverence for its traditions — would come into possession of the place. The thought was bitter — unbearable.

Once — more than twoscore years ago — the Judge had hoped that an heir might succeed to his name and estate. But with the passing of the one who could have made this a reality, this hope, too, had died. Better so, he comforted himself now; far better that the odium for failure to live up to Holmacres' heritage be his than that it should have been shifted to a son who would have borne his name.

He mounted the stairs. Just outside the door of his guests' room he found their shoes.

And that night — and for succeeding nights — he slept in the bed that had but one sheet.

But his guests at the breakfast table next morning probably thought that his only solicitude lay in planning for their well-being. He was sorry that, owing to 'Lijah's shiftlessness — the black rascal! — he had been compelled to make such short shift for them on the previous night. He hoped they had rested well.

After breakfast they found Grover Cleveland, freshly curried and rubbed till his coat shone like satin, hitched to the buggy ready for their trip. The vehicle itself bore signs of recent washing; the harness, too, one would have said had been freshly oiled.

"I wonder how we're going to begin talking business to a man who treats us like members of his family," the older stranger said as he climbed into the vehicle. "We'll have to use a lot of diplomacy."

"We'll just remember," the younger man reminded, "that we've come several hundred miles to secure a property at as favorable terms to ourselves as possible. And that business is business — always."

Judge Holmsted waited only long enough to see his guests off. Then he walked to one of the fields where a Negro was ploughing.

"Eph," he said, "I'll have to be using the mule for a few days."

"But, Judge, suh!" Eph stared, gaping. "Dis grass! It's plum' ram-pant since 'em las' rains, suh. Can't you see it's jus' nachelly chokin' de cotton to death?"

The Judge could see, plainly enough. The spindling stalks of cotton were struggling weakly through mazes of Johnson and Bermuda grasses. But he saw something else, too; something that Eph, being a recent comer, could not have seen or, seeing, could not have understood: there were guests beneath Judge Holmsted's roof.

It was the first time that he had ridden a mule since he was a boy. Often then, in a spirit of mischief, he had done so. Things had changed now. Horses . . . dogs . . . servants . . . gone. Everything! Everything save the will to be a hospitable host.

At the little bank in town he was courteously but firmly refused an additional loan. The bank officials liked the Judge — and sympathized with him — but his previous loans were still outstanding. And it was doubtful — exceedingly doubtful — that his crop that year would pay the cost of raising it.

But that evening, as he sat with his guests on the broad veranda, he was solicitous only as to the result of their investigations. Were they finding the hardwood timber of good quality? And was it in sufficient quantity to justify them in purchasing and logging it? He hoped this might be the case; he was looking forward with a great deal of pleasure to welcoming them as permanent neighbors.

He proved himself to be a raconteur of rare ability and charm. The grave-faced stranger seemed fascinated by his stories as he spoke of the days when steamboats from Mobile plied the Tombigbee daily. Now there were only one or two boats weekly. But then many were the gay parties that made the round trip. There was always a Negro orchestra on board and stately men and beautiful women, after the dining saloon had been cleared, danced the schottische and the polka until the early hours of morning. More than once, too, a steamer had been forced to pull in to the bank while two young blades went ashore and settled their hot-blooded quarrels according to the code. Judge Holmsted sighed reminiscently. Those had been wonderful days.

The air was soft with the softness of southern nights. There came to them, as they sat there, the odor of cape jasmine and the fainter but more caressing scent of honeysuckle. A light breeze rustled the leaves of the water oaks, shimmering now by the light of the full moon in a mantle of pure silver dust.

The younger stranger lighted a cigar and leaned back in his chair, sighing restfully. " Two weeks of this," he said, " and I shouldn't want to go home. You southern planters lead an enviable life, Judge."

" It's enchanting," his companion assented.

" We like it, sir — some of us," the Judge admitted. He spoke with a tinge of regret of former neighbors who, one by one, had been lured away by the cities. Many fine old places had been left to the care of tenants and had speedily gone to ruin. But the Holmsteds, being lovers of the land, had always lived close to it. " Maybe we are more firmly rooted in the soil than some of the others were," the Judge said.

" It seems to me, Judge," the grave-faced stranger offered, " that you have a wonderful place here for a stock farm. Aren't these native grasses — I believe you call them Johnson and Bermuda — good for grazing? "

" Excellent, sir."

" That's just what I'd do with this place if I owned it," the younger stranger broke in. He was more outspoken than his elderly companion. " I'd divide it into pastures with good fences, build up-to-date barns and pig houses, and stock it with blooded cattle and hogs. You've your grasses for spring and summer. And I understand that those river canebrakes make fine winter grazing."

" I may try something of the kind next year," the Judge admitted. " I've been thinking for some time of venturing along that line."

Venturing! Blooded cattle and hogs! Fences and barns, when the burning question was one of bare existence! Not that he had never had dreams. Many times he had pictured his broad lands dotted with droves of sleek cattle and herds of swine, with an income assured that would again crown Holmacres with its fair name for hospitality. But the realization of this dream would require money.

It was the next morning that a mocking bird, nesting in a near-by tree, awakened the serious-faced stranger with its early song. Arising, he crept softly to the window and stood listening. And suddenly, as he looked out, he started and stared fixedly. Then a dull red flush mounted slowly to his cheeks. He withdrew from the window even more softly than he had approached it and lay down again without wakening his companion.

But that morning brought consternation to Judge Holmsted. Modern plumbing had not been installed at Holmacres, and he remembered suddenly that his guests must shave. And there was one item that he had overlooked.

" I suppose, gentlemen," he remarked at the breakfast table, " that 'Lijah — you see I have to keep close check on him — brought you hot water? "

They admitted that he had not.

" He'll be the death of me yet," the Judge said, hopelessly, " if I don't wring his neck soon. He's getting more worthless every day."

The young stranger laughed. " You're more lenient with your servants, Judge, than we'd be in the North. They must attend to their duties there or they're discharged."

" But it's different with us, sir." The Judge smiled. " Take 'Lijah, for example. Been on the place all of his life — going on fifty years. I couldn't get rid of him. If I were to discharge him he'd refuse to stay discharged. He'd simply come sneaking back and I'd have to feed him."

The younger man's interest in 'Lijah was more intrigued than ever. Returning with his companion earlier than usual one evening, he sought out 'Bama. He was eager, he said, to see 'Lijah. But that worthy, as usual, failed to answer even when 'Bama, standing on the kitchen porch, called his name lustily several times.

" When does he sleep? " the stranger asked. " He doesn't seem to be around the place of nights."

" Sleep? Him sleep? You neentuh worry 'bout 'at, Cap'n. All 'Lijah needs is a sof' place on de shady side of a tree when

dey's somep'm needs doin' round de house. He'll 'tend to de
sleepin'. Dey's jus' two things 'Lijah's good foh: he de sleep-
lovin'es' an' de catfish-ketchin'es' nigguh you eveh seed."

" He's typical all right," the stranger laughed. " And I must
see him — I've simply got to see him before I leave."

Judge Holmsted found himself gradually forming a sneaking
fondness for his creation. Maybe it was because he was unconsciously bringing into being an ideal. For 'Lijah was just the
shiftless, work-dodging, cigar-pilfering type that the Judge
would have loved — the kind that would run rabbits with his
bird dogs — provided the Judge could afford the dogs — or slip
his pack of fox hounds out on cold autumn nights — if the Judge
should ever own a pack — for surreptitious 'coon and 'possum
hunting. Yes . . . that would be just like 'Lijah. Indolent,
grumbling always, complaining of a mis'ry in his side; absolutely
dependent, thoroughly undependable — and utterly likable. In
short, he would be perfect. The Judge even caught himself at
times murmuring aloud, " That trifling black rascal! "

But such things — oh, well! — they were dreams, visions that
an old man was seeing.

As the strangers showed no signs of terminating their visit,
'Bama, with visions of a rapidly depleted larder, began to experience a real concern. With only the Judge and herself to care for,
she could have made shift of some sort. Maybe a hint to Judge
Holmsted of the real state of affairs might not prove unavailing.
So she tried, very diplomatically, one evening at the supper
table, to sound a warning.

" Judge, suh," she remarked, meaningly, " 'Lijah is been
'mongst de chickens agi'n."

" What of it? " Judge Holmsted smiled on his guests. 'Lijah,
he explained, was probably giving a party for some of his friends.
" A few chickens, more or less, don't matter, do they, 'Bama? "

" But dese is *fattenin'* chickens, suh; de onlies' ones I had left."

" You don't mind 'Lijah entertaining his friends, do you? "
the talkative stranger asked.

" Not gen'ally; no, suh. But he's been gittin' entirely *too*
entertainin' lately."

" Doesn't he catch enough fish for his feasts? "

" Yessuh; he ketches plenty fish. But catfish, you knows,
is just a nigguh's reg'lar eatin' victuals. Dey uses de chickens
kind o' foh dessert."

"You must find his parties something of a drain on your resources."

"'Tain't no pahty, suh, he's givin' 'is time. It's just a shindig — a plain shindig."

The Judge explained that a shindig was a dance.

"Dance?" The younger stranger seemed amazed. "An old man like 'Lijah?"

"Him dance?" 'Bama gave answer. "Just de thoughts of a fiddle'll send him shufflin' his feets 'cross de flo' — right now! Age ain't purified him none."

'Bama, strictly orthodox in her religious beliefs, was patently outraged by this latest of the hapless 'Lijah's escapades, for as she left the room they heard her muttering:

"An' him wid gran'chillun! I's gwine to have him churched — I *sho'* is!"

Between themselves the strangers discussed the business which had brought them to Holmacres.

"It's showing up even better than the estimate we received," the older man said one evening.

"One of the richest deposits I ever saw," the other admitted.

When they went to their room he complained of not being in the mood for sleeping. The rays of that southern moon, he said, must have affected him. He felt restless; he'd walk round a bit.

Five minutes later he returned quietly to the house, mounted the stairs softly, undressed silently, and went to bed.

The next morning as they seated themselves at the breakfast table, 'Bama's voice, raised in loud and indignant self-communion, was heard in the kitchen.

"Co'se, he don't keer! Out dere diggin' yearthworms to go fishin' wid an' lettin' all 'em cows an' ca'fs git together! Don't make no diffe'nce to him if us *don't* have no milk foh de cawfee."

It was much better, 'Bama reasoned, to blame this lack on 'Lijah than be compelled to admit that their only cow, bitten by a snake two days previously, had died.

But the younger stranger, usually so talkative when reference was made to 'Lijah, was strangely silent now.

Another day, as the visitors were dressing in their room, the more taciturn one spoke of their business. "I wonder," he asked, "if the Judge knows anything about the value of the property?"

"Oh, yes!" The younger man's loquaciousness had returned. "He knows all about it. I was talking to 'Lijah only yesterday"

— he made sudden pretense of searching for something in his traveling bag — " and he said the Judge had received several offers for the property, but that he wasn't eager to sell. Saving it as a sort of nest egg, I was given to understand. In fact, 'Lijah said — "

" So, you've seen him? " At the first mention of the name, the serious-faced stranger had seemed surprised — almost startled. Then a look of comprehension — of complete and sympathetic understanding — lighted his grave features. And, as he smiled softly, tiny wrinkles creased the corners of his eyes. " What's 'Lijah like? "

" Just what I expected. Quite a character. Unique. He let me understand how these southern planters feel about parting with any of their landholdings. From what 'Lijah said, the Judge probably wouldn't even name a figure if we were to approach him on the matter. And don't forget that it would be fatal even to think of trying any haggling or ' jewing down.' He doesn't want for money, with this plantation bringing in a steady income and all the servants he needs. That's not even considering what he gets out of his law practice. Now, I'd suggest — "

" Just a moment! "

At the interruption the voluble young stranger looked up from his traveling bag. Something that he saw — maybe it was the quiet smile in his companion's eyes — sent an answering flash into his own.

" We're partners," the serious-faced man reminded him, " and ought to be frank with each other. Just how long have you known the actual conditions here? That 'Lijah is a myth? That it's the Judge who has been polishing our shoes — "

" And washing that damned old buggy! " The younger man's face was crimson. " And letting us have his saddle horse — the only one on the place — while he rode a mule! Think of it! That hospitable old aristocrat! Poverty-stricken! My God, I — " He stammered and stopped.

" We both understand, I guess." The quiet-spoken man extended his hand, which was grasped in silence.

That evening they announced to Judge Holmsted that, having finished their inspection, they were ready to return home. After thanking the Judge for his hospitality, the younger stranger broached the matter of business. They were not only timberland investors, it appeared, but dealt also in other property. But, as he tried diplomatically to come to the subject uppermost in his mind, he seemed strangely ill at ease for one accustomed to business deals of magnitude. And finally, instead of the tactful approach which he had planned, he came very bluntly to the point.

" There's a deposit of mica on that hill forty of yours, Judge," he said simply. " Would you care to sell it ? "

That old hill forty! Hope blossomed faintly in Judge Holmsted's breast. The strangers might — it was barely possible that they might — pay enough for that rocky, worthless waste to take care of that threatening interest note. If so, he was assured tenancy of his home for another six months. After that . . .

But the stranger was speaking again. " We realize, Judge, that, between gentlemen, there should be no haggling over such a thing as price. We've talked it over, my friend and I, and have decided to offer you just what the property is worth to us."

That faint gleam of hope flickered and died. Evidently the strangers considered the hill forty almost valueless. Foolish! Just an old man dreaming . . . Holmacres . . . home of his ancestors . . . home of hospitality. . . .

He heard the stranger's voice again. He was speaking rapidly. " We can offer you, for all rights to the land, fifty thousand dollars."

Fifty thousand dollars! One watching Judge Holmsted closely might have noticed a sudden throbbing of the blue veins at his temples; might have detected a slight tremor in the hand that went up, trying unconcernedly to stroke his gray goatee; might even have observed his other hand grip tightly for a moment the arm of the chair on which it rested. Maybe, in that brief instant, the Judge saw a dream fulfilled: broad fields fenced to pasture and dotted with sleek cattle and fat swine; bottom lands, yellow with ripening corn; barns and outhouses, as befitted a vast estate; Holmacres, with its doors once more flung wide. . . .

But whatever might have been his emotions, he gave no evidence of them, as he answered with his usual grave courtesy:

" So far as I know, gentlemen, the matter can be arranged."

When the strangers left next morning he expressed regret that he could not accompany them to town, since urgent matters necessitated his presence on the plantation. They could leave Grover Cleveland and the buggy at the livery stable in Wynnesborough. He would send 'Lijah for them.

After they had gone he seated himself before the old rosewood secretary. Maybe he dreamed again . . . of quail hunting during the crisp months of fall . . . of fox hounds in their kennels . . . of servants. Servants?

Suddenly he drew up a sheet of paper and began writing in a firm, precise script. And when he had finished he scanned what he had written:

" WANTED: Negro house servant, male, aged fifty, or thereabouts, for light work in plantation house. Must be willing to answer to the name of Elijah. Apply B. L. H. care *Clarion*."

SUGGESTIONS FOR STUDY

1. Vocabulary: garrulous, mirage, gourmand, entity, raconteur, cane-brakes, taciturn, loquaciousness, voluble, mica.

2. Did you notice how Judge Holmsted's high ideals of conduct unconsciously raised the standards of his guests? In some such way writers of " idealistic " literature claim that literature may help build the character of the reader.

3. Do you think this story is realistic or romantic? Why?

4. In what ways had the modern " go-getters " who were bringing prosperity to the community lowered its standards? Do you think that modern business methods necessarily lower standards?

5. What details make the story distinctly southern? Why is " Grover Cleveland " a good name for Judge Holmsted's horse?

6. The dramatized version Mr. Smith has made of this story would make a good play for your classroom or club.

7. Can you write a story of your community as it is today, introducing some character who will carry with him the flavor of the life of fifty years ago?

8. What similarities do you find to " A Municipal Report " ?

FOR FURTHER READING

" Prelude "

TO BUILD A FIRE [1]

By JACK LONDON (1876–1916)

" Jack London, California waif, water-front street gamin, bar-room ' tough ' and hoodlum, leader of the oyster pirates, deck hand on a North

[1] From *Lost Face* by Jack London. Reprinted by permission of The Macmillan Company, publishers.

Pacific sealer, mill worker, hobo, college student for a time, gold-seeker in Alaska during the first wild days of the Klondike rush, adventurer among the islands of the South Seas!" Surely here is a wealth of experience for a writer to draw upon for stories! London's stories are filled with an atmosphere which convinces his reader that authentic pictures of life are being painted. Written early in the present century, they embody both the localized realism and the journalistic style which first appeared between the years 1890 and 1900. Their virility and power make them epic in scope. They are "crisp and crackling and interesting, terse in style and vigorous of phrase," as he himself declared that stories should be. In this story notice how he piles detail upon detail to accomplish his effect. There are no digressions, no time is wasted in getting from introduction to conclusion. "Cold" is the fourth word, and the story ends with the phrase, "fire provider." In technique this is an almost perfect story. Give it a fair chance at your emotions by reading it through without an interruption.

Day had broken cold and gray, exceedingly cold and gray, when the man turned aside from the main Yukon trail and climbed the high earth bank, where a dim and little-traveled trail led eastward through the fat spruce timberland. It was a steep bank, and he paused for breath at the top, excusing the act to himself by looking at his watch. It was nine o'clock. There was no sun nor hint of sun, though there was not a cloud in the sky. It was a clear day, and yet there seemed an intangible pall over the face of things, a subtle gloom that made the day dark, and that was due to the absence of sun. This fact did not worry the man. He was used to the lack of sun. It had been days since he had seen the sun, and he knew that a few more days must pass before that cheerful orb, due south, would just peep above the skyline and dip immediately from view.

The man flung a look back along the way he had come. The Yukon lay a mile wide and hidden under three feet of ice. On top of this ice were as many feet of snow. It was all pure white, rolling in gentle undulations where the ice-jams of the freeze-up had formed. North and south, as far as his eye could see, it was unbroken white, save for a dark hair-line that curved and twisted from around the spruce-covered island to the south, and that curved and twisted away into the north, where it disappeared behind another spruce-covered island. This dark hair-line was the trail — the main trail — that led south five hundred miles to the Chilcoot Pass, Dyea, and salt water; and that led north seventy miles to Dawson, and still on to the north a thousand miles to Nulato, and finally to St. Michael on Bering Sea, a thousand miles and half a thousand more.

But all this — the mysterious, far-reaching hair-line trail, the absence of sun from the sky, the tremendous cold, and the strangeness and weirdness of it all — made no impression on the man. It was not because he was long used to it. He was a new-comer in the land, a *chechaquo,* and this was his first winter. The trouble with him was that he was without imagination. He was quick and alert in the things of life, but only in the things, and not in the significances. Fifty degrees below zero meant eighty-odd degrees of frost. Such fact impressed him as being cold and uncomfortable, and that was all. It did not lead him to meditate upon his frailty as a creature of temperature, and upon man's frailty in general, able only to live within certain narrow limits of heat and cold and from there on it did not lead him to the conjectural field of immortality and man's place in the universe. Fifty degrees below zero stood for a bite of frost that hurt and that must be guarded against by the use of mittens, earflaps, warm moccasins, and thick socks. Fifty degrees below zero was to him just precisely fifty degrees below zero. That there should be anything more to it than that was a thought that never entered his head.

As he turned to go on, he spat speculatively. There was a sharp, explosive crackle that startled him. He spat again. And again, in the air, before it could fall to the snow, the spittle crackled. He knew that at fifty below spittle crackled on the snow, but this spittle had crackled in the air. Undoubtedly it was colder than fifty below — how much colder he did not know. But the temperature did not matter. He was bound for the old claim on the left fork of Henderson Creek, where the boys were already. They had come over across the divide from the Indian Creek country, while he had come the roundabout way to take a look at the possibilities of getting out logs in the spring from the islands in the Yukon. He would be in to camp by six o'clock ; a bit after dark, it was true, but the boys would be there, a fire would be going, and a hot supper would be ready. As for lunch, he pressed his hand against the protruding bundle under his jacket. It was also under his shirt, wrapped up in a handkerchief and lying against the naked skin. It was the only way to keep the biscuits from freezing. He smiled agreeably to himself as he thought of those biscuits, each cut open and sopped in bacon grease, and each enclosing a generous slice of fried bacon.

He plunged in among the big spruce trees. The trail was faint. A foot of snow had fallen since the last sled had passed over, and he was glad he was without a sled, traveling light. In fact, he carried nothing but the lunch wrapped in the handkerchief. He was surprised, however, at the cold. It certainly was cold, he concluded, as he rubbed his numb nose and cheek bones with his mittened hand. He was a warm-whiskered man, but the hair on his face did not protect the high cheek bones and the eager nose that thrust itself aggressively into the frosty air.

At the man's heels trotted a dog, a big native husky, the proper wolf-dog, gray-coated and without any visible or temperamental difference from its brother, the wild wolf. The animal was depressed by the tremendous cold. It knew that it was no time for traveling. Its instinct told it a truer tale than was told to the man by the man's judgment. In reality, it was not merely colder than fifty below zero; it was colder than sixty below, than seventy below. It was seventy-five below zero. Since the freezing point is thirty-two above zero, it meant that one hundred and seven degrees of frost obtained. The dog did not know anything about thermometers. Possibly in its brain there was no sharp consciousness of a condition of very cold such as was in the man's brain. But the brute had its instinct. It experienced a vague but menacing apprehension that subdued it and made it slink along at the man's heels, and that made it question eagerly every unwonted movement of the man, as if expecting him to go into camp or to seek shelter somewhere and build a fire. The dog had learned fire, and it wanted fire, or else to burrow under the snow and cuddle its warmth away from the air.

The frozen moisture of its breathing had settled on its fur in a fine powder of frost, and especially were its jowls, muzzle, and eyelashes whitened by its crystalled breath. The man's red beard and mustache were likewise frosted, but more solidly, the deposit taking the form of ice and increasing with every warm, moist breath he exhaled. Also, the man was chewing tobacco, and the muzzle of ice held his lips so rigidly that he was unable to clear his chin when he expelled the juice. The result was that a crystal beard of the color and solidity of amber was increasing its length on his chin. If he fell down it would shatter itself, like glass, into brittle fragments. But he did not mind the appendage. It was the penalty all tobacco-chewers paid in that country, and he had been out before in two cold snaps. They had not been so cold as this, he knew, but by the spirit thermometer at Sixty Mile he knew they had been registered at fifty below and at fifty-five.

He held on through the level stretch of woods for several miles, crossed a wide flat of nigger-heads, and dropped down a bank to the frozen bed of a small stream. This was Henderson Creek, and he knew he was ten miles from the forks. He looked at his watch. It was ten o'clock. He was making four miles an hour, and he calculated that he would arrive at the forks at half-past twelve. He decided to celebrate that event by eating his lunch there.

The dog dropped in again at his heels, with a tail drooping discouragement, as the man swung along the creek bed. The furrow of the old sled trail was plainly visible, but a dozen inches of snow covered the marks of the last runners. In a month no man had come up or down that silent creek. The man held steadily on. He was not much given to thinking, and just then particularly he had nothing to think about save that he would eat lunch at the forks and that at six o'clock he would be in camp with the boys. There was nobody to talk to; and, had there been, speech would have been impossible because of the ice muzzle on his mouth. So he continued monotonously to chew tobacco and to increase the length of his amber beard.

Once in a while the thought reiterated itself that it was very cold and that he had never experienced such cold. As he walked along he rubbed his cheek bones and nose with the back of his mittened hand. He did this automatically, now and again changing hands. But rub as he would, the instant he stopped his cheek bones went numb, and the following instant the end of his nose went numb. He was sure to frost his cheeks; he knew that, and experienced a pang of regret that he had not devised a nose strap of the sort Bud wore in cold snaps. Such a strap passed across the cheeks, as well, and saved them. But it didn't matter much, after all. What were frosted cheeks? A bit painful, that was all; they were never serious.

Empty as the man's mind was of thoughts, he was keenly observant, and he noticed the changes in the creek, the curves and bends and timber-jams, and always he sharply noted where he placed his feet. Once, coming around a bend, he shied abruptly,

like a startled horse, curved away from the place where he had
been walking, and retreated several paces back along the trail.
The creek, he knew, was frozen clear to the bottom, — no creek
could contain water in that arctic winter, — but he knew also that
there were springs that bubbled out from the hillsides and ran
along under the snow and on top of the ice of the creek. He
knew that the coldest snaps never froze these springs, and he
knew likewise their danger. They were traps. They hid pools
of water under the snow that might be three inches deep, or three
feet. Sometimes a skin of ice half an inch thick covered them,
and in turn was covered by the snow. Sometimes there were
alternate layers of water and ice skin, so that when one broke
through he kept on breaking through for a while, sometimes
wetting himself to the waist.

That was why he had shied in such panic. He had felt the
give under his feet and heard the crackle of a snow-hidden ice
skin. And to get his feet wet in such a temperature meant trouble
and danger. At the very least it meant delay, for he would be
forced to stop and build a fire, and under its protection to bare
his feet while he dried his socks and moccasins. He stood and
studied the creek bed and its banks, and decided that the flow
of water came from the right. He reflected a while, rubbing his
nose and cheeks, then skirted to the left, stepping gingerly and
testing the footing for each step. Once clear of the danger, he
took a fresh chew of tobacco and swung along at his four-mile
gait.

In the course of the next two hours he came upon several similar traps. Usually the snow above the hidden pools had a sunken,
candied appearance that advertised the danger. Once again,
however, he had a close call; and once, suspecting danger, he compelled the dog to go on in front. The dog did not want to go. It
hung back until the man shoved it forward, and then it went
quickly across the white, unbroken surface. Suddenly it broke
through, floundered to one side, and got away to firmer footing.
It had wet its forefeet and legs, and almost immediately the water
that clung to it turned to ice. It made quick efforts to lick the
ice off its legs, then dropped down in the snow and began to bite
out the ice that had formed between the toes. This was a matter
of instinct. To permit the ice to remain would mean sore feet.
It did not know this. It merely obeyed the mysterious prompting that arose from the deep crypts of its being. But the man

knew, having achieved a judgment on the subject, and he removed the mitten from his right hand and helped tear out the ice particles. He did not expose his fingers more than a minute, and was astonished at the swift numbness that smote them. It certainly was cold. He pulled on the mitten hastily, and beat the hand savagely across his chest.

At twelve o'clock the day was at its brightest. Yet the sun was too far south on its winter journey to clear the horizon. The bulge of the earth intervened between it and Henderson Creek, where the man walked under a clear sky at noon and cast no shadow. At half-past twelve, to the minute, he arrived at the forks of the creek. He was pleased at the speed he had made. If he kept it up, he would certainly be with the boys by six. He unbuttoned his jacket and shirt and drew forth his lunch. The action consumed no more than a quarter of a minute, yet in that brief moment the numbness laid hold of the exposed fingers. He did not put the mitten on, but, instead, struck the fingers a dozen sharp smashes against his leg. Then he sat down on a snow-covered log to eat. The sting that followed upon the striking of his fingers against his leg ceased so quickly that he was startled. He had had no chance to take a bite of biscuit. He struck the fingers repeatedly and returned them to the mitten, baring the other hand for the purpose of eating. He tried to take a mouthful, but the ice muzzle prevented. He had forgotten to build a fire and thaw out. He chuckled at his foolishness, and as he chuckled he noted the numbness creeping into the exposed fingers. Also he noted that the stinging which had first come to his toes when he sat down was already passing away. He wondered whether the toes were warm or numb. He moved them inside the moccasins and decided that they were numb.

He pulled the mitten on hurriedly and stood up. He was a bit frightened. He stamped up and down until the stinging returned into the feet. It certainly was cold, was his thought. That man from Sulphur Creek had spoken the truth when telling how cold it sometimes got in the country. And he had laughed at him at the time! That showed one must not be too sure of things. There was no mistake about it, it *was* cold. He strode up and down, stamping his feet and threshing his arms, until reassured by the returning warmth. Then he got out matches and proceeded to make a fire. From the undergrowth, where high water of the previous spring had lodged a supply of seasoned twigs, he got his firewood. Working carefully from a small beginning, he soon had a roaring fire, over which he thawed the ice from his face and in the protection of which he ate his biscuits. For the moment the cold of space was outwitted. The dog took satisfaction in the fire, stretching out close enough for warmth and far enough away to escape being singed.

When the man had finished, he filled his pipe and took his comfortable time over a smoke. Then he pulled on his mittens, settled the ear-flaps of his cap firmly about his ears, and took the creek trail up the left fork. The dog was disappointed and yearned back toward the fire. This man did not know cold. Possibly all the generations of his ancestry had been ignorant of cold, of real cold, of cold one hundred and seven degrees below freezing point. But the dog knew; all its ancestry knew, and it had inherited the knowledge. And it knew that it was not good to walk abroad in such fearful cold. It was the time to lie snug in a hole in the snow and wait for a curtain of cloud to be drawn across the face of outer space whence this cold came. On the other hand, there was no keen intimacy between the dog and the man. The one was the toil-slave of the other, and the only caresses it had ever received were the caresses of the whip-lash and of harsh and menacing throat sounds that threatened the whip-lash. So the dog made no effort to communicate its apprehension to the man. It was not concerned in the welfare of the man; it was for its own sake that it yearned back toward the fire. But the man whistled, and spoke to it with the sound of whip-lashes, and the dog swung in at the man's heels and followed after.

The man took a chew of tobacco and proceeded to start a new amber beard. Also, his moist breath quickly powdered with white his mustache, eyebrows, and lashes. There did not seem to be so many springs on the left fork of the Henderson, and for half an hour the man saw no signs of any. And then it happened. At a place where there were no signs, where the soft, unbroken snow seemed to advertise solidity beneath, the man broke through. It was not deep. He wet himself halfway to the knees before he floundered out to the firm crust.

He was angry, and cursed his luck aloud. He had hoped to get into camp with the boys at six o'clock, and this would delay him an hour, for he would have to build a fire and dry out his foot-gear. This was imperative at that low temperature — he knew that much; and he turned aside to the bank, which he climbed. On top, tangled in the underbrush about the trunks of several small spruce trees, was a high-water deposit of dry firewood — sticks and twigs, principally, but also larger portions of seasoned branches and fine, dry, last year's grasses. He threw down several large pieces on top of the snow. This served for a foundation and prevented the young flame from drowning itself in the snow it otherwise would melt. The flame he got by touching a match to a small shred of birch-bark that he took from his pocket. This burned even more readily than paper. Placing it on the foundation, he fed the young flame with wisps of dry grass and with the tiniest dry twigs.

He worked slowly and carefully, keenly aware of his danger. Gradually, as the flame grew stronger, he increased the size of the twigs with which he fed it. He squatted in the snow, pulling the twigs out from their entanglement in the brush and feeding directly to the flame. He knew there must be no failure. When it is seventy-five below zero a man must not fail in his first attempt to build a fire — that is, if his feet are wet. If his feet are dry, and he fails, he can run along the trail for half a mile and restore his circulation. But the circulation of wet and freezing feet cannot be restored by running when it is seventy-five below. No matter how fast he runs, the wet feet will freeze the harder.

All this the man knew. The old-timer on Sulphur Creek had told him about it the previous fall, and now he was appreciating the advice. Already all sensation had gone out of his feet. To build the fire, he had been forced to remove his mittens, and the fingers had quickly gone numb. His pace of four miles an hour had kept his heart pumping blood to the surface of his body and to all the extremities. But the instant he stopped, the action of the pump eased down. The cold of space smote the unprotected tip of the planet, and he, being on that unprotected tip, received the full force of the blow. The blood of his body recoiled before it. The blood was alive, like the dog, and like the dog it wanted to hide away and cover itself up from the fearful cold. So long as he walked four miles an hour, he pumped that blood, willy-nilly, to the surface; but now it ebbed away and sank down into the recesses of his body. The extremities were the first to feel its absence. His wet feet froze the faster, and his exposed fingers numbed the faster, though they had not yet begun to freeze.

Nose and cheeks were already freezing, while the skin of all his body chilled as it lost its blood.

But he was safe. Toes and nose and cheeks would be only touched by the frost, for the fire was beginning to burn with strength. He was feeding it with twigs the size of his finger. In another minute he would be able to feed it with branches the size of his wrist, and then he could remove his wet foot-gear, and, while it dried, he could keep his naked feet warm by the fire, rubbing them at first, of course, with snow. The fire was a success. He was safe. He remembered the advice of the old-timer on Sulphur Creek, and smiled. The old-timer had been very serious in laying down the law that no man must travel alone in the Klondike after fifty below. Well, here he was; he had had the accident; he was alone; and he had saved himself. Those old-timers were rather womanish, some of them, he thought. All a man had to do was to keep his head, and he was all right. Any man who was a man could travel alone. But it was surprising the rapidity with which his cheeks and nose were freezing. And he had not thought his fingers could go lifeless in so short a time. Lifeless they were, for he could scarcely make them move together to grip a twig, and they seemed remote from his body and from him. When he touched a twig he had to look and see whether or not he had hold of it. The wires were pretty well down between him and his finger-ends.

All of which counted for little. There was the fire, snapping and crackling and promising life with every dancing flame. He started to untie his moccasins. They were coated with ice; the thick German socks were like sheaths of iron halfway to the knees; and the moccasin strings were like rods of steel all twisted and knotted as by some conflagration. For a moment he tugged with his numb fingers, then, realizing the folly of it, he drew his sheath-knife.

But before he could cut the strings, it happened. It was his own fault, or, rather, his mistake. He should not have built the fire under the spruce tree. He should have built it in the open. But it had been easier to pull the twigs from the brush and drop them directly on the fire. Now the tree under which he had done this carried a weight of snow on its boughs. No wind had blown for weeks, and each bough was fully freighted. Each time he had pulled a twig he had communicated a slight agitation to the tree — an imperceptible agitation, so far as he was concerned, but an agitation sufficient to bring about the disaster. High up in the tree one bough capsized its load of snow. This fell on the boughs beneath, capsizing them. This process continued, spreading out and involving the whole tree. It grew like an avalanche, and it descended without warning upon the man and the fire, and the fire was blotted out! Where it had burned was a mantle of fresh and disordered snow.

The man was shocked. It was as though he had just heard his own sentence of death. For a moment he sat and stared at the spot where the fire had been. Then he grew very calm. Perhaps the old-timer on Sulphur Creek was right. If he had only had a trail-mate he would have been in no danger now. The trail-mate could have built the fire. Well, it was up to him to build the fire over again, and this second time there must be no failure. Even if he succeeded, he would most likely lose some toes. His feet must be badly frozen by now, and there would be some time before the second fire was ready.

Such were his thoughts, but he did not sit and think them. He was busy all the time they were passing through his mind. He made a new foundation for a fire, this time in the open, where no treacherous tree could blot it out. Next he gathered dry grasses and tiny twigs from the high-water flotsam. He could not bring his fingers together to pull them out, but he was able to gather them by the handful. In this way he got many rotten twigs and bits of green moss that were undesirable, but it was the best he could do. He worked methodically, even collecting an armful of the larger branches to be used later when the fire gathered strength. And all the while the dog sat and watched him, a certain yearning wistfulness in its eyes, for it looked upon him as the fire-provider, and the fire was slow in coming.

When all was ready, the man reached in his pocket for a second piece of birch-bark. He knew the bark was there, and, though he could not feel it with his fingers, he could hear its crisp rustling as he fumbled for it. Try as he would, he could not clutch hold of it. And all the time, in his consciousness, was the knowledge that each instant his feet were freezing. This thought tended to put him in a panic, but he fought against it and kept calm. He pulled on his mittens with his teeth, and threshed his arms back and forth, beating his hands with all his might against his sides. He did this sitting down, and he stood up to do it; and all the while the dog sat in the snow, its wolf-brush of a tail curled around warmly over its forefeet, its sharp wolf ears pricked forward intently as it watched the man. And the man, as he beat and threshed with his arms and hands, felt a great surge of envy as he regarded the creature that was warm and secure in its natural covering.

After a time he was aware of the first far-away signals of sensation in his beaten fingers. The faint tingling grew stronger till it

HE FELT A GREAT SURGE OF ENVY AS HE REGARDED THE CREATURE

evolved into a stinging ache that was excruciating, but which the man hailed with satisfaction. He stripped the mitten from his right hand and fetched forth the birch-bark. The exposed fingers were quickly going numb again. Next he brought out his bunch of sulphur matches. But the tremendous cold had already driven the life out of his fingers. In his effort to separate one match from the others, the whole bunch fell in the snow. He tried to pick it out of the snow, but failed. The dead fingers could neither touch nor clutch. He was very careful. He drove the thought of his freezing feet, and nose, and cheeks, out of his mind, devoting his whole soul to the matches. He watched, using the sense of vision in place of that of touch, and when he saw his fingers on each side the bunch, he closed them — that is, he willed to close them, for the wires were down, and the fingers did not obey. He pulled the mitten on the right hand, and beat it fiercely against his knee. Then, with both mittened hands, he scooped the bunch of matches, along with much snow, into his lap. Yet he was no better off.

After some manipulation he managed to get the bunch between the heels of his mittened hands. In this fashion he carried it to his mouth. The ice crackled and snapped when by a violent effort he opened his mouth. He drew the lower jaw in, curled the upper lip out of the way, and scraped the bunch with his upper teeth in order to separate a match. He succeeded in getting one, which he dropped on his lap. He was no better off. He could not pick it up. Then he devised a way. He picked it up in his teeth and scratched it on his leg. Twenty times he scratched before he succeeded in lighting it. As it flamed he held it with his teeth to the birch-bark. But the burning brimstone went up his nostrils and into his lungs, causing him to cough spasmodically. The match fell into the snow and went out.

The old-timer on Sulphur Creek was right, he thought in the moment of controlled despair that ensued: after fifty below, a man should travel with a partner. He beat his hands, but failed in exciting any sensation. Suddenly he bared both hands, removing the mittens with his teeth. He caught the whole bunch between the heels of his hands. His arm muscles, not being frozen, enabled him to press the hand heels tightly against the matches. Then he scratched the bunch along his leg. It flared into flame, seventy sulphur matches at once! There was no wind to blow them out. He kept his head to one side to escape the strangling fumes, and held the blazing bunch to the birch-bark. As he so held it, he became aware of sensation in his hand. His flesh was burning. He could smell it. Deep down below the surface he could feel it. The sensation developed into pain that grew acute. And still he endured it, holding the flame of the matches clumsily to the bark that would not light readily because his own burning hands were in the way, absorbing most of the flame.

At last, when he could endure no more, he jerked his hands apart. The blazing matches fell sizzling into the snow, but the birch-bark was alight. He began laying dry grasses and the tiniest twigs on the flame. He could not pick and choose, for he had to lift the fuel between the heels of his hands. Small pieces of rotten wood and green moss clung to the twigs, and he bit them off as well as he could with his teeth. He cherished the flame carefully and awkwardly. It meant life, and it must not perish. The withdrawal of blood from the surface of his body now made him begin to shiver, and he grew more awkward. A large piece of green moss fell squarely on the little fire. He tried to poke it out with his fingers, but his shivering frame made him poke too far, and he disrupted the nucleus of the little fire, the burning grasses and tiny twigs separating and scattering. He tried to poke them together again, but, in spite of the tenseness of the effort, his shivering got away with him, and the twigs were hopelessly scattered. Each twig gushed a puff of smoke and went out. The fire-provider had failed. As he looked apathetically about him, his eyes chanced on the dog, sitting across the ruins of the fire from him, in the snow, making restless, hunching movements slightly lifting one forefoot and then the other, shifting its weight back and forth on them with wistful eagerness.

The sight of the dog put a wild idea into his head. He remembered the tale of the man, caught in a blizzard, who killed a steer and crawled inside the carcass, and so was saved. He would kill the dog and bury his hands in the warm body until the numbness went out of them. Then he could build another fire. He spoke to the dog, calling it to him; but in his voice was a strange note of fear that frightened the animal, who had never known the man to speak in such way before. Something was the matter, and its suspicious nature sensed danger — it knew not what danger, but somewhere, somehow, in its brain arose an apprehension of the man. It flattened its ears down at the sound of the man's voice, and its restless, hunching movements and the liftings and shiftings of its forefeet became more pronounced; but it would not come to the man. He got on his hands and knees and crawled toward the dog. This unusual posture again excited suspicion, and the animal sidled mincingly away.

The man sat up in the snow for a moment and struggled for calmness. Then he pulled on his mittens, by means of his teeth, and got upon his feet. He glanced down at first in order to assure himself that he was really standing up, for the absence of sensation in his feet left him unrelated to the earth. His erect position in itself started to drive the webs of suspicion from the dog's mind; and when he spoke peremptorily with the sound of whip-lashes in his voice, the dog rendered its customary allegiance and came to him. As it came within reaching distance, the man lost his control. His arms flashed out to the dog, and he experienced genuine surprise when he discovered that his hands could not clutch, that there was neither bend nor feeling in the fingers. He had forgotten for the moment that they were frozen and that they were freezing more and more. All this happened quickly, and before the animal could get away, he encircled its body with his arms. He sat down in the snow, and in this fashion held the dog, while it snarled and whined and struggled.

But it was all he could do, hold its body encircled in his arms and sit there. He realized that he could not kill the dog. There was no way to do it. With his helpless hands he could neither draw nor hold his sheath-knife nor throttle the animal. He released it, and it plunged wildly away, with tail between its legs, and still snarling. It halted forty feet away and surveyed him curiously, with ears sharply pricked forward. The man looked down at his hands in order to locate them, and found them hanging on the ends of his arms. It struck him as curious that one should have to use his eyes in order to find out where his hands were. He began threshing his arms back and forth, beating the mittened hands against his sides. He did this for five minutes, violently, and his heart pumped enough blood up to the surface to put a stop to his shivering. But no sensation was aroused in the hands. He had an impression that they hung like weights on the ends of his arms, but when he tried to run the impression down, he could not find it.

A certain fear of death, dull and oppressive, came to him. This fear quickly became poignant as he realized that it was no longer a mere matter of freezing his fingers and toes, or of losing his hands and feet, but that it was a matter of life and death, with the chances against him. This threw him into a panic, and he turned and ran up the creek-bed along the old dim trail. The dog joined in behind and kept up with him. He ran blindly, without intention, in fear such as he had never known in his life. Slowly, as he plowed and floundered through the snow, he began to see things again, — the banks of the creek, the old timber-jams, the leafless aspens, and the sky. The running made him feel better. He did not shiver. Maybe, if he ran on, his feet would thaw out; and, anyway, if he ran far enough, he would reach the camp and the boys. Without doubt he would lose some fingers and toes and some of his face; but the boys would take care of him, and save the rest of him when he got there. And at the same time there was another thought in his mind that said he would never get to the camp and the boys; that it was too many miles away, that the freezing had too great a start on him, and that he would soon be stiff and dead. This thought he kept in the background and refused to consider. Sometimes it pushed itself forward and demanded to be heard, but he thrust it back and strove to think of other things.

It struck him as curious that he could run at all on feet so frozen that he could not feel them when they struck the earth and took the weight of his body. He seemed to himself to skim along above the surface, and to have no connection with the earth. Somewhere he had once seen a winged Mercury, and he wondered if Mercury felt as he felt when skimming over the earth.

His theory of running until he reached camp and the boys had one flaw in it: he lacked the endurance. Several times he stumbled, and finally he tottered, crumpled up, and fell. When he tried to rise, he failed. He must sit and rest, he decided, and next time he would merely walk and keep on going. As he sat and regained his breath, he noted that he was feeling quite warm and comfortable. He was not shivering, and it even seemed that a warm glow had come to his chest and trunk. And yet, when he touched his nose or cheeks, there was no sensation. Running would not thaw them out. Nor would it thaw out his hands and feet. Then the thought came to him that the frozen portions of his body must be extending. He tried to keep this thought down, to forget it, to think of something else; he was aware of the panicky feeling that it caused, and he was afraid of the panic. But the thought asserted itself, and persisted, until it produced a vision of his body totally frozen. This was too much, and he made another wild run along the trail. Once he slowed down to a walk, but the thought of the freezing extending itself made him run again.

And all the time the dog ran with him, at his heels. When he fell down a second time, it curled its tail over its forefeet and sat in front of him, facing him, curiously eager and intent. The warmth and security of the animal angered him, and he cursed it till it flattened down its ears appeasingly. This time the shivering came more quickly upon the man. He was losing in his battle with the frost. It was creeping into his body from all sides. The thought of it drove him on, but he ran no more than a hundred feet, when he staggered and pitched headlong. It was his last panic. When he had recovered his breath and control, he sat up and entertained in his mind the conception of meeting death with dignity. However, the conception did not come to him in such terms. His idea of it was that he had been making a fool of himself, running around like a chicken with its head cut off — such was the simile that occurred to him. Well, he was bound to freeze anyway, and he might as well take it decently. With this new-found peace of mind came the first glimmerings of drowsiness. A good idea, he thought, to sleep off to death. It was like taking an anæsthetic. Freezing was not so bad as people thought. There were lots worse ways to die.

He pictured the boys finding his body next day. Suddenly he found himself with them, coming along the trail and looking for himself. And, still with them, he came around a turn in the trail and found himself lying in the snow. He did not belong with himself any more, for even then he was out of himself standing with the boys and looking at himself in the snow. It certainly was cold, was his thought. When he got back to the States, he could tell the folks what real cold was. He drifted on from this to a vision of the old-timer on Sulphur Creek. He could see him quite clearly, warm and comfortable, and smoking a pipe.

" You were right, old hoss; you were right," the man mumbled to the old-timer of Sulphur Creek.

Then the man drowsed off into what seemed to him the most comfortable and satisfying sleep he had ever known. The dog sat facing him and waiting. The brief day drew to a close in a long, slow twilight. There were no signs of a fire to be made, and, besides, never in the dog's experience had it known a man to sit like that in the snow and make no fire. As the twilight drew on, its eager yearning for the fire mastered it, and with a great lifting and shifting of forefeet, it whined softly, then flattened its ears down in anticipation of being chidden by the man. But the man remained silent. Later, the dog whined loudly. And still later it crept close to the man and caught the scent of death. This made the animal bristle and back away. A little longer it delayed, howling under the stars that leaped and danced and shone brightly in the cold sky. Then it turned and trotted up the trail in the direction of the camp it knew, where were the other food-providers and fire-providers.

SUGGESTIONS FOR STUDY

1. Why are there no hard words in this story?

2. What is the difference between "localized romance" and "localized realism"? List twenty details that add convincing atmosphere to this story. See introduction.

3. Name four of London's predecessors in the field of localized realism, and tell what part of the country each of them portrayed.

4. How would the quality of the story have been affected had the man been rescued?

5. What are the opposing forces of this plot? When were you sure that one had been triumphant in the struggle? How near the end of a good story will the reader know the outcome of the struggle?

6. What effect is obtained by not naming the man? Did Owen Wister name the hero in *The Virginian?* Do you know any other stories using this device?

7. What is Jack London's most famous book? Have you read *Martin Eden?* This book is mainly autobiographical.

8. Jack London was greatly influenced by the writings of Rudyard Kipling, an Englishman. Have you read any of Kipling's stories?

FOR FURTHER READING

INDIVIDUAL SHORT STORIES

" For the Love of Man "
" The Night-Born "
" All-Gold Canyon "
" Where the Trail Forks "
" That Spot "
" Into the Primitive "
" The White Silence "
" Love of Life "
" Thanksgiving at Slav Creek "
" Brown Wolf "

VOLUMES OF SHORT STORIES

Tales of the Fish Patrol
The Faith of Men
Children of the Frost
Lost Face
Moon-Face
The Son of the Wolf

LONG STORIES

The Call of the Wild
The Sea-Wolf
White Fang
The Cruise of the Snark

ENGLAND TO AMERICA

By MARGARET PRESCOTT MONTAGUE (1878–)

Here is a story of the World War. In 1919 when our country was just catching its breath after two years of fighting, this story appeared in the *Atlantic Monthly* and later won the O. Henry Memorial award for the best short story of that year. It commemorates not so much the fighting spirit of the men at the front as the " gameness " of those far behind the lines. It forgets for a moment the side of international relationship that has to do with presidents and kings and diplomats, and shows the intimacy that may grow between the people of various nations. In telling the story the author has followed the Henry James method of gradual illumination by which an originally mystifying situation is made clear. And, like Mrs. Wharton, she reveals the mental processes of cultivated people. But there is no satire in this story; the characters are all presented sympathetically.

Miss Montague lives in her native state of West Virginia. She has recently recorded in *Up Eel River* the exploits of Tony Beaver, the Paul Bunyan of the Appalachians. (See p. 481.)

I

" Lord, but English people are funny! "

This was the perplexed mental ejaculation that young Lieutenant Skipworth Cary, of Virginia, found his thoughts constantly reiterating during his stay in Devonshire. Had he been, he wondered, a confiding fool, to accept so trustingly Chev Sherwood's suggestion that he spend a part of his leave, at least, at Bishopsthorpe, where Chev's people lived? But why should he have anticipated any difficulty here, in this very corner of England which had bred his own ancestors, when he had always hit it off so splendidly with his English comrades at the Front? Here, however, though they were all awfully kind — at least, he was sure they meant to be kind — something was always bringing him up short: something that he could not lay hold of, but which made him feel like a blind man groping in a strange place, or worse, like a bull in a china-shop. He was prepared enough to find differences in the American and English points of view. But this thing that baffled him did not seem to have to do with that; it was something deeper, something very definite, he was sure — and yet, what was it? The worst of it was that he had a curious feeling as if they were all — that is, Lady Sherwood and Gerald; not Sir Charles so much — protecting him from himself — keeping him from making breaks, as he phrased it. That hurt and annoyed him, and piqued his vanity. Was he a social blunderer, and weren't a Virginia gentleman's manners to be trusted in England without leading-strings?

He had been at the Front for several months with the Royal Flying Corps, and when his leave came, his Flight Commander, Captain Cheviot Sherwood, discovering that he meant to spend it in England, where he hardly knew a soul, had said his people down in Devonshire would be jolly glad to have him stop with them; and Skipworth Cary, knowing that, if the circumstances had been reversed, his people down in Virginia would indeed have been jolly glad to entertain Captain Sherwood, had accepted unhesitatingly. The invitation had been seconded by a letter from Lady Sherwood — Chev's mother — and after a few days sight-seeing in London, he had come down to Bishopsthorpe, very eager to know his friend's family, feeling as he did about Chev himself. " He's the finest man that ever went up in the air," he had written home; and to his own family's disgust, his letters had been far more full of Chev Sherwood than they had been of Skipworth Cary.

And now here he was, and he almost wished himself away — wished almost that he was back again at the Front, carrying on under Chev. There, at least, you knew what you were up against. The job might be hard enough, but it wasn't baffling and queer, with hidden undercurrents that you couldn't chart. It seemed to him that this baffling feeling of constraint had rushed to meet him on the very threshold of the drawing-room, when he made his first appearance.

As he entered, he had a sudden sensation that they had been awaiting him in a strained expectancy, and that, as he appeared, they adjusted unseen masks and began to play-act at something. " But English people don't play-act very well," he commented to himself, reviewing the scene afterward.

Lady Sherwood had come forward and greeted him in a manner which would have been pleasant enough, if he had not, with quick sensitiveness, felt it to be forced. But perhaps that was English stiffness.

Then she had turned to her husband, who was standing staring into the fireplace, although, as it was June, there was no fire.

" Charles," she said, " here is Lieutenant Cary "; and her voice had a certain note in it which at home Cary and his sister Nancy were in the habit of designating " mother-making-dad-mind-his-manners."

At her words the old man — and Cary was startled to see how old and broken he was — turned round and held out his hand.

"How d'you do?" he said jerkily, "how d'you do?" and then turned abruptly back again to the fireplace.

"Hello! What's up! The old boy doesn't like me!" was Cary's quick, startled comment to himself.

He was so surprised by the look the other bent upon him that he involuntarily glanced across to a long mirror to see if there was anything wrong with his uniform. But no, that appeared to be all right. It was himself, then — or his country; perhaps the old sport didn't fall for Americans.

"And here is Gerald," Lady Sherwood went on in her low remote voice, which somehow made the Virginian feel very far away.

It was with genuine pleasure, though with some surprise, that he turned to greet Gerald Sherwood, Chev's younger brother, who had been, tradition in the corps said, as gallant and daring a flyer as Chev himself, until he'd got his in the face.

"I'm mighty glad to meet you," he said eagerly, in his pleasant, muffled southern voice, grasping the hand the other stretched out, and looking with deep respect at the scarred face and sightless eyes.

Gerald laughed a little, but it was a pleasant laugh, and his hand-clasp was friendly.

"That's real American, isn't it?" he said. "I ought to have remembered and said it first. Sorry."

Skipworth laughed too. "Well," he conceded, "we generally are glad to meet people in my country, and we don't care who says it first. But," he added, "I didn't think I'd have the luck to find you here."

He remembered that Chev had regretted that he probably wouldn't see Gerald, as the latter was at St. Dunstan's, where they were re-educating the blinded soldiers.

The other hesitated a moment, and then said rather awkwardly, "Oh, I'm just home for a little while; I only got here this morning, in fact."

Skipworth noted the hesitation. Did the old people get panicky at the thought of entertaining a wild man from Virginia, and send an S O S for Gerald? he wondered.

"We are so glad you could come to us," Lady Sherwood said rather hastily just then. And again he could not fail to note that she was prompting her husband.

The latter reluctantly turned round, and said, "Yes, yes, quite so. Welcome to Bishopsthorpe, my boy," as if his wife had pulled a string, and he responded mechanically, without quite knowing what he said. Then, as his eyes rested a moment on his guest, he looked as if he would like to bolt out of the room. He controlled himself, however, and, jerking round again to the fireplace, went on murmuring, " Yes, yes, yes," vaguely — just like the dormouse at the Mad Tea-Party, who went to sleep, saying, " Twinkle, twinkle, twinkle," Cary could not help thinking to himself.

But after all, it wasn't really funny, it was pathetic. Gosh, how doddering the poor old boy was! Skipworth wondered, with a sudden twist at his heart, if the war was playing the deuce with his home people, too. Was his own father going to pieces like this, and had his mother's gay vivacity fallen into that still remoteness of Lady Sherwood's? But of course not! The Carys hadn't suffered as the poor Sherwoods had, with their youngest son, Curtin, killed early in the war, and now Gerald knocked out so tragically. Lord, he thought, how they must all bank on Chev! And of course they would want to hear at once about him. " I left Chev as fit as anything, and he sent all sorts of messages," he reported, thinking it more discreet to deliver Chev's messages thus vaguely than to repeat his actual carefree remark, which had been, " Oh, tell 'em I'm jolly as a tick."

But evidently there was something wrong with the words as they were, for instantly he was aware of that curious sense of withdrawal on their part. Hastily reviewing them, he decided that they had sounded too familiar from a stranger and a younger man like himself. He supposed he ought not to have spoken of Chev by his first name. Gee, what sticklers they were! Wouldn't his family — dad and mother and Nancy — have fairly lapped up any messages from him, even if they had been delivered a bit awkwardly? However, he added, as a concession to their point of view, " But of course, you'll have had later news of Captain Sherwood."

To which, after a pause, Lady Sherwood responded, " Oh, yes," in that remote and colorless voice which might have meant anything or nothing.

At this point dinner was announced.

Lady Sherwood drew her husband away from the empty fireplace, and Gerald slipped his arm through the Virginian's, saying pleasantly, " I'm learning to carry on fairly well at St. Dunstan's, but I confess I still like to have a pilot."

To look at the tall young fellow beside him, whose scarred face was so reminiscent of Chev's untouched good looks, who had known all the immense freedom of the air, but who was now learning to carry on in the dark, moved Skipworth Carey to generous homage.

"You know my saying I'm glad to meet you isn't just American," he said half shyly, but warmly. "It's plain English, and the straight truth. I've wanted to meet you awfully. The oldsters are always holding up your glorious exploits to us newcomers. Withers never gets tired telling about that fight of yours with the four enemy planes. And besides," he rushed on eagerly, "I'm glad to have a chance to tell Chev's brother — Captain Sherwood's brother, I mean — what I think of him. Only as a matter of fact, I can't," he broke off with a laugh. "I can't put it exactly into words, but I tell you I'd follow that man straight into hell and out the other side — or go there alone if he told me to. He is the finest chap that ever flew."

And then he felt as if a cold douche had been flung in his face, for after a moment's pause, the other returned, "That's awfully good of you," in a voice so distant and formal that the Virginian could have kicked himself. What an ass he was to be so darned enthusiastic with an Englishman! He supposed it was bad form to show any pleasure over praise of a member of your family. Lord, if Chev got the V. C., he reckoned it would be awful to speak of it. Still, you would have thought Gerald might have stood for a little praise of him. But then, glancing sideways at his companion, he surprised on his face a look so strange and suffering that it came to him almost violently what it must be never to fly again; to be on the threshold of life, with endless days of blackness ahead. Good God! How cruel he had been to flaunt Chev in his face! In remorseful and hasty reparation he stumbled on, "But the old fellows are always having great discussions as to which was the best — you or your brother. Withers always maintains you were."

"Withers lies, then!" the other retorted. "I never touched Chev — never came within a mile of him, and never could have."

They reached the dinner-table with that, and young Cary found himself bewildered and uncomfortable. If Gerald hadn't liked praise of Chev, he had liked praise of himself even less, it seemed.

Dinner was not a success. The Virginian found that, if there was to be conversation, the burden of carrying it on was upon him, and gosh! they don't mind silences in this man's island, do they? he commented desperately to himself, thinking how different it was from America. Why, there they acted as if silence was an egg that had just been laid, and every one had to cackle at once to cover it up. But here the talk constantly fell to the ground, and nobody but himself seemed concerned to pick it up. His attempt to praise Chev had not been successful, and he could understand their not wanting to hear about flying and the war before Gerald.

So at last, in desperation, he wandered off into descriptions of America, finding to his relief, that he had struck the right note at last. They were glad to hear about the States, and Lady Sherwood inquired politely if the Indians still gave them much trouble; and when he assured her that in Virginia, except for the Pocahontas tribe, they were all pretty well subdued, she accepted his statement with complete innocency. And he was so delighted to find at last a subject to which they were evidently cordial, that he was quite carried away, and wound up by inviting them all to visit his family in Richmond, as soon as the war was over.

Gerald accepted at once, with enthusiasm; Lady Sherwood made polite murmurs, smiling at him in quite a warm and almost, indeed, maternal manner. Even Sir Charles, who had been staring at the food on his plate as if he did not quite know what to make of it, came to the surface long enough to mumble, " Yes, yes, very good idea. Countries must carry on together — What? "

But that was the only hit of the whole evening, and when the Virginian retired to his room, as he made an excuse to do early, he was so confused and depressed that he fell into an acute attack of homesickness.

Heavens, he thought, as he tumbled into bed, just suppose, now, this was little old Richmond, Virginia, U.S.A., instead of being Bishopsthorpe, Avery Cross near Wick, and all the rest of it! And at that, he grinned to himself. England wasn't such an all-fired big country that you'd think they'd have to ticket themselves with addresses a yard long, for fear they'd get lost — now, would you? Well, anyway, suppose it was Richmond, and his train just pulling into the Byrd Street Station. He stretched out luxuriously, and let his mind picture the whole familiar scene. The wind was blowing right, so there was the mellow homely smell of tobacco in the streets, and plenty of people all along the way to hail him with outstretched hands and shouts of " Hey, Skip Cary, when did you get back ? "   " Welcome home, my boy ! " " Well, will you *look* what the cat dragged in ! "   And so he came to his own front door-step, and, walking straight in, surprised the whole family at breakfast; and yes — doggone it ! if it wasn't Sunday, and they having waffles !   And after that his obliging fancy bore him up Franklin Street, through Monroe Park, and so to Miss Sally Berkeley's door.   He was sound asleep before he reached it, but in his dreams, light as a little bird, she came flying down the broad stairway to meet him, and —

But when he waked next morning, he did not find himself in Virginia, but in Devonshire, where, to his unbounded embarrassment, a white housemaid was putting up his curtains, and was whispering something about his bath.   And though he pretended profound slumber, he was well aware that people do not turn brick-red in their sleep.   And the problem of what was the matter with the Sherwood family was still before him.

II

" They're playing a game," he told himself after a few days. " That is, Lady Sherwood and Gerald are — poor old Sir Charles can't make much of a stab at it.   The game is to make me think they are awfully glad to have me, when in reality there's something about me, or something I do, that gets them on the raw."

He almost decided to make some excuse and get away; but after all, that was not easy.   In English novels, he remembered, they always had a wire calling them to London; but, darn it all ! the Sherwoods knew mighty well there wasn't any one in London who cared a hoot about him.

The thing that got his goat most, he told himself, was that they apparently didn't like his friendship with Chev.   Anyway they didn't seem to want him to talk about him; and whenever he tried to express his warm appreciation for all that the older man had done for him, he was instantly aware of a wall of reserve on their part, a holding of themselves aloof from him.   That puzzled and hurt him, and put him on his dignity.   He concluded that they thought it was cheeky of a youngster like him to think that a man like Chev could be his friend; and if that was the way they felt, he reckoned he'd jolly well better shut up about it.

But whatever it was that they didn't like about him, they

most certainly did want him to have a good time. He and his
pleasure appeared to be for the time being their chief consideration. And after the first day or so he began indeed to enjoy
himself extremely. For one thing, he came to love the atmosphere
of the old place and of the surrounding country, which he and
Gerald explored together. He liked to think that ancestors of
his own had been inheritors of these green lanes, and pleasant
mellow stretches. Then, too, after the first few days, he could
not help seeing that they really began to like him, which of
course was reassuring, and tapped his own warm friendliness,
which was always ready enough to be released. And besides, he
got by accident what he took to be a hint as to the trouble. He
was passing the half-open door of Lady Sherwood's morning-
room, when he heard Sir Charles's voice break out, " Good God,
Elizabeth, I don't see how you stand it! When I see him so
straight and fine-looking, and so untouched, beside our poor lad,
and think — and think — "

Skipworth hurried out of earshot, but now he understood that
look of aversion in the old man's eyes which had so startled
him at first. Of course, the poor old boy might easily hate the
sight of him beside Gerald. With Gerald himself he really got
along famously. He was a most delightful companion, full of
anecdotes and history of the countryside, every foot of which
he had apparently explored in the old days with Chev and the
younger brother, Curtin. Yet even with Gerald, Cary sometimes
felt that aloofness and reserve, and that older protective air that
they all showed him. Take, for instance, that afternoon when
they were lolling together on the grass in the park. The Virginian,
running on in his usual eager manner, had plunged without thinking into an account of a particularly daring bit of flying on Chev's
part, when suddenly he realized that Gerald had rolled over on
the grass and buried his face in his arms, and interrupted himself
awkwardly. " But, of course," he said, " he must have written
home about it himself."

" No, or if he did, I didn't hear of it. Go on," Gerald said in
a muffled voice.

A great rush of compassion and remorse overwhelmed the
Virginian, and he burst out penitently, " What a brute I am!
I'm always forgetting and running on about flying, when I know
it must hurt like the very devil! "

The other drew a difficult breath. " Yes," he admitted, " what

you say does hurt in a way — in a way you can't understand.
But all the same I like to hear you. Go on about Chev."

So Skipworth went on and finished his account, winding up,
" I don't believe there's another man in the service who could
have pulled it off — but I tell you your brother's one in a million."

" Good God, don't I know it ! " the other burst out. " We were
all three the jolliest pals together," he got out presently in a
choked voice, " Chev and the young un and I ; and now —— "

He did not finish, but Cary guessed his meaning. Now the
young un, Curtin, was dead, and Gerald himself knocked out.
But, heavens ! the Virginian thought, did Gerald think Chev
would go back on him now on account of his blindness ? Well,
you could everlastingly bet he wouldn't !

" Chev thinks the world and all of you ! " he cried in eager
defense of his friend's loyalty. " Lots of times when we're all
awfully jolly together, he makes some excuse and goes off by
himself ; and Withers told me it was because he was so frightfully cut up about you. Withers said he told him once that he'd
a lot rather have got it himself — so you can everlastingly bank
on him ! "

Gerald gave a terrible little gasp. " I — I knew he'd feel like
that," he got out. " We've always cared such a lot for each
other." And then he pressed his face harder than ever into the
grass, and his long body quivered all over. But not for long.
In a moment he took fierce hold on himself, muttering, " Well,
one must carry on, whatever happens," and apologized disjointedly. " What a fearful fool you must think me ! And —
and this isn't very pippy for you, old chap." Presently, after
that, he sat up, and said, brushing it all aside, " We're facing
the old moat, aren't we ? There's an interesting bit of tradition
about it that I must tell you."

And there you were, Cary thought : no matter how much
Gerald might be suffering from his misfortune, he must carry on
just the same, and see that his visitor had a pleasant time. It
made the Virginian feel like an outsider and very young, as if
he were not old enough for them to show him their real feelings.

Another thing that he noticed was that they did not seem to
want him to meet people. They never took him anywhere to
call, and if visitors came to the house, they showed an almost
panicky desire to get him out of the way. That again hurt his
pride. What in heaven's name was the matter with him anyway !

III

However, on the last afternoon of his stay at Bishopsthorpe, he told himself with a rather rueful grin that his manners must have improved a little, for they took him to tea at the rectory.

He was particularly glad to go there because, from certain jokes of Withers's, who had known the Sherwoods since boyhood, he gathered that Chev and the rector's daughter were engaged. And just as he would have liked Chev to meet Sally Berkeley, so he wanted to meet Miss Sybil Gaylord.

He had little hopes of having a tête-à-tête with her, but as it fell out he did. They were all in the rectory garden together, Gerald and the rector a little behind Miss Gaylord and himself, as they strolled down a long walk with high hedges bordering it. On the other side of the hedge Lady Sherwood and her hostess still sat at the tea-table, and then it was that Cary heard Mrs. Gaylord say distinctly, " I'm afraid the strain has been too much for you — you should have let us have him."

To which Lady Sherwood returned quickly, " Oh, no, that would have been impossible with —— "

" Come — come this way — I must show you the view from the arbor," Miss Gaylord broke in breathlessly; and laying a hand on his arm, she turned him abruptly into a side path.

Glancing down at her, the Southerner could not but note the panic and distress in her fair face. It was so obvious that the overheard words referred to him, and he was so bewildered by the whole situation, that he burst out impulsively, " I say, what *is* the matter with me? Why do they find me so hard to put up with? Is it something I do — or don't they like Americans? Honestly, I wish you'd tell me."

She stood still at that, looking at him, her blue eyes full of distress and concern.

" Oh, I am so sorry," she cried. " They would be so sorry to have you think anything like that."

" But what is it? " he persisted. " Don't they like Americans? "

" Oh, no, it isn't that — Oh, quite the contrary! " she returned eagerly.

" Then it's something about me they don't like? "

" Oh, no, no! Least of all, that — *don't* think that! " she begged.

"But what am I to think then?"

"Don't think anything just yet," she pleaded. "Wait a little, and you will understand."

She was so evidently distressed that he could not press her further; and fearing she might think him unappreciative, he said, "Well, whatever it is, it hasn't prevented me from having a ripping good time. They've seen to that, and just done everything for my pleasure."

She looked up quickly, and to his relief he saw that for once he had said the right thing.

"You have enjoyed it, then?" she questioned eagerly.

"Most awfully," he assured her warmly. "I shall always remember what a happy leave they gave me."

She gave a little sigh of satisfaction, "I am so glad," she said. "They wanted you to have a good time — that was what we all wanted."

He looked at her gratefully, thinking how sweet she was in her fair English beauty, and how good to care that he should have enjoyed his leave. How different she was too from Sally Berkeley — why she would have made two of his little girl! And how quiet! Sally Berkeley, with her quick glancing vivacity, would have been all around her and off again like a hummingbird before she could have uttered two words. And yet he was sure that they would have been friends, just as he and Chev were. Perhaps they all would be, after the war. And then he began to talk about Chev, being sure that, had the circumstances been reversed, Sally Berkeley would have wanted news of him. Instantly he was aware of a tense listening stillness on her part. That pleased him. Well, she did care for the old fellow all right, he thought; and though she made no response, averting her face, and plucking nervously at the leaves of the hedge as they passed slowly along, he went on pouring out his eager admiration for his friend.

At last they came to a seat in an arbor, from which one looked out upon a green beneficent landscape. It was an intimate secluded little spot — and oh, if Sally Berkeley were only there to sit beside him! And as he thought of this, it came to him whimsically that in all probability she must be longing for Chev, just as he was for Sally.

Dropping down on the bench beside her, he leaned over, and said with a friendly, almost brotherly, grin of understanding,

" I reckon you're wishing Captain Sherwood was sitting here, instead of Lieutenant Cary."

The minute the impulsive words were out of his mouth, he knew he had blundered, been awkward, and inexcusably intimate. She gave a little choked gasp, and her blue eyes stared up at him, wide and startled. Good heavens, what a break he had made!

HE KNEW HE HAD BLUNDERED

No wonder the Sherwoods couldn't trust him in company! There seemed no apology that he could offer in words, but at least, he thought, he would show her that he would not have intruded on her secret without being willing to share his with her. With awkward haste he put his hand into his breast pocket, and dragged forth the picture of Sally Berkeley he always carried there.

" This is the little girl I'm thinking about," he said, turning very red, yet boyishly determined to make amends, and also proudly confident of Sally Berkeley's charms. " I'd like mighty well for you two to know one another."

She took the picture in silence, and for a long moment stared down at the soft little face, so fearless, so confident and gay, that smiled appealingly back at her. Then she did something astonishing — something which seemed to him wholly un-English — and yet he thought it the sweetest thing he had ever seen. Cupping her strong hands about the picture with a quick protectiveness, she suddenly raised it to her lips, and kissed it lightly. " O little girl! " she cried, " I hope you will be very happy! "

The little involuntary act, so tender, so sisterly and spontaneous, touched the Virginian extremely.

" Thanks, awfully," he said unsteadily. " She'll think a lot of that, just as I do — and I know she'd wish you the same."

She made no reply to that, and as she handed the picture back to him, he saw that her hands were trembling, and he had a sudden conviction that, if she had been Sally Berkeley, her eyes would have been full of tears. As she was Sybil Gaylord, however, there were no tears there, only a look that he never forgot. The look of one much older, protective, maternal almost, and as if she were gazing back at Sally Berkeley and himself from a long way ahead on the road of life. He supposed it was the way most English people felt nowadays. He had surprised it so often on all their faces, that he could not help speaking of it.

" You all think we Americans are awfully young and raw, don't you? " he questioned.

" Oh, no, not that," she deprecated. " Young perhaps for these days, yes — but it is more that you — that your country is so — so unsuffered. And we don't want you to suffer! " she added quickly.

Yes, that was it! He understood now, and, heavens, how fine it was! Old England was wounded deep — deep. What she suffered herself she was too proud to show; but out of it she wrought a great maternal care for the newcomer. Yes, it *was* fine — he hoped his country would understand.

Miss Gaylord rose. " There are Gerald and father looking for you," she said, " and I must go now." She held out her hand. " Thank you for letting me see her picture, and for everything you said about Captain Sherwood — for *everything,* remember — I want you to remember."

With a light pressure of her fingers she was gone slipping away through the shrubbery, and he did not see her again.

IV

So he came to his last morning at Bishopsthorpe; and as he dressed, he wished it could have been different; that he were not still conscious of that baffling wall of reserve between himself and Chev's people, for whom, despite all, he had come to have a real affection.

In the breakfast-room he found them all assembled, and his last meal there seemed to him as constrained and difficult as any that had preceded it. It was over finally, however.

"I can never thank you enough for the splendid time I've had here," he said as he rose. "I'll be seeing Chev tomorrow, and I'll tell him all about everything."

Then he stopped dead. With a smothered exclamation, old Sir Charles had stumbled to his feet, knocking over his chair, and hurried blindly out of the room; and Gerald said, "*Mother!*" in a choked appeal.

As if it were a signal between them, Lady Sherwood pushed her chair back a little from the table, her long delicate fingers dropped together loosely in her lap; she gave a faint sigh as if a restraining mantle slipped from her shoulders, and, looking up at the youth before her, her fine pale face lighted with a kind of glory, she said, "No, dear lad, no. You can never tell Chev, for he is gone."

"*Gone!*" he cried.

"Yes," she nodded back at him, just above a whisper; and now her face quivered, and the tears began to rush down her cheeks.

"Not *dead!*" he cried. "Not Chev — not that! O my God, Gerald, not *that!*"

"Yes," Gerald said. "They got him two days after you left."

It was so overwhelming, so unexpected and shocking, above all so terrible, that the friend he had so greatly loved and admired was gone out of his life forever, that young Cary stumbled back into his seat, and, crumpling over, buried his face in his hands, making great uncouth gasps as he strove to choke back his grief.

Gerald groped hastily around the table, and flung an arm about his shoulders.

"Steady on, dear fellow, steady," he said, though his own voice broke.

"When did you hear?" Cary got out at last.

"We got the official notice just the day before you came — and Withers has written us particulars since."

"And you *let* me come in spite of it! And stay on, when every word I said about him must have — have fairly *crucified* each one of you! Oh, forgive me! forgive me!" he cried distractedly.

He saw it all now; he understood at last. It was not on Gerald's account that they could not talk of flying and of Chev, it was because — because their hearts were broken over Chev himself. "Oh, forgive me!" he gasped again.

"Dear lad, there is nothing to forgive," Lady Sherwood returned. "How could we help loving your generous praise of our poor darling? We loved it, and you for it; we wanted to hear it, but we were afraid. We were afraid we might break down, and that you would find out."

The tears were still running down her cheeks. She did not brush them away now; she seemed glad to have them there.

Sinking down on his knees, he caught her hands. "Why did you *let* me do such a horrible thing?" he cried. "Couldn't you have trusted me to understand? Couldn't you *see* I loved him just as you did — no, no!" he broke down humbly. "Of course I couldn't love him as his own people did. But you must have seen how I felt about him — how I admired him, and would have followed him anywhere — and *of course* if I had known, I should have gone away at once."

"Ah, but that was just what we were afraid of," she said quickly. "We were afraid you would go away and have a lonely leave somewhere. And in these days a boy's leave is so precious a thing that nothing must spoil it — *nothing*," she reiterated; and her tears fell upon his hands like a benediction. "But we didn't do it very well, I'm afraid," she went on presently, with gentle contrition. "You were too quick and understanding; you guessed there was something wrong. We were sorry not to manage better," she apologized.

"Oh, you wonderful, wonderful people!" he gasped. "Doing everything for my happiness, when all the time — all the time — "

His voice went out sharply, as his mind flashed back to scene after scene: to Gerald's long body lying quivering on the grass; to Sybil Gaylord wishing Sally Berkeley happiness out of her own tragedy; and to the high look on Lady Sherwood's face. They seemed to him themselves, and yet more than themselves — shining bits in the mosaic of a great nation. Disjointedly there passed through his mind familiar words — "these are they who have washed their garments — having come out of great tribulation." No wonder they seemed older.

"We — we couldn't have done it in America," he said humbly.

He had a desperate desire to get away to himself; to hide his face in his arms, and give vent to the tears that were stifling him; to weep for his lost friend, and for this great heartbreaking heroism of theirs.

" But why did you do it? " he persisted. " Was it because I was his friend? "

" Oh, it was much more than that," Gerald said quickly. " It was a matter of the two countries. Of course, we jolly well knew you didn't belong to us, and didn't want to, but for the life of us we couldn't help a sort of feeling that you did. And when America was in at last, and you fellows began to come, you seemed like our very own come back after many years, and," he added, a throb in his voice, " we were most awfully glad to see you — we wanted a chance to show you how England felt."

Skipworth Cary rose to his feet. The tears for his friend were still wet upon his lashes. Stooping, he took Lady Sherwood's hands in his and raised them to his lips. " As long as I live, I shall never forget," he said. " And others of us have seen it too in other ways — be sure America will never forget, either."

She looked up at his untouched youth out of her beautiful sad eyes, the exalted light still shining through her tears. " Yes," she said, " you see it was — I don't know exactly how to put it — but it was England to America."

SUGGESTIONS FOR STUDY

1. Did the ending surprise you? Did the author follow the rules about surprise endings? Support your answer by details.

2. What do you think was the author's purpose as suggested in the title? You may recall that " The Man Without a Country " was written during the Civil War. Do you know Hale's purpose in writing that famous story?

3. Read the story again. If you like it better the second time, what does that signify about the quality of the story? Do stories with surprise endings usually improve upon second reading? Why?

FOR FURTHER READING

VOLUMES OF STORIES	INDIVIDUAL STORIES
England to America	" Of Water and the Spirit "
Uncle Sam of Freedom Ridge	" What Mr. Grey Said "
Closed Doors	" Why It was W —— on the Eyes "
Up Eel River	" Gift "

FOOTFALLS

By WILBUR DANIEL STEELE (1886–   )

" This is not an easy story," says Mr. Steele in his first sentence; but
wherefore should we end with an easy story? When you have forgotten
many of the short stories of this collection, you will still remember Boaz
Negro, the blind Portuguese cobbler, listening through nine years for the
footfalls of *" that cachorra."* You will remember the " act of almost
incredible violence " with which the story ends. The author, Wilbur
Daniel Steele, belongs to both the North and the South, the East and the
West. He was born in North Carolina, graduated from the University of
Denver, studied art in Boston and New York, and now resides in Nan-
tucket, Massachusetts, in the midst of the Cape Cod life he portrays so
well in many of his stories. He has no recognized superior in the field of
the modern American short story.

This is not an easy story; not a road for tender or for casual
feet. Better the meadows. Let me warn you, it is as hard as
that old man's soul and as sunless as his eyes. It has its inception
in catastrophe, and its end in an act of almost incredible violence;
between them it tells barely how one long blind can become also
deaf and dumb.

He lived in one of those old Puritan sea towns where the strain
has come down austere and moribund, so that his act would not
be quite unbelievable. Except that the town is no longer Puritan
and Yankee. It has been betrayed; it has become an outpost
of the Portuguese islands.

This man, this blind cobbler himself, was a Portuguese from
St. Michael, in the Western Islands, and his name was Boaz
Negro.

He was happy. An unquenchable exuberance lived in him.
When he arose in the morning he made vast, as it were uncontrollable, gestures with his stout arms. He came into his shop
singing. His voice, strong and deep as the chest from which it
emanated, rolled out through the doorway and along the street,
and the fishermen, done with their morning work and lounging
and smoking along the wharves, said, " Boaz is to work already."
Then they came up to sit in the shop.

In that town a cobbler's shop is a club. One sees the interior
always dimly thronged. They sit on the benches watching the

artisan at his work for hours, and they talk about everything in the world. A cobbler is known by the company he keeps.

Boaz Negro kept young company. He would have nothing to do with the old. On his own head the gray hairs set thickly.

He had a grown son. But the benches in his shop were for the lusty and valiant young, men who could spend the night drinking, and then at three o'clock in the morning turn out in the rain and dark to pull at the weirs, sing songs, buffet one another among the slippery fish in the boat's bottom, and make loud jokes about the fundamental things, love and birth and death. Harkening to their boasts and strong prophecies, his breast heaved and his heart beat faster. He was a large, full-blooded fellow, fashioned for exploits; the flame in his darkness burned higher even to hear of them.

It is scarcely conceivable how Boaz Negro could have come through this much of his life still possessed of that unquenchable and priceless exuberance; how he would sing in the dawn; how, simply listening to the recital of deeds in gale or brawl, he could easily forget himself a blind man, tied to a shop and a last; easily make of himself a lusty young fellow breasting the sunlit and adventurous tide of life.

He had had a wife, whom he had loved. Fate, which had scourged him with the initial scourge of blindness, had seen fit to take his Angelina away. He had had four sons. Three, one after another, had been removed, leaving only Manuel, the youngest. Recovering slowly, with agony, from each of these recurrent blows, his unquenchable exuberance had lived. And there was another thing quite as extraordinary. He had never done anything but work, and that sort of thing may kill the flame where an abrupt catastrophe fails. Work in the dark. Work, work, work! And accompanied by privation; an almost miserly scale of personal economy. Yes, indeed, he had " skinned his fingers," especially in the earlier years. When it tells most.

How he had worked! Not alone in the daytime, but also sometimes, when orders were heavy, far into the night. It was strange for one, passing along that deserted street at midnight, to hear issuing from the black shop of Boaz Negro the rhythmical tap-tap-tap of hammer on wooden peg.

Nor was that sound all: no man in town could get far past that shop in his nocturnal wandering unobserved. No more than a dozen footfalls, and from the darkness Boaz's voice rolled forth, fraternal, stentorian, " Good night, Antone! " " Good night to you, Caleb Snow! "

To Boaz Negro it was still broad day.

Now, because of this, he was what might be called a substantial man. He owned his place, his shop, opening on the sidewalk, and behind it the dwelling-house with trellised galleries upstairs and down.

And there was always something for his son, a " piece for the pocket," a dollar-, five-, even a ten-dollar bill if he had " got to have it." Manuel was " a good boy." Boaz not only said this; he felt that he was assured of it in his understanding, to the infinite peace of his heart.

It was curious that he should be ignorant only of the one nearest to him. Not because he was physically blind. Be certain he knew more of other men and of other men's sons than they or their neighbors did. More, that is to say, of their hearts, their understandings, their idiosyncrasies, and their ultimate weight in the balance-pan of eternity.

His simple explanation of Manuel was that Manuel " wasn't too stout." To others he said this, and to himself. Manuel was not indeed too robust. How should he be vigorous when he never did anything to make him so? He never worked. Why should he work, when existence was provided for, and when there was always that " piece for the pocket " ? Even a ten-dollar bill on a Saturday night! No, Manuel " wasn't too stout."

In the shop they let it go at that. The missteps and frailties of every one else in the world were canvassed there with the most shameless publicity. But Boaz Negro was a blind man, and in a sense their host. Those reckless, strong young fellows respected and loved him. It was allowed to stand at that. Manuel was " a good boy." Which did not prevent them, by the way, from joining later in the general condemnation of that father's laxity — " the ruination of the boy! "

" He should have put him to work, that's what."

" He should have said to Manuel, ' Look here, if you want a dollar, go earn it first.' "

As a matter of fact, only one man ever gave Boaz the advice direct. That was Campbell Wood. And Wood never sat in that shop.

In every small town there is one young man who is spoken

of as "rising." As often as not he is not a native, but "from away."

In this town Campbell Wood was that man. He had come from another part of the state to take a place in the bank. He lived in the upper story of Boaz Negro's house, the ground floor now doing for Boaz and the meager remnant of his family. The old woman who came in to tidy up for the cobbler looked after Wood's rooms as well.

Dealing with Wood, one had first of all the sense of his incorruptibility. A little ruthless perhaps, as if one could imagine him, in defense of his integrity, cutting off his friend, cutting off his own hand, cutting off the very stream flowing out from the wellsprings of human kindness. An exaggeration, perhaps.

He was by long odds the most eligible young man in town; good looking in a spare, ruddy, sandy-haired Scottish fashion; important, incorruptible, "rising." But he took good care of his heart. Precisely that; like a sharp-eyed duenna to his own heart. One felt that here was the man, if ever was the man, who held his destiny in his own hand. Failing, of course, some quite gratuitous and unforeseeable catastrophe.

Not that he was not human, or even incapable of laughter or passion. He was, in a way, immensely accessible. He never clapped one on the shoulder; on the other hand, he never failed to speak. Not even to Boaz.

Returning from the bank in the afternoon, he had always a word for the cobbler. Passing out again to supper at his boarding-place, he had another, about the weather, the prospects of rain. And if Boaz were at work in the dark when he returned from an evening at the Board of Trade, there was a "Good night, Mr. Negro!"

On Boaz's part, his attitude toward his lodger was curious and paradoxical. He did not pretend to anything less than reverence for the young man's position; precisely on account of that position he was conscious toward Wood of a vague distrust. This was because he was an uneducated fellow.

To the uneducated the idea of large finance is as uncomfortable as the idea of the law. It must be said for Boaz that, responsive to Wood's unfailing civility, he fought against this sensation of dim and somehow shameful distrust.

Nevertheless his whole parental soul was in arms that evening, when, returning from the bank and finding the shop empty of loungers, Wood paused a moment to propose the bit of advice already referred to.

"Haven't you ever thought of having Manuel learn the trade?"

A suspicion, a kind of premonition, lighted the fires of defense.

"Shoemaking," said Boaz, "is good enough for a blind man."

"Oh, I don't know. At least it's better than doing nothing at all."

Boaz's hammer was still. He sat silent, monumental. Outwardly. For once his unfailing response had failed him, "Manuel ain't too stout, you know." Perhaps it had become suddenly inadequate.

He hated Wood; he despised Wood; more than ever before, a hundredfold more, quite abruptly, he distrusted Wood.

How could a man say such things as Wood had said? And where Manuel himself might hear!

Where Manuel *had* heard! Boaz's other emotions — hatred and contempt and distrust — were overshadowed. Sitting in darkness, no sound had come to his ears, no footfall, no infinitesimal creaking of a floor-plank. Yet by some sixth uncanny sense of the blind he was aware that Manuel was standing in the dusk of the entry joining the shop to the house.

Boaz made a Herculean effort. The voice came out of his throat, harsh, bitter, and loud enough to have carried ten times the distance to his son's ears.

"Manuel is a good boy!"

"Yes — h'm — yes — I suppose so."

Wood shifted his weight. He seemed uncomfortable.

"Well. I'll be running along, I — ugh! Heavens!"

Something was happening. Boaz heard exclamations, breathings, the rustle of sleeve-cloth in large, frantic, and futile graspings — all without understanding. Immediately there was an impact on the floor, and with it the unmistakable clink of metal. Boaz even heard that the metal was minted, and that the coins were gold. He understood. A coin-sack, gripped not quite carefully enough for a moment under the other's overcoat, had shifted, slipped, escaped, and fallen.

And Manuel had heard!

It was a dreadful moment for Boaz, dreadful in its native sense, as full of dread. Why? It was a moment of horrid revelation, ruthless clarification. His son, his link with the departed Angelina, that "good boy" — Manuel, standing in the shadow of the entry, visible alone to the blind, had heard the clink of falling gold, and — *and Boaz wished that he had not!*

There, amazing, disconcerting, destroying, stood the sudden fact.

Sitting as impassive and monumental as ever, his strong, bleached hands at rest on his work, round drops of sweat came out on Boaz's forehead. He scarcely took the sense of what Wood was saying. Only fragments.

A COIN-SACK HAD FALLEN

"Government money, understand — for the breakwater workings — huge — too many people know here, everywhere — don't trust the safe — tin safe — 'Noah's Ark' — give you my word — Heavens, no!"

It boiled down to this — the money, more money than was good for that antiquated "Noah's Ark" at the bank — and whose contemplated sojourn there overnight was public to too many minds — in short, Wood was not only incorruptible, he was canny. To what one of those minds, now, would it occur that he should take away that money bodily, under casual cover of

his coat, to his own lodgings behind the cobbler-shop of Boaz
Negro? For this one, this important night!

He was sorry the coin-sack had slipped, because he did not
like to have the responsibility of secret sharer cast upon any one,
even upon Boaz, even by accident. On the other hand, how
tremendously fortunate that it had been Boaz and not another.
So far as that went, Wood had no more anxiety now than before.
One incorruptible knows another.

"I'd trust you, Mr. Negro" (that was one of the fragments
which came and stuck in the cobbler's brain), "as far as I would
myself. As long as it's only you. I'm just going up here and
throw it under the bed. Oh, yes, certainly."

Boaz ate no supper. For the first time in his life food was dry
in his gullet. Even under those other successive crushing blows
of Fate the full and generous habit of his functionings had carried
on unabated; he had always eaten what was set before him.
Tonight, over his untouched plate, he watched Manuel with his
sightless eyes, keeping track of his every mouthful, word, in-
tonation, breath. What profit he expected to extract from this
catlike surveillance it is impossible to say.

When they arose from the supper-table Boaz made another
Herculean effort. "Manuel, you're a good boy!"

The formula had a quality of appeal, of despair, and of
command.

"Manuel, you should be short of money, maybe. Look, what's
this? A tenner? Well, there's a piece for the pocket; go and
enjoy yourself."

He would have been frightened had Manuel, upsetting tradition, declined the offering. With the morbid contrariness of
the human imagination, the boy's avid grasping gave him no
comfort.

He went out into the shop, where it was already dark, drew
to him his last, his tools, mallets, cutters, pegs, leather. And
having prepared to work, he remained idle. He found himself
listening.

It has been observed that the large phenomena of sunlight
and darkness were nothing to Boaz Negro. A busy night was
broad day. Yet there was a difference; he knew it with the
blind man's eyes, the ears.

Day was a vast confusion, or rather a wide fabric, of sounds;
great and little sounds all woven together, voices, footfalls, wheels,

far-off whistles and foghorns, flies buzzing in the sun. Night was another thing. Still there were voices and footfalls, but rarer, emerging from the large, pure body of silence as definite, surprising, and yet familiar entities.

Tonight there was an easterly wind, coming off the water and carrying the sound of waves. So far as other fugitive sounds were concerned it was the same as silence. The wind made little difference to the ears. It nullified, from one direction at least, the other two visual processes of the blind, the sense of touch and the sense of smell. It blew away from the shop, toward the living-house.

As has been said, Boaz found himself listening, scrutinizing with an extraordinary attention, this immense background of sound. He heard footfalls. The story of that night was written, for him, in footfalls.

He heard them moving about the house, the lower floor, prowling here, there, halting for long spaces, advancing, retreating softly on the planks. About this aimless, interminable perambulation there was something to twist the nerves, something led and at the same time driven like a succession of frail and indecisive charges.

Boaz lifted himself from his chair. All his impulse called him to make a stir, join battle, cast in the breach the re-enforcement of his presence, authority, good will. He sank back again; his hands fell down. The curious impotence of the spectator held him.

He heard footfalls, too, on the upper floor, a little fainter, borne to the inner rather than the outer ear, along the solid causeway of partitions and floor, the legs of his chair, the bony framework of his body. Very faint indeed. Sinking back easily into the background of the wind. They, too, came and went, this room, that, to the passage, the stair-head, and away. About them too there was the same quality of being led and at the same time of being driven.

Time went by. In his darkness it seemed to Boaz that hours must have passed. He heard voices. Together with the footfalls, that abrupt, brief, and (in view of Wood's position) astounding interchange of sentences made up his history of the night. Wood must have opened the door at the head of the stair; by the sound of his voice he would be standing there, peering below perhaps; perhaps listening.

" What's wrong down there? " he called. " Why don't you go to bed? "

After a moment, came Manuel's voice, " Ain't sleepy."

" Neither am I. Look here, do you like to play cards? "

" What kind? Euchre! I like euchre all right. Or pitch."

" Well, what would you say to coming up and having a game of euchre then, Manuel? If you can't sleep? "

" That'd be all right."

The lower footfalls ascended to join the footfalls on the upper floor. There was the sound of a door closing.

Boaz sat still. In the gloom he might have been taken for a piece of furniture, of machinery, an extraordinary lay figure, perhaps, for the trying on of the boots he made. He seemed scarcely to breathe, only the sweat starting from his brow giving him an aspect of life.

He ought to have run, and leaped up that inner stair and pounded with his fists on that door. He seemed unable to move. At rare intervals feet passed on the sidewalk outside, just at his elbow, so to say, and yet somehow, tonight, immeasurably far away. Beyond the orbit of the moon. He heard Rugg, the policeman, noting the silence of the shop, muttering, " Boaz is to bed tonight," as he passed.

The wind increased. It poured against the shop with its deep, continuous sound of a river. Submerged in its body, Boaz caught the note of the town bell striking midnight.

Once more, after a long time, he heard footfalls. He heard them coming around the corner of the shop from the house, footfalls half swallowed by the wind, passing discreetly, without haste, retreating, merging step by step with the huge, incessant background of the wind.

Boaz's muscles tightened all over him. He had the impulse to start up, to fling open the door, shout into the night, " What are you doing? Stop there! Say! What are you doing and where are you going? "

And as before, the curious impotence of the spectator held him motionless. He had not stirred in his chair. And those footfalls, upon which hinged, as it were, that momentous decade of his life, were gone.

There was nothing to listen for now. Yet he continued to listen. Once or twice, half arousing himself, he drew toward him his unfinished work. And then relapsed into immobility.

As has been said, the wind, making little difference to the ears, made all the difference in the world with the sense of feeling and the sense of smell. From the one important direction of the house. That is how it could come about that Boaz Negro could sit, waiting and listening to nothing in the shop and remain ignorant of disaster until the alarm had gone away and come back again, pounding, shouting, clanging.

"*Fire!*" he heard them bawling in the street. "*Fire! Fire!*" Only slowly did he understand that the fire was in his own house.

There is nothing stiller in the world than the skeleton of a house in the dawn after a fire. It is as if everything living, positive, violent, had been completely drained in the one flaming act of violence, leaving nothing but negation till the end of time. It is worse than a tomb. A monstrous stillness! Even the foot-falls of the searchers can not disturb it, for they are separate and superficial. In its presence they are almost frivolous.

Half an hour after dawn the searchers found the body, if what was left from that consuming ordeal might be called a body. The discovery came as a shock. It seemed incredible that the occupant of that house, no cripple or invalid but an able man in the prime of youth, should not have awakened and made good his escape. It was the upper floor which had caught; the stairs had stood to the last. It was beyond calculation. Even if he had been asleep!

And he had not been asleep. This second and infinitely more appalling discovery began to be known. Slowly. By a hint, a breath of rumor here; there an allusion, half taken back. The man, whose incinerated body still lay curled in its bed of cinders, had been dressed at the moment of disaster; even to the watch, the cuff-buttons, the studs, the very scarf-pin. Fully clothed to the last detail, precisely as those who had dealings at the bank might have seen Campbell Wood any week-day morning for the past eight months. A man does not sleep with his clothes on. The skull of the man had been broken, as if with a blunt instrument of iron. On the charred lacework of the floor lay the leg of an old andiron with which Boaz Negro and his Angelina had set up housekeeping in that new house.

It needed only Mr. Asa Whitelaw, coming up the street from that gaping "Noah's Ark" at the bank, to round out the scandalous circle of circumstance.

" Where is Manuel ? "

Boaz Negro still sat in his shop, impassive, monumental, his thick, hairy arms resting on the arms of his chair. The tools and materials of his work remained scattered about him, as his irresolute gathering of the night before had left them. Into his eyes no change could come. He had lost his house, the visible monument of all those years of " skinning his fingers." It would seem that he had lost his son. And he had lost something incalculably precious — that hitherto unquenchable exuberance of the man.

" Where is Manuel ? "

When he spoke his voice was unaccented and stale, like the voice of a man already dead.

" Yes, where is Manuel ? "

He had answered them with their own question.

" When did you last see him ? "

Neither he nor they seemed to take note of that profound irony.

" At supper."

" Tell us, Boaz ; you knew about this money ? "

The cobbler nodded his head.

" And did Manuel ? "

He might have taken sanctuary in a legal doubt. How did he know what Manuel knew ? Precisely ! As before, he nodded his head.

" After supper, Boaz, you were in the shop ? But you heard something ? "

He went on to tell them what he had heard : the footfalls, below and above, the extraordinary conversation which had broken for a moment the silence of the inner hall. The account was bare, the phrases monosyllabic. He reported only what had been registered on the sensitive tympanums of his ears, to the last whisper of footfalls stealing past the dark wall of the shop. Of all the formless tangle of thoughts, suspicions, interpretations, and the special and personal knowledge given to the blind which moved in his brain, he said nothing.

He shut his lips there. He felt himself on the defensive. Just as he distrusted the higher ramifications of finance (his house had gone down uninsured), so before the rites and processes of that inscrutable creature, the Law, he felt himself menaced by the invisible and the unknown, helpless, oppressed ; in an abject sense, skeptical.

" Keep clear of the Law ! " they had told him in his youth.

The monster his imagination had summoned up then still stood beside him in his age.

Having exhausted his monosyllabic and superficial evidence, they could move him no farther. He became deaf and dumb. He sat before them, an image cast in some immensely heavy stuff, inanimate. His lack of visible emotion impressed them. Remembering his exuberance, it was only the stranger to see him unmoving and unmoved. Only once did they catch sight of something beyond. As they were preparing to leave he opened his mouth. What he said was like a swan-song to the years of his exuberant happiness. Even now there was no color of expression in his words, which sounded mechanical.

"Now I have lost everything. My house. My last son. Even my honor. You would not think I would like to live. But I go to live. I go to work. That *cachorra,* one day he shall come back again, in the dark night, to have a look. I shall go to show you all. That *cachorra!*"

(And from that time on, it was noted, he never referred to the fugitive by any other name than *cachorra,* which is a kind of dog. "That *cachorra!*" As if he had forfeited the relationship not only of the family, but of the very genus, the very race! "That *cachorra!*")

He pronounced this resolution without passion. When they assured him that the culprit would come back again indeed, much sooner than he expected, "with a rope around his neck," he shook his head slowly.

"No, you shall not catch that *cachorra* now. But one day — "

There was something about its very colorlessness which made it sound oracular. It was at least prophetic. They searched, laid their traps, proceeded with all their placards, descriptions, rewards, clues, trails. But on Manuel Negro they never laid their hands.

Months passed and became years. Boaz Negro did not rebuild his house. He might have done so, out of his earnings, for upon himself he spent scarcely anything, reverting to his old habit of almost miserly economy. Yet perhaps it would have been harder after all. For his earnings were less and less. In that town a cobbler who sits in an empty shop is apt to want for trade. Folk take their boots to mend where they take their bodies to rest and their minds to be edified.

No longer did the walls of Boaz's shop resound to the boastful recollections of young men. Boaz had changed. He had become not only different, but opposite. A metaphor will do best. The spirit of Boaz Negro had been a meadowed hillside giving upon the open sea, the sun, the warm, wild winds from beyond the blue horizon. And covered with flowers, always hungry and thirsty for the sun and the fabulous wind and bright showers of rain. It had become an entrenched camp, lying silent, sullen, verdureless, under a gray sky. He stood solitary against the world. His approaches were closed. He was blind, and he was also deaf and dumb.

Against that what can young fellows do who wish for nothing but to rest themselves and talk about their friends and enemies? They had come and they had tried. They had raised their voices even higher than before. Their boasts had grown louder, more presumptuous, more preposterous, until, before the cold separation of that unmoving and as if contemptuous presence in the cobbler's chair, they burst of their own air, like toy balloons. And they went and left Boaz alone.

There was another thing which served, if not to keep them away, at least not to entice them back. That was the aspect of the place. It was not cheerful. It invited no one. In its way that fire-bitten ruin grew to be almost as great a scandal as the act itself had been. It was plainly an eyesore. A valuable property, on the town's main thoroughfare — and an eyesore! The neighboring owners protested.

Their protestations might as well have gone against a stone wall. That man was deaf and dumb. He had become, in a way, a kind of vegetable, for the quality of a vegetable is that, while it is endowed with life, it remains fixed in one spot. For years Boaz was scarcely seen to move foot out of that shop that was left him, a small, square, blistered promontory on the shores of ruin.

He must indeed have carried out some rudimentary sort of domestic programme under the débris at the rear (he certainly did not sleep or eat in the shop). One or two lower rooms were left fairly intact. The outward aspect of the place was formless; it grew to be no more than a mound in time; the charred timbers, one or two still standing, lean and naked against the sky, lost their blackness and faded to a silvery gray. It would have seemed strange, had they not grown accustomed to the thought, to imagine that blind man, like a mole, or some slow slug, turning himself mysteriously in the bowels of that gray mound — that time-silvered " eye-sore."

When they saw him, however, he was in the shop. They opened the door to take in their work (when other cobblers turned them off), and they saw him seated in his chair in the half darkness, his whole person, legs, torso, neck, head, as motionless as the vegetable of which we have spoken — only his hands and his bare arms endowed with visible life. The gloom had bleached the skin to the color of damp ivory, and against the background of his immobility they moved with a certain amazing monstrousness, interminably. No, they were never still. One wondered what they could be at. Surely he could not have had enough work now to keep those insatiable hands so monstrously in motion. Even far into the night. Tap-tap-tap! Blows continuous and powerful. On what? On nothing? On the bare iron last? And for what purpose? To what conceivable end?

Well, one could imagine those arms, growing paler, also growing thicker and more formidable with that unceasing labor; the muscles feeding themselves, omnivorously on their own waste, the cords toughening, the bone-tissues revitalizing themselves without end. One could imagine the whole aspiration of that mute and motionless man pouring itself out into those pallid arms, and the arms taking it up with a kind of blind greed. Storing it up. Against a day!

" That *cachorra!* One day — "

What were the thoughts of this man? What moved within that motionless cranium covered with long hair? Who can say? Behind everything, of course, stood that bitterness against the world — the blind world — blinder than he would ever be. And against " that *cachorra.*" But this was no longer a thought; it was the man.

Just as all muscular aspiration flowed into his arms, so all the energies of his senses turned to his ears. The man had become, you might say, two arms and two ears. Can you imagine a man listening, intently, through the waking hours of nine years?

Listening to footfalls. Marking with a special emphasis of concentration the beginning, rise, full passage, falling away, and dying of all footfalls. By day, by night, winter and summer and winter again. Unravelling the skein of footfalls passing up and down the street!

For three years he wondered when they would come. For the

next three years he wondered if they would ever come. It was during the last three that a doubt began to trouble him. It gnawed at his huge moral strength. Like a hidden seepage of water, it undermined (in anticipation) his terrible resolution. It was a sign, perhape of age, a slipping away of the reckless infallibility of youth.

Supposing, after all, that his ears should fail him. Supposing they were capable of being tricked, without his being able to know it. Supposing that that *cachorra* should come and go, and he, Boaz, living in some vast delusion, some unrealized distortion of memory, should let him pass unknown. Supposing precisely this thing had already happened!

Or the other way around. What if he should hear the footfalls coming, even into the very shop itself? What if he should be as sure of them as of his own soul? What, then, if he should strike? And what then, if it were not that *cachorra* after all? How many tens and hundreds of millions of people were there in the world? Was it possible for them all to have footfalls distinct and different?

Then they would take him and hang him. And that *cachorra* might then come and go at his own will, undisturbed.

As he sat there sometimes the sweat rolled down his nose, cold as rain.

Supposing!

Sometimes, quite suddenly, in broad day, in the booming silence of the night, he would start. Not outwardly. But beneath the pale integument of his skin all his muscles tightened and his nerves sang. His breathing stopped. It seemed almost as if his heart stopped.

What was it? Were those the feet, there, emerging faintly from the distance? Yes, there was something about them. Yes! Memory was in travail. Yes, yes, yes! No! How could he be sure? Ice ran down into his empty eyes. The footfalls were already passing. They were gone, swallowed up already by time and space. Had that been that *cachorra?*

Nothing in his life had been so hard to meet as this insidious drain of distrust in his own powers; this sense of a traitor within the walls. His iron-gray hair had turned white. It was always this now, from the beginning of the day to the end of the night: how was he to know? How was he to be inevitably, unshakably, sure?

Curiously, after all this purgatory of doubts, he did know them. For a moment at least, when he had heard them, he was sure.

It was on an evening of the winter holidays, the Portuguese festival of *Menin' Jesus*. Christ was born again in a hundred mangers on a hundred tiny altars; there was cake and wine; songs went shouting by to the accompaniment of mandolins and tramping feet. The wind blew cold under a clear sky. In all the houses there were lights; even in Boaz Negro's shop a lamp was lit just now, for a man had been in for a pair of boots which Boaz had patched. The man had gone out again. Boaz was thinking of blowing out the light. It meant nothing to him.

He leaned forward, judging the position of the lamp-chimney by the heat on his face, and puffed out his cheeks to blow. Then his cheeks collapsed suddenly, and he sat back again.

It was not odd that he had failed to hear the footfalls until they were actually within the door. A crowd of merry-makers was passing just then; their songs and tramping almost shook the shop.

Boaz sat back. Beneath his passive exterior his nerves thrummed; his muscles had grown as hard as wood. Yes! Yes! But no! He had heard nothing; no more than a single step, a single foot-pressure on the planks within the door. Dear God! He could not tell!

Going through the pain of an enormous effort, he opened his lips.

" What can I do for you? "

" Well, I — I don't know. To tell the truth — "

The voice was unfamiliar, but it might be assumed. Boaz held himself. His face remained blank, interrogating, slightly helpless.

" I am a little deaf," he said. " Come nearer."

The footfalls came half way across the intervening floor, and there appeared to hesitate. The voice, too, had a note of uncertainty.

" I was just looking around. I have a pair of — well, you mend shoes? "

Boaz nodded his head. It was not in response to the words, for they meant nothing. What he had heard was the footfalls on the floor.

Now he was sure. As has been said, for a moment at least after he had heard them he was unshakably sure. The congestion of his muscles had passed. He was at peace.

The voice became audible once more. Before the massive pre-occupation of the blind man it became still less certain of itself.

"Well, I haven't got the shoes with me. I was — just looking around."

It was amazing to Boaz, this miraculous sensation of peace.

"Wait!" Then, bending his head as if listening to the winter wind, "It's cold tonight. You've left the door open. But wait!" Leaning down, his hand fell on a rope's end hanging by the chair. The gesture was one continuous, undeviating movement of the hand. No hesitation. No groping. How many hundreds, how many thousands of times, had his hand schooled itself in that gesture!

A single strong pull. With a little *bang* the front door had swung to and latched itself. Not only the front door. The other door, leading to the rear, had closed too and latched itself with a little *bang*. And leaning forward from his chair, Boaz blew out the light.

There was not a sound in the shop. Outside, feet continued to go by, ringing on the frozen road; voices were lifted; the wind hustled about the corners of the wooden shell with a continuous, shrill note of whistling. All of this outside, as on another planet. Within the blackness of the shop the complete silence persisted.

Boaz listened. Sitting on the edge of his chair, half-crouching, his head, with its long, unkempt, white hair, bent slightly to one side, he concentrated upon this chambered silence the full power of his senses. He hardly breathed. The other person in that room could not be breathing at all, it seemed.

No, there was not a breath, not the stirring of a sole on wood, not the infinitesimal rustle of any fabric. It was as if in this utter stoppage of sound, even the blood had ceased to flow in the veins and arteries of that man, who was like a rat caught in a trap.

It was appalling even to Boaz; even to the cat. Listening became more than a labor. He began to have a fight against a growing impulse to shout out loud, to leap, sprawl forward without aim in that unstirred darkness — do something. Sweat rolled down from behind his ears, into his shirt-collar. He gripped the chair-arms. To keep quiet he sank his teeth into his lower lip. He would not! He would not!

And of a sudden he heard before him, in the center of the room, an outburst of breath, an outrush from lungs in the extremity of pain, thick, laborious, fearful. A coughing up of dammed air.

Pushing himself from the arms of the chair, Boaz leaped.

His fingers, passing swiftly through the air, closed on something. It was a sheaf of hair, bristly and thick. It was a man's beard.

On the road outside, up and down the street for a hundred yards, merry-making people turned to look at one another. With an abrupt cessation of laughter, of speech. Inquiringly. Even with an unconscious dilation of the pupils of their eyes.

" What was that ? "

There had been a scream. There could be no doubt of that. A single, long-drawn note. Immensely high-pitched. Not as if it were human.

" God's sake! What was that? Where'd it come from? "

Those nearest said it came from the cobbler-shop of Boaz Negro.

They went and tried the door. It was closed; even locked, as if for the night. There was no light behind the window-shade. But Boaz would not have a light. They beat on the door. No answer.

But from where, then, had that prolonged, as if animal, note come?

They ran about, pentrating into the side lanes, interrogating, prying. Coming back at last, inevitably, to the neighborhood of Boaz Negro's shop.

The body lay on the floor at Boaz's feet, where it had tumbled down slowly after a moment from the spasmodic embrace of his arms; those ivory-colored arms which had beaten so long upon the bare iron surface of the last. Blows continuous and powerful. It seemed incredible. They were so weak now. They could not have lifted the hammer now.

But that beard! That bristly, thick, square beard of a stranger!

His hands remembered it. Standing with his shoulders fallen forward and his weak arms hanging down, Boaz began to shiver. The whole thing was incredible. What was on the floor there, upheld in the vast gulf of darkness, he could not see. Neither could he hear it; smell it. Nor (if he did not move his foot) could he feel it. What he did not hear, smell, or touch did not exist. It was not there. Incredible!

But that beard! All the accumulated doubtings of those years fell down upon him. After all, the thing he had been so fearful of in his weak imaginings had happened. He had killed a stranger. He, Boaz Negro, had murdered an innocent man!

And all on account of that beard. His deep panic made him light-headed. He began to confuse cause and effect. If it were not for that beard, it would have been that *cachorra*.

On this basis he began to reason with a crazy directness. And to act. He went and pried open the door into the entry. From a shelf he took down his razor. A big, heavy-heeled strop. His hands began to hurry. And the mug, half full of soap. And water. It would have to be cold water. But after all, he thought (light-headedly), at this time of night —

Outside, they were at the shop again. The crowd's habit is to forget a thing quickly, once it is out of sight and hearing. But there had been something about that solitary cry which continued to bother them, even in memory. Where had it been? Where had it come from? And those who had stood nearest the cobbler-shop were heard again. They were certain now, dead certain. They could swear!

In the end they broke down the door.

If Boaz heard them he gave no sign. An absorption as complete as it was monstrous wrapped him. Kneeling in the glare of the lantern they had brought, as impervious as his own shadow sprawling behind him, he continued to shave the dead man on the floor.

No one touched him. Their minds and imaginations were arrested by the gigantic proportions of the act. The unfathomable presumption of the act. As throwing murder in their faces to the tune of a jig in a barber-shop. It is a fact that none of them so much as thought of touching him. No less than all of them, together with all other men, shorn of their imaginations — that is to say, the expressionless and imperturbable creature of the Law — would be sufficient to touch that ghastly man.

On the other hand, they could not leave him alone. They could not go away. They watched. They saw the damp, lather-soaked beard of that victimized stranger falling away, stroke by stroke of the flashing, heavy razor. The dead denuded by the blind!

It was seen that Boaz was about to speak. It was something important he was about to utter; something, one would say, fatal. The words would not come all at once. They swelled his cheeks out. His razor was arrested. Lifting his face, he encircled the watchers with a gaze at once of imploration and of command. As if he could see them. As if he could read his answer in the expressions of their faces.

" Tell me one thing now. Is it that *cachorra?* "

For the first time those men in the room made sounds. They shuffled their feet. It was as if an uncontrollable impulse to ejaculation, laughter, derision, forbidden by the presence of death, had gone down into their boot-soles.

"Manuel?" one of them said. "You mean *Manuel?*"

Boaz laid the razor down on the floor beside its work. He got up from his knees slowly, as if his joints hurt. He sat down in his chair, rested his hands on the arms, and once more encircled the company with his sightless gaze.

"Not Manuel. Manuel was a good boy. But tell me now, is it that *cachorra?*"

Here was something out of their calculations; something for them, mentally, to chew on. Mystification is a good thing sometimes. It gives to the brain a fillip, stirs memory, puts the gears of imagination in mesh. One man, an old, tobacco-chewing fellow, began to stare harder at the face on the floor. Something moved in his intellect.

"No, but look here now, by God—"

He had even stopped chewing. But he was forestalled by another.

"Say now, if it don't look like that fellow Wood, himself. The bank fellow — that was burned — remember? Himself."

"That *cachorra* was not burned. Not that Wood. You darned fool!"

Boaz spoke from his chair. They hardly knew his voice, emerging from its long silence; it was so didactic and arid.

"That *cachorra* was not burned. It was my boy that was burned. It was that *cachorra* called my boy upstairs. That *cachorra* killed my boy. That *cachorra* put his clothes on my boy, and he set my house on fire. I knew that all the time. Because when I heard those feet come out of my house and go away, I knew they were the feet of that *cachorra* from the bank. I did not know where he was going to. Something said to me — you better ask him where he is going to. But then I said, you are foolish. He had the money from the bank. I did not know. And then my house was on fire. No, it was not my boy that went away; it was that *cachorra* all the time. You darned fools! Did you think I was waiting for my own boy?"

"Now I show you all," he said at the end. "And now I can get hanged."

No one ever touched Boaz Negro for that murder. For murder

it was in the eye and letter of the Law. The Law in a small town is sometimes a curious creature; it is sometimes blind only in one eye.

Their minds and imaginations in that town were arrested by the romantic proportions of the act. Simply, no one took it up. I believe the man, Wood, was understood to have died of heart-failure.

When they asked Boaz why he had not told what he knew as to the identity of that fugitive in the night, he seemed to find it hard to say exactly. How could a man of no education define for them his own but half-denied misgivings about the Law, his sense of oppression, constraint, and awe, of being on the defensive, even, in an abject way, his skepticism? About his wanting, come what might, to "keep clear of the Law"?

He did say this, "You would have laughed at me."

And this, "If I told folk it was Wood went away, then I say he would not dare come back again."

That was the last. Very shortly he began to refuse to talk about the thing at all. The act was completed. Like the creature of fable, it had consumed itself. Out of that old man's consciousness it had departed. Amazingly. Like a dream dreamed out.

Slowly at first, in a makeshift, piece-at-a-time, poor man's way, Boaz commenced to rebuild his house. That "eyesore" vanished.

And slowly at first, like the miracle of a green shoot pressing out from the dead earth, that priceless and unquenchable exuberance of the man was seen returning. Unquenchable, after all.

SUGGESTIONS FOR STUDY

1. Vocabulary: moribund, weirs, stentorian, ruthless, duenna, canny, fillip.

2. If the ending surprised you, you have nobody but yourself to blame, for Mr. Steele has played the game fairly. Consider how absolutely wrong, after all, would have been the ending you expected. Read the story again and see how emphatically you were told that Wood was a villain and that he was preparing a trap.

3. What particular incident reminded you of Poe? Why is it more horrible than most of the passages in Poe?

4. Have any other characters in these stories been as real to you as Boaz Negro? If so, what ones?

5. In what way is Steele like Hawthorne?

6. Would you like to dramatize this story?

FOR FURTHER READING

" Land's End "	" Blue Murder "
" White Horse Winter "	" Autumn Bloom "
" Down on Their Knees "	" Lightning "
" The Yellow Cat "	

WHERE TO FIND AMERICAN SHORT STORIES

The better-known writers are usually represented by volumes of their published short stories. All of them may be found in one or more of the ways suggested below.

1. *The Best Short Stories of 1915, etc.*, a series of annual volumes made up of selections chosen from American magazines by Edward J. O'Brien.
2. *O. Henry Memorial Award Prize Stories of 1919, etc.*, a series of annual volumes similar to the above edited by Blanche Colton Williams.
3. *Representative American Short Stories*, edited by Alexander Jessup.
4. *Americans All*, edited by Benjamin Heydrick.
5. *Century Readings in the American Short Story*, edited by Fred Lewis Pattee.
6. *The Best American Humorous Stories*, edited by Alexander Jessup.
7. *The Great American Short Stories*, edited by William Dean Howells.

In case of trouble in finding a given story you can always consult the *Index to Short Stories* compiled by Ida Ten Eyck Firkins. This gives the place of original publication and every other work in which a given story may be found. All libraries have this volume. A comprehensive history of the American short story is *The Development of the American Short Story* by Fred Lewis Pattee.

Following is a list of American short stories recommended for further reading. Italicized titles are those of stories which will be found in volumes of the same name.

Allen, James Lane. *Flute and Violin*, " King Solomon of Kentucky," " Two Gentlemen of Kentucky "
Andrews, Mary Raymond Shipman. " The Counsel Assigned," " The Three Things," " The Perfect Tribute," " American, Sir! "
Bacon, Josephine Daskam. " Edgar, the Choir Boy Uncelestial "
Brown, Alice. *Meadow Grass*, " Farmer Eli's Vacation," " Rosy Balm," *Tiverton Tales, The Flying Teuton*

Cable, George W. *Old Creole Days,* " Jean-ah-Poquelin," " Posson Jone," " 'Tite Poulette," " Madame Delphine "

Clemens, Samuel (Mark Twain). " The Jumping Frog," " A Dog Story "

Cobb, Irvin S. *The Escape of Mr. Trimm,* " The Belled Buzzard," *Back Home* (stories of Old Judge Priest)

Cohen, Octavus Roy. *Polished Ebony, Come Seven, Black and Blue*

Craddock, Charles E. (Mary N. Murfree). *In the Tennessee Mountains*

Crane, Stephen. *The Little Regiment, The Open Boat*

Davis, Richard Harding. *The Bar Sinister, Gallegher, Ranson's Folly, Van Bibber and Others*

Deland, Margaret. *Old Chester Tales, Dr. Lavendar's People*

Ferber, Edna. *Cheerful, By Request. Roast Beef, Medium. Mother Knows Best*

Fisher, Dorothy Canfield. *Hillsboro People, Home Fires in France, Made-to-Order Stories, The Real Motive*

Freeman, Mary E. Wilkins. *A New England Nun, A Humble Romance, Wind in the Rosebush, Best Stories of Mary E. Wilkins* (ed. by H. W. Lanier)

Gale, Zona. *Friendship Village*

Garland, Hamlin. *Main-Travelled Roads, Other Main-Travelled Roads*

Hale, Edward Everett. " The Man Without a Country," " My Double and How He Undid Me "

Harris, Joel Chandler. " The Wonderful Tar Baby," " How a Witch Was Caught," " The Creature with No Claws "

Hurst, Fannie. *Humoresque, Every Soul Hath Its Song, Gaslight Sonatas*

James, Henry. " The Real Thing," *Daisy Miller*

Jewett, Sarah Orne. *A White Heron, A Native of Winby, Best Stories of Sarah Orne Jewett* (ed. by Willa Cather)

Kelly, Myra. *Little Citizens, Little Aliens*

Marshall, Edison. " The Elephant Remembers," " The Heart of Little Shikara "

O'Brien, Fitz-James. " The Diamond Lens," " What Was It? "

Singmaster, Elsie. *Bred in the Bone, Gettysburg,* " November the Nineteenth," " July the First "

Smith, F. Hopkinson. *Forty Minutes Late, A Gentleman Vagabond, The Other Fellow*

Stuart, Ruth McEnery. *Sonny, A Golden Wedding*

Suckow, Ruth. *Iowa Interiors*

Tarkington, Booth. *Penrod, Penrod and Sam, The Fascinating Stranger,* " Monsieur Beaucaire," " Stella Crozier "

Van Dyke, Henry. *The Blue Flower, The Ruling Passion, Half-Told Tales, The Unknown Quantity*

Wharton, Edith. *Xingu,* " The Triumph of Night "

White, Stewart Edward. *Blazed Trail Stories, Arizona Nights,* " The Two-Gun Man "

White, William Allen. *The Court of Boyville, In Our Town, The Real Issue*

Wister, Owen. *Red Men and White, When West Was West,* " Philosophy Four "

Wood, Frances Gilchrist. " Shoes," " Turkey Red "

Yezierska, Anzia. *Children of Loneliness, Hungry Hearts*

The Essay

If we were making a list of the things we really enjoy doing in this world, most of us would put near the top the simple, everyday act of sitting down and chatting with our best friends about things in general. Our minds are then comfortable and relaxed; our ideas flow without great effort. We may surprise ourselves occasionally by a sudden realization of how well we have been talking, or perhaps we may forget ourselves completely in listening to the engrossing conversation of a friend.

But to read an essay — ah, that is a different matter. Many a student in the presence of the word *essay* snaps his mind to with a click, resolving in advance to be either bored or irritated. Thus does he cut himself off from a great company of goodly companions. For your true essayist is simply an intimate friend without bodily substance. He is a genial ghost (or if you don't like that word — a spirit) who takes you fishing with him or hiking across the hills, or on a chilly, rainy day he invites you into his study where you toast your shins before his open fire and have much " good talk."

You are astonished at how well you come to know your essay friend in a short time. He has the advantage over the mere story-teller, or dramatist, for he can talk about himself. As one essayist says, " If I like cats and snowstorms, and you like cats and snowstorms, we are likely to come together on that mutual ground and clasp shadow hands across the page. But if you do not like cats and snowstorms, why then you will not like me, and we needn't bore each other, need we? " After all, our daily lives are full of essays. Wherever people are thrown together for an hour's chat, be it in train, hotel lobby, party, picnic, or what not, you will hear little essays in progress on

" The Weather," " What I Like to Eat," " How to Reduce," " Where to Spend a Vacation," " The Kind of People I Like," " The Best Make of Car," and so on and on.

Development of the essay as a literary form

To study the history of the essay you would have to go back many centuries and cross the ocean. A sixteenth century Frenchman, Montaigne, first used the word *essai* and wrote many witty ones. Bacon, Addison, and Lamb were famous English essayists long before the type had a chance to develop in America. In our Colonial and Revolutionary periods there was a great deal of prose written, but usually in the form of sermons, personal experiences, historical accounts, or political treatises rather than in the form we think of as the essay today. With the nineteenth century came the real beginning of the American essay with the great names of Irving, Emerson, Thoreau, Holmes, and Lowell, each of whom wrote a different variety. The first three you will encounter in the selections to follow; Holmes has been placed with Humorous Prose because he exemplified that even more than the typical essay; Lowell confined himself largely to literary criticism where he was unexcelled.

There is no real history of the development of the essay as there is with the short story. Every man goes his own gait and it is of interest only to know certain writers who have been outstanding essayists in the different fields of subject matter.

The magazine of America is the foster parent of the essay, giving it protection and nourishment. The typical magazine " article " is a kind of essay, while such magazines as *The Atlantic Monthly, Harper's, Scribner's,* and *The Century* give harborage to the familiar essay written with literary distinction, a form which finds scant welcome in those magazines appealing only to the masses.

Types of the essay

An *essay* means an *attempt,* and so it is comparatively short and never sets out to exhaust a subject but merely to touch on some interesting phase of it. The discussion of the essay by Carl Van Doren in this section will show you how unrestricted and varied its form may be. Naturally, there are a great many kinds of essays according to the purpose or the degree of seriousness in one's attempt. That which is a piece of glorified conversation for pure enjoyment is known as the personal or familiar essay. That which attempts to make the reader see a bit of nature, architecture, or human life through the eyes of the writer is clearly a descriptive essay. That which pronounces judgment upon a piece of literature or art would be called a critical essay. That which gives us an understanding of some particular human being is the character sketch, or if more extended, the biographical essay. That which meditates seriously on the great issues of life is the reflective or didactic essay. Other classifications might be added, but these are the common types, all of which are to be found among the selections which follow.

THE CENTURY

By CHRISTOPHER MORLEY (1890–   )

Christopher Morley is an excellent example of the link between that rather formless and uproarious thing which we have called " Humorous Prose " and the more unified, more delicately whimsical, and more finished type of humor in the typical familiar essay. The former expresses the often crude vigor of a new nation; the latter carries the flavor of an old-world civilization. Christopher Morley is an American in whom the English tradition is strong. Not only were his parents both born in England, but he himself, after getting his degree from Haverford College, Pennsylvania, continued his education as a Rhodes scholar at New College, Oxford. One need only read the delightful musings in his volumes called *Shandygaff, Mince Pie, Plum Pudding,* and *Pipefuls,* to realize the rich colorings taken on from his Oxford contacts, like the suffused browns of a seasoned meerschaum.

Upon his return to America he was variously connected with well-known publishing houses, magazines, and newspapers. For four years he conducted " The Bowling Green " column in the New York *Evening Post,* thus linking himself with the professional humorists. In recent years he has devoted himself to independent writing, and it must not be forgotten that he has produced distinctive novels, short stories, plays, and verse, as well as many volumes of essays.

But more worth while than knowing these mere facts *about* him, is knowing the man himself through his own words. In this example of one of his recent essays in *Off the Deep End* he will take you adventuring with him across the continent.

In New York we think of the Twentieth Century Limited as just a train, but in Chicago she is an institution. The Century, as she is affectionately and familiarly called out there, makes her departure from the La Salle Street station with something of the circumstance of a crack liner leaving her pier. Visitors stand

along the platform to see her off. Telephone booths, right beside
her shining brass observation balcony, are busy until the last
moment. There are even telephones in the observation car, disconnected at the final tick. That brass-railed platform at the end
of the train seems, in those parting instants, as romantic as a
Shakespearean set. The morale of the whole scene is magnificent. Porters have an air, and are double-tipped for it. The
railroad conductor and the Pullman conductor, both stout, elderly,
ruddy nabobs, confer like captain and staff captain on the bridge
of the *Mauretania*.[1] She pulls out on the tick, and leaps at once
into her long smooth stride. Behind you see the second section
following, the big locomotive fluttering two green flags. I don't
know how passengers, sitting softly in observation or club car, can
settle down so promptly to the *Illustrated London News* or
Liberty. It is all far too exciting.

And, just as in a big liner sailing from New York, as soon as
you are off lunch is served. Going along the corridors you are
thrilled by the intimate air of all those little compartments.
Yourself, a mere occupant of a lower in the usual type of sleeper,
feel a little humbled by those apartment-house cars that are all
private cabins. You meet the train stenographer; he asks for
your name " for the Train Register." " Oh," he says, " there's
a gentleman looking for you, Mr. Soandso, a friend of Mr. Blank."
(Mr. Blank has been your host in Chicago.) " What space have
you got?" *Space*, I have learned, is the technical term for your
location on a swell train. He tells me what Mr. Soandso's space
is, so I can look him up. I am abashed to admit that I didn't:
it was discourteous, but this was my first voyage in the Century
and I wanted to brood.

Her morale, I repeat, is magnificent. In the diner the steward
gives you a cheerful and apparently recognitory grin. " It's a
long time since we had the pleasure of having *you* with us," he
says, and of course I am subtly flattered to be thought an alumnus. The officers of this champion train are on generous terms
with regular patrons. My friend Mr. Blank, who is an epicure,
was once brought a parcel of codfish tongues by the conductor.
There are fresh flowers on each table: a rose, two carnations, and
a daffodil. The Century celebrates her twenty-fifth anniversary
this spring. I suppose when she makes her quarter-century run,

[1] One of the largest passenger ships on the Atlantic; companion ship of the
famous *Lusitania*, which was sunk during the World War.

on June 15, there will be big doings. All sorts of things have happened on the roads since 1902, and will happen by 1952; yet even in these spacious days of Tin Elizabeth the locomotive still gives us the greatest thrill. I hear much of King Ganaway, the Chicago photographer who has done marvelous pictures of engines. I hope he'll do the Century as she pulls out of La Salle Street on the morning of June 15th.

We make our first stop at Elkhart. It's fine to see a squad of oilers and coal-passers leap at the engine almost before she has come to a stop and begin hostlering her. You stroll up and down the platform for a brief inhale of windy March, try to savor the feeling of Indiana, the green little park, the Civil War statue. You admire the two rotund conductors, like Tweedledum and Tweedledee,[2] still conferring. Then we're off again. The Second Section pulls in just as we leave. Do they keep it up like that, nip and tuck, all night?

The sweet brown fields of Indiana recede behind us. Chew Mail Pouch, Chew Bag Pipes; red cows, red pigs, red barns. And, if you have been spending a few days with a typical Chicago host, you suddenly find yourself strangely and peaceably weary. I guess there's truth in what the railroad claims about the water-level route; certainly the running is amazingly smooth. Going back to your seat in the car *French Lake* you find a fat white pillow put there by a fat black porter. You oblique yourself into it. Your mind goes back to the wonders of that amazing city. An apartment high over the lake, a night of gale and sleet, grilled casement windows looking onto the foam of perilous lakes forlorn. The roar of that fresh-water surf sounds even above the roar of the fire in the great chimney throat. Like all genuine Chicagoans, my host believes in going nature one better. His logs are treated with chemicals, the flames are blue and silver and platinum color. In that gale and draught the fire burns through suddenly. You leave the room for a little while — when you come back it is all burned out; no softly glowing log to linger redly. In the elevator shafts of lake front apartments the gale screams a fierce Aeolian cry. I wish Shakespeare had known Chicago. And softly, with a little terror even, pondering these things, you fall asleep.

---

[2] Two things between which there is only the slightest distinction. The author was referring to the famous twins in Lewis Carroll's *Through the Looking-Glass*. In a dispute in the eighteenth century as to the relative merits of two musicians, the satirist, John Byrom, wrote a poem in which he dubbed the two men Tweedledum and Tweedledee.

You wake up just entering Toledo. Again a chance for a swig of air. You are thrilled by strange names on cars and engines — *Nickel Plate Road, Hocking Valley, Père Marquette.* You buy a Toledo paper. An ad amused me — *Girls, carry a spare.* Stocking, they mean. It appears that life in Toledo is hard on hosiery, for you are urged to buy stockings "Three to the pair." Then, if a run starts (says the ad) you take your spare from your purse and refill. — Just as I was losing myself in Ronald Fraser's *Flower Phantoms* (what an enchanting book!) I noticed a pleasant town. The porter came by. "What is this place?" I asked him. "This is Elyria," he said. That indeed had a Shakespearean sound. "What country, friends, is this?" "This is Illyria, lady." [3]

By dusk the train has settled down to so tranquil and domestic a routine that you have all the settled feeling of an ocean voyage. From the little compartments comes the sound of card-playing, bursts of cheerful mirth. Yet the Centurions are not too folksy, as on lesser trains. You are not approached, as I was on another limited once, to know if I'd make a fourth at bridge. I said I didn't play bridge. Well, how about poker said the other. I said I didn't play poker. "Do you play anything at all?" was his final attempt. Whatever it might have been I fear I'd have lost.

When you've had a light dinner, and read G. K. Chesterton [4] in the *Illustrated London News,* and remembered to put your watch an hour ahead, you'll find your berth made up. You fall asleep just as you come into Erie.

What happens between Erie and Albany I have no notion. Usually I don't sleep much on trains, but I thank the Century for some eight hours vanished forever from my life — hours of complete nothing, a capsule of eternity. You wake, being on the starboard side, to see a half moon riding in pale light over a faint rosy epilogue of dawn. You smoke a pipe and pensively overhaul your belongings. Somehow you've lost your collar button, but (like the girls of Toledo) you had a spare with you. Your pride over this makes you quite pleased with yourself. You nap for another hour or so, and then orange juice and scrambled eggs.

I was sorry to see the last of our relay of locomotives leave

[3] From Shakespeare's *Twelfth Night.* Illyria was the country in which Viola met with her adventures after her shipwreck.

[4] A noted English critic and essayist of the present day.

us at Harmon.[5] It would have been nice for her, I thought, to have had the honor of roaring us proudly to the very end. And I wouldn't have been myself, I reflected ruefully, if I hadn't immediately gone on to find a symbol in the matter. For it is just so with man throughout his life — he's frequently changing engines. For a while, Fun is his motive power; then Earning, or Ambition, or Love, or Family, all powerful moguls, keep him all steamed up. Perhaps it is the quiet electric engine, Peace, that brings him at last into his Grand Central Station.

SUGGESTIONS FOR STUDY

1. State some definite points learned about Christopher Morley in this essay which make you feel acquainted with him.
2. Find examples of clever touches of humor in the use of words such as "I am subtly flattered to be thought an *alumnus*."
3. How does he carry out the comparison to an ocean voyage after his first mention of the *Mauretania?*
4. How do you like the bit of life philosophy at the end?
5. Describe some train on which you have ridden.
6. Contrast the Century with a crowded local day coach.

FOR FURTHER READING

ESSAYS
Shandygaff
Mince Pie
Plum Pudding
Pipefuls
Off the Deep End
Forty-Four Essays

DRAMA
Collection of One-Act Plays

FICTION
Parnassus on Wheels
The Haunted Bookshop
Where the Blue Begins
Thunder on the Left

POETRY
Songs for a Little House
Chimney Smoke
Parson's Pleasure
Toulemonde

MARY WHITE

By WILLIAM ALLEN WHITE (1868–   )

If ever a literary man was identified through his whole life with a single town, that man is William Allen White, and the town is Emporia, Kansas.

---

[5] At Harmon, New York Central trains change from steam engines to electric.

His birth, his schooling, and his long career as owner and editor of the Emporia *Gazette* have forged such a strong link between his name and that of the town, that one hardly thinks of the one without the other. Through Mr. White's grasp of public affairs and penetrating editorials, his newspaper has attained an unusual reputation throughout the country. He has also written essays, short stories and novels. His two best-known pieces of fiction are *The Court of Boyville* and *A Certain Rich Man*.

It is not, however, as a publicist or novelist that we here consider him, but as a father. Probably no such remarkable obituary has ever appeared in a newspaper as the one he wrote for his own daughter. Composed when her loss was still fresh enough to have overwhelmed an ordinary man, it nevertheless reveals a self-command and depth of affection which rise above ordinary expressions of grief, and give to Mary White a lease of life far beyond her mortal years.

The Associated Press reports carrying the news of Mary White's death declared that it came as the result of a fall from a horse. How she would have hooted at that! She never fell from a horse in her life. Horses have fallen on her and with her — " I'm always trying to hold 'em in my lap," she used to say. But she was proud of few things, and one was that she could ride anything that had four legs and hair. Her death resulted not from a fall, but from a blow on the head which fractured her skull, and the blow came from the limb of an overhanging tree on the parking.

The last hour of her life was typical of its happiness. She came home from a day's work at school, topped off by a hard grind with the copy on the high school *Annual*, and felt that a ride would refresh her. She climbed into her khakis, chattering to her mother about the work she was doing, and hurried to get her horse and be out on the dirt roads for the country air and the radiant fields of the spring. As she rode through the town on an easy gallop she kept waving at passers-by. She knew every one in town. For a decade the little figure with the long pigtail and the red hair-ribbon has been familiar on the streets of Emporia, and she got in the way of speaking to those who nodded at her. She passed the Kerrs, walking the horse, in front of the Normal Library, and waved at them; passed another friend a few hundred feet farther on, and waved at her. The horse was walking, and as she turned into North Merchant Street she took off her cowboy hat, and the horse swung into a lope. She passed the Tripletts and waved her cowboy hat at them, still moving gaily north on Merchant Street. A *Gazette* carrier passed — a high school boy friend — and she waved at him, but with her bridle hand; the horse veered quickly, plunged into the parking where the low-hanging limb faced her, and, while she still looked back waving, the blow came. But she did not fall from the horse; she slipped off, dazed a bit, staggered and fell in a faint. She never quite recovered consciousness.

But she did not fall from the horse, neither was she riding fast. A year or so ago she used to go like the wind. But that habit was broken, and she used the horse to get into the open to get fresh, hard exercise, and to work off a certain surplus energy that welled up in her and needed a physical outlet. That need has been in her heart for years. It was back of the impulse that kept the dauntless little brown-clad figure on the streets and country roads of this community and built into a strong, muscular body what had been a frail and sickly frame during the first years of her life. But the riding gave her more than a body. It released a gay and hardy soul. She was the happiest thing in the world. And she was happy because she was enlarging her horizon. She came to know all sorts and conditions of men; Charley O'Brien, the traffic cop, was one of her best friends. W. L. Holtz, the Latin teacher, was another. Tom O'Connor, farmer-politician, and Rev. J. H. J. Rice, preacher and police judge, and Frank Beach, music master, were her special friends, and all the girls, black and white, above the track and below the track, in Pepville and Stringtown, were among her acquaintances. And she brought home riotous stories of her adventures. She loved to rollick; persiflage was her natural expression at home. Her humor was a continual bubble of joy. She seemed to think in hyperbole and metaphor. She was mischievous without malice, as full of faults as an old shoe. No angel was Mary White, but an easy girl to live with, for she never nursed a grouch five minutes in her life.

With all her eagerness for the out-of-doors, she loved books. On her table when she left her room were a book by Conrad, one by Galsworthy, *Creative Chemistry* by E. E. Slosson, and a Kipling book. She read Mark Twain, Dickens, and Kipling before she was ten — all of their writings. Wells and Arnold Bennett particularly amused and diverted her. She was entered as a student in Wellesley in 1922; was assistant editor of the high school *Annual* this year, and in line for election to the editorship of the *Annual* next year. She was a member of the executive committee of the high school Y. W. C. A.

Within the last two years she had begun to be moved by an ambition to draw. She began as most children do by scribbling, in her school books, funny pictures. She bought cartoon magazines and took a course — rather casually, naturally, for she was, after all, a child with no strong purposes — and this year she tasted the first fruits of success by having her pictures accepted by the high school *Annual.* But the thrill of delight she got when Mr. Ecord, of the Normal *Annual,* asked her to do the cartooning for that book this spring, was too beautiful for words. She fell to her work with all her enthusiastic heart. Her drawings were accepted, and her pride — always repressed by a lively sense of the ridiculousness of the figure she was cutting — was a really gorgeous thing to see. No successful artist ever drank a deeper draught of satisfaction than she took from the little fame her work was getting among her schoolfellows. In her glory, she almost forgot her horse — but never her car.

For she used the car as a jitney bus. It was her social life. She never had a " party " in all her nearly seventeen years — wouldn't have one; but she never drove a block in the car in her life that she didn't begin to fill the car with pick-ups! Everybody rode with Mary White — white and black, old and young, rich and poor, men and women. She liked nothing better than to fill the car full of long-legged high school boys and an occasional girl, and parade the town. She never had a " date," nor went to a dance, except once with her brother, Bill, and the " boy proposition " didn't interest her — yet. But young people — great spring-breaking, varnish-cracking, fender-bending, door-sagging carloads of " kids " gave her great pleasure. Her zests were keen. But the most fun she ever had in her life was acting as chairman of the committee that got up the big turkey dinner for the poor folks at the county home; scores of pies, gallons of slaw; jam, cakes, preserves, oranges, and a wilderness of turkey were loaded in the car and taken to the county home. And, being of a practical turn of mind, she risked her own Christmas dinner by staying to see that the poor folks actually got it all. Not that she was a cynic; she just disliked to tempt folks. While there, she found a blind colored uncle, very old, who could do nothing but make rag rugs, and she rustled up from her school friends rags enough to keep him busy for a season. The last

engagement she tried to make was to take the guests at the county
home out for a car ride. And the last endeavor of her life was
to try to get a rest room for colored girls in the high school.
She found one girl reading in the toilet, because there was no better place for a colored girl to loaf, and it inflamed her sense of
injustice and she became a nagging Harpy to those who, she
thought, could remedy the evil. The poor she had always with
her, and was glad of it. She hungered and thirsted for righteous-
ness; and was the most impious creature in the world. She
joined the Congregational Church without consulting her parents; not particularly for her soul's good. She never had a thrill
of piety in her life, and would have hooted at a " testimony."
But even as a little child she felt the church was an agency for
helping people to more of life's abundance, and she wanted to
help. She never wanted help for herself. Clothes meant little
to her. It was a fight to get a new rig on her; but eventually
a harder fight to get it off. She never wore a jewel and had no
ring but her high school class ring, and never asked for anything
but a wrist watch. She refused to have her hair up; though she
was nearly seventeen. " Mother," she protested, " you don't
know how much I get by with, in my braided pigtails, that I could
not with my hair up." Above every other passion of her life
was her passion not to grow up, to be a child. The tomboy in
her, which was big, seemed to loathe to be put away forever in
skirts. She was Peter Pan, who refused to grow up.

Her funeral yesterday at the Congregational Church was as
she would have wished it; no singing, no flowers save the big
bunch of roses from her Brother Bill's Harvard classmen —
Heavens, how proud that would have made her! and the red
roses from the *Gazette* force — in vases at her head and feet. A
short prayer, Paul's beautiful essay on " Love " from the Thirteenth Chapter of First Corinthians, some remarks about her democratic spirit by her friend, John H. J. Rice, pastor and police
judge, which she would have deprecated if she could, a prayer sent
down for her by her friend, Carl Nau, and opening the service the
slow, poignant movement from Beethoven's Moonlight Sonata,
which she loved, and closing the service a cutting from the joyously melancholy first movement of Tschaikowski's Pathetic
Symphony, which she liked to hear in certain moods on the
phonograph; then the Lord's Prayer by her friends in the high
school.

That was all.

For her pallbearers only her friends were chosen; her Latin teacher, W. L. Holtz; her high school principal, Rice Brown; her doctor, Frank Foncannon; her friend, W. W. Finney; her pal at the *Gazette* office, Walter Hughes; and her brother Bill. It would have made her smile to know that her friend, Charley O'Brien, the traffic cop, had been transferred from Sixth and Commercial to the corner near the church to direct her friends who came to bid her good-by.

SUGGESTIONS FOR STUDY

1. Give some of the details of Mary White's appearance and actions which make her seem like a real girl and not an idealized figure.

2. Would you have liked Mary as a classmate? Point out specific reasons for your answer.

3. To what general type of high school girl would you say she belonged?

4. How do her favorite authors match up with your own?

5. What was particularly appropriate about her funeral service?

6. Try writing a portrayal of one of your classmates in which vividness is achieved by intimate detail.

FOR FURTHER READING

ESSAYS

The Old Order Changeth

BIOGRAPHY

The Martial Adventures of Henry and Me
Life of Woodrow Wilson
Life of Calvin Coolidge
Masks in a Pageant

FICTION

The Court of Boyville
In Our Town
A Certain Rich Man
God's Puppets
In the Heart of a Fool

THE AUTHOR'S ACCOUNT OF HIMSELF

By WASHINGTON IRVING (1783–1859)

Inevitably when we turn back to the beginning of a prose type in American literature we strike Washington Irving. Certainly no picture of the American essay would be complete without the author of *The Sketch Book,* for it was this collection of essays and tales which first won for an American author the respect of Europe. Irving had that gift, indispensable to the familiar essayist, of being able to stand off and view himself impersonally with a twinkle in his eye. This is the way he accounts in a later work for the popularity of the earlier venture: "It has been a matter of marvel to my European readers that a man from the wilds of America should express himself in tolerable English. I was looked upon as something new and strange in literature; a kind of demi-savage with a feather in his hand instead of on his head; and there was a curiosity to hear what such a being had to say about civilized society."

In the following " Account of Himself," which opens *The Sketch Book,* the author has shown us a miniature of himself — his love of travel and adventure, of history and legend, his loyalty to America combined with his devotion to European tradition. We have a taste of his easy-rolling sentences and his sly digs of humor. All of these traits are illuminated and vivified as we turn the pages of *The Sketch Book,* written under the appropriate name of Geoffrey Crayon. Here he has drawn loving pictures of Stratford-on-Avon and Westminster Abbey at the same time that he has protested vigorously against English writers' disparagement of America. Legend is mingled with direct observation, story with essay. Such combinations are to be found again in *Bracebridge Hall,* purely English in setting, and in *The Alhambra,* based on his Spanish travels. All of these books are good examples of how slight is the line of demarcation between an essay and a story.

" I am of this mind with Homer, that as the snaile that crept out of her shel was turned eftsoons into a toad, and thereby was forced to make a stoole to sit on; so the traveller that stragleth from his owne country is in a short time transformed into so monstrous a shape, that he is faine to alter his mansion with his manners, and to live where he can, not where he would." — LYLY's *Euphues.*

I was always fond of visiting new scenes, and observing strange characters and manners. Even when a mere child I began my travels, and made many tours of discovery into foreign parts and unknown regions of my native city,[1] to the frequent alarm of my parents, and the emolument of the town-crier.[2] As I grew into boyhood, I extended the range of my observations. My holiday afternoons were spent in rambles about the surrounding country. I made myself familiar with all its places famous in history or fable. I knew every spot where a murder or robbery had been

[1] New York.
[2] In the eighteenth century the town-crier was a kind of animated newspaper, who served the purpose of the advertising sections of today.

committed, or a ghost seen. I visited the neighboring villages, and added greatly to my stock of knowledge by noting their habits and customs, and conversing with their sages and great men. I even journeyed one long summer's day to the summit of the most distant hill, whence I stretched my eye over many a mile of *terra incognita*,[3] and was astonished to find how vast a globe I inhabited.

This rambling propensity strengthened with my years. Books of voyages and travels became my passion, and in devouring their contents, I neglected the regular exercises of the school. How wistfully would I wander about the pier-heads in fine weather, and watch the parting ships, bound to distant climes — with what longing eyes would I gaze after their lessening sails, and waft myself in imagination to the ends of the earth!

Further reading and thinking, though they brought this vague inclination into more reasonable bounds, only served to make it more decided. I visited various parts of my own country; and had I been merely a lover of fine scenery, I should have felt little desire to seek elsewhere its gratification, for on no country have the charms of nature been more prodigally lavished. Her mighty lakes, like oceans of liquid silver; her mountains, with their bright aërial tints; her valleys, teeming with wild fertility; her tremendous cataracts, thundering in their solitudes; her boundless plains, waving with spontaneous verdure; her broad, deep rivers, rolling in solemn silence to the ocean; her trackless forests, where vegetation puts forth all its magnificence; her skies, kindling with the magic of summer clouds and glorious sunshine; — no, never need an American look beyond his own country for the sublime and beautiful of natural scenery.

But Europe held forth the charms of storied and poetical association. There were to be seen the masterpieces of art, the refinements of highly cultivated society, the quaint peculiarities of ancient and local custom. My native country was full of youthful promise: Europe was rich in the accumulated treasures of age. Her very ruins told the history of times gone by, and every moldering stone was a chronicle. I longed to wander over the scenes of renowned achievement — to tread, as it were, in the footsteps of antiquity — to loiter about the ruined castle — to meditate on the falling tower — to escape, in short, from the com-

---

[3] Unknown land.

HOW WISTFULLY WOULD I WANDER ABOUT THE PIER-HEADS

monplace realities of the present, and lose myself among the
shadowy grandeurs of the past.

I had, beside all this, an earnest desire to see the great men of
the earth. We have, it is true, our great men in America: not
a city but has an ample share of them. I have mingled among
them in my time, and been almost withered by the shade into
which they cast me; for there is nothing so baleful to a small man
as the shade of a great one, particularly the great man of a city.
But I was anxious to see the great men of Europe; for I had read
in the works of various philosophers, that all animals degenerated
in America, and man among the number. A great man of Europe,
thought I, must therefore be as superior to a great man of America
as a peak of the Alps to a highland of the Hudson; and in this
idea I was confirmed by observing the comparative importance
and swelling magnitude of many English travelers among us,
who, I was assured, were very little people in their own country.
I will visit this land of wonders, thought I, and see the gigantic
race from which I am degenerated.

It has been either my good or evil lot to have my roving passion
gratified. I have wandered through different countries, and witnessed many of the shifting scenes of life. I cannot say that
I have studied them with the eye of a philosopher; but rather
with the sauntering gaze with which humble lovers of the picturesque stroll from the window of one print-shop to another,
caught sometimes by the delineations of beauty, sometimes by
the distortions of caricature, and sometimes by the loveliness of
landscape. As it is the fashion for modern tourists to travel pencil
in hand, and bring home their portfolios filled with sketches, I am
disposed to get up a few for the entertainment of my friends.
When, however, I look over the hints and memorandums I have
taken down for the purpose, my heart almost fails me at finding
how my idle humor has led me aside from the great objects studied by every regular traveler who would make a book. I fear
I shall give equal disappointment with an unlucky landscape
painter, who had traveled on the continent, but, following the
bent of his vagrant inclination, had sketched in nooks, and corners, and by-places. His sketch-book was accordingly crowded
with cottages, and landscapes, and obscure ruins; but he had
neglected to paint St. Peter's, or the Coliseum; the cascade of
Terni, or the bay of Naples; and had not a single glacier or vol-
cano in his whole collection.

SUGGESTIONS FOR STUDY

1. How does Irving illustrate the proverb, "As the twig is bent, the tree is inclined " ?

2. What do you think would be his attitude today toward the slogan " See America First " ?

3. Is his attitude toward great men serious or humorous?

4. Would you enjoy a trip to Europe in the company of Irving? Why or why not?

FOR FURTHER READING

The Sketch Book: " English Writers on America," " Rural Life in England," " The Art of Book-Making," " The Country Church," " Westminster Abbey," " Five Christmas Sketches," " Stratford-on-Avon," " John Bull," " The Angler "

Bracebridge Hall: " The Busy Man," " Family Servants," " An Old Soldier," " Ready-Money Jack," " Bachelors," " May-Day Customs," " Popular Superstitions "

The Alhambra: " The Palace of the Alhambra," " Inhabitants of the Alhambra," " The Hall of Ambassadors," " The Court of Lions," " Public Fêtes of Granada," " A Fête in the Alhambra "

For Irving's stories see page 43.

GIFTS

By RALPH WALDO EMERSON (1803–1882)

Whether or not you have read a word written by Ralph Waldo Emerson, you must at least be familiar with his name, for he has left a deep imprint on American life. Schools, streets, and even cigars have been named for him. But how many who glibly bandy his name know the real man or can understand his message? It is not written so that " he who runs may read." His essays are not ice-cream sodas with which to beguile a warm afternoon, but rather, substantial beefsteaks intended for lusty chewing in gusty weather.

Emerson's life was bound up with Boston and the village of Concord, twenty miles out. The city was the place of his birth, his schooling, and his early ministry. But his real career, in which he spoke to the world for half a century, was in the village, where he was the center of the most remarkable literary group ever contained in this country by one small town.

With the tradition of a line of ministers behind him, it was inevitable that he should go to Harvard even though the untimely death of his father had left the large family an inheritance of poverty. Through the continuous efforts of his mother and of the boys themselves, four of the brothers went through college. Emerson once said that Toil, Want, Truth, and Mutual Faith were the four angels of his home. After graduation he taught school to earn money to attend the divinity school and finally at the age of twenty-three he was ordained as a Unitarian minister. Three years later he became associate pastor of the famous Old North Church of Boston in whose tower, in Revolutionary times, the signal lanterns had been hung for Paul Revere. But this apparent success was clouded by the death of his young wife and by a severe crisis in his mental life. The young preacher could not conscientiously agree with all the doctrines of his church. Rather than conceal the fact in order to retain his office, with characteristic honesty he stated his position openly and resigned from the church. Thus did he illustrate by an act which took considerable courage, the sincerity, self-reliance, and independence of thought which he later preached through his essays.

Fortunately his wife's estate left him an annual income of $1200. Meager as this seems to us today, it enabled him with a few other resources to live simply and happily in a comfortable big house in Concord, to marry a second time and rear a family, and to take an occasional trip abroad. Europe did not beckon Emerson in the same way that it did Irving. He cared little for the cathedrals, the literary shrines, or the legends. What meant the most to him was contact with the great thinkers of England, especially Thomas Carlyle, with whom he formed a permanent friendship, perpetuated for us in their published letters.

With ample leisure for meditation, Emerson was gradually drawn into lyceum lecturing, which was then attaining great popularity in this country. He became the most distinctive lecturer of his day, and people not only flocked to his public lectures, but even pursued him to his home, so that Concord became a kind of Mecca to the intellectuals of that day. The lectures were published from time to time, and thus it is that Emerson's essays, unlike most, were first prepared for oral delivery. More profoundly than other essays they deal with interpretations of life and thought. A swift glance at the titles will show this. Friendship, Love, Self-Reliance, Heroism, Character, Manners, Compensation — each treats of some quality of human life with a sincerity and wisdom which have won for their author such titles as seer, sage, and prophet.

It will help you in reading Emerson to understand that his unit of thought is generally the sentence, and not the paragraph as with most writers. You must therefore read slowly and let the complete meaning of each sentence sink in.

> Gifts of one who loved me, —
> 'Twas high time they came;
> When he ceased to love me,
> Time they stopped for shame.

It is said that the world is in a state of bankruptcy, that the world owes the world more than the world can pay, and ought to go into chancery, and be sold. I do not think this general insolvency, which involves in some sort all the population, to be the reason of the difficulty experienced at Christmas and New Year, and other times, in bestowing gifts; since it is always so pleasant to be generous, though very vexatious to pay debts. But the impediment lies in the choosing. If, at any time, it comes into

FLOWERS AND FRUITS ARE ALWAYS FIT PRESENTS

my head that a present is due from me to somebody, I am puzzled what to give, until the opportunity is gone. Flowers and fruits are always fit presents; — flowers, because they are a proud assertion that a ray of beauty outvalues all the utilities of the world. These gay natures contrast with the somewhat stern countenance of ordinary nature; they are like music heard out of a workhouse. Nature does not cocker [1] us: we are children, not pets: she is not fond [2]: everything is dealt to us without fear

---

[1] Spoil, coddle.   [2] In the sense of foolishly tender.

or favor, after severe universal laws. Yet these delicate flowers look like the frolic and interference of love and beauty. Men used to tell us that we love flattery, even though we are not deceived by it, because it shows that we are of importance enough to be courted. Something like that pleasure, the flowers give us: what am I to whom these sweet hints are addressed? Fruits are acceptable gifts, because they are the flower of commodities, and admit of fantastic values being attached to them. If a man should send to me to come a hundred miles to visit him, and should set before me a basket of fine summer fruit, I should think there was some proportion between the labor and the reward.

For common gifts, necessity makes pertinences and beauty every day, and one is glad when an imperative leaves him no option, since if the man at the door has no shoes you have not to consider whether you could procure him a paint-box. And as it is always pleasing to see a man eat bread, or drink water, in the house or out of doors, so it is always a great satisfaction to supply these first wants. Necessity does everything well. In our condition of universal dependence, it seems heroic to let the petitioner be the judge of his necessity, and to give all that is asked, though at great inconvenience. If it be a fantastic desire, it is better to leave to others the office of punishing him. I can think of many parts I should prefer playing to that of the Furies.[3] Next to things of necessity, the rule for a gift, which one of my friends prescribed, is, that we might convey to some person that which properly belonged to his character, and was easily associated with him in thought. But our tokens of compliment and love are for the most part barbarous. Rings and other jewels are not gifts, but apologies for gifts. The only gift is a portion of thyself. Thou must bleed for me. Therefore the poet brings his poem; the shepherd, his lamb; the farmer, corn; the miner, a gem; the sailor, coral and shells; the painter, his picture; the girl, a handkerchief of her own sewing. This is right and pleasing, for it restores society in so far to its primary basis, when a man's biography is conveyed in his gift, and every man's wealth is an index of his merit. But it is a cold, lifeless business when you go to the shops to buy me something, which does not represent your life and talent, but a goldsmith's. This is fit for kings, and rich men who represent kings, and a false state of property, to

[3] In Greek mythology, beings who punished the wicked.

make presents of gold and silver stuffs, as a kind of symbolical sin-offering, or payment of blackmail.

The law of benefits is a difficult channel, which requires careful sailing, or rude boats. It is not the office of a man to receive gifts. How dare you give them? We wish to be self-sustained. We do not quite forgive a giver. The hand that feeds us is in some danger of being bitten. We can receive anything from love, for that is a way of receiving it from ourselves; but not from any one who assumes to bestow. We sometimes hate the meat which we eat, because there seems something of degrading dependence in living by it.

> Brother, if Jove to thee a present make
> Take heed that from his hands thou nothing take.

We ask the whole. Nothing less will content us. We arraign society, if it do not give us, besides earth, and fire, and water, opportunity, love, reverence, and objects of veneration.

He is a good man who can receive a gift well. We are either glad or sorry at a gift, and both emotions are unbecoming. Some violence, I think, is done, some degradation borne, when I rejoice or grieve at a gift. I am sorry when my independence is invaded, or when a gift comes from such as do not know my spirit, and so the act is not supported; and if the gift pleases me overmuch, then I should be ashamed that the donor should read my heart, and see that I love his commodity and not him. The gift, to be true, must be the flowing of the giver unto me, correspondent to my flowing unto him. When the waters are at a level, then my goods pass to him, and his to me. All his are mine, all mine his. I say to him, " How can you give me this pot of oil, or this flagon of wine, when all your oil and wine is mine? " which belief of mine this gift seems to deny. Hence the fitness of beautiful, not useful things for gifts. This giving is flat usurpation, and therefore when the beneficiary is ungrateful, as all beneficiaries hate all Timons,[4] not at all considering the value of the gift, but looking back to the greater store it was taken from, I rather sympathize with the beneficiary than with the anger of my lord Timon. For the expectation of gratitude is mean, and is continually punished by the total insensibility of the obliged person. It is a great happiness to get off without injury and heart-burning from one

[4] The leading character in Shakespeare's play *Timon of Athens,* who spent his entire fortune on lavish gifts and was then spurned by those who had flattered him.

who has had the ill-luck to be served by you. It is a very onerous business, this of being served, and the debtor naturally wishes to give you a slap. A golden text for these gentlemen is that which I so admire in the Buddhist, who never thanks, and who says, " Do not flatter your benefactors."

The reason of these discords I conceive to be, that there is no commensurability between a man and any gift. You cannot give anything to a magnanimous person. After you have served him, he at once puts you in debt by his magnanimity. The service a man renders his friend is trivial and selfish, compared with the service he knows his friend stood in readiness to yield him, alike before he had begun to serve his friend, and now also. Compared with that good will I bear my friend, the benefit it is in my power to render him seems small. Besides, our action on each other, good as well as evil, is so incidental and at random, that we can seldom hear the acknowledgments of any person who would thank us for a benefit without some shame and humiliation. We can rarely strike a direct stroke, but must be content with an oblique one; we seldom have the satisfaction of yielding a direct benefit, which is directly received. But rectitude scatters favors on every side without knowing it, and receives with wonder the thanks of all people.

I fear to breathe any treason against the majesty of love, which is the genius and god of gifts, and to whom we must not affect to prescribe. Let him give kingdoms or flower-leaves indifferently. There are persons from whom we always expect fairy tokens; let us not cease to expect them. This is prerogative, and not to be limited by our municipal rules. For the rest, I like to see that we cannot be bought and sold. The best of hospitality and of generosity is also not in the will, but in fate. I find that I am not much to you; you do not need me; you do not feel me; then am I thrust out of doors, though you proffer me house and lands. No services are of any value, but only likeness. When I have attempted to join myself to others by services, it proved an intellectual trick — no more. They eat your service like apples, and leave you out. But love them, and they feel you, and delight in you all the time.

SUGGESTIONS FOR STUDY

1. Why does Emerson think that flowers and fruits are always fit presents?

2. Does he approve of giving necessaries? Jeweiry? Handkerchiefs?

3. Under what circumstances do you think he would approve or disapprove of the following as gifts: a check, winter underwear, a gold bracelet, a photograph, an embroidered lunchcloth, a corsage bouquet, a book of poetry, a necktie?

4. What difficulties does he see in receiving gifts?

5. In the light of this essay what criticisms can you make of some of our common practices in Christmas giving?

6. Do you disagree with Emerson on any points? If so, what?

SELECTIONS FROM OTHER EMERSON ESSAYS

Since Emerson's essays are rather rambling in construction, one can gain from quotations here and there an idea of his point of view, and a vivid impression of the great thoughts which have stirred the minds of men and women for almost a century.

FROM " NATURE "

It seems as if the day was not wholly profane in which we have given heed to some natural object. The fall of snowflakes in a still air, preserving to each crystal its perfect form; the blowing of sleet over a wide sheet of water, and over plains, the waving rye-field, the mimic waving of acres of houstonia,[1] whose innumerable florets whiten and ripple before the eye; the reflections of trees and flowers in glassy lakes; the musical steaming odorous south wind, which converts all trees to windharps; the crackling and spurting of hemlock in the flames; or of pine logs, which yield glory to the walls and faces in the sitting-room — these are the music and pictures of the most ancient religion. . . . We can find these enchantments without visiting the Como Lake, or the Madeira Islands. . . . In every landscape, the point of astonishment is the meeting of the sky and the earth, and that is seen from the first hillock as well as from the top of the Alleghanies. The stars at night stoop down over the brownest, homeliest common with all the spiritual magnificence which they shed on the Campagna, or on the marble deserts of Egypt. . . . The difference between landscape and landscape is small, but there is great difference in the beholders. . . . Nature cannot be surprised in undress. Beauty breaks in everywhere.

[1] A low, slender plant named for Dr. Houston, a naturalist.

FROM " MANNERS "

The gentleman is a man of truth, lord of his own actions, and expressing that lordship in his behavior, not in any manner dependent and servile either on persons, or opinions, or possessions. Beyond this fact of truth and real force, the word denotes good-nature or benevolence; manhood first and then gentleness. The popular notion certainly adds a condition of ease and fortune; but that is a natural result of personal force and love, that they should possess and dispense the goods of the world. In times of violence every eminent person must fall in with many opportunities to approve [2] his stoutness and worth; therefore every man's name that emerged at all from the mass in the feudal ages, rattles in our ear like a flourish of trumpets. But personal force never goes out of fashion. That is still paramount today, and in the moving crowd of good society, the men of valor and reality are known, and rise to their natural place. The competition is transferred from war to politics and trade, but the personal force appears readily enough in these new arenas. . . . My gentleman gives the law where he is; he will outpray saints in chapel, out-general veterans in the field, and outshine all courtesy in the hall. He is good company for pirates, and good with academicians. . . .

FROM " FRIENDSHIP "

A friend is a person with whom I may be sincere. Before him I may think aloud. I am arrived at last in the presence of a man so real and equal that I may drop even those undermost garments of dissimulation, courtesy, and second thought, which men never put off, and may deal with him with the simplicity and wholeness with which one chemical atom meets another. Sincerity is the luxury allowed, like diadems and authority, only to the highest rank, *that* being permitted to speak truth, as having none above it to court or conform unto. Every man alone is sincere. At the entrance of a second person, hypocrisy begins. We parry and fend the approach of our fellow man by compliments, by gossip, by amusements, by affairs. We cover up our thought from him under a hundred folds. . . . Almost every man we meet requires some civility, requires to be humored; — he has some fame, some talent, some whim of religion or philanthropy in his head that is

[2] Prove.

not to be questioned, and which spoils all conversation with him. But a friend is a sane man who exercises not my ingenuity but me. My friend gives me entertainment without requiring me to stoop, or to lisp, or to mask myself. A friend therefore is a sort of paradox in nature. I who alone am, I who see nothing in nature whose existence I can affirm with equal evidence to my own, behold now the semblance of my being, in all its height, variety, and curiosity, reiterated in a foreign form; so that a friend may well be reckoned the masterpiece of nature.

FROM " COMPENSATION "

The same dualism underlies the nature and condition of man. Every excess causes a defect; every defect an excess. Every sweet hath its sour; every evil its good. Every faculty which is a receiver of pleasure has an equal penalty for its abuse. It is to answer for its moderation with its life. For every grain of wit there is a grain of folly. For everything you have missed, you have gained something else; and for everything you gain, you lose something. If riches increase, they are increased that use them. If the gatherer gathers too much, nature takes out of the man what she puts into his chest; swells the estate, but kills the owner. Nature hates monopolies and exceptions. The waves of the sea do not more speedily seek a level from their loftiest tossing than the varieties of condition tend to equalize themselves. There is always some leveling circumstance that puts down the overbearing, the strong, the rich, the fortunate, substantially on the same ground with all others. . . .

The farmer imagines power and place are fine things. But the President has paid dear for his White House. It has commonly cost him all his peace, and the best of his manly attributes. To preserve for a short time so conspicuous an appearance before the world, he is content to eat dust before the real masters who stand erect behind the throne. Or do men desire the more substantial and permanent grandeur of genius? Neither has this an immunity. He who by force of will or of thought is great and overlooks thousands, has the responsibility of overlooking. With every influx of light comes new danger. Has he light? He must bear witness to the light, and always outrun that sympathy which gives him such keen satisfaction, by his fidelity to new revelations of the incessant soul.

FROM " SELF-RELIANCE "

There is a time in every man's education when he arrives at the conviction that envy is ignorance; that imitation is suicide; that he must take himself for better for worse as his portion; that though the wide universe is full of good, no kernel of nourishing corn can come to him but through his toil bestowed on that plot of ground which is given him to till. The power which resides in him is new in nature, and none but he knows what he can do, nor does he know until he has tried. . . .

Society everywhere is in conspiracy against the manhood of every one of its members. Society is a joint-stock company, in which the members agree for the better securing of his bread to each shareholder, to surrender the liberty and culture of the eater. The virtue in most request is conformity. Self-reliance is its aversion. It loves not realities and creators, but names and customs.

Whoso would be a man, must be a nonconformist. He who would gather immortal palms must not be hindered by the name of goodness, but must explore if it be goodness. Nothing is at last sacred but the integrity of your own mind. Absolve you to yourself, and you shall have the suffrage of the world. . . .

A foolish consistency is the hobgoblin of little minds, adored by little statesmen and philosophers and divines. With consistency a great soul has simply nothing to do. He may as well concern himself with his shadow on the wall. Speak what you think now in hard words, and tomorrow speak what tomorrow thinks in hard words again, though it contradict everything you said today. " Ah, so you shall be sure to be misunderstood." Is it so bad, then, to be misunderstood? Pythagoras was misunderstood, and Socrates, and Jesus, and Luther, and Copernicus, and Galileo, and Newton, and every pure and wise spirit that ever took flesh. To be great is to be misunderstood. . . .

The civilized man has built a coach, but has lost the use of his feet. He is supported on crutches, but lacks so much support of muscle. He has got a fine Geneva watch, but he has lost the skill to tell the hour by the sun. A Greenwich nautical almanac he has, and so being sure of the information when he wants it, the man in the street does not know a star in the sky. The solstice he does not observe; the equinox he knows as little; and the whole bright calendar of the year is without a dial in his mind.

His note-books impair his memory; his libraries overload his wit; the insurance-office increases the number of accidents; and it may be a question whether machinery does not encumber; whether we have not lost by refinement some energy, by a Christianity entrenched in establishments and forms some vigor of wild virtue. For every stoic was a stoic; but in Christendom, where is the Christian?

SUGGESTIONS FOR STUDY

1. Vocabulary: *Nature*, profane; *Friendship*, dissimulation, paradox, ingenuity, reiterated; *Compensation*, faculty; *Self-Reliance*, integrity, nonconformist, hobgoblin.

2. Name two or three persons conspicuous in public life today who you think could be called gentlemen according to Emerson's definition. Name two or three who could not. Defend your answers.

3. What difference is there between a friend as Emerson defines one and a friend in the common use of the word as an acquaintance? Do you think that most school friendships stand the test of Emerson's definition?

4. Give examples from your own experience to illustrate some of the general statements made about compensation. Would you agree with Emerson that there are *always* compensations in life? Give illustrations to prove your point. (See poem on compensation, p. 537.)

5. By what kind of people is Emerson's message of self-reliance most needed? Do you feel that it is needed in your high school? Is it needed generally in the country today? Prove your points by examples.

6. What dangers would there be to society if Emerson's words were taken too literally? From what you know of Emerson do you think he is sanctioning law-breaking? Why or why not?

7. Look up the lives of the great men mentioned at the end of the selection to find out in what ways they were misunderstood. Suggest other names of great men in history today who have been misunderstood.

8. Consider, not necessarily for class discussion, but in your own mind, ways in which Emerson's ideas in any of these essays might enter into your own attitudes or actions.

FOR FURTHER READING

If you have found the paragraphs from the essays challenging, try reading the entire essays. Others which might interest you if you like these are " Experience," " Character," " Politics," " Heroism," " Love," " The American Scholar." If you find the essays too difficult, you might enjoy *The Heart of Emerson's Journals*, where you will find bits of his philosophy interspersed with the daily happenings of his life.

For his poetry, see p. 535.

BRUTE NEIGHBORS

By HENRY DAVID THOREAU (1817–1862)

One of Emerson's friends (and indeed in the sense he meant in his essay) was Henry David Thoreau, a native of Concord. At one time Thoreau was also Emerson's gardener, thus demonstrating the simple democratic life of the village. Of course he was no ordinary gardener. By education he was a Harvard graduate; by inherited trade, a pencil maker; by disposition, the most complete illustration imaginable of Emerson's theory of independence and self-reliance. He did what he wanted when he wanted — read, studied, lectured, surveyed land, carpentered, tutored, helped to edit Emerson's paper the *Dial,* roamed up into Maine or Canada or out west, and occasionally fell back on pencil making. Once while in Minnesota he just naturally failed to appear at a reception given in his honor. In the light of ordinary social standards he may seem queer, but there is something delightfully refreshing in the simple naturalness and complete independence of the man.

Lover of freedom though he was, he once went to jail rather than pay a tax of which he disapproved. The story goes that Emerson called at the jail, and addressing him through the window said, " David, aren't you ashamed to be inside those bars? " Thoreau replied, " Mr. Emerson, aren't you ashamed to be *outside* these bars? " To the prisoner's great annoyance his relatives paid the tax for him and he was freed.

In 1854 Thoreau made an experiment in living in the woods which has become so famous that many people think of him as a hermit who spent all his life in the woods. On the contrary, the experiment lasted only two years, and during that period he made frequent excursions into town. Walden Pond, a beautiful little lake with high wooded shores, is only a few miles from Concord. Here Thoreau retired and built himself a hut for the purpose of having leisure and solitude for writing. Incidentally he proved that the money expenditure for giving himself a happy life was exceedingly small. " Most of the luxuries," he said, " and many of the so-called comforts of life, are not only not indispensable, but positive hindrances to the elevation of mankind." His carefully kept accounts show a cost of $28.12½ for the hut itself, and during eight months $8.74 for food, $8.40¾ for clothes, and $2.00 for oil and household utensils. He could earn a life of leisure by short periods of toil. " It is not necessary," he said, " that a man should earn his living by the sweat of his brow, unless he sweats easier than I do." Of course, he had no wife and children, which makes a difference; besides, the time was the middle of the nineteenth century.

The following extract from the book written about his experiment, *Walden,* shows the thoughtful observations he made of the wood life about him. He was the first of our American school of nature writers (except for Audubon, the student of birds). Not quite a scientific naturalist like his successors John Muir and William Beebe, Thoreau emphasized rather the philosophical basis of simple outdoor living.

It is remarkable how many creatures live wild and free though secret in the woods, and still sustain themselves in the neighborhood of towns, suspected by hunters only. How retired the otter manages to live here! He grows to be four feet long, as big as a small boy, perhaps without any human being getting a glimpse of him. I formerly saw the raccoon in the woods behind where my house is built, and probably still heard their whinnering at night. Commonly I rested an hour or two in the shade at noon, after planting, and ate my lunch, and read a little by a spring which was the source of a swamp and of a brook, oozing from under Brister's Hill, half a mile from my field. The approach to this was through a succession of descending grassy hollows, full of young pitch pines, into a larger wood about the swamp. There, in a very secluded and shaded spot, under a spreading white pine, there was yet a clean, firm sward to sit on. I had dug out the spring and made a well of clear gray water, where I could dip up a pailful without roiling it, and thither I went for this purpose almost every day in midsummer, when the pond was warmest. Thither, too, the woodcock led her brood, to probe the mud for worms, flying but a foot above them down the bank, while they ran in a troop beneath; but at last, spying me, she would leave her young and circle round and round me, nearer and nearer till within four or five feet, pretending broken wings and legs, to attract my attention, and get off her young, who would already have taken up their march, with faint, wiry peep, single file through the swamp, as she directed. Or I heard the peep of the young when I could not see the parent bird. There too the turtle doves sat over the spring, or fluttered from bough to bough of the soft white pines over my head; or the red squirrel, coursing down the nearest bough, was particularly familiar and inquisitive. You only need sit still long enough in some attractive spot in the woods that all its inhabitants may exhibit themselves to you by turns.

I was witness to events of a less peaceful character. One day when I went out to my wood-pile, or rather my pile of stumps, I observed two large ants, the one red, the other much larger, nearly half an inch long, and black, fiercely contending with one another. Having once got hold they never let go, but struggled and wrestled and rolled on the chips incessantly. Looking farther, I was surprised to find that the chips were covered with such combatants, that it was not a *duellum* [1] but a *bellum,* a war between two races of ants, the red always pitted against the black, and frequently two red ones to one black. The legions of these Myrmidons [2] covered all the hills and vales in my wood-yard, and the ground was already strewn with the dead and dying, both red and black. It was the only battle which I have ever witnessed, the only battle-field I ever trod while the battle was raging; internecine war; the red republicans on the one hand, and the black imperialists on the other. On every side they were engaged in deadly combat, yet without any noise that I could hear, and human soldiers never fought so resolutely. I watched a couple that were fast locked in each other's embraces, in a little sunny valley amid the chips, now at noonday prepared to fight till the sun went down, or life went out. The smaller red champion had fastened himself like a vice to his adversary's front, and through all the tumblings on that field never for an instant ceased to gnaw at one of his feelers near the root, having already caused the other to go by the board; while the stronger black one dashed him from side to side, and, as I saw on looking nearer, had already divested him of several of his members. They fought with more pertinacity than bulldogs. Neither manifested the least disposition to retreat. It was evident that their battle-cry was " Conquer or die." In the meanwhile there came along a single red ant on the hillside of this valley, evidently full of excitement, who either had dispatched his foe, or had not yet taken part in the battle; probably the latter, for he had lost none of his limbs; whose mother had charged him to return with his shield or upon it. Or perchance he was some Achilles,[3] who had nourished his wrath apart, and had now come to avenge or rescue his Patroclus. He saw this unequal combat from afar — for the blacks were nearly twice the size of the red — he drew near with rapid pace till he stood on his guard within half an inch of the combatants; then, watching his opportunity, he sprang upon the black warrior, and commenced his operations near the root of his right fore leg,

[1] A duel. *Bellum:* a war.   [2] The followers of Achilles in the Trojan war.
[3] In the *Iliad,* Achilles, the Greek hero, is represented as sulking in his tent over a hurt to his pride, but when his best friend, Patroclus, is killed, he forgets his wrath and re-enters the battle in his desire for vengeance.

leaving the foe to select among his own members; and so there were three united for life, as if a new kind of attraction had been invented which put all other locks and cements to shame. I should not have wondered by this time to find that they had their respective musical bands stationed on some eminent chip, and playing their national airs the while, to excite the slow and cheer the dying combatants. I was myself excited somewhat even as if they had been men. The more you think of it, the less the difference. And certainly there is not the fight recorded in Concord history, at least, if in the history of America, that will bear a moment's comparison with this, whether for the numbers engaged in it, or for the patriotism and heroism displayed. For numbers and for carnage it was an Austerlitz or Dresden.[4] Concord Fight [5]! Two killed on the patriots' side, and Luther Blanchard wounded! Why, here every ant was a Buttrick — " Fire! for God's sake, fire! " — and thousands shared the fate of Davis and Hosmer.[6] There was not one hireling there. I have no doubt that it was a principle they fought for, as much as our ancestors, and not to avoid a three-penny tax on their tea; and the results of this battle will be as important and memorable to those whom it concerns as those of the battle of Bunker Hill, at least.

I took up the chip on which the three I have particularly described were struggling, carried it into my house, and placed it under a tumbler on my window-sill, in order to see the issue. Holding a microscope to the first-mentioned red ant, I saw that, though he was assiduously gnawing at the near fore leg of his enemy, having severed his remaining feeler, his own breast was all torn away, exposing what vitals he had there to the jaws of the black warrior, whose breastplate was apparently too thick for him to pierce; and the dark carbuncles of the sufferer's eyes shone with ferocity such as war only could excite. They struggled half an hour longer under the tumbler, and when I looked again the black soldier had severed the heads of his foes from their bodies, and the still living heads were hanging on either side of him like ghastly trophies at his saddle-bow, still apparently as

---

4 Battles of Napoleon, attended by terrible loss of life. In the former, 42,000 were killed; in the latter between 7,000 and 8,000.

5 The battle of Concord, which with that of Lexington opened the American Revolution.

6 Natives of Concord participating in the fight, the latter two being the only ones killed.

firmly fastened as ever, and he was endeavoring with feeble struggles, being without feelers and with only the remnant of a leg, and I know not how many other wounds, to divest himself of them; which at length, after half an hour more, he accomplished. I raised the glass, and he went off over the window-sill in that crippled state. Whether he finally survived that combat, and spent the remainder of his days in some Hôtel des Invalides,[7] I do not know; but I thought that his industry would not be worth much thereafter. I never learned which party was victorious, nor the cause of the war; but I felt for the rest of that day as if I had had my feelings excited and harrowed by witnessing the struggle, the ferocity and carnage, of a human battle before my door.

Kirby and Spence [8] tell us that the battles of ants have long been celebrated and the date of them recorded, though they say that Huber is the only modern author who appears to have witnessed them. "Aeneas Sylvius," say they, "after giving a very circumstantial account of one contested with great obstinacy by a great and small species on the trunk of a pear tree," adds that "'this action was fought in the pontificate of Eugenius the Fourth, in the presence of Nicholas Pistoriensis, an eminent lawyer, who related the whole history of the battle with the greatest fidelity.' A similar engagement between great and small ants is recorded by Olaus Magnus, in which the small ones, being victorious, are said to have buried the bodies of their own soldiers, but left those of their giant enemies a prey to the birds. This event happened previous to the expulsion of the tyrant Christiern the Second from Sweden." The battle which I witnessed took place in the Presidency of Polk, five years before the passage of Webster's Fugitive-Slave Bill.

Many a village Bose, fit only to course a mud-turtle in a victualling cellar, sported his heavy quarters in the woods, without the knowledge of his master, and ineffectually smelled at old fox burrows and woodchucks' holes; led perchance by some slight cur which nimbly threaded the wood, and might still inspire a natural terror in its denizens; — now far behind his guide, barking like a canine bull toward some small squirrel which had treed itself for scrutiny, then, cantering off, bending the bushes with

7 Famous veterans' home in Paris.
8 English naturalists of the early nineteenth century. Huber was a Swiss naturalist of the same time. The other names given are of persons who lived in the fifteenth century.

his weight, imagining that he is on the track of some stray member of the jerbilla family. Once I was surprised to see a cat walking along the stony shore of the pond, for they rarely wander so far from home. The surprise was mutual. Nevertheless the most domestic cat, which has lain on a rug all her days, appears quite at home in the woods, and, by her sly and stealthy behavior, proves herself more native there than the regular inhabitants. Once, when berrying, I met with a cat with young kittens in the woods, quite wild, and they all, like their mother, had their backs up and were fiercely spitting at me. A few years before I lived in the woods there was what was called a " winged cat " in one of the farm-houses in Lincoln nearest the pond, Mr. Gilian Baker's. When I called to see her in June, 1842, she was gone a-hunting in the woods, as was her wont (I am not sure whether it was a male or female, and so use the more common pronoun), but her mistress told me that she came into the neighborhood a little more than a year before, in April, and was finally taken into their house; that she was of a dark brownish-gray color, with a white spot on her throat, and white feet, and had a large bushy tail like a fox; that in the winter the fur grew thick and flatted out along her sides, forming strips ten or twelve inches long by two and a half wide, and under her chin like a muff, the upper side loose, the under matted like felt, and in the spring these appendages dropped off. They gave me a pair of her " wings," which I keep still. There is no appearance of a membrane about them. Some thought it was part flying squirrel or some other wild animal, which is not impossible, for, according to naturalists, prolific hybrids have been produced by the union of the marten and domestic cat. This would have been the right kind of cat for me to keep, if I had kept any; for why should not a poet's cat be winged as well as his horse?

In the fall the loon (*Colymbus glacialis*) came, as usual, to moult and bathe in the pond, making the woods ring with his wild laughter before I had risen. At rumor of his arrival all the Mill-dam sportsmen are on the alert, in gigs and on foot, two by two and three by three, with patent rifles and conical balls and spyglasses. They come rustling through the woods like autumn leaves, at least ten men to one loon. Some station themselves on this side of the pond, some on that, for the poor bird cannot be omnipresent; if he dive here he must come up there. But now the kind October wind rises, rustling the leaves and rippling the surface of the water, so that no loon can be heard or seen, though his foes sweep the pond with spyglasses, and make the woods resound with their discharges. The waves generously rise and dash angrily, taking sides with all water-fowl, and our sportsmen must beat a retreat to town and shop and unfinished jobs. But they were too often successful. When I went to get a pail of water early in the morning I frequently saw this stately bird sailing out of my cove within a few rods. If I endeavored to overtake him in a boat, in order to see how he would maneuver, he would dive and be completely lost, so that I did not discover him again, sometimes, till the latter part of the day. But I was more than a match for him on the surface. He commonly went off in a rain.

As I was paddling along the north shore one very calm October afternoon, for such days especially they settle on to the lakes, like the milkweed down, having looked in vain over the pond for a loon, suddenly one, sailing out from the shore toward the middle a few rods in front of me, set up his wild laugh and betrayed himself. I pursued with a paddle and he dived, but when he came up I was nearer than before. He dived again, but I miscalculated the direction he would take, and we were fifty rods apart when he came to the surface this time, for I had helped to widen the interval; and again he laughed long and loud, and with more reason than before. He maneuvered so cunningly that I could not get within half a dozen rods of him. Each time, when he came to the surface, turning his head this way and that, he coolly surveyed the water and the land, and apparently chose his course so that he might come up where there was the widest expanse of water and at the greatest distance from the boat. It was surprising how quickly he made up his mind and put his resolve into execution. He led me at once to the widest part of the pond, and could not be driven from it. While he was thinking one thing in his brain, I was endeavoring to divine his thought in mine. It was a pretty game, played on the smooth surface of the pond, a man against a loon. Suddenly your adversary's checker disappears beneath the board, and the problem is to place yours nearest to where his will appear again. Sometimes he would come up unexpectedly on the opposite side of me, having apparently passed directly under the boat. So long-winded was he and so unweariable, that when he had swum farthest he would immediately plunge again, nevertheless; and then no wit could divine where in the deep pond, beneath the smooth surface, he might be speeding his way like a fish, for he had time and ability to visit the bottom of the pond in its deepest part. It is said that loons have been caught in the New York lakes eighty feet beneath the surface, with hooks set for trout — though Walden is deeper than that. How surprised must the fishes be to see this ungainly visitor from another sphere speeding his way amid their schools! Yet he appeared to know his course as surely under water as on the surface, and swam much faster there. Once or twice I saw a ripple where he approached the surface, just put his head out to reconnoitre, and instantly dived again. I found that it was as well for me to rest on my oars and wait his reappearing as to endeavor to calculate where he would rise; for again and again, when I was straining my eyes over the surface one way, I would suddenly be startled by his unearthly laugh behind me. But why, after displaying so much cunning, did he invariably betray himself the moment he came up by that loud laugh? Did not his white breast enough betray him? He was indeed a silly loon, I thought. I could commonly hear the plash of the water when he came up, and so also detected him. But after an hour he seemed as fresh as ever, dived as willingly, and swam yet farther than at first. It was surprising to see how serenely he sailed off with unruffled breast when he came to the surface, doing all the work with his webbed feet beneath. His usual note was this demoniac laughter, yet somewhat like that of a water-fowl; but occasionally, when he had balked me most successfully and come up a long way off, he uttered a long-drawn unearthly howl, probably more like that of a wolf than any bird; as when a beast puts his muzzle to the ground and deliberately howls. This was his looning — perhaps the wildest sound that is ever heard here, making the woods ring far and wide. I concluded that he laughed in derision of my efforts confident of his own resources. Though the sky was by this time overcast, the pond was so smooth that I could see where he broke the surface when I did not hear him. His white breast, the stillness of the air, and the smoothness of the water were all against him. At length, having come up fifty rods off, he uttered one of those prolonged howls, as if calling on the god of loons to aid him, and immediately there came a wind from the east and rippled the surface, and filled the whole air with misty rain, and I was impressed as if it were the prayer of the loon answered, and his god was angry with me; and so I left him disappearing far away on the tumultuous surface.

For hours, in fall days, I watched the ducks cunningly tack and veer and hold the middle of the pond, far from the sportsman; tricks which they will have less need to practice in Louisiana bayous. When compelled to rise they would sometimes circle round and round and over the pond at a considerable height, from which they could easily see to other ponds and the river, like black motes in the sky; and, when I thought they had gone off thither long since, they would settle down by a slanting flight of a quarter of a mile on to a distant part which was left free; but what beside safety they got by sailing in the middle of Walden I do not know, unless they love its water for the same reason that I do.

SUGGESTIONS FOR STUDY

1. Make a list of all the different living creatures which Thoreau has observed as indicated in this chapter. Do his observations seem to you wide or limited?

2. In the battle of the ants, how does the author make the ants seem human? How does he show his familiarity with history? With writings on natural science?

3. What evidence do you find of his attitude toward the hunters who came to Walden Pond? It would be interesting to have an informal class debate as to whether hunting for sport is justifiable.

4. When Thoreau records so exactly the time of his observation of the battle of the ants, do you think he was being serious or facetious?

FOR FURTHER READING

Walden, or Life in the Woods
A Week on the Concord and Merrimac Rivers
The Maine Woods
Cape Cod
The Heart of Thoreau's Journals. Edited by Odell Shepard.
See also page 340 in biography section.

VALENTINE VAGARIES

By Lafcadio Hearn (1850–1904)

Modern times have seen few more picturesque figures than Lafcadio Hearn. Born of an Irish father and a Greek mother on the island of Leucadia in the Ionian sea, and educated in England, he came to this country at the age of nineteen. He was by nature inclined to be solitary and found it difficult to gain a livelihood by writing. He went to Cincinnati and there worked at all sorts of jobs, including that of general houseman in a boarding house, but eventually he became connected with the *Enquirer* of that city. The articles he wrote were not signed and it is only recently (1924) that many of these writings were culled from the files of the newspaper. " Valentine Vagaries " is one of them, appearing there February 14, 1875. His later activities took him to New Orleans, and finally to Japan, where he became a naturalized Japanese and married a native woman. He changed his name to Yakumo Koizumi, secured a position as professor of English in the University of Tokio, and wrote many books, most of them having to do with his adopted country.

The antique loveliness of paganism is not yet dead, and today is sacred to Cytherea, the snow-limbed goddess, whose subtle sway, immortal as her beauty, will cease only with the death of the human race. Her altar fires died out in pale ashes nearly two thousand years ago; and the dust of her Cyprian and Paphian Roman worshipers mingles with the dust of her temples; and the colder sunshine of our modern world no longer kisses her graceful statues on the public places of modern cities. But the world today still bears her rosy yoke, and seems in nowise inclined to rebel. This is her festival — her beloved pagan festival, ancient as the age which taught that birds sought their mates upon this day of the month. Nominally this day is sacred to St. Valentine. But St. Valentine retired from the scene before the close of the eighteenth century, finding that naughty Aphrodite was altogether too much for him. No one ever finds the picture of the saint upon a love missive in these days; the image of some little-winged love-god, the mischievous son of Venus, is now stamped upon all.

But it is on the eve of St. Valentine that the fair goddess most strongly asserts her sway, descending to thrill the heart of the sleeping world with love dreams and love memories. It is the evening of all evenings, when dusty drawers are carefully opened; and faded letters, with the ghost of sweet perfume still clinging to them, are read by the flickering firelight; and a little lock of hair, tied about with soft threads of silk, is removed from its sacred resting-place in some jeweled locket, to be reverently kissed. This, too, is the evening of all evenings when lonely people dream of ideal homes, and strive to read their future fate in the fantastic light of dying fires; while the sleigh-bells tinkle without, and the white moonlight glitters upon the crystal leaves of those fairy frost trees which Winter loves to paint upon window-panes. The delicious rustle of a silken dress; the gentle mesmerism of soft eyes; the electric thrill of glossy curls touching one's cheek, together with the pleasant pressure of some dainty young head on one's shoulder; the clear, full curve of a rosy cheek, melting into the snow of a white neck; the sweet music of a silvery voice; the caress of a gentle little hand playing with one's beard — these are all appropriate subjects of meditation for St. Valentine's Eve.

The remembrance of one's first valentine, and the pleasurable emotions of mingled surprise and gladness and wonder which its receipt occasioned, is very apt to recur at this season of the year. It is the great dusting-day in Memory's most sacred chambers, when the outlines of long past scenes become once more vivid, and we again find ourselves humming melodies heard but once years before and forgotten; and the image of the first sweetheart, grown rather dingy and dusty for want of faithful attention, is again brushed up and retouched in spots where the colors had faded away. Many a one who peeped in his mirror last evening and found a sprinkling of gray in his beard despaired of making a home in the remote future, and cast a package of faded letters in the fire that he might enjoy the dismal pleasure of beholding his hopes and his romances die out in ashes. For who can deny that there is a real pleasure in dwelling upon one's sorrows, and fancying one's self the most miserable creature in the universe? But these are few. Young blood ever sparkles with warm bright hopes, and thousands of hearts beat somewhat faster from the mere anticipation of what might happen when certain love missives reached their destination. But today will be the Day of Blushes, when a thousand maidenly cheeks will wear the transient ruddiness that Venus loves. May the fair goddess grant that all honest hopes born of the hour be realized, and all evil wiles be baffled! Jove was wont to laugh at lovers' perjuries, but then Jove is dead; and the fairest of the Olympian immortals is alone truly immortal.

SUGGESTIONS FOR STUDY

1. Vocabulary: Cyprian, Paphian, Cytherea, Aphrodite.
2. You will find it interesting to look up the history of Valentine Day.
3. Also read or re-read Charles Lamb's " Valentine's Day " in the *Essays of Elia.*
4. What is the chief point made by the author?
5. How is the Saint's day observed by modern youth? Is the author's point still true? Or not?

FOR FURTHER READING

Glimpses of Unfamiliar Japan   *Out of the East*
Kokoro   *Fantastics and Other Fancies*

THE BUBBLE REPUTATION [1]

By WALTER PRICHARD EATON (1878–   )

A native of Malden, Massachusetts, and an alumnus of Harvard University, Walter Prichard Eaton is known principally as a dramatic critic, having served in that capacity on the New York *Tribune,* New York *Sun,* and the *American Magazine.* In his off hours he writes familiar essays for his own enjoyment — and the reader comes in for his share. Says Mr. Eaton in the foreword of one of his volumes: " It is not a little unfortunate that no one can attempt the essay form nowadays, more especially that type of essay which is personal, reminiscent, ' an open letter to whom it may concern,' without being accused of trying to write like Charles Lamb. Of course if we were ever accused of succeeding that would be another story! " Thus does he illustrate one of the prime requisites for the light essayist, the ability to poke a bit of fun at himself. The following essay from *Penguin Persons and Peppermints* has a pleasant intermingling of humor, irony, and philosophy.

A great dramatist is authority for the statement that —

" The evil that men do lives after them;
The good is oft interred with their bones." [2]

[1] The title is part of the famous " Seven Ages of Man " speech from *As You Like It.* " A soldier . . . seeking the bubble reputation, Even in the cannon's mouth."
[2] The quotation is from Mark Antony's famous funeral oration over the body of Julius Caesar in Shakespeare's play of that name.

That is no doubt in a measure true; yet it would be grossly unfair to blame personally certain great ones of the past for the evil that has lived after them and borne their names. For instance, it may be doubted whether Louis XIV of France was all that he should have been. His private life would hardly have escaped censure in Upper Montclair, N. J., or West Newton, Mass., and his public acts were not always calculated to promote social justice and universal brotherhood. But to blame him for all the gilt furniture which has ever since stood around the walls of hotel ballrooms and borne his name is a libel even on that lax and luxurious monarch. Yet such is his fate. You who are familiar with history, I who know next to nothing about it, are alike in this — when we hear the words *Louis XIV* we do not think of a great monarch with a powdered wig and a powdered mistress, of magnificent fountains and courtiers and ladies dancing the gavotte, of a brilliant court and striking epoch. Not at all. We think, both of us, of a gilt chair with a brocaded seat (slightly worn), and maybe a sofa to match. If you say that you don't, I must politely but firmly — well, differ with you.

Alas! poor Louis XIV was not the only worthy (or unworthy) of the past who has come down to the present, not as a personality but as a piece of furniture, a dog, a boot, or some other equally ignominious thing. Speaking of furniture, there's the Morris chair. The man who made the Morris chair was a great and good man — not because he made the Morris chair, but in spite of it! He composed haunting poems, he wrote lovely prose romances of the far-off days of knights and ladyes and magic spells, such as that hight *The Water of the Wondrous Isles,* a right brave book mayhap you have not perused, to your exceeding great loss, for beautiful it is and fair to read and full of the mighty desire of a man for a maid. Beside all this, he printed lovely books by other writers, and designed wall-paper, and painted pictures, and thundered against the deadening effect on men of mechanical toil, and in social theories was far in advance of his age. Such a man was William Morris — known today to the mass of mankind for one of the most accursed articles of furniture ever devised by human ingenuity gone astray! Every day, in a million homes, men and women sit in Morris chairs (made by machinery) and read Robert W. Chambers and Florence Barclay. Such, alas, is fame!

Then there was Queen Anne [3] — in many respects an estimable

[3] Queen of England, 1702–1714.

woman, though leaving much to be desired as a monarch. She had her Rooseveltian virtues, being the mother of seventeen children (none of whom lived to grow beyond infancy, to be sure) ; and she had what the world just now has come to regard as the monarchical vice of autocracy. In her reign science and literature flourished, though without much aid from her, and the English court buzzed with intrigue and politics. But speak the name Queen Anne aloud, and then tell me the picture you get. Is it a picture of the lady or her period? Is it a picture of Pope and Dryden sitting in a London coffee-house? No, it is not — that is, unless you are a very learned, or a very young, person. It is a picture of a horrible architectural monstrosity built about thirty or forty years ago in any American city or suburb, and bearing certain vague resemblances to a home for human beings. Whatever else Queen Anne was, she was not an architect, and she wasn't to blame for those houses, any more than she was to blame for Pope's " Essay on Man." But that doesn't count. She gets the blame, just the same. She is known forever now by those gables and that gingerbread, those shingles and stains.

She had a predecessor on the English throne by the name of Charles. Like Louis in France, he wasn't all he should have been, and there were those in his own day who didn't entirely approve of him. But it wasn't because of his dogs. However, if you mention King Charles now, it is a dog you think of — a small, eary dog, with somewhat splay feet and a seventeenth-century monarchical preference for the society of ladies and the softest cushion. Maybe the royal gentleman didn't deserve anything better of posterity; but, anyhow, that's what he got.

St. Bernhard [4] fared better. If one had to be remembered by a dog, what better dog could he select, save possibly an Airedale? Big, strong, faithful, wise, true to type for centuries, the most reliable of God's creatures (including Man by courtesy in that category), the St. Bernhard is a monument for — well, not for a king, and a king didn't get him; for a saint, rather. It is doubtful if the old monk is playing any lamentations on his harp.

But I'm not so sure about that peerless military leader, General A. E. Burnside.[5] When you have risen to lead an army

[4] Often spelled Bernard, a French monk of the twelfth century, one of the most eloquent preachers and influential abbots of his day.

[5] A general in the American Civil War. These whiskers, which came to be known as " side-burns," are now practically obsolete.

corps against your country's foes, when you have commanded men and sat your horse for a statue on the grounds of the state capitol or the intersection of Main and State Streets, it really is rather rough to be remembered for your whiskers. Of course, as a wit remarked of Shaw, no man is responsible for his relatives, but his whiskers are his own fault. Nevertheless, how is a great general to know that his military exploits will be forgotten, while his whiskers thunder down the ages, as it were, progressing in the course of time with the changing fashions from bank presidents to Presbyterian elders, and finally to stage butlers? At last even the stage butlers are shaving clean, and a stroke of the razor wipes out a military reputation, blasts a general's immortality! Fame is a fickle jade.

An artistic reputation lasts longer, and resists the barber, proving the superiority of the arts to militarism. "Van Dyke" is still a generally familiar appellation and sounds the same, no matter which way you spell it. Of course, there's no rhyme nor reason in it — artist and whiskers should be spelled the same way. Only they're not. "Something ought to be done about it." However, to resume. If you tell me John Jones has a Vandyke, I don't visualize John as an art-collector standing in his gallery in rapt contemplation of a masterpiece by the great Flemish painter. I visualize him as a man with a certain type of beard. I may later think of the master who put these beards upon his portraits. Then again, I may not. Exactly the same would be true if I told you John Jones had a Vandyke, instead of the other way about. Don't contradict me — you know it's so. It is nearly as difficult today to own a Van Dyke canvas as it is to paint one, but anybody can raise a Vandyke beard. In fact, many still do, and thus keep the master's memory green. "By their whiskers ye shall know them."

A military reputation, as we have already proved by the case of General Burnside, is a precarious thing. How many patrons of Atlantic City, I wonder, know the hero of the wars in the Low Countries and his greatest triumph by a certain hotel [6] on the Board Walk, and would be hard put to say which half of the hyphenated name was the general and which the battle? Then there was Wellington, who at one time threatened to be remem-

[6] The Marlborough-Blenheim. The Duke of Marlborough was a famous general of Queen Anne's reign who defeated the French at Blenheim in Bavaria in 1704.

bered for his boots, and Blücher [7] who still is remembered for his. A certain Massachusetts statesman (anybody elected to the Massachusetts House of Representatives is a statesman) once said that the greatest triumph of Napoleon was when Theodore Roosevelt stood silent at his tomb. This is witty, but like most witty sayings, not quite true. It was a great triumph, of course, but rather spectacular. The greatest triumphs are not showy. What actually proves Napoleon's greatness is the fact that he is still remembered as a commander after generations have selected from the tray of French pastry the delectable and indigestible morsel of sugar, flour, and lard that bears his name. To have a toothsome article of food named after you, and then to be still remembered for your actual achievements, is the ultimate test of human greatness. Only a Napoleon can meet it. Even Washington might not now be known as the father of his country if his pie had been a better one.

Who was King, for instance? Was he the cook, or the man cooked for? I fancy I knew once, but I have forgotten. But chicken à la King will live to perpetuate his name as long as there are chickens to be eaten and men to eat them. Even Sardou,[8] spectacular dramatist, for all his *Toscas* and *Fédoras* (and ten to one you think of Fedora as a hat!) lives for me, a dramatic critic, by virtue of eggs Victorien Sardou, a never-to-be-too-much-enjoyed concoction secured at the old Brevoort House in New York. He may actually have invented this recipe himself, for he was a great lover of the pleasures of the table. If so, it was his masterpiece. An egg is poached on the tender heart of an artichoke, and garnished with a peculiar yellow sauce, topped with a truffle. Around all four sides are laid little bunches of fresh asparagus tips. What is *Tosca* compared to this?

Then, of course, there was Mr. Baldwin. Who was Mr. Baldwin? The people of Wilmington, Mass., know, because there is a monument to the original tree in that town. But we don't know, any more than we know who Mr. Bartlett was, when we eat one of his pears, or Mr. Logan, father of the wine-red berry. In this case the Scripture is indeed verified, that by their fruits shall ye know them.

[7] The Duke of Wellington was the English general who defeated Napoleon in the battle of Waterloo, 1815. Blücher was another general in the same battle who headed the Prussian allies of the English.

[8] A French dramatist (1831–1908) whose many plays have been widely translated and acted in other countries.

Two or three times a year my wife gets certain clothes of mine from the closet and combs them for moths, hangs them flapping in the breeze for a while, and puts them back. Among the lot is a garment once much worn by congressmen, church ushers, and wedding guests, known to the fashion editors as " frock coats," and to normal human beings as Prince Alberts. Doubtless, in

the flux of styles (like a pendulum, styles swing forth and back again), the Prince Albert will once more be correct, and my wife's labor will not have been in vain, while the estimable consort of England's haircloth sofa and black-walnut bureau queen [9] will continue to be remembered of posterity by this outlandish garment. Poor man, after all, he achieved little else to be remembered by!

REMEMBERED BY THIS OUTLAND-
ISH GARMENT

And as for the queen herself, she will be remembered by a state of mind. Already " mid-Victorian " has little or nothing to do with Victoria, and is losing its suggestion, even, of a time-period. It is coming to stand for a mental and moral attitude — in fact, for priggishness and moral timidity. Queen Victoria was a great and good lady, and her home life was, as the two women so clearly pointed out when they left the theater, totally different from that of Cleopatra. But she is going to give her name to a mental attitude, just the same, even as the Philistines and the Puritans. It pays to pick the period you queen it over rather carefully. Elizabeth had better luck. To be Elizabethan is to be everything gay and dashing and out-doory and adventuresome, with insatiable curiosity and the gift of song. Of course, Shakespeare, Drake, Raleigh, ought to have the credit — but they don't get it, any more than Tennyson comes in on the Victorian discredit. The head that wears a crown may well lie uneasy.

[9] Victoria, Queen of England from 1837 to 1901. Her husband was Prince Albert of Saxe-Coburg-Gotha. He was known as the Prince Consort and had no recognized part in the government.

The memory of many a man has been perpetuated, all un-wittingly, by the manufacturers and advertising agencies. Here I tread on dangerous ground, but surely I shall not be accused of commercial collusion if I point out that so " generously good " a philanthropist as George W. Childs became a name literally in the mouth of thousands. He became a cigar. Then there was Lord Lister.[10] He, too, has become a name in the mouths of thousands — as a mouth wash. And how about the only daughter of the Prophet? [11] Fatima was her name.

Who was Lord Raglan, or was he a lord? He is a kind of overcoat sleeve now. Who was Mr. Mackintosh? Was it Lord Brougham,[12] too? Gasoline has extinguished his immortality. Gladstone [13] has become a bag, Gainsborough [14] is a hat. The beautiful Madame Pompadour,[15] beloved of kings, is a kind of hair-cut now. The Mikado of Japan is a joke, set to music, heavenly music, to be sure, but with its tongue in its angelic cheek. An operetta did that. You cannot think of the Mikado of Japan in terms of royal dignity. I defy you to try. Ko-ko and Katisha keep getting in the way, and you hear the pitty-pat of Yum-Yum's little feet, and the bounce of those elliptical billiard balls. Gilbert and Sullivan's operetta is perhaps the most potent document for democracy since the Communist Manifesto!

The other day I heard a woman say that she had got to begin banting. A nice verb, to bant, though not approved of by the dictionary, which scornfully terms it " humorous and colloquial." The humor, to be sure, is usually for other people, not for the person banting. Do you know, I wonder, the derivation of this word? It means, of course, to induce this too, too solid flesh to melt, by the careful avoidance of farinaceous, saccharine, and oily foods, and occasionally its meaning is stretched by the care-less to include also rolling on the bedroom floor fifteen times

[10] An English surgeon (1827–1912), the father of antiseptic surgery.
[11] Mohammed.
[12] The brougham named for him was a fashionable four-wheeled carriage drawn by two horses. The author is not quite right in saying that gasoline has extinguished his immortality, for there is a motor car modeled after the carriage which perpetuates his name.
[13] Famous prime minister under Queen Victoria.
[14] English portrait painter of the eighteenth century. His well-known por-trait of the Duchess of Devonshire wearing a large plumed hat gave rise to the term *Gainsborough hat*.
[15] Favorite of Louis XV of France in the eighteenth century.

before breakfast, and standing up twenty minutes after meals. Yet the word is derived from the name of William Banting, who was a London cabinet-maker. Cabinet-making is a worthy trade; indeed, it is one of the most appealing of all trades; in fact, it's not a trade, it's an art. I haven't a doubt that William made splendid furniture, especially chairs, for nobody appreciates a nice, roomy, strong chair like a fat man. I haven't a doubt that it was his ambition in life to be remembered for his furniture, even as the brothers Adam, as Chippendale, and Sheraton.[16] But it was not to be. In an unfortunate moment, William discovered that by eating fewer potatoes and cutting out two lumps of sugar from his tea he could take off some of the corpulence that troubled him. He told of his discovery — and the world knows him now as a method of getting number 44 ladies into a perfect 38. I have always felt sorry for William Banting. He is one of the tragic figures of history.

Of course, there are many more, if none other quite so poignant, but you must recall them for yourself. For some paragraphs now I have been working up to a climax of prophecy. I have been planning to predict what Kaiser William II will be noted for in the days that are to come. It seemed to me that would make rather a neat conclusion for this little essay. But, Gentle Reader, I've got to turn that job over to you, also. Not that the space is lacking, but after long and painful concentration I have been unable to think of anything bad enough. It may turn out that he will be known simply by the meek and nourishing kaiser roll on the breakfast table — the only surviving relic of a monarchical vocabulary in a peaceful and democratic universe. Perhaps, for him, that would be the bitterest fate of all, the ultimate irony.

SUGGESTIONS FOR STUDY

1. This essay is a serio-comic essay on fame. Can you think of other examples which prove the author's point?

2. Glance through the pages of some of our magazines which are heavily weighted with advertising and see how many commodities you can find which are named for famous people. Are there persons prominent in the world today whose names in future may be linked with something beside their legitimate title to fame? Give examples, or write a theme on the subject bringing Eaton's essay thoroughly up to date.

[16] English cabinet-makers of the eighteenth century.

FOR FURTHER READING

ON THE DRAMA

The American Stage of Today
At the New Theater and Others
Plays and Players
The Actor's Heritage
A Study of English Drama on the Stage

MISCELLANEOUS ESSAYS

Barn Doors and Byways
Green Trails and Upland Pastures
On the Edge of the Wilderness
Penguin Persons and Peppermints
Skyline Camps
A Bucolic Attitude

ONCE THERE WAS A FURNACE BOY

By CHARLES STEPHEN BROOKS (1878–   )

There are two points in common between Charles S. Brooks and the great English essayist Charles Lamb, who was born just about a hundred years earlier. One is their Christian name, and the other is the long servitude to business which preceded in each man's life the happy period of liberation from the office grind to give full devotion to writing.

Charles S. Brooks grew up in Cleveland, Ohio, graduated from Yale, and then naturally entered the printing firm which had been established by his family. After fifteen years of business life he retired and went to New York to engage in a literary career. Later he returned to Cleveland, for he says, " I like to live where people know me, where I do not need to explain myself, where I am accepted for what I am and not for what I do." Here he has done college teaching, built a little theater, and turned out numerous volumes, including a novel and several plays as well as his most characteristic form, the essay. His travels in England have formed the basis of some of his most delightful essays, but again we find the full flavor of the American scene, with reflections on the rapid changes in our manner of life, pictures of the Ohio country, and satires on the American strivings for bigness in everything. His style is distinctive, with well knit sentences, and he has an uncanny sense for the surprising but inevitably right word. The following essay is taken from *Like Summer's Cloud*.

It is lucky that nature proves a laggard in invention. With our restless enterprise it would push the stars forward near the earth and put reflectors on them. It would hang the clouds on a higher pole so that their curtain did not obscure the light. The moon, also, to a modern eye, is badly managed. Its movement is too eccentric. A man of shallow observation never knows its time of rising or in what quarter of the heavens it will appear. I am accustomed to catch it from my sleeping-porch, but it comes there on a whim. It grows ragged, also, through the month and lingers without profit until the sun is well advanced. It seems as if nature spent its ingenuity to light the day but left the night to shift for itself with a scheme of antiquated candles. And yet I think it lucky that nature is content with its outworn system, for something of the mystery of night is yet preserved. Even our theaters and movies with huge electric signs can do no more than hold at arm's length the amazing darkness in which we move. And on a housetop we are still the skippers of a black uncharted sea.

I was thinking of this lately and wondering if electricity had not taken much of the adventure out of life, out of childhood especially. Lately at a neighbor's, when the children were dispatched to bed, I could not detect in their eyes any of the half-fearful look of one who is about to encounter the mystery of darkness. They had but to snap a button at the foot of the stairs and follow a lighted path to bed. Only when safe and snug in the cavern of a blanket need the light go out. In common sense, of course, this is a better thing; but something — something slight, unexplainable and of cobweb texture is lost. Our houses are too secure to breed imagination. Their shadows are the cringing servants of a lamp, and their dark and ancient reign is done.

There are now no rooms of ticklish gloom with gas jets plugged and out of use, or with tipless jet that yields a bluish dreadful flame. No longer must an upper hallway be crossed with flickering candle that beckons to the shadows. There is no twilight beneath the stairs. The pantry, with spectral windows that chilled at bedtime our search for cookies, offers now no hidden nook for villainy. The flight of steps to the attic is innocence itself, and this dusty cavern underneath the roof is ceiled and set with harmless lamps.

Here once a bit of flooring had been removed — the wreckage of a plumber — and, by lying on the stomach and thrusting the head inside, one looked on a maze of pipes. A cambric theater was built about this trap in hopes that the genie of the lamp — for we planned Aladdin — might find it possible to descend within the hole. Here, also, when rain pattered on the slates and branches scratched the windows in a sudden gust, one fancied that his ship sailed furled against the tempest. On sunny days a shaft of light fell across the floor and revealed a thousand airplanes flying in the dust, but at night the attic was a place unspeakable. Did nature plan that we should always live in flaring light it would have fastened a chain upon the sun to hold its wandering foot. We shall see whether some touch of fancy that is bred in darkness may not have departed from our children.

Are there attics now where trunks and discarded furniture are piled, where the roof slopes off behind the clutter into undiscovered darkness? Do carpenters still leave holes where one may clamber above the rafters and sit in delight and fear? Are there broad upper shelves beneath the ceiling in clothes closets to which a child may climb on a narrowing ledge of projecting drawers and stow himself aloft like a pirate come ashore? Electricity has robbed childhood of a proper birthright.

CAREFUL NOT TO LOOK ACROSS MY SHOULDER

I was once the furnace boy, and I fetched the coal from a bin into which no daylight ever entered. It was a perilous spot even when the sun was up, but Egypt held not so black a night. It was my custom at the dangerous hour of nine o'clock to carry down a candle from the kitchen and to hold it in front to scatter the shadows at the turn. This tempted out an equal shadow at the rear, but I was careful not to look across my shoulder. The very flame crouched back for company as I walked as if it, too, feared encounter with the dark. At the foot of the stairs the gas meter ticked with sober haunted count, and a spark of red showed at the furnace door. I now set my candle on the stones with a drop of tallow to hold it upright and went about my stoking. But when I scooped the coal I often loosened the pile above and, when it rattled toward me, I retreated to the light for reassurance until the sound of it was done. It was a place to go on tiptoe, yet I cannot remember that it was all terror. A kind of wonder filled the basement in the night, and I descended softly from the kitchen with brave thoughts thumping in my heart.

And there was a hallway in the basement just off the laundry that led in darkness God knows where. Its forward end was piled in winter with the furniture that had been used upon the porch, and I have crawled on hands and knees through the crowded darkness hoping that it might issue on a cavern that ran beneath the city. A dim light entered from a grille and here, if anywhere, the Prisoner of Chillon [1] with a chain upon his ankle might thrust his nose for air. A window, also, had opened from the laundry to the yard; but a pantry had been built above and it was another door to undiscovered darkness. With such peril beneath the house, our sitting-room with lights and fire was a harbor from a storm. And down below, poking at the furnace with guttering candle, I heard the murmur of its voices and wondered how the family could sit in such security so thinly partitioned from the terrors of the dark.

But our houses now have banished danger; and children, although they tease to lengthen out the pleasures of the evening, go through placid hallways to bed.

SUGGESTIONS FOR STUDY

1. Do you agree that " Electricity has robbed childhood of a proper birthright "? Discuss.

2. Tell some of your own experiences in the dark.

3. Can you think of any modern improvements besides electricity which may have taken some of the romance out of life?

[1] In the sixteenth century Bonnivard, a Swiss patriot, was imprisoned for six years in the Castle of Chillon on Lake Geneva. His story has been made famous in a poem by Byron called " The Prisoner of Chillon," and the narrow dungeon that he is supposed to have occupied is still shown to visitors, along with the chains that bound him.

FOR FURTHER READING

Journeys to Bagdad   *A Thread of English Road*
There's Pippins and Cheese to Come   *Like Summer's Cloud*
Chimney-Pot Papers   *Roundabout to Canterbury*
Hints to Pilgrims   *Roads to the North*

VERMONT

By Dorothy Canfield Fisher (1879–   )

To read the essay which follows, we might suppose Dorothy Canfield Fisher to be a native of Vermont, but instead she was born and brought up in Lawrence, Kansas, where her father was president of the University. Later moves of her father took her to Ohio State University and Columbia University where she acquired B.A. and Ph.D. degrees, specialized in languages, wrote a textbook, and began her career as a short story writer. After her marriage to a former Columbia football captain, she and her husband chose to live on a farm near Arlington, Vermont, which has been their home ever since, except for periods of travel. During the World War, Mrs. Fisher accompanied her husband to France and did relief work among the wounded soldiers and the refugees, an experience reflected in her *Home Fires in France.* Mrs. Fisher's versatility is shown by the fact that she has done notable work as a novelist, short story writer, essayist, and translator. Vermont has furnished the scene for many of her stories, with Arlington disguised under the fictitious name Hillsboro. In this essay on Vermont, which appeared in *The Nation,* she has given us the full flavor of her adopted state — a picture of its sturdy farmers which may well make one stop and consider what are the real values in life.

Everybody knows that New York State is a glowing, queenly creature with a gold crown on her head and a flowing purple velvet cloak. The face of Louisiana is as familiar — dark-eyed, fascinating, temperamental. Virginia is a white-haired, dignified *grande dame* with ancient, well-mended fine lace and thin old silver spoons. Massachusetts is a man, a serious, middle-aged man, with a hard conscientious intelligent face, and hair thinned by intellectual application. And if I am not mistaken, Pennsylvania is a man too, a well-dressed business man, with plenty of money in his pockets and the consciousness of his prosperity written large on his smooth indoor face and in his kindly calculating eyes.

These state countenances are familiar to all of us, and many more; but back of this throng of affluent, thriving personalities, quite conscious of their own importance in the world, stands one, known to fewer Americans, lean, rather gaunt compared to the well-fed curves of the others, anything but fine, aristocratic, or picturesque. Yet the little group of mountaineers who know the physiognomy of Vermont from having grown up with it have the most crabbed, obstinate affection and respect for their state, which they see as a tall, powerful man, with thick gray hair, rough outdoor clothes, a sinewy axman's hand and arm, a humorous, candid, shrewd mouth and a weatherbeaten face from which look out the most quietly fearless eyes ever set in any man's head. They know there is little money in the pockets of that woodman's coat, but there is strength in the long, corded arm, and an unhurried sense of fun lies behind the ironic glint in the eyes, and the life animating all the quaint, strong, unspoiled personality is tinctured to its last fiber by an unenvious satisfaction with plain ways which is quite literally worth a million dollars to any possessor. Not to envy other people is an inheritance rich enough; but Vermont adds to that treasure the greater one of not being afraid. It seems incredible, in our modern world, so tormented with fears about its safety, that a whole stateful of people have no ground for apprehension; but that is true. The Vermonter is so used to the moral freedom of not dreading anything that he is hardly conscious of it. It is the breath he draws, this lack of fear; it is the marrow of his bones. Why should he be afraid of anybody or anything?

What are some of the things that other people fear? Well, most of them are afraid of being poor. This fear, rather more than love, is what makes the modern world go round. The Vermonter is not afraid of being poor because he is poor already and has been for a hundred and fifty years, and it hasn't hurt him a bit. To trade for money this lack of fear of poverty would seem to him the most idiotic of bargains, and if there is one thing on which he prides himself it is on not making poor bargains. This quality makes him by no means a favorite with people who try to organize the world along what they call "strictly business lines of industrial efficiency." Most of their operations are based on their certainty that people are afraid to be poor. We Vermonters often notice a considerable heat of exasperation in such devotees of industrialism when they encounter the natives of our state. We make no comment on this at the time, taking them in with the silent attentive observation which they furiously dub " bucolic stolidity "; but after they have gone back to the city we laugh to ourselves, and some old fellow among us hits on just the droll, ironic phrase to describe the encounter. For years afterwards, we quote this to the mystification of the outsider.

Another well-known and much-described fear is that of not keeping up with the social procession, of being obliged to step down a rung on the social ladder. This is another fear which stops short before it gets into Vermont. That small section of the country has never kept up with other people's processions and has found it no hardship to walk along at its own gait. And as for social ladders, any glimpse of a social ladder or of purely social distinctions moves a Vermonter to the unaffected, pitying, perhaps rather coarsely hearty mirth which white people feel at the sight of the complicated taboo of savage tribes. Of course, the Vermonter pays for his high-handed scoffing at sacred social distinctions by a rough plainness, not to say abruptness, of speech and manner which people from outside do not relish and which they describe in far from complimentary terms. This is a pity. But I dare say you can't have something for nothing morally, any more than materially, and perhaps it is not too high a price to pay for the total absence in our world of any sort of servility or overbearing arrogance or any sort of pretentiousness. Every man to his taste. We like it better the way we have it.

Another fear, perhaps the most corroding one in our world of possessors of material wealth, is the panic alarm at any glimpse of possible changes in the social fabric which may make things uncomfortable for possessors. The Latin poet who many years ago described the light-hearted stride of a poor man across a dark plain infested with robbers described the care-free gait at which Vermont moves through the uncertain and troubled modern world. Vermont, like some of the remote valleys in the Pyrenees, has always been too far out of the furiously swirling current of modern industrial life to be much affected by it or to dread its vagaries. For generations, now, when times get hard and manufactures are flat and deflated, and the mills in the industrial States around us are shut down, and the newspapers are talking about bankruptcies and bread-lines, the Vermont family, exactly as rich and exactly as poor as it ever was, remarks with a kindliness tinged with pride: " Well, we'd better ask Lem's folks up to stay a spell, till times get better. I guess it's pretty hard sledding for them." And when times get better and Lem's family leave the poor little frame farm-house which has been their refuge, and drive off down the steep stony road which is the first stage of their journey back to wages and movies, the Vermont family stand looking after them, still with friendliness.

They realize shrewdly that already they seem countrified to their mill-town, factory-hand guests, but this does not worry them: rather it makes an ironic quirk come into the corner of their mouths, as at the transparent absurdity of a child. They continue to stand and wave their hands with undiminished kindliness, this time tinged by an amused humor which would be distinctly unpalatable to the others if they could understand it. I am afraid there is an element of sinful pride in the granite-like comfort they take in the security given them by their plain tastes and ability to deal with life at first hand. No dependence on employers for them!

Another problem of which we read occasionally as bothering serious-minded folks in other parts is what to do with accumulated wealth. It bothers us as little as how to fight cobras. For the most part, society in Vermont is organized along the most obviously solid and natural lines, primitive and elemental. Everybody is working. Yes, working, you jeering step-lively outsiders, although Vermonters may not hit up the hectic pace of factory hands, and although some leisure for talking things over and reading the papers and cracking jokes about life, and going hunting and nutting is a necessity for Vermonters even if they are obliged to pay for it by the foregoing of sacred dollars. Almost everybody is working, and at the plainest, most visible, most understandable jobs, to raise food, or grind corn, or make shoes, or put houses together, or repair Fords, or teach children. It is very rare when anybody in Vermont fails to secure a fair amount of shelter and clothing and food and education; and it is equally rare when anybody secures very much more than that. There are, so to speak, no accumulated possessions at all.

But perhaps what Vermont is least afraid of, and what other people fear and hate most, is politics. You know as well as I do that most Americans are low in their minds about politics. They feel that politics is really beyond them, that they never will be able to get what they want through their political action. The "fatalism of the multitude" weighs like lead upon their hearts. When there are so many, what can one man do? Well, you see in Vermont there aren't so many. There isn't any multitude. Self-government may not be perfection there, any more than anywhere else, but it bears the closest, realest relationship to the citizens, and is not at all given over to professional politicians who are always below the level of the best voters. Vermonters see nothing in self-government (especially local self-government) inherently more complicated than keeping your bank book balanced. Perhaps this is because Vermont puts up as little as possible with that lazy substitute for self-government known as the "representative system," under which you tell somebody else to do the governing for you and not to bother you about it lest your money-making be disturbed. There is so little money to make in Vermont that few people are absorbed in making it. Nearly everybody has sufficient strength and time left over, and more than sufficient interest, to give to self-government. The Town Meeting is self-government, direct, articulate, personal. It is the annual assemblage not of the representatives of the governed, but of every one of the governed themselves. Anybody—you who are governed by a non-existing entity called "the county" cannot understand this, but it is true—anybody at all who does not like the way things are going in his town can stand up and say so, and propose a cure, as pungently as his command of his native tongue will allow. And Czar Public Opinion not only lets him do this, but rather admires a man who has something to say for his own point of view.

Every question concerning the welfare of the town, to the last forgotten valley in the mountains, is brought up at this open meeting and decided after loud and open discussion. When it is over and the teams and Fords and lean wiry men stream away from the Town Hall over the rutted roads in the sharp March air, they are all tingling with that wonderfully stimulating experience, having spoken their minds out freely on what concerns them. They step heavily in their great shoes through the mud, which on March-meeting Day is awful beyond belief, but they hold up their heads. They have settled their own affairs. The physical atmosphere of town meeting is rather strong with tobacco and sawdust and close air, but the moral atmosphere is like that on a mountain peak compared to any political life I ever saw elsewhere, either in France or in other American states. There is none of that stultifying, bored, cynical, disillusioned conviction that the rogues will beat the honest men again this time, as always. Not on your life! The honest men are on the job, with remarkably big and knotty fists, their dander ready to rise if somebody tries to put something over on them. And although they might not be able to cope with specially adroit political rogues, there is blessedly so little money involved in most Vermont operations that it is hardly worth the while of specially adroit rogues to frequent town meetings. The Vermonter has for a century and a half found self-government not so very daunting, and often the highest form of entertainment.

This tradition of looking the world in the eye and asking no odds of it, probably seems to the rest of you a rather curious tradition for a small, poor, rustic state with hardly a millionaire to its name, no political pull of any sort, and nothing to distinguish it in the eyes of the outside world. But all Vermonters know where it comes from, straight down from our forefathers who did look the world in the eye and made the world back down. With nothing on their side but their fearlessness and a sense of human rights as against property rights, they held out stoutly and successfully against oppression and injustice, though dressed up in all the fine names of " legality " and " loyalty to the organization of society."

Not many people outside Vermont know the dramatic story of the state's early life, but everybody inside the state does. There are fewer people in the whole state of Vermont than in the city of Buffalo, which is not at all huge as cities go now. But even at that, there are a good many men, women, and children in the state, over three hundred thousand. There is hardly one of this number who does not know about the history of the New Hampshire Grants, and how our great-grandfathers stood up against all the then existing British state for their naked human rights; and won the fight.

I know you are vague on this point, though you probably had it as a lesson one day in high school; so I will give you a sketch of it, compressed to a brevity which ought not to bore you too much. After the end of the French and Indian War, Vermont was safe ground for American settlers and the bolder spirits began to come in from New Hampshire and Connecticut. They settled, went through the terribly wearing toil of pioneers, felled trees, reclaimed land, drained swamps, built houses and mills, braved isolation, poverty, danger, health-breaking labor, and made Vermont a region of homes. They had learned to love it as we love it now, silently, undramatically, steadfastly, detesting any florid, highflown talk about it, burying our love in our hearts and pretending to outsiders that it is not there. Vermonters are not sentimental, articulate Celts, but hermetically sealed Yankees. But they live on this love for their homes and they have shown themselves quite ready to die for it.

Back there in the eighteenth century, just when the settlers had definitely proved that they could make homes out of the wilderness, they were informed that by a legal technicality the grants by which they held their land were not valid; and that the King of England authorized New York lawyers to send officers of the law to take the Vermont land away from the men who had reclaimed it. It was then to be given to soft-handed, well-to-do men, with political influence, who had no more rightful connection with that land than did the inhabitants of Peking. The Vermont settlers did not pretend to understand the law of that day. They only knew in their hearts that the land they had so painfully reclaimed, worked over, brought up their children on, was theirs, if anything ever belonged to anybody. A shout went up from Vermont to the New York officers of the law: " Just come and take it away, if you dare! " And they got down their long rifles, ran some bullets, and dried their powder.

The hated " York State men " tried to do this, ventured into the Vermont settlements, were roughly treated, and sent home. They were afraid to try it again and retreated to the Albany courts of law, which summoned the Vermonters to submit the matter to trial. With nothing but their inherent human rights back of them, the Vermonters went down to Albany (no true Vermonter can abide the name of Albany since then!) and there went through the solemn twaddle of a law trial, where the standards were not those of human rightness and fair dealing, but were drawn from yellow parchments. Of course the parchments won. That is their habit in law courts.

Ethan Allen was in Albany through this trial, to help the Vermonters. After the decision was rendered, he walked out of the law court, on his way home, surrounded by a mocking crowd of York State men. The whole history is so familiar to us Vermonters that any one of us would know just what is coming next in this episode. When, in speaking to a Vermont audience, you begin this story, you can see every backbone straighten as you go on in the phrases consecrated by time. "They shouted jeeringly at Allen: 'Now do you know you're beaten? Now will you lie down and give up?' Ethan Allen drew himself to the full height of his magnificent manhood" (we never use any less fine a phrase than this) "and cried out in a ringing voice, 'The gods of the mountains are not the gods of the plains,' and strode away leaving them silenced." (Here is where the speaker always has to wait for people to get through clapping.) He strode back to Vermont and organized a resistance. Was there ever a more absurd, pitiable, pretentious attempt? A handful of rough ignorant mountaineers without a legal leg to stand on, to try and defend themselves against the British law! And their only pretext, the preposterous one that they had earned what they held.

Well, to make a long and complicated story short, the rough handful of ignorant men did continue to hold the land they had earned, and we, their descendants, are living on it now. They did more. For fourteen years after that, those men, our great-grandfathers, ruled Vermont, free of any sovereignty, an independent republic on the continent of North America. You never heard that quaint and colorful fact about our little State, did you? Yes, for fourteen years they stood straight and strong on their own feet, owing allegiance to nothing in creation but their own consciences. They stood steady in a whirling, shifting world, and proved to their own satisfaction that to stand steady is not an impossible task.

Down to this day, down to the last corner of our green, wooded, mountain-bedecked State, we all stand steadier because of that memory back of us. Every foot of the land on which we live was held for us by the courage, almost absurd in its simple-heartedness, of our tall, lean, ironic grandfathers, and by their candid faith in the inherent strength of a just cause. They risked their fortunes and their lives on their faith in this principle: that those who work and create have certain sacred rights, no matter what laws may be, more than those who do nothing. With that principle as our main inheritance, we Vermonters can cock our feet up on the railing of the porch and with a tranquil heart read the news of the modern world and the frightened guessing of other folks at what is coming next!

SUGGESTIONS FOR STUDY

1. Vocabulary: physiognomy, devotees, bucolic stolidity, arrogance, vagaries, articulate, stultifying, hermetically sealed, preposterous.

2. Picture other states of the Union as persons in the way that Mrs. Fisher does in the first paragraph.

3. Make a list of the things which the author says the Vermonters are not afraid of. Are any of these common fears in your community? Discuss. Compare with Emerson's " Self-Reliance."

4. With what attitude toward the Vermonters does this essay leave you? Would you like to resemble them? Why or why not?

5. Write a character study of the people of your own school, city, or state.

FOR FURTHER READING

FICTION	ESSAYS
Hillsboro People	*Fellow Captains*
The Bent Twig	
The Brimming Cup	TRANSLATION
Home Fires in France	Papini's *Life of Christ*

A NOTE ON THE ESSAY

By CARL VAN DOREN (1885–   )

As a professor of English at the University of Illinois and at Columbia, as literary editor of *The Nation,* and as author of several books of literary criticism, Carl Van Doren has come to be known as one of our outstanding literary critics of today. In this little essay on the essay he not only shows you in lively fashion how the essay differs from other types of writing but introduces you in terse but telling phrases to many of the great essayists of England and America.

The sonnet has a standard form very much as a man has. Leave off the sestet of your sonnet and you do about what a god does when he leaves the legs off a man. The drama has a standard form very much as a rendezvous has. Write a drama in which no spark is exchanged between the audience and the action and you have done what fate does when it keeps lovers from their meeting. The novel has a standard form very much as a road has. You may set out anywhere you like and go wherever you please, at any gait, but you must go somewhere, or you have made what is no more a novel than some engineer's road would be a road if it had neither beginning, end, nor direction. But the essay! It may be of any length, breadth, depth, weight, density, color, savor, odor, appearance, importance, value, or uselessness which you can or will give it. The epigram bounds it on one side and the treatise on the other, but it has in its time encroached upon the territory of both of them, and it doubtless will do so again. Or, to look at the essay from another angle, it is bounded on one side by the hell-fire sermon and on the other by the geometrical demonstration; and yet it ranges easily between these extremes of heat and cold and occasionally steals from both of them. It differs from a letter by being written to more — happily a great many more — than one person. It differs from talk chiefly by being written at all.

Having to obey no regulations as to form, the essay is very free to choose its matter. The sonnet, by reason of its form, tends to deal with solemn and not with gay themes. The drama, for the same reason, tends to look for intense and not for casual incidents. The novel tends to feel that it must carry a considerable amount of human life on its back. The essay may be as fastidious as a collector of carved emeralds or as open-minded as a garbage-gatherer. Nothing human, as the platitude says, is alien to it. The essay, however, goes beyond the platitude and dares to choose matter from numerous non-human sources. Think of the naturalists and their essays. Think, further, of the range of topics for essayists at large. Theodore Roosevelt in an essay urges the strenuous life; Max Beerbohm in an essay defends cosmetics. De Quincey expounds the fine art of murder, Thoreau the pleasures of economy, William Law the blisses of prayer, Hudson the sense of smell in men and in animals, Schopenhauer the ugliness of women, Bacon the advantages of a garden, Plutarch the traits of curiosity, and A. C. Benson the felicity of having nothing much in the mind. All, in fact, an essayist needs to start with is something, anything, to say. He gets up each morning and finds the world spread out before him, as the world was spread out before Adam and Eve the day they left Paradise. With the cosmos, past, present, and future, to pick from, the essayist goes to work. If he finds a topic good enough he may write a good essay, no matter how he writes it.

He may. There is still, however, the question of his manner. Thousands of dull men have written millions of true things which no one but their proof-readers, wives, or pupils ever read. If each essayist could take out a patent on each subject into which he dips his pen, and could prevent any other pen from ever dipping into it after him, he might have better luck. But there are no monopolists in this department. Would research find in all the hoards of books or all the morgues of manuscripts a single observation which has never been made twice? Competition in such affairs is free and endless. The only law which gives an essayist a right to his material is the law which rules that the best man wins. The law does not say in what fashion he must be best. Any fashion will do. Let him be more sententious than others, like Bacon; or more harmonious, like Sir Thomas Browne; or more elegant, like Addison; or more direct, like Swift; or more hearty, like Fielding; or more whimsical, like Lamb; or more impassioned, like Hazlitt; or more encouraging, like Emerson; or more Olympian, like Arnold; or more funny, like Mark Twain; or more musical, like Pater; or more impish, like Max Beerbohm; or more devastating, like Mencken. Let the essayist be any of these things and he may have a copyright till some one takes it away from him. What matters is the manner. If he has good matter, he *may* write a good essay; if he has good manner he probably *will* write a good essay.

An essay is a communication. If the subject of the discourse were the whole affair, it would be enough for the essayist to be an adequate conduit. If the manner were the whole affair, any versatile fellow might try all the manners and have universal triumph. But back of matter and manner both lies the item which is really significant. The person who communicates, anything in any way, must be a person. His truth must have a tone, his speech must have a rhythm which are his and solely his. His knowledge or opinions must have lain long enough inside him to have taken root there; and when they come away they must bring some of the soil clinging to them. They must, too, have been shaped by that soil — as plants are which grow in cellars, on housetops, on hillsides, in the wide fields, under shade in forests. Many kinds of men, many kinds of essays! Important essays come from important men.

SUGGESTIONS FOR STUDY

1. At the beginning the sonnet is mentioned. You might make sure that you know what it is. See page 519.

2. How many of the proper names did you recognize? Which of them are American?

3. According to the author, what is absolutely necessary to make an essay entertaining? Apply his theory to those read in this book.

FOR FURTHER READING

The American Novel   *The Contemporary American Novel*

WALTER REED

By PAUL DE KRUIF (1890–   )

A bacteriologist with a marked literary style is in a position to give deserved publicity to a group of men too little known to the world as compared with the generals, authors, statesmen, and prize-fighters. These are the scientists. Such a man is Paul de Kruif who in *Microbe Hunters* can hold one spellbound with the drama of the world known only through the microscope, or show how the thrills of hunting invisible microbes in

Africa may exceed those of hunting big game. The success of this book led
him to write two other series of biographical essays, *Hunger Fighters* and
Seven Iron Men.

The following selection from *Microbe Hunters* concerns the fight made
by Walter Reed against yellow fever. It is a combination of the biographical essay, the scientific essay, and the lively narrative — hard to classify
but fascinating to read. Once you get into it, you will not care by what
name it is called — you will just read on and on.

Everybody is agreed that Walter Reed — head of the Yellow
Fever Commission — was a courteous man and a blameless one,
that he was a mild man and a logical: there is not one particle of
doubt he had to risk human lives; animals simply will not catch
yellow fever!

Then it is certain that the ex-lumberjack, James Carroll, was
perfectly ready to let go his own life to prove Reed's point, and
he was not too sentimental about the lives of others when *he*
needed to prove a point — which might and might not be what
you would call a major point.

All Cubans (who were on the spot and ought to know) are
agreed that those American soldiers who volunteered for the fate
of guinea-pigs were brave beyond imagining. All Americans who
were then in Cuba are sure that those Spanish immigrants
who volunteered for the fate of guinea-pigs were not brave, but
money-loving — for didn't each one of them get two hundred
dollars?

Of course you might protest that fate hit Jesse Lazear a hard
knock — but it was his own fault; why didn't he brush that mosquito off the back of his hand instead of letting her drink her fill?
Then, too, fate has been kind to his memory; the United States
Government named a Battery in Baltimore Harbor in his honor!
And that same government has been more than kind to his wife:
the widow Lazear gets a pension of fifteen hundred dollars a year!
You see, there are no arguments — and that makes it fun to tell
this story of yellow fever. And aside from the pleasure, it has
to be told: this history is absolutely necessary to the book of
Microbe Hunters. It vindicates Pasteur [1]! At last Pasteur, from
his handsome tomb in that basement in Paris, can tell the world:

[1] Louis Pasteur (1822–1895), French chemist who made extensive studies
in the theory of germs, inoculation, and sterilization. The process of producing
pasteurized milk is named for him. His work is described in earlier chapters of
Microbe Hunters.

"I told you so!" Because, in 1926, there is hardly enough of the poison of yellow fever left in the world to put on the points of six pins; in a few years there may not be a single speck of that virus left on earth — it will be as completely extinct as the dinosaurs — unless there is a catch in the fine gruesome experiments of Reed and his Spanish immigrants and American soldiers.

It was a grand coöperative fight, that scotching of the yellow jack. It was fought by a strange crew, and the fight was begun by a curious old man, with enviable mutton chop whiskers — his name was Doctor Carlos Finlay — who made an amazingly right guess, who was a terrible muddler at experiments, who was considered by all good Cubans and wise doctors to be a Theorizing Old Fool. What a crazy crank is Finlay, said everybody.

For everybody knew just how to fight that most panic-striking plague, yellow fever; everybody had a different idea of just how to combat it. You should fumigate silks and satins and possessions of folks before they *left* yellow fever towns — no! that is not enough: you should burn them. You should bury, burn, and utterly destroy these silks and satins and possessions before they *come into* yellow fever towns. It was wise not to shake hands with friends whose families were dying of yellow fever; it was perfectly safe to shake hands with them. It was best to burn down houses where yellow fever had lurked — no! it was enough to smoke them out with sulphur. But there was one thing nearly everybody in North, Central, and South America had been agreed upon for nearly two hundred years, and that was this: when folks of a town began to turn yellow and hiccup and vomit black, by scores, by hundreds, every day — the only thing to do was to get up and get out of that town. Because the yellow murderer had a way of crawling through walls and slithering along the ground and popping around corners — it could even pass through fires! — it could die and rise from the dead, that yellow murderer; and after everybody (including the very best physicians) had fought it by doing as many contrary things as they could think of as frankly as they could do them — the yellow jack kept on killing, until suddenly it got fed up with killing. In North America that always came with the frosts in the fall.

This was the state of scientific knowledge about yellow fever up to the year 1900. But from between his mutton chop whiskers Carlos Finlay of Habana howled in a scornful wilderness: "You are all wrong — yellow fever is caused by a mosquito!"

II

There was a bad state of affairs in San Cristobal de Habana in Cuba in 1900. The yellow jack had killed thousands more American soldiers than the bullets of the Spaniards had killed. And it wasn't like most diseases, which considerately pounce upon poor dirty people — it had killed more than one third of the officers of General Leonard Wood's staff, and staff officers — as all soldiers know — are the cleanest of all officers and the best protected. General Wood had thundered orders; Habana had been scrubbed; happy dirty Cubans had been made into unhappy clean Cubans — " No stone had been left unturned " — in vain! There was more yellow fever in Habana than there had been in twenty years!

Cablegrams from Habana to Washington, and on June 25th of 1900 Major Walter Reed came to Quemados in Cuba with orders to " give special attention to questions relating to the cause and prevention of yellow fever." It was a big order. Considering who the man Walter Reed was, it was altogether too big an order. Pasteur had tried it! Of course, in certain ways — though you would say they had nothing to do with hunting microbes — Walter Reed had qualifications. He was the best of soldiers; fourteen years and more he had served on the western plains and mountains; he had been a brave angel flying through blizzards to the bedsides of sick settlers — he had shunned the dangers of beer and bottle-pool in the officers' mess and resisted the seductions of poker. He had a strong moral nature. He was gentle. But it will take a genius to dig out this microbe of the yellow jack, you say — and are geniuses gentle? Just the same, you will see that this job needed particularly a strong moral nature, and then, besides, since 1891 Walter Reed *had* been doing a bit of microbe hunting. He had done some odd jobs of searching at the very best medical school under the most eminent professor of microbe hunting in America — and that professor had known Robert Koch,[2] intimately.

So Walter Reed came to Quemados, and as he went into the yellow fever hospital there, more than enough young American soldiers passed him, going out, on their backs, feet first. There were going to be plenty of cases to work on all right — fatal cases! Dr. James Carroll was with Walter Reed, and he was not

[2] A German doctor (1843–1910) who discovered the germs of tuberculosis and cholera. His work is described in an earlier chapter of *Microbe Hunters*.

what you would call gentle, but you will see in a moment what a soldier-searcher James Carroll was. And Reed found Jesse Lazear waiting for him — Lazear was a European-trained microbe hunter, aged thirty-four, with a wife and two babies in the States, and with doom in his eyes. Finally there was Aristides Agramonte (who was a Cuban) — it was to be his job to cut up the dead bodies, and very well he did that job, though he never became famous because he had had yellow fever already and so ran no risks. These four were the Yellow Fever Commission.

The first thing the Commission did was to fail to find any microbe whatever in the first eighteen cases of yellow fever that they probed into. There were many severe cases in those eighteen; there were four of those eighteen cases who died; there was not one of those eighteen cases that they didn't claw through from stem to gudgeon, so to speak, drawing blood, making cultures, cutting up the dead ones, making endless careful cultures — and not one bacillus [3] did they find. All the time — it was July and the very worst time for yellow fever — the soldiers were coming out of the hospital of Las Animas feet first. The Commission failed absolutely to find any cause, but that failure put them on the right track. That is one of the humors of microbe hunting — the way men make their finds! Theobald Smith [4] found out about those ticks because he had faith in certain farmers; Ronald Ross [5] found out the doings of those gray mosquitoes because Patrick Manson told him to; Grassi [6] discovered the zanzarone carrying malaria because he was patriotic. And now Walter Reed had failed in the very first part — and anybody would say it was the most important part — of his work. What to do? There was nothing to do. And so Reed had time to hear the voice of that Theorizing Old Fool, Dr. Carlos Finlay, of Habana, shouting: " Yellow fever is caused by a *mosquito!* "

The Commission went to call on Dr. Finlay, and that old gentleman — everybody had laughed at him, nobody had listened to him

[3] Disease germ.

[4] An American physician who discovered how Texas fever is spread among cattle by ticks.

[5] A medical officer of the English army in India, who studied the mosquito as a carrier of malaria germs.

[6] Battista Grassi, an Italian scientist who also studied the transmission of malaria germs. There was considerable controversy between these two men as to which was entitled to the discovery. Accounts of the work of the three men here mentioned are given in *Microbe Hunters*.

— was very glad to explain his fool theory to the Commission. He told them the ingenious but vague reasons why he thought it was mosquitoes carried yellow fever; he showed them records of those awful experiments, which would convince nobody; he gave them some little black eggs shaped like cigars and said: " Those are the eggs of the criminal! " And Walter Reed took those eggs, and gave them to Lazear, who had been in Italy and knew a thing or two about mosquitoes, and Lazear put the eggs into a warm place to hatch into wigglers, which presently wiggled themselves into extremely pretty mosquitoes, with silver markings on their backs — markings that looked like a lyre. Now Walter Reed had failed, but you have to give him credit for being a sharp-eyed man with plenty of common sense — and then too, as you will see, he was extraordinarily lucky. While he was failing to find bacilli, even in the dreadful cases, with bloodshot eyes and chests yellow as gold, with hiccups and with those prophetic retchings — while he was failing, Walter Reed noticed that the nurses who handled those cases, were soiled by those cases, never got yellow fever! They were non-immunes too, those nurses, but they didn't get yellow fever.

" If this disease were caused by a bacillus, like cholera, or plague, some of those nurses certainly should get it," argued Walter Reed to his Commission.

Then all kinds of strange tricks of yellow fever struck Walter Reed. He watched cases of the disease pop up most weirdly in Quemados. A man in a house in 102 Real Street came down with it; then it jumped around the corner to 20 General Lee Street, and from there it hopped across the road — and not one of these families had anything to do with each other, hadn't seen each other, even!

" That smells like something carrying the disease through the air to those houses," said Reed. There were various other exceedingly strange things about yellow fever — they had been discovered by an American, Carter. A man came down with yellow fever in a house. For two or three weeks nothing more happened — the man might die, he might have got better and gone away, but at the end of that two weeks, bang! a bunch of other cases broke out in that house. " That two weeks makes it look as if the virus were taking time to grow in some insect," said Reed, to his Commission, who thought it was silly, but they were soldiers.

" So we will try Finlay's notion about mosquitoes," said Walter

Reed, for all of the just-mentioned reasons, but particularly because there was nothing else for the Commission to do.

That was easy to say, but how to go on with it? Everybody knew perfectly well that you cannot give yellow fever to any animal — not even to a monkey or an ape. To make any kind of experiment to prove mosquitoes carry yellow fever you *must* have experimental animals, and that meant nothing more nor less than human animals. But give human beings yellow fever! In some epidemics — there were records of them! — eighty-five men out of a hundred died of it, in some fifty out of every hundred — almost never less than twenty out of every hundred. It would be murder! But that is where the strong moral nature of Walter Reed came to help him. Here was a blameless man, a Christian man, and a man — though he was mild — who was mad to help his fellow men. And if you could *prove* that yellow fever was *only* carried by mosquitoes!

So, on one hot night after a day among dying men at Pinar del Rio, he faced his Commission: " If the members of the Commission take the risk first — if they let themselves be bitten by mosquitoes that have fed on yellow fever cases, that will set an example to American soldiers, and then — " Reed looked at Lazear, and then at James Carroll.

" I am ready to take a bite," said Jesse Lazear, who had a wife and two small children.

" You can count on me, sir," said James Carroll, whose total assets were his searcher's brain, and his miserable pay as an assistant-surgeon in the army. (His liabilities were a wife and five children.)

III

Then Walter Reed (he had been called home to Washington to make a report on work done in the Spanish War) gave elaborate instructions to Carroll and Lazear and Agramonte. They were secret instructions, and savage instructions, when you consider the mild man he was. It was an immoral business — it was a breach of discipline in its way, for Walter Reed then had no permission from the high military authorities to start it. So Reed left for Washington, and Lazear and Carroll set off on the wildest, most daring journey any two microbe hunters had ever taken. Lazear? You could not see the doom in his eyes — the gleam of the searcher outshone it. Carroll? That was a soldier who cared neither for death nor courts-martial — Carroll was a microbe hunter of the great line.

Lazear went down between the rows of beds on which lay men, doomed men with faces yellow as the leaves of autumn, delirious men with bloodshot eyes. He bit those men with his silver-striped she-mosquitoes; carefully he carried these blood-filled beasts back to their glass homes, in which were little saucers of water and little lumps of sugar. Here the she-mosquitoes digested their meal of yellow fever blood, and buzzed a little, and waited for the test.

"We should remember malaria," Reed had told Lazear and Carroll. "In that disease it takes two or three weeks for the mosquito to become dangerous — maybe it's the same here."

But look at the bold face of Jesse Lazear, and tell me if that was a patient man! Not he. Somehow he collected seven volunteers, who so far as I can find have remained nameless, since the test was done in dark secrecy. To these seven men — whom for all I know he may have shanghaied — but first of all to himself, Lazear applied those mosquitoes who a few days before had fed on men who now were dead.

But alas, they all stayed as fit as fiddles, and that discouraged Lazear.

But there was James Carroll. For years he had been the right-hand man of Walter Reed. He had come into the army as a buck private and had been a corporal and a sergeant for years — obeying orders was burned into his very bones — and Major Reed had said: "Try mosquitoes!" What is more, what Major Reed thought was right, James Carroll thought was right, too, and Major Reed thought there was something in the notion of that Old Theorizing Fool. But in the army, thoughts are secondary — Major Reed had left them saying: "Try mosquitoes!"

So James Carroll reminded the discouraged Lazear: "I am ready!" He told Lazear to bring out the most dangerous mosquito in his collection — not one that had bitten only a single case, but he must use a mosquito that had bitten many cases — and they must be bad cases — of yellow fever. That mosquito must be as dangerous as possible! On the twenty-seventh of August, Jesse Lazear picked out what he thought to be his champion mosquito, and this creature, which had fed on four cases of yellow fever, two of them severe ones, settled down on the arm of James Carroll.

That soldier watched her while she felt around with her stinger. What did he think as he watched her swell into a bright balloon with his blood? Nobody knows. But he could think, what everybody knows: "I am forty-six years old, and in yellow fever the older the fewer — get better." He was forty-six years old. He had a wife and five children, but that evening James Carroll wrote to Walter Reed:

"If there is anything in the mosquito theory, I should get a good dose of yellow fever!" He did.

Two days later he felt tired and didn't want to visit patients in the yellow fever ward. Two days after that he was really sick: "I must have malaria!" he cried, and went to the laboratory under his own power, to squint at his own blood under the microscope. But no malaria. That night his eyes were bloodshot, his face a dusky red. The next morning Lazear packed Carroll off to the yellow fever wards, and there he lay, near to death for days and days. There was one minute when he thought his heart had stopped . . . and that, as you will see, was a bad minute for Assistant-Surgeon Carroll.

He always said those were the proudest days of his life. "I was the first case to come down with yellow fever after the experimental bite of a mosquito!" said Carroll.

Then there was that American private soldier they called "X.Y." — these outlaw searchers called him "X.Y.," though he was really William Dean, of Grand Rapids, Michigan. While James Carroll was having his first headaches, they bit this X.Y. with four mosquitoes — the one that nearly killed Carroll, and then three other silver-striped beauties besides, who had fed on six men that were fairly sick, and four men that were very sick with yellow fever and two men that died.

Now everything was fine with the experiments of Quemados. Eight men had been bitten, it is true, and were fit as fiddles — but the last two, James Carroll and X.Y., they were real experimental guinea-pigs, those two, they had both got yellow fever — and James Carroll's heart had nearly stopped, but now they were both getting better, and Carroll was on the heights, writing to Walter Reed, waiting proudly for his chief to come back — to show him the records. Only Jesse Lazear was a little cynical about these two cases, because Lazear was a fine experimenter, a tight one, a man who had to have every condition just so, like a real searcher — and, thought Lazear, "It is too bad, seeing the nerve of Carroll and X.Y.—but both of them exposed themselves in dangerous zones once or twice, before they came down. It wasn't an absolutely perfect experiment—it isn't sure that *my* mosquitoes gave them yellow fever!" So Lazear was skeptical, but orders were orders, and every afternoon he went to those rows of beds at Las Animas, in the room with the faint strange smell, and here he turned his test-tubes upside-down on the arms of boys with bloodshot eyes, and let his she-mosquitoes suck their fill. But September 13th was a bad day, it was an unlucky day for Jesse Lazear, for while he was at this silly job of feeding his mosquitoes, a stray mosquito settled down on the back of his hand. "Oh! that's nothing!" he thought. "That wouldn't be the right kind of mosquito anyway!" he muttered, and he let the mosquito drink her fill—though, mind you, she was a stray beast that lived in this ward where men were dying!

That was September 13th.

"On the evening of September 18th Dr. Lazear complained of feeling out of sorts, and had a chill at 8 P.M.," says a hospital record at Las Animas.

"September 19: Twelve o'clock noon," goes on that laconic record, "temperature 102.4 degrees, pulse 112. Eyes injected, face suffused." (That means bloodshot and red) ". . . 6 P.M. temperature 103.8 degrees, pulse, 106. Jaundice appeared on the third day. The subsequent history of this case was one of progressive and fatal yellow fever" (and the record softens a little), "the death of our lamented colleague having occurred on the evening of September 25, 1900."

IV

Then Reed came back to Cuba, and Carroll met him with enthusiasm, and Walter Reed was sad for Lazear, but very happy about those two successful cases of Carroll and X.Y.—and then, and then (brushing aside tears for Lazear) even in that there was the Hand of God, there was something for Science: "As Dr. Lazear was bitten by a mosquito while present in the wards of a yellow fever hospital," wrote Walter Reed, "one must, at least, admit the possibility of this insect's contamination by a previous bite of a yellow fever patient. This case of accidental infection therefore *cannot fail to be of interest.*"

"Now it is my turn to take the bite!" said Walter Reed, but he was fifty years old, and they persuaded him not to. "But we

must prove it! " he insisted, so gently, that, hearing his musical
voice and looking at his chin that did not stick out like the chin
of a he-man, you might think Walter Reed was wavering (after
all, here was one man dead out of three).

" But we must prove it," said that soft voice, and Reed went to
General Leonard Wood, and told him the exciting events that had
happened. Who could be less of a mollycoddle than this Wood?
And he gave Walter Reed permission to go as far as he liked. He
gave him money to build a camp of seven tents and two little
houses — to say nothing of a flagpole — but what was best of all,
Wood gave him money to buy men, who would get handsomely
paid for taking a sure one chance out of five of never having a
chance to spend that money! So Walter Reed said: " Thank you,
General," and one mile from Quemados they pitched seven tents
and raised a flagpole, and flew an American flag and called that
place Camp Lazear (three cheers for Lazear!), and you will see
what glorious things occurred there.

Now, nothing is more sure than this: that every man of the
great line of microbe hunters is different from every other man of
them, but every man Jack of them has one thing in common: they
are original. They were all original, excepting Walter Reed —
who you cannot say would be shot for his originality, seeing
that this business of mosquitoes and various bugs and ticks carrying diseases was very much in the air in those last ten years of the
nineteenth century. It was natural for a man to think of that!
But he was by all odds the most moral of the great line of microbe
hunters — aside from being a very thorough clean-cut experimenter — and now that Walter Reed's moral nature told him:
" You must kill men to save them! " he set out to plan a series of
air-tight tests — never was there a good man who thought of more
hellish and dastardly tests!

And he was exact. Every man about to be bit by a mosquito
must stay locked up for days and days and weeks, in that sun-
baked Camp Lazear — to keep him away from all danger of
accidental contact with yellow fever. There would be no catch
in these experiments! And then Walter Reed let it be known, to
the American soldiers in Cuba, that there was another war on, a
war for the saving of men — were there men who would volunteer?
Before the ink was dry on the announcements Private Kissenger of
Ohio stepped into his office, and with him came John J. Moran,
who wasn't even a soldier — he was a civilian clerk in the office

of General Fitzhugh Lee. " You can try it on us, sir ! " they told him.

Walter Reed was a thoroughly conscientious man. " But, men, do you realize the danger ? " And he told them of the headaches and the hiccups and the black vomit — and he told them of fearful epidemics in which not a man had lived to carry news or tell the horrors.

"We know," said Private Kissenger and John J. Moran of Ohio, " we volunteer solely for the cause of humanity and in the interest of science."

Then Walter Reed told them of the generosity of General Wood. A handsome sum of money they would get — two hundred, maybe three hundred dollars, if the silver-striped she-mosquitoes did things to them that would give them one chance out of five not to spend that money.

" The one condition on which we volunteer, sir," said Private Kissenger and civilian clerk John J. Moran of Ohio, " is that we get no compensation for it."

To the tip of his cap went the hand of Walter Reed (who was a major) : " Gentlemen, I salute you ! " And that day Kissenger and John J. Moran went into the preparatory quarantine, that would make them first-class, unquestionable guinea-pigs, above suspicion and beyond reproach. On the 5th of December Kissenger furnished nice full meals for five mosquitoes — two of them had bitten fatal cases fifteen days and nineteen days before. Presto ! Five days later he had the devil of a backache, two days more and he was turning yellow — it was a perfect case, and in his quarters Walter Reed thanked God, for Kissenger got better ! Then great days came to Reed and Carroll and Agramonte — for, if they weren't exactly overrun with young Americans who were ready to throw away their lives in the interest of science — and for humanity still there were ignorant people, just come to Cuba from Spain, who could very well use two hundred dollars. There were five of these mercenary fellows — whom I shall simply have to call " Spanish immigrants," or I could call them Man 1, 2, 3, and 4 — just as microbe hunters often mark animals : " Rabbit 1, 2, 3, and 4 — " anyway they were bitten, carefully, by mosquitoes who, when you take averages, were much more dangerous than machine gun bullets. They earned their two hundred dollars — for four out of five of them had nice typical (doctors would look scientific and call them beautiful) cases of yellow fever! It was a triumph! It was sure! Not one of these men had been anywhere near yellow fever — like so many mice they had been kept in their screened tents at Quemados. If they hadn't been ignorant immigrants — hardly more intelligent than animals, you might say — they might have been bored, because nothing had happened to them excepting — the stabs of silver-striped she-mosquitoes.

" Rejoice with me, sweetheart," Walter Reed wrote to his wife, " as, aside from the antitoxin of diphtheria and Koch's discovery of the tubercle bacillus, it will be regarded as the most important piece of work, scientifically, during the nineteenth century."

Walter Reed was so thorough that you can call him original, as original as any of the microbe hunters of the great line — for he was certainly original in his thoroughness. He might have called it a day — you would swear he was tempted to call it a day: eight men had got yellow fever from mosquito bites, and only one — what amazing luck! — had died.

" But can yellow fever be carried in any other way? " asked Reed.

Everybody believed that clothing and bedding and possessions of yellow fever victims were deadly — millions of dollars' worth of clothing and bedding had been destroyed; the Surgeon-General believed it; every eminent physician in America, North, South and Central (excepting that old fool Finlay) believed it. " But can it? " asked Reed, and while he was being so joyfully success-ful with Kissenger and Spaniards 1, 2, 3, and 4, carpenters came, and built two ugly little houses in Camp Lazear. House No. 1 was the nastier of these two little houses. It was fourteen feet by twenty, it had two doors cleverly arranged one back of the other so no mosquitoes could get into it, it had two windows looking south — they were on the same side as the door, so no draft could blow through that little house. Then it was furnished with a nice stove, to keep the temperature well above ninety, and there were tubs of water in the house — to keep the air as chokey as the hold of a ship in the tropics. So you see it was an uninhabitable little house — under the best of conditions — but now, on the thirtieth of November in 1900, sweating soldiers carried several tightly nailed suspicious-looking boxes, that came from the yellow fever wards of Las Animas — to make the house altogether cursed.

That night, of the thirtieth of November, Walter Reed and James Carroll were the witnesses of a miracle of bravery, for into this House No. 1 walked a young American doctor named Cooke, and two American soldiers, whose names — where are their monuments? — were Folk and Jernegan.

Those three men opened the tightly nailed, suspicious-looking boxes. They opened those boxes inside that house, in air already too sticky for proper breathing.

Phew! There were cursings, there were holdings of noses.

But they went on opening those boxes, and out of them Cooke and Folk and Jernegan took pillows, soiled with the black vomit of men dead of yellow fever; out of them they took sheets and blankets, dirty with the discharges of dying men past helping themselves. They beat those pillows and shook those sheets and blankets — "you must see the yellow fever poison is well spread around that room!" Walter Reed had told them. Then Cooke and Folk and Jernegan made up their little army cots with those pillows and blankets and sheets. They undressed. They lay down on those filthy beds. They tried to sleep — in that room fouler than the dankest of medieval dungeons. And Walter Reed and James Carroll guarded that little house, so tenderly, to see no mosquito got into it, and Folk and Cooke and Jernegan had the very best of food, you may be sure.

Night after night those three lay in that house, wondering perhaps about the welfare of the souls of their predecessors in those sheets and blankets. They lay there, wondering whether anything else besides mosquitoes (though mosquitoes hadn't even been proved to carry it then!) carried yellow fever. Then Walter Reed, who was a moral man and a thorough man, and James Carroll, who was a grim man, came to make their test a little more thorough. More boxes came to them from Las Animas — and when Cooke and Jernegan and Folk unpacked them, they had to rush out of their little house, it was so dreadful.

But they went back in, and they went to sleep.

For twenty nights — where are their monuments? — these three men stayed there, and then they were quarantined in a nice airy tent, to wait for their attack of yellow fever. But they gained weight. They felt fit as fiddles. They made vast jokes about their dirty house and their perilous sheets and blankets. They were happy as so many schoolboys when they heard Kissenger and those Spaniards (1, 2, 3, and 4) had really got the yellow jack after the mosquito bites. What a marvelous proof, you will say, but what a dastardly experiment — but for the insanely scientific

Walter Reed that most dastardly experiment was not marvelous enough! Three more American boys went in there, and for twenty nights slept in new unspeakable sheets and blankets — with this little refinement of the experiment : they slept in the very pajamas in which yellow fever victims had died. And then for twenty more nights three other American lads went into House No. 1, and slept that way — with this additional little refinement of the experiment: they slept on pillows covered with towels soaked with the blood of men whom the yellow jack had killed.

But they all stayed fit as fiddles! Not a soul of these nine men had so much as a touch of yellow fever! How wonderful is science, thought Walter Reed. " So," he wrote, " the bubble of the belief that clothing can transmit yellow fever was pricked by the first touch of human experimentation." Walter Reed was right. It is true, science is wonderful. But science is cruel, microbe hunting can be heartless, and that relentless devil that was the experimenter in Walter Reed kept asking: " But is your experiment really sound? " None of those men who slept in House No. 1 got yellow fever, that is true — but how do you know they were *susceptible* to yellow fever? Maybe they were naturally immune! Then Reed and Carroll, who had already asked as much of Folk and Jernegan as any captain has ever asked of any soldier — so it was that Reed and Carroll now shot virulent yellow fever blood under the skin of Jernegan, so it was they bit Folk with mosquitoes who had fed on fatal cases of yellow fever. They both came down with wracking pains and flushed faces and blood-shot eyes. They both came through their Valley of the Shadow. " Thank God," murmured Reed — but especially Walter Reed thanked God he had proved those two boys were not immune during those twenty hot stinking nights in House No. 1.

For these deeds Warren Gladsden Jernegan and Levi E. Folk were generously rewarded with a purse of three hundred dollars — which in those days was a lot of money.

While these tests were going on John J. Moran, that civilian clerk from Ohio, whom Walter Reed had paid the honor of a salute, was a very disappointed man. He had absolutely refused to be paid; he had volunteered in " the interest of science and for the cause of humanity," he had been bitten by those silver-striped Stegomyia mosquitoes (the bug experts just then thought this was the proper name for that mosquito) — he had been stabbed several times by several choice poisonous ones, but he hadn't come down with yellow fever, alas, he stayed fit as a fiddle. What to do with John J. Moran?

"I have it!" said Walter Reed. "This to do with John J. Moran!"

So there was built, close by that detestable little House No. 1, another little house, called House No. 2. That was a comfortable house! It had windows on the side opposite to its door, so that a fine trade wind played through it. It was cool. It had a nice clean cot in it, with steam-disinfected bedding. It would have been an excellent house for a consumptive to get better in. It was a thoroughly sanitary little house. Half way across the inside of it was a screen, from top to bottom, a fine-meshed screen that the tiniest mosquito found it impossible to fly through. At 12 o'clock noon on the twenty-first of December in 1900, this John J. Moran (who was a hog for these tests) "clad only in a nightshirt and fresh from a bath," walked into this healthy little house. Five minutes before Reed and Carroll had opened a glass jar in that room, and out of that jar flew fifteen she-mosquitoes, thirsty for blood, whining for a meal of blood, and each and every one of those fifteen mosquitoes, had fed, on various days before — on the blood of yellow-faced boys in the hospital of Las Animas.

Clad only in a nightshirt and fresh from a bath, Moran — who knows of him now? — walked into the healthy little room and lay down on his clean cot. In a minute that damned buzzing started round his head, in two minutes he was bitten, in the thirty minutes he lay there he was stabbed seven times — without even the satisfaction of smashing those mosquitoes. You remember Mr. Sola, whom Grassi tortured — he probably had his worried moments — but all Mr. Sola had to look forward to was a little attack of malaria and a good dose of curative quinine to get him out of it. But Moran? But John J. Moran was a hog for such tests! He was back there at four-thirty the same afternoon, to be bitten again, and once more the next day — to satisfy the rest of the hungry she-mosquitoes who hadn't found him the first day. In the other room of this house, with only a fine-meshed but perfect wire screen between them and Moran — and the mosquitoes — lay two other boys, and those two boys slept in that house safely for eighteen nights.

But Moran?

On Christmas morning of 1900, there was a fine present waiting for him — in his head, how that thumped — in his eyes, how red they were and how the light hurt them — in his bones, how tired they were! A nasty knock those mosquitoes had hit him and he came within a hair of dying but (thank God! murmured Walter Reed) he was saved, this Moran, to live the rest of his life in an obscurity he didn't deserve. So Moran had his wish — in the interest of science, and for humanity! So he, with Folk and Jernegan and Cooke and all those others proved that the dirty pest hole of a house (with no mosquitoes) was safe; and that the clean house (but with mosquitoes) was dangerous, so dangerous! So at last Walter Reed had every answer to his diabolical questions, and he wrote, in that old-fashioned prose of his: "The essential factor in the infection of a building with yellow fever is the presence therein of mosquitoes that have bitten cases of yellow fever."

It was so simple. It was true. That was all. That was that. And Walter Reed wrote to his wife:

"The prayer that has been mine for twenty years, that I might be permitted in some way or at some time to do something to alleviate human suffering has been granted! A thousand Happy New Years. . . . Hark, there go the twenty-four buglers in concert, all sounding taps for the old year!"

They were sounding taps, were those buglers, for the searcher that was Jesse Lazear, and for the scourge of yellow fever that could now be wiped from the earth.

SUGGESTIONS FOR STUDY

1. There are three outstanding features of interest in this essay: the human element, the scientific, and the lively style of the author. Watch for particularly good examples.

2. Of all the persons involved in the experiments, which ones did you find most interesting? Why?

3. Do you know of other great scientific discoveries that are of universal benefit to mankind? They would make good topics for oral reports to a class.

FOR FURTHER READING

Microbe Hunters
Hunger Fighters
Seven Iron Men

FOR FURTHER READINGS OF ESSAYS

Broun, Heywood. *Seeing Things at Night, Pieces of Hate*

Crothers, Samuel M. *Among Friends, The Cheerful Giver, The Dame School of Experience, The Gentle Reader*

Grayson, David (Ray Stannard Baker). *Adventures in Contentment, Adventures in Friendship, The Friendly Road, Great Possessions*

Holliday, Robert Cortes. *Broome Street Straws, Turns About Town, Walking Stick Papers*

Howells, William Dean. *Suburban Sketches, Imaginary Interviews, Impressions and Experiences*

Keller, Helen. *The World I Live In*

Lowell, James Russell. *My Study Windows*

Mabie, Hamilton Wright. *Backgrounds of Literature, Books and Culture, Under the Trees*

Marvel, Ik (Donald G. Mitchell). *Dream Life, Reveries of a Bachelor*

Palmer, George H. *Self-Cultivation in English*

Phelps, William Lyon. *As I Like It, Essays on Modern Novelists, Essays on Modern Dramatists, Happiness*

Repplier, Agnes. *Americans and Others, Essays in Miniature, In Our Convent Days, Points of Friction*

Roosevelt, Theodore. *American Ideals, The Strenuous Life*

Slosson, E. E. *Creative Chemistry*

van Dyke, Henry. *Camp Fires and Guide Posts, Days Off, Fisherman's Luck, Little Rivers*

Warner, Charles Dudley. *A-Hunting of the Deer, Backlog Studies, Being a Boy, My Summer in a Garden*

Warner, Frances Lester. *Endicott and I, Life's Minor Collisions, Surprising the Family and Other Peradventures*

NATURE ESSAYS

Beebe, William. *The Edge of the Jungle, Jungle Peace*

Burroughs, John. *Afoot and Afloat, Birds and Bees, Locusts and Wild Honey, Sharp Eyes*

Muir, John. *Our National Parks, Steep Trails, Travels in Alaska*

Sharp, Dallas Lore. *The Hills of Hingham, Roof and Meadow, The Whole Year Through, The Face of the Fields, A Watcher in the Woods*

White, Stewart Edward. *The Cabin, The Forest, The Mountains*

ADVENTUROUS EXPERIENCE

Aldrich, Mildred. *A Hilltop on the Marne*

Collier, Price. *England and the English from an American Point of View*

Franck, H. A. *Four Months Afoot in Spain, A Vagabond Journey Around the World*

Halliburton, Richard. *The Royal Road to Romance, The Glorious Adventure*

Jackson, Helen Hunt. *Glimpses of California and the Missions*

Smith, F. Hopkinson. *Gondola Days, In Dickens's Land, A White Umbrella in Mexico*

Street, Julian. *Abroad at Home*

COLLECTIONS OF ESSAYS

Atlantic Classics — First and Second Series

Brown, Sharon. *Essays of Our Times*

Chamberlain, Essie. *Essays Old and New*

Hastings, W. T. *Contemporary Essays*

Heydrick, B. A. *Types of the Essay*

Johnson, Burgess. *Essaying the Essay*

Knickerbocker, E. V. *Present-Day Essays*

Law, Frederick H. *Modern Essays and Stories, Modern Life and Thought, Science in Literature*

Lyman, R. L. *The Mind at Work*

McCullough and Burgum. *A Book of Modern Essays*

Morley, Christopher. *Modern Essays for Schools*

Rees, Byron J. *Modern American Prose Selections*

Tanner, W. M. *Essays and Essay Writing, Modern Familiar Essays*

Biography and Autobiography

The recent increase in the number and quality of biographies produced in America indicates that this type of literature has today reached a place of importance never attained before. Two thousand years ago Plutarch wrote his famous *Lives*. From that time till recent years only an occasional volume by sheer excellence pushed itself into public favor in competition with the more popular poetry, drama, or novel. But today biography is one of our most popular forms of literature.

Biography as "the Lives of Great Men."

Our first concept of biography is probably as the "lives of great men." Many biographies are just such stories of achievement. We all wish to know intimate details of our great military heroes, and we read the life stories of Washington, Jackson, Lee, Grant. By reading biographies of Hamilton, Jefferson, Daniel Webster, and Lincoln, we get near to the heart of America through acquaintance with her great statesmen. Literature becomes more lucid as we learn of the varied careers of our great authors, like Poe, Walt Whitman, Mark

Twain, and Jack London. The development of modern science and modern business can best be understood by reading the lives of Burbank, Edison, Carnegie, Ford, and Rockefeller.

The Older Conception of the Purpose of Biography

It used to be popular to write flattering " official " biographies of great men, leaving out their defects and glossing over their weaknesses. The biographers accepted whole-heartedly Longfellow's dictum:

> " Lives of great men all remind us
> We can make our lives sublime,
> And, departing, leave behind us,
> Footprints on the sands of time."

And they assumed that the inspiration from the career of a great man would be increased if the biographer stripped him of human weaknesses and made him into a heroic figure, wholly worthy of being accepted as an ideal. But there has been a reaction to this method.

The New Conception of Biography

The new biography is partly the result of the realistic movement in fiction and partly of a deep-seated conviction on the part of writers that biographies are more inspirational if the " great man " is not set upon too high a pedestal. Many modern biographers feel that the reader must not worship from afar, but must come to realize that the great man and he are similar after all, and that he, too, may some day perform mighty deeds as did the hero in the book. The reader knows he is not perfect, say these modern writers, and he must come to realize that the great of the world were not perfect, either, but that they rose to prominence in spite of weaknesses and moral imperfections similar to his own. It is not surprising that the exponents of this new type of realistic biography have antagonized numerous hero-worshippers by overemphasizing the defects of our great men. But we must remember that, after all, the earlier biographers helped to bring about these modern excesses by their own dishonest interpretations. You will find it worth your while to decide for yourselves whether you prefer the idealistic or the realistic treatment of biography. Perhaps you will discover that you get inspiration from both and can find a place for both in your reading.

Biography often Clarifies History

But the value of reading biography is not limited to the inspiration that comes from acquaintance with the careers of great men. Biography may, for instance, be an excellent approach to the study of history.   Thomas Carlyle, the famous English historian, in his great series of essays, *Heroes and Hero Worship,* declares, " Universal history is at bottom the history of the great men who have worked here."   To get at the truth of history, he says, we must study not movements and state papers, but the biographies of men.   And even if to us movements seem more important in the study of history than they did to Carlyle, we may still find biography the best entrance to that field.   As we read about the men, we see them moving before a background of activities and events, and we come to a better understanding of their times and the movements in which they were engaged.   American history, which is essentially the story of the moving frontier, is probably best told in the biographies of the pioneers, from Captain John Smith to Charles A. Lindbergh.   Sometimes the chief persons in the book are themselves in no sense prominent; indeed, in the case of some of our best biographies the leading character's one claim to immortality is the biography itself.   Particularly is this true of biography in the form of a diary or letters, such as *A Confederate Girl's Diary* by Sarah Morgan Dawson, or — most famous of all — *Two Years Before the Mast* by Richard Henry Dana, Jr.   Often books of this sort make the past living and real to us in a way that a straight history textbook never does.

Rubbing Elbows with the Great through Biography

Still another reason for reading biography is to enlarge our human sympathy and rid ourselves of unreasonable prejudices.   Often we dislike persons just because we do not know them; acquaintance brings understanding.   Read Booker T. Washington's *Up from Slavery* and come to a better understanding of the American Negro; read Rose Cohen's *Out of the Shadow* and learn to sympathize with the struggle of the foreigner in this country.   If you are a Northerner with any lingering traces of Civil War bitterness, read Thomas Nelson Page's *Robert E. Lee, Man and Soldier,* and grow to revere one of America's greatest sons, who sorrowfully fought against the flag he loved because he considered it his duty.   If you feel that the theater is a den of iniquity and actors are beyond the pale, let E. H. Sothern's *The Melancholy Tale of Me* tell you the fascinating story of a great artist and a true man, and at the same time reveal the rich, colorful life behind the footlights. If you find yourself becoming anti-any-group, read a good biography of one of its leaders. You will learn that " there are two sides to every question "; and you will grow into a much broader minded, more intelligent, more useful man or woman.

The Personal Inspiration of Good Biography

Perhaps the pleasantest feature of biography reading is that, while it is inspiring us to higher achievement, leading us into the study of history, or enlarging our sympathies, it is also making us acquainted with interesting personalities. Jackson's life may or may not arouse our latent capacity for leadership, but acquaintance with the man Jackson certainly adds spice to life. We may or may not care for the study of history as such, but Lincoln, Cleveland, and Roosevelt are worth-while friends to have at one's side throughout life. We may or may not shed prejudices through the reading of biography, but we cannot help enjoying broadening our acquaintance among other races, nationalities, and social classes. Interesting people! That is the center of biography. Buffalo Bill, P. T. Barnum, Mark Twain, Brigham Young! Clara Barton, Helen Keller, Jane Addams, Mary Antin! Joseph Jefferson, Edward Bok, Benjamin Franklin, Al Smith! Actors, authors, pioneers, statesmen! The list is endless.

Contemporary Biographers

Among our modern writers we find several who are achieving fame as professional biographers. Among these are Gamaliel Bradford, who paints " portraits " in words; William Roscoe Thayer, whose successful biographies include those of Washington, John Hay, and Roosevelt; M. R. Werner, who has made P. T. Barnum, Brigham Young, and William Jennings Bryan real people to us; and Carl Sandburg, whose *The Prairie Years* is a real addition to the long list of biographies of Lincoln.

Among the seven selections included in this book from seven American biographies, it is hoped that each student will find at least one that interests him sufficiently for him to wish to read the complete biography. And from this study and your supplementary reading it is further hoped that many of you will add biography to the list of types of literature you enjoy and that you will continue ever afterward to enrich your lives by forming the acquaintance of the fascinating personalities of American life.

SCHOOL LIFE [1]

By HAMLIN GARLAND (1860–

The winning of the West was not all covered wagons, buffalo hunts, and Indian raids. It included also years of hard, monotonous labor as the "homesteader" turned the virgin prairie into grain fields and fenced-in pastures. The literary historian of the pioneer farmer of the Middle West is Hamlin Garland. Mr. Garland began writing realistic stories of local color back in the '90's. In 1917 he published his great autobiography, *A Son of the Middle Border*. This book is an epic portrayal of pioneer life on the farms of Wisconsin, Iowa, and Dakota. It is a beautifully written book, Mr. Garland having revised many of its passages more than twenty times.

The chapter here presented is called "School Life," but in its accounts of well-digging, threshing, and prairie fires and blizzards it suggests the pioneering which is the core of *A Son of the Middle Border*. The description of the school life itself, with its rich detail of recess games, McGuffey's readers, feet itching from chilblains, and frozen lunches, illustrates the painstaking and vivid realism found throughout the entire book.

Our new house was completed during July but we did not move into it till in September. There was much to be done in way of building sheds, granaries, and corn-cribs and in this work father was both carpenter and stone-mason. An amusing incident comes to my mind in connection with the digging of our well.

Uncle David and I were "tending mason," and father was down in the well laying or trying to lay the curbing. It was a tedious and difficult job and he was about to give it up in despair when one of our neighbors, a quaint old Englishman named Barker, came driving along. He was one of these men who take a minute inquisitive interest in the affairs of others; therefore he pulled his team to a halt and came in.

Peering into the well he drawled out, "Hello, Garland. W'at ye doin' down there?"

"Tryin' to lay a curb," replied my father lifting a gloomy face, "and I guess it's too complicated for me."

"Nothin' easier," retorted the old man with a wink at my uncle, "jest putt two a-top o' one and one a-top o' two — and the

---

[1] From *A Son of the Middle Border* by Hamlin Garland. Reprinted by permission of The Macmillan Company, publishers.

big end out " — and with a broad grin on his red face he went
back to his team and drove away.

My father afterwards said, " I saw the whole process in a flash
of light. He had given me all the rule I needed. I laid the rest of
that wall without a particle of trouble."

Many times after this Barker stopped to offer advice, but he
never quite equaled the startling success of his rule for masonry.

The events of this harvest, even the process of moving into the
new house, are obscured in my mind by the clouds of smoke which
rose from calamitous fires all over the west. It was an unprece-
dentedly dry season, so that not merely the prairie but many
weedy cornfields burned. I had a good deal of time to meditate
upon this for I was again the plow-boy. Every day I drove away
from the rented farm to the new land where I was cross-cutting
the breaking, and the thickening haze through which the sun
shone with a hellish red glare, produced in me a growing
uneasiness which became terror when the news came to us that
Chicago was on fire. It seemed to me then that the earth was
about to go up in a flaming cloud just as my granddad had so
often prophesied.

This general sense of impending disaster was made keenly
personal by the destruction of Uncle David's stable with all his
horses. This building like most of the barns of the region was not
only roofed with straw but banked with straw, and it burned so
swiftly that David was trapped in a stall while trying to save one
of his teams. He saved himself by burrowing like a gigantic mole
through the side of the shed, and so, hatless, covered with dust and
chaff, emerged as if from a fiery burial after he had been given up
for dead.

This incident combined with others so filled my childish mind
that I lived in apprehension of similar disaster. I feared the hot
wind which roared up from the south, and I never entered our
own stable in the middle of the day without a sense of danger.
Then came the rains — the blessed rains — and put an end to my
fears.

In a week we had forgotten all the " conflagrations " except that
in Chicago. There was something grandiose and unforgettable in
the tales which told of the madly fleeing crowds in the narrow
streets. These accounts pushed back the walls of my universe
till its far edge included the ruined metropolis whose rebuilding
was of the highest importance to us, for it was not only the source

of all our supplies, but the great central market to which we sent
our corn and hogs and wheat.

My world was splendidly romantic. It was bounded on the west
by THE PLAINS with their Indians and buffalo; on the north by
THE GREAT WOODS, filled with thieves and counterfeiters; on the
south by OSAGE and CHICAGO; and on the east by HESPER, ONA-
LASKA, and BOSTON. A luminous trail ran from Dry Run Prairie
to Neshonoc — all else was " chaos and black night."

For seventy days I walked behind my plow on the new farm
while my father finished the harvest on the rented farm and moved
to the house on the knoll. It was lonely work for a boy of eleven
but there were frequent breaks in the monotony and I did not
greatly suffer. I disliked cross-cutting for the reason that the
unrotted sods would often pile up in front of the coulter and make
me a great deal of trouble. There is a certain pathos in the sight
of that small boy tugging and kicking at the stubborn turf in
the effort to free his plow. Such misfortunes loom large in a
lad's horizon.

One of the interludes, and a lovely one, was given over to gathering the hay from one of the wild meadows to the north of us.
Another was the threshing from the shock on the rented farm.
This was the first time we had seen this done and it interested us
keenly. A great many teams were necessary and the crew of men
was correspondingly large. Uncle David was again the thresher
with a fine new separator, and I would have enjoyed the season
with almost perfect contentment had it not been for the fact that
I was detailed to hold sacks for Daddy Fairbanks who was the
measurer.

Our first winter had been without much wind but our second
taught us the meaning of the word " blizzard " which we had
just begun to hear about. The winds of Wisconsin were " gentle
zephyrs " compared to the blasts which now swept down over the
plain to hammer upon our desolate little cabin and pile the drifts
around our sheds and granaries, and even my pioneer father was
forced to admit that the hills of Green's Coulee had their uses
after all.

One such storm which leaped upon us at the close of a warm
and beautiful day in February lasted for two days and three
nights, making life on the open prairie impossible even to the
strongest man. The thermometer fell to thirty degrees below
zero and the snow-laden air moving at a rate of eighty miles an

hour pressed upon the walls of our house with giant power. The sky of noon was darkened, so that we moved in a pallid half-light, and the windows thick with frost shut us in as if with gray shrouds.

Hour after hour those winds and snows in furious battle, howled and roared and whistled around our frail shelter, slashing at the windows and piping on the chimney, till it seemed as if the Lord Sun had been wholly blotted out and that the world would never again be warm. Twice each day my father made a desperate sally toward the stable to feed the imprisoned cows and horses or to replenish our fuel — for the remainder of the long pallid day he sat beside the fire with gloomy face. Even his indomitable spirit was awed by the fury of that storm.

So long and so continuously did those immitigable winds howl in our ears that their tumult persisted, in imagination, when on the third morning, we thawed holes in the thickened rime of the window panes and looked forth on a world silent as a marble sea and flaming with sunlight. My own relief was mingled with surprise — surprise to find the landscape so unchanged. True, the yard was piled high with drifts and the barns were almost lost to view but the far fields and the dark lines of Burr Oak Grove remained unchanged.

We met our schoolmates that day, like survivors of shipwreck, and for many days we listened to gruesome stories of disaster, tales of stages frozen deep in snow with all their passengers sitting in their seats, and of herders with their silent flocks around them, lying stark as granite among the hazel bushes in which they had sought shelter. It was long before we shook off the awe with which this tempest filled our hearts.

The schoolhouse which stood at the corner of our new farm was less than half a mile away, and yet on many of the winter days which followed, we found it quite far enough. Hattie was now thirteen, Frank nine and I a little past eleven, but nothing, except a blizzard such as I have described, could keep us away from school. Facing the cutting wind, wallowing through the drifts, battling like small intrepid animals, we often arrived at the door moaning with pain yet unsubdued, our ears frosted, our toes numb in our boots, to meet others in similar case around the roaring hot stove.

Often after we reached the schoolhouse another form of suffering overtook us in the " thawing out " process. Our fingers and toes, swollen with blood, ached and itched, and our ears burned.

Nearly all of us carried sloughing ears and scaling noses. Some of the pupils came two miles against these winds.

The natural result of all this exposure was, of course, chilblains! Every foot in the school was more or less touched with this disease, to which our elders alluded as if it were an amusing trifle, but to us it was no joke.

After getting thoroughly warmed up, along about the middle of the forenoon, there came into our feet a most intense itching and burning and aching, a sensation so acute that keeping still was impossible, and all over the room an uneasy shuffling and drumming arose as we pounded our throbbing heels against the floor or scraped our itching toes against the edge of our benches. The teacher understood and was kind enough to overlook this disorder.

The wonder is that any of us lived through that winter, for at recess, no matter what the weather might be, we flung ourselves out of doors to play " fox and geese " or " dare goal," until, damp with perspiration, we responded to the teacher's bell, and came pouring back into the entry ways to lay aside our wraps for another hour's study.

Our readers were almost the only counterchecks to the current of vulgarity and baseness which ran through the talk of the older boys, and I wish to acknowledge my deep obligation to Professor McGuffey, whoever he may have been, for the dignity and literary grace of his selections. From the pages of his readers I learned to know and love the poems of Scott, Byron, Southey, Wordsworth and a long line of the English masters. I got my first taste of Shakespeare from the selected scenes which I read in these books.

With terror as well as delight I rose to read " Lochiel's Warning," " The Battle of Waterloo " or " The Roman Captive." Marco Bozzaris and William Tell were alike glorious to me. I soon knew not only my own reader, the fourth, but all the selections in the fifth and sixth as well. I could follow almost word for word the recitations of the older pupils and at such times I forgot my squat little body and my mop of hair, and became imaginatively a page in the train of Ivanhoe, or a bowman in the army of Richard the Lion Heart battling the Saracen in the Holy Land.

With a high ideal of the way in which these grand selections should be read, I was scared almost voiceless when it came my turn to read them before the class. " STRIKE FOR YOUR ALTARS AND YOUR FIRES. STRIKE FOR THE GREEN GRAVES OF YOUR SIRES —

GOD AND YOUR NATIVE LAND," always reduced me to a trembling breathlessness. The sight of the emphatic print was a call to the best that was in me and yet I could not meet the test. Excess of desire to do it just right often brought a ludicrous gasp and I often fell back into my seat in disgrace, the titter of the girls adding to my pain.

Then there was the famous passage, " Did ye not hear it? " and the careless answer, " No, it was but the wind or the car rattling o'er the stony street." — I knew exactly how those opposing emotions should be expressed but to do it after I rose to my feet was impossible. Burton was even more terrified than I. Stricken blind as well as dumb he usually ended by helplessly staring at the words which, I conceive, had suddenly become a blur to him.

No matter, we were taught to feel the force of these poems and to reverence the genius that produced them, and that was worth while. Falstaff and Prince Hal, Henry and his wooing of Kate, Wolsey and his downfall, Shylock and his pound of flesh all became a part of our thinking and helped us to measure the large figures of our own literature, for Whittier, Bryant and Longfellow also had place in these volumes. It is probable that Professor McGuffey, being a southern man, did not value New England writers as highly as my grandmother did, nevertheless " Thanatopsis " was there and " The Village Blacksmith," and extracts from *The Deer Slayer* and *The Pilot* gave us a notion that in Cooper we had a novelist of weight and importance, one to put beside Scott and Dickens.

A by-product of my acquaintance with one of the older boys was a stack of copies of the *New York Weekly,* a paper filled with stories of noble life in England and hair-breadth escapes on the plain, a shrewd mixture, designed to meet the needs of the entire membership of a prairie household. The pleasure I took in these tales should fill me with shame, but it doesn't — I rejoice in the memory of it.

I soon began, also, to purchase and trade " Beadle's Dime Novels " and, to tell the truth, I took an exquisite delight in *Old Sleuth* and *Jack Harkaway.* My taste was catholic. I ranged from *Lady Gwendolin* to *Buckskin Bill* and so far as I can now distinguish one was quite as enthralling as the other. It is impossible for any print to be as magical to any boy these days as those weeklies were to me in 1871.

One day a singular test was made of us all. Through some

agency now lost to me my father was brought to subscribe for *The Hearth and Home* or some such paper for the farmer, and in this I read my first chronicle of everyday life.

In the midst of my dreams of lords and ladies, queens and dukes, I found myself deeply concerned with backwoods farming, spelling schools, protracted meetings, and the like familiar homely scenes. This serial (which involved my sister and myself in many a spat as to who should read it first) was *The Hoosier Schoolmaster,* by Edward Eggleston, and a perfectly successful attempt to interest western readers in a story of the middle border.

To us " Mandy " and " Bud Means," " Ralph Hartsook," the teacher, " Little Shocky," and sweet patient " Hannah," were as real as Cyrus Button and Daddy Fairbanks. We could hardly wait for the next number of the paper, so concerned were we about " Hannah " and " Ralph." We quoted old lady Means and we made bets on " Bud " in his fight with the villainous drover. I hardly knew where Indiana was in those days, but Eggleston's characters were near neighbors.

The illustrations were dreadful, even in my eyes, but the artist contrived to give a slight virginal charm to Hannah and a certain childish sweetness to Shocky, so that we accepted the more than mortal ugliness of old man Means and his daughter Mirandy (who simpered over her book at us as she did at Ralph), as a just interpretation of their worthlessness.

This book is a milestone in my literary progress as it is in the development of distinctive western fiction, and years afterward I was glad to say so to the aged author, who lived a long and honored life as a teacher and writer of fiction.

It was always too hot or too cold in our schoolroom and on certain days when a savage wind beat and clamored at the loose windows, the girls, humped and shivering, sat upon their feet to keep them warm, and the younger children with shawls over their shoulders sought permission to gather close about the stove.

Our dinner pails (stored in the entry way) were often frozen solid and it was necessary to thaw out our mince pie as well as our bread and butter by putting it on the stove. I recall, vividly, gnawing, dog-like, at the mollified outside of a doughnut while still its frosty heart made my teeth ache.

Happily all days were not like this. There were afternoons when the sun streamed warmly into the room, when long icicles formed on the eaves, adding a touch of grace to the desolate building, moments when the jingling bells of passing wood-sleighs expressed the natural cheer and buoyancy of our youthful hearts.

SUGGESTIONS FOR STUDY

1. Vocabulary: grandiose, interludes, intrepid, sloughing, Saracen, catholic.
2. What was the meaning of Barker's rule for masonry?
3. What spectacular fires or storms have you even seen?
4. What are the boundaries of your " world "?
5. Do you think your literary taste is " catholic "? Can you name any " milestones " in your " literary progress "?
6. Do you think the many hardships these boys and girls had to undergo to get an education were a help or a hindrance to them? Why?

FOR FURTHER READING

FICTION

Main-Traveled Roads
Other Main-Traveled Roads
Trail-Makers of the Middle Border

POETRY

Prairie Songs

BIOGRAPHY AND AUTOBIOGRAPHY

A Daughter of the Middle Border
Back-Trailers from the Middle Border
Ulysses S. Grant, His Life and Character

PROJECT OF ARRIVING AT MORAL PERFECTION

By Benjamin Franklin (1706–1790)

Franklin's *Autobiography* is generally recognized as of outstanding importance in American letters. In fact, of all the books written in America before 1800, it stands supreme and could least be spared from the libraries of modern America. It is one of the few books of which one is tempted to dare say, " These should be read by all Americans."

The *Autobiography* was written at different times from 1771 to 1789. The manuscript itself has had a strange and interesting history. The first edition was a French version of the first instalment, published in 1791. Garbled and distorted editions followed in both French and English, but not till 1874 was Franklin's own manuscript brought to light and published in a complete and accurate form.

The *Autobiography* is an honest account of Franklin's life up to 1757, portraying his weaknesses frankly and his strength with no false modesty.

The first section, written in the form of a letter to his son, is especially direct, simple, and candid. As one reads of Franklin's early life, his experiences as a printer, his travels, his military and civil offices, his writings, his inventions, and his scientific and philosophic interests, the reader understands why one modern biographer calls him " the many-sided Franklin." And as one reads of his open-mindedness, his practical business sense, his humor, his zest in living, and his sane adjustment to human limitations, the reader senses why another **modern** writer styles him " the first civilized American."

Of this masterpiece nothing is satisfactory but **the whole,** but the following chapter in which Franklin describes his attempt to arrive at " moral perfection " will reveal to you his breadth and his limitations, and also the delightful candor of his style.

It was about this time I conceived the bold and arduous project of arriving at moral perfection. I wished to live without committing any fault at any time; I would conquer all that either natural inclination, custom, or company might lead me into. As I knew, or thought I knew, what was right and wrong, I did not see why I might not always do the one and avoid the other. But I soon found I had undertaken a task of more difficulty than I had imagined. While my care was employed in guarding against one fault, I was often surprised by another; habit took the advantage of inattention; inclination was sometimes too strong for reason. I concluded, at length, that the mere speculative conviction that it was our interest to be completely virtuous was not sufficient to prevent our slipping; and that the contrary habits must be broken, and good ones acquired and established, before we can have any dependence on a steady, uniform rectitude of conduct. For this purpose I therefore contrived the following method.

In the various enumerations of the moral virtues I had met with in my reading, I found the catalogue more or less numerous, as different writers included more or fewer ideas under the same name. Temperance, for example, was by some confined to eating and drinking, while by others it was extended to mean the moderating every other pleasure, appetite, inclination, or passion, bodily or mental, even to our avarice and ambition. I proposed to myself, for the sake of clearness, to use rather more names, with fewer ideas annexed to each, than a few names with more ideas; and I included under thirteen names of virtues all that at that time occurred to me as necessary or desirable, and annexed to each a short precept, which fully expressed the extent I gave to its meaning.

These names of virtues, with their precepts were:

1. TEMPERANCE

Eat not to dullness; drink not to elevation.

2. SILENCE

Speak not but what may benefit others or yourself; avoid trifling conversation.

3. ORDER

Let all your things have their places; let each part of your business have its time.

4. RESOLUTION

Resolve to perform what you ought; perform without fail what you resolve.

5. FRUGALITY

Make no expense but to do good to others or yourself; i.e., waste nothing.

6. INDUSTRY

Lose no time; be always employed in something useful; cut off all unnecessary actions.

7. SINCERITY

Use no hurtful deceit; think innocently and justly; and, if you speak, speak accordingly.

8. JUSTICE

Wrong none by doing injuries, or omitting the benefits that are your duty.

9. MODERATION

Avoid extremes; forbear resenting injuries so much as you think they deserve.

10. CLEANLINESS

Tolerate no uncleanliness in body, clothes, or habitation.

11. TRANQUILLITY

Be not disturbed at trifles, or at accidents common or unavoidable.

12. CHASTITY

13. HUMILITY

Imitate Jesus and Socrates.

My intention being to acquire the *habitude* of all these virtues,
I judged it would be well not to distract my attention by attempting the whole at once, but to fix it on one of them at a time;
and, when I should be master of that, then to proceed to another,
and so on, till I should have gone through the thirteen; and as
the previous acquisition of some might facilitate the acquisition
of certain others, I arranged them with that view, as they stand
above. Temperance first, as it tends to procure that coolness
and clearness of head, which is so necessary where constant vigilance was to be kept up, and guard maintained against the un-
remitting attraction of ancient habits, and the force of perpetual
temptations. This being acquired and established, Silence would
be more easy; and my desire being to gain knowledge at the same
time that I improved in virtue, and considering that in conversation it was obtained rather by the use of the ears than of the
tongue, and therefore wishing to break a habit I was getting into
of prattling, punning, and joking, which only made me acceptable
to trifling company, I gave Silence the second place. This and
the next, Order, I expected would allow me more time for attending
to my project and my studies. Resolution, once become habitual,
would keep me firm in my endeavors to obtain all the subsequent
virtues; Frugality and Industry freeing me from my remaining
debt, and producing affluence and independence, would make
more easy the practice of Sincerity and Justice, etc., etc. Conceiving then, that, agreeably to the advice of Pythagoras in his
Golden Verses, daily examination would be necessary, I contrived
the following method for conducting that examination.

I made a little book, in which I allotted a page for each of the
virtues. I ruled each page with red ink, so as to have seven
columns, one for each day of the week, marking each column
with a letter for the day. I crossed these columns with thirteen
red lines, marking the beginning of each line with the first letter
of one of the virtues, on which line, and in its proper column, I
might mark, by a little black spot, every fault I found upon
examination to have been committed respecting that virtue upon
that day.

I determined to give a week's strict attention to each of the
virtues successively. Thus, in the first week, my great guard
was to avoid even the least offense against Temperance, leaving
the other virtues to their ordinary chance, only marking every
evening the faults of the day. Thus, if in the first week I could

Form of the Pages.

TEMPERANCE.							
EAT NOT TO DULLNESS; DRINK NOT TO ELEVATION.							
	S.	M.	T.	W.	T.	F.	S.
T.							
S.	*	*		*		*	
O.	* *	*	*		*	*	*
R.			*			*	
F.		*			*		
I.			*				
S.							
J.							
M.							
C.							
T.							
C.							
H.							

keep my first line, marked T, clear of spots, I supposed the habit of that virtue so much strengthened, and its opposite weakened, that I might venture extending my attention to include the next, and for the following week keep both lines clear of spots. Proceeding thus to the last, I could go through a course complete in thirteen weeks, and four courses in a year. And like him who, having a garden to weed, does not attempt to eradicate all the bad herbs at once, which would exceed his reach and his strength, but works on one of the beds at a time, and, having accomplished the first, proceeds to a second, so I should have, I hoped, the encouraging pleasure of seeing on my pages the progress I made in virtue, by clearing successively my lines of their spots, till in the end, by a number of courses, I should be happy in viewing a clean book, after a thirteen weeks' daily examination.

This my little book had for its motto these lines from Addison's
Cato:

> " Here will I hold. If there's a power above us
> (And that there is, all nature cries aloud
> Thro' all her works), He must delight in virtue;
> And that which he delights in must be happy."

Another from Cicero,

" O vitae Philosophia dux! O virtutum indagatrix expul-
trixque vitiorum! Unus dies, bene et ex praeceptis tuis actus,
peccanti immortalitati est anteponendus." [1]

Another from the *Proverbs* of Solomon, speaking of wisdom
or virtue:

" Length of days is in her right hand, and in her left hand
riches and honor. Her ways are ways of pleasantness, and all
her paths are peace." iii. 16, 17.

And conceiving God to be the fountain of wisdom, I thought
it right and necessary to solicit his assistance for obtaining it; to
this end I formed the following little prayer, which was prefixed
to my tables of examination, for daily use.

" O powerful Goodness! bountiful Father! merciful Guide!
Increase in me that wisdom which discovers my truest interest.
Strengthen my resolutions to perform what that wisdom dictates.
Accept my kind offices to thy other children as the only return in
my power for thy continual favors to me."

I used also sometimes a little prayer which I took from Thom-
son's poems, viz.:

> " Father of light and life, thou Good Supreme!
> O teach me what is good; teach me Thyself!
> Save me from folly, vanity, and vice,
> From every low pursuit; and fill my soul
> With knowledge, conscious peace, and virtue pure;
> Sacred, substantial, never-fading bliss! "

---

[1] " O Philosophy, guide of life! O detecter and judge of crimes! A single
day lived well and in accordance with your precepts is to be preferred to an
immortality of error."

The precept of Order requiring that *every part of my business should have its allotted time,* one page in my little book contained the following scheme of employment for the twenty-four hours of a natural day.

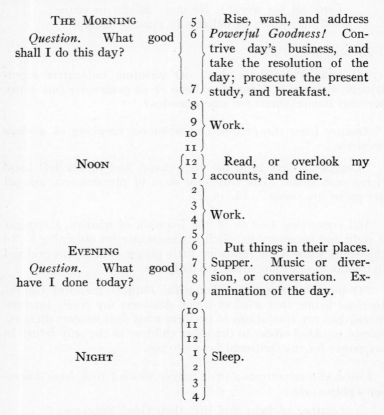

THE MORNING	5	Rise, wash, and address
Question. What good	6	*Powerful Goodness!* Contrive day's business, and take the resolution of the day; prosecute the present study, and breakfast.
shall I do this day?		
	7	
	8	
	9	Work.
	10	
	11	
NOON	12	Read, or overlook my accounts, and dine.
	1	
	2	
	3	Work.
	4	
	5	
EVENING	6	Put things in their places.
Question. What good	7	Supper. Music or diversion, or conversation. Examination of the day.
have I done today?	8	
	9	
	10	
	11	
	12	
NIGHT	1	Sleep.
	2	
	3	
	4	

I entered upon the execution of this plan for self-examination, and continued it with occasional intermissions for some time. I was surprised to find myself so much fuller of faults than I had imagined; but I had the satisfaction of seeing them diminish. To avoid the trouble of renewing now and then my little book, which, by scraping out the marks on the paper of old faults to make room for new ones in a new course, became full of holes, I transferred my tables and precepts to the ivory leaves of a memorandum book, on which the lines were drawn with red ink, that made a durable stain, and on those lines I marked my faults with a black lead pencil, which marks I could easily wipe out with a wet sponge. After a while I went through one course only in a year, and afterward only one in several years, till at length I omitted them entirely, being employed in voyages and business abroad, with a multiplicity of affairs that interfered; but I always carried my little book with me.

My scheme of Order gave me the most trouble; and I found that, though it might be practicable where a man's business was such as to leave him the disposition of his time, that of a journeyman printer, for instance, it was not possible to be exactly observed by a master, who must mix with the world, and often receive people of business at their own hours. Order, too, with regard to places for things, papers, etc., I found extremely difficult to acquire. I had not been early accustomed to it, and, having an exceeding good memory, I was not so sensible of the inconvenience attending want of method. This article, therefore, cost me so much painful attention, and my faults in it vexed me so much, and I made so little progress in amendment, and had such frequent relapses, that I was almost ready to give up the attempt, and content myself with a faulty character in that respect, like the man who, in buying an ax of a smith, my neighbor, desired to have the whole of its surface as bright as the edge. The smith consented to grind it bright for him if he would turn the wheel; he turned, while the smith pressed the broad face of the ax hard and heavily on the stone, which made the turning of it very fatiguing. The man came every now and then from the wheel to see how the work went on, and at length would take his ax as it was, without further grinding. " No," said the smith, " turn on, turn on; we shall have it bright by and by; as yet, it is only speckled." " Yes," says the man, " *but I think I like a speckled ax best*." And I believe this may have been the case with many, who, having, for want of some such means as I employed, found the difficulty of obtaining good and breaking bad habits in other points of vice and virtue, have given up the struggle, and concluded that *" a speckled ax was best ";* for something, that pretended to be reason, was every now and then suggesting to me that such extreme nicety as I exacted of myself might be a kind of foppery in morals, which, if it were known, would make me ridiculous; that a perfect character might be attended with the inconvenience of being envied and hated; and that a benevolent man should allow a few faults in himself, to keep his friends in countenance.

In truth, I found myself incorrigible with respect to Order; and now I am grown old, and my memory bad, I feel very sensibly the want of it. But, on the whole, though I never arrived at the perfection I had been so ambitious of obtaining, but fell far short of it, yet I was, by the endeavor, a better and a happier man than I otherwise should have been if I had not attempted it; as those who aim at perfect writing by imitating the engraved copies, though they never reach the wished-for excellence of those copies, their hand is mended by the endeavor.

It may be well my posterity should be informed that to this little artifice, with the blessing of God, their ancestor owed the constant felicity of his life, down to his 79th year, in which this is written. What reverses may attend the remainder is in the hand of Providence; but, if they arrive, the reflection on past happiness enjoyed ought to help his bearing them with more resignation. To Temperance he ascribes his long-continued health, and what is still left to him of a good constitution; to Industry and Frugality, the early easiness of his circumstances and acquisition of his fortune, with all that knowledge that enabled him to be a useful citizen, and obtained for him some degree of reputation among the learned; to Sincerity and Justice, the confidence of his country, and the honorable employs it conferred upon him; and to the joint influence of the whole mass of the virtues, even in the imperfect state he was able to acquire them, all that evenness of temper, and that cheerfulness in conversation, which makes his company still sought for, and agreeable even to his younger acquaintance. I hope, therefore, that some of my descendants may follow the example and reap the benefit.

It will be remarked that, though my scheme was not wholly without religion, there was in it no mark of any of the distinguishing tenets of any particular sect. I had purposely avoided them; for, being fully persuaded of the utility and excellency of my method, and that it might be serviceable to people in all religions, and intending some time or other to publish it, I would not have anything in it that should prejudice any one, of any sect, against it. I purposed writing a little comment on each virtue, in which I would have shown the advantages of possessing it, and the mischiefs attending its oppositive vice; and I should have called my book *The Art of Virtue,* because it would have shown the means and manner of obtaining virtue, which would have distinguished it from the mere exhortation to be good, that does not instruct and indicate the means, but is like the apostle's man of verbal charity, who only without showing to the naked and hungry how or where they might get clothes or victuals, exhorted them to be fed and clothed. — James ii. 15, 16.

But it so happened that my intention of writing and publishing this comment was never fulfilled. I did, indeed, from time to time, put down short hints of the sentiments, reasonings, etc., to be made use of in it, some of which I have still by me; but the necessary close attention to private business in the earlier part of my life, and public business since, have occasioned my postponing it; for, it being connected in my mind with *a great and extensive project,* that required the whole man to execute, and which an unforeseen succession of employs prevented my attending to, it has hitherto remained unfinished.

In this piece it was my design to explain and enforce this doctrine, that vicious actions are not hurtful because they are forbidden, but forbidden because they are hurtful, the nature of man alone considered; that it was, therefore, every one's interest to be virtuous who wished to be happy even in this world; and I should, from this circumstance (there being always in the world a number of rich merchants, nobility, states, and princes, who have need of honest instruments for the management of their affairs, and such being so rare), have endeavored to convince young persons that no qualities were so likely to make a poor man's fortune as those of probity and integrity.

My list of virtues contained at first but twelve; but a Quaker friend having kindly informed me that I was generally thought proud; that my pride showed itself frequently in conversation; that I was not content with being in the right when discussing any point, but was overbearing and rather insolent, of which he convinced me by mentioning several instances; I determined endeavoring to cure myself, if I could, of this vice or folly among the rest, and I added Humility to my list.

I cannot boast of much success in acquiring the *reality* of this virtue, but I had a good deal with regard to the *appearance* of it. I made it a rule to forbear all direct contradiction to the sentiments of others, and all positive assertion of my own. I even forbid myself, agreeably to the old laws of our Junto, the use of every word or expression in the language that imported a fixed opinion, such as *certainly, undoubtedly,* etc., and I adopted, instead of them, *I conceive, I apprehend,* or *I imagine* a thing to be so or so; or it *so appears to me at present.* When another asserted something that I thought an error, I denied myself the pleasure of contradicting him abruptly, and of showing immediately some absurdity in his proposition; and in answering I began by observing that in certain cases or circumstances his opinion would be right, but in the present case there *appeared* or *seemed* to me some difference, etc. I soon found the advantage of this change in my manner; the conversations I engaged in went on more pleasantly. The modest way in which I proposed my opinions procured them a readier reception and less contradiction; I had less mortification when I was found to be in the wrong, and I more easily prevailed with others to give up their mistakes and join with me when I happened to be in the right.

And this mode, which I at first put on with some violence to natural inclination, became at length so easy, and so habitual to me that perhaps for these fifty years past no one has ever heard a dogmatical expression escape me. And to this habit (after my character of integrity) I think it principally owing that I had early so much weight with my fellow-citizens when I proposed new institutions, or alterations in the old, and so much influence in public councils when I became a member; for I was but a bad speaker, never eloquent, subject to much hesitation in my choice of words, hardly correct in language, and yet I generally carried my points.

In reality, there is, perhaps, no one of our natural passions so hard to subdue as *pride.* Disguise it, struggle with it, beat it down, stifle it, mortify it as much as one pleases, it is still alive, and will every now and then peep out and show itself; you will see it, perhaps, often in this history; for, even if I could conceive that I had completely overcome it, I should probably be proud of my humility.

SUGGESTIONS FOR STUDY

1. Do you agree with Franklin that Temperance is the virtue to be first striven for? Why? Just what is meant by Temperance?

2. Which of Franklin's virtues seems to you the hardest to attain? Easiest? Most worth while? Least worth while?

3. What sort of Franklin does this chapter reveal to you?

4. What is the chief defect of Franklin's list of virtues? Make your own list, and see what improvements you can make.

FOR FURTHER READING

BIOGRAPHY

Dudley, Edward L. *Benjamin Franklin*

Fisher, Sidney G. *The True Benjamin Franklin*

Ford, Paul Leicester. *The Many-Sided Franklin*

Hubbard, Elbert. "Benjamin Franklin" (in *Little Journeys to the Homes of American Statesmen*)

Russell, Phillips. *Benjamin Franklin, the First Civilized American*

FICTION

Bacheller, Irving A. *In the Days of Poor Richard*

DRAMA

Benton, Rita. *Franklin and Other Plays*

Brougham, J. *Franklin* (in French's *Modern Standard Drama*)

Hague and Chalmers. *Benjamin Franklin* (in *Dramatic Moments in American History*)

Mackay, C. D. *Benjamin Franklin, Journeyman* (in Webber and Webster, *Short Plays for Junior and Senior High Schools*)

Wade, Mary Hazelton. *Benjamin Franklin, a Story and Play*

LEE IN DEFEAT

By THOMAS NELSON PAGE (1853–1922)

Few, if any, Americans deserve greater devotion and honor than Robert E. Lee (1807–1870). At the opening of the Civil War, this great military genius was offered the command of the Federal forces; but, standing true to his family traditions and his high concept of honor and duty, he turned his back upon certain renown, and allied his fortunes with those of his native Virginia. To know Lee is to understand the honesty of purpose, the gallant courage, the tragic despair, and the manly acceptance of unavoidable defeat that characterized the southern leaders of the Lost Cause.

From the many accounts of the life of Lee, we have selected a chapter by his fellow-Virginian, Thomas Nelson Page. Page, you will remember, was one of the followers of Bret Harte in the writing of local color stories, in which he pictured the romance of Old Virginia before the Civil War. He also won recognition as a novelist, his *Red Rock* being our best portrayal of the terrible conditions of Reconstruction days. In *Robert E. Lee,*

Man and Soldier Mr. Page expresses the same sympathetic understanding of southern character that we find in his fiction. This biography is well worth reading in its entirety, both because it is an excellent portrait of a noble American and because it is written in the pleasing style of one of our most eminent southern authors.

And now, having endeavored to picture Lee during those glorious campaigns which must, to the future student of military skill, place him among the first captains of history, I shall not invite attention further to Lee the soldier — to Lee the strategist — to Lee the victorious, but to a greater Lee — to Lee the defeated.

As glorious as were these campaigns, it is on the last act of the drama — the retreat from Petersburg, the surrender at Appomattox, and the dark period that followed that surrender — that we must look to see him at his best. His every act, his every word, showed how completely he had surrendered himself to Duty, and with what implicit obedience he followed the command of that " stern daughter of the voice of God."

" Are you sanguine of the result of the war? " asked Bishop Wilmer of him in the closing days of the struggle. His reply was :

" At present I am not concerned with results. God's will ought to be our aim, and I am quite contented that His designs should be accomplished and not mine."

On that last morning when his handful of worn and starving veterans had made their last charge, to find themselves shut in by ranks of serried steel, hemmed in by Grant's entire army, he faced the decree of Fate with as much constancy as though that decree were success, not doom.

" What will history say of the surrender of an army in the field? " asked an officer of his staff in passionate grief.

" Yes, I know they will say hard things of us; they will not understand that we were overwhelmed by numbers; but that is not the question, colonel. The question is, is it right to surrender this army? If it is right, then I will take all of the responsibility."

It was ever the note of duty that he sounded.

" You will take with you," he said to his army in his farewell address, " the satisfaction that proceeds from the consciousness of duty faithfully performed."

" We are conscious that we have humbly tried to do our duty," he said, a year or more after the war, when the clouds hung heavy over the South; " we may, therefore, with calm satisfaction trust in God and leave results to Him."

The sun which has shone in the morning, but has become obscured by clouds in the afternoon, sometimes breaks forth and at its setting shines with a greater splendor than it knew even at high noon.

So here. Sheathing his stainless sword, surrendering in the field the remnant of an army that had once been the most redoubtable body of fighting men of the century, the greatest captain, the noblest gentleman of our time, expecting to slip into the darkness of oblivion, suddenly stepped forth from the gloom of defeat into the splendor of perpetual fame.

I love to think of Grant as he appeared that April day at Appomattox: the simple soldier, the strenuous fighter who, though thrashed, was always ready to fight again; who, now though he had achieved the prize for which he had fought so hard and had paid so dearly, was so modest and so unassuming that but for his shoulder-straps and that yet better mark of rank, his generosity, he might not have been known as the victor. Southerners generally have long forgiven Grant all else for the magnanimity that he showed that day to Lee. By his orders no salutes of joy were fired, no public marks of exultation over his fallen foe were allowed. History contains no finer example of greatness. Not Alexander in his generous youth excelled him.

Yet, it is not more to the victor that Posterity will turn her gaze than to the vanquished, her admiration at the glory of the conqueror wellnigh lost in amazement at the dignity of the conquered.

Men who saw the defeated general when he came forth from the chamber where he had signed the articles of capitulation say that he paused a moment as his eyes rested once more on the Virginia hills, smote his hands together as though in some excess of inward agony, then mounted his gray horse, Traveler, and rode calmly away.

If that was the very Gethsemane of his trials, yet he must have had then one moment of supreme, if chastened, joy. As he rode quietly down the lane leading from the scene of capitulation, he passed into view of his men — of such as remained of them. The news of the surrender had got abroad and they were

waiting, grief-stricken and dejected, upon the hillsides, when
they caught sight of their old commander on the gray horse. Then
occurred one of the most notable scenes in the history of war.
In an instant they were about him, bare-headed, with tear-wet
faces; thronging him, kissing his hand, his boots, his saddle;
weeping; cheering him amid their tears; shouting his name to
the very skies. He said: " Men, we have fought through the war

THE DEFEATED GENERAL CAME FORTH

together. I have done my best for you. My heart is too full to
say more."

The cheers were heard afar off over the hills where the victorious army lay encamped, and awakened some anxiety. It was
a sound they well knew:

> " The voice once heard through Shiloh's woods,
>   And Chickamauga's solitudes,
> The fierce South cheering on her sons."

It was reported in some of the northern papers that it was the
sound of jubilation at the surrender. But it was not. It was the
voice of jubilation, yet not for surrender, but for the captain

who had surrendered their muskets but was still the commander of their hearts.

This is Lee's final victory and the highest tribute to the South: that the devotion of the South to him was greater in the hour of defeat than in that of victory. It is said that Napoleon was adored by the men of France, but hated by the women. It was not so with Lee. No victor ever came home to receive more signal evidences of devotion than this defeated general.

Richmond was in mourning. Since the Union army had entered her gates, every house had been closed as though it were the house of death. One afternoon, a few days after the surrender, Lee, on his gray horse, Traveler, attended by two or three officers, crossed the James and rode quietly up the street to his home on Franklin Street, where he dismounted. That evening it was noised abroad that General Lee had arrived; he had been seen to enter his house. Next morning the houses were open as usual; life began to flow in its accustomed channels. Those who were there have said that when General Lee returned they felt as safe as if he had had his whole army at his back.

His first recorded words on his arrival were a tribute to his successful opponent. " General Grant has acted with magnanimity," he said to some who spoke of the victor with bitterness. It was the keynote to his after life.

Indeed, from this record a few facts stand forth beyond all others: Lee's nobility and genius; the fortitude of the southern people; Grant's resolution and magnanimity, and the infinite valor of the American soldier.

Over forty years have gone by since that day in April when Lee, to avoid further useless sacrifice of life, surrendered himself and all that remained of the Army of Northern Virginia and gave his *parole d'honneur* to bear arms no more against the United States. To him, who with prescient mind had long borne in his bosom knowledge of the exhausted resources of the Confederacy, and had seen his redoubtable army, under the " policy of attrition," dwindle away to a mere ghost of its former self, it might well appear that he had failed, and, if he ever thought of his personal reputation, that he had lost the soldier's dearest prize; that Fame had turned her back and Fate usurped her place. Thenceforth he who had been the leader of armies, whose glorious achievements had filled the world, who had been the prop of a high-hearted nation's hope, was to walk the narrow byway of private life, defeated, impoverished, and possibly misunderstood.

But to us who have survived for the space of more than a generation, how different it appears. We know that Time, the redresser of wrongs, is steadily righting the act of unkind Fate; and Fame, firmly established in her high seat, is ever placing a richer laurel on his brow.

Yea, ride away, thou defeated general! Ride through the broken fragments of thy shattered army, ride through thy war-wasted land, amid thy desolate and stricken people. But know that thou art riding on Fame's highest way:

" This day shall see
Thy head wear sunlight and thy feet touch stars."

SUGGESTIONS FOR STUDY

1. Vocabulary: strategist, sanguine, serried, magnanimity, posterity, capitulation, prescient, attrition, Gethsemane.

2. To what extent is Lee accepted as a national hero today? Do you know about the statues of Lee at Gettysburg and in the Capitol at Washington? What is there remarkable about these tributes? What do they signify about the man Lee?

3. What is your opinion of a " good loser "? What is more important than winning?

4. What does Page's incidental picture of Grant indicate?

5. What stories or novels by Thomas Nelson Page have you read?

FOR FURTHER READING

ABOUT ROBERT E. LEE

Bradford, Gamaliel, *Lee, The American*

Dodd, William E., *Lincoln or Lee?*

Drinkwater, John, *Robert E. Lee*, a Drama

Gilman, Bradley, *Robert E. Lee*

Hamilton and Hamilton, *Life of Robert E. Lee for Boys and Girls*

Lee, R. E., *Recollections and Letters of General Robert E. Lee by His Son*

Masters, Edgar Lee, *Lee, a Dramatic Poem*

Wilson, Woodrow, *Robert E. Lee, an Interpretation*

BY THOMAS NELSON PAGE

Biography: *Thomas Jefferson*

Fiction: *In Ole Virginia; Red Rock; The Old Gentleman of the Black Stock*

PRACTICAL POLITICS

By Theodore Roosevelt (1858–1919)

"Teddy" Roosevelt was a vivid personality, with whom Americans associate many colorful expressions: the strenuous life, the Ananias Club, the Rough Riders, the Big Stick, the Square Deal. Most high school students are familiar with many striking features of his life: his battle for health in cowboy land, his Spanish-American War experiences, his career as President of the United States, his hunting expedition in Africa, and his spectacular leadership in the formation of the Progressive Party in 1912. But the following selection from his autobiography will present a new picture of the many-sided Roosevelt, that of the wealthy New York youth breaking into the arena of the lurid practical politics of 1880. You will find it a revelation of Roosevelt's character and also an even more enlightening revelation of political conditions fifty years ago.

Almost immediately after leaving Harvard in 1880 I began to take an interest in politics. I did not then believe, and I do not now believe, that any man should ever attempt to make politics his only career. It is a dreadful misfortune for a man to grow to feel that his whole livelihood and whole happiness depend upon his staying in office. Such a feeling prevents him from being of real service to the people while in office, and always puts him under the heaviest strain of pressure to barter his convictions for the sake of holding office. A man should have some other occupation — I had several other occupations — to which he can resort if at any time he is thrown out of office, or if at any time he finds it necessary to choose a course which will probably result in his being thrown out, unless he is willing to stay in at cost to his conscience.

At that day, in 1880, a young man of my bringing up and convictions could join only the Republican party, and join it I accordingly did. It was no simple thing to join it then. That was long before the era of ballot reform and the control of primaries; long before the era when we realized that the Government must take official notice of the deeds and acts of party organizations. The party was still treated as a private corporation, and in each district the organization formed a kind of social and political club. A man had to be regularly proposed for and elected into this club, just as into any other club. As a friend of mine picturesquely phrased it, I " had to break into the organization with a jimmy."

Under these circumstances there was some difficulty in joining the local organization, and considerable amusement and excitement to be obtained out of it after I had joined.

It was over thirty-three years ago that I thus became a member of the Twenty-first District Republican Association in the city of New York. The men I knew best were the men in the clubs of social pretension and the men of cultivated taste and easy life. When I began to make inquiries as to the whereabouts of the local Republican Association and the means of joining it, these men — and the big business men and lawyers also — laughed at me, and told me that politics were " low "; that the organizations were not controlled by " gentlemen "; that I would find them run by saloon-keepers, horse-car conductors, and the like, and not by men with any of whom I would come in contact outside; and, moreover, they assured me that the men I met would be rough and brutal and unpleasant to deal with. I answered that if this were so it merely meant that the people I knew did not belong to the governing class, and that the other people did —

and that I intended to be one of the governing class; that if they proved too hard-bit for me I supposed I would have to quit, but that I certainly would not quit until I had made the effort and found out whether I really was too weak to hold my own in the rough and tumble.

The Republican Association of which I became a member held its meetings in Morton Hall, a large, barn-like room over a saloon. Its furniture was of the canonical kind: dingy benches, spittoons, a dais at one end with a table and chair and a stout pitcher for iced water, and on the walls pictures of General Grant, and of Levi P. Morton, to whose generosity we owed the room. We had regular meetings once or twice a month, and between times the place was treated, at least on certain nights, as a kind of club-room. I went around there often enough to have the men get accustomed to me and to have me get accustomed to them, so that we began to speak the same language, and so that each could begin to live down in the other's mind what Bret Harte has called " the defective moral quality of being a stranger." It is not often that a man can make opportunities for himself. But he can put himself in such shape that when or if the opportunities come he is ready to take advantage of them. This was what happened to me in connection with my experiences in Morton Hall. I soon became on good terms with a number of the ordinary " heelers " and even some of the minor leaders. The big leader was Jake Hess, who treated me with rather distant affability. There were prominent lawyers and business men who belonged, but they took little part in the actual meetings. What they did was done elsewhere. The running of the machine was left to Jake Hess and his captains of tens and of hundreds.

Among these lesser captains I soon struck up a friendship with Joe Murray, a friendship which is as strong now as it was thirty-three years ago. He had been born in Ireland, but brought to New York by his parents when he was three or four years old, and, as he expressed it, " raised as a barefooted boy on First Avenue." When not eighteen he had enlisted in the Army of the Potomac and taken part in the campaign that closed the Civil War. Then he came back to First Avenue, and, being a fearless, powerful, energetic young fellow, careless and reckless, speedily grew to some prominence as leader of a gang. In that district, and at that time, politics was a rough business, and Tammany Hall held unquestioned sway. The district was overwhelmingly

Democratic, and Joe and his friends were Democrats who on election day performed the usual gang work for the local Democratic leader, whose business it was to favor and reward them in return. This same local leader, like many other greater leaders, became puffed up by prosperity, and forgot the instruments through which he had achieved prosperity. After one election he showed a callous indifference to the hard work of the gang and complete disregard of his before-election promises. He counted upon the resentment wearing itself out.

But Joe Murray was not a man who forgot. He explained to his gang his purposes and the necessity of being quiet. Accordingly they waited for their revenge until the next election day. They then, as Joe expressed it, decided " to vote furdest away from the leader " — I am using the language of Joe's youth — and the best way to do this was to vote the Republican ticket. In those days each party had a booth near the polling-place in each election district, where the party representative dispensed the party ballots. This had been a district in which, as a rule, very early in the day the Republican election leader had his hat knocked over his eyes and his booth kicked over and his ballots scattered; and then the size of the Democratic majority depended on an elastic appreciation of exactly how much was demanded from headquarters. But on this day things went differently. The gang, with a Roman sense of duty, took an active interest in seeing that the Republican was given his full rights. Moreover, they made the most energetic reprisals on their opponents, and as they were distinctly the tough and fighting element, justice came to her own with a whoop. Would-be repeaters were thrown out on their heads. Every person who could be cajoled or, I fear, intimidated, was given the Republican ticket, and the upshot was that at the end of the day a district which had never hitherto polled more than two or three per cent of its vote Republican broke about even between the two parties.

To Joe it had been merely an act of retribution in so far as it was not simply a spree. But the leaders at the Republican headquarters did not know this, and when they got over their paralyzed astonishment at the returns, they investigated to find out what it meant. Somebody told them that it represented the work of a young man named Joseph Murray. Accordingly they sent for him. The room in which they received him was doubtless some place like Morton Hall, and the men who received him were akin to those who had leadership in Morton Hall; but in Joe's eyes they stood for a higher civilization, for opportunity, for generous recognition of successful effort — in short, for all the things that an eager man desires. He was received and patted on the back by a man who was a great man to the world in which he lived. He was introduced to the audience as a young man whose achievement was such as to promise much for the future, and moreover he was given a place in the post office — as I have said, this was long before the day of Civil Service Reform.

Now, to the wrong kind of man all this might have meant nothing at all. But in Joe Murray's case it meant everything. He was by nature as straight a man, as fearless and as stanchly loyal, as any one whom I have ever met, a man to be trusted in any position demanding courage, integrity, and good faith. He did his duty in the public service, and became devotedly attached to the organization which he felt had given him his chance in life. When I knew him he was already making his way up; one of the proofs and evidences of which was that he owned a first-class racing trotter — " Alice Lane " — behind which he gave me more than one spin. During this first winter I grew to like Joe and his particular cronies. But I had no idea that they especially returned the liking, and in the first row we had in the organization (which arose over a movement, that I backed, to stand by a non-partisan method of street-cleaning) Joe and all his friends stood stiffly with the machine, and my side, the reform side, was left with only some half-dozen votes out of three or four hundred. I had expected no other outcome and took it good-humoredly.

Next fall, as the elections drew near, Joe thought he would like to make a drive at Jake Hess, and after considerable planning decided that his best chance lay in the fight for the nomination to the Assembly, the lower house of the Legislature. He picked me as the candidate with whom he would be most likely to win; and win he did. It was not my fight, it was Joe's; and it was to him that I owe my entry into politics. I had at that time neither the reputation nor the ability to have won the nomination for myself, and indeed never would have thought of trying for it.

Jake Hess was entirely good-humored about it. In spite of my being anti-machine, my relations with him had been friendly and human, and when he was beaten he turned in to help Joe elect me. At first they thought they would take me on a personal canvass through the saloons along Sixth Avenue. The canvass, however, did not last beyond the first saloon. I was introduced with proper solemnity to the saloon-keeper — a very important personage, for this was before the days when saloon-keepers became merely the mortgaged chattels of the brewers — and he began to cross-examine me, a little too much in the tone of one who was dealing with a suppliant for his favor. He said he expected that I would of course treat the liquor business fairly; to which I answered, none too cordially, that I hoped I should treat all interests fairly. He then said that he regarded the licenses as too high; to which I responded that I believed they were really not high enough, and that I should try to have them made higher. The conversation threatened to become stormy. Messrs. Murray and Hess, on some hastily improvised plea, took me out into the street, and then Joe explained to me that it was not worth my while staying in Sixth Avenue any longer, that I had better go right back to Fifth Avenue and attend to my friends there, and that he would look after my interests on Sixth Avenue. I was triumphantly elected.

Once before Joe had interfered in similar fashion and secured the nomination of an Assemblyman; and shortly after election he had grown to feel toward this Assemblyman that he must have fed on the meat which rendered Caesar proud, as he became inaccessible to the ordinary mortals whose place of resort was Morton Hall. He eyed me warily for a short time to see if I was likely in this respect to follow in my predecessor's footsteps. Finding that I did not, he and all my other friends and supporters assumed toward me the very pleasantest attitude that it was possible to assume. They did not ask me for a thing. They accepted as a matter of course the view that I was absolutely straight and was trying to do the best I could in the Legislature. They desired nothing except that I should make a success, and they supported me with hearty enthusiasm. I am a little at a loss to know quite how to express the quality in my relationship with Joe Murray and my other friends of this period which rendered that relationship so beneficial to me. When I went into politics at this time I was not conscious of going in with the set purpose to benefit other people, but of getting for myself a privilege to which I was entitled in common with other people. So it was in my relationship with these men. If there had lurked in the innermost recesses of my mind anywhere the thought that I was in some way a patron or a benefactor, or was doing something noble by taking part in politics, or that I expected the smallest consideration save what I could earn on my own merits, I am certain that somehow or other the existence of that feeling would have been known and resented. As a matter of fact, there was not the slightest temptation on my part to have any such feeling or any one of such feelings. I no more expected special consideration in politics than I would have expected it in the boxing ring. I wished to act squarely to others, and I wished to be able to show that I could hold my own as against others. The attitude of my new friends towards me was first one of polite reserve, and then that of friendly alliance. Afterwards I became admitted to comradeship, and then to leadership. I need hardly say how earnestly I believe that men should have a keen and lively sense of their obligations in politics, of their duty to help forward great causes, and to struggle for the betterment of conditions that are unjust to their fellows, the men and women who are less fortunate in life. But in addition to this feeling there must be a feeling of real fellowship with the other men and women engaged in the same task, fellowship of work, with fun to vary the work; for unless there is this feeling of fellowship, of common effort on an equal plane for a common end, it will be difficult to keep the relations wholesome and natural. To be patronized is as offensive as to be insulted. No one of us cares permanently to have some one else conscientiously striving to do him good; what we want is to work with that some one else for the good of both of us — any man will speedily find that other people can benefit him just as much as he can benefit them.

.   .   .   .

There are many debts that I owe Joe Murray, and some for which he was only unconsciously responsible. I do not think that a man is fit to do good work in our American democracy unless he is able to have a genuine fellow-feeling for, understanding of, and sympathy with his fellow-Americans, whatever their creed or their birthplace, the section in which they live, or the work which they do, provided they possess the only kind of Americanism that really counts, the Americanism of the spirit. It was no small help to me, in the effort to make myself a good citizen and good American, that the political associate with whom I was on closest and most intimate terms during my early years was a man born in Ireland, by creed a Catholic, with Joe Murray's upbringing; just as it helped me greatly at a later period to work for certain vitally necessary public needs with Arthur von Briesen, in whom the spirit of the " Acht-und-Vierziger " [1] idealists was embodied; just as my whole life was influenced by my long association with Jacob Riis, whom I am tempted to call the best American I ever knew, although he was already a young man when he came hither from Denmark.

I was elected to the Legislature in the fall of 1881, and found myself the youngest man in that body. I was reëlected the two following years. Like all young men and inexperienced members, I had considerable difficulty in teaching myself to speak. I profited much by the advice of a hard-headed old countryman — who was unconsciously paraphrasing the Duke of Wellington, who was himself doubtless paraphrasing somebody else. The advice ran: " Don't speak until you are sure you have something to say, and know just what it is; then say it, and sit down."

SUGGESTIONS FOR STUDY

1. What great changes have taken place in " practical politics " since 1880? To what extent was Roosevelt helpful in these changes?

2. How do you explain the union between politicians and liquor interests?

3. What is your opinion of Roosevelt's motives for entering politics?

4. Is there any type of American for whom you do not have a " genuine fellow-feeling "? Do you think you could justify this attitude on your part?

5. Roosevelt was himself a writer of no mean ability. What books by him have you read?

FOR FURTHER READING

ABOUT ROOSEVELT

Burroughs, John, *Camping and Tramping with Roosevelt*

Hagedorn, Herman, *The Boys' Life of Theodore Roosevelt*

Riis, Jacob, *Theodore Roosevelt, the Citizen*

Robinson, Corinne Roosevelt, *My Brother, Theodore Roosevelt*

Thayer, W. R., *Theodore Roosevelt*

Fiction and drama: Andrews, Mary R. S., *His Soul Goes Marching On;* Hagedorn, Herman, *The Rough Riders;* Lütkenhaus, Annie M., " A Modern Knight, Theodore Roosevelt " (in *New Plays for School Children*)

[1] " Forty-eighter " — referring to a group of German socialists active in 1848.

BY ROOSEVELT

American Ideals and Other Essays
A Book-Lover's Holidays in the
   Open
Good Hunting
Hunting the Grizzly
Life Histories of African Game
   Animals

The Strenuous Life
Theodore Roosevelt's Diaries of
   His Boyhood and Youth
Theodore Roosevelt's Letters to His
   Children
The Winning of the West

HENRY DAVID THOREAU

By J. ARTHUR MYERS (1888–   )

In *Adventures in American Literature* Thoreau's writing is represented in both the Essay and the Biography sections. From his own writings, personal as they are, the reader gets the idea that Thoreau was a sort of recluse who shunned man and all his habitations whenever possible, that he was one of those dreamers who thought so much about nature and all her works that the details of common life were utterly boresome, and that he was poor but not too proud to be supported by others. How wrong all these impressions are is told in the following lively sketch by Dr. Myers, lively in spite of the fact that it deals largely with the death of its subject. Several of the letters in the text have been abbreviated. The selection which follows is drawn from Dr. Myers' book, *Fighters of Fate*.

In the little town of Concord, with a population then of about two thousand people, John Thoreau and his wife, Cynthia Dunbar, lived; and there all their four children were born. Shortly after Henry was born, on July 12, 1817, the family moved to Chelmsford and then to Boston, where Henry's schooling began. They returned to Concord when he was six years old and there he lived for the remainder of his life.

His childhood was a most happy one. John Thoreau and his wife knew and loved the Concord woods, and took their children to them to study the birds and flowers. They were poor, but they made the best of what they had and so they never felt the pinch of poverty. They did without tea, coffee, sugar and other luxuries, that their girls might have the piano their musical tastes soon proved they needed, and that a college education might be provided for the youngest son.

Henry prepared for Harvard University in the Concord schools.

Even in his boyhood, every moment outside of school hours was spent with Nature, exploring all her marvelous wonders. He entered college at the age of sixteen, with the determination to win a scholarship in order to help the serious strain on the family resources. For periods during his college course he taught school, for though it was a comparatively small amount needed to maintain him at Harvard, it meant, nevertheless, much sacrifice on the part of his family.

He was an unusually good student of mathematics and the classics but instead of bending all his efforts to obtaining honors in these studies, he deliberately devoted much of his time to the college library, an opportunity to the country boy not to be neglected. He acquired the widespread knowledge of authors that was ever remarkable. He received the degree of Bachelor of Arts in 1837, without honors, but with an excellent fund of information not usually included in a college course.

The natural field open to a youth fresh from college was teaching and, for lack of a better opportunity, Thoreau took charge of the town school in Concord. This service was of short duration, since he refused to administer corporal chastisement and since the town did not feel that it was getting its money's worth without it. So he whipped six scholars and then resigned to find a place where such methods were not required.

The next year, with his adored brother, John, he took a position in the Concord Academy, and made of it a great success. John was the principal, while Henry had charge of the classical department. The scholars, in later life, remembered both brothers with affection and gratitude for the breadth and the quality of their instruction. The two were enough unlike to increase the interest and happiness of their relationship. During a summer vacation together on the river, John died very suddenly from lockjaw, resulting from a seemingly trifling cut received while shaving. The shock completely overwhelmed Henry, who for a long time was helpless and inconsolable.

At length Thoreau recovered his poise, but it seemed as though a part of himself had been torn away. He turned instinctively to Nature for healing and spent many hours in the woods. In the next few years he worked with his father in the pencil-making business. Thanks to Henry's persistence and careful study of the subject, the Thoreaus began the manufacture of a pencil similar to the good German sort, replacing the hard, gritty, inefficient leads then made in America.

In the year 1849 the process of electrotyping was invented in Boston. The man engaged in the business wanted the best lead available. Consequently he ordered the lead from John Thoreau, who guarded his method of making it very carefully. This increased their business materially, and eventually the making of lead for electrotypes became their principal trade, with the pencils as a mere side-line.

As soon as the business was on its way to prosperity Thoreau resigned his partnership with his father. He had few wants; plain food, strong clothing, and a telescope sufficed. He was a good gardener, mechanic, and emergency man, and he did all sorts of odd jobs both at home and among his friends. He wrote articles for magazines, which brought him little money, and books then hardly salable. Today they are esteemed as classics. His leading profession was that of land surveyor, and the farther it led him into the woods and fields the more he enjoyed it.

It is through his two years' encampment, on the shore of a small lake in the Walden Woods, a mile or so south of Concord, that Thoreau is best known to the world. His hermit life was not a protest against the luxury and restraint of society, nor a strict discipline of the soul imposed upon himself after the fashion of monks and saints. He went there to live a life of labor and study, free from interruption, and when he had exhausted the advantages of his solitude he left it. He edited his first book and satisfied himself that he was fit to be an author. The events and the thoughts of his life at Walden may be read in his book under that name.

The years he spent there were happy, wholesome years, expanding his whole future by their teaching. He left his retreat frequently, for his family were a little anxious and troubled for him, fearing the hardship and danger of his life at Walden. He came home often to see them and to help about the garden and the house, or to drop in at other friendly homes. While at Walden, the episode of his refusal to pay his poll-tax occurred. The slave-power had forced upon the country the war of invasion with Mexico. Ordinarily a good citizen, he felt that the government had sunk so low that the time had come for a rebellion of his own. When the town constable, himself a good friend, came to arrest him, he offered to pay Thoreau's tax for him, not understanding that his refusal was a matter of principle rather than of poverty. He spent a night in jail and, after dark, some unrecognized person left the tax money at the constable's door; whereupon, the next morning that worthy gentleman gladly sent Thoreau away.

Thoreau did not seek to be drawn into the question of slavery, but it came to his cabin door. He solved it as he felt right. He sheltered the fugitive slave, helped and guided him and others, later on becoming one of the managers of the Underground Railroad. Thoreau did not neglect his civic duties, in spite of the tax episode. He was aroused by the low moral tone of the country and, again and again, he left the quiet woods to speak in Concord and elsewhere for freedom of person, thought and conscience.

Music was his early and lifelong friend. His sisters made the home full of it; and the sweet tunes of Mrs. Hawthorne's music-box comforted him much in the lonely days after John's death. The songs of the birds were his sweetest music, and many a girl and boy owes to him the opening of a gate to almost fairy knowledge of the voices often unknown and unnoted by others.

His friends were many — their names known to all the world. He was often at the home of the Emersons and early formed deep and lasting friendships with Ellery Channing, Alcott, Hawthorne, Margaret Fuller, and Horace Greeley. He was acquainted with Daniel Webster and Walt Whitman, both of whom visited Concord. Ellery Channing, who perhaps knew him more intimately than any one else, said: "In his own home he was one of those characters who may be called 'household treasures'; always on the spot, with skilful eye and hand, to raise the best melons in the garden, plant the orchard with choicest trees, or act as extempore mechanic; fond of the pets, his sister's flowers, or sacred Tabby; kittens were his favorites; he would play with them by the half-hour. No whim or coldness, no absorption of his time by public or private business, deprived those to whom he belonged of his kindness and affection. He did the duties that lay nearest, and satisfied those in his immediate circle; and whatever the impression from the theoretical part of his writings, when the matter is probed to the bottom, good sense and good feeling will be detected in it."

Thoreau was but forty-four years old when he died. He contracted a chill by long stooping, in a wet snowstorm, engaged in counting the growth-rings on some old tree stumps. His tuberculosis became active. He lived a year and a half after this exposure and made a trip to Minnesota in the vain search for health. His reasons for going to Minnesota are brought out in the letters written by Thoreau to Harrison Blake:

" Mr. Blake, — I am still as much an invalid as when you and Brown were here, if not more of one, and at this rate there is danger that the cold weather may come again, before I get over my bronchitis. The doctor accordingly tells me that I must ' clear out ' to the West Indies, or elsewhere — he does not seem to care much where. But I decided against the West Indies, on account of their muggy heat in the summer, and the south of Europe, on account of the expense of time and money, and have at last concluded that it will be most expedient for me to try the air of Minnesota, say somewhere about St. Paul. I am only waiting to be well enough to start. Hope to get off within a week or ten days."

After reaching Minnesota, he wrote the following letter to F. B. Sanborn: " Mr. Sanborn, — I was very glad to find awaiting me, on my arrival here, on Sunday afternoon, a letter from you. I have performed this journey in a very dead and alive manner, but nothing has come so near waking me up as the receipt of letters from Concord. I read yours, and one from my sister (and Horace Mann, his four), near the top of a remarkable isolated bluff here, called Barn Bluff, or the Grange, or Redwing Bluff, some four hundred and fifty feet high, and half a mile long — a bit of the main bluff or bank standing alone. The top, as you know, rises to the general level of the surrounding country, the river having eaten out so much. Yet the valley just above and below this (we are at the head of Lake Pepin) must be three or four miles wide.

" The grand feature hereabouts is, of course, the Mississippi River. Too much can hardly be said of its grandeur, and of the beauty of this portion of it (from Dunleith, and probably from Rock Island to this place). St. Paul is a dozen miles below the Falls of St. Anthony, or near the head of uninterrupted navigation on the main stream, about two thousand miles from its mouth. There is not a ' rip ' below that, and the river is almost as wide in the upper as the lower part of its course. Steamers go up to the Sauk Rapids, above the Falls, near a hundred miles farther, and then you are fairly in the pine woods and lumbering country. Thus it flows from the pine to the palm.

"The lumber, as you know, is sawed chiefly at the Falls of St. Anthony (what is not rafted in the log to ports far below), having given rise to the towns of St. Anthony, Minneapolis, etc., etc. In coming up the river from Dunleith, you meet with great rafts of sawed lumber and of logs, twenty rods or more in length, by five or six wide, floating down, all from the pine region above the Falls. An old Maine lumberer, who has followed the same business here, tells me that the sources of the Mississippi were comparatively free from rocks and rapids, making easy work for them; but he thought that the timber was more knotty here than in Maine.

"It has chanced that about half of the men whom I have spoken with in Minnesota, whether travelers or settlers, were from Massachusetts."

After returning from Minnesota to Concord, Thoreau wrote to Daniel Ricketson as follows:

"Friend Ricketson,— When your last letter was written I was away in the far Northwest, in search of health. My cold turned to bronchitis, which made me a close prisoner up to the moment of my starting on that journey, early in May. As I had an incessant cough, my doctor told me that I must 'clear out'— to the West Indies, or elsewhere— so I selected Minnesota. I returned a few weeks ago, after a good deal of steady traveling, considerably, yet not essentially better; my cough still continuing. If I don't mend very quickly, I shall be obliged to go to another climate again very soon.

"My ordinary pursuits, both indoors and out, have been for the most part omitted, or seriously interrupted— walking, boating, scribbling, etc. Indeed, I have beeen sick so long that I have almost forgotten what it is to be well; and yet I feel that it is in all respects only my envelope. Channing and Emerson are as well as usual; but Alcott, I am sorry to say, has for some time been more or less confined by a lameness, perhaps of a neuralgic character, occasioned by carrying too great a weight on his back while gardening."

The last months he was confined to the house, but he was very brave and worked on his manuscript, until the end. A Calvinistic aunt, coming to see him, asked, "Henry, have you made your peace with God? " and the pleasant answer came, " I did not know we had ever quarreled, Aunt."

On December 19th, Thoreau's sister, Sophia, wrote a letter for him, replying to one from Daniel Ricketson. She said: " The air and exercise which he enjoyed during the fine autumn days were a benefit to him; he seemed stronger, had a good appetite, and was able to attend somewhat to his writings; but since the cold weather has come, his cough has increased and he is able to go out but seldom. Just now he is suffering from an attack of pleurisy, which confines him wholly to the house. His spirits did not fail him; he continues in his usual serene mood, which is very pleasant for his friends as well as himself. I am hoping for a short winter and early spring, that the invalid may again be out-of-doors."

The following is the last letter Thoreau ever wrote. He dictated it to his sister, in reply to a letter received from Myron Benton, in which Benton complimented him very highly on two of his books, *The Week* and *Walden*.

" Dear Sir: I thank you for your very kind letter, which, ever since I received it, I have intended to answer before I died, however briefly. I am encouraged to know, that, so far as you are concerned, I have not written my books in vain. I was particularly gratified, some years ago, when one of my friends and neighbors said, ' I wish you would write another book — write it for me.' He is actually more familiar with what I have written than I am myself.

" The verses you refer to, in Conway's *Dial*, were written by F. B. Sanborn, of this town. I never wrote for that journal.

" I am pleased when you say that in *The Week* you like especially ' those little snatches of poetry interspersed through the book,' for these, I suppose, are the least attractive to most readers. I have not been engaged in any particular work on botany, or the like, though, if I were to live, I should have much to report on natural history generally.

" You ask particularly after my health. I suppose that I have not many months to live; but, of course, I know nothing about it. I may add that I am enjoying existence as much as ever, and regret nothing.
　　　　　　　　　　　" Yours truly,
　　　　　　　　　　　　" Henry D. Thoreau,
　　　　　　　　　　　　" by Sophia E. Thoreau."

Thoreau died on May 6, 1862, and was buried in the village cemetery, " Sleepy Hollow," where many of his famous friends now lie beside him. Said one of them: "With Thoreau's life something went out of the Concord woods and fields and river that will never return. He so loved Nature, delighted in her every aspect, that he seemed to infuse himself into her."

SUGGESTIONS FOR STUDY

1. This sketch should be read in connection with " Brute Neighbors " in the Essay section of this book.

2. What were some of the activities of Thoreau other than writing about nature?

3. What can you say about his fighting spirit after he was attacked by disease?

4. In what famous cemetery is he buried? Why is it famous?

FOR FURTHER READING

ABOUT THOREAU

Atkinson, Justin B., *Henry Thoreau, the Cosmic Yankee*

Burroughs, John, "Another Word on Thoreau " (in his *The Last Harvest*)

Emerson, Edward Waldo, *Henry Thoreau as Remembered by a Young Friend*

Emerson, Ralph Waldo, *Biographical Sketch of Thoreau*

Hubbard, Elbert, "Henry David Thoreau " (in *Little Journeys to the Homes of Great Philosophers*)

Lowell, James Russell, " Thoreau " (in *My Study Windows*)

Marble, Annie Russell, *Thoreau, His Home, Friends, and Books*

For books by Thoreau, see page 252.

HAWTHORNE AT COLLEGE

By LLOYD MORRIS (1893–   )

In the introduction to "The Minister's Black Veil " you have already learned something about Hawthorne's life, and in this selection from Morris's *The Rebellious Puritan* (1927) you get an idea of how much friendships made at college can influence one's later life. All four of these college chums remained friends through life, and all of them became famous, each in his own way — one President of the United States, one a novelist and short story writer, one a poet, and one an officer in the navy. But what the author really emphasizes in this selection is the spirit of the youthful Hawthorne, modest and shy, yet definitely determined to carve out a career as a writer.

When in later life Nathaniel recollected the four years spent at Bowdoin College in Brunswick,[1] he revived an impression of inward excitement and outward placidity. His life at Bowdoin, as he recalled it, might well have been composed of two independent existences, so slender seemed the connection between its external events and its intimate significance.

It had begun with a long trip by stage-coach from Boston, during which he struck up an acquaintance with two New Hampshire lads, Franklin Pierce and Jonathan Cilley, also on their way to Bowdoin; they had later become his intimate friends. Then the little town of Brunswick; a ragged village, remote from the highways of travel, with dusty unshaded streets, a tavern, a church, and a handful of commonplace dwellings on the borders of the college grounds. The college itself; a few unlovely buildings into which an earnest faculty herded about one hundred students and attempted to infect them with the contagion of culture. In his studies Nathaniel had found it possible to indulge his preferences. He had disliked mathematics and philosophy, neglected them, and had not been ashamed of his frequent failures in recitation. He had distinguished himself in Latin and in English composition. In other branches he had lapsed into a comfortable mediocrity, and had displayed only one idiosyncrasy, a steadfast refusal to declaim in chapel, as had been required of all students. Admonitions, reproofs, and fines imposed by an outraged faculty had been without avail. In his later life in England, when the making of addresses had become a part of his official duties as American consul, Nathaniel remembered painfully his early dislike of public speaking and its cause. Once in Salem he had gone upon the schoolroom platform to declaim and had been loudly ridiculed by some older schoolmates. His mortification had been so extreme that for nearly half a century afterward he had been incapable of mounting a platform and facing an audience; and never in his life could he do so with a sense of pleasure and ease. But at college his delinquency in declamation had been punished at graduation; although he ranked eighteenth

[1] In Maine.

in a class of thirty-eight, he had been denied a part in the Commencement exercises, failing to win the privilege of " speaking in public upon the stage."

He had been indolent in his studies and he had not been amenable to the severe discipline imposed upon the students by the sensitive conscience of President Willam Allen. Card-playing for stakes and the drinking of wines or spirits were forbidden; he had indulged in both at the comfortable tavern conducted by respectable Miss Ward. On one occasion, at the end of his freshman year, all the card-players had been discovered and summoned to appear before the President; one had been expelled, two suspended, and the remaining delinquents, Nathaniel among them, had been fined and their misconduct reported to their families by President Allen. In his letter to Madam Hathorne,[2] the President had injudiciously remarked that perhaps Nathaniel " might not have gamed, were it not for the influence of a student whom we have dismissed from the college." Nathaniel's comment upon this had been pointed. " I was fully as willing to play as the person he suspects of having enticed me," he had informed his sister, " and would have been influenced by no one. I have a great mind to commence playing again, merely to show him that I scorn to be led astray by another." But the incident had not been lacking in effect. " I have involved myself in no ' foolish scrape,' as you say all my friends suppose," he had written to his sister, " but ever since my misfortune I have been as steady as a signpost and as sober as a deacon, have been in no ' blows ' this term, nor drank any kind of ' wine or strong drink.' So that your comparison of me to the ' prodigious son ' will hold good in nothing, except that I shall probably return penniless, for I have had no money these six weeks."

He had attached to himself, as companions rather than as friends, Franklin Pierce and Jonathan Cilley. Pierce was the son of a distinguished Revolutionary general, and his martial proclivities induced him to organize a military company at Bowdoin, which Nathaniel joined. The three had likewise joined the Athenaeum, the more radical of Bowdoin's two literary clubs, in the modest library of which, as Nathaniel always believed, he had spent the most productive hours of his college residence. He had met, but had not then become intimate with, a boy who was afterward destined to become a valuable friend, Henry Long-

[2] The original spelling.

fellow, who at fourteen was Bowdoin's youngest and most accomplished student. And, most important of all, he had found, in a youth named Horatio Bridge, an intimate companion and confidant with whom to share the troubled excitement of his inward life.

Until, in his seventeenth year, he met Horatio Bridge,[3] Nathaniel had formed no intimate relationships whatever. His two years of invalidism and subsequent year of residence in Maine had removed him from all contact with boys of his own age. His childhood and adolescence had been spent in an atmosphere almost exclusively feminine, dominated by the morbid sensibility of his mother. The household had been, as though under quarantine, isolated from all contact with the world. Within the house every member of the family maintained an all but complete solitude. They were obsessed by the past, and had told him the tragic history[4] of his family as a preparation for life. Its melancholy significance had been emphasized by their pride, embittered by an increasing adversity that testified to the efficacy of the curse that had been put upon them. He had therefore come to regard the world as hostile and contaminating; but his fear of it, nourished by every element of his environment, had only quickened his curiosity. This curiosity was further stimulated by his reading, which had familiarized him with the picture of life achieved in poetry and romance. He was eager for knowledge, but apprehensive of experience. At seventeen he was unsophisticated and exceptionally impressionable. He was sensitive, reticent, and abnormally introspective. He was painfully lonely, but scarcely realized it, for solitude had come to seem an inevitable condition of his existence.

Then, as it seemed to him at the time, a miracle had occurred. He had been introduced to Bridge one evening, and had been confused by the excitement with which the introduction was acknowledged. During the whole evening Bridge had never left his side; when others joined them, he became abruptly silent but never took his eyes from Nathaniel's face; when the gathering dispersed, Bridge had insisted upon making an appointment for the following day. His extraordinary attraction for this new

---

[3] Afterwards an officer in the navy.

[4] Hawthorne's original Puritan ancestor had been one of the judges in the Salem witchcraft trials, and the family story told how one of the victims had put a curse on the judge and all his descendants. Hawthorne's father, a sea captain, had died of fever in a distant port.

acquaintance had embarrassed Nathaniel. He knew that his classmates considered him handsome; he was aware that his face was not without beauty and his body not without grace; but no one had ever sought as positively as had Bridge to win his regard. For Bridge had not attempted to conceal his admiration; as their acquaintance ripened into intimacy Nathaniel learned what it is to be loved. In the beginning of their association he had been embarrassed by Bridge's ingenuous expression of affection. Every shy, wistful glance and every casual gesture was an avowal. Bridge's eyes sparkled when Nathaniel addressed him, and his voice took on unaccustomed tones of tenderness when he replied. Nathaniel's habitual reserve was intensified by his embarrassment; afterward he realized that to Bridge he must have seemed discouragingly remote and indifferent. But Bridge, with a prophetic intuition of Nathaniel's necessity, had persisted imperturbably until his overtures met with success. For notwithstanding his apparent hostility, Nathaniel was lonely in his inaccessibility, and he suffered in his nostalgia for the companion he had never possessed. He was grateful for Bridge's patient confidence in the birth of their friendship, and accepted with reticent pleasure Bridge's romantic devotion.

It was chiefly with Bridge that Nathaniel wandered in the countryside about Brunswick. The college stood at the edge of a wide tract of pine forest where footpaths wound through miles of fragrant shade, and a brook loitered on its way to the Androscoggin River. The two companions shot pigeons and gray squirrels in the woods and fished the little brook for trout. On spring days they often strolled over the fields and along the river to the falls, and lingered to watch the pine logs from distant forests plunge over the brink and tumble into the foaming pool beneath. Another frequented walk took them to Maquoit Bay, a remote inlet of Casco, where the air held a faintly perceptible tang of salt and a dilapidated wharf and an occasional desolate lumber-sloop reminded Nathaniel of the seacoast. In the long evening twilight, after tea, they often tramped the deserted road along the river, and it was on these evening strolls that Nathaniel became most communicative. Darkness seemed a promise of secrecy that impelled him to confidences, and one night he confided to Bridge his desire to become a writer. To this tentative [5] Bridge responded with enthusiasm, prophesying success and

[5] That is, trial confidence.

fame for Nathaniel as a writer of fiction. Of his conviction Bridge was able to give no rational account, but he reiterated his prophecy at every opportunity, and never with greater emphasis than when Nathaniel objected that he would never succeed in pleasing the public sufficiently to be supported in a literary career.

Nevertheless the encouragement so liberally given cheered Nathaniel, and hardened his wavering desire into firmness of purpose. He did not share Bridge's conviction, nor did he have any exceptional faith in his own abilities. To doubt was as natural to him as to believe was necessary. He considered himself excluded from the world and uninfluenced by its purposes and activities. But incommunicable even to Bridge and unacknowledged to himself he cherished a craving for fame and an ambition to achieve it; he wished to be isolated from the world, yet to affect it profoundly. He did not realize that this had been the ambition of his ancestors. Such as it was, it was sufficient to persuade him to resume the practice of writing.

In the summer of 1825 Nathaniel departed from Bowdoin, a slender, dark-haired youth whose eyes and sensitive lips and creamy skin produced the effect of beauty. He had profited by four years of college, having employed his time in acquiring, indolently and without effort, an acquaintance with literature and an ability to live among men. He had drawn to himself two friends and one intimate companion. He had, secretly and with trepidation, sketched out the draft of a novel and begun the labor of composition. And he had satisfied the expectations of his family; perhaps too well. The commendation of an uncle having preceded him from Brunswick, he wrote to his sister in an effort to modify their excessive ambition for him: " The family had before conceived much too high an opinion of my talents, and had probably formed expectations which I shall never realize. I have thought much upon the subject, and have finally come to the conclusion that I shall never make a distinguished figure in the world, and all I hope or wish is to plod along with the multitude. I do not say this for the purpose of drawing any flattery from you, but merely to set mother and the rest of you right upon a point where your partiality has led you astray. I did hope that Uncle Robert's opinion of me was nearer to the truth, as his deportment toward me never expressed a very high estimation of my abilities."

What he hoped for was freedom to gratify his own ambition, not that of his family.

SUGGESTIONS FOR STUDY

1. Vocabulary: placidity, mediocrity, indolent, morbid sensibility, introspective, nostalgia, trepidation.
2. Why did Hawthorne dislike public speaking? Was his reason a good one? Comment from your own experience in school.
3. What impression do you form of Bowdoin College in the old days? What do you know of Bowdoin today?
4. How do you learn of Hawthorne's desire to become a writer?
5. Which of the four friends became most famous? Of which one do you know least?

FOR FURTHER READING

Julian Hawthorne, *Hawthorne and His Wife*

Moncure Conway, *Hawthorne* (Great Writers Series)

G. E. Woodberry, *Nathaniel Hawthorne* (American Men of Letters Series)

For Hawthorne's stories, see page 58.

HERMAN MELVILLE WRITES "MOBY-DICK"

By LEWIS MUMFORD (1895–   )

Among the important biographies that appeared in 1929 was *Herman Melville,* by Lewis Mumford. Its importance lies not only in the fact that it is so excellently done, but that it appeared at the moment when the reading public of two continents was ready for a sound evaluation of a man and an author who had been almost completely forgotten. In his own day Herman Melville (1819–1891) had achieved a fair but not lasting recognition, chiefly because the sort of thing that he could do best, and did, was not in tune with the critical and reading taste of his day. He has always had his readers and admirers, but now, at the turn of the first quarter of the twentieth century, Melville's work, much of it, seems almost contemporary.

The selection from Chapter Six of Mr. Mumford's book tells how a troubled genius struggles over the composition of a masterpiece. Before he began to write *Moby-Dick* Melville had written *Typee, Omoo,* and other stories of the South Seas. He had just returned from a trip to England, where he had made favorable publishing connections, but Melville found this story of the white whale difficult because he wanted to make so much more of it than a mere adventure story. The novel was to embrace the whole of human life, its gropings and searchings after the impossible, and always ending in tragedy. That Melville was successful in his effort accounts for the book's failure to secure a wide popular sale, for the author's generation wanted none of his realistic pessimism. But today we find ourselves ready to understand and appreciate Melville as a first class literary personage.

It was time for Melville to begin work again. In February, 1850, he owed his publisher, Harper's, more than seven hundred dollars in advances not covered by royalties. He did what he could to reduce the scale of his living. In the spring, he left New York and went up to Broadhall with his family — the old homestead that his Grand-Uncle Thomas had sold when he emigrated to Ohio, had now been converted into an inn; his grandfather's old desk was still mildewing in the barn, and Melville brought it to light, cleaned it up for his own use, and sat down to it.

The Berkshires [1] were " home " for Melville quite as much as Albany or New York; perhaps more so, for he had a feeling for the open country and its ways. By October he had found a near-by farmstead, with a house that had been an inn during the eighteenth century, an apple orchard on the south side, broad hay fields to the north, and pasture rising back of the house to the west, which ended in a wood lot on the summit of the hill. The countryside was well cultivated. Maple trees lined the highroad on each side, the willows dropped lazily over the banks of the Housatonic and, on the poorer upland soils, where the amaranth grew, the white threads of birch trees stood out against the dark pattern of the woods. Pittsfield, a village with metropolitan pretensions, the capital of the Berkshires and the resort of palpable celebrities, was only two miles or so away by a road that led down the valley and across the river, past a sawmill, and through the parklike streets of the village itself.

Judge Shaw [2] advanced Melville funds on a friendly sort of mortgage to purchase Arrowhead; and Melville doubtless intended by modest and spasmodic farming, with a vegetable garden, hay fields, a wood lot, a cow, and a horse, to eke out the narrow income derived from his books. For a man in prime health there was nothing injudicious in this arrangement; winter leaves a considerable amount of free time from farm work, and,

---

[1] In Massachusetts.
[2] Melville's father-in-law.

with only a few hundred dollars in ready cash every year, Melville might have made a pretty good go of it. But there were handicaps. He had a wife and child to support; other children came presently, four in all; and Elizabeth Melville was a duffer as a housekeeper; try as she would, she could not cook without strain nor manage a servant; and her chief equipment for facing the work and the winter was an admirable set of party dresses and slippers. Melville's picked-up knowledge of cookery must have been called upon for service during the first weeks they were definitely on their own; and presently Mrs. Maria Melville and his sisters came to join the household, in order to teach Elizabeth the rudiments of the household arts. It was a humiliating experience for Elizabeth; but there was no help for it; to the end of her days she did not like housekeeping; the art of " managing " was apparently not in her. The many hands in Arrowhead doubtless made light work; they also made inroads upon the larder, and what the Melvilles gained in service they lost in supplies. The house itself was commodious in rooms, but cramped in space, since it did not so much exist in its own right, as it did as a sort of annex to the chimney, a vast brick structure, with a circumference of forty-eight feet at the base; the chimney was ample enough, but it swallowed wood on a winter day as a whale swallows little fishes, and the rooms that were left were none too large.

On any realistic canvas, this new move, with all its unexpected burdens, was a dubious one. But in 1850 Melville was at the top of his energies; the impetus from *Typee* and *Omoo* had not been lost; the reception in England had probably added to his confidence; and when he looked around him, the American scene itself reinforced his courage and his convictions, and gave him new strength.

Conceive of Melville in his new home, as he embarks upon the most extensive of his spiritual voyages. The furniture has been removed to his new house, the beds put up, the heavier articles shifted and re-shifted, and, by a month's work outdoors, the woodpile has grown and the hay been stowed into the hayloft. For the moment, all his relations are well poised, Barney is through the period of teething, Elizabeth has help in her housework, and the first tension of removal is over; Mr. Duyckinck [3] occasionally, with the most tactful sort of generosity, sends up

[3] Melville's literary adviser, connected with a publishing house.

a case of champagne in a wicker cradle or a fine bundle of cigars, or he suggests a review to be written. He even tries to nourish Melville's reputation by abetting some one who is writing about him in the papers and who wishes to publish a photograph of the famous author. Here alone Melville's pride rebuffs this rudimentary effort at an art which has become a loathsome sore in our own time; he refuses his picture. " The fact is," he explains, " almost everybody is having his ' mug ' engraved nowadays, so that this test of distinction is getting to be reversed; and therefore, to see one's ' mug ' in a magazine is presumptive evidence that he's a nobody. . . . I respectfully decline to be *oblivionated. . . .*" But when a journeyman painter made the rounds of the neighborhood Melville sat for him — and the portrait, which slightly resembles Allan's, remains a just punishment for his vanity.

Below the edge of Melville's horizon is this new friend, Nathaniel Hawthorne,[4] and, as he raises his eyes from the desk in his second-story chamber and looks through the single small window that faces the north, he sees the wide valley sweeping across to successive ridges of hills, dominated by Mt. Greylock — otherwise called, from the double hump in the ridge, Saddleback. The red clover that incarnadined the summer fields is gone; or rather, its color has mounted to the crown of the landscape; the maples are a still more glorious red. The spirits caper in the autumn air; there are glowing Byzantine days when the heavens reflect the hues of the October apples, when the sky is so ripe and ruddy it seems there must be harvest home for the angels and that Charles' Wain is heaped as high as Saddleback with autumn sheaves. The sunrises and the sunsets glow side by side in the woods, and momentarily moult in the falling leaves. Neither the Rhine nor the Moselle produces anything as heady as the landscape of the Berkshires in autumn. Now is the time to begin. When Melville writes his first words, " Call me Ishmael," he is writing out of his health and ecstasy; he himself is not an outcast, nor is his spirit drooping with the " hypos "; his first touch is a black one because his canvas demands it. He is about to build up a vast pyramid of contrasts, between the whiteness of external evil and the blackness of man's inner doom; and he faces this drama with his full powers.

---

[4] Melville's friendship with Hawthorne is one of the famous literary friendships in American literature.

The apples are gathered; the autumn plowing is done; Melville is at work. The mood of creation is upon him; he is ready not for one book but for fifty books; if Mr. Duyckinck would only send him about fifty fast-writing youths with an easy style, not averse to polishing their letters, he might set them all at work. " It is not so much the paucity, as the superabundance of material that seems to incapacitate modern authors," he had written that summer. In this autumn ferment, Melville has scarcely enough time to think about his future books separately; in lieu of using fifty youths, he must pack as much as possible into one book. Melville scarcely breaks his way through a chapter or two before he realizes that he has found his theme; and the only question is how to quarry this marble, how to get it out. " Youth," Melville said in another place, " must wholly quit, then, the quarry for a while; and not only go forth and get tools to use in the quarry, but must go and thoroughly discover architecture. Now the quarry-discoverer is long before the stone-cutter; and the stone-cutter is long before the architect; and the architect is long before the temple; for the temple is the crown of the world." His apprenticeship is at last definitely over; he is at work on the temple itself — such a temple as Dante, Shakespeare, Webster, Marlowe, Browne, might each in his way have conceived and designed.

The days go by; the leaves fall; the candlelight comes early; the mice creep into the cupboard and make nests for themselves in the woodpile; the wide meadows become as bleak as a gray sea. In this most inland scene, with only the Housatonic to connect him with the watery world, Melville still dreams of the sea; his thought centers on the sea, its creatures, its boats, its fish, its men, its deeper monsters. Oh! for a dash of salt spray! he cries; and as substitute he draws upon experience and memory for the savor. The days grow cold. Snow hems in the roof and chimney of Arrowhead. Melville has a sea-feeling all the more; when he looks out of his little window on rising, he feels as if he were looking out of his port-hole in the midst of the Atlantic; his room seems a ship's cabin, and at nights, when he wakes up and hears the wind shrieking, he can almost fancy there is too much sail on the house, and he had better go up on the roof and rig in the chimney. On a winter morning he rises at eight, helps his horse to his hay and the cow to her pumpkin, stands around to take in the grateful complacency of the cow, she moves her

jaws so mildly and with such sanctity; then, with his own breakfast over, he goes to his workroom and lights the fire, runs rapidly
through the MS. and starts to work. At half past two a knock
comes. He does not answer. Again the knock and again, till he
rises from his writing, almost mechanically, and resumes the
external round; feed for the horse and cow; then dinner; then
he rigs up his sleigh and goes off to the village for the mail, for
supplies, for a little friendly chaffer perhaps round the tavern
bar. So one day follows another on the surface; but within,
there is change and tumult. Melville, like Ahab, finds a creature tearing at his vitals, and that creature the thing he has
created.

"How then with me, writing of this Leviathan [5]? Unconsciously, my chirography expands into placard capitals. Give
me a condor's quill! Give me Vesuvius' crater for an inkstand.
Friends! hold my arms! For in the mere act of penning my
thoughts of this Leviathan, they weary me, and make me faint
with the outreaching comprehensiveness of sweep, as if to include
the whole circle of the sciences, and all the generations of whales,
and men, and mastodons, past, present, and to come, with all the
revolving panoramas of empire on earth, and throughout the
whole universe, not excluding its suburbs. Such, and so magni-
fying, is the virtue of a large and liberal theme! We expand to
its bulk. To produce a mighty volume you must choose a mighty
theme. No great and enduring volume can ever be written upon
the flea, though many there be who have tried it."

Such intensity of effort, so many hours of writing and reading,
are as exhausting as the direction of a battle; but there is no
lying up in winter quarters, no delegation of responsibility. The
writer does not live outside his book; the world, the familiar,
homely world, becomes a weak picture, and his imagination is
the body and blood of reality. Taking a book off the brain,
Melville exclaims while in the midst of it, "is akin to the ticklish
and dangerous business of taking an old painting off a panel: you
have to scrape off the whole brain in order to get at it with due
safety — and even then the painting may not be worth the
trouble." Well, *Moby-Dick* is worth the trouble; the very
writing of it becomes a powerful instrument in his own development. What absorbs so much of his time and life is not the book

[5] A fabled sea monster, here referring to Moby-Dick, the white whale of
the story.

alone, "but the primitive elementalizing of the strange stuff, which in the act of attempting the book, has upheaved and up-gushed in his soul. Two books are being writ; of which the world shall only see one, and that the bungled one. The larger book, and the infinitely better, is for . . . his own private shelf. That it is whose unfathomable cravings drunk his blood; the other only demands ink."

Melville knows he must not let up on this work; he flogs himself to get his uttermost into it; the application ruins his eyesight. This small aperture and northern light are bad for his eyes. No matter; he writes with one eye closed and the other blinking. By December, in the evening, he is exhausted: he spends the aftermath of the day in a sort of physical trance; but already his mind is anticipating the developments of the next day, and he is up early, and goes back to his task.

Spring comes; but it is no spring for Melville. He will not even be bothered for dinner. Some days he sits at his desk till 4:30 without writing a word; in the spring twilight, when the catkins of the maples glow in the mild sunset and the bluebirds dart about the field like unfettered flowers, he at last comes out and creeps about like an owl. If Melville plows and plants, he does it mechanically; his heart is not in it; and he is not nourished by it. In the midst of his writing, his soul reaches a pitch of exaltation, as it does defiantly in a terrible gale, when the hand is firmly on the wheel, and the dangerous seas that wash the decks do not loosen the hold; the letters that he writes to Hawthorne then are prophetic, and deep, and full of proud mastery.

But the soft milky air of June gets the better of Melville's humors; every breath of the warm earth, the spicy perfume of wild strawberries, the honeyed odor of the locust trees, the dank green fragrance of ferns, the sight of buttercups making the fields sunny even on dull days, or the daisies turning the high grass into the whitish green color of the ocean when the waves disperse on the beach, the warm feeling of animal contentment that the sun itself pours into a man — all these things renewed his energies and revived his spirits. Melville relaxed and refreshed himself in the sunlight, building an addition to the house, and plowing and sowing, and watching the green shoots rise. He does not doubt the reality of his black moments; for, as he tells Hawthorne, in the boundless, trackless, but still glorious wilderness of the universe, where he and Hawthorne are outposts, there are savage Indians as well as mosquitoes; still, one does not go on fighting them forever. As for the crotchety and overdoleful chimeras, " the like of you and me, and some others, forming a chain of God's outposts around the world, must be content to encounter now and then, and fight them as best we can."

Melville goes down to New York to see the first part of *Moby-Dick* through the press; but the oppressive, humid days in that Babylonish brick-kiln, and the long delays of the printers, disgust him; he comes back to the country, and purposes to end the book, if possible, reclining on the grass, or watching the clouds play on a summer afternoon around old Greylock, from the newly built porch he has added to the north side of the house, where the view lies. The tail of *Moby-Dick* is not cooked yet; though the hell-fire in which the book was broiled might not unreasonably have charred it before this. Melville's intention is sane enough, if only he had the leisure to cultivate the calm, grass-growing mood; but no, he must keep on patching and tinkering at his buildings. In July the hay waits for no author to finish his chapter; there are a hundred chores to keep him away from his book, still more from deep questions about the universe and its meaning, and evil, and truth, and all those aspects of reality that need a Hawthorne for perfect communication. There is no help for it; he must go back to New York to finish the book in a third-story room, where there is no cow to milk, no horse to feed, no sister or wife or mother to be a little hurt or concerned by his inattentiveness or moodiness.

" Dollars damn me," he wrote Hawthorne, " and the malicious devil is forever grinning in upon me, holding the door ajar. My dear Sir, a presentiment is upon me.— I shall at last be worn out and perish, like an old nutmeg-grater, grated to pieces by the constant attrition of the wood, that is, the nutmeg. What I feel most moved to write, that is banned — it will not pay. Yet, altogether write the *other* way I cannot. So the product is a final hash; and all my books are botches. . . . But I was talking about the ' whale.' As the fishermen say, ' he was in his flurry' when I left him some three weeks ago. I'm going to take him up by his jaw, however, before long and finish him up in some fashion or another. What's the use of elaborating what, in its very essence, is so short-lived as a modern book? Though I wrote the Gospels in this century, I should die in the gutter. What reputation H. M. has is horrible. Think of it! To go down to posterity as the man who lived among the cannibals.[6] When I speak of posterity in reference to myself, I only mean the babies who will probably be born in the moment immediately ensuing upon my giving up the ghost. . . . I shall go down to them in all likelihood. . . . I have come to regard this matter of Fame as the most transparent of all vanities. I read Solomon more and more, and every time see deeper and deeper and unspeakable meanings in him. I did not think of Fame, a year ago, as I do now. My development has all been within a few years past. I am like one of those seeds taken out of the Egyptian pyramids which, after being three thousand years a seed, and nothing but a seed, being planted in English soil, it developed itself, grew to greenness, and then fell to mold. So I. Until I was twenty-five, I had no development at all. From my twenty-fifth year I date my life. Three weeks have scarcely passed, at any time between then and now, that I have not unfolded within myself. But I feel that I am now come to the utmost leaf of the bulb, and that shortly the flower must fall to the mold."

If it was in a mood of confidence and creative delight that he sounded his depths in *Moby-Dick,* it was in this other mood, chastened, almost fearful, that his stripped ego rose to the surface after this extreme plunge. He had looked into the abyss; he was dizzy, terrified, appalled. His letters to Hawthorne have this mingled sense of awe and exaltation: they are the mood of the last part of *Moby-Dick*. Melville's notes to Mr. Duyckinck are still jocular and robust; they might be the words of the imperturbable Stubb or the jaunty Flask, but that is because Melville gave Mr. Duyckinck only a part of himself, the polite, free-and-easy, effervescent side, meant for appreciative eating and solicitous drinking, the side he doubtless turned to his family and housemates, when weariness did not bury him from their sight — the last people who could share or understand his quest, his insight, his triumph. There is no question of wearing a mask: both sides of Melville are authentic, but the deeper part of him, which would under happier circumstances have served as ballast and

---

[6] In *Typee,* the book which first won him fame, Melville recounts his experiences while living with a tribe of South Sea cannibals.

made him face the waves more steadily, claimed too much of his inner space. He lost buoyancy; the water crept above the waterline; the ship rode dangerously. Now, however, we are speaking of the consequences of Melville's writing *Moby-Dick*. The book itself was published towards the end of 1851 by Bentley, in England, and a little later in the same year by Harper's in New York.

Whether it was an angel or a devil that Melville had struggled with this long year, he had wrestled magnificently, and the book was done, the most important of Melville's books, and surely one of the most important books of the century.

SUGGESTIONS FOR STUDY

1. If you have never read *Typee* and *Omoo,* either one of them will be a good introduction to Melville.
2. Does the author of this sketch succeed in conveying to you a definite idea of a great genius at work?
3. This biography of Melville is a good example of what is often called the " newer " style of writing about great men. Do you note some of the differences between this and the other examples of biography in this section?

FOR FURTHER READING

ABOUT MELVILLE

Freeman, John, *Herman Melville*
Weaver, R. M., *Herman Melville, Mariner and Mystic*

BY MELVILLE

Typee
Omoo
Moby-Dick
John Marr, and Other Poems

FOR FURTHER READING OF BIOGRAPHY

Aldrich, Thomas Bailey: Aldrich, Mrs. T. B., *Crowding Memories;* Greenslet, Ferris, *Life of Thomas Bailey Aldrich*
Addams, Jane, *Twenty Years at Hull-House*
Alcott, Louisa H.: Cheney, E. D. (ed.), *Life and Letters of Louisa M. Alcott*
Antin, Mary, *The Promised Land*
Barnum, P. T., *Autobiography.* Werner, M. R., *Barnum*
Barton, Clara: Epler, P. H., *Life of Clara Barton*
Bok, Edward W., *The Americanization of Edward Bok*

Boone, Daniel: Thwaites, R. G., *Daniel Boone;* White, S. E., *Daniel Boone, Wilderness Scout*

Burroughs, John: Barrus, Clara, *John Burroughs, Boy and Man;* Sharp, Dallas Lore, *Boy's Life of John Burroughs*

Byrd, Richard E., *Skyward*

Cody, W. F. (" Buffalo Bill "), *Autobiography of Buffalo Bill*

Custer, General: Custer, Mrs. Elizabeth B., *Boots and Saddles*

Eastman, C. A., *An Indian Boyhood; From Deep Woods to Civilization*

Edison, Thomas Alva: Jones, F. A., *Thomas Alva Edison;* Meadowcroft, W. H., *A Boy's Life of Edison*

Grant, Ulysses S.: Hill, F. T., *On the Trail of Grant and Lee;* Nicolay, *Boy's Life of Grant*

Jefferson, Joseph, *Autobiography*

Keller, Helen, *The Story of My Life*

Lincoln, Abraham. For list of biographies, see page 459.

Lindbergh, Charles A.: Lindbergh, C. A., *We;* Keyhoe, D. E., *Flying with Lindbergh*

Lyon, Mary: Gilchrist, B. B., *Life of Mary Lyon*

Muir, John, *The Story of My Boyhood and Youth.* Young, S. Hall, *With Muir in Alaska*

Page, Walter H.: Hendrick, Burton J., *Life and Letters of Walter H. Page*

Palmer, Alice Freeman: Palmer, G. H., *The Life of Alice Freeman Palmer*

Parker, Carleton: Parker, Cornelia S., *An American Idyl*

Porter, William Sidney (O. Henry): Smith, C. Alphonso, *Life of O. Henry*

Pupin, Michael, *From Immigrant to Inventor*

Riis, Jacob, *The Making of an American*

Shaw, Anna H., *The Story of a Pioneer*

Skinner, Otis, *Footlights and Spotlights*

Sothern, E. H., *The Melancholy Tale of " Me "*

Steiner, Edward A., *Against the Current; From Alien to Citizen*

Stein, E. G., *My Mother and I*

Tarkington, Booth: Holliday, Robert C., *Booth Tarkington*

Twain, Mark (Samuel L. Clemens), *Autobiography.* Howells, William Dean, *My Mark Twain;* Paine, Albert Bigelow, *A Boy's Life of Mark Twain*

Washington, Booker T., *Up from Slavery*

Washington, George. For list of biographies, see p. 449.

Wiggin, Kate Douglas, *My Garden of Memory*

Wright Brothers: Charnley, M. V., *A Boy's Life of the Wright Brothers*

COLLECTIVE BIOGRAPHY

Beard, A. E. S., *Our Foreign-Born Citizens*

Bradford, Gamaliel, *American Portraits; Confederate Portraits; Damaged Souls; Portraits of Women*

Bridges, T. C., and Tiltman, H. H., *Heroes of Modern Adventure*
Fields, James T., *Yesterdays with Authors*
French, J. L., *Pioneers All*
Hubbard, Elbert, *Little Journeys to the Homes of American Statesmen*
Husband, Joseph, *Americans by Adoption*
Hyde, Marietta, *Modern Biography*
Law, F. H., *Modern Great Americans*
Parkman, M. R., *Fighters for Peace; Heroes of Today*
Seitz, Don C., *Uncommon Americans*

Humorous Prose

What makes you laugh?

Sometimes just an excess of good spirits, but more often spontaneous laughter bursts out at the sight of something incongruous, as a pompous fat man chasing his hat on a windy day; or it is caused by the exaggeration of something ordinary until it becomes ridiculous, as Charlie Chaplin's shoes. Broad farces on the stage and the Sunday newspaper " comics " belong to this variety of humor, while in literature similar effects are obtained by dialect, weird spelling, distorted grammar, and odd mannerisms of style. But unless there is an idea back of it all, something that touches upon the universal philosophy of the life of mankind, there is no lasting quality to that which makes one laugh. One person can laugh at only the most obvious jokes; another has that quick perception which enables him to see a world of quiet fun where the other merely looks blank.

Wit and Humor

A sense of humor is the oil which lubricates the grinding wheels of life; wit may be called the electric spark of life's engine. Wit appeals to the mind rather than to the emotions. It lies in language more than in character or situation. Certain words come together with an unexpected flash that illuminates an idea. Wit and humor are often so closely bound together that it is difficult to distinguish one from the other. Nor is it necessary to do so. As you continue to read this book you will find that humor is not confined to any one type of literature. Nearly every section has its sprinkling of humor, and this is as it should be in a study of American literature, which is richer in humor than that of any other country.

Benjamin Franklin the First American Humorist

Who started this American humor? As nearly as it is possible to tell, it was that famous self-starter, Benjamin Franklin. We may think of him as the earnest, industrious man, starting lightning rods, stoves, postal systems, circulating libraries, street lighting, paving, fire brigades, foreign diplomacy, and autobiography, but we must not forget that he also started *Poor Richard's Almanac* which taught the American rustic how to live sanely while tickling him with its homely wit. Poor Richard's descendants of today are the " colyum-ists " of our newspapers who help to brighten the day for the tired business man. It is not possible to discuss this phase of American humor in detail, but it is worth knowing that at the end of the last century Eugene Field was the quip-master on the Chicago *Daily News*, and that this century has been enlivened by such men as Bert Leston Taylor (B. L. T.) on the Chicago *Tribune*, Franklin P. Adams (F. P. A.) on the New York *World*, Don Marquis on the New York *Sun*, and Christopher Morley on the Philadelphia *Public Ledger* and the New York *Evening Post*.

Washington Irving's Literary Practical Joke

About fifty years after *Poor Richard's Almanac* stopped, the first great piece of American humor appeared, the *Knickerbocker History of New York* by Washington Irving. It is interesting to know that the man who later won recognition for American literature in Europe because of the elegance of his style should have begun his career by a huge sort of practical joke which set New York rocking with merriment.

The New England Humorists

During the first half of the nineteenth century American humor is best represented by two men of established literary reputation, James Russell Lowell and Oliver Wendell Holmes. Both were college men of the sophisticated Boston Brahmin group of intellectuals. Lowell gave voice to the folk-humor of Yankee characters, and in *The Biglow*

Papers he was the first to use dialect effectively. Holmes, on the other hand, exhibited typical Boston wit in a series of monologues first published in *The Atlantic Monthly.* Examples of the work of both writers will be found in this volume.

The Cracker Box Philosophers

While Irving, Lowell, and Holmes were displaying the wit and humor of men familiar with literary tradition, another vein of American humor was beginning to be worked. Racy, often boisterous, but always full of the flavor of a new people beginning to see its own " funny side," these so-called " Cracker Box Philosophers " portrayed the country store lounger, the rural politician, and local and contemporary problems. Today hardly any of them are read, and even the picturesque names some of them assumed are unfamiliar to the reader of today. Artemus Ward and Bill Nye are still readable, but who knows the works of Josh Billings, Petroleum V. Nasby, and Bill Arp, So-Called?

Mark Twain and Late Nineteenth Century Wits

In the '80's of the last century Mark Twain began to be known as a " funny " writer, but he rose above that and built himself a reputation as the foremost American humorist, a position that he still holds. With the last decade of the nineteenth century, and ever since, there has grown up a most generous crop of humorous writers, both in prose and poetry. It is possible merely to indicate here the trend of American humor by naming some of the outstanding figures. Eugene Field is today remembered for his poetry rather than his prose, although much of the latter is distinctly worth while. The turn of the century saw Finley Peter Dunne, " Mr. Dooley," at the height of his fame; then came George Ade with his *Fables in Slang.* Many writers with a gift of humor displayed it in ways other than merely being funny, in stories, for instance, like Bunner, Stockton, and others. A number of comic weeklies offered a market for jokes and short quips. The most famous were *Puck, Judge,* and *Life.*

Popular Contemporary Humorists

As we come down to our own day, the name that would occur first in the minds of most of us is that of Irvin Cobb, although he prefers to be considered a serious writer. He says, " Let a man turn out one piece of foolery that tickles the public in its short-ribs and from that hour he is branded as a humorist." Feeling as he does, it is too bad that he wrote *Speaking of Operations, A Plea for Old Cap Collier,* and many another " funny " piece. Readers looking for humor will not give him up, although at the present time he has succeeded in gaining full recognition as a serious writer.

One of the types of humor popular today is parody. By stretching the boundaries of American literature to include Canada, the foremost exponent of the type is Stephen Leacock. In the United States proper we have Donald Ogden Stewart and Robert C. Benchley. The danger in this kind of writing is that it is apt to be of temporary interest only. The same may be said of all writing that is a " take-off " on something, such as satire, burlesque, and caricature, all of them enjoying a tremendous vogue at the present time. The humor supposed to lie in dialect was for a long time taboo in magazines, but it is once more appearing. And slang, of course, is always with us. If it were not, how could we enjoy George Ade and Ring Lardner?

Types of Literary Humor

In reading the following selections you will find it interesting to be able to distinguish some of the special forms which humorists employ to make us laugh. Several of these are based on imitation. The parody, which has just been mentioned, produces a humorous effect by treating a subject, usually a trivial one, in the exact style of another piece, usually a serious one. For instance, Donald Ogden Stewart parodies the style of a book of etiquette; Ring Lardner, correspondence schools or the stage directions of some " highbrow " plays; Stephen Leacock, the general tone of the dime novel, detective story, and other forms of fiction. Parodies on poems often follow the exact wording of the original with just enough change to apply to the new subject.

The exact opposite of the parody is the travesty, which retains the subject of the original, but treats it in an extravagant or absurd style. It is not so common as the parody. Stewart combines both in his *Parody Outline of History.* The story of John Alden and Priscilla told in the manner of one of our ultra-modern writers is both a parody on that writer and a travesty on Longfellow's version.

Similar to these two is the burlesque which either treats a trivial subject in mock-heroic style, or a serious subject in frivolous vein. Irving's *Knickerbocker History* is a good illustration, for it uses both methods. Ade's Fables have elements of both the parody and the burlesque.

The satire holds a subject up to ridicule by pointing out its weaknesses and follies. This may be done rather sympathetically in a spirit of fun, or bitterly with intent to wound. The several examples of satire in this section are all of the goodnatured variety.

A caricature when applied to writing means the same as in drawing — a picture which exaggerates some special details. Thus *Hermione* is both a caricature and a satire.

A yarn is a rambling account of a highly improbable or even impossible experience, supposed to have happened to the speaker, and told as if it were absolute truth. This is one of the favorite devices of Mark Twain. By a little adjustment it may fall into the short story form as illustrated by Stockton's " The Widow's Cruise."

HERMIONE

By Don Marquis (1878–   )

Is it any wonder that a man with a name like Donald Robert Perry Marquis and a humorous turn of mind would become Don Marquis permanently? Like so many of our other humorists, he was born in the Mississippi valley. His birthplace was Walnut, Illinois, which he describes as " one of those towns that prop two cornfields apart." His young manhood was occupied with trying his hand at " almost all the trades and professions that flourished in Walnut and vicinity." This same pleasing variety was evident when he went to Washington, D. C., and combined a job in the census office with newspaper reporting and study in an art school. Later he assisted Joel Chandler Harris with *Uncle Remus's Magazine* in Atlanta, and finally settled down to a long career in New York newspaperdom, where his column, " The Sun Dial " in the New York *Sun,* made his reputation. Like many of our humorists Don Marquis has the gift of creating a vivid humorous character, but unlike most of them his fame rests on several widely differing types rather than just one. Among these, Hermione, the young lady who poses as being intellectual by merely skimming the surface of all the latest " movements," is unique in being the only feminine character to occupy this kind of position in American humor. Once when Don Marquis was lecturing before a large audience of young girls, he had quite a hard time of it until he began talking about Hermione. Suddenly everybody seemed to realize that they were all Hermiones more or less, even himself, and after that, according to his account, it was a merry party. Two extracts from *Hermione and Her Little Group of Serious Thinkers* follow.

PRISON REFORM AND POISE

Aren't you just crazy about prison reform? The most wonderful man talked to us — to our Little Group of Advanced Thinkers, you know — about it the other evening.

It made me feel that I'd be willing to do anything — simply anything! — to help those poor, unfortunate convicts. Collect money, you know, or give talks, or read books about them, or make any other sacrifice.

Even get them jobs. One ought to help them to start over again, you know.

Though as for hiring one of them myself, or rather getting Papa to — well, really, you know, one must draw the line somewhere!

But it's a perfectly fascinating subject to take up, prison reform is.

It gives one such a sense of brotherhood — and of service — It's so broadening, don't you know — taking up things like that.

And one must be broad. I ask myself every night before I go to bed: "Have I been broad today? Or have I failed?"

Though, of course, one can be too broad, don't you think?

What I mean is, one must not be so broad that one loses one's poise in the midst of things.

Poise! That is what this age needs!

I suppose you've heard wide-brimmed hats are coming in again?

THE SPIRIT OF CHRISTMAS

Isn't the Christmas festival just simply wonderful?

For days beforehand I feel so uplifted — so, well, otherworldly — if you know what I mean.

Isn't it just dreadful that any material considerations have to spoil such a sacred time?

It does seem to me that somehow we might free ourselves of worldliness and greediness and just rise to the spiritual significance of the day. If only we could!

And what a blessing it would be to the poor, tired shop girls if we could!

Though, of course, they, the shop girls, I mean, must be upheld even in their weariest moments by the thought that they are helping on the beautiful impulse of giving!

When they reflect that every article they sell is to be a gift from one thoughtful and loving heart to another they must forget the mere fatigue of the flesh and just feel the stimulus, the inspiration, the vibration!

There are gifts, I admit, that haven't the divine spark of love to hallow them, but after all there aren't so many of that sort. Love one another is the spirit of Christmas — and it prevails, whatever the skeptics may say to the contrary. And though it's a pity there has to be a material side to Christmas at all, it's so comforting, so ennobling to realize that back of the material gifts is Brotherly Love.

It quite reassures one about the state of the world; it certainly isn't getting worse with Brotherly Love and the Spirit of Giving animating everybody.

Of course, Christmas giving is a problem sometimes. It is so embarrassing when somebody you'd forgotten entirely sends you a present.

I always buy several extra things just for that emergency. Then, when an unexpected gift arrives, I can rush off a return gift so promptly that nobody'd ever dream I hadn't meant to send it all along.

And I always buy things I'd like to have myself, so that if they aren't needed for unexpected people they're still not wasted.

With all my spirituality, I have a practical side, you see.

All well-balanced natures have both the spiritual and the practical side. It's so essential, nowadays, to be well-balanced, and it's a great relief to me to find I can be practical. It saves me a lot of trouble, too, especially about this problem of Christmas giving.

I know the value of material things, for instance. And I never waste money giving more expensive presents to my friends than I receive from them. That's one of the advantages of having a well-balanced nature, a practical side.

And, anyway, the value of a gift is not in the cost of it. Quite cheap things, when they represent true thought and affection, are above rubies.

Mamma and Papa are going to get me a pearl necklace, just to circle the throat, but beautifully matched pearls. I wouldn't care for an ostentatiously long string of pearls anyway.

Poor, dear Papa says he really can't afford it — with times so hard, and those dear, pathetic Europeans on everybody's hands, you know — but Mamma made him understand how necessary beauty is to me, and he finally gave in.

Isn't it just wonderful how love rules us all at Christmas time?

SUGGESTIONS FOR STUDY

1. Make a list of good adjectives to describe Hermione. Does she amuse or annoy you? Did you ever know any one like her?

2. In her remarks on prison reform what weakness of logic common to human nature does she exhibit?

3. What are some fairly frequent practices in Christmas giving which are satirized in the second selection?

FOR FURTHER READING

HUMOR

Hermione and Her Little Group of Serious Thinkers
Prefaces
Noah an' Jonah an' Cap'n John Smith
The Old Soak, and Hail and Farewell

POEMS

Dreams and Dust
Poems and Portraits

SAYINGS OF POOR RICHARD

By BENJAMIN FRANKLIN (1706–1790)

Having had a taste of modern humor, let us now turn back to the early days of our nation and sample the wit of Benjamin Franklin, creator of the first great fictitious character to serve as a mouthpiece for his author's jests. In 1732 (the year of Washington's birth) Franklin began *Poor Richard's Almanac* by playing a practical joke on his only rival almanac-maker, Titus Leads, a quack astrologer. Poor Richard prophesied the death of this man the following October in accordance with the infallible stars. When Leeds protested violently, Poor Richard replied that he must be dead because the stars could not lie, and no living man would use such unchristian language or publish such an unworthy almanac. This trick had been played in England some years before by Jonathan Swift, author of *Gulliver's Travels,* but most Americans did not know about that, and accepted the incident as a huge joke.

The almanac continued in popularity for twenty-five years and many of its wise saws still live in American conversation. Many of them were combined into a kind of essay, entitled " The Way to Wealth," in which an old man, Father Abraham, quotes them to admonish a group of citizens complaining of the taxes. Franklin really borrowed largely from the wisdom of the ages, but often rephrased the maxims or put them into fresh metaphors. They are examples of wit rather than humor. Notice the neatness, the balance, and the clever contrasts, all of which go with brevity to form the soul of wit. They also illustrate Franklin's practical common sense, but show his limitations in that they fail to emphasize the spiritual and idealistic qualities. Franklin's feet were always planted firmly on the ground.

1. Experience keeps a dear school, but a fool will learn in no other.

2. If a man empties his purse into his head, no man can take it away from him. An investment in knowledge always pays the best interest.

3. A great talker may be no fool, but he is one who relies on him.

4. Tart words make no friends; a spoonful of honey will catch more flies than a gallon of vinegar.

5. Glass, china, and reputation are easily cracked and never well mended.

6. Early to bed and early to rise, makes a man healthy, wealthy, and wise.

7. A truly great man will neither trample on a worm nor sneak to an Emperor.

8. He that riseth late must trot all day, and shall scarce overtake his business at night; while laziness travels so slowly that poverty soon overtakes him. Drive thy business. Let it not drive thee.

9. A little neglect may breed great mischief; for want of a nail the shoe was lost; for want of a shoe the horse was lost; for want of a horse the rider was lost; for want of the rider the battle was lost.

10. If you would know the value of money, go and try to borrow some; he that goes a-borrowing goes a-sorrowing.

11. He that composes himself is wiser than he that composes books.

12. He that is of the opinion that money will do everything, may well be suspected of doing everything for money.

13. If a man could have half his wishes, he would double his troubles.

14. Creditors have better memories than debtors.

15. Don't think to hunt two hares with one dog.

16. A lie stands on one leg, truth on two.

17. A pair of good ears will drain dry a hundred tongues.

18. A plowman on his legs is higher than a gentleman on his knees.

19. Handle your tools without mittens; the cat in gloves catches no mice.

20. Now that I have a sheep and a cow everybody bids me good-morrow.

21. Silks and satins, scarlet and velvet, put out the kitchen fire.

SUGGESTIONS FOR STUDY

1. Be sure you understand the meaning of each of these sayings. The last seven are highly figurative. For each write a sentence in ordinary English to show the meaning.

2. Make a list of all the virtues preached by these sayings, such as thrift, perseverance, etc. What kind of virtues are emphasized? What kinds are conspicuous by their absence? Does your list verify or contradict the comment made at the end of the introductory remarks on Franklin?

3. Try your hand at writing some parodies on these sayings or some wise saws of your own which will apply to your school life.

FRANKLIN'S TOAST

Franklin was dining with a small party of distinguished gentlemen, when one of them said: " Here are three nationalities represented. I am French, and my friend here is English, and Mr. Franklin is an American. Let each one propose a toast."

It was agreed to and the Englishman's turn came first. He arose and in the tone of a Briton bold said, " Here's to Great Britain, the sun that gives light to all nations of the earth."

The Frenchman was rather taken aback at this; but he proposed, " Here's to France, the moon whose magic ray moves the tides of the world."

Franklin then arose, with an air of quaint modesty, and said, " Here's to our beloved George Washington, the Joshua of America, who commanded the sun and moon to stand still — and they obeyed."

FOR FURTHER READING

Autobiography

Collected Works: " Father Abraham's Speech," " Dialogue between Franklin and the Gout," " The Whistle," " The Ephemera," " On the Loss of Her American Squirrel," " Rules for Reducing a Great Empire to a Small One," " A Parable on Persecution "

Carl Holliday, *Wit and Humor of Colonial Days:* Chapter VI

IN THE DAYS OF WOUTER VAN TWILLER

By WASHINGTON IRVING (1783–1859)

Modern advertisers may not realize how much they are indebted to Washington Irving for methods in the preliminary advertising of a new product. During the months of October and November, 1809, there appeared in the New York *Evening Post* a series of notices and letters concerning the disappearance of one Diedrich Knickerbocker, a small elderly gentleman, who had left in his lodgings a " curious kind of written book." The landlord gave warning that he intended to publish this book in order to pay off the old gentleman's board bill in case of his non-appearance. A week later a publishing firm announced the approaching publication of *A History of New York* in two volumes, price three dollars, published to discharge the debts of the mysteriously vanished Mr. Diedrich Knickerbocker. The summary of its contents suggested a profound piece of scholarship " interspersed with philosophical speculations and moral precepts."

The book was prefaced by an account of the author from the pen of Seth Handaside, his landlord, and a statement by the author of the historical methods employed and of his own indebtedness to the New York Historical Society. After these solemn preliminaries, the book opened with an absurd description of the beginning of the world, and its readers soon realized that a hoax had been played on them. Reviewers hailed the book as " the wittiest our press has ever produced," but some members of the Historical Society and the old Dutch families were indignant at what they considered its ridicule of them. Forty years later Irving wrote an apology, for a later edition, showing how the term Knickerbocker had come to be used for everything from bread to insurance companies, and how the old Dutch families now prided themselves on being " genuine Knickerbockers." Irving truly contributed a new word to our language. The extract that follows is Chapter IV, Book III.

In this dulcet period of my history, when the beauteous island of Manna-hata [1] presented a scene, the very counterpart of those glowing pictures drawn of the golden reign of Saturn,[2] there was, as I have before observed, a happy ignorance, an honest simplicity prevalent among its inhabitants, which, were I even able to depict, would be but little understood by the degenerate age for which I am doomed to write. Even the female sex, those arch innovators upon the tranquillity, the honesty, and gray-beard customs of society, seemed for a while to conduct themselves with incredible sobriety and comeliness.

Their hair, untortured by the abominations of art, was scrupulously pomatumed back from their foreheads with a candle, and covered with a little cap of quilted calico, which fitted exactly to their heads. Their petticoats of linsey-woolsey [3] were striped with a variety of gorgeous dyes — though I must confess these gallant garments were rather short, scarce reaching below the knee; but then they made up in the number, which generally equaled that of the gentleman's small-clothes; and what is still more praiseworthy, they were all of their own manufacture — of which circumstance, as may well be supposed, they were not a little vain.

These were the honest days in which every woman stayed at home, read the Bible, and wore pockets — ay, and that too of a goodly size, fashioned with patchwork into many curious devices, and ostentatiously worn on the outside. These, in fact, were convenient receptacles, where all good housewives carefully stored away such things as they wished to have at hand; by which means they often came to be incredibly crammed; and I remember there was a story current, when I was a boy, that the lady of Wouter Van Twiller once had occasion to empty her right pocket in search of a wooden ladle, when the contents filled a couple of corn-baskets, and the utensil was discovered lying among some rubbish in one corner; — but we must not give too much faith to all these stories, the anecdotes of those remote periods being very subject to exaggeration.

Besides these notable pockets, they likewise wore scissors and pin-cushions suspended from their girdles by red ribands, or, among the more opulent and showy classes, by brass, and even silver chains — indubitable tokens of thrifty housewives and in-

---

[1] The Indian name for the island on which New York City is built.

[2] The Roman god of agriculture, who was supposed to have taught the primitive people how to harvest their grain.

[3] A cloth mixture of linen and wool.

dustrious spinsters. I cannot say much in vindication of the shortness of the petticoats [4]; it doubtless was introduced for the purpose of giving the stockings a chance to be seen, which were generally of blue worsted, with magnificent red clocks — or, perhaps, to display a well-turned ankle, and a neat, though serviceable foot, set off by a high-heeled leathern shoe, with a large and splendid silver buckle. Thus we find that the gentle sex in all ages have shown the same disposition to infringe a little upon the laws of decorum, in order to betray a lurking beauty, or gratify an innocent love of finery.

From the sketch here given, it will be seen that our good grandmothers differed considerably in their ideas of a fine figure from their scantily dressed descendants of the present day. A fine lady, in those times, waddled under more clothes, even on a fair summer's day, than would have clad the whole bevy of a modern ballroom. Nor were they the less admired by the gentlemen in consequence thereof. On the contrary, the greatness of a lover's passion seemed to increase in proportion to the magnitude of its object — and a voluminous damsel, arrayed in a dozen of petticoats, was declared by a Low-Dutch sonneteer of the province to be radiant as a sunflower, and luxuriant as a full-blown cabbage. Certain it is, that in those days the heart of a lover could not contain more than one lady at a time; whereas the heart of a modern gallant has often room enough to accommodate half a dozen. The reason of which I conclude to be, that either the hearts of the gentlemen have grown larger, or the persons of the ladies smaller: this, however, is a question for physiologists to determine.

But there was a secret charm in these petticoats, which, no doubt, entered into the consideration of the prudent gallants. The wardrobe of a lady was in those days her only fortune; and she who had a good stock of petticoats and stockings was as absolutely an heiress as is a Kamchatka [5] damsel with a store of bear-skins, or a Lapland [5] belle with a plenty of reindeer. The ladies, therefore, were very anxious to display these powerful attractions to the greatest advantage; and the best rooms in the house, instead of being adorned with caricatures of dame Nature, in water

[4] In Irving's day women wore skirts almost to the floor, cut on long, straight lines. It is this slim silhouette which he probably had in mind in speaking later of " their scantily dressed descendants."

[5] A peninsula of northeastern Asia. *Lapland:* a region in the extreme north of Europe.

colors and needlework, were always hung round with abundance of homespun garments, the manufacture and the property of the females — a piece of laudable ostentation that still prevails among the heiresses of our Dutch villages.

The gentlemen, in fact, who figured in the circles of the gay world in these ancient times, corresponded, in most particulars, with the beauteous damsels whose smiles they were ambitious to deserve. True it is, their merits would make but a very inconsiderable impression upon the heart of a modern fair: they neither drove their curricles,[6] nor sported their tandems,[7] for as yet those gaudy vehicles were not even dreamt of; neither did they distinguish themselves by their brilliancy at the table, and their consequent rencontres [8] with watchmen, for our forefathers were of too pacific a disposition to need those guardians of the night, every soul throughout the town being sound asleep before nine o'clock. Neither did they establish their claims to gentility at the expense of their tailors, for as yet those offenders against the pockets of society, and the tranquillity of all aspiring young gentlemen, were unknown in New Amsterdam; every good housewife made the clothes of her husband and family, and even the goede vrouw [9] of Van Twiller himself thought it no disparagement to cut out her husband's linsey-woolsey galligaskins.[10]

Not but what there were some two or three youngsters who manifested the first dawning of what is called fire and spirit; who held all labor in contempt; skulked about docks and market-places; loitered in the sunshine; squandered what little money they could procure at hustle-cap and chuck-farthing; swore, boxed, fought cocks, and raced their neighbors' horses; in short, who promised to be the wonder, the talk, and abomination of the town, had not their stylish career been unfortunately cut short by an affair of honor with a whipping-post.

Far other, however, was the truly fashionable gentleman of those days: his dress, which served for both morning and evening, street and drawing-room, was a linsey-woolsey coat, made, perhaps, by the fair hands of the mistress of his affections, and gallantly bedecked with abundance of large brass buttons; half a score of breeches heightened the proportions of his figure; his

---

6 Two-wheeled, two-horse carriages popular in Irving's day.
7 A vehicle with two horses, one in front of the other.
8 Encounters.
9 Dutch for "good wife."
10 Long, loose breeches.

shoes were decorated by enormous copper buckles; a low-crowned broad-rimmed hat overshadowed his burly visage; and his hair dangled down his back in a prodigious queue of eel-skin.

Thus equipped, he would manfully sally forth, with pipe in mouth, to besiege some fair damsel's obdurate heart — not such a pipe, good reader, as that which Acis did sweetly tune in praise of his Galatea,[11] but one of true Delft [12] manufacture, and furnished with a charge of fragrant tobacco. With this would he resolutely set himself down before the fortress, and rarely failed, in the process of time, to smoke the fair enemy into a surrender, upon honorable terms.

Such was the happy reign of Wouter Van Twiller, celebrated in many a long-forgotten song as the real golden age, the rest being nothing but counterfeit copper-washed coin. In that delightful period, a sweet and holy calm reigned over the whole province. The burgomaster smoked his pipe in peace; the substantial solace of his domestic cares, after her daily toils were done, sat soberly at the door, with her arms crossed over her apron of snowy white, without being insulted with ribald street-walkers or vagabond boys — those unlucky urchins who do so infest our streets, displaying, under the roses of youth, the thorns and briers of iniquity. Then it was that the lover with ten breeches, and the damsel with petticoats of half a score, indulged in all the innocent endearments of virtuous love, without fear and without reproach; for what had that virtue to fear, which was defended by a shield of good linsey-woolseys, equal at least to the seven bull-hides of the invincible Ajax? [13]

Ah, blissful and never to be forgotten age! when everything was better than it has ever been since, or ever will be again — when Buttermilk Channel was quite dry at low water — when the shad in the Hudson were all salmon — and when the moon shone with a pure and resplendent whiteness, instead of that melancholy yellow light which is the consequence of her sickening at the abominations she every night witnesses in this degenerate city!

Happy would it have been for New Amsterdam could it always have existed in this state of blissful ignorance and lowly simplicity; but, alas! the days of childhood are too sweet to last! Cities, like men, grow out of them in time, and are doomed alike

---

[11] Lovers in Greek mythology.
[12] A town in Holland famous for glazed earthenware.
[13] The most muscular Greek hero of the Trojan war.

to grow into the bustle, the cares, and miseries of the world. Let no man congratulate himself, when he beholds the child of his bosom or the city of his birth increasing in magnitude and importance — let the history of his own life teach him the dangers of the one, and this excellent little history of Mannahata convince him of the calamities of the other.

SUGGESTIONS FOR STUDY

1. Vocabulary: dulcet, innovators, pomatumed, ostentatiously, opulent, indubitable, vindictive, voluminous, laudable ostentation, prodigious queue.

2. What hints do you find that Irving moved in the fashionable life of his day?

3. Point out places where Irving makes use of the humor of contrast.

4. Write or give orally a humorous contrast between the early days of your school or community and the present.

5. Write a composition in which you imagine a person fifty years from now looking back at the present day and citing it as the era of true morality, or the opposite.

FOR FURTHER READING

See lists on page 43.

THE AUTOCRAT OF THE BREAKFAST TABLE

By OLIVER WENDELL HOLMES (1809–1894)

When a young man at the beginning of his medical career remarks, as did Oliver Wendell Holmes, " Small fevers gratefully accepted," we can see that he is a joker. Later when his reputation was firmly established and he was a medical lecturer at Harvard, his lively disposition and frequent quips even in the midst of a learned lecture made him highly popular with the students. Holmes was one of those persons who choose their ancestors well, for the Quincys, Bradstreets, and other famous New England families were branches on his family tree. The tree has continued to bear good fruit in Oliver Wendell Holmes, Jr., who has been called the " grand old man of the Supreme Court." Except for periods of study abroad, the whole of the long life of Holmes, Senior, was spent in Boston and Cambridge, where he was the acknowledged wit of the intellectual group. He it was who smilingly dubbed Boston " the hub of the universe " as a dig at the self-satisfaction of some of its citizens.

His great contribution to humorous prose is *The Autocrat of the Breakfast Table* series written for early numbers of *The Atlantic Monthly* at the request of his friend Lowell, its first editor. *The Autocrat* was followed by *The Professor* and later *The Poet at the Breakfast Table*. These papers, though often designated as essays, do not have the unity and completeness of essays, but belong to this same long line of American humorous prose. Like the *Knickerbocker History*, they have no real counterpart. They represent a series of conversations or rather a monologue — for the persons around the breakfast table, though distinct characters, figure largely as background for the autocrat's remarks. Disconnected indeed these conversations are, but surprising in the variety of topics and brilliance of language. The following extract from Part I is a fair example.

— You don't suppose that my remarks made at this table are like so many postage-stamps, do you — each to be only once uttered? If you do, you are mistaken. He must be a poor creature who does not often repeat himself. Imagine the author of the excellent piece of advice, "Know thyself," never alluding to that sentiment again during the course of a protracted existence! Why, the truths a man carries about with him are his tools; and do you think a carpenter is bound to use the same plane but once to smooth a knotty board with, or to hang up his hammer after it has driven its first nail? I shall never repeat a conversation, but an idea often. I shall use the same types when I like, but not commonly the same stereotypes.[1] A thought is often original, though you have uttered it a hundred times. It has come to you over a new route, by a new and express train of associations.

Sometimes, but rarely, one may be caught making the same speech twice over, and yet be held blameless. Thus, a certain lecturer, after performing in an inland city, where dwells a *littératrice*[2] of note, was invited to meet her and others over the social teacup. She pleasantly referred to his many wanderings in his new occupation. "Yes," he replied, "I am like the Huma, the bird that never lights, being always in the cars, as he is always on the wing." — Years elapsed. The lecturer visited the same place once more for the same purpose. Another social cup after the lecture, and a second meeting with the distinguished lady.

[1] Casts or plates used in printing. Here it means the exact unchangeable form.

[2] A literary woman. This incident actually occurred to Holmes at Hartford, Connecticut. The lady was Mrs. Sigourney, a well-known writer of that day.

"You are constantly going from place to place," she said. —
"Yes," he answered, "I am like the Huma" — and finished the
sentence as before.

What horrors, when it flashed over him that he had made this
fine speech, word for word, twice over! Yet it was not true, as
the lady might perhaps have fairly inferred, that he had em-
bellished his conversation with the Huma daily during that whole
interval of years. On the contrary, he had never once thought
of the odious fowl until the recurrence of precisely the same circumstances brought up precisely the same idea. He ought to have
been proud of the accuracy of his mental adjustments. Given
certain factors, and a sound brain should always evolve the same
fixed product with the certainty of Babbage's calculating machine.
— What a satire, by the way, is that machine on the mere
mathematician! A Frankenstein monster,[3] a thing without brains
and without heart, too stupid to make a blunder; which turns
out results like a corn-sheller, and never grows any wiser or
better, though it grind a thousand bushels of them!

I have an immense respect for a man of talents *plus* "the
mathematics." But the calculating power alone should seem to
be the least human of qualities, and to have the smallest amount
of reason in it; since a machine can be made to do the work of
three or four calculators, and better than any one of them. Sometimes I have been troubled that I had not a deeper intuitive
apprehension of the relations of numbers. But the triumph of
the ciphering hand-organ has consoled me. I always fancy I can
hear the wheels clicking in a calculator's brain. The power of
dealing with numbers is a kind of "detached lever" arrangement,
which may be put into a mighty poor watch. I suppose it is about
as common as the power of moving the ears voluntarily, which
is a moderately rare endowment.

— Little localized powers, and little narrow streaks of
specialized knowledge, are things men are very apt to be conceited about. Nature is very wise; but for this encouraging principle how many small talents and little accomplishments would
be neglected! Talk about conceit as much as you like, it is to
human character what salt is to the ocean; it keeps it sweet,
and renders it endurable. Say rather it is like the natural unguent

---

[3] Frankenstein was the hero of a novel by Mary Godwin Shelley. He
created a human monster who committed horrible crimes and finally destroyed
him.

of the sea-fowl's plumage, which enables him to shed the rain
that falls on him and the wave in which he dips. When one has
had *all* his conceit taken out of him, when he has lost *all* his
illusions, his feathers will soon soak through, and he will fly no
more.

"So you admire conceited people, do you?" said the young
lady who has come to the city to be finished off for — the duties
of life.

I am afraid you do not study logic at your school, my dear.
It does not follow that I wish to be pickled in brine because I like
a salt-water plunge at Nahant.[4] I say that conceit is just as
natural a thing to human minds as a center is to a circle. But
little-minded people's thoughts move in such small circles that
five minutes' conversation gives you an arc long enough to
determine their whole curve. An arc in the movement of a
large intellect does not sensibly differ from a straight line. Even
if it have the third vowel as its center, it does not soon betray it.
The highest thought, that is, is the most seemingly impersonal; it
does not obviously imply any individual center.

Audacious self-esteem, with good ground for it, is always imposing. What resplendent beauty that must have been which
could have authorized Phryne to "peel" in the way she did!
What fine speeches are those two: "*Non omnis moriar*,"[5] and
"I have taken all knowledge to be my province"![6] Even in
common people, conceit has the virtue of making them cheerful;
the man who thinks his wife, his baby, his house, his horse, his
dog, and himself severally unequaled is almost sure to be a good-
humored person, though liable to be tedious at times.

—What are the great faults of conversation? Want of ideas,
want of words, want of manners, are the principal ones, I suppose you think. I don't doubt it, but I will tell you what I have
found spoil more good talks than anything else — long arguments
on special points between people who differ on the fundamental
principles upon which these points depend. No men can have
satisfactory relations with each other until they have agreed on
certain *ultimata*[7] of belief not to be disturbed in ordinary conversation, and unless they have sense enough to trace the secondary questions depending upon these ultimate beliefs to their

---

[4] A coast town in Massachusetts.
[5] "I shall not wholly die," a quotation from Horace.
[6] From a letter by Francis Bacon.
[7] Final or fundamental matters.

source. In short, just as a written constitution is essential to the best social order, so a code of finalities is a necessary condition of profitable talk between two persons. Talking is like playing on the harp; there is as much in laying the hand on the strings to stop their vibrations as in twanging them to bring out their music.

— Do you mean to say the pun-question is not clearly settled in your minds? Let me lay down the law upon the subject. Life and language are alike sacred. Homicide and *verbicide* — that is, violent treatment of a word with fatal results to its legitimate meaning, which is its life — are alike forbidden. Manslaughter, which is the meaning of the one, is the same as man's laughter, which is the end of the other. A pun is *primâ facie* [8] an insult to the person you are talking with. It implies utter indifference to or sublime contempt for his remarks, no matter how serious. I speak of total depravity, and one says all that is written on the subject is deep raving. I have committed my self-respect by talking with such a person. I should like to commit him, but cannot, because he is a nuisance. Or I speak of geological convulsions, and he asks me what was the cosine of Noah's ark; also, whether the Deluge was not a deal huger than any modern inundation.

A pun does not commonly justify a blow in return. But if a blow were given for such cause, and death ensued, the jury would be judges both of the facts and of the pun, and might, if the latter were of an aggravated character, return a verdict of justifiable homicide. Thus, in a case lately decided before Miller, J., Doe presented Roe a subscription paper, and urged the claims of suffering humanity. Roe replied by asking, When charity was like a top? It was in evidence that Doe preserved a dignified silence. Roe then said, " When it begins to hum." Doe then — and not till then — struck Roe, and his head happening to hit a bound volume of the Monthly Rag-Bag and Stolen Miscellany, intense mortification ensued, with a fatal result. The chief laid down his notions of the law to his brother justices, who unanimously replied, " Jest so." The chief rejoined, that no man should jest so without being punished for it, and charged for the prisoner, who was acquitted, and the pun ordered to be burned by the sheriff. The bound volume was forfeited as a deodand,[9] but not claimed.

[8] At first view.
[9] Personal property that has been instrumental in the death of some one.

People that make puns are like wanton boys that put coppers on the railroad tracks. They amuse themselves and other children, but their little trick may upset a freight train of conversation for the sake of a battered witticism.

I will thank you, B. F., to bring down two books, of which I will mark the places on this slip of paper. (While he is gone, I may say that this boy, our landlady's youngest, is called Benjamin Franklin, after the celebrated philosopher of that name. A highly merited compliment.)

I wished to refer to two eminent authorities. Now be so good as to listen. The great moralist says: " To trifle with the vocabulary which is the vehicle of social intercourse is to tamper with the currency of human intelligence. He who would violate the sanctities of his mother tongue would invade the recesses of the paternal till without remorse, and repeat the banquet of Saturn [10] without an indigestion."

And, once more, listen to the historian. " The Puritans hated puns. The Bishops were notoriously addicted to them. The Lords Temporal carried them to the verge of license. Majesty itself must have its royal quibble. ' Ye be burly, my Lord of Burleigh,' said Queen Elizabeth, ' but ye shall make less stir in our realm than my Lord of Leicester.' The gravest wisdom and the highest breeding lent their sanction to the practice. Lord Bacon playfully declared himself a descendant of 'Og, the King of Bashan. Sir Philip Sidney, with his last breath, reproached the soldier who brought him water, for wasting a casque full upon a dying man. A courtier, who saw Othello performed at the Globe Theater, remarked, that the blackamoor was a brute, and not a man. ' Thou hast reason,' replied a great Lord, ' according to Plato his saying; for this be a two-legged animal *with* feathers.' The fatal habit became universal. The language was corrupted. The infection spread to the national conscience. Political double-dealings naturally grew out of verbal double meanings. The teeth of the new dragon were sown by the Cadmus [11] who introduced the alphabet of equivocation. What was levity in the time of the Tudors grew to regicide and revolution in the age of the Stuarts."

---

[10] The Greek god Saturn was said to have eaten his children.

[11] In Greek mythology, a troop of armed men sprang from the dragon's teeth sown by Cadmus and helped him found the city of Thebes. He was also supposed to have introduced the alphabet into Greece.

Who was that boarder that just whispered something about the Macaulay [12] flowers of literature? — There was a dead silence. — I said calmly, I shall henceforth consider any interruption by a pun as a hint to change my boarding-house. Do not plead my example. If *I* have used any such, it has been only as a Spartan father would show up·a drunken helot.[13] We have done with them.

SUGGESTIONS FOR STUDY

1. Be sure you understand the difference between *autocrat* and *aristocrat*. Both apply to Holmes, but not with the same meaning. Find examples in this selection which show in what sense he is an autocrat.

2. Do you agree with his opinion on mathematicians, conceit, conversational faults? Notice the variety of subjects discussed in this short selection. How many do you find in all?

3. In the passage on puns, Holmes says that they are forbidden and then he proceeds to make eleven puns in three pages. Can you find them all?

4. What do you think of puns as a form of wit?

FOR FURTHER READING

The Autocrat of the Breakfast Table: Chapters VII and XI
The Professor at the Breakfast Table
The Poet at the Breakfast Table: Chapters II and V
Over the Teacups
Pages from an Old Volume of Life: Chapter II

For poetry by Holmes, see page 595.

A BUSINESS LETTER

By Artemus Ward (Charles Farrar Browne, 1834–1867)

"He's the wuss speller I know of," said Artemus Ward of Chaucer in "At the Tomb of Shakespeare," one of his contributions to *Punch*. Ward belongs to a class of humorists who depended for much of their effect on outrageous spelling, a method not highly thought of at present except in dialect stories and poems. But there was a good deal more to Ward than merely taking unparalleled liberties with the English language,

[12] A British essayist and poet noted for his finished style.
[13] Lowest class among the Spartans.

as his admirers know. He had a genuine gift for conveying humorous ideas through both the spoken and written word.

Charles Farrar Browne, to call him by his real name, was born in Maine, from Puritan stock. Once, when asked about his Puritan ancestry, he said, " I think we came from Jerusalem, for my father's name was Levi and we had a Moses and a Nathan in the family, but my poor brother's name was Cyrus; so, perhaps, that makes us Persians." He learned the trade of printer and from that he advanced to reporter for various papers until in 1858 he reached Cleveland, where he got a job on the *Plain Dealer* where he conducted a humorous column. One of his office companions has left this picture of the humorist at work: " When writing, his gaunt form looked ridiculous enough. One leg hung over the arm of his chair like a great hook, while he would write away, sometimes laughing to himself. and then slapping the table in the excess of his mirth." He was fond of the circus, sideshow and all, and from this he conceived the idea of the " moral show " which he continued to use effectively at frequent intervals. Of course, the show existed only in his own imagination. " A Business Letter," which follows, was his first pronouncement and made him more than locally famous.

Browne was of a roving disposition. To gratify this, as well as to appeal to a wider and more profitable audience, he decided to try the lecture platform. He was a phenomenal success, for he was able to talk his particular line even more effectively than write it. The first lecture was entitled " The Babes in the Woods," and the second " Sixty Minutes in Africa." He repeated these many times, but they never were twice the same. He said, " One of the features of my entertainment is, that it contains so many things that don't have anything to do with it."

In 1866 he conceived the idea of going to England, where he repeated his American successes, but by this time tuberculosis had worn him down so that at the end of his seventh week, while giving his lecture on the Mormons, he had to leave the platform, and a short time thereafter he died.

One of the most ardent admirers of Artemus Ward was Abraham Lincoln, who would often break the tension of a solemn cabinet meeting during the war by reading aloud some comical extracts from Ward's early books.

To the Editor of the ——

Sir. — I'm movin' along — slowly along — down tords your place. My show at present consists of three moral Bares, a Kangaroo (a amoozin little Raskal — 'twould make you larf yerself to deth to see the little cuss jump up and squeal), wax figgers of G. Washington, Gen. Taylor, John Bunyan, Capt. Kidd, and Dr. Webster in the act of killin' Dr. Parkman, besides several miscellanyus moral wax statoots of celebrated piruts & murderers, &c., ekalled

by few & exceld by none. Now, Mr. Editor, scratch orf a few
lines sayin' how is the show bizness down to your place. I shall
have my hanbills dun at your offiss. Depend upon it. I want
you should git my hanbills up in flamin' stile. Also, git up a
tremenjus excitement in yr. paper 'bowt my onparaleld Show. We
must fetch the public somhow. We must wurk on their feelins.
Cum the moral on 'em strong. If it's a temperance community,
tell 'em I sined the pledge fifteen minutes arter Ise born, but on
the contery, ef your peple take their tods, say Mister Ward is as
Jenial a feller as we ever met, full of conwivIality, & the life an
sole of the Soshul Bored. Take, don't you? If you say any-
thin' abowt my show, say my snaiks is as harmliss as the new-
born Babe. What a interestin' study it is to see a zewolOgical
animil like a snaik under perfeck subjection! My Kangaroo is
the most larfable little cuss I ever saw. All for 15 cents. I am
anxyus to skewer your infloounce. I repeet in regard to them
hanbills, that I shall git 'em struck orf up to your printin' offiss.
My perlitercal sentiments agree with yourn exactly. I know thay
do, becawz I never saw a man whoos didn't.

Respectively yures,

A. WARD.

P.S. — You scratch my back & Ile scratch your back.

SUGGESTIONS FOR STUDY

1. In what way is this letter a satire on advertising? On the intelligence
of the public?

2. How does the spelling add to the humorous effect?

3. What in this letter do you think would especially appeal to Abraham
Lincoln?

FOR FURTHER READING

Selected Works carries an introduction by Albert Jay Nock, who edited
the volume.

Chapters III, V, and VI of *Why Lincoln Laughed*, by Russell H. Con-
well, contain interesting accounts of the relations between Ward and Lincoln, with selections from Ward's writings of which Lincoln was especially
fond.

AN UNEXPECTED ACQUAINTANCE

By MARK TWAIN (SAMUEL L. CLEMENS, 1835–1910)

High above the Mississippi River at Hannibal, Missouri, face turned toward the Turtle Island which is the scene for much of those greatest of boys' stories, *Huckleberry Finn* and *Tom Sawyer,* stands a bronze statue of Samuel Langhorne Clemens. And under the better-known name of Mark Twain, which he borrowed from the expression of a river pilot in sounding the shallows, is inscribed: " His religion was humanity and the whole world mourned for him when he died." Eulogist of Joan of Arc, wag, historian of the great river which flows at the feet of his effigy, and under all this one of the keenest philosophers America has produced, Mark Twain's fame extends around the world. In every office and in nearly every home are aging men and women whose faces brighten at the memory of Huck Finn and Tom Sawyer or Pudd'n'head Wilson; in Berlin, London, and Paris the drolleries of his *Tramp Abroad* and *Innocents Abroad* still make hundreds laugh. And the life of the creator of these characters and the writer of these books was as vari-colored and as interesting as the books themselves. You must read in Paine's *Life of Mark Twain* or in his own *Autobiography,* in *Life on the Mississippi,* or in *Roughing It,* how he lived Tom Sawyer's boyhood in Hannibal, Missouri; how he.struggled to become the best river pilot on the Mississippi; how he joined the California gold-seekers and missed a fortune by one pailful of water; how he " jumped into fame on the back of a Jumping Frog "; how he toured the Mediterranean and set the United States rocking with laughter at his resulting book, *The Innocents Abroad,* how this trip was the means of his meeting and marrying a beautiful young lady; how he built up a fortune through his writings and then lost it suddenly; how he paid all his debts by further writing and lecturing; how he was honored and acclaimed in his old age both here and abroad. To know Mark Twain is an experience no one can afford to miss.

His typical form of humor is the " yarn," an incredible incident told with due solemnity. In *The Innocents Abroad* much of the fun lies in the front of blank incredulity presented by the young Americans to the stories of the foreign guides, intended to impress them. This hilarious book shocked many Americans by its irreverence for the older civilization, but its great service besides affording amusement was to put to shame the insincere rhapsodizing of American tourists over anything and everything European. It marks the fresh point of view of the young western nation which, like many an adolescent, was no longer willing to swallow unquestioningly everything its elders tried to teach it.

The following experience, taken from *A Tramp Abroad,* is a good example of the " boomerang " joke which turns itself back on the joker.

Half of the summer horde in Switzerland is made up of English people; the other half is made up of many nationalities, the Germans leading and the Americans coming next. The Americans were not as numerous as I had expected they would be.

The 7.30 table d'hôte at the great Schweizerhof furnished a mighty array and variety of nationalities, but it offered a better opportunity to observe costumes than people, for the multitude sat at immensely long tables, and therefore the faces were mainly seen in perspective; but the breakfasts were served at small round tables, and then if one had the fortune to get a table in the midst of the assemblage he could have as many faces to study as he could desire. We used to try to guess out the nationalities, and generally succeeded tolerably well. Sometimes we tried to guess people's names; but that was a failure; that is a thing which probably requires a good deal of practice. We presently dropped it and gave our efforts to less difficult particulars. One morning I said —

" There is an American party."

Harris said —

" Yes — but name the State."

I named one State, Harris named another. We agreed upon one thing, however — that the young girl with the party was very beautiful, and very tastefully dressed. But we disagreed as to her age. I said she was eighteen, Harris said she was twenty. The dispute between us waxed warm and I finally said, with a pretense of being in earnest —

" Well, there is one way to settle the matter — I will go and ask her."

Harris said, sarcastically, " Certainly, that is the thing to do. All you need to do is to use the common formula over here: go and say, ' I'm an American! ' Of course she will be glad to see you."

Then he hinted that perhaps there was no great danger of my venturing to speak to her.

I said, " I was only talking — I didn't intend to approach her, but I see that you do not know what an intrepid person I am. I am not afraid of any woman that walks. I will go and speak to this young girl."

The thing I had in my mind was not difficult. I meant to address her in the most respectful way and ask her to pardon me if her strong resemblance to a former acquaintance of mine was de-

ceiving me; and when she should reply that the name I mentioned was not the name she bore, I meant to beg pardon
again, most respectfully, and retire. There would be no harm
done. I walked to her table, bowed to the gentleman, then
turned to her and was about to begin my little speech when she
exclaimed —

"I *knew* I wasn't mistaken — I told John it was you! John
said it probably wasn't, but I knew I was right. I said you
would recognize me presently and come over; and I'm glad you
did, for I shouldn't have felt much flattered if you had gone out
of this room without recognizing me. Sit down, sit down — how
odd it is — you are the last person I was ever expecting to see
again."

This was a stupefying surprise. It took my wits clear away,
for an instant. However, we shook hands cordially all around,
and I sat down. But truly this was the tightest place I ever was
in. I seemed to vaguely remember the girl's face, now, but I had
no idea where I had seen it before, or what name belonged with it.
I immediately tried to get up a diversion about Swiss scenery, to
keep her from launching into topics that might betray that I did
not know her, but it was of no use, she went right along upon
matters which interested her more:

"O dear, what a night that was, when the sea washed the
forward boats away — do you remember it?"

"Oh, *don't* I!" said I — but I didn't. I wished the sea had
washed the rudder and the smoke-stack and the captain away
— then I could have located this questioner.

"And don't you remember how frightened poor Mary was, and
how she cried?"

"Indeed I do!" said I. "Dear me, how it all comes back!"

I fervently wished it *would* come back — but my memory
was a blank. The wise way would have been to frankly own up;
but I could not bring myself to do that, after the young girl had
praised me so for recognizing her; so I went on, deeper and
deeper into the mire, hoping for a chance clue but never getting
one. The Unrecognizable continued, with vivacity —

"Do you know, George married Mary, after all?"

"Why, no! Did he?"

"Indeed he did. He said he did not believe she was half as
much to blame as her father was, and I thought he was right.
Didn't you?"

" Of course he was. It was a perfectly plain case. I always said so."

" Why, no, you didn't! — at least that summer."

" Oh, no, not that summer. No, you are perfectly right about that. It was the following winter that I said it."

" Well, as it turned out, Mary was not in the least to blame — it was all her father's fault — at least his and old Darley's."

It was necessary to say something, so I said —

" I always regarded Darley as a troublesome old thing."

" So he was, but then they always had a great affection for him, although he had so many eccentricities. You remember that when the weather was the least cold, he would try to come into the house."

I was rather afraid to proceed. Evidently Darley was not a man — he must be some other kind of animal — possibly a dog, maybe an elephant. However, tails are common to all animals, so I ventured to say —

" And what a tail he had!"

" *One!* He had a thousand!"

This was bewildering. I did not quite know what to say, so I only said —

" Yes, he *was* rather well fixed in the matter of tails."

" For a Negro, and a crazy one at that, I should say he was," said she.

It was getting pretty sultry for me. I said to myself, "Is it possible she is going to stop there, and wait for me to speak? If she does, the conversation is blocked. A Negro with a thousand tails is a topic which a person cannot talk upon fluently and instructively without more or less preparation. As to diving rashly into such a vast subject — "

But here, to my gratitude, she interrupted my thought by saying —

" Yes, when it came to tales of his crazy woes, there was simply no end to them if anybody would listen. His own quarters were comfortable enough, but when the weather was cold, the family were sure to have his company — nothing could keep him out of the house. But they always bore it kindly because he had saved Tom's life, years before. You remember Tom?"

" Oh, perfectly. Fine fellow he was, too."

" Yes, he was. And what a pretty little thing his child was!"

" You may well say that. I never saw a prettier child."

"I used to delight to pet it and dandle it and play with it."

"So did I."

"You named it. What *was* that name? I can't call it to mind."

It appeared to me that the ice was getting pretty thin, here. I would have given something to know what the child's sex was. However, I had the good luck to think of a name that would fit either sex, so I brought it out —

"I named it Frances."

"From a relative, I suppose? But you named the one that died, too — one that I never saw. What did you call that one?"

I was out of neutral names, but as the child was dead and she had never seen it, I thought I might risk a name for it and trust to luck. Therefore I said —

"I called that one Thomas Henry."

She said, musingly —

"That is very singular — very singular."

I sat still and let the cold sweat run down. I was in a good deal of trouble, but I believed I could worry through if she wouldn't ask me to name any more children. I wondered where the lightning was going to strike next. She was still ruminating over that last child's title, but presently she said —

"I have always been sorry you were away at the time — I would have had you name my child."

"*Your* child! Are you married?"

"I have been married thirteen years."

"Christened, you mean."

"No, married. The youth by your side is my son."

"It seems incredible — even impossible. I do not mean any harm by it, but would you mind telling me if you are any over eighteen? — that is to say, will you tell me how old you are?"

"I was just nineteen the day of the storm we were talking about. That was my birthday."

That did not help matters much, as I did not know the date of the storm. I tried to think of some non-committal thing to say, to keep up my end of the talk and render my poverty in the matter of reminiscences as little noticeable as possible, but I seemed to be about out of non-committal things. I was about to say, "You haven't changed a bit since then" — but that was risky. I thought of saying, "You have improved ever so much since then" — but that wouldn't answer, of course. I was about to try a shy at the weather, for a saving change, when the girl slipped in ahead of me and said —

" How I have enjoyed this talk over those happy old times, haven't you? "

" I never have spent such a half hour in all my life before ! " said I, with emotion; and I could have added, with a near approach to truth, "and I would rather be scalped than spend another one like it." I was holily grateful to be through with the ordeal, and was about to make my good-byes and get out, when the girl said —

" But there is one thing that is ever so puzzling to me."

" Why, what is that? "

" That dead child's name. What did you say it was? "

Here was another balmy place to be in: I had forgotten the child's name; I hadn't imagined it would be needed again. However, I had to pretend to know, anyway, so I said —

" Joseph William."

The youth at my side corrected me, and said —

" No — Thomas Henry."

I thanked him, in words, and said, with trepidation —

" O yes — I was thinking of another child that I named — I have named a great many, and I get them confused — this one *was* named Henry Thompson — "

" Thomas Henry," calmly interposed the boy.

I thanked him again, strictly in words, and stammered out —

" Thomas Henry — yes, Thomas Henry was the poor child's name. I named him for Thomas — er — Thomas Carlyle, the great author, you know — and Henry — er — er — Henry the Eighth. The parents were very grateful to have a child named Thomas Henry."

" That makes it more singular than ever," murmured my beautiful friend.

" Does it? Why? "

" Because when the parents speak of that child now, they always call it Susan Amelia."

That spiked my gun. I could not say anything. I was entirely out of verbal obliquities; to go further would be to lie, and that I would not do; so I simply sat still and suffered — sat mutely and resignedly there, and sizzled — for I was being slowly fried to death in my own blushes. Presently the enemy laughed a happy laugh and said —

"I *have* enjoyed this talk over old times, but you have not. I saw very soon that you were only pretending to know me, and so as I had wasted a compliment on you in the beginning, I made up my mind to punish you. And I have succeeded pretty well. I was glad to see that you knew George and Tom and Darley, for I had never heard of them before and therefore could not be sure that you had; and I was glad to learn the names of those imaginary children, too. One can get quite a fund of information out of you if one goes at it cleverly. Mary and the storm, and the sweeping away of the forward boats, were facts — all the rest was fiction. Mary was my sister; her full name was Mary ——. *Now* do you remember me?"

"Yes," I said, "I do remember you now; and you are as hard-hearted as you were thirteen years ago in that ship, else you wouldn't have punished me so. You haven't changed your nature nor your person, in any way at all; you look just as young as you did then, you are just as beautiful as you were then, and you have transmitted a deal of your comeliness to this fine boy. There — if that speech moves you any, let's fly the flag of truce, with the understanding that I am conquered and confess it."

All of which was agreed to and accomplished, on the spot. When I went back to Harris, I said —

"Now you see what a person with talent and address can do."

"Excuse me, I see what a person of colossal ignorance and simplicity can do. The idea of your going and intruding on a party of strangers, that way, and talking for half an hour — why, I never heard of a man in his right mind doing such a thing before. What did you say to them?"

"I never said any harm. I merely asked the girl what her name was."

"I don't doubt it. Upon my word I don't. I think you were capable of it. It was stupid in me to let you go over there and make such an exhibition of yourself. But you know I couldn't really believe you would do such an inexcusable thing. What will those people think of us? But how did you say it? — I mean the manner of it. I hope you were not abrupt."

"No, I was careful about that. I said, ' My friend and I would like to know what your name is, if you don't mind.' "

"No, that was not abrupt. There is a polish about it that does you infinite credit. And I am glad you put me in; that was a delicate attention which I appreciate at its full value. What did she do?"

"She didn't do anything in particular. She told me her name."

"Simply told you her name. Do you mean to say she did not show any surprise?"

"Well, now I come to think, she did show something; maybe it was surprise; I hadn't thought of that — I took it for gratification."

"Oh, undoubtedly you were right; it must have been gratification; it could not be otherwise than gratifying to be assaulted by a stranger with such a question as that. Then what did you do?"

"I offered my hand and the party gave me a shake."

"I saw it! I did not believe my own eyes, at the time. Did the gentleman say anything about cutting your throat?"

"No, they all seemed glad to see me, as far as I could judge."

"And do you know, I believe they were. I think they said to themselves, 'Doubtless this curiosity has got away from his keeper — let us amuse ourselves with him.' There is no other way of accounting for their facile docility. You sat down. Did they *ask* you to sit down?"

"No, they did not ask me, but I supposed they did not think of it."

"You have an unerring instinct. What else did you do? What did you talk about?"

"Well, I asked the girl how old she was."

"*Un*doubtedly. Your delicacy is beyond praise. Go on, go on — don't mind my apparent misery — I always look so when I am steeped in a profound and reverent joy. Go on — she told you her age?"

"Yes, she told me her age, and all about her mother, and her grandmother, and her other relations, and all about herself."

"Did she volunteer these statistics?"

"No, not exactly that. I asked the questions and she answered them."

"This is divine. Go on — it is not possible that you forgot to inquire into her politics?"

"No, I thought of that. She is a Democrat, her husband is a Republican, and both of them are Baptists."

"Her husband? Is that child married?"

"She is not a child. She is married, and that is her husband who is there with her."

" Has she any children? "

" Yes — seven and a half."

" That is impossible."

" No, she has them. She told me herself."

" Well, but seven and a *half?* How do you make out the half? Where does the half come in? "

" That is a child which she had by another husband — not this one but another one — so it is a step-child, and they do not count it full measure."

" Another husband? Has she had another husband? "

" Yes, four. This one is number four."

" I do not believe a word of it. It is impossible, upon its face. Is that boy there her brother? "

" No, that is her son. He is her youngest. He is not as old as he looks; he is only eleven and a half."

" These things are all manifestly impossible. This is a wretched business. It is a plain case: they simply took your measure, and concluded to fill you up. They seem to have succeeded. I am glad I am not in the mess; they may at least be charitable enough to think there ain't a pair of us. Are they going to stay here long? "

" No, they leave before noon."

" There is one man who is deeply grateful for that. How did you find out? You asked, I suppose? "

" No, along at first I inquired into their plans, in a general way, and they said they were going to be here a week, and make trips round about; but toward the end of the interview, when I said you and I would tour around with them with pleasure, and offered to bring you over and introduce you, they hesitated a little, and asked if you were from the same establishment that I was. I said you were, and then they said they had changed their mind and considered it necessary to start at once and visit a sick relative in Siberia."

" Ah me, you struck the summit! You struck the loftiest altitude of stupidity that human effort has ever reached. You shall have a monument of jackass's skulls as high as the Strassburg spire if you die before I do. They wanted to know if I was from the same ' establishment ' that you hail from, did they? What did they mean by ' establishment ' ? "

" I don't know; it never occurred to me to ask."

" Well, *I* know. They meant an asylum — an *idiot* asylum, do you understand? So they *do* think there's a pair of us, after all. Now what do you think of yourself?"

"Well, I don't know. I didn't know I was doing any harm; I didn't *mean* to do any harm. They were very nice people, and they seemed to like me."

Harris made some rude remarks and left for his bedroom — to break some furniture, he said. He was a singularly irascible man; any little thing would disturb his temper.

I had been well scorched by the young woman, but no matter, I took it out of Harris. One should always "get even" in some way, else the sore place will go on hurting.

SUGGESTIONS FOR STUDY

1. From what you have heard or read, do you think that tourists would be apt to do just the sort of thing shown here? Give reasons, one way or the other.

2. Describe Harris's thoughts or feelings as he saw his friend's actions.

3. At what point do you think the young lady realized that the gentleman visitor was bluffing?

4. How does the boy help in the humor of the situation?

5. Does the final talk with Harris add to the fun, or do you think the episode might have ended sooner? Discuss.

FOR FURTHER READING

PICTURES OF THE MISSISSIPPI AND
THE FAR WEST

WITH FOREIGN SETTINGS

Tom Sawyer

Huckleberry Finn

Life on the Mississippi

Roughing It

The Jumping Frog of Calaveras County

The Gilded Age

The Innocents Abroad

A Connecticut Yankee in King Arthur's Court

The Prince and the Pauper

A Tramp Abroad

Tom Sawyer Abroad

Personal Recollections of Joan of Arc

THE FABLE OF A WONDERFUL MEAL OF VITTLES

By GEORGE ADE (1866–   )

George Ade is an example of a man whose ambition in life was thwarted by one accidental lucky idea. He wanted to be a playwright and he did succeed in turning out some good comedy and light opera. But one day while attempting to enliven his modest column on a Chicago paper he hit upon the idea of a fable in slang. This clever novelty created such a popular demand for more that he has had to spend his time ever since turning out more and more fables for the newspaper syndicates, and the dramatist is quite lost sight of in the fabulist. The combination of the ancient stilted form of Aesop with the modern gaiety and unexpectedness of the slang phrase gives that contrast which we have already shown to be the essence of humor. The ridiculous moral tag pleases an age which condemns the moral tag in its serious literature. Ade uses slang artistically, never vulgarly or stupidly. He says, " There are niceties of distinction even when out on a slang debauch. . . . Besides, the so-called ' slang ' that romps so gaily into the homes and offices of the socially important is not slang at all. It is not the argot of a criminal element. . . . It is highly figurative speech, tinctured with the American spirit of playfulness — bantering, unconventional."

Once there were two Lads who grew up on adjoining Farms and were real Buddies, killing Garter Snakes together, popping Corn, tracking Rabbits in the Snow and often sleeping in the same Bed.

About the time they were big enough to pitch Hay, Henry heard the Siren Call of the City and beat it for the Bright Lights, while Ez continued to peg away on the old Home Place, with a growing Ambition to trade in Mules and feed a few Steers for the Chicago Market.

Strange as it may seem, Henry up in the City and Ez out in the Country both prospered, in spite of Congress.

Henry handled more Currency than Ez ever saw, but after he had paid the Rent for a Suite in the Shakedown Apartment Building and settled with the Japanese Servants and had given Checks to the Tradesmen and all of the perfumed Brigands who unloaded Stuff on the Wife, and remitted to various Clubs, he had just about as much left as Ez had after he bought an Outer Casing and paid his Taxes over at the Court House.

Although Henry had become more or less of a Rowdy-Dow,

with cloth tops for his Shoes and Ribbon on his Eye-Glasses, while Ez seldom experienced the protecting warmth of a Necktie, the Boys sort of kept tab on each other, exchanging occasional Letters and keeping alive the Bonfire which had been kindled on the sacred Altar of Friendship in the golden Days of Youth.

Henry lived among rumbling L trains, Street Cries, the tooting of Horns and the incessant roar of Street Traffic. Consequently his Dream of Paradise was to get out on an Island somewhere and lie in the shade of a Yama-Yama Tree where the Celestial Stillness would not be disturbed except by the lazy purring of the soft Breakers on a Coral Strand.

Ez lived out among the Hickories and Maples, where the harshest sound to fall upon the Ear was the bleating of a Spring Lamb or the call of a Cricket to his Mate at Eventide.

Consequently, his Idea of a beneficial Change was to occupy a Reserved Seat in the Big Top at a Performance given by Barnum and Bailey and the Ringling Brothers while the Band was playing and about 8 Acts were being put on simultaneously in Rings and on Elevated Platforms.

Henry often longed to connect up with Ez and talk over Old Times with him, but they never could agree on a Meeting-Place. Henry was always in favor of a Sanitarium while Ez preferred Atlantic City.

Once Ez happened to be in the City and Henry, wishing to give him a Jolly Day, took him up to the Club to play Auction. Ez was very sore, as he had planned to see the Follies, both afternoon and evening.

When Henry learned that Ez had acquired the Florida Habit he thought they could get together in the Winter and check up on their old Playmates back in Rhubarb Township, but there was nothing doing.

Ez picked out St. Petersburg because there were 80,000 People on the Street all of the time and every Day was like Thursday of County Fair Week.

He loved to hear the glad yelps of the Horse-Shoe Pitchers and mingle with the happy Jam at the Cafeteria and stand in line at the Movies and get a lot of glad thrills which seldom come to one who lives a half-mile back from State Road No. 27 on R. F. D. 3.

Henry had a place in Florida but it was concealed behind an

Orange Grove and was far removed from any other Habitation and was entirely surrounded by Signs reading as follows: Keep Out.

We all long for the Things we seldom get, as proven by the fact that so many Good People fall and fall hard when confronted by unusual but not unwelcome Temptations.

The Boston Young Man with Weak Eyes wants to be a Cow-Puncher and the Hired Hand employed near Beatrice, Nebraska, wants to go to Hollywood and play Valentino Parts.

Just to illustrate the big Idea, one day last Summer it happened that Ez was in the City and he met Henry who got ready to blow his Boyhood Friend to a swell Luncheon.

Henry arranged to have the Food served in a snug Corner entirely screened by Oleanders and Palms. The Chef received private Instructions to throw himself.

When the Visitor entered the far-famed establishment and found himself entirely protected from the Vulgar Gaze he knew that at last he was in the Headquarters for sure-enough Food. He was getting ready to order Oyster Stew with Dill Pickles but he was told that Henry had arranged everything.

" What is it? " he asked, gazing into the limpid Amber of the First Course.

" Turtle Soup," replied the Host.

" We shoot the Blame Things just for Practice, out our Way," said the Guest, " but if I went Home and told my Wife I'd been eatin' Turtle she wouldn't live with me."

So the Alsatian Nobleman hurried it away and substituted a Tid-Bit with Cray-Fish as the principal Ornament in the Ensemble.

" It's a Craw-Dabber! " exclaimed Ez. " I see Ten Million of them little Cusses every Spring but I wouldn't touch one with a Ten-Foot Pole."

To relieve the embarrassing Situation, Henry gave a Sign and the Menials came running with the Third Course, a tempting array of Frog Saddles.

" A Frog is a Reptile," said Ez, backing away from the Table. " I've heard they were Et but I never believed it. I can go out any Morning and gather a Car-Load."

The next Serving was Breast of Guinea Hen with Mushrooms under Glass on the Side.

" On my Farm I've got a lot of these Things," said the Guest, poking at the Guinea Hen timidly with his Fork. "We use them as Alarm Clocks, but I'd just as soon eat a Turkey Buzzard."

"How about the Mushrooms?"

"Eight People in our Township were poisoned this Summer from Foolin' with that Truck. My pasture's speckled with 'em, but we never pick 'em. Most of them are Toad-Stools. I tried a

"A FROG IS A REPTILE," SAID EZ

Real One once at a K. P. banquet. It tasted a good deal like a Rubber Glove."

The only remaining Item before Dessert was a tempting Salad of Water Cress.

The Guest identified it as something that grew in the Crick below the Spring and was commonly classified as Grass.

"Perhaps you had better order for Yourself," said Henry as the lowly Water Cress followed the other Courses into the Discard.

The Guest motioned the Waiter to come close and said: "If it's too late for Oysters give me a T-Bone Steak with Onions and a large Cup of Coffee."

MORAL: A Delicacy is something not raised in the same County.

SUGGESTIONS FOR STUDY

1. How does this fable illustrate the point made in the Introduction that humor relies largely on contrast for its effect. How many points of contrast can you find in this fable?

2. Is this fable true to actual life? Have you ever had experiences with relatives from an entirely different environment from your own, which would illustrate the principle of life here involved?

3. Select those details or those bits of slang which strike you as being especially amusing.

4. Read Aesop's " Fable of the Town Mouse and the Country Mouse " and find out in what ways Ade's fable resembles it. How is the point or " moral " different?

5. Try your hand at writing a fable in slang. Remember Ade's principles that the slang must not be vulgar nor just stupid stock expressions which mean nothing. It must be vivid, lively, and figurative.

6. Note how Ade's use of capital letters heightens the general effect.

FOR FURTHER READING

There are a number of volumes of Ade's fables published under slightly differing titles, such as *More Fables, Hand-Made Fables,* etc.

His published plays include *The County Chairman* and *The College Widow.*

LONG PANTS

By Irvin S. Cobb (1876–   )

Irvin S. Cobb has been called a " four-dimension " writer because after having won fame in the three dimensions of newspaper reporting, humorous prose, and short story writing, he ventured into the fourth dimension of the novel. Rarely can a man attain notable success in so many fields, but Irvin Cobb *is* rare. One of his rare qualities is the ability to stand off and view himself impersonally as a subject for laughter. Take, for instance, the opening of the autobiographical account he once wrote: " Irvin S. Cobb, of whom I have the honor to be whom, was born, successfully, in Paducah, Kentucky, almost exactly one hundred years after the signing of the Declaration of Independence, thus making it possible for future generations to celebrate both centennials simultaneously in 1976. He is a member of an old, or southern family, his family being fully as old as any southern family known. It extends back without a break to the Garden of Eden."

In his home town at the age of nineteen he became the youngest managing editor of a daily newspaper in the United States. His subsequent biography could easily become a tiresome enumeration of the newspapers and magazines to which he has contributed, and famous trials and war scenes which he has reported, but let us not have anything tiresome connected with Irvin Cobb's name. Better to read him and rejoice. Don't forget, however, that he himself would prefer to have you think of him as a short story writer than as a humorist. After you have read the following amusing account of his boyhood experiences, take a pleasant detour into his distinguished fiction.

Where I came from, they were not "trousers" nor yet were they "breeches," as counter-distinguished from "knee breeches." They were long pants — and putting them on did something to a boy. Something seemed to happen inside him. After that he was a different person and it was a different world. Perhaps I can come near to explaining the difference when I say that in his own eyes he became a more important person than he had been before, whereas, relatively speaking, the world became of less importance. It still was an interesting world; it shortly would become a romantic world, swimming in a tender, glowing mist edged with rainbow trimmings; but it no longer was an overpowering and an unconquerable world. It could be beaten by one coming at it in the right spirit and long pants. You felt that. You showed it.

As though it were yesterday I remember my own sensations, my own experiences on the date of the dedication of my young legs to long pants. One experience in particular do I remember. I'll come to that in a few minutes.

I remember that beforehand, from the hour when I won the parental consent for the great change, I was filled, like the fabled chameleon that got on the piece of Scotch plaid, with conflicting emotions. I was in a fever of joy over the approach of the promised event, and at the same time I was in a chill of apprehension, for I knew that until the novelty of my transformation had worn off I should be the victim of scandalizing remarks on the part of my contemporaries. For such was the ribald custom among us. The occasion of the first pair of long pants was likewise the occasion for gibes and scalding criticism. It took a very strongminded boy to pass, without suffering, through this period. To check the floods of juvenile ridicule at their sources took a boy with the reputation of being ready with his fists. I was neither; so in advance I was torn between dread and yearnings.

Encysted in my ointment was one considerable insect. I had set my heart upon an entire shift of wardrobe, including a mannish shirt with a separate collar. Crossing the line, I desired to cross

all the way over and be at once on the farther side, a grown-up
in outward appearance if not in years. I already had chosen the
model I wished to pattern myself on, sartorially.

This model was a person very much older than I. To me
he seemed almost incredibly old. He must have been all of
thirty-five. But in the sunset of his days, when properly he
should be through with the gauds and vanities of this life, he
plainly had springtime in his soul. He advertised it by his
dress.

I once had been privileged to see him in the act of disrobing.
He was put together so beautifully, with so many fascinating
hitches and catches and snaps. His cuffs — detachable and therefore doubly desirable — fastened to his sleeves with cunning metal
devices having levers and tiny springs to them and notched jaws.
The button-holed tab at the lower end of his shirt bosom was not
a mere superfluous adornment as with so many adults of our town.
With him it served a purpose. It latched to the top button of a
certain undergarment. His watch-chain was of woven horse-hair
and passed twice about his neck, being confined in front with a
clasp of precious gold. His scarf was kept snugly down by a
toothed mechanism which bit into the center plait of his shirt
and which also might be employed at meal times for retaining
the napkin on the bosom. In the knot of the tie itself was a splendid gorgeous horseshoe studded with diamonds, and for further
security a little gold chain ran from this blazing clump to a gold
safety pin that was set in the edge of his waistcoat vest. Nobody
would ever get his jewelry away from him without a struggle. His
key-ring, his pen-knife, and his match-safe were attached to a
much longer chain than the above — a chain which practically
encircled him amidships and disappeared into a fob pocket. He
had a yoke-shaped appliance of whalebone which slipped under
the lapel of his coat, holding it firmly to the breast. His gold-
mounted private toothpick was kept, when not in use, in a decorative little gold case. His collar was of a sort never encountered
nowadays. Glossy and white and glistening, it reared to a vast
height at the back, but was sharply divided at the front to give
the Adam's apple a chance. You cannot find such a collar in this
age. Practically the only way to get the effect would be to have
the tails starched and then put your shirt on upside down. His
sleeve garters had genteel rosettes and tiny fluted edges on them.
For a crowning touch his suspenders were of broad and embroid-

ered webbing with magnificent buckles and shining bosses set in the elastic parts, and there were pendant chains instead of the conventional leather straps affected by the plain people.

My hero's mind also was brilliant, to match his costume. I recall that it was he who said to me:

" Bud, did you get that letter? "

And when I, wriggling in a pleased embarrassment, pretended I had never heard the answer to the catch and, with an attempt to counterfeit innocence, said, "What letter?" he did not reply by saying, "Let her go, Gallagher!" according to the regular formula. No, instead of that, he instantly retorted, "Let her go, postal card!"

It left me, as you might say, stunned. The man was one of our leading drug clerks. He was the first person in town to wear a "chestnut bell" and ring it when somebody got off an old one. He would be!

So I envied him for all that he was and for all that he had on him, and particularly I envied him for his noble suspenders and the detachable cuffs. For the other manly ornamentations — the silver and gold contrivances and the whalebone dingus and the personal toothpick — I could wait; but it seemed to me that I must have a pair of those cuffs and a set of those suspenders to signalize my utter emancipation from the last lingering traces of a vanished juvenility. But the cuffs were denied me, becoming a fond future hope and dream. Nor, at the outset, was I given a complete "long-pants suit," with a vest and all; that lack was the chief dead fly in my Balm of Gilead. I still owned a roundabout jacket or two — scorned relics of a repugnant childhood — which must be worn out first. How I strove, by fair means and foul, to wear them out that autumn! But on me was bestowed a pair of long pants, built of gray jeans, very stiff and warranted to last out any season, and with them suspenders — not, 'tis true, the costly and luxurious suspenders I coveted, but nevertheless suspenders. The jeans was a sort of cloth very hard to wrinkle, but once wrinkled, guaranteed to remain so.

On a great day in the morning, a day destined forever after and forevermore to be marked in my mind with a bright-red asterisk, I drew on my long pants and, thrilled by the thought that never again would I button on breeches to the meridian of a "shirtwaist," I snapped my suspenders into place upon my shoulders; and then, leaving off my coat so that all might observe what wondrous thing had come to pass, I went forth, being proud and yet ashamed.

Through the forenoon I endured the stings and arrows of outrageous acquaintances. In the afternoon, immediately following the principal or midday meal, I met a boy who lived in the next street to ours. Across the years I see him haloed about with affectionate regards. Whatever became of him I cannot tell, but today

THE STINGS AND ARROWS OF OUTRAGEOUS ACQUAINTANCES

I look on him as Damon looked on Pythias, as Jesse looked on Frank. Alone out of all my group, he did not make fun of me that day. He accepted me without comment.

Another thing serves to solder the boyhood picture of him firmly in my memory. He was one of the most appropriately named persons I have known. Names do not often match their wearers. Take Sing Fat, now — of only moderate value to a Chinese merchant in San Francisco, but a perfect name for almost any grand opera tenor. This boy's name was Speck — Oliver Speck — which was suitable to start with, but had been elaborated by us into All-over Speckles, which was better, because he was the most vividly and extensively freckled human being I ever saw. You would have said that he must have been down in a freckle-mine when it blew up, and was one of the main victims.

Speckles suggested that evening we should visit a trained animal exhibition then showing on a vacant lot in the outskirts of town. This suited me. Earlier in the week, this being Saturday, I had come into possession of a large sum of money. I had earned a whole dollar for folding circulars at Mr. Jim Terrell's tobacco warehouse, and I had been spending my fortune, a dime at a time, on the tented attraction in question. In the light of maturer years I know now that originally it must have been a menagerie which had sloughed off from a circus that got into difficulties somewhere.

There was a performing elephant, and there was an educated ostrich — not highly educated, but of some surface culture — and a pet bear; and there were several cages containing animals that had never enjoyed the advantages of much learning. Some of them, you might almost say, were downright unrefined. In one large cage, though, was a trained lion, his mate being in an adjoining cage with her three newly-born cubs.

This lion had a special fascination for me. At the climax of the performance the dauntless keeper would enter the den and, forcing the great beast to squat on his haunches, would wrest the massive jaws apart and thrust his head into the vast mouth. Night after night the prospect of witnessing the feat brought me back. There was an even greater lure — I did so hope to be there the night the lion sneezed!

So I fell in with my good friend Speckles' plan. Then he superimposed on it a daring and revolutionary suggestion: Suppose we took a girl apiece along with us? He named the girls. One of them he had been squiring; the other I had from time to time looked upon with the distant and diffident eye of favor.

On any previous day I should instantly have rejected the proposition. Indignantly I should have asked him if he thought I was one of these here sissies, to be running around with girls? But the enclosing of my lower half in long pants was beginning to work a change in me all over. Already I could feel within me a gentle, insidious stirring, a motive mysterious and vague but by no means unpleasant. It was a thing which, by instinct, I felt might grow on me. I was willing to have it do so. Nay, experimentally I was ready to meet it half-way. Long pants were giving me courage. The suspenders helped, too.

All at once — thus quickly was the yeasty leaven at work in my being — it seemed to me a fitting thing that we two should escort two girls to the show that night. But I left it to my companion, he having had prior experience in these delicate matters, to make arrangements.

At eight o'clock, by secret appointment, we met these young ladies on a corner near the home of one of them. I was grateful for the fact that darkness and large shade trees sheltered the place of rendezvous. Few words were exchanged, none at all being offered by me. Four abreast, but keeping our distances, we started for the show grounds. When we met or overtook other pedestrians, Speckles and I would fall a few paces to the rear and march in a stiffened and stolid silence, leaving the paired-off girls to precede us and temporarily creating the impression that we were not with that giggling twain at all, but merely chanced to be going the same way that they were, merely happened to be walking just behind them. Then, when the danger passed, we would catch up and again make a carefully-spaced-off quartet of it. By such wise strategy we avoided detection until we were inside the tent, and after that, since the attendance was large, we merged with the other patrons, maintaining a loose sort of group formation which was not calculated to arouse suspicion touching on our relationships.

For a special Saturday night feature the management had augmented the program. The official announcer stated that the lion cubs would be taken from their mother's side and passed among the members of the audience, which, after growled protests from the lioness, was done. A few bolder spirits fondled the infant whelps — three woolly, smelly, awkward bundles of tawny fur, each being no longer and not much heavier than a full-grown house cat.

But the two girls shrank and shuddered. With one voice they declared that if one of these awful baby lions should so much as touch them they'd die on the spot.

" Shuckins ! " said Speckles valiantly. " I wouldn't be skeered to have one for a pet and teach him to do tricks and ever'thing.

Would you be skeered, Corn-Cob?'' (" Corn-Cob " was my nickname for intimates.)

I did not answer; my thoughts were elsewhere. My eyes had
fallen on a yellowish fur boa which a cousin of mine, a young
matron who stood with her husband a few yards away, was wearing over her shoulders, and at the sight a splendid whimsical
inspiration had popped, full-born, into my brain. Why not do
something to prove my resourcefulness as a practical joker, and
at the same time cure these timorous lady friends of ours of their
silly fears and, to top all, exhibit my native brilliancy and fertility
of intellect before the opposite sex? In knee-breeches I scarcely
should have dared entertain the bare thought of it, even. In the
dignity and estate of long pants I felt I dared do anything that
avowedly and radically was advanced or masculine. You see how
swiftly the spell continued to work in my blood.

Unobserved by my party, I slipped over and asked my cousin to
let me borrow her neckpiece for just a minute. She eyed me curiously, but surrendered it. Rolling it into a compact bundle, hairy
side out, I crept up behind that one of the two girls who was my
guest, and thrust the wadded pelt against her face and uttered
a quick, snarling, yelping, cat-like sound.

I learned about women from her! Also, in the next instant,
from her female companion. She screamed. The second one
screamed. They kept on screaming, both of them. It hardly
seemed possible that two young girls, neither being more than
twelve or thirteen years old, could scream so piercingly, so continuously, so rapidly, so calliopiously.

Neighbors of their own sex immediately caught the contagion;
these likewise, without reason, began screaming. Somebody —
but I think that stupid creature was a man — shouted out, " The
lions is loose! " Somebody else — and this one undoubtedly was
a man — yelled " Fire! " Somebody, as I now know, always does
yell " Fire! " in such cases. At this moment, also, the elephant
was so ill-advised as to start trumpeting in a strident and disconcerting manner.

Now the close-packed crowd was milling; now it was radiating
from its common center, and now, above all those other night-
marish sounds of pain and terror and panic, there arose sharp
sounds of tearing and rending, which were the sounds made by
the canvas sidewalls as they were ripped from their moorings.
The maddened multitude fell over guy ropes and tripped over

tent stakes and became entangled in choking, baffling tarpaulin folds. People ran into one another and fell down and got up again and fell some more. And some there were who were painfully trampled upon, and many lost their hats and had their garments damaged, and all were distracted and unhappy. Once outside, they scattered in every direction, carrying the alarm with them, and the word spread that the wild beasts had escaped and also that a conflagration raged on the Trimble Street commons; and the fire department turned out, adding to the confusion, and the police force came, and with the police a number of courageous citizen volunteers bearing firearms and other weapons.

But of these latter details I learned only by hearsay. For I no longer was present on the scene. I had been among the very earliest to go away from there. I was barely past my fourteenth birthday, but I knew enough to go and to keep on going. Hours later, on undressing, I found sandy loam in one of my pants pockets. I must have been leaning well over to the inner side when I turned that corner just below the show grounds.

In some quarters, after the excitement had abated, there was a disposition to blame me. At home, I was for days more or less of a pariah; abroad I was shunned by some and by some regarded as an outcast. I shall pass over the spanking that I got. It struck me as an impiety, indeed a thing bordering on the sacrilegious, that while wearing my first new pair of long pants I should be spanked. Still, it were better to have them on at the time than to have them off.

SUGGESTIONS FOR STUDY

1. What effect do you think the present style of putting long pants on very small boys will have upon the emotions of boys as described in this account? Will some other garment take the place of the long pants as the badge of manhood?

2. See if you can find in the family photograph album a picture of a man dressed in the style of the 70's such as Cobb describes as his "model." Comment on what changes have taken place in men's styles since then.

3. How does the attitude of this boy toward girls compare with that of most of the boys in your school?

4. How is the incident of the trained animal show worked up to an exciting climax? Point out the details in this incident and its results which make it especially funny.

5. Write an account of some experience you have had which made you feel suddenly grown up, or of some experience in which you " got into a scrape." Make it as funny as you can by attention to the details you include, slight exaggerations, and unexpected words.

FOR FURTHER READING

" Speaking of Operations — "
A Plea for Old Cap Collier
Eating in Two or Three Languages
" Here Comes the Bride — " and So Forth

The Life of the Party
Roughing It De Luxe
Those Times and These
Old Judge Priest
The Escape of Mr. Trimm

HOW TO WRITE SHORT STORIES
By RING LARDNER (1885–   )

" How to Write Short Stories " suggests a textbook, but the name of Ring Lardner is a guarantee that what follows is at least not of the ordinary textbook type. When, in 1924, he published a volume of his collected stories he chose the above title and added a " Preface " which is quite the most delicious bit in the book. This " Preface " follows.

A glimpse at the advertising columns of our leading magazines shows that whatever else this country may be shy of, there is certainly no lack of correspondence schools that learns you the art of short story writing. The most notorious of these schools makes the boast that one of their pupils cleaned up $5000.00 and no hundreds dollars writing short stories according to the system learnt in their course, though it don't say if that amount was cleaned up in one year or fifty.

However, for some reason another when you skin through the pages of high class periodicals, you don't very often find them cluttered up with stories that was written by boys or gals who had win their phi beta skeleton keys at this or that story-writing college. In fact, the most of the successful authors of the short fiction of today never went to no kind of a college, or if they did, they studied piano tuning or the barber trade. They could of got just as far in what I call the literary game if they had of stayed home those four years and helped mother carry out the empty bottles.

The answer is that you can't find no school in operation up to date, whether it be a general institution of learning or a school that specializes in story writing, which can make a great author out of a born druggist.

But a little group of our deeper drinkers has suggested that maybe boys and gals who wants to take up writing as their life work would be benefited if some person like I was to give them a few hints in regards to the technic of the short story, how to go about planning it and writing it, when and where to plant the love interest and climax, and finally how to market the finished product without leaving no bad taste in the mouth.

Well, then, it seems to me like the best method to use in giving out these hints is to try and describe my own personal procedure from the time I get inspired till the time the manuscript is loaded on to the trucks.

The first thing I generally always do is try and get hold of a catchy title, like for instance, " Basil Hargrave's Vermifuge," or " Fun at the Incinerating Plant." Then I set down to a desk or flat table of any kind and lay out 3 or 4 sheets of paper with as many different colored pencils and look at them cock-eyed a few moments before making a selection.

How to begin — or, as we professionals would say, " how to commence " — is the next question. It must be admitted that the method of approach (" L'approchement ") differs even among first class fictionists. For example, Blasco Ibañez usually starts his stories with a Spanish word, Jack Dempsey with an " I," and Charley Peterson with a couple of simple declarative sentences about his leading character, such as " Hazel Gooftree had just gone mah jong. She felt faint."

Personally it has been my observation that the reading public prefers short dialogue to any other kind of writing and I always aim to open my tale with two or three lines of conversation between characters — or, as I call them, my puppets — who are to play important rôles. I have often found that something one of these characters says, words I have perhaps unconsciously put into his or her mouth, directs my plot into channels deeper than I had planned and changes, for the better, the entire sense of my story.

To illustrate this, let us pretend that I have laid out a plot as follows : Two girls, Dorothy Abbott and Edith Quaver, are spending the heated term at a famous resort. The Prince of Wales visits the resort, but leaves on the next train. A day or two later, a Mexican reaches the place and looks for accommodations, but is unable to find a room without a bath. The two girls meet him at the public filling station and ask him for a contribution to their autograph album. To their amazement, he utters a terrible oath, spits in their general direction and hurries out of town. It is not until years later that two girls learn he is a notorious forger and realize how lucky they were after all.

Let us pretend that the above is the original plot. Then let us begin the writing with haphazard dialogue and see whither it leads:

"Where was you?" asked Edith Quaver.

"To the taxidermist's," replied Dorothy Abbott.

The two girls were spending the heated term at a famous watering trough. They had just been bathing and were now engaged in sorting dental floss.

"I am getting sick in tired of this place," went on Miss Quaver.

"It is mutual," said Miss Abbott, shying a cucumber at a passing paper-hanger.

There was a rap at their door and the maid's voice announced that company was awaiting them downstairs. The two girls went down and entered the music room. Garnett Whaledriver was at the piano and the girls tiptoed to the lounge.

The big Nordic, oblivious of their presence, allowed his fingers to form weird, fantastic minors before they strayed unconsciously into the first tones of Chopin's 121st Fugue for the Bass Drum.

From this beginning, a skilled writer could go most anywheres, but it would be my tendency to drop these three characters and take up the life of a mule in the Grand Canyon. The mule watches the trains come in from the east, he watches the trains come in from the west, and keeps wondering who is going to ride him. But she never finds out.

The love interest and climax would come when a man and a lady, both strangers, got to talking together on the train going back east.

"Well," said Mrs. Croot, for it was she, "what did you think of the Canyon?"

"Some cave," replied her escort.

"What a funny way to put it!" replied Mrs. Croot. "And now play me something."

Without a word, Warren took his place on the piano bench and at first allowed his fingers to form weird, fantastic chords on the black keys. Suddenly and with no seeming intention, he was in the midst of the second movement of Chopin's Twelfth Sonata for Flute and Cuspidor. Mrs. Croot felt faint.

That will give young writers an idea of how an apparently trivial thing such as a line of dialogue will upset an entire plot and lead an author far from the path he had pointed for himself. It will also serve as a model for beginners to follow in regards to style and technic. I will not insult my readers by going on with the story to its obvious conclusion. That simple task they can do for themselves, and it will be good practice.

So much for the planning and writing. Now for the marketing of the completed work. A good many young writers make the mistake of enclosing a stamped, self-addressed envelope, big enough for the manuscript to come back in. This is too much of a temptation to the editor.

Personally I have found it a good scheme to not even sign my name to the story, and when I have got it sealed up in its envelope and stamped and addressed, I take it to some town where I don't live and mail it from there. The editor has no idea who wrote the story, so how can he send it back? He is in a quandary.

In conclusion let me warn my pupils never to write their stories — or, as we professionals call them, "yarns" — on used paper. And never to write them on a post-card. And never to send them by telegraph (Morse code).

SUGGESTIONS FOR STUDY

1. Does the author's barbarous grammar add to the humor of the story? Find examples, put them into good English, and note the effect.

2. Select a short short story, like those that appear in *Collier's Weekly,* and change it into burlesque in Ring Lardner's manner.

3. If your teacher approves, write about some school affair in the same manner.

FOR FURTHER READING

The Story of a Wonder Man	*How to Write Short Stories*
Symptoms of Being 35	*The Love Nest and Other Stories*
What of It?	*Own Your Own Home*

CORRECT BEHAVIOR ON A PICNIC

By DONALD OGDEN STEWART (1894–   )

Among the younger humorists Donald Ogden Stewart has won an enviable position. His particular forte is to poke fun at some of the common foibles of all of us. In *Perfect Behavior,* from which the following is a section, he satirizes a class of books that have become annoyingly common in recent years, the How to Do books, more especially books on etiquette.

There often comes a time in the life of the members of " society " when they grow a little weary of the ceaseless round of teas, calls, and dinners, and for such I would not hesitate to recommend a " picnic."

A day spent in the " open," with the blue sky over one's head, is indeed a splendid tonic for jaded nerves. But one should not make the mistake of thinking that because he (or she) is " roughing it " for a day, he (or she) can therefore leave behind his (or her) " manners," for such is not the case. There is a distinct etiquette for picnics, and any one who disregards this fact is apt to find to his (or her) sorrow that the " shoe " in this case is decidedly " on the other foot."

A young man, for example, is often asked by a young lady to accompany her on a " family picnic." To this invitation he should, after some consideration, reply either " Yes " or " No," and if the former, he should present himself at the young lady's house promptly on the day set for the affair (usually Sunday).

A " family picnic " generally consists of a Buick, a father, a mother, a daughter, a small son, beef loaf, lettuce sandwiches, a young man (you), two blow-outs, one spare tire, and Aunt Florence.

The father drives with the small boy beside him; in the rear are the mother, the daughter, Aunt Florence, the thermos bottles, the lunch baskets, and you. As you take your seat you must remember that it is a distinct evidence of bad breeding to show in any way that you are conscious of the fact that the car has been standing for the last hour and forty-four minutes in the hot July sun.

" We're off! " cries father, pressing his foot on the self-starting pedal. Thirty minutes later you roll away from the curb and the picnic has begun. The intervening time has, of course, been profitably spent by you in walking to the nearest garage for two new spark-plugs.

It should be your duty, as guest, to see that the conversation in the rear seat is not allowed to lag. " It's a great day," you remark, as the car speeds along. " I think it's going to rain," replies Aunt Florence. " Not too fast, Will! " says mother. " Mother! " says the daughter.

Ten minutes later you should again remark, " My, what a wonderful day! " " Those clouds are gathering in the west," says Aunt Florence; " I think we had better put the top up." " I think this is the wrong road," says mother. " Dear, I know what I'm doing," replies father.

The secret in good conversation lies in discovering the " hobby " of the person with whom one is conversing, and a good talker always throws out several " feelers " in order to find out the things in which his partner is most interested. You should, therefore, next say to mother, " Don't you think this is a glorious day for a picnic? " to which she will reply, " Well, I'm sure this is the wrong road. Hadn't you better ask? " The husband will answer nothing, but Aunt Florence will murmur, " I think I felt a drop of rain, Will. If you don't put the top up now we'll all be drenched."

The husband will then stop the car, and you will proceed to put up the top. In doing this it is customary for the guest to get the second and third fingers of his right hand so severely pinched that he cannot use the hand for several days. As soon as the top is up and the rain curtains are in place, the sun will come out and you can at once get out and put the top down, taking care this time to ruin two fingers of the *left* hand.

No good conversationalist confines himself exclusively to one subject, and when you are once more " under way " you should remark to the mother, " I think that motoring is great fun, don't you, Mrs. Caldwell? " Her answer will be, " I wish you wouldn't drive so fast! " You should then smile and say to Aunt Florence, " Don't *you* think that motoring is great fun, Mrs. Lockwood? " As she is about to reply the left rear tire will blow out with a loud noise, and the car will come to with a bumping stop.

The etiquette of changing a tire is fairly simple. As soon as the " puncture " occurs one should at once remark, " Is there anything I can do? " This request should be repeated from time to time, always taking care however, that no one takes it at all seriously. The real duty of a young man who is a " guest " on a motor trip on which a " blow-out " occurs is, of course, to keep the ladies of the party amused during the delay. This can be accomplished by any of the conventional methods, such as card tricks, hand-springs, and other feats of athletic agility, or making funny jokes about the host who is at work on the tire.

When the damage has been repaired and the car is once more speeding along, leaving behind it mile after mile of dusty road as well as father's best " jack " and set of tire tools, the small boy will suddenly remark, " I'm hungry." His father will then reply, " We'll be at a fine place to eat in ten minutes." Thirty minutes later mother will remark, " Will, that looks like a good place for a picnic over there." The father will reply, " No — we're coming to a wonderful place — just trust me, Mary! " Twenty minutes later Aunt Florence will say, " Will, I think that grove over there would be fine for our lunch," to which the husband will reply, " We're almost at the place I know about — it's ideal for a picnic." Forty minutes after this father will stop the car and point to a clump of trees. " There," he will say, " what do you think of that? " " Oh, we can't eat *there!* " will be the answer of mother, daughter, and Aunt Florence. " Drive on a bit further — I think I know a place."

Three hours and thirty minutes later (i.e., four hours past your normal lunch hour) there will be another puncture and as the car stops beside a wheat field it will begin to rain, and the daughter will sigh, " Well, we might as well eat here." The " picnic " will then be held in the car, and nothing really quite carries one back to nature and primeval man as does warm lemonade and a lettuce sandwich in a Buick with the top up and side curtains on.

After lunch it will be time to return home, and after you and father have ruined your clothes in repairing punctures, the merry party will proceed on its way. The next morning, if you have not caught pneumonia, you will be able to go to your work greatly refreshed by your day's outing in the lap of old Mother Nature.

SUGGESTIONS FOR STUDY

1. What details make this sketch humorous?
2. Describe at some length the character of " mother " and " Aunt Florence."
3. From your own experience of picnics, can you verify the truth of the author's statements?
4. From such experiences, write an imitation of this sketch.

FOR FURTHER READING

A Parody Outline of History   *Aunt Polly's Story of Mankind*
Perfect Behavior   *The Crazy Fool*

FOR FURTHER READING OF HUMOROUS PROSE

Adeler, Max (Charles Heber Clark). *Out of the Hurly-Burly*
Bangs, John Kendrick. *Over the Plum-Pudding, The Inventions of the Idiot, The Houseboat on the Styx*
Benchley, Robert. *Love Conquers All, Of All Things, Pluck and Luck, The Early Worm, 20,000 Leagues Under the Sea, or David Copperfield*
Billings, Josh. *Complete Works*
Butler, Ellis Parker. *The Behind Legs of the 'Orse, and Other Stories, Ghosts What Ain't, Goat-Feathers, Pigs Is Pigs! Pups and Pies*
Chappell, George S. (Walter S. Traprock). *The Cruise of the Kawa, My Northern Exposure, Rollo in Society*
Dunne, Finley Peter. *Mr. Dooley in Peace and War, Mr. Dooley on Making a Will and Other Necessary Evils, Mr. Dooley Says, Mr. Dooley's Philosophy, Mr. Dooley in the Hearts of His Countrymen*
Fitch, George Helgeson. *At Good Old Siwash*
French, Joseph Lewis. *Sixty Years of American Humor*
Glass, Montague. *Potash and Perlmutter: Their Copartnership Ventures and Adventures*
Gross, Milt. *Nize Baby*
Hellman, Sam. *Low Bridge and Punk Pungs*
Herford, Oliver. *This Giddy Globe*
Holliday, Carl. *The Wit and Humor of Colonial Days, 1607–1800*
Johnson, Owen. *The Varmint, The Tennessee Shad*
Leacock, Stephen. *Behind the Beyond, Further Foolishness, Moonbeams from the Larger Lunacy, Nonsense Novels, Winnowed Wisdom, My Discovery of England, The Iron Man and the Tin Woman, with Other Such Futurities*
Locke, David Ross. *Struggles of Petroleum V. Nasby*
Masson, Tom, Editor, *Listen to These, Masterpieces of American Wit and Humor*
Nye, Edgar Wilson. *Bill Nye, His Own Life Story*
Paine, Albert Bigelow. *The Arkansaw Bear*
Upson, William Hazlitt. *Alexander Botts, Earthworm Tractors*
Ward, Christopher. *Gentleman into Goose*
Warner, Anne. *Susan Clegg and Her Friend Mrs. Lathrop*
Wilson, Harry Leon. *Ma Pettengill, Bunker Bean, Merton of the Movies*

Historic Milestones

History records; literature vivifies.

That in general is the difference in the purpose of the two forms of writing, though there is bound to be overlapping. The greatest historians have always written in a vivid and vigorous style and their works are included in accounts of our literature, while much literature is the best record that we have of times which have passed or are passing away. The historian must often draw upon literature for his source material; the author must often draw upon history for his background. But the historian must above all things be accurate; the writer of fiction or drama must above all be vivid and entertaining. For instance, Clyde Fitch changed and manipulated historical facts to increase the effectiveness of his drama *Nathan Hale*. Now we are to see how records of events or public documents which would ordinarily belong to the realm of history only, have been so clothed with vigorous or picturesque or beautiful or majestic language that they have become the joint property of history and literature. In our nation's life there have been many of these. Only a few of them can be here represented, but they serve to trace the pattern of the great crises through which our country has passed.

Colonial Period

First came the colonial period, an age of preparatory struggle, though not of immediate crisis. Though life itself was excitingly adventurous in those days, most of the so-called literature of that time consists of sermons, bad imitations of English poetry, and long chronicles which are dull for the modern young person, however interesting they may be to those who have made a special study of colonial times, or have lived among the scenes of our early history. The two journals here included, however, are marked by a readable sprightliness and vividness. Moreover, they go to show how the infant group of colonies was having as much trouble coördinating its parts as a baby has with its muscle movements. Virginia and North Carolina had no settled boundary line; a Boston woman regarded Connecticut as a foreign country.

The Revolution

When these disjointed segments were finally welded into one united whole through the first great crisis, the Revolution, we find among the many voices of the day three notable spokesmen whose words are unquestionably immortal: Patrick Henry, representing the fiery oratory which incited the timid to action; Thomas Jefferson, chief framer of the Declaration of Independence; and George Washington, sage counselor and shaper of future policies.

The Civil War

The second crisis, which threatened to rend the nation apart, had its one great spokesman, Abraham Lincoln, whose claim to greatness is all the more evident when we consider how great were some of the men above whom he towers in our memories today — Daniel Webster, John C. Calhoun, Henry Clay, and Edward Everett.

The World War

Finally, the third great crisis, involving our country along with all the other nations in a world cataclysm, produced the third of our war presidents, Woodrow Wilson, who spoke for a new principle of international living not yet fully accomplished or even fully understood.

Towards World Peace

Almost from time immemorial efforts towards universal peace were made, with what lack of success history tells us. So far as our own country was concerned, the principle of avoiding entangling alliances with foreign powers, as enunciated by Washington, and the pronouncement of the Monroe Doctrine, which warned those powers to keep " hands off " America, enabled us to preserve a state of peace with them, except for the War of 1812 and the War with Spain. Since the World War there have been determined efforts once more towards real world peace. The League of Nations, the World Court, the Kellogg-Briand Peace Pact, and the political machinery towards disarmament set in motion by Premier Macdonald and President Hoover in 1929, definitely point in the direction of the long-desired goal.

Colonization

HER PRIVATE JOURNAL

By SARAH KEMBLE KNIGHT (1666–1727)

In October, 1704, Madam Sarah Knight, a lady of Boston, undertook the hazardous journey from Boston to New York City on horseback. On the way, both to and from New York, she remained for some time at New Haven, Connecticut, and reached home again in March, 1705. The journey between Boston and New Haven, less than two hundred miles, took her almost a week in October and considerably longer on the return trip in winter. Today one can make it comfortably in six or seven hours by automobile and in less by fast train or airplane.

Soon after her return to Boston, Madam Knight opened a school in which it is supposed, though not established as a fact, that Benjamin Franklin was one of her pupils. It is said that she was an especially good teacher of composition. Noting her keenness of observation, liveliness of imagination, and quaintness of style, one can well believe the report. The original spelling and capitalization have been preserved in the printing of her journal.

STRANGE CUSTOMS OF CONNECTICUT

Saturday, Oct. 7th, wee sett out early in the Morning, and being something unaquainted with the way, having ask't it of some wee mett, they told us wee must Ride a mile or two and turne down a Lane on the Right hand; and by their Direction wee Rode on but not Yet comeing to the turning, we mett a Young fellow and ask't him how farr it was to the Lane which turn'd down towards Guilford. Hee said wee must Ride a little further, and turn down by the Corner of uncle Sams Lott. My Guide vented his Spleen at the Lubber; and we soon after came into the Rhode, and keeping still on, without any thing further Remarkabell, about two a clock afternoon we arrived at New Haven, where I was received with all Posible Respects and civility. Here I discharged Mr. Wheeler with a reward to his satisfaction, and took some time to rest after so long and toilsome a Journey; And Inform'd myselfe of the manners and customs of the place, and at the same time employed myselfe in the afair I went there upon.

They are Govern'd by the same Laws as wee in Boston, (or little differing,) thr'out this whole Colony of Connecticot, And much the same way of Church Government, and many of them good, Sociable people, and I hope Religious too: but a little too much Independant in their principalls, and, as I have been told, were formerly in their Zeal very Riggid in their Administrations towards such as their Lawes made Offenders, even to a harmless Kiss or Innocent merriment among Young people. Whipping being a frequent and counted an easy Punishment, about which, as other Crimes, the Judges were absolute in their Sentences. Their Diversions in this part of the Country are on Lecture days [1] and Training days mostly: on the former there is Riding from town to town.

And on training dayes The Youth divert themselves by Shooting at the Target, as they call it, (but it very much resembles a pillory,) where hee that hitts neerest the white has some yards of Red Ribbin presented him, which being tied to his hattband, the two ends streeming down his back, he is Led away in Triumph, with great applause, as the winners of the Olympiack Games.[2] They generally marry very young: the males oftener as I am told under twentie than above; they generally make public weddings, and have a way something singular (as they say) in some of them, viz. Just before Joyning hands the Bridegroom quitts

---

[1] Thursdays were so called because of the regular midweek religious lecture.

[2] The Greeks held great athletic festivals every four years beginning in 776 B.C., at Olympia. It is from these that the modern Olympic games take their name.

the place, who is soon followed by the Bridesmen, and as it were, dragg'd back to duty — being the reverse to the former practice among us, to steal Mrs. Bride.

There are great plenty of Oysters all along by the sea side, as farr as I Rode in the Collony, and those very good. And they Generally lived very well and comfortably in their famelies. But too Indulgent (especially the farmers) to their slaves: sufering too great familiarity from them, permitting them to sit at Table and eat with them, (as they say to save time,) and into the dish goes the black hoof as freely as the white hand. They told me that there was a farmer lived nere the Town where I lodgd who had some difference with his slave, concerning something the master had promised him and did not punctualy perform; which caused some hard words between them; But at length they put the matter to Arbitration and Bound themselves to stand to the award of such as they named — which done, the Arbitrators Having heard the Allegations of both parties, Order the master to pay 40s to black face, and acknowledge his fault. And so the matter ended: the poor master very honestly standing to the award.

There are every where in the Towns as I passed, a Number of Indians the Natives of the Country, and are the most salvage of all the salvages of that kind that I had ever Seen: little or no care taken (as I heard upon enquiry) to make them otherwise. They have in some places Landes of their owne, and Govern'd by Law's of their own making; — they marry many wives and at pleasure put them away, and on the least dislike or fickle humor, on either side, saying *stand away* to one another is a sufficient Divorce. And indeed those uncomely *Stand aways* are too much in Vougue among the English in this [Indulgent Colony] as their Records plentifully prove, and that on very trivial matters, of which some have been told me, but are not proper to be Related by a Female pen, tho some of that foolish sex have had too large a share in the story.

If the natives committ any crime on their own precincts among themselves, the English takes no Cognezens[3] of. But if on the English ground, they are punishable by our Laws. They mourn for their Dead by blacking their faces, and cutting their hair, after an Awkerd and frightfull manner; But can't bear You

[3] Cognizance. In other words, the English pay no attention to these crimes.

should mention the names of their dead Relations to them: they trade most for Rum, for which they'd hazzard their very lives; and the English fit them Generally as well, by seasoning it plentifully with water.

They give the title of merchant to every trader; who Rate their Goods according to the time and spetia [4] they pay in: viz. Pay, mony, Pay as mony, and trusting. *Pay* is Grain, Pork, Beef, &c. at prices sett by the General Court that Year; *mony* is pieces of Eight,[5] Ryalls, or Boston or Bay shillings (as they call them,) or Good hard money, as sometimes silver coin is termed by them; also Wampom, vizt. Indian beads which serves for change. *Pay as mony* is provisions, as aforesaid one Third cheaper then as the Assembly or General Court sets it; and *Trust* as they and the merchant agree for time.

Now, when the buyer comes to ask for a comodity, sometimes before the merchant answers that he has it, he sais, *is Your pay redy?* Perhaps the Chap Reply's Yes: what do You pay in? say's the merchant. The buyer having answered, then the price is set; as suppose he wants a sixpenny knife, in pay it is 12d — in pay as money eight pence, and hard money its own price, viz. 6d. It seems a very Intricate way of trade and what Lex Mercatoria [6] had not thought of.

Being at a merchants house, in come a tall country fellow, with his alfogeos [7] full of Tobacco; for they seldom Loose their Cudd, but keep Chewing and Spitting as long as they'r eyes are open, — he advanc't to the midle of the Room, makes an Awkward Nodd, and spitting a Large deal of Aromatick Tincture, he gave a scrape with his shovel like shoo, leaving a small shovel full of dirt on the floor, made a full stop, Hugging his own pretty Body with his hands under his arms, Stood staring rown'd him, like a Catt let out of a Baskett. At last, like the creature [8] Balamm Rode on, he opened his mouth and said: have You any Ribinen for Hatbands to sell I pray? The Questions and Answers about the pay being past, the Ribin is bro't and opened. Bumpkin [9] Simpers, cryes its confounded Gay I vow; and beckning to the door, in comes Jone Tawdry [9] dropping about 50 curtsees, and

---

[4] Specie, coin.
[5] Spanish dollars containing eight reals, worth ninety-six cents.
[6] The law of merchants.
[7] Spanish saddlebags, here humorously used for cheeks.
[8] A famous ass in the Bible, which could speak. Numbers xxii: 21–33.
[9] Humorous name for the country folk.

stands by him: hee shows her the Ribin. *Law, You,* sais shee, *its right Gent,*[10] do You, take it, *tis dreadfull pretty.* Then she enquires, *have you any hood silk I pray?* which being brought and bought, *Have You any thred silk to sew it with* says shee, which being accommodated with they Departed. They Generaly stand after they come in a great while speachless, and sometimes dont say a word till they are askt what they want, which I impute to the Awe they stand in of the merchants, who they are constantly almost Indebted too; and must take what they bring without Liberty to choose for themselves; but they serve them as well, making the merchants stay long enough for their pay.

We may Observe here the great necessity and bennifitt both of Education and Conversation; for these people have as Large a portion of mother witt, and sometimes a Larger, than those who have bin brought up in Citties; But for want of emprovements, Render themselves almost Ridiculos, as above. I should be glad if they would leave such follies, and am sure all that Love Clean Houses (at least) would be glad on't too.

They are generaly very plain in their dress, throuout all the Colony, as I saw, and follow one another in their modes; that You may know where they belong, especially the women, meet them where you will.

Their Chief Red Letter day is St. Election,[11] which is annually Observed according to Charter, to choose their Govenr: a blessing they can never be thankfull enough for, as they will find, if ever it be their hard fortune to loose it.[12] The present Govenor in Conecticott is the Honorable John Winthrop Esq. A Gentleman of an Ancient and Honourable Family, whose Father was Govenor here sometime before, and his Grand father had bin Govr of the Massachusetts. This gentleman is a very curteous and afable person, much Given to Hospitality, and has by his Good services Gain'd the affections of the people as much as any who had bin before him in that post.

HARDSHIPS OF TRAVEL

Decr. 6th. Being by this time well Recruited and rested after my Journy, my business lying unfinished by some concerns at

---

[10] A rustic abbreviation for genteel or elegant.

[11] A humorous way of indicating that an election was as religiously observed as a saint's day in a Catholic country.

[12] In Massachusetts the governor was appointed by the king, to the great dissatisfaction of the colony.

New York depending thereupon, my Kinsman, Mr. Thomas
Trowbridge of New Haven, must needs take a Journy there before
it could be accomplished, I resolved to go there in company with
him, and a man of the town which I engaged to wait on me there.
Accordingly, Dec. 6th we set out from New Haven, and about
11 the same morning came to Stratford ferry; which crossing,
about two miles on the other side Baited our horses and would
have eat a morsell ourselves, But the Pumpkin and Indian mixt
Bred had such an Aspect, and the Bare-legg'd Punch so awkerd or
rather Awfull a sound, that we left both, and proceeded forward,
and about seven at night come to Fairfield, where we met with
good entertainment and Lodg'd; and early next morning set
forward to Norowalk, from its halfe Indian name *North-walk,*
when about 12 at noon we arrived, and Had a Dinner of Fryed
Venison, very savoury. Landlady wanting some pepper in the
seasoning, bid the Girl hand her the spice in the little *Gay* cupp
on the shelfe. From hence we Hasted towards Rye, walking and
Leading our Horses neer a mile together, up a prodigios high
Hill; and so Riding till about nine at night, and there arrived
and took up our Lodgings at an ordinary,[13] which a French family
kept. Here being very hungry, I desired a fricasee, which the
Frenchman undertakeing, mannaged so contrary to my notion of
Cookery, that I hastned to Bed superless; And being shewd the
way up a pair of stairs which had such a narrow passage that
I had almost stopt by the Bulk of my Body; But arriving at my
apartment found it to be a little Lento[14] Chamber furnisht
amongst other Rubbbish with a High Bedd and a Low one, a Long
Table, a Bench and a Bottomless chair,—Little Miss went to
scratch up my Kennell[15] which Russelled as if shee'd bin in the
Barn amongst the Husks, and supose such was the contents of the
tickin—nevertheless being exceedingly weary, down I laid my
poor Carkes (never more tired) and found my Covering as scanty
as my Bed was hard. Annon I heard another Russelling noise in
The Room—called to know the matter—Little miss said shee
was making a bed for the men; who, when they were in Bed,
complained their leggs lay out of it by reason of its shortness—
my poor bones complained bitterly not being used to such Lodgings, and so did the man who was with us; and poor I made but

---

[13] An inn.
[14] A lean-to room, or one under a low sloping roof.
[15] Humorous for " shake up my mattress."

one Grone, which was from the time I went to bed to the time I Riss, which was about three in the morning, Setting up by the Fire till Light, and having discharged our ordinary [16] which was as dear as if we had had far Better fare—wee took our leave of Monsieur and about seven in the morn come to New Rochell a french town, where we had a good Breakfast. And in the strength of that about an how'r before sunsett got to York. Here I applyd myself to Mr. Burroughs, a merchant to whom I was recommended by my Kinsman Capt. Prout, and received great Civilities from him and his spouse, who were now both Deaf but very agreeable in their Conversation, Diverting me with pleasant stories of their knowledge in Brittan from whence they both come.

NEW YORK CITY

The Cittie of New York is a pleasant, well compacted place, situated on a Commodius River which is a fine harbour for shipping. The Buildings Brick Generaly, very stately and high, though not altogether like ours in Boston. The Bricks in some of the Houses are of divers Coullers and laid in Checkers, being glazed look very agreeable. The inside of them are neat to admiration, the wooden work, for only the walls are plasterd, and the Summers and Gist [17] are plained and kept very white scowr'd as so is all the partitions if made of Bords. The fire places have no Jambs (as ours have) But the Backs run flush with the walls, and the Hearth is of Tyles and is as farr out into the Room at the Ends as before the fire, which is Generally Five foot in the Low'r rooms, and the peice over where the mantle tree should be is made as ours with Joyners work, and as I supose is fasten'd to iron rodds inside. The House where the Vendue [18] was, had Chimney Corners like ours, and they and the hearths were laid with the finest tile that I ever see, and the stair cases laid all with white tile which is ever clean, and so are the walls of the Kitchen which had a Brick floor. They were making Great preparations to Receive their Govenor, Lord Cornbury from the Jerseys, and for that end raised the militia to Gard him on shore to the fort.

They are Generaly of the Church of England and have a New England Gentleman for their minister, and a very fine church

[16] Paid the bill.
[17] Supporting beams and joints.
[18] An auction sale which Madam Knight attended.

set out with all Customary requsites. There are also a Dutch and Divers Conventicles as they call them, viz. Baptist, Quakers, etc. They are not strict in keeping the Sabbath as in Boston and other places where I had bin, But seem to deal with great exactness as farr as I see or Deall with. They are sociable to one another and Curteos and Civill to strangers and fare well in their houses. The English go very fasheonable in their dress. But the Dutch, especially the middling sort, differ from our women, in their habitt go loose,[19] were French muches [20] which are like a Capp and a head band in one, leaving their ears bare, which are sett out with Jewells of a large size and many in number. And their fingers hoop't with Rings, some with large stones in them of many Coullers as were their pendants in their ears, which You should see very old women wear as well as Young.

PERILS OF THE RETURN TRIP

The next morning I Crossed the Ferry to Groton, having had the Honor of the Company, of Madam Livingston (who is the Govenors Daughter) and Mary Christophers and divers others to the boat — And that night Lodged at Stonington and had Rost Beef and pumpkin sause for supper. The next night at Haven's and had Rost fowle, and the next day wee come to a river which by Reason of The Freshetts coming down was swell'd so high wee feard it impassable and the rapid stream was very terryfying — However we must over and that in a small Cannoo. Mr. Rogers assuring me of his good Conduct,[21] I after a stay of near an how'r on the shore for consultation went into the Cannoo, and Mr. Rogers paddled about 100 yards up the Creek by the shore side, turned into the swift stream and dexterously steering her in a moment wee come to the other side as swiftly passing as an arrow shott out of the Bow by a strong arm. I staid on the shore till Hee returned to fetch our horses, which he caused to swim over himself bringing the furniture [22] in the Cannoo. But it is past my skill to express the Exceeding fright all their transactions formed in me. Wee were now in the colony of the Massachusetts and taking Lodgings at the first Inn we come too had a pretty difficult passage the next day which was the second of

19 Wear loose dresses.
20 Wear French caps.
21 Her guide assured her he could manage a canoe skilfully.
22 Saddles and traveling bags.

March by reason of the sloughy ways then thawed by the Sunn. Here I mett Capt. John Richards of Boston who was going home, So being very glad of his Company we Rode something harder than hitherto, and missing my way in going up a very steep Hill, my horse dropt down under me as Dead; this new surprize no little hurt me meeting it Just at the Entrance into Dedham from whence we intended to reach home that night. But was now obliged to gett another Hors there and leave my own, resolving for Boston that night if possible. But in going over the Causeway at Dedham the Bridge being overflowed by the high waters comming down I very narrowly escaped falling over into the river Hors and all which twas almost a miracle I did not — now it grew late in the afternoon and the people having very much discouraged us about the sloughy way which they said wee should find very difficult and hazardous it so wrought on mee being tired and dispirited and disapointed of my desires of going home that I agreed to Lodg there that night which wee did at the house of one Draper, and the next day being March 3d wee got safe home to Boston, where I found my aged and tender mother and my Dear and only Child in good health with open arms redy to receive me, and my kind relations and friends flocking in to welcome mee and hear the story of my transactions and travails I having this day bin five months from home and now I cannot fully express my Joy and Satisfaction. But desire sincearly to adore my Great Benefactor for thus graciously carying forth and returning in safety his unworthy handmaid.

SUGGESTIONS FOR STUDY

1. Point out evidence to show that Madam Knight considered Connecticut less advanced socially and intellectually than Massachusetts. On the other hand, did she find anything preferable to conditions in her own colony?

2. Write or tell any uncomfortable experiences you have had in traveling, with a humorous view of your predicaments. Or, contrast travel conditions of her day with ours.

3. You will find a modern account of Madam Knight and her journey in *Dames and Daughters of Colonial Days* by Geraldine Brooks. Report any additional matters of interest found in this.

A HISTORY OF THE DIVIDING LINE

By COLONEL WILLIAM BYRD (1674–1744)

Every high school student today knows about Rear Admiral Richard E. Byrd, the famous flier and arctic explorer. Not every one, however, knows that back in his line of ancestors was a Colonel William Byrd of Westover, Virginia, equally famous in his day for energy and initiative. Three successive generations in this renowned colonial family included the name of William Byrd. The first William came from England upon inheriting a Virginia estate from his uncle, became a leader in his community, and built up the largest fortune in the colony. The second, adding to his father's executive ability a cultivated literary taste through his London education, collected the finest private library in America at that time, consisting of about four thousand volumes. The third unfortunately lacked the power of his fathers and dissipated most of the fortune in mere pleasure.

William Byrd II had a charming, often witty, literary style quite unusual among colonial writers. Then too, he had something worth writing about. Among his other enterprises he was one of the commissioners in charge of establishing the Virginia-North Carolina boundary, long under dispute. Because of the forests and swamps, and the hostile attitude between the two colonies, this was a dangerous undertaking, which was, however, successfully accomplished. At the request of friends in England, Colonel Byrd worked up from the rough notes taken in the woods a more complete account of the dispute, which is called *History of the Dividing Line,* extracts from which follow. All his manuscripts were carefully copied and bound for preservation in his library, but were not printed until 1841, almost a century after his death.

CAMP LIFE

March 12, [*1728*]. . . . Our landlord[1] had a tolerable good house and clean furniture, and yet we could not be tempted to lodge in it. We chose rather to lie in the open field, for fear of growing too tender. A clear sky, spangled with stars, was our canopy which, being the last thing we saw before we fell asleep, gave us magnificent dreams. The truth of it is, we took so much pleasure in that natural kind of lodging that I think at the foot of the account mankind are great losers by the luxury of feather-beds and warm apartments.

The curiosity of beholding so new and withal so sweet a method

[1] A plantation owner named Ballance.

of encamping, brought one of the senators of North Carolina to make us a midnight visit. But he was so very clamorous in his commendations of it that the sentinel, not seeing his quality, either through his habit or behavior, had like to have treated him roughly.

After excusing the unseasonableness of his visit, and letting us know he was a Parliament man, he swore he was so taken with our lodging that he would set fire to his house as soon as he got home, and teach his wife and children to lie, like us, in the open field.

THE DISMAL SWAMP

March 14. Before nine of the clock this morning, the provisions, bedding, and other necessaries, were made up into packs for the men to carry on their shoulders into the Dismal. They were victualed for eight days at full allowance, nobody doubting but that would be abundantly sufficient to carry them through that inhospitable place; nor indeed was it possible for the poor fellows to stagger under more. As it was, their loads weighed from 60 to 70 pounds, in just proportion to the strength of those who were to bear them.

'Twould have been unconscionable to have saddled them with burthens heavier than that, when they were to lug them through a filthy bog which was hardly practicable with no burthen at all. Besides this luggage at their backs, they were obliged to measure the distance, mark the trees, and clear the way for the surveyors every step they went. It was really a pleasure to see with how much cheerfulness they undertook, and with how much spirit they went through all this drudgery. For their greater safety, the commissioners took care to furnish them with Peruvian bark, rhubarb, and hipocoacanah,[2] in case they might happen, in that wet journey, to be taken with fevers or fluxes.

Although there was no need of example to inflame persons already so cheerful, yet, to enter the people with better grace, the author and two more of the commissioners accompanied them half a mile into the Dismal. The skirts of it were thinly planted with dwarf reeds and gall-bushes but, when we got into the Dismal itself, we found the reeds grew there much taller and closer and, to mend the matter, was so interlaced with bamboo-briars that there was no scuffling through them without the help of pioneers. At the same time, we found the ground moist and trembling

2 Known today as ipecac.

under our feet like a quagmire, insomuch that it was an easy matter to run a ten-foot pole up to the head in it, without exerting
any uncommon strength to do it.

Two of the men, whose burthens were the least cumbersome,
had orders to march before with their tomahawks and clear the
way, in order to make an opening for the surveyors. By their
assistance we made a shift to push the line half a mile in three
hours, and then reached a small piece of firm land about 100 yards
wide standing up above the rest like an island. Here the people
were glad to lay down their loads and take a little refreshment,
while the happy man whose lot it was to carry the jug of rum
began already, like Aesop's bread-carriers,[3] to find it grow a good
deal lighter.

After reposing about an hour, the commissioners recommended
vigor and constancy to their fellow-travelers, by whom they were
answered with three cheerful huzzas in token of obedience. This
ceremony was no sooner over but they took up their burthens and
attended the motion of the surveyors who, though they worked
with all their might, could reach but one mile farther, the same
obstacles still attending them which they had met with in the
morning.

However small this distance may seem to such as are used to
travel at their ease, yet our poor men, who were obliged to work
with an unwieldy load at their backs, had reason to think it a long
way; especially in a bog where they had no firm footing, but
every step made a deep impression, which was instantly filled
with water. At the same time they were laboring with their
hands to cut down the reeds, which were ten feet high, their legs
were hampered with the briars. Besides, the weather happened
to be very warm, and the tallness of the reeds kept off every
friendly breeze from coming to refresh them. And, indeed, it was
a little provoking to hear the wind whistling among the branches
of the white cedars, which grew here and there amongst the reeds,
and at the same time not have the comfort to feel the least breath
of it.

In the meantime the three commissioners returned out of the
Dismal the same way they went in and, having joined their
brethren, proceeded that night as far as Mr. Wilson's.

[3] According to the fable the man who wanted the lightest burden on the
journey was laughed at for choosing the bread, which was the heaviest; but by
night the bread had all been distributed and he had only the empty basket to
carry.

This worthy person lives within sight of the Dismal, in the skirts whereof his stocks range and maintain themselves all the winter, and yet he knew as little of it as he did of *Terra Australis Incognita*.[4] He told us a Canterbury tale [5] of a North Briton whose curiosity spurred him a long way into this great desert, as he called it, near 20 years ago, but he having no compass, nor seeing the sun for several days together, wandered about till he was almost famished; but at last he bethought himself of a secret his countrymen make use of to pilot themselves in a dark day.

He took a fat louse out of his collar and exposed it to the open day on a piece of white paper which he brought along with him for his journal. The poor insect, having no eye-lids, turned himself about till he found the darkest part of the heavens, and so made the best of his way towards the north. By this direction he steered himself safe out, and gave such a frightful account of the monsters he saw and the distresses he underwent, that no mortal since has been hardy enough to go upon the like dangerous discovery.

NORTH CAROLINA PLANTATION LIFE

March 25. . . . In the mean time, we who stayed behind had nothing to do but to make the best observations we could upon that part of the country. The soil of our landlord's plantation, though none of the best, seemed more fertile than any thereabouts, where the ground is near as sandy as the deserts of Africa, and consequently barren. The road leading from thence to Edenton, being in distance about 27 miles, lies upon a ridge called Sandy Ridge, which is so wretchedly poor that it will not bring potatoes.

The pines in this part of the country are of a different species from those that grow in Virginia : their bearded leaves are much longer and their cones much larger. Each cell contains a seed of the size and figure of a black-eyed pea, which, shedding in November, is very good mast for hogs, and fattens them in a short time.

The smallest of these pines are full of cones, which are eight or nine inches long, and each affords commonly 60 or 70 seeds. This kind of mast has the advantage of all other by being more constant, and less liable to be nipped by the frost or eaten by the caterpillars. The trees also abound more with turpentine, and

---

[4] Unknown southern land, such as Byrd's descendant has lately explored.

[5] Here means an incredible tale. The *Canterbury Tales* were famous stories written by the first great English poet, Chaucer. The reference shows Byrd's literary education.

consequently yield more tar than either the yellow or the white pine; and for the same reason make more durable timber for building. The inhabitants hereabouts pick up knots of lightwood in abundance, which they burn into tar, and then carry it to Norfolk or Nansimond for a market. The tar made in this method is the less valuable because it is said to burn the cordage, though it is full as good for all other uses as that made in Sweden and Muscovy.

Surely there is no place in the world where the inhabitants live with less labor than in North Carolina. It approaches nearer to the description of Lubberland [6] than any other, by the great felicity of the climate, the easiness of raising provisions, and the slothfulness of the people.

Indian corn is of so great increase that a little pains will subsist a very large family with bread, and then they may have meat without any pains at all, by the help of the low grounds, and the great variety of mast that grows on the high-land. The men for their parts, just like the Indians, impose all the work upon the poor women. They make their wives rise out of their beds early in the morning, at the same time that they lie and snore till the sun has run one third of his course and dispersed all the unwholesome damps. Then, after stretching and yawning for half an hour, they light their pipes, and, under the protection of a cloud of smoke, venture out into the open air; though, if it happens to be never so little cold, they quickly return shivering into the chimney corner. When the weather is mild, they stand leaning with both their arms upon the corn-field fence, and gravely consider whether they had best go and take a small heat at the hoe: but generally find reasons to put it off till another time.

Thus they loiter away their lives, like Solomon's sluggard, [7] with their arms across, and at the winding up of the year scarcely have bread to eat.

To speak the truth, 'tis a thorough aversion to labor that makes people file off to North Carolina, where plenty and a warm sun confirm them in their disposition to laziness for their whole lives.

---

[6] A paradise for lazy fellows. The following comments on the natives show the antipathy between the aristocratic Virginians and the small farmers of North Carolina, who were largely ex-servants.

[7] King Solomon said, " Go to the ant, thou sluggard; consider her ways and be wise." Proverbs vi: 6.

A FALSE ELDORADO

October 10.[8] The day began very fortunately by killing a fat doe, and two brace of wild turkeys; so the plenty of the morning made amends for the short commons over night. One of the new men we brought out with us the last time was unfortunately heard to wish himself at home and, for that show of impatience, was publicly reprimanded at the head of the men, who were all drawn up to witness his disgrace.

He was asked how he came so soon to be tired of the company of so many brave fellows, and whether it was the danger or fatigue of the journey that disheartened him? This public reproof from thenceforward put an effectual stop to all complaints, and not a man amongst us after that pretended so much as to wish himself in paradise.

A small distance from our camp we crossed a pleasant stream of water called Cocquade Creek, and something more than a mile from thence our line intersected the south branch of Roanoke River the first time, which we called the Dan. It was about 200 yards wide where we forded it and, when we came over to the west side, we found the banks lined with a forest of tall canes that grew more than a furlong in depth. So that it cost us abundance of time and labor to cut a passage through them wide enough for our baggage.

In the mean time we had leisure to take a full view of this charming river. The stream, which was perfectly clear, ran down about two knots or two miles, an hour, when the water was at the lowest. The bottom was covered with a coarse gravel, spangled very thick with a shining substance that almost dazzled the eye, and the sand upon either shore sparkled with the same splendid particles.

At first sight, the sunbeams, giving a yellow cast to these spangles, made us fancy them to be gold-dust and, consequently, that all our fortunes were made. Such hopes as these were the less extravagant, because several rivers lying much about the same latitude with this have formerly abounded with fragments of that tempting metal. Witness the Tagus in Portugal, the Heber in Thrace, and the Pactolus in Lesser Asia; not to mention the rivers on the gold coast in Africa, which lie in a more southern climate.

[8] The work had had to be discontinued in the spring because of the rattlesnakes. It was resumed again in September.

But we soon found ourselves mistaken, and our gold dust dwindled into small flakes of isinglass. However, though this did not make the river so rich as we could wish, yet it made it exceedingly beautiful.

KILLING A BUFFALO

November 11. We had all been so refreshed by our day of rest that we decamped earlier than ordinary, and passed the several fords of Hico River. The woods were thick great part of this day's journey, so that we were forced to scuffle hard to advance seven miles, being equal in fatigue to double that distance of clear and open grounds.

We took up our quarters upon Sugartree Creek, in the same camp we had lain in when we came up, and happened to be entertained at supper with a rarity we had never had the fortune to meet with before during the whole expedition.

A little wide of this creek, one of the men had the luck to meet with a young buffalo of two years old. It was a bull which, not withstanding he was no older, was as big as an ordinary ox. His legs are very thick and very short, and his hoofs exceeding broad. His back rose into a kind of bunch a little above the shoulders, which I believe contributes not a little to that creature's enormous strength. His body is vastly deep from the shoulders to the brisket, sometimes six feet in those that are full grown. The portly figure of this animal is disgraced by a shabby little tail, not above 12 inches long. This he cocks up on end whenever he's in a passion and, instead of lowing or bellowing, grunts with no better grace than a hog.

The hair growing on his head and neck is long and shagged, and so soft that it will spin into thread not unlike mohair, which might be wove into a sort of camlet.[9] Some people have stockings knit of it that would have served an Israelite during his forty years' march through the wilderness.

Its horns are short and strong, of which the Indians make large spoons, which they say will split and fall to pieces whenever poison is put into them. Its color is a dirty brown, and its hide so thick that it is scarce penetrable. However, it makes very spongy sole leather by the ordinary method of tanning, though this fault might by good contrivance be mended.

[9] Fabric of camel's-hair.

As thick as this poor beast's hide was, a bullet made shift to enter it and fetch him down. It was found all alone, though buffaloes seldom are. They usually range about in herds, like other cattle, and, though they differ something in figure, are certainly of the same species. There are two reasons for this opinion: the flesh of both has exactly the same taste, and the mixed breed betwixt both, they say, will generate. All the difference I could perceive between the flesh of buffalo and common beef was that the flesh of the first was much yellower than that of the other, and the lean something tougher.

The men were so delighted with this new diet, that the gridiron and frying-pan had no more rest all night than a poor husband subject to curtain lectures. Buffaloes may be easily tamed when they are taken young. The best way to catch them is to carry a milch mare into the woods and, when you find a cow and a calf, to kill the cow and then, having catched the calf, to suckle it upon the mare. After once or twice sucking her, it will follow her home and become as gentle as another calf.

If we could get into a breed of them, they might be made very useful not only for the dairy by giving an ocean of milk, but also for drawing vast and cumbersome weights by their prodigious strength. These, with the other advantages I mentioned before, would make this sort of cattle more profitable to the owner than any other we are acquainted with, though they would need a world of provender.

SUGGESTIONS FOR STUDY

1. Point out evidences of Byrd's energy, of his sense of humor, of his London education.

2. Read Rear Admiral Richard E. Byrd's *Skyward* and see what similarities you can discover in the adventures and the personalities of the two men.

A New Nation

SPEECH IN THE VIRGINIA CONVENTION, 1775

By Patrick Henry (1736–1799)

The eighteenth century was notably an age of oratory. There were great issues at stake to call forth great speeches, and the classical education of that day developed a remarkably finished style. The period of our Revolutionary War produced an unusual galaxy of powerful speakers: in the North, James Otis, Samuel Adams, Josiah Quincy, Joseph Warren, John Adams, and Alexander Hamilton; in the South, Patrick Henry, Richard Henry Lee, William Pinkney, William Wirt, and John Randolph.

Among all the speeches of that day, none has quite equaled in quotability and reputation the "Liberty or Death" speech of Patrick Henry delivered before the Virginia Convention in March, 1775. For fifteen years, ever since James Otis had enunciated the famous "Taxation without representation is tyranny," the colonies had been protesting in vain against the high-handed measures of the British king. When the Virginia House of Burgesses was dissolved by the royal governor, it reassembled and a resolution was proposed that "Virginia be immediately put into a posture of defense." There was considerable opposition to this, many influential members believing that war was not only unnecessary but impracticable against the strong mother country.

At this point Patrick Henry arose. He was a great six-footer, rawboned, slightly stoop-shouldered, and totally indifferent to dress, but with that firm jaw, flashing blue eye, and power of personality which had hypnotized many a jury in his law practice, and which now so moved the conservative Burgesses that the resolution was passed.

Mr. President: —

No man thinks more highly than I do of the patriotism, as well as abilities, of the very worthy gentlemen who have just addressed the house. But different men often see the same subject in different lights; and, therefore, I hope it will not be thought disrespectful to those gentlemen, if, entertaining as I do opinions of a character very opposite to theirs, I shall speak forth my sentiments freely, and without reserve. This is no time for ceremony. The question before the house is one of awful moment to this country. For my own part, I consider it as nothing less than a question of freedom or slavery. And in proportion to the magnitude of the subject ought to be the freedom of the debate. It is only in this way that we can hope to arrive at truth, and fulfill the great responsibility which we hold to God and our country. Should I keep back my opinions at such a time, through fear of giving offense, I should consider myself as guilty of treason towards my country, and of an act of disloyalty toward the Majesty of Heaven, which I revere above all earthly kings.

Mr. President, it is natural to man to indulge in the illusions of hope. We are apt to shut our eyes against a painful truth, and listen to the song of that siren till she transforms us into beasts. Is this the part of wise men, engaged in a great and arduous struggle for liberty? Are we disposed to be of the number of those who having eyes see not, and having ears hear not, the things which so nearly concern their temporal salvation? For my part, whatever anguish of spirit it may cost, I am willing to know the whole truth; to know the worst and to provide for it.

I have but one lamp by which my feet are guided, and that is the lamp of experience. I know of no way of judging of the future but by the past. And judging by the past, I wish to know what there has been in the conduct of the British ministry for the last ten years, to justify those hopes with which gentlemen have been pleased to solace themselves and the house? Is it that insidious smile with which our petition has been lately received? Trust it not, sir: it will prove a snare to your feet. Suffer not yourselves to be betrayed with a kiss. Ask yourselves how this gracious reception of our petition comports with those warlike preparations which cover our waters and darken our land. Are fleets and armies necessary to a work of love and reconciliation? Have we shown ourselves so unwilling to be reconciled that force must be called in to win back our love? Let us not deceive ourselves, sir. These are the implements of war and subjugation — the last arguments to which kings resort. I ask gentlemen, sir, What means this martial array, if its purpose be not to force us to submission? Can gentlemen assign any other possible motive for it? Has Great Britain any enemy in this quarter of the world, to call for all this accumulation of navies and armies? No, sir, she has none. They are meant for us: they can be meant for no other. They are sent over to bind and rivet upon us those chains which the British ministry have been so long forging. And what have we to oppose to them? Shall we try argument? Sir, we have been trying that for the last ten years. Have we anything new to offer upon the subject? Nothing. We have held the subject up in every light of which it is capable; but it has been all in vain. Shall we resort to entreaty and humble supplication? What terms shall we find which have not been already exhausted? Let us not, I beseech you, sir, deceive ourselves longer.

Sir, we have done everything that could be done to avert the storm which is now coming on. We have petitioned; we have remonstrated; we have supplicated; we have prostrated ourselves before the throne, and have implored its interposition to arrest the tyrannical hands of the ministry and Parliament. Our petitions have been slighted; our remonstrances have produced additional violence and insult; our supplications have been disregarded; and we have been spurned with contempt from the foot of the throne! In vain, after these things, may we indulge the fond hope of peace and reconciliation. There is no longer any room for hope. If we wish to be free, if we mean to preserve inviolate those inestimable privileges for which we have been so long contending, if we mean not basely to abandon the noble struggle in which we have been so long engaged, and which we have pledged ourselves never to abandon until the glorious object of our contest shall be obtained — we must fight! I repeat it, sir, we must fight! An appeal to arms and to the God of Hosts is all that is left us!

They tell us, sir, that we are weak — unable to cope with so formidable an adversary. But when shall we be stronger? Will it be the next week, or the next year? Will it be when we are totally disarmed, and when a British guard shall be stationed in every house? Shall we gather strength by irresolution and inaction? Shall we acquire the means of effectual resistance by lying supinely on our backs, and hugging the delusive phantom of hope until our enemies shall have bound us hand and foot? Sir, we are not weak, if we make a proper use of those means which the God of nature hath placed in our power. Three millions of people, armed in the holy cause of liberty, and in such a country as that which we possess, are invincible by any force which our enemy can send against us. Besides, sir, we shall not fight our battles alone. There is a just God who presides over the destinies of nations, and who will raise up friends to fight our battles for us. The battle, sir, is not to the strong alone; it is to the vigilant, the active, the brave. Besides, sir, we have no election. If we were base enough to desire it, it is now too late to retire from the contest. There is no retreat but in submission and slavery! Our chains are forged! their clanking may be heard on the plains of Boston! The war is inevitable — and let it come! I repeat it, sir, let it come!

It is in vain, sir, to extenuate the matter. Gentlemen may cry, Peace, Peace — but there is no peace. The war is actually begun! The next gale that sweeps from the north will bring to our ears the clash of resounding arms! Our brethren are already in the field! Why stand we here idle? What is it that gentlemen wish? What would they have? Is life so dear, or peace so sweet, as to be purchased at the price of chains and slavery? Forbid it, Almighty God! I know not what course others may take; but as for me, give me liberty or give me death!

SUGGESTIONS FOR STUDY

1. The best way to study this speech is to practice reading it aloud, reproducing as far as you are able the spirit in which it was originally delivered. Be careful to avoid an exaggeration which becomes mere ranting. It would be interesting for the class to elect one member to deliver the speech before the class, preliminary to discussion of it. Another entertaining plan is to dramatize the Virginia Convention with students assigned to prepare speeches of reluctant Burgesses, to whom Patrick Henry may reply, concluding with a vote on the resolution.

2. Some of the rhetorical devices with which this speech abounds are repetition, the question and the exclamation, the balanced sentence, the figure of speech, and the climax. Can you find good examples of all of them? There are several touches of Biblical language which are also interesting to look for.

3. John Randolph said of Patrick Henry that he was Shakespeare and Garrick combined. Do you know what he meant by this?

THE DECLARATION OF INDEPENDENCE

By THOMAS JEFFERSON (1743–1826)

When the Second Continental Congress assembled in Philadelphia, May 19, 1775, there was already open war between the Colonies and Great Britain, but the actual establishment of an independent country was still far from the mind of most. Early in 1776 Thomas Paine issued a pamphlet called *Common Sense* in which he urged in terse, impelling sentences the necessity of breaking away from the British government. Paine was as fiery on paper as Patrick Henry had been in oratory. His pamphlet was the match to the dynamite of public opinion. The earlier idea of remaining British subjects went up in the explosion, and finally most of the members of Congress were convinced that complete separation from England was the only course to take. In June, 1776, a committee consisting of Thomas Jefferson, John Adams, Benjamin Franklin, Roger Sherman, and Robert R. Livingston was appointed to draft a declaration of independence. At the request of this committee Thomas Jefferson wrote the text, which, with a few changes by the committee, was presented to Congress, June 28. After several days of debate, the Declaration of Independence was formally adopted July 4, 1776.

Aside from its political import, this document is remarkable for the clearness, dignity, and beauty of its language. Its composer, Thomas Jefferson, showed this same gift for phraseology in all the state papers for which he was responsible.

When in the course of human events, it becomes necessary for one people to dissolve the political bands which have connected them with another, and to assume among the powers of the earth the separate and equal station to which the laws of nature and of nature's God entitle them, a decent respect to the opinions of mankind requires that they should declare the causes which impel them to the separation.

We hold these truths to be self-evident, that all men are created equal, that they are endowed by their Creator with certain in-alienable rights, that among these are life, liberty, and the pursuit of happiness. That to secure these rights, governments are insti-tuted among men, deriving their just powers from the consent of the governed. That whenever any form of government becomes destructive of these ends, it is the right of the people to alter or abolish it, and to institute new government, laying its foundation on such principles and organizing its powers in such form as to them shall seem most likely to effect their safety and happiness. Prudence indeed will dictate that governments long established should not be changed for light and transient causes; and ac-cordingly all experience hath shown, that mankind are more dis-posed to suffer, while evils are sufferable, than to right themselves by abolishing the forms to which they are accustomed. But when a long train of abuses and usurpations, pursuing invariably the same object, evinces a design to reduce them under absolute despotism, it is their right, it is their duty, to throw off such government and to provide new guards for their future security. Such has been the patient sufferance of these Colonies; and such is now the necessity which constrains them to alter their former systems of government. The history of the present king of Great Britain is a history of repeated injuries and usurpations, all having in direct object the establishment of an absolute tyranny over these States. To prove this let facts be submitted to a candid world.

[Here follows a long list of injustices suffered by the Colonies.]

In every stage of these oppressions we have petitioned for redress in the most humble terms. Our repeated petitions have been answered only by repeated injuries. A prince whose character is thus marked by every act which may define a tyrant, is unfit to be the ruler of a free people.

Nor have we been wanting in attention to our British brethren. We have warned them from time to time of attempts by their legislature to extend an unwarrantable jurisdiction over us. We have reminded them of the circumstances of our emigration and settlement here. We have appealed to their native justice and magnanimity, and we have conjured them by the ties of our common kindred to disavow these usurpations, which would inevitably interrupt our connection and correspondence. They too have been deaf to the voice of justice and of consanguinity. We must, therefore, acquiesce in the necessity which denounces our separation, and hold them as we hold the rest of mankind, enemies in war, in peace friends.

We, therefore, the representatives of the United States of America, in General Congress assembled, appealing to the Supreme Judge of the world for the rectitude of our intentions do, in the name, and by the authority of the good people of these Colonies, solemnly publish and declare, that these United Colonies are and of right ought to be free and independent States; that they are absolved from all allegiance to the British crown, and that all political connection between them and the State of Great Britain is and ought to be totally dissolved; and that as free and independent States, they have full power to levy war, conclude peace, contract alliances, establish commerce, and do all other acts and things which independent States may of right do. And for the support of this declaration, with a firm reliance on the protection of Divine Providence, we mutually pledge to each other our lives, our fortunes, and our sacred honor.

SUGGESTIONS FOR STUDY

1. Vocabulary: inalienable, usurpations, unwarrantable jurisdiction, magnanimity, consanguinity, acquiesce.

2. What oft-quoted phrases do you find here? In the popular mind the Declaration of Independence and the Constitution of the United States are sometimes confused. Do you find any phrases here which you had supposed were in the Constitution?

3. Is it true that all men are created entirely equal? In what sense did the writers of this document mean equal?

4. What part of this document might the Southern States have quoted to justify their secession from the Union in the Civil War?

5. What attitude is shown toward the British people?

FAREWELL ADDRESS

By George Washington (1732–1799)

It is said that no state document of our country has been so frequently printed as Washington's *Farewell Address*. Small wonder it is that the parting advice of one who had been the preëminent leader during days of military, economic, and political struggle should be sought again and again as successive questions of policy have arisen. By refusing a third term Washington set a precedent which has never been broken; by stating certain principles of action he set a high standard of national conduct which has never been forgotten. At the time of the World War the address was frequently revived and was quoted by both sides to prove that we should or should not go into the war, and that we should or should not join the League of Nations.

As Washington's second term drew to a close he put considerable thought upon his farewell words, submitting the first draft to Madison and Hamilton, and revising it carefully in the light of their suggestions. Students sometimes have a false mental picture of Washington delivering this address before a great concourse of people, but such was not the case. The so-called address was first given to the public in a Philadelphia newspaper, and was reprinted all over the country. One can see from the long, ponderous sentences that it was intended to be read rather than heard. Compare its dignified style with the sharp, terse sentences of Patrick Henry or the simplicity of Lincoln's phrases. It is not easy reading, but it is a challenge to you to bring all the powers of your mind to bear on a worth-while message.

TO THE PEOPLE OF THE UNITED STATES

September 17th, 1796

Friends and Fellow-Citizens,

The period for a new election of a citizen to administer the executive government of the United States being not far distant, and the time actually arrived when your thoughts must be employed in designating the person who is to be clothed with that important trust, it appears to me proper, especially as it may conduce to a more distinct expression of the public voice, that I should now apprise you of the resolution I have formed, to decline being considered among the number of those out of whom a choice is to be made.

I beg you, at the same time, to do me the justice to be assured that this resolution has not been taken without a strict regard to all the considerations appertaining to the relation which binds a dutiful citizen to his country; — and that, in withdrawing the tender of service, which silence in my situation might imply, I am influenced by no diminution of zeal for your future interest, no deficiency of grateful respect for your past kindness; but am supported by a full conviction that the step is compatible with both.

[In the five omitted paragraphs Washington says that he had been deterred from writing a similar address at the end of his first term only because of the critical state of public affairs at that time, but that present conditions justify his retirement. He expresses great gratitude for the confidence and support of his countrymen and introduces the main body of the address by saying that on this occasion he cannot refrain from offering some reflections of his own, " the disinterested warnings of a parting friend who can possibly have no personal motives to bias his counsels."]

Interwoven as is the love of liberty with every ligament of your hearts, no recommendation of mine is necessary to fortify or confirm the attachment.

The unity of government which constitutes you one people, is also now dear to you. It is justly so, for it is a main pillar in the edifice of your real independence; the support of your tranquillity at home, your peace abroad, of your safety, of your prosperity in every shape, of that very liberty which you so highly prize. But as it is easy to foresee that from different causes, and from different quarters, much pains will be taken, many artifices employed, to weaken in your minds the conviction of this truth; as this is the point in your political fortress against which the batteries of internal and external enemies will be most constantly and actively (though often covertly and insidiously) directed, it is of infinite moment that you should properly estimate the immense value of your national union to your collective and individual happiness; that you should cherish a cordial, habitual, and immovable attachment to it; accustoming yourselves to think and speak of it as of the Palladium [1] of your political safety and prosperity; watching for its preservation with jealous anx-

---

[1] A safeguard. It was originally an image of the goddess Pallas which was supposed to have fallen from heaven and to have protected Troy until the Greeks stole it and were thus able to capture the city.

iety; discountenancing whatever may suggest even a suspicion
that it can in any event be abandoned, and indignantly frowning
upon the first dawning of every attempt to alienate any portion
of our country from the rest, or to enfeeble the sacred ties which
now link together the various parts.

For this you have every inducement of sympathy and interest.
Citizens by birth or choice of a common country, that country
has a right to concentrate your affections. The name of
AMERICAN, which belongs to you in your national capacity, must
always exalt the just pride of patriotism more than any appellation derived from local discriminations. With slight shades of
difference you have the same religion, manners, habits, and
political principles. You have in a common cause fought and
triumphed together. The independence and liberty you possess
are the work of joint councils and joint efforts, of common dangers, sufferings, and successes.

But these considerations, however powerfully they address
themselves to your sensibility, are greatly outweighed by those
which apply more immediately to your interest. Here every portion of our country finds the most commanding motives for carefully guarding and preserving the union of the whole.

The North in an unrestrained intercourse with the South,
protected by the equal laws of a common government, finds in
the productions of the latter great additional resources of maritime and commercial enterprise and precious materials of manufacturing industry. The South in the same intercourse, benefiting
by the agency of the North, sees its agriculture grow and its
commerce expand. Turning partly into its own channels the
seamen of the North, it finds its particular navigation envigor-
ated; and while it contributes in different ways to nourish and
increase the general mass of the national navigation, it looks
forward to the protection of a maritime strength to which itself
is unequally adapted. The East, in a like intercourse with the
West,[2] already finds, and in the progressive improvement of interior communications by land and water will more and more
find, a valuable vent for the commodities which it brings from
abroad or manufactures at home. The West derives from the
East supplies requisite to its growth and comfort, and what is

---

[2] It must be remembered that in Washington's day the West was still east
of the Mississippi. The Appalachian Mountains might roughly be considered
the dividing line between the East and the West at that time.

perhaps of still greater consequence, it must of necessity owe the secure enjoyment of indispensable outlets for its own productions to the weight, influence, and the future maritime strength of the Atlantic side of the Union, directed by an indissoluble community of interest, as one nation. Any other tenure by which the West can hold this essential advantage, whether derived from its own separate strength, or from an apostate and unnatural connection with any foreign power,[3] must be intrinsically precarious.

While, then, every part of our country thus feels an immediate and particular interest in union, all the parts combined in the united mass of means and efforts cannot fail to find greater strength, greater resource, proportionably greater security from external danger, a less frequent interruption of their peace by foreign nations; and what is of inestimable value, they must derive from union an exemption from those broils and wars between themselves, which so frequently afflict neighboring countries not tied together by the same government, which their own rivalships alone would be sufficient to produce, but which opposite foreign alliances, attachments, and intrigues would stimulate and embitter. Hence, likewise, they will avoid the necessity of those overgrown military establishments which under any form of government are inauspicious to liberty, and which are to be regarded as particularly hostile to republican liberty. In this sense it is that your union ought to be considered as a main prop of your liberty, and that the love of the one ought to endear to you the preservation of the other.

[Washington continues the subject of the preservation of unity by pointing out some of the possible disturbances to it, such as geographical jealousies, lack of respect for the constitution and laws, usurpation of power by a small group, and too many innovations in government.]

I have already intimated to you the danger of parties in the state, with particular reference to the founding of them on geographical discriminations. Let me now take a more comprehensive view, and warn you in the most solemn manner against the baneful effects of the spirit of party generally.

This spirit, unfortunately, is inseparable from our nature, having its roots in the strongest passions of the human mind. It

[3] Because of the failure of the United States government to obtain from Spain navigation rights on the Mississippi, Kentucky and Tennessee had had secret intrigues with that country and had threatened to leave the Union.

exists under different shapes in all governments, more or less stifled, controlled, or repressed; but in those of the popular form it is seen in its greatest rankness, and is truly their worst enemy.

The alternate domination of one faction over another, sharpened by the spirit of revenge natural to party dissension, which in different ages and countries has perpetrated the most horrid enormities, is itself a frightful despotism. But this leads at length to a more formal and permanent despotism. The disorders and miseries which result, gradually incline the minds of men to seek security and repose in the absolute power of an individual; and sooner or later the chief of some prevailing faction,[4] more able or more fortunate than his competitors, turns this disposition to the purposes of his own elevation on the ruins of public liberty.

Without looking forward to an extremity of this kind (which nevertheless ought not to be entirely out of sight), the common and continual mischiefs of the spirit of party are sufficient to make it the interest and duty of a wise people to discourage and restrain it.

It serves always to distract the public councils and enfeeble the public administration. It agitates the community with ill-founded jealousies and false alarms, kindles the animosity of one part against another, foments occasionally riot and insurrection. It opens the doors to foreign influence and corruption,[5] which find a facilitated access to the government itself through the channels of party passions. Thus the policy and the will of one country are subjected to the policy and will of another.

There is an opinion that parties in free countries are useful checks upon the administration of the government, and serve to keep alive the spirit of liberty. This within certain limits is probably true; and in governments of a monarchical cast, patriotism may look with indulgence if not with favor upon the spirit of party. But in those of the popular character, in governments purely elective, it is a spirit not to be encouraged. From their natural tendency it is certain there will always be enough of that spirit for every salutary purpose. And there being constant

---

[4] What Washington feared for the United States actually happened in France within five years of this address when Napoleon gained complete control after the turbulent French Revolution.

[5] He was referring to the attempts of Genêt, minister from France, through direct appeals in the press to involve this country in an alliance with France against England. Washington had been greatly reviled in some quarters for insisting on neutrality.

danger of excess, the effort ought to be by force of public opinion to mitigate and assuage it. A fire not to be quenched, it demands a uniform vigilance to prevent its bursting into a flame, lest, instead of warming, it should consume.

It is important, likewise, that the habits of thinking in a free country should inspire caution in those entrusted with its administration, to confine themselves within their respective constitutional spheres, avoiding in the exercise of the powers of one department to encroach upon another. The spirit of encroachment tends to consolidate the powers of all the departments in one, and thus to create, whatever the form of government, a real despotism. A just estimate of that love of power and proneness to abuse it which predominates in the human heart, is sufficient to satisfy us of the truth of this position. The necessity of reciprocal checks in the exercise of political power, by dividing and distributing it into different depositories, and constituting each the guardian of the public weal against invasions by the others, has been evinced by experiments ancient and modern; some of them in our country and under our own eyes. To preserve them must be as necessary as to institute them. If in the opinion of the people the distribution or modification of the constitutional powers be in any particular wrong, let it be corrected by an amendment in the way which the Constitution designates. But let there be no change by usurpation; for though this, in one instance may be the instrument of good, it is the customary weapon by which free governments are destroyed. The precedent must always greatly overbalance in permanent evil any partial or transient benefit which the use can at any time yield.

Of all the dispositions and habits which lead to political prosperity, religion and morality are indispensable supports. In vain would that man claim the tribute of patriotism who should labor to subvert these great pillars of human happiness, these firmest props of the duties of men and citizens. The mere politician, equally with the pious man, ought to respect and to cherish them. A volume could not trace all their connections with private and public felicity. Let it simply be asked, where is the security for property, for reputation, for life, if the sense of religious obligation desert the oaths which are the instruments of investigation in courts of justice? And let us with caution indulge the supposition that morality can be maintained without religion. Whatever may be conceded to the influence of refined education on

minds of peculiar structure, reason and experience both forbid us
to expect that national morality can prevail in exclusion of
religious principle.

It is substantially true that virtue or morality is a necessary
spring of popular government. The rule indeed extends with
more or less force to every species of free government. Who that
is a sincere friend to it can look with indifference upon attempts
to shake the foundation of the fabric?

Promote then, as an object of primary importance, institutions
for the general diffusion of knowledge. In proportion as the
structure of a government gives force to public opinion, it is
essential that public opinion should be enlightened.

[A paragraph follows urging that public credit be cherished, and
pointing out some of the difficulties of establishing a fair taxation.]

Observe good faith and justice towards all nations; cultivate
peace and harmony with all. Religion and morality enjoin this
conduct; and can it be that good policy does not equally enjoin
it? It will be worthy of a free, enlightened, and, at no distant
period, a great nation, to give to mankind the magnanimous and
too novel example of a people always guided by an exalted justice
and benevolence. Who can doubt that in the course of time and
things the fruits of such a plan would richly repay any temporary
advantages which might be lost by a steady adherence to it? Can
it be that Providence has not connected the permanent felicity
of a nation with its virtue? The experiment, at least, is recommended by every sentiment which ennobles human nature. Alas!
is it rendered impossible by its vices?

In the execution of such a plan nothing is more essential than
that permanent, inveterate antipathies against particular nations,
and passionate attachments for others, should be excluded; and
that in place of them, just and amicable feelings towards all
should be cultivated. The nation which indulges towards another
an habitual hatred or an habitual fondness is in some degree a
slave. It is a slave to its animosity or to its affection, either of
which is sufficient to lead it astray from its duty and its interest.
Antipathy in one nation against another disposes each more
readily to offer insult and injury, to lay hold of slight causes of
umbrage, and to be haughty and intractable when accidental or
trifling occasions of dispute occur. Hence frequent collisions,
obstinate, envenomed and bloody contests. The nation prompted
by ill will and resentment sometimes impels to war the govern-

ment, contrary to the best calculations of policy. The government sometimes participates in the national propensity and adopts through passion what reason would reject; at other times it makes the animosity of the nation subservient to projects of hostility instigated by pride, ambition, and other sinister and pernicious motives. The peace often, sometimes perhaps the liberty, of nations has been the victim.

So likewise a passionate attachment of one nation for another produces a variety of evils. Sympathy for the favorite nation, facilitating the illusion of an imaginary common interest, in cases where no real common interest exists, and infusing into one the enmities of the other, betrays the former into a participation in the quarrels and wars of the latter, without adequate inducement or justification. It leads also to concessions to the favorite nation of privileges denied to others, which is apt doubly to injure the nation making the concessions; by unnecessarily parting with what ought to have been retained, and by exciting jealousy, ill will, and a disposition to retaliate, in the parties from whom equal privileges are withheld. And it gives to ambitious, corrupted, or deluded citizens [6] (who devote themselves to the favorite nation), facility to betray, or sacrifice the interests of their own country, without odium, sometimes even with popularity, gilding with the appearances of a virtuous sense of obligation, a commendable deference for public opinion, or a laudable zeal for public good, the base or foolish compliances of ambition, corruption, or infatuation.

As avenues to foreign influence in innumerable ways, such attachments are particularly alarming to the truly enlightened and independent patriot. How many opportunities do they afford to tamper with domestic factions, to practice the arts of seduction, to mislead public opinion, to influence or awe the public councils! Such an attachment of a small or weak, towards a great and powerful nation, dooms the former to be the satellite of the latter.

Against the insidious wiles of foreign influence, I conjure you to believe me, fellow-citizens, the jealousy of a free people ought to be constantly awake, since history and experience prove that foreign influence is one of the most baneful foes of republican government. But that jealousy, to be useful, must be impartial;

[6] He was referring here to the way Genêt had been received and encouraged by many Americans, though his methods violated every rule of diplomacy.

else it becomes the instrument of the very influence to be avoided, instead of a defense against it. Excessive partiality for one foreign nation and excessive dislike of another, cause those whom they actuate to see danger only on one side, and serve to veil and even second the arts of influence on the other. Real patriots, who may resist the intrigues of the favorite, are liable to become suspected and odious; while its tools and dupes usurp the applause and confidence of the people, to surrender their interests.

The great rule of conduct for us in regard to foreign nations is, in extending our commercial relations, to have with them as little political connection as possible. So far as we have already formed engagements, let them be fulfilled with perfect good faith. Here let us stop.

Europe has a set of primary interests, which to us have none, or a very remote relation. Hence she must be engaged in frequent controversies, the causes of which are essentially foreign to our concerns. Hence therefore it must be unwise in us to implicate ourselves by artificial ties in the ordinary vicissitudes of her politics, or the ordinary combinations and collisions of her friendships, or enmities.

Our detached and distant situation invites and enables us to pursue a different course. If we remain one people, under an efficient government, the period is not far off when we may defy material injury from external annoyance; when we may take such an attitude as will cause the neutrality we may at any time resolve upon, to be scrupulously respected; when belligerent nations, under the impossibility of making acquisitions upon us, will not lightly hazard the giving us provocation; when we may choose peace or war, as our interest guided by our justice shall counsel.

Why forego the advantages of so peculiar a situation? Why quit our own to stand upon foreign ground? Why, by interweaving our destiny with that of any part of Europe, entangle our peace and prosperity in the toils of European ambition, rivalship, interest, humor, or caprice?

It is our true policy to steer clear of permanent alliances with any portion of the foreign world; so far I mean as we are now at liberty to do it; for let me not be understood as capable of patronizing infidelity to existing engagements. I hold the maxim no less applicable to public than to private affairs, that honesty is always the best policy. I repeat it therefore, let those engagements be observed in their genuine sense. But in my opinion it is unnecessary and would be unwise to extend them.

Taking care always to keep ourselves by suitable establishments on a respectable defensive posture, we may safely trust to temporary alliances for extraordinary emergencies.

Harmony, liberal intercourse with all nations, are recommended by policy, humanity, and interest. But even our commercial policy should hold an equal and impartial hand; neither seeking nor granting exclusive favors or preferences; consulting the natural course of things; diffusing and diversifying by gentle means the streams of commerce, but forcing nothing; establishing with powers so disposed, in order to give trade a stable course, to define the rights of our merchants, and to enable the government to support them, conventional rules of intercourse, the best that present circumstances and mutual opinion will permit, but temporary, and liable to be from time to time abandoned or varied, as experience and circumstances shall dictate; constantly keeping in view that it is folly in one nation to look for disinterested favors from another; that it must pay with a portion of its independence for whatever it may accept under that character; that by such acceptance it may place itself in the condition of having given equivalents for nominal favors, and yet of being reproached with ingratitude for not giving more. There can be no greater error than to expect or calculate upon real favors from nation to nation. It is an illusion which experience must cure, which a just pride ought to discard.

In offering to you, my countrymen, these counsels of an old and affectionate friend, I dare not hope they will make the strong and lasting impression I could wish; that they will control the usual current of the passions, or prevent our nation from running the course which has hitherto marked the destiny of nations. But if I may even flatter myself that they may be productive of some partial benefit, some occasional good; that they may now and then recur to moderate the fury of party spirit, to warn against the mischiefs of foreign intrigue, to guard against the impostures of pretended patriotism; this hope will be a full recompense for the solicitude for your welfare, by which they have been dictated.

[The address is concluded by a further personal farewell referring to certain difficulties to his administration, the principles under which he has acted, and the happiness he anticipates as a private citizen enjoying " the benign influence of good laws under a free government, the ever favorite object of my heart, and the happy reward, as I trust, of our mutual cares, labors, and dangers."]

SUGGESTIONS FOR STUDY

1. One of the greatest difficulties in understanding this address is in the wording, but on the other hand you will seldom find within a single piece such a good opportunity to enlarge your vocabulary. Here are fifty unusual words in the order in which they appear. If you learn the meanings of these words before you begin the reading, you will find the address more readily understandable.

conduce	inauspicious	felicity	pernicious
diminution	baneful	magnanimous	retaliate
compatible	perpetrated	inveterate	odium
edifice	enormities	antipathies	laudable
artifices	foments	amicable	infatuation
covertly	facilitated	animosity	satellite
insidiously	salutary	umbrage	vicissitudes
appellation	mitigate	intractable	scrupulously
indissoluble	assuage	propensity	belligerent
apostate	proneness	subservient	diversifying
intrinsically	reciprocal	instigated	impostures
precarious	weal	sinister	solicitude
exemption	subvert		

You can get fun out of this by turning it into a contest. Divide your class into two sides. Let each team or a committee from the team compose a vocabulary test on half the words. Then each side can take the test composed by the other side and see which can make the highest score.

To make a vocabulary test, put each word into a short sentence, and follow this by three wrong meanings and one right meaning thus: " I discovered his *artifices,* paintings, tricks, mistakes, difficulties." Be sure to have each of the four possible meanings a word that is easily understood and that would make sense in the sentence. Be careful also to vary the order of the right meaning among the wrong meanings. These tests can be taken by underlining the correct synonym on mimeographed sheets or they can be taken orally in the form of a spell-down.

2. In order to understand this address fully, you must be able to realize the difference between the United States in Washington's day and in ours. It would be well to have brief reports from members of the class on such matters as the boundaries, population, political parties, conditions of commerce and manufacturing, condition of education, relationship

with England, France, and other foreign nations, and the number of republics in the world at that time, comparing all of them with conditions in our own day.

3. In the light of changed conditions which parts of Washington's advice do you think apply today and which do not? This affords good subject matter for informal debates.

4. The body of this address falls into two main parts: advice on home affairs and advice on foreign affairs. Make an outline of the points under each.

5. An interesting project for a class or committee would be the making of two small world maps, one for his day, one for ours, to show the increase of republics in the world. In both maps color absolute monarchies black, limited or constitutional monarchies gray, and republics white. You may be surprised at the results.

6. Washington warns emphatically against the dangers of long and decided affections or antipathies between nations. Can you think of any striking examples of this in the world's history or among countries today?

7. Washington's early biographers represented him as a kind of petrified saint with a halo. It is curious that four of the writers who have tried their hands at making him a more natural human being and clearing away the fiction have been themselves eminent writers of fiction. These four biographies, all of which are highly interesting reading, are Washington Irving's *Life of Washington,* Paul Leicester Ford's *The True George Washington,* Owen Wister's *The Seven Ages of Washington,* and Rupert Hughes's *George Washington, 1762–1777.*

Civil Strife

FAREWELL AT SPRINGFIELD

By ABRAHAM LINCOLN (1809–1865)

When Lincoln left Springfield, Illinois, in 1861, to take up his duties as President in Washington, he seemed to realize that Fate might never let him return. The scene of his departure has been vividly described by Carl Sandburg in his *Abraham Lincoln: The Prairie Years:* " A cold drizzle of rain was falling on the morning of February 11 when Lincoln and his party of fifteen were to leave Springfield on the eight o'clock at the Great Western Railway station. Chilly gray mist hung the circle of the prairie horizon. A short little locomotive with a flat-topped smokestack stood puffing with a baggage car and special passenger car hitched on; a railroad president and superintendent were on board. A thousand people crowded in and around the brick station, inside of which Lincoln was standing, and one by one came hundreds of old friends, shaking hands, wishing him luck and Godspeed, all faces solemn. Even Judge David Davis, weighing 350 pounds, wearing a new white silk hat, was a serious figure.

"A path was made for Lincoln from the station to his car; hands stretched out for one last handshake. He hadn't intended to make a speech; but on the platform of the car, as he turned and saw his home people, he took off his hat, stood perfectly still, and looked almost as he had at Bowling Green burial services when tears had to take the place of words. He raised a hand for silence. They stood with hats off. Then he said slowly, amid the soft gray drizzle from the sky:

" ' Friends, no one who has ever been placed in a like position can understand my feelings at this hour nor the impressive sadness I feel at this parting. For more than a quarter of a century I have lived among you, and during all that time I have received nothing but kindness at your hands. Here I have lived from my youth till now I am an old man. Here the most sacred trusts of earth were assumed; here all my children were born and one of them lies buried. To you, dear friends, I owe all that I have, all that I am. All the strange checkered past seems to crowd now upon my mind. Today I leave you; I go to assume a task more difficult than that which devolved upon General Washington. Unless the great God who assisted him shall be with and aid me, I must fail. But if the same omniscient mind and the same Almighty arm that directed and protected him shall guide and support me, I shall not fail; I shall succeed. Let us all pray that the God of our fathers may not forsake us now. To Him I commend you all. Permit me to ask that with equal sincerity and faith you will all invoke his wisdom and guidance for me. With these few words I must leave you — for how long I know not. Friends, one and all, I must now bid you an affectionate farewell.'

"Bells rang, there was a grinding of wheels, and the train moved and carried Lincoln away from Springfield. The tears were not yet dry on some faces when the train had faded into the gray to the east.

"Some of the crowd said afterward that Lincoln too was in tears, that tears ran down his face as he spoke that morning.

"And one of the crowd said there were no tears on Lincoln's face. ' But he had a face with dry tears,' said this one. ' He was a man who often had dry tears.' "

-R-M-B-

LETTER TO GENERAL JOSEPH HOOKER

By ABRAHAM LINCOLN (1809–1865)

During 1862 the Northern Army had suffered several defeats and Lincoln had had to remove both General McClellan and General Burnside. The man that he put in the command of the Army of the Potomac over the protest of Secretary Stanton and General Halleck was General Joseph Hooker, who had served under both of his predecessors, and had criticized both with great frankness. The next day after the appointment Lincoln sent General Hooker this remarkable letter which showed his directness, fearlessness, and understanding of men. It administers a rebuke at the same time that it shows confidence and encouragement.

I have placed you at the head of the Army of the Potomac. Of course I have done this upon what appear to me to be sufficient reasons, and yet I think it best for you to know that there are some things in regard to which I am not quite satisfied with you. I believe you to be a brave and skilful soldier, which, of course, I like. I also believe you do not mix politics with your profession, in which you are right. You have confidence in yourself, which is a valuable, if not an indispensable, quality. You are ambitious, which, within reasonable bounds, does good rather than harm; but I think that during General Burnside's command of the army you have taken counsel of your ambition, and thwarted him as much as you could, in which you did a great wrong to the country and to a most meritorious and honorable brother officer. I have heard, in such way as to believe it, of your recently saying that both the army and the Government needed a Dictator. Of course it was not for this, but in spite of it, that I have given you the command. Only those generals who gain successes can set up dictatorships. What I now ask of you is military success, and I will risk the dictatorship. The Government will support you to the utmost of its ability, which is neither more nor less than it has done and will do for all commanders. I much fear that the spirit which you have aided to infuse into the army, of criticizing their commander and withholding confidence from him, will now turn upon you. I shall assist you as far as I can to put it down. Neither you nor Napoleon, if he were alive again, could get any good out of an army while such a spirit prevails in it. And now, beware of rashness, but with energy and sleepless vigilance go forward, and give us victories.

PROCLAMATION FOR A NATIONAL FAST DAY

MARCH 30, 1863

By ABRAHAM LINCOLN (1809–1865)

General Hooker did not at once gain the victories which the President had asked for. All during the spring of 1863 the outlook was still dark. This proclamation suggests the prostrate spirit of the nation.

Whereas, the Senate of the United States, devoutly recognizing the supreme authority and just government of Almighty God in all the affairs of men and of nations, has by a resolution requested the President to designate and set apart a day for national prayer and humiliation:

And whereas, it is the duty of nations as well as of men to own their dependence upon the overruling power of God; to confess their sins and transgressions in humble sorrow, yet with assured hope that genuine repentance will lead to mercy and pardon; and to recognize the sublime truth, announced in the Holy

Scriptures and proven by all history, that those nations only are blessed whose God is the Lord:

And insomuch as we know that, by His divine law, nations, like individuals, are subjected to punishments and chastisements in this world, may we not justly fear that the awful calamity of civil war which now desolates the land may be but a punishment inflicted upon us for our presumptuous sins, to the needful end of our national reformation as a whole people? We have been the recipients of the choicest bounties of Heaven. We have been preserved, these many years, in peace and prosperity. We have grown in numbers, wealth, and power as no other nation has ever grown; but we have forgotten God. We have forgotten the gracious hand which preserved us in peace, and multiplied and enriched and strengthened us; and we have vainly imagined, in the deceitfulness of our hearts, that all these blessings were produced by some superior wisdom and virtue of our own. Intoxicated with unbroken success, we have become too self-sufficient to feel the necessity of redeeming and preserving grace, too proud to pray to the God that made us:

It behooves us, then, to humble ourselves before the offended Power, to confess our national sins, and to pray for clemency and forgiveness:

Now, therefore, in compliance with the request, and fully concurring in the views, of the Senate, I do by this my proclamation designate and set apart Thursday, the 30th day of April, 1863, as a day of national humiliation, fasting, and prayer. And I do hereby request all the people to abstain on that day from their ordinary secular pursuits, and to unite at their several places of public worship and their respective homes in keeping the day holy to the Lord, and devoted to the humble discharge of the religious duties proper to that solemn occasion. All this being done in sincerity and truth, let us then rest humbly in the hope authorized by the divine teachings, that the united cry of the nation will be heard on high, and answered with blessings no less than the pardon of our national sins, and the restoration of our now divided and suffering country to its former happy condition of unity and peace.

In witness, etc.

ABRAHAM LINCOLN

By the President:

WILLIAM H. SEWARD, Secretary of State

PROCLAMATION FOR THANKSGIVING

OCTOBER 3, 1863

By ABRAHAM LINCOLN (1809–1865)

In July, 1863, the tide of battle turned in favor of the Union armies with the victories of Gettysburg and Vicksburg. The country, therefore, was in fit mental state for a real Thanksgiving. This was the first year that there had been a national Thanksgiving Day with proclamation by the President. Before that time, proclamations had been issued only by the governors when their states so desired, and the feast had not been celebrated over the entire country. It is interesting to compare the language and tone of this one with the preceding proclamation for a fast day. It may also be interesting to you to observe future Thanksgiving Day Proclamations and compare their literary quality with this one of Lincoln's.

The year that is drawing toward its close has been filled with the blessings of fruitful fields and healthful skies. To these bounties, which are so constantly enjoyed that we are prone to forget the source from which they come, others have been added, which are of so extraordinary a nature that they cannot fail to penetrate and soften the heart which is habitually insensible to the ever-watchful providence of Almighty God.

In the midst of a civil war of unequaled magnitude and severity, which has sometimes seemed to foreign states to invite and provoke their aggressions, peace has been preserved with all nations, order has been maintained, the laws have been respected and obeyed, and harmony has prevailed everywhere, except in the theater of military conflict; while that theater has been greatly contracted by the advancing armies and navies of the Union.

Needful diversions of wealth and of strength from the fields of peaceful industry to the national defense have not arrested the plow, the shuttle, or the ship; the ax has enlarged the borders of our settlements, and the mines, as well of iron and coal as of the precious metals, have yielded even more abundantly than heretofore. Population has steadily increased, notwithstanding the waste that has been made in the camp, the siege, and the battlefield, and the country, rejoicing in the consciousness of augmented strength and vigor, is permitted to expect continuance of years with large increase of freedom.

No human counsel hath devised, nor hath any mortal hand worked out these great things. They are the gracious gifts of the most high God, who, while dealing with us in anger for our sins, hath nevertheless remembered mercy.

It has seemed to me fit and proper that they should be solemnly, reverently, and gratefully acknowledged as with one heart and one voice by the whole American people. I do, therefore, invite my fellow citizens in every part of the United States, and also those who are at sea and those who are sojourning in foreign lands, to set apart and observe the last Thursday of November next as a day of Thanksgiving and praise to our beneficent Father who dwelleth in the heavens. And I recommend to them that, while offering up the ascriptions justly due to Him for such singular deliverances and blessings, they do also, with humble penitence for our national perverseness and disobedience, commend to His tender care all those who have become widows, orphans, mourners, or sufferers in the lamentable civil strife in which we are unavoidably engaged, and fervently implore the interposition of the Almighty hand to heal the wounds of the nation, and to restore it, as soon as may be consistent with the Divine purposes, to the full enjoyment of peace, harmony, tranquillity, and union.

In testimony, etc.

A. LINCOLN

By the President:

WILLIAM H. SEWARD, Secretary of State

GETTYSBURG ADDRESS

NOVEMBER 19, 1863

By ABRAHAM LINCOLN (1809–1865)

Probably no speech of so few words has ever become so celebrated as Lincoln's " Gettysburg Address," or aroused such dispute as to how it was written, delivered, and received.

The victory of Gettysburg had been a costly one. More men had been killed than in any previous battle of the war. Scarcely had the echoes of the guns passed away when it was proposed by a citizen of Gettysburg that part of the battlefield be set apart for a national cemetery. There was immediate response from all over the North, the land was purchased, the date set for dedication, and Edward Everett, considered the greatest orator of his day, selected to be the main speaker. Six weeks later and apparently as an afterthought President Lincoln was asked " to set apart formally these grounds to their sacred use by a few appropriate remarks."

It was estimated that a hundred thousand persons from all parts of the country attended the ceremony. Edward Everett's address lasted for two hours and exhausted all the arts of oratory. Naturally the brevity of Lincoln's succeeding remarks paralyzed the crowd, which had scarcely begun to concentrate on his words when he sat down. The most authentic reports indicate that disappointment in the speech was general and that it was not until enthusiastic praise began to appear in British and other foreign reviews that this country realized the power and beauty contained in the brief span of words.

Four score and seven years ago our fathers brought forth on this continent a new nation, conceived in liberty, and dedicated to the proposition that all men are created equal.

Now we are engaged in a great civil war, testing whether that nation, or any nation so conceived and so dedicated, can long endure. We are met on a great battlefield of that war. We have come to dedicate a portion of that field as a final resting-place for those who here gave their lives that that nation might live. It is altogether fitting and proper that we should do this.

But in a larger sense we cannot dedicate, we cannot consecrate, we cannot hallow this ground. The brave men, living and dead, who struggled here have consecrated it, far above our poor power to add or detract. The world will little note nor long remember what we say here, but it can never forget what they did here. It is for us, the living, rather, to be dedicated here to the unfinished work which they who fought here have thus far so nobly advanced. It is rather for us to be here dedicated to the great task remaining before us — that from these honored dead we take increased devotion to that cause for which they gave the last full measure of devotion; that we here highly resolve that these dead shall not have died in vain; that this nation, under God, shall have a new birth of freedom; and that government of the people, by the people, and for the people, shall not perish from the earth.

SUGGESTIONS FOR STUDY

1. Read the address until you feel you " possess " it. It has a message for " us, the living " today.

2. Since so much controversy has gathered around the circumstances of the writing and delivery of this address, it would be interesting to have class reports on some of the varying accounts. Most persons gain their impressions of the circumstances of this speech from Mary Raymond Shipman Andrews's story " The Perfect Tribute," but unfortunately that story is fiction and many of its details are not true historically. The best accounts are *Lincoln at Gettysburg,* by Clark E. Carr, one of the commissioners of the cemetery, and Chapter XV of Vol. II of William E. Barton's *Life of Abraham Lincoln.* Both of these summarize the various bits of evidence, especially that from an article by John G. Nicolay in the *Century Magazine,* February 1894. A fiction story of the famous occasion is " November Nineteenth " by Elsie Singmaster, based on a tradition current in the neighborhood that Lincoln rode on a small horse.

SECOND INAUGURAL ADDRESS

MARCH 4, 1865

By ABRAHAM LINCOLN (1809–1865)

The morning of Lincoln's second inauguration was cold and stormy, but at noon the sun came out as the procession moved with dignity from the White House. Numbers of wounded soldiers were conspicuous in the great throng. The following comment upon the Second Inaugural Address was made by the London *Spectator* after the President's death: " We cannot read it without a renewed conviction that it is the noblest political document known to history, and should have for the nation and the statesmen he left behind him something of a sacred and almost prophetic character." The last paragraph of this speech and the entire Gettysburg Address are inscribed on opposite walls of the beautiful Lincoln Memorial at Washington.

Fellow-countrymen: At this second appearing to take the oath of the presidential office, there is less occasion for an extended address than there was at the first. Then a statement, somewhat in detail, of a course to be pursued, seemed fitting and proper. Now, at the expiration of four years, during which public declarations have been constantly called forth on every point and phase of the great contest which still absorbs the attention and engrosses the energies of the nation, little that is new could be presented. The progress of our arms, upon which all else chiefly depends, is as well known to the public as to myself; and it is, I trust, reasonably satisfactory and encouraging to all. With high hope for the future, no prediction in regard to it is ventured.

On the occasion corresponding to this four years ago, all thoughts were anxiously directed to an impending civil war. All dreaded it — all sought to avert it. While the inaugural address was being delivered from this place, devoted altogether to saving the Union without war, insurgent agents were in the city seeking to destroy it without war — seeking to dissolve the Union, and divide effects, by negotiation. Both parties deprecated war; but one of them would make war rather than let the nation survive; and the other would accept war rather than let it perish. And the war came.

One eighth of the whole population were colored slaves, not distributed generally over the Union, but localized in the southern part of it. These slaves constituted a peculiar and powerful interest. All knew that this interest was, somehow, the cause of the war. To strengthen, perpetuate, and extend this interest was the object for which the insurgents would rend the Union, even by war; while the government claimed no right to do more than to restrict the territorial enlargement of it.

Neither party expected for the war the magnitude or the duration which it has already attained. Neither anticipated that the cause of the conflict might cease with, or even before, the conflict itself should cease. Each looked for an easier triumph and a result less fundamental and astounding. Both read the same Bible, and pray to the same God; and each invokes His aid against the other. It may seem strange that any men should dare to ask a just God's assistance in wringing their bread from the sweat of other men's faces; but let us judge not, that we be not judged.[1] The prayers of both could not be answered — that of neither has been answered fully.

The Almighty has his own purposes. "Woe unto the world because of offenses! for it must needs be that offenses come; but woe to that man by whom the offense cometh."[2] If we shall suppose that American slavery is one of those offenses which in

[1] Matthew vii: 1.   [2] Matthew xviii: 7.

the providence of God, must needs come, but which, having continued through his appointed time, He now wills to remove, and that He gives to both North and South this terrible war, as the woe due to those by whom the offense came, shall we discern therein any departure from those divine attributes which the believers in a living God always ascribe to Him? Fondly do we hope — fervently do we pray — that this mighty scourge of war may speedily pass away. Yet, if God wills that it continue until all the wealth piled by the bondman's two hundred and fifty years of unrequited toil shall be sunk, and until every drop of blood drawn with the lash shall be paid by another drawn with the sword, as was said three thousand years ago, still it must be said, "The judgments of the Lord are true and righteous altogether." [3]

With malice toward none; with charity for all; with firmness in the right, as God gives us to see the right, let us strive on to finish the work we are in; to bind up the nation's wounds; to care for him who shall have borne the battle, and for his widow and his orphan — to do all which may achieve and cherish a just and lasting peace among ourselves, and with all nations.

FOR FURTHER READING ON ABRAHAM LINCOLN

Important biographies in order of their publication are as follows:

William H. Herndon, *Life of Lincoln* (1888)
Nicolay and Hay, *Life of Abraham Lincoln,* 10 volumes (1890)
Lord Charnwood, *Abraham Lincoln* (1916)
Ida M. Tarbell, *Life of Abraham Lincoln* (1916)
William E. Barton, *Life of Abraham Lincoln* (1925)
Carl Sandburg, *Abraham Lincoln, The Prairie Years* (1926)
Albert J. Beveridge, *Abraham Lincoln; 1809–1858* (1928)

Popular lives for young people are:

Helen Nicolay, *The Boy's Life of Abraham Lincoln*
Ida M. Tarbell, *Boy Scouts' Life of Lincoln*
Carl Sandburg, *Abe Lincoln Grows Up*
W. M. Thayer, *Abraham Lincoln, the Pioneer Boy*
C. C. Coffin, *Abraham Lincoln*
E. S. Brooks, *The True Story of Abraham Lincoln the American*
W. O. Stoddard, *The Boy Lincoln*

[3] Psalms xix: 9.

No single American has been the subject of so much writing as Abraham Lincoln. A bibliography made in 1925 contained 2680 separate items including writing of all sorts. Some of the best-known pieces of fiction, drama, and poetry about him are as follows:

Fiction

Ida M. Tarbell, " He Knew Lincoln "
Mary Raymond Shipman Andrews, " The Perfect Tribute "
———, " The Counsel Assigned "
Elsie Singmaster, " November Nineteenth "
Irving Bacheller, *A Man for the Ages*
Honoré M. Willsie, *Forever Free*

Drama

John Drinkwater, *Abraham Lincoln*

Poetry

William Cullen Bryant, " To the Memory of Abraham Lincoln "
James Russell Lowell, " Commemoration Ode " (Stanza VI)
Oliver Wendell Holmes, " Hymn on the Death of Lincoln "
Walt Whitman, " O Captain, My Captain! "
——— " Hush'd Be the Camps Today "
——— " When Lilacs Last in the Dooryard Bloomed "
Julia Ward Howe, " Crown His Blood-Stained Pillow "
Phoebe Cary, " Our Sun Hath Gone Down "
Lucy Larcom, " Tolling "
Richard Watson Gilder, " On the Life Mask of Abraham Lincoln "
Bayard Taylor, " The Gettysburg Ode " (Part)
Richard Henry Stoddard, " Abraham Lincoln "
Edwin Markham, " Lincoln, the Man of the People "
Edwin Arlington Robinson, " The Master "
Vachel Lindsay, " Abraham Lincoln Walks at Midnight "
Witter Bynner, " A Farmer Remembers Lincoln "
James Oppenheim, " The Lincoln Child "
John Gould Fletcher, " Lincoln "
Stephen Vincent Benét, " John Brown's Body " (Parts)

World War

THE WAR MESSAGE TO CONGRESS

APRIL 2, 1917

By WOODROW WILSON (1856–1924)

President Woodrow Wilson had passed little more than a year in the White House when in the summer of 1914 the World War began. Within a few weeks' time five of the greatest European powers had become involved, and lesser nations were later drawn in. The preservation of American neutrality in the face of a European upheaval caused President Wilson even more difficulty than it had Washington a century earlier. A vast number of immigrants from all the countries at war had become American citizens or lived here as though they were citizens. Nothing was more natural than that they should have sympathies for their home country as well as love for that of their adoption. In spite of much feeling for or against either the Allies or Germany, the great body of American people thought that we should keep decidedly out of the struggle.

In Wilson's second campaign for election his party had used the slogan, " He kept us out of war." Between the election and his second inauguration, however, events had so shaped themselves that the entrance of the United States into the war had become inevitable. For a man who had just been nationally hailed as the preserver of peace it was a delicate situation to have to propose a declaration of war to Congress and the nation. That the justice and necessity of the step might be made convincing, every circumstance had to be carefully explained and the principles governing our participation clearly set forth. Wilson was a master of language, and the following speech has already become one of the great documents of our nation. Four days after the message was spoken before Congress, war was declared by pronounced majorities.

I have called the Congress into extraordinary session because there are serious, very serious, choices of policy to be made, and made immediately, which it was neither right nor constitutionally permissible that I should assume the responsibility of making.

On the third of February last I officially laid before you the extraordinary announcement of the Imperial German Government that on and after the first day of February it was its purpose to put aside all restraints of law or of humanity and use its submarines to sink every vessel that sought to approach either the ports of Great Britain and Ireland or the western coasts of Europe or any of the ports controlled by the enemies of Germany within the Mediterranean. That had seemed to be the object of the German submarine warfare earlier in the war, but since April of last year the Imperial Government had somewhat restrained the commanders of its undersea craft in conformity with its promise then given to us that passenger boats should not be sunk and that due warning would be given to all other vessels which its submarines might seek to destroy, when no resistance was offered or escape attempted, and care taken that their crews were given at least a fair chance to save their lives in their open boats. The precautions taken were meager and haphazard enough, as was proved in distressing instance after instance in the progress of the cruel and unmanly business, but a certain degree of restraint was observed.

The new policy has swept every restriction aside. Vessels of every kind, whatever their flag, their character, their cargo, their destination, their errand, have been ruthlessly sent to the bottom without warning and without thought of help or mercy for those on board, the vessels of friendly neutrals along with those of belligerents. Even hospital ships and ships carrying relief to the sorely bereaved and stricken people of Belgium, though the latter were provided with safe conduct through the proscribed areas by the German Government itself and were distinguished by unmistakable marks of identity, have been sunk with the same reckless lack of compassion or of principle.

I was for a little while unable to believe that such things would in fact be done by any government that had hitherto subscribed to the humane practices of civilized nations. International law had its origin in the attempt to set up some law which would be respected and observed upon the seas, where no nation had right of dominion and where lay the free highways of the world. By painful stage after stage has that law been built up, with meager enough results, indeed, after all was accomplished that could be accomplished, but always with a clear view, at least, of what the heart and conscience of mankind demanded. This minimum of right the German Government has swept aside under the plea of retaliation and necessity and because it had no weapons which it could use at sea except these which it is impossible to employ as it is employing them without throwing to the winds all scruples of humanity or of respect for the world. I am not now thinking of the loss of property involved, immense and serious as that is, but only of the wanton and wholesale destruction of the lives of non-combatants, men, women, and children, engaged in pursuits which have always, even in the darkest periods of modern history, been deemed innocent and legitimate. Property can be paid for; the lives of peaceful and innocent people cannot be. The present German submarine warfare against commerce is a warfare against mankind.

It is a war against all nations. American ships have been sunk, American lives taken, in ways which it has stirred us very deeply to learn of, but the ships and people of other neutral and friendly nations have been sunk and overwhelmed in the waters in the same way. There has been no discrimination. The challenge is to all mankind. Each nation must decide for itself how it will meet it. The choice we make for ourselves must be made with a moderation of counsel and a temperateness of judgment befitting our character and our motives as a nation. We must put excited feeling away. Our motive will not be revenge or the victorious assertion of the physical might of the nation, but only the vindication of right, of human right, of which we are only a single champion.

When I addressed the Congress on the twenty-sixth of February last I thought that it would suffice to assert our neutral rights with arms, our right to keep our people safe against unlawful violence. But armed neutrality, it now appears, is impracticable. Because submarines are in effect outlaws when used as the German submarines have been used against merchant shipping, it is impossible to defend ships against their attacks as the law of nations has assumed that merchantmen would defend themselves against privateers or cruisers, visible craft giving chase upon the open sea.

It is common prudence in such circumstances, grim necessity indeed, to endeavor to destroy them before they have shown their own intention. They must be dealt with upon sight, if dealt with at all. The German Government denies the right of neutrals to use arms at all within the areas of the sea which it has proscribed, even in the defense of rights which no modern publicist has ever before questioned their right to defend. The intimation is conveyed that the armed guards which we have placed on our merchant ships will be treated as beyond the pale of law and subject to be dealt with as pirates would be. Armed neutrality is ineffectual enough at best; in such circumstances and in the face of such pretensions it is worse than ineffectual: it is likely only to produce what it was meant to prevent; it is practically certain to draw us into the war without either the rights or the effectiveness of belligerents.

There is one choice we cannot make, we are incapable of making; we will not choose the path of submission and suffer the most sacred rights of our nation and our people to be ignored or violated. The wrongs against which we now array ourselves are no common wrongs; they cut to the very roots of human life.

With a profound sense of the solemn and even tragical character of the step I am taking and of the grave responsibilities which it involves, but in unhesitating obedience to what I deem my constitutional duty, I advise that the Congress declare the recent course of the Imperial German Government to be in fact nothing less than war against the government and people of the United States; that it formally accept the status of belligerent which has thus been thrust upon it; and that it take immediate steps not only to put the country in a more thorough state of defense but also to exert all its power and employ all its resources to bring the Government of the German Empire to terms and end the war.

What this will involve is clear. It will involve the utmost practicable coöperation in counsel and action with the governments now at war with Germany, and, as incident to that, the extension to those governments of the most liberal financial credits, in order that our resources may so far as possible be added to theirs. It will involve the organization and mobilization of all the material resources of the country to supply the materials of war and serve the incidental needs of the nation in the most abundant and yet the most economical and efficient way possible. It will involve the immediate full equipment of the navy in all respects but particularly in supplying it with the best means of dealing with the enemy's submarines. It will involve the immediate addition to the armed forces of the United States already provided for by law in case of war of at least five hundred thousand men, who should, in my opinion, be chosen upon the principle of universal liability to service, and also the authorization of subsequent additional increments of equal force so soon as they may be needed and can be handled in training. It will involve also, of course, the granting of adequate credits to the Government, sustained, I hope, so far as they can equitably be sustained by the present generation, by well conceived taxation.

I say sustained so far as may be equitable by taxation because it seems to me that it would be most unwise to base the credits which will now be necessary entirely on money borrowed. It is our duty, I most respectfully urge, to protect our people so far as we may against the very serious hardships and evils which would be likely to arise out of the inflation which would be produced by vast loans.

In carrying out the measures by which these things are to be accomplished we should keep constantly in mind the wisdom of interfering as little as possible in our own preparation and in the equipment of our own military forces with the duty — for it will be a very practical duty — of supplying the nations already at war with Germany with the materials which they can obtain only from us or by our assistance. They are in the field and we should help them in every way to be effective there.

I shall take the liberty of suggesting, through the several executive departments of the Government, for the consideration of your committees, measures for the accomplishment of the several objects I have mentioned. I hope that it will be your pleasure to deal with them as having been framed after very careful thought by the branch of the Government upon which the responsibility of conducting the war and safeguarding the nation will most directly fall.

While we do these things, these deeply momentous things, let us be very clear, and make very clear to all the world, what our motives and our objects are. My own thought has not been driven from its habitual and normal course by the unhappy events of the last two months, and I do not believe that the thought of the nation has been altered or clouded by them. I have exactly the same things in mind now that I had in mind when I addressed the Senate on the twenty-second of January last; the same that I had in mind when I addressed the Congress on the third of February and on the twenty-sixth of February. Our object now, as then, is to vindicate the principles of peace and justice in the life of the world as against selfish and autocratic power, and to set up among the really free and self-governed peoples of the world such a concert of purpose and of action as will henceforth insure the observance of those principles.

Neutrality is no longer feasible or desirable where the peace of the world is involved and the freedom of its peoples, and the menace to that peace and freedom lies in the existence of autocratic governments backed by organized force which is controlled wholly by their will, not by the will of their people. We have seen the last of neutrality in such circumstances. We are at the beginning of an age in which it will be insisted that the same standards of conduct and of responsibility for wrong done shall be observed among nations and their governments that are observed among the individual citizens of civilized states.

We have no quarrel with the German people. We have no feeling towards them but one of sympathy and friendship. It was not upon their impulse that their government acted in entering this war. It was not with their previous knowledge or approval. It was a war determined upon as wars used to be determined upon in the old, unhappy days when peoples were nowhere consulted by their rulers and wars were provoked and waged in the interest of dynasties or of little groups of ambitious men who were accustomed to use their fellow men as pawns and tools. Self-governed nations do not fill their neighbor states with spies or set the course of intrigue to bring about some critical posture of affairs which will give them an opportunity to strike and make conquest. Such designs can be successfully worked out only under cover and where no one has the right to ask questions. Cunningly contrived plans of deception or aggression, carried, it may be, from generation to generation, can be worked out and kept from the light only within the privacy of courts or behind the carefully guarded confidences of a narrow and privileged class. They are happily impossible where public opinion commands and insists upon full information concerning all the nation's affairs.

A steadfast concert for peace can never be maintained except by a partnership of democratic nations. No autocratic government could be trusted to keep faith within it or observe its covenants. It must be a league of honor, a partnership of opinion. Intrigue would eat its vitals away; the plottings of inner circles who could plan what they would and render account to no one would be a corruption seated at its very heart. Only free peoples can hold their purpose and their honor steady to a common end and prefer the interests of mankind to any narrow interest of their own.

Does not every American feel that assurance has been added to our hope for the future peace of the world by the wonderful and heartening things that have been happening within the last few weeks in Russia? Russia was known by those who knew it best to have been always in fact democratic at heart, in all the vital habits of her thought, in all the intimate relationships of her people that spoke their natural instinct, their habitual attitude towards life. The autocracy that crowned the summit of her political structure, long as it had stood and terrible as was the reality of its power, was not in fact Russian in origin, character, or purpose; and now it has been shaken off and the great, generous Russian people have been added in all their naïve majesty and might to the forces that are fighting for freedom in the world, for justice, and for peace. Here is a fit partner for a League of Honor.

One of the things that has served to convince us that the Prussian autocracy was not and could never be our friend is that from the very outset of the present war it has filled our unsuspecting communities and even our offices of government with spies and set criminal intrigues everywhere afoot against our national unity of counsel, our peace within and without, our industries and our commerce. Indeed it is now evident that its spies were here even before the war began; and it is unhappily not a matter of conjecture but a fact proved in our courts of justice that the intrigues which have more than once come perilously near to disturbing the peace and dislocating the industries of the country have been carried on at the instigation, with the support, and even under the personal direction of official agents of the Imperial Government accredited to the Government of the United States. Even in checking these things and trying to extirpate them we have sought to put the most generous interpretation possible upon them because we knew that their source lay, not in any hostile feeling or purpose of the German people towards us (who were, no doubt, as ignorant of them as we ourselves were), but only in the selfish designs of a Government that did what it pleased and told its people nothing. But they played their part in serving to convince us at last that that Government entertains no real friendship for us and means to act against our peace and security at its convenience. That it means to stir up enemies against us at our very doors the intercepted note to the German Minister at Mexico City is eloquent evidence.

We are accepting this challenge of hostile purpose because we know that in such a government, following such methods, we can never have a friend; and that in the presence of its organized power, always lying in wait to accomplish we know not what purpose, there can be no assured security for the democratic governments of the world. We are now about to accept gauge of battle with this natural foe to liberty, and shall, if necessary, spend the whole force of the nation to check and nullify its pretensions and its power. We are glad, now that we see the facts with no veil of false pretense about them, to fight thus for the ultimate peace of the world and for the liberation of its peoples, the German peoples included: for the rights of nations great and small and the privilege of men everywhere to choose their way of life and of obedience.

The world must be made safe for democracy. Its peace must be planted upon the tested foundations of political liberty. We must have no selfish ends to serve. We desire no conquest, no dominion. We seek no indemnities for ourselves, no material compensation for the sacrifices we shall freely make. We are but one of the champions of the rights of mankind. We shall be satisfied when those rights have been made as secure as the faith and the freedom of nations can make them.

Just because we fight without rancor and without selfish object, seeking nothing for ourselves but what we shall wish to share with all free peoples, we shall, I feel confident, conduct our operations as belligerents without passion and ourselves observe with proud punctilio the principles of right and of fair play we profess to be fighting for.

I have said nothing of the governments allied with the Imperial Government of Germany because they have not made war upon us or challenged us to defend our right and our honor. The Austro-Hungarian Government has, indeed, avowed its unqualified indorsement and acceptance of the reckless and lawless submarine warfare adopted now without disguise by the Imperial German Government, and it has therefore not been possible for this Government to receive Count Tarnowski, the Ambassador recently accredited to this Government by the Imperial and Royal Government of Austria-Hungary; but that Government has not actually engaged in warfare against citizens of the United States on the seas, and I take the liberty, for the present at least, of postponing a discussion of our relations with the authorities at Vienna. We enter this war only where we are clearly forced into it because there are no other means of defending our rights.

It will be all the easier for us to conduct ourselves as belligerents in a high spirit of right and fairness because we act without animus, not in enmity towards a people or with the desire to bring any injury or disadvantage upon them, but only in armed opposition to an irresponsible government which has thrown aside all considerations of humanity and of right and is running amuck. We are, let me say again, the sincere friends of the German people, and shall desire nothing so much as the early reëstablishment of intimate relations of mutual advantage between us — however hard it may be for them, for the time being, to believe that this is spoken from our hearts. We have borne with their present government through all these bitter months because of that friendship — exercising a patience and forbearance which would otherwise have been impossible. We shall, happily, still have an opportunity to prove that friendship in our daily attitude and actions towards the millions of men and women of German birth and native sympathy who live among us and share our life, and we shall be proud to prove it towards all who are in fact loyal to their neighbors and to the Government in the hour of test. They are, most of them, as true and loyal Americans as if they had never known any other fealty or allegiance. They will be prompt to stand with us in rebuking and restraining the few who may be of a different mind and purpose. If there should be disloyalty, it will be dealt with with a firm hand of stern repression; but, if it lifts its head at all, it will lift it only here and there and without countenance except from a lawless and malignant few.

It is a distressing and oppressive duty, Gentlemen of the Congress, which I have performed in thus addressing you. There are, it may be, many months of fiery trial and sacrifice ahead of us. It is a fearful thing to lead this great peaceful people into war, into the most terrible and disastrous of all wars, civilization itself seeming to be in the balance. But the right is more precious than peace, and we shall fight for the things which we have always carried nearest our hearts — for democracy, for the right of those who submit to authority to have a voice in their own governments, for the rights and liberties of small nations, for a universal dominion of right by such a concert of free peoples as shall bring peace and safety to all nations and make the world itself at last free. To such a task we can dedicate our lives and our fortunes, everything that we are and everything that we have, with the pride of those who know that the day has come when America is privileged to spend her blood and her might for the principles that gave her birth and happiness and the peace which she has treasured. God helping her, she can do no other.

SUGGESTIONS FOR STUDY

1. Make a list of the immediate causes of the declaration of war as enumerated by President Wilson.

2. What specific plans for carrying on the war does he outline?

3. Mark passages in which he speaks of the spirit with which we should enter the war. How does his attitude compare with that of Patrick Henry? Of the Declaration of Independence?

4. What difference is there in Wilson's attitude toward the German Government and the German people? Compare the tone of the last two paragraphs with that of the end of Lincoln's Second Inaugural Address. It is of rather pathetic significance that in both cases our nation as a whole fell far short of the nobility of spirit indicated by its chief spokesmen, but this only serves to accentuate by contrast the loftiness of their visions.

A LEAGUE FOR PEACE

JANUARY 22, 1917

By WOODROW WILSON (1856–1924)

This speech, of which the first third is here omitted, was delivered before the Senate over two months before the War Message, but is here put last because it is the clearest statement made by President Wilson of the great forward-looking principles governing world peace. Although the United States refused to accept the detailed plan for the League of Nations which President Wilson fostered, although attempts at disarmament have so far proved unsuccessful, although world peace is far from being an established fact in the world today, nevertheless the principles here stated are at work, and have largely overthrown the old principle of the balance of power among nations which governed the eighteenth and nineteenth centuries. In this sense it is perhaps not too extravagant to say as did one of Wilson's admirers that this address is the " most important pronouncement of an American president since the Monroe Doctrine."

The equality of nations upon which peace must be founded if it is to last must be an equality of rights; the guarantees exchanged must neither recognize nor imply a difference between big nations and small, between those that are powerful and those that are weak. Right must be based upon the common strength, not upon the individual strength, of the nations upon whose concert peace will depend. Equality of territory or of resources there of course cannot be; nor any other sort of equality not gained in the ordinary peaceful and legitimate development of the peoples themselves. But no one asks or expects anything more than an equality of rights. Mankind is looking now for freedom of life, not for equipoises of power.

And there is a deeper thing involved than even equality of right among organized nations. No peace can last, or ought to last, which does not recognize and accept the principle that governments derive all their just powers from the consent of the governed, and that no right anywhere exists to hand peoples about from sovereignty to sovereignty as if they were property. I take it for granted, for instance, if I may venture upon a single example, that statesmen everywhere are agreed that there should be a united, independent, and autonomous Poland; and that henceforth inviolable security of life, of worship, and of industrial and social development should be guaranteed to all peoples who have lived hitherto under the power of governments devoted to a faith and purpose hostile to their own.

I speak of this, not because of any desire to exalt an abstract political principle which has always been held very dear by those who have sought to build up liberty in America, but for the same reason that I have spoken of the other conditions of peace which seem to me clearly indispensable — because I wish frankly to uncover realities. Any peace which does not recognize and accept this principle will inevitably be upset. It will not rest upon the affections or the convictions of mankind. The ferment of spirit of whole populations will fight subtly and constantly against it, and all the world will sympathize. The world can be at peace only if its life is stable, and there can be no stability where the will is in rebellion, where there is not tranquillity of spirit and a sense of justice, of freedom, and of right.

So far as practicable, moreover, every great people now struggling towards a full development of its resources and of its powers should be assured a direct outlet to the great highways of the sea. Where this cannot be done by the cession of territory, it can no doubt be done by the neutralization of direct rights of way under the general guarantee which will assure the peace itself. With a right comity of arrangement no nation need be shut away from free access to the open paths of the world's commerce.

And the paths of the sea must alike in law and in fact be free. The freedom of the seas is the *sine qua non* [1] of peace, equality, and coöperation. No doubt a somewhat radical reconsideration of many of the rules of international practice hitherto thought to be established may be necessary in order to make the seas indeed free and common in practically all circumstances for the use of mankind, but the motive for such changes is convincing and compelling. There can be no trust or intimacy between the peoples of the world without them. The free, constant, unthreatened intercourse of nations is an essential part of the process of peace and of development. It need not be difficult either to define or to secure the freedom of the seas if the governments of the world sincerely desire to come to an agreement concerning it.

It is a problem closely connected with the limitation of naval armaments and the coöperation of the navies of the world in keep-

---

[1] Latin for " without which not "; that is, something absolutely necessary.

ing the seas at once free and safe. And the question of limiting naval armaments opens the wider and perhaps more difficult question of the limitation of armies, and of all programs of military preparation. Difficult and delicate as these questions are, they must be faced with the utmost candor and decided in a spirit of real accommodation, if peace is to come with healing in its wings, and come to stay. Peace cannot be had without concession and sacrifice. There can be no sense of safety and equality among the nations if great preponderating armaments are henceforth to continue here and there to be built up and maintained. The statesmen of the world must plan for peace, and nations must adjust and accommodate their policy to it as they have planned for war and made ready for pitiless contest and rivalry. The question of armaments, whether on land or sea, is the most immediately and intensely practical question connected with the future fortunes of nations and of mankind.

I have spoken upon these great matters without reserve and with the utmost explicitness because it has seemed to me to be necessary if the world's yearning desire for peace was anywhere to find free voice and utterance. Perhaps I am the only person in high authority amongst all the peoples of the world who is at liberty to speak and hold nothing back. I am speaking as an individual, and yet I am speaking also, of course, as the responsible head of a great Government, and I feel confident that I have said what the people of the United States would wish me to say. May I not add that I hope and believe that I am in effect speaking for liberals and friends of humanity in every nation and of every program of liberty? I would fain believe that I am speaking for the silent mass of mankind everywhere who have as yet had no place or opportunity to speak their real hearts out concerning the death and ruin which they see has come already upon the persons and the homes they hold most dear.

And in holding out the expectation that the people and Government of the United States will join the other civilizations of the world in guaranteeing the permanence of peace upon such terms as I have named, I speak with the greater boldness and confidence because it is clear to every man who can think that there is in this promise no breach in either our traditions or our policy as a nation, but a fulfilment, rather, of all that we have professed or striven for.

I am proposing, as it were, that the nations should with one accord adopt the doctrine of President Monroe [2] as the doctrine of the world; that no nation should seek to extend its polity over any other nation or people, but that every people should be left free to determine its own polity, its own way of development, un-hindered, unthreatened, unafraid, the little along with the great and powerful.

I am proposing that all nations henceforth avoid entangling alliances [3] which would draw them into competitions of power, catch them in a net of intrigue and selfish rivalry, and disturb their own affairs with influences intruded from without. There is no entangling alliance in a concert of power. When all unite to act in the same sense and with the same purpose, all act in the common interest and are free to live their own lives under a common protection.

I am proposing government by the consent of the governed; that freedom of the seas which in international conference after conference representatives of the United States have urged with the eloquence of those who are the convinced disciples of liberty; and that moderation of armaments which makes of armies and navies a power for order merely, not an instrument of aggression or of selfish violence.

These are American principles, American policies. We could stand for no others. And they are also the principles and policies of forward-looking men and women everywhere, of every modern nation, of every enlightened community. They are the principles of mankind and must prevail.

SUGGESTIONS FOR STUDY

1. Vocabulary: equipoises, autonomous, inviolable, comity, prepon-derating.

2. In the second paragraph Poland is mentioned as an example. An interesting special report in class would be a brief account of the various partitions of Poland, among the nations in the past, and what restitution was made after the World War.

3. Find out what various conferences on disarmament have been held

[2] In 1823 President Monroe stated that the United States would not tolerate any attempt of European countries to do further colonization, or to oppress or control in any other manner the destiny of the independent govern-ments of the Western Hemisphere. See page 475.

[3] The phrase had been first used by Thomas Jefferson in his Inaugural Address, but the idea of course goes back to Washington's Farewell Address.

since the World War, and what the situation is today. The subject of
disarmament affords opportunity for a good class debate.

4. Look up the origin and development of the League of Nations, and
the part played in it by the United States.

5. Look up the proposed World Court and find out the latest developments.

6. For reading on the life of Wilson you will find the following books
valuable: W. E. Dodd, *Woodrow Wilson and His Work;* William Allen
White, *Woodrow Wilson;* Lucian L. Knight, *Woodrow Wilson, The
Dreamer and the Dream;* Ray Stannard Baker, *Life and Letters of Woodrow Wilson.*

World Peace

THE MONROE DOCTRINE

EXTRACT FROM PRESIDENT JAMES MONROE'S MESSAGE, DEC. 2, 1823

With the exception of the first of the Historic Milestones, all were concerned more or less with war. Washington in the " Farewell Address "
had asserted the policy of American non-interference in the affairs
of Europe, a policy which this country still holds to. On the other hand,
it has always been the part of the United States to take forward-looking
steps in the direction of world peace. When by the year 1822 the South
American countries had freed themselves from Spain and had been recognized by the United States as independent republics, there was a strong
sentiment in certain European countries to help Spain win them back,
and incidentally help themselves. This situation was the immediate cause
of the pronouncement of the Monroe Doctrine, for the most part in the
dignified and stately language of John Quincy Adams, Monroe's Secretary
of State.

The occasion has been judged proper for asserting, as a principle . . . that the American continents, by the free and independent condition which they have assumed and maintain, are
henceforth not to be considered as subjects for future colonization by any European powers. . . .   The citizens of the United
States cherish sentiments the most friendly in favor of the liberty
and happiness of their fellow men on that side of the Atlantic. In
the wars of the European powers in matters relating to themselves we have never taken any part, nor does it comport with
our policy to do so. It is only when our rights are invaded or se-

riously menaced that we resent injuries or make preparation for defense. With the movements in this hemisphere we are of necessity more immediately connected, and by causes which must be obvious to all enlightened and impartial observers. The political system of the allied powers is essentially different in this respect from that of America. This difference proceeds from that which exists in their respective governments; and to the defense of our own, which has been achieved by the loss of so much blood and treasure, and matured by the wisdom of their most enlightened citizens, and under which we have enjoyed unexampled felicity, this whole nation is devoted. We owe it, therefore, to candor and to the amicable relations existing between the United States and those powers to declare that we should consider any attempt on their part to extend their system to any portion of this hemisphere as dangerous to our peace and safety. With the existing colonies or dependencies of any European power we have not interfered and shall not interfere. But with the governments who have declared their independence and maintained it, and whose independence we have, on great consideration and on just principles, acknowledged, we could not view any interposition for the purpose of oppressing them, or controlling in any other manner their destiny, by any European power in any other light than as the manifestation of an unfriendly disposition toward the United States.

PRESIDENT CLEVELAND AND THE VENEZUELA BOUNDARY

The Monroe Doctrine had been called forth by the attitude of certain European nations towards the newly established republics of South America. In 1841 a dispute arose about a boundary line between Venezuela and British Guiana, and this continued, in spite of many efforts on the part of Venezuela to come to an agreement, until 1899. For a number of years the United States tried to get England to arbitrate, but to no avail. Developments at last led to a point where the United States had to tell England frankly that if she continued to press her claims upon Venezuelan territory it would be necessary for this country to invoke the principles of the Monroe Doctrine. After an exchange of many fruitless communications, President Grover Cleveland finally made the following statement in a message to Congress, December, 1895.

It may not be amiss to suggest that the doctrine upon which we stand is strong and sound, because its enforcement is important to our peace and safety as a nation, and is essential to the integrity of our free institutions and the tranquil maintenance of our distinctive form of government. It was intended to apply to every stage of our national life, and cannot become obsolete while our Republic endures. If the balance of power is justly a cause for jealous anxiety among the governments of the Old World and a subject for our absolute non-interference, none the less is the observance of the Monroe Doctrine of vital concern to our people and their Government. . . .

When such a report is made and accepted, it will, in my opinion, be the duty of the United States to resist by every means in its power, as a wilful aggression upon its rights and interests, the appropriation by Great Britain of any lands or the exercise of governmental jurisdiction over any territory which after investigation we have determined of right belongs to Venezuela.

THE PEACE PACT

By FRANK B. KELLOGG (1856–   )

What may well turn out to be the most significant milestone in the road to international peace is the so-called Paris Peace Pact, sponsored and promoted in this country by Frank B. Kellogg, Secretary of State under President Coolidge. It was signed in Paris on the twenty-eighth of August, 1928, and has since been accepted officially or by intention by nearly fifty of the world's governments.

Article I. The High Contracting Parties solemnly declare in the names of their respective peoples that they condemn recourse to war for the solution of international controversies, and renounce it as an instrument of national policy in their relations with one another.'
Article II. The High Contracting Parties agree that the settlement or solution of all disputes or conflicts of whatever nature or of whatever origin they may be which may arise among them shall never be sought except by pacific means.

FOR FURTHER READING OF SPEECHES

The following collections will help you to find further speeches of persons already mentioned and of numerous other prominent orators such as Daniel Webster, Henry Clay, William Jennings Bryan, Theodore Roosevelt, Elihu Root, and Franklin P. Lane.

Baker, E. W. *Great Speeches*
Blackstone. *The Best American Orations of Today*
Boardman, L. W. *Modern American Speeches*
Cody, Sherwin. *A Selection from the World's Greatest Orations*
Denny, J. V. *American Public Addresses*
Foerster and Pearson. *American Ideals*
Gauss, Christian. *Democracy Today*
Greenlaw, Edwin. *Builders of Democracy*
Long, A. W. *American Patriotic Prose*
O'Neill, J. M. *Modern Short Speeches*
Ringwalt, R. C. *American Oratory*
Shurter, E. D. *Masterpieces of Modern Oratory*
Speare and Norris. *Vital Forces in Current Events*
St. John and Noonan. *Landmarks of Liberty*
Stratton, Clarence. *Great American Speeches*
Watkins and Williams. *The Forum of Democracy*

Folk Literature

Many fascinating pieces of literature have not been created by individual authors, but, like Topsy, have " just growed." Even before there were any books, there were skilful story-tellers. Every heroic deed, every great battle, every romantic adventure was seized upon by the early bards as material for tales with which to while away the hours of leisure around the camp fire or in the great castles of the feudal barons. These stories, passed from one yarn-spinner to another, grew in strength and beauty, until finally some genius, usually a poet, told or sang the story so well that ever afterwards succeeding bards used many of his exact phrases and expressions. Thus the story assumed a definite form, was later written down, and became a part of our literary inheritance.

Such literature is called folk literature. Combined with the melodies, the dances, the drawings, and the religious ceremonies of any primitive people, it makes up folk lore, the name applied to the whole body of art and custom, the origin of which is too remote to be credited to known individuals.

We are so accustomed to think of folk literature in terms of ballad singers and medieval romance that it is somewhat startling to realize that there is much fascinating folk literature in America. Of course, we have inherited all the English folk tales and songs; and in America, especially among the Appalachian Mountain people, these have gone on developing with a peculiarly American twist; but, after all, these are still essentially English. There is, however, much folk literature in America which is our very own, the product of New World environments which were at least sufficiently like those of olden times to furnish the ingredients for the folk story or song. This either has been collected, or is being collected, and forms one of the most interesting sections of American literature.

The Negro Contribution.

The Negro quarters on the old southern plantations were ideal for the development of folk dance, song, and story. The tales that these uneducated slaves created for their own entertainment and with no thought of books or " the public," are charming revelations of their ideas, ideals, and shrewd insight into human nature. Joel Chandler Harris, who absorbed these stories from Negro mammies when a boy, first conceived the idea of recording them. He has put them into the mouth of an old darkey, Uncle Remus; but the " Uncle Remus stories " are not really a literary creation; they are rather recorded folk lore, and should be read from that point of view. The Negro religious songs are known as " spirituals," and their melodies are recognized as a real contribution to the world's music. The words are real folk lyrics, revealing the longings and aspirations of a whole race, looking beyond the bonds of slavery to a " home over Jordan," where the sorrows of this world would be no more. A recent novel and play, *Porgy*, by Dubose Heyward, vividly portrays the creation of these songs, showing how sorrow for a death, or fear of a great tornado, naturally found expression in song. When the song was good enough, it lived on.

The Lumberjacks

The lumberjacks, or shanty-boys, have also contributed both song and story to our literature. As the great army of lumberjacks have moved across our country from Maine to Washington, they have among them developed the great Paul Bunyan legend, so that America need not yield precedence to any nation when heroic deeds are mentioned. For what Odysseus, or Aeneas, or Beowulf, or Roland ever outdid our Paul in titanic achievement? Moreover, when the sturdy Swede lumberjacks sat around the shanty stove in the evenings, in addition to their yarn-spinners, they cherished their fiddlers and singers, and created some songs which are genuine revelations of their feelings and attitudes. These, as well as the Paul Bunyan stories, have been collected for us.

Cowboys, Sailors, and Soldiers

The lonely cowboys riding after their cattle, the sailors of the old sailboat days, the soldiers of our various wars, even the prisoners in

the penitentiaries, have all developed a sort of " community literature " which is genuine folk lore, for it is not created by one literary
artist, but is the product of a whole succession of story-tellers and
singers, each of whom has added his bit to the story or song until it
has become a revelation of the spirit of the whole group. And if we
wish to become acquainted with the real cowboy, or sailor, or soldier,
how much wiser it is to read the literature he has himself created to
express himself than to go to literature written about him by some
outsider!

The Uncle Remus stories, the Paul Bunyan tales, the spirituals, the
cowboy songs, the war-time ditties of the training camp, are all real
parts of our American literature, and there is no part more revealing
or fascinating.

One final word. We sometimes hear stories or songs called " folk
lore " because everybody knows them and they are a part of our
common heritage. This is a mistake. " Way Down Upon the
Swanee River " is not a folk song, but the studied creation of Stephen
C. Foster. " Rip Van Winkle " is not a folk story, but a literary production of Washington Irving. It is based upon a folk legend, but it
is not a legend itself. True folk literature is the product of many
authors; it has not merely appealed to many hearts, but has actually
come from the hearts of a whole group and reveals a whole people as
no single author's work ever can.

AN AMERICAN HERCULES

By JAMES STEVENS (1892–   )

James Stevens, who worked for many months in Washington and
Oregon and Idaho lumber camps, was just the right person to put into
permanent form the Paul Bunyan saga. This he has done in his book,
Paul Bunyan, which records many of the greatest stories, including
" The Winter of the Blue Snow," " The Sourdough Drive," and " The
Black Duck Dinner," the greatest yarn of all. This feast was so satisfying
that after it not a single logger was able to appear for supper. One made
an effort: at the call for supper " he appeared in the door of a bunkhouse,
stared dully for a moment and then staggered back into the darkness."
After reading the descriptions of the groaning boards on this historic
occasion, we wonder only that even one man had the courage to make the
tiniest move towards more food that day.

In " An American Hercules " Mr. Stevens has written especially for
Adventures in American Literature an account of the manner in which

the Paul Bunyan legend has developed; he has followed this with a hitherto-unrecorded yarn, almost, if not quite, the equal of "The Black Duck Dinner." In the introduction to his book, *Paul Bunyan*, Mr. Stevens says: "A Paul Bunyan bunkhouse service is a glory to hear, when it is spontaneous and in a proper setting; preferably around a big heated stove in the winter, when the wind is howling through crackling boughs outside, and the pungent smell of steaming wood drifts down from the drying lines above the stove. When a vasty spirit of the woods really moves the meeting a noble and expansive ecstasy of the soul is exhibited."

Draw up your chair, stranger.

Paul Bunyan, the mythical hero of the lumberjacks, is the supreme figure of American folk lore. Paul was a Herculean logger who combed his beard with a young pine tree; who skidded his timber with Babe the Blue Ox, a creature so vast that he measured forty-two ax handles and a plug of chewing tobacco between the horns; who operated a camp cookhouse where the flapjack griddle was greased by twenty-four Arabs — imported from the Sahara Desert because they could stand the heat — skating to and fro with slabs of bacon strapped to their feet; who tamed the Mississippi when it was young and wild by building river corrals and driving the river through their gates (the Great Lakes remain as evidence of this feat); who ruled the American country in the period when it was only a timberland. This epoch, according to the best authorities, began with the Winter of the Blue Snow and ended with the Spring the Rain Came up from China.

Here, indeed, is a full-bodied myth. The Paul Bunyan stories have been told in American logging camps since 1840. They are unquestionably of Canadian origin. There was a Paul Bunyan who won fame in the Papineau Rebellion of 1837. There is no evidence that the beginnings of the stories are beyond him. The other materials and characters of the myth, were developed out of the magic of bunkhouse nights; when the workday in the woods, or on the iced road, or on the drive, was done; when the camp men, isolated from all life but that of the woods, had no other outlet for their fancies than the creation of romances about their own life.

Thus Paul Bunyan, Babe the Blue Ox, Johnny Inkslinger, the timekeeper who figured with a fountain pen fed by hose lines from twenty-four barrels of ink, Hels Helson, the Big Swede and bull of the woods, who muddied the Missouri River forever with one spring bath, and many smaller characters, such as Hot Biscuit Slim, the cook, Shanty Boy, the bard, and Big Ole, the blacksmith, have been celebrated in logging camps from Bangor, Maine, to Portland, Oregon. The tall tale, the "whopper," is not confined, of course, to the lumber camps. It appears with the earliest accounts of the Appalachian pioneers. It is forever present in the best writings of Mark Twain. Other mythical heroes have won a certain fame, such as Tony Beaver of the Virginia mountains and Pecos Bill, the Southwestern *vaquero* [1] who once straddled a cyclone and rode it to a finish. But the myth of Paul Bunyan stands alone, possessing, as it does, its own time, place, and people.

The stories are told in this manner:

Supper is over in the logging camp, and the after-supper period of smoking and quiet is also done. A murmur of talk about the day's work rises from the gang around the heating stove. There is a strong smell of steaming wool from the drying lines. Blue pipe smoke drifts through the mellow light of the Rochester burners. A gust of frosty air blows in whenever the bunkhouse door is opened. Some logger ventures the opinion that this will be the hardest winter this part of the country has ever known. Weather talk runs on until some one states solemnly that "the weather ain't what she used to be. Gettin' old now, the weather is. Take the Year of the Two Winters, in Paul Bunyan's time. Yes, sir. Then. That year two winters come all at once. . . ."

Then there is a contest to see who can tell the tallest tale about cold weather in the day of Paul Bunyan.

Or it is a summer night, and the loggers are circling a smudge fire outside the bunkhouse. Mosquitoes swarm up from the swamp below camp. So mosquito stories are in order. Any man is free to invent new Paul Bunyan yarns himself, or he can repeat the stories heard from other bards. Occasionally some bard is so inspired that his creation is never forgotten, and becomes a permanent addition to the Paul Bunyan myth. Such is the story of the mammoth mosquitoes and their amazing experiences with Bum and Bill, Paul Bunyan's battling bees.

Here is the story.

It was in the Year of the Dry Summer that Paul Bunyan's loggers first encountered mosquitoes. That was the season Paul

---

[1] Cow-puncher.

Bunyan invented thunder. Day after day, week after week, month after month, the great hero-leader of the loggers toiled through experiments with all the sounds he could imagine. Just as cows, pigs, dogs, hens and ducks could be called, so could clouds be called, thought Paul Bunyan. Seventeen thousand various kinds of calls the great logger tried that summer before he hit on the sound of thunder. Then his labors were rewarded. Paul Bunyan had not thundered once before a stray cloud rolled up from the west. He thundered on, and by midnight so many clouds had gathered that the Dry Summer ended in a downpour that was a deluge instead of a rain. Ever since that parched season the weather has used the thunder which Paul Bunyan invented for it.

But Paul Bunyan had other troubles during this wretched summer. Time and again he had to quit his important labor of trying out sounds that would call up clouds and attend to small bothers, plagues, and worries. The most troublesome of all these troubles was the invasion of mosquitoes.

The mammoth mosquitoes came from the Tall Wolf country. There the tribe had experienced a devastating famine. For the larger it grew, the smaller became the tribe of tall wolves, the mammoth mosquitoes' natural prey. Eventually the last tall wolf was gone, and only a small company of female mosquitoes was left from the once vast and powerful insect tribe. These females were forced by hunger into migration. They were ready to fall and perish from exhaustion when they reached Paul Bunyan's loggers, who, stripped to the waist, were at work even on this, the hottest of the Dry Summer's days.

Paul Bunyan was afar from his loggers at the moment, pondering deeply on the problem of calling up the clouds. He failed to notice when the ring of axes and the drone of saws were hushed. Not until agonizing yells arose from his loggers did the hero-leader realize that a new trouble had come to camp. Then he saw that his men were struggling for their lives all through the timber five miles away. Two strides and one leap, and Paul Bunyan was on the scene of battle.

Many of his loggers were already white and faint from loss of blood, and the others were hacking desperately with their axes at the dodging, diving mosquitoes. Two of the mammoth winged females were sprawled lifelessly over some pine logs.

Others had paused in the fight to bind up their split bills. The battle raged on.

Paul Bunyan was so stirred with wrath at the sight that he unloosed a yell of astonishment and anger. The loggers, of course, were all lifted off their feet and then hurled to the ground by the force of that cyclonic voice; and the mammoth mosquitoes instantly took advantage of this and plunged on the loggers with bloodthirsty hums. Each one held down seven or more men at once and prepared to feast.

For a moment Paul Bunyan was in a panic. He thought of smashing the mosquitoes with smacks of his hand, but that would have crushed the loggers underneath. With a mighty effort, the great logger collected his wits. He had to think fast, and he did. Paul Bunyan was that kind of man. And at once he acted.

What he did was to call for Babe the Blue Ox, whose ears were so far from his muzzle that he couldn't hear himself snort. As he approached, Babe saw what was needed for the emergency. He did not wait for orders. Without even a glance at Paul, the Blue Ox did a squads right about, halted, straightened out his tail, and began to flirt the mosquitoes off the prone loggers with swishes of his huge tail brush. In one minute every frustrated mosquito was humming angrily in the air and the saved loggers were galloping for the protection of the bunkhouses. There they remained. All night the ravenous mammoth mosquitoes maintained a deafening and ominous hum over the bunkhouses. Paul Bunyan listened. He figured and planned, the ideas for sounds to call clouds forgotten for the moment. At dawn Paul Bunyan had a satisfying idea. He called for Johnny Inkslinger, his timekeeper and man of science.

"Johnny," said Paul, "you need a vacation."

"Yes, sir, Mr. Bunyan," said Johnny, but not very enthusiastically; for if there was anything he hated it was to leave his figures, his grand fountain pen and ink barrels.

"A vacation," Paul Bunyan repeated firmly. "So a vacation you shall take. A hunting vacation, Johnny. I'm going to send you bee-hunting."

"Mr. Bunyan," said Johnny Inkslinger, "I am a good hunter and I like to hunt. Why, once I found a moose who had died of old age, found his moldering bones, I did, and I tracked him to his birthplace. How's that for hunting, Mr. Bunyan?" said

Johnny proudly. But then he looked doubtful. " I don't know about hunting bees, though, Mr. Bunyan."

" You must not only hunt bees, Johnny. You must trap 'em and tame 'em."

" Now, Mr. Bunyan, that's asking a lot," protested Johnny Inkslinger. " I never did claim to be a bee-trapper, or a bee-tamer, either. Why pick on me, Mr. Bunyan? "

" Don't question orders, Johnny," said Paul Bunyan, kindly but sternly. " You pack up now for a vacation in the Mastodonic Clover country. Once there, hunt, trap, and tame the two fightingest, savagest, irritablest, cantankerousest bees you can find. Then trot 'em home to camp."

" Trot 'em, Mr. Bunyan? "

" Trot 'em, Johnny. Trot the bees."

" Yes, sir," said Johnny; and with a will, for he was sentimental about obeying orders.

When Johnny Inkslinger was sent by Paul Bunyan to do anything he did it. So he wasn't a day in the Mastodonic Clover country until he had hunted down, trapped, and tamed — as nearly as two such fighting, savage, irritable, and cantankerous bees could be tamed — the two famous battling bees, Bum and Bill. Johnny tamed the two bees so that they allowed him to chain their wings to their bodies. They also trusted him with their stingers, which he put in his knapsack. Then Johnny Inkslinger put calked boots on the bees' hind feet, trotted them out of the clover country, trotted them on over hill and dale, trotted them all the way to camp, just as Paul Bunyan had ordered.

Paul Bunyan had a great hive ready for the two warriors. When their wings were unchained, Bum and Bill took off their calked boots, stretched their legs, ate a hearty meal of lump sugar and turned in for a refreshing sleep. The next morning they buzzed for their stingers at sunup and showed in other ways that they were eager for battle. Paul Bunyan himself led them to the woods, for Johnny Inkslinger insisted on getting back to his figures at once.

Logging had been continued under the tail of Babe the Blue Ox. For three days he had been swishing the ravenous mammoth mosquitoes away from the loggers. He was so tail-weary that he welcomed Bum and Bill, the battling bees, with a joyful moo that shivered the timber for miles. The bees answered with buzzes of rage, and it required all of Paul Bunyan's bee-taming art to convince the fighting bees that Babe was a friend and not the enemy. Bum and Bill were still buzzing suspicion when they sighted the actual foe. Then, with a battle cry that sounded like the rasping roar of a bandsaw, Bum and Bill lit out in a bee line and charged in an irresistible attack. In seventeen seconds the bodies of seventeen mammoth mosquitoes crashed down into the timber, shattering scores of great pines into splinters. A thunderous hum of fear sounded from the survivors. They flew off in a panic. Pursued and pursuers vanished in the haze of the Dry Summer, which smothered the forest. Soon the hums of fear and the buzzes of rage were only faint murmurs among the far trees. Paul Bunyan's teeth shone through his beard in a smile of triumph.

" Yay, Babe! " he commanded the Blue Ox.

The logging went on.

Paul Bunyan brushed his hands and praised the saints that this mosquito trouble had been so easily ended. Then he returned to his great task of trying out sounds which would call up clouds. The labor engrossed the great logger to such a degree that the mosquito invasion vanished from his thoughts. He also forgot the two big battling bees who had driven the invaders from the logging camp. But Johnny Inkslinger did not forget. Often he raised his head from his books and held his fountain pen poised in the air, while the hose lines from the ink barrels gushed an inky flood to the office floor. This Johnny Inkslinger did not notice in such moments, for he was remembering his grand success as a bee-hunter, a bee-trapper, and a bee-tamer. It was one of the proudest memories of his life.

And often Johnny Inkslinger wondered what had become of the bees he had tamed, what had happened to the female mammoth mosquitoes Bum and Bill had driven from the camp. Weeks had passed, and still there was not a hum from the mosquitoes or a buzz from the bees.

Then, during such a moment of wondering and remembering, Johnny Inkslinger heard a sound from the distance that was nothing but a buzz-hum. He ran out of the office and peered into the heat haze. A small, dark cloud seemed to be moving toward the camp. Johnny watched and waited. The cloud grew larger. As it approached the loggers in the woods Johnny saw that the cloud was a vast swarm of giant insects. They hovered over the loggers for an instant, then dived without circling. And again agonizing yells rolled up from the timber and smote Paul Bunyan's ears.

"What's happened down there?" Paul Bunyan shouted.

"The mosquitoes have come back!" said Johnny Inkslinger.

"It's a new kind, then," said Paul Bunyan, coming on the run, and calling Babe the Blue Ox. "Look at 'em! They're bees!"

"They're mosquitoes," said Johnny. "Look at their bills!"

"But look at their stingers!"

"Sure enough," said Johnny Inkslinger, almost dumb with astonishment. "Why — why — Mr. Bunyan — they — "

"Look at 'em!" yelled Paul Bunyan. "Why, they got bills in front and stingers behind, and they're getting the loggers going and coming! You know what's happened? Those two bees have married the mosquitoes, that's what! And these are the offspring! Bills in front and stingers behind! Yay, Babe!"

And on Paul galloped with Babe the Blue Ox, who soon got his tail brush to working and let the loggers escape to the bunkhouses. But these mammoth insects which were half mosquito and half bee wouldn't be denied. They attacked the bunkhouses. One would stick his bill under one side of a shake on a bunkhouse roof, and his stinger under the other side; and then he would flap his wings until he had ripped off the shake; and the loggers would have to stand guard with pike poles and peavies to keep the savage insects from coming at them through the ripped roofs. Paul Bunyan saw that he needed to act quick. So he spent another night in figuring and planning. And, just as usual, he had a grand idea at daylight. He called for Johnny Inkslinger.

"Johnny," said Paul Bunyan, "we are going to carry sugar."

"Yes, Mr. Bunyan."

"We are going to throw some rafts together, Johnny, and then we are going to load the rafts with all the sugar in camp. After that we are going to rope the rafts together and have Babe the Blue Ox tow the whole raft fleet out into the middle of Lake Michigan."

Johnny Inkslinger never batted an eye. He knew the great logger too well to think that any of his ideas were foolish. So Johnny went to work without a word; and by noon the rafts were built, loaded, and roped together. Paul hitched Babe to the head raft of the fleet.

"Yay, Babe," he commanded.

And the Blue Ox bowed his neck, lumbered off, and straight to the center of Lake Michigan he towed the raft loads of sugar. Johnny Inkslinger stayed on shore. He watched and waited. Soon he saw all the mosquito-bees flying out over the lake after the rafts. Then Johnny Inkslinger realized what Paul Bunyan was up to.

" Oh, ain't he got a brain, though? " said Johnny Inkslinger worshipfully. " Oh, but ain't Paul Bunyan got a brain? "

And a brain Paul Bunyan certainly had. For he had figured that the bee blood in the hybrid insects would send them after the sugar. And he had figured that their mosquito blood would make them fill their stomachs till they were stuffed. And Paul Bunyan knew the weight of sugar. . . .

Sure enough, the mosquito-bees glutted themselves on sugar till they could hardly fly. Then Paul Bunyan started Babe on a run for the shore. The stuffed insects tried to follow. But lower and lower they flew; and soon, with anguished buzz-hums, they all sank into the waters of the great lake; and that was the last of them.

The camp of Paul Bunyan was never again troubled by mammoth mosquitoes, or by mammoth mosquito-bees, either. Bum and Bill at last returned to camp, and gave every appearance of being ashamed of themselves. Paul Bunyan did not reproach them, but gave them a home in a furnished hive; and thereafter Bum and Bill occupied themselves solely with making honey for the loggers' flapjacks. Their fighting days were done.

History does not state the fate of the female mammoth mosquitoes. Some authorities advance the idea that they flew to Asia. They point to the elephant to prove their contention. The elephant, they assert, is descended from the mammoth mosquito of Paul Bunyan's time. Other authorities ridicule this idea, asserting that the elephant is too small to be a descendant of the mammoth mosquito.

All such ideas and contentions are guesswork, however. And guesswork has no place in the history of Paul Bunyan.

SUGGESTIONS FOR STUDY

1. What other great heroes have been celebrated in folk tales? Which ones of these folk tales assumed the form of epic poems? Do you think the Paul Bunyan legend would make a good poem?

2. How much historic foundation is there for the Paul Bunyan legend? For the legends about the other heroes? The way an historic hero can become shrouded in fable and legend is excellently shown by Lloyd Lewis in his book *Myths After Lincoln*. Do you suppose that eventually the real Lincoln and the legendary Lincoln will ever become so completely merged as to be inseparable?

3. Which one of the short stories in this book had the same " whopper " flavor as the Paul Bunyan stories?

4. Tell to the class any other Paul Bunyan story you may have heard.

5. Margaret Prescott Montague has recorded the Tony Beaver legends of the Appalachian country in a book called *Up Eel River*. One of these stories, " The World's Funny Bone," has Paul Bunyan for a character.

THE BANKS OF THE LITTLE EAU PLEINE

LUMBERJACK SONG

Of a class with " Paul Bunyan " is the valuable collection of lumberjack literature, *Ballads and Songs of the Shanty-Boy,* collected and edited by Franz Rickaby, who spent seven years gathering the ballads and songs from men who were woodsmen in Michigan, Wisconsin, and Minnesota during the years between 1870 and 1900, which he calls the " Golden Age of American Lumbering." Most of the men who sang these songs for Mr. Rickaby were past man's allotted threescore years and ten, but they were all willing to sing, and eager to help in the preservation of the songs which had enlivened their evenings around the fire in the little shanty of the lumber camp. They took their singing seriously, closing their eyes for greater concentration, and either rocking nervously in their rocking-chairs or sitting bolt upright and stiff. The shanty-boy, Mr. Rickaby says, often dropped to a speaking voice for part or all of the song's last line, to indicate, probably, " That's all there is to that song." An acquaintance with this book adds to our picture of the lumber camp the popular " singer," and equally popular " fiddler," whose talents enabled them to hold their jobs at good pay and made them general favorites even if they " couldn't shovel snow and do it right." Mr. Rickaby, himself a " fiddler " of no mean ability, has recorded the tunes as well as the words of the old lumberjack ditties.

These songs were doubtless originally created consciously for entertainment, but in most cases the name of the author and the original words are unknown. Generally we have a version to which many singers have contributed. Sometimes the songs were sung by the group; sometimes the " singer " sang the verse and the men joined in the refrain; but usually the " singer," a man with a good voice, a good memory, and an inherent inclination to song, was responsible for the entire rendition. Through the memories of these " singers " Mr. Rickaby has been able to trace the old shanty songs, silent for some thirty years till his interest called them back to life.

The Banks of the Little Eau Pleine

One eve-ning last June as I ram-bled .. The green woods and val-leys a - mong. The mos-qui- to's notes were me - lod - ious, . . And so was the whip-poor-will's song. . . The frogs in the marsh-es were croak - ing, . . . The tree-toads were whist - ling for rain, . . . The par-tridg - es round me were drum - ming . . . On the banks of the Lit - tle Eau Pleine.

1   One evening last June as I rambled
     The green woods and valleys among,
     The mosquito's notes were melodious,
        And so was the whip-poor-will's song.

The frogs in the marshes were croaking,
  The tree-toads were whistling for rain,
And partridges round me were drumming,
  On the banks of the Little Eau Pleine.

2   The sun in the west was declining
      And tinging the tree-tops with red.
    My wandering feet bore me onward,
      Not caring whither they led.
    I happened to see a young school-ma'am.
      She mourned in a sorrowful strain,
    She mourned for a jolly young raftsman
      On the banks of the Little Eau Pleine.

3   Saying, " Alas, my dear Johnny has left me.
      I'm afraid I shall see him no more.
    He's down on the lower Wisconsin,
      He's pulling a fifty-foot oar.
    He went off on a fleet with Ross Gamble
      And has left me in sorrow and pain;
    And 'tis over two months since he started
      From the banks of the Little Eau Pleine."

4   I stepped up beside this young school-ma'am,
      And thus unto her I did say,
    " Why is it you're mourning so sadly
      While all nature is smiling and gay? "
    She said, " It is for a young raftsman
      For whom I so sadly complain.
    He has left me alone here to wander
      On the banks of the Little Eau Pleine."

5   " Will you please tell me what kind of clothing
      Your jolly young raftsman did wear?
    For I also belong to the river,
      And perhaps I have seen him somewhere.
    If to me you will plainly describe him,
      And tell me your young raftsman's name,
    Perhaps I can tell you the reason
      He's not back to the Little Eau Pleine."

6   " His pants were made out of two meal-sacks,
     With a patch a foot square on each knee.
His shirt and his jacket were dyed with
     The bark of a butternut tree.
He wore a large open-faced ticker
     With almost a yard of steel chain,
When he went away with Ross Gamble
     From the banks of the Little Eau Pleine.

7   " He wore a red sash round his middle,
     With an end hanging down at each side.
His shoes number ten were of cowhide,
     With heels about four inches wide.
His name it was Honest John Murphy,
     And on it there ne'er was a stain,
And he was as jolly a raftsman
     As was e'er on the Little Eau Pleine.

8   " He was stout and broad-shouldered and manly.
     His height was about six feet one.
His hair was inclined to be sandy,
     And his whiskers as red as the sun.
His age was somewhere about thirty,
     He neither was foolish nor vain.
He loved the bold Wisconsin River
     Was the reason he left the Eau Pleine."

9   " If John Murphy's the name of your raftsman,
     I used to know him very well.
But sad is the tale I must tell you:
     Your Johnny was drowned in the Dell.
They buried him 'neath a scrub Norway,
     You will never behold him again.
No stone marks the spot where your raftsman
     Sleeps far from the Little Eau Pleine."

10   When the school-ma'am heard this information,
     She fainted and fell as if dead.
I scooped up a hatful of water
     And poured it on top of her head.

She opened her eyes and looked wildly,
    As if she was nearly insane,
And I was afraid she would perish
    On the banks of the Little Eau Pleine.

11   "My curses attend you, Wisconsin!
    May your rapids and falls cease to roar.
May every tow-head and sand-bar
    Be as dry as a log schoolhouse floor.
May the willows upon all your islands
    Lie down like a field of ripe grain,
For taking my jolly young raftsman
    Away from the Little Eau Pleine.

12   "My curses light on you, Ross Gamble,
    For taking my Johnny away.
I hope that the ague will seize you,
    And shake you down into the clay.
May your lumber go down to the bottom,
    And never rise to the surface again.
You had no business taking John Murphy
    Away from the Little Eau Pleine.

13   "Now I will desert my vocation,
    I won't teach district school any more.
I will go to some place where I'll never
    Hear the squeak of a fifty-foot oar.
I will go to some far foreign country,
    To England, to France, or to Spain;
But I'll never forget Johnny Murphy
    Nor the banks of the Little Eau Pleine."

SUGGESTIONS FOR STUDY

1. Why are these verses literature even though they are in some ways very poor poetry?

2. Can you explain why many of the lumberjack songs are sentimental?

3. Did the curse at the end of the poem strike you as funny, or did you feel it was effective? How was it intended by the singer?

4. If the class is fortunate enough to have a fiddler who can sing, he should be able to bring to you the cumulating power in the tragic pathos of the ballad. Or perhaps one boy can fiddle while another sings, although

the effect is best when singer and fiddler are one. The song loses its effect when sung as a chorus, as it is essentially a tale to be told by one story-teller.

5. What old English ballads do you know? How are they like this one? How are they different?

6. The best collection of American folk songs is to be found in Carl Sandburg's *American Songbag*. If your class has it, you can make up several programs of American folk songs from all sources.

THE COWBOY'S DREAM

COWBOY SONG, TO THE AIR OF "MY BONNIE LIES OVER THE OCEAN"

Even more romantic than the lumberjack, and even richer in song, is the American cowboy. The cowboys sang as they drove their herds "up the trail" from the Texas plains to the nearest railroad in Kansas, or from the breeding grounds in Texas to the open ranges of Montana. And they sang as they guarded the cattle at night, riding round and round the herd, improvising cattle lullabies or "dogie songs" to soothe the cattle to sleep and to prevent stampedes.

The young American of today who gets his ideas of the cowboy from the typical Western movie has a very one-sided and distorted picture indeed. The songs of the cowboy, which have been collected by Mr. John A. Lomax into a book called *Cowboy Songs and Other Frontier Ballads,* reveal the true cowboy to us. He was a hard-working, serious-minded fellow, different from the familiar movie hero, who seems never to have any real work to do but is always free to scour the country to rescue maidens in distress or rid the community of eastern villains. Most of the songs in this book are sad and mournful, for the cowboy was lonesome and homesick. And the songs are full of a simple religion, a child-like faith reminiscent of boyhood homes, their mothers and sisters. One interesting feature which reminds us of the old English ballads is the glorification of the outlaw, but the hero is Jesse James instead of Robin Hood. Perhaps the outstanding qualities of the cowboy songs are their masculine vitality and direct simple honesty. Through them we learn to know the now vanishing western knight-errant as we can in no other way.

To get the full effect of this song the boys of the class should imagine themselves riding after cattle through a wide valley enclosed by the great western mountains. They have indulged themselves in the gay colors that all men love but only a few of the most courageous dare put on: big hats with gay beaded hat-bands, crimson handkerchiefs knotted at their throats, fancy belts, high-heeled boots with shining spurs. As the purple haze of evening descends upon the mountains, the best singer of the crowd begins to sing, without any instrument for accompaniment, as easily and as naturally as he rides. The rest join in the chorus. The chorus should be sung after every verse; one of the outstanding characteristics of these cowboy songs is their length. From Texas to Montana was a long ride.

> Last night as I lay on the prairie,
> And looked at the stars in the sky,
> I wondered if ever a cowboy
> Would drift to that sweet by and by.

> Roll on, roll on;
> Roll on, little dogies, roll on, roll on,
> Roll on, roll on;
> Roll on, little dogies, roll on.

> The road to that bright, happy region
> Is a dim, narrow trail, so they say;
> But the broad one that leads to perdition
> Is posted and blazed all the way.

They say there will be a great round-up,
And cowboys, like dogies, will stand,
To be marked by the Riders of Judgment
Who are posted and know every brand.

I know there's many a stray cowboy
Who'll be lost at the great, final sale,
When he might have gone in the green pastures
Had he known of the dim, narrow trail.

I wonder if ever a cowboy
Stood ready for that Judgment Day,
And could say to the Boss of the Riders,
" I'm ready, come drive me away."

For they, like the cows that are locoed,
Stampede at the sight of a hand,
Are dragged with a rope to the round-up,
Or get marked with some crooked man's brand.

And I'm scared that I'll be a stray yearling —
A maverick, unbranded on high —
And get cut in the bunch with the " rusties "
When the Boss of the Riders goes by.

For they tell of another big owner
Who's ne'er overstocked, so they say,
But who always makes room for the sinner
Who drifts from the strait, narrow way.

They say he will never forget you,
That he knows every action and look;
So, for safety, you'd better get branded,
Have your name in the great Tally Book.

SUGGESTIONS FOR STUDY

1. Vocabulary: dogies, blazed, round-up, locoed, yearling, maverick, cut, rusties, Tally Book.

2. What part of a cowboy's life does the song reveal? What characteristics of the cowboy?

3. What essential differences do you find between the cowboy and the lumberjack?

4. What difference would there be in the way the cowboys sang this song when riding after cattle or when sitting around the fire in the evening? Do you think it would make a good " cattle lullaby "? Why?

5. Did you ever think of singing as being essentially masculine? Why do you suppose the cowboys, soldiers, sailors, and lumberjacks all sang, while perhaps the boys of your English class did not wish to?

6. Get " Cowboy Songs " and sing some more of the songs in class. The songs that have original tunes are often very mournful and beautiful. See if you can find any jolly songs.

LEAVE HER, JOHNNY, LEAVE HER

SAILOR CHANTEY

Gone, like the romantic lumberjack and the lonesome cowboy, is the rough sailorman of the sailboat days a hundred years ago. But the lure of the sailor's life still draws us as it did the boy Franklin and young George Washington, both of whom just missed a career before the mast by parental intervention at the last moment. That the life was not all romance, however, is convincingly proved in Richard Henry Dana, Jr.'s record of his *Two Years Before the Mast* in the '40's, the best picture of sailor life in our literature.

The sailors sang as they worked. In fact, most of their songs were made up to fit the rhythmic motions of raising the anchor or hauling on the halyards.

Robert Frost, one of our greatest modern American poets (see p. 723), learned sailor chanteys as a boy along the waterfront at San Francisco. He treasured the melodies and words in his heart, and gave to Carl Sandburg's *American Songbag* his version of two of his favorites, " Whiskey Johnny " and " Blow the Man Down."

The chantey we have selected for this book is one the sailors sang when dropping anchor on returning to port after a long voyage. They used it to serve notice on the hated skipper that they were now free from his hard taskmastership and that he could look elsewhere for a new crew for his next voyage. The version in *The American Songbag* is called " Leave Her, Bullies, Leave Her." The one printed here is from Robert Frothingham's *Songs of the Sea*.

The song should be sung briskly and with marked rhythm.

Leave Her, Johnny, Leave Her

Moderately

Solo
Oh, the times are hard and the wag - es low,

Chorus
Leave her, John - ny, leave her! I'll pack my bag and

Chorus
go be - low; It's time for us to leave her.

Solo	Oh, the times are hard and the wages low,
Chorus	Leave her, Johnny, leave her!
Solo	I'll pack my bag and go below;
Chorus	It's time for us to leave her.

Solo	It's growl you may but go you must,
Chorus	Leave her, Johnny, leave her!
Solo	It matters not whether you're last or first,
Chorus	It's time for us to leave her.

Solo	I'm getting thin and growing sad,
Chorus	Leave her, Johnny, leave her!
Solo	Since first I joined this wooden-clad,
Chorus	It's time for us to leave her.

Solo	I thought I heard the second-mate say
Chorus	" Leave her, Johnny, leave her!
Solo	Just one more drag and then belay,
Chorus	It's time for us to leave her."

Solo	The work was hard, the voyage long,
Chorus	Leave her, Johnny, leave her!
Solo	The seas were high, the gales were strong,
Chorus	It's time for us to leave her.

Solo	The sails are furled, our work is done,
Chorus	Leave her, Johnny, leave her!
Solo	And now on shore, we'll have our fun,
Chorus	It's time for us to leave her.

SUGGESTIONS FOR STUDY

1. Vocabulary: wooden-clad, belay, furled.
2. What essential difference is there in the purpose of a sailor chantey and of a lumberjack song? A cowboy song? Which kind do you most enjoy singing?
3. What other sailor chanteys do you know?
4. In what ways are the cowboy, the lumberjack, and the sailor songs alike?
5. Notice how you must pronounce " first " to make the rhyme. Whittier deliberately put into his poems Yankee colloquial pronunciations, claiming they added to the local color. (See p. 566.) Do you agree with him?

NATHAN HALE

WAR BALLAD

In the World War, as in all wars, the soldiers sang as they marched and sang in the camps, while the civilians, bound together by the stress of the times, fostered community singing. Song writers created " Over There " and " Keep the Home-Fires Burning," and the soldiers piled up verse after verse of " Hinky Dinky Parley-Voo." One interesting folk-song of the World War is " Our Uncle Sammy He Needs the Infantry," sung to the same old Negro tune adopted years ago by the folk singers of " The Old Gray Mare She Ain't What She Used to Be."

The Spanish-American War, the Civil War, the Mexican War, the War of 1812, and the Revolution all contributed their quota of song to the American tradition. Many, like " The Battle Hymn of the Republic," are the work of single writers, but others, like " Yankee Doodle," come from the people.

The period of the Revolution gave us, besides the songs, some folk ballads with the genuine flavor of the old troubadours. Of these " Nathan Hale " is perhaps the most famous.

> The breezes went steadily through the tall pines,
>   A-saying " Oh hu-ush! " a-saying " Oh hu-ush! "
> As stilly stole by a bold legion of horse,
>   For Hale in the bush, for Hale in the bush.
>
> " Keep still! " said the thrush as she nestled her young,
>   In a nest by the road, in a nest by the road;
> " For the tyrants are near, and with them appear
>   What bodes us no good, what bodes us no good."
>
> The brave captain heard it and thought of his home,
>   In a cot by the brook, in a cot by the brook,
> With mother and sister and memories dear,
>   He so gaily forsook, he so gaily forsook.
>
> Cooling shades of the night were coming apace,
>   The tattoo had beat, the tattoo had beat:
> The noble one sprang from his dark lurking-place
>   To make his retreat, to make his retreat.
>
> He warily trod on the dry rustling leaves,
>   As he passed through the wood, as he passed through the wood,
> And silently gained his rude launch on the shore,
>   As she played with the flood, as she played with the flood.
>
> The guards of the camp, on that dark, dreary night,
>   Had a murderous will, had a murderous will:
> They took him and bore him afar from the shore,
>   To a hut on the hill, to a hut on the hill.
>
> No mother was there, nor a friend who could cheer,
>   In that little stone cell, in that little stone cell.
> But he trusted in love from his Father above:
>   In his heart all was well, in his heart all was well.
>
> An ominous owl with his solemn bass voice
>   Sat moaning hard by, sat moaning hard by:
> " The tyrant's proud minions most gladly rejoice,
>   For he must soon die, for he must soon die."

The brave fellow told them, no thing he restrained,
  The cruel gen'ral, the cruel gen'ral;
His errand from camp, of the ends to be gained;
  And said that was all, and said that was all.

They took him and bound him and bore him away,
  Down the hill's grassy side, down the hill's grassy side.
'Twas there the base hirelings, in royal array,
  His cause did deride, his cause did deride.

Five minutes were given, short moments, no more,
  For him to repent, for him to repent:
He prayed for his mother, he asked not another;
  To Heaven he went, to Heaven he went.

The faith of a martyr the tragedy showed,
  As he trod the last stage, as he trod the last stage;
And Britons will shudder at gallant Hale's blood,
  As his words do presage, as his words do presage:

" Thou pale king of terrors, thou life's gloomy foe,
  Go frighten the slave, go frighten the slave;
Tell tyrants to you their allegiance they owe:
  No fears for the brave, no fears for the brave."

SUGGESTIONS FOR STUDY

1. Look up ballads in a good encyclopedia. In what way is this ballad typical of the old English ballads? In what way is it better poetry than the shanty-boy ballad we studied?

2. Do you think this ballad is better sung or recited? Could you improvise a tune and sing it?

3. Is there anything in Clyde Fitch's *Nathan Hale* to remind you of this ballad?

4. List all the war songs you can think of from all our various wars. Then try to find out whether they are folk songs, or literary creations. There are interesting stories connected with many, such as " The Star-Spangled Banner," " Maryland, My Maryland," and " Dixie."

THE AWFUL FATE OF MR. WOLF

By JOEL CHANDLER HARRIS (1849–1908)

" Uncle Remus " is not a folk character; Joel Chandler Harris created him as a mouthpiece for the old plantation stories of the Negro slaves. Mr. Harris's own words explain the origin of this lovable old Negro: " He was not an invention of my own, but a human syndicate, I might say, of three or four old darkies whom I had known. I just walloped them together into one person and called him ' Uncle Remus.' You must remember that sometimes the Negro is a genuine and an original philosopher."

But the stories themselves are true folk literature. When questioned about their origin, Mr. Harris said, " All that I know — all that we Southerners know — about it, is that every old southern mammy in the South is full of these stories. One thing is certain — the Negroes did not get them from the whites: probably they are of remote African origin." So the " Uncle Remus stories " are genuine folk tales with Uncle Remus himself added by Joel Chandler Harris to bind the stories together that they may take their place as a part of our American literature.

Joel Chandler Harris was born in Georgia. At the age of thirteen he undertook to learn the printer's trade in the shop of the *Countryman,* a newspaper printed on a plantation. Here Harris became familiar with the curious myths and animal stories of the plantation Negro. Later, when he was working for the Atlanta *Constitution,* he created Uncle Remus and began telling these stories as a daily newspaper feature, like the familiar " column."

The stories made Harris famous. Five volumes of Uncle Remus stories have been published; but the best stories are in the first book, *Uncle Remus: His Songs and Sayings,* published in 1880, from which the following selection is taken.

In the Uncle Remus stories Harris has preserved carefully true Negro dialect, sentence structure, and vernacular. To appreciate its rich flavor and color, one need only compare it with the totally false Negro dialect in *Uncle Tom's Cabin.*

Uncle Remus was half-soling one of his shoes, and his Miss Sally's little boy had been handling his awls, his hammers, and his knives to such an extent that the old man was compelled to assume a threatening attitude; but peace reigned again, and the little boy perched himself on a chair, watching Uncle Remus driving in pegs.

" Folks w'at's allers pesterin' people, en bodderin' 'longer dat

w'at ain't dern, don't never come ter no good eend. Dar wuz
Brer Wolf; stidder mindin' un his own bizness, he hatter take
en go in pardnerships wid Brer Fox, en dey want skacely a minnit
in de day dat he want atter Brer Rabbit, en he kep' on en kep'
on twel fus' news you knowed he got kotch up wid — en he got
kotch up wid monstus bad."

"Goodness, Uncle Remus! I thought the Wolf let the Rabbit
alone, after he tried to fool him about the Fox being dead."

"Better lemme tell dish yer my way. Bimeby hit'll be yo'
bed time, en Miss Sally'll be a hollerin' atter you, en you'll be
a whimplin' roun', an den Mars John'll fetch up de re'r wid dat
ar strop w'at I made fer 'im."

The child laughed, and playfully shook his fist in the simple,
serious face of the venerable old darkey, but said no more. Uncle
Remus waited awhile to be sure there was to be no other demonstration, and then proceeded:

"Brer Rabbit ain't see no peace w'atsumever. He can't leave
home 'cep' Brer Wolf 'ud make a raid en tote off some er de
fambly. Brer Rabbit b'ilt 'im a straw house, en hit wuz tored
down; den he made a house outen pine-tops, en dat went de
same way; den he made 'im a bark house, en dat wuz raided on,
en eve'y time he los' a house he los' one er his chilluns. Las' Brer
Rabbit got mad, he did, en cust, en den he went off, he did, en
got some kyarpinters, en dey b'ilt 'im a plank house wid rock
foundashuns. Atter dat he could have some peace en quietness.
He could go out en pass de time er day wid his neighbors, en come
back en set by de fier, en smoke his pipe, en read de newspapers
same like enny man w'at got a fambly. He made a hole, he did,
in de cellar whar de little Rabbits could hide out w'en dar wuz
much uv a racket in de neighborhood, en de latch er de front do'
kotch on de inside. Brer Wolf, he see how de lan' lay, he did,
en he lay low. De little Rabbits was mighty skittish, but hit got
so dat cole chills ain't run up Brer Rabbit's back no mo' w'en
he heerd Brer Wolf go gallopin' by.

"Bimeby, one day w'en Brer Rabbit wuz fixin' fer ter call on
Miss Coon, he heerd a monstus fuss en clatter up de big road, en
'mos' 'fo' he could fix his years fer ter lissen, Brer Wolf run in
de do'. De little Rabbits dey went inter dere hole in de cellar,
dey did, like blowin' out a cannle. Brer Wolf wuz far'ly kivver'd
wid mud, en mighty nigh outer win'.

"'Oh, do pray save me, Brer Rabbit!' sez Brer Wolf, sezee.

' Do please, Brer Rabbit! de dogs is atter me, en dey'll t'ar me up.
Don't you year um comin'? Oh, do please save me, Brer Rabbit!
Hide me some'rs whar de dogs won't git me.'

"No quicker sed dan done.

"' Jump in dat big chist dar, Brer Wolf,' sez Brer Rabbit, sezee;
' jump in dar en make yo'se'f at home.'

"In jump Brer Wolf, down come the led, en inter de hasp
went de hook, en dar Mr. Wolf wuz. Den Brer Rabbit went
ter de lookin'-glass, he did, en wink at hisse'f, en den he draw'd
de rockin'-cheer in front er de fier, he did, en tuck a big chaw
terbarker."

"Tobacco, Uncle Remus?" asked the little boy, incredulously.

"Rabbit terbarker, honey. You know dis yer life ev'lastin'
w'at Miss Sally puts 'mong de cloze in de trunk; well, dat's rabbit
terbarker. Den Brer Rabbit sot dar long time, he did, turnin' his
mine over en wukken his thinkin' masheen. Bimeby he got up,
en sorter stir 'roun'. Den Brer Wolf open up:

"' Is de dogs all gone, Brer Rabbit?'

"' Seem like I hear one un um smellin' roun' de chimbly-
cornder des now.'

"Den Brer Rabbit git de kittle en fill it full er water, en put
it on de fier.

"' W'at you doin' now, Brer Rabbit?'

"' I'm fixin' fer ter make you a nice cup er tea, Brer Wolf.'

"Den Brer Rabbit went ter de cubberd en git de gimlet, en
commence for ter bo' little holes in de chist-led.

"' W'at you doin' now, Brer Rabbit?'

"' I'm a bo'in' little holes so you kin get bref, Brer Wolf.'

"Den Brer Rabbit went out en git some mo' wood, en fling it
on de fier.

"' W'at you doin' now, Brer Rabbit?'

"' I'm a chunkin' up de fier so you won't git cole, Brer Wolf.'

"Den Brer Rabbit went down inter de cellar en fotch out all
his chilluns.

"' W'at you doin' now, Brer Rabbit?'

"' I'm a tellin' my chilluns w'at a nice man you is, Brer Wolf.'

"En de chilluns, dey had ter put der han's on der moufs fer
ter keep fum laffin'. Den Brer Rabbit he got de kittle en commenced fer to po' de hot water on de chist-lid.

"' W'at dat I hear, Brer Rabbit?'

"' You hear de win' a blowin', Brer Wolf.'

" Den de water begin fer ter sif' thoo.

" ' W'at dat I feel, Brer Rabbit? '

" ' You feels de fleas a bitin', Brer Wolf.'

" ' Dey er bitin' mighty hard, Brer Rabbit.'

" ' Tu'n over on de udder side, Brer Wolf.'

" ' W'at dat I feel now, Brer Rabbit? '

" ' Still you feels de fleas, Brer Wolf.'

" ' Dey er eatin' me up, Brer Rabbit,' en dem wuz de las words er Brer Wolf, kase de scaldin' water done de bizness.

" Den Brer Rabbit call in his neighbors, he did, en dey hilt a reg'lar juberlee; en ef you go ter Brer Rabbit's house right now, I dunno but w'at you'll fine Brer Wolf's hide hangin' in de back-po'ch, en all bekaze he wuz so bizzy wid udder fo'kses doin's."

SUGGESTIONS FOR STUDY

1. Read the story aloud until you can make the dialect flow smoothly.

2. Have you ever seen the edition of *Uncle Remus: His Songs and Sayings* illustrated by Church? An edition in 1906 was illustrated by A. B. Frost. To what extent are illustrations in books important? With what other books do you associate the pictures of a definite illustrator?

3. From a literary standpoint how does Uncle Remus differ from Paul Bunyan?

4. You would enjoy reading *The Life and Letters of Joel Chandler Harris* by his daughter-in-law, Julia Collier Harris.

IT'S ME, O LORD

NEGRO SPIRITUAL

The slave song, or spiritual, is essentially dignified and at times noble, both in words and in music. Although spirituals often carry the decided rhythm that Negro music has given our popular American melodies, they should not be confused with music hall entertainment. They are the cry of a race in bondage, primitive, but serious and exalted.

For this book we have selected a simple spiritual, for the minor harmonies in some of the more complicated melodies make them too difficult for classroom purposes. But this is a song you can easily learn to sing. The melody was a favorite among the doughboys of the World War, who profaned it with words which carried a vigorous message of defiance to " Kaiser Bill."

In many ways "It's Me, O Lord" is a typical spiritual. It is strongly religious. It illustrates the endless repetition of lines, which is a common feature. The verse proper contains "leading lines" ("Tain't my mother or my father, but it's me, O Lord") followed by a response, "Standin' in the need of prayer." This form is common to the African songs from which the spirituals probably sprang, and is found in some of the best-known spirituals such as "Oh, Wasn't Dat a Wide Ribber" and "Swing Low, Sweet Chariot." The spiritual in this book also illustrates the development of the response into a full chorus, with which the congregation begins the singing, followed later by the leads and responses.

When you sing this song, let the richest, deepest voices carry the leads; let those who can sing tenor and other parts make harmonies; and try to get the spontaneity and freedom of the true spiritual. But, above all, remember that it is a religious song and do not "jazz" the rhythm. Keep to the camp-meeting mood.

I

It's me, it's me, it's me, O Lord, —
Standin' in the need of prayer.
It's me, it's me, it's me, O Lord, —
An' I'm standin' in the need of prayer, O Lord.
It's me it's me, it's me, O Lord, —
Standin' in the need of prayer.
It's me, it's me, it's me, O Lord, —
An' I'm standin' in the need of prayer.
Tain't my mother, or my father, but it's me, O Lord, —
Standin' in the need of prayer.
Tain't my mother, or my father, but it's me, O Lord, —
Standin' in the need of prayer.
It's me, it's me, it's me, O Lord, —
Standin' in the need of prayer.
It's me, it's me, it's me, O Lord, —
An' I'm standin' in the need of prayer.

II

It's me, it's me, it's me, O Lord, —
Standin' in the need of prayer.
It's me, it's me, it's me, O Lord, —
An' I'm standin' in the need of prayer, O Lord.
It's me, it's me, it's me, O Lord, —
Standin' in the need of prayer.

It's me, it's me, it's me, O Lord, —
An' I'm standin' in the need of prayer.
Tain't the deacon, or my leader, but it's me, O Lord, —
Standin' in the need of prayer.
Tain't the deacon, or my leader, but it's me, O Lord, —
Standin' in the need of prayer.
It's me, it's me, it's me, O Lord, —
Standin' in the need of prayer.
It's me, it's me, it's me, O Lord, —
An' I'm standin' in the need of prayer.

It's Me, O Lord

SUGGESTIONS FOR STUDY

1. What have you learned about the Negro race from a study of Negro folk literature?

2. Could you add appropriate " leads " for the song to the ones in the two stanzas here published?

3. In what ways has your study of folk literature made you realize that literature cannot be totally separated from other arts?

FOR FURTHER READING OF FOLK LITERATURE

Cox, John Harrington. *Folk Songs of the South*

Finger, Charles J. *Frontier Ballads*

Gray, Roland Palmer. *Songs and Ballads of the Maine Lumberjacks*

Harris, Joel Chandler. *Uncle Remus: His Songs and His Sayings. Nights with Uncle Remus*

Johnson, James Weldon and Rosamond. *The First and Second Books of American Negro Spirituals*

Lomax, John A. *Cowboy Songs, and Other Frontier Ballads. Songs of the Cattle Trail and Cow-Camp*

Lummis, Charles Fletcher. *Pueblo Indian Folk-Stories*

Mackaye, Percy. *Tall Tales from the Kentucky Mountains, Weather-goose Woo*

Montague, Margaret Prescott. *Up Eel River*

Morris, Cora. *Stories from Mythology, North American*

Parsons, Elsie Clews. *American Indian Life, by Several of Its Students*

Pound, Louise. *American Ballads and Songs*

Rickaby, Franz. *Ballads and Songs of the Shanty-Boy*

Sandburg, Carl. *The American Song-Bag*

Shephard, Esther. *Paul Bunyan*

Smith, Reed. *South Carolina Ballads*

Stevens, James. *Paul Bunyan*

Wadsworth, Wallace. *Paul Bunyan and His Great Blue Ox*

Poetry

Poetry is fairly easy to recognize but next to impossible to define. Even such good definition-makers as encyclopedias admit the difficulty, for one of them opens a long sentence full of abstract words with the apology, "Without attempting to define poetry — " The poets themselves (who should know, if anybody does) have tried to express this unexplainable quality of poetry. One says, "Poetry is the opening and closing of a door, leaving those who look through to guess what is seen during a moment" (Carl Sandburg). Another puts it this way, "Poetry is a language that tells us, through a more or less emotional reaction, something that cannot be said" (Edwin Arlington Robinson). Indefinable as poetry may be, it has elements that are commonly recognized. The first is the stirring of our emotions. "The right reader of a good poem can tell the moment it strikes him that he has taken an immortal wound — that he will never get over it" (Robert Frost). And again, "If I read a book and it makes my whole body so cold no fire can ever warm me, I know that it is poetry. If I feel physically as if the top of my head were taken off, I know that is poetry. These are the only ways I know it. Are there any other ways?" (Emily Dickinson.) These two statements sound rather terrible, but what the poets meant was that poetry in its best sense is something intensely personal and definitely individual. What may be poetry to me may not be poetry to you. Even more than the short story, the essay, and biography, poetry is not just a type of literature but also a frame of mind, a point of view, a scent in the air, a fleeting memory, a hidden force of nature which, like electricity, flashes into light when given the right contacts. If something is poetry to you it sends an invigorating current through your blood; if it leaves you unmoved, it is not poetry to you. The essence of poetry, then, is emotional appeal.

What stimulates the emotions? So far as poetry is concerned it is largely the imagination. The poet may start out with the rough clay of ordinary things seen every day, but before he has finished molding it, mental vision has far outstripped the merely physical. He has touched the imagination. With the magic spell of words he has clothed an idea with beauty. To realize this we need only take some poem that really moves us, state the idea in plain prose, and compare the two. Shorn of its wings, the prose version simply confronts us with a fact or a principle; it has lost its power to thrill or sway or uplift us.

Granting that emotion and the imagination are two of the essentials to poetry, what more is there? Besides mere words, how does the poet secure the final effect that he wishes to create? Again a direct answer eludes us, but we may say that without *rhythm* there can be no poetry. In a general way we all know what the word means. Its Greek original meant " measured motion," and in English poetry this is to a large extent produced by the more or less regular recurrence of accented and unaccented syllables. Ideas expressed in rhythmical language that stimulates the imagination and stirs the emotions constitute the essentials of poetry.

POETRY IN AMERICA

Styles come and go in poetry as well as in clothes. It is curious to see how poetry began in our country, how it has changed and developed. There is rhythm in its very history, for some ages have a great wave of poetry; others have marked the ebb, when little was being produced, but power was gathering for a new wave.

Colonial Period Barren of Poetry

It was almost two hundred years after the landing of the Pilgrims before a really fine poem was produced on this side of the Atlantic. There had been much writing of verse, but it lacked the magic touch which transforms mere rhyming into poetry. In 1640 the colonists had turned the Psalms into metrical form for singing in their services. Poets of the late colonial and Revolutionary periods attempted ambitious poetic dramas or great epic poems modeled upon the style of their English predecessors. Everything was ponderous and imitative. The Revolution called forth some mediocre songs, ballads, and satires on the British. Philip Freneau alone of all the poets before Bryant seemed to have a gift for the telling phrase and the point of view of a real poet. Some of his short poems like " The Indian Burying Ground " and " To a Honey Bee " are still read with pleasure.

Early Northern Poets the First Important Group

With the coming of William Cullen Bryant the first great wave of poetry began to roll in. Upon its crest rode Longfellow, Whittier, Holmes, and Lowell, poets you have undoubtedly known since childhood. Even Emerson and Thoreau, whose greatest messages were given in prose, contributed their share in metrical form, while innumerable minor poets sent their songs upon the air.

Most of these poets were still to a great extent imitative of Europe in spite of the fact that they used American themes. Longfellow perpetuated the legends of the Indians and the early settlers, but his " Hiawatha " was modeled upon the style of the Finnish epic, the *Kalevala,* and most of his narrative poems resemble the manner of Old World metrical tales. Whittier took his inspiration from the Scotch Burns, and is often compared to him in his simple pictures of rural life. Lowell and Holmes smack of the library and the gentlemanly ease of cultivated backgrounds even in picturing the New England rustic. All of these men were poets of distinct talent whose contributions have become a part of our American inheritance. You will study them in greater detail in this section, so that little need be said about them here. For pure originality these sturdy New Englanders were outstripped by two others of the same general period — Poe and Whitman.

Poe a Great Original Genius

Poe himself lived more vitally in the land of imagination than in the land of reality, where he was constantly failing to adapt himself to what his environment demanded of him. Consequently he was able to lift his readers with him into this dream world where pure poetry seemed enthroned. There is magic in his lines, and though he has given us the exact recipe for his incantations when he tells us how he built his poems, they remain magic just the same. In his work as literary critic on various magazines, Poe had occasion to review the writings of other poets. Unfortunately he involved himself in violent controversy especially against the firmly intrenched New England group. His greatest quarrel with the northern poets was on their moralizing, which he believed should have no place in poetry. " The immediate object of poetry is pleasure, not truth." Poetry is " the rhythmical creation of beauty." Humor is " antagonistical to that which is the soul of the muse proper." Sadness he declared the most poetic mood and the death of a beautiful woman the most perfect theme. Metrical imperfections called forth his scorn, as did a trite or empty meaning of a word. Many of his criticisms of contemporaries were deserved; many seemed unduly harsh. At least, however, Poe practiced what he preached and gave us a slender but technically unexcelled body of poetry which places him in the front rank.

Whitman's Originality and Realism

Whitman outdid even Poe in originality, for his poetry owes almost nothing to books and literary background, although he was not ignorant of them. Like a mighty prophet of old, he poured forth his torrent of powerful words, seizing for his material everything about him — himself, other men, the open road, the teeming city, the frightful war hospitals (where he was a nurse), a spider, the stars, Abraham Lincoln — whatever came into his ken. Poe removes us into a land that never was; Whitman plunges us into a land that most vitally is. Many persons find it hard to realize that Whitman was the contemporary of the New England poets because he seems so much more modern. Whitman's face was set toward the future instead of the past, and his own generation failed for many years to appreciate him. But his fame and influence have been steadily on the increase, and many poets of the present day look directly to him as the pioneer in the new realms of poetry which are opening up so rapidly.

Whitman Originates " Free Verse "

Whitman was the great emancipator of the form as well as the spirit of poetry. He it was who first cast aside the regular metrical forms for those larger untrammeled rhythms known as " free verse." To many ears this was not poetry at all, but prose printed in lines of varying length. The difference, however, between this poetry and ordinary prose can be felt after one has lived with it a while. The emotional quality, the repetition and assonance (similarity of sound, but not rhyme) the imaginative perceptions, all give the tone of a rhythmic chant. Strange to say, Whitman had no noteworthy disciples during his lifetime. It was not until almost twenty years after his death that " free verse " came into its own, and after a considerable fight for life succeeded in establishing itself as a recognized sister of metrical verse.

The Civil War and the Poets

To return to the period of the Civil War, one may well ask what effect that great struggle had upon the poetry of the land. Did it produce great poets and great poems? Of course there was the usual crop of war songs which will undoubtedly go ringing on through time long after the last vestige of feeling between the two sides has been wiped out. Many of these could almost be classed as folk songs, were it not that an author's name is attached to them; but the writers themselves are of no importance in the history of our poetry. No one today remembers the names of the writers of " Dixie," " My Maryland," " Tenting on the Old Camp Ground," " The Battle Cry of Freedom," " Stonewall Jackson's Way," and " Marching Through Georgia." One song alone is always associated with its author, perhaps because of the unusual fact that she was a woman. This is " The Battle Hymn of the Republic " by Julia Ward Howe. At the close of the war came that touchingly beautiful attempt to heal the wounds of war, " The Blue and the Gray " by Francis M. Finch. Of course the New England poets wrote freely about the war, especially the critical situations leading up to it. Whittier's anti-slavery poems, and Lowell's " Biglow Papers," " The Present Crisis," and " Commemoration Ode " form an intimate part of the history of the great struggle.

As for soldier-poets, men who were under fire, and at the same time had the fire of poetry burning in their bosoms, there is only one — a Southerner, Sidney Lanier. Nor would any one call him a war-poet, for whatever impress his painful experiences as soldier, prisoner, and refugee may have left on his memory, they left none on his poetry. Musician *par excellence,* and lover of beauty, of nature, of old legends, and of noble character, he turned his back completely on the nightmare of his early days. Only slight reflection of the war is given by Timrod and Hayne, also Southerners, who as war correspondents and aides-de-camp had intimate contacts with the action of the armies. On the northern side there is no one, though Whitman, the war nurse, has given us more than any one else a taste of what war means.

Years Following Civil War Meager in Poetry

After the Civil War the first great wave of poetry had broken and there was a long rolling back of the waters preparatory to another onslaught. The old poets were still writing in their last years, but no new ones seemed ready to take their places. Lanier flashed brilliantly for only a few years before death took him off. Emily Dickinson was as yet undiscovered, and her poems seem to belong to our century when they were published rather than to the nineteenth when she was secretly writing them. Thomas Bailey Aldrich represents the typical eastern poet of the time — at his best, delicately charming, but at his worst, weakly insignificant and lost in oriental affectations.

The West and Middle West Come into Poetry

Meanwhile things were beginning to happen in the West. Not only was romance being lived, it was also being recorded. Bret Harte, whose greater work was in fiction, and John Hay, whose greater work was in politics, both began to picture in lively verse the miner, the card-sharper, the claim-jumper, and others of the motley crew pouring into the western states. Edward Rowland Sill with his eastern background contributed a more polished note, mingled with western frankness. Joaquin Miller splashed in flamboyant colors the great panorama of the plains and the sierras.

Then the Middle West made itself heard in James Whitcomb Riley, transcribing Hoosier farm dialect, and Eugene Field, combining newspaper light verse, tender lullabies, and western dialect poems. In the last decade of the nineteenth century came two young revolutionists, Bliss Carman and Richard Hovey, who in their successive *Songs from Vagabondia* running over a period of six years turned poetry out of doors to roam over the hills and escape the conventionalities of civilization. Hovey died young, but Carman continued to write poetry with about the same theme until his death in 1929. About the same time William Vaughn Moody, another who died too young, spoke for American idealism in the crises of public life. Just at the end of the century Edwin Markham harnessed poetry to the cause of social justice in " The Man with the Hoe " and thereby opened up the whole field of industrial life as a theme for poetry.

Then for the first decade of the twentieth century poetry seemed to reach its lowest ebb. There simply was no poetry to speak of. But the waters were gathering for the second great wave of poetry which broke upon America in the second decade of the twentieth century.

Twentieth Century Brings Second Great Wave, " The New Poetry "

In 1912 there was established a little magazine of verse called *Poetry*. Hitherto unknown poets found encouragement between its covers. Strange kinds of poetry were fostered and began to develop. In the next few years volume after volume of poetry appeared on the market, and what was more, found a sale. " The new poetry " became a topic of general conversation like the weather and baseball. People had a hard time deciding whether the new poetry *was* poetry, and then whether or not they liked it. But upon all this controversy the new poetry thrived, and now it seems neither new nor startling — just part of our heritage of poetry, just the voice of our modern America speaking to us. Those poets who less than twenty years ago seemed dangerous revolutionists are now our accepted and established artists.

It is hard to know which of these new poets to put first in point of time. The very fact that Masters, Robinson, Amy Lowell, Frost, Sandburg, and Lindsay broke almost simultaneously upon the shore of poetry added to the effectiveness of all of them. In the five years between 1912 and our entrance into the World War in 1917, each of them had published a significant volume which set the pace for what was to follow. Each of the six has his own clearly marked individuality. Robinson and Frost hold to traditional verse forms but picture a new New England with startling insight.

The Imagists Wield Influence

Amy Lowell, the only one of the group who has died, pioneered in new verse forms and allied herself with the Imagists, a band of Englishmen and Americans who had distinct theories of poetry. Since the six tenets of the Imagists have had such widespread influence upon modern poetry and really sum up many of the important differences between nineteenth and twentieth century poetry even in the latter's more conservative forms, it is well to quote their creed:

1. To use the language of common speech, but to employ always the *exact* word, not the merely decorative word.

2. To create new rhythms as the expression of new moods. We do not insist upon " free verse " as the only method of writing poetry. . . . We do believe that the individuality of a poet may often be better expressed in free verse than in conventional forms.

3. To allow absolute freedom in the choice of subject.

4. To present an image (hence the name " Imagist "). We are not a school of painters, but we believe that poetry should render particulars exactly and not deal in vague generalities, however magnificent and sonorous.

5. To produce poetry that is hard and clear, never blurred or indefinite.

6. Finally, most of us believe that concentration is the very essence of poetry.

These principles are illustrated largely by Masters and Sandburg, both Illinois poets, who have made effective use of free verse, the crisp figure, and startling epithet, and the unlimited selection of subject matter, in their interpretations of the town, the city, and the plain. Lindsay, associated with them in his native state, is yet entirely different in his method, using a highly marked rhythm and numerous unusual devices to produce an intensely emotional musical effect.

The Youngest Contemporaries

These six are the most distinguished of our older contemporary poets. Among the great number of excellent younger singers only a few have been chosen to be here represented. Of the poets appearing in this book, John Neihardt stands out as a writer of epic rather than lyric poetry, perpetuating for posterity the deeds of the early hunters and trappers along our western rivers. Also of epic proportions is Stephen Vincent Benét's *John Brown's Body*, which does for the Civil War what no contemporary of the war period was able to do — gives us a stupendous picture of the whole struggle from North to South, from home to battlefield. Louis Untermeyer not only writes verse of pronounced merit, but has done more than any other poet to advance and interpret the work of others. Among the many women poets, Sara Teasdale, Edna St. Vincent Millay, and Elinor Wylie have unusual lyric gift. Nathalia Crane, phenomenal girl poet, is put at the end to beckon the rising generation into the realms of poetry.

Who knows what readers of this book may be her successors?

THE TECHNIQUE OF POETRY

In studying poetry it is helpful to know the various terms applying to the subject, so that one may more easily discuss the poems and understand what has been written about them.

Poetry falls naturally into three great classes: narrative, dramatic, and lyric. The first two both tell stories, narrative resembling the short story or novel in its method, dramatic being a play or at least a dialogue in verse. Lyric poetry expresses thought or feeling. Though it may suggest a story, it does not tell it outright.

Kinds of Narrative Poetry: the Epic

Narrative poetry has its subdivisions. The epic is a long narrative poem celebrating in dignified style the deeds of a hero. Among the European nations we find natural epics which grew up in the early days before printing, by word-of-mouth transmission from one bard to another. American literature has nothing of that kind but we have a few artificial or literary epics in which a specific author composes a poem based on the legends previously existing. Thus Longfellow's " Hiawatha " is an epic of the Indians, and Neihardt's " Song of Hugh Glass " of the hunters and trappers.

Metrical Tales

Shorter narrative poems corresponding to the prose short story and called variously metrical romances, metrical tales, or idylls, abound in American literature, especially in the works of Longfellow and Whittier. Longfellow's " Tales of a Wayside Inn " are probably the best known examples. In this book Lowell's " Vision of Sir Launfal " belongs to this class, though the preludes are distinctly lyrical.

Ballads

Still shorter stories in verse with such marked singing quality that they are almost like lyrics are called ballads. Back in medieval times these grew up naturally like epics, and we may still see the process going on in our American folk lore; but other ballads are definitely composed, such as Lowell's " The Courtin'," Sill's " The Fool's Prayer," and Edna Millay's " The Harp Weaver." Typical " ballad measure " is the four-line stanza with alternate rhymes, and three or four beats to a line. Variations of this pattern are of course found, and some ballads, like Whittier's " Skipper Ireson's Ride," are in much longer stanzas.

Dramatic poetry has never flourished in America. Longfellow's " Spanish Student " was a failure, and few of the older authors even attempted the form. In modern poetry, Edna Millay's " The King's Henchman " is almost unique in its vogue.

Kinds of Lyric Poetry: the Song

Lyric poetry is the form which has made itself most felt in America. Certain classifications can be made, but there are always lyrics which defy such labeling. The song is a simple little piece clearly intended for singing purposes. If of religious bent, it becomes a hymn. In this section you will find Emerson's " Concord Hymn," and Whittier's " Dear Lord and Father of Mankind."

Odes

The ode is a sustained poem of exalted mood, often irregular in metrical form. Timrod's " Ode " in this section is too short to be typical. Probably the two most famous odes in American literature (not included here because of their length and difficulty) are Lowell's " Commemoration Ode " and Moody's " Ode in Time of Hesitation."

The Elegy and the Epitaph

The elegy is a mournful poem usually on death. Similar to it is the dirge, or funeral song. Bryant's " Thanatopsis," Whitman's " Carol of Death," and Millay's " Dirge without Music " are examples. It is questionable whether a poem as cheerful in its attitude toward death as Lanier's " Stirrup-Cup " could properly be called an elegy. Frost's " The Death of the Hired Man " is an unusual type of elegy worked out through dialogue. Similar to the elegy and yet different is the epitaph, or inscription for the dead, of which Masters has made such surprising use in his *Spoon River Anthology*.

The Sonnet

The sonnet is the most restricted metrical form, being limited to fourteen lines. In the so-called Italian form there is a break in the thought between the first eight and the last six lines (called the *octave* and the *sestet*), a five-accent line, and an intricate rhyme scheme. The Shakespearean form is more flexible, usually in alternate rhyme, with a couplet at the end to clinch the idea. Perhaps because of this very challenge to ingenuity, the sonnet has been a great favorite with poets of all ages. Examples included in this book are Longfellow's "In the Churchyard at Tarrytown" and Edna Millay's "Dirge without Music."

DEFINITIONS OF TECHNICAL TERMS OF POETRY

Meter

Meter is an element of poetry which presents many possibilities of study. Of course it is more important to enjoy the swing of a poem than to analyze it, but sometimes one has the same curiosity which prompts the small boy to take the clock apart to see what makes it tick.

" Feet ": the Trochee

Lines of poetry are divided into "feet" with one accented syllable to every "foot." The marching of soldiers illustrates one of the common forms of measure. In starting his men out together the sergeant emphasizes the left foot thus: "LEFT, right, LEFT, right," or perhaps just "LEFT . . . LEFT . . . LEFT" omitting the unaccented syllable entirely. An example of this kind of meter is found in Longfellow's "Building of the Ship: "

> " Build me straight, O worthy Master,
> Stanch and strong, a goodly vessel."

There is a vigorous swing to this type of foot suggesting life and action. It is called the trochee, or trochaic foot.

The Iambic Foot

The reverse of this is the iambus, or iambic foot, in which the unaccented syllable comes first, followed by the accented syllable. Whittier's "Snowbound" illustrates it:

> " The sun that brief December day
> Rose cheerless over hills of gray,
> And, darkly circled, gave at noon
> A sadder light than waning moon."

This is the most commonly used foot in English poetry.

The Dactyl and the Anapest

Because of the alternate accents, the iambus and the trochee are marching feet, but there are others which are dancing feet. Could you imagine soldiers marching to waltz time? It couldn't be done. ONE, two, three, ONE, two, three. They would have to dance to it. By a queer twist of anatomy this foot is really a finger, for the Greeks called it a dactyl, or finger, because, of the three bones in that part of the hand, the first is long, the second and third short. When they wanted to reverse the accent and make it: one, two, THREE, one, two, THREE, they called it an anapest, which means striking back. In English poetry the dactyl is seldom found all by itself. Longfellow's " Evangeline " is one of the rare examples of prevailing dactylic measure.

" This is the forest primeval; but where are the hearts that beneath it
  Leaped like the roe, when it hears in the woodland the voice of the
    huntsman? "

Either the dactyl or the anapest, however, mixed with other feet, is frequently used in poems about rides, to simulate horses' hoof-beats. Thus we find the three-syllable foot in " Paul Revere's Ride," " The Deacon's Masterpiece," " Sheridan's Ride," and in the English poems, " The Charge of the Light Brigade " and " How They Brought the Good News from Ghent to Aix." The anapest is more likely to be found in its pure form, as in Poe's " Ulalume ":

" It was night in the lonesome October
  Of my most immemorial year."

Various Verse Forms

In all but the most sing-song of verse, we come across variations in the prevailing form of foot. The poet is governed by the higher laws of his sensitive ear, rather than by the mechanical laws of mathematics. There must, however, be a real swing evident in the variations, else the lines mark the amateur poet by their " limping feet."

Sometimes we wish to indicate the number of feet to a line, and the ancient Greeks have again supplied us with some technical terms: one foot, *monometer;* two feet, *dimeter;* three, *trimeter;* four, *tetrameter;* five, *pentameter;* six, *hexameter;* seven, *heptameter;* eight, *octameter.* Fortunately for our memories, these terms, with the exception of pentameter, are seldom used.

" Iambic pentameter," however, is such a common term that we need to understand that, if no other. This dignified five-foot line is the basis of the sonnet, of blank verse (meaning unrhymed verse, not to be confused with free verse) and of many stanza forms. Bryant's " Thanatopsis " and Frost's " Birches " are examples of blank verse. Robinson's " Richard Cory " shows a four-line stanza in iambic pentameter. Tetrameter is more often used than called by name. " Snowbound " is in iambic tetrameter rhymed in couplets; " Hiawatha " is in unrhymed trochaic tetrameter. Ballad measure alternates tetrameter and trimeter in a four-line stanza. Longfellow is almost unique among our poets for his use of the long and difficult hexameter as in " Evangeline " and " The Courtship of Miles Standish."

Knowledge of these matters is interesting and valuable after we have come to know and enjoy the poetry itself, but it can never be said to create a love for poetry, or in itself to make a poet.

Early Northern Poetry

The first significant movement in American poetry began in the North, but there is little that can be said to be distinctly characteristic of mere geography. During colonial times the students and scholars were brought up on the English poetry that was then the style, chiefly the school of Pope, Dryden, and their followers. Much of the verse of the colonials showed this, and since there were no geniuses here like Dryden and Pope, the American imitations were poor indeed. In 1798 there appeared in England a small volume of only twenty-nine poems, *Lyrical Ballads,* written by two young and almost unknown poets, Wordsworth and Coleridge. The Preface which introduced it was a definite challenge to the so-called Classical school of poetry, in which more attention was paid to *how* a thing was said than to *what* was said. Both nature and human nature were restored by the far-reaching influence of this Preface to their proper places as subjects for poetry.

In America there was a tendency to follow English models, and the conditions of life in this growing country, teeming with suggestions for romance, led to a ready acceptance of the new ideals of poetry. Most of the early poets, both North and South, followed the English traditions without trying to be distinctly national until the great question of slavery and the Civil War made them sound a new and distinctively American note. The style and mannerisms, however, still remained English, and it was not until the strongly individualistic work of Walt Whitman that American poetry came into its own as national in the widest and best sense.

PHILIP FRENEAU (1752–1832)

Freneau was a young man during the Revolution, active in literary propaganda against the British both before and during the war. He spent part of the war years in the West Indies in a commercial capacity and was once captured by the British and imprisoned for some months on a ship in New York harbor. This experience he used in his " The British Prison Ship." Most of his earlier poetry lacks interest today because of its partisan connections with events that were more important in Freneau's time than in ours. After the war he once more became an active journalist, and the three poems that follow are generally conceded to be his best. The first deals with the battle of Eutaw Springs. It has a dignity of meter and stateliness of thought not unlike the poetry of Thomas Gray. Sir Walter Scott, who died the same year as Freneau, thought sufficiently well of the twentieth line to use it in *Marmion,* with only one word changed. " The Wild Honeysuckle " is the first outstanding nature poem in American literature and should be thought of in connection with the nature poems of Wordsworth, the best of which were written but a few years after Freneau's. " The Indian Burying Ground " explains itself, but again it is worth noting that the English poet Thomas Campbell culled a line from it for his " O'Connor's Child." These English references are mentioned to prepare you for further remarks about the relations between the romantic poetry of America and that of England.

TO THE MEMORY OF THE BRAVE AMERICANS

UNDER GENERAL GREENE, IN SOUTH CAROLINA, WHO FELL IN THE
ACTION OF SEPTEMBER 8, 1781

> At Eutaw Springs the valiant died;
>   Their limbs with dust are covered o'er —
> Weep on, ye springs, your tearful tide;
>   How many heroes are no more!

> If in this wreck of ruin, they   5
>   Can yet be thought to claim a tear,
> O smite your gentle breast, and say
>   The friends of freedom slumber here!

Thou, who shalt trace this bloody plain,
 If goodness rules thy generous breast,   10
Sigh for the wasted rural reign;
 Sigh for the shepherds sunk to rest!

Stranger, their humble graves adorn;
 You too may fall, and ask a tear:
'Tis not the beauty of the morn   15
 That proves the evening shall be clear. —

They saw their injured country's woe,
 The flaming town, the wasted field;
Then rushed to meet the insulting foe;
 They took the spear — but left the shield. 20

Led by thy conquering genius, Greene,
 The Britons they compelled to fly;
None distant viewed the fatal plain,
 None grieved in such a cause to die —

But, like the Parthians famed of old,   25
 Who, flying, still their arrows threw,
These routed Britons, full as bold,
 Retreated, and retreating slew.

Now rest in peace our patriot band;
 Though far from nature's limits thrown, 30
We trust they find a happier land,
 A brighter sunshine of their own.

THE WILD HONEYSUCKLE

Fair flower, that dost so comely grow,
 Hid in this silent, dull retreat,
Untouched thy honied blossoms blow,
 Unseen thy little branches greet;
  No roving foot shall crush thee here,
  No busy hand provoke a tear.

By Nature's self in white arrayed,
  She bade thee shun the vulgar eye,
And planted here the guardian shade,
  And sent soft waters murmuring by;
    Thus quietly thy summer goes,
    Thy days declining to repose.

Smit with those charms, that must decay,
  I grieve to see your future doom;
They died — nor were those flowers more gay,
  The flowers that did in Eden bloom;
    Unpitying frosts and Autumn's power
    Shall leave no vestige of this flower.

From morning suns and evening dews
  At first thy little being came:
If nothing once, you nothing lose,
  For when you die you are the same;
    The space between is but an hour,
    The frail duration of a flower.

THE INDIAN BURYING GROUND

In spite of all the learned have said,
  I still my old opinion keep;
The posture that we give the dead
  Points out the soul's eternal sleep.

Not so the ancients of these lands; —   5
  The Indian, when from life released,
Again is seated with his friends,
  And shares again the joyous feast.

His imaged birds, and painted bowl,
  And venison, for a journey dressed,   10
Bespeak the nature of the soul,
  Activity, that knows no rest.

His bow for action ready bent,
    And arrows with a head of stone,
Can only mean that life is spent,   15
    And not the old ideas gone.

Thou, stranger, that shalt come this way,
    No fraud upon the dead commit —
Observe the swelling turf, and say
    They do not lie, but here they sit.   20

Here still a lofty rock remains,
    On which the curious eye may trace
(Now wasted half by wearing rains)
    The fancies of a ruder race.

Here still an aged elm aspires,   25
    Beneath whose far-projecting shade
(And which the shepherd still admires)
    The children of the forest played.

There oft a restless Indian queen
    (Pale Shebah with her braided hair)   30
And many a barbarous form is seen
    To chide the man that lingers there.

By midnight moons, o'er moistening dews,
    In habit for the chase arrayed,
The hunter still the deer pursues,   35
    The hunter and the deer, a shade!

And long shall timorous fancy see
    The painted chief, and pointed spear,
And reason's self shall bow the knee
    To shadows and delusions here.   40

SUGGESTIONS FOR STUDY

1. Compare the first poem with some stanzas of Gray's "Elegy." What similarities do you find?

2. Campbell's "Hohenlinden" (1802) is another English poem that offers an interesting parallel study.

3. Would you prefer a ballad of battle to this lyric of contemplation? If so, can you name such a ballad?

4. In " The Wild Honeysuckle " note particularly the last stanza. What do you make of it? As it turned out, American poets have always had a fondness for that sort of ending.

5. What is the Indian's idea of a hereafter, as depicted in the last poem?

FOR FURTHER READING [1]

" On a Honey-Bee "   " Arnold's Departure "
" The Caty-Did "   " The Northern Soldier "
" The Hurricane "

WILLIAM CULLEN BRYANT (1794–1878)

Fate played strange tricks with William Cullen Bryant. Born and bred in New England, he nevertheless spent two-thirds of his life in New York City. The portrait of Bryant best known to students of poetry shows him as a white-bearded patriarch, although the poems which entitle him to be called our first great American poet were all written before he was thirty-eight. A lover of the woods and the flowers, and by nature a meditative recluse, Bryant spent most of his life in the turmoil of a newspaper office. While still in his teens he made his reputation by " Thanatopsis," a melancholy poem on death, and then lived to the good old age of eighty-four.

When Bryant was seventeen years old he passed through a period of deep discouragement because of the failure of his plans to go to Yale. In this mood he read many of the English poems of melancholy popular at the time. Perhaps his mood was heightened by his own rather poor health and the fact that there was tuberculosis in the family. Under these circumstances he wrote " Thanatopsis." Six years later, in 1817, his father found the poem in a desk and submitted it to *The North American Review.* One of the editors said, " No one on this side of the Atlantic is capable of writing such verses," but when the authorship was verified the poem was published. In 1825, in Bryant's first volume of poems, " Thanatopsis " appeared in the version that follows.

THANATOPSIS

To him who in the love of Nature holds
Communion with her visible forms, she speaks
A various language; for his gayer hours
She has a voice of gladness, and a smile
And eloquence of beauty, and she glides   5

[1] The poems cited in this and later reading lists can generally be found in the anthologies in high school libraries.

Into his darker musings, with a mild
And healing sympathy, that steals away
Their sharpness, ere he is aware. When thoughts
Of the last bitter hour come like a blight
Over thy spirit, and sad images   10
Of the stern agony, and shroud, and pall,
And breathless darkness, and the narrow house,
Make thee to shudder and grow sick at heart; —
Go forth, under the open sky, and list
To Nature's teachings, while from all around —   15
Earth and her waters, and the depths of air —
Comes a still voice —
　　　　　　　　　Yet a few days, and thee
The all-beholding sun shall see no more
In all his course; nor yet in the cold ground,
Where thy pale form was laid with many tears,   20
Nor in the embrace of ocean, shall exist
Thy image. Earth, that nourished thee, shall claim
Thy growth, to be resolved to earth again,
And, lost each human trace, surrendering up
Thine individual being, shalt thou go   25
To mix forever with the elements,
To be a brother to the insensible rock
And to the sluggish clod, which the rude swain
Turns with his share, and treads upon. The oak
Shall send his roots abroad, and pierce thy mold.   30

　　Yet not to thine eternal resting-place
Shalt thou retire alone, nor couldst thou wish
Couch more magnificent. Thou shalt lie down
With patriarchs of the infant world — with kings,
The powerful of the earth — the wise, the good,   35
Fair forms, and hoary seers of ages past,
All in one mighty sepulcher. The hills
Rock-ribbed and ancient as the sun — the vales
Stretching in pensive quietness between;
The venerable woods — rivers that move   40
In majesty, and the complaining brooks
That make the meadows green; and, poured round all,
Old Ocean's gray and melancholy waste —

17. **Yet a few days:** This was the opening of the original poem.

Are but the solemn decorations all
Of the great tomb of man. The golden sun,   45
The planets, all the infinite host of heaven,
Are shining on the sad abodes of death
Through the still lapse of ages. All that tread
The globe are but a handful to the tribes
That slumber in its bosom. — Take the wings   50
Of morning, pierce the Barcan wilderness,
Or lose thyself in the continuous woods
Where rolls the Oregon, and hears no sound,
Save his own dashings — yet the dead are there;
And millions in those solitudes, since first   55
The flight of years began, have laid them down
In their last sleep — the dead reign there alone.
So shalt thou rest, and what if thou withdraw
In silence from the living, and no friend
Take note of thy departure? All that breathe   60
Will share thy destiny. The gay will laugh
When thou art gone, the solemn brood of care
Plod on, and each one as before will chase
His favorite phantom; yet all these shall leave
Their mirth and their employments, and shall come   65
And make their bed with thee. As the long train
Of ages glides away, the sons of men,
The youth in life's green spring, and he who goes
In the full strength of years, matron and maid,
The speechless babe, and the gray-headed man —   70
Shall one by one be gathered to thy side,
By those who in their turn shall follow them.

So live, that when thy summons comes to join
The innumerable caravan, which moves
To that mysterious realm, where each shall take   75
His chamber in the silent halls of death,
Thou go not, like the quarry-slave at night,
Scourged to his dungeon, but, sustained and soothed
By an unfaltering trust, approach thy grave,
Like one who wraps the drapery of his couch   80
About him, and lies down to pleasant dreams.

51. **Barcan:** pertaining to Barca, a district in Northern Africa on the
Mediterranean coast. 53. **Oregon:** now known as the Columbia River in
Oregon. 66. **And make their bed with thee:** This was the end of the original
poem.

SUGGESTIONS FOR STUDY

1. Vocabulary: pall, l. 11; patriarchs, l. 34; hoary seers, l. 36; sepulcher, l. 37; venerable, l. 40; scourged, l. 78.

2. What different messages does Nature have for us according to Stanza 1?

3. How does the view of death in line 17–20 contrast with that in lines 31–72?

4. Does the idea of companionship of the dead seem consoling to you?

5. In what spirit does the poet think we should approach death as shown in the last stanza?

6. Does the poet show his belief in life after death or ignore the subject?

TO A WATERFOWL

When Bryant as a young man was licensed to practice law he was confronted by the problem of where to open his office. One December day while tramping over the hills to consider the town of Plainfield, Massachusetts, he felt particularly depressed by the uncertainty of his future. As his biographer, John Bigelow, describes it, "The sun had already set, leaving behind it one of those brilliant seas of chrysolite and opal which often flood the New England skies, and while pausing to contemplate the rosy splendor with rapt adoration, a solitary bird made its winged way along the illuminated horizon. He watched the lovely wanderer until it was lost in the distance. He then went on with new strength and courage. When he reached the house where he was to stop for the night, he immediately sat down and wrote the lines ' To a Waterfowl,' the concluding verse of which will perpetuate to future ages the lesson on faith which the scene had impressed upon him."

Whither, midst falling dew,
While glow the heavens with the last steps of day,
Far, through their rosy depths, dost thou pursue
    Thy solitary way?

Vainly the fowler's eye   5
Might mark thy distant flight to do thee wrong,
As, darkly painted on the crimson sky,
    Thy figure floats along.

Seek'st thou the plashy brink
Of weedy lake, or marge of river wide,
Or where the rocking billows rise and sink   10
    On the chafed ocean-side?

There is a Power whose care
Teaches thy way along the pathless coast —
The desert and illimitable air —   15
    Lone wandering, but not lost.

All day thy wings have fanned,
At that far height, the cold, thin atmosphere,
Yet stoop not, weary, to the welcome land,
    Though the dark night is near.   20

And soon that toil shall end;
Soon shalt thou find a summer home, and rest,
And scream among thy fellows; reeds shall bend,
    Soon, o'er thy sheltered nest.

Thou'rt gone, the abyss of heaven   25
Hath swallowed up thy form; yet, on my heart
Deeply hath sunk the lesson thou hast given,
    And shall not soon depart.

He who, from zone to zone,
Guides through the boundless sky thy certain flight,   30
In the long way that I must tread alone
Will lead my steps aright.

SUGGESTIONS FOR STUDY

1. Vocabulary: plashy, l. 9; marge, l. 10; illimitable, l. 15; abyss, l. 25.
2. This poem has three parts: the picture presented to the poet's eye, his meditation about the bird, his application to his own life. Point out the stanzas which contain these.
3. In view of the circumstances under which the poem was written do you like or dislike the "moral tag"?
4. It is interesting to compare this poem with one written under similar circumstances by the Scotch poet, Robert Burns. In "To a Mouse" Burns reflected on his own life, but with what a different note!

THE BATTLE–FIELD

Bryant's early poems were about evenly divided in subject matter between death and nature, but some of his later poems, written after his more energetic life in New York had begun, present a stirring challenge and show the fine Puritan spirit which was his inheritance. The first line in the ninth stanza has become almost a proverb through frequent quoting.

Once this soft turf, this rivulet's sands,
    Were trampled by a hurrying crowd,
And fiery hearts and armèd hands
    Encountered in the battle-cloud.

Ah! never shall the land forget   5
    How gushed the life-blood of her brave;
Gushed, warm with hope and valor yet,
    Upon the soil they fought to save.

Now all is calm, and fresh, and still;
    Alone the chirp of flitting bird,   10
And talk of children on the hill,
    And bell of wandering kine, are heard.

No solemn host goes trailing by
  The black-mouthed gun and staggering wain;
Men start not at the battle-cry,   15
  Oh, be it never heard again!

Soon rested those who fought; but thou
  Who minglest in the harder strife
For truths which men receive not now,
  Thy warfare only ends with life.   20

A friendless warfare! lingering long
  Through weary day and weary year,
A wild and many-weaponed throng
  Hang on thy front, and flank, and rear.

Yet nerve thy spirit to the proof,   25
  And blench not at thy chosen lot.
The timid good may stand aloof,
  The sage may frown — yet faint thou not.

Nor heed the shaft too surely cast,
  The foul and hissing bolt of scorn;
For with thy side shall dwell, at last,   30
  The victory of endurance born.

Truth, crushed to earth, shall rise again;
  Th' eternal years of God are hers;
But Error, wounded, writhes in pain,   35
  And dies among his worshipers.

Yea, though thou lie upon the dust,
  When those who helped thee flee in fear,
Die full of hope and manly trust,
  Like those who fell in battle here.   40

Another hand thy sword shall wield,
  Another hand the standard wave,
Till from the trumpet's mouth is pealed
  The blast of triumph o'er thy grave.

SUGGESTIONS FOR STUDY

1. Vocabulary: wain, l. 14; blench, l. 26.
2. What two kinds of battles are contrasted?
3. In what way does this poem reflect the life of a man engaged in public affairs? List the different kinds of persons who may oppose him.
4. Can you see any similarity between the spirit of this poem and that of Lincoln's " Gettysburg Address "?
5. What consolation does this poem offer to a person who suffers defeat in a righteous cause?

FOR FURTHER READING

" To the Fringed Gentian "

" The Death of the Flowers "

" Robert of Lincoln "

" The Evening Wind "

" The Planting of the Apple Tree "

" A Forest Hymn "

" June "

" The Yellow Violet "

" Song of Marion's Men "

" Hymn of the City "

" Abraham Lincoln "

SUGGESTIONS FOR MEMORIZING

" Thanatopsis," especially the last stanza

" To a Waterfowl "

" The Battle-Field," especially the last three stanzas

RALPH WALDO EMERSON (1803–1882)

You have already met Emerson as an essayist, transcendentalist, and prophet. You will not be surprised, then, on meeting him as a poet to find him philosophizing in meter rather than creating moods or pictures as poets usually do. Some critics have even said that most of his poetry was not poetry at all; but on the other hand a few of his best-known pieces could not be sacrificed from our national literature. The " Concord Hymn," the most complete and faultless of his poems according to Oliver Wendell Holmes, was written for the dedication on July 4, 1837, of the monument to the " minute men " of the battle of Concord, which opened the American Revolution. Remember that Emerson's grandfather, a minister of that town, had watched the battle from the Old Manse, only a stone's throw from the bridge (the same Old Manse which Hawthorne later celebrated). Today the minute man may be seen through a leafy vista on the far side of the new stone arch which has replaced the original bridge of rough wood. On the base of the statue is inscribed the first stanza of the poem.

THE CONCORD HYMN

By the rude bridge that arched the flood,
    Their flag to April's breeze unfurled,
Here once the embattled farmers stood,
    And fired the shot heard round the world.

The foe long since in silence slept;
    Alike the conqueror silent sleeps;
And Time the ruined bridge has swept
    Down the dark stream which seaward creeps.

On this green bank, by this soft stream,
    We set today a votive stone;
That memory may their deed redeem,
    When, like our sires, our sons are gone.

Spirit, that made those heroes dare
    To die and leave their children free,
Bid Time and Nature gently spare
    The shaft we raise to them and thee.

SUGGESTIONS FOR STUDY

1. In what sense was "the shot heard round the world"? A map showing the number of republics in the world in that day and in ours would make this line have added significance.

2. To make the situation more vivid, look up the battle in a history book and read "Paul Revere's Ride."

3. Compare the spirit of this with that of Lincoln's "Gettysburg Address." What note struck by Lincoln at the end of his speech is not brought out in this dedication? What appeal is made here instead? To whom is it addressed?

A FABLE

A fable is a short tale in which the characters usually are animals but talk and act like human beings. There always is a moral or a lesson that stands out plainly. In the old fables this lesson is tacked on at

the end so that the reader cannot possibly miss it. As Emerson failed
to follow this old custom, why not make a sentence to tell the meaning?

> The mountain and the squirrel
> Had a quarrel,
> And the former called the latter " Little Prig ";
> Bun replied,
> " You are doubtless very big;
> But all sorts of things and weather
> Must be taken in together,
> To make up a year
> And a sphere.
> And I think it no disgrace
> To occupy my place.
> If I'm not so large as you,
> You are not so small as I,
> And not half so spry.
> I'll not deny you make
> A very pretty squirrel track;
> Talents differ; all is well and wisely put;
> If I cannot carry forests on my back,
> Neither can you crack a nut."

COMPENSATION

Emerson wrote two short poems and one long essay on this subject.
The idea of balance in human life was a favorite of his. In the first
stanza, when others are gay he is silent; in the second it is the reverse.

> Why should I keep holiday
> When other men have none?
> Why but because, when these are gay,
> I sit and mourn alone?
>
> And why, when mirth unseals all tongues,
> Should mine alone be dumb?
> Ah! late I spoke to silent throngs,
> And now their hour is come.

THE RHODORA

ON BEING ASKED, WHENCE IS THE FLOWER?

In this essay on *Nature* Emerson says that the "love of Beauty" is one of the nobler wants of man. While the natural beauty of nature and its forms delights the eye, the appreciation of beauty is also necessary for spiritual perfection. This thought of Emerson is strikingly similar to the theories of Wordsworth, expressed in many poems on flowers.

In May, when sea-winds pierced our solitudes,
I found the fresh Rhodora in the woods,
Spreading its leafless blooms in a damp nook,
To please the desert and the sluggish brook.
The purple petals, fallen in the pool,
Made the black water with their beauty gay;
Here might the red-bird come his plumes to cool,
And court the flower that cheapens his array.
Rhodora! if the sages ask thee why
This charm is wasted on the earth and sky,
Tell them, dear, that if eyes were made for seeing,
Then Beauty is its own excuse for being.
Why thou wert there, O rival of the rose!
I never thought to ask, I never knew;
But, in my simple ignorance, suppose
The self-same Power that brought me there brought you.

2. **Rhodora:** a shrub commonly found in New England, having large clusters of pink flowers shading into purple, which come out before the leaves in early spring. The original Greek meaning of the word was *rose*.

VOLUNTARIES III

The long poem "Voluntaries" contains five disconnected stanzas each treating of some act of the will in relation to the struggles of life. The third one of these is the most easily understood and the best known. The last four lines are frequently quoted.

In an age of fops and toys,
Wanting wisdom, void of right,
Who shall nerve heroic boys
To hazard all in Freedom's fight —

Break sharply off their jolly games,
Forsake their comrades gay,
And quit proud homes and youthful dames
For famine, toil, and fray?
Yet on the nimble air benign
Speed nimbler messages,
That waft the breath of grace divine
To hearts in sloth and ease.
So nigh is grandeur to our dust,
So near is God to man,
When Duty whispers low, *Thou must*,
The youth replies, *I can*.

SUGGESTIONS FOR STUDY

1. What is Emerson's attitude toward " the rising generation "?
2. In the light of Emerson's essays, what is the full significance of
" So near is God to man "?
3. How was the youth's response illustrated in the World War? How
is the sacrifice of self to duty illustrated in other situations than war?
(See De Kruif's *Microbe Hunters*, p. 278.)

EACH AND ALL

That each person or thing is dependent on all that surrounds it is
the theme of this poem. The poet builds up this idea through a number
of examples of the intangible influence of environment, closing with the
idea that truth cannot be entirely disassociated from beauty, much as the
English poet Keats had sung in his famous " Ode on a Grecian Urn " —
" Beauty is truth, truth beauty."

Little thinks, in the field, yon red-cloaked clown,
Of thee from the hill-top looking down;
The heifer that lows in the upland farm,
Far-heard, lows not thine ear to charm;
The sexton, tolling his bell at noon,   5
Deems not that great Napoleon
Stops his horse, and lists with delight,
Whilst his files sweep round yon Alpine height;
Nor knowest thou what argument
Thy life to thy neighbor's creed has lent.   10

All are needed by each one,
Nothing is fair or good alone.
I thought the sparrow's note from heaven,
Singing at dawn on the alder bough;
I brought him home, in his nest, at even;   15
He sings the song, but it pleases not now,
For I did not bring home the river and sky; —
He sang to my ear — they sang to my eye.
The delicate shells lay on the shore;
The bubbles of the latest wave   20
Fresh pearls to their enamel gave;
And the bellowing of the savage sea
Greeted their safe escape to me.
I wiped away the weeds and foam,
I fetched my sea-born treasures home;   25
But the poor, unsightly, noisome things
Had left their beauty on the shore
With the sun, and the sand, and the wild uproar.
The lover watched his graceful maid,
As 'mid the virgin train she strayed,   30
Nor knew her beauty's best attire
Was woven still by the snow-white choir.
At last she came to his hermitage,
Like the bird from the woodlands to the cage; —
The gay enchantment was undone,   35
A gentle wife, but fairy none.
Then I said, " I covet truth;
Beauty is unripe childhood's cheat;
I leave it behind with the games of youth " —
As I spoke, beneath my feet   40
The ground-pine curled its pretty wreath,
Running over the club-moss burrs;
I inhaled the violet's breath;
Around me stood the oaks and firs;
Pine-cones and acorns lay on the ground;   45
Over me soared the eternal sky,
Full of light and of deity;
Again I saw, again I heard,
The rolling river, the morning bird; —
Beauty through my senses stole;   50
I yielded myself to the perfect whole.

SUGGESTIONS FOR STUDY

1. Point out the examples given at the beginning of the poem of the unconscious influence of one person upon another. Discuss lines 9 and 10.

2. Point out examples of loss of charm through loss of environment. Can you give any examples of this from your own experience?

3. What makes the poet decide that "Beauty is unripe childhood's cheat"? Why does he change his mind?

4. In what kind of natural surroundings did Emerson yield himself "to the perfect whole"? Have you had a similar experience?

5. If you have read Emerson's *Self-Reliance* do you consider this idea of interdependence contradictory to it? Give your reasons.

FOR FURTHER READING

"The Humblebee"   "The Romany Girl"   "The Problem"
"The Snowstorm"   "Voluntaries"   "The Test"
"Forbearance"   "The Past"

HENRY WADSWORTH LONGFELLOW (1807–1882)

Since Longfellow is preëminently "the Children's Poet" you have doubtless already eaten heartily of the bountiful feast of story-poems which he has provided, and drunk of his clear-flowing lyrics. If you have never read "The Children's Hour," "The Village Blacksmith," "The Arrow and the Song," "Paul Revere's Ride," "Hiawatha," "Evangeline," and "The Courtship of Miles Standish," it is almost as if you had never jumped rope, played marbles, gone on picnics, or ridden in an automobile. You have just missed some of the common experiences which American boys and girls are assumed to have had. One of the greatest services which Longfellow rendered this country was to immortalize such early American figures as Paul Revere, Priscilla and John Alden (from whom, by the way, he was descended), to give us a semblance of a national Indian epic in "Hiawatha," and to perpetuate in verse the many historical legends of the early settlers as in "Evangeline." Your study as a maturing high school student may well be directed to some of the poems less commonly read than the foregoing.

Longfellow's life presents an unusually smooth path of education, financial ease, happiness, and popular acclaim, broken only by the tragic circumstances surrounding the death of each of his two wives. His boyhood was spent in Portland, Maine, where both the Longfellows and the Wadsworths were families of means and social standing. He made such a brilliant record at Bowdoin College that soon after graduation he was selected to fill a newly-created chair of modern languages in that college. Three years of study in various European countries, six years of teaching at Bowdoin, his marriage to a beautiful Portland girl, a call to Harvard College, and the chance for further European study, followed in happy succession. Then came the first tragedy when in the winter of their stay in Holland his young wife died and was buried far from home. This, with his lonely study of German mysticism and romance, lent a twilight tone to much of his later writing, a mingling of tender sentiment, quiet melancholy, and wistful dreaming of the past. Returning to Harvard he taught for eighteen years, married again, and settled down for the rest of his life in the beautiful colonial Craigie House in Cambridge, where today one can see his handsome study left just as it was during his lifetime. Sorrow visited him again when his second wife was accidentally burned to death, but his later years were brightened by his children about him, his happiness in writing, and the many honors heaped upon him. Noteworthy it is that he was the first American to be honored by a bust in the Poets' Corner of Westminster Abbey. But such a tribute after his death seems cold compared with that which came during his life, when the school children of Cambridge contributed their pennies to have carved for him an armchair from the wood of " the spreading chestnut tree."

HYMN TO THE NIGHT

This poem appeared in the volume *Voices of the Night,* published four years after the death of Longfellow's first wife. It shows the kind of consolation which came to him in this period of sadness.

'Ασπασίη, τρίλλιστος*

I heard the trailing garments of the Night
    Sweep through her marble halls!
. I saw her sable skirts all fringed with light
    From the celestial walls!

I felt her presence, by its spell of might,   5
    Stoop o'er me from above;
The calm, majestic presence of the Night,
    As of the one I love.

* " Welcome, thrice prayed for . . ." *Iliad,* viii, 488.

I heard the sounds of sorrow and delight,
   The manifold, soft chimes   10
That fill the haunted chambers of the Night,
   Like some old poet's rhymes. .

From the cool cisterns of the midnight air
   My spirit drank repose;
The fountain of perpetual peace flows there —   15
   From those deep cisterns flows.

O holy Night! from thee I learn to bear
   What man has borne before!
Thou layest thy finger on the lips of Care,
   And they complain no more.   20

Peace! Peace! Orestes-like I breathe this prayer!
   Descend with broad-winged flight,
The welcome, the thrice-prayed for, the most fair,
   The best-beloved Night!

SUGGESTIONS FOR STUDY

1. Point out the words or lines which seem to refer directly to the poet's recent bereavement.

2. Point out the words in the poem which have an effect of soothing or quieting the spirit. How does this extend the application of the poem to life in general?

3. What evidences do you find that Longfellow was a student of old literatures?

4. Read " Footsteps of Angels," written during the same period, which refers even more directly to the consoling power of his wife's spirit.

21. **Orestes:** a youth of Greek mythology, who prayed to Athene for peace from the pursuit of the Furies.

MAIDENHOOD

After the publication of his second volume of poems Longfellow wrote his father that he thought this and " Excelsior " were the best things he had done up to that time.

Maiden! with the meek, brown eyes,
In whose orbs a shadow lies
Like the dusk in evening skies!

Thou whose locks outshine the sun,
Golden tresses, wreathed in one,   5
As the braided streamlets run!

Standing, with reluctant feet,
Where the brook and river meet,
Womanhood and childhood fleet!

Gazing, with a timid glance,   10
On the brooklet's swift advance,
On the river's broad expanse!

Deep and still, that gliding stream
Beautiful to thee must seem,
As the river of a dream.   15

Then why pause with indecision
When bright angels in thy vision
Beckon thee to fields Elysian?

Seest thou shadows sailing by,
As the dove, with startled eye,   20
Sees the falcon's shadow fly?

Hearest thou voices on the shore,
That our ears perceive no more,
Deafened by the cataract's roar?

18. **Elysian:** In Greek mythology the Elysian fields were the abode of blest spirits after death.

O, thou child of many prayers!   25
Life hath quicksands — Life hath snares!
Care and age come unawares!

Like the swell of some sweet tune,
Morning rises into noon,
May glides onward into June.   30

Childhood is the bough, where slumbered
Birds and blossoms many-numbered; —
Age, that bough with snows encumbered.

Gather, then, each flower that grows,
When the young heart overflows,   35
To embalm that tent of snows.

Bear a lily in thy hand;
Gates of brass cannot withstand
One touch of that magic wand.

Bear through sorrow, wrong, and ruth,   40
In thy heart the dew of youth,
On thy lips the smile of truth.

O, that dew, like balm, shall steal
Into wounds, that cannot heal,
Even as sleep our eyes doth seal;   45

And that smile, like sunshine, dart
Into many a sunless heart,
For a smile of God thou art.

SUGGESTIONS FOR STUDY

1. Which lines picture the outward appearance of the maiden? Which, her mental state?

2. What possible reasons for the maiden's frame of mind are suggested by the poet's questions?

3. What advice does he give the maiden?

4. Why do you think he chooses a lily to be her magic wand? Point out other figures derived from nature which describe the life or the power of the maiden.

THE ARSENAL AT SPRINGFIELD

This impressive plea for peace was written long before the Civil
War. In the light of the two great struggles through which our country
has passed since then, and of the efforts to establish world peace today,
this poem has a real message for our twentieth century ears.

This is the Arsenal. From floor to ceiling,
 Like a huge organ, rise the burnished arms;
But from their silent pipes no anthem pealing
 Startles the villages with strange alarms.

Ah! what a sound will rise, how wild and dreary,   5
 When the death-angel touches those swift keys!
What loud lament and dismal Miserere
 Will mingle with their awful symphonies!

I hear even now the infinite fierce chorus,
 The cries of agony, the endless groan,   10
Which, through the ages that have gone before us,
 In long reverberations reach our own.

On helm and harness rings the Saxon hammer,
 Through Cimbric forest roars the Norseman's song,
And loud, amid the universal clamor,   15
 O'er distant deserts sounds the Tartar gong.

I hear the Florentine, who from his palace
 Wheels out his battle-bell with dreadful din,
And Aztec priests upon their teocallis
 Beat the wild war-drum made of serpent's skin;   20

The tumult of each sacked and burning village;
 The shout that every prayer for mercy drowns;
The soldiers' revels in the midst of pillage;
 The wail of famine in beleaguered towns;

1. **Arsenal:** In Springfield, Massachusetts. 7. **Miserere:** the first word in
the Latin version of the Psalm beginning "Have mercy upon me, O Lord!"
14. **Cimbric:** referring to the Cimbri, a tribe of Norsemen destroyed by the
Romans. 16. **Tartar:** The Tartars, a race of savage Orientals, swept over
Asia and most of Europe in the thirteenth century. 17. **Florentine:** The soldiers of Florence, Italy, in medieval times actually wheeled a great bell out
into the battlefield. 19. **Aztec:** a native race of Mexicans found and later
practically exterminated by the Spaniards. Their teocallis were flat-topped
pyramids of worship.

The bursting shell, the gateway wrenched asunder, 25
   The rattling musketry, the clashing blade;
And ever and anon, in tones of thunder,
   The diapason of the cannonade.

Is it, O man, with such discordant noises,
   With such accursèd instruments as these, 30
Thou drownest Nature's sweet and kindly voices,
   And jarrest the celestial harmonies?

Were half the power, that fills the world with terror,
   Were half the wealth, bestowed on camps and courts,
Given to redeem the human mind from error, 35
   There were no need of arsenals nor forts:

The warrior's name would be a name abhorrèd!
   And every nation, that should lift again
Its hand against a brother, on its forehead
   Would wear forevermore the curse of Cain! 40

Down the dark future, through long generations,
   The echoing sounds grow fainter and then cease;
And like a bell, with solemn, sweet vibrations,
   I hear once more the voice of Christ say, " Peace! "

Peace! and no longer from its brazen portals 45
   The blast of War's great organ shakes the skies!
But beautiful as songs of the immortals,
   The holy melodies of love arise.

SUGGESTIONS FOR STUDY

1. Vocabulary: symphonies, l. 8; reverberations, l. 12; diapason, l. 28; celestial, l. 32.

2. How is the idea of sound or music carried out through the entire poem? Can you see in what two ways the organ is the most fitting instrument with which to compare the arsenal?

3. What different ages and different parts of the world are brought into the poet's survey of war sounds? How does this strengthen his point?

4. What great plea does he make for peace? What attempts to establish universal peace have been made since Longfellow's day? Would you say it is established today?

40. **Cain:** a son of Adam and Eve who was cursed because he slew his brother, Abel. Genesis, iv.

IN THE CHURCHYARD AT TARRYTOWN

Longfellow had been much influenced by Washington Irving. His *Outre Mer* had been somewhat in the spirit of the *Sketch Book,* and the two men resembled each other in kindliness and courtliness of manner, interest in the legends of their own regions, and love of Old World traditions. Why is Indian Summer rather than winter the appropriate metaphor for Irving's last days? Could the last part be applied to Longfellow himself?

Here lies the gentle humorist, who died
　In the bright Indian Summer of his fame!
　A simple stone with but a date and name,
Marks his secluded resting-place beside
The river that he loved and glorified.
　Here in the autumn of his days he came,
　But the dry leaves of life were all aflame
With tints that brightened and were multiplied.

How sweet a life was his; how sweet a death!
　Living to wing with mirth the weary hours,
　Or with romantic tales the heart to cheer;
Dying to leave a memory like the breath
　Of summers full of sunshine and of showers,
　A grief and gladness in the atmosphere.

MY LOST YOUTH

When a man nearing fifty looks back on his youth it may be in a spirit of mournful despair or of happy reminiscence. Which do you think this is?

Longfellow was born in a great three-storied square house facing directly on the bay at Portland, Maine. Today the house is kept open as a memorial to the poet, but the neighborhood is greatly run down and the sparkling bay is filled in with made land covered by railroad tracks — a sorry sight indeed, could the poet see it. Of equal interest is the Wadsworth home on Portland's main business street, where Longfellow lived during his school days and wrote some of his early poems.

Often I think of the beautiful town
　That is seated by the sea;
Often in thought go up and down
The pleasant streets of that dear old town,

And my youth comes back to me.   5
   And a verse of a Lapland song
Is haunting my memory still:
" A boy's will is the wind's will,
And the thoughts of youth are long, long thoughts."

I can see the shadowy lines of its trees,   10
   And catch, in sudden gleams,
The sheen of the far-surrounding seas,
And islands that were the Hesperides
   Of all my boyish dreams.
     And the burden of that old song,   15
     It murmurs and whispers still:
     " A boy's will is the wind's will,
And the thoughts of youth are long, long thoughts."

I remember the black wharves and the slips,
   And the sea-tides tossing free;   20
And Spanish sailors with bearded lips,
And the beauty and mystery of the ships,
   And the magic of the sea.
     And the voice of that wayward song
     Is singing and saying still: 25
     " A boy's will is the wind's will,
And the thoughts of youth are long, long thoughts."

I remember the bulwarks by the shore,
   And the fort upon the hill;
The sunrise gun, with its hollow roar,   30
The drum-beat repeated o'er and o'er,
   And the bugle wild and shrill.
     And the music of that old song
     Throbs in my memory still:
     " A boy's will is the wind's will,   35
And the thoughts of youth are long, long thoughts."

13. **Hesperides:** in Greek mythology the maidens guarding the golden apples, or the island of the sunset on which they lived. From a certain high point in Portland one can get a magnificent view of the sunset across the bay. Perhaps the poet had this in mind.

I remember the sea-fight far away,
　　How it thundered o'er the tide!
And the dead captains, as they lay
In their graves, o'erlooking the tranquil bay   40
　　Where they in battle died.
　　　　And the sound of that mournful song
　　　　Goes through me with a thrill:
　　　　" A boy's will is the wind's will,
And the thoughts of youth are long, long thoughts."   45

I can see the breezy dome of groves,
　　The shadows of Deering's Woods;
And the friendships old and the early loves
Come back with a Sabbath sound, as of doves
　　In quiet neighborhoods.   50
　　　　And the verse of that sweet old song,
　　　　It flutters and murmurs still:
　　　　" A boy's will is the wind's will,
And the thoughts of youth are long, long thoughts."

I remember the gleams and glooms that dart   55
　　Across the school-boy's brain;
The song and the silence in the heart,
That in part are prophecies, and in part
　　Are longings wild and vain.
　　　　And the voice of that fitful song   60
　　　　Sings on, and is never still:
　　　　" A boy's will is the wind's will,
And the thoughts of youth are long, long thoughts."

There are things of which I may not speak;
　　There are dreams that cannot die;   65
There are thoughts that make the strong heart weak,
And bring a pallor into the cheek,
　　And a mist before the eye.
　　　　And the words of that fatal song
　　　　Come over me like a chill: 70
　　　　" A boy's will is the wind's will,
And the thoughts of youth are long, long thoughts."

37. **sea-fight far away:** an engagement between the American *Enterprise* and the English *Boxer* in 1813. Longfellow was six years old at the time. The two captains were actually buried side by side, as the poem suggests.

Strange to me now are the forms I meet
    When I visit the dear old town;
But the native air is pure and sweet, 75
And the trees that o'ershadow each well-known street,
    As they balance up and down,
        Are singing the beautiful song,
        Are sighing and whispering still:
        "A boy's will is the wind's will, 80
And the thoughts of youth are long, long thoughts."

And Deering's Woods are fresh and fair,
    And with joy that is almost pain
My heart goes back to wander there,
And among the dreams of the days that were, 85
    I find my lost youth again.
        And the strange and beautiful song,
        The groves are repeating it still:
        "A boy's will is the wind's will,
And the thoughts of youth are long, long thoughts." 90

SUGGESTIONS FOR STUDY

1. What are some of the dreams that you imagine the boy Longfellow had? What experiences in his life probably fulfilled some of these dreams?

2. How many items of his recollections have to do with the sea? Which of his memories seem to be those that would impress a boy rather than a girl?

3. Explain the meaning of the refrain running through this poem.

THE BUILDING OF THE SHIP

All of Longfellow's life was spent near the ship-building centers of Portland and Boston. He had probably watched the building and launching of many a vessel. In this poem he works out a three-fold analogy — the "Union," the name of the new ship; the union in marriage of the young builder with the master's daughter; and the union of states within our nation, which, in 1849, when this poem was published, was already being threatened with disruption. The last stanza rises to the height of a solemn pledge of loyalty.

" Build me straight, O worthy Master!
    Stanch and strong, a goodly vessel,
That shall laugh at all disaster,
    And with wave and whirlwind wrestle! "

The merchant's word   5
Delighted the Master heard;
For his heart was in his work, and the heart
Giveth grace unto every Art.
A quiet smile played round his lips,
As the eddies and dimples of the tide   10
Play round the bows of ships,
That steadily at anchor ride.
And with a voice that was full of glee,
He answered, " Ere long we will launch
A vessel as goodly, and strong, and stanch,   15
As ever weathered a wintry sea! "

And first with nicest skill and art,
Perfect and finished in every part,
A little model the Master wrought,
Which should be to the larger plan   20
What the child is to the man,
Its counterpart in miniature;
That with a hand more swift and sure
The greater labor might be brought
To answer to his inward thought.   25
And as he labored, his mind ran o'er
The various ships that were built of yore,
And above them all, and strangest of all,
Towered the Great Harry, crank and tall,
Whose picture was hanging on the wall,   30
With bows and stern raised high in air,
And balconies hanging here and there,
And signal lanterns and flags afloat,
And eight round towers, like those that frown
From some old castle, looking down   35

29. **Great Harry:** an English man-of-war built in the reign of Henry VII
and named for him. Its 1000 tons, thought tremendous then, now appear
insignificant beside modern vessels.

Upon the drawbridge and the moat.
And he said, with a smile, " Our ship, I wis,
Shall be of another form than this! "

It was of another form, indeed;
Built for freight, and yet for speed,   40
A beautiful and gallant craft;
Broad in the beam, that the stress of the blast,
Pressing down upon sail and mast,
Might not the sharp bows overwhelm;
Broad in the beam, but sloping aft   45
With graceful curve and slow degrees,
That she might be docile to the helm,
And that the currents of parted seas,
Closing behind, with mighty force,
Might aid and not impede her course.   50

In the ship-yard stood the Master,
    With the model of the vessel
That should laugh at all disaster,
    And with wave and whirlwind wrestle!

Covering many a rood of ground,   55
Lay the timber piled around;
Timber of chestnut, and elm, and oak,
And scattered here and there, with these,
The knarred and crooked cedar knees;
Brought from regions far away,   60
From Pascagoula's sunny bay,
And the banks of the roaring Roanoke!
Ah! what a wondrous thing it is
To note how many wheels of toil
One thought, one word, can set in motion!   65
There's not a ship that sails the ocean,
But every climate, every soil,
Must bring its tribute, great or small,
And help to build the wooden wall!

61. **Pascagoula:** a bay on the southern coast of Mississippi. 62. **Roanoke:** a river in North Carolina.

The sun was rising o'er the sea,   70
And long the level shadows lay,
As if they, too, the beams would be
Of some great, airy argosy,
Framed and launched in a single day.
That silent architect, the sun,   75
Had hewn and laid them every one,
Ere the work of man was yet begun.

Beside the Master, when he spoke,
A youth, against an anchor leaning,
Listened, to catch his slightest meaning.   80
Only the long waves, as they broke
In ripples on the pebbly beach,
Interrupted the old man's speech.

Beautiful they were, in sooth,
The old man and the fiery youth!   85
The old man, in whose busy brain
Many a ship that sailed the main
Was modeled o'er and o'er again; —
The fiery youth, who was to be
The heir of his dexterity,   90
The heir of his house, and his daughter's hand,
When he had built and launched from land
What the elder head had planned.

" Thus," said he, " will we build this ship!
Lay square the blocks upon the slip,   95
And follow well this plan of mine.
Choose the timbers with greatest care;
Of all that is unsound beware;
For only what is sound and strong
To this vessel shall belong.   100
Cedar of Maine and Georgia pine
Here together shall combine.
A goodly frame, and a goodly fame,
And the UNION be her name!
For the day that gives her to the sea   105
Shall give my daughter unto thee! "

The Master's word
Enraptured the young man heard;
And as he turned his face aside,
With a look of joy and a thrill of pride,   110
Standing before
Her father's door,
He saw the form of his promised bride.
The sun shone on her golden hair,
And her cheek was glowing fresh and fair,   115
With the breath of morn and the soft sea air,
Like a beauteous barge was she,
Still at rest on the sandy beach,
Just beyond the billow's reach;
But he   120
Was the restless, seething, stormy sea!

Ah, how skilful grows the hand
That obeyeth Love's command!
It is the heart, and not the brain,
That to the highest doth attain,   125
And he who followeth Love's behest
Far excelleth all the rest!

Thus with the rising of the sun
Was the noble task begun,
And soon throughout the ship-yard's bounds   130
Were heard the intermingled sounds
Of axes and of mallets, plied
With vigorous arms on every side;
Plied so deftly and so well,
That, ere the shadows of evening fell,   135
The keel of oak for a noble ship,
Scarfed and bolted, straight and strong,
Was lying ready, and stretched along
The blocks, well placed upon the slip.
Happy, thrice happy, every one   140
Who sees his labor well begun,
And not perplexed and multiplied,
By idly waiting for time and tide!

And when the hot, long day was o'er,
The young man at the Master's door   145
Sat with the maiden calm and still.
And, within the porch, a little more
Removed beyond the evening chill,
The father sat, and told them tales
Of wrecks in the great September gales,   150
Of pirates upon the Spanish Main,
And ships that never came back again,
The chance and change of a sailor's life,
Want and plenty, rest and strife,
His roving fancy, like the wind,   155
That nothing can stay and nothing can bind,
And the magic charm of foreign lands,
With shadows of palms, and shining sands,
Where the tumbling surf,
O'er the coral reefs of Madagascar   160
Washes the feet of the swarthy Lascar,
As he lies alone and asleep on the turf.
And the trembling maiden held her breath
At the tales of that awful, pitiless sea,
With all its terror and mystery,   165
The dim, dark sea, so like unto Death,
That divides and yet unites mankind!
And whenever the old man paused, a gleam
From the bowl of his pipe would awhile illume
The silent group in the twilight gloom,   170
And thoughtful faces as in a dream;
And for a moment one might mark
What had been hidden by the dark,
That the head of the maiden lay at rest,
Tenderly, on the young man's breast!   175

Day by day the vessel grew,
With timbers fashioned strong and true,
Stemson and keelson and sternson-knee,
Till, framed with perfect symmetry,

160. **Madagascar:** an island in the Indian Ocean. 161. **Lascar:** an East
Indian sailor. 178. **Stemson and keelson and sternson-knee:** supporting
timbers of various parts of the hull of the ship.

A skeleton ship rose up to view!   180
And around the bows and along the side
The heavy hammers and mallets plied,
Till after many a week, at length,
Wonderful for form and strength,
Sublime in its enormous bulk,   185
Loomed aloft the shadowy hulk!
And around it columns of smoke, upwreathing,
Rose from the boiling, bubbling, seething
Caldron, that glowed,
And overflowed   190
With the black tar, heated for the sheathing.
And amid the clamors
Of clattering hammers,
He who listened heard now and then
The song of the Master and his men: —   195

" Build me straight, O worthy Master,
    Stanch and strong, a goodly vessel,
That shall laugh at all disaster,
    And with wave and whirlwind wrestle! "

With oaken brace and copper band,   200
Lay the rudder on the sand,
That, like a thought, should have control
Over the movement of the whole;
And near it the anchor, whose giant hand
Would reach down and grapple with the land,   205
And immovable and fast
Hold the great ship against the bellowing blast!
And at the bows an image stood,
By a cunning artist carved in wood,
With robes of white, that far behind   210
Seemed to be fluttering in the wind.
It was not shaped in a classic mold,
Not like a nymph or goddess of old,
Or naiad rising from the water,
But modeled from the Master's daughter!   215
On many a dreary and misty night,
'Twill be seen by the rays of the signal light,

Speeding along through the rain and the dark,
Like a ghost in its snow-white sark,
The pilot of some phantom bark,   220
Guiding the vessel, in its flight,
By a path none other knows aright!

Behold, at last,
Each tall and tapering mast
Is swung into its place;   225
Shrouds and stays
Holding it firm and fast!

Long ago,
In the deer-haunted forests of Maine,
When upon mountain and plain   230
Lay the snow,
They fell — those lordly pines!
Those grand, majestic pines!
'Mid shouts and cheers
The jaded steers,   235
Panting beneath the goad,
Dragged down the weary, winding road
Those captive kings so straight and tall
To be shorn of their streaming hair,
And, naked and bare,   240
To feel the stress and the strain
Of the wind and the reeling main,
Whose roar
Would remind them forevermore
Of their native forests they should not see again. 245

And everywhere
The slender, graceful spars
Poise aloft in the air,
And at the masthead,
White, blue, and red,   250
A flag unrolls the stripes and stars.
Ah! when the wanderer, lonely, friendless
In foreign harbors shall behold
That flag unrolled,

'Twill be as a friendly hand 255
Stretched out from his native land,
Filling his heart with memories sweet and endless.

All is finished! and at length
Has come the bridal day
Of beauty and of strength. 260
Today the vessel shall be launched!
With fleecy clouds the sky is blanched,
And o'er the bay,
Slowly, in all his splendors dight,
The great sun rises to behold the sight. 265

The ocean old,
Centuries old,
Strong as youth, and as uncontrolled,
Paces restless to and fro,
Up and down the sands of gold. 270
His beating heart is not at rest;
And far and wide,
With ceaseless flow,
His beard of snow
Heaves with the heaving of his breast. 275

He waits impatient for his bride.
There she stands,
With her foot upon the sands,
Decked with flags and streamers gay,
In honor of her marriage day, 280
Her snow-white signals fluttering, blending,
Round her like a veil descending,
Ready to be
The bride of the gray, old sea.

On the deck another bride 285
Is standing by her lover's side.
Shadows from the flags and shrouds,
Like the shadows cast by clouds,
Broken by many a sunny fleck,
Fall around them on the deck. 290

The prayer is said,
The service read,
The joyous bridegroom bows his head;
And in tears the good old Master
Shakes the brown hand of his son,   295
Kisses his daughter's glowing cheek
In silence, for he cannot speak,
And ever faster
Down his own the tears begin to run.
The worthy pastor —   300
The shepherd of that wandering flock,
That has the ocean for its wold,
That has the vessel for its fold,
Leaping ever from rock to rock —
Spake, with accents mild and clear,   305
Words of warning, words of cheer,
But tedious to the bridegroom's ear.
He knew the chart
Of the sailor's heart,
All its pleasures and its griefs,   310
All its shallows and rocky reefs,
All those secret currents, that flow
With such resistless undertow,
And lift and drift, with terrible force,
The will from its moorings and its course.   315
Therefore he spake, and thus said he: —
" Like unto ships far off at sea,
Outward or homeward bound are we.
Before, behind, and all around,
Floats and swings the horizon's bound,   320
Seems at its distant rim to rise
And climb the crystal wall of the skies,
And then again to turn and sink,
As if we could slide from its outer brink.
Ah! it is not the sea,   325
It is not the sea that sinks and shelves,
But ourselves
That rock and rise
With endless and uneasy motion,
Now touching the very skies,   330
Now sinking into the depths of ocean.

Ah! if our souls but poise and swing
Like the compass in its brazen ring,
Ever level and ever true
To the toil and the task we have to do,   335
We shall sail securely, and safely reach
The Fortunate Isles, on whose shining beach
The sights we see, and the sounds we hear,
Will be those of joy and not of fear! "

Then the Master,   340
With a gesture of command,
Waved his hand;
And at the word,
Loud and sudden there was heard,
All around them and below,   345
The sound of hammers, blow on blow,
Knocking away the shores and spurs.
And see! she stirs!
She starts — she moves — she seems to feel
The thrill of life along her keel,   350
And, spurning with her foot the ground,
With one exulting, joyous bound,
She leaps into the ocean's arms!

And lo! from the assembled crowd
There rose a shout, prolonged and loud,   355
That to the ocean seemed to say,
" Take her, O bridegroom, old and gray,
Take her to thy protecting arms,
With all her youth and all her charms! "

How beautiful she is! How fair   360
She lies within those arms, that press
Her form with many a soft caress
Of tenderness and watchful care!
Sail forth into the sea, O ship!
Through wind and wave, right onward steer!   365
The moistened eye, the trembling lip,
Are not the signs of doubt or fear.

337. **Fortunate Isles:** home of the spirits of the blessèd after death.

Sail forth into the sea of life,
O gentle, loving, trusting wife,
And safe from all adversity   370
Upon the bosom of that sea
Thy comings and thy goings be!
For gentleness and love and trust
Prevail o'er angry wave and gust;
And in the wreck of noble lives   375
Something immortal still survives!

Thou, too, sail on, O Ship of State!
Sail on, O UNION, strong and great!
Humanity with all its fears,
With all the hopes of future years,   380
Is hanging breathless on thy fate!
We know what Master laid thy keel,
What Workmen wrought thy ribs of steel,
Who made each mast, and sail, and rope,
What anvils rang, what hammers beat,   385
In what a forge, and what a heat
Were shaped the anchors of thy hope!
Fear not each sudden sound and shock,
'Tis of the wave and not the rock;
'Tis but the flapping of the sail,   390
And not a rent made by the gale!
In spite of rock and tempest's roar,
In spite of false lights on the shore,
Sail on, nor fear to breast the sea!
Our hearts, our hopes, are all with thee,   395
Our hearts, our hopes, our prayers, our tears,
Our faith triumphant o'er our fears,
Are all with thee — are all with thee!

SUGGESTIONS FOR STUDY

1. Vocabulary: argosy, l. 73; dexterity, l. 90; slip, l. 95; scarfed and bolted, l. 137; naiad, l. 214; sark, l. 219; dight, l. 264; wold, l. 302.

2. Was the ship which forms the subject of the poem a warship or a merchant vessel? A wooden or a steel ship? A sailing vessel or a steamship? Prove your points.

3. From what different parts of the country were the materials brought? How does the poet link this up with the Ship of State?

4. How does the metrical form of this poem differ from the others by Longfellow in this book? From these poems and others of his you have read, would you say that his poems are unified or varied in the metrical forms used?

5. Point out a refrain which is repeated in the poem. How many times is it brought in? How is it varied each time?

6. There are two possible interpretations for *straight* in the first line. Do you think it means " Build me a goodly vessel, straight, stanch, and strong " or " Build me straightway (i.e. immediately) a goodly vessel, stanch and strong " ? Do *me* and *straight* have different meanings in lines 196–199 from those of the first stanza?

7. What figurative expressions do you find in the description of various parts of the vessel?

8. Describe the figurehead at the prow. " Drowne's Wooden Image " by Hawthorne, telling the story of a figurehead modeled after a living woman, would make interesting outside reading.

9. Put the minister's wedding sermon into your own words.

10. How is the triple analogy carried out in the last three stanzas? Find out from your history what some of the waves, winds, rocks, and false lights for the Union might have referred to in 1849.

THE BELLS OF SAN BLAS

Just a week before he died Longfellow wrote this, his last poem. It is typical of so much of his poetry with its romantic setting, its tender lingering over the past, and its bell music, that it seems a fitting swan song. Especially significant is the last stanza, which does not show the glorification of the past at the expense of the present and future, so characteristic of aged men, but rather the hopeful note of progress and coming light. " It is daybreak everywhere."

What say the Bells of San Blas
To the ships that southward pass
    From the harbor of Mazatlan?
To them it is nothing more
Than the sound of surf on the shore —   5
    Nothing more to master or man.

But to me, a dreamer of dreams,
To whom what is and what seems
    Are often one and the same —
The Bells of San Blas to me   10
Have a strange, wild melody,
    And are something more than a name.

For bells are the voice of the church;
They have tones that touch and search
    The hearts of young and old;   15
One sound to all, yet each
Lends a meaning to their speech,
    And the meaning is manifold.

They are a voice of the Past,
Of an age that is fading fast,   20
    Of a power austere and grand;
When the flag of Spain unfurled
Its folds o'er this western world,
    And the Priest was lord of the land.

The chapel that once looked down   25
On the little seaport town
    Has crumbled into the dust;
And on oaken beams below
The bells swing to and fro,
    And are green with mold and rust.   30

1. **San Blas:** name of the church or monastery. 3. **Mazatlan:** a town on the west coast of Mexico.

" Is, then, the old faith dead,"
They say, " and in its stead
   Is some new faith proclaimed,
That we are forced to remain
Naked to sun and rain,   35
   Unsheltered and ashamed?

" Once in our tower aloof
We rang over wall and roof
   Our warnings and our complaints;
And round about us there   40
The white doves filled the air,
   Like the white souls of the saints.

" The saints! Ah, have they grown
Forgetful of their own?
   Are they asleep, or dead,   45
That open to the sky
Their ruined Missions lie,
   No longer tenanted?

" Oh, bring us back once more
The vanished days of yore,   50
   When the world with faith was filled;
Bring back the fervid zeal,
The hearts of fire and steel,
   The hands that believe and build.

" Then from our tower again   55
We will send over land and main
   Our voices of command,
Like exiled kings who return
To their thrones, and the people learn
   That the Priest is lord of the land! "   60

O Bells of San Blas, in vain
Ye call back the Past again!
   The Past is deaf to your prayer;
Out of the shadows of night
The world rolls into light;   65
   It is daybreak everywhere.

FOR FURTHER READING

"The Psalm of Life"
"The Reaper and the Flowers"
"The Wreck of the Hesperus"
"The Village Blacksmith"
"The Skeleton in Armor"
"Excelsior"
"The Bridge"
"The Old Clock on the Stairs"
"The Arrow and the Song"
"The Builders"

"Children"
"The Children's Hour"
"The Ladder of St. Augustine"
"The Discoverer of the North Cape"
"Evangeline"
"The Courtship of Miles Standish"
"Hiawatha"
"The Tales of a Wayside Inn"

SUGGESTIONS FOR MEMORIZING

"The Arsenal at Springfield," especially the last four stanzas
The last stanza of "The Building of the Ship"

JOHN GREENLEAF WHITTIER (1807–1892)

Whittier presents a striking contrast to the other New England poets. Bryant, for instance, wrote his best poetry in youth before he became embroiled in newspaper life, whereas Whittier in his youth was too much engrossed in the Abolition cause to write much besides anti-slavery poems, editorials, and tracts, and thus his best poetry was produced after he was fifty. Emerson, Longfellow, Lowell, and Holmes were all college men with a long line of college-bred ancestors behind them (the Brahmin caste, as Holmes puts it); whereas Whittier, the Quaker farm boy, earned money for two terms in Haverhill Academy by cobbling. All the others traveled extensively, acquired valuable libraries, and lived in well-appointed or even handsome homes; whereas Whittier never crossed the ocean, was out of New England only for short periods, and even after the success of "Snowbound" had little extra money for luxuries. He was born at the old homestead described in "Snowbound" near Haverhill, Massachusetts, and was buried from his comfortable but unpretentious white frame house in Amesbury not twenty miles away. Thus he is more distinctly an American product than any of the other New Englanders, less molded and modified by Old World culture.

One marked influence from across the water did, however, reach him. In early life a volume of Burns's poems was lent him by his schoolmaster (not the one in "Snowbound"). The lyrics of this Scotch farm boy struck an answering chord in the New England farm boy, and spurred him on to write his first verses. Because of similarity in the pictures of country life drawn by the two poets, Whittier has often been called " The American Burns," but in character the two men were totally different.

Whittier's early interest in anti-slavery appears in his first printed poem, " The Exile's Departure," published in the paper edited by the famous Abolitionist, William Lloyd Garrison, with whom he later became closely acquainted. Early portraits of Whittier show the flashing dark eye and firm-set mouth of a born reformer. He threw himself heart and soul into the then unpopular cause of abolition. Several times he suffered from mob violence. Once in Philadelphia when his newspaper office was being sacked and burned, Whittier, disguised in a heavy cloak, apparently joined the marauders and thus cleverly saved some important papers in his desk. As the abolition movement grew in favor and Whittier's ringing poems won the popular fancy, he gradually took his place among the other New England writers, a place firmly established when he was asked to become a contributor to *The Atlantic Monthly*.

When we survey his life as a whole, the Civil War seems to cut it into two distinct parts. Before the war we think of him as a fiery soul struggling in the face of unpopularity, poverty, and ill health to champion his beloved cause. After the war we picture him as the gentle, white-bearded old Quaker, with his quaint *thee* and *thou,* visited by many admiring friends and receiving for a quarter of a century the plaudits of the nation.

ICHABOD

The title of this poem is an old Hebrew name meaning " the glory has departed." In the Bible story (Sam. iv, 21) a child was given this name because the ark of the Lord had been captured by the enemy and the high priest had died. Here Whittier applies the term to Daniel Webster, whose famous Seventh of March Speech, 1850, advocated compromise on the slavery question and thus made Whittier feel that the cause of Abolition had been sacrificed, and its high priest, Webster, had fallen. It is generally conceded by modern historians that Webster was unjustly condemned at the time and that his motive was purely to save the Union rather than to win the presidency. Whittier, who was, by the way, related to Webster, said himself that the poem was dictated by no partisan or personal enmity. " On the contrary, my admiration of the splendid personality and intellectual power of the great senator was never stronger than when I laid down his speech, and, in one of the saddest moments of my life, penned this protest."

So fallen! so lost! the light withdrawn
    Which once he wore!
The glory from his gray hairs gone
    Forevermore!

Revile him not — the Tempter hath   5
    A snare for all;
And pitying tears, not scorn and wrath,
    Befit his fall!

Oh, dumb be passion's stormy rage,
    When he who might   10
Have lighted up and led his age
    Falls back in night.

Scorn! would the angels laugh, to mark
    A bright soul driven,
Fiend-goaded, down the endless dark,   15
    From hope and heaven!

Let not the land once proud of him
    Insult him now,
Nor brand with deeper shame his dim,
    Dishonored brow.   20

But let its humbled sons, instead,
    From sea to lake,
A long lament, as for the dead,
    In sadness make.

Of all we loved and honored, naught   25
    Save power remains —
A fallen angel's pride of thought,
    Still strong in chains.

All else is gone; from those great eyes
    The soul has fled;   30
When faith is lost, when honor dies,
    The man is dead!

Then, pay the reverence of old days
    To his dead fame;
Walk backward, with averted gaze,   35
    And hide the shame!

SUGGESTIONS FOR STUDY

1. Look up in a history the conditions calling forth Webster's Seventh of March Speech, and find out just what he advocated about slavery.

2. Which spirit do we find in this poem — pity or scorn?   Which of these two would you most hate to have directed at you?

3. Read " The Lost Occasion," a poem written by Whittier about Webster after the latter's death.   Find out whether Whittier changed his opinion of the statesman after " Ichabod."

4. A poem similar in occasion and idea to " Ichabod " was written by Robert Browning about Wordsworth, called " The Lost Leader."   It would be interesting to compare these two poems to see whether the attitude toward the fallen idol is the same or different.

TELLING THE BEES

Whittier perpetuated in his poems many of the superstitions and legends of the New England countryside.   This one, based on the quaint idea that the bees must be told of a death in the family, else they would desert their hives, is full of the beauty and underlying sadness of the country.   The mourning lover, a year after Mary's death, lingers over the details of his first grief.   Though Whittier was an old man when he wrote this and was probably saddened by the death of his mother the previous year, he may also have been thinking of the faded romance of his own youth.

Here is the place; right over the hill
    Runs the path I took;
You can see the gap in the old wall still,
    And the stepping-stones in the shallow brook.

There is the house, with the gate red-barred,   5
    And the poplars tall;
And the barn's brown length, and the cattle-yard,
    And the white horns tossing above the wall.

There are the beehives ranged in the sun;
    And down by the brink   10
Of the brook are her poor flowers, weed-o'errun,
    Pansy and daffodil, rose and pink.

A year has gone, as the tortoise goes,
Heavy and slow;
And the same rose blows, and the same sun glows,   15
And the same brook sings of a year ago.

There's the same sweet clover-smell in the breeze;
And the June sun warm
Tangles his wings of fire in the trees,
Setting, as then, over Fernside farm.   20

I mind me how with a lover's care
From my Sunday coat
I brushed off the burrs, and smoothed my hair,
And cooled at the brookside my brow and throat.

Since we parted, a month had passed —   25
To love, a year;
Down through the beeches I looked at last
On the little red gate and the well-sweep near.

I can see it all now — the slantwise rain
Of light through the leaves,
The sundown's blaze on her window-pane,   30
The bloom of her roses under the eaves.

Just the same as a month before —
The house and the trees,
The barn's brown gable, the vine by the door —   35
Nothing changed but the hives of bees.

Before them, under the garden wall,
Forward and back,
Went drearily singing the chore-girl small,
Draping each hive with a shred of black.   40

Trembling, I listened: the summer sun
Had the chill of snow;
For I knew she was telling the bees of one
Gone on the journey we all must go!

Then I said to myself, " My Mary weeps 45
 For the dead today:
Haply her blind old grandsire sleeps
 The fret and the pain of his age away."

But her dog whined low; on the doorway sill,
 With his cane to his chin, 50
The old man sat; and the chore-girl still
 Sung to the bees stealing out and in.

And the song she was singing ever since
 In my ear sounds on: —
" Stay at home, pretty bees, fly not hence! 55
 Mistress Mary is dead and gone! "

SNOWBOUND

THE WINTER IDYL

After the close of the Civil War with the question of slavery settled,
Whittier's mind turned more toward personal reminiscence. Being a
bachelor he had lived in closer touch with the family of his boyhood

than he might have otherwise, and these home ties had recently been broken by the death of his mother and elder sister, and later his younger sister, Elizabeth. No one was left now but his brother, Matthew, and himself. What more natural than that he should write a memorial poem dedicated to the old household? The poem was published in 1866 and was immediately hailed as the greatest American pastoral poem.

Whittier gave a faithful account of the family circle and the farm life. Nothing is fictitious. The farmhouse, now about two centuries old, still stands just off the highway between Haverhill and Amesbury, carefully preserved by a Memorial Association. Here the visitor may see every detail as pictured, even the slanting well-sweep outside and the turkey-wing to brush up the hearth.

"As the Spirits of Darkness be stronger in the dark, so Good Spirits which be Angels of Light are augmented not only by the Divine light of the Sun, but also by our common Wood Fire: and as the Celestial Fire drives away dark spirits, so also this our Fire of Wood doth the same." — COR. AGRIPPA, *Occult Philosophy*, Book I, ch. v.

> " Announced by all the trumpets of the sky,
>   Arrives the snow, and, driving o'er the fields,
>   Seems nowhere to alight: the whited air
>   Hides hills and woods, the river, and the heaven,
>   And veils the farm-house at the garden's end.
>   The sled and traveler stopped, the courier's feet
>   Delayed, all friends shut out, the housemates sit
>   Around the radiant fireplace, enclosed
>   In a tumultuous privacy of storm."
>
>   — EMERSON, *The Snow Storm.*

The sun that brief December day
Rose cheerless over hills of gray,
And, darkly circled, gave at noon
A sadder light than waning moon.
Slow tracing down the thickening sky   5
Its mute and ominous prophecy,
A portent seeming less than threat,
It sank from sight before it set.
A chill no coat, however stout,
Of homespun stuff could quite shut out,   10

A hard, dull bitterness of cold,
   That checked, mid-vein, the circling race
   Of life-blood in the sharpened face,
The coming of the snowstorm told.
The wind blew east: we heard the roar   15
Of Ocean on his wintry shore,
And felt the strong pulse throbbing there
Beat with low rhythm our inland air.

Meanwhile we did our nightly chores —
Brought in the wood from out of doors,   20
Littered the stalls, and from the mows
Raked down the herd's-grass for the cows;
Heard the horse whinnying for his corn;
And, sharply clashing horn on horn,
Impatient down the stanchion rows   25
The cattle shake their walnut bows;
While, peering from his early perch
Upon the scaffold's pole of birch,
The cock his crested helmet bent
And down his querulous challenge sent.   30

Unwarmed by any sunset light
The gray day darkened into night,
A night made hoary with the swarm
And whirl-dance of the blinding storm,
As zigzag wavering to and fro,   35
Crossed and recrossed the wingèd snow:
And ere the early bedtime came
The white drift piled the window-frame,
And through the glass the clothes-line posts
Looked in like tall and sheeted ghosts.   40

So all night long the storm roared on:
The morning broke without a sun;
In tiny spherule traced with lines
Of Nature's geometric signs,
In starry flake and pellicle,   45
All day the hoary meteor fell;
And, when the second morning shone,

We looked upon a world unknown,
On nothing we could call our own.
Around the glistening wonder bent   50
The blue walls of the firmament,
No cloud above, no earth below —
A universe of sky and snow!
The old familiar sights of ours
Took marvelous shapes; strange domes and towers   55
Rose up where sty or corn-crib stood,
Or garden-wall, or belt of wood;
A smooth white mound the brush-pile showed,
A fenceless drift what once was road;
The bridle-post an old man sat   60
With loose-flung coat and high cocked hat;
The well-curb had a Chinese roof;
And even the long sweep, high aloof,
In its slant splendor, seemed to tell
Of Pisa's leaning miracle.   65

A prompt, decisive man, no breath
Our father wasted: " Boys, a path! "
Well pleased, (for when did farmer boy
Count such a summons less than joy?)
Our buskins on our feet we drew;   70
    With mittened hands, and caps drawn low,
    To guard our necks and ears from snow,
We cut the solid whiteness through.
And, where the drift was deepest, made
A tunnel walled and overlaid   75
With dazzling crystal: we had read
Of rare Aladdin's wondrous cave,
And to our own his name we gave,
With many a wish the luck were ours
To test his lamp's supernal powers.   80
We reached the barn with merry din,
And roused the prisoned brutes within.

62. well-curb had a Chinese roof: Whittier explained, when asked how
this could be, that a board had been placed across the curb to hold the
bucket and that this gave the roof effect. 65. Pisa's leaning miracle: a famous
slanting tower in Pisa, Italy. 70. buskins: a name for heavy boots derived
from the high-heeled boots worn by ancient Greek actors. 77. Aladdin: the
youth in the Arabian Nights who discovered great treasure in a cave through
the power of a magical lamp.

The old horse thrust his long head out,
And grave with wonder gazed about;
The cock his lusty greeting said,   85
And forth his speckled harem led;
The oxen lashed their tails, and hooked,
And mild reproach of hunger looked;
The hornèd patriarch of the sheep,
Like Egypt's Amun roused from sleep,   90
Shook his sage head with gesture mute,
And emphasized with stamp of foot.

All day the gusty north-wind bore
The loosening drift its breath before;
Low circling round its southern zone,   95
The sun through dazzling snow-mist shone.
No church-bell lent its Christian tone
To the savage air, no social smoke
Curled over woods of snow-hung oak.
A solitude made more intense   100
By dreary-voicèd elements,
The shrieking of the mindless wind,
The moaning tree-boughs swaying blind,
And on the glass the unmeaning beat
Of ghostly finger-tips of sleet.   105
Beyond the circle of our hearth
No welcome sound of toil or mirth
Unbound the spell, and testified
Of human life and thought outside.
We minded that the sharpest ear   110
The buried brooklet could not hear,
The music of whose liquid lip
Had been to us companionship,
And, in our lonely life, had grown
To have an almost human tone.   115

As night drew on, and, from the crest
Of wooded knolls that ridged the west,
The sun, a snow-blown traveler, sank
From sight beneath the smothering bank,

90. **Egypt's Amun:** An Egyptian god frequently represented with a ram's
head.

We piled with care our nightly stack   120
Of wood against the chimney-back —
The oaken log, green, huge, and thick,
And on its top the stout backstick;
The knotty forestick laid apart,
And filled between with curious art   125
The ragged brush; then, hovering near,
We watched the first red blaze appear,
Heard the sharp crackle, caught the gleam
On whitewashed wall and sagging beam,
Until the old, rude-furnished room   130
Burst, flower-like, into rosy bloom;
While radiant with a mimic flame
Outside the sparkling drift became,
And through the bare-boughed lilac-tree
Our own warm hearth seemed blazing free.   135
The crane and pendent trammels showed,
The Turks' heads on the andirons glowed;
While childish fancy, prompt to tell
The meaning of the miracle,
Whispered the old rime: " *Under the tree*   140
When fire outdoors burns merrily,
There the witches are making tea."

The moon above the eastern wood
Shone at its full; the hill-range stood
Transfigured in the silver flood,   145
Its blown snows flashing cold and keen,
Dead white, save where some sharp ravine
Took shadow, or the somber green
Of hemlocks turned to pitchy black
Against the whiteness at their back.   150
For such a world and such a night
Most fitting that unwarming light,
Which only seemed where'er it fell
To make the coldness visible.

Shut in from all the world without,   155
We sat the clean-winged hearth about,

137. **Turks' heads:** the design of the top of the andiron resembled a Turkish cap.   156. **clean-winged hearth:** a turkey-wing was used for a hearth broom.

Content to let the north-wind roar
In baffled rage at pane and door,
While the red logs before us beat
The frost-line back with tropic heat; 160
And ever, when a louder blast
Shook beam and rafter as it passed,
The merrier up its roaring draught
The great throat of the chimney laughed;
The house-dog on his paws outspread 165
Laid to the fire his drowsy head,
The cat's dark silhouette on the wall
A couchant tiger's seemed to fall;
And, for the winter fireside meet,
Between the andirons' straddling feet, 170
The mug of cider simmered slow,
The apples sputtered in a row,
And, close at hand, the basket stood
With nuts from brown October's wood.

What matter how the night behaved? 175
What matter how the north-wind raved?
Blow high, blow low, not all its snow
Could quench our hearth-fire's ruddy glow.
O Time and Change! — with hair as gray
As was my sire's that winter day, 180
How strange it seems, with so much gone
Of life and love, to still live on!
Ah, brother! only I and thou
Are left of all that circle now —
The dear home faces whereupon 185
That fitful firelight paled and shone.
Henceforward, listen as we will,
The voices of that hearth are still;
Look where we may, the wide earth o'er,
Those lighted faces smile no more. 190
We tread the paths their feet have worn,
  We sit beneath their orchard-trees,
  We hear, like them, the hum of bees
And rustle of the bladed corn;
We turn the pages that they read, 195
  Their written words we linger o'er,

But in the sun they cast no shade,
No voice is heard, no sign is made,
   No step is on the conscious floor!
Yet Love will dream, and Faith will trust,   200
(Since He who knows our need is just,)
That somehow, somewhere, meet we must.
Alas for him who never sees
The stars shine through his cypress-trees!
Who, hopeless, lays his dead away,   205
Nor looks to see the breaking day
Across the mournful marbles play!
Who hath not learned, in hours of faith,
   The truth to flesh and sense unknown,
That Life is ever lord of Death,   210
   And Love can never lose its own!

We sped the time with stories old,
Wrought puzzles out, and riddles told,
Or stammered from our school-book lore
" The chief of Gambia's golden shore."   215
How often since, when all the land
Was clay in Slavery's shaping hand,
As if a trumpet called, I've heard
Dame Mercy Warren's rousing word:
" *Does not the voice of reason cry,*   220
   Claim the first right which Nature gave,
From the red scourge of bondage fly,
   Nor deign to live a burdened slave! "
Our father rode again his ride
On Memphremagog's wooded side;   225
Sat down again to moose and samp
In trapper's hut and Indian camp;
Lived o'er the old idyllic ease
Beneath St. François' hemlock trees;
Again for him the moonlight shone   230
On Norman cap and bodiced zone;
Again he heard the violin play

215. **"The chief of Gambia's golden shore"**: a line from a popular poem
of the day called "The African Chief." This and the quotation of lines 220–
223 show the interest in anti-slavery in Whittier's boyhood.   225. **Memphremagog:** a lake between Vermont and Canada.   229. **St. François:** a river
in Quebec.   231. **Norman cap and bodiced zone:** dress of Canadian girls who
had come originally from Normandy, France.

Which led the village dance away,
And mingled in its merry whirl
The grandam and the laughing girl.   235
Or, nearer home, our steps he led
Where Salisbury's level marshes spread
　Mile-wide as flies the laden bee;
Where merry mowers, hale and strong,
Swept, scythe on scythe, their swaths along   240
　The low green prairies of the sea.
We shared the fishing off Boar's Head,
　And round the rocky Isles of Shoals
　The hake-broil on the driftwood coals;
The chowder on the sand-beach made,   245
Dipped by the hungry, steaming hot,
With spoons of clam-shell from the pot.
We heard the tales of witchcraft old,
And dream and sign and marvel told
To sleepy listeners as they lay   250
Stretched idly on the salted hay
Adrift along the winding shores,
When favoring breezes deigned to blow
The square sail of the gundalow,
And idle lay the useless oars.   255

Our mother, while she turned her wheel
Or ran the new-knit stocking-heel,
Told how the Indian hordes came down
At midnight on Cocheco town,
And how her own great-uncle bore   260
His cruel scalp-mark to fourscore.
Recalling, in her fitting phrase,
　So rich and picturesque and free,
　(The common unrimed poetry
Of simple life and country ways)   265
The story of her early days —
She made us welcome to her home;
Old hearths grew wide to give us room;
We stole with her a frightened look
At the gray wizard's conjuring-book,   270

237. **Salisbury:** a sea-coast town in northeastern Massachusetts. 242,
243. **Boar's Head, Isles of Shoals:** points along the coast north of Salisbury.
259. **Cocheco:** Indian name for Dover, New Hampshire.

The fame whereof went far and wide
Through all the simple countryside;
We heard the hawks at twilight play,
The boat-horn on Piscataqua,
The loon's weird laughter far away;   275
We fished her little trout-brook, knew
What flowers in wood and meadow grew,
What sunny hillsides autumn-brown
She climbed to shake the ripe nuts down,
Saw where in sheltered cove and bay   280
The ducks' black squadron anchored lay,
And heard the wild-geese calling loud
Beneath the gray November cloud.

Then, haply, with a look more grave,
And soberer tone, some tale she gave   285
From painful Sewel's ancient tome,
Beloved in every Quaker home,
Of faith fire-winged by martyrdom,
Or Chalkley's Journal, old and quaint —
Gentlest of skippers, rare sea-saint! —   290
Who, when the dreary calms prevailed,
And water-butt and bread-cask failed,
And cruel, hungry eyes pursued
His portly presence, mad for food,
With dark hints muttered under breath   295
Of casting lots for life or death,
Offered, if Heaven withheld supplies,
To be himself the sacrifice.
Then, suddenly, as if to save
The good man from his living grave,   300
A ripple on the water grew,
A school of porpoise flashed in view.
" Take, eat," he said, " and be content;
These fishes in my stead are sent
By Him who gave the tangled ram   305
To spare the child of Abraham."

274. **Piscataqua:** a river in Maine. The rhyme shows that they gave it a
rustic pronunciation. 286. **Sewel:** author of a history of the Quakers. *Painful* here means *pains-taking* rather than *unpleasant to read.* 289. **Chalkley:**
a traveling Quaker preacher. 306. **child of Abraham:** The story of how Isaac
was saved from sacrifice by the appearance of a ram is told in Genesis, xxii.

Our uncle, innocent of books,
Was rich in lore of fields and brooks,
The ancient teachers never dumb
Of Nature's unhoused lyceum.   310
In moons and tides and weather wise,
He read the clouds as prophecies,
And foul or fair could well divine,
By many an occult hint and sign,
Holding the cunning-warded keys   315
To all the woodcraft mysteries;
Himself to Nature's heart so near
That all her voices in his ear
Of beast or bird had meanings clear,
Like Apollonius of old,   320
Who knew the tales the sparrows told,
Or Hermes, who interpreted
What the sage cranes of Nilus said;
A simple, guileless, childlike man,
Content to live where life began;   325
Strong only on his native grounds,
The little world of sights and sounds
Whose girdle was the parish bounds,
Whereof his fondly partial pride
The common features magnified,   330
As Surrey hills to mountains grew
In White of Selborne's loving view —
He told how teal and loon he shot,
And how the eagle's eggs he got,
The feats on pond and river done,   335
The prodigies of rod and gun;
Till, warming with the tales he told,
Forgotten was the outside cold,
The bitter wind unheeded blew,
From ripening corn the pigeons flew,   340
The partridge drummed i' the wood, the mink

---

307. **Our uncle:** Moses, the bachelor brother of Whittier's father. 315.
cunning-warded keys: keys with notches nicely adjusted to fit different locks.
320. **Apollonius:** an ancient Greek sage, who was reputed to have known languages of birds and animals. 322. **Hermes:** the Greek name for the Egyptian
god, Thoth, who understood the wisdom of the sacred cranes of the Nile and
was often represented with a crane's beak. 332. **White of Selborne:** Gilbert
White, an English naturalist, who carefully recorded his observations.

Went fishing down the river-brink.
In fields with bean or clover gay,
The woodchuck, like a hermit gray,
　　Peered from the doorway of his cell;　　　345
The muskrat plied the mason's trade,
And tier by tier his mud-walls laid;
And from the shagbark overhead
　　The grizzled squirrel dropped his shell.

Next, the dear aunt, whose smile of cheer　　　350
And voice in dreams I see and hear —
The sweetest woman ever Fate
Perverse denied a household mate,
Who, lonely, homeless, not the less
Found peace in love's unselfishness,　　　355
And welcome wheresoe'er she went,
A calm and gracious element,
Whose presence seemed the sweet income
And womanly atmosphere of home —
Called up her girlhood memories,　　　360
The huskings and the apple-bees,
The sleigh-rides and the summer sails,
Weaving through all the poor details
And homespun warp of circumstance
A golden woof-thread of romance.　　　365
For well she kept her genial mood
And simple faith of maidenhood;
Before her still a cloud-land lay,
The mirage loomed across her way;
The morning dew, that dries so soon　　　370
With others, glistened at her noon;
Through years of toil and soil and care,
From glossy tress to thin gray hair,
All unprofaned she held apart
The virgin fancies of the heart.　　　375
Be shame to him of woman born
Who hath for such but thought of scorn.
There, too, our elder sister plied

350. **the dear aunt**: Aunt Mercy, his mother's sister, who always made her home with the Whittiers.

Her evening task the stand beside;
A full, rich nature, free to trust,   380
Truthful and almost sternly just,
Impulsive, earnest, prompt to act,
And make her generous thought a fact,
Keeping with many a light disguise
The secret of self-sacrifice.   385
O heart sore-tried! thou hast the best
That Heaven itself could give thee — rest,
Rest from all bitter thoughts and things!
 How many a poor one's blessing went
  With thee beneath the low green tent   390
Whose curtain never outward swings!

As one who held herself a part
Of all she saw, and let her heart
 Against the household bosom lean,
Upon the motley-braided mat   395
Our youngest and our dearest sat,
Lifting her large, sweet, asking eyes,
 Now bathed within the fadeless green
And holy peace of Paradise.
Oh, looking from some heavenly hill,   400
 Or from the shade of saintly palms,
 Or silver reach of river calms,
Do those large eyes behold me still?
With me one little year ago: —
The chill weight of the winter snow   405
 For months upon her grave has lain;
And now, when summer south-winds blow
 And brier and harebell bloom again,
I tread the pleasant paths we trod,
I see the violet-sprinkled sod   410
Whereon she leaned, too frail and weak
The hillside flowers she loved to seek,
Yet following me where'er I went

378. **elder sister:** Mary, who died five years before the poem was written. She was Mrs. Jacob Caldwell of Haverhill. 396. **Our youngest:** Elizabeth, the unmarried sister, who kept house for Whittier until she died about a year before the poem was written. As she too possessed some poetic gift, the brother and sister were most congenial, and the poet's mourning for her is most feelingly expressed.

With dark eyes full of love's content.
The birds are glad; the brier-rose fills 415
The air with sweetness; all the hills
Stretch green to June's unclouded sky;
But still I wait with ear and eye
For something gone which should be nigh,
A loss in all familiar things, 420
In flower that blooms, and bird that sings.
And yet, dear heart! remembering thee,
    Am I not richer than of old?
Safe in thy immortality,
    What change can reach the wealth I hold? 425
    What chance can mar the pearl and gold
Thy love hath left in trust with me?
And while in life's late afternoon,
    Where cool and long the shadows grow,
I walk to meet the night that soon 430
    Shall shape and shadow overflow,
I cannot feel that thou art far,
Since near at need the angels are;
And when the sunset gates unbar,
    Shall I not see thee waiting stand, 435
And, white against the evening star,
    The welcome of thy beckoning hand?

Brisk wielder of the birch and rule,
The master of the district school
Held at the fire his favored place, 440
Its warm glow lit a laughing face
Fresh-hued and fair, where scarce appeared
The uncertain prophecy of beard.
He teased the mitten-blinded cat,
Played cross-pins on my uncle's hat, 445
Sang songs, and told us what befalls
In classic Dartmouth's college halls.
Born the wild Northern hills among,
From whence his yeoman father wrung
By patient toil subsistence scant, 450
Not competence and yet not want,

438. **Brisk wielder of the birch and rule:** George Haskell was his name.
447. **Dartmouth:** a well-known New Hampshire college.

He early gained the power to pay
His cheerful, self-reliant way;
Could doff at ease his scholar's gown
To peddle wares from town to town;   455
Or through the long vacation's reach
In lonely lowland districts teach,
Where all the droll experience found
At stranger hearths in boarding round,
The moonlit skater's keen delight,   460
The sleigh-drive through the frosty night,
The rustic party, with its rough
Accompaniment of blind-man's-buff,
And whirling plate, and forfeits paid,
His winter task a pastime made.   465
Happy the snow-locked homes wherein
He tuned his merry violin,
Or played the athlete in the barn,
Or held the good dame's winding yarn,
Or mirth-provoking versions told   470
Of classic legends rare and old,
Wherein the scenes of Greece and Rome
Had all the commonplace of home,
And little seemed at best the odds
'Twixt Yankee pedlers and old gods;   475
Where Pindus-born Araxes took
The guise of any grist-mill brook,
And dread Olympus at his will
Became a huckleberry hill.

A careless boy that night he seemed;   480
  But at his desk he had the look
And air of one who wisely schemed,
  And hostage from the future took
  In trainèd thought and lore of book.
Large-brained, clear-eyed — of such as he   485
Shall Freedom's young apostles be,
Who, following in War's bloody trail,
Shall every lingering wrong assail;
All chains from limb and spirit strike,

476. **Pindus-born Araxes:** a river rising in the Pindus Mountains of Greece.
478. **Olympus:** a mountain supposed to be the home of the gods in ancient Greece.

Uplift the black and white alike;   490
Scatter before their swift advance
The darkness and the ignorance,
The pride, the lust, the squalid sloth,
Which nurtured Treason's monstrous growth,
Made murder pastime, and the hell   495
Of prison-torture possible;
The cruel lie of caste refute,
Old forms remold, and substitute
For Slavery's lash the freeman's will,
For blind routine, wise-handed skill;   500
A school-house plant on every hill,
Stretching in radiate nerve-lines thence
The quick wires of intelligence;
Till North and South together brought
Shall own the same electric thought,   505
In peace a common flag salute,
And, side by side in labor's free
And unresentful rivalry,
Harvest the fields wherein they fought.

Another guest that winter night   510
Flashed back from lustrous eyes the light.
Unmarked by time, and yet not young,
The honeyed music of her tongue
And words of meekness scarcely told
A nature passionate and bold,   515
Strong, self-concentered, spurning guide,
Its milder features dwarfed beside
Her unbent will's majestic pride.
She sat among us, at the best,
A not unfeared, half-welcome guest,   520
Rebuking with her cultured phrase
Our homeliness of words and ways.
A certain pard-like, treacherous grace
  Swayed the lithe limbs and drooped the lash,
  Lent the white teeth their dazzling flash;   525
  And under low brows, black with night,

510. **Another guest:** Harriet Livermore, a brilliant but eccentric woman, who went to Palestine believing that the second coming of Christ was near at hand. Here she lived for a while on Mount Lebanon with Lady Hester Stanhope, referred to in line 555 as the "crazy queen of Lebanon."

Rayed out at times a dangerous light;
The sharp heat-lightnings of her face
   Presaging ill to him whom Fate
Condemned to share her love or hate. 530
A woman tropical, intense
In thought and act, in soul and sense,
She blended in a like degree
The vixen and the devotee,
Revealing with each freak or feint 535
   The temper of Petruchio's Kate,
The raptures of Siena's saint.
Her tapering hand and rounded wrist
Had facile power to form a fist;
The warm, dark languish of her eyes 540
Was never safe from wrath's surprise.
Brows saintly calm and lips devout
Knew every change of scowl and pout;
And the sweet voice had notes more high
And shrill for social battle-cry. 545

Since then what old cathedral town
Has missed her pilgrim staff and gown,
What convent-gate has held its lock
Against the challenge of her knock!
Through Smyrna's plague-hushed thoroughfares, 550
Up sea-set Malta's rocky stairs,
Gray olive slopes of hills that hem
Thy tombs and shrines, Jerusalem,
Or startling on her desert throne
The crazy Queen of Lebanon 555
With claims fantastic as her own,
Her tireless feet have held their way;
And still, unrestful, bowed, and gray,
She watches under Eastern skies,
   With hope each day renewed and fresh, 560
   The Lord's quick coming in the flesh,
Whereof she dreams and prophesies!
Where'er her troubled path may be,

536. **Petruchio's Kate:** In Shakespeare's *The Taming of the Shrew*, Petruchio
tamed the hot-tempered Kate. 537. **Siena's saint:** St. Catherine of Italy,
who went into trances and made a vow of silence for three years.

The Lord's sweet pity with her go!
The outward wayward life we see,   565
  The hidden springs we may not know.
Nor is it given us to discern
  What threads the fatal sisters spun,
  Through what ancestral years has run
The sorrow with the woman born,   570
What forged her cruel chain of moods,
What set her feet in solitudes,   .
  And held the love within her mute,
What mingled madness in the blood,
  A life-long discord and annoy,   575
  Water of tears with oil of joy,
And hid within the folded bud
  Perversities of flower and fruit.
It is not ours to separate
The tangled skein of will and fate,   580
To show what metes and bounds should stand
Upon the soul's debatable land,
And between choice and Providence
Divide the circle of events;
But He who knows our frame is just,   585
  Merciful and compassionate,
And full of sweet assurances
And hope for all the language is,
That He remembereth we are dust!

At last the great logs, crumbling low,   590
Sent out a dull and duller glow,
The bull's-eye watch that hung in view,
Ticking its weary circuit through,
Pointed with mutely warning sign
Its black hand to the hour of nine.   595
That sign the pleasant circle broke:
My uncle ceased his pipe to smoke,
Knocked from its bowl the refuse gray
And laid it tenderly away,
Then roused himself to safely cover   600
The dull red brands with ashes over.

568. **fatal sisters:** the three fates of Greek mythology who spun the thread
of man's life and cut it at his death.

And while, with care, our mother laid
The work aside, her steps she stayed
One moment, seeking to express
Her grateful sense of happiness   605
For food and shelter, warmth and health,
And love's contentment more than wealth,
With simple wishes (not the weak,
Vain prayers which no fulfilment seek,
But such as warm the generous heart,   610
O'er-prompt to do with Heaven its part)
That none might lack, that bitter night,
For bread and clothing, warmth and light.

Within our beds awhile we heard
The wind that round the gables roared,   615
With now and then a ruder shock,
Which made our very bedsteads rock.
We heard the loosened clapboards tost,
The board-nails snapping in the frost;
And on us, through the unplastered wall,   620
Felt the light-sifted snow-flakes fall;
But sleep stole on, as sleep will do
When hearts are light and life is new;
Faint and more faint the murmurs grew,
Till in the summer-land of dreams   625
They softened to the sound of streams,
Low stir of leaves, and dip of oars,
And lapsing waves on quiet shores.

Next morn we wakened with the shout
Of merry voices high and clear;   630
And saw the teamsters drawing near
To break the drifted highways out.
Down the long hillside treading slow
We saw the half-buried oxen go,
Shaking the snow from heads uptost,   635
Their straining nostrils white with frost.
Before our door the straggling train
Drew up, an added team to gain.
The elders threshed their hands a-cold,

Passed, with the cider-mug, their jokes　　　640
　From lip to lip; the younger folks
Down the loose snow-banks, wrestling, rolled,
Then toiled again the cavalcade
　O'er windy hill, through clogged ravine,
　And woodland paths that wound between　　645
Low drooping pine-boughs winter-weighed.
From every barn a team afoot,
At every house a new recruit,
Where, drawn by Nature's subtlest law,
Haply the watchful young men saw　　　　650
Sweet doorway pictures of the curls
And curious eyes of merry girls,
Lifting their hands in mock defense
Against the snow-ball's compliments,
And reading in each missive tost　　　　655
The charm with Eden never lost.

We heard once more the sleigh-bells' sound;·
　And, following where the teamsters led,
The wise old Doctor went his round,
Just pausing at our door to say,　　　　660
In the brief autocratic way
Of one who, prompt at Duty's call,
Was free to urge her claim on all,
　That some poor neighbor sick abed
At night our mother's aid would need.　　665
For, one in generous thought and deed,
　What mattered in the sufferer's sight
　The Quaker matron's inward light,
The Doctor's mail of Calvin's creed?
All hearts confess the saints elect　　　670
　Who, twain in faith, in love agree,
And melt not in an acid sect
　The Christian pearl of charity!

So days went on: a week had passed
Since the great world was heard from last.　　675
The almanac we studied o'er,

---

669. **Calvin's creed:** The doctor was a Presbyterian, or follower of Calvin,
a French reformer.

Read and reread our little store
Of books and pamphlets, scarce a score;
One harmless novel, mostly hid
From younger eyes, a book forbid,   680
And poetry, (or good or bad,
A single book was all we had,)
Where Ellwood's meek, drab-skirted Muse,
    A stranger to the heathen Nine,
    Sang, with a somewhat nasal whine,   685
The wars of David and the Jews.
At last the floundering carrier bore
The village paper to our door.
Lo! broadening outward as we read,
To warmer zones the horizon spread;   690
In panoramic length unrolled
We saw the marvels that it told.
Before us passed the painted Creeks,
    And daft McGregor on his raids
    In Costa Rica's everglades.   695
And up Taygetos winding slow
Rode Ypsilanti's Mainote Greeks,
A Turk's head at each saddle bow!
Welcome to us its week-old news,
Its corner for the rustic Muse,   700
    Its monthly gauge of snow and rain,
Its record, mingling in a breath
The wedding bell and dirge of death;
Jest, anecdote, and love-lorn tale,
The latest culprit sent to jail;   705
Its hue and cry of stolen and lost,
Its vendue sales and goods at cost,
    And traffic calling loud for gain.
We felt the stir of hall and street,
The pulse of life that round us beat;   710
The chill embargo of the snow
Was melted in the genial glow;

683. **Ellwood's meek, drab-skirted Muse:** Thomas Ellwood was a Quaker poet; therefore his muse was clothed in gray. The "heathen Nine" in the next line were the Greek muses presiding over the arts. 694. **McGregor:** a Scotchman who attempted to found a colony in Costa Rica in 1822. The time of the poem is thus identified as being when Whittier was about fifteen. 697. **Ypsilanti:** a Greek patriot who led a struggle for independence against the Turks.

Wide swung again our ice-locked door,
And all the world was ours once more!

Clasp, Angel of the backward look   715
    And folded wings of ashen gray
    And voice of echoes far away,
The brazen covers of thy book;
The weird palimpsest old and vast,
Wherein thou hid'st the spectral past;   720
Where, closely mingling, pale and glow
The characters of joy and woe;
The monographs of outlived years,
Or smile-illumed or dim with tears,
    Green hills of life that slope to death,   725
And haunts of home, whose vistaed trees
Shade off to mournful cypresses
    With the white amaranths underneath.
Even while I look, I can but heed
    The restless sands' incessant fall,   730
Importunate hours that hours succeed,
Each clamorous with its own sharp need,
    And duty keeping pace with all.
Shut down and clasp the heavy lids;
I hear again the voice that bids   735
The dreamer leave his dream midway
For larger hopes and graver fears:
Life greatens in these later years,
The century's aloe flowers today!

Yet, haply, in some lull of life,   740
Some Truce of God which breaks its strife
The worldling's eyes shall gather dew,
    Dreaming in throngful city ways
Of winter joys his boyhood knew;
And dear and early friends — the few   745

719. **palimpsest:** a parchment written upon a second time after old writing
has been erased.   739. **century's aloe:** a shrub of the southwestern United
States supposed to flower only once in a hundred years.   The poet here refers
to the abolition of slavery, which he considers the crowning event of his century.   741. **Truce of God:** in medieval times an agreement to cease fighting
on certain days of the week.

Who yet remain — shall pause to view
These Flemish pictures of old days;
Sit with me by the homestead hearth,
And stretch the hands of memory forth
    To warm them at the wood-fire's blaze!   750
And thanks untraced to lips unknown
Shall greet me like the odors blown
From unseen meadows newly mown,
Or lilies floating in some pond,
Wood-fringed, the wayside gaze beyond;   755
The traveler owns the grateful sense
Of sweetness near, he knows not whence,
And, pausing, takes with forehead bare
The benediction of the air.

SUGGESTIONS FOR STUDY

1. In this poem there is little action except by suggestion. Verify this statement.

2. What were some of the signs of the coming storm?

3. What pleasant duties did the storm bring to the farm boys?

4. What pleasures may be had by those living where there is much snow?

5. If you live in a warm climate, name some pleasures denied to those living in the North.

6. Name all those who sat in front of the hearth on this particular evening.

7. The body of the poem consists of descriptions, characterizations, and reminiscences of the group by the fireside. It is suggested that each member of the group be described and told about in the pupil's own words. A good plan is for different pupils to take different characters.

8. After all have been described and discussed, select the one liked best by the class. This might be determined by debate and a vote of the class.

9. Which one is most sympathetically treated by the poet himself?

10. On the whole, what is your general reaction to the poem?

11. What other poems or stories do you know that are based on snow storms, or any other kind of storm?

747. **Flemish:** The painters of Flanders (now Belgium) in the fifteenth century were noted for their pictures of simple domestic life.

DEAR LORD AND FATHER OF MANKIND

In his old age Whittier gained a serenity of soul quite in contrast with the fiery spirit of his youth. His religious faith, strong as it always had been, took on added mellowness and beauty. It had always been simple, like the plain little Quaker church in Amesbury which he attended; here it becomes exalted. Today you can find this poem in many church hymnals.

Dear Lord and Father of mankind,
Forgive our feverish ways;
Reclothe us in our rightful mind;
In purer lives thy service find,
In deeper reverence, praise.

In simple trust like theirs who heard,
Beside the Syrian sea,
The gracious calling of the Lord,
Let us, like them, without a word,
Rise up and follow thee.

O Sabbath rest by Galilee!
O calm of hills above,
Where Jesus knelt to share with thee
The silence of eternity,
Interpreted by love.

Drop thy still dews of quietness,
Till all our strivings cease;
Take from our souls the strain and stress,
And let our ordered lives confess
The beauty of thy peace.

Breathe through the heats of our desire
Thy coolness and thy balm;
Let sense be dumb, let flesh retire;
Speak through the earthquake, wind, and fire,
O still small voice of calm!

24. **earthquake, wind, and fire:** a reference to the experience of the prophet Elijah in the wilderness. I Kings xix : 9–19.

FOR FURTHER READING

" The Barefoot Boy "

" In School Days "

" Maud Muller "

" Barbara Frietchie "

" Skipper Ireson's Ride "

" Barclay of Ury "

" The Angels of Buena Vista "

" Burns "

" The Pipes of Lucknow "

" My Playmates "

" The Trailing Arbutus "

" The Lost Occasion "

" Laus Deo "

" The Vanishers "

" The Eternal Goodness "

OLIVER WENDELL HOLMES (1809–1894)

You will doubtless like to renew acquaintance with Oliver Wendell Holmes, whom you have already met in the section of Humorous Prose. Before the genial doctor took up medicine, he had tried his hand at law, but he confessed later that his year at law school was " less profitable than it should have been " because of " the seduction of verse-writing." At this time, when he was just twenty-one, he gained for himself permanent fame, and for the United States the preservation of an historic relic, by writing " Old Ironsides." This poem was a vigorous protest against the destruction of the frigate *Constitution*, which had defeated the *Guerrière* in the War of 1812. At first published in the Boston *Advertiser*, the verses were later copied in newspapers and scattered on broadsides all over the country. Such indignation was aroused that the ship was saved, and has become an object of great interest in the Charlestown Navy Yard, just outside of Boston. Recently, because of its rotting timbers, it has been taken apart and restored to its original form as a national memorial.

OLD IRONSIDES

Ay, tear her tattered ensign down!
  Long has it waved on high,
And many an eye has danced to see
  That banner in the sky;
Beneath it rung the battle shout,
  And burst the cannon's roar; —
The meteor of the ocean air
  Shall sweep the clouds no more.

Her decks, once red with heroes' blood,
     Where knelt the vanquished foe,
When winds were hurrying o'er the flood,
     And waves were white below,
No more shall feel the victor's tread,
     Or know the conquered knee; —
The harpies of the shore shall pluck
     The eagle of the sea!

Oh, better that her shattered hulk
     Should sink beneath the wave;
Her thunders shook the mighty deep,
     And there should be her grave;
Nail to the mast her holy flag,
     Set every threadbare sail,
And give her to the god of storms,
     The lightning and the gale!

SUGGESTIONS FOR STUDY

1. Vocabulary: ensign, l. 1; meteor, l. 7; harpies, l. 15.
2. Why was the ship given the nickname " Old Ironsides "?
3. Look up the history of the *Constitution,* especially its fight with the *Guerrière,* and find out whether you think Holmes was justified in his indignation.
4. Who were " the harpies of the shore "?
5. Compare the three possible fates of the vessel: the proposed dismantling which called forth the poem, the fate preferred by Holmes, and what has actually happened to the vessel.
6. If you have seen the moving picture " Old Ironsides," discuss how it helps you to appreciate this poem.

TO AN INSECT

Six years after the printing of " Old Ironsides " Holmes obtained his medical degree and published his first volume of poems. His long career as a lecturer on medicine at Dartmouth and Harvard was punctuated by the publication of volumes of poetry even up to his seventy-ninth year. Holmes's humor is nowhere more evident than in his verse. " To an Insect " and " The Height of the Ridiculous " (see page 778) show him in rollicking mood, and further illustrate the fondness for playing on words which was conspicuous in the selection from *The Autocrat* on page 373.

I love to hear thine earnest voice,
    Wherever thou art hid,
Thou testy little dogmatist,
    Thou pretty Katydid!
Thou mindest me of gentlefolks —   5
    Old gentlefolks are they —
Thou say'st an undisputed thing
    In such a solemn way.

Thou art a female, Katydid!
    I know it by the trill   10
That quivers through thy piercing notes,
    So petulant and shrill;
I think there is a knot of you
    Beneath the hollow tree —
A knot of spinster Katydids —   15
    Do Katydids drink tea?

Oh, tell me where did Katy live,
    And what did Katy do?
And was she very fair and young,
    And yet so wicked, too?   20
Did Katy love a naughty man,
    Or kiss more cheeks than one?
I warrant Katy did no more
    Than many a Kate has done.

Dear me! I'll tell you all about   25
    My fuss with little Jane,
And Ann, with whom I used to walk
    So often down the lane,
And all that tore their locks of black,
    Or wet their eyes of blue —   30
Pray tell me, sweetest Katydid,
    What did poor Katy do?

Ah, no! the living oak shall crash,
    That stood for ages still,
The rock shall rend its mossy base   35
    And thunder down the hill,

Before the little Katydid
   Shall add one word, to tell
The mystic story of the maid
   Whose name she knows so well.   40

Peace to the ever-murmuring race!
   And when the latest one
Shall fold in death her feeble wings
   Beneath the autumn sun,
Then shall she raise her fainting voice   45
   And lift her drooping lid,
And then the child of future years
   Shall hear what Katy did.

SUGGESTIONS FOR STUDY

You would be interested to compare this poem with an earlier one called " To a Caty-did " by Philip Freneau, which may have suggested this idea to Holmes. Other poems have been addressed to insects: for instance, Freneau's " On a Honey-Bee," Emerson's " The Humble Bee," Whitman's " A Noiseless Patient Spider " (page 659), Keats's " On the Grasshopper and Cricket," and Leigh Hunt's " To the Grasshopper and the Cricket " (the last two being written in friendly competition). Probably the most humorous insect poem is Burns's " To a Louse," which ends with the much-quoted passage, " O wad some Power the giftie gie us, To see oursels as ithers see us! "

THE BOYS

Dr. Holmes's wit and engaging personality made him highly popular in Boston as an after-dinner speaker and writer of poems for special occasions. He once said of himself:

" I'm a florist in verse, and what *would* people say
If I came to a banquet without my bouquet? "

Probably the best known of these poems is " The Boys," written for the thirtieth reunion of his own Harvard Class of 1829, a class famous for the notable men it had produced.

Has there any old fellow got mixed with the boys?
If there has, take him out, without making a noise.
Hang the Almanac's cheat and the Catalogue's spite!
Old time is a liar! We're twenty tonight!

We're twenty! We're twenty! Who says we are more?   5
He's tipsy — young jackanapes! — show him the door!
" Gray temples at twenty? " — Yes! *white* if we please!
Where the snow-flakes fall thickest there's nothing can freeze!

Was it snowing I spoke of? Excuse the mistake!
Look close — you will not see a sign of a flake!   10
We want some new garlands for those we have shed —
And these are white roses in place of the red.

We've a trick, we young fellows, you may have been told,
Of talking (in public) as if we were old: —
That boy we call " Doctor," and this we call " Judge ";   15
It's a neat little fiction — of course it's all fudge.

That fellow's the " Speaker " — the one on the right;
" Mr. Mayor," my young one, how are you tonight?
That's our " Member of Congress," we say when we chaff;
There's the " Reverend " what's his name? — don't make **me**
    laugh.   20

That boy with the grave mathematical look
Made believe he had written a wonderful book,
And the ROYAL SOCIETY thought it was *true!*
So they chose him right in; a good joke it was, too!

There's a boy, we pretend, with a three-decker brain,   25
That could harness a team with a logical chain;
When he spoke for our manhood in syllabled fire,
We called him " The Justice," but now he's " The Squire."

And there's a nice youngster of excellent pith —
Fate tried to conceal him by naming him Smith;   30
But he shouted a song for the brave and the free —
Just read on his medal, " My country," " of thee! "

30. **Smith:** Samuel Francis Smith, author of "America." Note that this is
the only one called by name; and he is probably the only one whose name has
ever been heard by the average high school student of today. Any one who is
curious to identify the others can find them listed in the footnotes of the
Cambridge edition of Holmes's poems.

You hear that boy laughing? — You think he's all fun;
But the angels laugh, too, at the good he has done;
The children laugh loud as they troop to his call,   35
And the poor man that knows him laughs loudest of all!

Yes, we're boys — always playing with tongue or with pen —
And I sometimes have asked — Shall we ever be men?
Shall we always be youthful, and laughing, and gay,
Till the last dear companion drops smiling away?   40

Then here's to our boyhood, its gold and its gray!
The stars of its winter, the dews of its May!
And when we have done with our life-lasting toys,
Dear Father, take care of thy children, THE BOYS!

SUGGESTIONS FOR STUDY

1. Imagine that your class is having its thirtieth reunion banquet. Identify different members with the characters mentioned in this poem. Let each make a few remarks appropriate to his character. Then let a student who has memorized the poem deliver it as the climax of the program.

2. Write a prophecy for your class thirty years hence, or write reminiscences of your present school life as if for a thirtieth reunion of your class.

THE CHAMBERED NAUTILUS

You must not think of Dr. Holmes as merely " a funny man." This poem, which he preferred above all his writings and by which he hoped to be remembered, is one of the best-loved poems of aspiration in our national literature. He caught his idea from the shell of the nautilus, of which he had several specimens. In *The Autocrat of the Breakfast Table*, where this poem was originally published, the author describes " the ship of pearl " as " a series of enlarging compartments successively dwelt in by the animal that inhabits the shell, which is built in a widening spiral." The name *nautilus*, or sailor, grew out of the old belief that the little creature sailed by the gauzy wings which were really its tentacles.

This is the ship of pearl, which, poets feign,
    Sails the unshadowed main —
    The venturous bark that flings
On the sweet summer wind its purpled wings

In gulfs enchanted, where the Siren sings —   5
    And coral reefs lie bare,
Where the cold sea-maids rise to sun their streaming hair.

Its webs of living gauze no more unfurl;
    Wrecked is the ship of pearl!
    And every chambered cell,   10
Where its dim dreaming life was wont to dwell,
As the frail tenant shaped his growing shell,
    Before thee lies revealed —
Its irised ceiling rent, its sunless crypt unsealed!

Year after year beheld the silent toil   15
    That spread its lustrous coil;
    Still, as the spiral grew,
He left the past year's dwelling for the new,
Stole with soft step its shining archway through,
    Built up its idle door,   20
Stretched in his last-found home, and knew the old no more.

Thanks for the heavenly message brought by thee,
    Child of the wandering sea,
    Cast from her lap, forlorn!
From thy dead lips a clearer note is born   25.
Than ever Triton blew from wreathèd horn!
    While on my ear it rings,
Through the deep caves of thought I hear a voice that sings: —

Build thee more stately mansions, O my soul,
    As the swift seasons roll!   30
    Leave thy low-vaulted past!
Let each new temple, nobler than the last,
Shut thee from heaven with a dome more vast,
    Till thou at length art free,
Leaving thine outgrown shell by life's unresting sea!   35

5. **Siren:** in classical mythology, the sirens were sea-nymphs near the west coast of Italy who lured mariners to their death by their enchanting songs.   26. **Triton:** ancient sea-god whose lower part resembled a fish. He is usually represented as blowing a trumpet made of a sea-shell.

SUGGESTIONS FOR STUDY

1. Vocabulary: feign, l. 1; main, l. 2; irised ceiling, l. 14; crypt, l. 14; lustrous, l. 16.

2. If possible bring a picture, or better yet, a specimen of a nautilus shell to class to see just how it is formed.

3. Point out phrases or lines which show the delicate beauty of the shell.

4. Express in your own words the comparison made by the poet between the shell and man's life.

5. Read Chapter II in Smith's *What Can Literature Do For Me?* in which this poem is discussed with others by our major poets to show how literature voices our ideals.

6. Compare the idea of this poem with Longfellow's "The Ladder of St. Augustine" and "Excelsior," and with the first stanza of Tennyson's "In Memoriam." Which of the three figures of speech for man's aspiration appeals to you most strongly?

7. This poem has been made into a beautiful cantata by John S. Fearis. It is not too hard for high-school glee clubs. Have you ever heard it?

CONTENTMENT

In this poem Holmes pokes good-natured fun at himself, and through himself at all comfortable, middle-aged city-dwellers whose pocketbooks bulge sufficiently to enable them to satisfy their highly cultivated tastes. This was one of the poems which were scattered at intervals through .*The Autocrat* papers.

" Man wants but little here below."

Little I ask; my wants are few;
   I only wish a hut of stone,
(A *very plain* brown stone will do,)
   That I may call my own; —
And close at hand is such a one,   5
In yonder street that fronts the sun.

Plain food is quite enough for me;
   Three courses are as good as ten; —
If Nature can subsist on three,
   Thank Heaven for three. Amen!   10
I always thought cold victual nice; —
My *choice* would be vanilla-ice.

I care not much for gold or land; —
   Give me a mortgage here and there —
Some good bank-stock, some note of hand,   15
   Or trifling railroad share —
I only ask that Fortune send
A *little* more than I shall spend.

Honors are silly toys, I know,
   And titles are but empty names;   20
I would, *perhaps,* be Plenipo —
   But only near St. James;
I'm very sure I should not care
To fill our Gubernator's chair.

Jewels are baubles; 'tis a sin   25
   To care for such unfruitful things; —
One good-sized diamond in a pin —
   Some, *not so large,* in rings —
A ruby, and a pearl, or so,
Will do for me; — I laugh at show.   30

My dame should dress in cheap attire;
   (Good, heavy silks are never dear;)
I own perhaps I *might* desire
   Some shawls of true Cashmere —
Some marrowy crapes of China silk,   35
Like wrinkled skins on scalded milk.

I would not have the horse I drive
   So fast that folks must stop and stare;
An easy gait — two forty-five —
   Suits me; I do not care; —   40
Perhaps, for just a *single spurt,*
Some seconds less would do no hurt.

21. Plenipo: Minister Plenipotentiary, or ambassador. **22. St. James:**
the court of England. This is considered the highest diplomatic position
offered by the United States. **24. Gubernator's chair:** the office of governor of
Massachusetts. **34. Cashmere:** a district in India. **39. two forty-five:** speed
of a mile in two minutes and forty-five seconds.

Of pictures, I should like to own
　　Titians and Raphaels three or four,
I love so much their style and tone —
　　One Turner, and no more   45
(A landscape — foreground golden dirt —
The sunshine painted with a squirt).

Of books but few — some fifty score
　　For daily use, and bound for wear;
The rest upon an upper floor; —   50
　　Some *little* luxury *there*
Of red morocco's gilded gleam,
And vellum rich as country cream.

Busts, cameos, gems — such things as these,   55
　　Which others often show for pride,
I value for their power to please,
　　And selfish churls deride; —
One Stradivarius, I confess,
Two Meerschaums, I would fain possess.   60

Wealth's wasteful tricks I will not learn
　　Nor ape the glittering upstart fool; —
Shall not carved tables serve my turn,
　　But *all* must be of buhl?
Give grasping pomp its double share —   65
I ask but *one* recumbent chair.

Thus humble let me live and die,
　　Nor long for Midas' golden touch;

44. **Titian and Raphael:** famous Italian painters of the sixteenth century, whose paintings, when purchasable at all, bring fabulous prices. 46. **Turner:** an English painter of the nineteenth century, whose work commands very high prices. 54. **vellum:** fine parchment made of the skin of calves and used for manuscripts. Since it turns cream-color with age, this suggests very old and priceless manuscripts. 59. **Stradivarius:** a violin made by Antonio Stradivari, an Italian of the seventeenth century. These violins are now rare and are considered the most valuable in existence. 60. **Meerschaums:** pipes made of a light clay-like substance, which becomes richly tinted with age. 64. **buhl:** patterns of metal and tortoise shell inlaid in furniture: so named from the Frenchman who perfected the work. 68. **Midas:** a mythical king who had the power to turn everything he touched into gold.

If Heaven more generous gifts deny,
   I shall not miss them *much* —   70
Too grateful for the blessing lent
   Of simple tastes and mind content!

SUGGESTIONS FOR STUDY

1. This poem shows the fashions of Holmes's day. Try your hand at writing a modern " Contentment " (in prose probably) substituting details of our twentieth-century life which would express the satisfactions of a modern millionaire.

2. Contrast the " contentment " of Holmes with the simple living of Thoreau as described in early chapters of *Walden.*

FOR FURTHER READING

HUMOROUS	SERIOUS
" My Aunt "	" The Voiceless "
" The Last Leaf "	" The Two Armies "
" The Old Man Dreams "	" Non-Resistance "
" The Deacon's Masterpiece "	" Dorothy Q."
" How the Old Horse Won the Bet "	" Homesick in Heaven "
" On Lending a Punch-Bowl "	

SUGGESTIONS FOR MEMORIZING

  " Old Ironsides "
  " The Chambered Nautilus "
  " The Height of the Ridiculous." (See p. 778.)

JAMES RUSSELL LOWELL (1819–1891)

A man deserves credit enough for attaining distinction in any one field, but when he can become notable in four or five, he fills us with wonder. Such an all-round man was James Russell Lowell, poet, humorist, political writer, literary critic, editor, college professor, lecturer, and diplomat. His achievement in poetry may have suffered because of his variety of interests, but his versatility has earned for Lowell the title of our most representative man of letters.

Few men in our restless country spend their lives in the house where they were born, yet this was among Lowell's many distinctions. " Elmwood," the beautiful old mansion in its rich setting of greenery, was the outward symbol of how firmly the Lowell family was established in Cambridge, Massachusetts. To overtop all the other famous Lowells both before and after him is no small part of the record of this man.

Like Longfellow and Holmes, Lowell held for a long period of years a professorship at Harvard. Like Irving, he represented the United States in Spain and England. In addition to these achievements he was the pre-eminent literary critic of his day, the first editor of *The Atlantic Monthly* and later a co-editor of *The North American Review,* two of our most notable magazines. Yet all of these dignified positions did not prevent his vein of rich humor from bursting forth.

Lowell created Hosea Biglow, an illiterate but shrewd New England farmer, to give vent to his feelings on the Mexican War situation in 1848. These *Biglow Papers* have immortalized the Yankee twang. To add to the humor, the papers purported to have been edited by a minister, Homerus Wilbur, Esq., in whose elaborate footnotes Lowell satirized pedantic learning. A second series during the Civil War continued to express in homely fashion the ideas of New Englanders concerning the vital topics of the war. Many parts of the *Biglow Papers* are crowded with references unintelligible to high school students of today, but some of the verses will continue to delight young people for years to come. Among these " The Courtin' " is usually the favorite. The original version as here printed was later given some additional stanzas and printed in the Second Series of 1866, but many prefer the directness of this original version without its trimmings.

THE COURTIN'

Zekle crep' up, quite unbeknown,
    An' peeked in thru the winder,
An' there sot Huldy all alone,
    'ith no one nigh to hender.

Agin' the chimbly crooknecks hung,   5
    An' in amongst 'em rusted
The ole queen's-arm thet gran'ther Young
    Fetched back frum Concord busted.

The wannut logs shot sparkles out
    Towards the pootiest, bless her!   10
An' leetle fires danced all about
    The chiny on the dresser.

The very room, coz she wuz in,
    Looked warm frum floor to ceilin',
An' she looked full ez rosy agin   15
    Ez th' apples she wuz peelin'.

She heerd a foot an' knowed it, tu,
    A-raspin' on the scraper —
All ways to once her feelin's flew
    Like sparks in burnt-up paper.   20

He kin' o' l'itered on the mat,
    Some doubtfle o' the seekle;
His heart kep' goin' pitypat,
    But hern went pity Zekle.

An' yet she gin her cheer a jerk   25
    Ez though she wished him furder,
An' on her apples kep' to work
    Ez ef a wager spurred her.

" You want to see my Pa, I spose? "
    " Wal, no; I come designin' — "   30
" To see my Ma?   She's sprinklin' clo'es
    Agin tomorrow's i'nin'."

He stood a spell on one foot fust,
    Then stood a spell on tother.
An' on which one he felt the wust   35
    He couldn't ha' told ye, nuther.

Sez he, " I'd better call agin; "
    Sez she, " Think likely, *Mister;* "
The last word pricked him like a pin,
    An' — wal, he up and kist her.   40

When Ma bimeby upon 'em slips,
    Huldy sot pale ez ashes,
All kind o' smily round the lips
    An' teary round the lashes.

Her blood riz quick, though, like the tide 45
Down to the Bay o' Fundy,
An' all I know is they wuz cried
In meetin', come nex' Sunday.

47. **they wuz cried:** The banns (that is, the announcement of their approaching marriage) were read in church last Sunday.

WHAT MR. ROBINSON THINKS

This poem was called forth by a newspaper letter of a certain lawyer of Lowell, Massachusetts, named John P. Robinson. The author had no intention of attacking Robinson personally, but simply used his opinion on the election as an excuse for some pointed comment on the issues between the two candidates for governor, General Caleb Cushing, who had taken a prominent part in the Mexican War, and Governor George N. Briggs, who was up for reëlection. The satirical treatment of Robinson's opinion is evident.

Guvener B. is a sensible man;
He stays to his home an' looks arter his folks;
He draws his furrer ez straight ez he can,
An' into nobody's tater-patch pokes; —
But John P. 5
Robinson he
Sez he wunt vote fer Guvener B.

My! aint it terrible? Wut shall we du?
We can't never choose him o' course — thet's flat;
Guess we shall hev to come round, (don't you?) 10
An' go in fer thunder an' guns, an' all that;
But John P.
Robinson he
Sez he wunt vote fer Guvener B.

Gineral C. is a dreffle smart man: 15
He's ben on all sides thet give places or pelf;
But consistency still wuz a part of his plan —
He's been true to *one* party — an' that is himself; —
So John P.
Robinson he 20
Sez he shall vote fer Gineral C.

Gineral C. he goes in fer the war;
  He don't vally principle more 'n an old cud;
Wut did God make us raytional creeturs fer,
  But glory an' gunpowder, plunder an' blood?   25
    So John P.
    Robinson he
  Sez he shall vote fer Gineral C.

We were gittin' on nicely up here to our village,
  With good old idees o' wut's right an' wut aint,   30
We kind o' thought Christ went agin war an' pillage,
  An' thet eppyletts worn't the best mark of a saint,
    But John P.
    Robinson he
  Sez this kind o' thing's an exploded idee.   35

The side of our country must ollers be took,
  An' Presidunt Polk, you know, *he* is our country.
An' the angel thet writes all our sins in a book
  Puts the *debit* to him, an' to us the *per contry;*
    An' John P.   40
    Robinson he
  Sez this is his view o' the thing to a T.

Parson Wilbur he calls all these argimunts lies;
  Sez they're nothin' on airth but jest *fee, faw, fum:*
An' thet all this big talk of our destinies   45
  Is half on it ign'ance, an' t' other half rum,
    But John P.
    Robinson he
  Sez it aint no sech thing; an', of course, so must we.

Parson Wilbur sez *he* never heerd in his life   50
  Thet th' Apostles rigged out in their swaller-tail coats,
An' marched round in front of a drum an' a fife,

---

23. **vally:** value.   32. **eppyletts:** epaulets, shoulder ornaments worn by
officers of the army.   39. **debit:** debt.   39. **per contry:** credit on the opposite
side of the page.   The meaning is that we must always agree with what is done
by the country, as represented by the President.   If there is anything wrong
about it, the sin will be charged to his account, not ours.   43. **Parson Wilbur:**
This was the minister who was supposed to edit Hosea Biglow's verses.

To git some on 'em office, an' some on 'em votes,
   But John P.
   Robinson he   55
Sez they didn't know ever'thin' down in Judee.

Wal, it's a marcy we've gut folks to tell us
   The rights an' the wrongs o' these matters, I vow —
God sends country lawyers, an' other wise fellers,
   To start the world's team wen it gits in a slough;   60
      Fer John P.
      Robinson he
Sez the world 'll go right, ef he hollers out Gee!

THE VISION OF SIR LAUNFAL

Published the same year as the first series of the *Biglow Papers,* yet entirely different from them in treatment is " The Vision of Sir Launfal," probably the best known and most quoted poem by Lowell. In it may be traced the influence of his wife, Maria White, to whom he had been married only a few years when he wrote this. She too was a poet, and so ardent a believer in the brotherhood of man that she had succeeded in winning Lowell over from his scoffing attitude toward the Abolitionists.

The author's own note of explanation is helpful: " According to the mythology of the Romancers, the San Greal, or Holy Grail, was the cup out of which Jesus partook of the last supper with His disciples. It was brought into England by Joseph of Arimathea, and remained there, an object of pilgrimage and adoration, for many years in the keeping of his lineal descendants. It was incumbent upon those who had charge of it to be chaste in thought, word, and deed; but one of the keepers having broken this condition, the Holy Grail disappeared. From that time it was a favorite enterprise of the knights of King Arthur's court to go in search of it. Sir Galahad was at last successful in finding it, as may be read in the seventeenth book of the Romance of King Arthur. Tennyson has made Sir Galahad the subject of one of the most exquisite of his poems. The plot (if I may give that name to anything so slight) of the foregoing poem is my own, and to serve its purposes, I have enlarged the circle of competition in search of the miraculous cup in such a manner as to include, not only other persons than the heroes of the Round Table, but also a period of time subsequent to the date of King Arthur's reign."

PRELUDE TO PART FIRST

Over his keys the musing organist,
  Beginning doubtfully and far away,
First lets his fingers wander as they list,
  And builds a bridge from Dreamland for his lay.
Then, as the touch of his loved instrument   5
  Gives hope and fervor, nearer draws his theme,
First guessed by faint, auroral flushes sent
  Along the wavering vista of his dream.

Not only around our infancy
  Doth Heaven with all its splendors lie;   10
Daily, with souls that cringe and plot,
  We Sinais climb and know it not.

Over our manhood bend the skies;
  Against our fallen and traitor lives

9. **Not only around our infancy:** The English poet, Wordsworth, had
written, "Heaven lies about us in our infancy." Lowell disagreed that
Heaven was limited to our infancy. 12. **Sinais:** Mount Sinai was the place
where God gave Moses the Ten Commandments; Exodus, xix. Here it sym-
bolizes communion with Heaven. 14. This is the beginning of the vision,
which continues to Part II, l. 89.

The great winds utter prophecies;   15
  With our faint hearts the mountain strives;
Its arms outstretched, the druid wood
  Waits with its benedicite;
And to our age's drowsy blood
  Still shouts the inspiring sea.   20

Earth gets its price for what earth gives us:
  The beggar is taxed for a corner to die in,
The priest hath his fee who comes and shrives us.
  We bargain for the graves we lie in;
At the devil's booth are all things sold,   25
Each ounce of dross costs its ounce of gold;
  For a cap and bells our lives we pay,
Bubbles we buy with a whole soul's tasking.
  'Tis Heaven alone that is given away,
  'Tis only God may be had for the asking;   30
No price is set on the lavish summer;
June may be had by the poorest comer.

And what is so rare as a day in June?
  Then, if ever, come perfect days;
Then Heaven tries earth if it be in tune,   35
  And over it softly her warm ear lays;
Whether we look, or whether we listen,
We hear life murmur, or see it glisten;
  Every clod feels a stir of might,
    An instinct within it that reaches and towers,   40
  And groping blindly above it for light,
    Climbs to a soul in grass and flowers.
The flush of life may well be seen
  Thrilling back over hills and valleys;
The cowslip startles in meadows green,   45
  The buttercup catches the sun in its chalice,
And there's never a leaf or a blade too mean
  To be some happy creature's palace;
The little bird sits at his door in the sun,
  Atilt like a blossom among the leaves,   50

---

17. **druid:** ancient Celtic priests who held the oak sacred and worshiped in the woods. 18. **benedicite:** blessing. 27. **cap and bells:** the jingling head-dress of a king's jester; in other words, mere superficial pleasures.

And lets his illumined being o'errun
  With the deluge of summer it receives;
His mate feels the eggs beneath her wings,
And the heart in her dumb breast flutters and sings;
He sings to the wide world, and she to her nest —   55
In the nice ear of Nature which song is the best?

Now is the high-tide of the year,
  And whatever of life hath ebbed away
Comes flooding back with a ripply cheer
  Into every bare inlet and creek and bay.   60
Now the heart is so full that a drop overfills it;
We are happy now because God wills it.
No matter how barren the past may have been,
'Tis enough for us now that the leaves are green.
We sit in the warm shade and feel right well   65
How the sap creeps up and the blossoms swell;
We may shut our eyes, but we cannot help knowing
That skies are clear and grass is growing.
The breeze comes whispering in our ear
That dandelions are blossoming near,   70
    That maize has sprouted, that streams are flowing,
That the river is bluer than the sky,
That the robin is plastering his house hard by;
And if the breeze kept the good news back,
For other couriers we should not lack;   75
  We could guess it all by yon heifer's lowing —
And hark! how clear bold chanticleer,
Warmed with the new wine of the year,
    Tells all in his lusty crowing!

Joy comes, grief goes, we know not how;   80
Everything is happy now,
    Everything is upward striving.
'Tis as easy now for the heart to be true
As for grass to be green or skies to be blue —
    'Tis the natural way of living.   85
Who knows whither the clouds have fled?
  In the unscarred heaven they leave no wake;
And the eyes forget the tears they have shed,
  The heart forgets its sorrow and ache;

The soul partakes the season's youth, 90
 And the sulphurous rifts of passion and woe
Lie deep 'neath a silence pure and smooth,
 Like burnt-out craters healed with snow.
What wonder if Sir Launfal now
Remembered the keeping of his vow? 95

PART FIRST

I

" My golden spurs now bring to me,
 And bring to me my richest mail,
For tomorrow I go over land and sea
 In search of the Holy Grail.
Shall never a bed for me be spread, 100
Nor shall a pillow be under my head,
Till I begin my vow to keep.
Here on the rushes will I sleep,
And perchance there may come a vision true
Ere day create the world anew." 105
 Slowly Sir Launfal's eyes grew dim;
 Slumber fell like a cloud on him,
And into his soul the vision flew.

II

The crows flapped over by twos and threes;
In the pool drowsed the cattle up to their knees; 110
 The little birds sang as if it were
 The one day of summer in all the year;
And the very leaves seemed to sing on the trees.
The castle alone in the landscape lay
Like an outpost of winter, dull and gray; 115
'Twas the proudest hall in the North Countree,
And never its gates might opened be
Save to lord or lady of high degree.
Summer besieged it on every side,
But the churlish stone her assaults defied; 120

103. **rushes:** This is inside the castle, not outside. The floors were covered with rushes.

She could not scale the chilly wall,
Though around it for leagues her pavilions tall
Stretched left and right,
Over the hills and out of sight.
   Green and broad was every tent,   125
   And out of each a murmur went
Till the breeze fell off at night.

III

The drawbridge dropped with a surly clang,
And through the dark arch a charger sprang,
Bearing Sir Launfal, the maiden knight,   130
In his gilded mail, that flamed so bright
It seemed the dark castle had gathered all
Those shafts the fierce sun had shot over its wall
   In his siege of three hundred summers long,
And, binding them all in one blazing sheaf,   135
   Had cast them forth; so, young and strong,
And lightsome as a locust-leaf,
Sir Launfal flashed forth in his unscarred mail,
To seek in all climes for the Holy Grail.

IV

It was morning on hill and stream and tree,   140
   And morning in the young knight's heart;
Only the castle moodily
Rebuffed the gifts of the sunshine free,
   And gloomed by itself apart;
The season brimmed all other things up   145
Full as the rain fills the pitcher-plant's cup.

V

As Sir Launfal made morn through the darksome gate,
   He was 'ware of a leper, crouched by the same,
Who begged with his hand and moaned as he sate;
   And a loathing over Sir Launfal came.   150
The sunshine went out of his soul with a thrill,
   The flesh 'neath his armor 'gan shrink and crawl,
And midway its leap his heart stood still
   Like a frozen waterfall;

For this man, so foul and bent of stature,   155
Rasped harshly against his dainty nature,
And seemed the one blot on the summer morn —
So he tossed him a piece of gold in scorn.

VI

The leper raised not the gold from the dust:
" Better to me the poor man's crust,   160
Better the blessing of the poor,
Though I turn me empty from his door;
That is no true alms which the hand can hold;
He gives nothing but worthless gold
    Who gives from a sense of duty;   165
But he who gives but a slender mite,
And gives to that which is out of sight,
    That thread of the all-sustaining Beauty
Which runs through all and doth all unite —
The hand cannot clasp the whole of his alms,   170
The heart outstretches its eager palms,
For a god goes with it and makes it store
To the soul that was starving in darkness before."

PRELUDE TO PART SECOND

Down swept the chill wind from the mountain peak,
From the snow five thousand summers old;   175
On open wold and hilltop bleak
    It had gathered all the cold,
And whirled it like sleet on the wanderer's cheek.
It carried a shiver everywhere
From the unleafed boughs and pastures bare;   180
The little brook heard it and built a roof
'Neath which he could house him, winterproof;
All night by the white stars' frosty gleams
He groined his arches and matched his beams;
Slender and clear were his crystal spars   185
As the lashes of light that trim the stars;
He sculptured every summer delight
In his halls and chambers out of sight;
Sometimes his tinkling waters slipped
Down through a frost-leaved forest-crypt,   190

Long, sparkling aisles of steel-stemmed trees
Bending to counterfeit a breeze;
Sometimes the roof no fretwork knew
But silvery mosses that downward grew;
Sometimes it was carved in sharp relief   195
With quaint arabesques of ice-fern leaf;
Sometimes it was simply smooth and clear
For the gladness of heaven to shine through, and here
He had caught the nodding bulrush-tops
And hung them thickly with diamond-drops,   200
That crystaled the beams of moon and sun,
And made a star of every one.
No mortal builder's most rare device
Could match this winter-palace of ice;
'Twas as if every image that mirrored lay   205
In his depths serene through the summer day,
Each fleeting shadow of earth and sky,
    Lest the happy model should be lost,
Had been mimicked in fairy masonry
    By the elfin builders of the frost.   210

Within the hall are song and laughter;
    The cheeks of Christmas grow red and jolly;
And sprouting is every corbel and rafter
    With lightsome green of ivy and holly.
Through the deep gulf of the chimney wide   215
Wallows the Yule-log's roaring tide;
The broad flame-pennons droop and flap
    And belly and tug as a flag in the wind;
Like a locust shrills the imprisoned sap,
    Hunted to death in its galleries blind   220
And swift little troops of silent sparks,
Now pausing, now scattering away as in fear,
Go threading the soot-forest's tangled darks
    Like herds of startled deer.
But the wind without was eager and sharp;   225
Of Sir Launfal's gray hair it makes a harp,
    And rattles and wrings
    The icy strings,

213. **corbel:** bracket.

Singing, in dreary monotone,
A Christmas carol of its own,   230
Whose burden still, as he might guess,
Was " Shelterless, shelterless, shelterless! "

The voice of the seneschal flared like a torch
As he shouted the wanderer away from the porch,
And he sat in the gateway and saw all night   235
   The great hall-fire, so cheery and bold,
   Through the window-slits of the castle old,
Build out its piers of ruddy light
   Against the drift of the cold.

PART SECOND

I

There was never a leaf on bush or tree,   240
The bare boughs rattled shudderingly;
The river was dumb and could not speak,
   For the weaver Winter its shroud had spun;
A single crow on the tree-top bleak
   From his shining feathers shed off the cold sun;   245
Again it was morning, but shrunk and cold,
As if her veins were sapless and old,
And she rose up decrepitly
For a last dim look at earth and sea.

II

Sir Launfal turned from his own hard gate,   250
For another heir in his earldom sate;
An old, bent man, worn out and frail,
He came back from seeking the Holy Grail.
Little he recked of his earldom's loss;
No more on his surcoat was blazoned the cross;   255
But deep in his soul the sign he wore,
The badge of the suffering and the poor.

III

Sir Launfal's raiment thin and spare
Was idle mail 'gainst the barbèd air,

233. **seneschal:** steward.

For it was just at the Christmas time.   260
So he mused, as he sat, of a sunnier clime,
And sought for a shelter from cold and snow
In the light and warmth of long ago;
He sees the snake-like caravan crawl
O'er the edge of the desert, black and small,   265
Then nearer and nearer, till, one by one,
He can count the camels in the sun,
As over the red-hot sands they pass
To where, in its slender necklace of grass,
The little spring laughed and leaped in the shade,   270
And with its own self like an infant played,
And waved its signal of palms.

IV

" For Christ's sweet sake, I beg an alms " —
The happy camels may reach the spring,
But Sir Launfal sees naught save the gruesome thing,   275
The leper, lank as the rain-blanched bone,
That cowers beside him, a thing as lone
And white as the ice-isles of Northern seas
In the desolate horror of his disease.

V

And Sir Launfal said, " I behold in thee   280
An image of Him who died on the tree.
Thou also hast had thy crown of thorns;
Thou also hast had the world's buffets and scorns;
And to thy life were not denied
The wounds in the hands and feet and side.   285
Mild Mary's Son, acknowledge me;
Behold, through him, I give to Thee! "

VI

Then the soul of the leper stood up in his eyes
    And looked at Sir Launfal, and straightway he
Remembered in what a haughtier guise   290
    He had flung an alms to leprosie,
When he girt his young life up in gilded mail
And set forth in search of the Holy Grail.

The heart within him was ashes and dust;
He parted in twain his single crust,   295
He broke the ice on the streamlet's brink,
And gave the leper to eat and drink;
'Twas a moldy crust of coarse, brown bread,
  'Twas water out of a wooden bowl —
Yet with fine wheaten bread was the leper fed,   300
  And 'twas red wine he drank with his thirsty soul.

VII

As Sir Launfal mused with a downcast face,
A light shone round about the place;
The leper no longer crouched at his side,
But stood before him glorified,
Shining and tall and fair and straight   305
As the pillar that stood by the Beautiful Gate —
Himself the Gate whereby men can
Enter the temple of God in Man.

VIII

His words were shed softer than leaves from the pine,   310
And they fell on Sir Launfal as snows on the brine,
That mingle their softness and quiet in one
With the shaggy unrest they float down upon;
And the voice that was calmer than silence said,
" Lo, it is I, be not afraid!   315
In many climes, without avail,
Thou hast spent thy life for the Holy Grail;
Behold, it is here — this cup which thou
Didst fill at the streamlet for Me but now;
This crust is My body broken for thee;   320
This water His blood that died on the tree;
The Holy Supper is kept, indeed,
In whatso we share with another's need;
Not what we give, but what we share —
For the gift without the giver is bare;   325
Who gives himself with his alms feeds three —
Himself, his hungering neighbor, and Me."

307. **the Beautiful Gate:** a gate of the temple at Jerusalem (Acts, iii, 2).
308. **Himself the Gate:** Christ said, "I am the door." The leper had become
the Christ. 322. **Holy Supper:** the Last Supper of Christ and His disciples,
commemorated in the communion service of Christian churches.

IX

Sir Launfal awoke as from a swound:
" The Grail in my castle here is found!
Hang my idle armor up on the wall;   330
Let it be the spider's banquet hall.
He must be fenced with stronger mail
Who would seek and find the Holy Grail."

X

The castle gate stands open now,
    And the wanderer is welcome to the hall   335
As the hangbird is to the elm-tree bough.
    No longer scowl the turrets tall;
The summer's long siege at last is o'er.
When the first poor outcast went in at the door,
She entered with him in disguise,   340
And mastered the fortress by surprise.
There is no spot she loves so well on ground;
She lingers and smiles there the whole year round.
The meanest serf on Sir Launfal's land
Has hall and bower at his command;   345
And there's no poor man in the North Countree
But is lord of the earldom as much as he.

SUGGESTIONS FOR STUDY

PRELUDE TO PART FIRST

1. How does the organist compare with the poet approaching his theme? With yourself writing a theme for school?

2. Why are the first ideas called *auroral flushes?*

3. What proof does the poet give that we have contacts with Heaven all through our lives?

4. What kind of things must we pay for and what things are given away in this world?

5. In the famous description of the June day, pick out the details which suggest awakening and teeming life.

6. How would you answer the question in line 56?

7. What is the effect of such a day upon a person?

PART FIRST

1. Look up the part played by the vigil in the training of a knight. (Tappan, *When Knights were Bold*).

2. Beginning with Stanza II, the rest of the poem to Part Second, Stanza IX, is the vision Sir Launfal had on the night of his vigil. Describe the way he appears in the vision as he goes forth on his quest. You would enjoy reading a similar description of Sir Launcelot in Tennyson's "Lady of Shalott," Part III.

3. Why did the leper reject Sir Launfal's gift?

4. Have you read any other works in which lepers figure? *Ben Hur* by Lew Wallace and Stevenson's *Father Damien* are notable examples.

PRELUDE TO PART SECOND

1. Vocabulary: wold, l. 176; groined, l. 184; crypt, l. 190; arabesques, l. 196.

2. Mark the words and phrases which you think especially vivid in the famous description of winter.

3. Give example from your own observation of how the frost mimics the images of summer.

4. Explain the tradition of the Yule-log and other medieval Christmas customs which have come down to our own day. See Irving's "Christmas Sketches."

5. Point out the various figures of speech the poet uses in describing the great hall fire.

PART SECOND

1. Part Second is in direct contrast to Part First. See how many points of contrast you can find.

2. Why does the leper accept Sir Launfal's gift this time?

3. What miraculous transformation takes place? Explain the speech of the transformed leper in your own words.

4. Henry van Dyke's story "The Other Wise Man" expresses a similar idea. Have you read it?

5. What effect did the vision have on Sir Launfal at the end?

FOR FURTHER READING

THE HOLY GRAIL AND KNIGHTHOOD

Tennyson,
  "Sir Galahad"
  "The Holy Grail"
Lanier, *The Boy's King Arthur*

Pyle, *The Story of King Arthur and His Knights*
Tappan, *When Knights Were Bold*
Bulfinch, *The Age of Chivalry*

LOWELL'S POEMS

" The First Snowfall "
" She Came and Went "
" The Changeling "
" To a Dandelion "
" The Fatherland "
" Stanzas on Freedom "
" The Present Crisis "

" Rhoecus "
" The Singing Leaves "
" A Fable for Critics "
" The Shepherd of King Admetus "
" Commemoration   Ode "   (especially Stanza VI on Lincoln)

Early Southern Poetry

In this twentieth century geographical lines in literature have almost entirely disappeared. There are no great causes or movements that are distinctly sectional, and, while it is still possible to classify writers according to their origin, it is no longer done. In an earlier day conditions were different. The North and the South had definite opposing ideals of life and its practical problems. The West represented the last scenes of the pioneering spirit, coupled with the pursuit of gold in some places. It was therefore natural that literature should reflect to a considerable extent the conditions of life characteristic of each section.

The poets whose work appears in the following pages were Southerners by birth and, with the exception of Poe, were all connected with the Confederate cause and its aftermath. Today there is a most lively activity in poetry by writers of the South, but their work differs but little by virtue of that one fact. They are poets, not distinctly *Southern* poets, although a number select themes and subjects from their own native environment, or from the traditions and history of the older South. In this volume the work of these later Southerners will be found in its proper place among the " Twentieth Century Poets."

EDGAR ALLAN POE (1809–1849)

Though Edgar Allan Poe is here placed with Southern authors he is probably the least local of any of our writers. Scarcely a story or poem of his reflects a distinctly American setting, but rather an Old World background or " the misty mid-regions of Weir " — the pure realm of the imagination.

You have already realized, through Poe's stories, his curious ability to present unpleasant or even diseased mental states with gripping intensity. In his poetry he often enthralls the reader, but with even greater emotional hold, through the effect of rhythm. Poe was a master of verse form. The same mathematical quality in his mind which made him solve cryptograms, as in " The Gold Bug," led him to weigh and balance his syllables, calculate the effect of his choice of consonants, and so produce a flowing richness of sound which makes the poetry of his northern contemporaries often sound thin or unmusical. You have probably already read at some time his poem " The Bells," which is as pure an example of a " sound " poem as there is in our language. Here he reproduces the tonal effects of the silver, golden, brazen, and iron bells, largely by choice of consonants combined with certain vowels. One of his favorite devices is onomatopeia, the use of a word whose sound suggests its meaning, as " tintinnabulation " of the bells. In another familiar poem, " Annabel Lee," the frequent repetition of *n* and *l* would seldom be offered by a reader as the reason for his enjoyment of it, yet that has much to do with its melodious flow. All the devices of the poet for creating sound and mood effects were as carefully studied by Poe as color-mixing is studied by the painter. We might prefer to think that this poetry rolled out without effort from the inspired imagination of the poet, but unfortunately, the poet has told us with his own pen how he patterned his poems with careful deliberation and selection. The resulting impression, however, is one of sheer beauty and music.

You will not find morals in Poe's poems as in those of Bryant, Longfellow, and Whittier, but instead haunting strains which insinuate themselves into your memory.

TO HELEN

This is one of the earliest poems by Poe, inspired by his youthful admiration for Mrs. Jane Stith Stannard of Richmond, whom he later identified as " the first purely ideal love of my soul." Two lines of this poem are frequently quoted. Do you recognize them?

> Helen, thy beauty is to me
> Like those Nicean barks of yore,
> That gently, o'er a perfumed sea,
> The weary, way-worn wanderer bore
> To his own native shore.   5

2. **Nicean:** pertaining to Nicaea, a town of Asia Minor. Poe probably had no reason for referring to this town especially, but chose the word for its sound and its suggestion of a picturesque ancient ship.

On desperate seas long wont to roam,
 Thy hyacinth hair, thy classic face,
Thy Naiad airs have brought me home
 To the glory that was Greece,
 And the grandeur that was Rome.   10

Lo! in yon brilliant window-niche
 How statuelike I see thee stand,
The agate lamp within thy hand!
 Ah, Psyche, from the regions which
 Are Holy Land!   15

8. **Naiad:** in Greek mythology, a water-nymph. 14. **Psyche:** the Greek word for soul or mind derived from the myth of the Greek maiden beloved of Cupid. Poe uses the word again in "Ulalume," p. 633.

ISRAFEL

The aspirations of Poe expressed in this poem have so closely identified him with the name Israfel that it is often applied to him directly, as in Markham's poem on page 691.

"And the angel Israfel, whose heart-strings are a lute, and who has the sweetest voice of all God's creatures." — KORAN.

In Heaven a spirit doth dwell
 "Whose heart-strings are a lute";
None sing so wildly well
As the angel Israfel,
And the giddy stars (so legends tell)   5
Ceasing their hymns, attend the spell
 Of his voice, all mute.

Tottering above
 In her highest noon,
 The enamored moon   10
Blushes with love,
 While, to listen, the red levin
 (With the rapid Pleiades, even,
 Which were seven),
 Pauses in Heaven.   15

12. **levin:** a poetic name for lightning. 13. **Pleiades:** the Pleiades, a constellation.

And they say (the starry choir
  And the other listening things)
That Israfeli's fire
Is owing to that lyre
  By which he sits and sings —   20
The trembling living wire
Of those unusual strings.

But the skies that angel trod,
  Where deep thoughts are a duty —
Where Love's a grown-up God —   25
Where the Houri glances are
  Imbued with all the beauty
Which we worship in a star.

Therefore, thou art not wrong,
  Israfeli, who despisest   30
An unimpassioned song;
To thee the laurels belong,
  Best bard, because the wisest!
Merrily live, and long!

The ecstasies above   35
  With thy burning measures suit —
Thy grief, thy joy, thy hate, thy love,
  With the fervor of thy lute —
Well may the stars be mute!

Yes, Heaven is thine; but this   40
  Is a world of sweets and sours;
  Our flowers are merely — flowers,
And the shadow of thy perfect bliss
  Is the sunshine of ours.

If I could dwell   45
Where Israfel
  Hath dwelt, and he where I,

---

23. **But the skies that angel trod:** the meaning is clearer if the words are put in normal order — but that angel trod the skies. 26. **Houri:** a nymph of the Mohammedan Paradise. 32. **laurels:** crown or prize, because in ancient Greece poets were awarded crowns of laurel leaves.

He might not sing so wildly well
A mortal melody,
While a bolder note than this might swell   50
From my lyre within the sky.

SUGGESTIONS FOR STUDY

1. Be sure you know the meaning of enamored, l. 10; lyre, l. 19; imbued, l. 27; ecstasies, l. 35; fervor, l. 38; mortal, l. 49.

2. How does Poe emphasize the power and beauty of Israfel's song? How does he explain the reason for it?

3. What contrast does he point out between Israfel's surroundings and his own? What does he think might happen if they could change places?

4. Compare the ending of this poem with that of Shelley's "To a Skylark."

ELDORADO

"Eldorado" was one of the last poems written by Poe and is unusually sprightly. He had once more made severe resolutions about his habits and was planning to be married a second time; and it is possible that he may have had definite visions of an ideal toward which he was striving.

Gayly bedight,
A gallant knight,
In sunshine and in shadow,
Had journeyed long,
Singing a song,
In search of Eldorado.   5

But he grew old,
This knight so bold,
And o'er his heart a shadow
Fell as he found
No spot of ground   10
That looked like Eldorado.

And, as his strength
Failed him at length,
He met a pilgrim shadow;   15

6. **Eldorado:** literally, "the gilded," an imaginary place abounding in gold, supposed by the sixteenth-century Spaniards to be located in America. It has come to stand for any place abounding in wealth and opportunity.

"Shadow," said he,
"Where can it be,
This land of Eldorado?"

"Over the Mountains
Of the Moon,   20
Down the Valley of the Shadow,
Ride, boldly ride,"
The shade replied,
"If you seek for Eldorado!"

SUGGESTIONS FOR STUDY

1. If this little tale is applied to life, what might Eldorado stand for?
2. There are two possible interpretations of this poem. Do you think the shade meant that one never could reach his Eldorado, or that he could reach it only by being unafraid and riding boldly toward his goal? The first interpretation makes the shade cynical; the second, inspirational.

THE RAVEN

Poe had very definite beliefs as to the nature of poetry — that its essence should be beauty and that sadness was the mood most in keeping with poetic beauty. Therefore he said there was no subject more fitting for poetry than the death of a beautiful woman. Uninformed persons have sometimes thought that this poem grew out of Poe's sorrow for the death of his own wife, but unfortunately for that theory, the poem was published almost two years before his wife died. Since she was an invalid for many years, however, there must have been a dread in Poe's mind of losing her which stamped its impress upon the quality of the poem. Many of the effects of the poem were built up quite deliberately, Poe tells us, by the use of sonorous words, alliteration, internal rhyme, and repetition.

Once upon a midnight dreary, while I pondered, weak and weary,
Over many a quaint and curious volume of forgotten lore —
While I nodded, nearly napping, suddenly there came a tapping,
As of some one gently rapping, rapping at my chamber door.
"'Tis some visitor," I muttered, "tapping at my chamber door: 5
Only this and nothing more."

Ah, distinctly I remember it was in the bleak December,
And each separate dying ember wrought its ghost upon the floor.
Eagerly I wished the morrow; — vainly I had sought to borrow
From my books surcease of sorrow — sorrow for the lost Lenore,   10
For the rare and radiant maiden whom the angels name Lenore:
        Nameless here for evermore.

And the silken sad uncertain rustling of each purple curtain
Thrilled me — filled me with fantastic terrors never felt before;
So that now, to still the beating of my heart, I stood repeating   15
" 'Tis some visitor entreating entrance at my chamber door,
Some late visitor entreating entrance at my chamber door:
        This it is and nothing more."

Presently my soul grew stronger; hesitating then no longer,
" Sir," said I, " or Madam, truly your forgiveness I implore;   20
But the fact is I was napping, and so gently you came rapping,
And so faintly you came tapping, tapping at my chamber door,
That I scarce was sure I heard you " — here I opened wide the
        door: —
        Darkness there and nothing more.

Deep into that darkness peering, long I stood there wondering,
        fearing,   25
Doubting, dreaming dreams no mortals ever dared to dream before;
But the silence was unbroken, and the stillness gave no token,
And the only word there spoken was the whispered word, " Lenore? "
This I whispered, and an echo murmured back the word, " Lenore: "
        Merely this and nothing more.   30

Back into the chamber turning, all my soul within me burning,
Soon again I heard a tapping somewhat louder than before.
" Surely," said I, " surely that is something at my window lattice;
Let me see, then, what thereat is, and this mystery explore;
Let my heart be still a moment and this mystery explore: 35
        'Tis the wind and nothing more."

Open here I flung the shutter, when, with many a flirt and flutter,
In there stepped a stately Raven of the saintly days of yore.
Not the least obeisance made he; not a minute stopped or stayed he;

But, with mien of lord or lady, perched above my chamber door,   40
Perched upon a bust of Pallas just above my chamber door:
   Perched, and sat, and nothing more.

Then this ebony bird beguiling my sad fancy into smiling
By the grave and stern decorum of the countenance it wore —
" Though thy crest be shorn and shaven, thou," I said, " art sure
   no craven,   45
Ghastly grim and ancient Raven wandering from the Nightly shore:
Tell me what thy lordly name is on the Night's Plutonian shore! "
   Quoth the Raven, " Nevermore."

Much I marveled this ungainly fowl to hear discourse so plainly,
Though its answer little meaning — little relevancy bore;   50
For we cannot help agreeing that no living human being
Ever yet was blessed with seeing bird above his chamber door,
Bird or beast upon the sculptured bust above his chamber door,
   With such name as " Nevermore."

But the Raven, sitting lonely on the placid bust, spoke only   55
That one word, as if his soul in that one word he did outpoor.
Nothing further then he uttered, not a feather then he fluttered,
Till I scarcely more than muttered, — " Other friends have flown
   before;
On the morrow *he* will leave me, as my Hopes have flown before."
   Then the bird said, " Nevermore."   60

Startled at the stillness broken by reply so aptly spoken,
" Doubtless," said I, " what it utters is its only stock and store,
Caught from some unhappy master whom unmerciful Disaster
Followed fast and followed faster till his songs one burden bore:
Till the dirges of his Hope that melancholy burden bore   65
   Of ' Never — nevermore.' "

But the Raven still beguiling all my fancy into smiling,
Straight I wheeled a cushioned seat in front of bird and bust and
   door;
Then, upon the velvet sinking, I betook myself to linking
Fancy unto fancy, thinking what this ominous bird of yore,   70
What this grim, ungainly, ghastly, gaunt, and ominous bird of yore
   Meant in croaking " Nevermore."

41. **Pallas:** Pallas Athene, Greek goddess of wisdom, called Minerva by the
Romans. 47. **Plutonian:** referring to Pluto, the god who in Greek mythology
presided over the regions of the dead.

This I sat engaged in guessing, but no syllable expressing
To the fowl whose fiery eyes now burned into my bosom's core;
This and more I sat divining, with my head at ease reclining   75
On the cushion's velvet lining that the lamplight gloated o'er,
But whose velvet violet lining with the lamplight gloating o'er
    She shall press, ah, nevermore!

Then, methought, the air grew denser, perfumed from an unseen
    censer
Swung by seraphim whose foot-falls tinkled on the tufted floor. 80
" Wretch," I cried, " thy God hath lent thee — by these angels he
    hath sent thee
Respite — respite and nepenthe from thy memories of Lenore!
Quaff, oh quaff this kind nepenthe, and forget this lost Lenore! "
    Quoth the Raven, " Nevermore."

" Prophet! " said I, " thing of evil! prophet still, if bird or devil! 85
Whether Tempter sent, or whether tempest tossed thee here ashore,
Desolate yet all undaunted, on this desert land enchanted —
On this home by Horror haunted — tell me truly, I implore:
Is there — *is* there balm in Gilead? — tell me — tell me, I implore! "
    Quoth the Raven, " Nevermore."   90

" Prophet! " said I, " thing of evil — prophet still, if bird or devil!
By that Heaven that bends above us, by that God we both adore,
Tell this soul with sorrow laden if, within the distant Aidenn,
It shall clasp a sainted maiden whom the angels name Lenore:
Clasp a rare and radiant maiden whom the angels name Lenore! " 95
    Quoth the Raven, " Nevermore."

" Be that word our sign of parting, bird or fiend! " I shrieked, up-
    starting:
" Get thee back into the tempest and the Night's Plutonian shore!
Leave no black plume as a token of that lie thy soul hath spoken!
Leave my loneliness unbroken! quit the bust above my door! 100
Take thy beak from out my heart, and take thy form from off my
    door! "
    Quoth the Raven, " Nevermore."

82. **nepenthe:** a drug that destroys pain and brings forgetfulness. 89. **balm in Gilead:** balm is a healing lotion made in Gilead, a part of ancient Palestine. See Jeremiah viii: 22. It has become a common expression meaning relief for affliction. 93. **Aidenn:** from the Arabic for Eden.

And the Raven, never flitting, still is sitting, still is sitting
On the pallid bust of Pallas just above my chamber door;
And his eyes have all the seeming of a demon's that is dreaming, 105
And the lamp-light o'er him streaming throws his shadow on the
    floor:
And my soul from out that shadow that lies floating on the floor
    Shall be lifted — nevermore!

SUGGESTIONS FOR STUDY

1. Vocabulary: surcease, l. 10; fantastic, l. 14; obeisance, l. 39; mien, l. 40; decorum, l. 44; relevancy, l. 50; ominous, l. 70; censer, l. 79; seraphim, l. 80; pallid, l. 104.

2. What atmosphere and mood are established at the very beginning of the poem?

3. From the few effective details given, picture to yourself the kind of room in which this story is set. Contrast this with the bare cottage at Fordham where Poe's own wife died two years later.

4. What in the Raven's behavior makes the poem unusually gruesome and depressing? Of what in life is the Raven a symbol?

5. Find striking examples throughout of Poe's devices: internal rhyme, alliteration, and repetition.

6. In what other poems or stories of Poe do you find that the subject is the death of a beautiful woman? He has another poem called "Lenore." It would be interesting to compare this with "The Raven."

7. According to the poem, what was the reason for the writer's mournfulness?

8. Poe was fond of repeating words to emphasize an idea. Quote instances.

9. Which word suits the poem: sincere, sentimental, emotional.

ULALUME

Here is a poem which really did follow the death of Poe's wife, for it was published before the first anniversary of her loss after he had suffered a critical illness. It suggests a deeply despairing and almost disordered mind. Do not try to understand the exact meaning of every line, for it has baffled even the critics. Read it rather for the remarkable creation of a mood and the sonorous roll of the lines.

The skies they were ashen and sober;
   The leaves they were crispèd and sere —
   The leaves they were withering and sere;
It was night in the lonesome October
   Of my most immemorial year;   5
It was hard by the dim lake of Auber,
   In the misty mid region of Weir —
It was down by the dank tarn of Auber,
   In the ghoul-haunted woodland of Weir.

Here once, through an alley Titanic,   10
   Of cypress, I roamed with my Soul —
   Of cypress, with Psyche, my Soul.
These were days when my heart was volcanic
   As the scoriac rivers that roll —
   As the lavas that restlessly roll   15
Their sulphurous currents down Yaanek
   In the ultimate climes of the pole —
That groan as they roll down Mount Yaanek
   In the realms of the boreal pole.

Our talk had been serious and sober,   20
   But our thoughts they were palsied and sere —
   Our memories were treacherous and sere —
For we knew not the month was October,
   And we marked not the night of the year —
   (Ah, night of all nights in the year!)   25
We noted not the dim lake of Auber —
   (Though once we had journeyed down here) —
Remembered not the dank tarn of Auber,
   Nor the ghoul-haunted woodland of Weir.

And now, as the night was senescent   30
   And star-dials pointed to morn —
   As the star-dials hinted of morn —
At the end of our path a liquescent
   And nebulous luster was born,

6. **Auber;** 7. **Weir;** 16. **Yaanek:** These are all imaginary names made up by Poe for their sound and suggestive effect. 10. **Titanic:** referring to the Titans, a race of giants in Greek mythology. Here it suggests vastness. 11. **cypress:** a tree symbolizing mourning because so frequently planted in grave-yards. 12. **Psyche:** Greek for soul.

Out of which a miraculous crescent 35
  Arose with a duplicate horn —
Astarte's bediamonded crescent
  Distinct with its duplicate horn.

And I said — " She is warmer than Dian:
  She rolls through an ether of sighs — 40
  She revels in a region of sighs:
She has seen that the tears are not dry on
  These cheeks, where the worm never dies
And has come past the stars of the Lion
  To point us the path to the skies — 45
  To the Lethean peace of the skies —
Come up, in despite of the Lion,
  To shine on us with her bright eyes —
Come up through the lair of the Lion,
  With love in her luminous eyes." 50

But Psyche, uplifting her finger,
  Said — " Sadly this star I mistrust —
  Her pallor I strangely mistrust: —
Oh, hasten! — oh, let us not linger!
  Oh, fly! — let us fly! — for we must." 55
In terror she spoke, letting sink her
  Wings until they trailed in the dust —
In agony sobbed, letting sink her
  Plumes till they trailed in the dust —
  Till they sorrowfully trailed in the dust. 60

I replied — " This is nothing but dreaming;
  Let us on by this tremulous light!
  Let us bathe in this crystalline light!
Its Sibyllic splendor is beaming
  With Hope and in Beauty tonight: — 65
  See! — it flickers up the sky through the night!

---

37. **Astarte:** The Phoenician goddess of the moon. 39. **Dian:** Diana, the Roman goddess of the moon. 44. **Lion:** A Northern constellation pictured as a lion. 46. **Lethean:** referring to Lethe, the river of forgetfulness in the Greek regions of the dead. 64. **Sibyllic:** pertaining to the Sibyl, in Greek mythology a prophetess.

Ah, we safely may trust to its gleaming,
   And be sure it will lead us aright —
We safely may trust to a gleaming
   That cannot but guide us aright,   70
   Since it flickers up to Heaven through the night."

Thus I pacified Psyche and kissed her,
   And tempted her out of her gloom —
   And conquered her scruples and gloom;
And we passed to the end of the vista,   75
   But were stopped by the door of a tomb —
   By the door of a legended tomb;
And I said — " What is written, sweet sister,
   On the door of this legended tomb? "
   She replied — " Ulalume — Ulalume —   80
   'Tis the vault of thy lost Ulalume! "

Then my heart it grew ashen and sober
   As the leaves that were crispèd and sere —
   As the leaves that were withering and sere,
And I cried — " It was surely October   85
   On *this* very night of last year
   That I journeyed — I journeyed down here —
   That I brought a dread burden down here —
   On this night of all nights in the year,
   Ah, what demon has tempted me here?   90
Well I know, now, this dim lake of Auber —
   This misty mid region of Weir —
Well I know, now, this dank tarn of Auber,
   This ghoul-haunted woodland of Weir."

SUGGESTIONS FOR STUDY

1. Vocabulary: sere, l. 2; immemorial, l. 5; dank tarn, l. 8; ghoul, l. 9;
volcanic, l. 13; scoriac, l. 14; ultimate, l. 17; boreal, l. 19; senescent,
l. 30; liquescent, l. 33; nebulous, l. 34; luminous, l. 50; crystalline, l. 63.

2. How do the time of the year, the time of the night, and the surroundings of nature all contribute to the mood of the poem? How does
the moonlight betray the false hope that the poet had placed in it? What
warning had he had that the place was not a good one to be in?

3. What mood is suggested by the very sound of the name Ulalume? Look up the word ululate in the dictionary to find its present meaning and derivation. Does this throw any added light on Poe's choice of the name?

FOR FURTHER READING

" Annabel Lee "   " The Conqueror Worm "
" The Bells "   " Lenore "
" To One in Paradise "   " The Haunted Palace "

HENRY TIMROD (1829–1867)

The three poets who follow — Timrod, Hayne, and Lanier — are pathetic illustrations of what war does to destroy the gentler and finer arts of life, especially in the invaded territory. All three, by nature sensitive to beauty, rich in imagination, and full of literary promise, came out of their experiences in the Confederate Army with broken health, returned to poverty-stricken homes and surrendered their lives before their time to tuberculosis.

Henry Timrod and Paul Hayne were school chums and fellow-poets in Charleston, South Carolina, which before the war was the literary center of the South as Boston was of the North. Poverty, the war, and a seemingly unlucky star interfered with everything Timrod attempted — his college career, his struggle to become a professor, his first volume of poems, and his editorial work on a Southern newspaper. His only child, even, died when less than a year old. When the bankrupt newspaper was unable to pay him a dollar of salary for four months, he wrote thus ruefully to Hayne of the sale of his possessions: " We have — let me see — yes, we have eaten two silver pitchers, one or two dozen silver forks, several sofas, innumerable chairs, and a huge bedstead." Two visits to Hayne among the Georgia pines made a bright spot in his life before death overtook him shortly before his thirty-eighth birthday.

The first of the following poems commemorates the spirit of Timrod's native city under blockade during the early part of the war. Timrod was not a soldier but a war correspondent, and his stirring poems voiced the feelings of the Southerners through the long strife. The second poem, written only a few months before his death, combines Southern courtliness and dignity with the pathos of a lost cause.

CHARLESTON

Calm as that second summer which precedes
     The first fall of the snow,
In the broad sunlight of heroic deeds
     The City bides the foe.

As yet, behind their ramparts stern and proud,　　　　5
　　Her bolted thunders sleep —
Dark Sumter like a battlemented cloud
　　Looms o'er the solemn deep.

No Calpe frowns from lofty cliff or scar
　　To guard the holy strand;　　　　　　　　　　10
But Moultrie holds in leash her dogs of war
　　Above the level sand.

And down the dunes a thousand guns lie couched
　　Unseen beside the flood,
Like tigers in some Orient jungle crouched,　　　　15
　　That wait and watch for blood.

Meanwhile, through streets still echoing with trade,
　　Walk grave and thoughtful men
Whose hands may one day wield the patriot's blade
　　As lightly as the pen.　　　　　　　　　　　20

And maidens with such eyes as would grow dim
　　Over a bleeding hound
Seem each one to have caught the strength of him
　　Whose sword she sadly bound.

Thus girt without and garrisoned at home,　　　　25
　　Day patient following day,
Old Charleston looks from roof and spire and dome
　　Across her tranquil bay.

Ships, through a hundred foes, from Saxon lands
　　And spicy Indian ports　　　　　　　　　　30
Bring Saxon steel and iron to her hands
　　And Summer to her courts.

7. **Sumter:** a fort on Charleston harbor which had surrendered to the Southern forces, April 14, 1861. Lincoln immediately called for volunteers and the war was opened. 9. **Calpe:** the ancient Phoenician name for the rock of Gibraltar. 11. **Moultrie:** another fort held by the Southerners about two and a half miles along the coast. 29. **Saxon lands:** England and her possessions. British ships ran the Northern blockade to bring supplies to the besieged city.

But still, along yon dim Atlantic line
  The only hostile smoke
Creeps like a harmless mist above the brine   35
  From some frail, floating oak.

Shall the Spring dawn, and she, still clad in smiles
  And with an unscathed brow,
Rest in the strong arms of her palm-crowned isles
  As fair and free as now?   40

We know not: in the temple of the Fates
  God has inscribed her doom;
And, all untroubled in her faith, she waits
  The triumph or the tomb.

SUGGESTIONS FOR STUDY

1. Look up the history of the secession of South Carolina and the fall of Fort Sumter.
2. What effect did the blockade have upon the life of the South?
3. What is the spirit of the people of Charleston as represented by the poem? Point out specific lines.

ODE

SUNG AT THE OCCASION OF DECORATING THE GRAVES OF THE CONFEDERATE DEAD, AT MAGNOLIA CEMETERY, CHARLESTON, S. C., 1867

Sleep sweetly in your humble graves,
  Sleep, martyrs of a fallen cause;
Though yet no marble column craves
  The pilgrim here to pause.

In seeds of laurel in the earth   5
  The blossom of your fame is blown,
And somewhere, waiting for its birth,
  The shaft is in the stone!

3. **marble column:** today there is a marble and bronze monument in this cemetery in honor of the fallen soldiers.

Meanwhile, behalf the tardy years
   Which keep in trust your storied tombs,   10
Behold! your sisters bring their tears,
   And these memorial blooms.

Small tributes! but your shades will smile
   More proudly on these wreaths today,
Than when some cannon-molded pile   15
   Shall overlook this bay.

Stoop, angels, hither from the skies!
   There is no holier spot of ground
Than where defeated valor lies,
   By mourning beauty crowned!   20

SUGGESTIONS FOR STUDY

1. After the Civil War many memorial songs to the fallen soldiers were written. Since this was the most famous one from the Southern point of view, it is interesting to compare it with Lowell's more elaborate and difficult " Commemoration Ode " from the Northern point of view, and with the tender and lyrical " The Blue and the Gray " by Francis M. Finch, which represents the spirit of equal mourning for both sides and the healing of war hatreds.

2. Timrod in his life and disposition resembled somewhat the British poet, William Collins, whose " Ode Written in the Beginning of the Year 1746 " commemorates the British soldiers killed in the War of the Austrian Succession. This also makes an interesting comparison with Timrod's ode.

FOR FURTHER READING

" The Cotton Boll "   " A Cry to Arms "
" Spring "   " Serenade "
" A Common Thought "

10. **storied:** suggesting stories of valor. 15. **cannon-molded pile:** monuments to soldiers are often made from melted cannon.

PAUL HAMILTON HAYNE (1830–1886)

The contrast between the beginning and end of Hayne's life is conspicuous. Belonging to a distinguished and wealthy Charleston family, he was given every advantage of education and was a leader in the literary coterie of the city, with editorial positions on two prominent Southern magazines, and two volumes of poetry to his credit. Then came the war. Hayne was not physically strong enough for active service and thus became an aide on Governor Pickens's staff. Returning to poverty and a devastated home (his magnificent library had been burned), he moved his wife and son to the pines of Augusta, Georgia, where in a crude log cabin he passed the rest of his days struggling for health, and earning a slender income through his poems. Hayne writes less of the war and more about nature than Timrod. There is a dignified beauty in his pictures of the forests which reminds one of Bryant.

THE MOCKING BIRD

The mocking bird has been the frequent subject of both literature and music. Hayne has written another longer poem entitled "The Mocking Birds." Lanier, the next poet to be considered, also wrote one with the same title in the singular, in which he called the bird "yon trim Shakespeare on the tree." Audubon has given us a vivid prose account of the bird.

A golden pallor of voluptuous light
Filled the warm southern night:
The moon, clear orbed, above the sylvan scene
Moved like a stately queen,
So rife with conscious beauty all the while,   5
What could she do but smile
At her own perfect loveliness below,
Glassed in the tranquil flow
Of crystal fountains and unruffled streams?
Half lost in waking dreams,   10
As down in loneliest forest dell I strayed,
Lo! from a neighboring glade,
Flashed through the drifts of moonshine, swiftly came
A fairy shape of flame.
It rose in dazzling spirals overhead,   15
Whence to wild sweetness wed,

Poured marvelous melodies, silvery trill on trill;
The very leaves grew still
On the charmed trees to hearken; while for me,
Heart-trilled to ecstasy,   20
I followed — followed the bright shape that flew,
Still circling up the blue,
Till as a fountain that has reached its height
Falls back in sprays of light
Slowly dissolved, so that enrapturing lay   25
Divinely melts away
Through tremulous spaces to a music-mist,
Soon by the fitful breeze
How gently kissed
Into remote and tender silences.   30

SUGGESTIONS FOR STUDY

1. Vocabulary: pallor, voluptuous, l. 1; orbed, sylvan, l. 3; rife, l. 5; glade, l. 12; enrapturing lay, l. 25.

2. What suggestions of the color and habit of the mocking bird do you find in the poem?

3. What differences do you find in the rhythm of this and the following poem by Hayne?

4. If you are a bird-lover you will enjoy some other poems about birds: John B. Tabb, " To a Wood-Robin "; William E. Henley, " Birds in April " and " A Thrush Sings "; Witter Bynner, " To a Phoebe-Bird "; Hilda Conkling, " Pigeons Just Awake "; Louise Bogan, " The Crows "; Celia Thaxter, " The Sandpiper "; Harriet Monroe, " The Water Ouzel."

ASPECTS OF THE PINES

Tall, somber, grim, against the morning sky
   They rise, scarce touched by melancholy airs,
Which stir the fadeless foliage dreamfully,
   As if from realms of mystical despairs.

Tall, somber, grim, they stand with dusky gleams   5
   Brightening to gold within the woodland's core,
Beneath the gracious noontide's tranquil beams —
   But the weird winds of morning sigh no more.

A stillness, strange, divine, ineffable,
    Broods round and o'er them in the wind's surcease,   10
And on each tinted copse and shimmering dell
    Rests the mute rapture of deep-hearted peace.

Last, sunset comes — the solemn joy and might
    Borne from the West when cloudless day declines —
Low, flutelike breezes sweep the waves of light,   15
    And lifting dark green tresses of the pines,

Till every lock is luminous — gently float,
    Fraught with hale odors up the heavens afar
To faint when twilight on her virginal throat
    Wears for a gem the tremulous vesper star.   20

SUGGESTIONS FOR STUDY

1. Vocabulary: ineffable, l. 9; surcease, l. 10; copse, l. 11; luminous, l. 17; virginal, l. 19; vesper, l. 20.

2. At what different times of day are the pines described? How does their appearance differ at each time?

3. If you live in a pine country, observe whether the same aspects

are evident in your experience. If you do not live in a pine country, try to find some pictures of pines which will show you their appearance.

4. If you love the woods, you will want to read some other poems about them, such as: Bryant, " A Forest Hymn " and " Inscription for the Entrance to a Wood "; Richard Watson Gilder, " The Woods that Bring the Sunset Near "; Theodosia Garrison, " The Green Inn "; Joyce Kilmer, " Trees "; Robert Graves, " An English Wood "; Grace Hazard Conkling, " Maine Woods in Winter "; Margaret Widdemer, " Winter Branches."

FOR FURTHER READING

" Vicksburg "

" Rose and Thorn "

" Under the Pine " (in memory of Timrod)

" Midsummer in the South "

" Laocoön "

" Forgotten "

" A Little While I Fain Would Linger Yet "

SIDNEY LANIER (1842–1881)

Of the three Southern poets who passed through the Civil War, Sidney Lanier is decidedly the greatest. Besides, he has the distinction of being the only one of our important American poets who was also a professional musician. Yet how fitting it is that the two talents should be linked together in one person. One of Lanier's famous lines is " Music is love in search of a word." As a boy in Macon, Georgia, Sidney had played both the violin and the flute, but the latter became his real medium of expression. He carried it with him through the Civil War, where he fought on the Confederate side, and even concealed it up his sleeve when he was sent to a Northern prison. Later when he was a member of the Baltimore Symphony Orchestra, he was considered by many the world's greatest flute player. So impressed was he with the close relation between music and poetry that he wrote *The Science of English Verse* to show the correspondence between the measures of poetry and the bars in music. He believed that the poet, by a nice selection of sounds and syllables and the proper " tuning " of his words, could produce unusual musical effects. One of his most successful attempts at this, and, therefore, perhaps the best-known poem, is " The Song of the Chattahoochee." Even though you may have read this before just as a lovely song, there is an added pleasure in discovering how the poet worked out the pattern of the melody. After you have read it through first to get the idea — the temptations of the river to linger and the final call which it must answer — read the poem again (aloud, of course) and listen to the rippling sound of the lines.

SONG OF THE CHATTAHOOCHEE [1]

Out of the hills of Habersham,
  Down the valleys of Hall,
I hurry amain to reach the plain,
Run the rapid and leap the fall,
Split at the rock and together again,   5
Accept my bed, or narrow or wide,
And flee from folly on every side
With a lover's pain to attain the plain
  Far from the hills of Habersham,
  Far from the valleys of Hall.   10

All down the hills of Habersham,
  All through the valleys of Hall,
The rushes cried *Abide, abide,*
The wilful waterweeds held me thrall,
The laving laurel turned my tide,   15
The ferns and the fondling grass said *Stay,*
The dewberry dipped for to work delay,
And the little reeds sighed *Abide, abide,*
  Here in the hills of Habersham,
  Here in the valleys of Hall.   20

High o'er the hills of Habersham,
  Veiling the valleys of Hall,
The hickory told me manifold
Fair tales of shade, the poplar tall
Wrought me her shadowy self to hold,   25
The chestnut, the oak, the walnut, the pine,
Overleaning, with flickering meaning and sign,
Said, *Pass not, so cold, these manifold*
  Deep shades of the hills of Habersham,
  These glades in the valleys of Hall.   30

And oft in the hills of Habersham,
  And oft in the valleys of Hall,
The white quartz shone, and the smooth brook-stone
Did bar me of passage with friendly brawl,
And many a luminous jewel lone   35

[1] **Chattahoochee:** this river is in Georgia, Lanier's native state.

— Crystals clear or a-cloud with mist,
Ruby, garnet, and amethyst —
Made lures with the lights of streaming stone
  In the clefts of the hills of Habersham,
  In the beds of the valleys of Hall.   40

But oh, not the hills of Habersham,
  And oh, not the valleys of Hall
Avail: I am fain for to water the plain.
Downward the voices of Duty call —
Downward, to toil and be mixed with the main   45
The dry fields burn, and the mills are to turn,
And a myriad flowers mortally yearn,
And the lordly main from beyond the plain
  Calls o'er the hills of Habersham,
  Calls through the valleys of Hall.   50

SUGGESTIONS FOR STUDY

1. Vocabulary: amain, l. 3; laving, l. 15; myriad, l. 47.

2. Observe how neatly the second, third, and fourth stanzas each record a different kind of temptation to linger. Try to name a topic for each stanza of the poem.

3. Though Lanier does not point a moral directly as Bryant does in " To a Waterfowl " or Holmes in " The Chambered Nautilus," can you work out a parallel between this river and man's life which is implied in the poem?

4. This poem is unusually full of alliteration. See how many examples of it you can find. What particular consonants are used again and again?

5. Where is refrain used in the poem? Is the variation in the refrain pleasing or otherwise?

6. Compare the sound of this poem with Poe's " Ulalume," p. 633. What similar devices are used by the two poets? What noticeable difference is there between the two poems?

7. Read Tennyson's " The Brook " with which this is often compared. Which do you prefer in rhythm? in idea?

8. Many other rivers in Georgia have musical names: Savannah, Willacoochee, Altamaha. What geographical names in your own state might have poems built around them?

FROM THE FLATS

To a man who loved the hills and mountain streams as did Lanier, no wonder the Florida flats seemed unendurable. The effect of surrounding nature on man's spirit has often been a theme in American literature. Many have felt as Lanier did about the flats or prairies. Others have found beauty and variety in them.

What heartache — ne'er a hill!
Inexorable, vapid, vague and chill
The drear sand-levels drain my spirit low.
With one poor word they tell me all they know;
Whereat their stupid tongues, to tease my pain,   5
Do drawl it o'er again and o'er again.
They hurt my heart with griefs I cannot name:
    Always the same, the same.

Nature hath no surprise,
No ambuscade of beauty 'gainst mine eyes   10
From brake or lurking dell or deep defile;
No humors, frolic forms — this mile, that mile;
No rich reserves or happy-valley hopes
Beyond the bend of roads, the distant slopes.
Her fancy fails, her wild is all run tame: 15
    Ever the same, the same.

Oh might I through these tears
But glimpse some hill my Georgia high uprears,
Where white the quartz and pink the pebble shine,
The hickory heavenward strives, the muscadine   20
Swings o'er the slope, the oak's far-falling shade
Darkens the dogwood in the bottom-glade,
And down the hollow from a ferny nook
    Bright leaps a living brook!

SUGGESTIONS FOR STUDY

1. Vocabulary: inexorable, l. 2; vapid, l. 2; ambuscade, l. 10; muscadine, l. 20.

2. How many of the same musical devices of the first poem can you find in this one?

3. If you live in a flat country, tell how you are affected by it.

4. For a fine prose description of a prairie see Rölvaag's *Giants in the Earth*, Chapter 1. Carl Sandburg is our most notable poet of the prairies. See his volume, *Slabs of The Sunburnt West*.

BARNACLES

Barnacles are small sea creatures which cling to the sides of vessels and in sufficient number may greatly impede the progress of the ship. Here Lanier has made the parallel between the natural object and man's life more explicit than in " The Song of the Chattahoochee," but the underlying idea of the forward urge is the same.

My soul is sailing through the sea,
But the Past is heavy and hindereth me.
The Past hath crusted cumbrous shells
That hold the flesh of cold sea-mells
    About my soul.
The huge waves wash, the high waves roll,
Each barnacle clingeth and worketh dole
    And hindereth me from sailing!

Old Past let go, and drop i' the sea
Till fathomless waters cover thee!
For I am living but thou art dead;
Thou drawest back, I strive ahead
    The Day to find.
Thy shells unbind! Night comes behind,
I needs must hurry with the wind
    And trim me best for sailing!

SUGGESTIONS FOR STUDY

1. Vocabulary: cumbrous, l. 3; sea-mells, l. 4; dole, l. 7; fathomless, l. 10.

2. By reading an account of Lanier's life you will discover some of these barnacles which he felt holding him back.

3. What barnacles do you think impede the progress of our civilization?

THE STIRRUP–CUP

As a result of Lanier's imprisonment during the war, his health was greatly impaired, and the last few years of his life showed a struggle against consumption which reminds one of Robert Louis Stevenson. During this period he was delivering a series of lectures on English literature at Johns Hopkins University, Baltimore, and sometimes he kept his appointment when he was almost too weak to stand on the platform. His wife testifies that when he wrote the end of " Hymns of the Marshes " he was so near death as to be unable to lift his hand to his mouth, though he wrote it four years before he died. " The Stirrup-Cup " expresses the high-hearted courage with which he was able to meet death when it came to him at the age of thirty-nine.

Death, thou'rt a cordial old and rare:
Look how compounded, with what care!
Time got his wrinkles reaping thee
Sweet herbs from all antiquity.

David to thy distillage went, 5
Keats, and Gotama excellent,
Omar Khayyám, and Chaucer bright,
And Shakespeare for a king-delight.

Then, Time, let not a drop be spilt:
Hand me the cup whene'er thou wilt; 10
'Tis thy rich stirrup-cup to me;
I'll drink it down right smilingly.

SUGGESTIONS FOR STUDY

1. Vocabulary: cordial, l. 1; distillage, l. 5.

2. John Hay has written a poem by the same name which may be found in Rittenhouse's *Little Book of American Poets*. Have this read in class and contrast the attitude of the two poets.

5. **David:** King David, writer of the Psalms. 6. **Keats:** John Keats, the English poet, who died of consumption at twenty-six. 6. **Gotama:** Another name for Buddha, the founder of Buddhism, who lived in India in the sixth century before Christ. 7. **Omar Khayyám:** A Persian poet of the twelfth century; author of the "Rubaiyat." 7. **Chaucer:** Geoffrey Chaucer, the first notable English poet, who lived in the 14th century. 11. **stirrup-cup:** the last drink taken by a rider before getting into the stirrups for a long or dangerous ride.

3. Compare Lanier's attitude with that of Bryant in " Thanatopsis "
(p. 528); with Whitman's " Carol of Death."

4. What other poems on death do you know? Would you say that this
is a common or uncommon subject among poets?

FOR FURTHER READING

" Tampa Robins "   " The Marshes of Glynn "
" A Song of the Future "   " Evening Song "
" The Mocking Bird "   " A Ballad of Trees and the
" The Harlequin of Dreams "   Master "
" Corn "   " The Revenge of Hamish "
" Sunrise "   " Life and Song "

ABRAM J. RYAN (1839–1886)

Abram J. Ryan was a Catholic priest who served in the Confederate
army as a chaplain. " The Conquered Banner " was written at the end
of the war and expresses his sympathy for those who had fought and lost.
Like " The Star-Spangled Banner " and " Maryland, My Maryland," the
poem was written under the stress of great emotion at a single sitting.
It was first published in Father Ryan's own paper, *The Banner of the
South*.

THE CONQUERED BANNER

Furl that Banner, for 'tis weary;
Round its staff 'tis drooping dreary:
    Furl it, fold it — it is best;
For there's not a man to wave it,
And there's not a sword to save it,   5
And there's not one left to lave it
In the blood which heroes gave it,
And its foes now scorn and brave it:
    Furl it, hide it — let it rest!

Take that Banner down! 'tis tattered;   10
Broken is its staff and shattered;
And the valiant hosts are scattered,
    Over whom it floated high.

Oh, 'tis hard for us to fold it,
Hard to think there's none to hold it,   15
Hard that those who once unrolled it
  Now must furl it with a sigh!

Furl that Banner — furl it sadly!
Once ten thousands hailed it gladly,
And ten thousands wildly, madly,   20
  Swore it should forever wave;
Swore that foeman's sword should never
Hearts like theirs entwined dissever,
Till that flag should float forever
  O'er their freedom or their grave!   25

Furl it! for the hands that grasped it,
And the hearts that fondly clasped it,
  Cold and dead are lying low;
And that Banner — it is trailing,
While around it sounds the wailing   30
  Of its people in their woe.

For, though conquered, they adore it —
Love the cold, dead hands that bore it,
  Weep for those who fell before it,
Pardon those who trailed and tore it;   35
And oh, wildly they deplore it,
  Now to furl and fold it so!

Furl that Banner! True, 'tis gory,
Yet 'tis wreathed around with glory,
And 'twill live in song and story   40
  Though its folds are in the dust!
For its fame on brightest pages,
Penned by poets and by sages,
Shall go sounding down the ages —
  Furl its folds though now we must.   45

Furl that Banner, softly, slowly!
Treat it gently — it is holy,
  For it droops above the dead.
Touch it not — unfold it never,
Let it droop there, furled forever —   50
  For its people's hopes are fled!

Transition Poetry

To classify literature by periods is to a considerable extent arbitrary, its chief value lying in the convenience it affords to indicate the trends in thought and style as new writers appear on the literary horizon. The two earlier sections of poetry in this volume were comparatively easy to group because of periods naturally determined by dates in our history, but to tell exactly where one era ends and the other begins is impossible. Nor is it necessary. Long before the end of the last century it was evident that new voices in poetry were clamoring to be heard; there were new tendencies, as might be expected; the older poets had written their best work; new problems arose in our national, social, and cultural life, all of which were bound to be reflected in literature, prose as well as poetry.

The group of poets represented in this section showed in their work that they were trying to get away from the older tradition, which had in the main been romantic. Perhaps unconsciously on the part of some, they aimed at a poetry more closely affiliated with real life as each individual poet interpreted it. By far the most strident voice was that of Walt Whitman, the voice of a real pioneer, who broke away from the earlier traditions both in subject matter and style. He did not achieve immediate recognition in this country, but before he died he had the satisfaction of knowing that his " barbaric yawp " was being heard around the world. In general, Whitman and the rest aimed at what they considered realism, so that it becomes possible to group together such odd contrasts as Whitman, Emily Dickinson, Thomas Bailey Aldrich, Joaquin Miller, Eugene Field, James Whitcomb Riley, and others.

Walt Whitman (1819–1892)

Lowell and Whitman were born in the same year and died within a year of each other. There the parallel ends, for no two men could present a more complete contrast in the backgrounds and the trends of their lives than these two. Lowell was born into the established elegance of an old Cambridge family; Whitman came from humble farming and sea-faring folk on Long Island. Lowell was nurtured in college halls and libraries; Whitman roamed the streets of New York and rubbed elbows with human nature in all its varied forms. Lowell wrote a fine scholarly essay on " Democracy "; Whitman gave an unusual example of genuine democratic living. Lowell was honored by an ambassadorship to Eng-land; Whitman lost a minor government position because an official considered his poems immoral. Lowell's writings show a vein of rich humor; Whitman regarded life vigorously and vitally, but always seriously.

There are three periods in Whitman's life which you must understand before you can wholly realize his poetic message. His first forty years were spent largely in experimenting with life. During these years he was variously a printer, school teacher, newspaper editor, carpenter, wanderer, and perhaps most significant of all — loafer. " I loaf, and in-vite my soul," he says in one of his poems. It was not mere idleness, but that constructive, glorified loafing of which poets are made. A leisurely journey by train, stage, and river steamship took him to New Orleans and back by way of Niagara. He voluntarily gave up the oppor-tunity to make a good income at his father's trade of house-building. He printed the first edition of his own book of poems, *Leaves of Grass,* which nobody would buy. In the eyes of a practical man of the world he would have appeared to be a complete failure.

The second period of his life centered around the Civil War. When his younger brother was wounded, he went to Washington as a volunteer nurse, and ministered with the greatest affection and tenderness to hun-dreds of soldiers in the army hospital until he became infected with blood poison from dressing a wound. A long illness followed, but his splendid physique brought him back to health, and in 1865 he is thus described by one of his friends: " A man of striking masculine beauty — a poet — powerful and venerable in appearance; large, calm, superbly formed; oftenest clad in the careless, rough, and always picturesque costume of the common people; resembling and generally taken by strangers for some great mechanic or stevedore, or seaman, or grand laborer of one kind or another." It was at this time that he lost his first government position, as previously stated, but his friends arranged that another one should be quietly substituted.

The third period of his life was spent rather sedately, first at Washington until a paralytic stroke forced him to retire, and then at Camden, New Jersey, just across the river from Philadelphia, where the small but sufficient income from his books enabled him to buy a modest home. Here one can picture " The Good Gray Poet " as represented in Alexander's famous painting, touched with a spiritual grandeur in his sunset days. He designed his own mausoleum at Camden. Fittingly enough, it is a massive, rough-hewn gray stone grotto, half hidden in the thick ferns and shrubs of the hillside.

You cannot read Whitman with indifference. You will be either powerfully drawn or violently repelled by his utterances. Some of you will not even grant him the title of poet; some will find an impelling rhythm in his uneven lines. You will have your ideas of poetry challenged; you will be moved to argument; but you cannot go to sleep over Whitman. It is well to know before reading him just what his poetic principles are. He intentionally throws out " the entire stock in trade of rhyme-talking heroes and heroines and all the love-sick plots of customary poetry, and constructs his verse in a loose and free meter of his own." The rhythm is not like the regular beat of waves on the shore, but rather like the impetuous gusts of wind in March. As a later poet, Edgar Lee Masters, said, " Whitman roared in the pines." Ears accustomed to wave-beat rhythm need time to re-attune themselves. When *Leaves of Grass* first appeared, it was read only to be reviled. Not only the lack of tunefulness, but the supposedly unpoetic subject matter caused Whittier to throw the book in the fire. All the other poets seemed to feel similar disgust save Emerson, who, recognizing a true exemplar of his " Self-Reliance," wrote: " I find it the most extraordinary piece of wit and wisdom that America has yet contributed. . . . I give you joy of your free and brave thought. I have great joy in it. . . . I find the courage of treatment which so delights us, and which large perception only can inspire. I greet you at the beginning of a great career." It took many years for the " great career " to be recognized, but Whitman is now securely placed among such original and distinctly *American* personalities as Emerson, Mark Twain, and Lincoln.

ONE'S–SELF I SING

This poem Whitman placed first in his final revised edition of *Leaves of Grass*. In his thoroughly characteristic style he states the theme for practically all his poetry — man, of which he is merely one. The poem should not be confused with his much longer " Song of Myself."

> One's-self I sing, a simple separate person,
> Yet utter the word Democratic, the word En-Masse.

2. **En-Masse:** French for "in mass" or "as one body." Whitman was fond of thrusting an occasional French or Spanish word into a poem.

Of physiology from top to toe I sing,
Not physiognomy alone nor brain alone is worthy for the Muse,
  I say the Form complete is worthier far,
The Female equally with the Male I sing.

Of Life immense in passion, pulse, and power,
Cheerful, for freest action formed under the laws divine,
The Modern Man I sing.

SUGGESTIONS FOR STUDY

  1. Be sure to know the difference between *physiology* and *physiognomy*.
  2. What points of his theory of life and of poetry does the poem illustrate?

I HEAR AMERICA SINGING

Whitman's exaltation of " self " suggested in the preceding poem by no means indicates a self removed from the rest of mankind, but rather the self standing fearlessly and enthusiastically in the midst of mankind. This poem carries out the " En-Masse " idea of the preceding one. It is often cited as one of the best poems to voice in condensed form the spirit of America.

I hear America singing, the varied carols I hear,
Those of mechanics, each one singing his as it should be blithe and
    strong,
The carpenter singing his as he measures his plank or beam,
The mason singing his as he makes ready for work, or leaves off work,
The boatman singing what belongs to him in his boat, the deck-hand
    singing on the steamboat deck,
The shoemaker singing as he sits on his bench, the hatter singing as
    he stands,
The wood-cutter's song, the plowboy's on his way in the morning,
    or at noon intermission or at sundown,
The delicious singing of the mother, or of the young wife at work,
    or of the girl sewing or washing,
Each singing what belongs to him or her and to none else,
The day what belongs to the day — at night the party of young
    fellows, robust, friendly,
Singing with open mouths their strong melodious songs.

MANNAHATTA

Whitman loved the old Indian names. His native Long Island he preferred to call Paumanok, and his exuberant affection for his city, New
York, needed Mannahatta to express it. The name is of course perpetuated
in Manhattan Island, which forms the core of the city today.

I was asking for something specific and perfect for my city,
Whereupon lo! upsprang the aboriginal name.
Now I see what there is in a name, a word, liquid, sane, unruly,
      musical, self-sufficient,
I see that the word of my city is that word from of old,
Because I see that word nested in nests of water-bays, superb,   5
Rich, hemmed thick all around with sailships and steamships, an
      island sixteen miles long, solid-founded,
Numberless crowded streets, high growths of iron, slender, strong,
      light, splendidly uprising toward clear skies,
Tides swift and ample, well-loved by me, toward sundown,
The flowing sea-currents, the little islands, larger adjoining islands,
      the heights, the villas,
The countless masts, the white shore-steamers, the lighters, the
      ferry-boats, the black sea-steamers well modeled,   10
The down-town streets, the jobbers' houses of business, the houses
      of business of the ship-merchants and money-brokers, the river-
      streets,
Immigrants arriving, fifteen or twenty thousand in a week,
The carts hauling goods, the manly race of drivers of horses, the
      brown-faced sailors,
The summer air, the bright sun shining, and the sailing clouds aloft,
The winter snows, the sleigh-bells, the broken ice in the river,
      passing along up or down with the flood-tide or ebb-tide.   15
The mechanics of the city, the masters, well-formed, beautiful-faced,
      looking you straight in the eyes,
Trottoirs thronged, vehicles, Broadway, the women, the shops and
      shows,
A million people — manners free and superb — open voices — hos-
      pitality — the most courageous and friendly young men,
City of hurried and sparkling waters! city of spires and masts!
City nested in bays! my city!
                                                              20

17. **trottoirs:** French for *sidewalks*.

BEAT! BEAT! DRUMS!

The terrific upheaval which war brings into civilian life has never been more vividly pictured than in this poem. Here the irregularity of the meter serves to emphasize the general chaos, with the throb of the drums running throughout.

Beat! beat! drums! — blow! bugles! blow!
Through the windows — through doors — burst like a ruthless force,
Into the solemn church, and scatter the congregation,
Into the school where the scholar is studying;
Leave not the bridegroom quiet — no happiness must he have now
    with his bride,   5
Nor the peaceful farmer any peace, plowing his field or gathering
    his grain,
So fierce you whirr and pound you drums — so shrill you bugles blow.

Beat! beat! drums! — blow! bugles! blow!
Over the traffic of cities — over the rumble of wheels in the streets;
Are beds prepared for sleepers at night in the houses? no sleepers
    must sleep in those beds,   10
No bargainers' bargains by day — no brokers or speculators — would
    they continue?
Would the talkers be talking? would the singer attempt to sing?
Would the lawyer rise in the court to state his case before the judge?
Then rattle quicker, heavier drums — you bugles wilder blow.

Beat! beat! drums! — blow! bugles! blow!   15
Make no parley — stop for no expostulation,
Mind not the timid — mind not the weeper or prayer,
Mind not the old man beseeching the young man,
Let not the child's voice be heard, nor the mother's entreaties,
Make even the trestles to shake the dead where they lie awaiting
    the hearses,   20
So strong you thump O terrible drums — so loud you bugles blow.

THE CAROL OF DEATH

FROM " WHEN LILACS LAST IN THE DOORYARD BLOOMED "

It is natural that a man of Whitman's elemental vigor should have been greatly attracted by the personality of Abraham Lincoln. Of all the poets who have paid tribute to him none has sounded so feelingly the note of personal grief at his death as Whitman. When the news of the assassination came to the poet, he was at home with his mother. He tells us, " Not a mouthful was eaten all day by either of us. We each drank half a cup of coffee; that was all. Little was said. We got every newspaper, morning and evening, and the frequent extras of that period and passed them silently to each other." You have doubtless known for many years that poem of Whitman's so universally loved, " O Captain, My Captain! " A full and complete expression of his grief was given in the long poem, " When Lilacs Last in the Dooryard Bloomed." In this he pictures himself as finding consolation in the carol of a " gray-brown bird " among " the ghostly pines." " And the voice of my spirit tallied the song of the bird."

Come lovely and soothing death,
Undulate round the world, serenely arriving, arriving,
In the day, in the night, to all, to each,
Sooner or later delicate death.

Praised be the fathomless universe,
For life and joy, and for objects and knowledge curious,
And for love, sweet love — but praise! praise! praise!
For the sure-enwinding arms of cool-enfolding death.

Dark mother always gliding near with soft feet,
Have none chanted for thee a chant of fullest welcome?
Then I chant it for thee, I glorify thee above all,
I bring thee a song that when thou must indeed come, come
    unfalteringly.

Approach strong deliveress,
When it is so, when thou hast taken them, I joyously sing the dead,
Lost in the loving floating ocean of thee,
Laved in the flood of thy bliss O death.

From me to thee glad serenades,
Dances for thee I propose saluting thee, adornments and feastings
    for thee,
And the sights of the open landscape and the high-spread sky are
    fitting,
And life and the fields, and the huge and thoughtful night.

The night in silence under many a star,
The ocean shore and the husky whispering wave whose voice I know,
And the soul turning to thee O vast and well-veiled death,
And the body gratefully nestling close to thee.

Over the tree-tops I float thee a song,
Over the rising and sinking waves, over the myriad fields and the
    prairies wide,
Over the dense-packed cities all and the teeming wharves and ways,
I float this carol with joy, with joy to thee O death.

A NOISELESS PATIENT SPIDER

This poem represents the deeper spiritual quality of Whitman's later
poetry. It suggests the longings, the gropings of the soul for something
beyond itself. As you read the poem, keep in mind that this is the poet of
" One's-self I Sing," where he is seeking solidarity with mankind.

A noiseless patient spider,
I marked where on a little promontory it stood isolated,
Marked how to explore the vacant vast surrounding,
It launched forth filament, filament, filament, out of itself,
Ever unreeling them, ever tirelessly speeding them.

And you O my soul where you stand,
Surrounded, detached, in measureless oceans of space,
Ceaselessly musing, venturing, throwing, seeking the spheres to
    connect them,
Till the bridge you will need be formed, till the ductile anchor hold,
Till the gossamer thread you fling catch somewhere, O my soul.

GIVE ME THE SPLENDID SILENT SUN

Here we have the conflict in the poet's mind between his longing for the peace of nature and his love of pulsing life in the city even though it be during the horrors of war time. Which conquers? The repetitions and exclamations throughout are highly typical of Whitman's mode of expression.

I

Give me the splendid silent sun with all his beams full-dazzling,
Give me juicy autumnal fruit ripe and red from the orchard,
Give me a field where the unmowed grass grows,
Give me an arbor, give me the trellised grape,
Give me fresh corn and wheat, give me serene-moving animals
    teaching content,   5
Give me nights perfectly quiet as on high plateaus west of the
    Mississippi, and I looking up at the stars,
Give me odorous at sunrise a garden of beautiful flowers where I can
    walk undisturbed,
Give me for marriage a sweet-breathed woman of whom I should
    never tire,
Give me a perfect child, give me away aside from the noise of the
    world a rural domestic life,
Give me to warble spontaneous songs recluse by myself, for my own
    ears only,   10
Give me solitude, give me Nature, give me again O Nature your
    primal sanities!

These demanding to have them (tired with ceaseless excitement, and
    racked by the war-strife),
These to procure incessantly asking, rising in cries from my
    heart,
While yet incessantly asking still I adhere to my city,
Day upon day and year upon year O city, walking your streets,   15
Where you hold me enchained a certain time refusing to give me up,
Yet giving to make me glutted, enriched of soul, you give me forever
    faces;
(O I see what I sought to escape, confronting, reversing my cries,
I see my own soul trampling down what it asked for).

2

Keep your splendid silent sun,   20
Keep your woods O Nature, and the quiet places by the woods,
Keep your fields of clover and timothy, and your corn-fields and
    orchards,
Keep the blossoming buckwheat fields where the Ninth-month bees
    hum;
Give me faces and streets — give me these phantoms incessant and
    endless along the trottoirs!
Give me interminable eyes — give me women — give me comrades
    and lovers by the thousand!   25
Let me see new ones every day — let me hold new ones by the hand
    every day!
Give me such shows — give me the streets of Manhattan!
Give me Broadway, with the soldiers marching — give me the sound
    of the trumpets and drums!
(The soldiers in companies or regiments — some starting away,
    flushed and reckless,
Some, their time up, returning with thinned ranks, young, yet very
    old, worn, marching, noticing nothing);   30
Give me the shores and wharves heavy-fringed with black ships!
O such for me!   O an intense life, full to repletion and varied!
The life of the theater, bar-room, huge hotel, for me!
The saloon of the steamer! the crowded excursion for me! the
    torchlight procession!
The dense brigade bound for the war, with high piled military
    wagons following;   35
People, endless, streaming, with strong voices, passions, pageants,
Manhattan streets with their powerful throbs, with beating drums
    as now,
The endless and noisy chorus, the rustle and clank of muskets (even
    the sight of the wounded),
Manhattan crowds, with their turbulent musical chorus!
Manhattan faces and eyes forever for me.   40

24. **trottoirs:** sidewalks.

WHEN I HEARD THE LEARNED ASTRONOMER

Whitman's intense feeling for nature is caught in this poem and " Miracles " which follows. The quiet solemnity of the first is in contrast with the exuberance of the second.

When I heard the learned astronomer,
When the proofs, the figures, were ranged in columns before me,
When I was shown the charts and diagrams, to add, divide, and
    measure them,
When I sitting heard the astronomer where he lectured with much
    applause in the lecture-room,
How soon unaccountable I became tired and sick,
Till rising and gliding out I wandered off by myself,
In the mystical moist night-air, and from time to time,
Looked up in perfect silence at the stars.

MIRACLES

Why, who makes much of a miracle?
As to me I know of nothing else but miracles,
Whether I walk the streets of Manhattan,
Or dart my sight over the roofs of houses toward the sky,
Or wade with naked feet along the beach just in the edge of the water, 5
Or stand under trees in the woods,
Or talk by day with anyone I love,
Or sit at table at dinner with the rest,
Or look at strangers opposite me riding in the car,
Or watch honey-bees busy around the hive of a summer forenoon, 10
Or animals feeding in the fields,
Or birds, or the wonderfulness of insects in the air,
Or the wonderfulness of the sundown, or of stars shining so quiet
    and bright,
Or the exquisite delicate curve of the new moon in spring;
These with the rest, one and all, are to me miracles,   15
The whole referring, yet each distinct and in its place.
To me every hour of the night and dark is a miracle,
Every cubic inch of space is a miracle,
Every square yard of the surface of the earth is spread with the same,
Every foot of the interior swarms with the same.   20

To me the sea is a continual miracle,
The fishes that swim — the rocks — the motion of the waves — the
    ships with men in them,
What stranger miracles are there?

DAREST THOU NOW O SOUL

Darest thou now O soul,
Walk out with me toward the unknown region,
Where neither ground is for the feet nor any path to follow?

No map there, nor guide,
Nor voice sounding, nor touch of human hand,
Nor face with blooming flesh, nor lips, nor eyes, are in that land.

I know it not O soul,
Nor dost thou, all is a blank before us,
All waits undreamed of in that region, that inaccessible land.

Till when the ties loosen,
All but the ties eternal, Time and Space,
Nor darkness, gravitation, sense, nor any bounds bounding us.

Then we burst forth, we float,
In Time and Space O soul, prepared for them,
Equal, equipt at last, (O joy! O fruit of all!) them to fulfil O soul.

FOR FURTHER READING

" Crossing Brooklyn Ferry "
" Poets to Come "
" I Saw in Louisiana a Live-Oak Growing "
" As at Thy Portals Also Death "
" For You, O Democracy "
" Pioneers, O Pioneers! "
" Eighteen Sixty-One "
" Cavalry Crossing a Ford "
" Come Up from the Fields, Father "
" A Sight in Camp in the Daybreak Gray and Dim "
" The Wound-Dresser "
" To a Certain Civilian "
" Hushed Be the Camps Today "
" When Lilacs Last in the Dooryard Bloomed "
" O Captain, My Captain! "
" Old Salt Kossabone "
" The Last Invocation "

Emily Dickinson (1830–1886)

A few years ago an American anthologist called Emily Dickinson's poetry " perhaps the finest by a woman in the English language." An English critic in commenting on this remark said, " I quarrel only with his ' perhaps '." The strange thing about Emily Dickinson is that during her lifetime no one outside of her small circle of friends had ever heard of her. None of her poems saw publication until after her death in 1886. Gradually as slender volumes of her verse began to come out, her name acquired reputation, culminating with the publication of her complete poems and her *Life and Letters* in 1924. Today she is recognized as a distinct genius. Recent interest has been stirred by the discovery of one hundred and fifty poems which appeared during 1929 under the title of *Further Poems of Emily Dickinson.*

It has been said that her whole life could be told in three lines:

> Born in Amherst
> Lived in Amherst
> Died in Amherst

It is true that outwardly her life was restricted by this little Massachusetts town, but the adventures of her mind and spirit knew no narrow bounds. To read the life written by her niece, Martha Dickinson Bianchi, is to realize how richly imaginative a life may be that bears no mark of outward adventure. Though her poems are all very short and rather similar in verse form, they have remarkable power to startle the mind and challenge the imagination. Once catch the fascination of them and you must read on to find out what original thing she will say next. In view of her retired life, an appropriate poem for an introduction is: " I'm Nobody."

I'M NOBODY

> I'm nobody! Who are you?
>   Are you nobody too?
> Then there's a pair of us — don't tell!
>   They'd banish us, you know.

> How dreary to be somebody!
>   How public like a frog
> To tell your name the livelong day
>   To an admiring bog!

A WORD

A word is dead
When it is said
Some say.
I say it just
Begins to live
That day.

TO MAKE A PRAIRIE

To make a prairie it takes a clover
And one bee —
One clover, and a bee,
And revery.
The revery alone will do
If bees are few.

THE LITTLE STONE

How happy is the little stone
That rambles in the road alone,
And doesn't care about careers,
And exigencies never fears;
Whose coat of elemental brown
A passing universe put on;
And independent as the sun
Associates or glows alone,
Fulfilling absolute decree
In casual simplicity.

AN ALTERED LOOK ABOUT THE HILLS

An altered look about the hills;
A Tyrian light the village fills;
A wider sunrise in the dawn;
A deeper twilight on the lawn;

2. **Tyrian:** Ancient Tyre was famous for its manufacture of purple dye.

A print of a vermilion foot;   5
A purple finger on the slope;
A flippant fly upon the pane;
A spider at his trade again;
An added strut in chanticleer;
A flower expected everywhere;   10
An ax shrill singing in the woods;
Fern-odors on untraveled roads —
All this and more I cannot tell —
A furtive look you know as well,
And Nicodemus' mystery   15
Receives its annual reply.

15. **Nicodemus' mystery:** John iii: 1–12, Nicodemus' question was "How can a man be born again?" What is "the annual reply"?

SOME KEEP THE SABBATH

Some keep the Sabbath going to church:
   I keep it staying at home,
With a bobolink for a chorister,
   And an orchard for a dome.

Some keep the Sabbath in surplice,
   I just wear my wings,
And instead of tolling the bell for church,
   Our little sexton sings.

God preaches — a noted clergyman —
   And the sermon is never long;
So instead of getting to heaven at last,
   I'm going all along!

I NEVER SAW A MOOR

I never saw a moor,
   I never saw the sea;
Yet know I how the heather looks,
   And what a wave must be.

I never spoke with God,
  Nor visited in heaven;
Yet certain am I of the spot
  As if the chart were given.

THE SOUL SELECTS HER OWN SOCIETY

An experience of Emily Dickinson's girlhood colored her whole life and was largely responsible for her almost ascetic seclusion in her own home. While on a visit to Philadelphia she had fallen in love with a young man and he with her. The tragedy was that he was already married. Emily's decision was that they must never see each other again, and he took his wife and child across the continent. Except to her devoted sister-in-law she never referred directly to this painful experience, but many of her poems show the emotional scar which she covered up so unostentatiously with her charm and wit.

The soul selects her own society,
  Then shuts the door;
On her divine majority
  Obtrude no more.

Unmoved, she notes the chariot's pausing
  At her low gate;
Unmoved, an emperor is kneeling
  Upon her mat.

I've known her from an ample nation
  Choose one;
Then close the valves of her attention
  Like stone.

MY LIFE CLOSED TWICE

My life closed twice before its close;
  It yet remains to see
If immortality unveil
  A third event to me,

So huge, so hopeless to conceive,
    As these that twice befell.
Parting is all we know of heaven,
    And all we need of hell.

WE NEVER KNOW HOW HIGH

We never know how high we are
    Till we are called to rise;
And then, if we are true to plan,
    Our statures touch the skies.

The heroism we recite
    Would be a daily thing,
Did not ourselves the cubits warp
    For fear to be a king.

FOR FURTHER READING

Since Emily Dickinson's poems have no titles except their first lines,
the best way to do further reading of her work is simply to get a volume
of her poems and go on an exploring expedition.

THOMAS BAILEY ALDRICH (1836–1907)

Thomas Bailey Aldrich was born in New England, lived for some years
in the South, settled down in New York long enough to become intimate
with the literary lights of the time, and then returned to Boston in 1865.
He became definitely associated with the Boston group, including the foremost poets and prose writers of our earlier literature, and, like Lowell,
edited *The Atlantic Monthly* for some years. Aldrich's poems are characterized by exquisite finish rather than by depth of thought, and that is
one of the reasons why his fame as a poet never reached the heights of
his contemporaries. The two examples are fairly representative of his
poetic qualities. Today Aldrich is best known for his prose work, especially
his short stories.

MEMORY

My mind lets go a thousand things,
Like dates of wars and deaths of kings,
And yet recalls the very hour —
'Twas noon by yonder village tower,

And on the last blue noon in May —
The wind came briskly up this way,
Crisping the brook beside the road;
Then, pausing here, set down its load
Of pine-scents, and shook listlessly
Two petals from that wild-rose tree.

SUGGESTION FOR STUDY

Note how trivial was the thing which impressed itself on his memory compared with the things he forgot. Does your memory ever act so? Can you account for this in any way?

A SNOWFLAKE

Once he sang of summer,
Nothing but the summer;
Now he sings of winter,
Of winter bleak and drear;
Just because there's fallen
A snowflake on his forehead
He must go and fancy
'Tis winter all the year!

SUGGESTION FOR STUDY

Here an idea about life is conveyed through a figure. What do you think the snowflake represents? Is this man's attitude to be admired, pitied, or condemned?

FOR FURTHER READING

" Identity "
" When the Sultan Goes to Is-
pahan "

" Nocturne "
" Sonnets "

For fiction by Aldrich, see page 97.

EDWARD ROWLAND SILL (1841–1887)

Edward Rowland Sill, a Connecticut youth and Yale graduate, went West on account of his health and taught in the University of California. The combination of Eastern respect for tradition and Western scorn of it caused in him a mental conflict which led to uncertainty and loneliness expressed in many of his poems. Though the body of his writing is small, "The Fool's Prayer" and "Opportunity" have found a secure place in our literature.

THE FOOL'S PRAYER

The royal feast was done; the King
   Sought some new sport to banish care,
And to his jester cried: " Sir Fool,
   Kneel now, and make for us a prayer! "

The jester doffed his cap and bells,   5
   And stood the mocking court before;
They could not see the bitter smile
   Behind the painted grin he wore.

He bowed his head, and bent his knee
   Upon the Monarch's silken stool;   10
His pleading voice arose: " O Lord,
   Be merciful to me, a fool!

" No pity, Lord, could change the heart
   From red with wrong to white as wool;
The rod must heal the sin: but Lord,   15
   Be merciful to me, a fool!

" 'Tis not by guilt the onward sweep
   Of truth and right, O Lord, we stay;
'Tis by our follies that so long
   We hold the earth from heaven away.   20

" These clumsy feet, still in the mire,
   Go crushing blossoms without end;
These hard, well-meaning hands we thrust
   Among the heart-strings of a friend.

" The ill-timed truth we might have kept —   25
   Who knows how sharp it pierced and stung?
The word we had not sense to say —
   Who knows how grandly it had rung!

" Our faults no tenderness should ask,
   The chastening stripes must cleanse them all;   30
But for our blunders — oh, in shame
   Before the eyes of heaven we fall.

" Earth bears no balsam for mistakes;
   Men crown the knave, and scourge the tool
That did his will; but Thou, O Lord,   35
   Be merciful to me, a fool! "

The room was hushed; in silence rose
   The King, and sought his gardens cool,
And walked apart, and murmured low,
   " Be merciful to me, a fool! "   40

SUGGESTIONS FOR STUDY

1. What is the double meaning of " fool " in this poem?
2. What other contrasts in this poem make it especially touching?
3. In what way had the king been a fool?
4. Are most of us fools in this sense?

FOR FURTHER READING

" Opportunity "   " Life "
" Solitude "   " Dare You? "

JOAQUIN MILLER (1841–1913)

His real name was Cincinnatus Hiner Miller, and he said that he was born on the boundary line between Ohio and Indiana as his parents were trekking westward in a covered wagon. Whether that is strictly true or not does not matter much now; more important is the fact that he became the poet of the great movement west. Miller wrote a great amount of verse, most of it hardly worth noting, but he did write a few poems of decidedly solid merit. His ode, " Columbus," is known to every student, and the one printed here is characteristic of what he tried to do in honor of the pioneers to which his family belonged.

WESTWARD HO!

What strength! what strife! what rude unrest!
What shocks! what half-shaped armies met!
A mighty nation moving west,
With all its steely sinews set
Against the living forests.   Hear
The shouts, the shots of pioneer,
The rended forests, rolling wheels,
As if some half-checked army reels,
Recoils, redoubles, comes again,
Loud sounding like a hurricane.

O bearded, stalwart, westmost men,
So tower-like, so Gothic built!
A kingdom won without the guilt
Of studied battle, that hath been
Your blood's inheritance. . . .   Your heirs
Know not your tombs: the great plowshares
Cleave softly through the mellow loam
Where you have made eternal home,
And set no sign.   Your epitaphs
Are writ in furrows.   Beauty laughs
While through the green ways wandering
Beside her love slow gathering
White, starry-hearted May-time blooms
Above your lowly leveled tombs;
And then below the spotted sky
She stops, she leans, she wonders why
The ground is heaved and broken so,
And why the grasses darker grow
And droop and trail like wounded wing.

Yea, Time, the grand old harvester,
Has gathered you from wood and plain.
We call to you again, again;
The rush and rumble of the car
Comes back in answer.   Deep and wide
The wheels of progress have passed on;
The silent pioneer is gone.

His ghost is moving down the trees,
And now we push the memories
Of bluff bold men who dared and died
In foremost battle, quite aside.

JAMES WHITCOMB RILEY (1849–1916)

James Whitcomb Riley was undoubtedly the most popular American poet of the end of the nineteenth century. His verse suggests a combination of Longfellow and Lowell, for like the former, he was the poet of the children and of simple sentiment, while like the latter, he immortalized the rural dialect of his state. Riley, " the Hoosier poet," was born in Greenfield, Indiana, and always made his home in or near Indianapolis. He was not a farm boy, but the son of a prosperous lawyer who wished his son to follow in his footsteps. Like many of his literary predecessors, the young man found the attempted study distasteful, and ran away with a troupe of strolling actors. His services to the troupe were varied by coaching, poster-painting, and drum-beating, as well as acting. Then followed a newspaper career, and in his later life lecture tours and public readings from his poems. It is hard to associate the cheerful Riley with Poe, yet curiously enough, his youthful joke of publishing a poem " Leonainie " over the initials E. A. P. was accepted seriously by some persons as a genuine discovery.

At the age of thirty-three he began a series of dialect poems in the Indianapolis *Journal* signed by " Benj. F. Johnson, of Boone, the Hoosier poet." Unlike other famous pseudonyms, it did not stick to the poet, except for the last part, which seems to have become an invariable appositive to Riley's own name. The child dialect, pronounced rhythms, and homely vividness of such poems as " The Raggedy Man " and " Little Orphant Annie " make them popular with children, who today celebrate his birthday in schools throughout the country.

WHEN THE FROST IS ON THE PUNKIN [1]

When the frost is on the punkin and the fodder's in the shock,
And you hear the kyouck and gobble of the struttin' turkey-cock,
And the clackin' of the guineys, and the cluckin' of the hens,
And the rooster's hallylooer as he tiptoes on the fence;

[1] From *Neighborly Poems*, copyright 1897, 1925. Used by special permission of the publishers, The Bobbs-Merrill Company.

O, it's then the time a feller is a-feelin' at his best,   5
With the risin' sun to greet him from a night of peaceful rest,
As he leaves the house, bareheaded, and goes out to feed the stock,
When the frost is on the punkin and the fodder's in the shock.

They's something kindo' harty-like about the atmusfere
When the heat of summer's over and the coolin' fall is here —   10
Of course we miss the flowers, and the blossoms on the trees,
And the mumble of the hummin'-birds and buzzin' of the bees;
But the air's so appetizin'; and the landscape through the haze
Of a crisp and sunny morning of the airly autumn days
Is a pictur' that no painter has the colorin' to mock —   15
When the frost is on the punkin and the fodder's in the shock.

The husky, rusty russel of the tossels of the corn,
And the raspin' of the tangled leaves as golden as the morn;
The stubble in the furries — kindo' lonesome-like, but still
A-preachin' sermuns to us of the barns they growed to fill;   20
The strawstack in the medder, and the reaper in the shed;
The hosses in theyr stalls below — the clover overhead! —
O, it sets my hart a-clickin' like the tickin' of a clock,
When the frost is on the punkin and the fodder's in the shock.

Then your apples all is gethered, and the ones a feller keeps   25
Is poured around the cellar-floor in red and yaller heaps;
And your cider-makin's over, and your wimmern-folks is through
With theyr mince and apple-butter, and theyr souse and sausage too!
I don't know how to tell it — but ef such a thing could be
As the angels wantin' boardin', and they'd call around on *me* — 30
I'd want to 'commodate 'em — all the whole-indurin' flock —
When the frost is on the punkin and the fodder's in the shock.

FOR FURTHER READING

" Little Orphant Annie "   " Knee-Deep in June "
" The Raggedy Man "   " My Ruthers "
" The Old Swimmin' Hole "   " Wet-Weather Talk "
" Out to Old Aunt Mary's "   " A Life Lesson "
" The Old Man and Jim "   " An Old Sweetheart of Mine "
" When the Green Gits Back in the
      Trees "

EUGENE FIELD (1850–1895)

Though Field and Riley are often bracketed together because they were contemporary newspaper men and poets of childhood, their work shows numerous differences. Riley's dialect poems give us midwestern domestic life, and are always decidedly local in flavor; Field shows the influence of foreign literature in his translations, imitations of Horace, and his series of lullabies of all nations. Field was wittier than Riley and more original. He was one of the first newspaper columnists, and most of his poems were written primarily to fill his daily space. His newspaper connections were in St. Louis, the city of his birth, Chicago, and Denver. The following poems of childhood illustrate Field's characteristic pathos and humor.

LITTLE BOY BLUE

The little toy dog is covered with dust,
　　But sturdy and staunch he stands;
The little toy soldier is red with rust,
　　And his musket molds in his hands.
Time was when the little toy dog was new,
　　And the soldier was passing fair;
And that was the time when our Little Boy Blue
　　Kissed them and put them there.

" Now don't you go till I come," he said,
  " And don't you make any noise! "
So, toddling off to his trundle bed,
  He dreamt of the pretty toys;
And, as he was dreaming, an angel song
  Awakened our Little Boy Blue —
Oh! the years are many, the years are long,
  But the little toy friends are true!

Ay, faithful to Little Boy Blue they stand,
  Each in the same old place,
Awaiting the touch of a little hand,
  The smile of a little face;
And they wonder, as waiting the long years **through**
  In the dust of that little chair,
What has become of our Little Boy Blue,
  Since he kissed them and put them there.

THE LIMITATIONS OF YOUTH

I'd like to be a cowboy an' ride a firey hoss
  Way out into the big and boundless West;
I'd kill the bears an' catamounts an' wolves I come across,
  An' I'd pluck the bal' head eagle from his nest!
    With my pistols at my side,
    I would roam the prarers wide,
An' to scalp the savage Injun in his wigwam would I ride —
    If I darst; but I darsen't!

I'd like to go to Afriky an' hunt the lions there,
  An' the biggest ollyfunts you ever saw!
I would track the fierce gorilla to his equatorial lair,
  An' beard the cannybull that eats folks raw!
    I'd chase the pizen snakes
    An' the 'pottimus that makes
His nest down at the bottom of unfathomable lakes —
    If I darst; but I darsen't!

I would I were a pirut to sail the ocean blue,
  With a big black flag aflyin' overhead;
I would scour the billowy main with my gallant pirut crew
  An' dye the sea a gouty, gory red!

With my cutlass in my hand
On the quarterdeck I'd stand
And to deeds of heroism I'd incite my pirut band —
    If I darst; but I darsen't!

And, if I darst, I'd lick my pa for the times that he's licked me!
    I'd lick my brother an' my teacher, too!
I'd lick the fellers that call round on sister after tea,
    An' I'd keep on lickin' folks till I got through!
        You bet! I'd run away
        From my lessons to my play,
An' I'd shoo the hens, an' tease the cat, an' kiss the girls all day —
    If I darst; but I darsen't!

FOR FURTHER READING

POEMS OF CHILDHOOD

" Jest 'fore Christmas "
" Seein' Things "
" The Duel "
" The Lyttel Boy "
" Wynken, Blynken, and Nod "
" Our Biggest Fish "
" Krinken "
" The Little Peach "

WESTERN VERSE

" Casey's Table d'Hôte "
" Our Lady of the Mine "
" The Conversazzhyony "
" Prof. Vere de Blaw "
" Our Two Opinions "

BLISS CARMAN (1861–1929)

(William) Bliss Carman was an American in the most inclusive sense of the word, for he was born in Canada and retained his Canadian citizenship, but lived in the United States for more than forty years. His point of view was distinctly cosmopolitan, partly owing to his education in three countries — Canada, Great Britain, and the United States. From his first volume, *Low Tide on Grand Pré* (1893), to *Wild Garden* (1929) Carman's poetry struck an outdoor note, the natural scenery of the wild Northland of lakes and forests. This consistency of theme is fully demonstrated in the two poems that follow, the first written in youth and the other in old age.

Carman published many volumes, and the ones which established his reputation were three successive *Songs from Vagabondia*, written in collaboration with his friend Richard Hovey in the nineties. Both were strongly influenced by the revolt of youth against conventionalities of all kinds then manifest in all countries, especially in France, and both were enthusiastic followers of Whitman, except that they did not adopt his ideas about verse forms. The title of the poem, "Green Fire," is an Indian expression for the first young verdure in spring which seems to spread as quickly as fire over the earth.

THE JOYS OF THE ROAD

Now the joys of the road are chiefly these:
A crimson touch on the hard-wood trees;

A vagrant's morning wide and blue,
In early fall, when the wind walks, too;

A shadowy highway cool and brown,　　　　　　5
Alluring up and enticing down

From rippled water to dappled swamp,
From purple glory to scarlet pomp;

The outward eye, the quiet will,
And the striding heart from hill to hill;　　　10

The tempter apple over the fence;
The cobweb bloom on the yellow quince;

The palish asters along the wood —
A lyric touch of the solitude;

An open hand, an easy shoe,　　　　　　　　15
And a hope to make the day go through —

Another to sleep with, and a third
To wake me up at the voice of a bird;

The resonant far-listening morn,
And the hoarse whisper of the corn;　　　　20

The crickets mourning their comrades lost,
In the night's retreat from the gathering frost;

(Or is it their slogan, plaintive and shrill,
As they beat on their corselets, valiant still?)

A hunger fit for the kings of the sea,   25
And a loaf of bread for Dickon and me;

A thirst like that of the Thirsty Sword,
And a jug of cider on the board;

An idle noon, a bubbling spring,
The sea in the pine-tops murmuring;   30

A scrap of gossip at the ferry;
A comrade neither glum nor merry,

Asking nothing, revealing naught,
But minting his words from a fund of thought,

A keeper of silence eloquent,   35
Needy, yet royally well content,

Of the mettled breed, yet abhorring strife,
And full of the mellow juice of life,

A taster of wine, with an eye for a maid,
Never too bold, and never afraid,   40

Never heart-whole, never heart-sick
(These are the things I worship in Dick):

No fidget and no reformer, just
A calm observer of ought and must,

A lover of books, but a reader of man,   45
No cynic and no charlatan,

Who never defers and never demands,
But, smiling, takes the world in his hands —

Seeing it good as when God first saw
And gave it the weight of his will for law.   50

And O the joy that is never won,
But follows and follows the journeying sun,

By marsh and tide, by meadow and stream,
A will-o'-the-wind, a light-o'-dream,

Delusion afar, delight anear,   55
From morrow to morrow, from year to year,

A jack-o'-lantern, a fairy fire,
A dare, a bliss, and a desire!

The racy smell of the forest loam,
When the stealthy, sad-heart leaves go home;   60

(O leaves, O leaves, I am one with you,
Of the mold and the sun and the wind and the dew!)

The broad gold wake of the afternoon;
The silent fleck of the cold new moon;

The sound of the hollow sea's release   65
From stormy tumult to starry peace;

With only another league to wend;
And two brown arms at the journey's end!

These are the joys of the open road —
For him who travels without a load.   70

SUGGESTIONS FOR STUDY

1. After reading the poem, try to recall as many as possible of the "joys" of the road.

2. What is meant by "the joy that is never won," line 51?

3. Who was the "Dickon" (line 26) and "Dick" (line 42)? See Introduction.

GREEN FIRE

You will never know the glory of the coming of the spring
Till you look upon its magic in the North,
When the wilderness is waking in a mist of Magian green
To the everlasting wonder of new birth.

Here in a starry silence when the Manitou sent forth   5
His summons to the Keepers of the Word,
The pine-tops caught his whisper, and from the swampy lands
The shrilling frogs made answer as they heard.

Now the birches break in yellow against the morning blue,
The aspens are a wash of palest gold,   10
The tamaracks in young green are soft as drifted smoke
In the freshness of enchantment never told.

The open lakes are sparkling, the rivers running white
With rapids calling all along the trail,
And Wise-heart and Fond-heart, they know 'tis time to go   15
Where lonely valleys answer to their hail.

Old heart, dear heart, hold the glory dream!
There's a cabin in a clearing round the bend,
With pointed firs about it, a river at the door,
And hermit thrushes singing at day's end.   20

For the Master of the Open, the Spirit of the Wild,
Our guide in wisdom, beauty, and desire,
Is making the old medicine whose conjure name is Love,
And all the hills are smoky with Green Fire.

SUGGESTIONS FOR STUDY

1. Are Wise-heart and Fond-heart names of Indians, or do they stand for something else?

3. **Magian:** pertaining to the Magi, priests of Ancient Media and Persia. This does not refer to the Magi who brought gifts to the infant Christ, but rather to the supposition that Magi or wise men were sorcerers. The word here has the force of "miraculous." 5. **Manitou:** among the Algonquin Indians, one of the powers controlling natural phenomena. 6. **Keepers of the Word:** the Manitou's servants or messengers who carry out his commands. 23. **Medicine:** in the Indian sense of control over natural forces by magic.

2. Compare this with Carman's well known "A Vagabond Song" for the effect of color and the figurative use of smoke.

FOR FURTHER READING

"An April Morning" "Roadside Flowers"
"Autumn" "My Teachers"
"The Winter Scene" "The Juggler"
"Daisies" "Lord of the Far Horizons"

RICHARD HOVEY (1864–1900)

After reading "The Sea Gypsy" and "The Wander Lovers" by Richard Hovey in connection with the preceding poems by his friend Bliss Carman it becomes easy to understand why in their three joint volumes of *Songs from Vagabondia* it was often difficult to determine which of the two had written a particular poem. Of the two, Hovey gave promise of being the greater poet. Besides a number of volumes of poems chiefly lyrical he also wrote five plays on Arthurian subjects, a most ambitious attempt to deal with the story of King Arthur.

Richard Hovey was born in Normal, Illinois. In 1885 he graduated from Dartmouth, and then determined to be a preacher. Before he finished his course at Union Theological Seminary in New York he gave that idea up and entered journalism. This led to his writing plays, giving lectures, acting, and writing poetry. After spending some time in France in close association with the poet and dramatist Maeterlinck, some of whose work he translated, Hovey returned to this country and, just as he was settling down to a professorship in English at Barnard College, he died, like so many brilliant poets, at the early age of thirty-six.

THE SEA GYPSY

I am fevered with the sunset,
I am fretful with the bay,
For the wander-thirst is on me
And my soul is in Cathay.

There's a schooner in the offing,
With her topsails shot with fire,
And my heart has gone aboard her
For the Islands of Desire.

I must forth again tomorrow!
With the sunset I must be
Hull down on the trail of rapture
In the wonder of the sea.

THE WANDER LOVERS

Down the world with Marna!
That's the life for me!
Wandering with the wandering wind,
Vagabond and unconfined!
Roving with the roving rain   5
Its unboundaried domain!
Kith and kin of wander-kind,
Children of the sea!

Petrels of the sea-drift!
Swallows of the lea!   10
Arabs of the whole wide girth
Of the wind-encircled earth!
In all climes we pitch our tents,
Cronies of the elements,
With the secret lords of birth   15
Intimate and free.

All the seaboard knows us
From Fundy to the Keys;
Every bend and every creek
Of abundant Chesapeake;   20
Ardise hills and Newport coves
And the far-off orange groves,
Where Floridian oceans break,
Tropic tiger seas.

Down the world with Marna,   25
Tarrying there and here!
Just as much at home in Spain
As in Tangier or Touraine!
Shakespeare's Avon knows us well,
And the crags of Neufchâtel;   30
And the ancient Nile is fain
Of our coming near.

Down the world with Marna,
Daughter of the air!
Marna of the subtle grace,   35
And the vision in her face!
Moving in the measures trod
By the angels before God!
With her sky-blue eyes amaze
And her sea-blue hair!   40

Marna with the trees' life
In her veins a-stir!
Marna of the aspen heart
Where the sudden quivers start!
Quick-responsive, subtle, wild!   45
Artless as an artless child,
Spite of all her reach of art!
Oh, to roam with her!

Marna with the wind's will,
Daughter of the sea!   50
Marna of the quick disdain,
Starting at the dream of stain!
At a smile with love aglow,
At a frown a statued woe,
Standing pinnacled in pain   55
Till a kiss sets free!

Down the world with Marna,
Daughter of the fire!
Marna of the deathless hope,
Still alert to win new scope   60
Where the wings of life may spread
For the flight unhazarded!
Dreaming of the speech to cope
With the heart's desire!

Marna of the far quest   65
After the divine!
Striving ever for some goal
Past the blunder-god's control!

Dreaming of potential years
When no day shall dawn in fears!   70
That's the Marna of my soul,
Wander-bride of mine!

SUGGESTIONS FOR STUDY

1. Both of these poems, like " The Joys of the Road " by Carman, deal with wander-thirst. Which are more descriptive, Hovey's or Carman's?

2. Would you agree that Hovey is more definitely lyrical? Give reasons for your opinion.

3. What general similarity in the two Hovey poems? Prove this by quoting lines.

4. What explanation would you give of Marna? Illustrate by definite passages.

FOR FURTHER READING

" Unmanifest Destiny "   " Men of Dartmouth "
" The Call of the Bugles "   " At the Crossroads "
" Dartmouth Winter Song "   " At the End of the Day "

SOME FAMOUS POEMS OF THE NINETEENTH CENTURY

BEFORE THE CIVIL WAR

" Marco Bozzaris," Fitz-Greene Halleck
" The American Flag," Joseph Rodman Drake
" Hail, Columbia," Joseph Hopkinson
" The Star-Spangled Banner," Francis Scott Key
" The Old Oaken Bucket," Samuel Woodworth
" The Little Beach Bird," Richard Henry Dana
" Home, Sweet Home," John Howard Payne
" Woodman, Spare That Tree," George Pope Morris
" America," Samuel Francis Smith
" Ben Bolt," Thomas Dunn English
" Nearer Home," Phoebe Cary
" The Old Folks at Home," " My Old Kentucky Home," Stephen Collins
      Foster
" Hannah Binding Shoes," Lucy Larcom
" Columbia the Gem of the Ocean," Thomas à Becket

CONNECTED WITH THE CIVIL WAR

" My Maryland," James Ryder Randall
" The Battle Cry of Freedom," " Just before the Battle, Mother," " Tramp,
      Tramp, Tramp " — George F. Root

" Dixie," General Albert Pike
" The Battle Hymn of the Republic," Julia Ward Howe
" Tenting on the Old Camp Ground," Walter Kittredge
" Little Giffen," Francis Ticknor
" Marching Through Georgia," Henry Clay Work
" Sheridan's Ride," Thomas Buchanan Read
" When Johnny Comes Marching Home," Patrick Gilmore
" The Blue and the Gray," Francis M. Finch

AFTER THE CIVIL WAR

" The Sandpiper," Celia Thaxter
" Jim Bludso," John Hay
" Bedouin Song," Bayard Taylor
" Opportunity," John Ingalls
" Frost Tonight " Edith M. Thomas

Twentieth Century Poetry

With the passing of the great group of nineteenth century poets there followed a rather barren era, with the exception of Whitman and others who are called " Transition Poets " in this volume. It is not possible to label accurately any era of literature by the mere matter of dates, but in retrospect one can recognize movements. Hence Whitman, by dates a contemporary of most of the later nineteenth-century poets, is now seen to have been the harbinger of something different in American poetry. In the same way Edwin Markham, although born in 1852, struck one of the keynotes of later poetry before the turn of the century, and is therefore put at the beginning of the movement whose height may not yet have been reached. Of the poets represented in this section all are living and active except George Sterling, Amy Lowell, Alan Seeger, and Elinor Wylie. Many of them may produce work that will eclipse anything so far written in the first thirty years of this twentieth century.

The most distinctive note of the country so far has been lyric, although a few poets, like Neihardt, Robinson, and Stephen Vincent Benét, have succeeded in writing long poems that are epic at least in spirit, and, what is more important, interesting to the reader and highly poetic in form.

In contemplating the work of the poets of today and the exalted position they occupy in the literary world, it is pleasant to realize that in an age that is undoubtedly mechanized and dominantly in- dustrial, works of the imagination need not want that appreciation which is necessary for continuing the spiritual traditions without which the human race would be in a bad way indeed.

EDWIN MARKHAM (1852–   )

Edwin Markham, child of pioneer parents, spent his boyhood in Oregon and California. Not satisfied with his life of farming and bronco-riding on a cattle ranch, he determined to be a teacher and entered a California normal school, later acting as superintendent of schools for many years. Though he had been writing poetry of varying merit since childhood, he suddenly became famous when he was forty-seven years old with " The Man With the Hoe." Partly because the poem was a splendid challenging thing in itself, partly because at the end of the nineteenth century there was a great wave of interest in common workers, the poem had, and still has, tremendous vogue, being quoted in papers from west to east. The poem was suggested by Millet's notable painting of a French peasant lean- ing on his hoe. Markham's own words best show the interpretation he gave to the picture: " The Yeoman is the landed and well-to-do farmer, you need shed no tears for him. But here in the Millet picture is the opposite — the Hoeman: the land-less, the soul-blighted workman of the world, the dumb creature that has no time to rest, no time to think, no time for the hopes that make us men."

THE MAN WITH THE HOE

WRITTEN AFTER SEEING MILLET'S WORLD-FAMOUS PAINTING OF A
BRUTALIZED TOILER IN THE DEEP ABYSS OF LABOR

" God made man in his own image; in the image of God He made him." — *Genesis*.

Bowed by the weight of centuries he leans
Upon his hoe and gazes on the ground,
The emptiness of ages in his face,
And on his back the burden of the world.
Who made him dead to rapture and despair,   5
A thing that grieves not and that never hopes,
Stolid and stunned, a brother to the ox?
Who loosened and let down this brutal jaw?
Whose was the hand that slanted back this brow?
Whose breath blew out the light within this brain?   10

Is this the Thing the Lord God made and gave
To have dominion over sea and land;
To trace the stars and search the heavens for power;
To feel the passion of Eternity?
Is this the dream He dreamed who shaped the suns   15
And markt their ways upon the ancient deep?
Down all the caverns of Hell to their last gulf
There is no shape more terrible than this —
More tongued with cries against the world's blind greed —
More filled with signs and portents for the soul —   20
More packt with danger to the universe.

What gulfs between him and the seraphim!
Slave of the wheel of labor, what to him
Are Plato and the swing of Pleiades?
What the long reaches of the peaks of song,   25
The rift of dawn, the reddening of the rose?
Through this dread shape the suffering ages look;
Time's tragedy is in that aching stoop;
Through this dread shape humanity betrayed,
Plundered, profaned and disinherited,   30
Cries protest to the Powers that made the world,
A protest that is also prophecy.

O masters, lords and rulers in all lands,
Is this the handiwork you give to God,
This monstrous thing distorted and soul-quencht?   35
How will you ever straighten up this shape;
Touch it again with immortality;
Give back the upward looking and the light;
Rebuild in it the music and the dream;
Make right the immemorial infamies,   40
Perfidious wrongs, immedicable woes?

O masters, lords and rulers in all lands,
How will the future reckon with this Man?
How answer his brute question in that hour
When whirlwinds of rebellion shake all shores?   45

24. **Plato:** an ancient Greek philosopher whose idealistic views of man have greatly influenced the world.   24. **Pleiades:** a constellation of brilliant stars often referred to by poets.

How will it be with kingdoms and with kings —
With those who shaped him to the thing he is —
When this dumb Terror shall rise to judge the world,
After the silence of the centuries?

SUGGESTIONS FOR STUDY

1. Vocabulary: portents, l. 20; seraphim, l. 22; immemorial infamies, l. 40; perfidious, l. 41; immedicable, l. 41.

2. Point out words and details used to emphasize the picture of an utterly crushed being.

3. To whom are the questions of this poem addressed? In what way are these people held responsible?

4. What examples can you find in history of uprisings of peasants or other workers as suggested in line 45, "When whirlwinds of rebellion shake all shores"? Graphic pictures of such outbursts are to be found in Dickens's *Tale of Two Cities* and *Barnaby Rudge,* and Galsworthy's *Strife.*

5. Some critics have said that Millet never intended to portray such a hopeless creature but simply an honest workman resting. Bring copies of the picture to class and discuss which interpretation it suggests to you. These may be obtained from several of the publishers of inexpensive prints.

QUATRAINS

Markham, the thinker and teacher, has given us a number of quatrains which people like to stow away in their memories, such as these. How do you interpret the first one? Compare it with Emerson's idea in "Compensation" (p. 537).

EVEN SCALES

The robber is robbed by his riches;
    The tyrant is dragged by his chain;
The schemer is snared by his cunning;
    The slayer lies dead by the slain.

INBROTHERED

There is a destiny that makes us brothers:
    None goes his way alone;
All that we send into the lives of others
    Comes back into our own.

YOUR WHISPERED SECRET

You told it to your friend; his oath was deep;
Now, here's a question for your wisdom-shelf:
Why did you hope some other one would keep
The secret that you could not keep yourself?

A CRY FOR STRENGTH

Give me heart-touch with all that live,
And strength to speak my word;
But if that is denied me, give
The strength to live unheard.

PREPAREDNESS

For all your days prepare,
And meet them ever alike:
When you are the anvil, bear —
When you are the hammer, strike.

OUR ISRAFEL

IN MEMORY OF EDGAR ALLAN POE

When Edwin Markham submitted a poem on Poe to a competition sponsored by the Poe Cottage Association and entitled it " Our Israfel " he performed a master stroke. It is a beautiful conception to identify Poe himself with one of his own creations, but Mr. Markham did not stop with the title; throughout " Our Israfel " he gives an interpretation of the spirit of Poe, of the sadness of his soul, and of his eagerness for creating beauty through poetic expression. Small wonder that this poem was declared the best of five hundred submitted in the contest; it would have won had there been ten times as many.

The complete text of " Our Israfel " has never before appeared in any book, and it is with Mr. Markham's cordial permission that it is here printed. In the volume of his complete poems, to be published in 1931, it will no doubt occupy a prominent place, second only to " The Man With the Hoe."

" In Heaven a spirit doth dwell
' Whose heart-strings are a lute ';
None sing so wildly well
As the angel Israfel." — POE

I

The sad great gifts the austere Muses bring —
    Breathing on poets the immortal breath —
Were laid on him that he might darkly sing
    Of Beauty, Love, and Death.

They laid upon him dreams of high romance,   5
    A hunger for a loveliness more strange
Than earth can give in all her piteous chance,
    In all her changeless change.

They sent him dreams of beauty's starrier birth,
    Dreams of a beauty touched with tragic grief —   10
A wilder beauty than is known to earth,
    Where beauty is so brief.

They laid upon him music's trembling charm,
    The mystery of sound, of shaken air,
Whose touch can still the spirit or alarm —   15
    Build rapture, build despair.

They struck him with imagination's rod,
    The power that built these heavens that soar and seem —
These heavens that are the daring of some God
    Stirred by the lyric dream.   20

And then (for, oh, the Muses do not spare!)
    They set for him one final gift apart:
They gave him sorrow as a pack to bear,
    Sorrow to break the heart.

II

And so they called the poet into Time,   25
    The saddest and the proudest of the race
That ever came this way with sound of rhyme,
    In quest of Beauty's face.

      1. **Muses:** the goddesses of song and poetry.

He knew life's immemorial grief — the cry
   Of young Love with the ruined rainbow wings,   30
The pathos of the vanishing, the sigh
   Out of all mortal things.

For he was son to Proserpine, and she
   Drew his proud bark to many a secret shore
Of the dim continents whose names shall be   35
   Night and the Nevermore.

Steering toward Shadow with melodious helm,
   He touched with somber prow the wharves of Dis,
Exploring all the hushed and hollow realm
   This side the last abyss.   40

He knew, too, all the melancholy sounds
   That beat about the pale Lethean piers;
And in his side he felt the secret wounds
   Known to the lyric seers.

He mused among the gray sarcophagi,   45
   While far upon the rim of ruin fled
A host of hooded forms that hurried by
   With laughters to the dead.

He looked on cities in their crumbling hours,
   Where Death obscurely mumbles out his rune,   50
Hoary, remote, alone, where time-torn towers
   Hang spectral in the moon.

III

He walked our streets as on a lonely strand:
   His country was not here — it was afar.
Not here his home, not here his motherland,   55
   But in some statelier star.

Life was his exile, Earth his alien shore,
   And these were foreign faces that he passed;

33. **Proserpine:** in Greek mythology, the queen of the infernal regions. 38. **Dis:** an underworld city, mentioned in Dante's *Inferno*. 42. **Lethean:** producing forgetfulness. 45. **sarcophagi:** tombs. 50. **rune:** an Anglo-Saxon term for poem.

For he had other language, other lore,
   And he must home at last.   60

His country was not here, but in the isles
   Of Aiden ringed around with lustrous seas,
Where golden galleys skim the silver miles
   Or sleep upon the breeze.

And there were gardens where the waters sing   65
   In valleys of a many-colored grass,
Where strange-eyed birds go by on rainbow wing,
   And rose-pale maidens pass —

Gardens of hyacinths and asphodels,
   Inwoven with the sound of warbling rills,   70
With triple-tinted suns and lilied wells,
   Walled in by golden hills.

And there he built him palaces of song,
   Lifting their spires against the pallid moon,
With corridors where shapes of shadow throng   75
   When night is at her noon.

He sought his dream-love there by many names
   Of beauty and of wonder and of doom —
Lenore, Ligeia (burning like pale flames)
   Morella, Ulalume.   80

He trod high chambers lit with ruby light,
   And heard in the hush the ghostly arras stir,
And stir again, in the deep and secret night,
   With memories of her.

He knew the demon whispers in the deep,   85
   And songs of deathless love where seraphs are:
He saw the cliffs of Time, a ghostly heap,
   But over the cliffs a star!

    62. **Aiden:** Arabic form of the word for Eden.

IV

O poet, not for you the trampling street,
  The wrangling crowds that cry and clutch for gold;   90
And so you followed Beauty's flying feet
  Into the dim and old.

O poet, life was bitter to your heart:
  These stones have memories of the tears you shed:
Forgive the serpent tongue, the flying dart —   95
  Forgive us from the dead.

You sang your song; we gave you scorn for pay;
  For beauty's bread we gave a stone, and yet
Because our eyes were holden on the way,
  Remember to forget.   100

Sing, Israfel: you have your star at last,
  Your morning star; but we — we still must live!
So now that all is over, all is past,
  Forget, forget — forgive!

SUGGESTIONS FOR STUDY

1. " Our Israfel " naturally challenges comparison with " The Man with the Hoe." What general similarities do you find? Or differences?

2. Read Poe's poem once more and note how remarkably " Our Israfel " carries the theme which Markham chose.

3. From your knowledge of Poe's life and his work, find passages in " Our Israfel " that ring true and appropriate.

4. This poem, like " The Man with the Hoe," as well as Poe's " Israfel," are excellent for oral reading before a class.

FOR FURTHER READING

Markham has published four volumes of poetry: *The Gates of Paradise and Other Poems, The Shoes of Happiness and Other Poems, The Man with the Hoe and Other Poems,* and *Lincoln and Other Poems.* A complete edition of all his poems to date will be published in 1931.

98. This line echoes a passage from Matthew vii, 9: " For what man is there of you who, if his son ask for bread, will he give him a stone? "

The following poems are called to your special attention:

"In a Cornfield"

"A Blossoming Bough"

"The Wall Street Pit"

"A Creed"

"Lincoln, the Man of the People"

"Memory of Good Deeds"

"To Young America"

"Outwitted"

HENRY VAN DYKE (1852–   )

Dr. Henry van Dyke, poet, story writer, essayist, preacher, critic, lecturer, diplomat, professor, and lover of the great outdoors, was born in Germantown, Pennsylvania, of Dutch ancestry. He graduated from Princeton in 1873 and four years later from the Princeton Theological Seminary. For many years he was one of the foremost Presbyterian preachers of New York City, and then followed brilliant years as a Professor of English at Princeton, where he still lives as Professor Emeritus. In spite of the duties of his various professions, Dr. van Dyke has always found time to write, and his list of volumes of all sorts is imposing. Besides many books of poetry, he is the author of *Fisherman's Luck, Days Off, The Blue Flower, The Ruling Passion, A Study of Tennyson,* and a number of works pertaining to religion. His latest book is *The Man Behind the Book* (1929).

" God of the Open Air," the poem here given, represents two phases of the many-sided Van Dyke — his love of the open air and his deep sense of religion. In form the poem is an ode, and consists of a series of lyrics in different meters strung together, quite in the manner of the old Greek poets.

GOD OF THE OPEN AIR

I

Thou who hast made thy dwelling fair
   With flowers below, above with starry lights,
And set thine altars everywhere —
   On mountain heights,
In woodlands dim with many a dream,   5
   In valleys bright with springs,
And on the curving capes of every stream:
Thou who hast taken to thyself the wings
   Of morning, to abide
Upon the secret places of the sea,   10
   And on far islands, where the tide
Visits the beauty of untrodden shores,

Waiting for worshipers to come to thee
   In thy great out-of-doors!
To thee I turn, to thee I make my prayer,   15
   God of the open air.

II

Seeking for thee, the heart of man
   Lonely and longing ran,
In that first, solitary hour,
   When the mysterious power   20
To know and love the wonder of the morn
Was breathed within him, and his soul was born;
      And thou didst meet thy child,
      Not in some hidden shrine,
But in the freedom of the garden wild,   25
   And take his hand in thine —
There all day long in Paradise he walked,
And in the cool of evening with thee talked.

III

Lost, long ago, that garden bright and pure,
   Lost, that calm day too perfect to endure,   30
And lost the childlike love that worshiped and was sure!
   For men have dulled their eyes with sin,
And dimmed the light of heaven with doubt,
And built their temple walls to shut thee in,
And framed their iron creeds to shut thee out.   35
But not for thee the closing of the door,
   O Spirit unconfined!
   Thy ways are free
   As is the wandering wind,
And thou hast wooed thy children, to restore   40
   Their fellowship with thee,
In peace of soul and simpleness of mind.

IV

Joyful the heart that, when the flood rolled by,
Leaped up to see the rainbow in the sky;
And glad the pilgrim, in the lonely night,   45

---

43. **heart:** that of Noah. 45. **pilgrim:** Abraham, who on his way to
Canaan, stopped at Haran, a city in northern Mesopotamia. (Gen. xi, 31–32).

For whom the hills of Haran, tier on tier,
Built up a secret stairway to the height
Where stars like angel eyes were shining clear.
From mountain-peaks, in many a land and age,
    Disciples of the Persian seer   50
Have hailed the rising sun and worshiped thee;
And wayworn followers of the Indian sage
Have found the peace of God beneath a spreading tree.

v

But One, but One — ah, Son most dear,
    And perfect image of the Love Unseen —   55
Walked every day in pastures green,
And all his life the quiet waters by,
Reading their beauty with a tranquil eye.
To him the desert was a place prepared
    For weary hearts to rest;   60
The hillside was a temple blest;
The grassy vale a banquet-room
Where he could feed and comfort many a guest.
    With him the lily shared
The vital joy that breathes itself in bloom;   65
And every bird that sang beside the nest
Told of the love that broods o'er every living thing.
    He watched the shepherd bring
His flock at sundown to the welcome fold,
    The fisherman at daybreak fling   70
His net across the waters gray and cold,
And all day long the patient reaper swing
His curving sickle through the harvest-gold.
So through the world the foot-path way he trod,
Breathing the air of heaven in every breath;   75
And in the evening sacrifice of death
Beneath the open sky he gave his soul to God.
Him will I trust, and for my Master take;
Him will I follow; and for his dear sake,
    God of the open air,   80
    To thee I make my prayer.

---

50. **Persian seer:** Zoroaster, the prophet of the old Persian religion. 52. **Indian sage:** Buddha, who is said to have meditated many weeks under a tree.

VI

From the prison of anxious thought that greed has builded,
From the fetters that envy has wrought and pride has gilded,
From the noise of the crowded ways and the fierce confusion,
From the folly that wastes its days in a world of illusion,   85
(Ah, but the life is lost that frets and languishes there!)
I would escape and be free in the joy of the open air.
By the breadth of the blue that shines in silence o'er me,
By the length of the mountain-lines that stretch before me,
By the height of the cloud that sails, with rest in motion,   90
Over the plains and the vales to the measureless ocean,
(Oh, how the sight of the greater things enlarges the eyes!)
Draw me away from myself to the peace of the hills and skies.

While the tremulous leafy haze on the woodland is spreading,
And the bloom on the meadow betrays where May has been tread-
    ing;   95
While the birds on the branches above, and the brooks flowing under,
Are singing together of love in a world full of wonder,
(Lo, in the magic of springtime, dreams are changed into truth!)
Quicken my heart, and restore the beautiful hopes of youth.
By the faith that the wild-flowers show when they bloom unbid-
    den,   100
By the calm of the river's flow to a goal that is hidden,
By the strength of the tree that clings to its deep foundation,
By the courage of birds' light wings on the long migration,
(Wonderful spirit of trust that abides in Nature's breast!)
Teach me how to confide, and live my life, and rest.   105

For the comforting warmth of the sun that my body embraces,
For the cool of the waters that run through the shadowy places,
For the balm of the breezes that brush my face with their fingers,
For the vesper-hymn of the thrush when the twilight lingers,
For the long breath, the deep breath, the breath of a heart without
    care —   110
I will give thee thanks and adore thee, God of the open air!

VII

These are the gifts I ask
Of thee, Spirit serene:

Strength for the daily task,
Courage to face the road,   115
Good cheer to help me bear the traveler's load,
And, for the hours of rest that come between,
An inward joy in all things heard and seen.
These are the sins I fain
Would have thee take away: 120
Malice, and cold disdain,
Hot anger, sullen hate,
Scorn of the lowly, envy of the great,
And discontent that casts a shadow gray
On all the brightness of the common day.   125
These are the things I prize
And hold of dearest worth:
Light of the sapphire skies,
Peace of the silent hills,
Shelter of forests, comfort of the grass,   130
Music of birds, murmur of little rills,
Shadows of cloud that swiftly pass,
And, after showers,
The smell of flowers
And of the good brown earth,   135
And best of all, along the way, friendship and mirth.
So let me keep
These treasures of the humble heart
In true possession, owning them by love;
And when at last I can no longer move   140
Among them freely, but must part
From the green fields and from the waters clear,
Let me not creep
Into some darkened room and hide
From all that makes the world so bright and dear;   145
But throw the windows wide
To welcome in the light;
And while I clasp a well-belovèd hand,
Let me once more have sight
Of the deep sky and the far-smiling land —   150
Then gently fall on sleep,
And breathe my body back to Nature's care,
My spirit out to thee, God of the open air.

SUGGESTIONS FOR STUDY

1. The most satisfactory method of studying this ode is to take it by sections. The first is an invocation to God the creator. Find the theme or motive of the other sections.

2. This poem offers opportunity for the study of meter and rhyme. Note the variety of rhyme schemes, the different lengths of the lines, and so on.

3. This is an excellent poem for oral reading before a class.

FOR FURTHER READING

" Work "
" America for Me "
" An Angler's Wish "
" The Veery "

" The Lily of Yarrow "
" Four Things "
" The Song Sparrow "

EDWIN ARLINGTON ROBINSON (1869–   )

If Lanier can be called a musician in poetry, Edwin Arlington Robinson may be styled a portrait painter in poetry. A whole gallery of men is revealed to our eye and, better yet, to our imagination as we turn the pages of Robinson's books. Sometimes their whole souls are laid open to us, sometimes we catch only a suggestion beneath a suave exterior. Sometimes they are treated earnestly, sometimes half cynically, sometimes with whimsical tenderness. In every case they are made very real, very human. Robinson came from Maine, attended Harvard, and though he lives most of the time in New York, is distinctly associated with New England, where the " Tilbury Town " and the " Town Down the River " of his poems are located. He has thrice won the Pulitzer Prize and is by many considered the greatest living American poet today. Besides studying modern men he has turned his attention to the Arthurian legends and in his long poems, *Merlin, Launcelot,* and *Tristram,* has done the most extensive work based on these stories since Tennyson, though differing widely in treatment from the earlier poet. His latest volume is *Cavender's House* (1929).

MINIVER CHEEVY

Among modern poets only Edgar Lee Masters has equaled Robinson in incisive satire. Robinson has adhered more closely to standard poetic forms than Masters, but both show great skill in putting tersely particular traits of character. In this poem is sketched the type of man who dreams but never gets anywhere except to the bottle.

Miniver Cheevy, child of scorn,
    Grew lean while he assailed the seasons;
He wept that he was ever born,
    And he had reasons.

Miniver loved the days of old   5
    When swords were bright and steeds were prancing;
The vision of a warrior bold
    Would set him dancing.

Miniver sighed for what was not,
    And dreamed, and rested from his labors;   10
He dreamed of Thebes and Camelot,
    And Priam's neighbors.

Miniver mourned the ripe renown
    That made so many a name so fragrant;
He mourned Romance, now on the town,   15
    And Art, a vagrant.

Miniver loved the Medici,
    Albeit he had never seen one;
He would have sinned incessantly
    Could he have been one.   20

Miniver cursed the commonplace
    And eyed a khaki suit with loathing;
He missed the medieval grace
    Of iron clothing.

Miniver scorned the gold he sought,   25
    But sore annoyed was he without it;
Miniver thought, and thought, and thought
    And thought about it.

11. **Thebes:** a famous city of ancient Greece. 11. **Camelot:** the city of King Arthur and the Knights of the Round Table. 12. **Priam:** the king of Troy during the time the Greeks were besieging it. 17. **Medici:** a highly cultivated but often unprincipled family of Florence, Italy, in the fifteenth and sixteenth centuries.

Miniver Cheevy, born too late,
  Scratched his head and kept on thinking;   30
Miniver coughed, and called it fate,
  And kept on drinking.

SUGGESTIONS FOR STUDY

1. In what spirit does the poet present Miniver? How does he make you feel about him? Indicate lines to prove your points. Notice how the name is repeated at the beginning of each stanza.

2. Did you ever know any one like this? Would you call him a common type?

RICHARD CORY

" Richard Cory " represents almost the reverse of " Miniver Cheevy." Richard Cory seemed to be everything that any one could wish; Miniver Cheevy wished to be what nearly every one might want to be. He lived his dream life, and " kept on drinking," while Richard Cory went home one night and —

Whenever Richard Cory went down town,
  We people on the pavement looked at him:
He was a gentleman from sole to crown,
  Clean favored, and imperially slim.

And he was always quietly arrayed,
  And he was always human when he talked;
But still he fluttered pulses when he said,
  " Good-morning," and he glittered when he walked.

And he was rich — yes, richer than a king —
  And admirably schooled in every grace:
In fine, we thought he was everything
  To make us wish that we were in his place.

So on we worked, and waited for the light,
  And went without the meat, and cursed the bread;
And Richard Cory, one calm summer night,
  Went home and put a bullet through his head.

SUGGESTIONS FOR STUDY

1. Why does one gasp on reading the last two lines for the first time? What suppositions flock to your mind as to possible causes for Richard's deed?

2. Is such a situation possible in life? Is it common? What bit of philosophy about life does it suggest to your mind?

3. What verbs in the second stanza have unusual force and originality? Explain them.

4. How do you explain the first two lines of the last stanza?

BEWICK FINZER [1]

Bewick Finzer is a cousin to Miniver Cheevy and Richard Cory. He is a sad picture of the man who had achieved his dream, that of wealth, and cracked under the strain when he lost it. But he neither took to drink nor did he shoot himself; he kept up his futile dream and became a nuisance to his friends.

Time was when his half million drew
　The breath of six per cent;
But soon the worm of what-was-not
　Fed hard on his content;
And something crumbled in his brain　　　　5
　When his half million went.

Time passed, and filled along with his
　The place of many more;
Time came, and hardly one of us
　Had credence to restore,　　　　10
From what appeared one day, the man
　Whom we had known before.

The broken voice, the withered neck,
　The coat worn out with care,
The cleanliness of indigence,　　　　15
　The brilliance of despair,
The fond imponderable dreams
　Of affluence — all were there.

[1] From *The Man Against the Sky* by E. A. Robinson. Reprinted by permission of The Macmillan Company, publishers.

Poor Finzer, with his dreams and schemes,
Fares hard now in the race, 20
With heart and eye that have a task
When he looks in the face
Of one who might so easily
Have been in Finzer's place.

He comes unfailing for the loan 25
We give and then forget;
He comes, and probably for years
Will he be coming yet —
Familiar as an old mistake,
And futile as regret. 30

SUGGESTIONS FOR STUDY

1. Vocabulary: credence, l. 10; indigence, l. 15; imponderable, l. 17; affluence, l. 18; futile, l. 30.
2. How do you interpret " the worm of what-was-not "? Can you put into simple words just what happened to Finzer in the first stanza?
3. How do the people of the town regard Finzer now?
4. Which of the three men portrayed in these three poems do you consider most pathetic? Why?

THE MASTER

This is one of the many poems in our literature on Lincoln, though he is not mentioned by name. It is harder than most Lincoln poems and requires careful study. For the younger generation who hear only praises of Lincoln it is hard to realize that he was greatly reviled by many during his lifetime. In the house where he died in Washington there is preserved a collection of the newspaper cartoons of his day showing the many indignities and even abuses which were heaped upon him. Robinson assumes in this poem the point of view of those who had failed to appreciate Lincoln at first.

A flying word from here and there
Had sown the name at which we sneered,
But soon the name was everywhere,
To be reviled and then revered:

A presence to be loved and feared,   5
We cannot hide it, or deny
That we, the gentlemen who jeered,
May be forgotten by and by.

He came when days were perilous
And hearts of men were sore beguiled;   10
And having made his note of us,
He pondered and was reconciled.
Was ever master yet so mild
As he, and so untamable?
We doubted, even when he smiled,   15
Not knowing what he knew so well.

He knew that undeceiving fate
Would shame us whom he served unsought;
He knew that he must wince and wait —
The jest of those for whom he fought;   20
He knew devoutly what he thought
Of us and of our ridicule;
He knew that we must all be taught
Like little children in a school.

We gave a glamour to the task   25
That he encountered and saw through,
But little of us did he ask,
And little did we ever do.
And what appears if we review
The season when we railed and chaffed?   30
It is the face of one who knew
That we were learning while we laughed.

The face that in our vision feels
Again the venom that we flung,
Transfigured to the world reveals   35
The vigilance to which we clung.
Shrewd, hallowed, harassed, and among
The mysteries that are untold,
The face we see was never young,
Nor could it wholly have been old.   40

For he, to whom we had applied
Our shopman's test of age and worth,
Was elemental when he died,
As he was ancient at his birth:
The saddest among kings of earth,   45
Bowed with a galling crown, this man
Met rancor with a cryptic mirth,
Laconic — and Olympian.

The love, the grandeur, and the fame
Are bounded by the world alone;   50
The calm, the smoldering, and the flame
Of awful patience were his own:
With him they are forever flown
Past all our fond self-shadowings,
Wherewith we cumber the Unknown   55
As with inept, Icarian wings.

For we were not as other men:
'Twas ours to soar and his to see.
But we are coming down again,
And we shall come down pleasantly;   60
Nor shall we longer disagree
On what it is to be sublime,
But flourish in our perigee
And have one Titan at a time.

SUGGESTIONS FOR STUDY

1. Do you understand the following words: glamour, l. 25; harassed, l. 37; rancor, l. 47; cryptic, l. 47; laconic, l. 48; cumber, l. 55; inept, l. 56?

2. Can you find examples in Lincoln's life to carry out the contrasting idea of his being mild and yet untamable, ll. 13–14? Examples of how he met rancor with a cryptic mirth, l. 47?

3. Note all the places where Robinson describes Lincoln's face. Do the portraits and statues confirm these ideas?

48. **Olympian:** like the old Greek gods who dwelt on Mount Olympus. 56. **Icarian:** referring to Icarus, the first unsuccessful aeronaut. The story is that Icarus, a Greek boy, attempted to fly with wings invented by his father, but the sun melted the wax which fastened them and he was dashed to earth. 63. **perigee:** the point in the orbit of the moon where it is nearest the earth. The lines mean that we shall accept our own more lowly position and not attempt to set ourselves up above the one really great man. 64. **Titan:** one of a race of giants in Greek mythology.

FOR FURTHER READING

" Flammonde "   " The House on the Hill "
" John Gorham "   " Isaac and Archibald "
" An Old Story "   " Uncle Ananias "
" Ballade by the Fire "   " Mr. Flood's Party "

All of these may be found in Robinson's *Collected Poems.*

EDGAR LEE MASTERS (1869–   )

Imagine a book of poetry being a " best seller," shouldering out all the love stories, detective stories, travel books, and other kinds of prose which usually appear in that class. Yet that is just what happened in 1915 when the *Spoon River Anthology* appeared in the book shops. So original in its conception, so enticing in its varied pictures, so provocative of thought and discussion did it prove to be that every one just had to read it. Masters was an Illinois lawyer-poet who, like Markham, had been writing for years without creating a ripple of excitement. Too much of his verse had been merely a poor imitation of the English poets whom he had studied. Finally at the suggestion of his friend, William Marion Reedy, editor of *Reedy's Mirror,* he turned his attention to his own surroundings and produced a masterpiece. Through the reading of the *Greek Anthology,* a collection of ancient poems, he conceived the idea of a series of epitaphs of the inhabitants of a fictitious Illinois town written by the dead themselves. Reading this book is like being present at the Day of Judgment when the dead arise and the truth about their lives is set free. All the multiple experiences of a village life are here represented, the good and the bad crowded together, the joys and aspirations recorded, the bitterness and ironies reiterated, the misunderstandings and mysteries revealed. Mr. Robert Littell has well summarized the impression left after reading the book: " Their faces, less distinct than the gossip, detective work and idealistic generalization in which they swam, have long since disappeared. There were no characters, and what we mistook for such were case histories in the clinic of life's hospital, with Mr. Masters as surgeon rather than artist."

The names of the men and women one indeed forgets, but can one ever look again upon a cemetery in a small town or even the town itself without repeopling it in imagination with many of these lives?

Anne Rutledge is the only actual historical character among those which follow. She will be remembered as the sweetheart of Lincoln's early life, lost to him through death.

ANNE RUTLEDGE

Out of me unworthy and unknown
The vibrations of deathless music;
" With malice toward none, with charity for all."
Out of me the forgiveness of millions toward millions,
And the beneficent face of a nation
Shining with justice and truth.
I am Anne Rutledge who sleep beneath these weeds,
Beloved in life of Abraham Lincoln,
Wedded to him, not through union,
But through separation.
Bloom forever, O Republic,
From the dust of my bosom!

JOHN HORACE BURLESON

I won the prize essay at school
Here in the village,
And published a novel before I was twenty-five.
I went to the city for themes and to enrich my art;
There married the banker's daughter,   5
And later became president of the bank —
Always looking forward to some leisure
To write an epic novel of the war.
Meanwhile friend of the great, and lover of letters,
And host to Matthew Arnold and to Emerson.   10
An after-dinner speaker, writing essays
For local clubs. At last brought here —
My boyhood home, you know —
Not even a little tablet in Chicago
To keep my name alive.   15
How great it is to write the single line:
" Roll on, thou deep and dark blue Ocean, roll! "

10. **Matthew Arnold:** a noted English writer and lecturer, much entertained in America. 17. This line is one of the most frequently quoted lines
written by the English poet, Lord Byron.

MRS. GEORGE REECE

To this generation I would say:
Memorize some bit of verse of truth or beauty.
It may serve a turn in your life.
My husband had nothing to do
With the fall of the bank — he was only cashier.
The wreck was due to the president, Thomas Rhodes,
And his vain, unscrupulous son.
Yet my husband was sent to prison,
And I was left with the children,
To feed and clothe and school them.
And I did it, and sent them forth
Into the world all clean and strong,
And all through the wisdom of Pope, the poet:
" Act well your part, there all the honor lies."

GEORGE GRAY

I have studied many times
The marble which was chiseled for me —
A boat with a furled sail at rest in a harbor.
In truth it pictures not my destination
But my life.
For love was offered me and I shrank from its disillusionment;
Sorrow knocked at my door, but I was afraid;
Ambition called to me, but I dreaded the chances.
Yet all the while I hungered for meaning in my life
And now I know that we must lift the sail
And catch the winds of destiny
Wherever they drive the boat.
To put meaning in one's life may end in madness,
But life without meaning is the torture
Of restlessness and vague desire —
It is a boat longing for the sea and yet afraid.

JACOB GOODPASTURE

When Fort Sumter fell and the war came
I cried out in bitterness of soul:
" O glorious republic now no more! "
When they buried my soldier son
To the call of trumpets and the sound of drums
My heart broke beneath the weight
Of eighty years, and I cried:
" Oh, son who died in a cause unjust!
In the strife of Freedom slain! "
And I crept here under the grass.
And now from the battlements of time, behold:
Thrice thirty million souls being bound together
In the love of larger truth,
Rapt in the expectation of the birth
Of a new Beauty,
Sprung from Brotherhood and Wisdom.
I with eyes of spirit see the Transfiguration
Before you see it.
But ye infinite brood of golden eagles nesting ever higher,
Wheeling ever higher, the sunlight wooing
Of lofty places of Thought,
Forgive the blindness of the departed owl.

SUGGESTIONS FOR STUDY

1. Which of these persons represent the following things in life: apparent failure, but real success; apparent success, but hidden failure; courage, cowardice; clarification after death of misunderstanding during life?

2. Under what circumstances did Lincoln say the third line in " Anne Rutledge "? See p. 459.

3. Can you see any relation between the poems " George Gray " and " Eldorado " (p. 628)?

4. Where had Jacob Goodpasture's sympathies lain in the Civil War? On which side had his son fought?

5. Try writing an epitaph for yourself in the manner of the *Spoon River Anthology*.

SILENCE

None of the many volumes of poetry which Masters published after the *Spoon River Anthology* were as powerful, but in *Songs and Satires* (1916) is to be found one poem which ranks with his best. It is one of those impressive meditations which one doesn't wish to talk about after reading, but just think over in silence.

I have known the silence of the stars and of the sea,
And the silence of the city when it pauses,
And the silence of a man and a maid,
And the silence for which music alone finds the word,
And the silence of the woods before the winds of spring begin, 5
And the silence of the sick
When their eyes roam about the room.
And I ask: For the depths
Of what use is language?
A beast of the field moans a few times   10
When death takes its young.
And we are voiceless in the presence of realities—
We cannot speak.

A curious boy asks an old soldier
Sitting in front of the grocery store,   15
" How did you lose your leg? "
And the old soldier is struck with silence,
Or his mind flies away
Because he cannot concentrate it on Gettysburg.
It comes back jocosely   20
And he says, " A bear bit it off."
And the boy wonders, while the old soldier
Dumbly, feebly lives over
The flashes of guns, the thunder of cannon,
The shrieks of the slain,   25
And himself lying on the ground,
And the hospital surgeons, the knives,
And the long days in bed.
But if he could describe it all
He would be an artist.   30
But if he were an artist there would be deeper wounds
Which he could not describe.

There is the silence of a great hatred,
And the silence of a great love,
And the silence of a deep peace of mind,   35
And the silence of an embittered friendship,
There is the silence of a spiritual crisis,
Through which your soul, exquisitely tortured,
Comes with visions not to be uttered
Into a realm of higher life,   40
And the silence of the gods who understand each other without
    speech.
There is the silence of defeat.
There is the silence of those unjustly punished;
And the silence of the dying whose hand
Suddenly grips yours.   45
There is the silence between father and son,
When the father cannot explain his life,
Even though he be misunderstood for it.

There is the silence that comes between husband and wife;
There is the silence of those who have failed;   50
And the vast silence that covers
Broken nations and vanquished leaders.
There is the silence of Lincoln,
Thinking of the poverty of his youth.
And the silence of Napoleon   55
After Waterloo.
And the silence of Jeanne d'Arc
Saying amid the flames, " Blessèd Jesus " —
Revealing in two words all sorrow, all hope.
And there is the silence of age,   60
Too full of wisdom for the tongue to utter it
In words intelligible to those who have not lived
The great range of life.
And there is the silence of the dead.
If we who are in life cannot speak   65
Of profound experiences,
Why do you marvel that the dead
Do not tell you of death?
Their silence shall be interpreted
As we approach them.   70

SUGGESTIONS FOR STUDY

1. The poet gives many illustrations of moments of " silence." Can you add others?
2. What is meant by lines 31 and 32?
3. What does he say of the " silence of the dead " ?

FOR FURTHER READING

To get more satisfaction and better understanding out of *Spoon River Anthology* you should read other epitaphs. Some that you would enjoy are: Dorcas Gustine, the outspoken woman; Theodore the Poet and Petit the Poet, two opposite types who could be made to represent different types of poets in this book; Lucinda Matlock, the happy wife and mother; Hod Putt, who " went into bankruptcy " in an unusual way; Emily Sparks, the devoted teacher; Albert Scherding, the failure, whose children were all successful; Isaiah Beethoven, who had three months to live; Fiddler Jones, whose fiddling gave him no time to plow; Griffy the Cooper, who saw us all living in tubs. Perhaps the most impressive one in the book is Harry Wilmans, whose experience in the Philippine War is the most terrible arraignment against war that one could find.

GEORGE STERLING (1869–1926)

George Sterling was born on Long Island and educated in eastern schools, but in 1895 he went to California and lived there until his tragic death in 1926. He was a friend of Joaquin Miller, whom he visited at his mountain home, and of Ambrose Bierce, who praised the work of his young friend most extravagantly. The last known piece of writing by Sterling was an essay on Bierce, published as a preface to a volume of Bierce's short stories. The two poems that follow are characteristic lyrics in Sterling's best manner, one with a narrative touch, the other a simple but beautiful picture of death. Sterling published ten or more volumes of verse, the best of his shorter poems being brought together in *Selected Poems* (1923).

THE MASTER–MARINER [1]

My grandsire sailed three years from home,
    And slew unmoved the sounding whale:
Here on a windless beach I roam
    And watch far out the hardy sail.

[1] Copyrighted by A. M. Robertson.

The lions of the surf that cry
  Upon this lion-colored shore
On reefs of midnight met his eye:
  He knew their fangs as I their roar.

My grandsire sailed uncharted seas,
  And toll of all their leagues he took:
I scan the shallow bays at ease,
  And tell their colors in a book.

The anchor-chains his music made
  And wind in shrouds and running-gear:
The thrush at dawn beguiles my glade,
  And once, 'tis said, I woke to hear.

My grandsire in his ample fist
  The long harpoon upheld to men:
Behold obedient to my wrist
  A gray gull's-feather for my pen!

Upon my grandsire's leathern cheek
  Five zones their bitter bronze had set:
Some day their hazards L will seek,
  I promise me at times. Not yet.

I think my grandsire now would turn
  A mild but speculative eye
On me, my pen, and its concern,
  Then gaze again to sea — and sigh.

DIRGE [1]

FROM " LILITH "

O lay her gently where the lark is nesting
    And wingèd things are glad!
Tears end, and now begins the time of resting
    For her whose heart was sad.

Give roses, but a fairer bloom is taken.
    Strew lilies — she was one,
Gone in her silence to a place forsaken
    By roses and the sun.

Deep is her slumber at the last of sorrow,
    Of twilight and the rain.
Her eyes have closed forever on tomorrow
    And on tomorrow's pain.

CALE YOUNG RICE (1872–   )

Cale Young Rice was born in Kentucky, educated at Cumberland University and Harvard, and taught English for one year at his alma mater. Without having achieved much of a reputation as a poet, he nevertheless determined upon poetry as a career. He knew the sort of thing that he wanted to do and has consistently followed it out. A number of volumes of plays and verse have appeared since 1897, when he first made up his mind to be a professional poet, and it has become increasingly evident that he delights in careful workmanship rather than in profuse production. Among those who enjoy delicate fancies musically expressed he stands in high favor, and today, while not in any sense popular, he is considered one of our most appealing poets. "The Runaway" is typical of his best lyric style.

THE RUNAWAY

What are you doing, little day-moon,
    Over the April hill?
What are you doing, up so soon,

[1] Copyrighted by A. M. Robertson.

Climbing the sky with silver shoon?
What are you doing at half-past noon,
　　Slipping along so still?

Are you so eager, the heights unwon,
　　That you cannot wait,
But, unheeding of wind and sun,
Out of your nest of night must run,
Up where the day is far from done,
　　Shy little shadow-mate?

Up and away then — with young mists
　　Tripping, along the blue!
Dance and dally and promise trysts
Unto each that around you lists;
For, little moon, not a one but wists
　　April's the time to woo!

SUGGESTIONS FOR STUDY

1. What picture is suggested by the first stanza?
2. Why does the poet refer to the moon as " shy little shadow-mate "?
3. What is the point of the title of the poem?

FOR FURTHER READING

" The Young to the Old "　　" April "
" Civil War "　　　　　　　" Brother Beasts "
" The Mystic "

AMY LOWELL (1874–1925)

You will probably like Amy Lowell either tremendously or not at all. She seldom leaves her readers lukewarm. She belonged to the renowned Lowell family of Cambridge, which has already been mentioned under James Russell Lowell. The famous poet was a cousin of her grandfather; one of her brothers was a distinguished astronomer, and another is president of Harvard University. Miss Lowell's education was entirely individual through tutoring, extensive travel, and her own determined study of literature and verse technique after she decided at twenty-eight to become a poet. She did not try to rush into print but laid careful foundations for herself and issued her first volume ten years after she had come to this decision. It was not, however, until her second volume *Sword Blades and Poppy Seed* (1914) that her individual style was evident. She became the chief exponent of the Imagists and the promoter of " polyphonic prose."

Like other innovators Miss Lowell became the target for both witticism and abuse which gradually diminished as the public became more accustomed to her manner and realized that when she wished, she could be a master of the regular rhythms as well as of " free verse." Finally when her death came unexpectedly, through a paralytic stroke, the press was overflowing with praise of her inestimable contributions to American literature.

In addition to her original verse, Miss Lowell made detailed studies of foreign literatures, notably her English versions of Chinese poems, her critical essays on French poets, and her two-volume study of John Keats. Following the footsteps of her famous poet-relative she wrote *A Critical Fable* as a sequel to his *Fable for Critics*. Her *Tendencies in Modern American Poetry* presents six of our modern poets in a style which high school students can enjoy reading.

Here are two poems about persons. Note how different they are from the pictures given us by Masters and Robinson — no names attached, no probing into their past histories or their present characters, simply the impression upon the poetic imagination made by these opposite types, the aura as it were, surrounding the visible person.

A LADY

You are beautiful and faded
Like an old opera tune
Played upon a harpsichord;
Or like the sun-flooded silks
Of an eighteenth-century boudoir.
In your eyes
Smolder the fallen roses of out-lived minutes,
And the perfume of your soul
Is vague and suffusing,
With the pungence of sealed spice-jars.
Your half-tones delight me,
And I grow mad with gazing
At your blent colors.

My Vigor is a new-minted penny,
Which I cast at your feet.
Gather it up from the dust,
That its sparkle may amuse you.

MUSIC

The neighbor sits in his window and plays the flute.
From my bed I can hear him,
And the round notes flutter and tap about the room,
And hit against each other,
Blurring to unexpected chords.   5
It is very beautiful,
With the little flute-notes all about me,
In the darkness.

In the daytime,
The neighbor eats bread and onions with one hand   10
And copies music with the other.

He is fat and has a bald head,
So I do not look at him,
But run quickly past his window.
There is always the sky to look at,   15
Or the water in the well!

But when night comes and he plays his flute,
I think of him as a young man,
With gold seals hanging from his watch,
And a blue coat with silver buttons.   20
As I lie in my bed
The flute-notes push against my ears and lips,
And I go to sleep, dreaming.

SUGGESTIONS FOR STUDY

1. In the two preceding poems point out the contrast between the writer and the person observed.

2. Find evidence in both poems that the writer likes antique things.

3. Find examples in both poems of the methods of the Imagists. (See p. 516.)

PATTERNS

"Patterns" is a lyric poem, deeply emotional and personal, as a good lyric should be. There is more than a touch of the romantic in both the setting and the suggestions of a story, but the poet was not merely describ-

ing a woman in a beautiful garden, waiting for her lover, nor did she intend
to tell a story, although both of these elements are present.   These are
merely part of the " pattern," that is, the woman of the poem is figured
as being and doing what a highly sensitized and cultured person might be
expected to do under the circumstances.   Through it all the poet is also
expressing an attitude toward life, and that is the most important of all.

I walk down the garden paths,
And all the daffodils
Are blowing, and the bright blue squills.
I walk down the patterned garden paths
In my stiff brocaded gown.   5
With my powdered hair and jeweled fan,
I too am a rare
Pattern.   As I wander down
The garden paths.

My dress is richly figured,   10
And the train
Makes a pink and silver stain
On the gravel, and the thrift
Of the borders.
Just a plate of current fashion,   15
Tripping by in high-heeled, ribboned shoes.
Not a softness anywhere about me,
Only whale-bone and brocade.
And I sink on a seat in the shade
Of a lime tree.   For my passion   20
Wars against the stiff brocade.
The daffodils and squills
Flutter in the breeze
As they please.
And I weep;   25
For the lime tree is in blossom
And one small flower has dropped upon my bosom.

And the plashing of waterdrops
In the marble fountain
Comes down the garden paths.   30
The dripping never stops.
Underneath my stiffened gown

Is the softness of a woman bathing in a marble basin,
A basin in the midst of hedges grown
So thick, she cannot see her lover hiding.   35
But she guesses he is near,
And the sliding of the water
Seems the stroking of a dear
Hand upon her.
What is summer in a fine brocaded gown!   40
I should like to see it lying in a heap upon the ground.
All the pink and silver crumpled up on the ground.

I would be the pink and silver as I ran along the paths,
And he would stumble after,
Bewildered by my laughter.   45
I should see the sun flashing from his sword-hilt and the buckles on
    his shoes.
I would choose
To lead him in a maze along the patterned paths,
A bright and laughing maze for my heavy-booted lover,
Till he caught me in the shade,   50
And the buttons of his waistcoat bruised my body as he clasped me,
Aching, melting, unafraid.
With the shadows of the leaves and the sundrops,
And the plopping of the waterdrops,
All about us in the open afternoon —   55
I am very like to swoon
With the weight of this brocade,
For the sun sifts through the shade.

Underneath the fallen blossom
In my bosom   60
Is a letter I have hid.
It was brought to me this morning by a rider from the Duke.
" Madam, we regret to inform you that Lord Hartwell
Died in action Thursday se'nnight."
As I read it in the white morning sunlight,   65
The letters squirmed like snakes.
" Any answer, Madam? " said my footman,
" No," I told him.
" See that the messenger takes some refreshment.
No, no answer."   70

And I walked into the garden,
Up and down the patterned paths,
In my stiff, correct brocade.
The blue and yellow flowers stood up proudly in the sun,
Each one.
I stood upright too, 75
Held rigid to the pattern
By the stiffness of my gown.
Up and down I walked
Up and down.
In a month he would have been my husband. 80
In a month, here, underneath this lime,
We would have broke the pattern;
He for me, and I for him,
He as Colonel, I as Lady,
On this shady seat. 85
He had a whim
That sunlight carried blessing.
And I answered, " It shall be as you have said."
Now he is dead.
In summer and in winter I shall walk 90
Up and down
The patterned garden paths
In my stiff brocaded gown.
The squills and daffodils
Will give place to pillared roses, and to asters, and to snow. 95
I shall go
Up and down,
In my gown
Gorgeously arrayed,
Boned and stayed. 100
And the softness of my body will be guarded from embrace
By each button, hook, and lace.
For the man who should loose me is dead,
Fighting with the Duke in Flanders,
In a pattern called a war. 105
Christ! What are patterns for?

SUGGESTIONS FOR STUDY

1. Look up " pattern " in the dictionary and point out how it fits the idea of the poem.

2. Notice some of the careful details of description and how they add to the picture.

3. Tell, briefly, the story back of the picture.

4. This poem is typical of the best so-called free verse. Comment on the rhythm, the irregularity of the line lengths, the rhyme or lack of it, and the general effect of it all.

5. Did you find the poem difficult to read or understand? Make some definite statement.

6. What is meant by the last line?

FOR FURTHER READING

POEMS

" Lilacs "
" Purple Grackles "
" The Garden by Moonlight "
" Wind and Silver "
" Night Clouds "

" Bombardment "
" Red Slippers "
" The Taxi "
" Lacquer Prints and Chinoiseries "
" A Tulip Garden "

VOLUMES

Sword Blades and Poppy Seeds
A Dome of Many-Colored Glass
Men, Women, and Ghosts
Can Grande's Castle

Pictures of the Floating World
What's O'clock?
East Wind
Ballads for Sale

ROBERT FROST (1875–   )

Strange that a poet who represents the very essence of New England farm life and who never writes of anything else should have spent the first ten years of his life in San Francisco and have been named after the Southern general, Robert E. Lee! Yet Robert Frost was a genuine New Englander by ancestry and disposition, and those first ten years before the death of his father and his return East with his mother seem to have left no impression on his poetry. Neither did the mill town of Lawrence, Massachusetts, where he went to school and later worked as bobbin-boy in a mill. It was always the country that charmed him. Spasmodic attempts at a college education both at Dartmouth and Harvard were given up through lack of interest. He supported his family by various temporary jobs, teaching, cobbling, editing, and the like. Finally, his grandfather bought him a farm in New Hampshire where, for a number of years, he worked and wrote but was unable to get much published. The sale of the farm enabled him to move his family to England and it was there, strange to say, that his distinctly American volumes, *A Boy's Will* and *North of Boston,* were published and received acclamation. He returned to America with his literary reputation established, but with no desire to give up farming in the New England hills. Intervals of lecturing and of teaching at Amherst and the University of Michigan are the only breaks in his peaceful farm life.

More than any other living poet, Frost gives us pastoral poetry, not the artificial picture of country life viewed from a classical library, but the simple, genuine life he knows, expressed in the idiom of daily speech. It is the combination of this familiar speech with the rhythm of blank verse which marks the distinctive style of Frost's poetry. His subject matter is sometimes the minutely observed details of nature interpreted through human experience, sometimes the exploration of the minds of his farm people with their instincts, their terrors, their griefs, and often their dumb inertia.

THE PASTURE

" The Pasture " was printed as a motto at the beginning of *North of Boston* and may well serve as an invitation to become acquainted with the work of Robert Frost.

> I'm going out to clean the pasture spring;
> I'll only stop to rake the leaves away
> (And wait to watch the water clear, I may):
> I shan't be gone long. — You come too.
>
> I'm going out to fetch the little calf
> That's standing by the mother. It's so young,
> It totters when she licks it with her tongue.
> I shan't be gone long. — You come too.

BIRCHES

Birch trees are fairly common in many parts of the country, and many boys besides Robert Frost have no doubt swung on them, but to the poet who in retrospect sees the birches and recalls his boyhood delight in swinging on them, they are suggestive of some of the most fundamental problems of life. That sounds as though you were about to read something difficult and involved, but such is far from being the case. Just as the birch tree is an everyday sight, so is the language of the poet that of every day. Frost writes in a way that seems conversational, as though he were talking to a group of friends by a fireside, and that is one of the charms of his poetry.

When I see birches bend to left and right
Across the line of straighter darker trees,
I like to think some boy's been swinging them.
But swinging doesn't bend them down to stay.
Ice-storms do that. Often you must have seen them   5
Loaded with ice a sunny winter morning
After a rain. They click upon themselves
As the breeze rises, and turn many-colored
As the stir cracks and crazes their enamel.
Soon the sun's warmth makes them shed crystal shells   10

Shattering and avalanching on the snow-crust —
Such heaps of broken glass to sweep away
You'd think the inner dome of heaven had fallen.
They are dragged to the withered bracken by the load,
And they seem not to break; though, once they are bowed   15
So low for long, they never right themselves:
You may see their trunks arching in the woods
Years afterward, trailing their leaves on the ground
Like girls on hands and knees that throw their hair
Before them over their heads to dry in the sun.   20

But I was going to say when Truth broke in
With all her matter-of-fact about the ice-storm
I should prefer to have some boy bend them
As he went out and in to fetch the cows —
Some boy too far from town to learn baseball, 25
Whose only play was what he found himself,
Summer or winter, and could play alone.
One by one he subdued his father's trees
By riding them down over and over again
Until he took the stiffness out of them, 30
And not one but hung limp, not one was left
For him to conquer. He learned all there was
To learn about not launching out too soon
And so not carrying the tree away
Clear to the ground. He always kept his poise 35
To the top branches, climbing carefully
With the same pains you use to fill a cup
Up to the brim, and even above the brim.
Then he flung outward, feet first, with a swish,
Kicking his way down through the air to the ground. 40

So was I once myself a swinger of birches;
And so I dream of going back to be.
It's when I'm weary of considerations,
And life is too much like a pathless wood
Where your face burns and tickles with the cobwebs 45
Broken across it, and one eye is weeping
From a twig's having lashed across it open.
I'd like to get away from earth awhile
And then come back to it and begin over.

May no fate wilfully misunderstand me 50
And half grant what I wish and snatch me away
Not to return. Earth's the right place for love:
I don't know where it's likely to go better.
I'd like to go by climbing a birch-tree,
And climb black branches up a snow-white trunk 55
Toward heaven, till the tree could bear no more,
But dipped its top and set me down again.
That would be good both going and coming back.
One could do worse than be a swinger of birches.

SUGGESTIONS FOR STUDY

1. Compare the description of the ice storm with that of the snowstorm in " Snowbound." Have you seen both kinds of storms in your own experience? Which kind do you think makes the more beautiful transformation of the world?

2. Point out words and details which make the description of the birches especially vivid.

3. What application to his own life does the poet make at the end?

STOPPING BY WOODS ON A SNOWY EVENING

As the title suggests, this poem is mainly a picture, or perhaps an episode set within the picture. But to the poet there was much more, as you will see from the last three lines.

Whose woods these are I think I know.
His house is in the village though;
He will not see me stopping here
To watch his woods fill up with snow.

My little horse must think it queer
To stop without a farmhouse near
Between the woods and frozen lake
The darkest evening of the year.

He gives his harness bells a shake
To ask if there is some mistake.
The only other sound's the sweep
Of easy wind and downy flake.

The woods are lovely, dark and deep,
But I have promises to keep,
And miles to go before I sleep,
And miles to go before I sleep.

THE BIRTHPLACE

" The Birthplace " and the poem that follows it are both taken from Frost's latest volume, *West-Running Brook* (1928). In both may be noted the qualities already mentioned in connection with his other poems

— simplicity of language, concreteness of picture, and a final twist that is of the essence of life.

Here further up the mountain slope
Than there was ever any hope,
My father built, enclosed a spring,
Strung chains of walls round everything,
Subdued the growth of earth to grass,
And brought our various lives to pass.
A dozen boys and girls we were.
The mountain seemed to like the stir,
And made of us a little while —
With always something in her smile.
Today she wouldn't know our name.
(No girl's of course has stayed the same.)
The mountain pushed us off her knees.
And now her lap is full of trees.

A MINOR BIRD

I have wished a bird would fly away,
And not sing by my house all day;

Have clapped my hands at him from the door
When it seemed as if I could bear no more.

The fault must partly have been in me.
The bird was not to blame for his key.

And of course there must be something wrong
In wanting to silence any song.

THE DEATH OF THE HIRED MAN

This is the best of Frost's longer narrative poems. While there is a story, definite and tragic, there is no action; merely a conversation between a New England farmer and his wife. As always in Frost's work, there are graphic pictures which enhance the setting, and in this poem help to soften the sting of the tragedy that the reader feels to be impending. Frost, although so much of his poetry concerns the Yankee farmer, never uses dialect to create a rustic effect.

Mary sat musing on the lamp-flame at the table
Waiting for Warren. When she heard his step,
She ran on tip-toe down the darkened passage
To meet him in the doorway with the news
And put him on his guard. " Silas is back."   5
She pushed him outward with her through the door
And shut it after her. " Be kind," she said.
She took the market things from Warren's arms
And set them on the porch, then drew him down   10
To sit beside her on the wooden steps.

" When was I ever anything but kind to him?
But I'll not have the fellow back," he said.
" I told him so last haying, didn't I?
' If he left then,' I said, ' that ended it.'
What good is he? Who else will harbor him   15
At his age for the little he can do?
What help he is there's no depending on.
Off he goes always when I need him most.
' He thinks he ought to earn a little pay,
Enough at least to buy tobacco with,   20
So he won't have to beg and be beholden.'
' All right,' I say, ' I can't afford to pay
Any fixed wages, though I wish I could.'
' Some one else can.' ' Then some one else will have to.'
I shouldn't mind his bettering himself   25
If that was what it was. You can be certain,
When he begins like that, there's some one at him
Trying to coax him off with pocket-money —
In haying time, when any help is scarce.
In winter he comes back to us. I'm done."   30

' Sh! not so loud: he'll hear you," Mary said.

" I want him to: he'll have to soon or late."

" He's worn out. He's asleep beside the stove.
When I came up from Rowe's I found him here,
Huddled against the barn door fast asleep,   35
A miserable sight, and frightening, too —
You needn't smile — I didn't recognize him —

I wasn't looking for him — and he's changed.
Wait till you see."

                    " Where did you say he'd been? "

" He didn't say. I dragged him to the house,   40
And gave him tea and tried to make him smoke.
I tried to make him talk about his travels,
Nothing would do: he just kept nodding off."

" What did he say?   Did he say anything? "

" But little."

                    " Anything?   Mary, confess   45
He said he'd come to ditch the meadow for me."

" Warren! "

          " But did he?   I just want to know."

" Of course he did. What would you have him say?
Surely you wouldn't grudge the poor old man
Some humble way to save his self-respect.
He added, if you really care to know,   50
He meant to clear the upper pasture, too.
That sounds like something you have heard before?
Warren, I wish you could have heard the way
He jumbled everything. I stopped to look   55
Two or three times — he made me feel so queer —
To see if he was talking in his sleep.
He ran on Harold Wilson — you remember —
The boy you had in haying four years since.
He's finished school, and teaching in his college.   60
Silas declares you'll have to get him back.
He says they two will make a team for work:
Between them they will lay this farm as smooth!
The way he mixed that in with other things.
He thinks young Wilson a likely lad, though daft   65
On education — you know how they fought
All through July under the blazing sun,
Silas up on the cart to build the load,
Harold along beside to pitch it on."

" Yes, I took care to keep well out of earshot."   70

" Well, those days trouble Silas like a dream.
You wouldn't think they would. How some things linger!
Harold's young college boy's assurance piqued him.
After so many years he still keeps finding
Good arguments he sees he might have used.   75
I sympathize. I know just how it feels
To think of the right thing to say too late.
Harold's associated in his mind with Latin.
He asked me what I thought of Harold's saying
He studied Latin like the violin   80
Because he liked it — that an argument!
He said he couldn't make the boy believe
He could find water with a hazel prong —
Which showed how much good school had ever done him.
He wanted to go over that. But most of all   85
He thinks if he could have another chance
To teach him how to build a load of hay — "

" I know, that's Silas' one accomplishment.
He bundles every forkful in its place,
And tags and numbers it for future reference,   90
So he can find and easily dislodge it
In the unloading. Silas does that well.
He takes it out in bunches like birds' nests.
You never see him standing on the hay
He's trying to lift, straining to lift himself."   95

" He thinks if he could teach him that, he'd be
Some good perhaps to some one in the world.
He hates to see a boy the fool of books.
Poor Silas, so concerned for other folk,
And nothing to look backward to with pride,   100
And nothing to look forward to with hope,
So now and never any different."

Part of a moon was falling down the west,
Dragging the whole sky with it to the hills.
Its light poured softly in her lap. She saw   105

83. **find water with a hazel prong:** a farm superstition that a proper location for a well could be ascertained by walking around holding a branch in
front of one. The branch is supposed to bend down at the point where water is
to be found under the surface.

And spread her apron to it. She put out her hand
Among the harp-like morning-glory strings,
Taut with the dew from garden bed to eaves,
As if she played unheard the tenderness
That wrought on him beside her in the night.　110
" Warren," she said, " he has come home to die:
You needn't be afraid he'll leave you this time."

" Home," he mocked gently.

　　　　　　　　　　" Yes, what else but home?
It all depends on what you mean by home.
Of course he's nothing to us, any more　115
Than was the hound that came a stranger to us
Out of the woods, worn out upon the trail."

" Home is the place where, when you have to go there,
They have to take you in."

　　　　　　　　　　" I should have called it
Something you somehow haven't to deserve."　120

Warren leaned out and took a step or two,
Picked up a little stick, and brought it back
And broke it in his hand and tossed it by.
" Silas has better claim on us, you think,
Than on his brother?　Thirteen little miles　125
As the road winds would bring him to his door.
Silas has walked that far no doubt today.
Why didn't he go there?　His brother's rich,
A somebody — director in the bank."

" He never told us that."

　　　　　　　　　　" We know it though."　130

" I think his brother ought to help, of course.
I'll see to that if there is need. He ought of right
To take him in, and might be willing to —
He may be better than appearances.
But have some pity on Silas. Do you think　135
If he'd had any pride in claiming kin ·

Or anything he looked for from his brother,
He'd keep so still about him all this time? "

" I wonder what's between them."

        " I can tell you.
Silas is what he is — we wouldn't mind him —   140
But just the kind that kinsfolk can't abide.
He never did a thing so very bad.
He don't know why he isn't quite as good
As anyone. He won't be made ashamed
To please his brother, worthless though he is."   145

" I can't think Si ever hurt any one."

" No, but he hurt my heart the way he lay
And rolled his old head on that sharp-edged chair-back.
He wouldn't let me put him on the lounge.
You must go in and see what you can do.   150
I made the bed up for him there tonight.
You'll be surprised at him — how much he's broken.
His working days are done; I'm sure of it."

" I'd not be in a hurry to say that."

" I haven't been. Go, look, see for yourself.   155
But, Warren, please remember how it is:
He's come to help you ditch the meadow.
He has a plan. You mustn't laugh at him.
He may not speak of it, and then he may.
I'll sit and see if that small sailing cloud   160
Will hit or miss the moon."

       It hit the moon.
Then there were three, making a dim row,
The moon, the little silver cloud, and she.

Warren returned — too soon, it seemed to her,
Slipped to her side, caught up her hand and waited.   165

" Warren? " she questioned.

      " Dead," was all he answered.

SUGGESTIONS FOR STUDY

1. Notice how simple the vocabulary of this poem is. Probably there is not a single word in it with which you are unfamiliar. See whether you can find one.

2. In the second stanza, ll. 11–30, remember that Warren is saying all of this to his wife. Between whom is the conversation he is quoting?

3. What points of contrast do you find between Silas and Harold Wilson? Are these differences principally between youth and age, or between two kinds of background and education?

4. Study the two definitions of home, ll. 118–120. Which do you prefer?

5. What does the discussion about the rich brother, ll. 124–145, add to our understanding of Silas?

6. What do you learn of the character of Warren and Mary from their conversation?

7. What makes the end of the poem especially impressive?

8. This poem may be dramatized before the class if you have readers who can do it without spoiling the quiet pathos of the poem.

FOR FURTHER READING

POEMS

"The Tuft of Flowers"
"Reluctance"
"Mending Wall"
"The Runaway"
"To the Thawing Wind"
"After Apple Picking"

"A Prayer in Spring"
"A Hillside Thaw"
"The Cow in Apple Time"
"The Road not Taken"
"Brown's Descent, or the Willy-Nilly Ride"

VOLUMES

A Boy's Will
North of Boston
Mountain Interval

New Hampshire
West-Running Brook

CARL SANDBURG (1878–   )

If Masters can be said to have immortalized the small town, another Illinois poet, Carl Sandburg, has shown that poetry can express the spirit of the great ungainly city with its sharp contrasts of beauty and ugliness. Just as the Cambridge poets were fitted at Harvard for their literary careers, so Carl Sandburg was fitted to become the poet laureate of industrialism at the college of Hard Work where he took courses in being a barber-shop porter, a scene-shifter, a truck-handler, a potter's apprentice, a hotel dish-washer, a construction worker on a railroad, a harvest hand, soldier, and janitor. Incidentally, he did go to a small college in Illinois for a time, but that was not his real education. Naturally, his product turned out to be considerably different from that of Longfellow and Lowell. From the beginning Whitman has been his master as to both freedom of form and that vital facing of life which neither discards nor blinds itself to anything. A comparison of Whitman's " Mannahatta " (p. 656) and Sandburg's " Chicago " shows our two greatest cities, each championed in song like two mighty heroes of ancient days sung by their bards. One can almost imagine the chants intoned to the chords of a crude harp. Sandburg does, indeed, sing to the accompaniment of his guitar many of the folk songs he has collected.

When *Chicago Poems* was published in 1916, it created much violent opposition. Many people felt as Sidney Lanier did about Whitman when he defined the latter's poetry as " hugh raw collops slashed from the rump of poetry, and never mind gristle." But as Louis Untermeyer pointed out, we must remember " that Sandburg was only brutal when dealing with brutality; that beneath his toughness, he was one of the tenderest of living poets."

" Chicago," the title piece in *Chicago Poems*, was first published in *Poetry, a Magazine of Verse*. At that time it won a prize of two hundred dollars as being " the best poem written by a citizen of the United States during the year." It was the foundation stone of Sandburg's fame. Following is an extract from this famous poem.

CHICAGO

Hog Butcher for the World,
Tool Maker, Stacker of Wheat,
Player with Railroads and the Nation's Freight Handler;
Stormy, husky, brawling,
City of the Big Shoulders: 5
They tell me you are wicked and I believe them, for I have seen your
    painted women under the gas lamps luring the farm boys.
And they tell me you are crooked and I answer: Yes, it is true I have
    seen the gunman kill and go free to kill again.
And they tell me you are brutal and my reply is: On the faces of
    women and children I have seen the marks of wanton hunger.
And having answered so I turn once more to those who sneer at this
    my city, and I give them back the sneer and say to them:

Come and show me another city with lifted head singing so proud
    to be alive and coarse and strong and cunning.   10
Flinging magnetic curses amid the toil of piling job on job, here is a
    tall bold slugger set vivid against the little soft cities;
Fierce as a dog with tongue lapping for action, cunning as a savage
    pitted against the wilderness,
      Bareheaded,
      Shoveling,
      Wrecking,   15
      Planning,
      Building, breaking, rebuilding.
Under the smoke, dust all over his mouth, laughing with white teeth,
Under the terrible burden of destiny laughing as a young man laughs,
Laughing even as an ignorant fighter laughs who has never lost a
    battle,   20
Bragging and laughing that under his wrist is the pulse, and under
    his ribs the heart of the people,
            Laughing!
Laughing the stormy, husky, brawling laughter of Youth, half-naked,
    sweating, proud to be Hog Butcher, Tool Maker, Stacker of
    Wheat, Player with Railroads and Freight Handler to the
    Nation.

BUTTONS

    The effect of this as in so many of Sandburg's poems lies in a single sharp contrast, the parenthesis startling one like a flash-back in a moving picture. The scene is, of course, during the World War, but the poet's mental picture was probably reinforced by memories of his own experiences as a soldier in Porto Rico during the Spanish-American War.

I have been watching the war map slammed up for advertising in
    front of the newspaper office.
Buttons — red and yellow buttons — blue and black buttons — are
    shoved back and forth across the map.

A laughing young man, sunny with freckles,
Climbs a ladder, yells a joke to somebody in the crowd,
And then fixes a yellow button one inch west
And follows the yellow button with a black button one inch west.

(Ten thousand men and boys twist on their bodies in a red soak
    along a river edge,
Gasping of wounds, calling for water, some rattling death in their
    throats.)

Who would guess what it cost to move two buttons one inch on the
    war map here in front of the newspaper office where the freckle-
    faced young man is laughing at us?

GRASS

As a companion picture to the preceding poem we have this one showing
the healing power of nature over war. Note the unique way in which this
is suggested. The five battles mentioned were those involving the greatest
loss of human life in the Napoleonic, the Civil, and the World Wars.

Pile the bodies high at Austerlitz and Waterloo.
Shovel them under and let me work —
        I am the grass; I cover all.

And pile them high at Gettysburg
And pile them high at Ypres and Verdun.
Shovel them under and let me work.
Two years, ten years, and passengers ask the conductor:
        What place is this?
        Where are we now?

        I am the grass.
        Let me work.

A FENCE

The first three lines of this poem suggest only the workingman's resentment of exclusiveness; the last line lifts it into the realm of exquisite
imagination.

Now the stone house on the lake front is finished and the workmen
    are beginning the fence.
The palings are made of iron bars with steel points that can stab the
    life out of any man who falls on them.

As a fence, it is a masterpiece, and will shut off the rabble and all
vagabonds and hungry men and all wandering children looking
for a place to play.
Passing through the bars and over the steel points will go nothing
except Death and the Rain and Tomorrow.

CHILD OF THE ROMANS

Remembering that Sandburg has himself seen both the points of view
shown in this poem, we realize all the more keenly the underlying irony.
Sandburg's father worked on a railroad construction gang, as the poet
himself did for a short time.   The railroad theme recurs in a number of
his poems such as " Limited," " Omaha," and " Southern Pacific."

The dago shovelman sits by the railroad track
Eating a noon meal of bread and bologna.
   A train whirls by, and men and women at tables
   Alive with red roses and yellow jonquils,
   Eat steaks running with brown gravy,
    Strawberries and cream, éclairs and coffee.
The dago shovelman finishes the dry bread and bologna,

Washes it down with the dipper from the water-boy,
And goes back to the second half of a ten-hour day's work,
Keeping the road-bed so the roses and jonquils
Shake hardly at all in the cut glass vases
Standing slender on the tables in the dining car.

CLEAN CURTAINS

New neighbors came to the corner house at Congress and Green Streets.

The look of their clean white curtains was the same as the rim of a nun's bonnet.

One way was an oyster pail factory, one way they made candy, one way paper boxes, strawboard cartons.

The warehouse trucks shook the dust of the ways loose and the wheels whirled dust — there was dust of hoof and wagon wheel and rubber tire — dust of police and fire wagons — dust of the winds that circled at midnights and noon listening to no prayers.

" O mother, I know the heart of you," I sang passing the rim of a nun's bonnet — O white curtains — and people clean as the prayers of Jesus here in the faded ramshackle at Congress and Green.

Dust and the thundering trucks won — the barrages of the street wheels and the lawless wind took their way — was it five weeks or six the little mother, the new neighbors, battled and then took away the white prayers in the windows?

A COIN

" A Coin " and the three following poems all treat of money, yet in what different ways! " In a Back Alley " is among the many poetic tributes to Lincoln. The second commemorates the passing of the buffaloes from America. The third uses money as a symbol of fate. The fourth introduces it whimsically into an unusual nature lyric.

Your western heads here cast on money,
You are the two that fade away together,
   Partners in the mist.

Lunging buffalo shoulder,
Lean Indian face,
We who come after where you are gone
Salute your forms on the new nickel.

You are
To us:
The past.

Runners
On the prairie:
Good-by.

IN A BACK ALLEY

Remembrance for a great man is this:
The newsies are pitching pennies,
And on the copper disk is the man's face.
Dead lover of boys, what do you ask for now?

FATE

Fate comes with pennies or dollars.
An Indian head or the Goddess of Liberty: it is all the same to Fate.
One day copper, one day silver, and these are samples:
   The cry held back
   the kiss kept under
   the song choked down
   the wish never spoken.
They are pennies and dollars these.
The girl at the sink washing dishes knows them.
The girl who has breakfast in bed knows them.

WIND SONG

Long ago I learned how to sleep,
In an old apple orchard where the wind swept by, counting its money
    and throwing it away,
In a wind-gaunt orchard where the limbs forked out and listened or
    never listened at all,
In a passel of trees where the branches trapped the wind into
    whistling, " Who, who are you? "
I slept with my head in an elbow on a summer afternoon and there
    I took a sleep lesson.
Then I went away saying: I know why they sleep,
I know how they trap the tricky winds.
Long ago I learned how to listen to the singing wind and how to
    forget and how to hear the deep whine,
Slapping and lapsing under the day-blue and the night stars:
        Who, who are you?

        Who can ever forget
        listening to the wind go by,
        counting its money
        and throwing it away?

NIGHT STUFF

Listen a while, the moon is a lovely woman,
    a lonely woman, lost in a silver dress,
    lost in a circus rider's silver dress.

Listen a while, the lake by night is a lonely woman,
    a lovely woman, circled with birches and pines,
    mixing their green and white among stars
    shattered in spray clear nights.

I know the moon and lake have twisted the roots under my heart
    the same as a lonely woman, a lovely woman,
    in a silver dress, in a circus rider's silver dress.

PRAYERS OF STEEL

This poem returns to the industrial world and treats it with a fervency that is moving. It voices the aspiration of mighty building, of the slender white towers which are rising up everywhere in our great cities. Can you see any implication in it similar to Holmes's " Build thee more stately mansions, O my Soul " ?

Lay me on an anvil, O God.
Beat me and hammer me into a crowbar.
Let me pry loose old walls.
Let me lift and loosen old foundations.

Lay me on an anvil, O God.
Beat me and hammer me into a steel spike.
Drive me into the girders that hold a skyscraper together.
Take red-hot rivets and fasten me into the central girders.
Let me be the great nail holding a skyscraper through blue nights
    into white stars.

GOOD MORNING, AMERICA

In his latest book, *Good Morning, America*, Sandburg again treats of skyscrapers. The point of view is not from below toward the heights as in " Prayers of Steel," but from above downward. The reader is in the position of a dweller on Mount Olympus looking down at the phenomena created by " the little two-legged joker." Then comes the contemplation of the god of speed we have reared for ourselves, with the underlying suggestion of our self-imposed slavery to it. Sections 1 and 16 of the title poem follow.

I

In the evening there is a sunset sonata comes to the cities.
There is a march of little armies to the dwindling of drums.
The skyscrapers throw their tall lengths of walls into black bastions
    on the red west.
The skyscrapers fasten their perpendicular alphabets far across the
    changing silver triangles of stars and streets.

And who made 'em? Who made the skyscrapers?   5
Man made 'em, the little two-legged joker, Man.
Out of his head, out of his dreaming, scheming skypiece,
Out of proud little diagrams that danced softly in his head —
    Man made the skyscrapers.

With his two hands, with shovels, hammers, wheelbarrows, with
    engines, conveyors, signal whistles, with girders, molds, steel,
    concrete —   10
Climbing on scaffolds and falsework with blueprints, riding the
    beams and dangling in mid-air to call, Come on, boys —
                                 Man made the skyscrapers.

When one tall skyscraper is torn down
To make room for a taller one to go up,
Who takes down and puts up those two skyscrapers?   15
Man . . . the little two-legged joker . . . Man.

16

The silent litany of the workmen goes on —
Speed, speed, we are the makers of speed.
We make the flying, crying motors,
Clutches, brakes, and axles,   20
Gears, ignitions, accelerators,
Spokes and springs and shock absorbers.
The silent litany of the workmen goes on —
Speed, speed, we are the makers of speed;
Axles, clutches, levers, shovels,   25
We make the signals and lay the way —
    Speed, speed.

The trees come down to our tools.
We carve the wood to the wanted shape.
The whining propeller's song in the sky,   30
The steady drone of the overland truck,
Comes from our hands; us; the makers of speed.

Speed; the turbines crossing the Big Pond,
Every nut and bolt, every bar and screw,
Every fitted and whirling shaft,   35
They came from us, the makers,
Us, who know how,
Us, the high designers and the automatic feeders,
Us, with heads,
Us, with hands,   40
Us, on the long haul, the short flight,
We are the makers; lay the blame on us —
The makers of speed.

SUGGESTIONS FOR STUDY

1. In what ways do you find Sandburg's poems like Whitman's?   In what ways different?

2. Point out all the poems in this group in which Sandburg makes use of striking contrast.

3. In which poems has he used a common object as a symbol of some deeper truth of life?

4. Where do you find examples of his " brutal " use of language? Where of delicacy of language?

5. On the whole does Sandburg seem to be more concerned with giving us external pictures of industrial life or interpretations of its underlying significance?

FOR FURTHER READING

The best from the first four volumes of poems have been gathered in the volume *Selected Poems of Carl Sandburg*. Recommended individual poems are:

" Fog "
" Cool Tombs "
" Smoke and Steel "
" Smoke Rose Gold "
" Limited "
" Jazz Fantasia "
" Nocturne in a Deserted Brick-
     yard "
" Monotone "

" Work Gangs "
" Omaha "
" Southern Pacific "
" A. E. F."
" Losers "
" Flash Crimson "
" Buffalo Dusk "
" Three Pieces on the Smoke of
     Autumn "

VOLUMES

Chicago
Cornhuskers
Smoke and Steel

Slabs of the Sunburnt West
Good Morning, America

NICHOLAS VACHEL LINDSAY (1879–1931)

Vachel Lindsay is our modern American troubadour. He believes that poetry is made not for the eye, but for the ear, and he is spending his life journeying up and down the land singing his songs, much as did the ballad-singers in the days of knights and feudal castles. Sometimes he makes dignified tours from city to city or college to college, appearing quite properly on lecture-platform or at college chapel. But he has been known to throw convention to the winds, and set off boldly afoot across country with nothing to pay his way except his little pamphlet, *Rimes to be Traded for Bread.* Because Mr. Lindsay is essentially a singer, his poems must be chanted aloud in the Lindsay manner, or much of their appeal is lost. To help the reader, the poet has, in many of his longer poems, printed directions for reading by the side of his verses.

After graduating from high school in Springfield, Illinois, Mr. Lindsay attended Hiram College and art schools in Chicago and New York. Shortly he was back in his home town, preaching his gospel of beauty through an attempted Ruskin revival, and campaigning against civic unrighteousness and ugliness in his privately printed weekly *War Bulletin.* " Ugliness," he said, " is a kind of misgovernment." He has continued ever since to be a John the Baptist preaching to a materialistic and cynical age the Americanism of Walt Whitman and the beauty and art of Edgar Allan Poe.

Mr. Lindsay has written many delightful rhymes for children. He has developed " poem games " to which children dance, needing no other instrument to beat the rhythm except the human voice. He has sung songs about movie stars, and has written one whole prose volume on *The Art of the Motion Picture.* He has brought forth a Southern challenge to the New Englanders in his recent " The Virginians Are Coming Again." He has set to music the lives of picturesque and vivid Americans — Old Andrew Jackson, Bryan, John Brown, Johnny Appleseed, Alexander Campbell. But his poetry is too various to be divided into neat little pigeon-holes. The best of it has given Mr. Lindsay an international reputation as the modern American minstrel.

THE SANTA FE TRAIL [1]

A HUMORESQUE

One of Mr. Lindsay's prose books is called *Adventures While Preaching the Gospel of Beauty.* It relates his experience while tramping across country from Springfield, Illinois, to the Southwest by way of Kansas. " The Santa Fe Trail " is a souvenir of that trip. The poet-tramp sits on a milestone by the side of the road, while, in the form of cars labeled ·with the city pennants popular around 1912, " the United States goes by."

This time Mr. Lindsay gives the reader full directions. If you follow them, this poem will bring to the class a whole day of color and sound, beginning with sunrise and the first faint horn in the East, moving on

[1] From *Collected Poems* by Vachel Lindsay. Reprinted by permission of The Macmillan Company, publishers.

through screaming cars and freight-trains, and ending with the evening whispers of the prairie fairies hidden in the corn and grass. It is a poem of sharp contrasts, and demands oral rendition, utilizing the full range of the voice.

I asked the old Negro, "What is that bird that sings so well?" He answered: "That is the Rachel-Jane." "Hasn't it another name, lark, or thrush, or the like?" "No. Jus' Rachel-Jane."

I. IN WHICH A RACING AUTO COMES FROM THE EAST

This is the order of the music of the morning: —
First, from the far East comes but a crooning.
The crooning turns to a sunrise singing.
Hark to the *calm*-horn, *balm*-horn, *psalm*-horn.
Hark to the *faint*-horn, *quaint*-horn, *saint*-
horn. . . .   5

To be sung delicately, to an improvised tune.

Hark to the *pace*-horn, *chase*-horn, *race*-horn.
And the holy veil of the dawn has gone.
Swiftly the brazen car comes on.
It burns in the East as the sunrise burns.
I see great flashes where the far trail turns.   10
Its eyes are lamps like the eyes of dragons.
It drinks gasoline from big red flagons.
Butting through the delicate mists of the morning,
It comes like lightning, goes past roaring.
It will hail all the wind-mills, taunting, ringing, 15
Dodge the cyclones,
Count the milestones,
On through the ranges the prairie-dog tills —
Scooting past the cattle on the thousand hills. . . .
Ho for the tear-horn, scare-horn, dare-horn,   20
Ho for the *gay*-horn, *bark*-horn, *bay*-horn.
Ho for Kansas, land that restores us
When houses choke us, and great books bore us!
Sunrise Kansas, harvester's Kansas,
A million men have found you before us.   25

To be sung or read with great speed.

To be read or sung in a rolling bass, with some deliberation.

II. IN WHICH MANY AUTOS PASS WESTWARD

I want live things in their pride to remain.   *In an even, deliberate,*
I will not kill one grasshopper vain   *narrative manner.*
Though he eats a hole in my shirt like a door.
I let him out, give him one chance more.
Perhaps, while he gnaws my hat in his whim,   30
Grasshopper lyrics occur to him.

I am a tramp by the long trail's border,
Given to squalor, rags and disorder.
I nap and amble and yawn and look,
Write fool-thoughts in my grubby book,   35
Recite to the children, explore at my ease,
Work when I work, beg when I please,
Give crank-drawings, that make folks stare
To the half-grown boys in the sunset glare,
And get me a place to sleep in the hay   40
At the end of a live-and-let-live day.

I find in the stubble of the new-cut weeds
A whisper and a feasting, all one needs:
The whisper of the strawberries, white and red
Here where the new-cut weeds lie dead.   45

But I would not walk all alone till I die
Without some life-drunk horns going by.
Up round this apple-earth they come
Blasting the whispers of the morning dumb: —
Cars in a plain realistic row.   50
And fair dreams fade
When the raw horns blow.

On each snapping pennant
A big black name: —
The careering city   55
Whence each car came.
They tour from Memphis, Atlanta, Savannah,   *Like a train-caller in*
Tallahassee and Texarkana.   *a Union Depot.*
They tour from St. Louis, Columbus, Manistee,
They tour from Peoria, Davenport, Kankakee.   60

Cars from Concord, Niagara, Boston,
Cars from Topeka, Emporia, and Austin.
Cars from Chicago, Hannibal, Cairo.
Cars from Alton, Oswego, Toledo.
Cars from Buffalo, Kokomo, Delphi,   65
Cars from Lodi, Carmi, Loami.
Ho for Kansas, land that restores us
When houses choke us, and great books bore us!
While I watch the highroad
And look at the sky,   70
While I watch the clouds in amazing grandeur
Roll their legions without rain
Over the blistering Kansas plain —
While I sit by the milestone
And watch the sky,   75
The United States
Goes by.

Listen to the iron-horns, ripping, racking.   *To be given very harshly, with a snapping explosiveness.*
Listen to the quack-horns, slack and clacking.
Way down the road, trilling like a toad,   80
Here comes the *dice*-horn, here comes the *vice*-
   horn,
Here comes the *snarl*-horn, *brawl*-horn, *lewd*-horn,
Followed by the *prude*-horn, bleak and squeak-
   ing: —
(Some of them from Kansas, some of them from
   Kansas.)
Here comes the *hod*-horn, *plod*-horn, *sod*-horn, 85
Nevermore-to-*roam*-horn, *loam*-horn, *home*-horn.
(Some of them from Kansas, some of them from
   Kansas.)
       Far away the Rachel-Jane   *To be read or sung, well-nigh in a whisper.*
       Not defeated by the horns
       Sings amid a hedge of thorns: —   90
       " Love and life,
       Eternal youth —
       Sweet, sweet, sweet, sweet,
       Dew and glory,
       Love and truth,   95
       Sweet, sweet, sweet, sweet."

WHILE SMOKE-BLACK FREIGHTS ON THE DOUBLE-
TRACKED RAILROAD,
DRIVEN AS THOUGH BY THE FOUL-FIEND'S OX-GOAD,
SCREAMING TO THE WEST COAST, SCREAMING TO THE
EAST,
CARRY OFF A HARVEST, BRING BACK A FEAST,   100
HARVESTING MACHINERY AND HARNESS FOR THE
BEAST.
THE HAND-CARS WHIZ, AND RATTLE ON THE RAILS,
THE SUNLIGHT FLASHES ON THE TIN DINNER-
PAILS.

Louder and louder,
faster and faster.

And then, in an instant,
Ye modern men,   105
Behold the procession once again,
Listen to the iron-horns, ripping, racking,
Listen to the *wise*-horn, desperate-to-*advise* horn,
Listen to the *fast*-horn, *kill*-horn, *blast*-horn. . . .

In a rolling bass,
with increasing
deliberation.

With a snapping
explosiveness.

    Far away the Rachel-Jane   110
    Not defeated by the horns
    Sings amid a hedge of thorns: —
    " Love and life,
    Eternal youth,
    Sweet, sweet, sweet, sweet,   115
    Dew and glory,
    Love and truth.
    Sweet, sweet, sweet, sweet. "

To be sung or read
well-nigh in a
whisper.

The mufflers open on a score of cars
With wonderful thunder,   120
CRACK, CRACK, CRACK,
CRACK-CRACK, CRACK-CRACK,
CRACK-CRACK-CRACK, . . .
Listen to the gold-horn . . .
Old-horn . . .   125
Cold-horn . . .

To be brawled in the
beginning with a
snapping explosive-
ness, ending in a
languorous chant.

And all of the tunes, till the night comes down
On hay-stack, and ant-hill, and wind-bitten town.
Then far in the west, as in the beginning,
Dim in the distance, sweet in retreating,   130
Hark to the faint-horn, quaint-horn, saint-horn,
Hark to the calm-horn, balm-horn, psalm-
horn. . . .

To be sung to
exactly the same
whispered tune as
the first five lines.

They are hunting the goals that they under-
    stand: —
San Francisco and the brown sea sand.
My goal is the mystery the beggars win.   135
I am caught in the web the night-winds spin.
The edge of the wheat-ridge speaks to me.
I talk with the leaves of the mulberry tree.
And now I hear, as I sit all alone
In the dusk, by another big Santa Fe stone,   140
The souls of the tall corn gathering round
And the gay little souls of the grass in the ground.
Listen to the tale the cotton-wood tells.
Listen to the wind-mills, singing o'er the wells.
Listen to the whistling flutes without price   145
Of myriad prophets out of paradise.
Harken to the wonder
That the night-air carries. . . .
Listen . . . to . . . the . . . whisper . . .
Of . . . the . . . prairies . . . fairies   150
    Singing o'er the fairy plain: —
    "Sweet, sweet, sweet, sweet.
    Love and glory,
    Stars and rain,
    Sweet, sweet, sweet, sweet. . . ."   155

This section beginning sonorously, ending in a languorous whisper.

To the same whispered tune as the Rachel-Jane song — but very slowly.

SUGGESTIONS FOR STUDY

1. How many different kinds of horns does Mr. Lindsay name? Could you add to the list?
2. What details of the poet's life as a tramp do you find?
3. What indication is there in this poem that Mr. Lindsay is an artist as well as a poet?
4. What is the meaning of the message of the Rachel-Jane?
5. What is Mr. Lindsay's attitude towards the autoists he watches?

FOR FURTHER READING

"The Congo"
"Abraham Lincoln Walks at Midnight"
"The Moon's the North Wind's Cooky"
"Yet Gentle Will the Griffin Be"
"The Broncho That Would Not Be Broken"
"The Ghosts of the Buffaloes"
"In Praise of Johnny Appleseed"
"The Statue of Old Andrew Jackson"

" Bryan, Bryan, Bryan, Bryan " " The Potatoes' Dance "
" The Kallyope Yell "   " Simon Legree "
ᵡ The Virginians Are Coming   " General William Booth Enters
Again "   into Heaven "

JOHN G. NEIHARDT (1881–   )

Unfortunately, John G. Neihardt's greatest contribution to American literature cannot be reproduced here because of its length. For many years he has been at work building a great American epic, or cycle of heroic poems, dealing with the entire period of Western development from the year 1822, when Ashley and Henry of St. Louis ascended the Missouri River, to 1890 when Indian resistance on the plains ended. In preparation for this work he has spent many years with Indians, has interviewed many old-timers among the whites, and has made a careful search of historical records. Between 1915 and 1925 three sections of the cycle have appeared: *The Song of Three Friends*, *The Song of Hugh Glass* (published first, but second in the sequence of the epic), and *The Song of the Indian Wars*. The two short poems here presented, though lyrical in form, suggest the heroic qualities of the epic. The first is the cry of the strong man never to see his strength shrink from him; the second is, fittingly enough, concerned with the most loudly acclaimed national hero of our own day, Charles Lindbergh. It was published in the St. Louis *Post-Dispatch* during the Lindbergh celebration of July, 1927.

LET ME LIVE OUT MY YEARS [1]

Let me live out my years in heat of blood!
Let me die drunken with the dreamer's wine!
Let me not see this soul-house built of mud
Go toppling to the dust — a vacant shrine!

Let me go quickly like a candle light
Snuffed out just at the heyday of its glow!
Give me high noon — and let it then be night!
Thus would I go.

And grant me, when I face the grisly Thing,
One haughty cry to pierce the gray Perhaps!
O let me be a tune-swept fiddlestring
That feels the Master Melody — *and snaps!*

[1] From *The Quest* by John G. Neihardt. Reprinted by permission of The Macmillan Company, publishers.

THE LYRIC DEED

We sighed and said, The world's high purpose falters;
Here in the West the human hope is sold;
Behold, our cities are but monstrous altars
That reek in worship to the Beast of Gold!

Now no rapt silence hears the bard intoning;   5
Our lurid stacks paint out the ancient awe,
And lock-step millions to the motor's moaning
Are herded into Moloch's yawning maw.

With men we stoke our diabolic fires;
Of smithied hearts the soaring steel is made   10
To dwarf and darken all our godward spires
With drunken towers of Trade.

We said it, blinded with the sweat of duty,
And now, behold! emerging from the dark,
Winged with the old divinity of beauty,   15
Our living dream mounts morning like a lark!

Of common earth men wrought it, and of wonder;
With lightning have men bitted it and shod;
The throat of it is clothed with singing thunder —
And Lindbergh rides with God!   20

We have not known, but surely now we know it;
Not thus achieve venality and greed;
The dreaming doer is the master poet —
And lo, the perfect lyric in a deed!

The sunset and the world's new morning hear it;   25
Ecstatic in the rhythmic motor's roar,
Not seas shall sunder now the human spirit,
For space shall be no more!

FOR FURTHER READING

" The Song of Three Friends "
" The Song of Hugh Glass "
" The Song of the Indian Wars "

Sara Teasdale (1884–   )

As with Emily Dickinson, the chronicle of outward actions in the life of Sara Teasdale is of little importance compared with the inner action of thought and imagination. That she was born and educated in St. Louis, Missouri, traveled extensively, and lives in New York City becomes a matter of interest only in the sense of pinning down a lovely butterfly and identifying it with scientific tags. At least we have pinned her to a fact or two. Her best volumes, *Love Songs* (1917) and *Flame and Shadow* (1920), are filled with delicate bits like the following samples — elusive little flashes of emotion caught and molded for us like tiny figures in ivory. They are little coins for the memory such as she here describes.

THE COIN [1]

Into my heart's treasury
  I slipped a coin
That time cannot take
  Nor a thief purloin —
Oh, better than the minting
  Of a gold-crowned king
Is the safe-kept memory
  Of a lovely thing.

I SHALL NOT CARE [2]

When I am dead and over me bright April
  Shakes out her rain-drenched hair,
Though you should lean above me broken-hearted,
  I shall not care.

I shall have peace, as leafy trees are peaceful
  When rain bends down the bough;
And I shall be more silent and cold-hearted
  Than you are now.

---

[1] From *Flame and Shadow* by Sara Teasdale. Reprinted by permission of The Macmillan Company, publishers.
[2] From *Love Songs* by Sara Teasdale. Reprinted by permission of The Macmillan Company, publishers.

NIGHT SONG AT AMALFI [1]

I asked the heaven of stars
  What I should give my love —
It answered me with silence,
  Silence above.

I asked the darkened sea
  Down where the fishermen go —
It answered me with silence,
  Silence below.

Oh, I could give him weeping,
  Or I could give him song —
But how can I give silence
  My whole life long?

THE LONG HILL [2]

I must have passed the crest a while ago
  And now I am going down —
Strange to have crossed the crest and not to know,
  But the brambles were always catching the hem of my gown.

All the morning I thought how proud I should be
  To stand there straight as a queen,
Wrapped in the wind and the sun with the world under me —
  But the air was dull, there was little I could have seen.

It was nearly level along the beaten track
  And the brambles caught in my gown —
But it's no use now to think of turning back,
  The rest of the way will be only going down.

[1] From *Love Songs* by Sara Teasdale. Reprinted by permission of The Macmillan Company, publishers.
[2] From *Flame and Shadow* by Sara Teasdale. Reprinted by permission of The Macmillan Company, publishers.

SUGGESTIONS FOR STUDY

1. An undercurrent of sadness and wistfulness runs through many of Sara Teasdale's poems. Where do you find it here?

2. What situations can you imagine calling forth the feelings expressed in these poems?

3. What application of "The Long Hill" can you make to the life of a human being?

LOUIS UNTERMEYER (1885–   )

Louis Untermeyer has humorously branded himself as "the least educated writer in America," because his failure in mathematics prevented his graduation from a New York high school. In youth he dreamed of becoming a composer, but his compositions turned out to be in poetry rather than for the piano, as he had contemplated. Through twenty years of business life in a jewelry manufacturing establishment of New Jersey, he wrote and published his poetry, until in 1923 he retired from business to devote himself entirely to literature. He is known not only for his own vigorous, challenging lyrics, but for his literary parodies, translations, critical volumes, and especially his anthologies. The number and quality of the last two types make Louis Untermeyer the outstanding collector and interpreter of poetry in America today.

The first three of the following poems show nature from the point of view of the city man. The impact between nature and civilization displays ironic contrast in the first poem, interminable contest in the second, and the infinity of nature in the third.

TO A TELEGRAPH POLE

You should be done with blossoming by now.
Yet here are leaves closer than any bough
That welcomes ivy. True, you were a tree
And stood with others in a marching line,
Less regular than this, of spruce and pine
And boasted branches rather than a trunk.
This is your final winter, all arms shrunk
To one cross-bar bearing haphazardly
Four rusty strands. You cannot hope to feel
The electric sap run through those veins of steel

The birds know this; the birds have hoodwinked you,
Crowding about you as they used to do.
The rainy robins huddled on your wire
And those blackbirds with shoulders dipped in fire
Have made you dream these vines; these tendrils are
A last despair in green, familiar
To derelicts of earth as well as sea.
Do not believe them, there is mockery
In their cool little jets of song. They know
What every one but you learned long ago:
The stream of stories humming through your head
Is not your own. You dream. But you are dead.

LONG FEUD

Where, without bloodshed, can there be
A more relentless enmity
Than the long feud fought silently

Between man and the growing grass.
Man's the aggressor, for he has
Weapons to humble and harass

The impudent spears that charge upon
His sacred privacy of lawn.
He mows them down, and they are gone

Only to lie in wait, although
He builds above and digs below
Where never a root would dare to go.

His are the triumphs till the day
There's no more grass to cut away,
And, weary of labor, weary of play,

Having exhausted every whim,
He stretches out each conquering limb.
And then the small grass covers him.

THE STONE'S HYMN

Earthquakes prepared me, made my bed;
　Worlds rose within me, fell apart.
Now small lives move beneath and overhead,
　While unseen heavens open in my heart.

Beyond extremities of pain,
　I touch the very source of might.
Do I not drink the warm, impersonal rain,
　Feed on the lavish and indifferent light?

Here, in a permanent peace, I lie
　Till finity and all its shapes are done;
And sorrow is an air that passes by
　And death a little absence of the sun.

Content to wait while kingdoms crack
　And men conspire and planets climb,
I know no fear, no weariness, no lack,
　Who have eternity instead of time.

PRAYER

Emerson defines prayer as " the contemplation of facts from the highest point of view." In the light of that definition read this " Prayer " thoughtfully.

God, though this life is but a wraith
　Although we know not what we use,
Although we grope with little faith,
　Give me the heart to fight — and lose.

Ever insurgent let me be,
　Make me more daring than devout;
From sleek contentment keep me free,
　And fill me with a buoyant doubt.

Open my eyes to visions girt
　　With beauty, and with wonder lit —
But let me always see the dirt,
　　And all that spawn and die in it.

Open my ears to music; let
　　Me thrill with Spring's first flutes and drums —
But never let me dare forget
　　The bitter ballad of the slums.

From compromise and things half done,
　　Keep me, with stern and stubborn pride;
And when, at last, the fight is won,
　　God, keep me still unsatisfied.

SUGGESTIONS FOR STUDY

1. Compare " Long Feud " with Sandburg's " Grass " (p. 737).
2. Compare " The Stone's Hymn " with Emily Dickinson's " How Happy Is the Little Stone " (p. 665).
3. In " Prayer " why does the poet want to " see the dirt," hear the " bitter ballads," and remain " still unsatisfied "?

FOR FURTHER READING

" Caliban in the Coal Mines "　　　　" Disenchantment "
" Landscapes "　　　　　　　　　" Prayer for This House "
" Hands "

DuBose Heyward (1885–　　)

Dubose Heyward was born in Charleston, South Carolina, and still lives there, one of the South's most outstanding writers of today. All of his work, both in poetry and fiction, is distinctly southern in atmosphere and setting. His novel *Porgy* (1925) was a literary sensation and when dramatized by the author and his wife it became even more of a sensation as a play. Of all writers who introduce the Negro into their work, none has been so successful as Heyward.

" The Mountain Woman " portrays realistically the sort of episode that one would wish to think of as not being possible. Unfortunately, there are still sections of the country where women must do hard work and men will engage in illegal pursuits and get drunk. The resignation of the woman of the mountain, slightly alleviated by a touch of sentiment, makes the poem seem all the sadder.

THE MOUNTAIN WOMAN [1]

Among the sullen peaks she stood at bay
And paid life's hard account from her small store.
Knowing the code of mountain wives, she bore
The burden of the days without a sigh;
And, sharp against the somber winter sky,
I saw her drive her steers afield that day.

Hers was the hand that sunk the furrows deep
Across the rocky, grudging southern slope.
At first youth left her face, and later hope;
Yet through each mocking spring and barren fall,
She reared her lusty brood, and gave them all
That gladder wives and mothers love to keep.

[1] From *Skylines and Horizons* by Dubose Heyward. Reprinted by permission of The Macmillan Company, publishers.

And when the sheriff shot her eldest son
Beside his still, so well she knew her part,
She gave no healing tears to ease her heart;
But took the blow upstanding, with her eyes
As drear and bitter as the winter skies.
Seeing her then, I thought that she had won.

But yesterday her man returned too soon
And found her tending, with reverent touch,
One scarlet bloom; and, having drunk too much,
He snatched its flame and quenched it in the dirt.
Then, like a creature with a mortal hurt,
She fell, and wept away the afternoon.

ELINOR WYLIE (1886–1928)

Elinor Wylie (Mrs. William Rose Benét) was almost as distinguished
a writer of prose as of verse, but she was primarily thought of as a poet.
Her first volume, *Nets to Catch the Wind* (1921), established her reputation, and her succeeding volumes more than bore out the promise of the
first. Just prior to her untimely death in 1928 she had completed a new
volume for the press, *Angels and Earthly Creatures* (1929). "Sea Lullaby" and "Escape" are taken from her first book, and "Nonsense
Rhyme" from the last. Her work is always highly finished technically
and yet deeply emotional as well as personal. One has the feeling that
she is groping for some means of escape from the heavy problems of
existence. This comes out in perhaps the lightest poem she ever wrote,
"Escape." In "Sea Lullaby" she presents a sharp picture of the saturnine
cruelty of the sea. The title of "Nonsense Rhyme" indicates the real
theme only by suggesting its opposite. *Jennifer Lorn* (1923), *The Vene-
tian Glass Nephew* (1925), and *The Orphan Angel* (1926) are her three
best known novels, although she has written several others.

SEA LULLABY

The old moon is tarnished
With smoke of the flood,
The dead leaves are varnished
With color like blood,

A treacherous smiler
With teeth white as milk,
A savage beguiler
In sheathings of silk,

The sea creeps to pillage,
She leaps on her prey;
A child of the village
Was murdered today.

She came up to meet him
In a smooth golden cloak,
She choked him and beat him
To death, for a joke.

Her bright locks were tangled,
She shouted for joy,
With one hand she strangled
A strong little boy.

Now in silence she lingers
Beside him all night
To wash her long fingers
In silvery light.

ESCAPE

When foxes eat the last gold grape,
And the last white antelope is killed,
I shall stop fighting and escape
Into a little house I'll build.

But first I'll shrink to fairy size,
With a whisper no one understands,
Making blind moons of all your eyes,
And muddy roads of all your hands.

And you may grope for me in vain
In hollows under the mangrove root,
Or where, in apple-scented rain,
The silver wasp-nests hang like fruit.

NONSENSE RHYME

Whatever's good or bad or both
Is surely better than the none;
There's grace in either love or loathe;
Sunlight, or freckles on the sun.

The worst and best are both inclined
To snap like vixens at the truth;
But, O, beware the middle mind
That purrs and never shows a tooth!

Beware the smooth ambiguous smile
That never pulls the lips apart;
Salt of pure and pepper of vile
Must season the extremer heart.

A pinch of fair, a pinch of foul,
And bad and good make best of all;
Beware the moderated soul
That climbs no fractional inch to fall.

Reason's a rabbit in a hutch,
And ectasy's a were-wolf's ghost;
But, O, beware the nothing-much
And welcome madness and the most!

FOR FURTHER READING

" The Eagle and the Mole "   " Pretty Words "
" Velvet Shoes "   " The Puritan's Ballad "
" Bells in the Rain "

ALAN SEEGER (1888–1916)

" I Have a Rendezvous with Death " is one of the finest poems that came out of the World War, and is no doubt the one poem by which Alan Seeger will be remembered. He began to write verse while still at Harvard, and a few years after his graduation in 1910 he felt that Paris offered a more satisfactory background for literary work than this country. That is how he happened to be in Paris at the outbreak of the war, and, with many other foreign students who loved France and lived there, he early enlisted in the Foreign Legion, which saw almost continuous service throughout the long struggle. He died in action in July, 1916. While most of his verse is of the kind that showed promise, the one here given has genuine merits beyond the tragic theme and the sentiment that naturally flows from the author's death. In connection with this poem one thinks of the young English poet, Rupert Brooke, whose fate was similar to that of Seeger, and of the Canadian, John McCrae, author of " In Flanders Fields," who also died in the war.

I HAVE A RENDEZVOUS WITH DEATH

I have a rendezvous with Death
At some disputed barricade,
When Spring comes back with rustling shade
And apple-blossoms fill the air —
I have a rendezvous with Death
When Spring brings back blue days and fair.

It may be he shall take my hand
And lead me into his dark land
And close my eyes and quench my breath —
It may be I shall pass him still.
I have a rendezvous with Death
On some scarred slope of battered hill,
When Spring comes round again this year
And the first meadow-flowers appear.

God knows 'twere better to be deep
Pillowed in silk and scented down,
Where Love throbs out in blissful sleep,
Pulse nigh to pulse and breath to breath,
Where hushed awakenings are dear. . . .
But I've a rendezvous with Death
At midnight in some flaming town,
When Spring trips north again this year,
And I to my pledged word am true,
I shall not fail that rendezvous.

SUGGESTIONS FOR STUDY

1. Be sure to know what the word " rendezvous " means.
2. Name the three places where he thinks the rendezvous may have to be kept.

3. Why would it be particularly tragic for a poet to have to die in spring? Point out some proof of this from the poem.

HERVEY ALLEN (1889–   )

Hervey Allen was born in Pittsburgh, educated at the United States Naval Academy, the University of Pittsburgh, and Harvard. After returning from service in France during the war he went south, where he lived from 1919 to 1924. He became a friend of Dubose Heyward, and together they founded the Poetry Society of South Carolina which has done a great deal to develop an interest in poetry, especially that of the South. Allen and Heyward collaborated on a volume of verse, *Carolina Chansons* (1922). While Allen can not strictly be called a Southerner, he is nevertheless definitely connected with the group of poets that has made Charleston one of the literary centers of the South. "Palmetto Town" presents a picture of Old Charleston seen through the eyes of the poet from the point of view of the present. Hervey Allen has published a number of volumes of poems, a biography of Poe under the title of *Israfel,* and one novel, *Toward the Flame* (1926). At present he is on the English faculty of Columbia University.

PALMETTO TOWN [1]

Sea-island winds sweep through Palmetto Town,
Bringing with piney tang the old romance
Of pirates and of smuggling gentlemen;
And tongues as languorous as southern France
Flow down her streets like water-talk at fords;   5
While through iron gates where pickaninnies sprawl,
The sound floats back, in rippled banjo chords,
From lush magnolia shade where mockers call.
Mornings, the flower-women hawk their wares —
Bronze caryatids of a genial race,   10
Bearing the bloom-heaped baskets on their heads;
Lithe, with their arms akimbo in wide grace,
Their jasmine nods jestingly at cares —
Turbaned they are, deep-chested, straight and tall,

[1] From *Carolina Chansons* by Dubose Heyward and Hervey Allen. Reprinted by permission of The Macmillan Company, publishers.

1. **Palmetto Town:** Charleston, S. C.   10. **caryatids:** statues of women used as columns.

Bandying old English words now seldom heard,   15
But sweet as Provençal.
Dreams peer like prisoners through her harp-like gates,
From molten gardens mottled with gray-gloom,
Where lichened sundials shadow ancient dates,
And deep piazzas loom.   20
Fringing her quays are frayed palmetto posts,
Where clipper ships once moored along the ways,
And fanlight doorways, sunstruck with old ghosts,
Sicken with loves of her lost yesterdays.
Often I halt upon some gabled walk,   25
Thinking I see the ear-ringed *picaroons,*
Slashed with a sash or Spanish *folderols,*
Gambling for moidores or for gold doubloons.
But they have gone where night goes after day,
And the old streets are gay with whistled tunes,   30
Bright with the lilt of scarlet parasols,
Carried by honey-voiced young octoroons.

16. **Provençal:** a section of southern France. 26. **picaroons:** pirates. 27.
folderois: bits of finery. 28. **moidores:** Portuguese gold coins worth about
seven dollars. A doubloon was originally worth sixteen.

CHRISTOPHER MORLEY (1890–   )

Morley, like so many of the younger generation of poets, likes to put
a single definite impression into a few terse but graphic lines. Hardly
anything could be more prosaic than an inkwell in a post office, yet the
eight lines that follow will forever give us a different idea of the scene
common to every post office in the country. For other works by Morley,
see pages 219 and 223.

TO A POST OFFICE INKWELL

How many humble hearts have dipped
In you and scrawled their manuscript!
Have shared their secrets, told their cares,
Their curious and quaint affairs!

Your pool of ink, your scratchy pen
Have moved the lives of unborn men,
And watched young people, breathing hard,
Put Heaven on a postal card.

EDNA ST. VINCENT MILLAY (1892–   )

Edna St. Vincent Millay comes from a poetry-writing family, for her mother and sister have also published volumes of verse. She was born in Rockland, Maine, and her early life was spent in New England. When she was nineteen, she wrote " Renascence," a poem of such remarkable spiritual insight that she was at once heralded as a coming poet. This poem was the title-piece in her first volume published in 1917, the same year that she left Vassar College. Since then she has published four other slender but significant volumes of poetry, several short plays in verse, and *The King's Henchman*, a libretto to the opera by Deems Taylor. This is a notable attempt to establish the hitherto undeveloped form of grand opera in America. Aside from its musical setting the libretto has taken its own place as a splendid poetic drama. Miss Millay's flowing melody is evident in her short lyrics. Observe the unusual back-wash of rhyme in the middle of each stanza of " The Spring and the Fall." In her earlier poems one finds often exuberance of life, occasionally pertness, but more frequently than either a kind of lyric wistfulness, a pathos with the quality of Irish folk-lore. This is especially noticeable in *The Harp-Weaver*. In her latest volume, *The Buck in the Snow*, from which " Dirge without Music " is taken, there is a growing bitterness at the injustices and tragedies of life.

LAMENT [1]

The poignancy of this poem lies in the twist of the last line, which comes like a cold shiver at the heart after the matter-of-fact tone of the first part.

> Listen, children:
> Your father is dead.
> From his old coats
> I'll make you little jackets;
> I'll make you little trousers
> From his old pants.
> There'll be in his pockets
> Things he used to put there,
> Keys and pennies

[1] From *Second April,* published by Harper and Brothers; copyright 1921 by Edna St. Vincent Millay.

Covered with tobacco;
Dan shall have the pennies
To save in his bank;
Anne shall have the keys
To make a pretty noise with.
Life must go on,
And the dead be forgotten;
Life must go on,
Though good men die;
Anne, eat your breakfast;
Dan, take your medicine;
Life must go on;
I forget just why.

THE SPRING AND THE FALL [1]

In the spring of the year, in the spring of the year,
I walked the road beside my dear.
The trees were black where the bark was wet.
I see them yet, in the spring of the year.
He broke me a bough of the blossoming peach
That was out of the way and hard to reach.

In the fall of the year, in the fall of the year,
I walked the road beside my dear.
The rooks went up with a raucous trill.
I hear them still, in the fall of the year.
He laughed at all I dared to praise,
And broke my heart, in little ways.

Year be springing or year be falling,
The bark will drip and the birds be calling.
There's much that's fine to see and hear
In the spring of a year, in the fall of a year.
'Tis not love's going hurts my days,
But that it went in little ways.

[1] From *The Harp-Weaver and Other Poems,* published by Harper and
Brothers; copyright 1920, 1921, 1922, 1923 by Edna St. Vincent Millay.

DIRGE WITHOUT MUSIC [1]

I am not resigned to the shutting away of loving hearts in the hard
    ground.
So it is, and so it will be, for so it has been time out of mind:
Into the darkness they go, the wise and the lovely; crowned
With lilies and with laurel they go; but I am not resigned.

Lovers and thinkers, into the earth with you.
Be one with the dull, the indiscriminate dust.
A fragment of what you felt, of what you knew,
A formula, a phrase remains — but the best is lost.

The answers quick and keen, the honest look, the laughter, the love,
They are gone; they are gone to feed the roses. Elegant and curled
Is the blossom; fragrant is the blossom. I know. But I do not
    approve.
More precious was the light in your eyes than all the roses of the
    world.

Down, down, down into the darkness of the grave
Gently they go, the beautiful, the tender, the kind;
Quietly they go, the intelligent, the witty, the brave.
I know. But I do not approve. And I am not resigned.

SUGGESTIONS FOR STUDY

1. This is one of the most recent poems on death in our literature. Contrast it with " Thanatopsis " of a century ago, and " The Stirrup-Cup "
and " Darest Thou Now, O Soul " of half a century ago. Which of all of
them seems to you the best way to look at death?

2. Do you think that these poems express in any way the feelings of
their respective generations or just the feelings of these individual poets?

FOR FURTHER READING

" God's World "   " Portrait of a Neighbor "
" Autumn Chant "   " Departure "
" My Heart, Being Hungry "   " The Curse "
" When the Year Grows Old "   " The Concert "
" Renascence "   " Aria Da Capo " (one-act play)
" The Pear Tree "   " The King's Henchman "
" Wild Swans "   " The Harp-Weaver "

[1] From *The Buck in the Snow*, published by Harper and Brothers; copyright 1928 by Edna St. Vincent Millay.

George O'Neil (1898–   )

The Hôtel des Invalides is an old public building in Paris used as a military museum, a home for old soldiers, and, more interesting to the world, it contains the specially built tomb of Napoleon Bonaparte. The " esplanade " is a level space in front of the building, and it is from this point of view that the poet describes his scene and voices his impression. George O'Neil, born in St. Louis, is one of the younger poets who has been interested in fostering what is often called the " new " poetry. His style is terse, trenchant, and forceful.

IN THE ESPLANADE DES INVALIDES

Towers and domes and minarets,
A river twisted like a rope of gold,
A city flashing on a lilt of hills
In April as the leaves unfold.

Fretted with buds, the chestnuts shake,
Blur even more that tenderness of blue
That curves ungarlanded, a canopy
Of softness to let silver through.

Amber, not air, to breathe today.
The walks are stippled with a frail design.
Life has its value in a touch of hands,
Bright purpose and a way benign.

Under a dome — an emperor. . . .
Ambition has its quiet place at last.
Let us not turn to seek abundant gloom,
To twinge beneath grandeur and the past.

Their monument shall stand a time.
The hour is vague, ineffable, and sweet.
Under the budding trees an old man stands
Charming the sparrows from the street.

LEAH RACHEL YOFFIE

Miss Yoffie was born in Ekaterinodar, the Russian Caucasus, and brought to this country at the age of nine. She was educated in the public schools of St. Louis and at Washington University of the same city. She graduated from the university in 1911 and has since broadened her scholarship by attending Columbia and the University of Pennsylvania, and by considerable travel abroad. At present Miss Yoffie is a teacher of English in Soldan High School of St. Louis. She is intensely interested in Jewish folk lore and the beliefs and customs of the Yiddish-speaking Jews, about all of which she has written a great deal. "The Lost Vision," from her *Dark Altar Stairs* (1926), is a reminiscent picture of her native Russia as contrasted with "the New World streets" of the country of her adoption.

THE LOST VISION

Vast stretch of steppe that billows to the sky,
And pale-blue poppies creeping through the grain,
Thick streaks of amber under clouds piled high,
And dark fir forests brooding in the rain:

From these gray steppes that gave me birth I drew
An open vision, wide and large as they,
Stretching as far as where the heron flew,
To seek the summer in a southern bay.

Now, bound and crowded in the New World streets
By dirty tenements that push and prey
On sky and cloud and sun, what far hope beats,
What dream thrusts out the business of the day?

How soon my youth was mauled by steel and stone!
I, too, have learned to live for bread alone.

STEPHEN VINCENT BENÉT (1898–   )

Next to Lee, Stonewall Jackson was undoubtedly the South's most popular general in the Civil War. He was loved by his friends and admired by his enemies, and today the story of his unfortunate death is perhaps even more gripping than it was during the hectic war years. The account given in the following extract from *John Brown's Body* presents an unforgettable picture of the man as he was and the traits of character that led to his end. The long and rather straggling epic, *John Brown's Body* (1928) is the first serious attempt to present an impartial view in poetry of the struggle between the states. Instead of telling his story in continuous narrative the author has taken a number of typical characters, some real, some fictional, and placed them in scenes that were significant of the trend of events in the war. None of these episodes gives such a sense of complete unity by itself as this particular one.

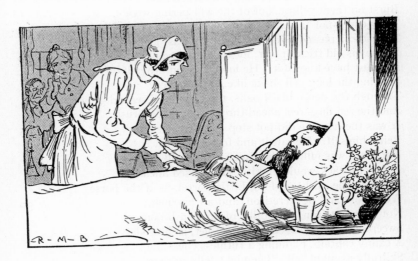

THE DEATH OF STONEWALL JACKSON

FROM "JOHN BROWN'S BODY"

In the dense heart of the thicketed Wilderness,
Stonewall Jackson lies dying for four long days.
They have cut off his arm, they have tried such arts as they know,
But no arts can save him.
     When he was hit
By the blind chance bullet-spatter from his own lines,   5
In the night, in the darkness, they stole him off from the field
To keep the men from knowing, but the men knew.
The dogs in the house will know when there's something wrong.
You do not have to tell them.

                    He marched his men
That grim first day across the whole Union front   10
To strike a sleepy right wing with a sudden stone
And roll it up — it was his old trick of war
That Lee and he could play like finger and thumb!
It was the last time they played so.
                   When the blue-coated
Unprepared ranks of Howard saw that storm,   15
Heralded by wild rabbits and frightened deer,
Burst on them yelling, out of the whispering woods,
They could not face it. Some men died where they stood,
The storm passed over the rest. It was Jackson's storm,
It was his old trick of war, for the last time played.   20
He must have known it. He loosed it and drove it on,
Hearing the long yell shake like an Indian cry
Through the dense black oaks, the clumps of second-growth pine,
And the red flags reel ahead through the underbrush.
It was the hour he did not stop to taste,   25
Being himself. He saw it and found it good,
But night was falling, the Union center still held,
Another attack would end it. He pressed ahead
Through the dusk, pushing Little Sorrel, as if the horse
Were iron, and he were iron, and all his men   30
Not men but iron, the stalks of an iron broom
Sweeping a dirt floor clean — and yet, as he rode,
A canny captain, planning a ruthless chess
Skilfully as night fell. The night fell too soon.
It is hard to tell your friend from your enemy   35
In such a night. So he rode too far in advance
And, turning back toward his lines, unrecognized,
Was fired upon in the night, in the stumbling darkness,
By his own men. He had ridden such rides before
Often enough and taken the chance of them,   40
But this chance was his bane.
                  He lay on the bed
After the arm had been lopped from him, grim and silent,
Refusing importunate Death with terrible eyes.
Death was a servant and Death was a sulky dog
And Death crouched down by the Lord in the Lord's own time, 45
But he still had work to finish that Death would spoil.
He would live in spite of that servant.

Now and then
He spoke, with the old curt justice that never once
Denied himself or his foe or any other
The rigid due they deserved, as he saw that due.   50
He spoke of himself and his storm. " A successful movement.
I think the most successful I ever made."
— He had heard that long yell shake like an Indian cry
Through the ragged woods and seen his flags go ahead.
Later on, they brought him a stately letter from Lee   55
That said in Lee's gracious way, " You have only lost
Your left arm, I my right."
                    The dour mouth opened.
" Better ten Jacksons should fall than one Lee," it said
And closed again, while the heart went on with its task
Of beating off foolish, unnecessary Death.   60

The slow time wore. They had to tell him at last
That he must die. The doctors were brave enough,
No doubt, but they looked awhile at the man on the bed
And summoned his wife to do it. So she told him.
He would not believe at first. Then he lay awhile   65
Silent, while some slow, vast reversal of skies
Went on in the dying brain. At last he spoke.
" All right," he said.
                    She opened the Bible and read.
It was spring outside the window, the air was warm,
The rough, plank house was full enough of the spring.   70
They had had a good life together, those two middle-aged
Calm people, one reading aloud now, the other silent.
They had passed hard schools. They were in love with each other
And had been for many years. Now the tale was told.
They had been poor and odd, found each other trusty,   75
Begotten children, prayed, disliked to be parted,
Had family jokes, known weather and other matters,
Planned for an age: they were famous now, he was dying.

The clock moved on, the delirium began.
The watchers listened, trying to catch the words;   80
Some awed, one broken-hearted, a few, no doubt,
Not glad to be there precisely, but in a way

Glad that, if it must happen, they could be there.
It is a human emotion.
                    The dying man
Went back at first to his battles, as soldiers do.   85
He was pushing a new advance
With the old impatience and skill, over tangled ground,
A cloudy drive that did not move as he willed
Though he had it clear in his mind. They were slow today.
" Tell A. P. Hill to push them — push the attack —   90
Get up the guns! "
                    The cloudy assault dispersed.
There were no more cannon. The ground was plain enough now.

He lay silent, seeing it so, while the watchers listened.
He had been dying once, but that was a dream.
The ground was plain enough now.   95
He roused himself and spoke in a different voice.
" Let us cross the river," he said, " and rest under the shade of
    the trees."

SUGGESTIONS FOR STUDY

1. Note how the poet states his theme in the first four lines.
2. State definitely how Jackson met his death.
3. Point out the traits of character emphasized in the poem.
4. How did the wounded general react to the announcement that he
could not live?
5. Why did the few watchers want to be with him to the end?
6. What is the most graphic picture in the poem?
7. Why a " different voice " in the second last line?

FOR FURTHER READING

" John Brown's Body "   " Portrait of a Boy "
" The Mountain Whippoorwill "   " Lonely Burial "

NATHALIA CRANE (1913–   )

Among the rising generation there is a certain New York girl who bids
fair to take her place with the notable poets of our century. At the date
of publication of this book Nathalia Crane is just the age of many of
the boys and girls who will be studying it, but she has had a national repu-

tation as a poet for five years, ever since her volume, *The Janitor's Boy*, was published when she was ten and a half. After *Lava Lane* appeared in 1925, she was invited to join the British Society of Authors and Playwrights. The honor was all the more remarkable in view of the fact that she was the first American poet since Walt Whitman to receive such an invitation. Her poetry combines a childlike buoyancy and sly humor with a remarkable vocabulary, literary background, and interpretive sense.

THE READING BOY

He is carved in alabaster, he is called the Reading Boy.
A cross-legged little pagan, pondering o'er the Siege of Troy;
He's a miniature Adonis, with a bandeau round his head,
And he's reading late and early when he ought to be in bed.

He cons an ancient manuscript, he scanneth as a sage,
But with all his mighty reading never yet hath turned a page;
Never alabaster side glance at the turtle in the bowl,
Never alabaster wiggle, though I know he has a soul.

I have watched him late and early, just an image out of Rome,
And politely offered bookmarks to divert him from that tome;
Yea, with aggravating gestures sought to turn aside his face,
But not for pots of honey could you make him lose his place.

There he sits in sweet perfection that the chisel did unveil,
With the rapture of an angel up against a lively tale.
But I'd give an old maid's ransom just to see that little wretch
Discard that Trojan magazine, and give a real good stretch.

FOR FURTHER READING

POEMS	VOLUMES
" The Flathouse Roof "	*The Janitor's Boy*
" The Vacant Lot "	*Lava Lane*
" The Swinging Stair "	
" The Gossips "	

COLLECTIONS OF POETRY

Broadhurst and Rhodes. *Verse for Patriots*
Braithwaite, William S. B. *Anthology of Magazine Verse* (issued annually)

3. **Adonis:** in Greek mythology a beautiful youth beloved by Venus.

Bryan, G. S. *Poems of Country Life*
Clark, G. H. *A Treasury of War Poetry*
Cunliffe, John W. *Poems of the Great War*
Davis, Mary G. *The Girls' Book of Verse*
Fish, Helen D. *The Boys' Book of Verse*
Gayley and Flaherty. *Poetry of the People*
Law, F. H. *Selections from American Poetry*
Leonard, S. A. *Poems of the War and Peace*
Markham, Edwin. *The Book of Poetry* (Volume I, *American*)
Mims and Payne. *Southern Prose and Poetry*
Monroe and Henderson. *The New Poetry*
Page, Curtis H. *Chief American Poets*
Repplier, Agnes. *A Book of Famous Verse*
Richards, Mrs. Waldo. *The Melody of Earth. High-Tide. Star Points*
Rittenhouse, Jessie. *The Little Book of American Poets. The Little Book of Modern Verse* (3 volumes)
Sanders and Nelson. *Chief Modern Poets of England and America*
Schauffler, R. H. *The Poetry Cure*
Stevenson, Burton. *Famous Single Poems. Home Book of Verse. Home Book of Verse for Young People*
Untermeyer, Louis. *Modern American Poetry. This Singing World. Yesterday and Today*
Wilkinson, Marguerite. *Contemporary Poetry. New Voices*

OTHER POETS OF THE TWENTIETH CENTURY

The best way for high school students to become acquainted with the many excellent poets of the present is to read widely in the anthologies listed above. Poets frequently represented in these collections are:

Conrad Aiken, "H. D." (Hilda Doolittle, Mrs. Richard Aldington), William Rose Benét, Witter Bynner, Madison Cawein, Grace Hazard Conkling, Hilda Conkling, Adelaide Crapsey, Countee Cullen, Thomas Augustine Daly, Paul Laurence Dunbar, John Gould Fletcher, Theodosia Garrison, Fannie Stearns Davis (Mrs. Augustus M. Gifford), Louise Imogen Guiney, Herman Hagedorn, Joyce Kilmer, Aline Murray Kilmer, Alfred Kreymborg, Richard Le Gallienne, Harriet Monroe, Ezra Pound, Lizette Woodworth Reese, Lew R. Sarett, Robert Haven Schauffler, Clinton Scollard, Frank Dempster Sherman, Eunice Tietjens (Mrs. Cloyd Head), Jean Starr Untermeyer, Margaret Widdemer

Humorous Poetry

Humor is a comparatively recent phenomenon in American literature. In the early Puritan days, down through the period of colonization and the tempestuous, serious-minded, early days of the Republic, there was little room in literature or life for the play of light-hearted wit. Toward the middle of the nineteenth century Boston and Cambridge had become the intellectual center of the country. In this period of long beards, serious mien, and philosophic attitudes the son of one of Boston's proudest families graduated with the most famous of Harvard classes. Everything about Dr. Oliver Wendell Holmes was eminent — his family, his classmates, his practice — all of which might have conspired to make him one of the Men of Measured Merriment (Sinclair Lewis's name for men in high places so bowed down by their cares that they are afraid to smile). The merriment in "The One-Hoss Shay" is not by any means measured, and it has given its author a clear title to being the first polished, civilized wit in America.

Out in the boisterous West things were going far from smoothly, but these pioneering folk had a streak of rough humor, such as Will Rogers today exemplifies, not apparent in the sterner Puritans. Therefore we find Mark Twain immortalizing the mischief-maker, Tom Sawyer, and the renegade Huck. We find Bret Harte catching the humorous side of California mining-camps in his dialect verse. But until late in the century there was no considerable body of humor characteristically American, such as the weekly magazine *Punch* embodies for the Englishman.

Then came the avalanche of newspaper writing. In Chicago, Eugene Field started a column in the *Daily News*. At first he was the only known member of his species. Today columnists are legion; and it is they, together with their brothers under the skin, the staff writers on such periodicals as *Life, Judge,* and *The New Yorker,* who are building up a distinctive brand of American humor. Many of these men have published full-length books. Don Marquis's *archy and mehitabel* is one example which points the way to the emergence of a true American humor, drawing not only on slapstick but on light irony and satire as well. Of the humorous poets represented in this section four are newspaper men.

THE HEIGHT OF THE RIDICULOUS

By OLIVER WENDELL HOLMES (1809–1894)

I wrote some lines once on a time
  In wondrous merry mood,
And thought, as usual, men would say
  They were exceeding good.

They were so queer, so very queer,   5
  I laughed as I would die;
Albeit, in the general way,
  A sober man am I.

I called my servant, and he came;
  How kind it was of him   10
To mind a slender man like me,
  He of the mighty limb!

" These to the printer," I exclaimed,
  And, in my humorous way,
I added (as a trifling jest),   15
  " There'll be the devil to pay."

He took the paper, and I watched,
  And saw him peep within;
At the first line he read, his face
  Was all upon the grin.   20

He read the next; the grin grew broad,
   And shot from ear to ear;
He read the third; a chuckling noise
   I now began to hear.

The fourth; he broke into a roar;   25
   The fifth; his waistband split;
The sixth; he burst five buttons off,
   And tumbled in a fit.

Ten days and nights, with sleepless eye,
   I watched that wretched man,   30
And since, I never dare to write
   As funny as I can.

PLAIN LANGUAGE FROM TRUTHFUL JAMES

TABLE MOUNTAIN, 1870

By BRET HARTE (1839–1902)

Which I wish to remark,
   And my language is plain,
That for ways that are dark
   And for tricks that are vain,
The heathen Chinee is peculiar,   5
   Which the same I would rise to explain.

Ah Sin was his name;
   And I shall not deny,
In regard to the same,
   What that name might imply;   10
But his smile it was pensive and childlike,
   As I frequent remarked to Bill Nye.

It was August the third,
   And quite soft was the skies;
Which it might be inferred   15
   That Ah Sin was likewise;
Yet he played it that day upon William
   And me in a way I despise.

Which we had a small game,
   And Ah Sin took a hand:
It was Euchre. The same   20
   He did not understand;
But he smiled as he sat by the table,
   With the smile that was childlike and bland.

Yet the cards they were stocked   25
   In a way that I grieve,
And my feelings were shocked
   At the state of Nye's sleeve,
Which was stuffed full of aces and bowers,
   And the same with intent to deceive.   30

But the hands that were played
   By that heathen Chinee,
And the points that he made,
   Were quite frightful to see —
Till at last he put down a right bower,   35
   Which the same Nye had dealt unto me.

Then I looked up at Nye,
   And he gazed upon me;
And he rose with a sigh,
   And said, " Can this be?   40
We are ruined by Chinese cheap labor," —
   And he went for that heathen Chinee.

In the scene that ensued
   I did not take a hand,
But the floor it was strewed   45
   Like the leaves on the strand
With the cards that Ah Sin had been hiding,
   In the game " he did not understand."

In his sleeves, which were long,
   He had twenty-four packs —
Which was coming it strong,   50
   Yet I state but the facts;
And we found on his nails, which were taper,
   What is frequent in tapers — that's wax.

Which is why I remark,   55
  And my language is plain,
That for ways that are dark
  And for tricks that are vain,
The heathen Chinee is peculiar —
  Which the same I am free to maintain.   60

THE AHKOOND OF SWAT

By GEORGE T. LANIGAN (1845–1886)

" The Ahkoond of Swat is Dead." — London papers of Jan. 22, 1878.

What, what, what,
  What's the news from Swat?
  Sad news,
  Bad news,
Comes by the cable led
Through the Indian Ocean's bed,

Through the Persian Gulf, the Red
Sea and the Med-
Iterranean — he's dead;
The Ahkoond is dead.

For the Ahkoond I mourn,
  Who wouldn't?
He strove to disregard the message stern,
  But he Ahkoodn't.
Dead, dead, dead;
  (Sorrow, Swats!)
Swats wha hae wi' Ahkoond bled,
Swats whom he hath often led
Onward to a gory bed,
  Or to victory,
    As the case might be,
      Sorrow, Swats!
Tears shed,
  Shed tears like water.
Your great Ahkoond is dead!
  That Swats the matter!

Mourn, city of Swat,
Your great Ahkoond is not
But laid 'mid worms to rot.
His mortal part alone, his soul was caught
  (Because he was a good Ahkoond)
  Up to the bosom of Mahound.
Though earthy walls his frame surround
(For ever hallowed be the ground!)
And skeptics mock the lowly mound
And say " He's now of no Ahkoond! "
  His soul is in the skies —
The azure skies that bend above his loved
  Metropolis of Swat.
He sees with larger, other eyes,
Athwart all earthly mysteries —
  He knows what's Swat.

Let Swat bury the great Ahkoond
  With a noise of mourning and of lamentation!
Let Swat bury the great Ahkoond
  With the noise of the mourning of the Swattish nation!
Fallen is at length
Its tower of strength;
Its sun is dimmed ere it had nooned;
Dead lies the great Ahkoond,
The great Ahkoond of Swat
Is not!

CANDOR

OCTOBER — A WOOD

By H. C. BUNNER (1855–1896)

" I know what you're going to say," she said,
  And she stood up looking uncommonly tall;
  " You are going to speak of the hectic fall,
And say you're sorry the summer's dead.
  And no other summer was like it, you know,
  And can I imagine what made it so?
Now aren't you, honestly? " " Yes," I said.

" I know what you're going to say," she said;
    " You are going to ask if I forget
    That day in June when the woods were wet,
And you carried me " — here she dropped her head —
    " Over the creek; you are going to say,
    Do I remember that horrid day.
Now aren't you, honestly? "   " Yes," I said.

" I know what you're going to say," she said;
    " You are going to say that since that time
    You have rather tended to run to rhyme,
And " — her clear glance fell and her cheek grew red —
    " And I have noticed your tone was queer? —
    Why, everybody has seen it here! —
Now, aren't you, honestly? "   " Yes," I said.

" I know what you're going to say," I said;
    " You're going to say you've been much annoyed,
    And I'm short of tact — you will say devoid —
And I'm clumsy and awkward, and call me Ted,
    And I bear abuse like a dear old lamb,
    And you'll have me anyway, just as I am,
Now aren't you, honestly? "   " Ye-es," she said.

HOW THE FEUD STARTED

By ARTHUR GUITERMAN (1871-   )

Before there were Pineapples, Peaches, or Plums,
The Dog and the Cat were Companions and Chums.

(They lived in a Highly Respectable Grotto,
Where " God Bless Our Home " was their Favorite Motto.)

The Dog had a Parchment, a Parchment had he,
Proclaiming his Right to be Happy and Free.

(This Charter was signed by the Patriarch Noah,
And Witnessed in Form by the Goat and the Boa.)

The Dog went a-hunting on Mount Ararat;
The Parchment he left in the Care of the Cat.

(His Trust in the Cat was Complete and Abiding.
The Dog, then as ever, was Much Too Confiding.)

The Cat, who was always a Rover in Soul,
Grew bored with the Cavern and went for a Stroll.

(Beguiled by the Song of the Birds in the Bowers,
He ambled and rambled for Hours and Hours.)

Then out from their Crannies the Mouse People crept,
And lunched on the Parchment that Puss should have kept.

(They flocked with their Children, their Nephews and Nieces;
They shredded the Charter and ate up the Pieces.)

When Home came the Dog near the Close of the Day,
The Last of his Freedom was whisking away!

(He Leaped! — but the Tails disappeared in a Flicker.
The Dog may be Quick, but the Mouse Folk are quicker.)

When Home strolled the Cat as the Twilight grew dim,
The Dog paid the Utmost Attention to *Him!*

(The Cat, who in Climbing was always a Leader,
Escaped by a Whisker and ran up a Cedar.)

So, seeking his Vengeance — and justly, at that,
The Dog, through the Ages, still chases the Cat.

(The Cat, with Equivalent Justification,
Has chosen the Mouse as his favorite Ration.)

REAL BASEBALL

By ARTHUR GUITERMAN

Our center field had golden locks,
    Our left was short and fat,
And Hal was in the pitcher's box
    And George behind the bat.

We took the field without a word,
  And grim was every face,
With Bob at first and Will at third
  And me at second base.

Among the green New Hampshire hills
  Of forests then unhewn,
We played that game of countless thrills
  Through all the afternoon,

Until against the azure sky
  Arose a mighty shout!
'Twas I who gripped that arching fly
  And put the last man out!

And still where gallant deeds are done
  I tell the tale anew:
Our rivals' score was thirty-one
  And ours was fifty-two!

TWO 'MERICANA MEN

By THOMAS AUGUSTINE DALY (1871–   )

Beeg Irish cop dat walks hees beat
  By dees peanutta stan',
First two, t'ree week w'en we are meet
  Ees call me " Dagoman."
An' we'n he see how mad I gat,   5
  Wheech eesa pleass heem, too,
Wan day he say: " W'at's matter dat,
  Ain't ' Dago ' name for you?
Dat's 'Mericana name, you know,
  For man from Eetaly;   10
Eet ees no harm for call you so,
  Den why be mad weeth me? "

First time he talka deesa way
  I am too mad for speak,
But nexta time I justa say: 15
  " All righta, Meester Meeck! "

O! my, I nevva hear bayfore
  Sooch langwadge like he say;
An' he don't look at me no more
  For mebbe two, t'ree day.   20
But pretta soon agen I see
  Das beeg poleecaman
Dat com' an' growl an' say to me:
  " Hallo, Eyetalian!
Now, mebbe so you gon' deny   25
  Dat dat's a name for you."
I smila back, an' mak' reply:
  " No, Irish, dat's a true."
" Ha! Joe," he cry, " you theenk dat we
  Should call you 'Merican? "   30
" Dat's gooda 'nough," I say, " for me,
  Eef dat's w'at you are, Dan."

So now all times we speaka so
  Like gooda 'Merican:
He say to me, " Good morna, Joe,"   35
  I say, " Good morna, Dan."

THE SAME OLD STORY

By JAMES J. MONTAGUE (1873–   )

When Julius Caesar went to town
  To purchase steaks and chops and such,
He tried to beat the butchers down
  And swore their prices were too much.
" Two cents a pound for steak," he roared,
  " Why, man, that's nothing short of crime.
You butchers are a greedy horde,
  It cost but one in Noah's time! "

When Ollie Cromwell went to shop
  For beef and mutton and the like,
He said if prices didn't drop
  He'd spit the butchers on a spike.

"Six cents a pound for steak," he said.
"It's more than honest men can pay.
You folks are robbers, on the dead,
It cost but two in Caesar's day!"

Today when we go out and find
That beef is eighty cents a pound,
We tarry there and speak our mind
And scatter savage words around.
'Twas ever thus, in every age,
In every time and clime and season
The price of meat has made men rage
And always with abundant reason.

IT HAPPENS, OFTEN

By EDWIN MEADE ROBINSON (1878–   )

There was a man in our town
Whose Christian name was Jim;
He stepped into a pot of glue,
And fell and broke his limb.

The doctors tried to set it,
But still it would not mend;
He limped about, and would, no doubt,
Be limping to the end,

But on a day it happened
He walked abroad, and then
He stepped into some other glue,
And broke his leg again.

And when his leg was mended,
And he was out once more,
Both leg and man were stronger than
They'd ever been before!

So, when I broke my heart, once,
I thought of Mister Jim —
I went and broke it once again,
Now I'm as well as him!

THE BALLAD OF TWO LAME MEN

By Franklin P. Adams (1881–   )

As I was strolling a-down the street,
  In an utterly random way,
A couple of men I chanced to meet
  And a piteous pair were they.

Their limbs were bent, their heads awry,
  They seemed two sorry freaks;
And I spake them thus, oh, thus spake I,
  In the manner of Percy's Reliques:

" O have ye been to the footballe-field
  And maimèd been and bent?
Or gat ye hurts that never healed
  In a railway's accident?

" O have ye been to the bloudy wars?
  O have ye been through a wreck?
O whence are come these wounds and scars,
  And the crick of the back and neck? "

" We haena been to the footballe-field
  Nor maimèd been nor bent.
Nor gat we hurts that never healed
  In a railway's accident.

" We haena been to the bloudy wars,
  We haena been in a wreck,
And yet we have these wounds and scars,
  And the crick of the back and neck."

" O tell me, tell me, my sad-eyed men,
  Gif ye haena been to wars,
Whence ever these bruises came, and when
  Acquired ye those dredesome scars? "

Then up and spake me those gentil sirs:
  " By goddiswoundes, we are
The sixth and seventh passengers
  Of a seven-passenger car."

THOSE TWO BOYS

By FRANKLIN P. ADAMS

When Bill was a lad he was terribly bad.
  He worried his parents a lot;
He'd lie and he'd swear and pull little girls' hair;
  His boyhood was naught but a blot.

At play and in school he would fracture each rule —
  In mischief from autumn to spring;
And the villagers knew when to manhood he grew
  He would never amount to a thing.

When Jim was a child he was not very wild;
  He was known as a good little boy;
He was honest and bright and the teachers' delight —
  To his father and mother a joy.

All the neighbors were sure that his virtue'd endure,
  That his life would be free of a spot;
They were certain that Jim had a great head on him
  And that Jim would amount to a lot.

And Jim grew to manhood and honor and fame
  And bears a good name;
While Bill is shut up in a dark prison cell —
  You never can tell.

THE DURABLE BON MOT

By KEITH PRESTON (1884–1927)

When Whistler's strongest colors fade,
  When inks and canvas rot,
Those jokes on Oscar Wilde he made
  Will dog him unforgot.

For gags still set the world agog
  When fame begins to flag,
And, like the tail that wagged the dog,
  The smart tale dogs the wag.

ANY ONE WILL DO

ANONYMOUS

A maiden once, of certain age,
To catch a husband did engage;
But, having passed the prime of life
In striving to become a wife
Without success, she thought it time
To mend the follies of her prime.

Departing from the usual course
Of paint and such like for resource,
With all her might this ancient maid
Beneath an oak-tree knelt and prayed;
Unconscious that a grave old owl
Was perched above — the mousing fowl!

" Oh, give! a husband give! " she cried,
" While yet I may become a bride;
Soon will my day of grace be o'er,
And then, like many maids before,
I'll die without an early love,
And none to meet me there above!

" Oh, 'tis a fate too hard to bear!
Then answer this my humble prayer,
And oh, a husband give to me! "
Just then the owl from out the tree
In deep bass tones cried, " Who — Who — Who! "
" Who, Lord?   And dost Thou ask me who?
Why any one, good Lord, will do."

THE HUMORIST

By KEITH PRESTON

He must not laugh at his own wheeze:
A snuff box has no right to sneeze.

AMERICAN LIMERICKS

A silly young fellow named Hyde
In a funeral procession was spied;
  When asked, " Who is dead? "
  He giggled and said,
" I don't know; I just came for the ride."

There was a young person named Tate
Who went out to dine at 8.8,
  But I will not relate
  What that person named Tate
And his tête-à-tête ate at 8.8.

A certain young fellow named Beebe
Wished to wed with a lady named Phoebe.
  " But," said he, " I must see
  What the clerical fee
Be before Phoebe be Phoebe Beebe."

FOR FURTHER READING OF HUMOROUS POETRY

Adams, Charles Follen. *Yawcob Strauss, and Other Poems*
Adams, Franklin Pierce. *Something Else Again, So there!, The Second Conning-Tower Book, Tobogganing on Parnassus*
Burdette, Robert J. *Chimes from a Jester's Bells, Smiles Yoked with Sighs, The Silver Trumpets*
Burgess, Gelett. *Rubaiyat of Omar Cayenne, The Gaze of Youth*
Carryl, Charles Edward. *Davy and the Goblin, The Admiral's Caravan*
Carryl, Guy Wetmore. *Fables for the Frivolous, Grimm Tales Made Gay, Mother Goose for Grown-Ups*
Daly, Thomas Augustine. *Canzoni and Songs of Wedlock, Carmina, Little Polly's Pomes, Madrigali, McAroni Ballads*

Foss, Sam Walter. *Back Country Poems, Songs of the Average Man, The Volunteer Organist, Whiffs from Wild Meadows*

Guiterman, Arthur. *The Ballad-Maker's Pack, Ballads of Old New York, Song and Laughter, The Laughing Muse, The Light Guitar, The Mirthful Lyre, A Poet's Proverbs, Wildwood Fables*

Hay, John. *Pike County Ballads*

Herford, Oliver. *A Kitten's Garden of Verses, Rubaiyat of a Persian Kitten, Jingle Jungles*

Lanigan, George T. *Canadian Ballads, Fables by G. Washington Aesop*

Leland, Charles Godfrey. *Hans Breitmann's Ballads*

Marquis, Don. *archy and mehitable, Noah an' Jonah an' Cap'n John Smith, Poems and Portraits, Sonnets to a Red-Haired Lady, and Famous Love Affairs*

Montague, James J. *More Truth than Poetry*

Parker, Dorothy. *Enough Rope, Sunset Gun*

Preston, Keith. *Splinters, Pot Shots from Pegasus, Types of Pan*

Robinson, Edwin Meade. *Mere Melodies, Piping and Panning*

Roche, James Jeffrey. *Songs and Satires*

Russell, Irwin. *Christmas Night in the Quarters and Other Poems*

Sherman, Frank Dempster and Bangs, John Kendrick. *New Waggings of Old Tales*

Stuart, Ruth McEnery. *Daddy-do-Funny*

Taylor, Bert Leston. *Motley Measures, A Penny Whistle Together with the Babette Ballads*

Webb, Charles Henry. *John Paul's Book; Parodies, Prose and Verse; Vagrom Verse*

Wells, Carolyn. *Idle Idyls*

Humorous poems may also be found among the poems of the following authors, the poetry of each of whom, except Riley, may be obtained complete in a single volume:

Bunner, Henry Cuyler
Dunbar, Paul Laurence
Field, Eugene
Harte, Bret
Holmes, Oliver Wendell

Lowell, James Russell
Morley, Christopher
Riley, James Whitcomb
Saxe, John G.
Sherman, Frank Dempster

ANTHOLOGIES

Daly, Thomas Augustine. *Little Book of American Humorous Verse*

Duffield, publisher, *Book of American Humor in Prose and Verse*

Herford, Oliver, *Poems from " Life "*

Knowles, F. L. *The Poetry of American Wit and Humor*

Matthews, Brander. *American Familiar Verse*

Morley, Christopher. *Bowling Green, an Anthology of Verse*

Paget, R. L. *The Poetry of American Wit and Humor*
Preston, Keith. *Column Poets*
Stone & Co., Herbert S., publisher. *A Book of American Humorous Verse*
Wells, Carolyn. *A Nonsense Anthology, Such Nonsense! an Anthology,
A Whimsey Anthology, A Parody Anthology, A Satire Anthology,
Book of American Limericks, Book of Humorous Verse, Outline of
Humor, Being a True Chronicle from Prehistoric Ages to the Twen-
tieth Century, Vers de Société Anthology*

Drama

The word *drama* is used for any composition in prose or poetry which through dialogue and action tells a story. Sometimes action alone is employed and then it is called *pantomime*. If the lines are sung and the story is tragic it is grand opera. Ordinarily, however, the word *play* is used for any stage production in which the dialogue is actually spoken by actors who interpret on a stage the story as written by the author. Today the term *drama* must be extended to include both the moving and the talking pictures. In all forms of dramatic presentation there must be some sort of story, which, as given on a stage, or what in the movies corresponds to a stage, affords entertainment to an audience.

Dialogue the Core of Dramatic Art

Aside from the movies, the core of dramatic art is the dialogue as spoken by the characters and the action necessary to the development of the story. In order to appreciate and enjoy a play one must adjust himself to certain conventions, particularly such as help to overcome the limitations of the stage setting and the time available for the unfolding of the plot. Costumes and scenery help considerably, but they are only secondary to the action and the dialogue. Stage convention allows time to be condensed; events happen faster than in real life; and the dialogue is restricted to what helps to carry forward the plot, making it more clean cut and direct than in actual real life talk. The events or incidents represent only the high spots in the story, but these, together with the dialogue and action, must for the moment create the impression that what is presented on the stage is a cross section of life; and above all and always, a stage presentation must be interesting. If it fails in that it fails completely.

Plays Must Have Audience Value

Just what it is that makes a play interesting is difficult to explain. It may be the skill of the dramatist in constructing his play as to plot and dialogue; it may be the art of the producer who provides suitable scenery, appropriate costumes, and competent actors; or it may be the personality and talent of the actors. When all of these are combined there should be no doubt of the success of the production, but such is not by any means always the case. Plays have been known to fail under what seemed ideal conditions. On the other hand, it has happened that a poor play became a success because celebrated actors were entrusted with the important rôles; a good play frequently succeeds even when given by mediocre actors; and it has not been uncommon for a poor play with only ordinary acting to become a smashing " hit." The only test is production before an audience.

Types of the Drama

For the purpose of studying the drama it is well to learn how to distinguish between the various kinds of plays. In the so-called classic drama of ancient Greece and Rome, all plays were classified as either tragedies or comedies. A *tragedy* was a play that ended in disaster, usually the death of the leading character or characters. A *comedy* was a play that not only ended without a death but was full of humorous situations, the most humorous often being the discomfiture of the " hero." When Shakespeare's plays were first printed they were labeled comedies, tragedies, and histories, but today that threefold classification has been generally dropped. Plays are spoken of as comedies and tragedies, with some minor variations. For instance, if a comedy is hilariously and uproariously overdone it is called a *farce*. This form is most common in one-act plays and apt to be found on a vaudeville program. If a play presents a succession of sensational situations and unexpected happenings, with a generous dash of pathos and humor, it is a *melodrama*. In the American drama " Uncle Tom's Cabin," " East Lynne," and " The Old

Homestead " are famous examples. Nowadays the term melodrama has fallen into disrepute because it has come to be applied to all sorts of cheap claptrap overacted plays, more especially the " mystery " and crime plays that are to be found both on the regular stage and in the movies. It should be borne in mind that a genuine melodrama, honestly produced and well acted, is a thoroughly worthy representative of dramatic art. Many of Shakespeare's plays fall within the category of the melodrama.

The Joy of Reading Plays

It is hardly possible that any one reading this note or studying this book has not gone to a play of some kind; but it is not at all unlikely that a considerable number do not for some reason or other go to plays frequently, aside from the motion and talking pictures. In either case, in order to get the kind of knowledge about plays necessary for the cultured mind, it is essential that the student form the habit of reading them. Reading plays may be almost as interesting as seeing them on a regular stage. With a fair knowledge of dramatic technique gained from some actual attendance at plays or by study, it becomes possible for the reader to construct in his own mind an imaginative presentation of the play he is reading. Often indeed this may be an improvement over an actual performance because the reader is able to make his own version the way he thinks it should be by visualizing the characters, hearing how they talk, and seeing them go through the action as they interpret the plot. This is certainly better than seeing a play poorly produced.

Motion Pictures and the Drama

In the history of the drama great revolutions have usually occurred within a comparatively short time. The era of the ancient classic drama was brief, both in Greece and Rome, while the Elizabethan drama fell within a hundred years. The first thirty years of the twentieth century have seen many transformations in dramatic art in all countries in which a native drama flourished, the most significant being the rise and the marvelous development of the motion picture, a development that played havoc with the regular stage. With all its shortcomings, and they are many, the moving pictures can not be ignored as a form of dramatic entertainment, although they do not fall within the province of the present discussion, with the exception of their most recent development.

What Will Talking Pictures Do to the Stage?

The " talkies," to give them their colloquial name, as an adjunct to the movies may well transform the whole dramatic situation once more. Their improvement in the course of a single year has been remarkable. Aside from the removal of some of the most obvious technical defects, they are valiantly hitting at the most flagrant abuses of the older movies, such as the cheap emotionalism of the average silent movie and the acting which so often was nothing more than a fashion show. With the substitution of the regular drama acted by professional stage actors the talking motion picture has possibilities that can not even be guessed at. Already it is possible for the most remote community to see and hear the best plays adequately presented by the foremost actors of the day, a condition heretofore denied to literally hundreds of thousands of people. How all this will affect the regular stage remains to be seen.

THE DRAMA IN AMERICA

In the study of American literature no subject is more difficult of approach than that of the drama, the chief reason for which is the dearth of plays of genuine literary merit as contrasted with the tremendous activity of play writing and play acting that has been going on in this country from early times to the present. Plays are primarily written to be acted on a stage, and to be successful they must be entertaining; but to be entertaining they do not necessarily have to be of high literary merit, as that term is generally understood. Many a play, in former times as well as today, owed its success chiefly to what may be called theatrical values, that is, to its theme or story, to special occasions or what may be called timeliness, to the actors who spoke the lines and interpreted them through action, and at times even to the manner of stage presentation. To see and hear actors on a stage telling and acting a story, with all the trimmings that the art of dramatic production can supply, is often amply sufficient to carry a poor play to comparative success, a success that is legitimate enough but does not imply literary value. So the difficulty remains.

Factors that Contribute to a Successful Play

In all these respects the American drama and its history is no different from what it has been in all countries. In mere quantity there is no comparison between the number of plays produced and those that have survived because of literary qualities. In a study of the drama, therefore, it becomes necessary to think not only of the plays themselves but of the theater and its history, of the business of producing, and of the art of acting, each one of which is interesting but again not particularly literary. A play to be literary must have the same qualities that any other form of writing must possess if it is to be considered as part of enduring literature. If the story is not basically true to life, if the writing is slovenly, or if the characterization is muffed, the play is not literature, although good acting and adequate stagecraft may carry it to a temporary success in the theater.

The First American Play

With these general considerations in mind it becomes possible to sketch the history of the American drama from a point of view that is fair both to literature and to the stage. The earlier part of American dramatic history is mostly that of stage productions, and these began in the colonies before the end of the seventeenth century. The first recorded performance of a play in English was in 1665. The play bore the fascinating title of *Ye Bare and Ye Cubb,* but nothing more is known except that the three producers were haled into court and acquitted of whatever the offense may have been. This happened in Virginia, one of the states that was particularly broadminded on the subject of plays, as was the South generally. In the North, however, the drama had rough sledding until after the Revolution, for the Puritan and Quaker traditions were definitely hostile to the theater and to everything that smacked of worldly entertainment.

First American Players

There are records of early dramatic performances at schools and colleges and by semi-professional companies, but the first real theatrical company opened for business in Philadelphia in 1749, and the following year the same company gave a season in New York. Later they went south and for a time Virginia and Maryland became the theatrical center of the country. It was at Williamsburg that the famous Hallam Company started its long career as a producing organization, beginning in 1752 and continuing with many vicissitudes and frequent reorganizations until the end of the century. The members originally were all English, the most prominent being of the Hallam family, professional London actors. This company gave an amazing number of plays, both tragedies and comedies, including many of Shakespeare's and the popular successes of the eighteenth century English stage. From the South they went to New York, and later to Philadelphia. In both cities there was much opposition, but the Hallams seemed able to surmount all narrow-minded obstacles, for they built theaters in all the cities in which they acted. When opposition, usually from the churches, became too strong in one place they moved to another. It was this company which gave the first of two performances of the first play written by an American, *The Prince of Parthia* by Thomas Godfrey (1736–1763). Godfrey had finished the play in 1759 and submitted it to the company, but they did not bring it out until April 24, 1767, four years after the author's death. Its only other recorded performance was a revival staged in 1915 by a men's dramatic organization of the University of Pennsylvania.

The Drama During the American Revolution

The company became known as the American Company and kept on playing until, in 1774, all acting was prohibited in the colonies. The following year they moved to the West Indies where they remained until after the Revolution. The Revolution of course halted what would have been the normal development of the American drama. While there were many plays written by both Tories and Patriots, they are not especially important except as satires of the leaders of both sides, often exceedingly clever and always intensely partisan. With the coming of peace, interest in stage productions was revived. Many of the new plays, based on the war, as was natural, for every war brings its aftermath of plays, were surprisingly good. In 1787 the American Company, now once more at the John Street Theater in New York, produced the first comedy written by an American for the stage. This was *The Contrast,* by Royall Tyler (1757–1826), a satire on the New England point of view toward the drama and other provincialisms. The play was a success both in New York and in Philadelphia, but when it came to Boston it had to be advertised as " A Moral Lecture in five parts." Since the eighteenth century it has been revived a number of times, its most recent production being in 1917. Unlike *The Prince of Parthia,* the earliest American tragedy, *The Contrast* was written in prose.

William Dunlap, First American Producer

Prejudice against the theater gradually disappeared, with the exception of New England, and the American Company began to have formidable rivals. There was tremendous activity in play writing and a remarkable number of plays saw actual production. In those distant days a play was considered a success if it ran a week consecutively, and if it could be revived at short intervals. Dissension in the American Company caused a split-up and the managership fell to William Dunlap (1766–1839). He wrote and produced comedies, tragedies, farces, spectacles, and operas — in fact, everything that could be given on a stage. Of his more than fifty plays and adaptations, *André*, the first American tragedy based on American history, remains his best. In his *History of the American Theater*, the one great source book for the story of the American theater up to 1832, he records the fact that in September, 1809, Mr. and Mrs. David Poe were acting in a Monk Lewis play, " The Specter." Their son Edgar had been born the previous January.

John Howard Payne, another Important Early Dramatist

The only other figure worthy of mention in this sketch of the early drama is that of John Howard Payne (1791–1852). Like Dunlap, Payne wrote or adapted a vast number of plays, comedies, tragedies, farces, and operas. Feeling that it was impossible for an American to succeed in his own country, Payne went to London, where most of his plays were first produced. American companies, however, played them as fast as they could get them, but owing to the lack of laws governing rights to literary work the author received no compensation. But for all of Payne's eminence in the drama of his day, he would hardly be remembered today outside of stage history were it not for the song of " Home, Sweet Home," in a play called *Clari, or the Maid of Milan*. Largely because of the song, this play was a great success on the Covent Garden stage in London, where it was first produced in 1823, and in New York in the same year.

" Uncle Tom's Cabin " a Perennial Success

The reader will note that so far there has been practically nothing said about the literary value of the work of the dramatists discussed. Success on the stage came without that, and throughout the first half of the nineteenth century certain types of plays were constantly recurring, such as the historical, the domestic comedy and tragedy, romantic melodrama of every variety, and even plays built on politics. American history furnished an astonishing amount of material, from John Smith and Pocahontas, the Indians of the North, West, and

South, border warfare, the Revolution, down to the problems of the new nation as late as 1850. About that time the greatest political and social problem ever faced by the country began to be prominent in written work. That was Negro slavery. *Uncle Tom's Cabin* was published in 1852 and a dramatic version was produced the same year. It failed after eleven nights, but another version in the same year was played more than two hundred nights, a record run in those days and a good one at any time. For a time Joseph Jefferson played a minor part in it. In the course of a short time numerous other versions appeared, and it is still to be seen in stock companies today. The play of " Uncle Tom's Cabin " is an example of the kind of dramatic and literary horror that has had a stage success probably unequaled by anything else in the story of the acted drama. This is due to its emotional appeal, its mechanical devices in creating certain effects, such as Eliza crossing most realistic ice with her sawdust babe clasped to her breast, the howling bloodhounds, Topsy, Uncle Tom himself, and above all, Little Eva ascending to heaven by the wire and pulley route. This last absurdity was once played by a Miss Smith, better known today as Mary Pickford.

Regional Dramas and Comedies of Manners Introduced After Civil War

In the last decades before the Civil War other types of plays developed, especially one that may be called the drama of local color or regional drama. This was mostly comedy that emphasized or exaggerated various localisms, from the Yankee to the Hoosier; again, it might be New York or Philadelphia that was held up to laughter. At the same time there was considerable interest in so-called social comedy, or the comedy of manners, much of which was satiric. The most representative play of this type was *Fashion,* by Anna Cora Ogden, also known as Mrs. Mowatt and later as Mrs. Ritchie, produced in 1845. It remains the best play of its kind and its time because it was clean and wholesome as well as genuine in its motives and realistic in its characterizations. In 1917 the Drama League of New York gave a performance of certain scenes from plays of historic interest in the American drama, one of which was from *Fashion.* This was approved so highly by the audience that it was repeated at subsequent performances. It has since been played by student organizations at the University of Chicago and the University of Pennsylvania, and on the professional stage.

Joseph Jefferson and His Domestic Drama, "Rip Van Winkle"

Of domestic dramas before the Civil War the most important is *Rip Van Winkle* as adapted and acted by Joseph Jefferson. Irving's story appeared in 1819, and within ten years two stage versions were produced. In the second and more successful of the two, three members of the Jefferson family had minor parts. The play was revised from time to time, with some one or more of the Jeffersons in it, but it was the third Joseph Jefferson (1829–1905) who gave the play distinction and made it part of American stage history. In 1859 he made an adaptation from the earlier versions and acted the part of Rip the same year, but the play known to theater-goers of more recent days was not made until 1865. In that year Joe Jefferson was in London and there obtained the assistance of the Irish dramatist Dion Boucicault in making the play over once more. In September, 1865, it was produced at the Adelphi Theater in London and ran for one hundred and seventy nights. A year later Jefferson brought his play to America, producing it first in New York and then all over the United States. Joe Jefferson acted in plays other than *Rip Van Winkle*, but he is definitely identified with the character of Rip, whom he continued to impersonate until 1904, a year before his death.

Boker the First American Playwright of Literary Standing

With the mention of the name of George Henry Boker (1823–1890) the student is at last introduced to a dramatist whose work is of real literary merit. Boker was a Philadelphian, a man of wealth and the highest social standing, a graduate of Princeton, and an energetic student of literature, especially that of foreign countries. He became distinguished as a poet, and in the latter part of his life as a diplomat. In the drama he is best in tragedy, his greatest being *Francesca da Rimini,* based upon a famous Italian story which has frequently appealed to dramatists, both before Boker's day and since. Boker's play afforded the American actor Lawrence Barrett his finest opportunity in character acting. In the original company of Barrett was Otis Skinner, who, in 1901, revived the play with himself in the old Barrett rôle. The mention of Mr. Skinner is of interest because he is still, in the year 1930, active on the stage. But this is getting ahead too fast, for *Francesca da Rimini* was actually written in 1853 and was first played two years later.

Dion Boucicault Inaugurates Traveling Companies After the Civil War

The life of Dion Boucicault (1820–1890) was almost exactly contemporaneous with that of Boker, but there the similarity ends. Boucicault was born in Ireland, spent four years in France, came to America, went to London, and finally returned to America, where he exerted a powerful influence in the dramatic world. He was a writer of plays, an actor and a producer — and tremendously active in each line. His chief connection with literary drama was the knack he had of turning novels and short stories into plays, among them *Nicholas Nickleby* and *The Cricket on the Hearth* by Dickens, and part of Scott's *Heart of Midlothian*. At the time of his death he was dramatizing Bret Harte's short story, " The Luck of Roaring Camp." A second important connection with the drama was his introduction of Irish plays. As a producer he was responsible for the road show, that is, traveling companies instead of traveling " stars " who would head local stock companies. While this innovation was of inestimable advantage to audiences, it was far less so to playwrights, for a traveling company, producing only a single play, reduced the market for new plays. The story of these traveling companies can not be told here with the exception of the fact that in recent years they have been threatened with extinction by the advent of the moving pictures and the high cost of transportation, and, one may add parenthetically, by the salaries paid to the leading stars. A valiant attempt to preserve good stage drama in the larger cities is being made (1930) by the Theater Guild of New York, but what the new talking pictures will do to the regular drama, traveling and otherwise, is still to be seen.

The Importance of William Dean Howells

From this point on the discussion will be confined to a few of the greatest names around whom the development of the later drama has been and is centered. It is to be regretted that it is not possible to do more than mention some of the great actors and actresses who have played no insignificant part in the history of our drama since the Civil War. When Mark Twain and Bret Harte were public idols the drama turned to comedy and the western frontier types. During the nineties, when the historical novel flourished, it was the practice to dramatize them, and later, with the advent of realism in fiction, the plays reflected this realistic tendency. Great impetus was given to the movement by the novels of William Dean Howells (1837–1920) and the series of light comedies into which he introduced the same photographic realism of character that was typical of his fiction. Most of his plays and farces are quite readable today, especially *The Mouse Trap*, *The Sleeping Car*, and *Five O'Clock Tea*.

David Belasco, Producer and Dramatist

With the exception of Clyde Fitch, the dramatists whose work remains to be discussed are all living and for the most part active in their profession. David Belasco (1853–   ) is best known as a producer, although he has acted and his hand has appeared in many plays as collaborator or adapter. His first important collaboration was with John Luther Long, the novelist, whose story, *Madame Butterfly*, was turned into a play, successfully acted in this country and in London. In the first night London audience was the Italian composer Puccini, and this led directly to the composition of one of the most famous grand operas of this century. Two years later, in 1902, Long and Belasco produced *The Darling of the Gods*, also a Japanese story, and again acted by Blanche Bates, an actress then at the height of her powers. Other plays by Belasco are *The Return of Peter Grimm* (1911) and *Kiki* (1921). Belasco is particularly noted for the attention he has always given to his methods of production, which, for perfection of realistic detail, have scarcely if ever been equaled in this country.

William Gillette, Actor and Playwright

Just as Belasco is usually thought of as a producer, so William Gillette (1855–   ) stands out primarily as an actor, although he has written and adapted many plays. *Held by the Enemy* (1898) and *Secret Service* (1898) are both plays with a Civil War background, proving that the American public responds to patriotic drama if well constructed and adequately presented. *Sherlock Holmes* (1899) is one of several plays made over from popular fiction of the day.

Augustus Thomas an Outstanding Figure

Belasco came from the far West, Gillette from New England, and Augustus Thomas (1857–   ) from the Middle West. After considerable amateur and semi-professional experience as actor, producer, and writer in his native city of St. Louis, Thomas, like all workers in the drama, went to New York. Augustus Thomas was definitely interested in what was still a problem back in the nineties — a complete unification of all parts of the country, especially the South with the North. He conceived the idea of writing a series of regional plays under the titles of various states, beginning with *Alabama* in 1898, and continuing with *Arizona* in 1899, *Colorado* in 1901, and *In Mizzoura* in 1916. The second is still performed by stock companies. Thomas's most successful play was *The Witching Hour* (1916) and his best *The Copperhead* (1918).

Clyde Fitch Features the " Period Play "

The closing decade of the nineteenth century and the opening of the twentieth saw the almost spectacular career of Clyde Fitch (1865–1909). His first play, *Beau Brummell* (1890), was suggested by the famous dramatic critic William Winter and acted by Richard Mansfield, America's foremost actor. After such an auspicious beginning Fitch continued to write plays with an almost frenzied activity, some thirty in all, until his untimely death. His special forte was the social play of manners, often tinged with historical background, or what was then called the " period " play. His plays based on American history are *Nathan Hale* (1899), *Barbara Frietchie* (1900), and *Major André* (1903). Of his remaining plays *The Truth* (1907) and *The City* (1909) are perhaps the best. For further discussion of Fitch see page 850.

Some Contemporary Dramatists

The first quarter of the twentieth century has seen many innovations in the drama, some of which at least are decidedly in the direction of improvement. More attention is placed upon literary value, partially due to better copyright laws which encourage the publishing of plays for the reader. Among recent and contemporary playwrights whose work is noteworthy from this angle are William Vaughn Moody (1869–1910), Percy MacKaye (1875–), Booth Tarkington (1869–), and Eugene O'Neill (1888–). The last two are discussed in connection with their plays printed in this volume.

The " Little Theater " Movement

Since the movies sounded the death-knell of the traveling company, the need for the drama has found expression throughout the country in various ways. In many cities stock companies have been revived. Schools and colleges have increased their interest in the drama, and students all over the land are writing and producing. But probably most important of all has been the growth of the " Little Theater " movement. Over three thousand of these " Little Theaters " exist in our country, fostered by real lovers of the drama, courageous and independent, keeping alive the best of the old and giving an opportunity often denied by the commercial theater for the production of the new. Several of them have achieved signal success. The Provincetown Players in Massachusetts, to which Eugene O'Neill for a time attached himself, has been of real importance in the development of American play writing. And the Theater Guild of New York City, started as a " Little Theater," has developed a distinguished repertory which it is now extending to the larger cities. The Little Theater movement has been especially important in the development of the one-act play, which, being shorter and less exacting in its requirements than the regulation full-length drama, more nearly matches the needs and the abilities of amateur actors. With the commercial theater in the metropolises, the " Little Theater " across the country, the interest of school and college dramatic societies, and the as-yet-unplumbed possibilities of the " talkies," the situation in American drama today is more than encouraging.

The Future of the American Drama

What the future holds we may only guess, but we can not help feeling that the great interest in drama all over the United States may reasonably be compared to the period of growing interest which resulted in the unexcelled drama of the Elizabethan Age. And if we are approaching the " golden age " of American drama, each of you may have a share in it, if not as writer or actor, at least as audience. That is a real share, for no great art ever flourishes without an intelligent and appreciative following.

THE TRYSTING PLACE[1]

By BOOTH TARKINGTON (1869–   )

Our first play is a one-act comedy dealing with modern life. It is put at the beginning because it contains only familiar material. In the humorous situation developed there is nothing strange or difficult to come between you and the fun Mr. Tarkington has created for your enjoyment.

Booth Tarkington has written so many different kinds of things that we scarcely know how to classify him. In fact, he has in no uncertain terms emphatically protested against any attempt at classification at all. We have already learned that he wrote novels and short stories, and now we find that he deserves consideration as a dramatist.

Booth Tarkington was born in Indiana and as a boy cultivated the friendship of the much older James Whitcomb Riley, the Hoosier poet. One of Tarkington's boyhood heroes was Jesse James. It is a long cry from Jesse James to William Dean Howells, whom Mr. Tarkington considers the greatest influence that American letters has produced; but perhaps that very distance is a good gauge of the breadth of Mr. Tarkington's literary interests.

At Princeton University "Tark" won popularity by his good fellowship and modesty, and acquired fame by rendering in his splendid bass voice a blood-curdling version of Kipling's "Danny Deever." Princeton men of his college generation declare that whenever there was an evening "sing" on the steps of historic Nassau Hall, the climax of the evening was sure to be this particular "stunt" of "Tark's," of which the men never tired.

Booth Tarkington should be added to Thomas Bailey Aldrich and Mark Twain as the best creators of the American boy in literature. You doubtless are already familiar with the *Penrod* stories. *Seventeen*, both as novel and play, and the comedy *Clarence* are two of our best delineations of the boy of high school age.

The Trysting Place illustrates Mr. Tarkington's ability to portray young America humorously, yet sympathetically. There is not much for you to do with this little comedy except enjoy it, laugh at it, and perhaps act it. But your enjoyment of this play, and of future plays as well, will depend upon your ability to adapt yourself to stage conventions and to see the play in action. So set your imagination to work. Keep the stage picture before you, and get the combination of action and word as if you were seeing the play from across the footlights.

THE PEOPLE AS THEY COME INTO THE PLAY

MRS. CURTIS, *The Young Woman, twenty-five or perhaps even a little older*

LANCELOT BRIGGS, *The Boy, slim and obviously under twenty*

MRS. BRIGGS, *his mother, a handsome woman of forty-five or fifty*

JESSIE, *his sister, a pretty girl of about twenty*

RUPERT SMITH, *The Young Man, about twenty-five*

MR. INGOLDSBY, *a man of fifty-five, or, possibly, sixty*

THE MYSTERIOUS VOICE, *male and adult*

The scene is a room just off the " lounge " of a hotel in the country. However, this is not a " country hotel "; but, on the contrary, one of those vast and elaborate houses of entertainment that affect an expensive simplicity in what is called the colonial manner, and ask to be visited — by those financially able to do so — in the general interest of health and the outdoor life. The wall at the back of the stage is broken only by symmetrically spaced pilasters of an ivory color; each of the side walls is broken in the same manner; but here the pilasters help to frame two rather broad entrances, one at the right and one at the left, and beyond these entrances, on both sides, we have glimpses of the two corridors that lead to them. There are a few old prints — or new prints from old plates — upon the walls; and there are flowering plants on stands in the corners. The furniture consists of some chintz-covered easy-chairs, a light wicker settee with a chintz cushion and a valance that reaches the floor; and there are two wicker tables with a vase of jonquils upon each of them. In the rear right-hand corner of the room, near the stand of plants, there is a tropical-looking chair, wicker, with a back of monstrous size — a Philippine Island chair — and in the opposite corner is its mate.

Dance music is heard from a distant orchestra. Just after the rise of the curtain two people come in together from the left — a young woman of twenty-five, or perhaps she is even a little older, and a slim boy obviously under twenty. She is rather elaborate in her afternoon indoor dress, but none the less effectively pretty; he is of a scrubbed and sleeked youthfulness, in white trousers, a short black coat and dancing shoes; and from the moment of his first appearance he is seen to be in an extremity of love. He leans as near the young woman as he can; his eyes search her face yearningly and without intermission; he caroms into her slightly as they come in, and repeats

*the carom unwittingly. They have evidently just come from the
dancing floor and are a little flushed; she fans herself with her handkerchief and he fans her with his. They are heard talking before
they enter: " Oh, let's do find some place to sit down! " she is saying; and he, simultaneously: " Oh, wasn't that divine! You dance
just simply divinely! " These speeches " bring them on."*

The Young Woman. Here's a place we can sit down! [*She immediately drops into a chair.*]

The Boy. Yes, this is a lovely place, where nobody is at all. It's
the only quiet place in the hotel: you never see more than two people
here at a time, because it's kind of off, like this. That's why I
wanted to walk this way. [*Sitting on a lounge and leaning toward
her.*] Isn't it divine to be in a place where nobody is at *all?*

The Young Woman. [*Still fanning herself*] Why, you and I are
here.

The Boy. Yes; but I mean nobody else at all. We're practically
all alone, practically.

The Young Woman. [*Laughing as she waves her hand to indicate
the spacious corridors to the right and left*] Alone? Why, there
are at least three hundred people in this hotel.

The Boy. Yes, but they're all either outdoors, or dancin', or
havin' tea, right now. It's practically the same as being alone. It is
— practically, I mean.

The Young Woman. Yes, I've noticed that it was a rather secluded spot myself. [*She glances about the room thoughtfully, then
turns to him, smiling.*] Don't you want to run and dance with some
of those pretty young girls your own age?

The Boy. [*With pained earnestness*] Them? My goodness, no!

The Young Woman. Oh, but that isn't normal, is it?

The Boy. I'm not normal. I don't want to be normal.

The Young Woman. Well, but it would only be natural for you
to like those pretty young things, so — Well, *do* run and dance with
one of 'em. Won't you, please?

The Boy. [*Interrupting*] No. They haven't got any experience
of life. What I like is a woman that's had some experience of life,
like you.

The Young Woman. But at your age —

The Boy. Age hasn't got anything to do with it. The thing that
brings a man and a woman together, it's when they have about the
same amount of experience of life.

The Young Woman. [*Absently*] You think that's it, Mr. Briggs? [*She looks about the room thoughtfully as she speaks.*]

Mr. Briggs. [*With intense seriousness*] I know it is. I had that feeling the minute I was introduced to you, night before last in the lobby — right by the third column beyond the office news stand, at a quarter after nine o'clock in the evening.

The Young Woman. You did?

Mr. Briggs. It came over me, and I felt kind of — [*he swallows*] kind of drawn to you, Missuz — Missuz — Missuz — [*He seems to hesitate somewhat emotionally.*]

The Young Woman. My name is Mrs. Curtis. You seem to have forgotten it.

Mr. Briggs. [*Swallowing again*] I haven't. I know it's Curtis. The trouble is, it kind of upsets me to call you *Missuz* Curtis. I thought it was Miss Curtis when I was introduced to you. I didn't know your name was Missuz — Missuz —Missuz Curtis till the clerk told me, early the next morning.

Mrs. Curtis. [*Frowning a little*] The clerk told you?

Mr. Briggs. Yes. I asked him if he'd noticed whether you'd gone in to breakfast yet. He said, " You mean Missuz — Missuz Curtis? " Then I knew you must be married. [*He shakes his head ruefully.*]

Mrs. Curtis. [*Smiling*] Well?

Mr. Briggs. [*Thoughtfully*] Well, it can't be helped.

Mrs. Curtis. I suppose not.

Mr. Briggs. [*Brightening a little*] Well, anyhow, I had that — that sort of *drawn* feeling toward you, the way I *would* get toward a woman that's had some experience of life; but a hotel like this is no place to explain feelings like that. You can't when you're dancing — not the way you want to — and all the rest of the time you had some o' those *old* men hangin' around, or else my mother and sister wanted me for something; because a hotel like this — why, it's terrible the way a young man's mother and sister want him to do somep'n for 'em *all* the time; so this is the first chance I've had.

Mrs. Curtis. [*Rather urgently*] Don't you really think you'd better be dancing with some of those young things yonder?

Mr. Briggs. [*Puzzled*] Think I'd *better* be?

Mrs. Curtis. Yes; I do really wish you would. Wouldn't it be a lot more fun than explaining something, as you said, to me?

Mr. Briggs. [*Hurriedly*] No. No, it wouldn't. I want to explain how I feel about you.

Mrs. Curtis. Please go and dance, Mr. Briggs. I think it would be *much* better if you —

Mr. Briggs. [*Rapidly*] No, it wouldn't. I want to explain how I feel about you, so you'll understand. It's like this, Missuz [*swallowing again*] Missuz Curtis. I never used to think I'd ever get to feeling this way about — about somebody that was married, but it — it came over me before I knew you *were* married. I already *was* feeling this way before he said, " You mean — you mean Missuz Curtis? " It'd already — [*he swallows*] happened to me before I knew you were a — a married woman. [*Shaking his head.*] I certainly never *did* think I'd feel this way about a married woman.

Mrs. Curtis. But I'm not — not as you mean it. I'm a widow, Mr. Briggs.

Mr. Briggs. [*As in a dim perplexity*] A wid — You're a widow? [*He jumps up suddenly, greatly amazed.*] Oh, my!

Mrs. Curtis. What's the matter?

Mr. Briggs. Oh, my!

Mrs. Curtis. What is it?

Mr. Briggs. I guess I've got to get used to the idea of it. First I thought you weren't married, and then I was just gettin' used to the idea that you *were,* and now — well, I s'pose it's a good deal better, your bein' a widow, though, except — except for —

Mrs. Curtis. Except for?

Mr. Briggs. [*Hurriedly*] Oh, I didn't mean except for your husband! I didn't mean your bein' a widow was better for — [*He checks himself and swallows.*]

Mrs. Curtis. Oh!

Mr. Briggs. [*Frowning with thought*] No. I meant more on account of the way my family treats me. My mother and sister — well, to tell the truth, they always seem to think I'm about four years old. They can't seem to *realize;* and when I go and tell 'em you're a *widow* —

Mrs. Curtis. You think they'll be interested in hearing it? I haven't even met them.

Mr. Briggs. No, but — but of course they've been *talkin'* about you quite a good deal.

Mrs. Curtis. They have?

Mr. Briggs. You know how people are in a hotel like this: wondering who everybody else *is,* and whether some woman's some old man's wife or his daughter or just a trained nurse, and all so on. Of course my family noticed *you* right away and then after I *met* you of course then they said a *lot* more about you. Golly! [*He shakes his head, indicating that the comment has been unfavorable.*]

Mrs. Curtis. Oh, indeed!

Mr. Briggs. [*Ruefully*] They watch me like a hawk, and I know what they'll say now! When I tell 'em you're a widow, I mean.

Mrs. Curtis. Do you?

Mr. Briggs. [*Shaking his head*] I certainly never thought myself I would ever get to feeling this way about a widow *either!*

Mrs. Curtis. Don't you *really* think you'd better run and dance with one of those —

Mr. Briggs. [*Absently*] No. [*Turning to her suddenly.*] I was goin' to ask you — well, of course, in a — a technical way, so to speak, I mean in a strickly technical way, so to speak, I'm not exactly of age yet, and I suppose I'd have to get my mother's consent, because *she's* a widow, too, and got herself appointed my guardian besides; and the truth is, she's a pretty cold-hearted, bossy kind of a woman, and it's goin' to be a big difficulty gettin' her to see this thing right.

Mrs. Curtis. To see *what* right?

Mr. Briggs. The way I feel about you. I know it's goin' to be difficult, because I started to talk a little about it last night to my mother and my sister — her name's Jessie — and they behaved — well, they behaved a good deal like two fiends.

Mrs. Curtis. They did?

Mr. Briggs. I told 'em they didn't know you, and they *haven't* even *met* you, but they treated me like a — a mere *jest;* and then they got so critical, the way they talked about you, it might be better if they didn't see me with you again for a few days. I can't stand the way they talk after they see me with you.

Mrs. Curtis. Indeed!

Mr. Briggs. Well, what I was saying: I can't touch my principal till I'm twenty-one on account of the way my father went and tied up his will; but of course my mother and sister think a good many'll be after me on account of it; but, anyhow, I *have* got to feeling this way, and I know I'll *never* get over it, so what I wanted to ask you — well, it's — it's — [*he swallows*] it's just this: I know you *are* a widow and everything like that, but would you be willing to — [*he swallows*] well, of course I don't know how long since you lost your first husband —

Mrs. Curtis. [*Incredulously*] What! [*She rises.*]

Mr. Briggs. I mean I — I don't know how you *would* feel about gettin' married again yet, even if I didn't have my own difficulties about it, but — but —

Mrs. Curtis. [*With increased incredulity*] Are you *proposing* to me, Mr. Briggs?

Mr. Briggs. Well — uh — yes. [*Then, looking beyond her down the corridor on the right.*] Oh, goodness. They watch me like a hawk! Here comes my mother! [*Dismayed, he turns to the left.*]

Mrs. Curtis. [*As he turns*] Perhaps it was time!

Mr. Briggs. [*Dismally*] There's my sister Jessie!

Mrs. Curtis. What of it?

Mr. Briggs. [*Hastily*] I told you they behave like two fiends when they see me with you. [*Glancing right and left nervously.*] Well, excuse me. [*With perfect gravity he kneels at one end of the settee, which is in the rear, a little left of " center."*] It'll be a good deal better if they don't see me, I expect. [*He promptly crawls under the settee, and the valance conceals him entirely. From this invisibility, he appeals with pathetic urgency in a hoarse whisper*]: They'll prob'ly go right on. *Please* wait! Or — if you *haf* to go, come *back!*

> [MRS. CURTIS *stands dumbfounded for a moment; and then, controlling a tendency to laugh immoderately, she turns to examine a print on the left wall as* MR. BRIGGS'S MOTHER *enters from the right.* MRS. BRIGGS *is a handsome woman of forty-five or fifty, not now in a gracious mood. She comes in decisively, halts, and stares at* MRS. CURTIS' *back. Then she looks over the room in an annoyed and puzzled manner.* MR. BRIGGS'S *sister* JESSIE *comes in from the left. She is a pretty girl of about twenty, but her expression is now rather cross. Her dress and equipment show that she has just come in from the golf course.*]

Jessie. [*Calling as she comes in*] Lancelot! [*She halts, puzzled, and looks inquiringly at her mother.*] Mamma, where's Lancelot? I was sure I saw him in here just a second ago.

Mrs. Briggs. [*Grimly*] So was I. [*After looking at each other, they turn their heads simultaneously and stare at* MRS. CURTIS, *who appears to be interested in the print.*] It's very odd!

Jessie. Yes, very.

> [*The two again look at each other, and at a little distance appear to consult telepathically, without any change of ex-*

pression; then they turn once more to look at Mrs.
Curtis.]

Mrs. Briggs. I beg your pardon, but I'm under the impression
that you have met my son.

Mrs. Curtis. [*Turning*] Yes?

Jessie. Wasn't he here just now?

Mrs. Curtis. Yes, he was.

Mrs. Briggs. Would you be good enough to tell me, did he leave
here to go to his room?

Mrs. Curtis. [*Casually*] I don't think so; he didn't say so. [*She
gives them a little nod, smiling politely, and goes out at the left.
They stare after her.*]

Jessie. [*Still staring after* Mrs. Curtis] She's a very bold type.

Mrs. Briggs. [*Seating herself on the settee*] Very.

Jessie. [*Turning to her*] I don't see how that little goose got
away. You were coming from that direction and I from just yonder.
I suppose he thought we'd say something that would embarrass him
before her.

Mrs. Briggs. I suppose she's thirty-five. I've heard of such people, but I never saw one before.

Jessie. I regard her as distinctly the dangerous type of adven-
turess.

Mrs. Briggs. Certainly. In the first place, her not having told
the child frankly that she's a widow. One of the clerks told *me* she
was.

Jessie. Oh, she did that to flatter him into believing he's a real
grown-up " man of the world " having an " affair " !

Mrs. Briggs. So that when he's sufficiently entangled she can tell
him she's a widow — and by that time we don't know *what* he'd do!
A country justice of the peace probably!

Jessie. Last night, when we were trying to teach him a little common sense about strange people in hotels, what was it he said she
was? " An angel! " — oh, yes! — " One of heaven's highest angels."

Mrs. Briggs. [*Grimly*] He said he wouldn't " listen to one of
heaven's highest angels gettin' talked against by a lot o' women! "
I'm sure they heard him in the next suite. [*She rises.*] I suppose
you'd better go and see where he slipped out to, Jessie. Of course,
he'll try to find *her* again as soon as he can.

Jessie. [*Dropping into a chair*] I played three times round the
course. Do you mind if I just sit here a while and rest?

Mrs. Briggs. Then why don't you go to your room?

Jessie. [*Laughing feebly*] I'm just too tired. I will in a minute. [*With a gesture toward the left entrance.*] Hadn't you better —

Mrs. Briggs. Keep her in sight? Yes. That's easier than trying to keep *him* in sight. You're going up to your room right away, aren't you?

Jessie. Yes, in only a minute. I really think you'd better go, Mamma. He might —

Mrs. Briggs. No, I'll see to that! [*She goes out.*]

[JESSIE *stares after her for a moment, glances at a wrist watch, then rises and looks down the corridor beyond the entrance at the right. She appears to derive some satisfaction from what she sees there, returns to her chair and sits in a carefully graceful attitude, her expression demure. A moment later a young man — he is about twenty-five — comes in rather nervously from the right. He pauses near the entrance.*]

The Young Man. You!

Jessie. [*Softly*] You!

The Young Man. Is your mother —

Jessie. She's gone.

The Young Man. [*Nervously advancing*] I — I —

Jessie. I was afraid maybe we couldn't have this nook to ourselves, after all. My absurd little brother was in here, hanging about that dreadful Mrs. Curtis, and I was afraid they wouldn't go away; but Mamma scared 'em both off providentially.

The Young Man. [*Moving a chair close to hers and sitting*] And so we're alone! [*He speaks with a sentimental hushedness.*] All alone!

Jessie. All alone, Rupert! This is the only place in the hotel where you *can* be by yourself a while. That's why I said to meet here.

Rupert. [*Nervously*] You don't think your mother'll be back for a while?

Jessie. No; she won't.

Rupert. She hasn't found out I've come, has she?

Jessie. She hasn't the remotest idea, thank heaven! Nobody dreams you're within hundreds of miles of here. That's one advantage of a big hotel.

Rupert. Darling —

Jessie. Yes, darling?

[*The settee moves slightly at this, but it is behind them and they do not see it.*]

Rupert.   I can't understand why your mother dislikes me so.

Jessie.   [*Gravely*] Well, I suppose her feeling about you is — well, she *says* it's because you're rather poor and I'm — not.

Rupert.   But what makes her think I care about you because you're not?

Jessie.   Well —

Rupert.   [*Leaning toward her and lowering his voice*] Darling, there's something I want to ask you —

Jessie.   [*Leaning toward him and almost whispering*] Yes, dearest, what is it?

[*The settee slowly moves nearer them as their voices become more indistinct.*]

Rupert.   I want to ask you —

Jessie.   Yes?

Rupert.   [*With hushed tenderness*] Do you *really* love me, dearest?

Jessie.   [*Gazing upward, tranced*] Oh, dearest, I do!

[*The settee goes back to where it came from.*]

Rupert.   But you don't think your mother'll ever change her mind about me?

Jessie.   She never does change her mind.

Rupert.   Then what can we do?

Jessie.   [*In a low voice*] Darling, there's something I wouldn't say for anything in the world to anybody but you.

[*The settee again approaches slightly.*]

Rupert.   Yes?

Jessie.   I think Mamma really knows you're not mercenary, but the *real* reason for her opposition to you is pretty selfish. I think it's because she doesn't want me to marry and go away and leave her alone in the world.

Rupert.   But she wouldn't be. She'd still have the companionship of your young brother.

Jessie.   [*Shaking her head*] That'd be the same as none. Lancelot seems to have scarcely *any* sense, you see.

[*The settee once more retires.*]

Rupert.   Then I don't see what possible hope —

Jessie. [*Warning him as she sees someone approaching in the corridor to the right*] Sh-h-h!

Rupert. [*Following her gaze*] Who *is* that old chap?

Jessie. It's old Mr. Ingoldsby. He's some old friend of Mamma's that happened to turn up here.

Rupert. [*Moving as if to withdraw*] I'd better —

Jessie. [*Quickly*] No; he doesn't know you. Sit still. [*She turns toward* Mr. Ingoldsby *with a smile as he enters.*] Good afternoon, Mr. Ingoldsby. Did you do it in eighty-five again today?

[Ingoldsby *is a man of fifty-five or, possibly, sixty. He wears neat knickerbockers and is otherwise sprightly in his outdoor attire. He smiles rather absently as he replies.*]

Ingoldsby. Eighty-five? No, I — ah — no. I didn't go round today. Ah — has Mrs. Briggs been here?

Jessie. Here?

Ingoldsby. Yes, I mean — ah — here.

Jessie. I think she's somewhere looking for Lancelot.

Ingoldsby. Yes? Ah — I —

Jessie. Is there something you'd like me to tell her when I see her?

Ingoldsby. [*Going toward the left entrance*] No; I — I — [*He glances at his watch, and looks absently at* Jessie.] No, I believe I — ah — [*He departs.*]

Rupert. Well, I *do* hope nobody else'll come poking about like that, because I —

Jessie. No, darling; we're alone again now.

Rupert. Darling —

Jessie. Yes, darling?

Rupert. We've had such difficulties in managing our little interviews; it does seem a precious thing to be near you again.

Jessie. Oh, it does!

Rupert. If we could only go away together, where it could *always* be like this —

Jessie. [*Dreamily*] Yes, with the world shut out.

Rupert. Why can't we —

Jessie. Hush, darling. [*She sees someone approaching in the corridor on the left. He looks dolefully in that direction.*]

Jessie. It's that dreadful woman.

Rupert. I don't know her.

Jessie. She's been trying to entangle Lancelot, and he's com-

pletely lost what slight intelligence he *had*, the little ninny! She's
old enough to be his mother.

[*The settee makes a slight convulsive movement.*]

Rupert. Sh! She'll hear you.

[MRS. CURTIS *enters from the left. She looks about, with a faint
embarrassment.* JESSIE *stares at her, then speaks coldly.*]

Jessie. I beg your pardon. Did you leave something when you
were here with my little brother?

Mrs. Curtis. [*Smiling constrainedly*] Did you happen to see a pair
of white gloves?

[RUPERT *rises and looks in his chair.*]

Jessie. No. There aren't any here.

Mrs. Curtis. I *may* have left them anywhere of course. [*To*
RUPERT] Don't bother, please. I thought just possibly — [*She
stoops slightly and looks behind the settee, and her expression shows
a considerable illumination.*] If I *had* left anything here I just
wanted to see if it was still —

Jessie. No; there aren't any gloves here. [*She speaks in a sharp
whisper to* RUPERT.] Sit down! [*He does so. Their backs are
toward* MRS. CURTIS.]

Mrs. Curtis. No. They don't seem to be. I'm sorry to have
disturbed you.

[*She moves toward the left entrance as she speaks. The settee
follows her. She checks it with a sudden commanding push.*]

Jessie. I hardly think my little brother will come back *here*.
My mother went to look for him.

Mrs. Curtis. [*Politely*] No doubt she's found him by this time.

[*She looks from the settee to* JESSIE *and* RUPERT, *and back again;
and her eyes widen with an intense inward struggle.*]

Jessie. [*Turning to look at her coolly*] Was there anything else?

Mrs. Curtis. [*After a moment, during which her inward struggle
prevents her from replying*] Oh — oh, no! I'm so sorry to have
disturbed you! [*Her voice threatens to break and she goes out
hurriedly, at the left.*]

Jessie. [*Staring after her*] Absolutely brazen! She came back
after that idiot *boy!* Thought *he'd* probably come back!

Rupert. Darling —

Jessie. [*Turning to him eagerly*] Yes, darling —

Rupert. [*Looking over her shoulder*] Oh, my goodness! [*He speaks with intense anguish.*]

Jessie. [*Seizing his hand feverishly*] What's the matter, darling?

Rupert. [*Rising*] It's your mother! [*He strides hastily backward out of sight from the left entrance.*]

Jessie. Oh, murder!

Rupert. She didn't see me, but she will if I try to go out there. [*He points to the right entrance.*]

Jessie. She's coming!

Rupert. This is awful! [*His despairing eye falls upon the huge Philippine chair in the left rear corner of the room; he rushes to it, turns it round, with its back toward the front, and sits in it, concealed from view. He speaks in a hoarse whisper.*] Darling —

Jessie. Hush! [*She has checked an impulse to rise and fly; and now, affecting carelessness, she brushes her left sleeve with her right hand, crosses her knees, swings her foot, whistles an operatic air and looks at the ceiling. MRS. BRIGGS enters at the left, frowning. JESSIE addresses her cheerfully.*] Back again, Mamma? Where's Lancelot?

Mrs. Briggs. [*In an annoyed tone*] I don't know. I thought you were going straight to your room.

Jessie. Oh, I am.

Mrs. Briggs. Have you just been sitting here alone?

Jessie. Mrs. Curtis came back a minute ago looking for the child.

Mrs. Briggs. Yes; I saw *her*. Wasn't any one else —

Jessie. [*Carelessly*] Oh, yes; that Mr. Ingoldsby was here, too.

Mrs. Briggs. He was? [*She looks at her watch and then toward the corridor on the left.*] You told me you were very tired and were going straight to your room.

Jessie. [*Casually*] Oh, well, I feel rested now.

Mrs. Briggs. You should lie down before dressing for dinner.

Jessie. Why don't *you* do that, Mamma? You know how it brightens you up.

Mrs. Briggs. [*Frowning*] Brightens me up? Really!

Jessie. Oh, I don't mean like a *terribly* aged person; but a nap every day's a good thing for everybody.

Mrs. Briggs. [*Stiffly*] I *took* a nap after lunch. Really, it's time you went.

Jessie. Oh, I'll just sit around a while longer. I rather like to just sit around and do nothing, like this.

Mrs. Briggs. You *said* you were going, and you ought to do things when you say you're going to do them.

Jessie. But *why?* Why can't I just sit around here a little longer if I want to?

Mrs. Briggs. Because you said you —

Jessie. Oh, what if I did! Haven't I got a right to change my mind?

Mrs. Briggs. I insist on your lying down for half an hour before you dress for dinner. What makes you so obstinate about it? Have you any *reason* for wishing not to do this simple thing? Is there anything you're trying to conceal from me, Jessie?

Jessie. [*Rising hastily*] Certainly not!

Mrs. Briggs. [*Severely*] You haven't any particular reason for staying here and not going to your room as you said you would?

Jessie. No!

Mrs. Briggs. Then —

Jessie. Oh, I'll go; but I don't understand why you make such a point of it!

Mrs. Briggs. [*A little flustered*] A point of it? I? I'm not making a point of it! I don't at all, except — except for your health.

Jessie. [*Going*] My *health!* [*She halts.*] What nonsense!

Mrs. Briggs. Your health is the only thing to consider. You've started; why don't you *go?*

Jessie. But what's the *hurry?*

Mrs. Briggs. Hurry? Oh, none! I just meant, as you *are* going, why shouldn't you *go* out and get it over?

Jessie. What makes you so queer?

Mrs. Briggs. [*With quiet severity*] Queer? You call your mother queer? It seems to me you're the one that's behaving queerly. Jessie, is there anything you're trying to —

Jessie. No! Don't get so upset. I'll go!

[*She goes out at the left.* Mrs. Briggs *stares after her for a moment; looks in the opposite direction; then seats herself upon the settee, and from the midst of a handkerchief which she has crumpled in her hand produces a small gold vanity box. She opens it, gazes in the tiny mirror, touches her hair, glances right and left, and uses a diminutive powder puff quickly; then she closes the box, conceals it in her handkerchief again, and hums a song to herself.* Mr. Ingoldsby *enters at the left. He has an air slightly embarrassed.*]

Mrs. Briggs. [*As if surprised*] Oh!

Ingoldsby. Ah — I was here a while ago. I was a little ear-lier than our — our appointment; if I may call it so. [*He laughs nervously.*]

Mrs. Briggs. [*Smiling*] Well, I suppose it *could* be called an appointment — in a way.

Ingoldsby. I — I thought — that is, I've noticed this was about the only place in the hotel where there aren't usually a lot of people. I suggested it because — because I had something to say — ah — I mean that I thought it would be as well to say it in private — as it were. That is, if we were alone together, I — ah — that is to say, it's something I couldn't very well say in — in pub-lic, so to speak. I mean it would be difficult with other people present.

Mrs. Briggs. [*Smiling nervously*] Is it something very mysteri-ous, Mr. Ingoldsby?

Ingoldsby. I wish you wouldn't call me that.

Mrs. Briggs. [*Seriously*] You want me to call you Henry?

Ingoldsby. You did once.

Mrs. Briggs. [*Rising in some agitation*] Yes, but that was pretty long ago.

Ingoldsby. [*Sharply*] I called you Fannie then.

Mrs. Briggs. [*More agitated*] I don't think we should ever refer to it. When an episode is as long buried as —

Ingoldsby. [*His own agitation increasing*] Episode? See here, Fannie; you know why I stayed a bachelor. You do know.

Mrs. Briggs. [*Protesting quickly*] No, no! I have no responsi-bility for that!

Ingoldsby. Haven't you? When you broke your engagement to me —

Mrs. Briggs. [*Crying out, though she suppresses the loudness of her voice*] It was a misunderstanding, Henry.

Ingoldsby. It was not. I've held my peace in silence all these years because of my principles. I wouldn't refer to such things with you when you had become a married woman. But I can speak now. You deliberately broke off with me —

Mrs. Briggs. [*Choking*] I didn't!

Ingoldsby. [*With a suppressed passion*] You did! [*He paces the floor as he goes on.*] You decided Lance Briggs was the better man, and you sent me my ring and letters without a single word explaining why you did it.

Mrs. Briggs. Oh!

Ingoldsby. You did!

Mrs. Briggs. Is it fair to attack me with that now?

Ingoldsby. Fair? How *dare* you speak of *fairness* to *me?*

Mrs. Briggs. But you *knew* why I did it.

Ingoldsby. [*Bitterly*] I did indeed! It was simply because you were of a fickle nature. Of course you didn't have the courage to explain *that.*

Mrs. Briggs. [*With great emotion*] But you don't know the pressure, the awful pressure my mother brought to bear on me. She simply *made* me marry him, Henry. It was night and day, day and night, week in, week out —

Ingoldsby. And you never for one moment had the simple bravery, the simple *loyalty* to the man you'd given your word to —

Mrs. Briggs. I was worn out. I was —

Ingoldsby. You didn't care enough for me to —

Mrs. Briggs. I *did!*

Ingoldsby. No! No! No!

Mrs. Briggs. [*Piteously*] Henry, you *must* listen to me! [*She puts her hand on his arm.*]

Ingoldsby. [*Moving away from her*] Why didn't you say that *then?* Why didn't —

Mrs. Briggs. I loved you — I did, Henry! I simply let my mother break my will and wreck our two lives.

Ingoldsby. What folly! You were perfectly happy with Briggs. I don't know *how* many people told me you were.

Mrs. Briggs. I did my duty, and I tried to do it cheerfully; but the scar was always there, Henry.

Ingoldsby. [*Harshly*] I don't believe it!

Mrs. Briggs. [*Plaintively*] It was, Henry. [*She sinks into the chair* JESSIE *has occupied.*]

Ingoldsby. [*Swallowing*] What?

Mrs. Briggs. [*Feebly*] It was, Henry — the scar was always there. [*Her head droops.*]

[*He walks across the room, then returns to her and looks down upon her.*]

Ingoldsby. [*Swallowing*] Do you know what my life has been?

Mrs. Briggs. [*Tremulously, not looking up*] I — I heard you became very — very prosperous in — in real estate.

Ingoldsby. Yes. What's that to fill a man's life? Look at the

difference! You have children to be a comfort to you in your —
your — as you approach middle age. I have nothing.

Mrs. Briggs. [*Pathetically, still looking down*] Oh, I'm sure you
have something.

Ingoldsby. I tell you I have nothing — nothing in the world
to make life worth living, not a thing on earth! [*He glances about,
then sits beside her and speaks in a very low voice.*] Fannie —
Fannie —

[*The settee approaches a little nearer.*]

Mrs. Briggs. [*Also in a very low voice*] Well?

Ingoldsby. Fannie — I — I — Fannie — I — [*His emotion is
difficult to control and his voice fades out into a murmur of several
slight incoherent sounds, whereupon the settee again moves slightly
closer.*]

Mrs. Briggs. Yes, Henry?

Ingoldsby. You said your life was wrecked, though you bore it
dutifully and — and cheerfully. Mine — *my* life — it was withered!

Mrs. Briggs. [*Murmuring*] Oh — Henry!

Ingoldsby. But, after all, our lives aren't over.

Mrs. Briggs. [*Shaking her down-bent head and protesting in a
weak voice*] Oh, no, no! Don't begin to talk that way.

Ingoldsby. Fannie, I never got over it. As time went on, I took
up my work and tried to do my part in the world, but — but I never
got over it, Fannie. I'm not over it now.

Mrs. Briggs. [*Turning to him mournfully*] Oh, yes, you are!

Ingoldsby. [*Shaking his head*] I'm not. I still — I still — I still
— I still —

[*The settee again moves a little nearer.*]

Mrs. Briggs. No, no.

Ingoldsby. I do. I still — I still —

Mrs. Briggs. [*In a faint and tearful protest*] No, you don't, Henry.
You only think you do.

Ingoldsby. No, I really do. I — I — I care for you yet, Fannie.

Mrs. Briggs. [*Recovering herself enough to smile faintly as she
shakes her head*] Oh, my, no!

Ingoldsby. Fannie, let's — let's save these years that we still
have before us. Let's try to make up for that old mistake.

Mrs. Briggs. [*Becoming a little brisker*] Why, how — how —
why, we — why, I couldn't think of such a thing!

Ingoldsby. [*Solemnly*] Fannie, I ask you to marry me.

[*She stares at him; the settee moves an inch nearer.*]

Mrs. Briggs. What?

Ingoldsby. I ask you to marry me.

Mrs. Briggs. Why, good gracious! I wouldn't have my children know that anybody had said such a thing to me for all the kingdoms on earth!

Ingoldsby. [*Earnestly*] They needn't know it till afterwards.

Mrs. Briggs. [*Breathlessly*] Afterwards? After — after —

Ingoldsby. You're not going to wreck us both *again,* are you, Fannie?

Mrs. Briggs. [*As in amazement*] Why, if I'd dreamed you were going to say anything like *this* to me when you asked me to meet you here this afternoon —

Ingoldsby. [*Solemnly*] Fannie, I want you to give me your answer, and to do it now. What do you say?

Mrs. Briggs. [*Feebly, with her hand to her breast*] Oh, my!

Ingoldsby. Yes; you must.

Mrs. Briggs. But I haven't had time to *think!* Why, I wouldn't have anybody know about this for —

Ingoldsby. I want my answer, Fannie — Fannie *dear!*

Mrs. Briggs. [*Blankly*] Oh, dear!

Ingoldsby. Fannie, *dearest!* [*He takes her hand.*]

Mrs. Briggs. Oh, I wouldn't have anybody know this —

Ingoldsby. Dearest, dearest Fannie!

Mrs. Briggs. Why, I wouldn't have anybody know that we —

[*They are interrupted by a voice from a mysterious and invisible source. It is a male and adult voice, loudly and emphatically affecting to clear the throat of its origin in the manner of a person wishing to attract the attention of some other person.*]

The Mysterious Voice. A-hem! A-a-a-*hem!*

Mrs. Briggs. [*Leaping in her chair*] Good heavens!

Ingoldsby. [*Jumping up*] What was that?

Mrs. Briggs. [*Rising*] Why, it was a man's voice.

Ingoldsby. It was right here in the room with us.

Mrs. Briggs. [*Sinking into her chair*] Oh, murder!

Ingoldsby. [*Staring about the room, notices the Philippine chair with its back turned to the front*] There's somebody sitting in that chair! [*He starts toward it angrily, but is checked by a suppressed scream from Mrs. Briggs.*]

Mrs. Briggs. Don't! I'd *much* rather never know who it is. [*Rising.*] Let's get away! [*She totters.*]

Ingoldsby. [*Undecided, but very angry*] We ought to know who's spying on us like this.

Mrs. Briggs. [*Clutching at him*] Oh!

The Mysterious Voice. [*Indignantly*] I'm not spying! This is a public room in a public hotel —

Mrs. Briggs. [*Moaning*] Oh!

The Mysterious Voice. [*Continuing*] Any guest of this hotel has a right to sit here in peace, and if you *will* go on talking about your private affairs in a public room —

Mrs. Briggs. [*Leaning on* INGOLDSBY'S *arm*] Oh, my!

The Mysterious Voice. [*Continuing heatedly*] Why, it's your own fault, not mine. I was only warning you not to go any further. I've heard enough of other people's affairs for one afternoon, anyhow.

Mrs. Briggs. [*Almost hysterically*] Oh, let's go! [*She swings the reluctant and angry* INGOLDSBY *toward the left entrance.*] Let's go!

Ingoldsby. [*Turning to call back angrily*] I don't know who you are, sir; but when I've seen this lady to a — a place of safety — I *intend* to know. I'll be *back* here, sir.

The Mysterious Voice. Fine!

Mrs. Briggs. Oh, mercy! [*She moves hastily away from* IN- GOLDSBY *as* JESSIE *suddenly comes in, from the left, confronting them.*]

Jessie. [*Halting sharply*] What in the world's the matter?

Mrs. Briggs. [*In a shaking voice*] Nothing! Nothing at all, Jessie. Why should you think anything's the matter?

Jessie. Why, you're all upset!

Mrs. Briggs. [*Trying hard to seem lightly amused, and failing*] Not at all — not at all! I was just sitting here a moment with Mr. Ingoldsby, chatting over old times and — and then we decided to leave. We decided to leave — that's all. I — I'm — [*Suddenly she starts, and with an incoherent exclamation looks behind her. Then she faces* JESSIE *and, with a painful effort to smile, completes her sentence.*] I'm all right.

Jessie. Yes, you seem so. Mr. Ingoldsby, will you kindly tell me what you've been saying to my mother to upset her so?

Mrs. Briggs. But I'm not —

Ingoldsby. [*Checking her sharply*] Miss Briggs, I should not be likely to say anything disrespectful to my old and dear friend, your mother. [*Looking around angrily.*] The truth is, there's an eaves-dropping scoundrel concealed in this room, and I —

Jessie. [*Alarmed*] What! Oh, I'm sure there isn't.

Ingoldsby. There is! An eavesdropping —

The Mysterious Voice. [*Angrily*] This is a public room, I told you. How can *I* help it if you —

Ingoldsby. I can't stand this. He's behind that chair.

[*He breaks away from* MRS. BRIGGS *and* JESSIE, *who both clutch at him.*]

Jessie. [*Crying out*] Don't! *Please* don't!

Mrs. Briggs. [*Simultaneously*] Henry! *Don't!*

[*But* INGOLDSBY *has already reached the Philippine chair that has its back turned toward the front of the stage; he seizes* RUPERT *by the collar and drags him forth.* RUPERT *is horrified.*]

Ingoldsby. Come out of there, you scoundrel. Come out to the light of day.

Rupert. [*Hastily*] I didn't do it. It wasn't *me.*

Mrs. Briggs. Rupert Smith!

Jessie. [*Dolefully*] Oh, goodness!

Ingoldsby. [*Hotly*] What do you mean by terrorizing a lady?

Rupert. I didn't! I didn't say a *word!* I *was* behind there, but I couldn't help it. It wasn't *my* voice talking to you.

Ingoldsby. Then who was it?

The Mysterious Voice. If you're anxious for more witnesses, I suggest that you look under the settee.

Mrs. Briggs. [*Changing her mind as she is in the act of sinking down upon the settee*] What!

Jessie. Look at it!

[MRS. BRIGGS *screams faintly, as the settee moves rapidly to the left entrance, evidently meaning to leave the room.*]

Ingoldsby. [*To* RUPERT] Stop that thing! Catch it!

[*They seize the settee just as it is disappearing into the corridor. They drag it back into the room.*]

Rupert. [*Trying to lift the settee*] Come out from under there!

Ingoldsby. Come out, now!

The Settee. I won't! You lea' me alone!

Ingoldsby. Both together now — heave!

[*They heave, and the settee yields, disclosing* LANCELOT *with his previously smooth hair disheveled and his clothes well rumpled.*]

Mrs. Briggs. [*Astonished*] Lancelot! Oh, gracious me!

Ingoldsby. [*To* LANCELOT] Shame on you!

Rupert. Yes, shame on you!

Lancelot. [*Resentfully*] Well, you *would* get me; but I'll make you sorry you did it, both of you! [*He rises, brushing himself and adjusting his attire.*]

Ingoldsby. [*Irritably*] Don't you know better than to frighten ladies and eavesdrop and —

Lancelot. [*Warmly*] I was abs'lootly honorable, because I couldn't help it, and you none of you ever gave me a single chance to get away. *My* conduct is the only one here that hasn't got a stain on it or anything. [*He turns hotly upon* MRS. BRIGGS *and* JESSIE.] I got nothing to reproach myself with, but I'd just like to know what either of you got to say for yourselves *now* about the way you been talkin' about Mrs. Curtis? If you either of you ever just *dare* to soil your lips with even her *name* again, why, I know more *things* —

Mrs. Briggs. Be quiet, Lancelot.

Lancelot. Quiet? *Me?* [*He laughs shortly with an irony he could not express in words.*] In the first place, don't call me Lancelot any more. You know how I hate that name, and I been tryin' to break you of it long enough — and now I will! I don't care what you call me, but don't call me *that!*

Jessie. [*Pointing to the settee*] How long were you under there?

Lancelot. [*Sternly*] Long enough to get mighty tired of hearin' people callin' each other " Darling "! Good gracious! You don't think I *enjoyed* it, do you? Why, what I heard while I was under there — well, I got a pretty strong constitution, but —

Mrs. Briggs. Hush! Oh, me!

Ingoldsby. The voice that spoke didn't sound like Lancelot's voice —

Lancelot. [*Turning upon him ominously*] Did you hear me say not to call me Lancelot? I mean you, too.

Ingoldsby. [*With hasty meekness*] I'll call you anything you like; but I want to know who it was that *spoke.* You say it wasn't you —

Lancelot. [*Very emphatically*] No, it wasn't. I wouldn't 'a' told you to look under the settee, would I?

Ingoldsby. [*With a gesture toward* RUPERT] And this gentleman says it wasn't he.

Rupert. Why, it spoke again after I came out.

Ingoldsby. [*Quite bewildered*] So it did. Then who —

Lancelot. I don't care who it was; what I want to point out, right here and now, before we go any further, why, I'm in a position to say that I got some plans for my future life and I don't expect to have any intaference with 'em from my family, or from anybody that wants to *join* my family either. All up to now, I've spent my life in a dependent position, so to speak, but after what's happened here lately, and knowin' all the *things* I *do* know —

[*His voice has risen during this oration, and* JESSIE, *after a glance to the left entrance, attempts to moderate him.*]

Jessie. Hush! There's somebody —

Lancelot. I don't care *who's* comin', I'm goin' to say my say. I expect to settle my own future in my own way, and any lady that I may decide to make *another* member of this family —

Jessie. Hush!

[*The eyes of Lancelot follow hers to the left entrance and his stern manner is instantly softened.*]

Lancelot. It's her.

[MRS. CURTIS *comes in, but stops uncertainly near the entrance.*]

Mrs. Curtis. Oh! I'm afraid I — [*She turns to go.*]

Lancelot. Wait. I was just talkin' to 'em about you.

Mrs. Curtis. You were, Mr. Briggs?

Lancelot. [*To the others, reprovingly*] *She* never calls me Lancelot. Missuz — Missuz Curtis, I didn't have to tell 'em; they'd already found out you were a widow. We don't need to bother about that anyway.

Mrs. Curtis. *We* don't?

Lancelot. I've found out a good *many* things since I saw you, and I'm goin' to tell you the whole biznuss.

Mrs. Briggs. Shame!

Jessie. [*With a despairing laugh*] What would it matter? There's somebody *else* here that knows " the whole biznuss "!

Mrs. Curtis. [*Struck by this*] What did you say, Miss Briggs?

Ingoldsby. [*Warmly*] She made a sensible remark, madam. There is a person concealed in this room —

Mrs. Curtis. [*Impulsively*] Oh, dear! How did you know?

All the Others. What?

Mrs. Curtis. Nothing.

Ingoldsby. All right! [*To* RUPERT.] I think I know now where he is, and I'm going to have him out.

Mrs. Curtis. [*Gasping, then imploringly*] Please stop!

Ingoldsby. [*Halting*] Why?

Mrs. Curtis. [*Weakly*] It's a friend of mine.

Lancelot. [*Apprehensively*] A friend of yours?

Mrs. Curtis. I — I'll answer for him. He'll never mention — ah — anything. He really wouldn't be interested. He doesn't know any of you.

The Mysterious Voice. No; and doesn't care to!

Ingoldsby. [*Angrily*] Now, I *will* —

Mrs. Curtis. Please don't!

Ingoldsby. I mean to know who he is.

Mrs. Curtis. [*Pleading*] Please! If you found him, you'd only see a total stranger to you. But he *wouldn't* be a stranger to quite a lot of people in this hotel that *I* know.

Ingoldsby. [*Now shaking his head*] I'm afraid I don't see it.

Mrs. Curtis. [*In a faltering voice*] He's just here for one day and we — we didn't want any one to know it. I had so many engagements I could only take a short walk in the country with him this morning and — and promise to meet him here at five this afternoon.

Lancelot. [*Who has been staring at her painfully*] But — but — see here!

Mrs. Curtis. Yes, I tried to get you to run away and dance with some nice young thing.

Lancelot. [*Pathetically*] So you could be here with — him?

Mrs. Curtis. I — I believe so.

Lancelot. [*Dismally*] Oh, my!

Ingoldsby. Madam, what you say doesn't excuse this person's eavesdropping.

The Mysterious Voice. [*Belligerently*] Why doesn't it? A lady's got a right to keep her engagement a secret as long as she wants to, hasn't she? There are people in this hotel that would know all about it if they saw her with me. [*With some bitterness.*] That's why she said to meet her here, because it's so quiet!

Ingoldsby. That doesn't excuse —

The Mysterious Voice. It's more your fault than anybody else's. I was awake all last night on a noisy train, and I was quietly *asleep* here — till you woke me up.

Ingoldsby. Till *who* woke you up?

The Mysterious Voice. Till *you* did. I never knew a man that made so much noise about proposing a second marriage.

Jessie. [*Amazed*] Oh, Mamma!

Mrs. Briggs. [*With severe dignity*] I'll speak to you and Mr. Rupert Smith after dinner. Henry, I don't see the propriety of continuing an argument with this interloper, whoever he may be. [*She takes* INGOLDSBY'S *arm.*]

Jessie. No. Let's *do* get away from here! [*She moves toward the left entrance with* RUPERT.]

Ingoldsby. [*Looking back, as he follows with* MRS. BRIGGS; *speaks reprovingly*] I hope you have some shame for your conduct, sir.

The Mysterious Voice. Bless you, my children!

Ingoldsby. [*Infuriated*] Now, I'll— [*He turns to go back.*]

Mrs. Briggs. [*Restraining him*] Henry!

[*They go out the left entrance.* JESSIE *and* RUPERT *have passed out into the corridor.*]

Lancelot. Did he say "a lady's got a right to keep her—her *engagement*—a secret"?

Mrs. Curtis. Yes.

Lancelot. To—to—to you?

Mrs. Curtis. Yes, dear.

Lancelot. [*Piteously*] Oh—oh, pshaw!

Mrs. Briggs. [*Calling back*] Lancelot!

Lancelot. [*Meekly*] Yes'm.

[*He goes dismally across to the left entrance and pauses.* INGOLDSBY *and* MRS. BRIGGS *have withdrawn, preceding him.*]

Mrs. Curtis. [*As he pauses*] What is it, Mr. Briggs?

Lancelot. [*Swallowing*] Noth—nothin'. [*He goes out.*]

Mrs. Curtis. [*Turning, after a moment's faintly smiling meditation*] You poor thing!

The Mysterious Voice. [*In an aggrieved tone*] Well, I should say I am!

[*She goes to the Philippine chair, near the right rear corner, and, moving a smaller chair close to it, seats herself and addresses the invisible person, who is evidently sitting in the shelter of the big chair.*]

Mrs. Curtis. After all, there's nobody else here just *now,* darling.
The Mysterious Voice. No. We're alone, darling.
Mrs. Curtis. You poor darling!

[*She glances about, then impulsively leans behind the huge back of the Philippine chair as the curtain descends.*]

SUGGESTIONS FOR STUDY

1. Be sure to visualize the characters, especially the boy.
2. How many threads of plot do you find? Name them.
3. How do they all get tangled up together?
4. Did you have any difficulty in keeping them separate in your mind? Make some comments on plot as you find it in this play.
5. Were there any surprises? If so, name them and comment on how you think they would be played on a stage.
6. Which character do you consider the most interesting? The most realistic?
7. Were you fully prepared for the Mysterious Voice at the end?
8. Would the ending have been more interesting if the Voice had been identified? Comment on the ending.
9. If you have never read the author's novel, *Seventeen,* this would be a good time to read it.

FOR FURTHER READING

ONE-ACT PLAYS
Station YYYY
The Travelers

FULL-LENGTH PLAYS
The Man from Home (in collaboration with H. L. Wilson)
Clarence
The Intimate Strangers

PLAYS MADE FROM STORIES AND NOVELS
Monsieur Beaucaire
Seventeen

WHERE THE CROSS IS MADE

By EUGENE O'NEILL (1888–   )

It is too early to assert definitely that Eugene O'Neill is the greatest dramatist that this country has produced, but contemporary opinion and the continued success of his plays certainly point in that direction. At the present writing (1930) O'Neill shares with Bernard Shaw, J. M. Barrie, and Gabriele d'Annunzio the honor of being one of the four outstanding living playwrights, and of the four he is by far the youngest. O'Neill was born in New York, and educated at various schools until he entered Princeton with the class of 1910. At the end of one year he was suspended and never returned. For the next four years he vagabonded in Central and South America, returning to New York. By this time he was an able seaman and served for a time on transatlantic liners. His first direct connection with the theater came as actor in a minor part of *Monte Cristo,* a play made famous by his father, the well-known James O'Neill. While recovering in a sanatorium from an attack of tuberculosis he gave serious attention to the study and writing of plays, one of which is still considered among the best of his one-act pieces, *Bound East for Cardiff.* A year in Professor Baker's drama class at Harvard finally determined his career. He was connected with the Provincetown Players, for whom he provided one-act plays, a form which he brought to an artistic level never before attained in this country.

Where the Cross Is Made (1918) is one of the plays written for the Provincetown group, later expanded into a full-length play, which, in spite of a powerful opening scene showing the shipwrecked sailors with their treasure on the desert island, was not successful. In the original form here printed it is possible to form an accurate idea of the O'Neill type of play. There is strong characterization, convincing atmosphere, and realistic dialogue, all important in an interesting stage production. In addition there is the pervading mysticism which the author is fond of giving to many of his plays, both long and short.

Besides those mentioned, other one-act plays by O'Neill are: *Ile* (1917), *The Moon of the Caribbees* (1918), and *In the Zone* (1917). Full-length plays are: *Beyond the Horizon* (1920), *The Emperor Jones* (1920), *Anna Christie* (1921), *The Great God Brown* (1925), *Marco Millions* (1927), and *Strange Interlude* (1928). All of O'Neill's plays are published and easily obtainable at any library.

CHARACTERS

CAPTAIN ISAIAH BARTLETT
NAT BARTLETT, *his son*
SUE BARTLETT, *his daughter*
DOCTOR HIGGINS
SILAS HORNE, *mate* ⎫
CATES, *bo'sun* ⎬ *of the schooner* Mary Allen
JIMMY KANAKA, *harpooner* ⎭

SCENE. *Captain Bartlett's " cabin " — a room erected as a lookout post at the top of his house situated on a high point of land on the California coast. The inside of the compartment is fitted up like the captain's cabin of a deep-sea sailing vessel. On the left, forward, a porthole. Farther back, the stairs of the companion-way. Still farther, two more portholes. In the rear, left, a marble-topped sideboard with a ship's lantern on it. In the rear, center, a door opening on stairs which lead to the lower house. A cot with a blanket is placed against the wall to the right of the door. In the right wall, five portholes. Directly under them, a wooden bench. In front of the bench, a long table with two straight-backed chairs, one in front, the other to the left of it. A cheap, dark-colored rug is on the floor. In the ceiling, midway from front to rear, a skylight extending from opposite the door to above the left edge of the table. In the right extremity of the skylight is placed a floating ship's compass. The light from the binnacle sheds over this from above and seeps down into the room, casting a vague globular shadow of the compass on the floor.*

The time is an early hour of a clear windy night in the fall of the year 1900. Moonlight, winnowed by the wind which moans in the stubborn angles of the old house, creeps wearily in through the port-holes and rests like tired dust in circular patches upon the floor and table. An insistent monotone of thundering surf, muffled and far-off, is borne upward from the beach below.

After the curtain rises the door in the rear is opened slowly and the head and shoulders of NAT BARTLETT *appear over the sill. He casts a quick glance about the room, and seeing no one there, ascends the remaining steps and enters. He makes a sign to some one in the darkness beneath: " All right, Doctor."* DOCTOR HIGGINS *follows him into the room and, closing the door, stands looking with great curiosity around him. He is a slight, medium-sized professional-looking man of about thirty-five.* NAT BARTLETT *is very tall, gaunt, and loose-framed. His right arm has been ampu-tated at the shoulder and the sleeve on that side of the heavy mackinaw he wears hangs flabbily or flaps against his body as he moves. He appears much older than his thirty years. His shoulders have a weary stoop as if worn down by the burden of his massive head with its heavy shock of tangled black hair. His face is long, bony, and sallow, with deep-set black eyes, a large aquiline nose, a wide thin-lipped mouth shadowed by an unkempt bristle of mustache. His voice is low and deep with a penetrating, hollow, metallic quality. In addition to the mackinaw, he wears corduroy trousers stuffed down into high laced boots.*

Nat. Can you see, Doctor?

Higgins. [*In the too-casual tones which betray an inward uneasiness*] Yes — perfectly — don't trouble. The moonlight is so bright ——

Nat. Luckily. [*Walking slowly toward the table*] He doesn't want any light — lately — only the one from the binnacle there.

Higgins. He? Ah — you mean your father?

Nat. [*Impatiently*] Who else?

Higgins. [*A bit startled — gazing around him in embarrassment*] I suppose this is all meant to be like a ship's cabin?

Nat. Yes — as I warned you.

Higgins. [*In surprise*] Warned me? Why, warned? I think it's very natural — and interesting — this whim of his.

Nat. [*Meaningly*] Interesting, it may be.

Higgins. And he lives up here, you said — never comes down?

Nat. Never — for the past three years. My sister brings his food up to him. [*He sits down in the chair to the left of the table.*] There's a lantern on the sideboard there, Doctor. Bring it over and sit down. We'll make a light. I'll ask your pardon for bringing you to this room on the roof — but — no one'll hear us here; and by seeing for yourself the mad way he lives —— Understand that I want you to get all the facts — just that, facts! — and for that light is necessary. Without that — they become dreams up here — dreams, Doctor.

Higgins. [*With a relieved smile carries over the lantern*] It is a trifle spooky.

Nat. [*Not seeming to notice this remark*] He won't take any note of this light. His eyes are too busy — out there. [*He flings his left arm in a wide gesture seaward.*] And if he does notice — well, let him come down. You're bound to see him sooner or later. [*He scratches a match and lights the lantern.*]

Higgins. Where is — he?

Nat. [*Pointing upward*] Up on the poop. Sit down, man! He'll not come — yet awhile.

Higgins. [*Sitting gingerly on the chair in front of table*] Then he has the roof too rigged up like a ship?

Nat. I told you he had. Like a deck, yes. A wheel, compass, binnacle light, the companionway there [*he points*], a bridge to pace up and down on — *and keep watch.* If the wind wasn't so high you'd hear him now — back and forth — all the livelong night. [*With a sudden harshness*] Didn't I tell you he's mad?

Higgins. [*With a professional air*] That was nothing new I've heard that about him from all sides since I first came to the asylum yonder. You say he only walks at night — up there?

Nat. Only at night, yes. [*Grimly*] The things he wants to see can't be made out in daylight — dreams and such.

Higgins. But just what is he trying to see? Does any one know? Does he tell?

Nat. [*Impatiently*] Why, every one knows what Father looks for, man! The ship, of course.

Higgins. What ship?

Nat. His ship — the *Mary Allen* — named for my dead mother.

Higgins. But — I don't understand —— Is the ship long over-due — or what?

Nat. Lost in a hurricane off the Celebes with all on board — three years ago!

Higgins. [*Wonderingly*] Ah. [*After a pause*] But your father still clings to a doubt ——

Nat. There is no doubt for him or any one else to cling to. She was sighted bottom up, a complete wreck, by the whaler *John Slocum*. That was two weeks after the storm. They sent a boat out to read her name.

Higgins. And hasn't your father ever heard ——

Nat. He was the first to hear, naturally. Oh, he *knows* right enough, if that's what you're driving at. [*He bends toward the doctor — intensely*.] He *knows*, Doctor, he *knows* — but he won't *believe*. He can't — and keep living.

Higgins. [*Impatiently*] Come, Mr. Bartlett, let's get down to brass tacks. You didn't drag me up here to make things more obscure, did you? Let's have the facts you spoke of. I'll need them to give sympathetic treatment to his case when we get him to the asylum.

Nat. [*Anxiously — lowering his voice*] And you'll come to take him away tonight — for sure?

Higgins. Twenty minutes after I leave here I'll be back in the car. That's positive.

Nat. And you know your way through the house?

Higgins. Certainly, I remember — but I don't see ——

Nat. The outside door will be left open for you. You must come right up. My sister and I will be here -- with him. And you understand —— Neither of us knows anything about this. The authorities have been complained to — not by us, mind — but by some one. He must never know ——

Higgins. Yes, yes — but still I don't —— Is he liable to prove violent?

Nat. No — no. He's quiet always — too quiet; but he might do something — anything — if he knows ——

Higgins. Rely on me not to tell him, then; but I'll bring along two attendants in case —— [*He breaks off and continues in matter-of-fact tones.*] And now for the facts in this case, if you don't mind, Mr. Bartlett.

Nat. [*Shaking his head — moodily*] There are cases where facts —— Well, here goes — the brass tacks. My father was a whaling captain as his father before him. The last trip he made was seven years ago. He expected to be gone two years. It was four before we saw him again. His ship had been wrecked in the Indian Ocean. He and six others managed to reach a small island on the fringe of the Archipelago — an island barren as hell, Doctor — after seven days in an open boat. The rest of the whaling crew never were heard from again — gone to the sharks. Of the six who reached the island with my father only three were alive when a fleet of Malay canoes picked them up, mad from thirst and starvation, the four of them. These four men finally reached Frisco. [*With great emphasis*] They were my father; Silas Horne, the mate; Cates the bo'sun, and Jimmy Kanaka, a Hawaiian harpooner. Those four! [*With a forced laugh*] There are facts for you. It was all in the papers at the time — my father's story.

Higgins. But what of the other three who were on the island?

Nat. [*Harshly*] Died of exposure, perhaps. Mad and jumped into the sea, perhaps. That was the told story. Another was whispered — killed and eaten, perhaps! But gone — vanished — that, undeniably. That was the fact. For the rest — who knows? And what does it matter?

Higgins. [*With a shudder*] I should think it would matter — a lot.

Nat. [*Fiercely*] We're dealing with facts, Doctor! [*With a laugh*] And here are some more for you. My father brought the three down to this house with him — Horne and Cates and Jimmy Kanaka. We hardly recognized my father. He had been through hell and looked it. His hair was white. But you'll see for yourself — soon. And the others — they were all a bit queer, too — mad, if you will. [*He laughs again.*] So much for the facts, Doctor. They leave off there and the dreams begin.

Higgins. [*Doubtfully*] It would seem — the facts are enough.

Nat. Wait. [*He resumes deliberately.*] One day my father sent for me and in the presence of the others told me the dream. I was to be heir to the secret. Their second day on the island, he said, they discovered in a sheltered inlet the rotten, water-logged hulk of a Malay prau — a proper war-prau such as the pirates used to use. She had been there rotting — God knows how long. The crew had vanished — God knows where, for there was no sign on the island that man had ever touched there. The Kanakas went over the prau — they're devils for staying under water, you know — and they found — in two chests —— [*He leans back in his chair and smiles ironically.*] Guess what, Doctor?

Higgins. [*With an answering smile*] Treasure, of course.

Nat. [*Leaning forward and pointing his finger accusingly at the other*] You see! The root of belief is in you, too! [*Then he leans back with a hollow chuckle.*] Why, yes. Treasure, to be sure. What else? They landed it and — you can guess the rest, too — diamonds, emeralds, gold ornaments — innumerable, of course. Why limit the stuff of dreams? Ha-ha! [*He laughs sardonically as if mocking himself.*]

Higgins. [*Deeply interested*] And then?

Nat. They began to go mad — hunger, thirst, and the rest — and they began to forget. Oh, they forgot a lot, and lucky for them they did, probably. But my father realizing, as he told me, what was happening to them, insisted that while they still knew what they were doing they should — guess again now, Doctor. Ha-ha!

Higgins. Bury the treasure?

Nat. [*Ironically*] Simple, isn't it? Ha-ha. And then they made a map — the same old dream, you see — with a charred stick, and my father had care of it. They were picked up soon after, mad as hatters, as I have told you, by some Malays. [*He drops his mocking and adopts a calm, deliberate tone again.*] But the map isn't a dream, Doctor. We're coming back to facts again. [*He reaches into the pocket of his mackinaw and pulls out a crumpled paper.*] Here. [*He spreads it out on the table.*]

Higgins. [*Craning his neck eagerly*] Dammit! This is interesting. The treasure, I suppose, is where ——

Nat. Where the cross is made.

Higgins. And here are the signatures, I see. And that sign?

Nat. Jimmy Kanaka's. He couldn't write.

Higgins. And below? That's yours, isn't it?

Nat. As heir to the secret, yes. We all signed it here the morning the *Mary Allen,* the schooner my father had mortgaged this house to fit out, set sail to bring back the treasure. Ha-ha.

Higgins. The ship he's still looking for — that was lost three years ago?

Nat. The *Mary Allen,* yes. The other three men sailed away on her. Only father and the mate knew the approximate location of the island — and I — as heir. It's —— [*He hesitates, frowning.*] No matter. I'll keep the mad secret. My father wanted to go with them — but my mother was dying. I dared not go either.

Higgins. Then you wanted to go? You believed in the treasure then?

Nat. Of course. Ha-ha. How could I help it? I believed until my mother's death. Then *he* became mad, entirely mad. He built this cabin — to wait in — and he suspected my growing doubt as time went on. So, as final proof, he gave me a thing he had kept hidden from them all — a sample of the richest of the treasure. Ha-ha. Behold! [*He takes from his pocket a heavy bracelet thickly studded with stones and throws it on the table near the lantern.*]

Higgins. [*Picking it up with eager curiosity — as if in spite of himself*] Real jewels?

Nat. Ha-ha! You want to believe, too. No — paste and brass — Malay ornaments.

Higgins. You had it looked over?

Nat. Like a fool, yes. [*He puts it back in his pocket and shakes his head as if throwing off a burden.*] Now you know why he's mad — waiting for that ship — and why in the end I had to ask you to take him away where he'll be safe. The mortgage — the price of that ship — is to be foreclosed. We have to move, my sister and I. We can't take him with us. She is to be married soon. Perhaps away from the sight of the sea he may ——

Higgins. [*Perfunctorily*] Let's hope for the best. And I fully appreciate your position. [*He gets up, smiling.*] And thank you for the interesting story. I'll know how to humor him when he raves about treasure.

Nat. [*Somberly*] He is quiet always — too quiet. He only walks to and fro — watching ——

Higgins. Well, I must go. You think it's best to take him tonight?

Nat. [*Persuasively*] Yes, Doctor. The neighbors — they're far away but — for my sister's sake — you understand.

Higgins. I see. It must be hard on her — this sort of thing — Well — [*He goes to the door, which* NAT *opens for him.*] I'll return presently. [*He starts to descend.*]

Nat. [*Urgently*] Don't fail us, Doctor. And come right up. He'll be here.

[*He closes the door and tiptoes carefully to the companion-way. He ascends it a few steps and remains for a moment listening for some sound from above. Then he goes over to the table, turning the lantern very low, and sits down, resting his elbows, his chin on his hands, staring somberly before him. The door in the rear is slowly opened. It creaks slightly and* NAT *jumps to his feet — in a thick voice of terror*] Who's there? [*The door swings wide open, revealing* SUE BARTLETT. *She ascends into the room and shuts the door behind her. She is a tall, slender woman of twenty-five, with a pale, sad face framed in a mass of dark red hair. This hair furnishes the only touch of color about her. Her full lips are pale; the blue of her wistful wide eyes is fading into a twilight gray. Her voice is low and melancholy. She wears a dark wrapper and slippers.*]

Sue. [*Stands and looks at her brother accusingly*] It's only I. What are you afraid of?

Nat. [*Averts his eyes and sinks back on his chair again*] Nothing. I didn't know — I thought you were in your room.

Sue. [*Comes to the table*] I was reading. Then I heard some one come down the stairs and go out. Who was it? [*With sudden terror*] It wasn't — Father?

Nat. No. He's up there — watching — as he always is.

Sue. [*Sitting down — insistently*] Who was it?

Nat. [*Evasively*] A man — I know.

Sue. What man? What is he? You're holding something back. Tell me.

Nat. [*Raising his eyes defiantly*] A doctor.

Sue. [*Alarmed*] Oh! [*With quick intuition*] You brought him up here — so that I wouldn't know!

Nat. [*Doggedly*] No. I took him up here to see how things were — to ask him about Father.

Sue. [*As if afraid of the answer she will get*] Is he one of them — from the asylum? Oh, Nat, you haven't ——

Nat. [*Interrupting her — hoarsely*] No, no! Be still.

Sue. That would be — the last horror.

Nat. [*Defiantly*] Why? You always say that. What could be more horrible than things as they are? I believe — it would be better for him — away — where he couldn't see the sea. He'll forget his mad idea of waiting for a lost ship and a treasure that never was. [*As if trying to convince himself — vehemently*] I believe this!

Sue. [*Reproachfully*] You don't, Nat. You know he'd die if he hadn't the sea to live with.

Nat. [*Bitterly*] And you know old Smith will foreclose the mortgage. Is that nothing? We cannot pay. He came yesterday and talked with me. He knows the place is his — to all purposes. He talked as if we were merely his tenants, curse him! And he swore he'd foreclose immediately unless ——

Sue. [*Eagerly*] What?

Nat. [*In a hard voice*] Unless we have — Father — taken away.

Sue. [*In anguish*] Oh! But why, why? What is Father to him?

Nat. The value of the property — our home which is his, Smith's. The neighbors are afraid. They pass by on the road at nights coming back to their farms from the town. They see *him* up there walking back and forth — waving his arms against the sky. They're afraid. They talk of a complaint. They say for his own good he must be taken away. They even whisper the house is haunted. Old Smith is afraid of his property. He thinks that *he* may set fire to the house — do anything ——

Sue. [*Despairingly*] But you told him how foolish that was, didn't you? That Father is quiet, always quiet.

Nat. What's the use of telling — when they believe — when they're afraid? [SUE *hides her face in her hands — a pause —* NAT *whispers hoarsely.*] I've been afraid myself — at times.

Sue. Oh, Nat! Of what?

Nat. [*Violently*] Oh, him and the sea he calls to! Of the damned sea he forced me on as a boy — the sea that robbed me of my arm and made me the broken thing I am!

Sue. [*Pleadingly*] You can't blame Father — for your misfortune.

Nat. He took me from school and forced me on his ship, didn't he? What would I have been now but an ignorant sailor like him if he had had his way? No. It's the sea I should not blame, that foiled him by taking my arm and then throwing me ashore — another one of *his* wrecks!

Sue. [*With a sob*] You're bitter, Nat — and hard. It was so long ago. Why can't you forget?

Nat. [*Bitterly*] Forget! You can talk! When Tom comes from this voyage you'll be married and out of this with life before you — a captain's wife as our mother was. I wish you joy.

Sue. [*Supplicatingly*] And you'll come with us, Nat — and Father, too — and then ——

Nat. Would you saddle your young husband with a madman and a cripple? [*Fiercely*] No, no, not I! [*Vindictively*] And not him, either! [*With sudden meaning — deliberately*] I've got to stay here. My book is three-fourths done — my book that will set me free! But I know, I feel, as sure as I stand here living before you, that I must finish it here. It could not live for me outside of this house where it was born. [*Staring at her fixedly*] So I will stay — in spite of hell! [*Sue sobs hopelessly. After a pause he continues.*] Old Smith told me I could live here indefinitely without paying — as caretaker — if ——

Sue. [*Fearfully — like a whispered echo*] If?

Nat. [*Staring at her — in a hard voice*] If I have *him* sent — where he'll no longer harm himself — nor others.

Sue. [*With horrified dread*] No — no, Nat! For our dead mother's sake.

Nat. [*Struggling*] Did I say I had? Why do you look at me — like that?

Sue. Nat! Nat! For our mother's sake!

Nat. [*In terror*] Stop! Stop! She's dead — and at peace. Would you bring her tired soul back to him again to be bruised and wounded?

Sue. Nat!

Nat. [*Clutching at his throat as though to strangle something within him — hoarsely*] Sue! Have mercy! [*His sister stares at him with dread foreboding.* NAT *calms himself with an effort and continues deliberately.*] Smith said he would give two thousand cash if I would sell the place to him — and he would let me stay, rent-free, as caretaker.

Sue. [*Scornfully*] Two thousand! Why, over and above the mortgage it's worth ——

Nat. It's not what it's worth. It's what one can get, cash — for my book — for freedom!

Sue. So that's why he wants Father sent away, the wretch! He must know the will Father made ——

Nat. Gives the place to me. Yes, he knows. I told him.

Sue. [*Dully*] Ah, how vile men are!

Nat. [*Persuasively*] If it were to be done — if it were, I say — there'd be half for you for your wedding portion. That's fair.

Sue. [*Horrified*] Blood-money! Do you think I could touch it?

Nat. [*Persuasively*] It would be only fair. I'd give it you.

Sue. My God, Nat, are you trying to bribe me?

Nat. No. It's yours in all fairness. [*With a twisted smile*] You forget I'm heir to the treasure, too, and can afford to be generous. Ha-ha.

Sue. [*Alarmed*] Nat! You're so strange. You're sick, Nat. You couldn't talk this way if you were yourself. Oh, we must go away from here — you and father and I! Let Smith foreclose. There'll be something over the mortgage; and we'll move to some little house — by the sea so that father ——

Nat. [*Fiercely*] Can keep up his mad game with me — whispering dreams in my ear — pointing out to sea — mocking me with stuff like this! [*He takes the bracelet from his pocket. The sight of it infuriates him and he hurls it into a corner, exclaiming in a terrible voice.*] No! No! It's too late for dreams now. It's too late; I've put them behind me tonight — forever!

Sue. [*Looks at him and suddenly understands that what she dreads has come to pass — letting her head fall on her outstretched arms with a long moan*] Then — you've done it! You've sold him! Oh, Nat, you're cursed!

Nat. [*With a terrified glance at the roof above*] Ssshh! What are you saying? He'll be better off — away from the sea.

Sue. [*Dully*] You've sold him.

Nat. [*Wildly*] No! No! [*He takes the map from his pocket.*] Listen, Sue! For God's sake, listen to me! See! The map of the island. [*He spreads it out on the table.*] And the treasure — where the cross is made. [*He gulps and his words pour out incoherently.*] I've carried it about for years. Is that nothing? You don't know what it means. It stands between me and my book. It's stood between me and life — driving me mad! *He* taught me to wait and hope with him — wait and hope — day after day. He made me doubt my brain and give the lie to my eyes — when hope was dead — when I knew it was all a dream — I couldn't kill it! [*His eyes starting from his head*] God forgive me, I still believe! And that's mad — mad, do you hear?

Sue. [*Looking at him with horror*] And that is why — you hate him!

Nat. No, I don't —— [*Then in a sudden frenzy*] Yes! I do hate him! He's stolen my brain! I've got to free myself, can't you see, from him — and his madness.

Sue. [*Terrified — appealingly*] Nat! Don't! You talk as if ——

Nat. [*With a wild laugh*] As if I were mad? You're right — but I'll be mad no more! See! [*He opens the lantern and sets fire to the map in his hand. When he shuts the lantern again it flickers and goes out. They watch the paper burn with fascinated eyes as he talks.*] See how I free myself and become sane. And now for facts, as the doctor said. I lied to you about him. He was a doctor from the asylum. See how it burns! It must all be destroyed — this poisonous madness. Yes, I lied to you — see — it's gone — the last speck — and the only other map is the one Silas Horne took to the bottom of the sea with him. [*He lets the ash fall to the floor and crushes it with his foot.*] Gone! I'm free of it — at last! [*His face is very pale, but he goes on calmly.*] Yes, I sold him, if you will — to save my soul. They're coming from the asylum to get him —— [*There is a loud, muffled cry from above, which sounds like "Sail-ho," and a stamping of feet. The slide to the companion-way above is slid back with a bang. A gust of air tears down into the room. NAT and SUE have jumped to their feet and stand petrified. CAPTAIN BARTLETT tramps down the stairs.*]

Nat. [*With a shudder*] God! Did he hear?

Sue. Ssshh! [*CAPTAIN BARTLETT comes into the room. He bears a striking resemblance to his son, but his face is more stern and formidable, his form more robust, erect and muscular. His mass of hair is pure white, his bristly mustache the same, contrasting with the weather-beaten leather color of his furrowed face. Bushy gray brows overhang the obsessed glare of his fierce dark eyes. He wears a heavy, double-breasted blue coat, pants of the same material, and rubber boots turned down from the knee.*]

Bartlett. [*In a state of mad exultation strides toward his son and points an accusing finger at him. NAT shrinks backward a step.*] Bin thinkin' me mad, did ye? Thinkin' it for the past three years,

ye bin — ever since them fools on the *Slocum* tattled their damn lie
o' the *Mary Allen* bein' a wreck.

Nat. [*Swallowing hard — chokingly*] No —— Father — I ——

Bartlett. Don't lie, ye whelp! You that I'd made my heir —
aimin' to git me out o' the way! Aimin' to put me behind the bars
o' the jail for mad folk!

Sue. Father — no!

Bartlett. [*Waving his hand for her to be silent*] Not you, girl,
not you. You're your mother.

" DON'T LIE, YE WHELP! "

Nat. [*Very pale*] Father — do you think — I ——

Bartlett. [*Fiercely*] A lie in your eyes! I bin a-readin' 'em.
My curse on you!

Sue. Father! Don't!

Bartlett. Leave me be, girl. He believed, didn't he? And ain't
he turned traitor — mockin' at me and sayin' it's all a lie — mockin'
at himself, too, for bein' a fool to believe in dreams, as he calls 'em.

Nat. [*Placatingly*] You're wrong, Father. I do believe.

Bartlett. [*Triumphantly*] Aye, now ye do! Who wouldn't credit
their own eyes?

Nat. [*Mystified*] Eyes?

Bartlett. Have ye not seen her, then? Did ye not hear me hail?

Nat. [*Confusedly*] Hail? I heard a shout. But — hail what? — seen what?

Bartlett. [*Grimly*] Aye, now's your punishment, Judas. [*Explosively*] The *Mary Allen,* ye blind fool, come back from the Southern Seas — come back as I swore she must!

Sue. [*Trying to soothe him*] Father! Be quiet. It's nothing.

Bartlett. [*Not heeding her — his eyes fixed hypnotically on his son's*] Turned the pint a half hour back — the *Mary Allen* loaded with gold as I swore she would be — carryin' her lowers — not a reef in 'em — makin' port, boy, as I swore she must — too late for traitors, boy, too late! — droppin' her anchor just when I hailed her.

Nat. [*A haunted, fascinated look in his eyes, which are fixed immovably on his father's*] The *Mary Allen!* But how do you know?

Bartlett. Not know my own ship! 'Tis you 're mad!

Nat. But at night — some other schooner ——

Bartlett. No other, I say! The *Mary Allen* — clear in the moonlight. And heed this: D'you call to mind the signal I gave to Silas Horne if he made this port o' a night?

Nat. [*Slowly*] A red and a green light at the mainmast-head.

Bartlett. [*Triumphantly*] Then look out if ye dare! [*He goes to porthole, left forward.*] Ye can see it plain from here. [*Commandingly*] Will ye believe your eyes? Look — and then call me mad! [NAT *peers through the porthole and starts back, a dumbfounded expression on his face.*]

Nat. [*Slowly*] A red and a green at the mainmast-head. Yes — clear as day.

Sue. [*With a worried look at him*] Let me see. [*She goes to the porthole.*]

Bartlett. [*To his son with fierce satisfaction*] Aye, ye see now clear enough — too late for you. [NAT *stares at him spellbound.*] And from above I saw Horne and Cates and Jimmy Kanaka plain on the deck in the moonlight lookin' up at me. Come! [*He strides to the companionway, followed by* NAT. *The two of them ascend.* SUE *turns from the porthole, an expression of frightened bewilderment on her face. She shakes her head sadly. A loud "Mary Allen, ahoy!" comes from above in* BARLETT'S *voice, followed like an echo by the same hail from* NAT. SUE *covers her face with her hands, shuddering.* NAT *comes down the companionway, his eyes wild and exulting.*]

Sue. [*Brokenly*] He's bad tonight, Nat. You're right to humor him. It's the best thing.

Nat. [*Savagely*] Humor him? What in hell do you mean?

Sue. [*Pointing to the porthole*] There's nothing there, Nat. There's not a ship in harbor.

Nat. You're a fool — or blind! The *Mary Allen's* there in plain sight of any one, with the red and the green signal-lights. Those fools lied about her being wrecked. And I've been a fool, too.

Sue. But, Nat, there's nothing. [*She goes over to the porthole again.*] Not a ship. See.

Nat. I saw, I tell you! From above it's all plain. [*He turns from her and goes back to his seat by the table.* Sue *follows him, pleading frightenedly.*]

Sue. Nat! You mustn't let this —— You're all excited and trembling, Nat. [*She puts a soothing hand on his forehead.*]

Nat. [*Pushing her away from him roughly*] You blind fool!

[Bartlett *comes down the steps of the companionway. His face is transfigured with the ecstasy of a dream come true.*]

Bartlett. They've lowered a boat — the three — Horne and Cates and Jimmy Kanaka. They're a-rowin' ashore. I heard the oars in the locks. Listen! [*A pause*]

Nat. [*Excitedly*] I hear!

Sue. [*Who has taken the chair by her brother — in a warning whisper*] It's the wind and sea you hear, Nat. Please!

Bartlett. [*Suddenly*] Hark! They've landed. They're back on earth again as I swore they'd come back. They'll be a-comin' up the path now. [*He stands in an attitude of rigid attention.* Nat *strains forward in his chair. The sound of the wind and sea suddenly ceases and there is a heavy silence. A dense green glow floods slowly in rhythmic waves like a liquid into the room — as of great depths of the sea faintly penetrated by light.*]

Nat. [*Catching at his sister's hand — chokingly*] See how the light changes! Green and gold! [*He shivers.*] Deep under the sea! I've been drowned for years! [*Hysterically*] Save me! Save me!

Sue. [*Patting his hand comfortingly*] Only the moonlight, Nat. It hasn't changed. Be quiet, dear, it's nothing. [*The green light grows deeper and deeper.*]

Bartlett. [*In a crooning, monotonous tone*] They move slowly

— slowly. They're heavy, I know, heavy — the two chests. Hark! They're below at the door. You hear?

Nat. [*Starting to his feet*] I hear! I left the door open.

Bartlett. For them?

Nat. For them.

Sue. [*Shuddering*] Ssshh! [*The sound of a door being heavily slammed is heard from way down in the house.*]

Nat. [*To his sister — excitedly*] There! You hear?

Sue. A shutter in the wind.

Nat. There is no wind.

Bartlett. Up they come! Up, bullies! They're heavy — heavy! [*The padding of bare feet sounds from the floor below — then comes up the stairs.*]

Nat. You hear them now?

Sue. Only the rats running about. It's nothing, Nat.

Bartlett. [*Rushing to the door and throwing it open*] Come in, lads, come in! — and welcome home! [*The forms of* SILAS HORNE, CATES, *and* JIMMY KANAKA *rise noiselessly into the room from the stairs. The last two carry heavy inlaid chests.* HORNE *is a parrot-nosed, angular old man dressed in gray cotton trousers and a singlet torn open across his hairy chest.* JIMMY *is a tall, sinewy, bronzed young Kanaka. He wears only a breech-cloth.* CATES *is squat and stout and is dressed in dungaree pants and a shredded white sailor's blouse, stained with iron-rust. All are in their bare feet. Water drips from their soaked and rotten clothes. Their hair is matted, intertwined with slimy strands of seaweed. Their eyes, as they glide silently into the room, stare frightfully wide at nothing. Their flesh in the green light has the suggestion of decomposition. Their bodies sway limply, nervelessly, rhythmically as if to the pulse of long swells of the deep sea.*]

Nat. [*Making a step toward them*] See! [*Frenziedly*] Welcome home, boys.

Sue. [*Grabbing his arm*] Sit down, Nat. It's nothing. There's no one there. Father — sit down!

Bartlett. [*Grinning at the three and putting his finger to his lips*] Not here, boys, not here — not before him. [*He points to his son.*] He has no right, now. Come. The treasure is ours only. We'll go away with it together. Come. [*He goes to the companionway. The three follow. At the foot of it* HORNE *puts a swaying hand on his shoulder and with the other holds out a piece of paper to him.* BARTLETT *takes it and chuckles exultantly.*] That's right —

for him — that's right! [*He ascends. The figures sway up after him.*]

Nat. [*Frenziedly*] Wait! [*He struggles toward the companionway.*]

Sue. [*Trying to hold him back*] Nat — don't! Father — come back!

Nat. Father! [*He flings her away from him and rushes up the companionway. He pounds against the slide, which seems to have been shut down on him.*]

Sue. [*Hysterically — runs wildly to the door in rear*] Help! help! [*As she gets to the door* DOCTOR HIGGINS *appears, hurrying up the stairs.*]

Higgins. [*Excitedly*] Just a moment, Miss. What's the matter?

Sue. [*With a gasp*] My father — up there!

Higgins. I can't see — where's my flash? Ah. [*He flashes it on her terror-stricken face, then quickly around the room. The green glow disappears. The wind and sea are heard again. Clear moonlight floods through the portholes.* HIGGINS *springs to the companionway.* NAT *is still pounding.*] Here, Bartlett. Let me try.

Nat. [*Coming down — looking dully at the doctor*] They've locked it. I can't get up.

Higgins. [*Looks up — in an astonished voice*] What's the matter, Bartlett? It's all open. [*He starts to ascend.*]

Nat. [*In a voice of warning*] Look out, man. Look out for them!

Higgins. [*Calls down from above*] Them? Who? There's no one here. [*Suddenly — in alarm*] Come up! Lend a hand here! He's fainted! [NAT *goes up slowly.* SUE *goes over and lights the lantern, then hurries back to the foot of the companionway with it. There is a scuffling noise from above. They reappear, carrying* CAPTAIN BARTLETT'S *body.*]

Higgins. Easy now! [*They lay him on the couch in rear.* SUE *sets the lantern down by the couch.* HIGGINS *bends and listens for a heart-beat. Then he rises, shaking his head.*] I'm sorry ——

Sue. [*Dully*] Dead?

Higgins. [*Nodding*] Heart failure, I should judge. [*With an attempt at consolation*] Perhaps it's better so, if ——

Nat. [*As if in a trance*] There was something Horne handed him. Did you see?

Sue. [*Wringing her hands*] Oh, Nat, be still! He's dead. [*To* HIGGINS *with pitiful appeal*] Please go — go ——

Higgins. There's nothing I can do?

Sue. Go — please —— [*Higgins bows stiffly and goes out.* NAT *moves slowly to his father's body, as if attracted by some irresistible fascination.*]

Nat. Didn't you see? Horne handed him something.

Sue. [*Sobbing*] Nat! Nat! Come away! Don't touch him, Nat! Come away. [*But her brother does not heed her. His gaze is fixed on his father's right hand, which hangs downward over the side of the couch. He pounces on it and, forcing the clenched fingers open with a great effort, secures a crumpled ball of paper.*]

Nat. [*Flourishing it above his head with a shout of triumph*] See! [*He bends down and spreads it out in the light of the lantern.*] The map of the island! Look! It isn't lost for me after all! There's still a chance — *my* chance! [*With mad, solemn decision*] When the house is sold I'll go — and I'll find it! Look! It's written here in his handwriting: "The treasure is buried where the cross is made."

Sue. [*Covering her face with her hands — brokenly*] Oh, God. Come away, Nat! Come away!

[*The Curtain Falls*]

SUGGESTIONS FOR STUDY

1. Although this play may seem difficult to act, it is not. In fact, it has been called "fool-proof" for amateur actors. What tends to make this opinion correct?

2. Who is the dominating character among the Bartletts? Who is the weak character? Who is the sane character? Which of the three is the most tragic? Why?

3. Do you think Nat was mad at the beginning of the play? Give evidence for your answer.

4. In what way is this play more realistic than *Nathan Hale?* In what way less so?

5. Point out places where O'Neill uses sound and light to achieve his effects.

6. In what way do you think O'Neill resembles Hawthorne? Poe?

7. What suggestion do you have of harrowing experiences Captain Bartlett had been through? It is interesting to try to reconstruct the events leading up to the scene of this play and then to read *Gold* and get O'Neill's version of them.

FOR FURTHER READING

ONE-ACT PLAYS

Thirst, and Other One-Act Plays
*The Moon of the Caribbees and
    Other Plays of the Sea*

LONG PLAYS

Beyond the Horizon
The Emperor Jones
Gold
Marco Millions

NATHAN HALE

By CLYDE FITCH (1865–1909)

Clyde Fitch was born in Elmira, New York, and educated at various schools before entering Amherst in 1882. As a boy he took an interest in things dramatic, such as organizing groups of children to give perform-ances and shows. At college he took an active part in college dramatics, writing plays, directing them, designing costumes, and every phase that went with productions, including acting. He was a frequent contributor to the college magazine and eventually became the Class Poet. When he came to New York in 1886 he made his way by writing, private teaching, and observing the theaters. He was unusually fortunate in being prac-tically commissioned to write his first play, *Beau Brummell,* for the great actor, Richard Mansfield. This remains as one of the outstanding plays not only of the American stage but of the last decade of the nine-teenth century. It is easy to understand that such a start was bound to bring success, and for the next twenty years Clyde Fitch occupied a posi-tion in the forefront of the American drama.

It happened that historical plays were the vogue, and Fitch turned out a number that were successful. Among them are *Major André, Barbara Frietchie,* and *Nathan Hale,* the last of which is printed in this book. In all of them he took liberties with historical facts, as all dramatists do, but he was always true to the spirit of the times he tried to portray and the essential character of his leading figures.

While Fitch's plays are not produced at the present time, they have at least three qualities that give them a guarantee of some permanence as literature. The first is their clever dialogue. The second is the realistic presentation of human relationships, for the author was a genius in sensing and recording the social values of the period or scene that he was portraying. The third is the dramatic power of his characterization. In most of his plays Fitch makes his leading character the embodiment of some abstract virtue, and through the character dramatizes that virtue effectively. In *Nathan Hale,* for instance, the hero is the incarnation of patriotism. Fitch was fortunate in having famous actors and actresses interpret his important rôles, both in America and in London. Among them were Richard Mansfield, Otis Skinner, Julia Marlowe, Madame Modjeska, Olga Nethersole, Leo Ditrichstein, and Maxine Elliott.

As you read this play, keep steadily in mind that the acid test of drama is its acting value. A play is a good play if it is good as it comes across the footlights; often such a play does not " read well " at all unless the reader has learned to take into account the dramatic conventions and to picture the characters in action upon the stage as he reads. As you read *Nathan Hale*, try to improve your ability along this line. If you do, the reading of drama will become one of the greatest pleasures literature can afford you.

CHARACTERS

NATHAN HALE (*Yale, 1773*)
GUY FITZROY
LIEUT. COL. KNOWLTON
CAPT. ADAMS
CUNNINGHAM
EBENEZER LEBANON
TOM ADAMS
WILLIAM HULL (*Yale, 1773*)
The Jefferson Boy
The Talbot Boy
JASPER
Sentinel
Three Soldiers
ALICE ADAMS
MISTRESS KNOWLTON
ANGELICA KNOWLTON
THE WIDOW CHICHESTER
 Schoolboys, schoolgirls, soldiers, townsmen and townswomen

ACT I

The Union Grammar Schoolhouse, New London, Connecticut, in 1775. It is a simple room with a door on the left side. At the back are two smallish windows through which are seen trees and the blue sky; between them is a big blackboard. At the right of the room is a small, slightly raised platform on which is the teacher's desk; on the latter are papers, quill pens, an old inkwell, pamphlets, and books. A large globe of the world stands beside the platform. On the wall behind hangs a " birch." In front of the platform, and to one side, is a three-legged dunce's stool, unoccupied for the present.

Two long, low benches for the classes are placed beneath the black-board, and the desks and benches for the scholars are placed on the left, facing the teacher's platform. It is toward noon of a sunny day, and the music of " Yankee Doodle" is in the air. As the curtain rises a very badly drawn, absurd picture is seen on the blackboard, representing the boys on the ice pond of Boston Common, with their thumbs to their noses, driving away the British army! ALICE ADAMS *is by the blackboard finishing this drawing.* MISS ADAMS *is one of the older pupils, somewhat of a hoyden, already a little of a woman, lovely to look upon, and altogether a charming, natural girl full of high spirits. All the scholars are half out of their places and they are laughing, shouting, talking, and gesticulating. Above the din, a* BOY's *voice is heard.*

Talbot Boy. [*In warning*] Quick, Alice! Teacher!

[*There is a wild scramble for their places, and just as* LEBANON *enters sudden silence reigns. All pretend to be absorbed in their books, but keep one eye on* LEBANON *and the black-board, till he, following their glances, discovers the draw-ing.*]

Lebanon. [*A prim and youthful assistant teacher, with a pompous manner, intended to deceive his pupils*] Who drew that picture? [*There is silence.*] Who drew this picture? [*No one replies, and only a few suppressed giggles are heard.*] I will keep you all after hours till the boy confesses.

Alice. [*Interrupts mischievously*] Perhaps it was a *girl*, sir. [*The children giggle and snicker.*]

Lebanon. No interruptions! I will keep you all in till the boy confesses. [LEBANON *looks about expectantly; nobody speaks.*] I am in earnest.

Talbot Boy. It wasn't a boy, it was Alice Adams.

[*The scholars hiss and cry " Shame! Shame! "*]

Lebanon. Miss Alice Adams, stand up. [ALICE *rises.*] Is that true?

Alice. [*Biting her lips to keep from laughing*] Yes, sir.

Lebanon. [*To* ALICE] Sit down. [*She does so, very leisurely. — To the Boy*] Well, Master Talbot, you deserve to be punished more than Miss Adams, for telling on a fellow pupil, and on a girl, too. I shall report you both to Mr. Hale.

Tom Adams. [ALICE's *younger brother*] Please tell him I did it, sir, instead of my sister. Mr. Hale's always punishing Alice.

Alice. No, Mr. Lebanon, that wouldn't be fair, sir. Besides, I want Mr. Hale to know how well I can draw. [*Smiling mischievously. All the scholars laugh.*]

Lebanon. [*Raps on the table*] Silence! That is enough. We will now begin the session in the usual manner by singing " God Save the King." [*A knock on the door. All the scholars are excited and curious.*] Master Adams, please open the door. [TOM *goes to the door and opens it; all the children looking over the tops of their books curiously.*] Everybody's eyes on their books. [*Each one holds his book up before his face between him or her and* LEBANON.]

[MRS. KNOWLTON *and* ANGELICA *enter.* MRS. KNOWLTON *is a handsome, but rather voluble and nervous lady, an undeterminated trifle past middle age. Her daughter,* ANGELICA, *is a pretty, quaint little creature, with a sentimental bearing; she is dressed in the top of the fashion.* LEBANON *rises and* TOM *returns to his place.*]

Alice. [*Half rising in surprise, and sitting again immediately*] Well! Angelica Knowlton! What are you doing here?

Lebanon. [*Raps on his desk with his ruler*] Miss Adams! [ANGELICA *throws* ALICE *a kiss.*]

Mrs. Knowlton. Is this Mr. Hale?

[ALICE *gives a litle explosion of laughter, which is at once followed by giggles from all the children.* LEBANON *raps again sharply.*]

Lebanon. No, madam, I am Mr. Lebanon, Mr. Hale's assistant.

[ALICE *coughs very importantly.*]

Mrs. Knowlton. I wrote Mr. Hale I would visit his schoolhouse today with my daughter, Angelica, to arrange for her becoming a pupil. [*Bringing* ANGELICA *slightly forward with one hand;* ANGELICA *is embarrassed, and plays nervously with her parasol.*] Her cousin, Miss Adams, is already a scholar, and it will be well for the girls to be together. Angelica, dear, stop fiddling with your parasol, you make my nerves quite jumpy!

Lebanon. Mr. Hale will be here in one moment, madam. Won't you be seated, meanwhile?

Mrs. Knowlton. Thank you, yes. Be careful of your dress, when you sit, Angelica — don't make any more creases than are absolutely necessary.

[They sit carefully in chairs placed for them by LEBANON *beside the desk.]*

Lebanon. Your daughter is a most intelligent appearing young lady, madam. I look forward with pleasure to instructing her.

Mrs. Knowlton. Thank you, sir, but it's only fair to tell you her appearances are deceitful. She is painfully backward in everything but spelling, and her spelling's a disgrace to the family. Angelica, dear, untie your bonnet strings; you'll get a double chin in no time if you're not more careful!

*[*ALICE ADAMS *lifts her hand.]*

Lebanon. What is it, Miss Adams?

Alice. Please may I go and kiss my aunt and cousin how d' you do?

[The scholars giggle softly.]

Mrs. Knowlton. That will not be at all necessary, Mr. Lebanon.

Lebanon. You must wait until recess, Miss Adams. Now, attention, please!

[The scholars all shut their books, which they have made a pretence of studying, and rise without noise.]

Mrs. Knowlton. *[To* ANGELICA*]* Do you like this teacher, my darling?

Angelica. I think he is beautiful, mother.

Mrs. Knowlton. Well, that is scarcely the adjective I should use; *harmless* would be better I think. Cross your feet, my dear, it looks much more ladylike.

Lebanon. *[Rising]* Ready! *[He strikes a tuning fork on the desk, motions three times with his finger, and at the third stroke all begin to sing " God Save the King."* MRS. KNOWLTON *and* ANGELICA *rise and sing. All sing except* TOM ADAMS. *After the first line,* LEBANON *stops them.]* Stop! Thomas Adams is not singing. Now, *everyone*, mind, and Thomas, if you don't sing, it will be five raps on the knuckles. *[All sing except* TOM, *two lines;* LEBANON *again stops them.]* Thomas Adams, come forward! *[*TOM *comes slowly forward.]* I am ashamed of you, being disobedient in this manner, before your esteemed relative, too. What do you mean, sir?

Tom. I won't sing " God Save the King."

Lebanon. And why not?

Tom. Because I hate him and his red coats. Hip! Hip! I say, for the Boston Indians, and Hooray for their tea-party! [*There is a low suppressed murmur of approval from the scholars, and a loud "Oh!" of astonishment from* ANGELICA.]

Lebanon. We'll see if we can't *make* you sing. Hold out your hand. [TOM. *holds out his hand, and* LEBANON *takes up his ruler.*]

Angelica. Oh— [*She cries out and rises involuntarily.*] Oh, please, Mr. Teacher—

Lebanon. [*After a moment's hesitation*] I cannot be deaf to the voice of beauty. [*Bowing to* ANGELICA, *he lays down the ruler.*]

Mrs. Knowlton. Child, compose your nerves; watch your mother!

Tom. Oh, you can whack me if you want. But when Mr. Hale's here, he don't punish me for not singing.

Lebanon. He doesn't? How's that?

Tom. No, sir. He said he didn't blame me!

Lebanon. Mr. Hale said that?

Tom. Yes, sir, and he said he had half a mind not to sing it himself any longer.

Lebanon. That's treason! We'll see about that when Mr. Hale arrives.

[TOM *goes back to his seat.*]

Mrs. Knowlton. Does Mr. Hale never come to the schoolhouse till toward noon? — Angelica! [*She motions aside to* ANGELICA *to pull down her skirts — that her ankles are showing.*]

Lebanon. No, madam. Only there was a rumor today that there had been bloodshed between the British and Americans at Concord, and Mr. Hale is at the Post waiting for news.

The Talbot Boy. [*With his eyes turned toward one of the windows*] Please, sir, here comes Mr. Hale now.

Lebanon. Very well. You will all please begin again and sing, whether Master Adams sings or not.

Tom. [*Who has been straining to see out*] Mr. Hale is out of breath, and he's wondrous excited!

[LEBANON *raps for them to sing, and strikes tuning fork. The children sing — all except* TOM — *through three lines, when* HALE *enters, excited.*]

Hale. [*Lifting his hand*] Stop that singing! [*The children stop.*]
Lebanon. Why is that, Mr. Hale?

Hale. I won't have my school sing any more anthems to that tyrant!

Lebanon. We will be punished for treason. Will you kindly notice the drawing on the board?

Hale. Hello! Hello! [*Laughing*] What is it?

The Jefferson Boy. It's our boys, sir, in Boston, driving the red coats off the Common.

Lebanon. I have left the punishment for *you* to fix on, sir.

Hale. Punishment! Punishment! Not a bit of it! Give the boy who did it a prize. Listen to me, boys and girls — how many of you are Whigs? Say " Aye." [*All but the* TALBOT BOY *raise their right hands and shout " Aye!* "] Who's a Tory?

Talbot Boy. Aye! [*Raising his right hand, but he takes it down quickly as all the others hiss him.*]

Hale. I make all the boys here " Sons of Liberty."[1] And all the *girls* too! Listen to me, boys and girls! Two days ago, eight hundred Britishers left Boston for Concord to capture our military stores there! —

All the Scholars. Boo! [*Groans.*]

Hale. But the Yankees were too smart for them! I want you to give three cheers for Paul Revere, — Ready!

All. Hip, hip, hip, hooray!

Tom. [*Excitedly*] What did he do, sir?

Hale. He rode like mad to Lexington and warned the people there, and all the farmers on the way, and other men rode in other directions, and when the Britishers came back to Lexington from Concord — [*Stops for breath.*]

All the School. [*Excited, and rising in disorder*] Yes — yes —

Hale. [*Continues in crescendo*] They found Minute Men by every fence, inside each house, behind every rock and tree! and the Americans chased those Regulars clean back to Boston, — at least what was left of them, for the British lost two hundred and seventy-three men, and we only eighty-eight! [*The whole school breaks loose in shouting, — whistles, catcalls, cries, applause, jumping up on their chairs and desks, etc.* LEBANON *tries in vain to quell the tumult; finally* HALE *comes to his rescue and silences the scholars; he turns to* LEBANON *questioningly.*]

Lebanon. Excuse me, Mr. Hale, there are visitors present; Mrs. Knowlton, the lady who wrote you yesterday.

Hale. Madam. [*Bows.*]

---

[1] A famous club of the day.

Mrs. Knowlton. [*Who has risen, curtseys*] Sir! Angelica, rise and curtsey. [*To* HALE] My daughter, of whom I wrote you, sir, [HALE *bows and* ANGELICA *curtseys.*] Angelica — what a curtsey! Who'd ever think you'd been taught all the fashionable attainments at a guinea a quarter?

Hale. I'm afraid you find us rather upside down this morning, madam. But I assure you it's nothing compared to what's going on in Boston, where the public schools were closed several days last week.

Mrs. Knowlton. So I heard, sir, which was one of my reasons for selecting New London. Sit down, Angelica. [ANGELICA *sits.*]

Hale. Excuse me one moment, madam. [*To* LEBANON] Take Miss —

Angelica. Angelica, sir.

Hale. Miss Angelica to one side, and inquire about her studies.

Lebanon. This way, Miss. [*They go beside the window up the stage.*]

Hale. Miss Alice Adams, please come forward. [ALICE *rises and comes to* HALE *in front of desk; she assumes an air of innocence, but with a mischievous and conscious twinkle in her eye when she looks at* HALE.] It will be a great pleasure for you, I am sure, to have your cousin with you.

Alice. [*Sweetly and conventionally*] Yes, Mr. Hale. [*She looks into his face, and deliberately winks mischievously at him, biting back a smile.*]

Hale. [*Coming nearer her and whispers*] Can I keep you in at recess? Have you done something I may punish you for?

Alice. Yes, sir. *I* drew the picture.

Hale. [*Delighted*] Good!

Alice. But I'm afraid you've spoiled it all by not disapproving.

Hale. Not a bit of it! As *you've* done it, I'll disapprove mightily! [*Smiles lovingly at her, and adds, as he goes back to his desk*] Very well, that is all, Miss Adams. I will give you an opportunity to talk with your aunt and cousin during recess.

Alice. [*About to go, turns back disappointedly, and speaks to him aside*] What — aren't you going to punish me?

Hale. [*Aside to her*] Certainly, that is only to blind the others. You know I'm obliged to change my mind rather suddenly about this picture. [ALICE *goes back to her seat.*] Mr. Lebanon! [LEBANON *joins* HALE *and they talk together aside.*]

Angelica. [*Joining her mother*] Oh, mother, he is really beautiful!

He says I know a great deal. [*She stands by her mother, with one arm about* Mrs. Knowlton.]

Mrs. Knowlton. Humph! He must be a fool. One of your mitts is off, child! Why is that?

Angelica. [*Drawing her hand away*] He wanted to kiss my hand.

Mrs. Knowlton. Put on your mitt, this minute — and remember this, my dear: you are not here to learn coquetry, but arithmetic, — the French *language* if you like, but not French *manners!*

Hale. In honor of the day, we will omit the first recitation, and recess will begin at once. [*A general movement and suppressed murmur of pleasure from all the scholars.*] One moment, however; on second thoughts, I have decided this picture — ahem — is, after all, very reprehensible. The perpetrator must suffer. Who is the culprit — she — he [*Correcting himself quickly*] must be punished.

Tom. [*Before any one else can speak, rises*] I did it, sir.

Alice. [*Rising*] No, sir, it was I!

Hale. Miss Adams, I am *surprised!* And deeply as it pains me, I must keep you in during recess.

Tom. It's a shame! [*Turns to school*] He's always doing it!

Hale. Silence, Master Adams! Ten minutes' recess. [*All the scholars rise, get their hats and caps from pegs on the wall, and go out talking and laughing gaily, except* Tom, *who goes out slowly, angry; and* Alice, *who remains behind.*]

Mrs. Knowlton. [*To* Angelica, *as the scholars are leaving*] I think he is rather strict with your cousin. You'll have to mind your P's and Q's, my dear.

Angelica. I don't like him one-half as much as Mr. Lebanon.

Mrs. Knowlton. [*Snapping her fingers on* Angelica's *shoulder*] Tut, my bird! Enough of that person.

Hale. [*Rising and turning to* Mrs. Knowlton] Madam, if you will allow Mr. Lebanon, he will escort you and your daughter about the playgrounds.

Mrs. Knowlton. [*Rising*] Thank you! Can my daughter remain today, sir? Angelica, straighten your fichu strings. You do give me the fidgets!

Hale. Certainly, madam. Mr. Lebanon — [*Lebanon offers his arm to* Mrs. Knowlton, *who takes it after a curtsey to* Mr. Hale.]

Mrs. Knowlton. Come, Angelica, and don't drop your mantilla! [Angelica, *after a curtsey, takes* Mrs. Knowlton's *hand and they go out — all three.* Hale *and* Alice *watch them closely till they are off and the door closes behind them, then both give a sigh of relief, and smile,* ALICE *rising and* HALE *going to her.*]

Hale. [*Very happy*] Well? [*Takes her two hands in his.*]

Alice. [*Also very happy*] Well? [HALE *sits on desk before her,* ALICE *back in her seat.*]

Hale. I'm afraid your brother is becoming unruly. I'll not be able to keep you in at recess much longer. You see you're not half bad enough. [*Smiling*] I ought *not* to punish you, and all the scholars will soon be perceiving that.

Alice. I try my best to think of something really bad to do, but my very wickedest things are always failures, and turn out so namby-pamby and half-way good, — I'm ashamed.

Hale. [*Impulsively*] You darling!

Alice. [*Laughing; delighted, but drawing back in mock fear, and holding her arithmetic open between them*] Mr. Hale!

Hale. [*Seriously, passionately, taking the book from her unconsciously and throwing it aside*] Alice, did a young man ever tell you that he loved you?

Alice. Yes, sir, — [*taking up her geography*] several have. [*Looking down into the book.*]

Hale. What!

Alice. [*Looks up at him coyly, then down again into her book*] And one of them three times.

Hale. [*Closing the book in her hands and holding it closed so she will look at him*] I'll keep you in three recesses in succession — one for each time.

Alice. [*Looks straight into his eyes*] Then I wish he'd asked me twice as often.

Hale. Alice!

Alice. It was my cousin Fitzroy! He says he will persist till he wins, and mother says he will.

Hale. And you — do you like this cousin Fitzroy?

Alice. If I say I like him, will you keep me in another recess?

Hale. [*Moodily*] I'll keep you in a dozen.

Alice. Then I *love* him!

Hale. [*Forgetting everything but her words, and leaving her*] Alice — Alice — go, join the others. I'll never keep you in again.

Alice. No — no — you *must!* [*She throws away the geography.*] You promised if I would say I liked my cousin Fitzroy, you'd keep me in a dozen recesses. [HALE *goes back to her.*] It isn't treating me fair.

Hale. Do you know what I wish? I wish life were one long recess and I could keep you in with me forever.

Alice. [*Shyly looking down, speaks softly, naïvely*] Well — why — don't — you — sir?

Hale. [*Eagerly, delighted*] May I?

Alice. As if you didn't *know* you could. Only there is one thing —

Hale. [*Tenderly*] What is it?

Alice. When we're married, I think it's only fair that *I* should turn the tables, and sometimes *keep you in!*

Hale. Agreed! I'll tell you what —

Alice. [*Interrupting*] Oh! I have an idea.

Hale. So have I. . . . I wonder if they're not the same?

Alice. I'll try again to do something really naughty!

Hale. And I will keep you after school.

Alice. [*Rises*] *My* idea — and then you will walk home with me —

Hale. *My* idea, too! And I will ask your father today!

Alice. [*With a half-mocking curtsey*] And if he won't give me to you, you will kindly take me all the same, sir.

[*The school-bell rings outside.*]

Hale. Here come the scholars! You love me, Alice?

Alice. Yes.

Hale. Half as much as I love you?

Alice. No, *twice* as much!

Hale. That couldn't be. My love for you is full of all the flowers that ever bloomed! of all the songs the birds have ever sung! of all the kisses the stars have given the sky since night was made. [*He kisses her.*]

[*The door opens and the scholars enter.* HALE *goes quickly to his desk.* ALICE *buries her face in a book.* ANGELICA *and* LEBANON *enter together, after the scholars.*

Lebanon. Mr. Hale, I think I had best point out to Miss Knowlton what her lessons will be — and shall she sit next to Miss Adams, sir?

Hale. Yes. And the first class in grammar will now come forward.

[*Seven scholars come forward and take their places on the forms in front of* HALE, *and while they are doing so* LEBANON *has arranged* ANGELICA *at a desk in front of* ALICE.]

Lebanon. This will be your desk, Miss Angelica.

Angelica. Thank you, sir. Can I see you from here?

Lebanon. Yes, I always occupy Mr. Hale's chair. But you mustn't look at me *all* the time, young lady.

Angelica. I'll try not to, sir. [*She sighs.* HALE *begins to hear his class.* LEBANON *bends over* ANGELICA, *opening several books, marking places in them for her, etc. He is showing her where her lessons are to be.*]

Hale. Master Tom Adams.

Tom. [*Rising*] Yes, sir.

Hale. The positive, comparative, and superlative of good?

Tom. Good, better, best.

Hale. Yes. I wish you'd try and act on one or two of those in school. [TOM *sits, grinning.*] Master Talbot! [TALBOT BOY *rises.*] Positive, comparative, and superlative of sick?

Talbot Boy. [*Who lisps*] Thick —— —— ?

Hale. Well? [*Pause*] Why, any boy half as old as you could answer that. There's our little visitor, Master Jefferson there, I'll wager he knows it. Master Jefferson! [*The* JEFFERSON BOY *comes forward.*] Positive, comparative, and superlative of sick?

The Jefferson Boy. Sick — [*Pause*] Worse — [*Longer pause*] Dead! [*The school laughs.*]

Hale. [*Laughing*] That's a good answer for the son of a doctor to make. [*He nods to the boy to sit, and he does so.*] What is it? [*He looks about and sees* ANGELICA *and* LEBANON *engrossed in each other behind a grammar book.*] Miss Angelica —[ANGELICA *and* LEBANON *start.*] Can *you* give it to us?

Angelica. [*Timidly, rising*] I love — you love — he or she loves. [*The school giggles.*]

Hale. That was hardly my question, Miss Angelica. [*She sits, embarrassed. A slight commotion is heard outside.*] What I asked was — [*The door bursts open and* FITZROY *enters. He is a young handsome fellow of about twenty-five, in the uniform of a British officer; he is excited, and somewhat loud and noisy.*]

Fitzroy. Is this the Union Grammar School?

Hale. [*Rising*] Yes!

Fitzroy. I have been sent here by General Gage, who is in Boston, to hold a meeting of your townspeople who are loyal to King George.

Hale. What for?

Fitzroy. Boston is in a state of siege. The rebels who chased the Regulars through Lexington have been joined by other colonists around, and have cut the town completely off from all communication, except by sea. This state of affairs is nothing else than war, and Great Britain calls upon her loyal children!

Hale. And my schoolhouse?

Fitzroy. Is where the meeting is to be held, at once.

Hale. [*Coming down from platform*] A *Tory* meeting! Here! Have you been properly empowered?

Fitzroy. [*Flourishing a paper*] Yes, here is my permit. A crier is going about the town now, calling the men to meet within the hour.

Hale. A Tory meeting here! [*He turns to the school.*] Then we'll get out, eh, boys?

All the School. Yes — yes!

Fitzroy. What — are you all *rebels* here? [*Looking over the school*]

Tom. No! We're " Sons of Liberty! "

Fitzroy. Damn you! [HALE *interrupts him with a gesture, motioning to the girls on their side of the room.* FITZROY *takes off his bearskin hat and bows gracefully.*] I'll warrant the young ladies favor the British — What, Alice, — you here? You will allow me, sir? [HALE *bows assent, but not too pleased, and* FITZROY *goes to* ALICE.]

Hale. What do you say now, Mr. Lebanon? Are *you* going to stay for this meeting?

Lebanon. No, sir-ee. I am going out to buy a gun.

Angelica. [*Gives an unconscious cry, and forgetting herself and her surroundings, rises frightened, crying,*] Oh, no, Mr. Lebanon, oh, no, no, no!

Hale. Don't be alarmed, Miss Knowlton! I doubt if he ever uses it.

Angelica. Make him promise me, sir, he'll never carry it loaded!

Hale. [*After a jealous look at* ALICE *and* FITZROY, *who are talking together at one side, turns to the school*] Boys! I have a proposition to make. What do you say to joining a small volunteer company with me at your head? Every boy over fifteen eligible.

Boys. Yes — yes!

The Jefferson Boy. Please, Mr. Hale, make it boys over 'leven.

Hale. We'll make you drummer-boy, Master Jefferson. Come — all boys who want to join, sign this paper. [*They all crowd around the desk and sign, the constant murmur of their voices being heard through the following scene.* FITZROY *and* ALICE *come down stage together,* ALICE *leading,* FITZROY *following.*]

Alice. Please do not ask me that again. I tell you, you can *never* persuade me. Nor can my mother influence me the least in this. Twenty mothers couldn't make my heart beat for you, if you can't make it beat yourself. And even if I did love you — [*She adds quickly*] which I *don't* — I'd let my heart *break* before I'd marry a man who is willing to take up arms against his own country!

Fitzroy. That's a girl's reasoning. England is too great a power to be defeated by an upstart little government like the American, and when she wins, those of us who have stood by her will be rewarded! These poor rebel fools will have their every penny confiscated, while I have a grant of land, promotion in the army — who knows, perhaps a *title*. Don't refuse me again too quickly!

Alice. Too quickly! There are no words short enough for me to use. You may *sell* your country for money and power, if you like, but you can't buy *me* with it, also. And that's the last word I'll ever say to you, Guy Fitzroy.

Fitzroy. Huh! You'll change your mind some day! I mean to *have* you — do you hear me? If I can't beg or buy you, then I'll steal. You know what I'm like when I'm in my cups! Some day when I've made up my mind I can't wait any longer, I'll drink myself mad for you, and then beware of me. You remember that evening two months ago, after your mother's punch, when I dragged you behind the window curtain and kissed you against your will on your arms and neck and lips till you called for help? Remember that, and don't think you can refuse me carelessly, and have it done with. No, watch for me. [*She stands facing him haughtily, showing her disgust for him. There is a moment's pause in which he gazes passionately and determinedly at her.* FITZROY *by a gesture and a toss of his head, as much as to say, "We'll see, I am sure to win," breaks the pause and the feeling of the scene, looking at his watch and speaking as boys go back in single file to their places, having signed the volunteer roll-call.*] It only lacks fifteen minutes of noon; I must be off. I will be back, Mr. Hale, for the meeting at twelve. How many of you boys wish to stay and rally round King George's flag? [*He waits for some sign from the boys. There is only silence.*] You little fools! [*He turns to* HALE.] Is this *your* teaching?

Hale. Not altogether, though I've done my best, sir. There is a gentleman in the Virginia Assembly who said " Caesar " — [*He looks at boys with a look and nod of invitation to join him, and they all finish with him heartily.*] " Caesar had his Brutus, Charles the First his Cromwell, and George III " — [TOM *throws up his cap.*]

Fitzroy. [*Loudly*] Treason — this is treason!

Hale. " George III may profit by their example." That's what Patrick Henry said.

Fitzroy. Fortunate for him he went no farther!

Hale. Oh, he is still moving! I think he will go far enough before he stops.

Fitzroy. He may go up! [*With a motion across the throat, of hanging*] See that the house is ready for us. [HALE *nods.* FITZROY *looks hard at* ALICE, *then says*] Good day to you all! [*and goes out.*]

Hale. The school will assemble tomorrow as usual. Of course, if there's really any fighting to be done I shall go, and the boys who are too young to go with me —

The Jefferson Boy. None of us are, sir.

All the Boys. None of us! none of us!

Hale. Ah, I'm *proud* of you! Proud of you all! But your parents have something to say; and for the girls and the younger boys we must find another teacher.

Lebanon. I will stay, Mr. Hale. I feel it's my duty.

Hale. [*Amused*] Ahem! Very well — that is settled then. For today the school is now dismissed, except Miss Alice Adams, who must remain behind.

Tom. [*Rises, angrily*] What for? She hasn't done anything — she hasn't had a chance to do anything. You kept her in all recess, and you shan't keep her in again! [ALICE *and* HALE *are secretly amused. The school looks on surprised and excited.*]

Hale. Look here, Master Adams, what right have you to say as to what shall or shall not be done in this school?

Tom. She's my sister, and you're always punishing her, and I won't have it!

Hale. [*Amused*] Oh, won't you?

Tom. No, sir, I won't! She never does anything worth being punished for. You've got a grudge against her; all the boys have seen it! Haven't you, boys? Go on, speak out — haven't you seen it? [*Turning to the boys, who murmur, rather timidly*] Yes.

Hale. Really — May I ask who is master here? School is dismissed, except Miss Alice Adams — she remains behind.

Tom. [*Excited, coming out from his seat to in front of the benches*] I say she shan't!

Hale. And I say it's none of your business, sir, and she shall.

Tom. [*Off his head with excitement*] She shan't! [*Beginning to take off his coat.*] Will you fight it out with me? Come on — a fair fight!

Alice. Tom!

> [*The school rise and go out slowly with* LEBANON, *but casting curious looks behind them as they go.* ALICE, HALE, *and* TOM *are left behind.*]

Hale. I will leave it with Miss Adams herself whether she does as I say, or not.

Tom. Come on, Alice, come on with me.

Alice. No, I prefer to stay.

Tom. Bah — just like a girl! Very well, then *I* shall stay, too. [HALE *and* ALICE *look surprised and disappointed, yet secretly amused.*] Every time you punish my sister, you'll have to punish me now. If she stays behind, I stay too, to keep her company. [*Behind* TOM'S *back* ALICE *and* HALE *exchange amused and puzzled looks and affectionate signals. Finally* HALE *has an idea.*]

Hale. Tom, come here, — go to the blackboard. [TOM *goes sullenly to the board.*] I think we'll have a little Latin out of you. Write the present tense of the Latin word to love. [TOM *sneers, but with a piece of chalk writes,*

> " Amo, *I love,*
> Amas, *Thou lovest,*
> Amat, *He —* "

is interrupted.] Never mind the " he or she "; just make it " she." [TOM *puts an " s " in front of the " he," making it " she," and adds " loves."* TOM *looks sullen and rather foolish, not understanding.* HALE *goes to board and taking a piece of chalk adds after first line " ALICE," and also to end of second line " ALICE "; he adds to third line " me," and signs it " NATHAN HALE." The blackboard then reads:* —

> " Amo, *I love* ALICE,
> Amas, *Thou lovest* ALICE,
> Amat, *She loves —* me.
>   NATHAN HALE."]

Tom. [*Embarrassed, surprised, not altogether pleased*] What — I don't believe it — it isn't true!

Alice. [*Rising and coming forward*] Yes, it is, Tom.

Tom. Well, I'll be blowed! — [*He stops short, crimson in the face, and rushes from the room.* HALE *goes toward* ALICE *with his arms outstretched to embrace her;* ALICE *goes into his arms — a long embrace and kiss; a loud tattoo on a drum outside startles them.*]

Hale. The Tory meeting!

Alice. Fitzroy will be back. I don't want to see him!

Hale. Quick — we'll go by the window! [*Putting a chair under the window, he jumps onto chair and out; then leans in the window and holds out his hands to* ALICE, *who is on the chair.*] And if tomorrow another drum makes me a soldier — ?

Alice. It will make me a soldier's sweetheart!

Hale. Come. [*She gets out of the window with his help, and with loud drum tattoo and bugle call, the Stage is left empty, and the Curtain Falls.*]

ACT II

September, 1776. At COLONEL KNOWLTON'S *house on Harlem Heights. A large, general room with white walls and columns. The furniture of the room is heavy mahogany upholstered in crimson brocade, this latter material also hanging in curtains at the windows. Life-sized portraits by Copley and Stuart, of* COLONEL *and* MRS. KNOWLTON *at the time of their marriage, hang on each side of the room. A broad window at back shows the brick wall of the garden, and through a tall, ornamental, iron gate is caught a glimpse of the river.* MRS. KNOWLTON *is nervously looking out of the window. She comes from the window, pulls the bell-rope, and returns agitatedly to window. A happy old colored servant in a light blue and silver livery enters in answer.*

Servant. Yaas, m'm?

Mrs. Knowlton. Oh, Jasper, how long since Miss Angelica went out?

Servant. I dunno, m'm.

Mrs. Knowlton. It isn't safe for her to go out alone, Jasper.

Servant. No, m'm.

Mrs. Knowlton. [*Looking again out of window*] And I've expressly forbidden her.

Servant. Yaas, m'm.

Mrs. Knowlton. [*Turning and coming back excitedly on her toes*] And you don't know?

Servant. Dunno nothing, m'm.

Mrs. Knowlton. And the other servants?

Servant. None of the servants in this hyah house, m'm, dunno nothing whatsomever what ole Jasper dunno.

[COLONEL KNOWLTON *enters hurriedly. He is a tall, striking-looking man, aquiline features, and iron-gray hair. He is strong in character, brave in spirit, and affectionate in heart. He is dressed in the blue and buff uniform of a Revolutionary Colonel.*]

Colonel Knowlton. [*Speaks as he enters*] Ah, Martha, that's good I've found you!

Servant. [*Eagerly*] Beg pardon, sah, but am thar any news, Colonel?

Colonel Knowlton. Yes, Jasper. You servants must turn all our rooms into bedchambers by tonight. [*Sits heavily on the sofa as if he were tired.*]

Mrs. Knowlton. What! [*Going to him and sitting beside him on the sofa*]

[*Jasper leaves the room, taking the Colonel's sword and hat.*]

Colonel Knowlton. The army has abandoned the city, under Washington's orders, to take a position here, on Harlem Heights. Washington is making his own headquarters at the house of Robert Murray, on Murray Hill, and we must take in all the staff officers we can.

Mrs. Knowlton. [*Brushing the dust off his shoulders, and holding his arm affectionately*] Well, I'm glad of a chance to be of some sort of use, even if it's only to turn the house into a tavern! Have we abandoned the city entirely?

Colonel Knowlton. No, General Putnam is there with four thousand men. But every one who can is leaving. The sick have been sent over to Paulus Hook.[1] I told Captain Adams he should stay with us, and he brings Alice with him.

Mrs. Knowlton. That's most desirable for Angelica. This Lebanon person proposed for her again to me this morning! He doesn't seem to understand the meaning of the word " No." The next time *you'd* better say it and see if he *will* understand.

Colonel Knowlton. What is there against Mr. Lebanon? — where is Angelica?

[1] Now Jersey City.

Mrs. Knowlton. I don't know, and I'm that worried. [*Rises and goes again to the window.*] She's been gone two hours, and she didn't wear her pattens.

Jasper. [*Enters, announcing*] Captain Adams, sah, and Missy.

[Colonel Knowlton *rises as* Captain Adams *and* Alice *come in.* Alice *looks much more of a young lady than in the first act, and very charming in a full blue and white dress, big hat, and black silk pelisse for traveling. Her father,* Captain Adams, *is a portly, dignified, good-hearted man, older than* Colonel Knowlton, *and like him in colonial uniform.* Captain Adams *kisses* Mrs. Knowlton, *then goes to* Knowlton, *while* Alice *kisses* Mrs. Knowlton.]

Mrs. Knowlton. I'm so glad you came, too, Alice. Angelica is worrying me terribly. [*Helping* Alice *off with her pelisse. The two women go up the stage together.*]

Captain Adams. I've been seeing about the public stores which are being taken to Dobbs Ferry. General Washington tells me he has asked you to hold a conference here today.

Colonel Knowlton. Yes. [*Turning to* Mrs. Knowlton] We must prepare this room, Martha.

Mrs. Knowlton. What is the conference for?

Colonel Knowlton. We must discover, in some way, what the enemy's plans are.

Captain Adams. Yes, what are these damned British going to do? We *must* know. The army is becoming more and more demoralized every day.

Alice. Only to think! We've heard our soldiers are actually in need of the barest necessities of clothing, and there are practically no blankets. [*During* Alice's *speech,* Mrs. Knowlton *goes to the door at left, opens it and listens for* Angelica. *Closes it and comes back.*]

Mrs. Knowlton. No blankets — and the winter coming! Well! I was married with six pairs, and mother was married with six, and Angelica shan't be married at all — at least not till this war's over! So there's three times six, — eighteen pairs for the Continental soldiers — bless their hearts! Alice, how about young Fitzroy? It's rumored again you're going to marry him. [*Crossing to* Alice *as she speaks her name. At the same time the two men go a few steps up the stage and talk together confidentially.*]

Alice. Oh, that rumor spreads every time I refuse him; and I did again by post, yesterday.

Mrs. Knowlton. I'm glad of it! He's nothing like Captain Hale's equal. People aren't through talking yet of *his* gallant capture of the British sloop in the East River!

Colonel Knowlton. Hale's done a hundred brave things since then! The eyes of the whole army are upon him.

Alice. [*Very happy and proud*] I know something very few are aware of. Not long ago the men of his company, whose term of service had expired, determined to leave the ranks, and he offered to give them his pay if they would only remain a certain time longer. [*The two men come forward.*]

Captain Adams. Good heavens! What, my daughter doesn't know about Captain Hale! —

Alice. [*Beseeching*] Father!

Captain Adams. [*Smiling*] If you allow Alice, she will spend the day discanting on Captain Hale's merits. As for Fitzroy, he's a blackguard. They say he would like to join the Americans now, but don't dare, because he killed one of his old friends in a drunken brawl, and he's afraid he'd get strung for it.

Colonel Knowlton. And just at present, Martha, Captain Adams would probably be pleased to go to his room.

Mrs. Knowlton. By all means. This way, Captain. Alice, I will return for you in a moment. You must share with Angelica, now the house is to be turned into a barracks.

Colonel Knowlton. Be careful you girls don't do any wounding on your own account. We've no men to spare. [ALICE *laughs.* MRS. KNOWLTON *and* CAPTAIN ADAMS *go out by the door, left.* ALICE *stops* COLONEL KNOWLTON, *as he is about to follow. She pantomimes him to come back, pushes him down onto the sofa — she is behind it — and with her arms about his neck, speaks cajolingly.*]

Alice. Uncle Knowlton?

Colonel Knowlton. Yes, my dear.

Alice. Have you any news of Captain Hale?

Colonel Knowlton. How long is it since you have seen him?

Alice. Much too long, and I've made up my mind not to have it any more.

Colonel Knowlton. That's right, don't trust him. In Connecticut, where he's been, the girls are far too pretty. [*Insinuatingly, bending his head back and looking up at her humorously*]

Alice. [*Jealously*] You've heard some stories of him?

Colonel Knowlton. [*Teasing her*] Ahem! Far be it from me to expose a fellow soldier.

Alice. Uncle Knowlton, I'm ashamed of you! An old man like you!

Colonel Knowlton. Oh, not so old!

Alice. What do you know?

Colonel Knowlton. [*Rising*] Nothing, my dear. I was only jesting. [*Starting to go*]

Alice. I'm not so sure of that. Wait a minute! [*Coming from behind the sofa to him, she seizes hold of him by a button on the breast of his coat, taking a pair of scissors from the table — the house bell is heard.*]

Colonel Knowlton. What are you doing?

Alice. Getting a soldier's button to make Captain Hale jealous with! He shan't think he is the only one to flirt.

[JASPER *enters from the hall in answer to the house bell and crosses the room to the door which leads to upstairs.*]

Colonel Knowlton. We soldiers don't *give* buttons away — we sell them!

Alice. Oh, I'm going to kiss you! You're quite old enough for that, [*She kisses him.*] but, when I tell Nathan about it, I shall pretend you were somebody else, and young, and good looking!

[JASPER, *who has watched them by the doorway, right, chuckles, and goes out.*]

Colonel Knowlton. Well, you can tell him today if you like! — [*For a second* ALICE *cannot speak for surprise and joy; then she catches her breath and cries,*]

Alice. He's coming here!

Colonel Knowlton. Yes. [*Nods his head violently.*]

Alice. Oh! [*She cries out for very happiness, and running across the room throws herself in an ecstasy of joy upon the sofa; then quickly jumps up and runs back to* COLONEL KNOWLTON.] I'll kiss you again for that good news. [*Starts to kiss him; changes her mind.*] No, I won't, either!

Colonel Knowlton. No, you must save all the rest of your kisses for Captain Hale!

Alice. Oh, dear no! Yours weren't at all the kind I give him. You know there are two kinds of visits, — those we make because we want to see people, and those we make on strangers, or after a

party, whether we want to or not. The latter are called *duty visits!*
Well? — Do you understand?

Colonel Knowlton. No, not in the least.

Alice. Stupid! Your *kiss* was a *duty visit.* [*With a low mocking
curtsey*] What hour is he coming?

Colonel Knowlton. I won't tell you, Miss! I won't give you another party, all for that one little duty visit. [*And he starts to go
out by the door, left.*]

Mrs. Knowlton. [*Off the stage, left, calls*] Thomas!

Colonel Knowlton. Coming, Martha! [*He closes the door behind him.*]

Alice. [*Dances half-way around the room, singing,*]

> " Nathan is coming, today, today!
> Nathan is coming today, today! " etc., etc.

[*Till she reaches the mirror on the wall at the left. She examines
herself critically in the glass, still singing, takes a rose from a vase
and puts it in her hair, retouches her toilet where she can, and pinches
her cheeks to make them red.*] Oh, dear, I wish I were prettier! I
wonder what those Connecticut girls are like! —

[ANGELICA *appears outside the window, and thrusts her head in.*]

Angelica. [*Whispers*] Alice!

Alice. [*Startled*] Oh! Angelica!

Angelica. Sh! . . . don't look — turn your head the other way.

Alice. What in the world — !

Angelica. Sh — Go on — Please. . . . [ALICE *turns her
back to the window.* ANGELICA *beckons, off left, and runs past
the window, followed by* LEBANON, *quickly. The front door
is heard to slam.* ANGELICA *puts her head in at the doorway,
right.*]

Alice. What's the matter?

Angelica. Alice! Matter! Matter enough! I'm married!!

Alice. [*Loudly*] What!!

Angelica. [*Frightened*] Sh! Where is mother?

Alice. Upstairs.

Angelica. Very well. [*Speaks over her shoulder.*] Come along,
darling! [*She enters, followed by* LEBANON, *dressed in Continental
uniform. He wears a white wedding favor, and carries a gun awkwardly.*] I'm a married woman, Alice! [*She turns and directs
*ALICE'S *attention to* LEBANON, *on whom she gazes lovingly.*] Isn't
he beautiful in his soldier clothes? [LEBANON *smiles, embarrassed*

but happy, and goes to shake hands with ALICE.]   Go on, you can
kiss him, Alice. I won't be jealous, just this once on our wedding
day!

Lebanon.   [*To* ANGELICA] No, really, thank you, Precious, but
I'd rather not. [*To* ALICE] You don't mind?

Alice.   [*Smiling*] Oh, no, pray don't put yourself out for
me!

Angelica.   [*Aside ·to* LEBANON] You've hurt her feelings. [*She
tries to take his arm, but it is his right in which he carries his gun.
Aloud*] Hold your gun in your other hand, I want to take your
arm. [*He changes his gun awkwardly. They stand together, arm
in arm, her head on his shoulder, and she gives a happy sigh.*] Alice,
will you break it to mother, at once?

Alice.   Mercy! I forgot about that. It's an elopement!

Angelica.   Yes, and in the day time! I hated to do without a
moon, but I could never get away evenings.

Alice.   Does your mother suspect?

Angelica.   Not a sign. She refused Ebenezer again this morning!

Mrs. Knowlton.   [*Calls from off stage, left*] Alice! [*All start.*
ANGELICA *and* LEBANON *show abject terror, and, " grabbing " for
each other, cling together.*]

Angelica.   Oh, she's coming! Save us. Alice, save us!

Alice.   Quick! Go back into the hall. [*Starts pushing them out.*]

Lebanon.   Do it gently, Miss Alice.

Angelica.   Yes, mother couldn't stand too great a shock. [*They go
out, right.* ALICE *takes a ribbon out of the little bag she carries, and
putting* COLONEL KNOWLTON'S *button on it, ties it around her neck,
as* MRS. KNOWLTON *comes into the room.*]

Mrs. Knowlton.   I heard voices. What did they want?

Alice.   [*Embarrassed, but amused*] They desired me to tell you,
as gently as possible, that they — that she — that he — well, that
you are a *mother-in-law!*

Mrs. Knowlton.   What do you mean, child, by calling me names?

Alice.   Angelica —

Mrs. Knowlton.   Angelica! — Mother-in-law — Alice, don't tell
me! Give me air! Give me air!

Alice.   [*Fanning her*] Air!

Mrs. Knowlton.   No! no! I mean something to sit on. Angelica
— my baby! hasn't made herself miserable for life? [*Sitting in a
chair which* ALICE *brings forward for her*]

Alice.   No! She's married.

Mrs. Knowlton. It's the same thing! Who was the wicked child's accomplice? [*She suddenly realizes, and rises.*] It wasn't — it wasn't — that — [*She chokes.*] that — *that!* —

Alice. Lebanon!

Mrs. Knowlton. No! [*Her legs give way, owing to her emotions, and she sits suddenly in the chair.*] I won't believe it! Those children! I'll spank them both and put them to bed! No! I won't do that either! Where are they?

Alice. In the hall.

Mrs. Knowlton. [*Rises and gestures tragically*] Call them!

Alice. [*Going to the door, right*] You won't be cruel to her — [MRS. KNOWLTON *breathes hard through her tightly compressed lips.*] Angelica! [ANGELICA *and* LEBANON *enter timidly.*]

Angelica. Mother!

Mrs. Knowlton. Don't come near me! I — you undutiful child! [*She begins to break down and tears threaten her; — to* LEBANON] As for you, sir — words fail me — I [*She breaks down completely, and turns to* ANGELICA.] Oh, come to my arms! [*The last is meant for* ANGELICA *only, but* LEBANON *takes it for himself also. Both* ANGELICA *and* LEBANON *go to* MRS. KNOWLTON'S *arms, but she repulses* LEBANON.] Not you, sir! Not *you!* [*And enfolds* ANGELICA.] My little girl! Why did you? — [*Crying.*]

Angelica. [*Herself a little tearful*] He said he'd go fight if I'd marry him! And I heard so much of our needing soldiers; I did it, a little, for the sake of the country!

Mrs. Knowlton. Rubbish! Come to my room! —

Angelica. Look at him, mother! And I wouldn't marry him till he put them all on! Gun and all!

Lebanon. [*Timidly*] Mother!

Mrs. Knowlton. [*Turning*] *What!!* How dare you, sir!

Lebanon. Please be a mother to me, just for a few minutes. I'm going off to fight this evening.

Mrs. Knowlton. [*Witheringly*] Fight! You?

Lebanon. Yes, I said to my wife — [*These words very proudly.* ANGELICA *also straightens up at them, and* MRS. KNOWLTON *gasps angrily.*] Let's begin with your mother, and if I'm not afraid before her, I'll be that much encouraged toward facing the British. [AN-GELICA, *seizing* LEBANON'S *free hand, says* "Come," *and the two kneel at* MRS. KNOWLTON'S *feet, in the manner of old-fashioned story books.*]

Angelica. Forgive him, mother, for the sake of the country?

Mrs. Knowlton. Hm! We'll see — [*She goes out saying,*] Come, Angelica! [ANGELICA *follows her out, beckoning to* LEBANON *to follow, which he does, pushed forward by* ALICE. ALICE *is left alone.* JASPER *enters from the right.*]

Jasper. Has Colonel Knowlton gone out, Missy?

Alice. No, Jasper.

Jasper. 'Cause thah's a young Captain Hale hyah to pay his respecks.

Alice. Captain Hale!

Jasper. Yaas, Missy.

Alice. Then never you mind about Colonel Knowlton, Jasper; *I* will take all the respects that gentleman has to pay!

Jasper. La, Missy! Is you sweet on him? [*Opens door.*] This way, sah! Hyah's a young lady says as how she's been waiting up sence sunrise foa you!

Alice. Jasper! [*Hale enters.*]

Hale. [*Seeing her, is very much surprised*] Alice! [*He rushes to her and takes her in his arms.*]

Jasper. [*By the door, right, with much feeling*] Dat's right, kiss on, ma honeys! Smack each other straight from the heart. It does ole Jasper good to see you. Thah's a little yaller gal lying out in the graveyard, yonder, dat knows ole Jasper was fond of kissing, too! [ALICE *and* HALE *finish their embrace, and sit side by side on the sofa. They are unconscious of* JASPER'S *presence, who lingers to enjoy their love, unable to tear himself away. He speaks softly to himself.*] Don't stop, ma honeys, don't stop!

Hale. I had no hint I should find you here. [*Taking her hand*]

Alice. Father brought me today.

Jasper. [*Taking a step nearer to them behind the sofa*] Bress their little souls!

Hale. I have just come down from Connecticut — a lovely part of the country. [ALICE *draws her hand away.*]

Alice. Yes. I've heard of you there.

Jasper. [*Coming in earshot, disappointed*] Oh, go on, ma honeys, don't stop! Kiss again, jes' for ole Jasper's sake!

Alice. Jasper!

Hale. What do you want, Jasper?

Jasper. Want to see you kiss again, Cappen. It warms ma ole heart, it does.

Hale. [*Laughing*] I'll warm something else for you, if you don't get out!

Jasper. You don' mind ole Jasper, Cappen? Why, I done see the nobles' in the lan' kiss right yah in this very room!

Hale. Well, you go away now. You have kissing on the brain.

Jasper. Maybe I has, Cappen, but I'd a deal sight rather have it on the lips! You ain't the on'y sojer anyway, Cappen, what Missy's kissed. Take ole Jasper's word for dat, you ain't the on'y one this very day, you take ole Jasper's word for dat! [*Chuckling*]

Alice. [*Leading* JASPER *on to make* HALE *jealous*] Why, Jasper, where were you?

Jasper. I was jes' comin' in, Missy, and jes' goin' out. I shet my eyes tight, but they would squint, honey! Jasper's ears anyway are jes' as sartin as stealin' to hear kissin' goin' on anywhere round these hyah parts. [*He goes out, right.*]

Hale. Is that true? [ALICE *looks at him, smiling provokingly, and playing with the military button on the ribbon around her neck, to call his attention to it. He sees the button.*] Whose — [*He stops himself, resolved not to ask her about it; but he can't take his eyes off it.*]

Alice. I wish to ask a question or two. How many young ladies did you see in Connecticut?

Hale. [*Moodily*] I don't know. What soldier's button is that you wear on your neck?

Alice. What young ladies have you made love to, since we've been separated?

Hale. Whom did you kiss today, before me?

Alice. Confess!

Hale. Whom?

Alice. [*Rises*] Captain Hale, [*With a curtsey*] I'm not your pupil any longer, to be catechised so!

Hale. [*Rises also*] Very well! Please tell your uncle, Colonel Knowlton, I am here to see him.

Alice. Captain Hale, [*Another curtsey*] I shan't do any such thing.

Hale. Then I'll go find him myself. [*Going toward the door, left*]

Alice. [*Running before him*] No, you won't — Captain Hale — [*Going before the door and barring his way*]

Hale. Give me that button. [*His eyes on it*]

Alice. [*Leaning against the door-frame*] Not for worlds! [*Kissing it.*]

Hale. [*Looking about the room*] I'll climb out the window. [ALICE *runs to prevent him, and gets to the window first.*]

Alice. Do, if you like, but I shan't follow you *this time!*

Hale. Ah, you remember that day in the schoolhouse when you promised to be a soldier's sweetheart? I didn't know you meant a whole regiment's.

Alice. [*Coming away from the window, indignant*] How dare you! Leave my house!

Hale. Whose house?

Alice. I mean — my uncle's house.

Hale. Which way may I go? The way I came?

Alice [*Witheringly*] Yes, back to your Connecticut young ladies!

Hale. Thank you! [*Bows, and steps out of the low window.* ALICE *stands listening a moment, then hurries to the window and leans out, calling.*]

Alice. Nathan! Nathan! Where are you going?

Hale. Where you sent me — to — ahem! — Connecticut!

Alice. Are there so many pretty girls there?

Hale. There isn't a petticoat in the State — at least there wasn't for my eyes!

Alice. Then come back! Come back! Quickly! [NATHAN *reappears outside the window.*]

Hale. Aren't you ashamed of yourself?

Alice. No!

Hale. [*Laughingly*] Then I won't come back!

Alice. Very well, sir, don't!

Hale. What reward will you give me, if I do?

Alice. [*Thinks a second*] This *button!*

Hale. Good! [*Putting his hands on window ledge, springs in. He holds out his hand for the button.*] Give it to me!

Alice. [*Teasing, pretends to be sad and repentant*] First I must make a confession.

Hale. [*Depressed*] Go on.

Alice. And tell you *whom* I kissed.

Hale. [*More depressed*] Well?

Alice. You'll forgive me?

Hale. [*Desperate, between his teeth*] Yes!

Alice. [*Looks up, smiling mischievously*] It was *Uncle Knowlton!* [HALE *starts, looks at her a moment, comprehends, then laughs.*]

Hale. You little devil, you! To tease your true love out of his wits. But I will make you regret it — I have been very ill in Connecticut.

Alice. That's why you were there so long! [*All her teasing humor vanishes, and for the rest of the act* ALICE *is serious. From this moment in the play the woman in her slowly and finally usurps the girl.*]

Hale. Yes. As soon as I was able I came on here. I've been out of the fighting long enough.

Alice. Fighting! Is there to be another battle at once? Is that what this conference is for?

Hale. I don't know, but we must attack or we'll be driven entirely out of New York, as we were out of Boston.

Alice. General Washington has twenty thousand men!

Hale. Yes, with no arms for half of them, and two-thirds undrilled. Good Heavens, the patient courage of that man! Each defeat, he says, only trains his men the better, and fits them for winning victory in the end! But General Howe has crossed now to Long Island with thirty thousand British soldiers.

Alice. Oh, this dreadful war! When will it end?

Hale. Not till we've won our freedom, or every man among us is dead or jailed!

Alice. That's the horror that comes to me at night, Nathan. I see you starving, choking, in some black hole, with one of those brutes of a red-coat over you, or worse — lying on the battlefield, wounded, dying, and *away from me!* There's one horrible dream that comes to me often! It came again last week! I'm in an orchard, and the trees are pink and white with blossoms, and the birds are singing, and the air is sweet with spring; then great clouds of smoke drift through, and the little birds drop dead from their branches, and the pink petals fall blood-red on the white face of a soldier lying on the ground, and it's you — [*In a hysterical frenzy*] you!! And — then I wake up, and oh, my God! I'm afraid some day it will happen! Nathan! Nathan!

Hale. My darling, my darling! It's only a war dream, such as comes to every one in times like these! [*Taking her in his arms and comforting her*]

Alice. Yes, and how often they prove true! Oh, Nathan, must you go on fighting?

Hale. Alice!

Alice. Yes, yes, of course you must. I know we need every man we have and more! Ah, if only I were one, to fight by your side, or even a drummer-boy to lead you on! [*She adds with a slight smile, and a momentary return to her girlish humor, and quickly, in a confidential tone, as if she were telling a secret,*] I would be very *careful* where *I led you!* Not where the danger was greatest, I'll warrant! [*She returns to her former serious mood.*] Nathan, listen. Promise me one thing, — that when you do go back to the fighting, you won't expose yourself unnecessarily.

Hale. [*Smiling*] My dear little woman, I don't know what you mean!

Alice. Yes, you do! You must! It *isn't* a foolish thing I'm asking! And I ask it for your love of me! You must fight, of course, and I want you to fight bravely — you couldn't do otherwise, that you've proved time and again! Well, let it be so! Fight bravely! But promise me you won't let yourself be carried away into leading some forlorn hope, that you won't risk your precious life just to encourage others! Remember, it's my life now! Don't volunteer to do more than your duty as a soldier demands, — not more, for my sake. Don't willingly place the life I claim for mine in any jeopardy your honor as a soldier does not make imperative. Will you promise me that?

Hale. Yes, dear, I will promise you that.

Alice. That you won't risk your life unnecessarily! Swear it to me!

Hale. [*Smiling*] By what?

Alice. [*Very serious*] By your love for me, and mine for you.

Hale. [*Serious*] I swear it!

Alice. Ah, God bless you! [*In the greatest relief, and with joy, she goes to embrace him, but they stand apart, startled by a loud knocking of the iron knocker on the front door of the house.*]

Hale. The men, beginning to come for the conference!

Alice. Oh, I wish I could stay! Can't I stay?

Hale. No. No women can be present.

Alice. If I asked Uncle?

Hale. He hasn't the power!

[COLONEL KNOWLTON *and* CAPTAIN ADAMS *come into the room from upstairs.*]

Colonel Knowlton. Ah, Hale, you're in good time! [*Shakes his hand, and* HALE *passes on and shakes* CAPTAIN ADAMS'S *hand, as* JASPER *ushers in three other men in uniform, who are greeted cordially by* COLONEL KNOWLTON, *and who pass on in turn to* CAPTAIN

ADAMS *and* HALE, *with whom each also shakes hands. Meanwhile,*
ALICE, *seeing she is unobserved, steals to the big window recess, where
she conceals herself behind the curtains. While the men are greeting
each other with the ordinary phrases,* JASPER *speaks at the door,
right.*]

Jasper. [*Shaking his head*] What a pity Colonel Knowlton was
down already! Ole Jasper was jes' a countin' on gittin' another kiss!
[*Starts to go out, but stops to hold door open, saying,*] This way,
gemmen, if you please. [HULL, *a handsome young officer,* HALE'S
age, and another man in uniform enter. They greet, first COLONEL
KNOWLTON *and then the others.*]

Colonel Knowlton. Jasper, arrange the chairs and table for us.

Jasper. Yaas, sir. [*He goes about the room arranging chairs
and talking aloud to himself. Places table for* COLONEL KNOWLTON
*at right, with a chair behind it, and groups the other chairs in a semi-
circle on the left. Three more men come in together and two separately, each one shaking hands all around, and always with* COLONEL
KNOWLTON *first.*] Lor' save us, ef I knows how to arrange chahs
for dis hyah meetin'! It ain't exackly a gospel meetin', no yetwise
a funeral. Mo' like a funeral 'n anything else, I reckon! Funeral
o' dat tha British Lion. [*Moving the table*] Dat's the place for the
corpse. [*Placing a chair behind*] Dat's fo' the preacher, and these
hyah other chahs — [*With a final arrangement of the chairs*] is fo'
de mourners! Guess dey's mighty glad to get red o' sech a pesky
ole relation, seems as ef she want de mother country, but mo' like
de mother-in-law country, to ole Jasper's mind. [*At this moment*
COLONEL KNOWLTON, *looking up, sees that all is ready.*]

Colonel Knowlton. [*With a motion to the men, and to the chairs*]
Brother soldiers! [*They take their places in the chairs according to
their military rank,* HALE *in the last row behind all the others.*
COLONEL KNOWLTON *takes his chair behind the table.* JASPER *draws
the heavy brocade curtains in front of the window recess, and in so
doing discovers* ALICE. *He starts, but, with her finger on her lips,
she motions him to be silent. None of the others know she is there.*
TOM ADAMS *enters in Continental soldier's uniform. He gives the
military salute.*]

Tom. Uncle, may I be present?

Colonel Knowlton. Yes, my boy, if no one has any objection. [*He
looks at the other men, but they all murmur,* " Oh, no, no," *and
*" Certainly not," *and* TOM *takes his place beside* HALE *at the back.*]
That is all, Jasper, and we are not to be interrupted.

Jasper. Yaas, sir.

Colonel Knowlton. Not on pain of imprisonment, Jasper.

Jasper. Nobody's not gwine to get into this hyah room, Colonel, with ole Jasper outside the door, not even King George hisself, honey.

[*With a stolen look toward the window where* ALICE *is hiding, he goes out, right. A moment's important silence. The men are all composed, serious.*]

Colonel Knowlton. [*Who has taken a letter from his pocket*] Gentlemen, I will first read you portions of a letter from General Washington to General Heath, forwarded to me with the request from headquarters that I should summon you here today. [*He reads.*] "The fate of the whole war depends upon obtaining intelligence of the enemy's motions; I do most earnestly entreat you and General Clinton to exert yourselves to accomplish this most desirable end. I was never more uneasy than on account of my want of knowledge on this score. *It is vital.*" [*He closes the letter, and places it in his breast pocket.*] Gentlemen, General Heath, General Clinton, and General Washington together have decided there is but one thing to be done. [*A moment's pause*] A competent person must be sent, in *disguise,* into the British camp on Long Island to find out these secrets on which depends *everything!* It must be a man with some experience in military affairs, with some scientific knowledge, a man of education, one with a quick eye, a cool head, and courage — *unflinching courage!* He will need tact and caution, and, above all, he must be one in whose judgment and fidelity the American Nation may have implicit confidence! I have summoned those men associated with me in the command of our army whom I personally think capable of meeting all these requirements. To the man who offers his services, in compensation for the risks he must run, is given the opportunity of serving his country supremely! Does any one of the men of this company now before me volunteer? [*He ends solemnly and most impressively. There is a long pause, the men do not move, and keep their faces set, staring before them. After waiting in vain for some one to speak,* KNOWLTON *continues.*] Not one? Have I pleaded so feebly in behalf of my country then? Or have I failed in placing her dire necessity before you? Surely you don't need me to tell you how our Continental Army is weak, wasted, unfed, unclothed, unsupplied with ammunition. We could not stand a long siege, nor can we stand a sudden combined attack. We must know beforehand and escape from both, should either be planned! After fighting bravely, as we have, are we to lose all we have gained, the *liberty* within our grasp, at this late day? No! One of you *will* come forward! What is it your country asks of you? Only to be a hero!

Hull. No! To be a spy! [*A murmur of assent from the men*]

Captain Adams. There's not a man amongst us who wouldn't lead a handful of men against a regiment of the English! who wouldn't fight for liberty in the very mouth of the cannon! but this is a request not meant for men like us.

Hull. [*Looking at the other men*] We are all true patriots here, I take it!

All. Aye! Aye! Patriots!

Hull. [*Appealing to the men*] Are we the men to be called on to play a part which every nation looks upon with scorn and contumely?

All. No! No!

Hull. [*Turning again to* KNOWLTON] I would give my *life* for my country, but not my *honor!*

All. Hear! Hear!

Colonel Knowlton. But, do you understand? Do you realize all that's at stake?

All. Yes! Yes!

Colonel Knowlton. Then surely one of you *will* come forward in response to this desperate appeal from your chief. In the name of Washington, I ask for a volunteer! [*He waits. Silence again. He rises.*] Men! Listen to me! Shall our fathers and brothers killed on the field of battle be sacrificed for nothing? Will you stand still beside their dead bodies and see our hero, George Washington, shot down before your eyes as a traitor? Will you accept oppression again and give up Liberty now you've won it? Or is there, in the name of God, one man among you to come forward with his *life and his honor* in his hands to lay down, if needs be, for his country? [*After a short pause,* HALE *rises, pale, but calm.*]

Hale. I will undertake it! [*General surprise not unmixed with consternation, and all murmur, questioningly, "*HALE!*" A short pause.*]

Colonel Knowlton. Captain Nathan Hale — [HALE *comes forward.*]

Captain Adams. [*Interrupting, rises*] I protest against allowing Captain Hale to go on this errand!

Hull. And I!

All. And I! And I!

Captain Adams. Captain Hale is too valuable a member of the army for us to risk losing. [*He turns to* HALE.] Hale, you can't do this! You haven't the right to sacrifice the brilliant prospects of your life! The hopes of your family, of your friends, of us, your fellow-soldiers? Let some one else volunteer; you must withdraw your offer. [*A second's pause. All look at* HALE *questioningly.*]

Hale. [*Quietly*] Colonel Knowlton, I repeat my offer!

Captain Adams. [*Rising, excitedly*] No! We are all opposed to it! Surely we have some influence with you! It is to certain death that you are needlessly exposing yourself!

Hale. Needlessly?

Hull. [*Also rising, excitedly*] It is to more than certain death, it is to an ignominious one! Captain Hale, as a member of your own regiment, I ask you not to undertake this! [HALE *shakes his head simply.*] We will find some one else! Some one who can be more easily spared. [*Here he loses his manner of soldier, and speaks impulsively as a boy.*] Nathan — dear old man! — We were schoolboys together, and for the love we bore each other then, and have ever since, for the love of all those who love you and whom you hold dear, I beg you to listen to me!

Hale. [*Looks at* HULL *with a smile of affection and gratitude, and turns to* KNOWLTON] I understand, sir, there is no one else ready to perform this business?

Colonel Knowlton. I must confess there is no one, Captain.

Hale. Then I say again, I will go.

Tom. [*Hurrying forward*] Mr. Hale! — Sir! — Captain! [*Seizes* HALE'S *hand.*] For the sake of my sis — [*He is interrupted quickly and suddenly by* HALE, *who places his hand on his mouth to prevent his speaking the rest.* HALE *takes a long breath, sets his face, then gives* TOM'S *hand a mighty grip, and puts him behind him.*]

Hale. [*Who is much moved, but gradually controls himself*] Gentlemen, I thank you all for the affection you have shown me, but I think I owe to my country the accomplishment of an object so important and so much desired by the commander of her armies. I am fully sensible of the consequences of discovery and capture in such a situation, but I hold that every kind of service necessary for the public good becomes *honorable* by being *necessary!* And my country's claims upon me are imperious!

[*Unnoticed by the men,* ALICE *draws aside the curtains and comes slowly forward during* COLONEL KNOWLTON'S *following speech.*]

Colonel Knowlton. [*Rises, and going to* HALE, *shakes his hand with deep feeling*] Manly, wise, and patriotic words, sir, which I am sure your country will not forget! I — I will call for you this afternoon to appear before Washington. Gentlemen, this conference is finished. [*A general movement of the men is immediately arrested by* ALICE'S *voice.*]

Alice. No! It is not!

Captain Adams. Alice! [ALICE *is white, haggard, " beside herself." She is oblivious of all but* HALE. *She goes to him, and, seizing his wrist, holds it in a tight but trembling grasp.*]

Alice. [*In a low, hoarse whisper*] Your promise to me! Your promise!

Hale. [*Surprised*] Do you hold me to it?

Alice. Yes!

Hale. Then I must break it!

Alice. No! I refuse to free you. You have given two years of your life to your country. It must give me the rest. It's my share! It's my right! [*She holds out her two arms toward him.*]

Hale. Still, I must do my duty.

Alice. [*Her hands drop to her side.*] And what about your duty to me!

Hale. [*Takes one of her hands, and holds it in his own*] Could you love a coward?

Alice. Yes, if he were a coward for my sake.

Hale. I don't believe you!

Alice. It is true, and if you love me you'll stay!

Hale. If — *if* I love you!

Alice. Yes, *if* you love me! Choose! If you go on this mission, it is the end of our love! Choose! [*She draws away her hand.*]

Hale. There can be no such choice, — it would be an insult to believe you.

Alice. [*In tearful, despairing entreaty*] You heard them — it's to *death* you're going.

Hale. Perhaps —

Alice. [*In a whisper*] You *will* go?

Hale. I must!

Alice. [*A wild cry*] Then I hate you!

Hale. And I *love you,* and always will so long as a heart beats in my body. [*He wishes to embrace her.*]

Alice. No! [*She draws back her head, her eyes blazing, she is momentarily insane with fear and grief and love.* HALE *bows his head and slowly goes from the room.* ALICE, *with a faint, heart-broken cry, sinks limply to the floor, her father hurrying to her as the Curtain Falls.*]

ACT III

SCENE I

September, 1776. Long Island, opposite Norwalk. The WIDOW CHICHESTER'S *Inn. Time: Night. A party of British officers and soldiers, including* CUNNINGHAM, *and also some men in civilian's dress are discovered drinking, the* WIDOW *serving them. At the curtain they are singing a jolly drinking song. As the* WIDOW *refills each mug, each soldier takes some slight liberty with her, pinches her arm, or puts his arm about her waist, or kisses her wrist, or " nips " her cheek; she takes it all good-naturedly, laughing, and sometimes slapping them, or pushing them away, and joining them in their song. At the end of the song* FITZROY *swaggers in by the door on the right. He is greeted with shouts and cheers. The* WIDOW *has gone behind the bar.*

Cunningham. [*Seated on the corner of the table, which is at the left*] Here's a man for a toast! A toast, Major!

All the Soldiers. [*Rapping the table with their mugs*] A toast! A toast!

Fitzroy. For God's sake, give me stuff to drink it in! [*Leaning with his back against the bar*] I've a hell's thirst in my throat. [*The* WIDOW *is ready, as he speaks, to fill his glass across the bar. As she is filling it he kisses her roughly, and she, to elude him, moves and thus spills half the liquor; he tries to seize her, but she pushes him off.*]

Widow. Enough of that! Kiss the liquor — it's your equal! [*The soldiers are laughing, singing, and filling their mugs.*]

Fitzroy. Ain't she coy, the Widow Chic! Well, boys — here you are to our Royal Master! Long life to King George!

Widow and All. [*Holding up their glasses and rising*] Long life to King George! Hip! Hip! [*All drink, and then sit down again, some of the men going on with the song.*]

Fitzroy. Here's another!

Cunningham. Give us a wench this time!

All. Yes, a wench! Give us a wench's name!

First Soldier. Yes, if you can't give us the wench herself, give us her name!

Fitzroy. [*By their table*] What's the matter with the Widow for a wench? [*All laugh, including* FITZROY, *who jeers derisively.*]

Widow. [*Coming to* FITZROY] You're a gallant soldier to poke fun at the woman who supplies you with drink! I've been hugged many a time by *your* betters! [*A general murmur of approval from the soldiers,* " Right for the widdy! " *etc., etc.*]

Fitzroy. [*Bowing low, with mock courtesy, and taking his hat off as he bows*] I ask pardon of your Highness! [*All guffaw. She makes a mocking bob curtsey and goes back to the bar.*]

Cunningham. Go on with the toast, we're thirsty.

All. [*Shouting and pounding on the table*] Your toast! Your toast! [*As they shout,* HALE *enters, from the right, very quietly and goes to the bar. He is dressed in a citizen's dress of brown cloth and a broad-brimmed hat. No notice is taken of him except by the* WIDOW, *who gives him a mug and a drink and watches him a little curiously through the scene.*]

Fitzroy. Here's death to George Washington!

All. Hurrah! Death to George Washington!

[HALE *has suddenly fixed his eyes on* FITZROY, *and shows that he finds something familiar in his voice and manner, and is trying to recall him.* HALE *has, at the giving of this toast, lost control of his muscles for a moment, — lost hold of his mug, it drops, and the liquor spills. As the others put their mugs down,* HALE *is stooping to pick up his. The noise when he dropped the mug and his following action bring him into notice. He comes forward as* FITZROY *goes up stage.*]

Cunningham. Hello! Who's this?

All. Hello! Hello! [FITZROY *doesn't pay much attention; he is talking with the* WIDOW *at the bar.*]

Hale. Gentlemen, I am an American, loyal to the King, but of very small account to His Majesty.

Cunningham. [*Tipping back his chair*] What's your name?

Hale. Daniel Beacon.

First Soldier. What's your business here?

Hale. I'm a teacher, but the Americans drove me out of my school.

Cunningham. [*Crossing behind* HALE *to the bar, where he gets another drink*] For your loyalty, eh?

Hale. Yes — for my loyalty.

First Soldier. [*Bringing his fist down hard on the table*] The damned rebels!

Hale. I am in hopes I can find a position of some sort over here.

Widow. [*Who has been half listening*] Can't you teach these soldiers something? Lord knows they're ignorant enough. [*Comes out from behind the bar and places a big flagon of wine on the table. Takes away the empty flagon.*]

First Soldier. Widdy! Widdy! [*All laugh.* FITZROY *joins them again.*]

Widow. [*Behind the men at table*] Well, have you heard what the Major here says — you drunken, lazy sots?

Cunningham. What's that?

Fitzroy. General Howe's new plans. [*The men lean over the table to hear.*]

Cunningham. Are we to make a move? [FITZROY *nods his head impressively several times. The men look at each other and nod their heads.*]

Widow. [*Poking* CUNNINGHAM *with her elbow*] Bad news for you, lazy! Lord! How the fellow does love the rear rank.

Cunningham. Shut up! Let's hear the news!

Widow. You've a nice way of speaking to ladies!

Cunningham. [*Growls in disgust*] Bah!

Fitzroy. It comes straight from headquarters! [*The men gather more closely about* FITZROY, HALE *with them, with calm, pale face, showing his suppressed excitement.* FITZROY *continues in lower tones.*] General Howe is going to force his way up the Hudson and get to the north of New York Island. [*An instantaneous expression of fear crosses* HALE'S *face.*]

Cunningham. [*Grunts*] Huh! What's that for?

Widow. Ninny!

Fitzroy. Use your brains!

Widow. [*Laughing*] Use his *what?*

Fitzroy. Hush, Widow Chic! If we can get to the north of New York Island without their being warned, we'll catch Washington and cage what is practically the whole American army! They'll have to surrender or fight under odds they can never withstand.

First Soldier. Well! What's to prevent the scheme?

Fitzroy. Nothing, unless the Americans should be warned.

Cunningham. If they have an inkling of it they can prevent us getting up the Hudson, eh?

Fitzroy. Precisely. In any case if they're warned it won't be tried, because Washington wouldn't be trapped and after all Washington is the man we want to get hold of.

Cunningham. Wring Washington's damned neck, and we won't have any more of this crying for liberty!

Fitzroy. The expedition is planned for tomorrow night, and there's practically no chance for him to be warned before then.

First Soldier. Have you authority for this, sir?

Fitzroy. The orders are being issued now, — it's been an open secret among the men for two days. Down at the Ferry Station the betting is this business finishes the rebellion. [*The* WIDOW, *in answer to a signal from one of the men, comes out from behind the bar, with another flagon of wine.*] They're giving big odds.

Cunningham. Can't finish it too soon to please me. [*Rises unsteadily*] Fighting's dangerous work!

Widow. [*Filling his cup*] That's a brave soldier for ye!

Cunningham. Shut up, damn you!

Widow. I'll shut when I please.

Cunningham. You'll shut when I say! You old *hag!*

Widow. "Hag!" [*Slaps his face*]

Cunningham. Hell! [*Throws the wine in his mug in her face.* HALE, *who has sprung up, knocks his mug out of his hand with a blow.*]

Hale. You coward! [*All the soldiers show excitement. Several rise.* WIDOW *goes to the bar, wiping the wine from her face; she is crying, but soon controls herself.*]

Cunningham. What damn business is it of yours?

Hale. It's every man's business to protect a woman from a brute!

Cunningham. Hear the pretty teaching gentleman quote from his reader!

Fitzroy. [*Rises. He has noticed* HALE *for the first time.*] Who is this?

Hale. Daniel Beacon.

Cunningham. A teacher the Rebs have driven out of New York.

Fitzroy. [*Who has looked at* HALE *curiously, turns to the* WIDOW] Have you ever seen him before?

Widow. Not to my knowledge.

Fitzroy. [*At the bar with the* WIDOW] There's a something about him damn familiar to me. I'm suspicious! Here you, Beacon, how do we know you're not some Rebel sneak?

All. [*Rising*] What's that?

Cunningham. That's true enough! What's your opinions?

All. Make him speak! Make him speak. [*A general movement among the soldiers*]

Fitzroy. Yes, if you *are* a loyalist, give us a taste of your sentiments!

" THERE'S A SOMETHING ABOUT HIM DAMN FAMILIAR "

Cunningham. A toast will do! Give us a toast! [FITZROY *turns aside to the* WIDOW.]

All. [*In a general movement, seizing* HALE *they put him on top of table.*] Come on, give us a toast!

Fitzroy. [*To the* WIDOW] I'm suspicious of this fellow! I've seen him somewhere before. [*He looks at* HALE *attentively, unable to recall him.*]

All. Give us a rouser! There you are! Now give us something hot!

Cunningham. A toast for the King, and then one with a wench in it.

Hale. Here's a health to King George! May right triumph and wrong suffer defeat!

All. Hip! Hip! To the King! [*All drink except* HALE, *who only pretends, which* FITZROY, *who is watching intently, notices.*]

Fitzroy. [*To the* WIDOW] He didn't drink! I am sure of it!

Widow. No! *I* think he *did!*

Cunningham. Now for the wench!

Hale. To the Widow Chic — God bless her. [*All laugh except* CUNNINGHAM, *who says,* "Bah!" *and ostentatiously spills his liquor on the floor.*]

Hale and All. The Widow Chic! Hip! Hip! [*All drink, and then the soldiers take* HALE *down, and all talk together, slapping each other on the back, drinking, starting another song, etc.* HALE *sits by the table.*]

Fitzroy. [*To the* WIDOW, *suddenly*] By God! Now I know! [*In a voice of conviction and alarm*]

Widow. [*Frightened by his voice and manner*] What?

Fitzroy. Who he is! He's my girl's white-livered lover, one named Hale!

Widow. Are you sure?

Fitzroy. Almost, — and if I'm right, he's doing spy's work here! Get plenty of liquor; if we can drug him he may disclose himself! Anyway, we'll loosen his tongue! [WIDOW *exits at back, with an empty flagon.* FITZROY *joins* HALE *and the other soldiers as he does so,* HALE *rises; he has grown uneasy under* FITZROY'S *scrutiny.*]

Hale. Well, gentlemen, I must retire for the night. I haven't a soldier's throat for wine.

Cunningham. Good! So much the better — the more for us! [HALE *goes toward the door at back;* FITZROY, *from the right, goes at the same time to meet him. They meet at the door, back.*]

Fitzroy. Still, won't you stay and have a game with us?

Hale. I think you must excuse me.

Fitzroy. [*Angry*] You're afraid to stay, you're afraid to drink, for fear we'll find out the truth as to who you are! [*The* WIDOW *comes in with more liquor, puts it on the table, and takes the empty flagon to the bar.*]

Hale. [*Laughs*] Oh, that's it, is it! Very well, then I'll stay! [*He sits again at the table. The soldiers start up singing "The Three Grenadiers." They all sing and drink.*]

Fitzroy. [*Interrupts them*] Stop singing a moment! Fill up, everybody! I have a bumper or two to give in honor of our *guest* here! [*He stands on a chair with one foot on the table, watching*

HALE *closely.*] Here's to New London, Connecticut, and the school-house there!

Cunningham. Damn silly toast!

Hale. Never you mind, it's an excuse for a drink! [*All repeat the first part of toast, but they are getting thick-tongued, and all come to grief over the word "Connecticut."* HALE *has answered* FITZROY'S *look without flinching, but has managed to spill his liquor. All refill their glasses, singing.*]

Fitzroy. Here's another for you. The toast of a sly wench, and a prim one, who flaunts a damned Yankee lover in my face! But I've kissed her lips already, and before I'm through with her, if she won't be my wife, by God, I'll have her anyway. Drink to my success with the prettiest maid in the colonies! — Alice Adams!

All. To Alice Adams! Hip! Hip! [*All hold up their glasses with loud cries and then drink.* HALE *again manages to spill his liquor and pretends to drink.* FITZROY *jumps down from the chair and table to beside* HALE.]

Fitzroy. [*Loudly, fiercely to* HALE] You didn't drink! I watched your damned throat and not a drop went down it! [*General movement of the soldiers. All rise; excitement.*]

All. Show us your cup! Show us your cup! [HALE, *with a sneering laugh, holds his glass above his head and turns it upside down; it is empty.*]

Cunningham. What's the matter with you? He knows good liquor when he tastes it! [*All laugh drunkenly; general movement again. All retake their seats, and continue singing.* HALE *looks defiantly in* FITZROY'S *face, and throws his cup on the floor.*]

Hale. Good night, gentlemen!

All. [*Drunkenly*] Good night, good night! [HALE *goes out by the door at back, shown by the* WIDOW, *who exits with him, taking a candle. One of the soldiers is asleep;* CUNNINGHAM *is on the floor; another under the table; they are singing in a sleepy, drunken way.* FITZROY *writes a letter rapidly on paper, which he finds on the corner of the bar. When he is finished,*]

Cunningham. [*On the floor, his head and arms on the chair, whining*] I'm thirsty! Won't some kind person please give me a drink?

Fitzroy. [*Kicking him with his foot to make him get up*] Get up, I say! I have an errand for you!

Cunningham. [*Rising, steadies himself against the chair.*] What is it?

Fitzroy. This man is a spy —

Cunningham. Hurrah! [*Waves the arm with which he was steadying himself, almost loses his balance.*] We'll hang him up to the first tree!

Fitzroy. Wait! We must prove it first, and I have thought of a plan. Take a horse and ride like hell to the Ferry Station. Cross to New York and give this letter to General Howe. He will see that you are conducted to a Colonel Knowlton's house, with a letter from him to a young lady who is staying there.

Cunningham. [*Who is a little drunk, throwing back his shoulders and swaggering a bit*] A young lady! Ah, Major, you've hit on the right man for your business this time.

Fitzroy. Don't interrupt, you drunken fool! but listen to what I am telling you. The letter will say that Captain Nathan Hale is here wounded and wishes to see his sweetheart, Alice Adams, before he dies. If you are questioned corroborate that, you understand! A young man named Hale is here wounded? That's who the fellow upstairs is, I'm very well nigh certain! The girl's in love with him, she'll come! and if it is Hale we've got here, we're likely to know it — if it isn't, well, no harm done!

Cunningham. Very pretty! Just the kind of business I like.

Fitzroy. Your password on this side will be "Love." Are you sober enough to remember that?

Cunningham. [*In a maudlin voice*] "Love!" You do me an injustice, Major! [*With a half-tipsy effort at dignity*]

Fitzroy. Mind you don't speak *my* name. You come at *General Howe's* orders.

Cunningham. Diplomacy was always my forte. Fighting's much too common work!

Fitzroy. Go on now. There's no time to be lost! I want the girl here by daybreak, before the dog's up and off.

Cunningham. You guarantee, Major, that the girl's pretty?

Fitzroy. [*Turning on him*] What! None of that! She's my property! You'd better not forget that. No poaching on my preserves!

Cunningham. [*Dogged*] I understand, sir. [*Salutes and exits. All the soldiers are asleep. The* WIDOW *comes back.* FITZROY *turns a chair to face the fire.*]

Fitzroy. Bring more liquor. [*He throws himself into the chair.*]

Widow. More? at this hour?

Fitzroy. [*Loosening his neck gear*] Yes, enough to last till morn-

ing. [*To himself*] I warned her some day I would set to and drink
myself mad for her! and the time's come! [*The stage darkens.*]

SCENE II

Outside the WIDOW CHICHESTER'S. *Very early the next morning.
The scene represents the front of the house, a low, rambling structure of gray stone, with a porch and a gabled roof, in which is the
window of* FITZROY'S *bedroom. There is a well-sweep on the left,
and a signpost beside the road. There are trees and shrubs on each
side. It is just at sunrise. As dawn begins a cock is heard crowing
behind the house, answered by a second cock and by others. The
sun rises and floods the scene.*

The WIDOW *is heard unbolting the door, and comes out on to the
porch, carrying the mugs of the night before, which she has washed
and which she places on a bench in the sun. A bugle call is heard,
and while she is arranging the mugs, three soldiers come out from
the house.*

The Three Soldiers. [*On the porch, saluting with elaborate politeness*] Good morning, Widow Chic.

Widow. [*Imitating their salute*] God bless you and King George!
[*The soldiers leave porch and start off, right.*] Where are you off
to this early?

First Soldier. [*As he speaks, all three stop and turn.*] On picket
duty, between here and the Ferry Station. The Major's orders.
[FITZROY *appears in the upstairs window, opening the shutters; he is
without his coat; he is disheveled and bloated; he looks as if he had
not been to bed.*]

Fitzroy. Here you men! No loitering! You've no time to lose!
Remember you're to pass no one but the girl, Alice Adams, with
Cunningham. If she's brought any one with her, man, woman, or
child, don't let 'em pass.

The Three Soldiers. [*Salute*] Yes, sir. [*They start to go.*]

Fitzroy. Burnham!

First Soldier. [*Salutes*] Yes, sir?

Fitzroy. Have you your bugle with you?

First Soldier. Yes, sir.

Fitzroy. Well, you change with Smith, then; take his position
nearest to the Ferry, and sound a warning the moment they pass,
that I may know *here* they're coming, and be ready.

First Soldier. [*Salutes*] Yes, sir.

Fitzroy. That's all. [*The three soldiers salute and go off down the road, right.* FITZROY *calls*,] Widow Chic!

Widow. [*Coming down from the porch, and looking up at* FITZROY] Yes, Major.

Fitzroy. We're going to have some pretty sport here presently.

Widow. I hope it's no harm to the young teacher who took my part last night, sir.

Fitzroy. Damme! You're sweet on him, too! He's quite a lady-killer.

[*He laughs satirically and disappears from the window, leaving the shutters open.* HALE *opens the door and comes out on to the porch.*]

Hale. Good morning, madam.

Widow. [*With a curtsey*] Good morning, sir; the Lord bless you and King George.

Hale. Ahem! By the way, where is my horse? Has she had a good night?

Widow. She's tethered right there, sir. [*Pointing off, right*] In the bushes. It's the best I could do, having no barn. I told the boy to feed her the first thing, sir. [HALE *goes to the right as she speaks. The* WIDOW *stands watching him.*]

Hale. [*Passes out of sight among the trees and bushes.*] Ah! Betsy, old girl! [*He is heard patting the horse.*] How is it, eh? Had a good night, my beauty? Hungry? Oh, no, you've had your breakfast, haven't you? [*He is heard patting her again.*] That's good! Be ready to start in a few minutes now. [*He comes back into sight.*] Will you kindly ask the boy to saddle her at once, madam?

[FITZROY *comes out on to the porch.*]

Widow. Certainly, sir. [*Goes into the house.*]

Fitzroy. Good morning.

Hale. Good morning.

Fitzroy. [*Leaning against a pillar of the porch*] I have a pleasant surprise for you.

Hale. [*Suspicious, walking slowly across the stage to hide his nervousness*] That is a sufficient surprise in itself.

Fitzroy. I am expecting a visitor for you every moment now.

Hale. [*Involuntarily stops a second and turns*] A visitor? [*He continues walking.*]

Fitzroy. For you.

Hale. [*More suspicious, but on his guard*] Who?

Fitzroy. Alice Adams. [HALE *does not make any movement, but he cannot avoid an expression of mingled fear and surprise flashing across his face — it is so slight that though* FITZROY *does see it, he cannot be sure that it is anything.* HALE *continues to walk, returning from left to right.* FITZROY *comes down from the porch and meets* HALE *as he crosses.*] You change color.

Hale. [*Quietly, himself again completely*] Do I? [*Walks on toward right.*]

Fitzroy. [*Looking after him*] Yes — Nathan Hale!

Hale. [*Walks on with his back to* FITZROY] Nathan what?

Fitzroy. Nathan Hale! And you are here stealing information of our movements for the rebel army! If I can only prove it — [*He is interrupted.*]

Hale. [*Turning sharply*] If!

Fitzroy. And I will prove it!

Hale. [*Walking towards* FITZROY, *now from right*] Indeed! How?

Fitzroy. If Cunningham has carried out my instructions, he has gone to Alice with a note from General Howe saying that Nathan Hale is wounded and dying here and wishes to see her! I think that will bring her readily enough — in which case we ought to hear them pass the sentinels any moment now! [*A short pause,* FITZROY *watching for the effect on* HALE *of every word he speaks. They stand face to face.*]

Hale. And who is Nathan Hale?

Fitzroy. A damned rebel fool the girl's sweet on. If you *are* he, and she is brought face to face with you, alive, whom she fears to find dead, she's sure to make some sign of recognition, if I know women, and that sign will cost you your life!

Hale. It's a dastardly trick to make such use of a woman.

Fitzroy. All's fair in love and war, and this is a case of both, for I love the girl, too.

Hale. And if I'm not — [*Hesitates*] what's his name — [FITZROY *sneers.*] the man you think me?

Fitzroy. Oh, well then, no harm's done. Meanwhile you needn't try to get away before she comes. I've placed pickets all about with orders who's to pass and not. [*The* WIDOW *comes from the house carrying a horse's saddle.*]

Widow. That boy's gone to the village; I will have to saddle your horse, myself, sir. [*Going toward the right*]

Fitzroy. [*Passing behind* HALE *to the* WIDOW.] I'm hungry,

Widow Chic! Is there a swallow of coffee and a bite of bread ready? I haven't time for more. [*With a meaning look toward* HALE]

Widow. Yes, in the kitchen.

Fitzroy. [*Goes on to the porch, and there turns on the steps to say to* HALE] Don't be alarmed, I won't miss your meeting; I shall be on hand. [*Goes into the house.*]

Hale. [*Quickly going after* WIDOW. *In half-lowered tones and showing suspense and suppressed excitement*] Madam!

Widow. Yes, sir?

Hale. [*Taking her by the arm kindly*] Dear madam, you thanked me last night for striking that dog of a soldier who had his cup raised against you —

Widow. Ah, sir, it's many a day since I've been protected by any man, let alone a handsome young beau like you, sir. [*With a curtsey*]

Hale. [*Bows*] Thank you, madam. Will you also do me a favor in return?

Widow. That I will, sir.

Hale. Then quick, leave the saddle by the horse to arrange on your return, and go a bit down the road toward the Ferry Station. Wait there! When you see Cunningham —

Widow. The brute who wanted to strike me!

Hale. Yes! — riding along with a girl, make some motion to her, wave your hand or kerchief or something. Do anything to attract her attention, if possible, without attracting his, and at the same time place your fingers on your lips — so! [*Showing her*] You don't understand! and neither will she, perhaps. But a life is at stake, and it's a chance, and my only one —

Widow. Wave my hand, and do so?

Hale. Yes. She is the girl I love, madam, and I ask you to do this for me.

Widow. And sir, I will. [HALE *starts and listens as if he heard something.*]

Hale. Quick! Run, for the love of God, or you may be too late! [*The* WIDOW *hurries off, right. The saddle is heard falling in the bushes where she throws it.* HALE *shakes his head doubtfully as to the success of his plan; he goes to the right and speaks to the horse.*] Betty! Ah! Bless your heart! Be ready, old girl. I may need you soon to race away from death with! Be ready, old girl. [*During the end of this speech* FITZROY *comes out on to the porch carrying a coffee bowl in his hand, from which he drinks. He doesn't hear* HALE's *words.*]

Fitzroy. That's a good horse of yours, Mr. Beacon. [*Drinks the coffee.* HALE *starts very slightly and turns, looks scornfully at* FITZROY, *and crosses stage slowly.*] Our friends are late! [*He starts to drink again, but just as the bowl touches his lips, a far-off bugle call of warning is heard. Both* HALE *and* FITZROY *start and stand still, except that very slowly the hand with the bowl sinks down from* FITZROY's *lips, as the head very slowly lifts, his eyes wide open, a smile of expectant triumph on his face.* HALE *is at the left,* FITZROY *is on the porch steps, as the bugle stops.* FITZROY *hurls away the bowl, from which some coffee is spilled and which is broken as it strikes, while he cries out,*] They're coming! [*He comes down the steps.*]

Second Picket's Voice. [*Off stage, right, at a far distance*] Who goes there?

Cunningham. [*Far off*] Charles Cunningham, with Miss Alice Adams, on private business.

Second Picket. Your password?

Cunningham. " Love! " [*In a sneering voice.* FITZROY *listens till* CUNNINGHAM's *reply is finished, then turns quickly to look at* HALE, *whose face shows nothing. The sound of the horse's hoofs is heard coming nearer and nearer. After a few seconds the third picket is heard.*]

Third Picket. [*Off stage at a distance*] Who goes there?

Cunningham. [*Nearer*] Charles Cunningham, with Miss Alice Adams, on private business.

Third Picket. Your password?

Cunningham. [*Again in a sneering voice*] " Love! " [*The horse's hoofs are heard coming closer and then stop. There is the noise of dismounting in the bushes.*] Here! just tie these safe! Come along now, Miss! [CUNNINGHAM *and* ALICE *come on, right.* ALICE's *eyes fall first on* FITZROY.]

Alice. You here! [FITZROY *doesn't answer, but turning his face and eyes to* HALE *directs with his hand* ALICE's *gaze in that direction, and then he quickly turns his eyes upon* ALICE, *to watch her face. She very slowly follows his glance to* HALE, *rests her eyes on his a full minute without making any recognition, and then turns to* CUNNINGHAM.]

Alice. Where is Captain Hale? Why don't you take me to him at once?

Fitzroy. [*In a rage*] She's been warned! Who's spoiled my plot! [*Going menacingly to* CUNNINGHAM. *At this action there is one moment when unseen,* ALICE *and* NATHAN'S *eyes can seek each other, but only for a moment.*]

Cunningham. Not I! It has spoiled my fun, too.

Fitzroy. [*To* ALICE] That's your lover, and you know it. I only saw him a few moments in his schoolhouse, but I can't have so bad a memory for a face as all that. [WIDOW *is heard singing " The Three Grenadiers " in the bushes at right, where she is tying the horses.*]

Alice. They told me Captain Hale was here and dying! Who played this trick on me? [*Looking blankly at* HALE *and then at* CUNNINGHAM *and* FITZROY]

Fitzroy. Well, isn't he here? [*Motioning to* HALE]

Alice. [*To* FITZROY] It was *you*, of course! You who have forced me to this ride through the night, half dead with fear, and all for a lie! Well, mark my word, you will lose your commission for this! Rebels or no rebels, we have our rights as human beings, and General Howe is a gentleman who will be the first to punish a trick like you have played on a woman!

Fitzroy. [*Going to* ALICE] We'll see what General Howe will do when I give into his hands a man who has been stealing information of our movements for the rebel army, who has been working for the destruction of the King's men, and I will do this yet! You've been warned by some one! I'll question the pickets, and if I find one of them the traitor — [*To* HALE, *crossing before* ALICE] he'll hang ahead of you to let the devil know you're coming. [*A look at* HALE, *then he recrosses before* ALICE *to* CUNNINGHAM.] There are men picketed all about — you need not hang around unless you want to. [*Aside to* CUNNINGHAM] I shall steal back behind the house and watch them from inside — make some excuse to go in, too. I want you ready by the door. [*He goes off, right.*]

Alice. [*To* CUNNINGHAM, *going toward him*] Aren't you going to take me back?

Cunningham. Well, not just this minute, Mistress. I've a hankering for some breakfast, when the Widow Chic comes back. [*He crosses behind her, strolls about in earshot and out, keeping an eye on them every other moment. He goes first to the old well, at the left.*]

Hale. [*To* ALICE] You were brought here, Mistress — ?

Alice. [*With a curtsey*] Adams, sir.

Hale. Adams, to see Captain Hale? I used to know him; he taught the same school with me. [*He adds quickly in a low voice,* CUNNINGHAM *being out of hearing,*] A woman warned you?

Alice. [*Low, quickly*] Yes! [*Then aloud, in a conventional voice, as* CUNNINGHAM *moves*] I was his scholar once.

Hale. You were?

Alice. Yes, in many things, but most of all in — *love!* [*Added in an undertone. In their conversation they keep a constant lookout about them, and when they see themselves out of* CUNNINGHAM'S *hearing, they drop their voices a little and speak seriously. In* ALICE'S *speech just now, for instance, she adds the word " love" in a voice full of emotion and sentiment, seeing* CUNNINGHAM *is for the moment out of hearing.*]

Hale. [*Softly, lovingly*] Alice! [CUNNINGHAM *approaches.*] You found him a good teacher? [CUNNINGHAM *goes on to the porch and opens the top part of the door; he leans on lower part, looking in; he is in earshot of the two, which they perceive.*]

Alice. Yes, in *love* only too proficient!

Hale. Oh, well — that was because of course he was enamored desperately of you!

Alice. [*Coquettishly*] He pretended so!

Hale. [*Seriously*] And didn't you believe him?

Alice. Oh, I did, at first —

Hale. [*With difficulty keeping the anxiety out of his voice*] Only at first! [CUNNINGHAM *passes on out of hearing.*] No — no — Alice, you didn't really doubt me! [ALICE *cannot answer, because the* WIDOW, *singing, enters at this moment, and* CUNNINGHAM *draws near again.*]

Widow. [*To* CUNNINGHAM] Well, you brute, your horses are well pastured.

Cunningham. I give you damns for thanks! Have you food for a brave soldier in the house?

Widow. No, but I've scraps for a coward who strikes women. Come in and eat, if you wish. I don't let starve even dogs! [*Enters the house.*]

Cunningham. Seeing you press me! [*Laughing, follows her in. Since the* WIDOW'S *entrance,* FITZROY *has appeared cautiously in the second story window, and leaning his arm out softly has caught hold of the shutters and bowed them shut. He watches behind them.* ALICE *sits on the porch steps, pretending to be bored, and* HALE *moves about with affected nonchalance. The moment they are apparently alone on the scene, they approach each other, but cautiously.*]

Hale. [*Anxious*] Did this Hale prove himself unworthy of you by some cowardly action? Had you any reason to doubt his passion?

Alice. He broke his word to me; that made me doubt his love.

Hale. But you are still betrothed to him?

Alice. Oh, no; when he broke faith, then I broke troth.

Hale. Yet you came this journey here to see him.

Alice. Out of pity — they told me he was dying.

Hale. [*Low voice*] Are you in earnest? Was it pity, or was it love?

Alice. [*With a frightened look about her, ignores his question.*] I can't imagine how they took you for the other gentleman — Captain Hale is taller; you, I think, are short.

Hale. [*A little sensitive*] Short?

Alice. I don't want to hurt your feelings, but it's only fair to you, sir, in this dilemma, to be frank. It may save your life.

Hale. [*Distressed, anxious, lest she loves him no longer*] You came to Captain Hale then only out of pity?

Alice. Out of pity, yes! And now " out of pity " I hope this ruffian will take me back.

Hale. [*In a low voice, his passion threatening to overmaster him*] No, no, say it isn't true! You love me still?

Alice. [*In a low voice*] Be careful, the very trees have ears!

Hale. If they have hearts of wood they'll break to hear you! [*Leaning over her*]

Alice. [*Loud voice, frightened, for fear they are being overheard*] Let me pass, sir!

Hale. [*Desperate, in a low voice full of passionate love*] No! Look! We're alone! They're at their breakfast — you drive me mad — only let me know the truth! You love me?

Alice. Yes!

Hale. [*His pent-up passion mastering him*] My darling! For just one moment. [*Opening his arms, she goes into them, and as they embrace* FITZROY *throws open the shutters of his window and leaning out cries,*]

Fitzroy. I arrest you, *Nathan Hale —*

Alice. [*Cries out*] My God!

Fitzroy. —In the name of the King, for a spy! [*At the mo-*

ment that he has thrown open the shutters with a bang, CUNNINGHAM
*has thrown open the door below and stands on the porch leveling his
musket at* HALE.]

Alice. [*Cries out*] Nathan!

Fitzroy. [*Calls down to* CUNNINGHAM] If he attempts to escape,
fire. [*Climbing out of the window on to the roof of the porch, and
flinging himself off by one of the pillars*] At last! I've won! Before
today's sun sets, you will be hanged to a tree out yonder, Nathan
Hale, and the birds can come and peck out the love for her in your
dead heart. For she'll be mine! [ALICE *starts, frightened, with a
low gasp.*]

Hale. Yours!

Fitzroy. Mine! [*To* ALICE] You remember I told you once,
sometime I'd make up my mind I'd waited long enough for you?
Well, so help me God, I made up my mind to that last night!
[*To* HALE] You leave her behind! But you leave her in
my arms! [*Seizing* ALICE *in his arms and forcing her into an
embrace*]

Alice. You brute! [*Fighting in his arms.* CUNNINGHAM *has put
his hand on* HALE'S *shoulder to keep him from going to her rescue.*
HALE *has shown by the movement of his eyes that he is taking in the
situation, the places of every one, etc.*]

Fitzroy. Look! [*And he bends* ALICE'S *head back upon her
shoulder to kiss her on the lips.*]

Hale. Blackguard! [*With a blow of his right arm he knocks*
CUNNINGHAM *on the head, who, falling, hits his head against the
pillar of the porch and is stunned. Meanwhile, the moment he has
hit* CUNNINGHAM, HALE *has sprung upon* FITZROY, *and with one
hand over his mouth has bent his head back with the other until he
has released* ALICE. HALE *then throws* FITZROY *down, and seizing*
ALICE *about the waist dashes off with her to the right, where his
horse is.* FITZROY *rises and runs to* CUNNINGHAM, *kicks him to get
his gun, which has fallen under him.*]

Fitzroy. [*Beside himself with rage*] Get up! Get up! You fool!
[*Horse's hoofs heard starting off*]

Third Picket's Voice. [*Off stage*] Who goes there?

Fitzroy. [*Stops, looks up, and gives a triumphant cry*] Ah! The
picket! They're caught! They're caught!

Hale. Returning with Alice Adams on private business.

Picket. The password.

Hale. " Love! "

Fitzroy. Damnation! Of course he heard! [*Runs off, right, yelling*] Fire on them! Fire! for God's sake, fire!

[*A shot is heard, followed by a loud defiant laugh from* HALE, *and an echoed " Love," as the clatter of horse's hoofs dies away, and the Curtain Falls.*]

A SECOND ENDING TO THE ACT

It was found on performing the Play that this ending of the Act, in which HALE'S *pent-up passion overcame his control and made him expose himself to* FITZROY, *did not, as the theatrical phrase is, " carry over the footlights." In consequence a new ending of the Act was devised, which proved to be more effective theatrically. In this second ending* JASPER *follows his mistress, and after* ALICE *has failed to recognize* NATHAN, FITZROY, *concealed upstairs, hears the servant being stopped and questioned by the pickets. The* MAJOR *orders* JASPER *brought into the presence of himself,* ALICE, *and* HALE, *and this time his scheme is successful; for* JASPER, *unwarned, recognizes* HALE, *and from the recognition the remainder of the Act is the same.*

ACT IV

SCENE I

Saturday night, September 21, 1776. The tent of a British officer. Above the tent is seen the deep blue sky full of stars, on each side are trees and bushes. There is every little while the noise of a company of soldiers encamped close by. HALE *is seated at a table inside the tent writing letters by candlelight.* CUNNINGHAM *is outside the tent, on guard.* CUNNINGHAM'S *head is plastered, where he struck it in falling when* HALE *felled him.* CUNNINGHAM *paces slowly up and down.*

Cunningham. Writing the history of your life?
Hale. [*Writing, without looking up*] I am writing a letter to my mother and sister.
Cunningham. Yankees, like yourself, I presume!
Hale. [*Still writing*] Please God!
Cunningham. I suppose you're making a pretty story out of your capture!

Hale. No, I'm only telling the truth — that I got the best of two pretty big men, yourself and Fitzroy. [*Half smiling. This is said not at all in the spirit of boasting, but only to ridicule* CUNNINGHAM.]

Cunningham. Yes, and don't forget to add how you were captured by the picket close to the Ferry Station.

Hale. [*Looks up*] Yes, because, hearing Fitzroy's cries, the picket threatened if I didn't stop he'd shoot the girl with me.

Cunningham. It was a narrow escape for us!

Hale. [*With a half-smile*] But too broad for me! [*Continues his writing*]

Cunningham. What else are you saying?

Hale. [*Writing*] Oh, that I was taken before General Howe, who probably only does what he feels his duty, although he condemns me without a trial!

Cunningham. Yes, but with plenty of evidence against you, thanks to us witnesses and the papers found in your shoes, too!

Hale. [*Smiling a little*] True, I walked on very slippery ground, didn't I? [*He comes out of the tent.*] However, you didn't find all the papers.

Cunningham. [*Surprised, changes his position*] What do you mean?

Hale. Oh, the men were so taken up with me they didn't see my friend and confederate Hempstead, who was waiting by the Ferry Station! I don't mind telling you, now he is out of danger, the only paper that was of immediate importance — the plan of General Howe's attack on Washington and upper New York — wrapped nicely in a leather pouch, I dropped in the bushes by the roadside when I was arrested. [*He walks a few steps toward* CUNNINGHAM *and stops. He adds cunningly, trying to get information out of him*] That's why the attempt to force the Hudson was a failure!

Cunningham. [*On his guard*] Oh! was there such an attempt?

Hale. [*Goes nearer* CUNNINGHAM, *desperately anxious to know*] Wasn't there?

Cunningham. [*Sneers*] Don't you wish you knew! Go on — make haste with your scribbling! [*Crosses before* HALE *to the other side*]

Hale. [*Reëntering the tent and taking up his letter*] I have finished. I do not find your presence inspiring. Have you a knife?

Cunningham. Yes.

Hale. Will you lend it me?

Cunningham. No! What do you want it for?

Hale. My mother — [*His voice breaks; he turns his back to* CUNNINGHAM.] poor little woman — wants a bit of my hair. [*He controls himself.*] Lend me your knife that I may send it to her.

Cunningham. [*Coming to* HALE] Yes! That's a fine dodge! And have you cut your throat and cheat the gallows! [*Getting out his knife*] I'll cut it off for you, shall I?

Hale. Thank you. [*Holding his head ready, and with his right hand choosing a lock*]

Cunningham. [*Cuts it off roughly*] There! [*Gives it to him.*]

Hale. [*Puts the hair in the letter; starts to fold it*] May I have a chaplain attend me?

Cunningham. A what?

Hale. A minister — a preacher!

Cunningham. No! Give me your letter if it's finished. [HALE *comes out from the tent and hands him the letter.* CUNNINGHAM *opens the letter.*]

Hale. How dare you open that!

Cunningham. [*Sneeringly*] How " dare " I?

Hale. You shall not read it!

Cunningham. Shan't I!

Hale. [*Coming nearer* CUNNINGHAM] No! That letter is my good-by to my mother, whom for the sake of my country I have robbed of her " boy." It is sacred to her eyes only!

Cunningham. Is it! [*Spreads it open to read.*]

Hale. [*Springs toward him, his hand on the letter*] Stop! There's the mark of one blow I've given you on your forehead now. Dare to read that letter, and I'll keep it company with another! I mean it! I'm not afraid, with death waiting for me outside in the orchard!

Cunningham. Either I read it, or it isn't sent. Take your choice! [HALE *looks at* CUNNINGHAM *a moment — a look of disgust.*]

Hale. [*He drops* CUNNINGHAM'S *wrist.*] Read it! [*He walks up and down as* CUNNINGHAM *reads. He goes to right; speaks to some one outside.*] Sentinel!

Sentinel. [*Who speaks with a strong Irish accent, outside*] Yis surr! [*The* SENTINEL *comes on.*]

Hale. Ask the men to sing something, will you?

Sentinel. They haven't sung tonight purrposely, surr, fearing it would disturb you.

Hale. Thank them for me, and say I'd like a song! Something gay! [*His voice breaks on the word " gay."*]

Sentinel. Yis, surr, but I'm afraid the soldiers haven't much spirits tonight. They're regretting the woruk of sunrise, surr.

Hale. Well — let them sing anything, only beg them sing — *till* sunrise!

Sentinel. Yis, surr. [HALE *turns.* CUNNINGHAM *has finished reading letter; he has grown furious as he reads. The* SENTINEL *exits.*]

Cunningham. Hell fires! Do you think I'll let these damned heroics be read by the Americans! By our Lady! they shall never know through me they had a rebel amongst them with such a spirit. [*He tears the letter into pieces before* HALE. *The soldiers are heard singing, outside, "Drink to me only with thine eyes."*]

Hale. You cur! Not to send a dying man's love home! [*Goes into the tent*]

Cunningham. I'll make a coward of you yet, damn you!

Hale. You mean you'll do your best to make me seem one! God knows the worst I have to suffer is to spend my last hours with a brute like you. How can a man give his thoughts to heaven with the devil standing by and spitting in his face! [*The* SENTINEL *comes on and salutes.* CUNNINGHAM *speaks with him.*]

Cunningham. Hale, you have visitors. Will you see them?

Hale. Who are they?

Cunningham. [*To the* SENTINEL] Say he refuses to see them.

Hale. That's a lie! I haven't refused! Who are they?

Cunningham. They come from General Howe!

Hale. Fitzroy! I refuse to receive him.

Cunningham. [*To the* SENTINEL] Say he refuses to receive them.

Sentinel. But it's not Major Fitzroy, surr; it's a lady.

Hale. What! [*On his guard now*]

Cunningham. [*To the* SENTINEL] Damn you, hold your tongue!

Sentinel. I was told to ansurr all the prisoner's quistions, surr.

Hale. [*To* CUNNINGHAM, *coming out of the tent*] You'd cheat me of every comfort, would you? [*To* SENTINEL] Is the lady young or —

Sentinel. [*Interrupting*] Young, surr.

Hale. [*Under his breath, scarcely daring to believe himself or the soldier, yet hoping*] Alice! [*To the* SENTINEL] Is she alone?

Sentinel. No, surr, a maid and a young man.

Hale. [*Again under his breath*] Tom!

Sentinel. [*Continues*] The young gintleman wishes to see you for a moment fust alone.

Hale. Quickly! Show him in!

Sentinel. Yis, surr. [*He exits.*]

Hale. [*To* CUNNINGHAM] What a dog's heart you must have to wish to keep even this from me!

Cunningham. Say what you like, one thing is true: I'm here on guard, and any comfort that you have with your sweetheart must be in my presence. [*He chuckles.*] I shall be here to *share* your kisses with you. [*Goes to right and sits on the stump of a tree there. The soldiers sing " Barbara Allen." The* SENTINEL *shows in* TOM ADAMS.*]

Tom. Nathan!

Hale. Tom! [*Taking his hand,* TOM *throws his arm about* NATHAN'S *shoulder, and burying his head sobs a boy's tears,* NATHAN *comforting him, for a moment, then.*]

Tom. Nathan, you *saved* the States!

Hale. [*Excited*] What do you mean? Was there an attack made on Harlem Heights?

Tom. Yes!

Hale. And Washington? — Good God, don't tell me he was captured!

Tom. [*More excited*] No, of course not — thanks to your information!

Hale. [*More excited*] Hempstead got it, then?

Tom. Yes; after the men went off with you he searched the spot, thinking perhaps he might find something in the bushes, and he did! he came across your wallet!

Hale. [*With joy*] Ah!

Tom. So, when the British tried to steal up the Hudson that night, they found us ready and waiting — [*He takes off his hat with the manner of paying homage, of being bareheaded in* HALE'S *presence.*] your name on everybody's lips, your example in their hearts!

Hale. [*Stopping* TOM *modestly*] And if you hadn't been warned? [*Putting his two hands on* TOM'S *shoulders.*]

Tom. It would have been the end of us, Nathan. Washington himself says so!

Hale. [*As if to himself, dropping his hands, half turning*] I'm glad I shan't die for nothing.

Tom. Nothing? Oh! Even if your mission had been a failure your example has already worked wonders — your bravery has inspired the army with new courage!

Hale. [*Taking his arm and walking up and down with him*] Sh! None of that. Talk to me about Alice. She is here?

Tom. General Howe has given her permission to see you, but only for five minutes. Can you bear it? Will you bear it for her sake? [*They stop.*]

Hale. Yes.

Tom. [*Looking at* CUNNINGHAM] Is this the man Cunningham? [HALE *nods.*] Alice told me about him; we heard he was your guard, and she has General Howe's permission to choose any other soldier to take his place inside the tent. [HALE *looks at* CUNNINGHAM *with a smile.*]

Cunningham. [*Rising. To the* SENTINEL, *who is standing at one side*] Have you such orders?

Sentinel. [*Stepping forward, salutes*] Yis, surr.

Hale. [*To the* SENTINEL] Very well, we'll ask *you* to stay in place of Cunningham.

Sentinel. Yis, surr.

Tom. [*To* CUNNINGHAM] Then you can take me to my sister — now, at once. [CUNNINGHAM *crosses to* HALE *and speaks to him.*]

Cunningham. I'll be back on the minute when your time is finished. [*He goes out with* TOM, *right.*]

Sentinel. [*To* HALE] I undershtand, surr. Don't think of me a minute. I must shtay in the tint, of course, but if iver a man could git away from his body, I'll promise you to git away from moine! [HALE *smiles his thanks and shakes the* SENTINEL's *hand. The soldiers sing the air of what is now called " Believe Me If All Those Endearing Young Charms."* HALE *stands listening for the sound of* ALICE's *coming. The* SENTINEL *retires to the farther corner of the tent and stands with arms folded, his back toward* HALE. TOM *comes on first, bringing* ALICE. *As they come into* HALE's *presence,* ALICE *glides from out of* TOM's *keeping, and her brother leaves the two together. They stand looking at each other a moment without moving, and then both make a quick movement to meet. As their arms touch in the commencement of their embrace, they remain in that position a few moments, looking into each other's eyes. Then they embrace,* HALE *clasping her tight in his arms and pressing a long kiss upon her lips. They remain a few moments in this position, silent and immovable. Then they slowly loosen their arms — though not altogether discontinuing the embrace — until they take their first position and again gaze into each other's faces.* ALICE *sways, about to fall, faint from the effort to control her emotions, and* HALE *gently leads her to the tree stump at right. He kneels beside her so that she can rest against him with her arms about his neck. After a moment, keeping her arms still tight about him,* ALICE *makes several ineffectual efforts to speak, but her quivering lips refuse to form any words, and her breath comes with difficulty.* HALE *shakes his head with a sad smile, as if to say, " No, don't try to speak. There are no words for us." And again they embrace. At this moment, while* ALICE *is clasped again tight in* HALE'S *arms, the* SENTINEL, *who has his watch in his hand, slowly comes out from the tent.* TOM *also reënters, but* HALE *and* ALICE *are oblivious.* TOM *goes softly to them and touches* ALICE *very gently on the arm, resting his hand there. She starts violently, with a hysterical drawing in of her breath, an expression of fear and horror, as she knows this is the final moment of parting.* HALE *also starts slightly, rising, and his muscles grow rigid. He clasps and kisses her once more, but only for a second. They both are unconscious of* TOM, *of everything but each other.* TOM *takes her firmly from* HALE *and leads her out, her eyes fixed upon* HALE'S *eyes, their arms outstretched toward each other. After a few paces she breaks forcibly away from* TOM, *and with a wild cry of " No! no! " locks her hands about* HALE'S *neck.* TOM *draws her away again and leads her backward from the scene, her eyes dry now and her breath coming in short, loud, horror-stricken gasps.* HALE *holds in his hand a red rose she wore on her breast, and thinking more of her than of himself, whispers, as she goes, "* Be brave! be brave! " *The light is being slowly lowered, till, as* ALICE *disappears, the stage is in total darkness.*]

SCENE II

COLONEL RUTGER'S *orchard, the next morning. The scene is an orchard whose trees are heavy with red and yellow fruit. The center tree has a heavy dark branch jutting out, which is the gallows; from this branch all the leaves and the little branches have been chopped off; a heavy coil of rope with a noose hangs from it, and against the trunk of the tree leans a ladder. It is the moment before dawn, and slowly at the back through the trees is seen a purple streak, which changes to crimson as the sun creeps up. A dim gray haze next fills the stage, and through this gradually breaks the rising sun. The birds begin to wake, and suddenly there is heard the loud, deep-toned, single toll of a bell, followed by a roll of muffled drums in the distance. Slowly the orchard fills with murmuring, whispering people;*

men and women coming up through the trees make a semicircle amongst them, about the gallows tree, but at a good distance. The

"ONLY ONE LIFE"

bell tolls at intervals, and muffled drums are heard between the twittering and happy songs of birds. There is the sound of musketry, of drums beating a funeral march, which gets nearer, and finally a company of British soldiers marches in, led by FITZROY, NATHAN HALE *in their midst, walking alone, his hands tied behind his back. As he comes forward the people are absolutely silent, and a girl in the front row of the spectators falls forward in a dead faint. She is quickly carried out by two bystanders.* HALE *is led to the foot of the tree before the ladder. The soldiers are in double lines on either side.*

Fitzroy. [*To* HALE] Nathan Hale, have you anything to say? We are ready to hear your last dying speech and confession! [HALE *is standing, looking up, his lips moving slightly, as if in prayer. He remains in this position a moment, and then, with a sigh of relief and rest, looks upon the sympathetic faces of the people about him, with almost a smile on his face.*]

Hale. I only regret that I have but one life to lose for my country!

[FITZROY *makes a couple of steps toward him;* HALE *turns and places one foot on the lower rung of the ladder, as the Curtain Falls.*]

SUGGESTIONS FOR STUDY

ACT I

1. The first act of a play should introduce the main characters, commence the struggle between the two opposing forces in the plot, and, by the creation of atmosphere, start the desired emotional reactions in the audience. Show that Act I does these things.

2. Since Nathan Hale is the hero and since he meets a tragic death, the actor of this part must never lose his dignity and descend to low comedy. If in this first act the actor fails to hold to an innate dignity and seriousness, he will find it almost impossible to carry later scenes. Point out dangerous places from this standpoint.

3. What purpose is served by the introduction of the characters Lebanon and Angelica? In what way are they essentially different from Hale and Alice? Why are their parts difficult to act?

4. If you were given the part of Mrs. Knowlton, what would you try to make of the part?

5. What danger must be guarded against by the actor of the part of Fitzroy?

6. Point out places in the act which border on farce. On melodrama. Careful acting must keep these places from getting out of bounds.

7. How can you defend the introduction into this play of stilted sentences like " I cannot be deaf to the voice of beauty " and " I wish life were one long recess "?

8. At the end of Act I do you wish to go on and finish the play? If so, what holds your interest?

ACT II

1. The attitude of the soldiers in this act towards a spy is of course not true to life. What did Fitch gain in dramatic value by this departure from realism? What part of the action is impossible without it?

2. Do Alice and Hale seem like real people to you? This creation of convincing human relationships is perhaps Fitch's chief claim to greatness. Of course a great deal depends on the actors, but Fitch gives them real opportunities.

3. What does Jasper add to the act besides humor?

4. If you were acting the part of one of the extra soldiers at the conference how could you aid in producing the proper effect in this scene? How might you hinder? Remember that every one on the stage is important.

5. If the scene with Mrs. Knowlton, Lebanon, and Angelica should be made to lean somewhat towards farce, how would the following love scene between Hale and Alice be affected?

6. What do you think of Fitch's ability to write stage directions?

7. Compare your interest in the play at the end of Act II with that at the end of Act I.

ACT III, SCENE 1

1. In what way have you been prepared for the degradation of Fitzroy?

2. What is the dramatic purpose of the coarseness in this scene? Do you think Fitch was interested in realism or in dramatic effect? What plays of the World War have you seen that went to great length in portraying the degrading effect of war?

3. What sort of interpretation should the actress make of the part of Widow Chic? What information should the audience get from her speech, " No! *I* think he *did!* "?

4. Which should be uppermost in this scene, humor, tenseness, or rowdiness?

5. What is meant in theater slang by the word *hokum?* Where do you find any " hokum " in this scene? Do you feel that the introduction of " hokum " is justified in good drama? Why?

ACT III, SCENE 2

1. What dramatic purpose is served by the device of the bugles?

2. The talk off-stage to the horse is the weakest incident in the play dramatically and is very difficult to make seem real in the acting. Why?

3. What human emotions are effectively portrayed in this scene?

4. Notice how reasonable it seemed that the Widow should help Hale. How has Fitch accomplished this?

5. Why was the ending of this scene unsatisfactory to the audience? What do you think of the ending that was substituted? Would you have liked to have Alice betray Hale? You might try your hand at a good ending of your own.

ACT IV, SCENE 1

1. Why do you think Hale wanted the knife?

2. What is gained by the introduction of music? Do you know the songs mentioned? Why are they effective?

3. What false note could the sentry strike in his last speech? How can he contribute to the desired effect?

4. What do you think of the part of Tom Adams considered as a whole?

5. What abstract quality is personified in Cunningham?

6. How could amateurs put across the ending of this scene? Either one of two possible extremes of acting would be fatal. Can you describe them?

ACT IV, SCENE 2

1. Why is this scene necessary? Upon what does its effectiveness depend? Do you consider it difficult to present? Why?

2. Is this play a tragedy? Why? What difference would have been made in final impression if the last scene had been omitted?

3. What would you consider the climax of the play?

4. What human emotions are effectively portrayed in this scene?

5. Look up the facts in the life of the real Nathan Hale and see how much liberty Fitch took with them. In what sense is the play true to history? How much liberty with history do you think an author is entitled to take?

FOR FURTHER READING

Beau Brummell   The Climbers
Barbara Frietchie   The Truth
Captain Jinks of the Horse Marines

FOR FURTHER READING OF PLAYS

FULL-LENGTH PLAYS

Austin, Mary. *The Arrowmaker*
Belasco, David. *The Return of Peter Grimm*
Broadhurst, George H. *The Man of the Hour*
Brown, Alice. *Children of Earth*
Crothers, Rachel. *He and She*
Forbes, James. *The Famous Mrs. Fair*
Gale, Zona. *Miss Lulu Bett*
Gillette, William. *Held by the Enemy. Secret Service*
Hazelton and Benrimo. *The Yellow Jacket*
Housman, Laurence. *The Chinese Lantern*
Housman and Barker. *Prunella*
Housum, Robert. *The Gypsy Trail*
Howard, Bronson. *Shenandoah*
Kaufman and Connelly. *Dulcy. Merton of the Movies*
Kelly, George. *The Show-Off. Craig's Wife*
Klein, Charles. *The Lion and the Mouse*
Mackaye, Percy. *The Scarecrow. The Canterbury Pilgrims. A Thousand Years Ago. Jeanne d'Arc*
Millay, Edna St. Vincent. *The King's Henchman*
Moody, William Vaughn. *The Great Divide. The Faith Healer*
Peabody, Josephine Preston. *The Piper. Marlowe. The Wolf of Gubbio*
Pollock, Channing. *The Fool. The Enemy*

Smith, Harry James. *A Tailor-Made Man. Mrs. Bumpstead-Leigh*
Smith, Winchell. *The Boomerang. The Fortune Hunter*
Thomas, Augustus. *The Witching Hour. The Copperhead. As a Man Thinks*
Van Dyke, Henry. *The House of Rimmon*

PLAYS BY ENGLISHMEN ABOUT AMERICA

Drinkwater, John. *Abraham Lincoln. Robert E. Lee*
Zangwill, Israel. *The Melting Pot*

ONE-ACT PLAYS

Bangs, John Kendrick. *A Proposal under Difficulties. The Real Thing*
Brown, Alice. *Joint Owners in Spain*
Bynner, Witter. *The Little King*
Cameron, Margaret. *The Teeth of the Gift Horse. The Burglar*
Cowles, Albert. *The Killer.*
Davis, Richard Harding. *Miss Civilization. The Zone Police*
Dix, Beulah Marie. *Allison's Lad*
Downs, Oliphant. *The Maker of Dreams*
Firkins, Oscar W. *Two Passengers for Chelsea and Other Plays*
Gale, Zona. *Neighbors. Uncle Jimmy*
Gerstenberg, Alice. *Overtones. The Pot Boiler. The Unseen.* (In *Ten One-Act Plays*)
Glaspell, Susan. *Trifles* (in *Short Plays*)
Goodman, Kenneth Sawyer. *Dust of the Road*
Green, Paul. *The Last of the Lowries*
Hawkridge, Winifred. *The Florist Shop*
Howells, William Dean. *The Parlor Car. The Sleeping Car. The Mouse-Trap.* (In *Polite Farces*)
Kreymborg, Alfred. *Manikin and Minikin. Lima Beans.* (In *Puppet Plays*)
Mackay, Constance D. *The Beau of Bath. The Christmas Guest. The Silver Lining*
MacMillan, Mary. *The Shadowed Star. A Fan and Two Candlesticks. The Ring*
McFadden, Elizabeth. *Why the Chimes Rang*
Millay, Edna St. Vincent. *Aria da Capo*
Morley, Christopher. *Good Theater. Thursday Evening. The Rehearsal*
Oliver, Margaret Scott. *The Turtle Dove*
Peabody, Josephine Preston. *Fortune and Men's Eyes*
Walker, Stuart. *Six Who Pass While the Lentils Boil. Sir David Wears a Crown. Nevertheless.* (*Portmanteau Adaptations, Portmanteau Plays*)

Tompkins, Frank G. *Sham*
Wolff, Oscar M. *Where But in America?*

COLLECTIONS OF PLAYS EMPHASIZING AMERICAN PLAYS

Baker, G. P. *Modern American Plays.*
Cohen, Helen L. *Longer Plays by Modern Authors. One-Act Plays. More One-Act Plays*
Dickinson, T. H. *Chief Contemporary Dramatists. Representative One-Act Plays*
Knickerbocker, E. V. *Twelve Plays. Plays for Classroom Interpretation*
Koch, F. H. *Carolina Folk-Plays*
Leonard, S. A. *Atlantic Book of Modern Plays*
Mayorga, Margaret G. *Representative Plays by American Authors*
Moses, Montrose. *Representative American Dramas*
Quinn, A. H. *Contemporary American Plays. Representative American Plays*
Shay, Frank. *Twenty Contemporary One-Act Plays*
Webber and Webster. *Short Plays for Junior and Senior High Schools. Short Plays for Young People. One-Act Plays*

HISTORY OF AMERICAN LITERATURE
A REVIEW AND RE-INTERPRETATION

Chapter I

COLONIAL AND REVOLUTIONARY LITERATURE

In the various sections of this book you have become acquainted with a goodly portion of the writings of our country, and have been able to trace the development of the individual types. One more thing remains to be done. Just as the miscellaneous parts of the engine, the chassis, the wheels, and the body of an automobile are assembled and bolted together before we can have a complete unit, so these miscellaneous writings, authors, and types which have taken on shape in your mind can be welded into one unified impression of American literature as a whole.

American history records the transplanting of European civilization into a wilderness and its transformation by the new environment. The history of American literature is the history of the inherited European literary traditions as modified by the westward-moving American frontier. Thus we must go back to the earliest days and briefly view the kind of people who first came to American shores. At the beginning of the seventeenth century two widely differing types were living side by side in England, but not on particularly friendly terms: in fact, by the middle of the century they came to open blows and brought about a civil war in that country. These two types are usually called the Puritan and the Cavalier. The Puritans were a serious-minded middle-class group, whose innate love of freedom caused them to resent the authority of the Church of England over their religious views, and the so-called " divine right of kings" over their civic liberties. The Cavaliers were the upholders of king and established church. They represented largely the aristocratic classes with their followers. Their attitude toward life was gayer, more urbane, more dashing than that of the Puritans. The early colonies in the North and in the South were formed respectively by representatives of these two types. Almost from the first the writings of both Cavalier and Puritan in America were distinctly local, the primitive surroundings strongly coloring the descriptions of personal experiences. Literary excellence was lacking in the writings of men whose chief work was to transform a wilderness into a habitable country.

COLONIAL LITERATURE

Writings of Southern Colonies. In 1607 a group of English adventurers of the Cavalier party established the colony of Jamestown in Virginia, though they had no intention of settling permanently in the new country. A miscellaneous lot of impoverished "gentlemen" who wanted to get rich quick and return to the gay life of London, they nevertheless were thoroughly imbued with the spirit of adventure that was characteristic of the Elizabethan period in England. Their leader was Captain John Smith (1560–1631). He wrote an account of the experiences of himself and his followers under the pretentious title, *A True Relation of such occurrences and accidents of noate as hath hapned in Virginia since the first planting of that Collony, which is now resident in the South part thereof, till the*

CAPTAIN JOHN SMITH
Who saved him from death at the hands of Indians?

last returne from thence. Written by Captaine John Smith Coronell of the said Collony, to a worshipful friend of his in England. Published in England in 1608, this was the first book written in America.

A True Relation, as it is usually called, was only one of several books written by Smith on the general subject of Virginia. Both he and his men had adventures galore, and they lost nothing in Smith's telling. It is in his last book that he tells the best-known adventure. In the hands of the Indians, John Smith had every reason to believe that he was about to be executed. "A long consultation was held, but the conclusion was, two great stones were brought before Powhatan: then as many as could laid hands on him [Smith], dragged him to them, and thereon laid his head, and being ready with their clubs, to beat out his brains, Pocahontas, the King's dearest daughter, when no entreaty could prevail, got his head in her arms, and laid her own upon his to save him from death; whereat the Emperor was contented he should live to make him hatchets and her bells, beads, and copper."

In a letter dated 1610, William Strachey, an employee of the company that controlled the affairs in Virginia, wrote *A True Repertory* of a shipwreck on the island of Bermuda. Nothing much is known about Strachey, and this letter would not be particularly important if it were not generally believed that Shakespeare got a hint from it for his play *The Tempest.*

In spite of a bad start, the Virginia adventure continued, and by 1728 Colonel William Byrd (1674–1744) found it desirable or interesting to write an account of the territorial problems that had arisen between Virginia and North Carolina under the title of *A History of the Dividing Line.* (See page 424.)

Writings of the Northern Colonies. As in the South, the earliest writing in the North was more or less historical, and largely personal in point of view. The first of these works was the *History of the Plymouth Plantation,* by William Bradford (1590–1657), begun on the " Mayflower " and carried down to 1647. It gives an excellent statement of the Puritans' ideals and what they hoped to achieve in the New World. In 1630 the Massachusetts Bay Colony was founded by Governor John Winthrop (1588–1649), a graduate of Cambridge and a successful lawyer in England. His *History of New England* tells the story of the first nineteen years of the settlements in the vicinity of Boston. Readers of today find this interesting in spots because of the author's fondness for recording of marvelous portents and monstrous happenings, from which he invariably drew a lesson.

The Mathers. In settlements so intensely religious as those of New England the theologians became prolific writers. The names of Increase and Cotton Mather, father and son, loom large, both because of the enormous volume of their work and because of their social and intellectual position in the colonies. Increase Mather (1639–1723) was president of Harvard, which was founded in 1636, and Cotton Mather (1663–1728) was the preacher of North Church. Both were connected with the Salem witchcraft scandals. Cotton Mather's most important works are *The Ecclesiastical History of New England* and *Wonders of the Invisible Universe,* but there are nearly four hundred sermons, essays, and other works from which to choose.

The narrowness of the Mather type of New Englander was slightly offset by such men as Roger Williams (1608–1683), who wrote and preached in defence of free thought and freedom of conscience, and John Eliot (1604–1690), who became the first Indian missionary, and translated part of the Bible into Indian dialects.

Jonathan Edwards (1703–1758). The greatest theologian was Jonathan Edwards. Born in Connecticut, a graduate of Yale, and later president of Princeton, he became the typical preacher of Christian dogma as it was understood by the narrow clergy of that era. His sermons were often great tirades against sin, with an impassioned plea for repentance. He constantly warned his hearers that they were in immediate danger of being damned to Hell by an angry God. In addition to his long sermons he wrote treatises on philosophic subjects. The most famous as well as the most profound of these tracts is *The Freedom of the Will.* While today his doctrines are considered old-fashioned, it is worth knowing that the colonies so early produced an intellectual giant.

Early Poetic Efforts. No real poetry was produced in the colonies prior to Philip Freneau. In 1640 the Psalms were turned into meter by John Eliot and others, to facilitate their use as songs. These were often monstrous concoctions, so that in the *Bay Psalm Book* may be found the following:

> Because there they that us away
>   led in captivitee
> Required of us a song, and thus
>   askt mirth, us waste who laid,
> Sing us among a Sion's song,
>   unto us then they said.

When the Puritan child went to school he started with the *New England Primer,* in which the alphabet was in rhyme, beginning

MICHAEL WIGGLESWORTH

In Adam's fall
We sinned all,

and ending

Zacchaeus, he
Did climb the Tree
His Lord to see.

G — As runs the *Glass* Mans life doth pass.

H — My *Book* and *Heart* Shall never part.

J — *Job* feels the Rod Yet blesses GOD.

K — Our *K I N G* the good No man of blood.

L — The *Lion* bold The *Lamb* doth hold.

M — The *Moon* gives light In time of night.

NEW ENGLAND PRIMER (G-M)

N — *Nightingales* sing In Time of Spring.

O — The *Royal Oak* it was the Tree That sav'd His Royal Majestie.

P — *Peter* denies His Lord and cries

Q — Queen *Esther* comes in Royal State To Save the JEWS from dismal Fate

R — *Rachol* doth mour. For her first born.

S — *Samuel* anoints Whom God appoints

NEW ENGLAND PRIMER (N-S)

Anne Bradstreet (1612–1672). The first woman who won a literary reputation in this country was Mrs. Anne Bradstreet, hailed by her London publisher as " The Tenth Muse Lately Sprung Up in America." In a definite literary environment, she might have produced a few real poems in her four-hundred-page volume. She seemed vaguely to sense that poetry was lying dormant in the American scene, but she was unable to get away from her few English and French models, so her verses are stilted, highly religious, and wholly uninteresting today except as curiosities.

Michael Wigglesworth (1631–1705). There were other serious attempts at poetry. In 1662 Michael Wigglesworth, a Puritan minister, wrote a long, gloomy, and terrifying poem entitled " The Day of Doom." It is mere doggerel, but its expression of the Puritan's attitude towards sin and redemption accounts for its continued popularity through a hundred years. In England at about the same time John Milton was writing his epic poem *Paradise*

Lost, which sets forth the same attitude, but with exalted poetic grandeur.

Sarah Kemble Knight (1652–1730). A woman whose literary reputation has fared better is Sarah Kemble Knight. Her work is discussed and illustrated on page 415. She did not write to establish a literary reputation, but merely to record her interesting experiences in the form of a diary.

Thomas Godfrey (1736–1763). A Philadelphian, Thomas Godfrey, wrote the first play in verse to be produced on the Colonial stage. This was " The Prince of Parthia," a tragedy. It was a youthful work, in the manner of Dryden and Pope; and had he not died at the age of twenty-seven he might have developed a distinctively individual style. Some critics give him the honor of having been the first real American poet.

LITERATURE OF THE REVOLUTION

By " Revolutionary " is meant the literature that definitely falls within the period of the American Revolution. Most of this literature was closely identified with the struggle.

Benjamin Franklin, the Link Between Two Periods (1706–1790). Because of his intimate connection with the long struggle for independence, Franklin is usually associated with this period. It must be remembered, however, that his most famous writings are distinctly a part of Colonial rather than of Revolutionary literature, for they were either published long before the war, or else reminiscent of his youth, though written in the quieter days after the war. Thus he stands as a link between the two periods. His career is one of the most fascinating in all history.

" A wit and philosopher, rich in learning, charming in manners, ripe in the wisdom of this world, resourceful in dealing with men and events, he was one of the most delightful as he was one of the greatest men produced by the English race in the eighteenth century." (Parrington). For Franklin's writing was merely a sideline, another way of using up his apparently boundless energy; but had he not achieved distinction as a moralist, scientist, inventor, diplomat, and patriotic statesman, he would still rank as America's first great man of letters. From another angle he may be regarded as typifying the poor boy who carved out a career for himself by taking advantage of the opportunities offered by a rising country. After migrating from Boston to Philadelphia Franklin set up his own print shop.

Here in 1732 he began the publication of *Poor Richard's Almanac,* which was issued regularly for twenty-five years and had a phenomenal sale. It is noted for its wit and humor, its homely doctrines of common sense as applied to daily living, and its uncompromising morality. Franklin had the knack of phrasing or rephrasing maxims in a way that struck home. Examples will be found on page 366. In 1728 Franklin founded the *Pennsylvania Gazette,* the only journal in this country that has had a continuous existence from Colonial times to the present day. Many will recognize it readily under its modern name, *The Saturday Evening Post.* However, the *Autobiography* constitutes Franklin's title to literary fame. He wrote five chapters in 1771, and the rest between 1784 and 1789. Unfortunately only a small part of his life is told, down to 1757. (See page 308.)

Literature of the Struggle. Franklin's life covered the period of American history when the ideals of freedom were being formed and carried to a happy fruition. In those exciting days there was little time for a purely literary life. Orators like James Otis (1725–1783) in Boston and Patrick Henry (1736–1799) in Virginia were shouting their cries, the one, "A man's house is his castle," the other, "Give me liberty or give me death." (See page 435.) Thomas Paine (1737–1809) of Philadelphia was a noted and fiery pamphleteer, the equivalent of a modern magazine writer, and his *Common Sense* (1776) helped to mold popular sentiment towards a favorable reception of the *Declaration of Independence,* written by Thomas Jefferson (1743–1826) and promulgated six months later. The first of Paine's series of papers, called *The Crisis,* begins with the familiar words, "These are the times that try men's souls." About the same

Poor Richard, 1733.

AN

Almanack

For the Year of Christ

1733,

Being the First after LEAP YEAR:

And makes since the Creation Years
By the Account of the Eastern Greeks   7241
By the Latin Church, when ☉ ent. ♈   6932
By the Computation of W.W.   5742
By the Roman Chronology   5682
By the Jewish Rabbies   5494

Wherein is contained

The Lunations, Eclipses, Judgment of the Weather, Spring Tides, Planets Motions & mutual Aspects, Sun and Moon's Rising and Setting, Length of Days, Time of High Water, Fairs, Courts, and observable Days.

Fitted to the Latitude of Forty Degrees, and a Meridian of Five Hours West from London, but may without sensible Error, serve all the adjacent Places, even from Newfoundland to South Carolina.

By RICHARD SAUNDERS, Philom.

PHILADELPHIA:

Printed and sold by B. FRANKLIN, at the New Printing Office near the Market.

The Third Impression.

Historical Society of Pennsylvania

TITLE PAGE OF THE FIRST
"POOR RICHARD'S ALMANAC"

First American best-seller, averaging 10,000 copies annually time Franklin warned the colonies that " we must all hang together or we shall all hang separately." The speeches and pamphlets of many others are a part of the history of those stirring times, and some have considerable literary merit. Many state papers, especially the *Declaration of Independence* (see page 435), rank as literature.

BENJAMIN FRANKLIN

The genial gentleman of the kite, Poor Richard, the *Autobiography,* and idol of France

There was, besides, the flood of songs and ballads that a war usually brings forth, most of them not worth remembering. The most famous is " Yankee Doodle," and the best is " Nathan Hale." (See page 500.) Francis Hopkinson (1737–1791), a signer of the Declaration of Independence, wrote a humorous political satire in verse, " The Battle of the Kegs." A group of poets in Hartford, Connecticut, achieved temporary fame as the " Hartford Wits," the most noted being three Yale men, John Trumbull (1750–1831), Joel Barlow (1754–1813), and Timothy Dwight (1752–1817). Trumbull wrote " McFingal," a mock-heroic poem important at the time as war propaganda. Barlow is known for his epic, " The Columbiad," greatly admired in its day. Dwight, a grandson of Jonathan Edwards and a chaplain in the army, wrote poems and essays, and eventually became president of Yale.

POST-WAR LITERATURE

When the war for independence had been won, the immediate problem was the kind of government that was to be established. There were two distinct points of view: one favored a weak central government and was sponsored by Jefferson and his party; the other was in favor of a strong central government controlled by the aristocrats, and was advocated by Alexander Hamilton, James Madison, John Jay, and others.

The latter group, chiefly Hamilton (1757–1804), wrote a series of political essays, collectively known as *The Federalist,* which had much to do with the Constitution as finally adopted. The most famous political classic of this period is Washington's "Farewell Address." (See page 438.)

Charles Brockden Brown (1771–1810). After the war, near the turn of the century, both readers and writers began to take interest in what may be called "pure literature," that is, literature not bound up with special occasions or special causes. Perhaps the first writer who may be called strictly professional was Charles Brockden Brown of Philadelphia. He was chiefly a hack writer, but is remembered as the first American novelist of any consequence. His first novel, *Wieland,* appeared in 1798. All of Brown's novels are marked by complicated plots, weird characters, and horrible happenings. In *Wieland,* for instance, his terror-compelling devices are three in number: spontaneous combustion of the father of the two main characters, the ventriloquism of Carwin, and the religious mania of Wieland that drove him to sacrifice his entire family. Brown had the ability to tell single episodes with considerable power, and he anticipated Cooper in his fondness for and skill in description.

THOMAS JEFFERSON

Aristocrat and democrat, author of the Declaration of Independence

St. John de Crèvecœur (1735–1813). He was born in France, lived in England, and emigrated to the colonies, where he became a successful farmer, first in Pennsylvania and later in New York. During the war he remained loyal to England and suffered many hardships. He finally had to leave the country in 1780. In London he sold a manuscript entitled *Letters from an American Farmer,* published in 1782. While this received recognition both in France and in England, it was not until 1925 that the full manuscript was published in this country. It is now held to be one of the best pieces of writing of the period. A short selection follows.

WHAT IS AN AMERICAN?

What then is the American, this new man? He is either an European, or the descendant of an European, hence that strange mixture of blood, which you will find in no other country. I could point out to you a family whose grandfather was an Englishman, whose wife was Dutch, whose son married a French woman, and whose present four sons have now four wives of different nations. *He* is an American, who, leaving behind him all his ancient prejudices and manners, receives new ones from the new mode of life he has embraced, the new government he obeys, and the new rank he holds. He becomes an American by being received in the broad lap of our great *Alma Mater*. Here individuals of all nations are melted into a new race of men, whose labors and posterity will one day cause great changes in the world. Americans are the western pilgrims, who are carrying along with them that great mass of arts, sciences, vigor, and industry which began long since in the east; they will finish the great circle. The Americans were once scattered all over Europe; here they are incorporated into one of the finest systems of population which has ever appeared, and which will hereafter become distinct by the power of the different climates they inhabit. The American ought therefore to love this country much better than that wherein either he or his forefathers were born. Here the rewards of his industry follow with equal steps the progress of his labor; his labor is founded on the basis of nature, *self-interest;* can it want a stronger allurement? Wives and children, who before in vain demanded of him a morsel of bread, now, fat and frolicsome, gladly help their father to clear those fields whence exuberant crops are to arise to feed and to clothe them all; without any part being claimed, either by a despotic prince, a rich abbot, or a mighty lord. Here religion demands but little of him; a small voluntary salary to the minister, and gratitude to God; can he refuse these? The American is a new man, who acts upon new principles; he must therefore entertain new ideas, and form new opinions. From involuntary idleness, servile dependence, penury, and useless labor, he has passed to toils of a very different nature, rewarded by ample subsistence. — This is an American.

Philip Freneau (1752–1832). The poetry of Philip Freneau fittingly closes the early period of our literature and begins the new. His long life fell within the Revolution and the post-war eras, and is typical of the active minds of those days. He graduated from Princeton in 1771, and in the same class with James Madison. He was a teacher, journalist, farmer, and adventurer. Only a few of his poems during the war had any considerable literary merit, but he wrote voluminously all his life, and today he enjoys a secure niche in American literature as our first real poet.

Summary. Throughout the early part of this period neither Cavaliers nor Puritans produced much of literary value. Men recorded personal experiences connected with founding a home in the new country. Since religion played an important part in the exodus of many Colonists from England, it was natural that nearly everything written prior to the time when separation from the home country became an issue should be deeply colored by the doctrines of the various sects that settled here. There was no poetry of consequence prior to Freneau, no fiction before Brown, and no drama before Godfrey. Franklin stands unique among the writers who tried to give readers enjoyment as well as information and instruction. The Revolution brought out good oratory, much special pleading in the form of propaganda, and essays of a high order in *The Federalist*. Crèvecœur shares with Franklin the distinction of writing entertainingly though intent on special pleading. As the new era dawned, Freneau wrote the first poems of literary excellence.

IN THIS VOLUME

PAGE

1. The Project of Arriving at Moral Perfection (Benjamin Franklin) 308
2. Sayings of Poor Richard (Benjamin Franklin) 366
3. Her Private Journal (Sarah Kemble Knight) 415
4. A History of the Dividing Line (William Byrd) . . . 424
5. Speech in the Virginia Convention (Patrick Henry) . . . 430
6. Declaration of Independence (Thomas Jefferson) . . . 435
7. Farewell Address (George Washington) 438
8. Nathan Hale (Anonymous) 500
9. To the Memory of Brave Americans (Philip Freneau) . . . 524
10. The Wild Honeysuckle (Philip Freneau) 525
11. The Indian Burying Ground (Philip Freneau) . . . 526

STUDY QUESTIONS

1. What two types of people transplanted from England laid the foundations of American literature?

2. Illustrate by examples the adventurous spirit shown in the literature of the Southern Colonies.

3. What different spirit or mood is evident in New England? Illustrate.

4. How did the Colonists rank as poets? Justify your answer.

5. In what way is Benjamin Franklin a link between two periods? Discuss his two chief literary contributions.

6. How is the Revolutionary War reflected in literature?

7. What writers at the end of this period show the beginning of interest in imaginative literature? To what extent are they read today?

Chapter II

THE BEGINNINGS OF
AMERICAN LITERARY PRESTIGE

Of the writers discussed in the previous chapter, Charles Brockden Brown and Philip Freneau remained active in the early years of the new century. Political affairs had so shaped themselves that the country was rapidly developing. Writers were no longer drawn by the lure of propaganda and began to devote their efforts to imaginative literature, that is, literature intended primarily for enjoyment.

The Romantic Revival in America. Along with the English writers of the early nineteenth century, American authors were energized by the Romantic Revival in literature. Their writings are deeply saturated with the influences of this great movement, and can be fully understood only through a comprehension of it. The Romantic Revival may be thought of, perhaps, as the literary flowering of the American and the French Revolutions. It represents the reaction against the English literary leaders of the eighteenth century, who, in their zeal to achieve clarity of expression and beauty of language, had exalted authority to a point incompatible with individualistic expression. These eighteenth-century " classicists " had written grammars, compiled a dictionary, set up czars over the language, and developed literary criticism. They had decided upon the " correct " way to compose every type of literature and to phrase every type of thought. Naturally the spirit of freedom abroad in the world came to grips with this standardization of language and literature, and in the Romantic Revival proclaimed the gospel of individual liberty for every writer.

Washington Irving (1783–1859). Irving was born in New York City, which at that time boasted a population of twenty-three thousand inhabitants. Though small, the city had its full quota of attractions, especially for an imaginative boy brought up in a cultured family. There were the old Dutch houses and the curious traditions connected with the original settlers; there was the Hudson river with its glorious scenery on both sides, and Indians not far away; and there was the life of the city itself, of which Irving was as fond as the most confirmed " Broadwayite " today. But there was also school, and, while he was a devoted reader, he was a poor student. Because of frail health he was indulged by his parents and was not sent to Columbia College, as his older brothers had been. He settled down to a half-hearted study of law, but a nervous breakdown necessitated a trip to Europe.

Before this trip he had already written for the papers a number of essays in the manner of Addison's *Spectator* under the name of " Jonathan Oldstyle." On his return to New York he joined his brother and James K. Paulding in founding a bi-weekly paper, *Salmagundi,* to which he contributed liberally throughout its life of one year. Meanwhile he had begun work on the *Knickerbocker History of New York,* published in 1809. (See page 368.) In the same year Matilda Hoffman, his fiancée died, and those of romantic leanings will find it interesting to know that Irving remained a bachelor and that in all his subsequent travels he carried with him Matilda's Bible.

When Irving's brothers failed in business he found himself in England without adequate funds, but within a year the first edition of the *Sketch Book* was published (1819) in New York, and the following year an enlarged edition was published in London. Its success was immediate and complete. The editor of *Blackwood's Magazine* expressed what seems to have been the general opinion

BROADWAY FROM THE BOWLING GREEN

Washington Irving was in Spain when this print was made, but he must often have walked through the Green when it looked like this

in England at the time, that Irving was " by far the greatest genius that has arisen on the literary horizon of the new world." This opinion was confirmed by *Bracebridge Hall* and *Tales of a Traveler* which followed the *Sketch Book* at two-year intervals, and, like it, were made up of essays, sketches, and short stories.

The next three years Irving spent in Spain and there, through the American Ambassador, he was given the privilege of using some newly found papers on Columbus which provided material for two volumes on the great discoverer. More interesting today are *The Conquest of Granada* (1829) and *The Alhambra* (1832), dealing with the Moors in Spain. The latter, written much in the manner of the *Sketch Book*, was not completed until Irving's return to London. He stayed in England for another year and then returned to America, practically all his best literary work done. Both famous and financially successful, Irving purchased a home at Tarrytown and named it " Sunnyside," intending to spend the rest of his life there in literary leisure. There were only two breaks; one, a tour of the United States, which gave him material for three books not now important, the other, four years (1842–1846) spent in Spain as American Ambassador. Back once more at Sunnyside, he lived his remaining years as he had planned, and the only literary work

JAMES FENIMORE COOPER

His *Leatherstocking Tales* still thrill American boys and girls

of any consequence was *Oliver Goldsmith* (1849) and his *Life of George Washington* (1855–1859) in eight volumes. He died in 1859 and was buried in the Sleepy Hollow cemetery.

James Fenimore Cooper (1789–1851). Cooper was born in New Jersey, but most of his life was spent on the shores of Lake Otsego in New York where his father had built a large mansion on the frontier, around which there grew up the village of Cooperstown. In its early days, when Cooper was an impressionable boy, hunters and trappers used this village as a trading-post. The surrounding woods were full of Indians and wild game, and the frontiersmen and Indians told the boy many stirring tales about the earlier and wilder life. No doubt his first ambitions were to be a trapper or an Indian scout, but his father had determined that his son was to go to Yale, and at thirteen he went. It seems that he had difficulty in adjusting himself to college routine and college rules as they were at that time, and it is remarkable that young Cooper lasted until his third year before he was dismissed.

Desiring to enter the navy, he served a year in the merchant marine, at that time the prerequisite to becoming a midshipman; but three years later he resigned at his wife's request. Although he spent many years abroad and in New York City, the greater part of his life was centered around his old home at Cooperstown.

Cooper had no idea of becoming a literary man, but he was a great reader, and the story goes that his first novel, *Precaution* (1820), was written because of his disgust with the current English fiction. *Precaution* was a poor imitation of the novels which had bored him. The scene was laid in England, about which he knew nothing at first hand. Some friends urged him to write a story laid nearer home but he doubted the sense of this because he could not conceive that Americans would be interested in things which were a part of their everyday life. However, he took his cue from a local story about a Revolutionary spy, and the result was *The Spy* (1821). Its immediate success in this country and in Europe finally determined him to make writing his career. The next novel was *The Pioneers* (1823), the first of the Leatherstocking Tales to be written but destined to be next to the last of the series, considering chronologically the career of the leading character. In 1826 came *The Last of the Mohicans,* his best novel, and then he and his family went to Europe. He stayed seven years, writing vigorously all the time, novels of his native land, novels set in Europe, and stories of the sea. Everywhere he went he found himself well known and popular.

Unfortunately this popularity did not follow him back to America. On his return, the contrast between the older civilization of Europe and the crudity of young New York led Cooper to write some bitter attacks on the manners and customs of his country in the guise of novels. However true his criticisms were, they were not tactful. Newspapers raged; Cooper replied in kind. He became involved in a series of libel suits in which he acted as his own lawyer. He won his cases, but lost his popularity. At the age of sixty-two he died, a thoroughly embittered man.

Of Cooper's more than thirty novels only about ten are read today, but had he written nothing more than the Leatherstocking Tales he would still rank high among American novelists. For these Indian stories his early life gave him abundant first-hand material, and he used it with a touch of real genius. He wisely emphasized the adventures of his hero and his Indians instead of following the traditional style of the current romances which stressed the love story. Cooper was exceptionally unskilled in delineating feminine characters, and in his best stories he bothered little about them. In Leatherstocking, or Natty Bumppo, Cooper created a thoroughly original character, one typical of the passing frontier. What is more, the author made his hero romantically interesting, so interesting that all writers of Indian stories since have been more than tempted to follow Cooper. When the series was finished Cooper had carried his hero, Leatherstocking, from youth to the grave. The correct order of the stories chronologically is: *The Deerslayer* (1841), *The Last of the Mohicans* (1826), *The Pathfinder* (1840), *The Pioneers* (1823), and *The Prairie* (1827). Of his sea stories the two best are *The Pilot* (1824) and *The Red Rover* (1828).

William Cullen Bryant (1794–1878). While Bryant spent the last fifty years of his long life in New York City, his career as a poet definitely belongs to New England, where he was born and

WILLIAM CULLEN BRYANT
"Belated Puritan," poet, and editor

where he wrote practically all of the poetry upon which his fame rests. Bryant was of Puritan ancestry and of Puritan bringing-up. That meant rigorous study of the Bible from infancy, and an essentially serious view of life. Bryant appended moral tags to most of his poems, and many are filled with thoughts, common enough to the Puritan, of death and the hereafter. If there had been no more to Bryant than this deeply religious note he would be known today as a minor poet and not as the first great poet of American literature, but his reflective nature was distinctly susceptible to the beauties and charm of Nature. Like Wordsworth he believed that a calm contemplation of Nature went a long way in healing the temporal ills of life. Brought up amid the beautiful scenery of western Massachusetts, he absorbed enough to enable him to draw on it in his poetic work for the rest of his life. Some of the strange contrasts of Bryant's life will be found in the introduction to his poems on page 528.

Edgar Allan Poe (1809–1849). While Irving, Cooper, and Bryant were giving literary prestige to New York, Edgar Allan Poe was independently writing both poetry and prose that in sheer brilliance and originality outdistanced the work of all his contemporaries. Although born in Boston, he was really a Southerner in spirit and sympathy, but so far as his work is concerned he belonged to no section. Most of it might have been written as well in Kambalu as in Baltimore, Richmond, Philadelphia, and New York, the cities in which he did nearly all of his writing. Poe was a solitary figure. He belonged to no group and he had few literary friends, owing in part to a personality that was unattractive to many people and habits that were unconventional. Nevertheless, he received recognition from Irving in New York and Lowell in Boston, but sincere friendships with those already in high places in American literature seem to have been impossible to Poe.

The essential details of Poe's life may be found in connection with the selections in this volume. (See pages 58–60, 624–625.) How or when he determined to make his way in the field of literature is not known, but when his connection with the Allans was finally broken he lived for a while in Baltimore, actively engaged in the writing of short stories which he submitted to papers in various cities. Desperately in need of money, he entered many of the prize contests popular in that period to advertise budding magazines. Poe at last won a hundred dollars for " Ms. Found in a Bottle," published in the Baltimore *Saturday Visitor* in 1833.

In 1833 he was offered an editorial position on the *Southern Literary Messenger,* the foremost literary magazine of the South, and in less than a year he was its editor. His writings found a sympathetic public; he was happily married; everything seemed to be going well. But Poe could not endure prosperity without falling back into dissipated habits, and the owner of the magazine discharged him. For several years he vacillated between Richmond and New York in the hope of making connections with some journal, but in the end he settled in Philadelphia for six years, notable for " The Gold Bug " and his first volume of stories. In this period too, Poe was prolific of penetrating book-reviews and critical articles, the most famous of which was his review of Hawthorne's *Twice-Told Tales* (see page 943) in *Graham's Magazine* (1842).

To be a critic is to be a reviewer of other writers' work. This type of work too often smacks of journalism, that is, work of temporary interest only. Our magazines and newspapers today are full of this kind of writing, some of it remarkably good. Some of it finds its way into books. A good critic must have a sound intellectual background, based on wide reading, and a sense of values. He should be concerned chiefly in discovering what an author is trying to say and how he says it. He should not permit personal likes and dislikes to warp his judgments. In this lies Poe's chief defect as a critic — he sometimes let his prejudices rule. But his keen analytical powers, his sure and profound knowledge of the underlying principles of the poetic and narrative arts, and a gifted pen lent distinction to his critical work. One of the pleasantest statements that one can make of Poe in the sphere of criticism is that he was eminently sane and fair in his criticism of his chief rival, Hawthorne. He recognized fully the splendid genius of the great New Englander, although he was heartily out of sympathy with the Puritan tradition on which much of Hawthorne's work was founded. To Bryant, the moralist who was also a prophet of beauty, Poe gave high praise. His friendship with Lowell and the cordiality with which they corresponded about literary matters were unhappily spoiled by Poe's unfair interpretation of a reference to himself in " The Fable for Critics." Poe had a negative reaction to Longfellow, and waged a long war of words with those of Longfellow's friends who rose in defence of their favorite.

In 1844 the Poe family moved to Fordham, then a suburb of New York, where Poe hoped that his frail invalid wife might recuperate.

POE'S COTTAGE AT FORDHAM

Where Annabel Lee died and was re-created

In spite of constant money troubles, lack of a position, and his wife's illness, Poe was always writing and somehow obtained minor or temporary employment on a magazine or newspaper. By this time Poe was well known in literary circles; he had made many enemies for himself through his critical attacks, and though his short stories had aroused much favorable comment, he was not in any sense popular.

In 1845 " The Raven " appeared in the New York *Evening Mirror,* and Poe for once achieved widespread fame, although no financial rewards followed. The poem was reprinted throughout the country, but for lack of proper copyright protection Poe received no money for

" The Raven " except the small sum that went with first publication. This same year he at last managed to buy a magazine for himself, but the venture died within a year. Poe was always intent on seeing his works in book form, and in the course of the year 1845 published another volume of stories and one of poems. Throughout 1846 Poe and his wife were both ill, and the family suffered actual privation. The climax came with the death of his wife in 1847, with most disastrous consequences for Poe. Poverty continued its pinch, but presently there was relief and Poe once more went on with his literary labors. Some of these were mere hack work, but Poe's last year is memorable in literature for the final revision of " The Bells " and for the writing of one of his most universally popular poems, as well as his last, " Annabel Lee," in which he expresses his agony over the tragic death of his young wife. He visited Richmond in the summer of 1849 to complete arrangements to marry the sweetheart of his boyhood, the former Miss Royster, but then the widow Shelton. On his way back to New York he stopped over in Baltimore, where he was later found dying in a tavern. The exact circumstances of his death have never been satisfactorily cleared up.

Herman Melville (1819–1891). In all literatures certain names stand out bravely among those who have written great books, but the books themselves are known to comparatively few. Among such, in the literature of this country, was Herman Melville. Until recently interest in Melville was tepid indeed; but there has always been a small group of enthusiasts, large enough, however, to keep his books in print. These clamored loyally for a fairer recognition of a writer whom they proclaimed as one of the world's major novelists. Several biographies appeared, and new and better editions of his novels were published, until today it is possible to judge whether Melville deserves the high recognition denied him by his own age.

Melville was born in New York City in 1819. Because of the commercial failure of his father, he received no college education and went to work on a farm. Like Irving, the youthful Melville was fond of lingering on the docks to watch the ships come and go. He longed to go to sea and at the age of eighteen made a trip to Liverpool. Upon his return he taught for several years and then enlisted as a common sailor on a whaling ship out of New Bedford. On account of bad treatment on this ship, a not uncommon experience for sailors in those days, Melville and a friend deserted the ship in the South Seas, on the Island of Nukuheva, one of the Marquesas. After a remarkable four months' captivity among cannibals they were rescued, and after some more roving experiences Melville returned to the United States in 1844.

With this background of unusual experience the young man of twenty-five set about writing his first book, based on the cannibal island adventure, and called it *Typee* (1845), the name of the valley where he had been a captive. The success of *Typee* brought a sequel, *Omoo* (1846), carrying the Marquesas adventure to its conclusion. Much speculation was aroused as to the accuracy of the facts, and how much of the story was to be considered fiction, a matter that remains unsolved to this day.

Melville wrote three more novels before the appearance of his greatest romance, *Moby-Dick* (1851), a profound novel based in part on his experience in a whaling ship. The circumstances under which this was written are given in the chapter from Mumford's biography of Melville on page 346. His own generation did not understand or appreciate *Moby-Dick*.

After *Moby-Dick* Melville wrote other novels, a number of short stories, and poetry, but he never again reached the high level of his earlier work. No one realized more than Melville himself that his powers had fallen off. For some years he traveled about a great deal, lecturing at times, or taking trips to far places. He finally settled down in New York where he had received a position in the Custom House. During those years he wrote hardly anything, and this sketch may be concluded with the first sentence of Lewis Mumford's biography: " When Herman Melville died in 1891, the literary journal of the day, *The Critic*, did not even know who he was," to which may be added the same writer's final sentences: " The day of Herman Melville's vision is now in the beginning. It hangs like a cloud over the horizon at dawn; and as the sun rises, it will become more radiant, and more a part of the living day." Whether this optimistic estimate of Melville's true stature as one of America's literary giants will gain universal acceptance remains to be seen.

Minor Writers. Among the minor writers of this period were Joseph Rodman Drake (1795–1820) and Fitz-Greene Halleck (1790–1867), intimate friends who styled themselves " The Croakers," and wrote much verse together. Separately each wrote a few pieces that are well known today. " The American Flag " by Drake appears in nearly every school book, and " The Culprit Fay " is known by title, at least. As a poem " The American Flag " is vastly inferior to the other; but it is shorter, which may account for its greater popularity. Drake died young, and the elegiac verses " On the

Death of Joseph Rodman Drake " by his friend Halleck are superior to anything either of them wrote. The opening lines show that the poem was inspired by genuine feeling:

> " Green be the turf above thee,
> Friend of my better days!
> None knew thee but to love thee,
> Nor named thee but to praise."

But in spite of this excellent short poem, Halleck is better known for " Marco Bozzaris " (1827), a poem that lends itself to spirited recitation and is still declaimed by budding orators.

In this era there were a number of writers remembered chiefly for some one work. John James Audubon (1780–1851), the " father of ornithology," for *The Birds of America;* William H. Prescott (1796–1859) for his histories of Mexico and Peru; Samuel Woodworth (1785–1842) for " The Old Oaken Bucket "; Francis Scott Key (1779–1843) for " The Star-Spangled Banner " (1814); John Howard Payne (1792–1852) for " Home, Sweet Home! " (1823); and Samuel Francis Smith (1808–1895) for " America " (1832).

Summary. In the earlier part of the century American authors, under the stimulus of the Romantic Revival, produced the first great imaginative writing in America. Irving was the first essayist and short-story writer; Cooper, the first novelist of real importance; and Bryant, the first major poet. Irving's *Knickerbocker History* and *Sketch Book,* emanating from New York, made that city the temporary literary center of the country. Both of those books, together with his other works, made Irving the first American literary man who gained full recognition in Europe. He was also the first American given a diplomatic post solely because of his work in literature. Cooper was not only the first novelist whose books are still read for genuine intrinsic interest, but he created Leatherstocking, one of the best-remembered characters in fiction. He made his Indians storybook creatures, but his conception of them is the one that most people still have. Bryant, in spite of the small amount of poetry he wrote in his eighty-four years of life, still ranks among the major American poets because of the high seriousness and beauty of both his thought and his style.

The career of Poe stands out unique in the history of American literature. While influenced by the Romantic Movement, he nevertheless struck out boldly along original lines in both prose and poetry. His poetry is characterized by its sheerly imaginative quality, that is, it is not inspired by Nature, nor is it narrative, nor does it have any local flavor. In his short stories he was equally original, and he laid down, by precept and example, the laws which have largely determined what the modern short story has become, both in this country and abroad. As a critic he wrote illuminating essays, many of them reviews of the work of others, in which he elaborated his literary theories with a brilliance and concreteness never before attained in this country. Not only that, he also analyzed his own work and his methods. While it is a fact that he wrote much that has no particular value, it remains true that a writer must be judged by his highest accomplishment, and in poetry, short stories, and criticism, the three fields cultivated by Poe, there is a fair amount that ranks with the highest.

Melville, in his own day and until the last ten or twenty years, had been considered a minor author. His greatest novel, *Moby-Dick,* is being put forward by many modern critics as an imaginative work of profound grandeur. Both *Moby-Dick* and *Typee,* the story of his romantic experiences in the South Seas, are growing in popular esteem. This period, like all periods, had its minor writers, most of whom are remembered for some one poem or book.

IN THIS VOLUME

PAGE

1. In the Days of Wouter Van Twiller (Washington Irving) . . 368
2. The Author's Account of Himself (Washington Irving) . . 228
3. The Devil and Tom Walker (Washington Irving) 30
4. The Monroe Doctrine (James Monroe) 475
5. Thanatopsis (William Cullen Bryant) 528
6. To a Waterfowl (William Cullen Bryant) 531
7. The Battle-Field (William Cullen Bryant) 533
8. To Helen (Edgar Allan Poe) 625
9. Israfel (Edgar Allan Poe) 626
10. Eldorado (Edgar Allan Poe) 628
11. Ulalume (Edgar Allan Poe) 633
12. The Raven (Edgar Allan Poe) 629
13. The Tell-tale Heart (Edgar Allan Poe) 58

STUDY QUESTIONS

1. State in your own words what Romanticism is.

2. With what parts of the United States and Europe is Irving's life connected? Name books which reflect his experiences in these places.

3. What different types of literature did Irving write? What aspects of his personality are shown in his writings?

4. How did Cooper's early training and disposition differ from Irving's? How was he regarded abroad and at home?

5. What are some of Cooper's favorite subjects for fiction? Name his most famous character and some of the books centering around this person.

6. Between what two parts of the East was Bryant's life divided? Which of these environments had the greater influence on his poetry?

7. What qualities lift Bryant's poetry above that of any poet preceding him? What was his favorite type of subject matter?

8. Point out several ways in which Poe's life was extraordinary. How does his personality differ from that of the others in this chapter?

9. What were his theories on the short story? On poetry? How does he rank among American authors today?

10. Point out how these men all contributed to the reputation of American literature abroad.

11. What other writers are included in this chapter? Which of these have diminished reputation since their own day? Which have increased reputation? Tell what each is known for.

Chapter III

TRANSCENDENTALISM IN THE EARLY
NINETEENTH CENTURY

In the early part of the nineteenth century the little village of Concord near Boston became the center of one of our most interesting groups of intellectual pioneers, bearing the formidable name of Transcendentalists. To understand them we must realize that they are a combination of the old Puritanism and the new Romanticism. The Puritanism of Cotton Mather and Jonathan Edwards had undergone considerable modification by the nineteenth century. Many of the churches of New England had become Unitarian and denied the theology of their forebears. This little group possessed the Puritan characteristics of seriousness, respect for intellectual achievement and a sense of intimacy with God, but had in addition such qualities of the Romanticists as strongly marked individuality which discarded outworn traditions, an intense feeling for God in Nature, and a keen appreciation of labor and the simple life. " Plain living and high thinking " was their motto. They believed that God's manifestation of Himself in Nature included human nature, and that the spark of the divine planted in every man was to be the only real guide of his life, in place of church authorities, creeds, or the Bible.

It was to be expected that there would be striking personalities among the Transcendentalists. Besides Emerson, their most influential leader, there were Thoreau, philosopher of Nature, and radical; Margaret Fuller, the most picturesque woman among them; and Louisa Alcott's father, whose school of philosophy proved a poor financial support for his family.

The Dial and Brook Farm. Two immediate fruits of the movement were the establishment of a magazine, *The Dial*, in which the new doctrines were expounded, and the Brook Farm experiment in plain living and high thinking. The magazine, edited by Margaret Fuller, ran from 1840 to 1844, and contained much of Emerson's prose and poetry, as well as many contributions by Thoreau, Bronson Alcott, and other leaders in the movement. Brook Farm was one of many attempts in the world's history to establish an ideal community where all were to share equally in everyday labor and high intellectual living. Under the leadership of George Ripley a farm of about two hundred acres was purchased nine miles out of Boston. Among the literary group there were, besides Ripley and Miss Fuller, Charles A. Dana, afterwards the famous editor of the New York *Sun,* George William Curtis, who also attained a certain distinction later as a literary man, and Hawthorne, who stayed only part of the six years (1841–1847) during which the experiment dragged on. Hawthorne's novel, *The Blithedale Romance,* gives a fictional presentation of life at Brook Farm. Both *The Dial* and Brook Farm were manifestations of transcendentalism in that they stressed the determination of individuals to live their own lives free from all the old restraints. Because of these beliefs many of the Transcendentalists became active in the protest against slavery, which was beginning to agitate New England in this period.

Ralph Waldo Emerson (1803–1882). Of all the Transcendentalists Emerson was the most illustrious as well as the most consistent. He never lost sight of the central doctrine of the movement — that man must work out his own individual destiny through an understanding of Nature, and that Nature is the only safe source of all inspiration. He came by this doctrine of individualism partly by inheritance. Some of his ancestors had been active in Revolutionary days; more immediately, his father and grandfather had been Unitarian ministers and therefore also in protest against the settled convictions of an established church. An early ancestor had helped in founding Concord, which was the home of the Emersons, although Ralph Waldo was born in Boston in 1803. For the details of Emerson's life see page 233.

RALPH WALDO EMERSON

He definitely wrote for the "younger generation"

Emerson's Prose. While he was still in college Emerson had formed the habit of jotting down ideas as they occurred to him. Many of these notes he later used in his lectures and essays. His first book was *Nature* (1836), and in this small volume Emerson voiced the rudiments of all his later philosophy of idealism as based on the contemplation of Nature. The following year he delivered his famous address, "The American Scholar," astounding his auditors by his almost militant plea for strong individualism as distinguished from subservient submission to established ideas and customs. "We will walk on our own feet; we will work with our own hands; we will speak our own minds," was the core of the address. For many years he traveled back and forth throughout the land delivering his lectures, many of which he afterwards arranged for

Halliday Historical Photograph Company

EMERSON'S STUDY, CONCORD

Rare and beautiful thoughts blossomed here

publication as essays. In 1841 and 1844 he published his volumes, *Essays, First Series* and *Essays, Second Series,* the first of which contains those destined to remain favorites, such as "Self-Reliance," "Friendship," "Compensation," and the "Over-Soul." Other volumes are *The Conduct of Life, Representative Men, English Traits,* and *Society and Solitude.* In the essay "Civilization," from the last-named volume, occurs the well-known passage, "Now that is the wisdom of a man, in every instance of his labor to hitch his wagon to a star, and see his chore done by the gods themselves."

Emerson's prose works are intensely inspirational, always optimistic, and constantly insistent that mind is superior to material things. He definitely preached to the young, it being his wish " to help the young soul, add energy, inspire hope, and blow the coals into a useful flame." His style is extremely sententious, that is, each sentence is so closely packed with thought that it stands by itself. This apparent lack of strict coherence makes his work somewhat difficult at first, but once the majestic swing is caught, the reader is carried along by its spiritual surge even though he may not be quite certain of exact meanings.

Emerson's Poetry. Like Bryant, Emerson wrote comparatively little poetry, but it is even in quality, although lacking the poetic graces of the earlier poet. As in the essays, Emerson idealizes Nature as man's chief source of genuine pleasure and sincere inspiration. His poetry is, in fact, a fine exposition of Transcendentalism. Again as in the essays, some passages at first reading seem vague because of the pithy thought. Furthermore, Emerson, just the contrary to Poe, sacrificed the music of his lines to the thought. He had remarkable skill in putting into a few lines what other poets would have put into a long poem; hence there are no really long poems in Emerson, and no narrative poems.

Nathaniel Hawthorne (1804–1864). Like Emerson, Hawthorne came of early Puritan stock. He was born in Salem on July 4, 1804. On account of the death of his father Hawthorne was educated by his uncles, graduating from Bowdoin in 1825. (For details of his life and friendships at college see pages 44 and 341–346.) Upon his return to Salem he lived a rather solitary life for twelve years, writing much, destroying much, publishing little, but gradually perfecting a literary style. His lack of success was most discouraging, but his loyal friends constantly urged him on. In 1836 he collected a volume of such stories as had been printed in little-known papers and magazines under an assumed name, and this he called *Twice-Told Tales*. Enlarged in 1842, it was the volume that called forth the famous review by Poe which contains his own ideas of what a short story ought to be. (See page 934.)

Through the political influence of his friend Pierce, later President of the United States, Hawthorne was given a position in the Custom House of Boston, and afterwards in the one at Salem. The two appointments covered, in all, about six years. Between the appointments he had joined the Brook Farm experiment in the hope that it would provide an ideal home for himself and Sophia Peabody, to whom he was engaged. He invested a thousand dollars in Brook Farm, but stayed only a little over a year because he found that it was not that kind of life that he wanted. He then married and moved to Concord into the Old Manse, where he wrote *Mosses from an Old Manse* (1846), a collection of short stories similar to *Twice-Told*

NATHANIEL HAWTHORNE

The man who would not be a doctor, a lawyer, or a preacher and live by men's ills

Tales. These two volumes, together with *The Snow Image* (1852), contain the short stories upon which Hawthorne's fame chiefly rests.

His appointment to the Salem Custom House necessitated his living in Salem, but when he once more lost his position through a political change in Washington, Hawthorne returned to Concord to live in the house now called the "Wayside." The new enforced leisure he employed to write *The Scarlet Letter*, generally considered the best of his long romances. In 1853 Franklin Pierce, then President of the United States, appointed his friend Hawthorne to the position of consul at Liverpool. This, together with the success of *The Scarlet Letter*, at last settled the financial problems of Hawthorne. After four years at Liverpool he resigned. Then followed several years in Rome, where he gathered material for his last long novel, *The Marble Faun* (1860), written after his return to Concord. During his sojourn in Europe he had also written *The House of the Seven Gables* (1851), and *The Blithedale Romance* (1852). Much earlier he had written several series of stories for children, the *Wonder Book* and *Grandfather's Chair*. After 1860 his health failed rapidly, and in 1864 Franklin Pierce persuaded him that a trip into the White Mountains would be good for him. The two friends proceeded by way of Plymouth, where they spent the night. In the morning Hawthorne was found dead. His old Bowdoin classmate, Longfellow, wrote

" There in seclusion and remote from men,
The Wizard hand lies cold."

Hawthorne as a Transcendentalist. Living in the thick of the movement, with all his most intimate friends and neighbors actively engaged in propagandizing it, Hawthorne could not help being profoundly influenced by Transcendentalism. He did not, however, go about preaching the new doctrine nor did he obtrusively use it in his fiction. No one familiar with his stories would accuse Hawthorne of being an optimistic idealist like Emerson, nor was he a direct worshiper of Nature like Thoreau, but rather an interpreter of human relationships. He sought adjustment to an existing world by an interpretation of the past. One of his constant themes is the effect of sin upon conscience. He was particularly concerned with the ideas of compensation and self-reliance, two of the central tenets of the Transcendentalists. Readers of *The Scarlet Letter* will at once know what is meant, and these same ideas form the themes of many of his best stories. While his subject matter is chiefly early Puritan New England, and his themes are stern and tragic, the interpretations are clothed with an enduring richness and beauty.

The Short Stories. Many of the best of Hawthorne's short stories are based on the history of New England or closely related to it. Among these are " The Gray Champion," " Lady Eleanore's Mantle," " The Maypole of Merry Mount," " Drowne's Wooden Image," and " Endicott's Red Cross." Another type of which he was particularly fond was the apologue or allegory, in which he brought out some great truth or lesson by means of a symbol. Readers will at once think of " Dr. Heidegger's Experiment," " The Great Stone Face," and " The Great Carbuncle." Still another type is closely allied to the essay, like some of the sketches of Irving; " A Rill from the Town Pump " and " Sights from a Steeple " are examples. Students interested in studying stories by types will find it worth while to think of Hawthorne's from this point of view, and at the same time they will find it interesting to note that while he was taking old-time subjects he interpreted life from a strictly modern angle, that is, the angle of Transcendentalism. In his children's stories, he re-tells old stories for the instruction and entertainment of the young.

The Romances. Most of Hawthorne's short stories were written before he turned to the long novel, and his readers could have felt little surprise when they found that the setting and the characters in *The Scarlet Letter* (1850) were strikingly similar to those of many of the shorter works. " Endicott's Red Cross " contained more than a hint for the new book. The author takes his reader back to the days of the bigoted Puritans, many of whom would have approved of the theme although they would have condemned the fictional form, while none of them would have agreed with the conclusion. The theme is strictly in line with transcendentalism because it shows acutely how the law of compensation works out. Sin is punished here and now, but Hawthorne's vivid artistic imagination created a beautiful romance out of a drab situation, and combined the ethical spirit of the earlier Puritans with the more rational interpretations of the modern thinker. *The Scarlet Letter* is one of the great novels of all literature.

The scene of *The House of the Seven Gables* (1851) is laid in Salem, and the story presents the problem of heredity — how a curse

Essex Institute

THE HOUSE OF THE SEVEN GABLES, SALEM

Made famous by Hawthorne's story

laid on a family is at last expiated. This idea attracted Hawthorne because the actions of one of his ancestors, a Salem witchcraft judge, had placed a curse on the Hawthorne family; at least, that was the tradition. The theme again is that " the wrong-doing of one generation lives into the successive ones." Although there is gloom and tragedy in the story, it is relieved by touches of humor and a happy ending.

The Blithedale Romance (1852) was admittedly based on Hawthorne's reminiscences of the life at Brook Farm. Many of the characters can be readily identified, and certain of the main episodes were taken from actual happenings. While the story lacks a theme of the usual Hawthorne type, there is strong character portrayal in the heroine, and a dramatic ending in her death by drowning.

In his last long novel, *The Marble Faun,* Hawthorne uses fully the romantic associations of Rome. Here recur his favorite themes of evil brooding over characters and the dire consequences of sin.

Henry David Thoreau (1817–1862). The life of Thoreau has already been given in other parts of this book. (See pages 244, 333–340.) As a Transcendentalist he was a close follower and disciple of Emerson. He desired leisure to read, study, loaf, observe, and write. By keeping himself as free as possible from all worldly encumbrances, he achieved his ideal to a remarkable extent. He described himself by saying, " I am a mystic, a Transcendentalist, and a natural philosopher." He believed that real happiness could be attained only through close and intimate contact with Nature, and he practiced what he preached, instead of only talking about it.

Thoreau's first book, *A Week on the Concord and Merrimac Rivers* (1849), is a record of a week's adventures with his brother in a rowboat. He was always indefatigable in taking minute notes on his observations, and in this book he did more. Having been a teacher, he seemed to think that he must instruct as well as entertain, and that tendency no doubt accounted in part for the small sale of the book. His sense of humor enabled him to say, " I have now a library of nearly nine hundred volumes, over seven hundred of which were written by myself."

Walden (1854) fared better, and deservedly. It is full of detailed and interesting experiences of natural life in the woods, and there is no preaching. The extract printed in this volume is typical. Thoreau's solitary life as described in *Walden* may seem tame enough to this bustling twentieth century, but in spite of all the fanfare of a mechanized age, this book continues to be read and enjoyed by those who take delight in the personality and work of a genuine poet-naturalist. After Thoreau's death a number of other books were made from his voluminous journal, but *Walden* merits our chief attention.

Summary. Transcendentalism was a unique movement of protest against the tyrannies of convention which had so long bound New England to Puritan traditions. It was an intellectual declaration of independence for the individual. It was also a plea for the simple life. Although the attempt to put theory into practice at Brook

Farm failed, Transcendentalism had an undoubted influence on the moral outlook upon life, and it is worth while to remember that the life around Concord, the home of Transcendentalism, was exceptionally clean and wholesome. While there was much that was drawn from Europe, especially from the romantic movement in Eng-

Halliday Historical Photograph Company

OLD NORTH BRIDGE, CONCORD

What famous literary men must have crossed here?

land, the American phase of Transcendentalism was first a natural growth on American soil, and the influence from abroad came later and functioned chiefly as an added stimulus. The movement inspired the three great writers discussed here, and in addition profoundly influenced the work of most of the New England contemporaries of Emerson, Hawthorne, and Thoreau.

IN THIS VOLUME

PAGE

1. The Minister's Black Veil (Nathaniel Hawthorne) . . . 44
2. Gifts (Ralph Waldo Emerson) 233
3. Selections from Other Essays (Ralph Waldo Emerson) . . . 239
4. Brute Neighbors (Henry David Thoreau) 244
5. The Concord Hymn (Ralph Waldo Emerson) 536
6. A Fable (Ralph Waldo Emerson) 536
7. Compensation (Ralph Waldo Emerson) 537

8. The Rhodora (Ralph Waldo Emerson) 538
9. Voluntaries (III) (Ralph Waldo Emerson) 538
10. Each and All (Ralph Waldo Emerson) 539

STUDY QUESTIONS

1. Explain Transcendentalism. Discuss some of the experiments tried by the Transcendentalists of New England.

2. What attitudes and incidents in Emerson's life show the influence of Transcendentalism?

3. What two types of literature did Emerson write? What were some of his favorite beliefs as set forth in his writings?

4. What circumstances of Hawthorne's life contributed to his serious-mindedness?

5. Point out his main types of writing, with good examples of each. How do the subject matter and style of his stories differ from those of Poe's?

6. How did Thoreau demonstrate his individualism?

7. Point out all the circumstances that justify considering these writers together in one chapter.

Chapter IV

THE LITERATURE OF
CULTURE AND SCHOLARSHIP

Henry Wadsworth Longfellow (1807–1882). The name of Longfellow is definitely linked with the Boston-Cambridge group of nineteenth-century literary men although he was nearly thirty years old before he settled permanently in that city. For the details of his life see the introduction to his poems on pages 541–542.

He was fond of books, an early favorite being Irving's *Sketch Book,* one of the most talked-of new books when Longfellow was a boy of twelve. He scribbled verses while still a school boy, and at least one saw publication in a local newspaper. While still an undergraduate he formed the idea of achieving fame as a writer and said so to his father in a letter, but the older man, himself a lawyer, declared positively that there was no chance to make a living in the profession of letters and that the boy was to aim in the direction of the law, and this he did. Fortunately he was offered a newly created position at Bowdoin as teacher of modern languages, and in preparation for this he spent three years (1826–1829) in Europe. He was attracted most by the Latin countries, spending considerable time in France, Italy, and Spain, where he met Washington Irving. To Germany he gave only a few months. Always a conscientious student, and with a natural flair for languages, he easily mastered those which he was preparing to teach. He never became a great scholar, but his idea that languages were to be studied because of the great literatures which they embody rather than as mere scholastic training must have been a boon to his students when he took up his professorship at Bowdoin in the autumn of 1829.

In those days the teaching of modern languages was still in its infancy, with but few textbooks available; so Longfellow, always taking his work seriously, prepared his own texts. He also began to write for *The North American Review,* and he lectured; but aside from some translations of Spanish poems, he gave no sign of becoming anything other than a successful teacher of languages. In 1835 he published a small volume of his European experiences, *Outre-Mer*, somewhat in the manner of Irving, and the same year he was offered the chair of modern languages at Harvard. This necessitated another sojourn in Europe, a short one, but it had far-reaching effects on Longfellow. This time he gave most of his attention to the languages and the literatures of the Scandinavian countries, as well as the German. Germany was still in the after-glow of its romantic period, partially reflected in America by the Transcendental movement already discussed. His interest in the romantic movement was deepened by the death of his wife in Holland, and the effects of both can easily be traced in the poems he now began to write, afterwards published in the volume *Voices of the Night*, containing such well-known poems as " The Reaper and the Flowers " and " The Psalm of Life."

Throughout these years he had given up the compiling of textbooks and devoted his time more and more to the writing of poetry, for which he found an immediate and wide audience. In 1842 he made a third trip to Europe, and on his way back wrote a number of anti-slavery poems, the first indication of his deep concern about that vexa-

HENRY WADSWORTH LONGFELLOW
England has given him a bust in Westminster Abbey, an honor rarely accorded to Americans

tious problem. However, he never took much active interest in the Abolition movement. Outwardly he lived a placid life in Cambridge, marred only by the tragic death of his second wife by accidental burning in 1861. By this time he had published most of the long narrative poems that are still universally read and admired, " Evangeline," " The Courtship of Miles Standish," and " Hiawatha," besides a great number of his shorter works. These story poems, together with shorter ones, like the " Tales of a Wayside Inn," constitute one of Longfellow's surest claims to a lasting fame among readers of poetry.

Like many great poets, including Browning and Tennyson, Longfellow gave some time to the writing of plays, and with just as little success. His last great poetic effort was the translation of Dante's *Divine Comedy,* a long work published in three volumes.

Qualities as a Poet. If a poet's greatness depended on wide and continued reading Longfellow would easily be America's greatest poet, as he unquestionably is the most popular with the general public. With changes in styles of thought, his reputation with the critics has suffered considerable eclipse. On the other hand, one must not conclude, as some critics have done, that wide appeal is a sure sign of inferiority. Although he does inevitably preach a lesson, although his attitudes are generally sentimental, although his poetic diction occasionally slips into the commonplace, nevertheless he succeeds by his competence as a poetic craftsman and his grace in touching the emotions simply and effectively, as in " The Village Blacksmith," " The Psalm of Life," " The Day is Done," " The Bridge," and literally dozens of other poems. Possibly his greatest service to American letters has been the preservation of American legends through his narrative poems such as " Hiawatha " and " Evangeline."

All in all, Longfellow has expressed in melodious poetry the feelings of the average person about home and children, as in " The Children's Hour "; romantic love, as in " The Courtship of Miles Standish "; and the glow of patriotism, as in " Paul Revere's Ride " and in the conclusion to " The Building of the Ship." Throughout his work there is the gentle flow of homely virtues and there are many lesson-pointing passages that have had a large influence in molding the character of the young.

Oliver Wendell Holmes (1809–1894). Of the Boston-Cambridge group of writers none lived a more placid life than Holmes, and he did so from conscious choice. Most of them were deeply moved by the issues that led to the Civil War and used their pens one way or another, but Holmes deliberately refused to join the Abolition party, nor did he allow himself to become overheated in any argument about slavery or anything else. To him life was to be enjoyed to the full, and he chose his own way of doing so.

His father was a Congregational clergyman in Cambridge, and there Holmes was born in 1809. He entered Harvard with the class of 1829, a class that contained a number of young men who achieved considerable fame in their time, although the only two now readily remembered are Holmes and Samuel Francis Smith, the author of

" America." The class also has the distinction of being the most " poetized " in all college history, for Holmes wrote a poem for every class reunion from 1851 to 1889, the most famous being " The Boys " (page 598). Through all his school and college days he was addicted to writing verses, but he considered it no more than a harmless diversion and he had no thought of making literature a profes-

OLIVER WENDELL HOLMES

The genial "Autocrat of the Breakfast Table"

sion, and never did. On graduating from Harvard he at first studied law, like Longfellow, but gave it up in favor of medicine. At the age of twenty-one he wrote " Old Ironsides," and caused a national sensation. To complete his medical studies Holmes went to Europe for several years, and then received his degree from Harvard. Since his practice was only fair, he accepted a teaching position at Dartmouth, later becoming Professor of Anatomy at Harvard, where he remained for thirty-five years.

Holmes had of course kept on writing verses, and in 1836 published a slim volume which contained many of the poems for which he is now remembered, " Old Ironsides," " The Height of the Ridiculous," " My Aunt," and " The Last Leaf," among others. His real entry into literature, always as a sideline, came in 1857 when *The Atlantic Monthly* was established in Boston with James Russell Lowell as editor. He had promised Lowell that he would contribute a serial to the new magazine, and that is how *The Autocrat of the Breakfast Table* came to be written. In this series of essays a number of his famous poems first appeared, notably " The Chambered Nautilus " and " The Deacon's Masterpiece, or The One-Hoss Shay." It is more than likely that Holmes's place in American literature will be determined by the works so far mentioned. The later essays entitled *The Professor at the Breakfast Table* (1860) and *The Poet at the Breakfast Table* (1870), as well as others which he contributed to the *Atlantic,* lack the vigor and originality of the *Autocrat.*

Holmes's Qualities as a Writer. Holmes's literary work suffers from a characteristic that made him a most charming personality — his genial sense of humor. Humor is a delightful gift, but no guarantee of permanent literary fame. No one knew this better than Holmes himself, and he said that he should like to be remembered by the altogether serious poem, " The Chambered Nautilus." Many readers prefer " The Last Leaf," which in spite of a humorous slant is yet serious enough. More frequently than his contemporaries, Holmes was called on to write an " occasional " poem, that is, a poem for the commemorating of some special occasion. Above all, such poems must be amusing, unless the occasion be a serious one, and Holmes was a master at writing for sheer entertainment.

In writing prose articles for the *Atlantic* he was considerably influenced by the English essayists, Addison and Steele, in their *Spectator Papers*. The interest of the Autocrat lies in his faculty for spinning out long monologues in a conversational tone, humorous or otherwise, on topics ranging from Shakespeare to cats. In this series of essays the noted Holmes wit (not excluding puns) sparkled freely. While much of the interest lies in local allusions and contemporary happenings, there is enough in the *Autocrat* to make it likable to this day, especially if the reader enjoys smoothly flowing colloquial prose. Holmes was also intensely local, and was no doubt speaking for himself when he had the Autocrat say, " Boston State House is the hub of the Solar System."

James Russell Lowell (1819–1891). Lowell is perhaps of equal importance with Hawthorne and Emerson, although less read by the average person than either of the other two. To many he is known chiefly as the author of " The Vision of Sir Launfal," whereas in his own day he stood out as America's first distinguished literary critic, a great political scientist, a scholar and teacher, a diplomat, and the first important American satirist. Like Holmes, he was born in Cambridge; he lived there all his life, and died in the house in which he was born. He came from an illustrious New England family, and like Longfellow and Holmes, studied law when he graduated from Harvard; but unlike the other two he actually became a lawyer, although he never practiced. He was early drawn to versifying, especially after he met Miss Maria White, a poetess and the sister of a classmate. To her he addressed many sonnets, and thirty-five of these, together with some thirty other poems, were published in 1841 under the title *A Year's Life*. Three years later he married Miss White.

In 1845 he joined the Abolitionists and remained steadfast in the anti-slavery cause until the Civil War was over. The first series of the *Biglow Papers* was written to protest against the Mexican War, which Lowell identified with the extension of slavery. The year 1848 was Lowell's greatest in poetry, for he published, besides the *Biglow Papers*, " A Fable for Critics " and " The Vision of Sir Launfal," the poems by which he is best known.

JAMES RUSSELL LOWELL

Poet, professor, editor, and ambassador

When Longfellow resigned his professorship at Harvard, Lowell was chosen as his successor, but the pleasure he derived from this appointment was shadowed by the death of his wife in 1853. Three of his four children had already died. To Lowell, the poet, the death of his wife was disastrous, for on only a few occasions afterward did he rise to the level of his earlier work. However, he taught with enthusiasm and retained his chair at Harvard for twenty years. During these years he wrote much prose; most of it found publication in *The Atlantic Monthly,* of which he was one of the founders (1857) and the first editor. At times Lowell " endeavored to express the American idea," in both its political and its literary aspects. He claimed, and justly, that American writers were too closely bound by tradition from over the sea. He was always an ardent pleader for deeper culture, both literary, artistic, and social. The final and perhaps greatest work that came from his contact with the war was the " Commemoration Ode " in 1865, in honor of Harvard students who had fallen in the Civil War. This contains a splendid tribute to Lincoln.

In 1872 he gave up his teaching position at Harvard and went abroad for two years. Although pleasantly received and granted the usual honorary degrees from both Oxford and Cambridge, he was not accorded the enthusiasm previously turned loose for Longfellow and Holmes. Five years later he was honored by being appointed Minister to Spain, and later Ambassador to England, the highest diplomatic post in the American foreign service. He retained this position until the election of a Democratic President (Cleveland) in 1885 and then returned home. He enjoyed great personal popularity and was in constant demand as a speaker for all sorts of occasions. He continued to write, but the old zest was gone. He lived a happy life, with books, with his family, and among congenial friends. The last year and a half of his life he suffered from a painful malady, but his naturally cheerful temperament kept his spirits up, as is shown by his letters during this time. He died in 1891.

Qualities as a Writer. Most readers, especially younger ones, know Lowell best as the author of " The Vision of Sir Launfal." His famous satire, " A Fable for Critics," contains comments in poetry on American writers, for the most part clever and witty but without malice. Poe seems to have been the only one to take offence. Lowell was one of the first American authors to write in dialect. In the *Biglow Papers* he tried to present the New England Yankee speech, but today readers find it increasingly difficult to read more than selected fragments with genuine pleasure. Detached bits, like those in this volume (page 608), are diverting enough, but the reader soon loses interest in the prose parts.

One feature of Lowell's work stands out prominently — his extraordinary versatility in both prose and poetry. He was an excellent scholar, and the one difficulty for younger readers is that his essays fairly bristle with learning.

A sense of humor is always a delight in literature. Like Holmes, Lowell was extremely witty, but wit is likely to be of only temporary interest, and to derive that largely from being coupled with the personality of the author. Even as a young man he had a tendency to turn everything into a jest, but in essays, speeches, and especially in his letters he gave free rein to his talent. Punning is generally considered a feeble form of wit, but Lowell's age condoned it and he did not hesitate to indulge. On the eve of departing for Europe he wrote to a friend, " My plan is to sit down in Florence — till I have cut my eye(talian) teeth. *Tusc*any must be a good place for that." Clever and amusing, if not done too often. But punning is only a minor feature of Lowell's writing, and his fame does not rest upon his humor. He was a man of high ideals and of genuine patriotism in the best sense of that term, and an able critic.

Richard Henry Dana, Jr. (1815–1882). Another member of the Cambridge-Boston group of cultivated gentlemen was Richard Henry Dana. Today he is remembered for one book, *Two Years Before the Mast* (1841). Like Melville, Dana sailed the seas largely for sheer adventure, and both found it. Melville had kept no notes of his voyagings into the South Seas, and when he came to write *Typee* he trusted to memory, and called upon his imagination. Dana, on the other hand, kept copious notes, and while still at sea he wrote out much of the story. On his return journey to Boston the finished manuscript, with some of his luggage, was lost. Fortunately he had retained his original notes, and he rewrote the book while completing his law course at Harvard.

When he started his two years' cruise around Cape Horn he was not yet twenty years old, and still an undergraduate at Harvard. It might be expected that youthful enthusiasm, or, as it turned out, righteous indignation at the treatment of sailors on board ship, would color his narrative, but he took his note-book as the basis for his account of life at sea in the days of the sailing vessels. Sticking to facts gave his narrative all the romance it needed. One of his motives in writing the book was to make known to the public the harsh treatment of sailors. By means of the book, which is conceded to rank as a classic of the sea, and later through his efforts as a lawyer, many reforms were brought about before the age of steam changed conditions.

THE HISTORIANS

In the nineteenth century there were four historians whose work has sufficient literary merit to give them a place in American literature not unlike that of Macaulay in England. All four were born in Massachusetts, all were graduates of Harvard, and all four gave practically their whole lives to the particular work which gives them a place in history and in literature. Each chose a field widely different from those of the others.

William Hickling Prescott (1796–1859). Prescott chose as his field of study and writing the history of the Spanish in America. This interesting subject had never been given much attention until Irving, while in Spain, gathered much valuable material; but when Irving learned of Prescott's plans he generously turned his own notes over to him. Much original investigation had to be done, however, and Prescott was handicapped from the start because he was almost blind. While a student at Harvard he had been struck in the eye by a piece of bread thoughtlessly thrown across the boarding-house table. Luckily Prescott was wealthy, and throughout his life maintained readers and private secretaries to help him. After much preliminary study and ten years of writing he published the first of his histories, *Ferdinand and Isabella* (1837). Six years later came the *History of the Conquest of Mexico* (1843), containing the fascinating story of the incredible adventures of Cortez in destroying the marvelous and picturesque civilization of the Aztecs. This was followed by the *History of the Conquest of Peru* (1847), in which the exploits of Pizarro among the Incas of Peru are related. Prescott rounded out his work on the Spaniards with the *History of the Reign of Philip the Second* (1858).

Since Prescott's day much light has been shed on the period which he made his life work, and naturally many of his facts and judgments have had to be revised, but nevertheless his books, full of remarkable descriptions and vivid bits of narration, are as exciting today as they ever were.

George Bancroft (1800–1891). Bancroft wrote a voluminous *History of the United States,* eight volumes of which appeared before the Civil War and two afterward. At different times he served as a public official, once as Secretary of the Navy in 1845, and later as Minister to England, and again as Minister to Germany. His only other work, a *History of the Formation of the Constitution of the United States,* was published when he was over eighty years old. His work is scholarly, but his minute detail and florid style are hardly to the taste of the modern reader.

John Lothrop Motley (1814–1877). Motley graduated from Harvard in 1831, and continued his studies in Germany for two years. On his return he took up the law but did not like it. Instead, he spent much time writing two novels which were failures. He entered the diplomatic service and held various minor posts until in his later life he became Minister first to Austria and then to England.

In 1851 he set out for Europe to prepare himself to write a history of the Netherlands. After five years of active study and research he wrote the three works by which he is known today, *The Rise of the Dutch Republic, History of the United Netherlands,* and *The Life and Death of John of Barneveld.* Motley was attracted to the Netherlands by his intense interest in the struggle for human liberty; he saw in the struggle of the Dutch countries a parallel to that of America.

Motley is sometimes accused of being prejudiced, especially against the Spaniards and the Catholics, but he regarded his work not as an isolated piece of historical work on the Dutch, but as a chapter in the history of human liberty. In the Netherlands it happened that the Spaniards, the opposing force, were Catholics; but he was equally critical of the Calvinists when it was they who infringed on human liberties. Like Carlyle, whom Motley greatly admired, he believed that history at bottom is the biographies of great men. His central hero is William of Orange; his central villains are the Duke of Alva and Philip the Second of Spain.

Francis Parkman (1823–1893). As a boy Parkman became interested in the French and Indian War and decided to write a history of it. He was a frail child and, in the hope of strengthening himself, he frequently exercised too strenuously and thus impaired his health further. Only two years out of Harvard, Parkman took a trip west over the Rockies to Oregon. On the way he hunted buffalo, met hostile Indians, and lived for a time in a Sioux camp.

His first work was *The Oregon Trail* (1849), an account of his adventures and observations on this trip. In reading this good book it becomes plain that Parkman's chief interest lay in the Indians and their relations to the white man. In his later books, to which he gave the general title *France and England in North America,* his interest narrowed down to the struggles between the English and the French (the latter with their Indian allies) for supremacy in America. He took great pains to be accurate, but he never forgot that a book to be interesting needed more than mere accuracy. His prose style is both clear and simple, although it lacks the brilliancy of Prescott and the passion of Motley. To the student of today the most readable of his books are, in addition to *The Oregon Trail, The Conspiracy of Pontiac* and *Montcalm and Wolfe.*

Summary. Longfellow, Holmes, and Lowell are not the greatest American poets but they may truthfully be called the most significantly American. As poets they rank below Edgar Allan Poe and Walt Whitman and some of our twentieth-century poets; but with Emerson, Hawthorne, and Thoreau, they formed the group that gave this country its first great impulse in literature. While none of the Boston-Cambridge group was directly connected with the Transcendental movement, all were greatly influenced by it. All were born in New England, educated there, and lived in Boston or its vicinity the greater part of their lives. All three wrote both prose and poetry, but only Holmes and Lowell wrote prose that is still read. They were teachers of unusual caliber. All were college bred, and all traveled abroad. Longfellow and Holmes were opposed to slavery but were willing to let others do the heavier service, while Lowell worked actively for Abolition. They had unusual ability in the difficult art of writing narrative verse. All three had charming personalities. Holmes and Lowell bubbled with an exuberant sense of humor, a trait which both carried over into their literary work. Of the group, Longfellow was the most popular in his day, and has remained so. In common with most American poets of the nineteenth century all were fond of pointing their poems with a lesson or a moral. While none of them rank with Shakespeare, Milton, Tennyson, Browning, Poe, or Whitman, all of them wrote much excellent poetry quite worth reading and liking. It is likely that the prose writings of Holmes and Lowell will withstand the corroding of time better than their poems. Notable prose was also contributed by the minor members of this cultivated and scholarly group — the four historians and Dana.

IN THIS VOLUME

PAGE

1. The Autocrat of the Breakfast Table (Oliver Wendell Holmes)   373
2. The Boys (Oliver Wendell Holmes)   508
3. Hymn to the Night (Henry Wadsworth Longfellow)   .   .   542
4. Maidenhood (Henry Wadsworth Longfellow)   544
5. The Arsenal at Springfield (Henry Wadsworth Longfellow)   .   546
6. In the Churchyard at Tarrytown (Henry Wadsworth Longfellow)   548
7. My Lost Youth (Henry Wadsworth Longfellow)   .   .   .   548
8. The Building of the Ship (Henry Wadsworth Longfellow)   .   551
9. The Bells of San Blas (Henry Wadsworth Longfellow)   .   .   563
10. Old Ironsides (Oliver Wendell Holmes)   595
11. To an Insect (Oliver Wendell Holmes)   596
12. Contentment (Oliver Wendell Holmes)   602
13. The Chambered Nautilus (Oliver Wendell Holmes)   .   .   606
14. The Courtin' (James Russell Lowell)   606
15. What Mr. Robinson Thinks (James Russell Lowell)   .   .   608
16. The Vision of Sir Launfal (James Russell Lowell)   .   .   610
17. The Height of the Ridiculous (Oliver Wendell Holmes)   .   .   778

STUDY QUESTIONS

1. How did Longfellow's occupation have an effect upon his poetry? How did his travels affect it? Name some of his poems which have preserved traditions and legends of our country.

2. What did the general public of Longfellow's day think of his poetic ability? Has this changed to any great extent? What points do critics of today object to in Longfellow's poetry? Do you know any critic of his own day who was hostile toward him? Discuss your own attitude toward Longfellow.

3. How did Holmes's occupation and connection with Harvard University differ from Longfellow's? How was Holmes especially suited by disposition for the writing of " occasional verse " ? Give examples.

4. How did Holmes differ from Longfellow in the relative importance of his prose and poetry?

5. Why may Lowell be said to represent the culture of Boston and Cambridge even more typically than Longfellow and Holmes? Compare and contrast his foreign experiences with those of the other two. Discuss his various fields of distinction.

6. Mention works of Lowell to illustrate the wide variety of his poetry and prose. What is his best-known poem today? Show how dialect literature was fostered by Lowell. (See p. 606.)

7. What justifies our considering Longfellow, Holmes, and Lowell as a distinct " group " of writers? What sets them off from the group composed of Emerson, Hawthorne, and Thoreau?

8. Name important minor writers of the cultivated Boston group of writers. Summarize the fields of interest of the great historians. Why are they entitled to be considered in a history of literature?

Chapter V

AMERICAN LITERATURE AND THE CIVIL WAR

During the " Golden Age " of New England literature, discussed in the preceding two chapters, the North and the South had come to grips on the questions of slavery and disunion, matters so vital that the dispute could be settled only by a great Civil War. This second great crisis in our national life had, like the first, its literary expression in various forms.

John Greenleaf Whittier (1807–1892). The greatest anti-slavery poet was the Massachusetts Quaker, John Greenleaf Whittier. For the details of his life see the introduction to his poems on page 566.

JOHN GREENLEAF WHITTIER

Poet of rural New England

Among his American contemporaries the name at once suggested by Whittier's is that of Longfellow. Both were exceptionally good in writing story poems; both chose subjects from everyday life which would be easily understandable and interesting to common people; and both moralized, Whittier more often than Longfellow. On the other hand, Longfellow was much more of a literary artist, that is to say, he paid more attention to the technical details of poetry than Whittier did.

Whittier's reputation as a poet will probably have to stand on rather few poems. " The Barefoot Boy," " Maud Muller," and " Barbara Frietchie " will in all likelihood remain stand-bys in school books. " In School Days " has a sentimental appeal that will keep it alive, although as a poem it is much inferior to the others. Whittier's best poetry is to be found in " Snow-Bound " and the series called *The Tent on the Beach*. " Snow-Bound " is as thoroughly picturesque and as adequately representative of New England farm life as Burns' " Cotter's Saturday Night " is of Scotch. Both poems are highly descriptive and in both skilful characterizations relieve the dead level of description. The Burns poem is, however, only one hundred and eighty-nine lines long, while that of Whittier is seven hundred and thirty-five. This contrast is noted here because of one of the main criticisms leveled at Whittier, that of a too great diffuseness. While the charge is true of many of his poems, it fails in the case of " Snow-Bound." The

Essex Institute

BIRTHPLACE OF WHITTIER, HAVERHILL

easy meter, the simple language, and the well-known details of everyday life serve to hold the reader to the end.

In Longfellow's *Tales of a Wayside Inn* seven persons are supposed to have taken refuge from a storm in a Sudbury inn, and they while away the time by telling stories, an old device to give greater vividness to the manner of presentation. In *The Tent on the Beach* (1867) Whittier used a similar scheme, having three persons instead of seven, and the place is Salisbury Beach. As in the Longfellow poem, the persons here are frankly real, in this instance James T. Fields, Bayard Taylor, and Whittier.

This brief discussion of Whittier may close with the poet's description of himself:

" And one there was, a dreamer born,
    Who, with a mission to fulfil,
Had left the Muses' haunts to turn
    The crank of an opinion-mill,
Making his rustic reed of song
    A weapon in the war with wrong."

Harriet Beecher Stowe (1811–1896). Of all the books directly connected with the Civil War, none exceeded in importance *Uncle Tom's Cabin,* by Harriet Beecher Stowe. The daughter of Lyman Beecher, the sister of Henry Ward Beecher (both famous preachers), and eventually the wife of Professor Stowe, of Lane Theological Seminary, the author of *Uncle Tom's Cabin* had a strong religious background in her training and environment. She began to write while quite young, but it was not until she lived in Cincinnati, to which city the family had moved when her father became head of a seminary there, that she became definitely interested in the problem of slavery. She began to gather facts and material for her work during a short period of actual observation in slave territory, but the book was written after she moved to Brunswick, Maine, where her husband had become a professor at Bowdoin College.

Whittier's Home Association

THE DESK IN WHITTIER'S HOME, AMESBURY

On this the poet wrote *Snowbound*

Uncle Tom's Cabin was published serially in *The National Era,* a journal of Washington, D. C., to which Whittier also was for a time a contributor. When the novel appeared in book form in 1852 it found a public already excited about slavery. In a remarkably short time the influence of *Uncle Tom's Cabin* was felt throughout the civilized world, and within a decade it was directly responsible for bringing about the emancipation of the serfs in Russia (1861). In this country its dramatic appeal was at once capitalized by turning it into a play (see page 801). After more than three-quarters of a century the book is still read and the play still acted.

Uncle Tom's Cabin heightened the already tense feeling in both North and South, and in that way was undoubtedly a strong factor in hastening on the Civil War. Sold by the millions, translated into every literary language, and having a profound influence on the attitude of the world toward the institution of slavery, *Uncle Tom's Cabin* cannot be dismissed by saying that its sentimentality was maudlin in spots, that its facts were exaggerated and untrue to the life it tried to portray, and that it lacked true artistry. Behind the story lay a sincere and righteous passion, which Mrs. Stowe was able to convey to her readers.

MEN OF PUBLIC AFFAIRS

Up to 1850 there was much discussion in Congress about the question of states' rights, and it was with this phase of politics that slavery became associated, involving ultimately the doctrine of the right of secession. Four famous orators, in Congress and out of it, bore the brunt of the debates on the subject: one from Massachusetts, two from South Carolina, and one from Kentucky.

Daniel Webster (1782–1852) was born in New Hampshire and educated at Dartmouth College, but his political career began in Boston. By his defence of Dartmouth in a famous case of law, and by the first " Bunker Hill " oration in 1825, he achieved early fame as a constitutional lawyer and an orator. He was twice Senator from Massachusetts, and twice Secretary of State. In 1830 Robert Y. Hayne (1791–1839), Senator from South Carolina, boldly proclaimed the doctrine of Nullification — that a state could " judge of the violation of the Constitution by the Federal Government," and it was in response to this that Webster delivered his greatest speech, known as the " Reply to Hayne." He took the stand that on the question of slavery the states could decide, but that they could not pass on matters involving the Constitution. He closed with the deathless words, " Liberty *and* Union, now and forever, one and inseparable."

By 1833 Hayne had been succeeded in the Senate by John C. Calhoun, who continued firm in the doctrine of his predecessor, and Webster again defended the position he had taken against Hayne, enunciating more eloquently than before that the people " alone are sovereign," and that " the majority must govern."

As the years went on the struggle continued in Congress and out of it, and in 1850 Henry Clay, then Senator from Kentucky, offered a compromise measure by which it was hoped that the Union might be saved. In defence of this measure Webster delivered his last great speech, known as the " Seventh of March " speech, in which he reiterated his position on slavery. During the seventeen years that had elapsed since the " Reply to Hayne " the question of slavery had come to the fore in all discussions of states' rights, and the public thought for a time that Webster had gone over to the opposition. It was this speech that made Whittier write " Ichabod " (see page 567).

Abraham Lincoln (1809–1865). While the national Congress was struggling with these constitutional problems a young man was coming into local fame as a lawyer and politician in Illinois. With little formal education but with intense personal effort Abraham Lincoln had slowly prepared himself for the great rôle he was destined to play in American history and in American literature. Earlier in this volume a great deal has been said of Lincoln (449–459) and a number of selections from his best-known works have been given.

Lincoln's Literary Significance. Lincoln's speeches, proclamations, and state papers constitute one of America's most precious literary heritages. " The style is the man," and Lincoln's prose style reflects with the faithfulness of a mirror the shining simplicity of the man, his logical mind, his homely wit, and his all-embracing humanity.

The importance of Lincoln in American literature lies not only in the power and literary excellence of " The Gettysburg Address " and " The Letter to Mrs. Bixby," but also in the inspiration which men of literature have found, and still are finding, in the drama of his life and the depths of his character. No other single figure has appealed so strongly to writers. Poets, biographers, essayists, orators, preachers, and artists have found him an apparently inexhaustible fountain of inspiration. If there is any one person that stands for Americanism at its best, it is Abraham Lincoln.

Edward Everett Hale (1822–1909). In addition to the orators, the war also produced Edward Everett Hale, one of the most voluminous writers in this country. His collected works fill ten large volumes, and consist of all types of writing except poetry. He was a Unitarian preacher, a lecturer, a reformer, a historian, and a writer of short stories. It is in the last capacity that he will be remembered in literature. Two of his short stories are known to most readers.

" My Double and How He Undid Me " is one of America's best
humorous short stories, and " The Man Without a Country " has
become a standard " classic " of American literature. The latter
appeared in 1863 when the Civil War was at its height, and although
the battles of Gettysburg and Vicksburg had been fought and won,
the Union cause seemed at its low ebb. The morale of the country
was sadly shaken, and this story was just what people needed to
restore their faith. In it Hale portrayed with great power how
miserable is a " man without a country." Hale's public activities
continued to the end of his long life, and during his last years he
was chaplain to the United States Senate.

HUMOR

The " Cracker-Box Philosophers." Even in the dark and
troubled days of the Civil War, the American sense of humor could
not entirely be repressed. The " Cracker-Box Philosophers " brought
off their digs at politicians and stay-at-homes, and portrayed the
funny side of public events. Most of their sallies were written in
one local dialect or another and hence are not widely read today.
But Artemus Ward and Bill Nye are still readable. (See page 379.)

A GROUP OF SOUTHERN POETS

Among the poets Whittier and Lowell for a considerable period
devoted most of their talents to the anti-slavery movement in the
North, while the others, although opposed to slavery, wrote only
occasional pieces definitely bearing on the great question. None
actually went to war as did these Southerners.

Henry Timrod (1829–1867). Timrod was born in Charleston, South Carolina, and attended the University of Georgia for a
time until compelled to leave because of ill health. Like Irving,
Bryant, and others, he tried the law but gave it up in favor of
literature. He wrote for the *Southern Literary Messenger,* the magazine made famous by Poe, and published a small volume of poems
just before the outbreak of the war. He enlisted early but his frail
physique allowed him little more activity than that of newspaper
correspondent. He wrote a number of stirring war poems, such as
" Charleston," " The Cotton Boll," and others, but he also is remembered for a small number of Nature lyrics. Sherman's march to the
sea carried away with it the newspaper office in which Timrod worked,

and at the close of the war he was practically destitute and hopelessly ill. His last poem was " At Magnolia Cemetery," in honor of the Confederate dead.

Paul Hamilton Hayne (1830–1886). Hayne was also born in Charleston, of a wealthy family. He was the nephew of Robert Y. Hayne, already mentioned in connection with Webster. After graduation from Charleston College he studied law, but like his friend Timrod he abandoned it in favor of literature. His career was successfully launched, but when the war came he enlisted and served chiefly on the governor's staff. Again like Timrod, his health failed, and the war ruined him financially. His war lyrics are uninteresting but his Nature poems, two of which are printed in this volume (see page 642), reveal a genuine lyric gift. For the last twenty years of his life he lived in a rough cottage which he called " Copse Hill," near Augusta, Georgia, and it was there that he wrote his best poetry.

William Gilmore Simms (1806–1870). Simms, like Timrod and Hayne, was a native of Charleston. Born of poor parents, Simms had little formal schooling, but by sheer will-power he gained literary recognition and became the head of a considerable group of writers in Charleston. Instead of confining himself to poetry, he would write prodigiously on any marketable topic. His competent stories of adventure won him such recognition that some call him " the Cooper of the South." As with his two friends Timrod and Hayne, the war carried away what property he had accumulated, and he found it impossible to adjust himself to the changed conditions. Today he is known generally only for his poetry, and in the South he is regarded warmly because of his intense love for his native section.

Abram Joseph Ryan (1839–1886). Father Ryan, as he is usually called, was born in Norfolk, Virginia. He became a Catholic priest and was chaplain in the Confederate army. After the war he was engaged in religious journalism. " The Conquered Banner," printed on page 650, is the one poem by which he is remembered today.

Sidney Lanier (1842–1881). Of the Southern poets, none has made a stronger impress on American literature than Sidney Lanier, Poe alone excepted. He was born in Macon, Georgia, and attended Oglethorpe University. After his graduation he taught there for a year, and then, in 1861, he enlisted in the Confederate army and served throughout the war, although for the last five months he was a prisoner at Point Lookout, Maryland.

The story of the Lanier family after the war is that of many thousands of others. Cultured and prosperous before the war, and impoverished after, there was the eternal question of what to do. Like Hayne and Timrod, Lanier's health was broken down and he never entirely recovered from his prison experience. He wandered from place to place, in search of health and of some opportunity to make a living. In 1867 he published *Tiger Lilies,* a novel of the war. He taught for a short period, and practiced law with his father, but in 1873 he decided on an artistic career. As he was a musician of considerable talent and had the ability to play almost any instrument, he was given a place as flutist in the Peabody Orchestra of Baltimore. The following year he published his first poem, " Corn," which brought his work to the attention of Bayard Taylor, and " The Symphony," written in 1875, led Taylor to secure for Lanier the privilege of writing a cantata for the Centennial Exposition in Philadelphia in 1876.

SIDNEY LANIER

Poet and musician of the period after the Civil War

The whole published work of Lanier is considerable in bulk, but today his poems overshadow everything else. Unlike many other Southern poets, Lanier successfully combated post-war evils and made himself not only a poet of the South but definitely an American poet of the first water. While his best-known poems, with the exception of " The Symphony," are Southern in setting, they are countrywide, not local, in appeal. He used onomatopoeia skilfully; that is, he made the sound of the words and the rhythm of the poem conform to his theme. For example read aloud his " Song of the Chattahoochee " (page 645). It is generally conceded that his great poem is " The Symphony," of which he himself said, " I personify each instrument in the orchestra, and make them discuss various deep social questions of the times, in the progress of the music." The theme of the poem is a protest against the commercialism of the age in so far as it tends to destroy the spiritual sense of the good and the beautiful. His last poem, " Sunrise," written on his death-bed, is packed with beautiful word-pictures and poetic overtones. The sheer beauty of this last poem suggests that had he lived longer he might easily have ranked with the highest. As it is, he stands out as the greatest poet of the South, and the first to adapt himself to the new conditions that the South had to face after the war.

CIVIL WAR BALLADS AND SONGS

The Civil War, like all wars, had its quota of ballads and songs, some of which are still remembered either for the words or for the music. One of the earliest was " Maryland! My Maryland! " by James Ryder Randall, a native of Baltimore living in Louisiana. It was written when he heard of the attack in Baltimore on the Massachusetts troops, April 19, 1861, in which the first blood of the war was shed.

Everybody, North and South, knows the melody of " Dixie," but probably few know the name of the author, or rather authors, of this famous ballad. The original version was written by Daniel D. Emmett, of Ohio, for a minstrel show. It quickly became popular on the stage, and various sets of words were written to fit the melody. The version found in books today is that by Albert H. Pike, a New Englander living in Arkansas, who had it published in the Natchez *Courier* in 1861. His version is literary enough but lacks the snap of Emmett's words.

Other poems by Southerners are " Carolina " and " Charleston " (see page 637) by Henry Timrod, " The Sword of Robert Lee " by Father Ryan, " Little Giffen " by Francis O. Ticknor, and " South Carolina to the States of the North " by Paul Hamilton Hayne.

An old religious camp-meeting song furnished the music for " John Brown's Body," one of the earliest and most popular of the war songs of the North. It is not known who wrote it, for again there are different versions, and, as in the case of " Dixie," the melody caught the popular ear. The song was sung by a Massachusetts regiment as it marched down Broadway, in New York City, on its way to the front in 1861. In an effort to improve the song Julia Ward Howe wrote " The Battle Hymn of the Republic," using the melody of " John Brown's Body " as its basis. Even then the soldiers preferred the earlier version, and more recently Stephen Vincent Benét used " John Brown's Body " as the title of his long epic of the Civil War (see page 771).

Among the poems of the North are " Sheridan's Ride " by Thomas Buchanan Read, " The Battle-Cry of Freedom " by George F. Root, " On Board the Cumberland " by George Henry Boker, and " The High Tide at Gettysburg " (written after the war) by W. H. Thompson.

In 1867 the women of Columbus, Mississippi, decorated the graves of Union soldiers at the same time that they decorated those of their own soldiers, and this episode furnished the theme of " The Blue and the Gray " by Francis M. Finch, ending with

> " Love and tears for the Blue;
> Tears and love for the Gray."

Summary.   The greatest anti-slavery poet was the Massachusetts Quaker, John Greenleaf Whittier, who, in his zeal to promote his cause, suffered persecution and barely escaped martyrdom. Whittier is of course, important in our literature as the poet of rural New England and of the dignity and calm of the Quaker religion; but his activities as an Abolitionist form the most colorful part of his life.

Harriet Beecher Stowe's novel, *Uncle Tom's Cabin,* proved to be propaganda of the most inflammatory sort, and she was called by Lincoln " the little woman who caused a great war." In the United States Senate Robert Y. Hayne and John C. Calhoun, both of South Carolina, presented able oratorical defenses of the Southern point of view. Their leading opponent was Daniel Webster, senator from Massachusetts, whose brilliant speeches have earned him the foremost place among American orators. In the actual conflict itself the leading figure was Abraham Lincoln. His simple, sincere English has no rival in our literature. Edward Everett Hale's " The Man Without a Country," conceived as propaganda to promote recruiting in the North, retains a distinguished place in American fiction. During the war flourished " The Cracker-Box Philosophers." A pathetic aftermath of the Civil War is found in the broken health, hard struggle against poverty, and early deaths of three promising Southern poets, Henry Timrod, Paul Hamilton Hayne, and Sidney Lanier. Of the three, Lanier made the greatest contribution; several of his poems have enduring qualities. Many songs of Civil War days are still popular favorites.

IN THIS VOLUME

PAGE

 1. A Business Letter (Artemus Ward) 379
 2. Farewell at Springfield (Abraham Lincoln) 449
 3. Letter to General Hooker (Abraham Lincoln) 451
 4. Proclamation for National Fast Day (Abraham Lincoln) . . 452
 5. Proclamation for a National Thanksgiving (Abraham Lincoln) . 454
 6. Gettysburg Address (Abraham Lincoln) 455
 7. Second Inaugural Address 457
 8. Ichabod (John Greenleaf Whittier) 567
 9. Telling the Bees (John Greenleaf Whittier) 569
10. Snow-Bound (John Greenleaf Whittier) 571
11. Dear Lord and Father of Mankind (John Greenleaf Whittier) . 594
12. Charleston (Henry Timrod) 637
13. Ode on the Decoration of Graves (Henry Timrod) . . . 639
14. The Mocking Bird (Paul Hamilton Hayne) 641
15. Aspects of the Pines (Paul Hamilton Hayne) 642
16. Song of the Chattahoochee (Sidney Lanier) 645
17. From the Flats (Sidney Lanier) 647
18. Barnacles (Sidney Lanier) 648
19. The Stirrup-Cup (Sidney Lanier) 649
20. The Conquered Banner (Abram Joseph Ryan) 650

STUDY QUESTIONS

1. How is Whittier different in background and education from the writers of the preceding chapter? What circumstances and influences in his life largely determined the kind of poetry he wrote?

2. Point out how the poetry of Whittier's early life differed from that of his later life. What is his greatest poem? What qualities of this poem give it continued popularity? What points of similarity can you find between Longfellow's and Whittier's poetry? What points of difference?

3. Name several of the orators of the Civil War period, pointing out on which side of the question their sympathies lay. Who is now considered the greatest spokesman of this period?

4. Summarize Lincoln's position in American literature.

5. What entitles Edward Everett Hale to a place in literary history?

6. Were the Southern poets as a whole affected by the war, or not? Prove your answer.

7. What other occupations besides literature did Lanier have which showed some effect on his writings?

8. What is the outstanding novel connected with the Civil War? Point out its strong and its weak points.

9. Name as many familiar lyrics of the Civil War as you can. Which of these are still sung rather generally? Which seem to have faded into the past? (See also pp. 685–6.)

Chapter VI

WALT WHITMAN AND EMILY DICKINSON —
INDIVIDUALISTS

The one poet to write effectively of the Civil War from actual experience was Walt Whitman, the war nurse; but the daring unconventionality and original structure of his compositions were later so influential in our modern American poetry that he cannot be considered primarily a war poet. He is the essence of a deeper Americanism; and it is significant that our modern poets acclaim Whitman and Poe as our two greatest poets, essentially " modern " in their artistic standards, opposites though they be.

Walt Whitman (1819–1892). Prior to 1900, American literary history was enlivened by two stormy petrels, both strongly individualistic, both independent, and both writing poetry that was strikingly original. The parallelism may be continued by saying that these two poets received the recognition of the foremost critics of Europe before those of their own country, and that to this day they are regarded in Europe as America's most original and greatest poets. In the case of Edgar Allan Poe it was his career that was stormy; in that of Walt Whitman it was the poetry that roused a storm which has not yet died down. Today no one denies Poe a place among the greatest poets, but Whitman's niche among the great is still vigorously disputed in many quarters. In general, the majority of the best critical minds in this country enthusiastically applaud Whitman's poetry. That it is daringly original is certain; that it has been a tremendous force in the breaking down of poetical traditions is equally certain; and, while much of it may not be poetry at all, as his enemies declare, there can be no doubt that a considerable body of it is destined to rank among the best yet written in America. For the details of Whitman's life see page 653.

Whitman's Backgrounds. As a young man Whitman read a great deal, especially Emerson and the other Transcendentalists. Their philosophy appealed to him because it cried out for new conceptions of the meaning of life, and especially for a revision of religious beliefs, a problem to which Whitman had given much thought. Being uneducated himself, he wanted to bring the newer thought to the common people. As early as 1847 he had begun to phrase his ideas, but before he ventured into print he rewrote his lines many times because he wanted to convey his thoughts in a form that would attract common folk. The first edition of *Leaves of Grass* was therefore not printed until 1855 and consisted of only twelve poems and a preface. This is now regarded as an epoch-making book, but like so many influential works, it was unnoticed at the time except by a few critics to whom Whitman sent copies.

WALT WHITMAN

The father of modern American poetry

Whitman's Poetic Credo. The preface to *Leaves of Grass* announced Whitman's new and radical theories of poetry, declared for emancipation from existing forms, and maintained that thought should take precedence over style. His poems, though intensely personal, convey a sense of certainty concerning the dignity of man that is almost arrogant. When he began his first poem with the line, " I celebrate myself, and sing myself," he meant that he was a symbol for all mankind, a single atom in a boundless universe. In this poem, afterwards entitled " Song of Myself," and expanded to 1347 lines in its final version, he glorifies mankind and declares himself the poet of all classes, from the humblest to the highest. Whitman asks questions about the mysteries of the universe and about God, but he always comes back to the individual and the life here and now. He defies death by saying, " It is idle to try to alarm me," and speaks of life as " the leavings of many deaths." To God he says, " Listener up there! what have you to confide in me? " And again, " Talk honestly, no one else hears you, and I stay only a minute longer," and in this connection he declares near the end of the poem,

" I too am not a bit tamed, I too am untranslatable,
I sound my barbaric yawp over the roofs of the world."

And finally, if you have lived your life eagerly, zestfully, if you have done your day's work honestly, why worry? " I depart as air," he says almost brazenly, " I shake my white locks at the runaway sun." And, " If you want me again look for me under your boot-soles."

In the preface to *Leaves of Grass* Whitman makes a strong plea for Americanism in poetry as well as for individualism. " The genius of the United States is best shown in the common people, and the American poet must express their life. He must love the earth and the sun and the animals. . . . He is at one with the universe, and feels the harmony of things with man. . . . The poet must be a champion of political liberty. He must recognize that the actual facts of the American republic are superior to fiction and romance. . . . The great poet is marked by unconstraint and defiance of precedent. . . . General laws rule, and these make for happiness." (These sentences are taken from Bliss Perry's summary of Whitman's Preface.)

The most revolutionary feature of this uncouth volume, however, was not the spirit of the poetry but the form in which it was written. No rhyme, rough meter if any, lines of unequal length, and weird spelling, all of which added to the blatant egoism of the poems, should have made *Leaves of Grass* a literary sensation. When the book remained almost unnoticed, Whitman himself wrote a number of reviews anonymously, in one of which he states that he followed no model. " The style of these poems, therefore, is simply their own style. . . . Nature may have given the hint to the author of *Leaves of Grass,* but there exists no book or fragment of a book which can have given the hint to them." The fact is that Whitman set down his thoughts much as Emerson did — just as they happened to occur to him. Although he perhaps owed a great deal to Emerson's poetic prose, Whitman practically invented a new method of expression, since known as " free verse." He deliberately persisted in free verse, and only in his later years or on special occasions did he fall into more regular and more orthodox measures.

Emerson's immediate and generous praise gave Whitman tremendous satisfaction because it came to him as approval from a teacher. The Transcendental group saw in Whitman an important recruit, and he was visited not only by Emerson but by Bronson Alcott, and Thoreau.

Whitman and the Civil War. Up to the Civil War Whitman's poetry had much to do with the physical life of the human body. But his experiences as a war nurse aroused a consciousness of soul that had heretofore not been stressed in his verses. The miserable wretchedness of the hospitals appealed so strongly to his sympathies that he continued as a volunteer helper until the end of the war. His experiences were recorded in a notebook and in letters to his mother, many of them later printed in *Specimen Days* (1865), one of the two important prose works by Whitman. The other is *Democratic Vistas*.

The war stirred Whitman's poetic powers more deeply than anything else. In 1866 he published *Drum-Taps,* which is the poetic counterpart of *Specimen Days*. He sensed and expressed the tragic realities of the war and the nobility of human beings under its stress better than any other poet. The assassination of Lincoln while *Specimen Days* was in press called forth two of Whitman's best poems, " O Captain! My Captain!," and " When Lilacs Last in the Dooryard Bloomed." Both of these poems were incorporated later in the volume *Drum-Taps*. In spite of its power, however, the book received little notice except from the few. Among his disciples in our own country the poet could now count John Burroughs, and in England he was favorably regarded by a number of well-known literary men and women, including Swinburne, Tennyson, and others.

After the war Whitman was given a government position in the Department of the Interior, but when the head of the Department found that his clerk was the author of what many people thought an indecent book, *Leaves of Grass,* he dismissed him. This episode brought Whitman's young friend W. D. O'Connor, a journalist, to his defence in a pamphlet entitled *The Good Gray Poet*. In defending *Leaves of Grass* O'Connor says, " It is all our own! The nation is in it! In form a series of chants, in substance it is an epic of America. It is distinctly and utterly American. Without model, without imitation, without reminiscence, it is evolved entirely from our own polity and popular life." This states exactly what Whitman had always hoped to be — the poet of all America. But the common people heard him not.

Qualities as a Poet. Whitman was a revolutionist in poetry, and like all revolutionists he had, and still has, his devoted followers and his bitter enemies. He wanted to be the singer of democracy, of the great inarticulate mass of humanity, and spoke of himself as a typical representative. At first one is repelled by his constant use of the personal pronoun " I," but this resentment passes after his great idea of the oneness of humanity becomes apparent. His admirers regard him as a prophet and a seer, his haters as blatant and ignorant. Those are extreme opinions, and as the years pass his enemies become fewer. Some details of his life were not wholly admirable, but one forgets those in experiencing the impact of his mighty thoughts and the surging, subtle music of his lines.

Today there is little negative criticism of his free verse. In his earlier poems the rhythm is much cruder and rougher than in his later ones. " The Carol of Death " (page 658) shows how powerful a metric swing he could attain. Some of his titles are in themselves sheer poetry, especially " Out of the Cradle Endlessly Rocking " and "When Lilacs Last in the Dooryard Bloomed." While no poet has directly imitated his characteristic chanting long lines, the newer and so-called modernistic forms of free verse hark back to him. In Whitman there is a world of realism, of the here and now. He used common, even vulgar, words and forsook utterly the " pretty words " and classical allusions of conventional poetry. He belongs to the school of nature writers, to the out of doors. Above all, he chanted his highly significant ethical message to his countrymen — the message to look to themselves if life was to have meaning beyond mere animalism.

In summary, one may quote Louis Untermeyer: [1]

" The final estimate of Whitman's work is yet to be written. Whitman's very universality has defeated his commentators. To the craftsmen, Whitman's chief contribution is his form. Hailing him as the father of the free verse movement, they placed their emphasis on his flexible sonority, his orchestral *timbre* and tidal rhythms, his piling up of details into a symphonic structure. To the philosophers, he is the first of modern prophets; a rhapsodic mystic with a magnificently vulgar sense of democracy. To the psychologist, he is the most revealing of autobiographers. ' Whoever touches this book, touches a man,' he wrote, and celebrating himself — hearty, gross, noble, ' sane and sensual to the core ' — he celebrated humanity."

Emily Dickinson (1830–1886). Whitman had no forerunners and, until the twentieth century, few followers — he belonged to no coterie; he was the great trumpeter of change, an individualist. Emily Dickinson has been characterized as " an epigrammatic Walt Whitman " and in her own original way she was a remarkable, isolated genius. Unlike Whitman, however, she wrote to please herself and a small circle of intimate friends. She cared nothing for the

[1] From his preface to Whitman in *Modern Poetry: American and British,* p. 50.

democratic mob. For the explanation of her cloistered life at Amherst see the introduction to her poems on page 664 and page 667.

Emily Dickinson wrote in short snatches for the most part; quick revelations of a single mood, an odd fancy, or a deep thought, often only four short lines, rarely as many as twenty-four. Her poems are miniature in size but profound in depth of vision. She wrote chiefly on four subjects — love, nature, life, death — and not a trite or hackneyed line is to be found in her work. Up to the time of her death she refused to publish, but many of her verses (five hundred in all) had been sent to friends and relatives and a few got into print. Four years after her death Thomas Wentworth Higginson, a friend of the family, edited the first of her published volumes. Her work commands interest because it was strikingly different from that of her immediate contemporaries, because it was untouched by outer influences, and because in the last twenty years it has gained a wide and increasingly enthusiastic audience. Her poetry will probably outlast that of any other poet of her own generation except Whitman.

Summary. Two individualists, Walt Whitman and Emily Dickinson, experienced the Civil War. Whitman was deeply stirred and his poetry was invigorated by his war experiences. On Emily Dickinson the war had no perceptible effect. Whitman's poetic credo, announced and propagandized vehemently by him, and his unconventional, powerful poems have won him the title, " Father of Modern American Poetry." Emily Dickinson's fragmentary, delicate lyrics have come to be considered ageless. Both contained the seeds of modernity and may be hailed as prophetic of the second great wave of poetic achievement, which came in the twentieth century.

IN THIS VOLUME

		PAGE
1.	One's Self I Sing (Walt Whitman)	654
2.	I Hear America Singing (Walt Whitman)	655
3.	Mannahatta (Walt Whitman)	656
4.	Beat! Beat! Drums! (Walt Whitman)	657
5.	The Carol of Death (Walt Whitman)	658
6.	A Noiseless Patient Spider (Walt Whitman)	659
7.	Give Me the Splendid Silent Sun (Walt Whitman)	660
8.	Miracles (Walt Whitman)	662
9.	When I Heard the Learned Astronomer (Walt Whitman)	662
10.	Darest Thou Now O Soul (Walt Whitman)	663
11.	Ten Poems (Emily Dickinson)	664–8

STUDY QUESTIONS

1. Point out what circumstances in the life of Whitman fitted him to be the poet of democracy. Show what connection he had with the Civil War and how this is reflected in his poems.

2. How has Whitman been regarded variously by other poets of his day, by critics, by the reading public at large, by poets of the twentieth century? What elements in his poetry cause him to be severely criticized by some or highly praised by others?

3. How is Whitman distinctly different from the other poets in the section, Transition Poetry, pages 652–686? What other American writers have had strongly marked individualities which enabled them to make very original contributions to our literature?

4. Re-read the poems of Emily Dickinson in this book and state whether you think her as great an individualist as Whitman. Be specific.

Chapter VII

THE WESTERN FRONTIER MOVEMENT

Soon after the close of the Civil War the western frontier again became a major influence in our literature. Released from four years of concentration upon a great military struggle, American life expanded in every direction. Now came the culmination of that great western migration which had followed the discovery of gold in California in 1849, and which had been halted by the war. The covered wagon was superseded by great transcontinental railroads, and the conquest of the West was rapidly concluded. Within a half-century the American frontier moved from the Mississippi River to disappear at the shores of the Pacific Ocean. The farm life on the prairie, traffic on the Mississippi, the conquest of the buffalo-covered plains, the romance of the trail of the covered wagons, the struggles with the Indians, the magnificent distances and gorgeous scenery of the Rockies, all furnished writers with native materials for some of our most important literature. Indeed, so definitely American and original is much of this writing that with it American literature is said to have come of age.

Prior to the war, nearly all the chief American authors came from somewhere along the Atlantic seaboard, and most of their work was deeply tinged by the influence of traditional English literature. The conditions that brought on the war, and those that followed it, created an America vastly different from that of the middle of the century, and sections of the country hitherto silent began to find expression, especially in the newspapers. The rigors of a highly real war to a large extent stifled the older romanticism. Sketches, stories, and poems in dialect represented the tendency toward " regional " material, often called " local color." At first this literature was strongly flavored with humor of a type that often was slightly coarse and usually based on exaggeration. During and immediately after the war this humor was frequently satiric, but later it became sheer farce, humor for the sake of being funny.

This new humor and new-found zest in colorful localisms hailed from the far West but quickly took root also in the South and Middle West and finally in New England. After 1849 many went to California to get rich quick and then return east to enjoy their wealth, not unlike the founders of Jamestown. Others were drifters, going from place to place for the sheer adventure of it. The population increased so fast that the law was unable to control it. Freedom meant the abandonment that goes with unrestrained individualism. Gambling, rum, and vice of every variety flourished prodigiously. Quarrels were settled on the spot with gun or knife. Such a life could not fail to be picturesque and interesting. It first became articulate in the newspaper; this meant journalism, which, however crude, demanded some sort of education on the part of those who produced the papers. Local journalism in California afforded opportunities that were destined in at least two instances to bring international fame to local writers, Bret Harte and Mark Twain, the one hailing from the East, the other from Missouri.

Mark Twain (Samuel Langhorne Clemens, 1835–1910). The Clemens family was one of thousands that in the early days could not resist the lure of the West, always hoping to better themselves by moving on. Their history was not unlike that of the Lincolns, the Boones, and the Garlands. From Virginia to Tennessee to Missouri, John Clemens at last halted in the crude village of Florida, some fifty miles beyond the Mississippi River in Missouri. There Samuel Clemens was born, but he grew up in Hannibal, a river town about a hundred miles north of St. Louis. In 1847 his father died and the boy worked on his brother's newspaper in Hannibal for some years until his restlessness carried him east to Philadelphia and New York.

Homesickness for the river, however, brought him back to the Mississippi valley. Readers of *Tom Sawyer* and *Huckleberry Finn* will understand what an important part the great river played in the imagination of young Clemens. Once on a trip down the river he made the acquaintance of Horace Bixby, the most famous of all Mississippi pilots, and before the boat reached New Orleans Sam Clemens had apprenticed himself to learn the pilot's business. During his four years' service on the river he became a licensed and trusted pilot, and quite unconsciously laid up a treasure-house of future literary material. Many years later he said, " In that brief, sharp schooling I got personally and familiarly acquainted with all the different types of human nature that are to be found in fiction, biography, or history."

After a brief experience as a Confederate soldier, Clemens took a position with his brother in Carson City, Nevada. Here he zestfully entered into the life of the West, prospecting for gold and silver, and plunging into all sorts of wildcat schemes for getting rich quick. After a year of this, with no tangible financial results, he became a reporter for the Virginia City *Enterprise,* and it was on this job that he first used the signature "Mark Twain," a common expression on the river boats of his day.

MARK TWAIN
The outstanding writer of the Western Frontier Movement

Later he reported for various papers in San Francisco, at that time the literary center of the west coast. When Bret Harte became editor of *The Californian,* Clemens was appointed to the staff. In after years he gave Bret Harte the chief credit for having "trimmed and trained and schooled" him into a style that was literary, instead of permitting him to remain "an awkward utterer of coarse grotesqueness."

In 1865, while he and a friend were out on a prospecting expedition, he heard a story which he later wrote out under the title of "Jim Smiley and His Jumping Frog," and sent to the New York *Saturday Express.* Its success was immediate and made Mark Twain's name known throughout the country. The story became the title piece of his first published volume in 1867.

After a period of successful lecturing in San Francisco, Clemens returned east and sailed with a special excursion party for a five months' trip on what is today called the "Mediterranean cruise." He had made a contract with the New York *Tribune* and the *Alta California* to report the trip in a series of letters. The literary result of this "picnic," as he called it in the Preface, was *The Innocents Abroad* (1869), a tremendous popular success and as delightful today as it was when first published. Although humorous, it is a frank and honest work, a real book of travels but vastly different from

Longfellow's poetic flutings in *Outre Mer*. Mark Twain refused to rhapsodize over the hitherto sacred relics, landmarks, works of art, and historical associations unless he really felt impressed. Much of his apparent irreverence is nothing but the refreshing comments of an honest person who refuses to have his feelings dictated to him.

On this momentous trip Clemens met a young man whose sister, Olivia Langdon, he married three years later. Becoming prosperous, he built a magnificent house in Hartford, Connecticut, where he had as near neighbors two of his best friends, Charles Dudley Warner and the Reverend Joseph Twichell (better known as the original of Harris in *A Tramp Abroad*). The fortune Clemens had made by his writings and by backing the publication of *The Personal Memoirs of General Grant* was later lost by the failure of the publishing house and also that of a type-setting machine he had financed. He faced his bankrupt position stoically, and by writing and lecturing made good all the losses, although legally he could have side-stepped them. In later life he traveled extensively, made hosts of friends everywhere, and received honorary degrees from Yale, Oxford, and the University of Missouri. On his seventieth birthday five years before his death, he was given a remarkable testimonial dinner in New York at which an unusually large number of distinguished people were present.

As a man, Mark Twain was a striking figure, especially in his later years when his shock of hair was entirely white, and when he dressed at all times in white suits. The drooping moustache seemed to fit in well with the peculiar slow drawl with which he spoke. In his lectures the serious manner in which he delivered his apparently spontaneous witticisms and waggery gave his hearers an unforgettable experience.

Mark Twain's Writings. Mark Twain's reputation was established by his humor, and though in later life he matured into a penetrating and sometimes cynical observer of life, he never lost his ability to make people laugh. After the crudeness of his early burlesques had been modified, partly through Bret Harte's influence, Clemens produced a remarkable array of varied and fascinating books. The great writings of his middle years fall into two main classes: the informal narrative of actual experience, and fiction based on actual experience. Each class is represented by three distinctive books.

Informal narrative is represented by *The Innocents Abroad* (1869), *Roughing It* (1872), and *Life on the Mississippi* (1883). The first has already been discussed. It fulfilled Whitman's plea that our literature be honestly American instead of merely an echo of traditions from across the sea or an imitation of the works of earlier American writers. *A Tramp Abroad* (1880), a later account of the American in Europe, belongs with it in subject matter, but is less unified than the earlier work, containing many isolated episodes. One of the best of these is given on page 382. Another is " The Awful German Language," which always won special applause when delivered from the lecture platform in Mark Twain's inimitable drawl. *Roughing It* is entitled to a permanent place in American literature because it records graphically an era of American life which is definitely past. In spite of its droll exaggerations and distortion of facts, it presents a vivid picture of the glamorously romantic West of the late sixties. *Life on the Mississippi* likewise preserves for us a picture of river-piloting which never regained after the war its previously important place in American life.

The three pieces of fiction based on personal experience are *The Gilded Age* (1873), *Tom Sawyer* (1876), and *The Adventures of Huckleberry Finn* (1884). The first of these, written in collaboration with his friend Charles Dudley Warner, can be forgiven its defects of plot for the sake of its portrayal of life along the Mississippi and the masterly characterization of Colonel Sellers, one of the outstanding creations of American fiction. *Tom Sawyer* was deservedly much more successful. Several years before, Thomas Bailey Aldrich had given the first realistic presentation of boy life in *The Story of a Bad Boy*, but Mark Twain went him one better and produced a story which firmly established the boy as a subject for literature, and which in half a century has lost none of its charm for both children and adults. *Huckleberry Finn* was originally planned as a sequel to *Tom Sawyer*, but unlike most sequels it became a greater book than its predecessor. In the meantime Clemens had re-visited the Mississippi. How much this influenced his plan is not known, but Huck instead of Tom became the hero, and Huck's own inimitable narrative of his adventures with Nigger Jim, told with the convincing realism one finds in *Robinson Crusoe*, lifts this book into the realm of great fiction.

Not all of Mark Twain's books, however, are based on personal experience. In his later years history furnished the basis for his juvenile story, *The Prince and the Pauper* (1881), in which the Prince, later Edward VI, accidentally exchanges places with his double, a London slums boy, with consequently astounding experiences for both of them. *A Connecticut Yankee in King Arthur's Court* (1889) burlesques the old stories of the golden age of chivalry by showing how a modern Yankee outwits the magicians of King Arthur's court by the application of modern science and native common sense. Under its fun, the book is also a biting satire of the whole monarchical and social caste system of Europe, to which Clemens attributed many of the evils of the present. It shows a strange intermingling of farcical situations with scenes of pathos and horror. A popular moving picture and a successful Broadway musical comedy have been based on Mark Twain's " Connecticut Yankee."

The Personal Recollections of Joan of Arc (1896) forms an interesting contrast to *The Connecticut Yankee*. From boyhood Mark Twain had been profoundly moved by the story of Joan. Fearing that his serious tribute to her would be taken as a joke by a public accustomed to mirth in his books, he published the biography anonymously. He always considered it his best work, although few of the critics or the reading public would agree. Some resented the blending of fact and fiction, and the treatment of the supernatural, which seems out of keeping with the typical Mark Twain attitude of Yankee common sense.

Clemens' later writings include *Pudd'nhead Wilson* (1894), a return to the Mississippi scene and the passing of slavery; *The Man that Corrupted Hadleyburg* (1899), illustrating the deeper satire of his later life; and his fascinating and startling *Autobiography,* written shortly before his death. The total volume of his writings is tremendous, ranging from the broad humor of his earlier productions to vivid description, lively fiction, penetrating satire, and occasional sublimity.

REGIONAL WRITERS

As already noted, after the Civil War there was spirited literary activity in all sections of the country. Much of both the poetry and the prose was humorous, but progressing journalism afforded an almost unlimited market for every kind of writing, from the serial novel to the pungent paragraph. It was fiction, however, that now came to be in demand, especially the short story. While the short story had been continuously written since the days of Hawthorne and Poe, the new tendency was in the direction of the regional or local-color story. Dialect and local-color poems also increased in popularity. The strongest impetus to local color came from the Far West, but it quickly spread over the whole country, in the short story and in longer fiction and poetry as well.

" The Pike." In the mining districts of the Far West a new type of American character was developed, and was later discovered by writers. This was " the Pike." Bayard Taylor described him as follows: " A Pike, in California dialect, is a native of Missouri, Arkansas, northern Texas, or southern Illinois. . . . He is the Anglo-Saxon relapsed into semi-barbarism. He is long, lathy, and sallow; he expectorates vehemently; he takes naturally to whiskey. . . ." Readers of Mark Twain, Bret Harte, and John Hay will instantly recognize this type. While well known by the name " Pike " in the West, he did not become a figure in literature until Bret Harte and John Hay made him famous the world over.

Bret Harte (1839–1902). Francis Bret Harte was born in Albany, New York. His father, a college professor, intended that the boy should have a regular college training. Frail health, however, made that seem inadvisable, and his education was obtained instead through an omnivorous devouring of books. At first his favorite authors were Irving and Dickens, and he later had an equal fondness for French and Spanish romances. At the death of his father, he unwillingly accompanied his mother to California to join an older brother who had been smitten with the gold fever. The trip to California in those days was made by sea and across the Isthmus of Panama — an adventure for any traveler, and especially for a boy of fifteen.

Bret Harte worked at miscellaneous jobs — in the mining camps, in clerical positions and teaching, and eventually as typesetter in newspaper offices. From there he graduated into journalism proper, writing sketches and poems, and, at the same time, making friends in Grub Street. While he was secretary to the San Francisco mint he definitely entered upon a literary career.

His early sketches were in the romantic manner of Irving, with a dash of Hawthorne, and his poems smacked of Longfellow. As a journalist, his work was undistinguished. The first number of *The Overland Monthly,* brought out in 1868 and bearing his name as editor, was wholly conventional — a real sister to its near namesake in Boston, *The Atlantic Monthly.* But Bret Harte, sensing that the thing was not quite right, had an idea to remedy it — an idea which not only brought him literary fame, but which led to the most important element in the advance of the American short story since Irving and Poe.

Bret Harte's earlier works had shown a tendency to portray the life and times around him; other writers, including Mark Twain, whose " Jumping Frog of Calaveras County " had recently appeared, were also unconsciously writing in this new manner. Bret Harte now decided to make his magazine a mirror of the stirring life and times about him. His poem, " Plain Language from Truthful James," better known as " The Heathen Chinee," was tremendously popular. (See page 779.) This encouraged him to print other poems which he had hesitated to make public because of their unconventionality. Among them were " Dow's Flat," " Jim," and " Chiquita," all of which were distinctly " Pike " poems. In reality, the " Chinee " was a foreigner turned into a " Pike," which made him all the more interesting. As a poet, Bret Harte will be remembered chiefly for these " Pike " poems.

His stories also did much toward winning Harte a real reputation in both Europe and America. " The Outcasts of Poker Flat," " Tennessee's Partner," and many others were popular, and his most characteristic volume is *The Luck of Roaring Camp and Other Stories,* published in 1870.

BRET HARTE

He first used local color in the short story

It was during this year that *The Atlantic Monthly* offered Bret Harte $10,000 to come east and write for it for a year. He accepted gladly — a born and bred Easterner, he had never, in his seventeen years in California, become a thorough Westerner. The gay dress-suit life of the big eastern cities thrilled him and wiped out any thoughts he may have had of returning to the West. It also brought on many expenses which the earnings from his writings could not cover, and, finding himself financially embarrassed, he was forced to accept a position in the United States consular service. His first appointment was to Germany, and he was later sent to Glasgow, where it was said he could be found any place but in his office. When he was relieved of his duties, he went to England, where he died in 1902.

Away from the thrilling environment of California in the days when gold-mining was still uppermost in the minds of the adventure-some, and so much a part of the life of its inhabitants, Bret Harte lost some of his old characteristic skill in making his background — " local color " — an inevitable part of his tale. His stories of the mining camp romanticized the rough, lawless fellow who was a social outcast, who wanted gold only to be able to enjoy its immediate pleasure in the saloon or gambling hall, but whose innate better self was perceived by Bret Harte and brought into action in his stories. The best of these stories, the ones that really " rang true," were written on the spot, and it is the stories in *The Luck of Roaring Camp* that should determine his final reputation.

John Hay (1838–1905). The fact that *Pike County Ballads,* by John Hay, was published the same year (1871) as Harte's *East and West Poems,* the volume containing Harte's " Pike " poems, gave rise to some controversy as to which was the first to bring the " Pike " into poetry. Hay was born in Indiana, but at thirteen he went to live with relatives in Pike County, Illinois, where he was thrown in among the river type of Westerners for three years. He attended Brown University and then studied law in the office of his uncle in Springfield, Illinois. At times during this period he wrote poems, but always in the manner of Longfellow and others whom he had come to admire during his stay in the East. When Lincoln went to Washington he took Hay with him as one of his secretaries. Then Hay served in the War, occupied diplomatic posts abroad, and later became a journalist in New York. Hay had written much verse by this time, but none that matters much except what he contributed to magazines during his journalistic career in New York. Two small volumes contained, among other poems, the few really stirring Pike ballads, and it is said that Hay always deplored the unexpected notice that was taken of these dialect verses. But it is quite possible that the poet Hay will always be remembered as the author of " Jim Bludso " and " Little Breeches." Later in life he wrote an exhaustive biography of Lincoln in collaboration with John G. Nicolay, and served as Secretary of State under McKinley.

Joaquin Miller (1841–1913) was one of the most picturesque fig-ures in American literature and a distinctly individual poet in the sense that what he wrote dealt with personal experiences — hair-raising experiences, especially as he told them. He emigrated west in a covered wagon and settled in Oregon. His life reads better than any Wild West fiction, but it can only be summarized here. With little education other than wide reading Miller plunged into the life of the Wild West. At one time or another in his varied career he was teacher, lawyer, adventurer in Nicaragua, judge, gold miner, and express messenger in Idaho; but throughout all these experiences he had his mind set on poetry. In 1869, back in Oregon, he published a small volume of his verses, *Joaquin et al*, and this he thought might serve as an entering wedge into the literary circles of San Francisco. To make sure, he went there in person, but was both surprised and hurt when he was received coldly. Harte as editor of the *Overland* did next to nothing for him. In New York and London he had similar receptions at first. No publisher would print his poetry, so he published a part of his work, at his own expense, under the title of *Pacific Poems*. Like Whitman, he flooded the offices of the reviewers with copies, and with almost startling results. While Whitman had to wait ten years and more for recognition, Miller became famous overnight, and in a short time a regular edition of his poems was published under the title *Songs of the Sierras*.

Throughout the rest of a long life this picturesque eccentric continued to write poems, many of them not even good doggerel. His best work is based on his frontier experiences. Such are " Exodus for Oregon " and " Westward Ho! " (see page 672). He was a poet of the " great open spaces "; and in some of his work achieved a sweep that carries the reader with him, as in the opening lines of "Kit Carson's Ride ":

> " Room, room to turn around in, to breathe and be free,
> To grow to be a giant, to sail as at sea
> With the speed of the wind on a steed with his mane
> To the wind."

Most students know his " Columbus," with its haunting refrain, " Sail on! sail on! and on! " During his last years Miller lived a solitary life in a cabin he had built in the hills near San Francisco.

THE SOUTH

After the West, the first strong notes came from the South.

George W. Cable (1844–1925) was born in New Orleans and lived there until 1884. He served two years in the Confederate army and after the war he had the same difficulty in finding ways of making a living that fell to the lot of so many Southerners. He finally became a reporter for the *Picayune* of his native city, and that led to his writing short stories about the Creoles, a term used in Louisiana to designate the descendants of the early Spanish and French settlers. Cable's first book, *Old Creole Days* (1879), was a collection of short stories written in the native dialect, a mixture of French and English. It contained such well known stories as " Posson Jone," " Sieur George," and in later editions, " Madame Delphine." It remains his most popular book, in spite of the present-day dislike for dialect. Historically it ranks with the California stories of Bret Harte because it opened up an entirely new region for local-color fiction, but has not quite the intrinsic interest of *The Luck of Roaring Camp*. His best long novel is *The Grandissimes* (1880), a work of high romance, excellent in its characterizations, full of dramatic incidents, and replete with humor. In 1884 Cable moved to New England, but he wisely continued to draw his material from his native state and city.

Joel Chandler Harris (1848–1908) was born in Georgia and described himself as " an uncultured Georgia cracker." As a boy he worked as a typesetter for a country newspaper and lived on the plantation of the owner who had many slaves. From these simple folk he learned the Negro dialect and listened to their many anecdotes. When he had once discovered the value of these stories as literary material he deliberately gathered more, and Harris is today widely known for his transcriptions of these folk stories. In addition to inventing a new variety of fable in his tales of Brer Rabbit, Brer Fox, and others, he created a unique character in Uncle Remus. With the publication of *Uncle Remus: His Songs and His Sayings* (1880) a new type of regional fiction was added to the literature of the country. Harris wrote other things besides the four Uncle Remus volumes, but they are for the most part eclipsed by his own novel creation.

Mary N. Murfree (1850–1922) under the name of " Charles Egbert Craddock " contributed her first story of the Tennessee mountains to *The Atlantic Monthly* in 1878. The masculine name of the author and the distinctly masculine nature of the material of the stories, as well as its treatment, easily deceived editors and publishers for a long while. With her first volume, *In the Tennessee Mountains* (1884), another region was added to the rapidly expanding domain of the local-color stories.

Thomas Nelson Page (1853–1922), a graduate of Washington and Lee University and a practicing lawyer in Richmond, did for Virginia what Bret Harte had done for California, Cable for Louisiana, and Miss Murfree for Tennessee. He portrayed the life of the Old South before the war, a life full of romantic glamour. The editors of *The Century Magazine* hesitated to publish his first story, " Marse Chan," because of its Negro dialect, although dialect stories were much in vogue. But it finally appeared in 1884. As it turned out, Page's stories of the old Southern chivalry and faithful family darkies proved immensely popular. With the publication of *In Ole Virginia* (1887) Page found himself a recognized writer of short stories. In his novel *Red Rock* he portrays the stirring Reconstruction days in the South following the Civil War. Today he is not read so widely, but the stories in this first volume still furnish good reading. His biography of General Lee is one of his notable pieces of work. (See page 319.)

THE MIDDLE WEST

Edward Eggleston (1837–1902). Edward Eggleston is remembered chiefly for one book, *The Hoosier Schoolmaster* (1874). Eggleston was born in Indiana, and in this book he presented for the first time in fiction the life of the Middle West. He was able to portray the Hoosier through dialect and manners so entertainingly that the book remains a landmark in American fiction. Eggleston wrote other books, but the *Schoolmaster* alone survives.

A Forerunner of Riley. In noting literary tendencies it is often necessary to turn to writers once in the high tide of popularity, but now forgotten. Among such is Will Carleton (1845–1912), who reached the ears of the common people with more success than Whitman. Carleton contributed to the papers and the magazines poems saturated with the sure-fire sentimentalities that would appeal to the crowd. A few titles from *Farm Ballads* (1873) will indicate the type: " Betsey and I Are Out," " Gone with a Handsomer Man," " The House Where We Were Wed," " Why Should They Kill My Baby," and " Over the Hill to the Poor-house." The opening lines of the last one are,

" Over the hill to the poor-house I'm trudgin' my weary way —
I, a woman of seventy, and only a trifle gray — "

Carleton wrote many volumes of such verse, and before his death in 1912 over six hundred thousand copies of his books had been sold.

James Whitcomb Riley (1849–1916). Carleton serves to introduce James Whitcomb Riley, who worked the same mine as Carleton but produced a higher grade of ore. For the details of his life see page 673.

In Riley's poems there is much homely sentiment, but he surpassed Carleton in metrical lilt. Genuine melody is characteristic of the

JAMES WHITCOMB RILEY
The hoosier poet

Hoosier poet. He was also strong in devising titles that grip the simplest and deepest emotions of people, such as "The Old Swimmin'-Hole," "An Old Sweetheart of Mine," and a number of others that played up the word "old." That sort of thing always catches the popular ear, and does not necessarily mean that the work is poor in quality. The work of Carleton had too little poetic merit to survive beyond his day, but Riley bids fair to retain the affection of American readers for some time to come.

Eugene Field (1850–1895). Another Middle Western poet of humor, pathos, and sentiment was Eugene Field. He was born in St. Louis and attended three colleges without ever graduating. Then there was some hilarious travel abroad, followed by newspaper work in St. Louis, Kansas City, Denver, and Chicago. In 1883 he became a columnist with the Chicago *News*, a type of newspaper writer just then coming to the front. He called his column "Sharps and Flats," and here most of his poems and prose first appeared. A columnist must be entertaining; he must furnish daily laughs. Field could sparkle with a gay abandon, and it is in the field of humor that he ranks highest. Like most successful humorists, he could plumb the depths of pathos, and many readers prefer a mixture of the two. "Little Boy Blue" (page 675) gave Field a national vogue, and as a poet of childhood few match him. He had a family of eight children and was a devoted father, so there is a ring of genuineness about his child poetry. Field, however, had an unfortunate tendency to be a practical joker, and it is not always possible to know whether he is serious or whether he is only pretending. His paraphrases of the Roman poet Horace are among his most delightful pieces, if you happen to know Horace. Of the whole group of columnists that have become popular since Field's day the one that most resembles him is Franklin Pierce Adams, the " F. P. A." of the New York *World* (page 788).

WOMEN WRITERS OF THE ATLANTIC AND PACIFIC COASTS

Sarah Orne Jewett (1849–1905) extended the domain of the local-color short story by writing sketches of village life on the coast of Maine. Her favorite type of character was a person who no longer took an active part in the life of the present, whose chief activity was " reminiscing " of the good old days. Retired sea captains, elderly maiden ladies, men and women who had once belonged to a reigning social set, and the common villagers are the characters met with in her stories. There is rarely any plot and nothing exciting ever happens. Miss Jewett was the earliest of a number of women writers of New England who once more put that region on the literary map. Her first volume, *Deephaven,* was published in 1877, and before the end of the century a number of volumes followed, of which the best known is *The Country of the Pointed Firs.*

Helen Hunt Jackson (1831–1885). Helen Hunt Jackson (" H. H.") came under the invigorating influence of the Frontier movement but reflected it in an unusual way — propaganda for the Indian. Born in Amherst, Massachusetts, she went to Colorado and then to California, where her New England sensibilities were outraged by the disgraceful treatment long accorded the North American Indian. In *A Century of Dishonor,* considered by many her most able book, she exposed the white man's atrocities. But her most popular work (1884) was the novel, *Ramona,* an idealization of the California Indian and the Spaniard.

REGIONAL STORIES OF THE NINETIES

As the nineteenth century entered its last decade, the dialects, quaint characters, and colorful localisms of other regions began to be exploited. In 1891 Hamlin Garland (1860–   ) published *Main-Traveled Roads,* stories of the agricultural districts of the northern Middle West (see also page 301), and in the same year James Lane Allen (1849–1925) introduced Kentucky into fiction with *Flute and Violin, and Other Kentucky Tales and Romances.* Both Garland and Allen published many more volumes, but neither has ever surpassed his earlier short stories. Allen's novels, *The Choir Invisible* and *The Reign of Law,* enjoyed considerable popularity, as did his earlier short novels, *The Kentucky Cardinal* and *Aftermath,* but " The White Cowl " and " King Solomon of Kentucky," two of the short stories from his first volume, are likely to be read long after his sentimental longer stories are forgotten.

Twentieth Century Effects. The frontier movement had its echoes far into the twentieth century. Owen Wister's *The Virginian* is a delightful series of related stories — almost a novel — about the Western cowboy, the " last romantic figure on our soil," as Wister himself calls him. *Giants in the Earth* by O. E. Rölvaag is another even more recent example of the tremendous influence the frontier has had on our literature. Willa Cather and other contemporary novelists and short-story writers reveal the Frontier in certain phases of their work.

HAMLIN GARLAND

Of *Middle Border* renown

Summary. The exciting, two-fisted life of the Western frontier had invigorating and far-reaching effects on American literature. Its most towering interpreter was Mark Twain. He and Bret Harte startled the reading public by the fresh vitality of their California stories and it demanded more. It is worth noting that Mark Twain ceased being a regional writer — unless one wants to extend his " region " to include the world. Harte, on the other hand, rarely departed from his first scenes, and never with success. His stories of California continued to be in demand, but in retrospect one must admit that his really great stories are fewer than a dozen. John Hay, as well as Harte, caught and imprisoned the " Pike," typical frontier character, in their humorous dialect poems. Humor, dialect, and local color characterized the beginnings of the frontier movement in literature. But with popularity came the demand from magazines and newspapers for short fiction and poems, and every corner of the country was heard from. Joaquin Miller celebrated the Rockies and his own incredible experiences in occasionally inspired verse. Riley intoned melodiously the homely Hoosier virtues. Eugene Field sparkled humor in his column one day and played on pathos with exquisite children's poetry the next. In the South Cable, Harris, Miss Murfree, and Page found a superabundance of color, humor, and eccentricity for their stories. Eggleston's one good book defined " the Hoosier schoolmaster," and Garland and Allen continued the thread unbroken in the Middle West. Miss Jewett was the outstanding woman " local colorist " in New England and Mrs. Jackson on the Pacific Coast. Even in the twentieth century the frontier, most distinctive and peculiarly American of literary movements, fires the creative imaginations of our writers.

IN THIS VOLUME

PAGE

1. An Ingénue of the Sierras (Bret Harte) 79
2. School Life (Hamlin Garland) 301
3. Lee in Defeat (Thomas Nelson Page) 319
4. An Unexpected Acquaintance (Mark Twain) 382
5. An American Hercules (James Stevens) 481
6. The Banks of the Little Eau Pleine 491
7. The Cowboy's Dream 495
8. The Awful Fate of Mr. Wolf (Joel Chandler Harris) . . . 503
9. It's Me, O Lord 506
10. Westward Ho! (Joaquin Miller) 672
11. When the Frost Is on the Punkin (James Whitcomb Riley) . . 673
12. Little Boy Blue (Eugene Field) 675
13. The Limitations of Youth (Eugene Field) 676
14. Plain Language from Truthful James (Bret Harte) 779

STUDY QUESTIONS

1. Point out experiences in different parts of this country and Europe that were significant in the life of Mark Twain. Link up well-known books he wrote with these different experiences.

2. By what devices did Mark Twain produce his humorous effects? What elements in Mark Twain's writings caused him to rise above the other humorists of his day? Which of his books are most strongly marked by humor? Which are more serious? Which contain sharp satire on general social conditions?

3. In what ways did the lives of Mark Twain and Bret Harte touch each other? Which attained greater fame eventually?

4. What type of fiction did Bret Harte introduce? Show how the influence of this was far-reaching. What kind of characters recur most fre-

quently in his writings? Would you say that the proportion of his total work on which his fame rests is large or small?

5. Name as many other authors as you can who represent the westward-moving frontier after the Civil War. In what ways would the literature of this movement necessarily differ from that of the older New England group? Illustrate by specific examples.

6. Locate geographically all the regional writers mentioned in this chapter and point out the chief contributions of each to the understanding we have of the various regions of our country.

Chapter VIII

THE BEGINNINGS OF REALISM

The treatment of the locality by Bret Harte and his immediate followers was partially romantic, with a selection of details which cast a glamour over the life depicted. It was natural that the Southern writers, especially Cable and Page, should follow this tone, since love of the picturesque and the gallant had been their literary inheritance since the days of Captain John Smith; and even in the North the romantic dye tinged the stories of Sarah Orne Jewett. But frontier literature was partially realistic — it attempted to present real characters in an actual setting, and with the frontier movement the more realistic view of life gradually gained ascendance. William Dean Howells, the great apostle of realism, and his many followers advocated that the writer should view the life about him dispassionately and depict it exactly as he sees it, without bias and without glamour. One may say that there was no fundamental contradiction between these two literary movements of the seventies, eighties, and nineties.

William Dean Howells (1837–1920). Howells was born in Ohio two years after Mark Twain in Missouri. Both had little formal schooling, both grew up with small-town " gangs," both were early associated with the business of printing, and both educated themselves by reading widely, and after they met in later life the two men became intimate friends. Howells was at first greatly drawn toward the writing of poetry, trying to imitate the Englishman Pope and the German Heine. Though some of his poetry eventually got into *The Atlantic Monthly*, his literary reputation rests on his prose.

In 1861 he was given the consulship at Venice, and this first sojourn resulted in his two earliest books, based on experiences and travels in Europe. After his return to America in 1865 Howells began to write for *The Nation* and *The Atlantic Monthly;* eventually he became editor of the latter, a position which he held until 1881. By this time he had made many friends and literary contacts, was active in the encouragement of young authors, and through his critical articles, began to have a direct influence on American fiction. He was severe with the romancers and cordial to realists. He insisted that literature picture life as it actually is and that it must not be permitted flights of fancy. Howells did not mean that all actual happenings have to be recorded, but that those that are recorded must be quite possible, better yet, probable, and in the highest form of realism, inevitable. Howells knew what everyone knows, that events so extraordinary as to be unbelievable often occur in real life, but these he declared unsuitable for fiction, simply because they are unbelievable.

It is not possible to follow in detail the long literary career of Howells, distinguished in criticism, in fiction, and to a lesser degree in the drama. He was easily the foremost critic and essayist of his day. After leaving *The Atlantic Monthly* he became an editorial contributor to *Harper's Magazine*. His first novel, *No Love Lost,* appeared in 1869, and, strangely enough, it was in verse. *Their Wedding Journey* (1871) is usually called a novel, but is rather a minutely detailed account of a trip, and its importance lies in its narrative method. It was really an example of what he thought ought to be the realistic style in fiction. In *A Chance Acquaintance* (1873) he showed how this style could be made the medium of telling a story interestingly. The novel was a success and remains one of the author's most favored stories. Others followed until in 1882 *A Modern Instance* won him a definite place among American novelists. *The Rise of Silas Lapham* (1884), picturing a self-made man and his vicissitudes of fortune, is the Howells story most read today. The experiences of the Lapham family may seem somewhat mild when compared with those of the noisy industrial adventurers of the present, but the strong and wholesome character of Silas appeals even though it is portrayed quietly. With the publication of *A Hazard of New Fortunes* (1889) the author broadened his scope by deserting the New England setting for that of New York. This was perhaps one of the reasons why the novel was more successful than his earlier stories. Of the stories written by Howells in the twentieth century the only one that needs to be mentioned is *The Kentons* (1902), sometimes described as the technically perfect novel. While that may be true, it does not necessarily mean that it is the author's best. Although Howells is still too close to the present generation to be assessed with finality, one is on firm ground in saying that during his long literary career a book from his pen was always an event.

For many years Howells was fondly called the " Dean of American Letters." He was unusually gifted for friendship, charming in personality, kind and helpful to his younger contemporaries, gentle in manner, and an unfailing believer in the independent Americanism that came to the fore after the Civil War. As a writer of realistic fiction his greatest weakness was a reluctance to look at the darker and more sinister aspects of life, which are just as real as the others. While he undoubtedly portrayed life faithfully as he perceived it, his perception was limited by his respect for fastidious New England culture. He kept his realism respectable by restricting it to the nobler phases of life. That perhaps explains why Howells the man is more highly regarded than Howells the novelist. Many readers know him best as a critic or as a writer of charming travel books. Still others prefer him for his series of one-act comedies which admirably and interestingly illustrate his manner of telling stories. He also wrote a number of books of reminiscences, both of his own life and those of others. The best of these is *My Mark Twain* (1910) and the last, written at the age of eighty, is *Years of My Youth* (1916).

Henry James (1843–1916). James was born in New York, received a rather desultory education in this country and in Europe, dabbled with the study of law at Harvard, and early began to contribute critical articles to various magazines and journals, including the inevitable *Atlantic Monthly* which Howells was editing at that time. His family was highly sophisticated, and James made none of the democratic contacts with life characteristic of Howells and Mark Twain. Most of Howells's novels have their background in America — and Mark Twain is always an American, even when writing of foreign scenes and subjects; but James was from the first irresistibly drawn to Europe, especially England.

Like Howells, James was greatly interested in the technique of writing, so much so that he became one of the most difficult of all novelists to read. He wrote realistically about life, but it was the life of culture and ease in which he found himself in both America and Europe. He added the psychological element to realism. In his stories one finds house parties or teas among the social world with their interminable small talk, but the author probes the inner workings of the mind and brings out some human problem by analyzing what he sees and hears in these gatherings. Of outward action there is little, but he often makes his reader aware of intense psychological struggle beneath the smooth surface of social intercourse.

In 1875 James finally decided to make Europe his permanent home. He chose Paris first, but after a year settled in England. By that time he had published a number of short stories and novelettes, and from these it is easy to see the sort of thing that interested him most — the problem of internationalism. While he cared little for America, he cared a great deal about the American and his reactions among cultivated Europeans. His first important novel on this tack was *The American* (1877) in which the hero is a rich, self-made American placed in a Parisian society that baffles him at first and eventually snubs him. *Daisy Miller* (1879) portrays a young woman who by her forward conduct scandalizes the European society in which she finds herself. In the *Portrait of a Lady* (1881) the heroine again is an American in a foreign setting, but the real story consists for the most part of what goes on in her mind as she decides which one of three suitors she ought to marry, and of her conduct after marriage when she discovers that she has not married the right one.

With each succeeding novel the style of James became more complex and the details of the narrative of less importance, until there was not much " story " left. This applies particularly to *The Wings of a Dove* (1902) and *The Golden Bowl* (1904). But in the intervening year *The Ambassadors* was published and is thought by many, including the author himself, to be his best work. To his five volumes of short stories James brought the same interest in motives, his preoccupation with inner conflicts, and neat workmanship.

After having lived in England for forty years James regarded himself as more of an Englishman than an American, but he retained his native citizenship until 1915. In that year he became a naturalized British subject, chiefly to show his approval of the course of Great Britain in the conduct of the Great War. He died the following year.

Neither Howells nor James was ever in any sense popular but they did accumulate followers and set literary styles. In their own day the most exciting fiction was that of the local colorists and regional writers, and with this the work of Howells and James could not compete for general popularity.

The Problem Novel. Another type of realistic novel that appeared after the Civil War was the problem novel, or, as it might be called more appropriately today, the novel dealing with some sort of propaganda on public policy. In 1884 *The Bread-Winners* caused something of a sensation because it took up the labor problem. It was published anonymously but later its authorship was acknowl-

edged by John Hay. *John Ward, Preacher* (1888) by Margaret
Deland treats of a domestic situation created when an orthodox
clergyman marries a wife who is broadminded. The discussion that
this novel aroused was made more intense because in England Mrs.
Humphry Ward's *Robert Elsmere* appeared at the same time and
dealt with the same problem except that in the English story the
husband strays from orthodoxy. The same year, 1888, saw the publication of Edward Bellamy's *Looking Backward, 2000–1887,* a story
that reminds one of Mark Twain's *Connecticut Yankee* published
two years later, although in Bellamy's book there is nothing humorous or satirical. *Looking Backward* has a form of communism for
its theme, and it was immensely popular all over the world. Anyone
reading the story today will find it of interest to note our progress, or
our lack of progress, toward the ideal state as outlined by Bellamy.

The Historical Novel. In the last ten years of the nineteenth
century came a revival of interest in the romantic historical novel,
partly as a reaction to realism and due partly to the success of Stevenson's *Kidnapped* (1886). In 1894 Anthony Hope, another English
writer, published *The Prisoner of Zenda,* a swashbuckling romance
that was soon widely imitated both in England and in America.
With these English novels successful in both countries, the fiction
counters became loaded down with historical romances with an
American setting.

Francis Marion Crawford (1854–1909) was one of the most
prolific writers of historical novels. He wrote forty-five stories,
nearly all full-length novels, for he despised the short story as a form
of literary art. He was born in Italy, but was educated in the United
States. However, he spent most of his life abroad, traveling in
civilized and uncivilized countries. Several of his novels were written both in French and in English, and, as one would expect, his settings are in foreign countries. In 1883 he took up permanent residence in Italy. His second novel, *Dr. Claudius,* brought Crawford
an invitation from Thomas Bailey Aldrich, then editor of *The Atlantic Monthly,* to write a serial for that magazine. *A Roman
Singer* (1884) was the result. Crawford was fond of the historical
novel, and the ones known best today are of that type. Readers
who want to test Crawford's fiction would do well to begin with
Saracinesca (1887), which is one of four dealing with the history of
one Roman family; or with *Via Crucis* (1899), which deals with
the crusades. If one likes these he is likely to read more.

Ben Hur (1880) by Lew Wallace is an historical novel set within the life and times of Christ in the Holy Land. In recent years this novel has proved immensely popular with the devotees of the moving pictures, and is widely read today.

Among historical novels that were marked successes in their day and that are still read by people who are fond of the type are James Lane Allen's *The Choir Invisible* (1897), S. Weir Mitchell's *Hugh Wynne, Free Quaker* (1897), Mary Johnston's *Prisoners of Hope* (1898) and *To Have and to Hold* (1899), Paul Leicester Ford's *Janice Meredith* (1899), Charles Major's *When Knighthood Was in Flower* (1898), Winston Churchill's *Richard Carvel* (1899), Booth Tarkington's *Monsieur Beaucaire* (1900), and Maurice Thompson's *Alice of Old Vincennes* (1900). *Monsieur Beaucaire* is probably the best of them all. Not all of these are historical novels in the strictest sense of the word, but they do depend largely upon a background that is laid in the past. Some of these writers continued to write after the turn of the century when new forces were already at work. Of these writers Mary Johnston is the only one who has strictly adhered to her original formula, and she has failed to hold her readers.

The Drama Reflects Realism. Howells brought his realistic technique to the writing of plays as well as fiction, and achieved just as signal an influence on American drama. For a fuller discussion of realism in the theater review the introduction to drama on pages 794 to 806. During these years the better plays moved from sentimentality and exaggerated melodrama towards realistic action, characters, dialogues, and stage settings under the leadership of Clyde Fitch, William Gillette, Augustus Thomas, William Vaughn Moody, and David Belasco. In the drama too there was a reaction to realism in the form of an increased demand for historical and period plays. Clyde Fitch was the outstanding writer of this type (see page 850).

EASTERN CULTURE

In the East a type of writing, not primarily realistic nor affected considerably by the Western frontier movement, was embodied in the stories of Thomas Bailey Aldrich, Frank R. Stockton, and Henry Cuyler Bunner. These three writers were frankly mere entertainers, reviving Poe's art of the short story in a lighter vein, with a flash of French brilliance. They added refinement to our humor, and " cleverness " to our literature. The poetry of Edward Rowland Sill, Aldrich, Bliss Carman, and Richard Hovey and the fiction of Louisa May Alcott seemed similarly unaffected by either of the two dominant literary trends of the late nineteenth century.

Louisa May Alcott (1833–1888).   Miss Alcott continued the New England tradition of plain living and high thinking, apparently not influenced by Howells and his realistic theories.   Although she was born in Germantown, Pennsylvania, in 1833, she lived most of her life in New England.   *Little Women,* the most popular of her works, contains her ideals of pure living, serious thinking, noble aspirations, simple and healthful joys.   It is in reality her own auto-biography.   In 1920, fifty years after this book was first published, over twenty-five thousand copies were reported sold during that year. Her other volumes, too, continue in popularity.   These include *Little Men, An Old-fashioned Girl, Eight Cousins,* and *Rose in Bloom.*   It can truthfully be said that Louisa May Alcott in her books about real, wholesome people not only influenced the lives of many men and women but also created a demand for children's books which took a lasting hold upon the thought and imagination of young-sters by teaching good living in a manner that was real and intensely interesting.

FRANK R. STOCKTON

Creator of short stories and master of the preposterous

Frank R. Stockton (1834–1902). In Stockton's work there is no special pleading of causes, domestic or political, moral or religious. Stockton literally exemplified the idea of F. Marion Crawford that a novelist should be a "public amuser."   Readers of this book are already familiar with Stockton's short stories (see page 65), and they constitute his best work.   In his novels, as in his short stories, Stockton liked to take an absurdly impossible situation and treat it with the utmost seriousness.   Short stories like "The Widow's Cruise" and "The Lady or the Tiger?" show how entertaining Stockton could make his situations and how he handled them; but in longer stories, like *Rudder Grange* (1879) and its sequels there is rather too much of it, even though these novels depend for their effect on the sequence of episodes in the manner of the shorter stories.   By far the best of these longer stories are the shortest, *The Casting Away of Mrs. Lecks and Mrs. Aleshine*

(1886), a rollicking account of two staid Pennsylvania ladies ship-wrecked in the South Seas, who float in life-preservers to an un-inhabited island. Stockton had a fondness for pirates, and interested readers will find *The Adventures of Captain Horn* to their liking, although he does not introduce Captain Kidd or any other famous story-book pirates.

Henry Cuyler Bunner (1855–1896). Although born in Oswego, New York, Bunner belongs to New York City, where he was reared and educated. After a short fling in business he turned to newspaper work. When, in 1877, a German-American humorous weekly called *Puck* decided to print an edition in English, Bunner was chosen its editor. It is the business of a humorous paper to be funny, and to that end Bunner devoted himself both as editor and as a writer of verse and stories. Before long *Puck* was the foremost humorous weekly in this country. Bunner was a delightful personality and a great reader, and had a fondness for New York and its countless oddities — queer restaurants, foreign quarters, and the types of char-acters that haunted both.

Bunner frequently used in his stories the " surprise " ending to gain his purpose. This now common device was tried upon the read-ing public by Thomas Bailey Aldrich in the seventies and at once became a popular fad.

After his marriage Bunner moved to a New Jersey suburb and many of his later stories have a country atmosphere. Bunner made no secret of his adoration for Maupassant. He even went so far as to paraphrase a number of his stories, giving them an American set-ting and casting them in a lighter vein. Concise, crisp narrative was what he admired in the Frenchman, and this he hoped to attain by these paraphrases. Bunner conclusively proves by his work that a terse vigorous style can be as effective for humor as for the somber aims of Maupassant. Bunner did much experimenting in adapting French methods to the American situation and finally worked out a satisfactory form in his brief sketches, contained in *Short Sixes* (1890) and *More Short Sixes* (1894). See " A Sisterly Scheme " on page 116.

Thomas Bailey Aldrich (1836–1907). Aldrich was born in New Hampshire and engaged in journalism in New York for a number of years. After writing much verse which he himself omitted from his collected works, he finally went to Boston, and eventually became edi-tor of *The Atlantic Monthly*. He had a hard time getting away from the influence of the poets beloved in his youth, especially Keats and

Tennyson and Longfellow. Only in his later years did he write more virile lyrics based on the life of the day. He was a conscientious workman, aiming at technical perfection. His attitude may be indicated by mentioning his dislike for the early Kipling. Today Aldrich is perhaps best known for his short stories. (See page 97.) He made an important contribution to the technique of the short story when he introduced the' surprise ending. Aldrich made the first notable American contribution to " boy " literature with his tale laid in Portsmouth, N. H., *The Story of A Bad Boy*. Who has not read this delightful story?

Edward Rowland Sill (1841–1887) and William Vaughn Moody (1869–1910) are two poets who may be placed together because they both had a tendency to delve into the philosophic backgrounds of human origin and destiny, a problem much discussed in their day because of the effects of science on religious beliefs. Moody also contributed *The Great Divide* and a few other notable plays.

Poets of Vagabondia. Two poets, Bliss Carman (1861–1929) and Richard Hovey (1864–1900), have already been discussed together on page 677. Their work represents Eastern culture at its best. Both men were highly educated and both had come in contact with the later nineteenth-century tendencies in Europe, but instead of falling under European influences, they struck out boldly to write lyrics that were meant to put the glow of romance into real life. Hovey's " Sea Gypsy " (page 682) reminds one of the English poet Masefield, and no other American poet has equaled him in songs of conviviality. The famous " Stein Song " is in reality part of a long poem, " Spring: an Ode." The mere titles of the volumes written in conjunction with Carman, *Songs from Vagabondia* and *More Songs from Vagabondia,* indicate the spirit of these two poets. The third volume, *Last Songs from Vagabondia,* was published in the year of Hovey's death. Carman kept on producing fine ringing lyrics until his death in 1929. Both poets acknowledged Whitman as their master, although a glance at the form of their poems shows that it was the independent spirit of Whitman rather than his individual style of expression that they followed.

FORERUNNERS OF THE NEW REALISM

Stephen Crane (1871–1900). Among the many uncertainties about the work of Stephen Crane there is none about his intense realism. Writing when the public demanded romance primarily, he had difficulty in finding a wide and appreciative audience. One should know what to expect from a young and zealous newspaper man who was also a disciple of Tolstoi and Zola, but not many readers of the day were familiar with the Russian and the Frenchman. Nevertheless *The Red Badge of Courage* (1895) was one of the literary sensations of the nineties. Its theme is the reaction of a young recruit on going into his first battle, and the amazing thing is that Crane had never been near a battle, so that the story is created absolutely from the writer's imagination. So far as is known, no soldier has ever denied the sensations described so realistically in the story, while many veterans came forward to testify to its literal truth. Crane wrote a great deal in his short life, was a war correspondent in the Spanish-American War, lived for a time in England where he was fortunate in having the sincere friendship of Joseph Conrad, and died before his powers were fully matured. Crane's short stories, contained in *Open Boat* (1898) and *Whilomville Stories* (1900) may be enjoyed for their conscientious avoidance of sentimentality and clear progression to a single final effect. Crane was the forerunner of the newer realism which portrayed the bitter and the dark side of life as well as the pleasant and agreeable realities. He expanded Howells' concept of realism beyond the limits of respectability.

Ambrose Bierce (1842–1913). Another forerunner of the new realism in fiction was Ambrose Bierce. For the details of his embittered life and mysteriously romantic death see page 108. His vivid creative abilities were expressed not only in the meaty paragraphs of his newspaper column but in the grim, unflinching realism of his studies of horror. " A Horseman in the Sky " (page 108) is a typical example of Bierce's ability to make the flesh creep. *In the Midst of Life* (1891) and *Can Such Things Be?* (1893) " entitle him to his own niche in the chamber of literary horrors."

Summary. Howells contributed the most considerable and influential body of realistic writings in the nineteenth century, in fiction and to a lesser extent in drama. To Howells' realism James added the psychological element. The problem novels, though few in number, were an outgrowth of the movement toward realism. As a reaction to realism came a flood of popular romances and some worthwhile historical novels. A group of cultured Eastern short-story writers — Stockton, Bunner, Aldrich — were not affected by realism. They wrote primarily to entertain. Carman, Hovey, Sill, and Moody were similarly unaffected. Louisa May Alcott continued the New England tradition in her autobiographical novel, *Little Women*. The influence of realism was apparent in the writing and production of better American plays. Toward the end of the century Crane and Bierce widened the concept of realism and sounded the keynote for the twentieth century.

IN THIS VOLUME

		PAGE
1. The Widow's Cruise (Frank R. Stockton)		65
2. A Struggle for Life (T. B. Aldrich)		97
3. A Horseman in the Sky (Ambrose Bierce)		108
4. A Sisterly Scheme (H. C. Bunner)		116
5. Memory (Thomas Bailey Aldrich)		668
6. A Snowflake (Thomas Bailey Aldrich)		669
7. The Fool's Prayer (Edward Rowland Sill)		670
8. The Joys of the Road (Bliss Carman)		678
9. Green Fire (Bliss Carman)		681
10. The Sea Gypsy (Richard Hovey)		682
11. The Wander Lovers (Richard Hovey)		683
12. The Ahkoond of Swat (George T. Lanigan)		781
13. Candor (H. C. Bunner)		782
14. Nathan Hale (Clyde Fitch)		850

STUDY QUESTIONS

1. State in your own words Howells's concept of realistic writing. What did James add to it?

2. What other influences were at work on the writers of the late nineteenth century?

3. What writers seemed to be unaffected by realism? Name three authors whose work showed a reaction against realism.

4. How did Crane's realism differ fundamentally from Howells's?

5. What writers of today would you mention as carrying on the Howells-James tradition?

6. Name one type of literature influenced by realism; one type not influenced.

Chapter IX

THE AMERICAN NOVEL OF THE TWENTIETH CENTURY

The dominant concept that determines the basic attitudes of the serious twentieth-century novelists has been realism; but it is realism modified and varied by the interplay of new personalities and new social forces. Immigrants had been flocking to our shores creating a new kind of frontier within the established civilization of the Eastern cities. Population centers were becoming congested; great fortunes were piling up; labor and capital were wrestling with each other. The industrial world by offering outlet for ambitions and energies no longer directed toward territorial expansion has become our latest frontier. In its first phase the new realism picked up the realism of Howells and James, broadening it to include violence and brutality as well as honesty and frankness. Frank Norris and Jack London continued the red-blooded tradition instituted by Crane and Bierce. The second phase is a marriage of realistic method to social propaganda, exemplified by Upton Sinclair, Winston Churchill, and others. Sinclair Lewis contributed several novels of social attack, made forceful by their painstaking piling up of realistic detail. The third major phase came after the World War in the disillusion of such writers as Floyd Dell and Ernest Hemingway. The local colorists, romancers, and frontier writers were still producing in the new century, but the methods of even these writers reveal the dominance of realism.

Frank Norris (1870–1902) was an almost exact contemporary of Stephen Crane. He learned from Kipling the important lesson that in order to write realistically one must secure his facts and backgrounds upon the spot. He was particularly impatient with the local colorists because of their restricted range of material. Despite *McTeague* (1899), a powerful and depressing novel, not much was heard of Norris until the publication of *The Octopus* in 1901. This was the first of a proposed series of three novels that were to deal in the epic manner with the subject of the production of wheat and how it finally reached the consumer. *The Octopus* tells with much realistic detail of the raising and harvesting of wheat in California under agricultural conditions made oppressive to the farmers by the merciless control of the railroad trust symbolized as the Octopus. The second novel in the series was *The Pit* (1903), dealing with the distribution of wheat through the Chicago grain market. The last one was to be called *The Wolf*, and in this the idea was to be the relief of European famine by American wheat. *The Wolf* was never written and Norris did not live to see the success of *The Pit* either as a novel or on the stage, where it was enthusiastically received. Both of these novels carried further the trend in American realistic fiction that tended towards propaganda, or the problem novel.

Jack London (1876–1916). The son of a frontier trapper and scout, Jack London was born into an adventurous environment in which he could not long resist the temptation of roving in search of adventure and experience. He lived on the west coast, and had become an oyster-pirate and a common sailor by the time he was seventeen. After several trips to the Far East in ships where the spirit of adventure was considerably cooled by hard labor, London became a tramp throughout the United States and Canada, with a jump to the Klondike during the gold rush. Meanwhile he had become a Socialist and a defender of the working classes. At last

Brown Brothers

JACK LONDON

A characteristic snapshot of the author of *The Call of the Wild*, taken beside the ship's wheel

he determined to write and set to work to master the art; the details of this labor are told in his book *Martin Eden*. He has written of his travels and adventures in graphic style, but he has never surpassed *The Call of the Wild* (1903), a glorious animal novel based upon his experiences in the Klondike, and *The Sea-Wolf* (1904), which deals with a sea captain thoroughly devilish in his cruelty. However, many readers like *White Fang* (1905) and *The Cruise of the Snark* (1911) equally well.

Upton Sinclair (1878–   ). Sinclair has been for many years an active propagandist for Socialism of a radical type, not in the sense of destruction, but for exposing the truth in modern industrial and social life. He became famous largely because of one novel, *The Jungle* (1906), in which he exposed the horrible conditions of the Chicago stock-yards. As a story it is not especially interesting, but it still grips its readers by its grimly realistic descriptions and its earnest appeal for the reform of an intolerable situation. It was directly responsible for legislation in the United States Congress to ameliorate the evils so truthfully presented. Sinclair has written many stories and essays since *The Jungle,* two of the best known being *The Brass Check* (1919) and *Boston* (1929).

Ernest Poole (1880–   ). In 1915 *The Harbor* by Ernest Poole seemed to indicate that a new novelist of major importance had made his appearance. Poole, after his graduation from Princeton, had become intensely interested in social problems, especially those having to do with child labor. He assisted Upton Sinclair in the Chicago investigations that resulted in *The Jungle.* Instead of imitating his friend's grim realism, however, Poole wrote an interesting story about New York, emphasizing the life on the docks with which he had long been familiar. While he maintained a high degree of realism, his material and his style in *The Harbor* smack of romance. Poole has written ten or more novels since *The Harbor,* but it remains his best book despite the fact that *His Family* was awarded the Pulitzer Prize in 1917.

Theodore Dreiser (1871–   ). While Crane, Norris, and London were producing successful realistic work, Theodore Dreiser published *Sister Carrie* (1900), causing thereby a mild flurry. Dreiser lacks the stylistic charm of the others, but he has persisted in analyzing keenly and realistically human motives in the seamier sides of life. Among the half-dozen or more novels by Dreiser there is not a single one that can stand on its merits purely as a story, but his followers claim that as a portrayer of certain phases of modern life he is the supreme master. His best work, the colossal *An American Tragedy* (1926), shows a youth, a weakling, under the crumpling impact of modern conditions. No depressing detail is missing, but the total effect is undeniably powerful.

Winston Churchill (1871–   ). Churchill has already been mentioned among the historical romancers prominent when the nineteenth century was turning into the twentieth. He has never quite forsaken romance although in his later novels he has introduced certain modern problems which most readers prefer to read about in books other than novels. *The Crossing* (1904) partly resembles his two earlier and more successful novels, *Richard Carvel* (1899), which deals with the Revolution, and *The Crisis* (1901), a Civil War story. In *The Crossing* the author took up the westward advance of the frontier. Churchill has never been strictly a professional novelist but rather a man of affairs who writes novels because he is deeply interested in certain ideas or problems that he thinks are of moral importance. The three novels mentioned were the result of Churchill's honest faith in his country's growth and development. That this faith became somewhat strained is indicated by *Coniston* (1906), a novel in which the moving force is the political " boss " whose sinister power spells corruption. Unfortunately the author's sense of romance spoils the realism of this story, for he ends it like the popular movie of today, with the villain transformed by the love of a girl. Churchill was active in the politics of New Hampshire, his adopted state, and actively fought the powers of corruption, but not always successfully. Meanwhile he was writing *Mr. Crewe's Career* (1908), another political novel. After 1908 his interest in active politics waned and he turned to other problems. *A Modern Chronicle* (1910) deals with divorce, *The Inside of the Cup* (1913) with religion, *A Far Country* (1915) with the entanglements of a corporation lawyer in crooked " big business," and *The Dwelling-Place of Light* (1917) with woman in modern industry. Since 1917 Churchill has written no novels and has definitely stated that he will write no more. Whether this is due to a feeling of failure to realize social reform through his novels one can not say. During his writing career a new book by him was always received with interest by the reading public. Critics were inclined to give him favorable notice because he was obviously a careful workman, never spending less than two years on a story. His sincerity and earnestness stand out conspicuously in all his novels, but there is no denying that his later stories, devoid of historical setting, lack the interest that readers found in his earlier work.

Sinclair Lewis (1885–   ). Among the younger novelists none created more of a furore than Sinclair Lewis when in 1920 *Main Street* was published. This piece of powerful realism continued the attack on the small town begun by Edgar Lee Masters in *The Spoon River Anthology* (1915). Lewis was born in Sauk Center, Minnesota a community which he no doubt used in part for his picture of Gopher Prairie in *Main Street*, although the setting is sufficiently composite to fit many small American towns. In spite of considerable resentment the book sold in huge quantities and made Lewis one of the foremost novelists of the day. In 1922 he continued his attack on another stratum of American society with *Babbitt*. The title is the name of the chief character, a typical Rotarian business man of a Middle Western city. As a story it is vastly superior to *Main Street* and much more convincing. *Arrowsmith* (1925) is a study of certain phases of science and the medical profession; the characters themselves are of importance for reasons other than those of satire. *Elmer Gantry* (1927) and *Dodsworth* (1929) are generally considered inferior to the first three. Lewis's style is verbose and he is given to cataloguing minute details in order to create a realistic picture. He has added two significant terms to the English language, " Main Street " and " Babbitt."

SINCLAIR LEWIS

The contemporary novelist who coined two new expressions. Do you know them?

Booth Tarkington (1869–   ) might properly be discussed as a short-story writer, a dramatist, or a novelist, because he has done much creditable work in all three fields. In the selection in this book he is represented as a dramatist only (page 807). He has been an extremely prolific author, perhaps too much so, but he has succeeded in making nearly everything he has written interesting even though the interest is temporary. He prefers being considered a novelist, for he has been careful to write his best-known short stories in such a way that they could be strung together to form a more or less connected long novel, and they have been so published. This is true of the two or three volumes of Penrod stories and *Seventeen* (1916). Tarkington began as a romancer with *The Gentleman from Indiana* (1899), followed by *Monsieur Beaucaire* (1900), which is probably the best historical romance yet written in this country. He, like so many of his contemporaries, became interested in social reform and took an interest in local politics to the extent of being elected to the state legislature. The literary results of this experience are a series of short stories collected under the title of *In the Arena* (1905). He was also conscious of the trend of realism in fiction and in some of his novels he clearly showed that he tried to give a semblance of reality to somewhat sugary romances. In *Penrod* (1914) and *Penrod and Sam* (1916) he presented a modernized Tom Sawyer, and these two books probably remain his most popular stories, though their appeal is stronger to adults than to boys of the age of Penrod. The puppy love motive of *Seventeen*, drawn out into a long story, also interests adults more than the group it satirizes. In *The Turmoil* (1915) and *The Magnificent Ambersons* (1918) Tarkington took a fling at modern industrialism and the social problems that go with it, but both are spoiled in spots by sentimentalism, especially in their endings. His best novel is *Alice Adams* (1921) in which for once the author carries a plot to its logical conclusion, although it would have been comparatively easy to give it the traditional happy ending so much beloved by movie audiences. The

BOOTH TARKINGTON
Of *Penrod* fame

realism of this story is simple and direct, there is humor and pathos, and there is suspense well sustained to the end. Both *Alice Adams* and *The Magnificent Ambersons* received the Pulitzer Prize. It seems impossible that the author of *Alice Adams* should have written such trivial books as *The Plutocrat* (1927), and *Claire Ambler* (1928). In *Penrod Jashber* (1929) an attempt has been made to build upon his earlier Penrod stories. Any résumé of the works of Booth Tarkington brings out the startling fact that among all his novels there are only a few that stand out conspicuously, and none of these is truly great. All his books are wholesome in tone, abounding in humor and satire without bitterness.

   James Branch Cabell (1879–   ). Cabell was born and educated in Virginia and continues to live there. His most enthusiastic admirers declare him the most original genius in the modern novel;

his most violent detractors claim that he is of no consequence at all as an original writer. As a setting for his novels he has created the imaginary land of Poictesme, based upon romantic mediæval chivalry, and has peopled it with characters from his own imagination to symbolize his ideas. He is a romancer — but with an individual twist. He does not profess to write for entertainment only but to bring out by irony, satire, and by what many consider humor, the foibles and pet delusions of mankind. He is the complete master of a prose style so smooth, so mellifluous, that, reading much of it, one feels as though he had been drowned in a barrel of honey. A collection of essays and sketches, *Beyond Life* (1919), should be read by anyone who is eager to understand Cabell.

Joseph Hergesheimer (1880–   ). Hergesheimer has written two or three novels of the first importance among American works of fiction. He was born in Pennsylvania and continues to make his home in West Chester. Among his better stories only the scene of *The Three Black Pennys* (1917) is laid there. The book is really a series of three stories, each dealing with a phase of the development of the iron industry under the Pennys through three generations. It is a powerful piece of work and many critics consider it his best. *Java Head*, which disputes the supremacy of *The Three Black Pennys*, is laid in Salem, Massachusetts, in the days when that interesting city was still one of the greatest of shipping centers. The story centers about the complications arising in old-fashioned Salem from the return of a seaman with a Chinese wife. In *Balisand* (1924) Hergesheimer turned to post-Revolutionary Virginia. The first third of the book is excellent, but later weaknesses make it inferior to *Linda Condon* (1919). He has also written short stories, many of them excellent; and travel books somewhat in the form of fiction; his latest book, *Swords and Roses* (1929), is practically history.

James Boyd (1888–   ). Boyd is a Princeton man who has achieved substantial recognition. His first novel, *Drums* (1926), is a reversion to historical fiction and deals with North Carolina during the Revolutionary period. His second book, *Marching On* (1927), which has met with equal success, centers around the Civil War.

WOMEN NOVELISTS

Since 1900 women writers have in increasing numbers made notable contributions to the American novel. Some of the more notable among these are Gertrude Atherton, Edith Wharton, Anne Douglas

Sedgwick, Ellen Glasgow, Zona Gale, Willa Cather, and Dorothy Canfield Fisher.

Gertrude Atherton (1857–   ). Mrs. Atherton was born in California and lives there when she is not traveling abroad. In spite of the fact that she is away from her native state so much, a large part of her work has to do with California. She has written a great many novels, some of which came into the " best seller " class, but her only considerable contribution to literature is *The Conqueror* (1902), a novel based upon the career of Alexander Hamilton.

Edith Wharton (1862–   ). Mrs. Wharton ranks in the first flight of women novelists. Born in New York City, she belongs to a family of wealth and social standing. Ten years of apprenticeship in the writing craft prefaced the publication of her first book, *The Greater Inclination* (1899), a collection of short stories. This was followed by her first novel, *The Touchstone* (1900), and a second volume of short stories, *Crucial Instances* (1901). These books brought favorable comments from Henry James and led to a life-long friendship between the two writers. They belonged to the same stratum of society, and in Mrs. Wharton's stories one meets essentially the same type of characters with the same problems that are found in James. She early declared herself a wholehearted disciple of James and his psychological realism. Most of her novels and short stories deal with the highly civilized life of the larger cities, especially New York, although she often leads her characters to Europe and back. Her style is epigrammatic, ironic, and vividly pictorial, though she is not indebted to James for these qualities.

It is not possible to mention all the novels of Mrs. Wharton, but it may be said that they are all on a high and general level of excellence, the first alone excepted. Her first popular success was *The House of Mirth* (1905), and her best novel is *The Age of Innocence* (1920), which pictures the New York and the social problems of Mrs. Wharton's girlhood. In *The Custom of the Country* (1913) and *The Children* (1928) the problem of divorce plays an important part in the complications of the plot. Her latest novel, *Hudson River Bracketed* (1929), returns to an earlier New York.

Like James, Mrs. Wharton has had a particular fondness for the long short story, or the novelette, a form of fiction not favored by many important American writers. The book generally acknowledged as her masterpiece is in this form, *Ethan Frome* (1911). Interestingly enough, this story is not laid in New York and does not deal with the upper classes. Ethan Frome is a New England farmer who becomes tragically involved in a triangle for which there is no solution.

Anne Douglas Sedgwick (1873–   ). Anne Douglas Sedgwick was born in New Jersey, lived for a short period in Ohio, and at the age of nine years was taken to Europe to be educated. She is married to Basil de Sélincourt, an Englishman, and has rarely revisited her own country. She may therefore be included among American expatriate authors. She has written many novels, most of them interesting in plot and convincing in characterization. She lacks the intensity and satire of Mrs. Wharton, and is more given to romantic touches. Her two biggest successes were *Adrienne Toner* (1922), which has an American heroine, and *The Little French Girl* (1924), one of the best post-war novels in English.

Ellen Glasgow (1874–   ). Ellen Glasgow was born in Virginia and has consistently made her home there. Most of her novels deal with Virginia, the earlier ones being of the local-color type, though not in the same sense as those of Thomas Nelson Page. While she wrote of the days before and during the Civil War, there was none of the sort of thing so much beloved by the South — the glamour of the old plantation life or the narrow provincialism of the upper classes in the cities. She has never had much patience with social class barriers and, under the influence of post-war realism, in her best novels, *Barren Ground* (1925) and *The Romantic Comedians* (1926), she deals somewhat satirically with situations that arise when Southern pride is pricked in its social conventions.

Zona Gale (1874–   ). Zona Gale published her first novel in 1906 and her second in 1911. Between those two dates were three collections of short stories, all based upon the social life of a small Wisconsin town to which Miss Gale gave the name of Friendship Village. Had she written nothing besides these mild local-color stories she would deserve some slight attention as a writer of short fiction, but in 1920 *Miss Lulu Bett* appeared and disclosed practically a new writer. Lulu Bett, while still a small-town character, is a strong personality of universal interest. The book, written in a sharp trenchant style quite different from Miss Gale's earlier work, lent itself readily to dramatization. As a play it won the Pulitzer Prize in 1921.

Willa Cather (1876–   ) was born in Virginia but lived her early life in Nebraska, was educated there, and made it the scene of her first novels. The material of these stories draws on the life of the Middle Western farming pioneers. Miss Cather's pioneers are frequently foreigners or persons of foreign ancestry, and of all the writers of fiction today none excels her in the power of strong characterization. Her realism is expressed in a simple direct manner. Her first real success was *My Ántonia* (1918), which with *O Pioneers!* makes a strong contribution to the literature of frontier life. *One of Ours,* awarded the Pulitzer Prize for 1923, owes much of its appeal to its World War situation. *The Professor's House* (1926), while strong in characterization, is poorly knit in plot. It leaves an impression of frustration, as the author probably intended. *Death Comes for the Archbishop* (1927) is laid in the New Mexico of the late nineteenth century and deals with the careers of two missionary priests and their problems in trying to make the church function properly in a territory which is poorly organized. Miss Cather has also written a number of excellent short stories, and in these her characters are for the most part artists, a strange variation from her immigrant pioneers. The best of these are in the volume *Youth and the Bright Medusa* (1920). Miss Cather holds an enviable place in the regard of both the critics and the general public.

DOROTHY CANFIELD

A quiet lady of New England. Born in Kansas, she is a dyed-in-the-wool New Englander

Dorothy Canfield Fisher (1879–   ). Born in Kansas, educated in Ohio, Mrs. Fisher is nevertheless a true New Englander. She lives in Vermont. Her published volumes are almost equally divided between novels and short stories, of which the novels are the more important. The first to attract attention was *The Squirrel Cage* (1912), and the first to achieve wide recognition was *The Bent Twig* (1915). Both of these are domestic novels dealing with household life in a small town. In her later stories she has continued to emphasize family life as it is touched by social problems, especially the life of families in small communities in which some member feels a sense of repression. Her best novel of this type is *The Brimming Cup* (1921) in which a wife and mother is made to feel that the life she lives is futile as compared with what it would be in the larger world. The best feature of *The Brimming Cup* is the portrayal of the mother and her relationship with her children in a number of situations that could easily have been spoiled by a too indulgent sentimentalism. Mrs. Fisher's later books continue to be of the domestic type. *Her Son's Wife* (1926) gives an unusual slant to the mother-in-law problem.

Post-War Disillusion. Realism after the World War took the form of protest against the herd-like tendencies of the middle class and against their sentimentalism. The " hard-boiled " novels of Floyd Dell, John Dos Passos, and Ernest Hemingway illustrate this tendency.

Younger novelists. Besides the writers either mentioned or discussed there are many others whom it is not possible to estimate at this time. It is more than probable that such newer writers as Elizabeth Madox Roberts, Thornton Wilder, Dubose Heyward, Julia Peterkin, Robert Nathan, Anne Parrish, Ruth Suckow, Glenway Westcott, Louis Bromfield, and others will be heard from favorably. A class of novelists omitted entirely in the discussion is that which deals with the more recent immigrants, such as Abraham Cahan and Anzia Yezierska. Writers of detective fiction have also been left out of this discussion, as have the sentimentalists, who are copiously prominent always. The novelists who are more particularly noted for their short stories will be taken up in the next chapter.

Summary. The types of the novel produced in the last twenty years of the nineteenth century have continued into the twentieth century, although some of the writers of the former period are still living and writing. The sophisticated realism of Howells and James is still distinctly noticeable in the work of Edith Wharton, considered one of the foremost living American novelists. The consciously brutal realism started by Stephen Crane and carried further by Norris, London, and Dreiser was one phase of the dominant newer realistic trend. The second phase of the new realism is shown by Sinclair, Churchill, and Lewis, among others, in the novels of social criticism. Willa Cather has adapted with less exaggeration the realism of Howells and James to modern conditions. The women novelists are making notable contributions. The writers of romance were definitely influenced by the wave of realism. They chose material that was more or less romantic and then attempted to treat it realistically. The most successful of these undoubtedly are Booth Tarkington and Joseph Hergesheimer. Among younger novelists who have done particularly promising work in the field of the historical novel is James Boyd.   The third phase of the newer realism, the post-war disillusion, is manifest in many writers.

STUDY QUESTIONS

1. What three chief forms did realism take in the twentieth century? Name one exponent of each.

2. How have the romantic novelists reflected the newer realism?

3. Which of the women novelists have contributed the most notable work?

4. Can you name some of the new social forces which paved the way for the newer realists?

5. Which novelists in this chapter have blended local color with realism?   Which are romancers with a realistic method?

Chapter X

THE TWENTIETH–CENTURY SHORT STORY

The earlier history of the American short story is given at the beginning of this volume (see page 9), and many of the writers discussed in previous chapters were active in the field of the short story, especially the novelists, for a number of the foremost novelists of the century are also among the best short-story writers. Since their short stories are of the same general type as their novels, their shorter work will not be discussed separately here. Among them are Edith Wharton, Willa Cather, Zona Gale, Joseph Hergesheimer, Jack London, Booth Tarkington, and others. On the other hand, many of the writers about to be discussed are also notable for their novels, but less so than for their short stories.

With the last decades of the nineteenth century the short story became so increasingly popular — because the rapid development of the American newspapers and magazines offered almost limitless opportunity for quick publication — that the writing of short stories became almost an industry instead of an art. The prevailing mode in the eighties was local color, at first with a romantic slant, but soon influenced by all the forces that made the novel what it has become today. In a sense, local color was a form of realism, and it was easy for men like Henry James to adapt their ideas of style to the newer vogue. Stockton, Aldrich, and Bunner also paved the way by contributing advances in technique to the modern burst of short-story writing.

In order to link up the past with the tendencies of today the work of two important local colorists has been left for discussion here because both are living and have published much in the present century. They are Alice Brown and Mary E. Wilkins Freeman, both New Englanders, who have written their best work about the section in which they were born and reared.

Alice Brown (1857–   ) published *Meadow-Grass,* her first volume of short stories, in 1895, and followed it with *Tiverton Tales* in 1899. These two volumes contain her most distinctive tales, although she has added seven volumes in the present century, the latest, *Homespun and Gold,* bearing the date 1920. She has written novels, essays, plays, travel sketches, and biography, but she remains best known for her short stories. Unlike some of her contemporaries in local-color fiction, Miss Brown definitely adjusted herself to the newer tendencies, so that her later work is comparatively free from some of the things the modern reader dislikes, such as exaggerated dialect. Her latest volume, *Dear Old Templeton,* a novel, appeared in 1927.

Mary E. Wilkins Freeman (1862–1930), like Alice Brown, was considerably influenced by the work of Sarah Orne Jewett, but of all the New England local colorists she is the least sentimental. She owes much, too, to Henry James's influence. Mrs. Freeman has published a number of novels and many collections of short stories, among which the best are *A Humble Romance* (1887) and *A New England Nun* (1891). Eleven volumes of short stories bear twentieth-century dates, the most recent that of 1918. At least two of her short stories are known to most readers, " The Revolt of Mother " and " A Village Singer." These two stories illustrate an outstanding characteristic of her work, an emphasis upon women protagonists, usually the long-suffering variety that rebels, successfully, against intolerable conditions or an environment that tends toward repression. Unlike her contemporaries in New England stories, Mrs. Freeman often introduces an element of the bitter into her realism, and in that sense she belongs more to the later period of the short story than to the earlier.

In the sketch that follows, the authors will be taken up more or less chronologically, with brief statements concerning the kind of work for which each one is noted, and in order to simplify the task of selection, only those whose work has appeared in book form will be considered.

O. Henry (William Sidney Porter) (1862–1910). Any study of the twentieth-century short story must inevitably begin with O. Henry. In spite of a present-day tendency among the more sophisticated critics to belittle the genius of O. Henry by emphasizing his shortcomings, he still is America's most popular short-story writer. While that does not mean that he is the best, it does mean that he has the ability to entertain. His influence has been enormous on the present generation of writers, many of whom have been flagrant imitators of his worst characteristics, such as the trenchant phrase, the claptrap devices for creating a humorous effect, coincidence, and the surprise ending.   In O. Henry these are used so cleverly as a rule that the reader is willing to overlook them in the general effect. In the hands of lesser writers, however, they often become trash. An author must be judged by his best work, and O. Henry wrote more good short stories than any writer of the day.   He also wrote an almost incredible number of poor ones, but so successful were his stories that publishers literally hounded him for his work.

O. HENRY

He is largely responsible for the short-story craze of the present day

So far as is known, O. Henry's first short story was accepted by a New York publisher in 1897.   Prior to that he had done desultory writing in Austin and Houston, Texas, where he was engaged in various activities, including banking.   Owing to some irregularities in the Austin bank, in all probability not criminal, O. Henry found himself in a penitentiary, and in two years of enforced leisure he perfected the style that gave him literary fame.   In 1902 he went to New York, where he spent most of his few remaining years.

The published volumes of O. Henry contain more than two hundred and fifty short stories, not including the sketches which make a haphazard continuous story of *Cabbages and Kings*.   Most of these were written after he came to New York and were contributed to various magazines and newspapers.   In a period of about two years and a half the New York *World* alone printed one hundred and thirteen of his short stories.   These figures are interesting solely because they show O. Henry's rapid creative powers, a rapidity that precluded all possibility of making many masterpieces.   He used the same plots over and over again.   His characters tend to be types, but he always gave distinctive individuality to the particular representative of a type in a given story.   While shop-girls are always shop-girls, and hoboes are hoboes, O. Henry was able to contrive incidents and plots that make the reader forget that the characters involved are similar to ones about which he has read before. Other favorite types are stenographers, crooks of every variety, policemen, aspiring artists, and that large class of city dwellers which has to struggle along on small incomes. While most of his better stories are laid in New York, a number of them are not. " A Municipal Report," printed in this volume (page 126), is laid in Nashville, Tennessee, and this story is often considered his best. He drew heavily from his experiences in the Southwest, and many of his crook types he found at close range among the inmates of the penitentiary. His own native South also furnished material.

O. Henry wrote in a style that was obviously intended to be realistic. The reader is quite convinced, at least while under the spell of the story, that criminals, clerks, and cowboys actually do talk as O. Henry makes them talk. But with all this realistic material and the mannerisms of realism in style, the stories of O. Henry are distinctly romantic in impression, and that is one of the many reasons for his continued popularity.

Henry van Dyke (1852–   ). Dr. Van Dyke is best known as a man of letters in the widest sense of that term, having published numerous volumes of essays, sermons, poems, sketches, and stories. Two short-story collections, *The Ruling Passion* (1901) and *The Blue Flower* (1902) give him a definite place among the short-story writers. " The First Christmas Tree " and " The Story of the Other Wise Man " are almost universally known, and are quite typical. He believes that every form of literature should convey a definite meaning. In all of his stories this is plain, although he himself decries the idea of a story's being written with the moral in evidence, for if the story is well done the meaning will be obvious to the reader.

Margaret Deland (1857–   ) achieved literary prominence by her first novel, *John Ward, Preacher* (1888), but she continues to be best known for her short stories, especially those which are laid in " Old Chester," the fictional name for the town of Manchester, near Pittsburgh, where she was born. Mrs. Deland did for this town the same sort of thing that Zona Gale did for " Friendship Village " in Wisconsin, and Dorothy Canfield Fisher for " Hillsboro " in Vermont. Her stories also remind the reader of the realistic local color of Alice Brown and Mrs. Freeman. In her early stories Mrs. Deland introduced the town and its people, starting with *Old Chester Tales* (1898) and continuing with other volumes down to *New Friends in*

Old Chester (1924). While the chief character of these stories, Dr. Lavendar, is her best individual creation, the chief interest centers about the women, as in the work of Zona Gale, Mrs. Freeman, and Dorothy Canfield Fisher. Her work in the novel form, *The Iron Woman* and *The Awakening of Helena Richie*, for instance, is not inferior to her shorter pieces. In spite of the withering effects of the numerous blasts that have been directed against the village type of stories by such writers as Sinclair Lewis, E. W. Howe, and Edgar Lee Masters, the stories of Mrs. Deland, while old-fashioned in a sense, are still widely read.

Richard Harding Davis (1864–1916), slightly younger than O. Henry, had published eight volumes of short stories before O. Henry went to New York. O. Henry is usually credited with being the foremost exponent of the journalistic style in the modern short story, although he never was a real journalist. Davis was first, last, and all the time an active journalist. After studying, more or less, at three colleges he became a newspaper reporter in Philadelphia. His first great chance came with the Johnstown flood, so that at the age of twenty-four he found himself a national figure as a star reporter. While doing strenuous newspaper work he was also constantly writing novels and short stories. He had become the most famous interviewer of celebrities, a large number of whom either were or became his personal friends, for a tremendous capacity for friendships was one of Davis's outstanding personal traits. Davis was a strikingly handsome man and a fastidious dresser. He himself said that he lost his position on *The Philadelphia Record* because he wore gloves on cold days.

One might easily draw the conclusion that the material for his stories would be based chiefly on his world-wide experiences as a traveler and reporter, or on his life in society. In reaching this conclusion, however, one must be careful to remember that the life of a reporter brings him into close contact with the seamier as well as the smoother sides of life. As a result of this experience, his best short stories deal with material not unlike that of O. Henry, except that the point of view is essentially different. O. Henry wrote as one of the class of people whom he was depicting, while Davis maintained a reportorial attitude in a manner similar to that of Kipling. Crooks and dwellers in the slums and along the docks find their place in Davis's stories, as well as the fashionable men of society, and of course characters and episodes from the world of journalism.

His first great short-story success was " Gallegher," a newspaper story published in *Scribner's Magazine* in 1890. From 1891 until the year after his death came a steady stream of work — eighteen volumes of short stories and many novels. He touched practically every type of the short story of his day — detective, boy, love, humor, crook, society, animal, political, psychic, and adventure. Their settings cover the world, both sea and land. The mere quantity of his literary work was amazing, and considering this the quality is remarkably high. However, Davis, like O. Henry, has been hard hit by critics of today, but for different reasons. Readers of Kipling and Stevenson will be ready to admit that Davis learned a great deal from his two favorite authors, but that is no literary crime. The chief fault of Davis is his intense journalistic method, which in terms of story-writing means that he was often if not usually melodramatic. As in news " stories," he liked to create the purple patches which made stories " smashing hits." This newspaper style also had the superficiality of rapid composition. Like O. Henry, he often tried to make his stories realistic by means of his characters' speech, but he remained always a romancer. A delightful feature of all his work is his youthful spirit and he is at his best when his characters are boys or young men.

From the point of view of artistic story-writing Davis ranks lower than either O. Henry or Booth Tarkington, but he wrote many stories that have not lost their interest. His first success, " Gallegher," in 1890, was directly based upon his connection with the Philadelphia *Press* and is a story of newspaper reporting. His last story, " The Deserter," (1916) is laid in Salonika, where Davis was a special correspondent in the World War. Besides these two, his varied types are best represented by the many stories of Van Bibber, the New York society man; " My Disreputable Friend, Mr. Raegen," a story of the slums; " Ranson's Folly," a western story; " A Derelict," a sea story; " The Bar Sinister," one of the best dog stories in American literature; " The Card Sharp," an English story; " Somewhere in France," a war story; " The Boy Scout "; and " In the Fog," a " long short story " laid in London.

William Allen White (1868–   ) has written a number of stories that belong to the older style of Middle Western local color, mixed somewhat with politics and economics, both of which subjects he has discussed in works other than his short stories. He is at his best in stories about children, especially boys. These are to be found in *In Our Town* (1912) and *The Court of Boyville* (1916).

White's fine novel, *A Certain Rich Man,* and his charming essays also furnish enjoyable reading.

Mary Raymond Shipman Andrews is one of the prolific women writers of the short story, having published no fewer than twenty volumes since 1902. Her work is extremely uneven, probably because of her interest in various " causes " which she allows to color her stories. She is an ardent propagandist of patriotism. The volumes that contain her best stories are *The Perfect Tribute* (1906) and *The Lifted Bandage* (1910). The title story of the first volume made her a notable figure in the contemporary short story.

Mary Austin (1868–   ). A patriot in a different sense is Mary Austin. She lived for years among the Indians, studying their manners, customs, language, and what may be called their literature. She has written novels, essays, and short stories, most of the last concerning either the Indians or the Far West. Her best volume of short stories is *The Basket Woman* (1904).

Sherwood Anderson (1876–   ) is one of the writers of the present day who is highly praised by certain types of critics and denounced by others. Whatever the final judgment may be, he has been a tremendous force in the fiction of today, more perhaps by sheer personality than by actual production. He is one of those writers whose work is constantly hailed as being full of promise. His published volumes of short stories are *Winesburg, Ohio* (1919), *The Triumph of the Egg* (1921), and *Horses and Men* (1923). Many of his stories are not yet collected into volumes. The position he has attained in modern American literature is due to his method of writing. It is characterized by a sturdy independence, special attention to graphic realism, and deep interest in the development of character in lives that seem of little or no importance in the general scheme of things. He writes novels, essays, and poems, and he has also written an autobiography.

Irvin S. Cobb (1876–   ) is one of the foremost living exponents of the journalistic style, a sort of composite O. Henry and Richard Harding Davis, not so good as the former but better than the latter. Add a generous dash of Mark Twain, and Irvin Cobb emerges. In Cobb's stories the reader gets the feeling that the author is personally present and directing his story. Cobb's greatest weakness is his cleverness and an absolutely irrepressible sense of humor. He has himself lamented the fact that when one has been funny in a single instance he is forever looked to for a laugh. And yet he is much more than a mere mountebank whose chief business is to

amuse audiences by clever tricks.   Of Cobb it may be said that
when he is good he is remarkably good, but when he is bad he is
deplorable.   It happens that Cobb's best stories are not funny,
although the greater number have a humorous slant.   The story
that made his name in the short-story field is " The Belled Buzzard,"
and one of his best stories is " Boys Will Be Boys."   Neither of
these is funny.   Even when he writes in his most humorous vein there
is one thing that he takes seriously and that is a proper understanding between the North and the South, a theme to which he returns
again and again.   Irvin Cobb has never been able to get entirely out
of journalism; nevertheless he may fairly be said to enjoy a contemporary fame not unlike that of O. Henry and Richard Harding
Davis in their day.   It is also possible that he will yet write stories
better than any he has written, although recently he has sidetracked
himself into the field of the novel.   The volumes containing his best
short stories are *Old Judge Priest* (1916), *Local Color* (1916), and
From Place to Place (1920).

Margaret Prescott Montague (1878–   ) has published novels
but is more widely known for her short stories dealing with patriotic
themes.   " England to America," printed in this volume (page 176),
is her best, although " Uncle Sam of Freedom Ridge " is a close second.   Both are based on the same general idea, that of international
understanding.   The first is laid in England, the other in this country, although its theme is the League of Nations.   Her published volumes of short stories are under the titles given above.

Katherine Fullerton Gerould (1879–   ) is in the direct line
of Henry James and Edith Wharton.   Like both, Mrs. Gerould is
highly intellectual.   She lives in the cultivated society of Princeton
University, where her husband is a professor of English.   She writes
brilliantly for the most part, so much so that the essence of the story
is often spread out rather thinly.   Her best stories are contained in
Vain Oblations (1914) and *The Great Tradition* (1915).

Konrad Bercovici (1882–   ), a Roumanian by birth and an
American by adoption, has written many stories about his native
land, the best having to do with the nomad gypsies and their picturesque life and customs.   Needless to say, his material is essentially romantic and he wisely plays up to it in his style and point
of view.   The volumes containing his best stories are *Ghitza* (1921),
Murdo (1923), and *Iliana* (1924).

Struthers Burt (1882–   ) began his writing career at the age of
sixteen as a reporter on the Philadelphia *Times,* but this was because

he was marking time before entering Princeton with the class of 1904. He later studied at Oxford and returned to Princeton as an instructor. He spent his summers in the West, wandered around a good deal, and finally became interested in cattle ranching in Wyoming and Idaho. His best stories are a mixture of the analytical method of Henry James and Mrs. Wharton and the material of Bret Harte. His first story, "The Water-Hole," appeared in *Scribner's Magazine* in 1915, and it is doubtful whether he has since written anything better. If he has, it is "Each in His Generation," written in 1920 and awarded the O. Henry Memorial prize for that year. The first story was laid in the wilds of Arizona and the second in the sophisticated society of New York. His stories are collected in *John O'May and Other Stories* (1918) and *Chance Encounters* (1921).

Ring Lardner (1885–   ) is a slangy, humorous writer who is highly thought of by some critics because of his penetrating social satire. He writes too much to be good at all times, but readers find him amusing and that is something in these days when real humorists are scarce. The selection printed in this volume (page 405) is the preface to his book *How to Write Short Stories,* really a collection of what he thinks are his best short stories. His gift for catching — and burlesquing — the American language "as she is spoke" is little short of astounding.

Wilbur Daniel Steele (1886–   ) is generally conceded first place among modern short-story writers. Three times he has been awarded the O. Henry Memorial prize, once for his general excellence in the field and not for a particular story. Steele was born in Greensboro, North Carolina, the birthplace of O. Henry. As a small child he lived for a time in Germany, but his formal education was entirely obtained in Denver. He had determined to be an artist and pursued studies in that direction in Boston, Paris, and New York, but although he had considerable talent as an illustrator, he gave up art as a career and turned to story-writing. "A White Horse Winter," published in *The Atlantic Monthly* in 1912, was the first of a series of stories laid in the Provincetown district of Massachusetts, where there is a considerable sprinkling of Portuguese sailors and their descendants. Most of his best stories belong to this period or are laid on Cape Cod, a district that is also exploited in the novels of Joseph Lincoln, though in a much paler manner. Steele's stories emphasize a background that is uncommon and he fits his characters carefully into it, always with a remarkable economy in the use of his material. He pays much attention to style and is strong in the presentation of vivid pictures, particularly of the sea in storm. During the war he was with the United States destroyers on the coast of France, and this provided material for some of his late stories. He visited northern Africa for the purpose of acquiring a different setting, the result of which was *The Shame Dance* (1923); but for his most characteristic as well as his best stories the reader must turn to the earlier volume, *Land's End* (1918) and the later *Urkey's Island* (1926). Steele has never been interested in quantity production, and his stories always appear in the better magazines. He has also written novels but so far he has not been particularly successful in that field. Probably his three best stories are " Ching, Ching, Chinaman," " For They Know Not What They Do," and " Footfalls " (see page 193). In his later work he seems to carry to extremes his ideas about economy of style, so that the stories lack the artistic brilliance of many of his early ones, but Mr. Steele is a comparatively young man, and the position he occupies in American fiction will continue to make his work of importance even though he should not excel what he has already done.

Edna Ferber (1887–) was a journalist before she definitely decided to write fiction. She published her first short story in 1910, and since then she has written much, not only in the shorter form but in the novel also. In her second story she introduced Emma McChesney, a traveling " salesman." The adventures of this character fill three of her collected volumes. In many of her stories she used character types not unlike those of O. Henry, except that they hail from Chicago instead of New York. Her best story is " The Gay Old Dog," and her best volumes of collections *Roast Beef Medium* (1913), *Personality Plus* (1914), and *Cheerful — by Request* (1918). In recent years she has given more attention to novels and plays than to the short story. *So Big* brought her more prestige than her short stories. In *Show Boat* (1926) she follows Mark Twain's favorite path, the Mississippi. Both stories have appeared in motion pictures.

Fannie Hurst (1889–) is a typical product of this age of machine-made writing, and that is not said in disparagement of her work. Though born in Hamilton, Ohio, Fannie Hurst really belongs to St. Louis, where she went through high school and Washington University. Both at school and at college she contributed to student publications, and had a few short sketches published in *Reedy's Mirror*, the foremost literary weekly of the Middle West. It was only after she went to New York, however, that Miss Hurst really arrived. While she might deny the influence of O. Henry, she doubtless owes a great deal to him. In the first place, she adopted his type of character for her best work — the New York shop-girl and the working girls who live in tenements and boarding houses. She obtained much of her material by living among them. Especially strong is her work that has to do with the second generation of Jewish immigrants. Like Hergesheimer and Steele, she has lately developed mannerisms of style sometimes bewildering. Recently she has tried to turn her short-story gifts to the novel. *A President Is Born* has won considerable approval. The volumes containing her best short stories are *Just Around the Corner* (1914), *Every Soul Hath Its Song* (1916), *Humoresque* (1919).

Ben Ames Williams (1889–   ), another of the younger writers who follow the journalistic style of O. Henry, has written a number of good stories but only a few of the highest excellence. His best stories, such as " Sheener," (see page 20) and " They Grind Exceeding Small " are collected in his only important volume, *Thrifty Stock* (1923). The pathos of narrow or stunted experience forms the theme of many of these, and the surprise ending is frequently used.

Summary. The writers discussed in this chapter are not by any means all who have done or are doing good work in the short story. Some, like Edgar Valentine Smith, have not yet published their work in volumes and so they have been omitted. The selection of the authors has been somewhat arbitrary, as must necessarily be the case in a short work like this. Nearly every intelligent reader of books and magazines will probably wonder why some of his particular favorites have been omitted and some of his pet dislikes included. No reader can keep up with short-story production in magazines, and in spite of numerous anthologies and textbooks, many a good story will remain buried in some magazine. Quantity production and set formulas long ago overtook the short story. The vogue of the short story was bound to bring about standardization of methods of production, as in any industry, and this at least seems to guarantee a considerable amount of good material even though little, if any, of superlative quality. The demand for the happy ending is less stringent today than it was a decade ago, but it still functions in the majority of editorial offices, since the object of most story readers is to pass a pleasant half-hour. But the fact remains, nevertheless, that the best fiction, including the short story, is of the serious type, though not necessarily tragic. Occasionally a writer transcends the formula. Nothing is more delightful than a really humorous story, yet comparatively few humorous short stories are to be found among the most famous. In general, the American short story has remained romantic among the popular writers, although in many instances the language is realistic; but realism of the sterner sort is to be found only in a few major writers whose appeal, paradoxically, is to the intellectual minority.

IN THIS VOLUME

		PAGE
1. Sheener (Ben Ames Williams)	. . . .	20
2. A Municipal Report (O. Henry)	. . . .	126
3. 'Lijah (Edgar Valentine Smith)	. . . .	142
4. To Build a Fire (Jack London)	. . . .	159
5. England to America (Margaret Prescott Montague)	. . . .	176
6. Footfalls (Wilbur Daniel Steele)	. . . .	193

STUDY QUESTIONS

1. Explain what the statement, "the writing of short stories has become almost an industry, not an art," means to you. Is it true? If so, why?

2. Which of the writers mentioned in this chapter would you classify as primarily journalistic? Which realistic?

3. Name three reasons for the phenomenal popularity of O. Henry's stories.

4. How did O. Henry's early life and background influence the development of his short-story methods?

5. What three living short-story writers seem most likely, in your opinion, to contribute the finest work in the next ten years?

Chapter XI

TWENTIETH-CENTURY POETRY

Just before the World War the seed which Whitman had sown began to sprout and the fruit of a new poetry ripened. Like some of Burbank's products, this new fruit showed the results of several engraftings. Romanticism caused it to break with old rules and experiment with " free verse "; realism turned its attention toward industrial life in subject matter; the new feeling for psychology made it probe into man's inner motives. Individual poets such as Robinson, Frost, Masters, Sandburg, and Lindsay represent these elements in varying degrees, but the movement as a whole contains them all.

The causes of the poetry revival are several. American poets, reacting against the Victorianism of Tennyson and Browning, relinquished the influence of the English tradition to stand, as Whitman had pleaded, on their own feet. The definite transition of America from a country predominantly agricultural to one industrial and urban called for new forms of poetic interpretation and expression. A complex and experimental age found its corollary in a complex and experimental poetry. The " spineless " lyrics of the Victorian age and of our own latter nineteenth century would not meet the new demands made by the twentieth century.

Mr. Louis Untermeyer, in his preface to " Modern American Poetry," [1] has best summarized the new spirit.

" Most of the poets represented in these pages have found a fresh and vigorous material in a world of honest and often harsh reality. They respond to the spirit of their times; not only have their views changed, their vision has been widened to include things unknown to the poet of yesterday. They have learned to distinguish real beauty from mere prettiness; to wring loveliness out of squalor; to find wonder in neglected places.

" And with the use of the material of everyday life, there has come a further simplification: the use of the language of everyday speech. The stilted and mouth-filling phrases have been practically discarded

---

[1] *Modern Poetry: American and British* (1928), pp. 46 et seq.

in favor of words that are part of our daily vocabulary. It would be hard at present to find a representative poet employing such awkward and outworn abbreviations as *'twixt, 'mongst, ope;* such evidences of poor padding as *adown, did go, doth smile;* such dull rubber-stamps (*clichés* is the French term) as *heavenly blue, roseate glow, golden hope, girlish grace, gentle breeze,* etc. The *peradventures, forsooths* and *mayhaps* have disappeared. And as the speech of the modern poet has grown less elaborate, so have the patterns that embody it. Not necessarily discarding rhyme, regular rhythm or any of the musical assets of the older poets, the forms have grown more flexible; the intricate versification has given way to simpler diction, direct vision, and lines that reflect and suggest the tones of animated or exalted speech. The result of this has been a great gain both in sincerity and intensity; it has enabled the poet of today to put greater emphasis on his emotion rather than on the cloak that covers it."

Without going into detail, it may be said that the new movement in poetry was once more simply the result of man's eager interest in himself, not necessarily in the boisterous manner of Whitman, but in himself as an individual living here and now, and finding expression in the language that he actually used in his everyday environment. In the meantime the work of Whitman was beginning to achieve wider recognition. Poets began to throw aside more and more the older manners of expression and no longer conformed to the sacred traditions of poetic form, such as regular rhythm and rhyme. Magazines began to feature poetry, and in 1912 *Poetry: A Magazine of Verse* was founded by Harriet Monroe in Chicago, for the distinct purpose of fostering the newer tendencies. This magazine, besides a number of others more or less similar, flourishes today and has been a powerful force in promoting and influencing the writing and the reading of poetry.

As was to be expected, there was much freakishness in the continual effort to be " different," but the merely bizarre has been eliminated, and today there is no longer any reason for adhering to the peculiar names given to the various phases of the poetry since 1910. Today such expressions as " imagism," " symbolism," " empiricism," and " vorticism " have little or no significance to the reader of poetry. All that really matters is that there has been a great resurgence of poetry, that much of it is fine, and that in this age of speed, machinery, clatter, and bustle there exists a zest for the reading of poetry rarely equalled in any other age.

Edwin Markham (1852–　　). Like Mark Twain's "Jumping Frog" and Bret Harte's "Heathen Chinee," "The Man with the Hoe" by Edwin Markham hailed from California. His earlier poems of protest had been in the traditional manner, but suddenly he seemed inspired by the tragedy of "man's inhumanity to man" and in particular by the hopelessness of the struggle of the ordinary laborer. While the Millet painting which served directly as Markham's inspiration was well known, it is today much better known because of the poem. The lines of "The Man with the Hoe" were a challenge to civilization, and Markham's voice was heard round the world. The spirit of Whitman had at last been taken in hand by a competent writer and it seemed fair to hope that poetry was about to resume its proper place in literature.

Not infrequently a writer achieves a single masterpiece without being able to follow it up, but after only two years Markham wrote "Lincoln, the Man of the People," and became definitely recognized as the champion of the common man. When it seemed that Markham's reputation was to rest upon these two masterpieces he wrote "Our Israfel," selected as the best poem on Poe in a competition promoted by the Poe Cottage Association in 1924. This poem, so different in theme and treatment from the other two, nevertheless takes its place as a third great work by Edwin Markham. (See page 691.)

Henry van Dyke (1852–　　) was born in the same year as Edwin Markham, but no two contemporaries could be more unlike. Markham was born, raised, and educated in the Far West when that section of the country was still in its pioneering state; van Dyke belongs to the cultured East where he was born and educated, and where, all his life, he has been associated with the higher stratum of society. Poetry has always been one of Dr. van Dyke's pleasantest avocations, his favorite themes being taken from nature and religion, frequently in combination as in "God of the Open Air" (page 696). He represents the older traditions in poetry and has never been worried by any of the newer "isms."

NEW POETS OF NEW ENGLAND

Robinson and Frost are real New Englanders but the New England they portray and analyze is vastly different from that of Longfellow and Emerson. Both recognize the diminishing energy of the section. Robinson turns his remarkable analytical powers on the failures and eccentrics in New England's hamlets. Although melancholy in tinge, his poetry conveys an exhilarating sense of glory in the spectacle of human tragedy. Frost, too, draws upon New England and regards the life there with just as realistic eye, but takes more joy in the simple life of the farmer and townsfolk.

Edwin Arlington Robinson (1869–   ). Robinson suggests the newest and best among the poets of the modern revival, but readers who think that in his work they will find apt illustration of all the varied and freak forms by which the movement was unfortunately characterized will be disappointed. In his verse forms he is the strictest traditionalist, his favorites being blank verse and the sonnet, while the five-stress four-line or other stanza does excellent service for his shorter poems. It should be remembered, however, that Robinson was writing and publishing poetry twenty years or more before the "new poetry" was heard of.

Robinson stands out as an analyst of human nature, particularly of the minds of futile and beaten men. In some respects his deep-probing poems resemble Browning's dramatic monologues, without the English poet's prolixity. One also thinks of Thomas Hardy in connection with certain phases of the work of Robinson, though his pessimism is expressed with sharper irony than that of Hardy; but Robinson is not an echo of any poet, English or American.

Macmillan

EDWIN ARLINGTON ROBINSON

A Harvard man, he has worked in the New York subways and written such exquisite poetry as *Tristram*

In his search for material Robinson has relied for the most part on his own observation and experience, but like so many other poets, he has not disdained the legends of Camelot and has made use of them on three different occasions, the first in *Merlin* (1917), and the others in *Lancelot* (1920) and *Tristram* (1927). His treatment of Arthurian themes differs little from his other work, for it is the individual human problem that interests him always. In each instance it is the disintegration of character and not the story with which Robinson is mainly concerned.

Robinson began to publish in 1897 and by 1921 he had enough poems to his credit to justify *Collected Poems*. This volume was awarded the Pulitzer Prize for that year. Since then a number of volumes have appeared, the latest being *Cavender's House* (1929), a fairly long single poem. He has steadily maintained an unusually high level in his work, with no falling off in quality. While not a popular poet in the ordinary meaning which is based on sales, the demand for his books has been sufficient to enable him to remain a professional poet.

Robert Frost (1875–   ). Frost belongs to New England although he was born in San Francisco. For the details of his life and his early struggles see page 723. In 1913 *A Boy's Will* was off the press, and in 1914 *North of Boston*, both first published in England, created something of a sensation both in England and in America. When he returned to this country Frost was hailed as one of the major living poets. Since then he has published *Mountain Interval* (1916), *New Hampshire* (1923), and *West-Running Brook* (1928), all of which have steadily added to his reputation. Along with Robinson he shares the highest contemporary fame among American poets.

Robert Frost has gathered the material for his poems from his New England life and environment, chiefly from the country and the farm. Always he maintains a common-sense point of view. In his work, characters are not analyzed with the psychological acumen of Robinson, who almost absolutely strips them from their background; quite the contrary, in fact. " The Death of the Hired Man " (page 728) is typical, showing the life of the farmer with keen realism, yet at the same time the three characters stand out boldly and accurately. The language is that which the New England farmer actually speaks, molded into noble blank verse. To appreciate the work of Frost it is necessary to catch the spirit in which he writes. An ordinary setting chiseled into beauty through the medium of speech realistically human, a familiar object, human or otherwise, a common experience — the result a poem. Frost makes no effort to bring out a moral or a lesson, but usually the reader will find a definite meaning if he cares to look for it.

THREE NEW POETS OF THE MIDDLE WEST

Even more drastically than Robinson and Frost the three chief poets of the Middle West carry out the new spirit in poetry. Masters exposed all the many currents of the typical Middle West town; Sandburg caught the violence and the cosmopolitan, hectic life of Chicago; and Lindsay, a poet of the people, turned syncopation and the modern wanderlust to the ends of poetry.

Edgar Lee Masters (1869–   ) was trained as a lawyer and practiced in Chicago. Before this he had lived in a small Illinois village and had gone through the ordinary process of education. He was fond of the nineteenth-century poets and early began to write in imitation of them. Prior to 1914 he had published a number of small and undistinguished volumes. For a discussion of the *Spoon River Anthology* and how Masters came to write it see page 708. This volume became a best seller and raised a storm of controversy. It was recognized as a bitter attack on the cramping conditions of small-town life, on the impossibility of achieving ideals, on the scandals common to all but a few such towns. All this naturally raised questions about living people in similar towns, and Masters was attacked as a scandalmonger by those who wanted

Macmillan

EDGAR LEE MASTERS

He started his career as a lawyer, but has achieved fame with his *Spoon River Anthology*

to believe in the conventional beauty and purity of the smaller community in contrast with the city. Masters is above all a satirist, and the style of these poems is swift, biting, and irregular. He paid attention chiefly to the ideas he wanted to bring out, and if a line lacked a foot or two it mattered little. He has since published a number of volumes of poetry and prose, but he has not been able to repeat his first success, except in a few individual poems, one of which is "Silence" (page 712).

Carl Sandburg (1878–   ). Sandburg is the poet laureate of Chicago and the western prairies. For biographical details see page 734. Although he published a small pamphlet of his poems in 1902, he remained unknown as a poet until 1914 when *Poetry: A Magazine of Verse* featured a small number of his poems, one of which was " Chicago " (page 735). This poem literally shrieked Chicago at the world, and when *Chicago Poems* (1916) appeared both the book and the poet were widely and sometimes violently discussed. Like Frost, Sandburg uses the language of the ordinary man as actually spoken, but the ordinary man of Sandburg is a different person and speaks a different language — strong, powerful, simple, direct, sometimes coarse, frequently slangy, and always colloquial. He is a modernized Whitman describing the multiform activities of a great city.

CARL SANDBURG

Dynamic poet-laureate of Chicago and the prairies

In form the work of Sandburg resembles that of Whitman. Rhyme and obvious rhythms are practically discarded. He depends upon cadence of phrase and underlying emotion for his chief effects. Unlike Robinson and Frost, Carl Sandburg has a definite feeling for the under dog, and he frequently rails at the unequal distribution of wealth and the political dangers underlying the social conditions produced by modern industrialism, although in his later work he takes a broader view of the situation as a whole. Some of Sandburg's best poems come from his deep fury, powerfully expressed, against war. Besides poetry Sandburg has written the Rootabaga stories for children, and a life of Lincoln.

Vachel Lindsay (1879–   ). For biographical details of Lindsay's life see page 744.

His first volume, *General Booth Enters Heaven* (1913), gained him wide acceptance as a poet of the new school. In it one finds the language of the people, racy and noisy, and one sees the Salvation

Army general go to his reward to the singing of an Army hymn, the clatter of the tambourine, and the booming of the drum. *The Congo and Other Poems* (1914) contains his most distinctive poems. Both "The Congo" and "The Santa Fe Trail" (page 745) speed along (or creep) to the accompaniment of inimitable sound effects. Both were written to be recited orally. Lindsay has himself recited or chanted them from one end of the country to the other.

But Lindsay has not limited his poetry to rhythmic chants. His striking portraits of folk characters such as Johnny Appleseed, and of popular heroes such as John L. Sullivan and John P. Altgeld, and his "Abraham Lincoln Walks at Midnight," which is universally admired because it links the spirit of Lincoln with the World War and quietly voices the sentiments of many who lived through those hectic days — these prevent such easy pigeonholing. In 1923 Lindsay published

Macmillan

VACHEL LINDSAY

Migratory art student, settlement worker, ballad singer, poet

a volume of his collected poems, and while he no doubt will continue to write many more, it is possible, judging from his later output, that he may have written his most characteristic works.

NIEHARDT, BENÉT, AND UNTERMEYER

John G. Niehardt (1881–   ). Niehardt studied the folk-lore of the Omaha Indians for years and produced three long poems, *The Song of Hugh Glass* (1915), *The Song of the Three Friends* (1919), and *The Song of the Indian Wars* (1926), part of a series of long poems celebrating the winning of the West by the pioneers.

Stephen Vincent Benét (1898–   ). Until publication of *John Brown's Body* (1928) Benét was considered a promising young writer of short lyrics running to the fanciful and the bizarre. But his powerful epic of the Civil War revealed a poetic talent well able to portray the titanic conflict of North and South with moving beauty. It is notable that both Benét and Niehardt have won esteem by their epics in an age that seems, on the whole, to prefer short lyrics and dramatic poetry.

Doubleday, Doran

STEPHEN VINCENT BENÉT

He went to Paris, stayed a year, and returned with the nearest approach to a national epic that America possesses

Louis Untermeyer (1885–   ), poet, critic, and anthologist, writes four varieties of poetry — parodies, translations, critical collections, and poetry. This is his own classification. He also admits that his early work was influenced by Heine, Housman, and Henley. This is merely another way of saying that he tried to make his verse sturdily independent. In his early work he frequently used over-robust language, but more recently he has ceased to be " dependent on loud adjectives or merely muscular epithets." These are his own words,

and it is also possible to agree cordially that *Burning Bush* (1928) " is far the quietest and surest of his poetry." Three of the selections in this volume are from *Burning Bush* and were suggested by him personally as the best for representing his latest work. (See pages 755, 758.) Recently Untermeyer has extended his lively literary activities to prose, with an historical novel, *Moses* (1929), and a first-rate book of travel, *Blue Rhine, Black Forest* (1930), already to his credit. He is also the author of a handbook, *Forms of Poetry.*

LOUIS UNTERMEYER

Why does he style himself " the uneducated poet "? See p. 755

THE WOMEN POETS

Amy Lowell (1874–1925). Miss Lowell was trained in the best cultural traditions of Boston. For the details of her life see page 717. With her second volume in 1914, *Sword Blades and Poppy Seed*, it was evident that Miss Lowell had joined the group of militant Imagists. From this time on, especially after the publication of her third book of poems, *Men, Women, and Ghosts* (1916), she devoted her forceful energies and strong personality to propagandizing for the new poetry. Without question Amy Lowell was during her lifetime the foremost figure in the new poetry movement, as much by her essays and lectures as by actual poetic achievement. " Patterns," probably the best Imagist poem, was written by her, but on the whole the number of distinctive poems by Miss Lowell is small. In her later volumes she made much of " polyphonic prose," a form of imagism that never had much following. Like all aggressive innovators, Amy Lowell stirred up much controversy and ridicule, but she lived long enough to see that her ideas had taken root and to see many who had originally laughed at her work about-face and openly admire.

Moffett Studios

AMY LOWELL

At " Sevenells " in Brookline, Massachusetts, she lived a peaceful existence, undisturbed by controversy over her polyphonic prose and imagist poetry

Sara Teasdale (1884–   ). Miss Teasdale has brought almost to perfection her intensely feminine short lyrics. Her favorite themes of love, nature, and death are framed with phrasing of unusual restraint, so that every word scores heavily. She is typically modern in her openness and frankness. For additional details see page 753.

Edna St. Vincent Millay (1892–   ). Miss Millay easily ranks among the foremost of contemporary lyricists. Too young to be in the thick of early controversies about the new poetry, she has never been worried by experimentation in poetic technique, nor has she devoted any time to propaganda. Nevertheless she is typical of her generation in her insistence upon simplicity of expression, more in the quiet manner of Frost and not with the noise and tumult of Sandburg and Lindsay, and with more singing quality than any of them. Miss Millay's reputation was established by " Renascence,"

Macmillan and E. O. Hoppé

SARA TEASDALE

Delicate craftsmanship and authentic loveliness distinguish her lyrics

a serious brooding poem especially remarkable because of her youth. She was barely twenty at the time. This was printed in her first volume, *Renascence* (1917). Besides the title poem, this volume contains " God's World " and some of her best sonnets. In her second book, *A Few Figs from Thistles* (1920), she adulterated her lyric powers with flippant cynicism, but *Second April* (1921) confirms her alliance with the new spirit — the joy of living and loving here and now. *The Harp-Weaver and Other Poems* (1924) is notable for the title poem

and its sonnets, a form in which Miss Millay excels, and there is sounded a distinctly increasing disillusionment. Her latest volume, *The Buck in the Snow* (1928), conveys the same impression. Besides these volumes of poems, Miss Millay has written short stories, plays, and the libretto of one grand opera.

Elinor Wylie (1886–1928) was a more versatile writer than her feminine contemporaries, Sara Teasdale and Edna St. Vincent Millay. Her poetic style lacks the simplicity of Miss Millay and she is more forceful than Miss Teasdale by

Brandt and Brandt

EDNA ST. VINCENT MILLAY
Her lyric notes prevail

virtue of an emotionalism which seems severely curbed. Often there is a staccato movement to her lines, most effective in the poems which are either somber or pessimistic. Her first volume, *Nets to Catch the Wind* (1921), small though it was, clearly indicated that a new major lyric poet had arrived. In her last volume, *Angels and Earthly Creatures* (1929), published shortly after her death, pessimism is the chief note, but there was no falling off in technique. Her three novels also exhibit her close attention to a distinctly personal style and are admired by readers who enjoy adroit use of language.

Summary. In response to Whitman's trumpet call, and in answer to the new poetry needs which were brought to the fore by changing social conditions, the new poetry came in a great wave. Twentieth-century poets expanded the traditional verse forms, although many continued to use rhyme and conventional rhythms, claimed the whole complex structure of American society for their subject matter, and insisted on realism of phrasing and approach. Of the new masters, Frost and Robinson represent New England; Masters, Sandburg, and Lindsay, the Middle West; and Amy Lowell, Sara Teasdale, Elinor Wylie, and Edna St. Vincent Millay easily stand out among the many women poets. Amy Lowell and Louis Untermeyer have done the most in an " extra-poetic " way to establish the new spirit. Niehardt and Benét will be remembered for their fine epics.

IN THIS VOLUME

See the section Twentieth-Century Poetry, pages 687 to 776.

STUDY QUESTIONS

1. Name three causes of the poetry revival in the twentieth century.

2. What would you say are the cardinal principles of the contemporary poetic credo?

3. How does the realism of Frost and Robinson principally differ from that of Sandburg?

4. Did the new poets win a more complete victory in the field of poetic subject matter or in the field of verse form? State the arguments on both sides.

5. Do you consider the new poets " romantic at heart " ?

6. Which of the poets mentioned in this chapter still use conventional rhyme? and which use conventional rhythm?

Chapter XII

OTHER TWENTIETH-CENTURY LITERATURE

The modern drama, humorous writers of today, and the authors of biographies and autobiographies have been fully discussed in the prefatory essays to those sections. There remain, however, a number of writers who for one reason or another do not seem to belong definitely with any special group, and these will be taken up briefly here.

NATURE WRITERS

Since Thoreau a few naturalists have revealed a sufficiently literary touch to merit inclusion in a history of literature.

John Burroughs (1837–1921). Unquestionably the foremost among these few was John Burroughs. He was born and reared on a farm in New York, and worked for the government for twenty years (1864–1884), but his fondness for outdoor life, with its birds and flowers, was always his chief passion. While a government clerk in Washington he wrote his first book, *Wake-Robin* (1871), and sixteen more of a similar nature appeared between that time and the year of his death. Since then three additional collections have been made up from his miscellaneous papers. He also wrote three volumes of poems, and a few biographies, one on his friend Walt Whitman and another on Audubon. So large a body of writing on practically the same theme must be of differing merit, and it happens that the volumes most read today are his earliest. Besides the one already mentioned there are *Winter Sunshine* (1875), *Birds and Poets* (1877), and *Locusts and Wild Honey* (1877). One of the qualities that keep the work of Burroughs fresh and readable is the poetic imagination with which he was able to see all objects in Nature, and a style aptly in keeping with it.

John Muir (1838–1914). Muir was born in Scotland but was reared on a farm in Wisconsin, whither his parents had come as immigrants. He was more of a scientific naturalist than Burroughs, but equally sensitive to the glow that the outdoors imparts. Primarily a botanist, a zoölogist, and a geologist, he had a remarkable zest for the pursuit of knowledge through direct observation. He made long trips, his favorite region being the Pacific coast, especially the Sierra Nevada Mountains. In *The Story of My Boyhood and Youth* (1913) he tells how the life about him on the Wisconsin farm stirred him into an enthusiasm for Nature and how he started on his career. The book is one of the most interesting autobiographies in the language. Other characteristic works are *A Thousand-Mile Walk to the Gulf* (1916), *My First Summer in the Sierras* (1911), and *Travels in Alaska* (1915). These indicate the range of his travels and the extent of his curiosity. The life of John Muir forms a most interesting contrast to that of Burroughs, who was content to live almost entirely at one place.

Ernest Thompson Seton (1860–   ). Seton was born in England but spent his boyhood and youth in the Canadian backwoods and the western plains of this country. He helped in the organization of the Boy Scouts, and has gone the length and breadth of the country lecturing in behalf of this movement, on his adventures in the West, and on the wild animals that are his chief interest. The range of his topics is indicated by the titles of some of his books: *Wild Animals I Have Known* (1898), *The Biography of a Grizzly* (1900), *Lives of the Hunted* (1901), and *Wild Animals at Home* (1913).

Dallas Lore Sharp (1870–1929). After being educated for the ministry and preaching three years Sharp became a librarian, was on the staff of *The Youth's Companion* for several years, and was professor of English in Boston University until his death in 1929. His books have to do with one aspect or another of Nature. The first was *Wild Life Near Home* (1901). Other characteristic titles are *Where Rolls the Oregon* (1914), and *The Spirit of the Hive* (1925). He has written many others, but these indicate the range of his interests. He writes in a style that is vivid with details of his particular subject, and an enthusiasm that is infectious.

William Beebe (1877–   ) differs distinctly from preceding nature writers. He is definitely a practicing scientist, his specialty being ornithology, the science of birds. He is one of a number of great American scientists who have been enabled to carry on their investigations through the American Museum of Natural History in New York. Beebe is mentioned here not because of his fame as a scientist but because he has written a number of books on his favorite topics that are literary as well as scientific. He writes not only about birds but also about his many adventures and researches in this country and elsewhere, in a quick-flowing prose style. *Two Bird-Lovers in Mexico* (1905), *Jungle Peace* (1918), *Jungle Days* (1925), and *Pheasant Jungles* (1927) are a few of his best books. In recent years he has carried on investigations under the sea, doing the actual diving himself. The results have been most remarkable, and no book of adventure stories can equal *The Arcturus Adventure* (1926) and *Beneath Tropic Seas* (1928).

INFORMAL ESSAYISTS

The informal essay is the free, untrammeled expression of an author's personality or opinion, usually on a subject connected with everyday life rather than one requiring profound thought or scholarship. (See also pages 217–219.) Many of the authors discussed in this book have written informal essays, but those here chosen for special attention are best known for this particular form of writing.

Edgar W. Howe (1854–   ), or Ed Howe, as he is familiarly called began his literary career as a novelist with *The Story of a Country Town*. But he has also proved his worth in the field of the essay by his *Daily Notes of a Trip Around the World* (1907) and by *Ventures in Common Sense* (1924). His home is in Atchison, Kansas, where he is owner and publisher of *E. W. Howe's Monthly*.

Agnes Repplier (1858–   ) holds the unique position in American literature of being a woman who has won high honors by the writing of essays alone. While other women, such as Dorothy Canfield Fisher (page 267), have done highly creditable work in essay writing, this has usually been a side-line, and their greater reputation rests on fiction, drama, or poetry. Miss Repplier's parents were French, but she was born in Philadelphia. Her convent education was supplemented by degrees from several eastern universities. Since her first book of essays, *Books and Men* (1888), she has issued more than a dozen delightful volumes, keen in perception, incisive in language, tasteful and individual in style. Only a few, scattered over her long career, are: *Essays in Miniature* (1892), *In the Dozy Hours* (1894), *In Our Convent Days* (1905), *A Happy Half Century* (1908), *Americans and Others* (1912), *Points of Friction* (1920), *Under Dispute* (1924).

Samuel McChord Crothers (1857–1927), like Henry van Dyke, was a clergyman by profession, having been pastor of the First

Unitarian Church of Cambridge, Massachusetts, for over thirty years. He was, however, a New Englander by adoption rather than by birth, for he was born in Oswego, Illinois, and his early pastorates were in California and Nevada. His indebtedness to Charles Lamb and the eighteenth-century essayists is suggested by the title of his first volume, *The Gentle Reader* (1903). Like Miss Repplier, he has issued volumes of essays at intervals of two or three years over a long period of time. Some of them are *The Pardoner's Wallet* (1905), *By the Christmas Fire* (1908), *Humanly Speaking* (1912), *The Dame School of Experience* (1920), and *The Cheerful Giver* (1923). His essays have a rich vein of humor, and appeal to persons of scholarly attainments and literary background.

Ray Stannard Baker (1870–   ) is known under his own name as former editor of *McClure's Magazine* and *The American Magazine,* and as Director of the Press Bureau of the American Peace Commission to Paris in 1919 after the war. He is better known to the reading public, however, as " David Grayson," a pseudonym under which he has written several volumes of essays on country life, which display a cheerful philosophy, pleasing and comprehensible to the average reader. The titles, *Adventures in Contentment* (1907), *Adventures in Friendship* (1910), *The Friendly Road* (1913), and *Great Possessions* (1917), suggest his genial, optimistic attitude.

Charles S. Brooks (1878–   ) and **Walter Prichard Eaton** (1878–   ) have already been discussed and represented by selections in the Essay Section. (See pages 263 and 255.) They resemble each other in the wide variety of their subjects and the vivacity of their style. Their essays are usually easier reading than those of Miss Repplier and Dr. Crothers, but have a more scholarly background than David Grayson's. Both are great travelers and have made wide use of their experiences in their essays, but Brooks' inclination is toward the European scene, while Eaton's is toward adventure in the outdoors. Some of their titles are suggestive of these differences. Witness Brooks' *Chimney Pot Papers* (1919), *Hints to Pilgrims* (1921) and *Roundabout to Canterbury* (1926); and in contrast, Eaton's *Green Trails and Upland Pastures* (1917), *Skyline Camps* (1922), and *A Bucolic Attitude* (1926). Eaton has also done a great deal of work in dramatic criticism.

Christopher Morley (1890–   ), unlike the others of this group, has written considerable fiction and poetry, but his chief reputation rests on his essay writing, for which he seems better fitted in style and personality. His experience as a Rhodes Scholar at Oxford gave a distinctly English flavor to his earlier volumes, but throughout all of them there is evident the keen observation, geniality, and ready humor of the born informal essayist. (See page 219.)

THE CRITICAL ESSAYISTS

The essay which pronounces critical judgment on literature probably appeals less to high school students than any other type in this book, because it is less concrete, and presupposes a wider literary experience than the student is likely to have before he enters college. Therefore the critical essay will be treated briefly.

WOODROW WILSON

American protagonist for world peace, one time President of Princeton University, later President of the United States, and distinguished man of letters

Paul Elmer More (1864–) is perhaps the most profound of the literary critics living today. He was born in St. Louis, holds degrees from five universities, has taught at Harvard and Bryn Mawr, and has been on the editorial staff of *The Independent,* the New York *Evening Post,* and *The Nation.* Since 1904 he has published at intervals eleven volumes in a series known as the *Shelburne Essays,* in which he has painted a vast canvas of literary celebrities. Out of more than a hundred of these, however, only about a dozen treat of American subjects. Stuart Sherman has wittily said of him, " If W. D. Howells was the dean of our fiction, Mr. More is the bishop of our criticism."

William Lyon Phelps (1865–   ), a native of New Haven, Connecticut, has remained in the city of his birth, having been on the faculty of Yale University since 1892. The list of his publications is astonishingly long, covering essays on the novel, the drama, poetry, and a large number of individual writers both in English and foreign literatures. *As I Like It* (1923) is the clever title of a series of brief comments and literary gossip originally appearing in

Scribner's Magazine. Adventures and Confessions (1926) turns more to the field of religion and philosophy. *Happiness* (1927) discusses pertinently the essential values of life.

Stuart P. Sherman (1881–1927) was an Iowan by birth but a New Englander by education at Williams and Harvard. He carried the New England tradition back to the Middle West, where he served for many years in the English departments of Northwestern University and the University of Illinois. He was also the literary editor of the New York *Herald-Tribune*. Until just before his death Sherman was a conservative critic, looking askance at the modern tendency to picture the dregs of life, and urging the older virtues of dignity and reserve. In addition to his critical volumes such as *Americans* (1922), *Points of View* (1924), *Critical Woodcuts* (1926), and *Main Stream* (1927), he has written some charming personal essays, *My Dear Cornelia* (1924) and *Letters to a Lady in the Country* (1925).

LEWIS MUMFORD

Philosopher, critic, biographer of Melville

H. L. Mencken (1880–   ). In strong contrast to Sherman stands the leader of radical criticism, H. L. Mencken, who has been likened to a gadfly because of the stings he has administered to all phases of American life through his magazine, *The American Mercury*. Mencken is the sworn foe of sentiment, smugness, and mediocrity. No tradition of literature is safe from his pen, and his ideas as set forth in a series of volumes called *Prejudices* (1919–1922) will stimulate or irritate according to the reader's preconceived notions and attitudes. His prose style, bombastic, consciously irritating, but none the less effective, has been widely imitated.

Carl Van Doren (1885–   ), a native of Illinois and a graduate of the university of that state, has been editor of *The Nation* and *The Century Magazine,* and is now editor-in-chief of the Literary Guild. He is a serious student of literature and has done much to put in easily available form estimates of the work of recent writers. Notable volumes of his are *The American Novel* (1921), *Contem-*

porary American Novelists (1922), *Many Minds* (1924), and *The Ninth Wave* (1926). (See page 276 for selection.)

BIOGRAPHY AND AUTOBIOGRAPHY

The importance of the twentieth century as an age of biography has already been discussed (see page 297). Writers of biographies have been so numerous and so often engaged in other types of writing that it is hard to select special ones for emphasis.

PAUL DE KRUIF

His books relate the incredibly romantic stories of the hard-headed men of science

Henry Adams (1838–1918). In 1918 there appeared the most notable and most discussed auto-biography of the twentieth century, *The Education of Henry Adams.* The author belonged to the fourth generation of the famous Adams family. His father was Charles Francis Adams, minister to England; his grandfather was John Quincy Adams, and his great-grandfather John Adams, both Presidents of the United States. Henry Adams presents with ironic force the disadvantage of a background and education such as his for meeting the problems of modern life.

Gamaliel Bradford (1867–   ). In contrast to Adams, whose reputation rests largely on a single challenging work, we find another scion of an aristocratic Boston family bombarding the reader with an astonishing series of biographies written in an unusually clear and trenchant style. Gamaliel Bradford can be said to be more distinctly a biographer by profession than any one else who is doing that type of work today. His books fall into certain interesting groups. His first trilogy centered around the Civil War with *Lee the American* (1912), *Confederate Portraits* (1914), and *Union Portraits* (1926). Then came his interest in women's lives with *Portraits of Women* (1916) and *Portraits of American Women* (1919), followed after an interval by *Wives* (1925). The third group suggests the world's unsuccessful ones with *Damaged Souls* (1923) and *Bare Souls* (1924). Such opposite types as *Darwin* (1926) and *Dwight L. Moody* (1927) have occupied his attention most recently.

Paul de Kruif (1890–   ). A younger man, Paul de Kruif (see page 278), has introduced an original note into biography by his lives of men who have won distinction in fields too little celebrated in literature. *Microbe Hunters* (1926), *Hunger Fighters* (1928), and *Seven Iron Men* (1929) are his suggestive titles. These lives are told with the descriptive power, the suspense, and the use of climax which we usually associate with fiction. They emphasize the romance and drama of the great world changes stirring underneath the surface of everyday living.

WRITERS OF HUMOR

The last years of the nineteenth century gave birth to two outstanding humorous creations which were to continue in popularity far into the twentieth century. These were *Fables in Slang* by George Ade (1866–   ) and *Mr. Dooley* by Finley Peter Dunne (1867–   ). The first has been discussed and illustrated (see page 392). The second is the Irish character through whose mouth Dunne commented on American life and politics to the delight of the American people. It has been said that if all other records of the first decade of this century were to be lost, we could still have a pretty complete idea of its public affairs through the comments of Mr. Dooley. Numerous volumes with *Mr. Dooley* as part of the title were collected and published between 1898 and 1919.

Other writers of humor flourishing in this century have been discussed in the Humor Section and need only be reassembled here. Don Marquis, Christopher Morley, Bert Leston Taylor (B. L. T.), and Franklin P. Adams (F. P. A.) are the outstanding columnists who keep the public merry through the daily papers. Robert Benchley, Stephen Leacock (Canadian), and Donald Ogden Stewart have specialized largely in parody, and have each issued many volumes which have attained great popularity. Irvin Cobb can scarcely escape his preëminence as a humorist, though he prefers to be considered a writer of fiction.

Summary. With its many varied types of literature, its freedom from old traditions, its large number of vigorous young writers, and its rapidly changing conditions provocative of expression, our twen-

tieth century, now having passed almost a third of its life, bids fair
to stand out in the eyes of the future as one of the great creative
periods in American literature.

IN THIS VOLUME

Drama

1. The Trysting Place (Booth Tarkington) 807
2. Where the Cross Is Made (Eugene O'Neill) 831

Essays

1. The Century (Christopher Morley) 219
2. Mary White (William Allen White) 223
3. Valentine Vagaries (Lafcadio Hearn) 253
4. The Bubble Reputation (Walter Prichard Eaton) 255
5. Once There Was a Furnace Boy (Charles S. Brooks) . . . 263
6. Vermont (Dorothy Canfield Fisher) 267
7. A Note on the Essay (Carl Van Doren) 276
8. Walter Reed (Paul de Kruif) 278

Biography and Autobiography

1. Practical Politics (Theodore Roosevelt) 325
2. Henry David Thoreau (J. Arthur Myers) 333
3. Hawthorne at College (Lloyd Morris) 340
4. Herman Melville Writes *Moby-Dick* (Lewis Mumford) . . . 346

Humorous Prose

1. Hermione (" Prison Reform " and " The Spirit of Christmas ")
   (Don Marquis) 362–4
2. The Fable of the Wonderful Meal of Vittles (George Ade) . . 392
3. Long Pants (Irvin Cobb) 396
4. How to Write Short Stories (Ring Lardner) 405
5. Correct Behavior on a Picnic (Donald Ogden Stewart) . . . 409

State Papers

1. The War Message (Woodrow Wilson) 461
2. A League for Peace (Woodrow Wilson) 471
3. The Peace Pact (Frank B. Kellogg) 477

STUDY QUESTIONS

1. How many types of literature are discussed in this chapter? Name one outstanding writer of each type.

2. What signs are there that contemporary prose will stand high in the estimation of posterity?

3. What names would you add to those given under the heading of "Informal Essayists"? For those under the heading, "Critical Essayists"?

4. What humorous writers stand out today?

NOVELS FOR HOME READING

GOOD ENTERTAINMENT: THRILLS, LAUGHS, AND TEARS

Mark Twain. *Tom Sawyer. Huckleberry Finn*
Owen Johnson. *The Varmint*
Booth Tarkington. *Seventeen. The Plutocrat*
Harry Leon Wilson. *Merton of the Movies*
E. N. Westcott. *David Harum*
Frank R. Stockton. *The Casting Away of Mrs. Lecks and Mrs. Aleshine.*
    Rudder Grange. The Adventures of Captain Horn
Thomas Nelson Page. *The Old Gentleman of the Black Stock*
Frances Hodgson Burnett. *T. Tembarom*
James Lane Allen. *A Kentucky Cardinal*
Richard Harding Davis. *Soldiers of Fortune*

HISTORICAL NOVELS WITH FOREIGN SETTINGS

Mark Twain. *The Prince and the Pauper. A Connecticut Yankee in*
    King Arthur's Court
Lew Wallace. *Ben Hur*
William Stearns Davis. *A Friend of Caesar. The Beauty of the Purple*
Charles Major. *Dorothy Vernon of Haddon Hall. When Knighthood*
    Was in Flower
F. Marion Crawford. *In the Palace of the King*
Booth Tarkington. *Monsieur Beaucaire* (novelette)

THE STORY OF AMERICA
Colonial Days

Mary Johnston. *To Have and to Hold*
James Fenimore Cooper. *The Deerslayer. The Last of the Mohicans.*
    The Pathfinder
Irving Bacheller. *In the Days of Poor Richard*

The Revolution

James Fenimore Cooper. *The Pilot. The Spy*
Winston Churchill. *Richard Carvel*
Paul Leicester Ford. *Janice Meredith*
S. Weir Mitchell. *Hugh Wynne, Free Quaker*
James Boyd. *Drums*
Gertrude Atherton. *The Conqueror*

From the Revolution to the Civil War

Mark Twain. *The Gilded Age*
Helen Hunt Jackson. *Ramona*
Winston Churchill. *The Crossing*
Edna Ferber. *Show Boat*
Herman Melville. *Moby-Dick*. *Typee*
Joseph Hergesheimer. *Java Head*
Stewart Edward White. *Gold*

The Civil War and Reconstruction

F. Hopkinson Smith. *Colonel Carter of Cartersville*
Irving Bacheller. *A Man for the Ages*
Winston Churchill. *The Crisis*
Honoré Willsie Morrow. *Benefits Forgot*
John Fox, Jr. *The Little Shepherd of Kingdom Come*
James Boyd. *Marching On*
Thomas Nelson Page. *Red Rock*
Owen Wister. *Lady Baltimore*

The Later Frontier

Hamlin Garland. *Trail-Makers of the Middle Border*
Willa Cather. *My Antonia*. *Death Comes for the Archbishop*
Stewart Edward White. *The Blazed Trail*. *The River Man*
Owen Wister. *The Virginian*
O. E. Rölvaag. *Giants in the Earth*

Modern American Life

Frank Norris. *The Pit*
Booth Tarkington. *The Magnificent Ambersons*
Sinclair Lewis. *Main Street*
Owen Johnson. *Stover at Yale*
William Allen White. *A Certain Rich Man*
F. Hopkinson Smith. *Caleb West, Master Diver*

These novels tend to emphasize certain kinds of environment typical of modern life. The list immediately following also includes many novels of modern life, but with emphasis more upon character development.

NOVELS OF CHARACTER DEVELOPMENT
Youth and Romance

Booth Tarkington. *The Turmoil*. *Alice Adams*
Dorothy Canfield Fisher. *The Bent Twig*

Henry Sydnor Harrison. *Queed*
Edna Ferber. *So Big*
Ernest Poole. *The Harbor*

MORE MATURE STUDIES

Nathaniel Hawthorne. *The House of the Seven Gables. The Scarlet Letter. The Marble Faun*
William Dean Howells. *The Rise of Silas Lapham. A Modern Instance*
Henry James. *The American. A Portrait of a Lady*
Winston Churchill. *Coniston*
Paul Leicester Ford. *The Honorable Peter Stirling*
Margaret Deland. *The Iron Woman*
Edith Wharton. *Ethan Frome*
Zona Gale. *Miss Lulu Bett*
Sinclair Lewis. *Babbitt. Arrowsmith*

REFERENCE BOOKS ON AMERICAN LITERATURE

The following books contain critical, biographical, or historical material on American literature. In addition to these there are many short histories of American literature intended for high school use, and the standard work, The Cambridge History of American Literature, which is most usable for high school students in its abridged one-volume form.

Baldwin, Charles C. *The Men Who Make Our Novels*
Boynton, Percy H. *Some Contemporary Americans. More Contemporary Americans*
Burton, Richard. *Literary Leaders of America*
Cook, H. W. *Our Poets of Today*
Cooper, Frederick T. *Some American Short-Story Tellers*
Curtis, George W. *Literary and Social Essays*
Dickinson, Thomas H. *Playwrights of the New American Theater*
Farrar, John. *The Literary Spotlight*
Fields, Annie. *Authors and Friends*
Foerster, Norman. *American Criticism. Nature in American Literature. The Reinterpretation of American Literature*
Halsey, Francis W. *American Authors and Their Homes. Authors of Our Day in Their Homes. Women Authors of Our Day in Their Homes*
Hansen, Harry. *Midwest Portraits*
Harkins, E. F. *Famous Authors*
Haweis, H. R. *American Humorists*
Hazard, Lucy. *The Frontier in American Literature*
Higginson, Thomas Wentworth. *Contemporaries*
Howe, M. A. D. *American Bookmen*

Howells, William Dean. *My Literary Friends and Acquaintance*
Karsner, David. *Sixteen Authors to One*
Lowell, Amy. *Tendencies in Modern American Poetry*
Mabie, Hamilton Wright. *American Ideals, Character, and Life*
Mackay, Constance D. *The Little Theater in the United States*
Macy, John. *The Spirit of American Literature*
Manly, J. M. and Rickert, Edith. *Contemporary American Literature*
Moses, Montrose. *The American Dramatist. Literature of the South*
Overton, Grant. *American Nights Entertainment. Cargoes for Crusoes.*
The Women Who Make Our Novels
Parrington, Vernon L. *Main Currents in American Thought*
Pattee, Fred L. *The Development of the American Short Story. A History of American Literature since 1870*
Perry, Bliss. *The American Spirit in Literature*
Phelps, William Lyon. *Howells, James, Bryant, and Other Essays. Some Makers of American Literature. Essays on Modern Dramatists. Essays on Modern Novelists*
Raymond, Charles H. *Story Lives of Master Writers*
Rittenhouse, Jessie. *The Younger American Poets*
Sherman, Stuart P. *Americans. The Main Stream*
Smith, C. Alphonso. *Southern Literary Studies. What Can Literature Do for Me?*
Squire, John. *Contemporary American Authors*
Ticknor, Caroline. *Glimpses of Authors*
Trent and Erskine. *Great American Writers*
Untermeyer, Louis. *American Poetry since 1900*
Van Doren, Carl. *The American Novel. The Contemporary American Novel. Many Minds*
Van Doren, Carl and Mark. *American and British Literature since 1890*
Vedder. *American Writers of Today*
Wendell, Barrett. *A Literary History of America*
Whitcomb. *Chronological Outlines of American Literature*
Williams, Blanche C. *Our Short Story Writers*
Williams, Stanley T. *The American Spirit in Letters*
Woodberry, George E. *America in Literature. Literary Memoirs of the Nineteenth Century*

Howells, William Dean. My Literary Passions; Literary Friends and Acquaintance.

Keiser, Albert. Aliens author in One.

Lowell, Amy. Tendencies in Modern American Poetry.

Mason, Hamilton Wright. American Drama, Character, and Life.

Markey, Constance D. The Little Thackerays (or Locked Stage.)

Macy, John. The Spirit of American Literature.

Manly, J. M. and Rickert, Edith. Contemporary American Literature.

Moses, Montrose. The American Dramatist. Literature of the South.

Overton, Grant. American Nights Entertainment. Cargoes for Crusoe.
    The Women Who Make Our Novels.

Parrington, Vernon L. Main Currents in American Thought.

Pattee, Fred L. The Development of the American Short Story. A His-
    tory of American Literature since 1870.

Perry, Bliss. The American Spirit in Literature.

Phelps, William Lyon. Howells, James, Bryant and Other Essays. Some
    Makers of American Literature. Essays on Modern Dramatists.
    Essays on Modern Novelists.

Raymond, Charles H. Story-Telling of Writer (Writers.)

Rittenhouse, Jessie. Editor, Anthologies, Anthologue.

Sherman, Stuart P. Americans. The Main Stream.

Smith, C. Alphonso. Southern Literary ... With Our Literature
    We for Art.

Squire, John. Contemporary American Authors.

Tichenor, Caroline. Changing of America.

Trent and Erskine. Great American Writers.

Untermeyer, Louis. American Poetry since 1900.

Van Doren, Carl. The American Novel. The Contemporary American
    Novel. Many Minds.

Van Doren, Carl and Mark. American and British Literature since
    1890.

Weber. American History by Today.

Wendell, Barrett. A Literary History of America.

Whitcomb. A Geographical Outline of American Literature.

Williams, Blanche C. Our Short Story Writers.

Williams, Stanley T. The American Spirit in Letters.

Woodberry, George E. America in Literature. A Study of Letters in the
    Nineteenth Century.

DICTIONARY OF WORDS, NAMES, AND PHRASES

This Glossary contains pronunciations and definitions for the more important of the harder and comparatively unusual terms used in this book. For each word the definition is limited to the use of that word in this volume. For a word already explained in a footnote in the body of the book, only the pronunciation is given here, and reference is made to the page where the explanation may be found. For words with more than one accepted pronunciation, the most usual pronunciation is given.

The diacritical markings used are very simple: āce, senâte, râre, băt, fäther, sofà, ĕvent, ēven, ĕnd, mothēr, fīnd, sĭt, rōpe, ŏmit, côrd, hŏt, ūnit, ûnite, bûrn, cŭt, bo͞ot, fo͝ot.

In a few foreign words the exact pronunciation is not quite achieved.

A

abashed (à băsht'). Ashamed guiltily; embarrassed

abetting (à bĕt'ĭng). Encouraging; supporting; upholding, usually used in a bad sense

abyss (à bĭs'). Bottomless gulf or pit

accouterment (ă ko͞o'tēr mĕnt). All objects of a soldier's personal outfit except clothing and weapons

Achilles (à kĭl'ēz). Page 246

acquiesce (ăk wĭ ĕs'). Consent, or rest satisfied

adolescence (ăd ồ lĕs'ĕns). Youth, or the period of life between 12 and 21

Adonis (à dō'nĭs). A beautiful youth, in classical myth, beloved by Aphrodite. Hence, any handsome young man

Aeneas (ē nē'ăs). Trojan hero of Vergil's *Aeneid;* the fabled originator of the Roman race

Aeolian (ē ō'lĭ ăn). Pertaining to the wind or Aeolus, god of the winds

affluence (ăf'lo͞o ĕns). An abundant supply of anything, usually of wealth

aide-de-camp (ād'dē kămp). An officer attached to the person of a leader

Aidenn (ā'dĕn). Page 632

akimbo (à kĭm'bō). Arms akimbo — hands on hips and elbows turned outward

alabaster (ăl'à bàs tēr). A hard white stone

Aladdin (à lăd'ĭn). Page 574

Alhambra (ăl hăm'brà). The fortified palace of the Moorish kings at Granada, Spain

Alma Mater (ăl'mà mā'tēr). Latin, meaning fostering mother. Hence, one's school

aloe (ăl'ō). Page 592

amain (à mān'). With full force; at great speed

amaranth (ăm'à rănth). A plant bearing flowers of green, purple, or crimson

ambiguous (ăm bĭg'û ŭs). Capable of more than one meaning

ambuscade (ăm bŭs kād'). A lying in wait, concealed, for the purpose of attacking an enemy by surprise ameliorate (á mēl′yŏ rāt). Make better; improve

amenable (á mē′nȧ b'l). Willing to yield; easy to lead

amicable (ăm′ĭ kȧ b'l). Friendly; peaceable

amuck (á mŭk′). In a frenzied, murderous manner

animosity (ăn i mŏs′ĭ tĭ). Hostility; hatred

animus (ăn′ĭ mŭs). Moving spirit; intention, especially a hostile one

anonymous (á nŏn′ĭ mŭs). Of unknown authorship

ante-bellum (ăn′tē-bĕl′ŭm). Before the war

antecedents (ăn tē sēd′ĕnts). Those who had lived before him

anthologist (ăn thŏl′ŏ jĭst). Compiler of beautiful passages of many authors into a single volume

antipathy (ăn tĭp′á thĭ). Distaste, dislike

Aphrodite (ăf rŏ dī′tē). The Greek goddess of love and beauty

Apollonius (á pŏl lōn′ĭ ŭs). Page 581

apostate (á pŏs′tāt). Faithless renegade

appellation (ăp ĕ lā shŭn). Name; title

Appomattox (ăp ŏ măt′ŭks). Place where Lee surrendered to Grant, 1865

arabesque (ăr á bĕsk′). A fanciful Arabic ornament

Ararat, Mt. (ăr′á răt). Famous mountain in Armenia, on which Noah's Ark came to rest after the deluge

archipelago (är kĭ pĕl′á gō). Group of many islands

argosy (är′gŏ sĭ). Large merchant vessel

argot (är′gō *or* är′gŏt). Secret language, usually of thieves or vagabonds

arras (ăr′ăs). A screen or hangings of rich, figured fabric

arrogance (ăr′ō găns). Pride; insolence

articulate (är tĭk′ů lāt). Uttered with distinctness

artifice (är′tĭ fĭs). Trick

asphodel (ăs′fŏ dĕl). A flower often referred to in poetry, usually the daffodil or narcissus

assonance (ăs′ŏ năns). Resemblance of sound

assuage (ă swāj′). Ease, soften, reduce

Astarte (ăs tär′tē). Page 635

attrition (ă trĭsh′ŭn). State of being worn down

Austerlitz (ôs′tēr lĭts). Page 247

autonomous (ô tŏn′ŏ mŭs). Independent in government

B

bacillus (bȧ sĭl′ŭs). A type of microbe

bacteriologist   (băk tē rĭ ŏl′ŏ jĭst). Scientist who specializes in the study of microbes

bane (bān). Ruin

bard (bärd). Poet

Bashan (bā′shăn). A district in Palestine, east of the Jordan, noted for its richness

bedight (bē dīt′). Ornamented or adorned

Belcher (bĕl′chēr), Jonathan. American colonial governor

beleaguered   (bē lē′gērd). Surrounded or shut in by an armed force

belligerent (bĕ lĭj′ēr ĕnt). Engaged in warfare

benedicite (bĕ nĕ dī′sĭ tĭ). Page 612

Beowulf (bā′ŏ wŏŏlf). Mythical hero of the Anglo-Saxon epic poem of the same name

Bermuda (bēr mū′dȧ). Group of islands in the Atlantic Ocean, belonging to Great Britain

binnacle (bĭn′á k'l). Case for ship's compass

bittern (bĭt′ērn). A member of the heron family

blench (blĕnch). Shrink back

Blücher (blē'kēr), Gebhard Leberecht von (1742–1819). Page 259

boreal (bō'rē ăl). Pertaining to Boreas, the north wind, hence to the north generally

boudoir (boo'dwär). A lady's private room

Bowdoin (bō'dĭn) College. Founded 1794, in Brunswick, Maine

Brahmin (brä'mĭn). A member of the four upper castes or classes in India

Briand (brē än'). A modern French statesman

Broadway. A street in the heart of the theatrical district of New York City

bronco (brŏng'kō). Mustang, nearly wild horse. Often spelled broncho

brougham (broo'ŭm). Page 261

Brown, John. An American, active to the point of revolution, in the anti-slavery movement

buccaneering (bŭk à nēr'ĭng). Pirating

bucolic stolidity (bŭ kŏl'ĭk). Rustic calm or stupidity

Buddha (bood'à). Meaning the awakened or enlightened, the surname given to the Hindu sage Gautama Siddhartha, who founded the religion of Buddhism

buhl (bool). Furniture decorated with metal inlay

bumpkin (bŭmp'kĭn). Page 418

buoyancy (boi'ăn sĭ). Power or tendency to float.

burlesque (bûr lĕsk'). Humorous imitation

Byzantine (bĭ zăn'tĭn). Relating to Constantinople or the Eastern Roman Empire

C

Calaveras (kăl à vā'ràs). County in California

calliope (kă lī'ō pē). A mechanical organ run by steam, used in circus parades

Calpe (kăl'pē). Page 638

Camelot (kăm'ĕ lŏt). Page 702

Campagna (käm pä'nyä). The large plain surrounding Rome, Italy

cane-brake. A dense growth of giant sugar-cane

canine (kà nīn'). Pertaining to the dog

canny (kăn'ĭ). Shrewd; thrifty

caparison (kà păr'ĭ sŭn). Decorative harness or trappings of a horse

capitulation (kà pĭt ū lā'shŭn). A surrender upon terms agreed upon

carbine (kär'bīn). A short, light rifle; formerly, a musket used chiefly by cavalry

carbuncle (kär'bŭng k'l). A mythical stone supposed to give off light in the dark; a deep red garnet

caricature (kăr'ĭ kà tŭr). A picture which exaggerates peculiarities

Carnegie (kär nĕg'ĭ), Andrew. American manufacturer and philanthropist

carrion (kăr'ĭ ŭn). Dead or decaying flesh

caryatid (kăr ĭ ăt'ĭd). A column in the form of a sculptured female figure, used to support roof

cashmere (kăsh'mēr). Page 603

cataclysm (kăt'à klĭzm). A sudden and overwhelming change

catamount (kăt'à mount). The cougar or panther

Cathay (kă thā'). Ancient name for China

Catholic. General; universal in application

catkin. Usually a pussywillow or cat-tail

cavalcade (kăv ăl kād'). A company of persons on the march; a parade

celestial (sē lĕs'chăl). Heavenly; divine

censer (sĕn'sēr). A vessel for burning incense or perfume

centennial (sĕn tĕn'ĭ ăl). The hundredth anniversary

chalice (chăl'ĭs). A drinking cup

chancery (chăn'sēr ĭ). The jurisdiction of a court of equity; bankruptcy

chantey (shăn'tĭ). A song of sailors, to a marked rhythm, to ease labor

chanticleer (chăn'tĭ klēr). A rooster

charlatan (shär'lȧ tăn). A pretender, one who makes false claims or boasts

chassis (shăs'ĭ). A bare frame for any vehicle

chaste (chāst). Virtuous; good

chastisement (chăs'tĭz mĕnt). Punishment

Chaucer, Geoffrey (chô'sēr, jĕf'rĭ). Page 649

Chilcoot (chĭl'kōōt) Pass. Just north of Skagway, Alaska

Chillon (shĭl lŏn). Page 266

chirography (kī rŏg'rȧ fĭ). Style or character of handwriting

chrysolite (krĭs'ȯ līt). A yellow stone

churl (chûrl). A rude, low-bred fellow

Cicero (sĭs'ēr ō), Marcus Tullius (106–43 B.C.). Roman lawyer and orator of distinction

cimbric (sĭm'brĭk). Page 546

classicist (klăs'ĭ sĭst). One who maintains the classic style and emphasizes the importance of correct form

Cleopatra (klē ȯ pā'trȧ). Queen of Egypt

clergy (klēr'jĭ). The whole body of men set apart by ordination for the service of God in the Christian church

cloistered (klois'tērd). Shut away from the world, as in a convent

cognizance (kŏg'nĭ zăns). Knowledge, notice

colloquial (kŏl lō'kwĭ ăl). Belonging to common usage as apart from classical

comity (kŏm'ĭ tĭ). Courtesy, consideration, friendliness

commensurability (kŏ mĕn shōō rȧ bĭl'ĭ tĭ). Reducibility to a common measure

Como, Lake (kō'mō). A lake of north Italy, celebrated for its beauty

compatible (kŏm păt'ĭ b'l). Mutually suitable and agreeable

condor (kŏn'dŏr). A very large South American vulture

conduce (kŏn dūs'). Lead

conduit (kŏn'dĭt). A means for conducting a substance or idea

consanguinity (kŏn săng gwĭn'ĭ tĭ). Blood relationship

contemporary (kŏn tĕm'pȯ rā rĭ). Existing or occurring at the same time

Copernicus (kȯ pûr'nĭ kŭs), Nicholas (1473–1543). A celebrated Prussian astronomer and mathematician

copse (kŏps). A thicket of bushes, or a wood of small trees

corbel (kôr'bĕl). Page 617

cordial (kôr'jăl). A sweet alcoholic liquor

corroborate (kȯ rŏb'ȯ rāt). Make more sure or evident

corsage (kôr sȧzh'). The waist of a woman's dress

cosine (kō'sīn). A term used in higher mathematics, in reference to angles and arcs

cosmopolitan (kŏz mȯ pŏl'ĭ tăn). Not limited to any geographic region

cosmos (kŏz'mŏs). The universe considered as a system

coterie (kō'tē rĭ). A set of persons who meet for some purpose

couchant (kouch'ănt). Crouching, with the head held up

coulee (kōō' lē). A deep gulch

coulter (kōl'tēr). A steel blade attached to the beam of a plow to cut sod

covertly (kŭv'ērt lĭ). Secretly

craven (krā'v'n). A base coward

credence (krē'dĕns). Belief; confidence based upon other than personal knowledge

credulity (krē dū'lĭ tĭ). A disposition to believe on slight or uncertain evidence crypt (krĭpt). A secret recess or vault

cryptic (krĭp'tĭc). Hidden or secret

cryptogram (krĭp'tō grăm). A message written in secret characters, or having a hidden meaning

cubit (kū'bĭt). An ancient measure of length, usually from the tips of the fingers to the elbow

cumbrous (kŭm'brŭs). Burdensome

curricle (kŭr'ĭ k'l). Page 371

cynic (sĭn'ĭk). One who disbelieves and sneers at moral worth

Cyprian (sĭp'rĭ ăn). Native to the island of Cyprus, in the Mediterranean Sea

Cytherea (sĭth ēr ē'à). A name applied to Venus because she was said to have risen from the waves near the island of Cythera

D

dais (dā'ĭs). A raised platform

Damon (dā'mŏn). An ancient Greek, famous for his friendship with Pythias

dank. Cold and moist

declamation (dĕk là mā'shŭn). The act of delivering a memorized speech in public

decorum (dĕ kō'rŭm). Propriety

decrepit (dĕ krĕp'ĭt). Enfeebled, worn-out

delirium tremens (dĕ lĭr'ĭ ŭm trē'mĕnz). Extreme trembling of hands and feet and terrifying hallucinations of sight and hearing, caused by excessive drinking of alcoholic liquors

deluge (dĕl'ūj). Flood

demi (dĕm'ĭ). Half

deodand (dē'ŏ dănd). Page 377

depravity (dĕ prăv'ĭ tĭ). Wickedness, corruption

deprecate (dĕp're kāt). Express disapproval of

despotism (dĕs'pŏt ĭsm). Unlimited authority

desultory (dĕs'ŭl tô rĭ). Passing aimlessly from one thing to another

dexterity (dĕks tĕr'ĭ tĭ). Skill; cleverness

diabolic (dī à bŏl'ĭk). Very wicked; like the devil; infernal

diapason (dī à pā'zŏn). Full range of an instrument

didactic (dī dăk'tĭk). Intended to instruct or edify

dight (dīt). Dressed or adorned

digression (dī grĕsh'ŭn). A turning aside from the main course

dilemma (dĭ lĕm'à). A state of things in which evils or obstacles present themselves on every side, and it is difficult to determine what course to pursue

diminution (dĭm ĭ nū'shŭn). Reduction

dinosaur (dī'nŏ sôr). Gigantic reptile of prehistoric times

dirge (dērj). A song of grief and mourning

disheveled (dĭ shĕv'ĕld). Disordered; in a state of confusion

disparagement (dĭs păr'àj mĕnt). Slighting or undervaluing

dissimulation (dĭ sĭm ŭ lā'shŭn). False pretension, hypocrisy

diversifying (dĭ vûr'sĭ fī ĭng). Giving variety to

docile (dŏs'ĭl). Easy to manage

doggerel (dôg'ēr ĕl). Ill-made verse

dogma (dôg'mà). A settled opinion or conviction

dole (dōl). Woe, grief

draught (dràft). A current of air; a drink

dross (drôs). Impurity in melted metal, slag

druid (drōō'ĭd). Page 612

ductile (dŭk'tĭl). Capable of being drawn into wire or thread

duenna (dū ĕn'à). An older or married woman who is employed to guard a younger one

dulcet (dŭl'sĕt). Agreeable to the taste or hearing

Dyea (dī'à). Alaskan village near Skagway

E

eccentricity (ĕk sĕn trĭs'ĭ tĭ). State of being strikingly different

edifice (ĕd'ĭ fĭs). A building, especially one that is large and imposing

effervescent (ĕf ēr vĕs'ĕnt). Giving off bubbles of gas

eftsoons (ĕft sōōnz'). Speedily, quickly

ego (ĕg'ō). Self

Eldorado (ĕl dŏ rä'dō). Any region rich in gold. Page 628

elegiac (ĕl ē jĭ'ăk). Of the nature of an elegy, or poem about death

embargo (ĕm bär'gō). Prohibition of vessels or goods from leaving port

emeritus (ē mĕr'ĭ tŭs). Honorably retired from active duty but retaining title

emolument (ē mŏl'û mĕnt). Salary or fee

encysted (ĕn sĭst'ĕd). Enclosed in a membranous sac

en masse (än mäs'). Page 654

enmity (ĕn'mĭ tĭ). Hatred

enormity (ē nôr'mĭ tĭ). Something very large; a great evil

ensign (ĕn'sīn). Flag

entity (ĕn'tĭ tĭ). Anything that really exists

envenomed (ĕn vĕn'ŭmd). Full of poison or bitterness

epicure (ĕp ĭ kūr). One who cultivates a taste for eating and drinking

epigram (ĕp'ĭ grăm). A pithy phrasing of a shrewd observation

epilogue (ĕp'ĭ lŏg). Concluding passage of a speech, play, or poem

epitaph (ĕp'ĭ tàf). Inscription on a tomb or monument

epithet (ĕp'ĭ thĕt). Phrase or word aptly describing some quality

epitomized (ē pĭt'ŏ mīzd). Described concisely; summarized

equipoise (ē'kwĭ poiz). Balance

equivocation (ē kwĭv ŏ kā'shŭn). Deceit, prevarication

Esperanto (ĕs pĕ rän'tō). An artificial language intended to be universal, having phonetic spelling

exemption (ĕg zĕmp'shŭn). The act of freeing from an obligation

exigency (ĕk'sĭ jĕn sĭ). A case that is urgent

exodus (ĕk'sŏ dŭs). Departure

exordium (ĕg zôr'dĭ ŭm). Introductory part of discourse or written composition

expectorate (ĕks pĕk'tŏ rāt). Spit

extemporized (ĕks tĕm'pŏ rīzd). Prepared on short notice without proper materials

extenuate (ĕks tĕn'ū āt). Represent as less blameworthy than it might be

extirpate (ĕks'tēr pāt). Destroy altogether; root up

exuberance (ĕgz ū'bēr ăns). Unlimited supply of energy and life

F

facetious (fà sē'shŭs). Droll, funny, waggish

facilitate (fà sĭl'ĭ tāt). Make more easy, free from hindrance

factotum (făk tō'tŭm). A person employed to do all kinds of work

faculty (făk'ŭl tĭ). Any one power of the mind

farinaceous (făr ĭ nā'shŭs). Mealy; made of meal or flour

fastidious (făs tĭd'ĭ ŭs). Hard to please, overnice, squeamish

fathomless (făth'ŭm lĕs). Immeasurable

feign (fān). Pretend

felicity (fē lĭs'ĭ tĭ). Well-founded happiness; complete comfort

feudal (fū'dăl). Pertaining to the relation of lord and vassal in medieval times

fillip (fĭl'ĭp). Stimulation

finite (fī'nīt). Having limits

Flanders. A region of western Europe, lying partly in Belgium, Holland and France

Flemish (flĕm'ĭsh). Pertaining to

Flanders, in Belgium, or the people thereof

fleur-de-lis (flûr dē lē'). Flower of the lily, the emblem of the former royal family in France

floret (flō'rĕt). One of the small flowers that make up a larger one

foible (foi'b'l). Personal weakness; slight fault

foppery (fŏp'ēr ĭ). The conduct of a dandy

frustration (frŭs trā'shŭn). Disappointment, defeat

Fugitive Slave Law. Passed in 1850, providing that a slave fleeing from his master was to be captured and restored

Fundy, Bay of. Between Nova Scotia and New Brunswick on the Atlantic coast of Canada. Noted for high tides

furtively (fûr'tĭv lĭ). Slyly

futile (fū'tĭl). Useless

G

Galahad (găl'à hăd), Sir. The purest of Arthur's knights

Galatea (găl à tē'à). Page 372

Galileo (gă lĭ lē'ō) (1564–1642). Famous Italian astronomer, mathematician, philosopher

galligaskins (găl ĭ găs'kĭnz). Page 371

Galsworthy (gôlz'wûr thĭ), John (1867–1933). English novelist and playwright

Garrison, William Lloyd (1804–1879). An American philanthropist active in the abolition of human slavery

garrulous (găr'ŏŏ lŭs). Talking much, especially about trivial things

gatling (găt'lĭng). A machine gun named after the American inventor, R. J. Gatling

genealogy (jĕn ē ăl'ŏ jĭ). History of a family or group

genial (jē'nĭ ăl). Cheerful and sympathetic, cordial, pleasant

Gethsemane (gĕth sĕm'à nē). A garden near Jerusalem, where Christ endured his agony, and was betrayed

ghoul (gōōl). An evil spirit supposed to prey on dead human bodies

Gilbert and Sullivan. A team of composers of such famous comic operas as "The Mikado" and "Pinafore"

Gilead (gĭl'ē ăd). A rich district of Palestine

glade (glād). An open space in a wood

gossamer (gŏs'à mēr). A single thread of spider silk, or a filmy tangle of such threads

Gotama (gō tä'mà). Page 649

Gothic (gŏth'ĭk). Pertaining to the pointed type of medieval architecture prevalent in western Europe

gourmand (gōōr'mänd). A greedy or ravenous eater

Grail (grāl), Holy. A legendary cup which appears in the Arthurian tales. Supposedly the cup used by Christ in the Last Supper. This cup is also supposed to have received Christ's blood when he was pierced in the side on the cross

Granada (grà nä'dà). A city and province of southern Spain, one time a stronghold of the Moors

grandiose (grăn'dĭ ōs). Impressive, grand, pompous

Greenwich (grĕn'ĭdj). A borough of the city of London, seat of the Royal Observatory

grilled (grĭld). Barred

groined (groind). Built so as to form intersected arches

gubernator (gū'bēr nä tŏr). Page 603

Guerrière (gĕr ĭ ĕr'). An American battleship in the War of 1812

guinea (gĭn'ĭ). An English coin worth about five dollars

gundalow (gŭn'dĕ lō). A barge

H

Habaña (hä bän'yä). Spanish form of Havana, capital of Cuba

hake-broil. Codfish cooked over open fire

halyards (hăl yērdz). Ropes for hoisting sail or flag

Haran (hă'răn). District and town in northern Mesopotamia

harassed (hăr'ăst). Worried

harpsichord (härp'sĭ kôrd). An old-fashioned stringed instrument, forerunner of the piano

harpy (här'pĭ). A winged monster, with the head and body of a woman and the feet of a bird.

heeler. A disreputable hanger-on of a political boss

helot (hĕl'ŏt). Page 379

Hercules (hēr'kū lēz). The national hero of Greece, doer of superhuman feats

heritage (hĕr'ĭ tāj). That which is passed down to one from one's ancestors

Hermes (hēr'mēz). Page 581

hermetically (hēr mĕt'ĭk ăl lĭ) sealed. Sealed to the exclusion of air; air-tight

Hesperides (hĕs pĕr'ĭ dēz). Page 549

Hiawatha (hī a wô'thà). The Indian hero of Longfellow's poem of like name

hieroglyphics (hī ēr ŏ glĭf'ĭks). Egyptian picture writing

hight (hīt). Named

hoary (hōr'ĭ). White with age

hobgoblin (hŏb'gŏb lĭn). Any imaginary cause of terror or dread

homicide (hŏm'ĭ sīd). The killing of one human being by another

hostlering (hŏs'lēr ĭng). Performing as a stableman or groom

Hotel Des Invalides (ō tĕl'dā zăn'và-lēd). Page 248

Houri (hoō'rĭ). Page 627

Houstonia (hūs tō'nĭ à). Page 239

I

Icarian (ī kā'rĭ ăn). Page 707

Ichabod (ĭk'à bŏd). Page 567

idiosyncrasy (ĭd ĭ ō sĭng'krà sĭ). Characteristic peculiarity of an individual

idyl (ī'dĭl). A short poem of simple life or rustic scenes

ignominious (ĭg nō mĭn'ĭ ŭs). Dishonoring, shameful

illimitable (ĭl lĭm'ĭt à b'l). Boundless

Illyria (ĭl lĭ'rĭ à). Page 222

immedicable (ĭ mĕd'ĭ kà b'l). Incurable

immemorial (ĭm ĕ mō'rĭ ăl). Older than memory can reach

imperturbable (ĭm pēr tûr'bà b'l). Not capable of being excited

impetus (ĭm'pē tŭs). Momentum, or the starting force

imposture (ĭm pŏs'tûr). Deception by false pretenses

impregnable (ĭm prĕg'nà b'l). Incapable of being captured, unconquerable

inalienable (ĭn āl'yĕn à b'l). Not transferable, cannot be taken away

inauspicious (ĭn ôs pĭsh'ŭs). Boding ill, unfortunate

Inca (ĭng'kà). The ruling class of the Peruvian Indian Empire destroyed by Pizarro

incantation (ĭn kăn tā'shŭn). The saying or singing of magical words

incarnadined (ĭn kär'nà dĭnd). Dyed red or flesh-color

incongruity (ĭn kŏn groō'ĭ tĭ). That which is out of harmony

incorrigible (ĭn kŏr'ĭ jĭ b'l). Bad, irreclaimable

increment (ĭn'krĕ mĕnt). Act of growing, enlargement

indigence (ĭn'dĭ jĕns). Poverty

indissoluble (ĭn dĭ sŏl'û b'l). Not capable of being dissolved

indolent (ĭn'dō lĕnt). Lazy

indubitable (ĭn dū'bĭ tà b'l). Certain; unquestionably true

ineffable (ĭn ĕf'à b'l). Unspeakable, unutterable

inept (ĭn ĕpt'). Not fit or suitable

inexorable (ĭn ek'sō rà b'l). Unyielding, unrelenting

infatuation (ĭn făt ū ā'shŭn). Extravagant or unreasonable love

ingénue (ăn zhā nü'). An innocent young girl

ingenuous (ĭn jĕn'ū ŭs). Frank, open, unsuspicious

ingenuity (ĭn jĕ nū'ĭ tĭ). Aptness, cleverness, skill

innovator (ĭn'ō vā tôr). One who introduces new things

inopportune (ĭn ŏp ŏr tūn'). Unsuitable, unseasonable

insatiable (ĭn sā'shĭ à b'l). Incapable of being satisfied

insidiously (ĭn sĭd'ĭ ŭs lĭ). Treacherously

instigate (ĭn'stĭ gāt). Urge, especially to evil

insurgent (ĭn sûr'jĕnt). Rebel

integrity (ĭn tĕg'rĭ tĭ). Honesty

interlocutor (ĭn tēr lŏk'ū tēr). One who takes part in a dialogue; a talker

interloper (ĭn'tēr lō pēr). Intruder

interlude (ĭn'tēr lūd). Time between events

internecine (ĭn tēr nē'sĭn). Involving mutual slaughter, deadly

intractable (ĭn trăk'tà b'l). Unruly, unmanageable

intrepid (ĭn trĕp'ĭd). Brave; daring

intrinsically (ĭn trĭn'sĭ kăl lĭ). Inherently, really, truly

introspective (ĭn trō spĕk'tĭv). Tending to analyze one's own thoughts

intuitive (ĭn tū'ĭ tĭv). Seen by the mind immediately

inundation (ĭn ŭn dā'shŭn). Overflow, flood, deluge

inveterate (ĭn vĕt'ēr āt). Habitual

inviolable (ĭn vī'ō là b'l). Not to be harmed or broken

Ionic (ī ŏn'ĭk). One form of Greek architecture; heavy, massive

ipecac (ĭp'ē kăk). A medicine given to cause vomiting

irascible (ĭ răs'ĭ b'l). Easily provoked, hot-tempered

irised (ī'rĭsd). Delicately colored with many hues. Iris is the Goddess of the Rainbow

Ishmael (ĭsh'mā ĕl). A son of Abraham, and the legendary founder of Arabian culture

J

jackanapes (jăk'à nāps). An impertinent fellow

jade (jād). A worthless person, especially a low woman

Joshua (jŏsh'ū à). Great general of the Hebrew nation

Jove (jōv). The Latin name of the Greek Zeus, the supreme god of the classic religions

jurisdiction (jōō rĭs dĭk'shŭn). Lawful power or right to exercise authority

K

Kamchatka (kàm chàt'kà). Page 370

keelson (kĕl'sŭn). Page 556

Keys. The Florida Keys, islands in the Gulf of Mexico off the tip of Florida

khaki (kä'kē). Dust or ash color, used for soldiers' service uniforms

Khayyam (kī yäm'), Omar. Page 649. Omar, the Tent-Maker

knarred (närd). Knotty, gnarled

Koch (kōk), Robert. Page 281

Koran (kō'răn). The sacred scriptures of Mohammedans

L

laconic (là kŏn'ĭk). Saying a great deal in a few words

lagniappe (lăn'nyăp). In Louisiana, a trifling present given to customers by tradesmen

Land Bank. A system by which the province advanced money on mortgages on land

languorous (lăng'gēr ŭs). In a state of tender dreaminess

Lascar (lăs'kàr). Page 556

laudable (lôd'à b'l). Worthy of praise

laurels (lô'rĕlz). Page 627

laving (lāv ĭng). Washing, bathing

Lebanon (lĕb'à nŏn). Page 587

Leicester (lĕs'tēr). Page 378

lento (lēn'tōō). Page 420

lethargic (lĕ thär'jĭk). Morbidly drowsy, sleepy

Lethean (lĕ thē'ăn). Page 635

Leviathan (lĕ vī'à thăn). Page 351

levin (lĕv'ĭn). Page 626

levity (lĕv'ĭ tĭ). Lack of gravity and earnestness

libretto (lĭ brĕt'ō). The text, or words, for an opera or some other long piece of music for singing

lichened (lī'kĕnd). Covered with lichen, a type of moss or fungus

liquescent (lĭ kwĕs'ĕnt). Becoming a liquid, melting

litany (lĭt'à nĭ). A solemn hymn or prayer of supplication

localism (lō'kăl ĭzm). A local idiom or peculiarity of speaking

locoed (lō'kōd). Affected with loco disease caused by cattle eating loco weed. They become mad and delirious

loquacious (lō kwā'shŭs). Given to talking; talkative

luminous (lū'mĭ nŭs). Shining, brilliant, bright

lustrous (lŭs'trŭs). Having luster, sheen, or brilliancy

lyceum (lī sē'ŭm). A school or place of instruction

M

Madeira Islands (mà dē'rà). Islands in Atlantic Ocean near Morocco in northern Africa

Magian (mā'jĭ ăn). Page 681

magnanimity (măg nà nĭm'ĭ tĭ). Generous and courageous spirit, above meanness

malignant (mà lĭg'nănt). Evil, rebellious

mall (môl). Public walk; shaded walk. Original was The Mall, St. James' Park, London, fashionable promenade

mangrove (măng'grōv). A tropical tree or shrub

Manitou (măn'ĭ tōō). Page 681

maritime (măr'ĭ tīm). Pertaining to the sea or navigation

mastodon (măs'tō dŏn). An extinct species of elephants

Mauretania (mô rē tā'nĭ à).Page 220

maverick (măv'ēr ĭk). An unbranded calf

Mazatlan (mä zät län'). Page 564

Mecca (mĕk'à). An Arabian city, birthplace of Mohammed and holy city of Moslems

Medici (mĕd'ē chē). Page 702

mediocre (mē dĭ ō'kēr). Of middle quality, neither very good nor very bad

Meerschaum (mēr'shôm). A pipe made of a fine white clay-like mineral

Memphremagog (mĕm frē mā'gŏg). Page 578

mercenary (mûr'sē nā rĭ). Greedy of gain, sordid, selfish

mesmerism (mĕz'mēr ĭzm). An early development of hypnotism

metaphor (mĕt'à fŏr). A figure of speech presenting an implied comparison

meteor (mē'tē ŏr). A heavenly body in rapid motion

mica (mī'kà). Minerals which may be separated into thin elastic leaves, varying from colorless, pale brown or yellow to gray or black. The transparent forms are commonly known as isinglass.

Midas (mī'dàs). Page 604

mien (mēn). Manner, demeanor, carriage

Millet (mē yā'), Jean François. Famous French painter

mirage (mē räzh'). An optical illusion; objects which seem to exist, but are not present except as we imagine them

mitigate (mĭt'ĭ gāt). Lessen

Moloch (mō'lŏk). A Semitic deity, whose worship was accompanied by human sacrifice

monologue (mŏn'ō lŏg). A long speech by one person

monopolies (mō nŏp'ō lĭz). A complete right or privilege over a certain product or market

Montmartre (môn màr'tr'). Section of Paris, France, on a hill above the Seine

morass (mō răs'). A tract of soft, wet ground, a marsh, a swamp

morbid (môr'bĭd). Of gloomy or unwholesome nature

moribund (môr'ĭ bŭnd). In a dying state, near death

Moselle (mō zĕl'). A river in France

Moultrie (mōl'trĭ). Page 638

munificent (mū nĭf'ĭ sĕnt). Enormous, bounteous, lavish

muscadine (mŭs'kà dĭn). A grape of southern United States

Muscovy (mŭs'kō vĭ). Old name for Russia

muse (mūz). A goddess who presides over the arts and sciences

myriad (mĭr'ĭ ăd). Consisting of a great, but indefinite number

Myrmidons (mûr'mĭ dŏnz). Page 246

N

nabob (nā'bŏb). An East Indian official given to luxurious dress; hence, anyone who wears a gorgeous uniform

Nahant (nà hănt'). Page 376

naiad (nā'yăd or nī'ăd). Page 626

naïve (nä ēv'). Having unaffected simplicity

nautilus (nô'tĭ lŭs). A type of shellfish

nebulous (nĕb'ū lŭs). Cloudy, hazy, misty

nepenthe (nĕ pĕn'thē). Page 632

Nicean (nī sē'àn). Page 625

Nicodemus (nĭk ō dē'mŭs). Page 666

noblesse oblige (nō blĕs' ō blēzh'). Page 22

nonconformist (nôn kŏn fôrm'ĭst). One who does not abide by some established custom or doctrine

nonpareil (nŏn pà rĕl'). Having no equal

nostalgia (nŏs tăl'jĭ à). Homesickness

nullify (nŭl'ĭ fī). Make of no consequence

O

obdurate (ŏb'dû răt or ŏb dû'răt). Hardened in feelings, rugged, rough

obeisance (ŏ bā'săns). A gesture in token of respect or homage

obelisk (ŏb'ē lĭsk). A pointed pillar. Egyptian obelisks are commonly covered with hieroglyphic writing, recording the achievements of kings.

obliterate (ŏb lĭt'ēr āt). Blot out, make indistinct

obsolete (ŏb'sŏ lēt). No longer in use

occult (ŏk ŭlt'). Secret, concealed

octoroon (ŏk tŏ rōōn'). Offspring of a quadroon and a white person; hence, a person one-eighth negro

odium (ō'dĭ ŭm). Stigma, disgrace

Odysseus (ŏ dĭs'ūs). Greek hero, commonly known as Ulysses

Olympian (ŏ lĭm'pĭ ăn). God-like

ominous (ŏm'ĭ nŭs). Foreshadowing evil

omnipotent (ŏm nĭp'ō tĕnt). All-powerful

omnipresent (ŏm nĭ prĕz'ĕnt). Present in all places at the same time

omniscient (ŏm nĭsh'ĕnt). Possessed of universal knowledge; all-knowing

omnivorous (ŏm nĭv'ō rŭs). Eating both animal and vegetable food; greedy

onomatopœia (ŏn ŏ măt ŏ pē'yà). Formation of words in imitation of natural sounds. Examples: buzz, hiss, clash

opulent (ŏp'ū lĕnt). Wealthy, rich

Orestes (ŏ rĕs'tēz). Page 543

ornithology (ôr nǐ thŏl'ō jǐ). Branch of zoölogy which treats of birds

ostentatious (ŏs tĕn tā'shŭs). Loud, conspicuous

P

palimpsest (păl'ǐmp sĕst). Page 592

pall (pôl). A covering for a coffin

Palladium (pă lā'dǐ ŭm). Page 439

pallid (păl'ǐd). Pale

pallor (păl'ŏr). Paleness

palpable (păl'pà b'l). Tangible, noticeable, obvious

pantomime (păn'tō mīm). A dramatic performance without words

Paphian (pā'fǐ ăn). Pertaining to Paphos, an ancient city of Cyprus, famed for a temple of Venus

paradox (păr'à dŏks). A seemingly contradictory sentiment

paraphrase (păr'à frāz). A free translation, or restatement in another manner

par excellence (pàr ĕk sĕ läns'). French phrase, meaning pre-eminently

pariah (pä'rǐ à *or* pà rī'à). A low-caste member of India and Burma; an outcast, one despised by society

parsimony (pär'sǐ mŏ nǐ). Stinginess; refusal to spend even though there is plenty of money

Pascagoula (păs kà gōō'là). Page 553

Pasteur (pàs tûr'). Page 279

patriarch (pā'trǐ ärk). Ruler of family or tribe

Patroclus (pà trō'klŭs). In Greek legend, a friend of Achilles

paucity (pô'sǐ tǐ). Smallness of number or quantity

pedantic (pĕ dăn'tǐk). Making a needless display of learning

pelisse (pĕ lēs'). A long outer garment for men or women

pellicle (pĕl'ǐ k'l). A thin skin or film

perambulation (pĕr ăm bū lā'shŭn). A tour on foot

perfidious (pēr fǐd'ǐ ŭs). Faithless, treacherous, false to trust

perigee (pĕr'ǐ jē). Page 707

peripatetic (pĕr ǐ pà tĕt'ǐk). Traveling or going from place to place

pernicious (pēr nǐsh'ŭs). Destructive, intending evil

perpetrate (pûr'pē trāt). To commit a crime or offense

persiflage (pĕr sĕ fläzh'). Frivolous or bantering talk

pertinacity (pûr tǐ năs'ǐ tǐ). Unyielding perseverance

pertinence (pûr'tǐ nĕns). Fitness of matter in hand

perversity (pēr vûr'sǐ tǐ). State or quality of being wilfully wrong

petrels (pĕt'rĕlz). Sea birds

petulant (pĕt'ū lănt). Ill-humored, complaining

Philistine (fǐ lǐs'tǐn). One of the enemies of the ancient Hebrew people. The term is used today to denote a person outside the influence of culture; one who thinks that wealth measures success.

Phryne (frī'nē). A Grecian beauty

physiognomy (fǐz ǐ ŏg'nŏ mǐ). The reading of character or disposition by study of features of a face

picaroon (pǐk à rōōn'). Page 765

pillory (pǐl'ŏ rǐ). A device for public punishment

pique (pēk). To hurt or offend

Pisa (pē'zä). Page 574

placidity (plà sǐd'ǐ tǐ). Calmness, serenity, mildness

plashy (plăsh'ǐ). Abounding in puddles; splashy

platitude (plăt'ǐ tūd). That which is flat, dull, stale, or trite

Pleiades (plē'yà dēz). Page 626

plighted (plīt'ĕd). Promised or pledged. A man's plighted wife is the girl to whom he is engaged to be married.

Pocahontas (pō kà hŏn'tàs). An Indian princess, made famous by Captain John Smith's story of the way she saved his life

polychromatic (pŏl ǐ krŏ măt'ǐk).

Showing a variety or a change of colors

pomatum (pŏ mā'tŭm). A perfumed ointment

portent (pōr'tĕnt). An omen or sign

posterity (pŏs tĕr'ĭ tĭ). Descendants

Potter's Field. A public burial place for unknown persons, paupers, and criminals

precarious (prē kā'rĭ ŭs). Uncertain, insecure

preponderating (prē pŏn'dēr ăt ĭng). Most important

preposterous (prē pŏs'tēr ŭs). Contrary to nature, reason, or common sense

prerequisite (prē rĕk'wĭ zĭt). Previously required; necessary as a preliminary to a proposed end

prerogative (prē rŏg'à tĭv). Superior in privilege; having right of precedence

presage (prĕ sāj'). Foretell or foreshadow

prescient (prē'shĭ ĕnt). Foreknowing, foreseeing

Priam (prī'ăm). Page 702

prima facie (prī'mà fā'shĭ ē). Page 372

primal (prī'măl). First in importance, original

probity (prō'bĭ tĭ). Tried virtue, honesty, moral excellence

proclivity (prō klĭv'ĭ tĭ). Inclination or tendency

prodigiously (prō dĭj'ŭs lĭ). Enormously, astonishingly

profane (prŏ fān'). To abuse or be disrespectful toward

prolific (prō lĭf'ĭk). Fruitful or productive

prolixity (prō lĭk'sĭ tĭ). Quality of being unduly long drawn out

proneness (prōn'nĕs). Mental inclination

propensity (prō pĕn'sĭ tĭ). Natural inclination; disposition

propitiate (prō pĭsh'ĭ āt). To remove displeasure from, or to make favorable

Proserpine (prō sēr'pĭ nà). Page 693

protagonist (prō tăg'ō nĭst). One who takes the lead in any matter

provençal (prō vän sàl'). Page 765

pseudonym (sū'dŏ nĭm). A fictitious name; pen name

Psyche (sī'kē). Page 626

punctilio (pŭngk tĭl'ĭ ō). Formal exactness

Pythagoras (pĭ thăg'ō răs). Greek philosopher and mathematician

Q

quagmire (quăg'mīr). Soft, wet, miry land, which shakes or yields under the foot

querulous (kwĕr'ŏŏ lŭs). Apt to find fault, habitually complaining

queue (kū). A long line

quixotic (kwĭk sŏt'ĭk). Romantic to extravagance

R

raconteur (rà kôn tûr'). A storyteller

rancor (răng'kēr). Malignity or spite, malice, hatred

ratiocination (răsh ĭ ŏs ĭ nā'shŭn). The mental process of exact thinking

raucous (rô'kŭs). Hoarse, harsh, rough

reciprocal (rē sĭp'rŏ kăl). Interchangeable, complementary

reconnoiter (rĕk ŏ noi'tēr). To make a preliminary survey before acting

rectitude (rĕk'tĭ tūd). Rightness or correctness of judgment or principle

regicide (rĕj'ĭ sīd). The murder of a king

reiterate (rē ĭt'ēr āt). To repeat over and over again

relevancy (rĕl'ĕ văn sĭ). Proper application to the matter at hand

rendezvous (rän'dĕ vōō). Meeting place

repertory (rĕp'ēr tō rĭ). A list, index, or catalogue

reprehensible (rĕp rē hĕn'sĭ b'l). Blamable, censurable

retaliate (rē tăl'ĭ āt). To return like for like, to repay by similar actions

retrospect (rĕt'rō spĕkt). A look back in thought

reverberation (rē vûr bēr ā'shŭn). Echo

ribald (rĭb'ăld). Low, coarse, obscene

rife (rīf). Numerous, abounding, existing generally

Roosevelt (Rōz'vĕlt). Neither President by this name pronounced it Rōōz'velt

rudder (rŭd'ēr). A piece of wood used to steer a boat

ruthless (rōōth'lĕss). Without pity or mercy

S

saccharine (săk'á rĭn). Unduly sweet

saga (sä'gà). An ancient legend, tale, or history

sagacity (sà găs'ĭ tĭ). Shrewd insight

salient (sā'lĭ ĕnt). The point projecting farthest into the enemy's territory

Salisbury (sôlz'bēr ĭ). Page 579

salon (sà lông). An apartment for the reception of company

salutary (săl'ū tā rĭ). Healthful; wholesome

sanctity (săngk'tĭ tĭ). Holiness, sacredness, saintliness

sanctuary (săngk'tū ā rĭ). Protection, shelter, or refuge

sanguine (săng'gwĭn). Confident, inclined to be hopeful and cheerful

Saracen (săr'à sĕn). A wanderer of the desert between Syria and Arabia, an Arab

sarcophagus (sär kŏf'à gŭs). A coffin which is placed in the open air, or tomb where it may be seen. Plural: sarcophagi

Sardou (sàr dōō'). Page 259

sark (särk). A shirt or garment

sartorial (sär tō'rĭ ăl). Pertaining to a tailor or his work

satellite (săt'ĕ līt). A heavenly body, revolving around a larger one

satire (săt'īr). Holding up of errors or abuses or folly to ridicule

saturnine (săt'ŭr nīn). Heavy, dull. From the name Saturn in old chemistry, meaning lead

Scheherazade (shĕ hā rà zä'dĕ). Page 21

Schopenhauer (shō'pĕn hou ēr), Arthur. German philosopher (1788–1860)

scoriac (skō'rĭ ăk). Full of rock refuse

scotching (skŏch'ĭng). Wounding slightly

scourge (skûrj). Whip or flog

scrupulously (skrōō'pů lŭs lĭ). Conscientiously

seer (sēr). Prophet, wise man

senescent (sē nĕs'ĕnt). Growing old

seneschal (sĕn'ĕ shăl). Page 618

sententious (sĕn tĕn'shŭs). Full of meaning; energetic in expression

sepulcher (sĕp'ŭl kēr). A tomb, burial vault

seraph (sĕr'ăf). One of an order of celestial beings, a type of angel. Plural: seraphim

sere (sēr). Dry; withered

serried (sĕr'ĭd). Crowded, compact, dense

sestet (sĕs'tĕt). The last six lines of a sonnet; or any six-line verse

Sheraton (shĕr'à tŏn). Page 262

shrive (shrīv). To hear confession and give absolution

Sibyllic (sĭ bĭl'ĭk). Page 635

Sinai (sī'nī). Page 611

sine qua non (sī'nē quā nŏn). Page 472

sinister (sĭn'ĭs tēr). Boding evil

slough (slŭf). To cast off as a snake does its skin

solicitude (sō lĭs'ĭ tūd). Anxiety, uneasiness of mind

solstice (sŏl'stĭs). The day on which the sun is farthest from the equator, north or south

sonata (sŏ nä'tà). An instrumental musical composition

sonorous (sō nō'rŭs). Loud or impressive in sound

sophisticated (sō fĭs'tĭ kāt ĕd). Experienced in the artificial phases of life, worldly-wise

Spartan (spär'tăn). Pertaining to ancient Sparta, noted for valor and bravery of citizens; hence, hardy, undaunted

spherule (sfĕr'ōōl). A little sphere

splay foot (splā'fŏŏt). A foot that is abnormally flattened and spread out

squill (skwĭl). A European garden flower

stanchion (stăn'shŭn). Upright pass to secure cattle in stalls

starboard (stär'bōrd). The right side of a ship when one stands facing the bow

stentorian (stĕn tō'rĭ ăn). Extremely loud. From Stentor, a loud-voiced herald in the *Iliad*

stereotypes (stĕr'ē ō tīpz). Page 374

stoically (stō'ĭ kă lĭ). In a manner indicating indifference to passion or pain

Stradivarius (străd ĭ vā'rĭ ŭs). Page 604

strategy (străt'ē jĭ). The science of directing military movements

stratum (strā'tŭm). Layer of rock or tissue

strident (strī'dĕnt). Harsh-sounding, shrill

stultify (stŭl'tĭ fī). To make foolish

suavity (swä'vĭ tĭ). Ease or confidence of position, pleasantness of manner

subservient (sŭb sûrv'ĭ ĕnt). Useful in an inferior capacity, subordinate

subtle (sŭt'l). Delicate, fine

subvert (sŭb vûrt'). To overthrow or destroy

superscription (sū pēr skrĭp'shŭn). Address on letters or the like

supinely (sū pīn'lĭ). Negligently, drowsily, indolently, listlessly

surcease (sŭr sēs'). Cessation, stop, end

surplice (sûr'plĭs). Outer vestment worn by Roman Catholic and Anglican clergy

surreptitious (sŭr ĕp tĭsh'ŭs). Under cover, done secretly

surtout (sŭr tōōt' *or* sŭr tōō'). A man's coat to be worn over his other garments

Swat (swät). A territory and river in India

sylvan (sĭl'văn). Country-like, rural, rustic

symphony (sĭm'fō nĭ). A harmony of sounds

synod (sĭn'ŭd). A formal meeting to consult and decide on church matters

T

taboo (tà bōō'). Set apart or forbidden

taciturn (tăs'ĭ tûrn). Habitually silent; not given to conversation

Tangier (tăn jēr'). Town in Morocco, Africa

tarn (tärn). A small mountain lake or pool

tarpaulin (tär pô'lĭn). Waterproof canvas for coverings

Taygetos (tå ĭj'ĕ tōs). A group of stars

technique (tĕk nēk'). Method or style of performance in any art

temporal (tĕm'pō răl). Worldly; limited in time

tenet (tĕn'ĕt). An opinion, principle or dogma

teocallis (tē ō kăl'ĭz). Page 546

termagant (tēr'mà gănt). A boisterous, quarrelsome, scolding woman

Thanatopsis (thăn à tŏp'sĭs). A meditation on death

theologian (thē ō lō'jĭ ăn). A person versed in the study of religion

thoroughbred (thŭr'ō brĕd). Of unmixed blood

Thrace (thrās). Ancient Roman province

tirade (tī'rād). A long speech marked by intemperate and harsh language

Titan (tī'tăn). Page 707

Titanic (tī tăn'ĭk). Page 634

Titian (tĭsh'ăn). Page 604

tome (tōm). A ponderous volume

Touraine (tōō rān'). City in ancient France

trekking (trĕk'ĭng). Hauling or drawing; traveling

trenchant (trĕn'chănt). Keen, biting, severe

trepidation (trĕp ĭ dā'shŭn). A trembling or quivering; a state of terror

Trinidad (trĭn'ĭ dăd). Small, rocky, volcanic island in south Atlantic Ocean

trite (trīt). Commonplace, overused

Triton (trī'tŏn). Page 601

trochaic (trō kā'ĭk). Page 520

trochee (trō'kē). Page 520

trottoir (trôt wàr'). Page 656

truffle (trŭf'l). A European mushroom which grows underground, and is usually dug up by hogs trained for that purpose

trundle bed (trŭn'd'l). A low bed that can be pushed under a higher one

Tschaikowski (chī kôf'skē). Russian composer

tumbril (tŭm'brĭl). A farmer's dump cart or wagon, also one used to convey condemned persons to the guillotine during the French Revolution

turnpike. A road maintained by the payment of toll

U

ultimata (ŭl tĭ mā'tà). Page 376

ultimate (ŭl'tĭ mǎt). Arrived at as a last result

umbrage (ŭm'brāj). Shade, shadow; hence, injured pride

undulate (ŭn'dū lāt). To move in wavelike manner

unguent (ŭng'gwĕnt). A salve or ointment

Unitarian (ū nĭ tā'rĭ ăn). One who denies the Holy Trinity and believes in God as one person

unrequited (ŭn rē kwīt'ĕd). Not returned, not repaid

urbane (ûr bān'). Courteous in manners, refined

usurer (ū'zhū rēr). One who lends money at an extremely high rate

usurpation (ū zûr pā'shŭn). Unauthorized exercise of powers belonging to another

V

vacillated (văs ĭ lāt'ĕd). Wavered, swerved

vagary (và gā'rĭ). A wild or fanciful freak, a whim

valance (văl'ĕns). A curtain or drapery from couch or bed to floor

vapid (văp'ĭd). Having lost its life or spirit; dead; insipid

vaquero (vä kā'rō). Page 483

vellum (vĕl'ŭm). Page 604

venality (vē năl'ĭ tĭ). Use of services or offices for reward

vendue (vĕn dū'). Page 421

veneration (vĕn ēr ā'shŭn). Highest degree of respect or reverence

Venus (vē'nŭs). Roman Goddess of Beauty, known as Aphrodite among the Greeks

verbicide (vĕr'bĭ sīd). The misuse of a word

Verdun (vēr dŭn'). A battlefield of the World War in France

verdure (vûr'dŭr). Greenness; freshness of vegetation

verisimilitude (vĕr ĭ sĭ mĭl'ĭ tūd). The appearance of truth

vesper (vĕs'pēr). Evening

vicissitude (vĭ sĭs'ĭ tūd). A complete change of circumstances

vindication (vĭn dĭ kā'shŭn). Defense; justification against denial

vindictive (vĭn dĭk'tĭv). Inclined to hold a grudge

virginal (vûr'jĭ năl). Pure, undefiled, unsullied

virus (vī'rŭs). Poison or contagion of infectious disease

volcanic (vŏl kăn′ĭk). Explosive

voluble (vŏl′ū b′l). Fluent in speech

voluminous (vȯ lū′mĭ nŭs). Of great volume or bulk

voluptuous (vȯ lŭp′tū ŭs). Full of sensual delight and pleasure; luxurious

W

wain (wān). A wagon or cart

weal (wēl). Prosperity, happiness

weir (wēr). A fence of stakes, brushwood, or the like, set in a stream, tideway, or inlet of the sea, for taking fish

werewolf (wēr′wo͝olf). A creature, half human and half wolf

wold (wōld). An open lowland

wont (wŭnt). Accustomed, habituated, used

wraith (rāth). An apparition of a living person, a specter

Y

Ypres (ē′pr). A battlefield of the World War in Flanders

INDEX

Adams, Franklin P., 359, 1051; poems, 788–9
Adams, Henry, 1050
Ade, George, 360, 361, 1051; *Fable,* 392
Ahkoond of Swat, The, George T. Lanigan, 781
Alcott, Bronson, 940
Alcott, Louisa May, 1003
Aldrich, Thomas Bailey, 7, 14, 515, 1002, 1004; story, 97; poems, 668–669
Allen, Hervey, poem, 764
Allen, James Lane, 16, 993, 1002
Altered Look about the Hills, An, Emily Dickinson, 665
American Hercules, An, James Stevens, 481
American Limericks, 791
Anderson, Sherwood, 1026
Andrews, Mary Raymond Shipman, 1026
Anne Rutledge, Edgar Lee Masters, 709
Any One Will Do, anon., 790
Arsenal at Springfield, The, H. W. Longfellow, 546
Aspects of the Pines, Paul Hamilton Hayne, 642
Atherton, Gertrude, 1015
Audubon, John James, 937
Austin, Mary, 1026
Author's Account of Himself, Washington Irving, 228
Autocrat of the Breakfast Table, The, Oliver Wendell Holmes, 373
Awful Fate of Mr. Wolf, The, Joel Chandler Harris, 503

Baker, Ray Stannard, 1047
Ballad of Two Lame Men, The, Franklin P. Adams, 788
Bancroft, George, 958
Banks of the Little Eau Pleine, The, 490
Barlow, Joel, 924
Barnacles, Sidney Lanier, 648
Barrett, Lawrence, 802

Bates, Blanche, 804
Battle-Field, The, William Cullen Bryant, 533
Beat! Beat! Drums, Walt Whitman, 657
Beebe, William, 1045
Belasco, David, 804, 1002
Bellamy, Edward, 1001
Bells of San Blas, The, H. W. Longfellow, 563
Benét, Stephen Vincent, 517, 1042; poem, 770
Benchley, Robert C., 361, 1051
Bercovici, Konrad, 1027
Bewick Finzer, E. A. Robinson, 704
Bierce, Ambrose, 15, 1006; story, 108
Birches, Robert Frost, 724
Birthplace, The, Robert Frost, 727
Boker, George Henry, 802, 971
Boucicault, Dion, 802–803
Boyd, James, 1014
Boyd, Thomas, 1019
Boys, The, O. W. Holmes, 598
Bradford, Gamaliel, 300, 1050
Bradford, William, 919
Bradstreet, Anne, 921
Bromfield, Louis, 1018
Brooks, Charles Stephen, 1047; essay, 263
Brown, Alice, 1020
Brown, Charles Brockden, 925
Brute Neighbors, H. D. Thoreau, 244
Bryant, William Cullen, 512, 519, 522, 932; poems, 528–534
Bubble Reputation, The, Walter Prichard Eaton, 255
Building of the Ship, The, H. W. Longfellow, 551
Bunner, H. C., 14, 15, 1002, 1004; story, 116; poem, 782
Burroughs, John, 1044
Burt, Struthers, 1027
Business Letter, A, Artemus Ward, 379
Buttons, Carl Sandburg, 736
Byrd, Rear-Admiral Richard E., 6
Byrd, Col. William, 6; selection, 424

Cabell, James Branch, 1013
Cable, George W., 13, 989
Cahan, Abraham, 1018
Candor, H. C. Bunner, 782
Carleton, Will, 989
Carman, Bliss, 515, 1002, 1005; poems, 677–682
Carol of Death, The, Walt Whitman, 658
Cather, Willa, 994, 1016
Century, The, Christopher Morley, 219
Chambered Nautilus, The, O. W. Holmes, 600
Charleston, Henry Timrod, 637
Chicago, Carl Sandburg, 735
Child of the Romans, Carl Sandburg, 738
Churchill, Winston, 1002, 1010
Clean Curtains, Carl Sandburg, 739
Clemens, S. L. (Mark Twain), 5, 7, 14, 215, 981–983; story, 382
Cleveland, Grover, selection, 476
Cobb, Irvin S., 360, 361, 1026; selection, 396
Cohen, Rose, 299
Coin, A, Carl Sandburg, 740
Coin, The, Sara Teasdale, 753
Compensation (poem), R. W. Emerson, 537
Concord Hymn, The, R. W. Emerson, 536
Conquered Banner, The, Abram J. Ryan, 650
Contentment, O. W. Holmes, 602
Cooke, Rose Terry, 12
Cooper, James Fenimore, 7, 930–932
Correct Behavior on a Picnic, Donald Ogden Stewart, 409
Courtin', The, James Russell Lowell, 606
Cowboy's Dream, The, 495
Crane, Nathalia, 517; poem, 774
Crane, Stephen, 16, 1005
Crawford, F. Marion, 1001
Crèvecœur, St. John de, 925
Crothers, Samuel McChord, 1046
Curtis, George William, 941

Daley, Thomas Augustine, poem, 785
Dana, Charles A., 941
Dana, Richard Henry, Jr., 299, 498, 956
Darest Thou Now O Soul, Walt Whitman, 663
Davis, Richard Harding, 16, 1024
Dawson, Sarah Morgan, 299

Dear Lord and Father of Mankind, J. G. Whittier, 594
Death of Stonewall Jackson, The, Stephen Vincent Benét, 771
Death of the Hired Man, The, Robert Frost, 728
Declaration of Independence, The, Thomas Jefferson, 435
De Kruif, Paul, 1051; essay, 278
Deland, Margaret, 16, 1001, 1023
Dell, Floyd, 1008, 1018
Devil and Tom Walker, The, Washington Irving, 30
Dickinson, Emily, 510, 977; poems, 664–668
Dirge, George Sterling, 716
Dirge without Music, Edna St. Vincent Millay, 768
Dos Passos, John, 1018
Drake, Joseph Rodman, 936
Dreiser, Theodore, 1010
Dunlap, William, 799–800
Dunne, Finley Peter, 360, 1051
Durable Bon Mot, The, Keith Preston, 789
Dwight, Timothy, 924

Each and All, R. W. Emerson, 539
Eaton, Walter Prichard, 1047; essay, 255
Edwards, Jonathan, 920
Eggleston, Edward, 991
Eldorado, Edgar Allan Poe, 628
Emerson, Ralph Waldo, 5, 512, 519, 941–943; essays, 233; poems, 535–541
Emmett, Daniel D., 970
England to America, M. P. Montague, 176
Escape, Elinor Wylie, 761
Essays, Selections from, Emerson, 239

Fable, A, R. W. Emerson, 536
Fable of the Wonderful Meal of Vittles, The, George Ade, 392
Farewell Addresses, George Washington, 438
Farewell at Springfield, Abraham Lincoln, 449
Fate, Carl Sandburg, 740
Fence, A, Carl Sandburg, 737
Ferber, Edna, 1029
Field, Eugene, 359, 515; poems, 675–677, 992
Finch, Francis M., 514, 971
Fisher, Dorothy Canfield, 1017; essay, 267

Fitch, Clyde, 413, 502, 805, 1002; play, 850
Fool's Prayer, The, Edward Rowland Sill, 670
Footfalls, Wilbur Daniel Steele, 193
Ford, Paul Leicester, 1002
Franklin, Benjamin, 359, 922; autobiography, 308; Poor Richard, 365
Freeman, Mary E. Wilkins, 16, 1021
Freneau, Philip, 512, 926; poems, 524–528
From the Flats, Sidney Lanier, 647
Frost, Robert, 498, 510, 516, 519, 522, 1036; poems, 723–34
Fuller, Margaret, 940

Gale, Zona, 1016
Garland, Hamlin, 16, 993; autobiography, 301
George Gray, Edgar Lee Masters, 710
Gerould, Katherine Fullerton, 1027
Gettysburg Address, Abraham Lincoln, 455
Gifts, R. W. Emerson, 233
Gillette, William, 804, 1002
Give Me the Splendid Silent Sun, Walt Whitman, 660
Glasgow, Ellen, 1016
God of the Open Air, Henry van Dyke, 696
Godfrey, Thomas, 799, 922
Good Morning, America, Carl Sandburg, 742
Grass, Carl Sandburg, 737
Green Fire, Bliss Carman, 681
Guiterman, Arthur, poems, 783–785

Hale, Edward Everett, 12, 967
Halleck, Fitz-Greene, 936
Hamilton, Alexander, 924
Harris, Joel Chandler, 8, 480, 990; story, 503
Harte, F. Bret, 13, 515, 803, 982, 986–988; story, 79; poem, 779
Hawthorne, Nathaniel, 10, 943–945; story by, 44; biography of, 340
Hawthorne at College, Lloyd Morris, 340
Hay, John, 515, 988, 1001
Hayne, Paul Hamilton, 514, 968, 970; poems, 641–644
Hearn, Lafcadio, essay, 253
Height of the Ridiculous, The, O. W. Holmes, 778
Hemingway, Ernest, 1008, 1018
Henry David Thoreau, J. Arthur Myers, 333
Henry, O., 5, 16, 17, 1021; story, 126

Henry, Patrick, speech, 431
Hergesheimer, Joseph, 1014
Herman Melville Writes "Moby-Dick," Lewis Mumford, 346
Hermione, Don Marquis, 362
Her Private Journal, Sarah Kemble Knight, 415
Heyward, Dubose, 480, 1018; poem, 758
History of the Dividing Line, A, Col. William Byrd, 424
Holmes, Oliver Wendell, 359, 360, 512, 952–954; "The Autocrat," 373; poems, 595–605, 778
Hopkinson, Francis, 924
Horseman in the Sky, A, Ambrose Bierce, 108
Hovey, Richard, 515, 1002, 1005; poems, 682–5
How the Feud Started, Arthur Guiterman, 783
How to Write Short Stories, Ring Lardner, 405
Howe, Edgar W., 1046
Howe, Julia Ward, 514, 970
Howells, William Dean, 16, 295, 803–804, 997–999
Humorist, The, Keith Preston, 791
Hurst, Fannie, 1029
Hymn to the Night, H. W. Longfellow, 542

Ichabod, J. G. Whittier, 567
I Have a Rendezvous with Death, Alan Seeger, 763
I Hear America Singing, Walt Whitman, 655
I'm Nobody, Emily Dickinson, 664
In a Back Alley, Carl Sandburg, 739
Indian Burying Ground, The, Philip Freneau, 526
I Never Saw a Moor, Emily Dickinson, 666
Ingénue of the Sierras, An, Bret Harte, 79
In the Churchyard at Tarrytown, H. W. Longfellow, 548
In the Days of Wouter Van Twiller, Washington Irving, 368
In the Esplanade des Invalides, George O'Neil, 769
Irving, Washington, 10, 928–930; story, 30; essay, 228; humorous selection, 368
I Shall Not Care, Sara Teasdale, 753
Israfel, Edgar Allan Poe, 626
It's Me, O Lord, 506

Jacob Goodpasture, Edgar Lee Masters, 711
Jackson, Helen Hunt, 993
James, Henry, 15, 999
Jefferson, Joseph, 802
Jefferson, Thomas, 923; *Declaration of Independence,* 435
Jewett, Sarah Orne, 13, 993
John Horace Burleson, Edgar Lee Masters, 709
Johnston, Mary, 1002
Joys of the Road, The, Bliss Carman, 678

Kellogg, Frank B., *Peace Pact,* 477
Key, Francis Scott, 937
Knight, Sarah Kemble, 6, 922; *Journal,* 415

Lady, A, Amy Lowell, 718
Lament, Edna St. Vincent Millay, 766
Lanier, Sidney, 514, 519, 968–970; poems, 644–650
Lanigan, George T., poem, 781
Lardner, Ring, 361, 1028; selection, 405
Leacock, Stephen, 361, 1051
League for Peace, Address on, Woodrow Wilson, 471
Leave Her, Johnny, Leave Her, 498
Lee in Defeat, Thomas Nelson Page, 319
Let Me Live Out My Years, John G. Neihardt, 751
Letter to Gen. Hooker, Abraham Lincoln, 451
Lewis, Sinclair, 1018
'Lijah, Edgar Valentine Smith, 142
Limitations of Youth, The, Eugene Field, 676
Lincoln, Abraham, 966; selections, 449, 451, 452, 454, 455, 457
Lindsay, Vachel, 516; poem, 745
Little Boy Blue, Eugene Field, 675
Little Stone, The, Emily Dickinson, 665
London, Jack, 5, 16, 1009; story, 159
Long, John Luther, 804
Longfellow, H. W., 512, 518, 520, 522, 951–953; poems, 541–566
Long Feud, Louis Untermeyer, 756
Long Hill, The, Sara Teasdale, 754
Long Pants, Irvin S. Cobb, 396
Lowell, Amy, 516, 1041; poems, 717–723
Lost Vision, The, Leah Rachel Yoffie, 770

Lowell, James Russell, 295, 359, 512, 514, 518, 519, 954–956; poems, 605–623
Lyric Deed, The, John G. Neihardt, 752

Maidenhood, H. W. Longfellow, 544
Major, Charles, 1002
Man with the Hoe, The, Edwin Markham, 688
Mannahatta, Walt Whitman, 656
Mansfield, Richard, 805
Markham, Edwin, 515, 1034; poems, 688–695
Marquis, Don, 359, 1051; selection, 362
Mary White, William Allen White, 223
Master, The, Edwin Arlington Robinson, 705
Master-Mariner, The, George Sterling, 714
Masters, Edgar Lee, 5, 516, 519, 1037; poems, 708–714
Mather, Increase and Cotton, 919
Melville, Herman, 12, 935–936; biographical sketch, 346
Memory, Thomas Bailey Aldrich, 668
Mencken, H. L., 1049
Millay, Edna St. Vincent, 517, 518, 519, 520, 1041; poems, 766–768
Miller, Joaquin, 515, 988; poems, 671–673
Minister's Black Veil, The, Nathaniel Hawthorne, 44
Miniver Cheevy, E. A. Robinson, 701
Minor Bird, A, Robert Frost, 728
Miracles, Walt Whitman, 662
Mitchell, S. Weir, 1002
Mocking Bird, The, Paul Hamilton Hayne, 641
Monroe, James, *Monroe Doctrine,* 475
Monroe Doctrine, The, James Monroe, 475
Montague, James J., poem, 786
Montague, Margaret Prescott, 17, 490, 509, 1027; story, 176
Moody, William Vaughn, 515, 519, 805, 1002, 1005
More, Paul Elmer, 1048
Morley, Christopher, 359, 1047, 1051; essay, 219; poem, 765
Morris, Lloyd, biography of Hawthorne, 340
Motley, Jahn Lothrop, 958
Mountain Woman, The, Dubose Heyward, 759
Mrs. George Reece, Edgar Lee Masters, 710

Muir, John, 1044
Mumford, Lewis, biography of Melville, 346
Murfee, Mary N., 990
Municipal Report, A, O. Henry, 126
Music, Amy Lowell, 719
Myers, J. Arthur, biography of Thoreau, 333
My Life Closed Twice, Emily Dickinson, 667
My Lost Youth, H. W. Longfellow, 548

Nathan Hale (ballad), 500
Nathan Hale (play), Clyde Fitch, 850
Nathan, Robert, 1018
Neihardt, John, 517, 518; poems, 751–752
New England Primer, The, 920
Night Song at Amalfi, Sara Teasdale, 754
Night Stuff, Carl Sandburg, 741
Noiseless, Patient Spider, A, Walt Whitman, 659
Nonsense Rhyme, Elinor Wylie, 762
Norris, Frank, 1008
Note on the Essay, A, Carl Van Doren, 276
Nye, Edgar W., 360, 966

O'Brien, Fitz-James, 12
Ode, Henry Timrod, 639
Ogden, Anna Cora, 801
Old Ironsides, O. W. Holmes, 595
Once There Was a Furnace Boy, Charles Stephen Brooks, 263
O'Neil, George, poem, 769
O'Neill, Eugene, 805, 806; play, 831
One's Self I Sing, Walt Whitman, 654
Our Israfel, Edwin Markham, 691

Page, Thomas Nelson, 13, 299, 990; biography of Lee, 319
Paine, Thomas, 932
Palmetto Town, Hervey Allen, 764
Parkman, Francis, 959
Parrish, Anne, 1018
Pasture, The, Robert Frost, 724
Patterns, Amy Lowell, 719
Payne, John Howard, 800, 937
Peace Pact, Frank B. Kellogg, 477
Peterkin, Julia, 1018
Phelps, William Lyon, 1048
Plain Language from Truthful James, Bret Harte, 779
Poe, Edgar Allan, 10–12, 18, 19, 512,

513, 521, 932–935; story, 58; poems, 624–636
Poe, Mr. and Mrs. David, 800
Poole, Ernest, 1010
Porter, William Sidney, *see* Henry, O.
Practical Politics, Theodore Roosevelt, 325
Prayer, Louis Untermeyer, 757
Prayers of Steel, Carl Sandburg, 742
Prescott, William Hickling, 937, 957
Preston, Keith, poems, 789, 791
Proclamation for National Fast Day, Abraham Lincoln, 452
Proclamation for Thanksgiving, Abraham Lincoln, 454
Project of Arriving at Moral Perfection, Benjamin Franklin, 308

Quatrains, Edwin Markham, 690

Randall, James Ryder, 970
Raven, The, Edgar Allan Poe, 629
Read, Thomas Buchanan, 971
Reading Boy, The, Nathalia Crane, 775
Real Baseball, Arthur Guiterman, 784
Repplier, Agnes, 295, 1046
Rhodora, The, R. W. Emerson, 538
Rice, Cale Young, poem, 716
Richard Cory, E. A. Robinson, 703
Rickaby, Franz, 490
Riley, James Whitcomb, 515, 991; poem, 673
Roberts, Elizabeth Madox, 1018
Robinson, Edwin Arlington, 510, 516, 522, 1035; poems, 701–708
Robinson, Edwin Meade, poems, 787
Rölvaag, O. E., 994
Roosevelt, Theodore, 295; autobiography, 325
Root, George F., 971
Runaway, The, Cale Young Rice, 716
Ryan, Abram J., 968, 970; poem, 650

Same Old Story, The, James J. Montague, 786
Sandburg, Carl, 300, 495, 509, 510, 516, 1037; poems, 734–44
Santa Fe Trail, The, Vachel Lindsay, 745
Sayings of Poor Richard, Benjamin Franklin, 365
School Life, Hamlin Garland, 301
Sea Gypsy, The, Richard Hovey, 682
Sea Lullaby, Elinor Wylie, 760
Second Inaugural Address, Abraham Lincoln, 457

Sedgwick, Anne Douglas, 1016
Seeger, Alan, poem, 762
Seton, Ernest Thompson, 1045
Sharp, Dallas Lore, 1045
Sheener, Ben Ames Williams, 20
Sherman, Stuart P., 1049
Silence, Edgar Lee Masters, 712
Sill, Edward Rowland, 515, 518, 1002, 1005; poem, 670
Simms, William Gilmore, 968
Sinclair, Upton, 1010
Sisterly Scheme, A, H. C. Bunner, 116
Smith, Captain John, 918
Smith, Edgar Valentine, 17, 1030; story, 142
Smith, Samuel Francis, 937, 952
Snowbound, J. G. Whittier, 571
Snowflake, A, Thomas Bailey Aldrich, 669
Some Keep the Sabbath, Emily Dickinson, 666
Song of the Chattahoochee, Sidney Lanier, 645
Sothern, E. H., 299
Soul Selects Her Own Society, The, Emily Dickinson, 667
Speech in the Virginia Convention, Patrick Henry, 431
Spring and the Fall, The, Edna St. Vincent Millay, 767
Steele, Wilbur Daniel, 17, 1028; story, 193
Sterling, George, poems, 714–716
Stevens, James, Paul Bunyan story, 481
Stewart, Donald Ogden, 361, 1051; selection, 409
Stirrup-Cup, The, Sidney Lanier, 649
Stockton, Frank R., 14, 15, 1002, 1003; story, 65
Stone's Hymn, The, Louis Untermeyer, 757
Stopping by Woods, Robert Frost, 727
Stowe, Harriet Beecher, 964; *Uncle Tom's Cabin,* 801, 964
Strachey, William, 910
Struggle for Life, A, T. B. Aldrich, 97
Suckow, Ruth, 1018

Tarkington, Booth, 805, 1002, 1012; play, 807
Taylor, Bert Leston, 359, 1051
Teasdale, Sara, 517, 1041; poems, 753–755
Telling the Bees, J. G. Whittier, 569

Tell-Tale Heart, The, Edgar Allan Poe, 58
Thanatopsis, William Cullen Bryant, 528
Thayer, William Roscoe, 300
Thomas, Augustus, 804, 1002
Thompson, Maurice, 1002
Thompson, W. H., 971
Thoreau, Henry David, 512, 940, 947; essay by, 244; biography of, 333
Those Two Boys, Franklin P. Adams, 789
Ticknor, Francis O., 970
Timrod, Henry, 514, 519, 967, 970; poems, 637–640
To an Insect, O. W. Holmes, 596
To a Post Office Inkwell, Christopher Morley, 765
To a Telegraph Pole, Louis Untermeyer, 755
To a Waterfowl, William Cullen Bryant, 531
To Build a Fire, Jack London, 159
To Helen, Edgar Allan Poe, 625
To Make a Prairie, Emily Dickinson, 665
To the Memory of Brave Americans, Philip Freneau, 524
Trumbull, John, 924
Trysting Place, The, Booth Tarkington, 807
Twain, Mark, *see* Clemens, S. L.
Two 'Mericana Men, Thomas A. Daly, 785
Tyler, Royall, 799

Ulalume, Edgar Allan Poe, 633
Unexpected Acquaintance, An, Mark Twain, 382
Untermeyer, Louis, 517, 1040; poems, 755–758

Valentine Vagaries, Lafcadio Hearn, 253
Van Doren, Carl, 1049; essay, 276
van Dyke, Henry, 215, 295, 1023, 1034; poem, 696–701
Venezuela Boundary Message, Grover Cleveland, 476
Vermont, Dorothy Canfield Fisher, 267
Vision of Sir Launfal, The, James Russell Lowell, 610
Voluntaries III, R. W. Emerson, 538

Wallace, Lew, 1001
Walter Reed, Paul de Kruif, 278

Wander Lovers, The, Richard Hovey, 683

Ward, Artemus, 360, 966; *A Business Letter,* 379

War Message to Congress, The, Woodrow Wilson, 461

Washington, Booker T., 299

Washington, George, *Farewell Address,* 438

Webster, Daniel, 965

We Never Know How High, Emily Dickinson, 668

Werner, M. R., 300

Westcott, Glenway, 1018

Westward Ho! Joaquin Miller, 672

Wharton, Edith, 1015

What Mr. Robinson Thinks, James Russell Lowell, 608

When I Heard the Learned Astronomer, Walt Whitman, 662

When the Frost Is on the Punkin, James Whitcomb Riley, 673

Where the Cross Is Made, Eugene O'Neill, 831

White, William Allen, 1025; essay, 223

Whitman, Walt, 512, 513, 514, 519, 973–977; poems, 652–663

Whittier, J. G., 512, 519, 962–964; poems, 566–594

Widow's Cruise, The, Frank R. Stockton, 65

Wigglesworth, Michael, 921

Wilder, Thornton, 1018

Wild Honeysuckle, The, Philip Freneau, 525

Williams, Ben Ames, 17, 1030; story, 20

Wilson, Harry Leon, 412

Wilson, Woodrow, selections, 461, 471

Wind Song, Carl Sandburg, 741

Winter, William, 805

Winthrop, John, 919

Wister, Owen, 994

Woodworth, Samuel, 937

Word, A, Emily Dickinson, 665

Wylie, Elinor, 517, 1042; poems, 760–762

Yezierska, Anzia, 1018

Yoffie, Leah Rachel, poem, 770